Children's Needs: Psychological Perspectives

Children's Needs: Psychological Perspectives

Edited by

Alex Thomas
Port Clinton City Schools
Port Clinton, Ohio

Jeff Grimes
Department of Education
Des Moines, Iowa

The National Association of School Psychologists
Silver Spring, Maryland

First printing: 1987
Second printing: 1994

Published by The National Association of School Psychologists
8455 Colesville Road, Suite 1000
Silver Spring, MD 20910

ISBN 0-932955-05-3

Printed in the the United States of America

Acknowledgments

We are indebted to Cathy Telzrow, Dan Reschly, Judy Fulwider, Lawrence Moran, and Darla Guth for their participation in this project.

A particular note of acknowledgment is extended to the Port Clinton City Schools (Dennis Rectenwald, Superintendent) and the Iowa Department of Education (Frank Vance, Chief of Bureau of Special Education) for fostering a professional environment supportive of the editorial involvement necessary for this book's completion.

We also thank the following individuals for their assistance in reviewing chapters for *Children's Needs: Psychological Perspectives:*

Tucker Anderson (GA)
Wray Brabham (LA)
Cinda C. Cannon (UT)
Julia Hickman Clark (TX)
Elizabeth Bull Danielson (MN)
Beth Doll (WI)
Nancy Enders (MD)
Dennis M. Flanagan (PA)
Virginia A. Francis (ID)
Jane Gallagher (ME)
Richard G. Games (NY)
Gail S. Gibson (AL)
Tad Greene (WI)
Michael Heaney (NY)
Janet Ann Hertig (WI)
Ron Kral (WI)
Megan Kromer (TX)
Hans Langner (NE)
Linda Leal (IL)
Marissa Manlove (IN)
Calvin O. Matthews (AL)
Robert Matuozzi (NY)
Mike Radice (OH)
Mary Ann Rafoth (IL)
Gay Rosenthal (MN)
Gary Ross-Reynolds (LA)
Jane Ross-Reynolds (LA)
David Sanville (CA)
Dale R. Schlemmer (MI)
Mary F. Schneider (IL)
Janet Werner Shelver (SD)
Robert O. Smith (VA)
William O. Sullivan (SC)
Linda S. Williamson (IA)
Thomas A. Wood (TX)

Introduction

Children's Needs: Psychological Perspectives acknowledges the diverse contributions to a child's success at school. As our society's demographics change, as we become more technologically involved, and as family patterns and cultural values re-orient to these changes, the contributors to a child's school success expand beyond the narrow view of the classroom or purely intra-student characteristics. Children bring to school various physical, family, social, and emotional characteristics which have as much to do with school success as teacher quality, school climate, their intelligence, and/or motivation. As helping professionals in the schools, we must broaden our own perspective to encompass these diverse issues effecting the development of children. This book is a small step in that acknowledgment. As school psychologists, we need to look beyond purely psychometric orientation and place the child in context relative to the outside contributors which effect school experience.

We fervently hope the material contained in this effort will assist in expanding that perspective through which children's school success will be enhanced.

Alex Thomas
Jeff Grimes

From NASP Publications Policy Handbook

Contents

Children and Access/Visitation Arrangements

Susan Kennell[1]
New Orleans, Louisiana

Steven I. Pfeiffer
Ochsner Clinic and Alton Ochsner Medical Foundation, New Orleans

BACKGROUND

Divorce in the United States is almost as prevalent as marriage itself. Certain problems relating to this growing phenomenon are associated with the ongoing care and status of children following a breakdown of the family unit. Children are affected physically and psychologically by parental separation and divorce, and researchers are beginning to examine the impact of such disequilibrium on children's subsequent mental health and educational attainment. Currently, the nation is struggling to cope with the upsurge of family dissolution and its concomitant effect on children, but as yet little research has focused on the issues of child custody and visitation/access. Surprisingly, despite increased divorce rates in the past 25 years, custodial and visitation arrangements have altered very little. Documentation of the results of specific custodial and visitation dispositions needs further investigation.

The prediction of the early 1970s that 30–40% of children born in the decade would experience divorce in their homes has sadly come to pass. Beginning in 1973, one million new children each year experienced the breakup of their family (Wallerstein, 1983). Estimates suggest that 40% of current U.S. marriages will ultimately end in divorce if the divorce rate stabilizes at the 1974 level (Heatherington, 1979). This figure translates into approximately 2 million divorces a year.

Approximately 90% of the children of divorce remain in their mother's custody. Historically, this differs from the pre-1920s assumption that all children should go to the father as head of the family. Changing sociopolitical and economic factors emphasized the mother as caretaker, and most courts then begin to take the position that children belong to the biological mother. In addition, judges assumed that the stability of a single home was preferable to children shuttling back and forth between feuding parents. Goldstein, Freud, and Solnit (1973) fortified the court's stance of sole custody by emphasizing the importance of a secure attachment with one adult caretaker. Additionally, these three authors advocated that the custodial parent should have the right to deny visits by the noncustodial parent to ensure the sustained stability of a child's life.

Recent economic forces and the women's movement have together altered woman's role within the family as more females, including divorcees, are entering the work force. Sixty percent of divorced women now work outside the home. As a result, many divorced parents are opting for more shared roles in child rearing and are choosing joint custody arrangements, where it is permissible by state law. Joint custody, in which parents share caretaker responsibilities, challenges traditional custody arrangements with a delegated custodial parent and rights for visitation.

Given the prevalence of divorce, changing parental roles, and the subsequent effects on children, child custody decisions and visitation schedules are difficult challenges for both the mental health field and the judicial system. Custody decisions must consider legal equity, parental responsibilities, and psychological well-being. The courts tend to favor custody rulings that are enforceable and that appear to promote the best interests of the child. In any proceeding where the custody of a minor child is at issue, statutes provide that the court may make any order that seems necessary or proper. The authority of the court to hear custody cases resulting from divorce is assumed.

Derdeyn and Scott (1984) have outlined four rules commonly followed by the court in deciding custody disputes:

1. A young child should be placed in the custody of his mother.
2. A girl should be placed in her mother's custody, while a boy should be placed in his father's custody if he no longer requires his mother's constant care.
3. If the child is old enough to form an intelligent judgment, his choice of custodian will be given consideration.
4. It is nearly unvarying practice to grant the rights of visitation to the parent not having custody.

Visitation will be refused only if it may result in serious harm to the child. A biological parent has the right to custody of the child unless he or she is shown to be unfit to perform the duties custody imposes.

Another provocative point of view on custody decisions was offered by Goldstein et al. (1973). Their proposed suggestions for the reform of child placement statutes and practices were based on psychoanalytic thinking, the following three explicit values being stated unambiguously: First, the child's needs should be foremost in legal proceedings; second, parents have a right to privacy in the way they raise their children; and third, the biological parent does not inherently have an unconditional right to custody but the "psychological parent" (caretaker/adult with whom the child has formed the most significant psychological bond/attachment) should be given legal priority in custody decisions.

[1]The authors enjoyed joint responsibility for the development and writing of this chapter.

Benedek and Benedek (1979) outlined the State of Michigan's set of guidelines for awarding custody. These include assessing the nature of the emotional ties between the competing parties; the location of each parent (and whether the living arrangements are stable); the length of time the child has lived in one stable environment; the desirability of maintaining continuity; the needs of the child for shelter, food, education, and medical care; and the "reasonable" preference of the child.

A contemporary trend is for mental health professionals to assist the court in evaluating parental capabilities. For example, Gardner (1982) states, "Our training and experience enable us to be particularly sensitive to the kinds of childrearing considerations that are scrutinized in custody litigation. Our understanding of psychopathological problems enables us to assess better than the courts the parental qualities being evaluated in such conflicts." McDermott (1970) has devised a parent–child interaction test. This instrument measures a child's attachment to each parent by assessing degree of comfort, initiative, spontaneity, fantasy expressions, range of feelings, and separation behavior; and the parents' attachment to the child by their empathy, sensitivity, discipline, guidance, consistency, patience, intellectual stimulation, facilitation of emotional expression and spontaneity, physical closeness, encouragement, and acceptance.

The literature suggests that there are many competing forces within the custody/visitation process. It is widely accepted, however, that the suggestion by Goldstein et al. (1973) that decisions should be made expediently helps children and that "the least detrimental alternative" is a reasonable and pragmatic philosophy. Because of the many interacting variables and the often arbitrary structure of custodial dispositions, Gardner (1982) concluded that there is no *completely* satisfactory solution to custodial problems when there is a divorce.

Types of Custody Arrangements

In most situations, four custody plans are the usual and legitimized options available for divorcing families. They are governed, however, by state law and therefore may vary nationwide.

Sole Custody. Sole custody is an arrangement in which one parent has custody of the child(ren) and the other parent has visitation privileges. This is the most traditional arrangement utilized by courts and parents. In this situation, the custodial parent makes the majority of the child's daily life decisions. However, both parents may jointly make broader decisions regarding the child's education, religion, etc. Commonly, a specific schedule of visitation is included in the separation agreement and divorce decree such as "Father will pick up the child on alternate weekends from Friday at 6:00 p.m. until Sunday at 2:00 p.m." This schedule does not encourage flexibility but hopes the parents will insure the child's best interests should conditions warrant unexpected changes. This schedule, undoubtedly, cannot take into consideration the unpredictable events of life and appears to work optimally when the custodial arrangements simulates a joint custody pattern (Gardner, 1982).

The sole custody plan is often utilized by the court when parents have demonstrated an inability to cooperate sufficiently and/or need the judicial system to act as a mediator. The specificity of its structure then becomes a useful tool and guideline for parents' equitable rights. Mental health consultants, judges, and the parents themselves must recognize the underlying receptivity of each parent toward access and appreciate the importance of the continuing relationship between the child and both parents.

Divided/Shared Custody. This is a less common custodial arrangement and is a relatively unusual plan. In this situation, the child spends have of the time with one parent and half with the other (such as 6 months with one parent and 6 months with the other parent). Each parent generally has reciprocal visitation privileges. Commonly, it is most workable when both parents live in the same same school district. If not, this creates a tremendous upheaval for the child in the school and neighborhood. One somewhat unwieldly option is for the parents to alternate in and out of the home and the child to remain in the same house. Unfortunately, the "rotating" parents soon come to feel unanchored and dizzy with this arrangement.

Split Custody. In this decree, the children are divided between both parents. One or more child(ren) live permanently with one parent and one or more live with the other parent.The most obvious controversial aspect of this plan centers on the many reasons for keeping siblings together. It is agreed that siblings often provide mutual support and a sense of continuity during the dissolution of a family.

One advantage of this plan is that each parent has full access to one or more of the children. Gardner (1982) described a family in which both parents were expatriates and both returned to their native land following the divorce. Each parent took a child of the same sex, and this seemed to be an appropriate option for this particular family.

Joint Custody (Coparenting, Cocustody). This arrangement refers to the situation in which both parents have equal responsibilities and rights regarding the upbringing of their child(ren). One parent's rights are not superior to the other's. In this situation the children can and often do live in both homes. The emphasis of joint custody is not equal time but rather on equal opportunities for the parent to be involved in rearing their children.

The joint custody plan has grown in popularity since the 1920s. It also has stirred controversy owing to its many risks as well as its many potential advantages. Consequently, this option is not available in all states.

The advantages of joint custody include a diminishment in the power that one parent can exert over the other, elimination of sexual discrimination, and sharing of the "good-guy and bad-guy" roles often set up by children. There may be financial disadvantages because it is necessary to establish child facilities in each home. Mental health practitioners also question the possible long-term deleterious effects on children, especially when the plan is initiated with children under the age of 4 years, who may be confused by the arrangement.

Types of Access

Another component of custody is access to the child by the noncustodial parent (joint custody excluded). There exists disagreement in the literature regarding the relative benefits of access. Access is best evaluated not by an analysis of visits per unit of time but rather as an overall pattern of visiting.The following classification system allows the quality of contact to be assessed (Hirst & Smiley, 1984):

Free access: Unrestricted contact between the child and the noncustodial parent, where access occurs as a response to the needs of the child.

Flexible regular access: The child sees the noncustodial parent on a regular basis, such as on weekends or alternate weekends and one midweek evening. An understanding exists between the parents that the regular arrangement can be modified and renegotiated when necessary.

Rigid regular access: Similar to the regular arrangement described above, except that little latitude is allowed for variation or modification.

Irregular or occasional access: There is no set pattern for access, visitation occurring on a sporadic or occasional basis, usually at the convenience and instigation of the noncustodial parent. Generally, access is not more regular because one or both parties are reluctant to maintain closer contact, because the custodial parent is less supportive of visitation, or because either parent has moved to another geographical location. This type of access is often marked by occasional contact by letter or telephone.

No access: There is no longer contact between the noncustodial parent and the child(ren). Usually, but not always, these are cases in which the noncustodial parent has abandoned the family.

PUTTING ACCESS/VISITATION ARRANGEMENTS IN PERSPECTIVE

Children's Response to Access/Visitation

Regardless of the delegated custody/visitation plan, children have the extraordinary task of adjusting to the many changes imposed by separation and divorce. Intrapsychic distress and intrafamilial disequilibrium typically extend into the child's life for at least 2 years. Wallerstein (1983) likens the child's experience of divorce to that of a child who loses a parent through death or community disaster. The custody/visitation plan plays an important role in a child's adjustment following divorce. Therefore, it seems critical to evaluate children's perceptions of visitation.

Research by Rosen (1977) is consistent with the impressions of most practitioners that children find the option of free access most desirable. Children themselves report that one source of frustration and unhappiness is restricted access to parents. Of 92 children of divorce interviewed by Rosen (1977), 52 indicated a clear preference for free access, whereas 12 children preferred a regulated form of access, 9 wanted to see their noncustodial parent only occasionally, and 4 refused to see the other parent at all. Statements such as the following were reported by Rosen: "Regulated access would have put me against my mother; I'd have hated it . . . . If there was something to talk to your mother about and you had to wait 'til the weekend, you'd forget and the problems get buried . . . . I want the freedom of going any time I like" (page 25).

Jacobson (1978) found that children who spent little time with their fathers during the year after the marital breakup were more likely to develop psychological problems than those children who had more frequent contact. Preschoolers in particular are considered to be most vulnerable to the deleterious effects of separation, divorce, and visitation issues. Their level of cognitive development precludes an accurate integration of events, and this is further complicated by any confusion or lack of understanding about the breakup, as related to their psychosexual and psychosocial stage of development.

The findings cited by Wallerstein (1983) suggest a significant relationship between depression in both younger children and adolescents experiencing divorce and limited visitation with their fathers. Conversely, positive self-esteem in all children, especially older boys, was correlated with a positive father–child relationship that included an ongoing, regular visitation schedule. Wallerstein (1983) found that the extent of a father's visiting is greatly influenced by his feeling about the divorce itself, by the age of the children, and by the children's responsiveness. The mother's attitude toward visits made by her ex-spouse is, surprisingly enough, less significant than expected. Research indicated that fathers are likely to visit younger children more regularly than they are to visit their older children. A trend toward reduced visits occurred more often with children between the ages of 9 and 12 years.

Access/Visitation Patterns

Wallerstein (1983) and Warshak and Santrock (1983) have conducted long-term investigations of visitation patterns. Wallerstein (1983) studied 60 divorcing families (consisting of 131 children and adolescents) over a 5-year period. She observed patterns of visiting immediately after separation and at 1 year following divorce. The most common visitation arrangement consisted of a few hours a day, only 25% of all children staying overnight or for a full weekend visit. "At the outset, the visiting at the noncustodial parent's house is often inadequate, for extended visits and early visits tend to be uneasy, tense or on the run. Also, new partners, some of whom have children, are likely to be present during these early visits, and children may feel aggrieved because their access to the parent has been blocked" (Wallerstein, 1983, p. 245). Only one-fifth of the children were satisfied with the access situation. In addition, children clearly protested that the common pattern of "reasonable" visitation (most commonly visits on alternate weekends) was not enough.

Warshak and Santrock (1983) studied 64 families undergoing divorce with children aged 6–11 years. They concluded that over two-thirds of their sample of children of divorce felt that the frequency of visitation was not meeting their needs. Sixty-two percent requested more visits and only three children wanted fewer visits. In addition, their data consistently reported a higher frequency of socially adjusted behavior in children living with their same-sex parent than those living with the opposite-sex parent. Girls in father-custody families were more likely to experience symptoms of separation anxiety. There was also evidence that children living with the opposite-sex parent experienced discontent with the infrequency of contact with the noncustodial parent. Additionally, they found that considerable satisfaction was expressed concerning the quality of the visits. About one-half of the children considered the noncustodial parent as "nicer to be with" since the divorce. This is consistent with Kelly and Wallerstein's 1977) findings that 5 years after divorce children continued to be reasonably content with their visits to their noncustodial parent.

Taken together, the literature on visitation/access suggests the importance of reinforcing an ongoing relationship between children and their noncustodial parents. A second and obviously interrelated implication is children's expressed dissatisfaction with infrequent visitation arrangements.

Conceptualizing Children's Adjustment to Access

Kurdek (1981) provides a useful framework for conceptualizing children's divorce adjustment based on Bronfrenbrenner's (1979) ecological model. This ecosystemic framework (Table 1) can be readily applied to exploring the implications of various types of access arrangements.

The framework consists of four interrelated systemic levels. The *ontogenic system* addresses the child's emotional and intellectual competencies for dealing with psychosocial stress. Included within this first level are the child's temperament, sex, intelligence level, emotional stability, and interpersonal reasoning capacity. The *microsystem* is the next dimension that can assist in conceptualizing a child's adjustment to divorce and access. At this level of abstraction we are interested in examining each parent's relationship with the child; their competence, comfort, and skill at parenting;the degree of concordance between ex-spouses regarding discipline and the child management techniques and philosophy; and the level of interparent conflict.

The third level is the *exosystem,* which consists of the relative stability of the postdivorce environment. Relevant factors include availability of social supports, financial resources, and childcare and after-school programs. The birth of a child in the noncustodial parent's new family or the remarriage of either party, for example, are two exosystem factors that frequently are associated with a falling off in contact between the noncustodial parent and child.

The final level is the *macrosystem,* which reminds us of the sociocultural and political fabric within which

TABLE 1

Framework for Conceptualizing Children's Adjustment to Divorce: Implications for Access/Visitation Arrangements

Ontogenic System	Microsystem	Exosystem	Macrosystem
The child's competencies for dealing with stress	Each parent's level of personal functioning	Relative stability of the postdivorce environment	Cultural beliefs, attitudes, and views about divorce, parenting, childrearing techniques, children's rights
Age and sex	Parenting competence	Availability of social supports	
Temperament	Degree of congruence regarding childrearing and discipline	Financial resources, legal services, housing, childcare and after-school programs	
Cognitive–developmental level	Noncustodial kin network		
Locus of control	Extent of cordiality and support between expouses		
Ego strength			
Interpersonal reasoning			
Ability to infer motives and feelings			

**Note:* Based on Bronfrenbrenner (1979) and Kurdek (1981)

divorce and postdivorce visitation are woven. For example, in some situations following divorce, the relationship that develops between the visiting parent, in most cases the father, and the child becomes considerably closer than that which existed before, perhaps because of how the noncustodial parent defines his new role.

A recent case in which the authors employed family therapy illustrates the usefulness of this framework which was used in evaluating the child's adjustment to her parents' divorce and subsequent access arrangement. Blythe was referred because of a decline in her level of school achievement, difficulty in concentrating, and withdrawing, depressive behaviors. An initial family diagnostic interview revealed an otherwise verbally precocious and intelligent 8-year-old girl who presented as vulnerable and emotionally needy, fearful that she would never see her father again, longing for her departed parent, and unrealistically nostalgic for her intact family. This girl's first drawing (Figure 1) was obtained during an early individual interview; she explained, "The big ole cat is sitting there thinking about feasting on some chicken legs or fish . . . while the mamma mouse and her little kids are trying to sneak by. The mamma mouse is thinking about getting swallowed by the big ole cat! And the babies are thinking about their daddy, who is too busy behind his big ole desk and can't get away to help his family!"

Blythe's father intentionally distanced himself emotionally from his daughter to be less vulnerable, while at the same time he permitted his unremitting hostility toward his ex-spouse to be expressed in disappointing his daughter with cancelled visits and unanswered telephone calls. Blythe's depression, conflicted loyalties, and guilt, her feelings of rejection, and her mourning reactions further distanced her from her father — who was unable to comfortably deal with his daughter's symptomatic responses. These *microsystem* issues were eloquently depicted in the child's kinetic family drawing (Figure 2). Note that this child depicted herself in the picture as frustrated in not being able to make any telephone contact with her father; the foreboding telephone poles overshadow the drawing and suggest this child's need for increased contact with her estranged parent.

Blythe's limited access to her father was based both on his busy work schedule and emotional unavailability to his daughter because of unresolved negative feelings toward his ex-spouse. Intervention would need to focus not only on the child (the *ontogenic system*), but on how to help the father regain enough self-esteem and ego strength to reestablish contact with his daughter (the *microsystem*), while also securing environmental supports to make visits easier (the *exosystem*).

ALTERNATIVE ACTIONS

Intervention strategies for the divorcing family can be complex and need to be individually tailored. School psychologists are in the unique position to aid the child of the divorcing family directly, as well as indirectly, through the personnel within the school system who work with the child. The aforementioned framework, utilizing the four interrelated dimensions, provides a set of strategies for both prevention of, or early intervention in, problems specific to visitation and access.

The Ontogenic System

Children who frequently turn to their parents for support additionally turn to teachers and friends. This suggests that a child who does not reach out when experiencing excessive psychosocial stress may become psychologically stranded. This provides a rationale for the design of child-oriented, school-based intervention programs.

Preventive measures for children in the school itself might include preparation for the parental separation and divorce and subsequent experience of visitation. Encouraging these children to explore their feelings and eliciting fantasized material and expectations regarding access are most advantageous. Elucidation of typical physical arrangements of visitation/custody are reassuring to the child. Identifying and accepting the children's feelings are also beneficial. Reasonable goals might include an increased level of overall functioning for the children, with an emphasis on greater interpersonal reasoning and internal locus of control — two psychological constructs that would be expected to facilitate the children's adjustment to the access arrangement with the noncustodial parent.

These objectives can be implemented within a setounseling. ting of individual or group cIndividual counseling is obviously the most intensive intervention in which the school psychologist can engage. Children's divorce group therapy is an effective modality; it provides an universalization experience for the child. Sharing similar experiences with peers promotes reality testing and fosters a supportive environment. Issues related to visitation and its concomitant problems can be discussed. Kurdek (1981) stated that children whose parents are divorced often find other children whose parents are divorced to be of great assistance in dealing with divorce-related concerns.

If the school psychologist is aware of a pending separation/divorce that will entail a visitation arrangement it is beneficial to alert school personnel. For example, teachers could be encouraged to enhance the child's self-esteem and reduce depressive symptoms during this stressful period. Consultation with a focus on assisting teachers in noting signs of increased inattention and distractibility, decreased learning, narcissistic disequilibrium, and lowered frustration tolerance might prevent future failure for this child.

Bibliotherapy is also quite useful, particularly with the burgeoning divorce literature geared to varying developmental stages of children (see the annotated bibliography for children and adolescents). Appropriate child-oriented literature helps the student identify and clarify ambivalent or uncomfortable feelings. Bibliotherapy is appropriate in individual or group counseling, or even when incorporated into regular classroom meetings.

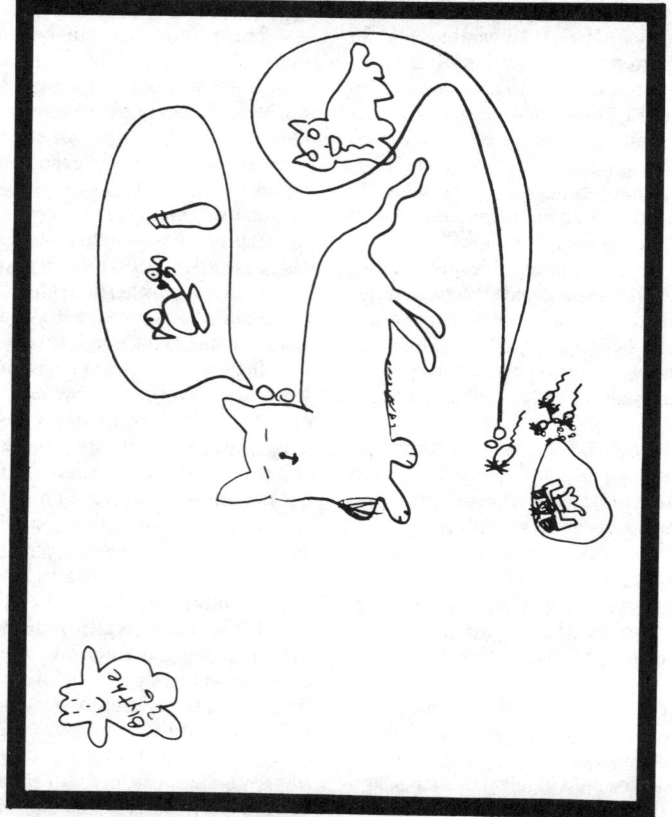

FIGURE 1

First drawing by 8-year-old girl separated from her father as a result of divorce.

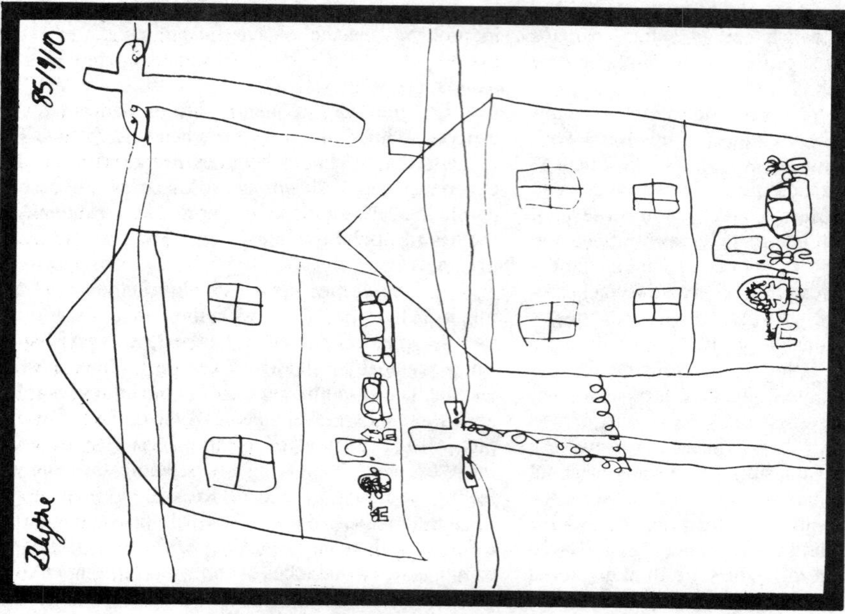

FIGURE 2

Later kinetic family drawing by the same 8-year-old girl who drew Figure 1.

The Microsystem

Therapeutic intervention for parents prior to, during, and following divorce lends support, stabilization, and important insights into the rebuilding of a family unit. The divorce adjustment of parents is positively related to their preparation for the divorce and their emotional distance from their former spouse, the extent of social interaction with family, friends, and other important individuals in their social network, and the establishment of new intimate relationships (Pais & White, 1979; Spanier & Anderson, 1979).

The family should be encouraged to notify school personnel or the school psychologist when separation appears imminent. Schools become a critical linkage system because behavioral changes in children can be identified and school-based services can be initiated. Brief individual, parent, or family therapy can be initiated. Anticipatory guidance meetings are particularly useful for parents before problems become magnified or calcified. Explaining the divorce to the child, issues related to visitation schedules, and concomitant concerns are important topics that could be addressed in anticipatory guidance meetings.

Goldstein and Solnit (1984) have advocated the creation by spouses of visitation plans that would then be submitted to the divorce court. A referral to a divorce mediator or mental health practitioner who specializes in divorce counseling might be appropriate. Issues for mediation and divorce counseling typically involve preparation for economic changes and child custody arrangements. Just as divorce is an ever changing process, mediation often requires a series of renegotiations to adequately meet family members' changing needs. Successful mediation should plan ahead for the family life cycle as children grow and visitation/custody and economic conditions change. For example,what might be an appropriate visitation plan for a 2-year-old boy, 4-hour time periods with his father, might not be in the child's interests in later years as his father becomes more comfortable as a single parent and as the older boy's psychological need for male identification becomes more evident. Ideally, mediation should empower people to conceptualize their own "map of their future" and promote a spirit of collaborative problem solving regarding visitation arrangements.

Optimally, visitation should be individually tailored and include long-range thinking and periodic revisions. Once visitation is established, subtle modifications can be made to avert problems. School psychologists can appropriately guide parents through situations requiring minor adjustments. For instance, arrival and departure periods of visits with the noncustodial parent can be problematic and painful for both parent and child. A suggestion from the school psychologist such as changing the drop-off time and place to a "neutral buffer zone" can minimize the often uncomfortable entry and exit period of visitation while still honoring the legal decree. For example, for weekend visits, noncustodial parents can keep their children on Sunday evening and return them to school the following Monday morning; the children then return to the custodial parent's home after school on Monday afternoon. Two additional ways of reducing the intensity of the pain and sadness of the repeated separation of child and noncustodial parent is for the noncustodial parent to have one of the child's friends over on occasion for planned, structured activities that defuse intense feelings and help to diminish the child's acting-out behavior.

Children often seem emotionally insatiable for the noncustodial parent's attention as a result of the family breakup, and this can be exacerbated by very brief visits. A school psychologist sensitive to the issue of the length of visits might advise extending the visits to help normalize the visitation experience for the child. With the exclusion of infants, all other children seem to respond more favorably to longer visitation periods with their noncustodial parents.

In visitation situations new challenges and responsibilities may arise; parental roles and discipline become more difficult. Mothers may have previously abdicated the disciplinarian role to their spouses and now find themselves in the often uncomfortable position of sole disciplinarian. Likewise, fathers who had taken primarily an authoritarian role with their children may be unfamiliar with the more nurturing stance that is natural to visits with their child(ren). Bedtime and bathtime rituals may now necessitate increased time and attention. The school psychologist can suggest ways to reduce the likelihood of uncomfortable or stressful experiences between parent and child.

Another common custody/visitation concern is the problem of children's divided loyalty to their parents. School psychologists need to advise and guide parents regarding this often problematic issue. Children used as parental weapons, spies, or informers ultimately bring unhappiness to the entire family. Again, these and other related problems can be effectively dealt with in short-term group counseling or couples' groups.

Bibliotherapy for parents, as with children, becomes a helpful aid for those who may be particularly comfortable reading about the process of divorce and visitation and may welcome concrete and tangible advice (see the Annotated Bibliography).

The Exosystem

Tangible services within the community can be used as support for both the custodial and the noncustodial parent. Childcare providers, after-school programs, and volunteer grandparents are three services that are important for children of divorce. Male teachers or older male student "big brothers" can be particularly helpful role models for those boys whose fathers may be unavailable for anything more than infrequent visits.

Divorcing adults may require financial planners and accountants as well as homemaking services to accommodate changing parental roles. Academic and job counseling also becomes imperative for those parents who must return to work or school. The school psychologist should have at hand a list of resources within the community to offer to divorcing parents. Finally bibliography, community libraries, community talks, and workshops are helpful sources of education.

The Macrosystem

Schools can help sensitize society and alleviate the crippling stigma that divorce can impose on families. Information about the divorce process, custody, and visitation issues should be provided through all levels of the educational system. School psychologists are in a unique position to provide workshops to teachers, school counselors, administrators, and parent groups within the community. School psychologists should attempt to identify consultants within the community who might be in a position to periodically provide school systems with organizational development services related to prevention and early management of problems encountered as the result of divorce and visitation arrangements.

School psychologists could also develop a liaison with religious organizations, which often provide support and information to interested parents and families. Libraries also offer an atmosphere for increased knowledge about divorce, and the school psychologist may want to provide the community library with updated lists of recent children's and adult literature on divorce.

SUMMARY

Divorce is a complex sociocultural and psychological phenomenon that brings with it difficult problems when children are part of the divorcing family. Although joint custody is an attractive alternative with great face validity, the majority of children of divorce find themselves in sole custody in connection with one of five access/visitation arrangements. The school psychologist is in a unique position to educate the school system and community about divorce and visitation and its effect on children, reduce the likelihood of visitation-related school learning and behavior problems, and provide strategic psychotherapeutic intervention before visitation-related problems become chronic.

REFERENCES

Benedek, E. P., & Benedek, R. S. (1979). Joint custody: Solution or illusion? *American Journal of Psychiatry, 136,* 1540–1544.

Bronfrenbrenner, U. (1979). *The ecology of human development.* Cambridge, MA: Harvard University Press.

Derdeyn, A. P., & Scott, E. (1984). Joint custody: A critical analysis and appraisal. *American Journal of Orthopsychiatry, 54,* 199–209.

Gardner, R. A. (1982). *Family evaluation in child custody litigation.* Cresskill, NJ: Creative Therapeutics.

Goldstein, J., Freud, A., & Solnit, A. J. (1973). *Beyond the best interests of the child.* New York: Free Press.

Goldstein, S., & Solnit, A. J. (1984). *Divorce and your child.* New Haven: Yale University Press.

Heatherington, E. M. (1979). Divorce: A child's perspective. *American Psychologist, 34,* 851–858.

Hirst, S. R., & Smiley, G. W. (1984). The access dilemma —A study of access patterns following marriage breakdown. *Conciliation Courts Review, 22,* 41–52.

Jacobson, D. (1978). The impact of marital separation/divorce on children: Interparent hostility and child adjustment. *Journal of Divorce, 2,* 3–19.

Kelly, J. B., & Wallerstein, J. S. (1977). Part-time parent, part-time child: Visiting after divorce. *Journal of Child Psychology, 6,* 51–54.

Kurdek, L. A. (1981). An integrative perspective on children's divorce adjustment. *American Psychologist, 36,* 856–866.

Kurdek, L. A. (Ed.) (1983). *Children and divorce: New directions for child development,* (Vol. 19, pp. 26–46). San Francisco: Jossey-Bass.

McDermott, J. F. (1970). Divorce and its psychiatric sequelae in children. *Archives of General Psychiatry, 23,* 421–427.

Pais, J., & White, P. (1979). Family redefinition: A review of the literature toward a model of divorce adjustment. *Journal of Divorce, 2,* 271–282.

Rosen, R. (1977). Children of divorce: What they feel about access and other aspects of the divorce experience. *Journal of Clinical Child Psychology, 6,* 24–27.

Spanier, G. B., & Anderson, E. A. (1979). The impact of the legal system on adjustment to marital separation. *Journal of Marriage and Family, 41,* 605–613.

Wallerstein, J. S. (1983). Separation, divorce, and remarriage. In M. Levine et al. (Eds.), *Developmental behavioral pediatrics* (pp. 241–255). Philadelphia: Saunders.

Warshak, R. A., & Santrock, J. W. (1983). The impact of divorce in father-custody and mother-custody homes: The child's perspective. In E. Callahan & K. McClouskey (Eds.), *Lifespan developmental psychology: Nonnormative life events.* New York: Academic.

BIBLIOGRAPHY: PROFESSIONALS AND PARENTS

Solnit, A., & Goldstein, S. (1984). *Divorce and your child.* New Haven: Yale University Press.
An updated and pragmatic view of divorce that is clearly written, with relevant discussion of child custody, mediation, and access/visitation. The book is essentially a manual for parents, with many useful guidelines that both practitioners and parents can follow.

Wallerstein, J., & Kelly, J. (1980). *Surviving the breakup: How children and parents cope with divorce.* New York: Basic Books.
Written by the foremost authorities on the long-term effects of divorce and access, this knowledgeable book offers in-depth research and clinical information for the practitioner. Of particular relevance is the chapter entitled "The Visiting Parent," which discusses critical topics such as why visits are so hard, what barriers discourage visiting, and what factors contribute to a positive access relationship.

BIBLIOGRAPHY: CHILDREN AND ADOLESCENTS

Gardner, R. A. (1970). *The boys and girls book about divorce.* New York: Bantam Books.
A book specifically for children, written by a well-known child psychiatrist. Dr. Gardner addresses the many, often confusing, feelings that children may experience when their parents divorce. He also provides good, practical advice for many problems that children of divorce encounter, including issues of access/visitation.

Majid, K., & Schreibman, W. (1980). *Divorce is . . . a kid's coloring book.* Gretna, LA: Pelican.
A charming little coloring book that provides the preschool-age and young child with a vehicle for dealing with 25 issues about divorce. Topics that are addressed include feelings, dating, discipline, remarriage, and visitation. The book also includes a brief introductory guide for parents.

Children and Adoption

Candice A. Hughes
Toronto, Canada

BACKGROUND

Adoption is a social service for children who, unable to be reared by their birth parents, are provided a new permanent family. This entails the establishment of a legal relationship with the same mutual rights and obligations that exist between children and their birthparents (Child Welfare League of America, 1973). Although federal data collection on adoption ceased in 1973, the Children's Home Society of California recently estimated that 1 of every 5 people are affected by adoption — as an adopted child (adoptee), adoptive parent (adopter), the birthparent of a child relinquished for adoption, or a relative of any one of these (cited in Melina, 1985).

Historically, this process of family formation began in primitive times. Adoption laws and procedures have evolved in response to societal changes and in recognition of the concerns of those directly involved in the adoption experience (Sorosky, Baran, & Pannor, 1984). Recently, the institution of adoption has undergone significant changes regarding the values and philosophies of adoption professionals, procedures, types of adoptees and adopters, and the behaviors of the adoptive participants (Berman & Bufferd, 1986; Dukette, 1984).

The greatest number of adoptions in the United States occurred during the post–World War II period, peaking with the adoption of 175,000 children in 1970 (Klibanoff & Klibanoff, 1973; National Committee for Adoption, 1985). During this period, meeting the needs of adoptive parents was emphasized by providing them a child that could best substitute for the biological child they could not have (Silverman & Feigelman, 1977). This generally was a healthy, white infant. A secondary emphasis was, by sealing confidential records and severing contact with the birth parents, to allow the child to develop within the new home environment and the birthmother to resume her life (Dukette, 1984).

Since the 1960s, marked changes have occurred in adoption practices; many of these have mirrored larger societal issues and events. In general, these changes in adoption procedures have reflected an increased emphasis on the legal rights and psychological well-being of the child rather than the needs of the birthparents or adoptive parents (Berman & Bufferd, 1986; Dukette, 1984; Silverman & Feigelman, 1977).

Approximately 10–15% of the married couples in the United States are estimated to be unable to conceive; 2 million of these couples are seeking to adopt a child (Kraft et al., 1980; National Committee on Adoption, 1985). The reality they face is a severely limited number of available, healthy, white babies. This is due to birth control advances, legalized abortions, and the fact that although 250,000 children are born out of wedlock annually, the lessened stigma of illegitimacy and the greater availability of social support services have led birthmothers to increasingly reject adoption planning in favor of remaining their child's parent (Berman & Bufferd, 1986; Deyken, Campbell, & Patti, 1984; Folkenberg, 1985; Silverman & Feigelman, 1977). As a result, adoptive parents have become more flexible regarding the types of children they are willing to adopt (Silverman & Feigelman, 1977).

Adoption professionals have become increasingly aware of the negative impact that placement in institutions or a series of foster homes has on the development of children (Berman & Bufferd, 1986). This has led to greater efforts to place children for adoption who are handicapped, older, or of minority backgrounds in nontraditional adoptive settings in which parents may be single, of different racial or cultural backgrounds, with biological children of their own, or foster parents (Coyne & Brown, 1985; Feigelman & Silverman, 1977; Silverman & Feigelman, 1977).

A third key change during this time period has been the public emergence of concerns and feelings about the adoption experience by those involved in it (Berman & Bufferd, 1986). Much of this has centered on the impact on adoptees of their permanent separation from their birthparents and biological heritage (Feigelman & Silverman, 1986; Sorosky et al., 1984). Recognizing the importance of this issue, many adoption agencies have modified their practices to better provide adoptees with nonconfidential information about their biological backgrounds. Such changes have included providing adoptive parents with more comprehensive social, genetic, and medical histories of the birthparents, and the establishment of mutual consent adoption registries in 18 states that allow adult adoptees and birthparents to register with the state or agency in order to obtain identifying information about each other when all parties are in agreement (National Committee for Adoption, 1985).

Additionally, some adoptees have also sought information about their biological backgrounds via legal challenges to sealed adoption records. A few (only 1–2% of all adoptees) actually engage in searches for their birthparents (Dukette, 1984; National Committee for Adoption, 1985; Sorosky et al., 1984).

Various adoption procedures exist for the placement of children in adoptive homes. The most prevalent is the use of an adoption agency, wherein adoption professionals work with birthparents to help them make adoption plans for their child, and with adoptive candidates, to evaluate their parental capabilities and their individual and marital adjustment. Traditionally, adoption agency procedures have been closed, and no contact and very little information was shared between these two sets of parents. Recent publicity about adoptee rights and concerns has led to the establishment of procedures by which an exchange of information occurs between the two sets of parents, within varying degrees of confidentiality (Dukette, 1984; Martin, 1980; Sorich & Siebert, 1982). Alternative procedures are independent or private adoptions in which an intermediary, such as a doctor, lawyer, or minister, helps birthparents find adoptive parents for their children, and legally prohibited black market adoptions, in which birthparents directly sell their baby to adoptive parents for profit (Johnson, 1986; Martin, 1980).

The Adoption Triangle

At the core of any adoption is a triangle composed of the birthparents, the adoptee, and the adoptive parents (Sorosky et al., 1984). Adoption represents both a solution and a dilemma for each of the triangle members (Dukette, 1984; Johnson, 1986). This fact may create the frequent recurrence of strong needs, intense emotions, and unresolved conflicts for each of the participants during the course of the adoption experience.

Birthparents generally are young unwed adolescents who, faced with the dilemma of pregnancy, must decide whether they should make an adoption decision for their child and legally sever any further parental rights (Berman & Bufferd, 1986). However, they may also be older single or married individuals who decide that they cannot remain in a parental role for their child for any of a number of reasons, or they may be deceased. Adoption represents a solution for birthparents, as it assures them that their child will be provided a permanent family. It also is a dilemma as their decision to choose adoption prohibits their future involvement in the development of their child (Deyken et al., 1984; Millen & Roll, 1985).

Adoptive parents generally are infertile couples, relatives of the adoptee, or couples with one or more biological children who wish to enlarge their families. Other categories of adopters include those who are single, older, foster parents, stepparents, handicapped, or homosexual (Martin, 1980; Melina, 1985). Compared to the biological parents of children the same age as the adoptees, adoptive parents, particularly those who are infertile, tend to be older, better-educated, and from higher socioeconomic backgrounds (Bachrach, 1983; Berman & Bufferd, 1986; Klibanoff & Klibanoff, 1973). Adoption provides a child to these parents, yet it also presents the dilemma of how to deal with their adoptee's need for knowledge about their birthparents and heritage.

Adoptees receive through adoption a permanent family, but they lost their direct linkage with their biological heritage. They may either be related to their adoptive parents or not. (The focus of this chapter is on nonrelated adoptions.) There were 141,861 reported adoptions in 1982 in the United States; 91,141 represented related adoptions and 50,720 were nonrelated (National Committee on Adoption, 1985).

It is estimated that approximately 900,000 children currently live with nonrelated adoptive families in the United States (Bachrach, 1983). Previously, the majority of these adoptees were white infants; more recently they have included children who are older, from other races or countries, and from foster or institutional placements, as well as children who are physically, mentally, or emotionally handicapped. During the period 1968–1984, transnational adoptions, the placement of foreign-born children with U.S. citizens, increased from 1,126 to 8,327. Most of these children were from Asia and Latin America (National Committee for Adoption, 1985; Silverman & Feigelman, 1977). Transracial adoptions, whereby children of one racial group are adopted by parents of a different racial background, were unknown prior to the 1960s, but peaked in 1971 with 2,474 such placements and then declined to approximately 831 in 1975 (Silverman & Feigelman, 1977).

School personnel involved with children who are adopted need to know that they must work with and/or understand all members of the adoption triangle, not just the adoptee. They may find themselves working with adoptees who are experiencing problems related to school, with their adoptive families, or with their own personal growth and identity. They most likely will also work with the adoptee's parents and adoptive siblings to help them deal with adoption-related issues. Finally, the birthparents serve as an invisible but significant aspect of any work with adoptees and their families. Additionally, the prevalence of teenage pregnancies may require school personnel to work with adolescent birthparents regarding their decision to relinquish their child for adoption (Folkenberg, 1985; Millen & Roll, 1985).

DEVELOPMENT

Each member of the adoption triangle may face

adoption-related developmental tasks, issues, and conflicts that must be successfully addressed for psychological well-being (Berman & Bufferd, 1986; Deyken et al., 1984). Theoretical perspectives that have been employed in the adoption literature to describe the psychodynamics inherent in the adoption process for these participants include psychoanalytic, ethological, social role, and systems theory (Berman & Bufferd, 1986; Brodzinsky, Schechter, Braff, & Singer, 1984; Kirk, 1964; Wieder, 1978).

Those espousing a psychoanalytic view believe that adoptees may be vulnerable to psychological maladjustment due to doubts surrounding the circumstances of their birth and are more likely to experience identity formation difficulties because they have two, rather than one, set of parents with whom to identify (Katz, 1980; Wieder, 1978). Ethological theorists such as Bowlby (1969) address the relevancy of early child–parent attachment to later child development. Adoptees placed in infancy with affectionate, caring adoptive parents would be at less risk for later psychological problems than those raised by many caretakers in institutions or a series of foster homes with minimal opportunities for the development of adult–child attachments (Brodzinsky, Schechter, & Braff, 1984).

Employing social role theory, Kirk (1964) linked adoptee adjustment problems to the failure of adoptive parents to recognize and accept the special character of their parental status. He argued that this "rejection-of-difference" coping style prohibits effective communication among family members about significant adoption issues. Finally, Berman and Bufferd (1986) have addressed adoption issues from a systems perspective, stressing the importance of the interactive effects among the adoption triangle members regarding the core issue of loss that each has experienced as a result of the adoption experience. Emotional conflicts, ambivalence, and coping difficulties associated with these individual losses can recur for each member during the course of the adoptee's development.

The Adoptee–Developmental Perspective

In general, the primary developmental tasks and cycles for adoptees do not differ from those facing non-adoptees. However, four unique development-related issues that adoptees do experience are (a) the loss of their birthparents, (b) identity formation without a visible biological foundation, (c) loss of a genealogical linkage, and (d) understanding and acceptance of their adoptive status. These issues tend to be present to varying degrees for most adoptees and, if not satisfactorily addressed, may recur at times of stress and loss, may impair their psychological functioning, and may interfere with their ability to establish interpersonal relationships (Berman & Bufferd, 1986; Dukette, 1984; Wieder, 1978).

Some adoptees have difficulty understanding and coping with the loss and unavailability of their birthparents (Berman & Bufferd, 1986). Finding that it is difficult to comprehend why adoption was chosen for them, they might feel abandoned and rejected. They may cope by directing their feelings inwardly as depression, anger, and guilt or outwardly in the form of expressions of anger and rejecting behavior toward their absent birthparents or their adoptive parents. Residual fears of further rejection frequently influence the behavior standards they set for themselves and their parents. They may develop maladaptive coping strategies, such as nonachievement and acting-out behavior, to test whether their adoptive parents will reject them; alternatively, they may become overachievers to guard against this.

All children must establish a self-identity that facilitates their attainment of goal-directed independent functioning in adulthood. A significant aspect of identity formation includes the comparison of oneself with other family members on a number of dimensions, such as physical appearance, personal interests, and special skills and talents. Adoptees are handicapped by the lack of these biological markers and must rely on their emerging competencies and the nurturance and cooperation provided by their adoptive families to establish their identities (Wieder, 1978). Some adoptees experience a strong need to have information about, and even meet, their birthparents before they believe they can accomplish this task (Sorosky et al., 1975, 1984).

Closely related to the issue of identity formation are the genealogical concerns of adoptees, their need for a biological perspective with respect to their past and future (Berman & Bufferd, 1986; Sorosky et al., 1984). These may reflect interest about one's heritage or real concerns and anxieties about medical or mental health actors in their background that may impact on their decision to marry or have children. To address these genealogical concerns, some adoptees develop elaborate family romances about their biological heritage, whereas others actively seek information about, and sometimes contact with, their birthparents or other biological relatives. Adoptees may become involved in a loyalty conflict between the reality of their adoptive parents and the fantasy they have developed about their birthparents, creating a dilemma as to how much they can share these genealogical concern with their adoptive parents, who may perceive this as a threat to their own parental functioning and self-concept (Wieder, 1978).

A primary task for adoptees is to understand and accept the uniqueness of their adoptive status (Dukette, 1984; Wieder, 1978). The degree to which this task is accomplished is significant as it can affect their general development and their interpersonal behavior. Thus, the acceptance by adoptees of their status of adopted child may influence whether a search for birthparents occurs, how others are told of their adoptive status, and whether they meet with success in the formation of social and family relationships (Wieder, 1978).

The critical periods for the successful resolution of these adoptive issues have been identified. Bonding and attachment with adoptive parents in early childhood establishes an atmosphere of trust and communication within families that allows the revelation to adoptees of their adoptive status and permits their need for information about their birthparents and heritage to be addressed openly and cooperatively by all members of the family.

During latency and the preadolescent years, adoptees develop an understanding of their adoptive status and what it implies, birth socially and legally; this understanding follows social cognition developmental patterns (Brodzinsky, 1984; Brodzinsky, Singer, & Braff, 1984). Whereas very young children may not be able to differentiate adoption from birth as a means of family formation, preadolescents are very aware of the difference and what it entails but do not realize that there is a legal basis that makes adoption permanent. As a result, children at this age may become overly concerned about the tenuousness of their family situations, experience threatening fantasies in which they are reclaimed by birthparents or rejected by their adoptive parents, and exhibit behavior that tests the permanency of their family relationships (Brodzinsky, 1984).

Adolescence has been identified as the period of greatest stress and vulnerability for adoptees (Berman & Bufferd, 1986; Mackie, 1982; Pannor & Nerlove, 1977; Sorosky et al., 1974, 1984), particularly for the primary development tasks of this age — identity formation and separation from one's parents. Unresolved issues related to their birthparents' decision of adoption for them and their acceptance of their adoptive status, as well as the quality of the relationship they have with their adoptive parents, can significantly affect the outcome of this stage. Problems that may occur at this stage include excessive fantasies about the birthparents or behavioral identification with them and rejection of the adoptive parents. This is exacerbated when adoptive parents make insinuating remarks about their birthparents. Adoptees who have developed a strong vicarious identification with missing parents may duplicate the negative characteristics of their birthparents that have been communicated to them, which may result in pregnancy or acting-out behavior. Some adoptees become obsessed with the need to acquire details about their heritage, sometimes even deciding to search for their missing parents. Unsuccessful resolution of these issues during adolescence may lead to alienation from the adoptive family and the lack of an integrated self-identity.

Atypical adoptees — transracial, transnational, older, and handicapped children, as well as foster children and stepchildren — face developmental issues related to their unique adoptive status (Wieder, 1978). Transracial and transnational adoptees need to establish their individual identities and satisfy their genealogical concerns despite marked physical dissimilarities with their adoptive parents and the fact that they are reared in cultures that differ significantly from their own biological heritage (Katz, 1974; Morin, 1977; Silverman & Feigelman, 1981). Older adoptees, placed in adoptive homes beyond their infancy, and foster children who have been placed over time with more than one caretaker, may experience problems in attachment with adoptive parents and the development of other relationships. Some of these children enter the adoptive situation with poor self-concepts and maladaptive coping mechanisms because of negative experiences with their previous placements (Katz, 1980). Handicapped children must not only cope with the developmental tasks related to adoption but also those related to their handicapping conditions (Coyne & Brown, 1985). Finally, adopted stepchildren may need to cope with issues of abandonment and rejection regarding the fact that a birthparent with whom they had a previous relationship has legally severed the ties between them (Melina, 1968a).

Adoptive Parents & Families — Developmental Perspective

As with biological parents, adoptive parents must, and do, provide parenting behaviors that allow the healthy development of their children (Marquis & Detweiler, 1985). However, the particular psychological tasks that many adoptive parents face are (a) resolution of emotional conflicts associated with their infertility, (b) acceptance of adoption as their form of family formation, (c) accepting and constructively incorporating into their parenting behavior the existence of their child's birthparents, and (d) deciding how and when to share the fact of the adoptive status of their child with others (Berman & Bufferd, (1986; Kirk, 1964; Klibanoff & Klibanoff, 1973; Kraft et al., 1980). Adoptive parents' inability to resolve these issues may compromise their parenting skills and the development of a constructive relationship with their adopted children. The emotions and conflicts these tasks arouse may reemerge during the developmental cycles of both adoptees and their parents as well as at times of unnatural stress and vulnerability.

To many adoptive parents, infertility represents the loss of the opportunity to have a biological child (Berman & Bufferd, 1986). Most couples respond to their infertility with a series of emotional reactions, including an initial denial of their condition, subsequent anger, and hopefully a subsequent acceptance of their condition and the need to seek alternative means of family formation (Kraft et al., 1980). Many of the procedures of the adoption process serve as painful reminders of their infertility. Their inability to conceive reemerges as an issue with their adoptee's sexual development (Berman & Bufferd, 1986). For example, adoptees' attainment of puberty and subsequent childbearing reinforce for adoptive parents that they were deprived of a significant life experience and the loss of a future genealogical perspective for themselves. Adoptive parents who have resolved the emotional conflict associated with their infertility have been found to have more effective parenting skills than those who have not (Kraft et al., 1980).

Kirk (1964) identified the process of becoming parents as more difficult for adopters than for biological parents. He emphasized that unless adoptive parents recognize and accept the difference of this method of family formation, they will tend to use denial when dealing with the issues that they and their adopted child will experience. Rather than seeking biological linkages with their children, such as similarities in physical appearance or intelligence, adoptive parents must work to develop relationships with their children that are built on trust and communication. Thus, successful adoptive parents tend to hold an environmental perspective that their nurturance will contribute to the adoptee's development more than the genetic factors that the child brings to the adoptive situation (L. R. Melina, personal communication, May 2, 1986).

Adoptive parents must deal with the reality of the birthparents throughout their adoptee's development, particularly since many of the unique issues of adoptees center on their biological background (Berman & Bufferd, 1986; Pannor & Nerlove, 1977). Adoptive parents' attitudes and feelings about the birthparents will influence their parenting behavior and the way they perceive and help their children understand and accept both their biological heritage and their adoptive status (Katz, 1980). Thus, they must decide when and what to reveal to adoptees about their adoptive status and be ready to respond to questions that adoptees may raise regarding their birthparents, particularly the adoption decision. When genealogical and identity formation issues become paramount for the adoptee, the adoptive parents may fear that they will lose the love and relationship they have with a child who is seeking resolution of these issues (Mackie, 1982). Parents who participate in, rather than resist, these activities by their children are less likely to experience mutual alienation and rejection at this time.

Adoptive parents must also decide when to inform others, such as nuclear and extended family members, neighbors, and school personnel, that their child is adopted. They must also decide how much they should share about their child's biological background, and how to respond to innocent, but painful remarks and questions conveyed by others to either themselves or their adopted child (Johnson, 1986; Klibanoff & Klibanoff, 1973).

Atypical adoptive parents may experience unique issues, tasks, and problems regarding the adoption process. Single adoptive parents may lack both nuclear and extended family supports to help them cope with the development of their children (Feigelman & Silverman, 1977). Foster parents, particularly those uncertain about adopting their child, may avoid developing a strong relationship with the child (Melina, 1986b). Those who have adopted children of different races and cultures may have to cope with physical differences as well as external sources of prejudice directed toward their family (Katz, 1974; Silverman & Feigelman, 1981). Finally, adopters who already have biological children and those who adopt older children must strive to ease the entry and establishment of the child into existing family structures (Borgman, 1982; Katz, 1977).

Birthparents — Developmental Perspective

Traditional adoptive practices assumed that choosing adoption for a child would enable birthparents to resume their life with limited residual emotional difficulties. However, limited research on this topic has revealed that some birthparents experience a period of bereavement over the loss of their child, guilt for their adoption decision, and anxiety and concern about their child's development (Deykin et al., 1984; Giaccardo, 1986; Millen & Roll, 1985; Sorosky et al., 1984). Resolution of these issues influences the future course of their development in life as well as their reactions if their child seeks to initiate a meeting with them upon reaching adulthood.

Adoption Problems and Failures

Problems in and failure of an adoption experience can be an emotionally wrenching process for all members of the adoption triangle, particularly the adoptee and the adoptive parents (Rooney, 1979). Neither the prevalence of problematic adoptive situations nor the frequency of adoptees' referrals for mental health services has been conclusively established in the adoption research literature (Brodzinsky, Schechter, Braff, & Singer, 1984). However, concern about the high rate of adoption failures with certain types of adoptees has led to recent efforts to modify adoption practices so as to enhance the probability of successful adoption (Coyne & Brown, 1985; Zwimpfer, 1983).

Unaddressed or unresolved adoption-related developmental tasks may precipitate the development of emotional or learning problems in adoptees or the breakdown of an adoption experience for an entire family. Stress factors within the adoptive situation such as illness, death, divorce, addictive behavior, or the birth of a handicapped sibling may make adoptive families particularly vulnerable to failure. Finally, demographic and personal characteristics of adoptees and adopters may contribute to adoption-related problems (Zwimpfer, 1983).

PUTTING ADOPTION IN PERSPECTIVE

Adoption Research

Adoption has been investigated along several lines of inquiry (Marion & Hayes, 1975). These have included demographic studies of the adoptive participants (Bachrach, 1983), postadoption longitudinal studies (Jaffe & Fanshel, 1970; Lahti, 1982), and comparative studies of adopted and nonadopted children regarding variables such as achievement (Bridgewater, 1984), emotional and academic adjustment (Brodzinsky, Schechter, Braff, & Singer, 1984; Marquis & Detweiler, 1985; Silver, 1970),and differences in understanding of the concept of adoption (Brodzinsky, Singer, & Braff, 1984).

Much of the research on adoption has focused on genetic versus environmental issues, or the degree of similarity between adopted children and their biological and adoptive families (parents, siblings) on a number of traits (Bohman, 1981; Melina, 1986c, 1986d, 1986e). Those that have been investigated include (a) intelligence (Baker, DeFries, & Fulker, 1983; Horn, 1983; Munsinger, 1975; Scarr & Weinberg, 1983), (b) personality traits and disturbances (Loehlin, Willerman, & Horn, 1982, 1985; Scarr, Webber, Weinberg, & Wittig, 1983), (c) vocational interests and choices (Grotevant, 1979; Grotevant, Scarr, & Weinberg, 1977), and (d) crime (Mednick, 1985).

Recently, the focus of adoption research has expanded to investigate changing procedures (Borgman, 1982), problematic adoptions (Coyne & Brown, 1985; Zwimpfer, 1983), and atypical adoption situations such as those with transracial and transnational adoptees (Joe, 1978; Silverman & Feigelman, 1981), single-parent adopters (Feigelman & Silverman, 1977), and foster parent adopters (Melina, 1986b; Meezan & Shireman, 1985). The effects of sealed records, meetings of adoptees and birthparents, and the emotional experiences of adoptive participants have also been studied (Feigelman & Silverman, 1986; Sorosky et al., 1984).

Several conclusions can be derived from this research that are relevant to school personnel working with adoptive situations. The first is that genetic influences have been verified in the comparative studies of adoptees with their biological and adoptive families on most of the variables measured (Melina, 1986c, 1986d, 1986e). Thus, data for adoptees have been found to be more highly correlated with data for biological parents than adoptive parents on factors such as intelligence, personality, temperament, interests, and a criminal tendency (Grotevant, 1979; Loehlin, Willerman, & Horn, 1982, 1985; Mednick, 1985; Munsinger, 1975). However, this conclusion must be interpreted cautiously, as correlations between adoptees and their biological families on measured traits have been small to moderate, suggesting the presence of other mediating variables between the genetic and environmental influences. It has been suggested that adoptive environments serve to optimize adoptees' genetic potential developmentally. Thus, many adoptees develop better in their adoptive home environment than they would have in their biological environment, particularly if the intelligence, achievement, or behavior standards were low or substantially different in the latter (Melina, 1986c, 1986d, 1986e).

Several researchers (e.g., Eiduson & Livermore, 1953; Silver, 1970; Taichert & Harvin, 1975) have reported that adoptees do not perform as well as non-adopted children in areas of academic achievement or emotional adjustment (cited in Brodzinsky, Schechter, Braff, & Singer, 1984). This research has been criticized for its predominant use of clinical populations, namely, children referred for mental health services. The limited research with nonclinical adoptee populations suggests that they may have a higher risk than nonadoptees for the development of academic or emotional difficulties, yet as a whole they tend to fall well within the mainstream in behavior and performance (Bridgewater, 1984; Brodzinsky, Schechter, Braff, & Singer, 1984; Marquis & Detweiler, 1985). Thus, some adoptees may be more fearful or more active than other children but not to the extent that they are phobic or hyperactive.

A child's age at the time of placement for adoption has emerged as a key variable regarding successful adoptive experience in research investigating single-parent adopters, transracial adoption, and hard-to-place children (Feigelman & Silverman, 1977; Katz, 1980; Silverman & Feigelman, 1977, 1981). The implications for this are straightforward. Adoption personnel should strive to place children for adoption at the earliest age possible, particularly when atypical factors are present in the adoptive situation. School personnel should also attend to the significance of this age factor in their assessment and intervention work with adoptees and their families, as some older adoptees may come to their new family and school situations with minimal socialization or academic skills and with residual effects of earlier emotional trauma or abuse.

A final research conclusion relates to the necessity of carefully considering the adoptive parents' and the adoptees' tolerance for stress and degree of vulnerability when placing children for adoption. Zwimpfer's research (1983) of demographic factors associated with adoption breakdown, and Feigelman and Silverman's research on atypical adoptive situations (single-parent adopters; transracial and hard-to-place adoptees) indicate that vulnerable children have been placed too often with equally vulnerable parents or families, thereby precipitating adoption problems and failures. School personnel working with dysfunctional adoptees or their families should carefully attend to their characteristics and try to help them to develop functional coping skills for their adoptive situations. For example, adoptive parents should be helped to apply generally approved parenting skills, such as consistent discipline and listening skills, with their children.

School-Related Adoption Issues

Despite the plethora of adoption research, there has been limited attention to the problems that adoptees and their families experience regarding school. Also absent are studies of adoptive parents' expectations regarding their children's academic performance in school. Several school-related problems can be identified that may be experienced by members of the adoption triangle.

One problem for adoptees is the assignment of tasks that they cannot complete owing to their adoptive status, such as the development of a family tree. Adoptees most likely will experience emotional reactions to this task and have difficulty deciding how or whether to complete it. Advising them on alternative ways to complete such tasks can be very helpful.

Another challenge is the attention adoptees may receive about their adoptive status from other children and adults in the school. This might consist of benign, but recurrent references to them as "adopted" by staff members, teasing and scapegoating behavior by their peers, or various forms of adoption-focused prejudice and rejection, particularly if they are a racial or cultural minority group member. Recurrent adoption-focused attention may affect adoptees' self-concept and personal coping skills. Thus, they must learn how to assertively communicate to others that such attention makes them uncomfortable.

Parents and adopters, and sometimes birthparents, must also determine when it is appropriate to disclose adoption information to others in the school. They must decide the appropriate occasions and content of such sharing as well as the appropriate recipient of this information. Adoptees need to learn how much self-disclosure is appropriate with peers and teachers. Those who share too much or too frequently may be perceived as attention-seeking. Those who never report their adoptive status in situations when doing so may be advantageous, such as upon assignment of schoolwork requiring genealogical information, also need to help with this issue. Adoptive parents need to ascertain the possible influence of shared adoption information on teachers' expectations, attitudes, and behavior regarding their child. Adolescent birthparents who have chosen adoption for their child and are still attending school may exhibit learning and behavior problems linked to their unresolved emotions about this decision. If the severity of their problems warrant counseling, disciplinary action, or even referral to special services personnel for evaluation, they must decide how much they will disclose about the decision they made.

A fourth issue relates to the attitudes, stereotypes, expectations, and attributions of school personnel about adoption, with which adoptees and their parents must contend. Adoptees and adoptive parents need to identify instances of staff negativism regarding adoption and learn to communicate their reactions to this as well as help these adults view adoption more positively.

Finally, the expectations and behavior of adoptive parents regarding their children's school performance and behavior may emerge as an issue. Adoptive parents often strive to be perfect parents and to maintain standards regarding the development of their child that are more appropriate to the nurture than the nature component of the adoption (Berman & Bufferd, 1986; Pannor & Nerlove, 1977). These parental traits may become problemsome if they result in overexpectations for the child or denial of any problems that occur.

ALTERNATIVE ACTIONS

The unique developmental issues and tasks and potential problems of members of an adoption triangle suggest the advisability of a prevention-oriented consultative approach to working with adoptive participants in school settings (Caplan, 1964; Katz, 1980). The primary, secondary, and tertiary levels of prevention delineated by Caplan (1964) can be provided within the four-level framework of school consultation services proposed by Meyers (1973): (a) direct service to the child, (b) indirect service to the child, (c) service to the teacher (parent), and (d) service to the organization.

Primary Prevention Activities

The purpose of primary prevention is to reduce the occurrence of disorders in a given population (Caplan, 1964). Related to adoption, this would constitute prevention work to avoid the emergence of adoption problems that might arise from unsatisfactory resolution of the predictable developmental issues and tasks that have been identified for adoption triangle members. Directed to those immediately touched by adoption, and to the adults and children in the school, the goals of primary prevention adoption work would include (a) the elimination of negative experiences and interactions with others that may cumulatively affect the psychological well-being of persons involved in adoption, (b) increased awareness, knowledge, and understanding by others in the school about adoption, and (c) expanded knowledge of resources, support systems, and action alternatives for persons involved in adoption.

Special services personnel might best facilitate this level of prevention by providing consultative services to the larger school organization about adoption. One effort could be in-service sessions for teachers to expand their knowledge about and attitudes toward this matter, and to alert them to the implications of certain behaviors, such as the language they use about and to those involved in adoption. For example, a phrase such as "chosen child" can imply a behavioral standard that adoptees feel they must always strive to achieve (Klibanoff & Klibanoff, 1973). The inclusion of a unit on adoption in the social studies, home economics, or sex education curriculum of the school system can help students learn that this is an alternative, positive method of family formation (Social Science Education Consortium, 1980). Larger societal issues such as change in family structures due to divorce and single parenting can be utilized to make this topic more relevant to children. A final organizational preventive approach would be the inclusion of fiction and nonfiction books in school libraries that are related to adoption and would serve to make this concept more familiar and acceptable to schoolchildren.

Support groups can be established within the school system if there are enough adoptive parents, adoptees, or birthparents to warrant this. Such groups would have an educational focus of helping the participants prepare for the adoptive developmental issues and tasks they will most likely encounter (Cordell, Nathan, & Krymow, 1985; Pannor & Nerlove, 1977). These groups might be limited to only one leg of the adoptive triangle or they may be mixed groups to provide a sharing of concerns and information between the various participants in adoption.

Parents, adoptees, and birthparents can also be encouraged to join the local and national adoptive organizations that exist to provide them with information and social support services. The North American Council on Adoptable Children and the National Committee for Adoption are two of the largest national organizations.

Secondary Prevention

The goal of secondary prevention is to reduce the duration of the occurrence of a disorder in a population (Caplan, 1964). This would apply to adoptive participants who exhibit maladaptive behaviors that may evolve into a permanent handicap if unaddressed. Immediate goals of this prevention effort would be to increase the coping skills of the adoptive families and to reduce their presenting problems. Inappropriate behavior in a new adoptive family of an older adoptee with a history of previous placement failures or unexpected stresses upon a marginally functional adoptive family (death, trauma) may require secondary prevention work. Consultative efforts might be directed to helping a teacher improve the socialization skills of an older adoptee in the school or to helping adoptive parents maintain or improve their parenting skills during times of stress.

Consultative efforts might also be directed to teachers if their lack of knowledge, skills, or objectivity about adoption are contributing to an adoptee's school difficulties. Teachers might be encouraged to review their past experiences with adoption to help them understand and alter their behavior and expectations regarding adoption.

Tertiary Prevention

Tertiary preventive work is directed toward reducing impaired functioning created by certain disorders within a population (Caplan, 1964). In the case of adoption, this may relate to work with families or individual adoptees who are experiencing significant emotional or academic difficulties. Special services personnel would most likely engage in consultation efforts that constitute direct services to the client, through assessment and therapeutic activities.

Decisions to refer, assess, and perhaps classify an adoptee as educationally handicapped should be carefully made only after all prereferral intervention efforts have been exhausted. The developmental tasks and issues of both typical and atypical adoptees and their families should be considered in all such decision making. For example, the assessment of a recently placed older adoptee might yield a significant ability–achievement disparity that reflects the child's early history of deprivation and the fact that the child's energies are being currently expended on adjusting to a new environment rather than on academic behavior; such a finding would negate the existence of a true handicapping condition. Alternatively, the child might appear emotionally disturbed because of poor social skills or maladaptive coping skills that have been situationally created. Interventions that help older adoptees adapt to new settings and address their developmental gaps should be tried before any referrals for assessment.

Therapeutic counseling services may be determined to be appropriate for the adoptive family members regarding school-related issues. For example, school mental health professionals may find it necessary to work with adoptees and their families on issues such as discrepancies between parental expectations and adoptee performance or adoptee truancy that are directly linked to their adoptive history. Specific therapeutic treatment issues unique to adoption, such as the interactive effects of each adoptive member's sense of loss, adoptive parenting fears, or some adoptees' preoccupation with their biological heritage, should be addressed in these sessions (Berman & Bufferd, 1978; Pannor & Nerlove, 1977). School personnel must, when providing these services, remember that adoption-related dilemmas arise in the context of general development and family functioning; thus, the unique issues that adoption may present should always be integrated and interpreted within this context in any therapeutic situation. Finally, the existing services of adoption agencies for adoptive families should be recommended whenever referral for mental health services outside the school system appears necessary.

SUMMARY

School personnel involved with adopted children must recognize that any adoption experience entails a triangle composed of three groups of participants, the adoptee, the birthparents, and the adoptive parents. It is important to recognize that each of these participants may serve as critical influences in their work with a given adopted child. Research has identified unique developmental issues and tasks facing participants in adoption that must be resolved for their psychological well-being. Failure to do so may result in problemsome experiences or failure of adoption. It is suggested that a prevention-oriented focus, employing a consultation framework, be utilized in work with adoptive participants.

REFERENCES

Bachrach, C. A. (1983). Adoption as a means of family formation: Data from the National Survey of Family Growth. *Journal of Marriage and Family, 45,* 859–865.

Baker, L. A., DeFries, J. C., & Fulker, D. W. (1983). Longitudinal stability of cognitive ability in the Colorado Adoption Project. *Child Development, 54,* 290–297.

Berman, L. C., & Bufferd, R. K. (1986). Family treatment to address loss in adoptive families. *Social Casework, 67,* 3–11.

Bohman, M. (1981). The interaction of heredity and childhood environment: Some adoption studies. *Journal of Child Psychology and Psychiatry, 22,* 195–200.

Borgman, R. 91982). The consequences of open and closed adoption for older children. *Child Welfare, 61,* 217–226.

Bowlby, J. (1969). *Attachment and loss. Vol. I: Attachment.* New York: Basic Books.

Bridgewater, C. A. (1984). Adoptees' lesser achievements. *Psychology Today, 18,* 12.

Brodzinsky, D. M. (1984). New perspectives on adoption revelation. *Early Child Development and Care, 18,* 105–118.

Brodzinsky, D. M., Schechter, D. E., Braff, A. M., & Singer, L. M. (1984). Psychological and academic adjustment in adopted children. *Journal of Consulting and Clinical Psychology, 52,* 582–590.

Brodzinsky, D. M., Singer, L. M., & Braff, A. M. (1984). Children's understanding of adoption. *Child Development, 55,* 869–878.

Caplan, G. (1964). *Principles of preventive psychiatry.* New York: Basic Books.

Child Welfare League of America. (1973). *Standards for adoption service: Revised* (rev. ed.). New York: Child Welfare League of America.

Cordell, A. S., Nathan, C., & Krymow, V. P. (1985). Group counseling for children adopted at older ages. *Child Welfare, 64,* 113-123.

Coyne, A., & Brown, M. E. (1985). Developmentally disabled children can be adopted. *Child Welfare, 64,* 607–615.

Deyken, E. Y., Campbell, L., & Patti, P. (1984). The postadoption experience of surrendering parents. *American Journal of Orthopsychiatry, 54,* 271–280,

Dukette, R. (1984). Value issues in present-day adoptions. *Child Welfare, 63,* 233-243.

Feigelman, W., & Silverman, A. R. (1977). Single parent adoptions. *Social Casework, 58,* 418–425.

Feigelman, W., & Silverman, A. R. (1986). Adoptive parents, adolescents, and the sealed record controversy. *Social Casework, 67,* 219–226.

Folkenberg, J. (1985). Teen pregnancy: Who opts for adoption? *Psychology Today, 19,* 16.

Giaccardo, D. (1986). Giving up your baby can be the right thing to do — but that doesn't make it easy. *People Weekly, 25,* 86–88.

Grotevant, H. D. (1979). Environmental influences on vocational interest development in adolescents from adoptive and biological families. *Child Development, 50,* 854–860.

Grotevant, H. D., Scarr, S., & Weinberg, R. A. (1977). Patterns of interest similarity in adoptive and biological families. *Journal of Personality and Social Psychology, 35,* 667–679.

Horn, J. M. (1983). The Texas Adoption Project: Adopted children and their intellectual resemblance to biological and adoptive parents. *Child Development, 54,* 268–275.

Jaffe, B., & Fanshel, D. (1970). *How they fared in adoption: A follow-up study.* New York: Columbia University Press.

Joe, B. (1978). In defense of intercountry adoption. *Social Service Review, 52,* 1–19.

Johnson, B. (1986). Mr. Stork delivers. *People Weekly, 25,* 78–85.

Katz, L. 91974). Transracial adoption: Some guidelines. *Child Welfare, 53,* 180–187.

Katz, L. (1977). Older child adoptive placements: A time of family crisis. *Child Welfare, 56,* 165–171.

Katz, L. (1980). Adoption counseling as a preventive mental health specialty. *Child Welfare, 59,* 161–167.

Kirk, H. D. (1964). *Shared fate: A theory of adoption and mental health.* New York: Free Press.

Klibanoff, S., & Klibanoff, E. (1973). *Let's talk about adoption.* Boston: Little, Brown.

Kraft, A. D., Palombo, J., Mitchell, D., Dean, C., Meyers, S., & Schmidt, A. W. (1980). The psychological dimensions of infertility. *American Journal of Orthopsychiatry, 50,* 618 –628.

Lahti, L. (1982). Follow-up study of foster children in permanent placements. *Social Service Review, 56,* 556–571.

Loehlin, J. C., Willerman, L., & Horn, J. M. (1982). Personality resemblances between unwed mothers and their adopted-away offspring. *Journal of Personality and Social Psychology, 42,* 1089–1099.

Loehlin, J. C., Willerman, L., & Horn, J. M. (1985). Personality resemblances in adoptive families when the children are late-adolescent or adult. *Journal of Personality and Social Psychology, 48,* 376–392.

Mackie, A. J. (1982). Families of adopted adolescents. *Journal of Adolescence, 5,* 167–178.

Marion, T. S., & Hayes, A. (1975). An updated cross-cultural literature review on adoption: Implications for future interventions. JSAS: *Catalog of Selected Documents in Psychology, 5,* 332. (MS No. 1106)

Marquis, K. S., & Detweiler, R. A. (1985). Does adopted mean different? An attributional analysis. *Journal of Personality and Social Psychology, 48,* 1054–1106.

Martin, C. (1980). *Beating the adoption game.* La Jolla, CA: Oak Tree.

Mednick, S. (1985). Crime in the family tree. *Psychology Today, 19,* 58–61.

Meezan, W., & Shireman, J. F. (1985). *Care and commitment: Foster parent adoption decisions.* New York: State University of New York Press.

Melina, L. R. (1985). Journalists give guidelines on adoption. *Adopted Child, 4*(12), 1–3.

Melina, L. R. (1986a). Caution urged in adopting stepchild. *Adopted Child, 5*(1), 1–4.

Melina, L. R. (1986b). Some foster parents expect to adopt. *Adopted Child, 5*(4), 1–3.

Melina, R. (1986c). Vocational interests influenced by adoption. *Adopted Child, 5*(5), 1.

Melina, L. (1986d). Biology plays significant role in intelligence. *Adopted Child, 5*(5), 2.

Melina, L. (1986e). Child's personality unlikely to resemble parents'. *Adopted Child, 5*(5), 3–4.

Meyers, J. (1973). A consultation model for school psychological services. *Journal of School Psychology, 11,* 5–15.

Millen, L., & Roll, S. (1985). Solomon's mothers: A special case of pathological bereavement. *American Journal of Orthopsychiatry, 55,* 411–418.

Morin, R. J. (1977). Black child, white parents: A beginning biography. *Child Welfare, 56,* 576–583.

Munsinger, H. (1975). The adopted child's IQ: A critical review. *Psychological Bulletin, 82,* 623–659.

National Committee on Adoption. (1985). *Adoption factbook: United States data: Issues, Regulations, and Resources.* Washington, DC: National Committee on Adoption.

Pannor, R., Baran, A., & Sorosky, A. D. (1978). Birth parents who relinquished babies for adoption revisited. *Family Process, 17,* 329–337.

Pannor, R., & Nerlove, E. A. (1977). Fostering understanding between adolescents and adoptive parents through group experiences. *Child Welfare, 56,* 537–545.

Rooney, R. (1979, March 4). When child adoption doesn't work. *Parade, 23,* 29.

Scarr, S., Webber, P. L., Weinberg, R. A., & Wittig, M. A. (1981). Personality resemblance among adolescents and their parents in biologically related and adoptive families. *Journal of Personality and Social Psychology, 40,* 885–898.

Scarr, S., & Weinberg, R. A. (1983). The Minnesota adoption studies: Genetic differences and malleability. *Child Development, 54,* 260–267.

Silver, L. B. (1970). Frequency of adoption in children with the neurological learning disability syndrome. *Journal of Learning Disabilities, 3,* 306–310.

Silverman, A. R. & Feigelman, W. (1977). Some factors affecting the adoption of minority children. *Social Casework, 58,* 554--561.

Silverman, A. R., & Feigelman, W. (1981). The adjustment of black children adopted by white families. *Social Casework, 62,* 529–536.

Social Science Education Consortium. (1980). *Adoption builds families.* Boulder, CO: Author. (855 Broadway, Boulder, CO 80302)

Sorich, C. J., & Siebert, R. (1982). Toward humanizing adoption. *Child Welfare, 61,* 207–216.

Sorosky, A. D., Baran, A., & Pannor, R. (1975). Identity conflicts in adoptees. *American Journal of Orthopsychiatry, 45,* 12–27.

Sorosky, A. D., Baran, A., & Pannor, R. (1984). *The adoption triangle: Sealed or open records: How they affect adoptees, birth parents, and adoptive parents.* (2nd ed.). New York: Anchor Press/Doubleday.

Wieder, H. (1978). Special problems in the psychoanalysis of adopted children. In J. Glenn (Ed.), *Child analysis and therapy* (pp. 557–577). New York: Jason Aronson.

Zwimpfer, D. M. (1983). Indicators of adoption breakdown. *Social Casework, 64,* 169–177.

BIBLIOGRAPHY: PROFESSIONALS

Feigelman, W., & Silverman, A. S. (1983). *Chosen children: New patterns of adoptive relationships.* New York: Praeger.
Presents the authors' research on current adoption issues, including the adjustment of adoptees, the importance of support to adoptive parents, transracial and intercountry adoptions, and single-parent adoptions.

Jewett, C. L. (1982). *Helping children cope with separation and loss.* Harvard, MA: Harvard Common Press.
Focuses on the feelings of grieving children, including those who are adopted, and describes ways to help children resolve their losses.

Kirk, H. D. (1984). *Shared fate: A theory and method of adoptive relationships* (rev. ed.) and Kirk, H. D. (1985). *Adoptive kinship: A modern institution in need of reform* (rev. ed.). Brentwood Bay, BC: Ben-Simon Publications. (P.O. Box 318, Brentwood Bay, BC, Canada VOS 1AO)
These books describe the unique psychosocial and legal relationships that exist in adoptive families.

Social Science Education Consortium. (1980). *Adoption builds families.* Boulder, CO: Author.
This three-level curriculum project developed for use in social studies or home economics has kits with activities and books. The first level, "Family Development," geared for primary grade levels, costs $24.95. The second level, "Decisions About Self and The Family," geared to high school students, costs $32.95 for the kit; a resource book, "Readings on Adoption," is available for $1.50. The third level, "Understanding Adoption: Resources and Activities for Teaching Adults About Adoption," is useful for teacher in-service, parent groups,and adult education; the cost of this kit is $14.95. (Address: 855 Broadway, Boulder, CO 80302)

Sorosky, A. D., Baran, A., & Pannor, R. (1984). *The adoption triangle: Sealed or open records: How they affect adoptees, birth parents, and adoptive parents* (2nd ed.). Garden City, NY: Anchor Press/Doubleday.
Presents the authors' research on issues regarding sealed adoption records for participants in adoption. It provides very thoughtful insights into the effect of adoption on adoptees, adoptive parents, and birthparents.

BIBLIOGRAPHY: PARENTS

Johnson, P. I. (1983). *Perspectives on a grafted tree: Thoughts of those touched by adoption.* Fort Wayne, IN: Perspectives Press.
A collection of poetry by and for those who have been involved with adoption. The content addresses the differing aspects of the adoption process. Written to provide an understanding of the feelings adoption triangle members experience, it is useful to share with adoptees as they develop.

Melina, L. R. (Editor & Publisher). *The Adopted Child.*
This is a monthly newsletter that addresses unique and different situations that develop for families formed by adoption. It contains adoption-focused advice, book reviews, and reports on research. (Order from: Lois Melina, P.O. Box 9362, Moscow, ID 83843)

Melina, L. R. (1986). *Raising adopted children.* New York: Harper and Row.
A sourcebook of information and advice about adoption-related issues that parents may experience with their children. The author has drawn from her own experiences as an adoptive mother and from the recent adoption research in the child development, psychology, sociology, and medical literature.

RESOURCES

North American Council on Adoptable Children, P.O. Box 14808, Minneapolis, MN 55414.
This is a nonprofit organization that advocates the adoption of children with special needs. It is a good source to contact for information about other adoptive parent support groups in the United States and Canada.

The National Committee on Adoption, 2025 M St., NW, Suite 512, Washington, DC 20036.
This is an umbrella organization of adoption agencies that lobbies on adoption issues, serves as an information clearinghouse, and provides an Adoption Hotline in the Washington, DC area (202-463-7563).

Post Adoption Center for Education and Research (PACER), 477 Fifteenth St., Room 200, Oakland, CA 94612.
This organization provides educational sessions and publishes information about the adoption experiences of adoptees, birthparents, and adoptive parents.

BIBLIOGRAPHY: CHILDREN

Cochran-Smith, M. (1984). *What is real? An adoptive parents' guide to children's books.* (Available from Linda Ritter, R.D. 22000, Mohnton, PA 19450)
This is a list of fiction and nonfiction children's books dealing with adoption.

Krementz, J. (1982). *How it feels to be adopted.* New York: Knopf.
This book written for adolescents, profiles 19 children, aged 8–16 years, who describe their feelings about adoption. It allows adoptees to learn that their feelings and experiences are not unusual.

Livingston, C. (1978). *Why was I adopted?* Secaucus, NJ: Lyle Stuart.
This book covers many of the reasons children are placed for adoption.

Powledge, F. (1982). *So you're adopted.* New York: Scribner's.
This book is about adolescent adoption issues.

Rosenberg, M. B. (1984). *Being adopted.* New York: Lothrup, Lee & Shepard.
This book profiles three preteen children who are racially or culturally different from members of their adoptive families.

Children and Aggressive Behavior

Leland Zlomke
Beatrice State Developmental Center, Nebraska

Wayne C. Piersel
The University of Nebraska–Lincoln

BACKGROUND

Scope

Aggressive behavior demonstrated by the nation's children has been an often voiced concern during the past 30 years. In recent years, parents, professional educators, the general public, and elected officials have expressed increasing disturbance over the violence that is demonstrated in the schools. A nationwide study conducted in 1977 by the National Institute of Education (NIE) revealed how commonplace assaultive behavior has become in our school systems. The results of this study support earlier findings that 36% of all assaults on urban teenagers occur within the schools. This study suggests that a typical secondary school student has about 1 chance in 80 of being attacked while on schoolgrounds. This risk to students was found to decline as the school and its surrounding area becomes less densely populated.

Furthermore, recent studies based on reports by special education teachers of behaviorally disordered students found that 29% of the students displayed extremely aggressive behavior at least weekly (Ruhl & Hughes, 1985).

The NIE report also revealed that each month 1% of the secondary school teachers sustained a physical attack at school. These reported attacks were of sufficient severity to require medical treatment in 19% of the cases. Kaufman (1981) stated that every classroom teacher can expect at least one very volatile and aggressive student in his or her classroom. Given these facts, it is not surprising that aggressive behavior was ranked as the most disturbing behavior in a survey of Texas elementary school teachers (Coleman & Gilliam, 1983). The risk of assault on teachers, as on students, is less in smaller schools and communities.

Definition of Aggressive Behavior

At first glance, it appears that aggressive behavior is easy to define. Many professionals, as well as parents, intuitively claim to "know it when we see it." However, the identification becomes less clear in cases of noncompliant and of extreme forms of assertive behavior that can have the appearance and effects of aggressive behavior. Bandura (1973) has observed that whether a particular behavior is determined to be aggressive depends on a variety of considerations, including the following: (a) the characteristics of the behavior (e.g., destruction of property, verbal assault, physical assault, verbal and gestural threats of assault) independent of the effects on the intended recipient; (b) the intensity of the behavior (e.g., talking loudly or rapidly, number of pushes, the severity of a physical blow); (c) the expressions of pain or injury or escape behavior by the recipient of the aggressive behavior; (d) the intentions (apparent or perceived) of the perpetrator of the act; (e) the characteristics of the observer (i.e., sex, race, socioeconomic status, own history of aggressive and nonaggressive behavior, etc.); and (f) characteristics of the aggressor (the same as those listed for the observer).

Labeling an act as aggressive, therefore, depends for some individuals on criteria inherent in the behavior;

for others the situation may be the critical component, or the characteristics of the aggressor may be most salient. In many instances when a child or youth is labeled aggressive by an adult, the aggressive content originate in the eye of the viewer.

Most professionals define aggression as any behavior that results in personal injury or in destruction of property. Personal injury can be either physical or psychological or both. This definition in the context of the above-mentioned six points can serve to distinguish aggressive behavior from noncompliance and overtly assertive behavior. Noncompliant behavior is defined as the failure of an individual to heed an appropriate directive to change his or her activities. It should be noted that for many professionals both aggressive and noncompliant behavior are incorporated under the broader category of "conduct disorder." It should also be clear that the act of an individual causing harm to himself or herself (self-injurious behavior) is also defined as aggressive behavior. However, this chapter will confine its discussion to outward-directed aggressive behavior.

Impact on Children

Given the commonplace occurrence of aggressive behavior demonstrated by children and youth in the schools, the impact that this behavior has on students is immense. As to long-range development, a study by Robbins (1966) showed that children who had been referred to a mental health center for aggressive or other antisocial behavior were much more likely to demonstrate severe psychological problems as adults approximately 30 years later. In addition, more immediate effects can be noted for the aggressive child, including (a) poor peer relationships, (b) inadequately developed social skills, and (c) special education placement. Deleterious effects on the victims of aggression can also be noted including injury, withdrawal, and increased anxiety.

With the implementation of P.L. 94-142 and development of special education services for children with behavior problems earlier intervention is now possible. However, even given this early intervention, short-term social and psychological impacts remain. The student who displays significantly deviant levels of aggressive behavior is likely to be referred for assessment and possible special education placement. Such outcomes are often required owing to the deleterious effects that aggressive behavior has on the regular classroom environment, among which are (a) the risk of injury to staff and students, (b) disruption of the learning environment because of the inordinate amount of teacher time required by the aggressive student, and (c) the generally increased levels of anxiety and confusion in an environment in which students act out aggressively.

Special education out-of-class placement can have a negative effect on a student's socialization with peers, academic achievement, and self-perception. Additionally, Ruhl and Hughes (1985) noted that aggressive behavior in special education classrooms for the behaviorally impaired or disordered continued at inappropriately high levels.

Aggressive and assaultive behavior among school-age children have become commonplace in our school system, with several implications for educational professionals and parents. First, technology is needed to define when excessive aggression is present. Second, an understanding of aggression from several theoretical perspectives is required to allow for a thorough understanding of aggressive acting out by individual children. Third, providers of childcare require a systematic procedure for problem-solving in cases of situational-specific aggressive incidents. Finally, multiple methodologies are needed for prevention and intervention in instances of aggressive behavior. It is clear that educators and parents must become familiar with the means of effectively dealing with aggression if the risks to students and teachers are to be diminished.

DEVELOPMENT

Factors Relating to Aggressive Behavior in Children

Numerous attempts have been made to identify the important differences between families of normal (non-aggressive) children and families of aggressive children. The research has generally failed to provide any clear data that yield convincing conclusions. However, the recent research has provided useful information on family interaction styles (Patterson, Reid, Jones, & Conger, 1975). Their analysis of data gathered during observations of families in their homes suggests the following:

1. The interaction in families of aggressive children was characterized by higher frequencies of negative and hostile exchanges; the interactions in normal families involved mutually rewarding reciprocal interactions.
2. Aggressive children had engaged more frequently in irritating and aversive behaviors toward their parents, the parents responding primarily with aversive control methods (e.g., hitting, yelling, threats). Thus, it appears that aggressive children live in families that can be characterized by negative interactions and coercion on the part of all family members.

Other researchers have noted that consistency of discipline, a supportive atmosphere of the family, and (negatively) family breakup are factors that are strongly related to aggressive behavior in children. Extreme forms of parental behavior appear to be implicated in the development of aggression. Parenting styles most frequently linked to aggression are: (a) inconsistent rule setting and application of discipline; (b) exercise of control in an erratic and permissive manner and (c) contradictory setting of behavioral standards, families where parenting figures which might occur, for example, if a mother is permissive and a father is rigid and restrictive. A child's temperament may also be an interactive, contributing factor. Given the complexity of aggressive behavior, it is quite likely that there is no single or even predominant cause. The development of aggressive behavior in a particular child will, as with most problems, reflect the unique combinations of variables present in that child's history and the current setting.

It is critical to understanding aggressive behavior to know what is typical and is to be expected. Furthermore, it is necessary to appreciate the developmental implications of aggressive behavior. For example, tantrums are to be expected during the ages of 3 to 5 or 6 years. However, the fact that tantrums are expected does not imply that adults should not manage them. On the contrary, we need to very carefully manager tantrum behavior. The point to be made is that aggression is a developmental problem to be managed as is the acquisition of reading skills or the learning of social skills. When assessing behavior that is potentially aggressive, it is important to compare the target youth to other youth of the same age and sex in the same setting.

Causal Models of Aggressive Behavior

As with any cluster of inappropriate behaviors, there is interest in the many "whys" of the behavior. Why children physically and psychologically hurt others, why they intimidate or threaten to hurt others, and why they persist in their aggressive behavior are questions requiring answers. Although there is no unanimity among psychologists concerning the causes of aggression and why it continues, three major theories have evolved, each of which views the acquisition, maintenance, and control of aggression from very different perspectives. These theories — (a) the biological/psychological, (b) the instinctual/intrapsychic, and (c) the learned response theories — and their respective components are presented in Table 1 and Figure 1.

Examination of each one of these theories reveals a variety of strengths and weaknesses in their particular assumptions. In support of the first-mentioned are findings that manipulation of genetic factors can produce increasingly aggressive generations. Additionally, there is evidence that neurochemical adjustments can induce or reduce aggressive behavior (Achenbach, 1982). For example, Delgado (1969) reported evidence demonstrating the control of aggression through the delivery of electrical impulses to specific parts of the brain. Such evidence makes it clear that psychobiological factors play a role in an individual's tendency to respond aggressively. However, these factors do not account for the selection and application of the specific aggressive behaviors in particular situations and toward identified targets.

As an alternative to the biological explanation, Freudian psychoanalytic drive theory has been employed to explain aggression. However, the tenets of Freud and others that form the basis of psychodynamic theories of aggression have failed to obtain empirical support. At best, drive theories such as frustration–aggression (Dollard, Doob, Miller, Mowrer, & Sears, 1939) have shown that frustration and other drives *can,* but do not *necessarily,* produce aggressive behavior. The explanation of aggression by factors such as instincts, drives, and "psychic energy" are interesting but do not lead to the development of useful applied interventions (Kaufman, 1981). However, the explanation for aggressive behavior presented by competition theories and ideas have accumulated overwhelming empirical support.

Finally, the learned response theory, a general theory explaining aggressive behavior, involves a learning approach to the development and maintenance of aggression. In particular, the social learning/behavior analysis theory of aggression developed by Bandura (1973) outlines aggression as a result of a multifaceted system. Included in this system are three controlling events: antecedents (setting events), consequences (actions/feedback following behavior), and cognitive events (thoughts and perceptions). Social learning theory incorporates several of the previously discussed theoretical factors. Included among its components are psychobiological predeterminations and individual discomforts due to emotional arousal generated by frustrations, drives, previous experiences, and thoughts. However, social learning theory places its greatest emphasis on an individual's prior experience. The predispositions determined by one's prior experiences have a definite role in the control of individual responses to situational-specific events.

The major factors that determine aggressive responding in individuals have been identified through

TABLE 1

Components of the Theories of the Causes of Aggression

Theories	Major components
Biological/psychological	Genetically organized, instinctual behavior Response to hormonal/biochemical actions Neurological electrical impulses
Instinctual/intrapsychic	Basic instinctual drive attributed to either aggression or frustration Expression of uncontrolled primitive impulses Response to alleviate the discomfort of a state of frustration
Learned response	Acquired through modeling of aggressive behavior by others Frequency is increased and strengthened by rewards for aggressive behavior Repeated practice of aggression in an accepting environment Reduced anxiety through aggressive behavior

FIGURE 1

Motivational determinants of aggression in instinct, drive, and social learning models.

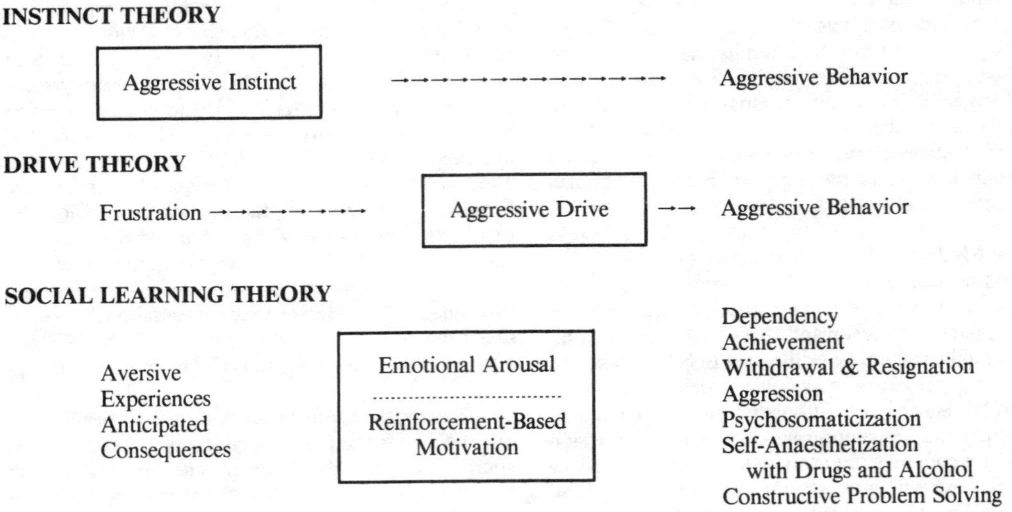

INSTINCT THEORY

Aggressive Instinct → Aggressive Behavior

DRIVE THEORY

Frustration → Aggressive Drive → Aggressive Behavior

SOCIAL LEARNING THEORY

Aversive Experiences
Anticipated Consequences

Emotional Arousal
Reinforcement-Based Motivation

Dependency
Achievement
Withdrawal & Resignation
Aggression
Psychosomaticization
Self-Anaesthetization with Drugs and Alcohol
Constructive Problem Solving

Note: From *Aggression: A Social learning analysis* (p. 54), by A. Bandura, 1973. Englewood Cliffs, NJ: Prentice-Hall. Copyright 1973, by Prentice-Hall. Reprinted by permission.

numerous research efforts, which have been reviewed by Bandura (1973). Among these are the following:

1. Aggression is a learned response that is often acquired through observation of aggressive responses being modeled by others. This modeling is most powerful when the behavior is being displayed by significant others.
2. Aggressive behavior will increase if such behavior is reinforced in a variety of ways (rewards, social status, escape from or avoidance of unpleasant situations, control of environment). Aggressive behavior also increases if it is consistently allowed to continue without aversive consequences.
3. Aggressive behavior is likely to occur when children undergo negative experiences such as personal assaults, physical threats, or frustration of desires.
4. Aggression can be maintained by the thoughts, perceptions and beliefs that an individual uses to justify aggressive behavior.

PUTTING CHILDREN'S AGGRESSIVE BEHAVIOR IN PERSPECTIVE

Assessment Considerations

For this chapter, the purposes of conducting an assessment are to: (a) identify and refine our definition's problems; (b) determine the severity of the problems, (c) describe the needs of the child and the environment, (d) identify relevant information concerning events that influence the problem, (e) establish specific treatment objectives, (f) develop and implement a particular intervention. To assess the nature and severity of a school child's aggressive behavior and its psychological and environmental origins *with an eye to eventual treatment,* three techniques are typically utilized: (a) behavioral interviewing; (b) behavior checklists completed by teachers, parents, and individual children; and (c) direct observation.

The *behavioral interview* is one of the most frequently utilized assessment techniques (O'Leary & Johnson, 1979). A systematic series of interviews of parents, teachers, and individual children are conducted to define the problems, gather information facilitating analysis, and generate an intervention to eliminate targeted aggressive behaviors and teach prosocial skills. Indeed, Helton, Workman, and Matuszek (1982) noted that the purposes of assessment in any social–environmental problem area is to: (a) specify the problem, (b) determine its severity, (c) describe the needs of the child, (d) state specific treatment objectives, and develop and implement a specific intervention.

Behavior checklists such as the Child Behavior Checklists, which are made up of teacher, parent, and self-report versions (Achenbach & Edelbrock, 1986), assist in establishing the prevalence of the problems, the number of the problems, and the severity of the problems. Behavior checklists can also serve to identify other problem areas in addition to aggression and as an evaluation tool to assess globally the progress that is being made.

Behavioral interviewing is utilized primarily to refine problem definitions, functional analysis of the defined problem(s), and develop and implement a treatment. Follow-up interviews also serve as an informal evaluation tool concerning progress that is being made.

Behavioral observation serves a number of functions in identifying problems and developing effective treatment plans. It provides an objective measure of the problems identified as well as information on the circumstances under which aggressive behavior occurs. Behavioral observation provides objective data to utilize in evaluating the effects of implemented treatment procedures.

Projective assessment techniques are not viewed as particularly helpful in providing meaningful information concerning aggressive behavior and how to develop effective interventions. Doke and Flippo (1983) noted that projective techniques have little use and, in fact, may actually provide misleading information. They also noted that projective techniques are very time-consuming to administer, score, and interpret and that environmental observation and interviewing provide a greater amount of more meaningful information in less time. A final limitation of projective assessment techniques is that they assess the child's behavior without providing information on the context in which aggression occurs.

To assess aggressive behavior, then, it appears to be most valuable to utilize the method that focuses upon the settings and circumstances of the aggressive responses. This is especially important since aggressive behavior frequently occurs only during specific conditions. Thus, assessment needs to be able to link ecological variables in the immediate context in which the aggressive behavior occurs.

Applied Behavior Analysis

Applied behavior analysis is a strategy that is frequently used to measure and monitor aggressive behavior in children, in a social learning conceptual framework. The measurement of behavior relies heavily on observation of instances of actual responses that are collected over time and across settings, in specific social situations and environments. Concrete knowledge of the child's responses to specific stimuli can lead directly to the design of effective treatments.

A wide variety of techniques for measuring and interpreting behavioral samples are available (Alberto & Troutman, 1982). Along with these techniques a thorough knowledge of behavioral principles, as well as applied creativity, is needed to develop and implement the most efficacious intervention (Epps, 1985; Martin & Pear, 1978).

One of the primary advantages to applied behavior analysis is the acquisition of pre- and post-intervention measures of behavior. With these measures available for review, small changes in behavior become apparent and can be used to evaluate the effectiveness of the intervention. Areas that may require revision of specific procedures are also available. Because aggressive behavior is a continuum that includes both appropriate and inappropriate responses, a measurement of total absence versus presence of aggressive behavior is inappropriate. Therefore, a system sensitive to variation in the frequency, intensity, or duration of exhibited behavior is necessary in order to evaluate progress.

Table 2, on page 25, displays the basic process of applied behavior analysis as it might be applied to aggressive behavioral concerns for third grade students.

Several key areas of information are provided through applied behavior analysis. The behavior of concern is quantified and understood in relation to the student's environment and social relationships, determination having been made in regard to whether the behavior is a limiting factor to the student or is primarily a problem of perception by significant adults in the environment. When it has been determined that the behavior is a limiting factor to the individual student and a valid concern of interested adults, alternative interventions are considered for implementation.

ALTERNATIVE ACTIONS

Once the decision has been reached to intervene in an aggressive child's environment, a process is needed to assist in the selection of a specific intervention. Many factors come into play when such a selection is being considered, each of which requires a careful analysis. If incorrect decisions are made at the treatment selection stage, the impact of future interventions at best will be less than maximally effective and at worst will lead to exacerbation of the target behavior.

The first factor requiring consideration is the level of dangerousness posed by the behavior. If the behavior is of sufficient intensity and/or frequency to pose a significant threat of injury to the student or others, treatments that provide for immediate suppression of the behavior and maximum protection of others in the environment are indicated. In conjunction with these safety and deceleration interventions in the development of competing appropriate alternative behaviors is mandatory. However, if the behavior is of less immediate concern due to safety issues, a less intrusive intervention may be more appropriate.

Individual differences among the major parties to the treatment procedures also warrant consideration. The idiosyncracies of both the student and the major intervenor are the primary significant personal factors affecting the ultimate success of the intervention. The particular characteristics of students undergoing treatment that require assessment include reinforcement preferences, ability to delay reinforcement, reactivity to control issues, likely response to deceleration procedures, cognitive abilities, and available alternative social skills. Any intervention will need, at a minimum, to partially address these issues in order to be an effective behavior change strategy.

Given an intervention that is tailored to the individual student, attention must then turn to variation in the characteristics of intervenor. Issues of concern in this area include personal preferences for types of treatment procedures, biases acquired from past experiences, motivation to apply the intervention, degree of consistency likely to be applied, and the relationship between the student and the intervenor. Even given a superlatively well-designed intervention procedure that very adequately addresses individual student differences, there will be little or no success if the intervenor does not accept or use the procedure presented. Without successfully dealing with intervenor differences and preferences, the procedures will not be successful and very possibly never be implemented.

In the selection of an intervention, the specific components of the target behavior also warrant consideration. Martin and Pear (1978) listed three primary characteristics of target behaviors that require evaluation in the process of intervention planning: (a) behavioral deficit, (b) behavioral excess, and (c) stimulus control alterations. The general procedures ultimately selected will depend heavily upon which of the above characteristics is the primary contributor to the behavior problem. Other important factors of the target behavior that need consideration prior to intervention planning are the intensity, frequency, and duration of the episodes. Each of these factors is found on a wide continuum of expression. Each factor, therefore, requires close scrutiny and creative application of procedures for the development of maximally effective interventions. The precise intervention developed for eliminating aggressive behavior and teaching an appropriate prosocial behavior will vary depending on the unique features of the individual and the problem. Typically one or more of the following procedures will be utilized.

1. Modeling of nonaggressive behaviors in response to aggression-provoking situations, by adults and peers. The models can be live or video recordings of the adaptive behavioral episodes.

2. The aggressive person can be guided in the practice of nonaggressive behaviors in actual situations. Such activities as role playing and rehearsal in "hypothetical" situations can also be employed. For example, an aggressive youth can practice alternative, acceptable responses to being teased on the playground.

3. Nonaggressive, appropriate behavior demonstrated in aggression-provoking situations can be rewarded. For example, turning away in the fact of teasing, and not losing one's temper and yelling in a game of kickball when hit by the ball are both especially commendable appropriate alternative responses in persons who in such situations might ordinarily express aggressive behavior.

4. For selected types of aggression such as temper tantrums and verbal intimidation, the use of extinction may be effective. For example, withholding the reward of "giving in" to a temper tantrum or "ignoring a threat" removes one of the primary incentives for such aggressive behavior.

5. Punishment of aggressive behavior by presenting an aversive stimulus, withdrawing a positive reinforcer (e.g., taking away earned points or portions of a weekly allowance or denial of a privilege), or placing the student in time out (i.e., brief isolation from the ongoing activities and reinforcing activities) can be utilized. It does need to be noted that punishment is difficult to correctly implement and may create additional problems if done in isolation from other components of treatment.

Aggressive behavior is primarily viewed as a to the learned-response theory. In the context of that analysis, it logically follows that teaching a student new behaviors and demonstrating that these new behaviors are more adaptive will eliminate the nonadaptive aggressive behaviors.

Given that punishment is a frequently employed technique at home and at school, we want to make some specific comments regarding its use to eliminate aggressive behavior. It is essential to remember that punishment occurs at a high rate in most settings and is frequently administered inappropriately. The use of physical punishment (spanking) or yelling can serve as a model for future aggression. Table 3 lists several considerations that will help make punishment procedures more effective and humane in controlling aggressive behavior.

Two additional concerns must be addressed and resolved prior to effective intervention planning. The concern is the matter of environmental factors: available space and how it is divided, social context, physical factors (heat, light, noise, etc.), and density of extraneous stimuli. These factors can have a significant if not ruinous impact on the possible success of an intervention. The final concern to be addressed is that of available resources. Resources include personnel time, money, reinforcers, equipment, and materials. Each set of procedures require different levels of support and resources for complete implementation. The attempted implementation of an intervention by procedures requiring resources that simply are not available is clearly destined for failure.

Many excellent references are available for selecting and developing appropriate interventions. These references provide the needed in-depth discussion and support to allow the intervenor the use of an appropriate behavior analysis procedure. Several of the references are listed and briefly discussed in the annotated bibliography.

SUMMARY

Irritating behavior is an every day occurrence in the lives of students and the adults who work with them. Aggressive behavior is a more extreme form of irritating behavior that not only disrupts the environment and inflicts pain on others but also, over time, causes the aggressive person to lose the capacity to act appropriately. Aggressive behavior can become an increasingly self-maintained phenomenon. It is important to realize that prevention of aggressive behavior in a student involves careful analysis and management of the day-to-day behavior of adults in the particular child's environment. School and home environments need to be structured to minimize the circumstances in which aggressive behavior is modeled and observed. Furthermore, the reinforcing consequences of aggressive behavior need to be minimized. The use of aggressive punishment will tend to increase aggressive behavior. The provision of structure, clear statement of expectations,

TABLE 2

An Analysis of Aggressive Behavior of a Boy in a Third-Grade Classroom

Setting/events before aggressive behavior	Aggressive behavior	Events occurring after aggressive behavior
Play in low-structure, unsupervised playground (recess)	Kicks and pushes others	Is stood up against fence; verbally reprimanded in front of peers
Cafeteria, eating lunch; in hallway	Throws food, utensils; pushes, bullies others	Gets attention from peers; other students complain; teacher talks to him
Father loses temper, curses, hits him	Curses	Peers give attention and report him to teacher
Peers tease him	Curses, yells, chases	Peers continue to tease; some students get caught by him
Teacher makes demand concerning difficult task	Refuses to comply, talks back	Peer attention; avoids doing difficult task
Before acceptable behavior	**Appropriate behavior**	**Events following appropriate behavior**
Structured, supervised playground, & activities	Plays, interacts cooperatively	Accepted by peers; receives teacher compliments
Lunch room organized, good behavior contract	Eats lunch	Has more time at recess; earns reward, praise
Walking in hallway	Arrives at destination	Receives compliments for promptness; earns free time
Father calmly discusses son's misbehavior	Listens, verbalizes alternative behavior	Does not curse in presence of peers
Peers tease students; teacher makes request, offering assistance, verbalizes verbalizes need to attempt task and consequences	Ignores peers; complies with request	Teasing decreases; experiences satisfaction for effort; teacher acknowledges effort

TABLE 3

Considerations in the Effective Use of Punishment

1. Punishment should only be utilized when more positive methods prove ineffective and when the continuation of the aggressive behavior will result in more harm than the punishment being implemented.
2. Punishment must be implemented matter-of-factly in a preplanned manner. Adults who are angry should not implement punishment. Moralizing and threats should not accompany or follow punishment.
3. Punishment should be implemented fairly, consistently, and immediately following the aggressive behavior.
4. Punishment should be administered by individuals who are involved with the student in positive relationships and by adults who observe or experience the problem. The adults who administer punishment need also to be involved in administering positive rewards for appropriate behavior.
5. Punishment needs to be reasonable in intensity and related to the aggressive behavior, for example, restoring or replacing a broken object when an item is broken during a tantrum. There are many punishment procedures such as positive practice, restoration, restitution, and response cost, that can be effectively linked to the aggressive response and logically fit into the ecology of the setting.
6. Punishment appears to be most effective when applied early in the chain or sequence of behaviors.
7. Punishment must be implemented only under conditions in which there is an active program in place to teach the student alternative, adaptive behaviors. The use of self-management techniques such as self-monitoring, self-reinforcement, self-evaluation, and rehearsal may be considered.

consistent enforcement of positive and negative consequences, and opportunities to develop alternative behaviors to replace aggressive behaviors constitute the basis of teaching prosocial behavior. In essence, the most effective approach to preventing and eliminating aggressive behavior is effective classroom teaching and effective parenting.

REFERENCES

Achenbach, T. M. (1982). *Developmental psychopathology.* New York: Harper and Row.

Achenbach, T., & Edelbrock, C. (1986). *Manual for the child behavior checklist and revised child behavior profile.* Burlington, VT: University of Vermont, Department of Psychiatry.

Alberto, P. A., & Troutman, A. C. (1982). *Applied behavior analysis for teachers: Influencing student performance.* Columbus, OH: Merrill.

Bandura, A. (1973). *Aggression: A social learning analysis.* Englewood Cliffs, NJ: Prentice-Hall.

Coleman, M. C., & Gilliam, J. E. (1983). Disturbing behaviors in the classroom: A survey of teacher attitudes. *Journal of Special Education, 17*(2), 121–129.

Delgado, J. M. (1969). *Physical control of the mind: Toward a psychocivilized society.* New York: Harper and Row.

Doke, L. A., & Flippo, J. R. (1983). Aggressive and oppositional behavior. In T. H. Ollendick & M. Hersen (Eds.), *Handbook of child psychopathology* (pp. 323–356). New York: Plenum.

Dollard, J., Doob, L. W., Miller, N. E., Mowrer, O. H., & Sears, R. R. (1939). *Frustration and aggression.* New Haven, CT: Yale University Press.

Fehrenback, P. A., & Thelen, M. H. (1982). Behavioral approaches to the treatment of aggressive disorders. *Behavior Modification, 6*(4), 465–497.

Helton, G. B., Workman, E. A., & Matuszek, P. A. (1982). *Psychoeducational assessment: Integrating concepts and techniques.* New York: Grune & Stratton.

Kauffman, J. M. (1981). *Characteristics of children's behavior disorders* (2nd ed.). Columbus, OH: Merrill.

Martin, G., & Pear, J. (1978). *Behavior modification: What it is and how to do it.* Englewood Cliffs, NJ: Prentice-Hall.

National Institute of Education (U. S. Department of Health, Education & Welfare). (1977). *Safe school study: Vol. 2. Executive summary.* Washington, DC: Author. (ERIC Document Reproduction Service No. ED149-466)

O'Leary, K. D., & Johnson, S. B. (1979). Psychological assessment. In H. C. Quay & J. S. Werry (Eds.), *Psychopathological disorders of childhood* (2nd ed.). New York: Wiley.

Patterson, G. R., Reid, J. B., Jones, R. R., & Congen, R. E. (1975). *A social learning approach to family intervention: Vol. 1. Families with aggressive children.* Eugene OR: Castalia.

Robins, L. N. (1966). *Deviant children grown up.* Baltimore, MD: Williams & Wilkins.

Ross, A. O. (1980). *Psychological disorders of children: A behavioral approach to theory, research, and therapy* (2nd ed.). New York: McGraw-Hill.

Ruhl, K. L., & Hughes, C. A. (1985, February). The nature and extent of aggression in special education settings serving behaviorally disordered students. *Behavioral Disorders,* pp. 95–104.

BIBLIOGRAPHY: PROFESSIONALS

Alberto, P. A., & Troutman, A. C. (1982). *Applied behavior analysis for teachers: Influencing student performance.* Columbus, OH: Merrill.
An excellent resource for professionals seeking to learn the basic techniques and procedures of behavior analysis and intervention with children. The major emphasis of the book is to define terminology, explain behavioral concepts, and guide the reader through practical intervention processes integrating theory, research, and practice. Many case examples are routinely provided.

Forehand, R. L., & McMahon, R. J. (1981). *Helping the noncompliant child: A clinician's guide to parent training.* New York: Guilford.
Noncompliance is one of the most frequent presenting problems designated by parents and teachers who refer children for additional assistance. A thorough discussion of assessment, standard treatment procedures, and adjunctive treatment strategies, and a review of related empirical literature are presented within the context of a social learning model. Although this text is intended for professionals to use in their work with children, it is also very appropriate for the use of teachers who might refer to in management of their classrooms.

Kauffman, J. M. (1981). *Characteristics of children's behavior disorders* (2nd ed.). Columbus, OH: Merrill.
Chapter 8 focuses on aggression as it is evidenced in children. The chapter presents a well-organized and outstanding discussion of the definition, measurement, causal factors, and control of aggressive behavior displayed by children.

Kerr, M. M., & Nelson, C. M. (1983). *Strategies for managing behavior problems in the classroom.* Columbus, OH: Merrill.
A pragmatic textbook written for the special educator or classroom teacher. As such, this text contains a discussion of basic classroom management principles, behavioral assessment approaches, and numerous procedural considerations. In addition to an excellent chapter on managing aggressive behavior, there are also chapters on socially immature and inadequate behaviors, social withdrawal, and self-stimulatory and self-injurious behaviors. The major strength of this text is its clear writing and use of numerous examples.

Martin, G., & Pear, J. (1978). *Behavior modification: What it is and how to do it.* Englewood Cliffs, NJ: Prentice-Hall.
Provides comprehensive information on the basic principles of behavior modification as well as presenting applied intervention to technology in an easy-to-read and practical format. Ample use of case studies and examples aid understanding. The provision of study exercises and questions make this text an excellent teaching reference.

Millman, H. L., Schaefer, C. E., & Cohen, J. J. (1981). *Therapies for school behavior problems: A handbook of practical interventions.* San Francisco: Jossey-Bass.
Chapter 5 focuses on disturbed peer relationships. Problems with aggressive responding to peers is a major section of the chapter. Several diverse practical interventions are described in a case study format. Intervention procedures for both individual students and classrooms are presented along with additional suggested readings.

Wolfengang, C. H., & Glickman, C. D. (1986). *Solving discipline problems: Strategies for classroom teachers.* Newton, MA: Allyn and Bacon.
Attempts to provide teachers with a variety of models and related techniques on dealing with behavior problems in the classroom. The text includes chapters on teacher effectiveness training, transactional analysis, Drieker's social discipline model, reality therapy, behavior modification, Canter's assertive discipline, and others. The intent of the authors is to provide teachers with practical techniques within various theoretical frameworks.

BIBLIOGRAPHY: PARENTS

Christophersen, E. R. (1984). *Little people: Guidelines for common sense child rearing.* Austin, TX: Pro-Ed.
Aggression as a topic is not covered in this book; however, the book contains excellent instruction in general parenting skills and intervention techniques for use with young children. Guidelines are presented on praise, monitoring, discipline, and specific approaches to a wide variety of inappropriate behavior.

Green, C. (1984). *Toddler taming: A survival guide for parents.* New York: Fawcett Columbine.
A good reference for all parents regardless of their parenting skills. It is an enjoyable and informative text that briefly address a wide variety of minor common parenting concerns. The book looks at problems involving emotional, social, behavioral, and minor biological aspects of good parenting.

Patterson, G. R. (1975). *Families: Applications of social learning to family life.* Champaign, IL: Research Press.
Chapter 12 provides a brief overview of childhood aggression within a family system and from a social learning perspective. The remainder of the text provides a review of the basics of social learning and behavior modification relating to common problems displayed by children. This is a good reference for the older child.

Children and Allergies

Steve Scofield
Indianapolis, Indiana

BACKGROUND

The National Institute of Allergy and Infectious Disease estimates that 1 of every 5 children who visit a pediatrician has an allergic disorder. Children with acute respiratory conditions, including asthma, account for 61.3% of school absenteeism that is due to health-related factors each year (Young, 1980). The stress of completing missed work assignments, the limitation on participation in social and educational activities, the financial burden of the physicians' services on the family, and the depletion of the child's physical and emotional energy due to the allergies is formidable.

The term *allergy* was originated by Dr. Clemens von Pirquet in 1906 to describe an "altered reaction" of the immune system (Galvin, Keim, & Conway, 1984). This reaction is attributed to a substance or substances against which the immune system does not usually react. These substances, called allergens, are various, the most common allergens being certain weeds, tree pollens, grasses, mold spores, animal dander, foods, plants, metals, insect stings, and drugs. For an allergy-prone person, initial exposure to an allergen results in the production of antibodies to attack these harmless invaders, as if they were a harmful virus or bacterium. These antibodies, called immunoglobulin E (IgE), become attached to the outer surface of mast cells, which are abundant in the lining of the nose, throat, lungs, digestive tract, skin, or on basophils, which are found in the blood. An allergic reaction occurs upon re-exposure to the allergen, when the IgE antibodies that were produced to react against it, cause histamine to be released from the adjoining mast cells. The histamine causes the various symptoms of the allergy. An allergic reaction can vary with the concentration and duration of the exposure to the allergen (Graber, 1983) and can either occur immediately, within minutes or several hours, or after a delay, such as within several days, depending on the mechanism of the reaction. Allergies can also be aggravated by strong emotions and irritants such as tobacco smoke and common cold germs (Graber, 1983; Young, 1980).

DEVELOPMENT

In Table 1 some of the more common allergies are presented along with some of their symptoms. Allergic reactions that are the subject of considerable controversy in the medical profession are not listed. This would include the works of Crook (1980), Mayron (1979), Rapp (1978, 1979), and Mandell (1979), who suggest that there can be allergies of the nervous system, purporting a direct relationship between allergies and learning or behavior problems in children. One of the more common cerebral allergic reactions is described as the "tension–fatigue syndrome," which is reported to be evidenced by periods of "allergic tension" with symptoms of restlessness, hyperkinesis, emotional instability, insomnia and by "allergic fatigue," which is manifested by listlessness and constant tiredness (Speer, 1954). There continues to be a need for more controlled studies before a cause–effect relationship between allergies and such behavior in children can be confirmed (National Institute of Allergy and Infectious Diseases [NIAID], 1984).

Another area of controversy is the use of the term allergy to describe the reaction in children to dyes and food additives by supporters of the Feingold theory (1973). While there is some support for the position that large doses of food coloring produce behavior changes in children, owing to a "drug-like" effect, an allergic reaction has not been proven (Shapiro, 1981; NIAID, 1984).

The listing of symptoms in Table 1 are direct, observable consequences of allergies. However, the secondary ailments that have an impact upon a child's social, emotional, physical, and educational development are also immense.

For example, serious otitis media, which is an inflammation of the middle ear with fluid accumulation that is often caused by allergies, can result in temporary hearing loss and permanent damage. Ghowskis, Savger, and Decker (1986) reviewed the literature and suggested that the temporary hearing loss due to otitis media has a negative impact upon children's intellectual, academic, auditory processing, and language development. The temporary loss of hearing can also affect children's classroom performance and social development, as they may tend to withdraw and become inattentive in the classroom (Galvin, Keim, & Conway, 1984).

An asthmatic child may live in constant fear of an asthmatic attack and experience a lack of independence and feelings of inferiority related to the restriction of activities needed to avoid an attack, all of which may eventually result in lowered self-concept. For example, the child may need to limit his or her participation in physical activities, field trips, and botany classes; vocational classes that involve woodworking; welding fumes, grinding dust, or paint fumes; and other activities that may expose the child to offending allergens. An oxygen imbalance may be caused by a recurrent upper respiratory disorder, causing fatigue and mental sluggishness,

TABLE 1
Allergies and Their Symptoms

Allergy	Symptoms
Allergic asthma	Shortness of breath, wheezing, and dry coughing.
Allergic rhinitis (hay fever)	Sneezing, runny nose, watery eyes, nasal stuffiness, mouth breathing, "allergic shiners,"* and a nose crease due to upward rubbing of the nose (allergic salute).
Atopic dermatitis (eczema)	A rash appearing in the creases of skin, and intense itching.
Intestinal disorders due to food allergies	Abdominal pain, diarrhea, vomiting, constipation, colic, and indigestion.
Serous otitis media	Fullness in ear, temporary hearing loss, and ear popping.
Contact dermatitis	Skin rash, itching, and swelling resulting from contact with offending substance (poison ivy, poison oak, and certain metals, for example).
Urticaria (hives)	Welts that appear like mosquito bites with surrounded redness and itch intensely.
Stinging insect	Anaphylaxis†, dizziness, weakness, large local swelling, sneezing, nausea, diarrhea, shock and unconsciousness.
Drug	Anaphylaxis†, swelling of body parts, fever, pain in the joints, and skin reactions.

* A bluish discoloration below the eyes.

† An extreme allergic reaction with symptoms that include skin reactions, vomiting, abdominal cramps, diarrhea, extreme breathing difficulties, drop in blood pressure, shock, and possible death.

and hindering a child's performance in physical activities (Galvin, Keim, & Conway, 1984).

When a child's gastrointestinal tract is involved, which is common in food allergies, the digestive system may not properly absorb minerals, resulting in irritability and loss of appetite (Galvin, Keim, & Conway, 1984). Adjustments in school lunches may also be needed if the child is allergic to a particular food or food group.

Skin allergy can cause children's skin to itch or burn, making them uncomfortable and disturbed about their appearance.

There are also possible side effects of medications that are frequently given to children with allergies. For example, antihistamines can cause drowsiness and abdominal symptoms, and decongestants can cause nervousness, dizziness, nausea, awareness of heartbeat, and stimulation of the central nervous system, all of which can easily affect the ability to function optimally in school (Golbert, 1981).Corticosteroid therapy has been reported to shorten attention span, indirectly affecting memory (Schraa & Dirks, 1982).

The myth that allergies are psychosomatic, "all in the head," can thwart the need for emotional support for the illness.Support by a child's family may fluctuate, owing to the parents' inability to adjust to the psychological needs of their allergic child, as well as the possible financial burden the medical bills may place on the family. Siblings may also become jealous of the allergic child, with whom the family must make adjustments in family outings and activities. On the other hand, family members may tend to overprotect the allergic-prone in fear of an attack, possibly leading to manipulation by the child for attention or to guilt feelings resulting from awareness that the family must make the unwanted adjustments (Graber, 1983; Young, 1980).

PUTTING CHILDREN'S ALLERGIES IN PERSPECTIVE

When a child displays symptoms of allergies, it is appropriate for the school psychologist to investigate whether interventions have been made for the child and to determine their impact upon the child's life. If the parents are not aware of the possibility that their child may indeed have an allergy, the school psychologist can appropriately help them make a referral. Prior to a referral, however, the school psychologist may want to interview the parents: positive responses from the following questions would support a referral.

1. Is there a history of allergies in the family?
2. Does the child experience itching, sneezing, or coughing when around animals?
3. Did the child have colic or persistent diaper rash as an infant?
4. Does the child frequently rub his or her nose or eyes?
5. Other than when having a cold, does the child have a chronic runny nose or repeated sneezing?
6. Have the parents noticed the child frequently breathing with his or her mouth open?
7. Has the child experienced diarrhea, "gas," or a rash after eating certain foods?

ALTERNATIVE ACTIONS

When determining if a child has an allergic condition, the physician can use information gathered from a personal and family history, the child's environment, information from a physical examination coupled with data from allergy testing, and other laboratory testing in an effort to pinpoint the cause. For example, a skin test can be used in which suspected allergens are either applied to a scratch or a puncture on the skin, or injected under the skin. If the patient is allergic to the substance the immune system will usually react, producing a small raised area surrounded by redness. If asthma is suspected, the child may be asked to inhale or ingest possible allergens, and in most cases the allergenic substance produces variations in breathing ability in an allergic asthmatic.

If the results of the examinations indicate that the child is allergic, removal of the offending allergen is usually recommended. Relief of the symptoms with medications and immunotherapy or "allergy shots," which attempt to prevent the allergic reaction, may also be utilized.

Open communication between the home, school, and physician is perhaps one of the most important factors in the development of an allergy program (McGovern, Peirce, & Lee, 1971). The more information that school personnel have regarding a child's allergy, the more effective the allergy program will be. Appropriate information would include the following: (a) the allergic substance(s); (b) any activities that need to be modified or avoided; (c) whether preferential seating is needed because, for example, of a temporary hearing loss; (d) the child's medications and possible side effects; (e) how to get in contact with the parents and doctor during school hours; and (f) the symptoms of an attack and actions that need to be taken during an attack (Graber, 1983).

To assist allergic children in coping with their problem, between 1979 and 1981 a program was developed in the Scottsdale, Arizona public schools in which prevention, in addition to intervention, was emphasized. In addition to providing school personnel with an understanding of the etiology of allergies through in-services training, the program also proposed regulations regarding environmental controls, home–school communication, adaptation of physical education activities, limitation of allergic materials in the schools, and excused participation from activities that entail contact with known allergens. The program also outlined procedures to follow when a child displayed symptoms of an asthmatic attack and symptoms of an insect allergy reaction.

SUMMARY

The medical aspects of a child's learning needs,

particularly when a variety of factors appear to be involved, are often overlooked by the school psychologist during evaluation, despite common sense reasoning that a child's behavior and school performance are often affected by physical ailments. Therefore, before the determination is made that a child has a handicap and is in need of special education services or intervention, the school psychologist has an obligation to investigate the physical factors that may be contributing to the problems. Some of the areas that have been delineated as factors involved in the case of children with allergies include the following: increased school absenteeism, depleted physical energy, curtailment of classroom performance, inhibited social development, avoidance of certain activities, and side effects of allergy medications.

Therefore, while there is considerable controversy regarding a direct relationship between allergies and learning and behavior problems in children, there does tend to be support for the premise that allergy symptoms exacerbate a child's learning and behavior problems (McLoughlin, Nall, & Petrosko, 1985). Given that allergies affect one of every 6 persons in the United States (Young, 1980), and given the impact of allergies upon a child's social, emotional,and educational development, there is a need, when a child is having difficulties in school, to consider the importance of any allergic disorder and to determine how the allergy may be affecting the child's ability to cope with the demands of schooling.

REFERENCES

Anderson, J. A., & Sogn, D. D. (Eds.). (1984). *Adverse reactions to foods* (NIH Publication No. 84-2442). Washington, DC: U.S. Government Printing Office.

Asthma & Allergy Foundation of America. (1985). *The potential for quackery and questionable treatment in asthma and allergy medicine.* Washington, DC: Author.

Crook, W. G., (1980). Can what a child eats make him dull, stupid, or hyperactive? *Journal of Learning Disabilities, 13*(5), 53–58.

Feingold, B. F. (1973). Food additives and child development [Editorial]. *Hospital Practice, 8*(10), 11–21.

Galvin, E. S., Keim, R. E., & Conway, T. P. (1984, January–February). Children and allergies: Some effects and treatment. *Children Today,* pp. 31–33.

Ghowskis, B. S., Savger, D. D., & Decker, T. N. (1986). Otitis media: Effect on a child's learning. *Academic Therapy, 21*(3), 283–290.

Golbert, T. M. (1981). Allergic diseases and their treatment. In The Asthma & Allergy Foundation of America & C. T. Craig (Eds.), *The allergy encyclopedia.* New York: New American Library.

Graber, R. F. (1983). *Parents book of childhood allergies.* New York: Ballantine Books.

Joseph, L. (1973). *A doctor discusses allergy: Facts and fiction.* Chicago: Budlong.

Mandell, M., & Scanlon, L. W. (1979). *Dr. Mandell's 5-day allergy relief system.* New York: Pocket Books.

Mayron, L. W. (1979). Allergy, learning and behavior problems. *Journal of Learning Disabilities, 12*(1), 41–49.

McGovern, J. P., Peirce, K. E., & Lee, R. E. (1971). The allergic child and his challenge to the school. *Clinical Pediatrics, 10*(11), 636–644.

McLoughlin, J. A., Nall, M., & Petrosko, J. (1985). Allergies and learning disabilities. *Learning Disability Quarterly, 8*(4), 255–259.

Rapp, D. (1978). Does diet affect hyperactivity? *Journal of Learning Disabilities, 12*(6), 56–62.

Rapp, D. (1979). *Allergies and the hyperactive child.* New York: Simon & Schuster.

Scherr, M. S. (Eds.). (1979–1981). *Allergy information kit for school personnel of Scottsdale Public Schools.* Scottsdale, AZ: Scottsdale Public Schools.

Schraa, J. C., & Dirks, J. F. (1982). The influence of corticosteroids and theophylline on cerebral function. *Chest 82*(2), 181–185.

Shapiro, G. (1981). Allergy research. In The Asthma & Allergy Foundation of America & C. T. Craig (Eds.), *The allergy encyclopedia.* New York: New American Library.

Speer, F. (1954). Allergic tension fatigue in children. *Annals of Allergy, 12,* 168–171.

Young, P. (1980). *Asthma and allergies: An optimistic future* (NIH Publication No. 80-388). Washington, DC: U.S. Government Printing Office.

BIBLIOGRAPHY: PROFESSIONALS

Anderson, J. A., & Sogn, D. D. (Eds.). (1984). *Adverse reactions to foods* (NIH Publication No. 84-2442). Washington, DC: U.S. Government Printing Office.
Written for physicians on the diagnosis and treatment of food allergies and other adverse reactions to foods, this book provides a thorough review of the current research on this controversial topic.

Craig, T., & The Asthma & Allergy Foundation of America (Eds.). (1981). *The allergy encyclopedia.* New York: New American Library.
This book presents a medical guide to the causes, symptoms, and treatments of allergies. It is also an excellent resource for information regarding various allergy clinics, camps, and organizations within the United States.

Young, P. (1980). *Asthma and allergies: An optimistic future* (NIH Publication No. 80-388). Washington, DC: U.S. Government Printing Office.
Based on the Report of the Task Force on Asthma and other Allergic Diseases by the National Institute of Allergy and Infections Diseases, this publication provides the reader with a thorough understanding of the social and economic effects of allergies, the basic mechanism of allergic diseases, and the various types of allergies.

BIBLIOGRAPHY: PARENTS

Graber, R. F. (1983). *Parents book of childhood allergies.* New York: Ballantine Books.
Written for parents with children who have allergies, this book provides the parents with an understanding of allergies, the therapies that are used by physicians, what to do during an allergic emergency, and how to help a child at school.

Lewis, G. E., Rachelefsy, G., Lewis, M. A., & Sota, A. (1979). *ACT (asthma care training) for kids.* Washington, DC: The Asthma & Allergy Foundation of America.
This program was designed for asthmatic children aged 7–12, with the goal of teaching asthmatic children self-management skills. It also functions as a support resource for parents. Detailed lesson plans are provided for each of five 1-hour sessions for both children and parents.

RESOURCES

American Academy of Allergy and Immunology
611 East Well Street
Milwaukee, WI 53202
(414) 272-6071

Asthma & Allergy Foundation of America
1302 18th Street, NW, Suite 303
Washington, DC 20036
(202) 293-2950

Children and Anger

Richard C. Bowers, Jr.
Heartland Education Agency, Johnston, Iowa

BACKGROUND

What does a child who has problems dealing with anger look like? Typically we picture a child throwing a tantrum: tense, scowling, yelling, shaking, hitting, or making threats. Some may be described as having a "chip on their shoulder"; others are seen as "exploders," whose anger appears suddenly and violently. Usually it is the behavioral excesses that draw attention; the anger is too intense, too frequent, or both. Yet many children having problems dealing with angry feelings seem very normal and never show their "tempers."

What is anger? Anger is a conflictive emotion that can be viewed at three levels: the physical, the behavioral, and the cognitive. Physically, anger often takes the form of increased muscle tension and adrenaline flow. Behaviorally, anger can be seen in clenched fists or in tantrum behaviors such as kicking and pounding. Cognitively, anger involves a person's perceptions and interpretations of the behavior of others. For example, if someone steals your parking space you might think to yourself, "No one is going to do that and get away with it! I am going to flatten their tires!" If you then flatten their tires and perhaps tried to flatten the other driver as well, you have gone past anger to active aggression. Anger is the emotion; aggression is the action.

Annoyance and anger also differ. We are usually annoyed at inanimate objects; the pens that run out of ink; needless paperwork, etc. Anger, however, is a social emotion. It involves some type of conflict between people.

Is getting angry normal? Yes! Anger has a definite social function in defining and resolving conflicts. It can be a dynamic, constructive force in relationships by allowing for the airing of differences. Although it is extremely important to inhibit anger in small, isolated, interdependent cultures, our society tends to celebrate anger and aggression through sports and the media. An example often referred to by children who have anger-control problems is professional "wrestling." The display of anger and threats before the bouts is seen as real to some children, and they resolve their conflicts in similar ways. Anger is also a normal part of the grieving process, either because of the death of a loved one or through divorce or separation. Anger can also be a normal reaction to abuse or to illness.

Even within small towns there are minicultures or "tribes" in which excessive anger and violence are daily occurrences. Most schools have groups of children in which being good at anger and aggression is important in defining social status. An almost constant stream of threats and challenges helps to determine the "pecking order" for the title of the "toughest dude." Treating children from these groups or from families in which anger and violence are everyday events can be extremely challenging.

Would it be better if children did not get angry? Because getting angry is normal and because it can contribute to good social relationships, children who are overcontrolled and do not allow themselves to get angry have an anger problem, too. Rather than having a behavioral excess, these children have a behavioral deficit. The therapeutic goal is to teach them to be assertive, to speak up for themselves (see "Assertiveness," in this volume). These children are not often referred to school psychologists because they do not cause problems. But children who do not let others know about their anger often get angry at themselves for not being assertive. This can lead to a loss of self-esteem and possibly depression.

So, anger is a normal part of the social lives of children. Learning to handle the emotion effectively is an important developmental task. However, some of the ways anger is handled by parents or portrayed in the media make learning the appropriate skills problematic. Anger problems seem to fall into two categories: (a) an excess of anger that often shows itself in tantrums or explosive behavior, and (b) a behavioral deficit consisting of the inability to express anger. School psychologists who attempt to treat anger disorders have to be aware of the unique individual and the social reasons for anger, how anger develops, how it is manifested, and the normal expressions of the emotion.

DEVELOPMENT

Little has been written about how anger develops or what is to be expected among various age groups. Goodenough (1931) and Gesell, Ilg, Ames, and Bullis (1977) described typical patterns of behavior based on observation and case study. Manifestations of anger change from thrashing about in infancy to tantrums at 18 months. The frequency of anger outbursts or tantrums peaks in the third year (the "terrible two's") and starts to decline. The length of this tantrum phase is approximately 1 year. As language skills develop, the children become more adept at substituting verbal for physical aggression and demonstrate more self-control. Typically the average tantrum lasts under 5 minutes (see "Temper Tantrums," in this volume).

Averill (1982) studied the everyday expression of adult anger. These findings may be useful in assessing the social environment of children referred for anger problems. Eighty-five percent of the subjects reported being angry at least once a week. The most frequent target was a friend or loved-one. The objective of the anger was not to do harm, but to change the environmental conditions causing the anger. Anger was usually aroused by some perceived wrong. It could be viewed as a form of problem solving, because nonaggressive responses such as talking things over were just as common as aggressive acts. Physical aggression was rarely reported. Verbal aggression and/or denial of benefits (e.g., affection) were the most typical responses. Afterwards, a generally negative mood prevailed, but the outcome was rated by both the angry person and the target of the anger as being positive. An airing of differences resulted in a more dynamic relationship. No real differences were found between men and women in the ways they dealt with anger.

Cummings, Zahn-Waxler, and Radke-Yarrow (1984) studied the developmental changes in a child's perception of others' anger in the home.Toddlers usually responded to such anger by crying, smiling, laughing, excitement, or angry yelling. School-age children responded with less overt expressions of emotion. The school-age children were able to engage in purposeful interventions such as comforting. Whereas toddlers tended to hit or scold, school-age children tried to find ways to resolve the conflict. The authors noted that in these normal middle-class homes incidents of anger were two to three times more likely to occur than incidents of affection.

The cultural rules of anger are taught to young children by what Averill (1982) called "paradigm scenarios." Such scenarios are typical events of the child's life, such as getting punished or watching parents fight. Also, scenarios can be experienced indirectly through stories. Through these interactions with parents and other important figures children learn how to feel and express anger. If the parents have difficulty handling anger,then so may the child.

To summarize, we have little information about what constitutes "normal" child behavior when it comes to anger other than our common-sense notions. How anger is expressed is learned by watching or listening to others and varies greatly within and across cultures. Anger that results in physical aggression is rare, so its occurrence is a cause of real concern. As children get older, they begin to rely on their verbal skills to express their own anger or to mediate angry disputes among others.

PUTTING CHILDREN'S ANGER IN PERSPECTIVE

Earlier, the point was made that children with anger problems fall into two broad categories: those with excessive amounts of the emotion and those who often express too little and appear timid and weak to others. The latter group are dealt with elsewhere in this volume. Therefore, the focus of the suggestions offered below will be on children who have excessive anger.

When a parent or teacher refers a student to the school psychologist, the first task is to define and evaluate the situation. Several things need to be explored: (a) the severity of the problem, (b) factors that may be causing anger such as academic frustration, grieving, illness, abuse, problems with peers, and (c) what skills and attitudes the child, the family, and the school can bring to the planned treatment.

Generally, direct assessment of the problem behavior and the setting in which it occurs is the most useful. Normative measures are available (Feindler & Fremouw, 1983). These measures may be useful in documenting a problem's severity, but perhaps not as helpful as comparing specific behaviors with those of the natural peer group. Useful data include frequency of anger outbursts, ratings of the emotional intensity, and descriptions of how the anger is displayed (threats? tantrums? tears?). Analysis of the setting would include time of day, type of activity (playground? small group?), and reactions of students and teachers. The same type of information can be collected for other children so that the child's behavior can be compared directly with his or her peer group.

Sitting down with children, going through some of the problem episodes, and examining their perceptions of the incidents is very useful. Most children who have temper outbursts see problems in ways that make them angrier and do not have a good "library" of coping strategies.

If they can be obtained, self-monitoring and self-evaluation data offer valuable insights to the therapist and to the children themselves. This "hassle log" (Feindler & Fremouw, 1983) should list when they get angry, who was involved, and the reason. The thoughts that were going through their head at the time (self-statements) and their evaluation of how well the problem was resolved should be included, too. Interviewing the families, the teachers, and the referred students themselves will be helpful in evaluating the social context of the anger, as well as helping in the identification of stressors that may aggravate or provoke anger.

ALTERNATIVE ACTIONS

Generally, in working with these children parents and teachers should try to keep their composure. Being seen as approachable and open is important. In their intervention, school psychologists should have the adults discuss a child's behavior and its effects on others when the child is calm. Children should be praised for those times when they are not angry. Children whose anger tends to be explosive can be allowed to leave the room temporarily to regain their composure. Usually they can feel the explosion coming and can avoid an incident if allowed some space. Adults should take the initiative in suggesting this to the students.

If further treatment is necessary, the recommended approaches fall into three categories: stress-inoculation training (cognitive–behavior modification), behavioral, and social skills training. In selecting a treatment approach one must keep in mind the severity of the problem, the child's age, the child's ability to accomplish the demands of the treatment, and the level of cooperation from the client and others that must be involved.

Stress-inoculation training (Feindler & Fremouw, 1983; Novaco, 1975, 1976, 1977a, 1977b; Schlichter, Jeffrey, & Horan, 1979) has the advantage of being comprehensive in its attention to the cognitive, physical, and behavioral responses of anger. The approach requires the youth's cooperation and some ability to self-monitor and self-evaluate.

Behavioral approaches focus strictly on modifying observable actions. The behavioral umbrella covers many techniques and strategies and has the advantage of being applicable to young or nonverbal children as well as uncooperative clients. Social skills training stresses the improvement of social competence through the direct teaching of appropriate social behaviors. The following section will describe stress-inoculation, behavioral, and social skills approaches, as well as other useful intervention techniques.

Stress-Inoculation Training

Rationale. Anger is viewed as a complex emotion expressed in three ways: cognitively, physiologically, and behaviorally. The cognitive expression deals with the cultural and personal "rules" defining when and how to get angry. An individual's self-statements, attributions, and expectations contribute to the arousal and expression of anger. Physiologically, muscle tension contributes to the anger response by acting as a cue that anger is developing. Also, too much tension can help trigger an aggressive response.

Observers interpret others' feelings through their overt behaviors, and these same behaviors help dictate the outcome of an anger episode. If one starts to shout, makes angry gestures, gets red-faced, and walks toward the target of the anger, the incident is likely to escalate. Likewise, if one acts unassertively and retreats when angry, the provocation is not really resolved and the perceived outcome is failure.

Approach. Although it can be done with individuals, stress-inoculation training is enriched by small-group work. Getting the voluntary cooperation of all participants is crucial. Feindler and Fremouw (1983) noted that cooperation can usually be elicited by pointing out the natural consequences of anger like unpopularity, punishment at home or at school, or even arrest. In some cases, however, anger is an adaptive response, and the motivation for change is indeed small. In those instances, to describe the training as a way of increasing self-control as well as the control of others (through assertiveness) is helpful. Clients would be less likely to be manipulated by others, thereby increasing their personal power. Reinforcers for participation in treatment can be used as long as they do not undermine the needed emphasis on inner-directedness and self-control.

Step One: Cognitive Preparation. The first step in the treatment procedure is to educate the client about the nature of anger and to develop an awareness of their personal responses to provocation. The self-awareness can be enhanced through the use of a "hassle log" or imagery techniques such as "running a movie," which involves recalling anger episodes as accurately as possible during a treatment session (Meichenbaum, 1976). These techniques help the client examine the frequency, duration, intensity, and bodily sensations of anger. Also obtained are descriptions of the typical targets, reasons for provocation, and ratings of how successful the anger episode was in meeting the client's objectives. In addition this phase usually involves finding out the differences between anger and aggression, understanding the three components of the anger response, calling attention to tension as a cue to anger, emphasizing the importance of self-statements, and introducing the coping strategies.

Step Two: Skill Acquisition. The second step of training involves learning the needed cognitive, physical, and behavioral coping skills and rehearsing them. Cognitive coping skills emphasize keeping a task orientation during anger episodes and the development of a library of coping self-statements. The task orientation concept is aided by viewing an anger episode as unfolding in four stages: (a) preparing for provocation, (b) impact and confrontation, (c) coping with arousal, and (d) self-assessment and reinforcement. Each client develops his or her own self-statements for each stage. Some examples:

Stage 1 — preparation: I know what's coming and I know I can handle it. Try to keep a sense of humor.
Stage 2 — impact: Keep relaxing. No point in getting mad. I've got the situation under control.
Stage 3 —coping: Relax, take deep breaths. Keep the lid on, don't let him get me angry. The tension is a signal to cope.

Stage 4 — reflection: The more I practice the better I'll get. It worked! I can handle it!

Besides cognitive coping skills, physical coping skills need to be learned. This involves teaching deep muscle relaxation and relaxation imagery as well as emphasizing the importance of maintaining a sense of humor. Relaxation is important because it is incompatible with the tension brought about by anger.

Commercial materials are available to help people learn to relax. Basically they teach how to get comfortable, breathe deeply and slowly, and begin tensing and relaxing various muscle groups. For example, clients might be told to make a fist with both hands, relax, and to note the sensation of relaxation. The same sequence is applied to muscles in the arms, head, trunk, and legs. Daily practice is encouraged. Asking clients to imagine being in the most peaceful spot they know helps in relaxation, too. For example, many children picture themselves walking through the woods with the sunlight filtering through the leaves, the sounds of birds chirping, and the smell of damp leaves. As the ability to relax improves, a quicker version of the relaxation program can be taught, in which the student is instructed to breathe deeply and to "let go" all of the body's tensions.

Finally, behavioral response training emphasizes changing provocative behavior such as fist clenching and shouting. Clients can be taught assertive behaviors that will help them reach their goals without anger. One technique often taught is called "broken record"; it involves the calm repetition of a request until it is carried out (see "Assertiveness," in this volume, for other ideas).

Step Three: Applied Practice. The third step in stress-inoculation training is to apply the coping strategies listed above in an escalating series of provocative encounters. The encounters are first presented imaginally and then discussed. For example, referred students could imagine they were angry at a friend for borrowing a tape and not returning it. They would be instructed to break the incident down into the four stages and to practice aloud the coping self-statements during each stage. They would also practice relaxation and imagine what overt behaviors they would use. This would be followed by a discussion with the psychologist and/or group members that would include praise and feedback. As the students progressed they could imagine themselves encountering and coping with more difficult situations such as with parents or teachers.

This imagination phase should be followed with actual role playing of provocative situations followed by the feedback session. The use of video recordings is often very useful at this stage. Including some of the real targets of anger such as teachers, parents, or administrators in the role playing adds realism and helps those adults understand the coping process.

The continued use of a "hassle log" aids the training effect, as does the use of homework assignments. Such assignments are often aimed at the use of specific coping strategies such as relaxation or the use of certain self-statements.

The use of stress-inoculation training in the *prevention* of anger problems has worked successfully with police and probation officers (Novaco, 1977, 1980). Parents of problem children, teachers, and administrators are groups that might benefit from such training, too.

Behavior Modification Strategies

Many different strategies fall under the umbrella of behaviorism such as extinction programs, reinforcement strategies and schedules, token economies, etc. These techniques would target only observable behavior, not cognitive behavior, for change. Many programs could be designed to deal with children with anger control problems. Presented below are just some of the possible ways of dealing with children having anger control problems. Think of them as blueprints whose details can (and should!) be altered to fit each child's individual circumstances.

Imagine John, a third grader, has been referred to you for help because he seems to have problems controlling his temper. After meeting with the parents and the teacher to discuss the problem, you observe John in his class and find that he averages about one incident every 30 minutes in which he angrily yells at another student or gestures as if he were going to hit someone. By observing several other classmates at random you find that they only yell or gesture once every two days. Other students seem to steer clear of him. Indeed, when you examine the peer nominations from his classmates, you find he is the least liked and they do not like to play with him on the playground.

After reviewing the data with the teacher and the parents, you agree that a real problem does exist and you jointly plan an intervention strategy. The day is divided into 30-minute segments (13 in all). If John can refrain from yelling or making angry gestures during a 30-minute segment, he will receive 100 points (1,300 total points possible per day). In addition, the teacher will commend him when he acts appropriately. John will keep a record of these points at his desk.

If John becomes angry, he will receive no points for that segment. If he becomes angry during a segment and loses the points, he can earn back 25 points by staying calm the rest of the segment. However, if he has two or more incidents during the period he receives no points. A reasonable point goal for the day is decided, perhaps 500. If John makes 500 points that day he will receive a small surprise like a game time, a snack, or a story, etc. In addition, if he meets his goal he is to take a note home to his parents who provide praise and access to a rewarding activity. No note means no praise and no special activity. His parents should encourage him to try harder the next day.

The plan is introduced to John. He likes it and he has some ideas for reinforcers. As the plan is put into action the point goal is gradually raised, the 30 minute segments become 60 minutes; later it becomes daily. Bonuses could be added for having perfect days.

Another approach is to use mediated essays (Blackwood, 1970; MacPherson, Candee, & Hohman,

1974) as a response cost, but with a cognitive twist. The mediated essay is a prepared paragraph that specifies the rewards and punishments resulting from a particular behavior. A sequence of four sections outlines what the child has done wrong ("I got angry and yelled"); why it was wrong ("Yelling is a bad way of getting what I want and others will not want to play with me"); what should have been done ("I could quietly ask for something or bargain for it; I can try relaxing"); and the consequences of appropriate behavior ("If I keep my temper and act politely others will like me more").

When the targeted behavior appears, the child must copy the essay as a response cost. Of course, some adaptive self-talk is included in the process. In John's case each time he becomes angry he is asked to copy the short essay. When his behavior is appropriate, he receives compliments from the teacher or other adults who may be observing.

Some teachers have objected to using writing assignments as punishers. But in this case the assignment is tailored to the problem and is not the useless "write your name 1,000 times." The paragraphs could be read to an aide or principal, too.

Behavioral contracting is another approach worth considering. Sometimes anger erupts when rules and/or consequences are not clearly specified or are applied inconsistently. Through a process of negotiation between the child and his parents or school personnel rules and consequences can be written out. The frequency of arguments is reduced for two reasons: (a) There is less room for disagreement because the rules and consequences are now clearly specified; and (b) the child and family learn something about the negotiating process as a way of solving disputes. It is crucial that the contract specify the positive consequences of appropriate behavior, such as an allowance. After all,would you sign a contract that specified your job duties and penalties for not performing, but said nothing about how much you were to be paid?

Social Skills Training

Social skills training emphasizes the development of social competence through the acquisition of certain crucial social behaviors. The skillstreaming approach (Goldstein, Sprafkin, Gershaw, & Klein, 1980) utilizes task analysis, role playing, feedback, and reinforcement techniques in the training program. Typically a skill is introduced such as "Controlling Your Temper." Following a brief discussion of what constitutes good anger control, the teacher demonstrates the wrong way and the right way to handle anger. Each skill is broken down into several components (count to 10; think of your choices — walk away or relax; act out your best choice). Following a discussion of the teacher's demonstration and the listing of the components of the skill, students role-play the skill. At first they might pause and list the steps as they proceed through the role-play. Feedback is provided by group members. Participation is reinforced verbally and with tokens.

The main difficulty with such programs has been in generalizing results outside the classroom. Treatment effects can be enhanced through the use of homework assignments or planned interactions in the community. The child who is good at listening, giving compliments, accepting criticism, and other important social skills seems less likely to use anger to solve problems.

SUMMARY

Anger is a complex emotion that is expressed at three levels: the cognitive, the somatic, and the behavioral. When used appropriately it serves to energize individuals and relationships, leads to a sense of control, and acts as a cue to utilize coping skills. Excessive anger can lead to loss of important relationships and even incarceration. The rules for the feeling and expression of anger appear to be culturally determined, sometimes leading to misunderstanding when different cultures try to interact. Even within a small community there are minicultures or tribes whose rules on the handling of anger may drastically differ from those of other nearby social groups. There are no apparent sex differences in the frequency of anger episodes, the reasons for anger, or in the effect of that anger.

Little is known about the developmental phases of anger. Observers have noted that tantrums are usually the expression of a want or desire and appear during the second year, reach a peak by age 3, and are decreasing by age 4. The tantrum phase lasts about 1 year. Children also change in their reactions to anger in the home. School-age children have been found to be much less likely to express any emotion when anger is being expressed and are better at trying to arbitrate the dispute.

Assessment is best when it directly relates to the treatment. Self-monitoring and self-evaluation and behavioral observations are accurate, reliable, and have treatment validity.

Several treatment approaches have been used to modify anger responses. Stress-inoculation training emphasizes the acquisition of coping skills, including adaptive self-statements and relaxation in a three stage format: (a) cognitive preparation, (b) skills acquisition, and (c) applications practice. It is possible to use this approach in a preventative program applied to teachers, administrators, and parents of problem children. Behavior modification strategies are often useful with nonverbal or noncompliant youngsters. Behavioral contracts can be used to reduce the need for anger by clearly specifying expectations and consequences. Also, learning negotiating skills makes anger less likely to occur. Social skills training has the further value of systematically teaching and reinforcing various behaviors that enhance one's sense of social competence and of reducing the need to rely on anger to resolve problems.

Even considering our advances in the technology of treating angry children, the basic helping tool is still listening. Angry children need adults who are open and who can respond with empathy, calm, and understanding.

REFERENCES

Averill, J. R. (1982). *Anger and aggression: An essay on emotion.* New York: Springer-Verlag.

Blackwood, R. O. (1970). The operant conditioning of verbally mediated self-control in the classroom. *Journal of School Psychology, 8,* 251–258.

Cummings, E. M., Zahn-Waxler, C., & Radke-Yarrow, M. (1984). Developmental changes in children's reactions to anger in the home. *Journal of Child Psychology and Psychiatry, 25,* 63–74.

Feindler, E. L., & Fremouw, W. J. (1983). Stress inoculation training for adolescent anger problems. In D. Meichenbaum & M. E. Jaremko (Eds.), *Stress reduction and prevention* (pp. 451–485). New York: Plenum.

Gesell, A., Ilg, F. L., Ames, L. B., & Bullis, G. E. (1977). *The child from five to ten* (rev. ed.). New York: Harper & Row.

Goldstein, A. P., Sprafkin, R. P., Gershaw, N. J., & Klein, P. (1980). *Skillstreaming the adolescent: A structured learning approach to teaching prosocial skills.* Champaign, IL: Research Press.

Goodenough, F. L. (1931). *Anger in young children* (Monograph Series No. 9). Minneapolis: The University of Minnesota Press, Institute of Child Welfare.

MacPherson, E. M., Candee, B. L., & Hohman, F. J. (1974). A comparison of three methods for eliminating disruptive lunchroom behavior. *Journal of Applied Behavior Analysis, 7,* 287–297.

Meichenbaum, D. (1976). A self-instructional approach to stress management: A proposal for stress inoculation training. In C. Spielberger & I. Sarason (Eds.), *Stress and anxiety in modern life.* New York: Winston.

Novaco, R. W. (1975). *Anger control: The development and evaluation of an experimental treatment.* Lexington, MA: Lexington Books.

Novaco, R. W. (1976). Treatment of chronic anger through cognitive and relaxation controls. *Journal of Consulting and Clinical Psychology, 44,* 681.

Novaco, R. W. (1977a). Stress-inoculation: A cognitive therapy for anger and its application to a case of depression. *Journal of Consulting and Clinical Psychology, 45,* 600–608.

Novaco, R. W. (1977b). A stress-inoculation approach to anger management in the training of law enforcement officers. *American Journal of Community Psychology, 5,* 527–546.

Novaco, R. W. (1980). The training of probation counselors for anger problems. *Journal of Counseling Psychology, 27,* 385–390.

Schlichter, K., Jeffrey, J. J. (1979). *Effects of stress inoculation training on the anger management skills of institutionalized juvenile delinquents* (Report No. CG 013 634). Paper presented at the Annual Meeting of the American Educational Research Association, San Francisco. (ERIC Document Reproduction Service No. ED 173 727)

BIBLIOGRAPHY: PROFESSIONALS

Averill, J. R. (1982). *Anger and aggression: An essay on emotion.* New York: Springer-Verlag.

The most comprehensive discussion of anger available. Examines anger from theoretical, cultural, legal, and historical views. Reports results of several research projects. Written from the social-constructivist point of view.

Feindler, E. L., & Fremouw, W. J. (1983). Stress inoculation training for adolescent anger problems. In D. Meichenbaum & M. E. Jaremko (Eds.), *Stress reduction and prevention* (pp. 451–485). New York: Plenum.

Provides an excellent description of a stress-inoculation program for adolescent anger control problems. Contains information on many helpful strategies to aid the treatment effect. Reviews several research reports dealing with this treatment approach.

Novaco, R. W. (1975). *Anger control: The development and evaluation of an experimental treatment.* Lexington, MA: Lexington Books.

Describes in detail the cognitive–behavior modification approach to anger control. Reviews research in anger control and describes outcome of treatment for college-age group.

Southern, S., & Smith, R. L. (1980). Managing stress and anxiety in the classroom. *Catalyst for Change, 10,* 4–7.

Describes sources of stress and anger in the classroom and explains the cognitive–behavioral approach to dealing with the stress. Would be useful for teachers to read, also.

BIBLIOGRAPHY: PARENTS

Tavris, C. (1982). *Anger: The misunderstood emotion.* New York: Simon & Schuster.

Tavris takes a critical look at the common theories and myths of anger and its treatment.

BIBLIOGRAPHY: CHILDREN

Smith, R. E. (1975). *When I say no, I feel guilty.* New York: Bantam Books.

This book contains information on assertiveness for teenagers.

Morris-Vann, A. M. (1979). *Once upon a time: A guide to the use of bibliotherapy with children.* Southfield, MI: Aid-U Publishing Co.

This reference contains listings of books for children and is organized by problem (e.g., anger, divorce), age of student, and reading level of the material.

Children and Anorexia and Bulimia

Joseph P. Irilli
Niles City Schools, Ohio

Cathy J. Carty
Kent State University

BACKGROUND

Eating disorders, namely, anorexia nervosa and bulimia (also called bulimarexia nervosa), have shown a dramatic increase in the past decade. The age of onset for these devastating problems is primarily at the junior and senior high school levels, the population with which the school psychologist has direct contact.

Eating disorders are found primarily among young women; however, males involved in sports, gymnastics, and dance are also prone to the syndrome. It is not completely known how widespread the disorder is, but many researchers suggest the syndrome may affect 18–20% of the students in this age range (Bayer & Baker, 1983; Kinoy, 1984). That means the significance equals or exceeds all other low- and high-incidence handicapping conditions with which school psychologists typically deal. Several current studies suggest the incidence among males to be 5–10%. Crisp and Toms suggested the occurrence of anorexia to be 1 of 15 males (Anderson, 1983).

Some school psychologists may not consider that diagnosing eating disorders is their responsibility when serving students. Possibly because of the typical school psychologist's limited experience with these maladies, it seems that eating disorders in the schools are poorly understood. However, second only to the immediate family, school psychologists are in the best position to diagnose eating disorders.

The syndrome has been recognized for more than 100 years, yet modern research still does not agree on its cause. There are broad cultural and societal implications for eating disorders among our students. Personality characteristics include depression, anxiety, compulsive neurotic tendencies, fear of rejection, low self-concept, and distorted body image.

The causes of eating disorders are generally attributed to psychological and social factors. Parental and sibling relationships are also variables to consider. Major life stresses and changes can initiate eating disorders in those who are susceptible. Some data exist that suggest that in a few cases physical factors are to be suspected. Medical causes cannot be ruled out and require medical consultation; however, evidence strongly points to emotional disturbance as the usual root cause.

DEVELOPMENT

The physical symptoms of anorexia and bulimia are varied. While all symptoms may not be readily observable, many would suggest that there are eight general signs that can be detected (Golden & Saker, 1984; Halmi & Falk, 1981; Weiner, 1985).

1. It is not uncommon for anorexics to lose 25% of their body weight within a few months. In an attempt to hide their extreme weight loss, anorectic students often resort to wearing layers of loose-fitting clothing.
2. Weight loss of this magnitude causes hypothermia and the layers of clothing can also serve the purpose of insulating the body against heat loss. Anorectics often complain of being cold. Interestingly, the body in this state will often grow fine body hair called lanugo to conserve body heat, thus signaling hormonal changes.
3. Many eating-disordered persons abuse laxatives and diuretics. Coupled with insufficient food and fluid intake, intestinal tract disturbances are often seen. Normal bowel movements become infrequent and painful.
4. Amenorrhea sets in once the female anorectic has lost approximately 18% of her body fat. Cessation of menstruation is caused by hormonal level disturbance that often characterizes anorectics.
5. Poor hair texture and fingernail quality is found among eating-disordered persons because of protein deprivation. Often eating-disordered patients lose their hair.
6. Eating-disordered persons exhibit dry skin and rashes because they suffer from dehydration. Protein deficiencies further add to the poor skin condition.
7. Poor nutrition, together with vomiting, negatively affect dental health. The hydrochloric acid that is present in the stomach, when vomited, will erode tooth enamel, causing dental caries.
8. Poor sleep patterns are often seen in eating-disordered persons. Consequently, fatigue and poor concentration are evident.

Emotional and perceptual symptoms are generally more subtle than physical characteristics. Close observation of behavior often discloses the signs of an eating-disorder in a student. It should be cautioned that not all affected students display all the symptoms or feelings.

1. Distorted body image and an intense fear of getting fat are symptoms in these students. Even in an emaciated state, anorectics feel fat in spite of their critical condition. The bulimic tends to be self-critical, feeling thighs, hips, and abdomen are disproportionately fat.
2. Extreme sensitivity is often seen among these students. Situations are generally overpersonalized and they view relatively benign events as threatening or negative.

3. Poor self-concept and low self-esteem are common expressions in these students.Because they are often unable to think clearly, owing to biological changes, eating-disordered students are often irrational and unable to make decisions. Suicidal ideation is often present.

4. Depression and masked anger are symptoms often displayed by these students. Repression of anger is their way of hiding real feelings to protect themselves from rejection.

5. Perfectionism and unrealistic goals of excellence are manifestations that are outwardly displayed in the form of dietary abuse. The misuse of diuretics and laxatives becomes a method to hasten weight loss in an attempt to gain perfection of bodily form. These students feel that they have poor self-control, and believe that bulimia or anorexia offers them the power of control over their body.

6. Preferred food lists are commonly found among eating-disordered students. Extremely knowledgeable about calorie content of foods, they compose lists of "good" and "bad" foods. Eventually, the "bad" food list is overly inclusive, leaving them with few foods that they will accept (Anorexia Nervosa and Associated Disorders [ANAD], 1985; Humphries et al., 1982; Inbody & Ellis, 1985; Peters et al., 1984).

The diagnosis of anorexia, according to the DSM III, is based on the following assumptions:

> 1. Intense fear of becoming obese, which does not diminish as weight loss progresses.
> 2. Disturbance of body image, e.g., claiming to "feel fat" even when emaciated.
> 3. Weight loss of at least 25% of original body weight or, if under 18 years of age, weight loss from original body weight plus projected weight gain expected from growth charts may be combined to make the 25%.
> 4. Refusal to maintain body weight over a minimal normal weight for age and height.
> 5. No known physical illness that would account for the weight loss. (APA, 1980, p. 69)

The diagnostic criteria for bulimia are as follows, according to the DSM III:

> 1. Recurrent episodes of binge eating (rapid consumption of a large amount of food in a discrete period of time, usually less than two hours).
> 2. At least three of the following: (a) consumption of high-caloric, easily ingested food during a binge; (b) Inconspicuous eating during a binge; (c) termination of such eating episodes by abdominal pain, sleep, social interruption, or self-induced vomiting; (d) repeated attempts to lose weight by severely restrictive diets, self-induced vomiting, or use of cathartics or diuretics; and (e) frequent weight fluctuations greater than 10 pounds due to alternating binges and fasts.
> 3. Awareness that the eating pattern is abnormal and fear of not being able to stop eating voluntarily.
> 4. Depressed mood and self-depracating thoughts following eating binges.
> 5. The bulimic episodes are not due to anorexia nervosa or any known physical disorder. (APA, 1980, p. 71)

The criteria for clinical diagnosis includes "loss of 20% of body weight; loss of the menstrual period; thinning hair; dry, flaking skin; constipation; lanugo — a downy growth of body hair; lowered blood pressure; lowered body temperature; lowered chloride levels (if vomiting); lowered potassium levels (if vomiting); and lowered pulse rate" (Garner & Garfinkel, 1985; Jacobson, 1985; Piazza & Piazza, 1978).

In order for effective treatment to begin, the factors responsible for initiating and perpetuating the eating disorder must be recognized. While they differ for each individual, many observers believe that the disorder tends to occur more often in children who come from overprotective families. Others cite as causes such circumstances as deep mother–daughter conflict, family instability, divorce, troubled sibling relationships, and chemical dependency. Adolescents who are confronted with these problems and never develop an eating disorder can be seen as fortunate, as lucky persons who are protected by their outgoing personalities and the strength provided within their families (Erichsen, 1986).

An increasing number of adolescents, not so lucky, develop eating disorders. The eating disorder becomes their cry for help. "Their own expectations and those of others may have combined to overwhelm them. They are undergoing an intense adolescent identity crisis, trying to establish who or what they are before feeling strong enough to continue to the next stage of their development" (Erichsen, 1986, p. 171). This becomes a time when their family not only needs to be reassuring, but also needs to develop firmness and refuse to be manipulated. Eating-disordered adolescents need to realize that their family members have joined together to help them overcome their disorder (Erichsen, 1986).

As an eating disorder continues to progress, the adolescent tends to withdraw from the family. This withdrawal is especially noticed in the case of a mother who has previously been overinvolved in her daughter's life, and who may become filled with anger, guilt, and despair at her daughter's refusal to eat meals she has painstakingly prepared. It is at this time that such a mother needs to remember to "use her head and keep her heart firmly under control" (Erichsen, 1986, p. 170). "An anorexic needs to feel that her mother is on her side rather than at her side. She needs her mother to be firmly behind her so that she cannot take a step backwards rather than to actually push her forwards" (Erichsen, 1986, p. 183).

However, it must be kept in mind, according to Erichsen (1986), that the mother of an eating-disordered individual

> has no devoted cooperation from anyone, no mutual understanding or support, painful emotional involvement and no time off. She is on duty 24 hours a day, seven days a week, often for years on end. She is the target for every kind of criticism, with no real opportunity to give her opinion on how the eating disorder may have developed, and never, under any circumstances, is she given the benefit of the doubt. (p. 97)

The eating-disordered adolescent is unable to see the frustration, confusion, and pain her mother is going through. One day she wants her mother constantly at her side, to be her best friend; the next day she totally withdraws from her as if she were her worst enemy. This may be brought on by her mother's social activity and involvement. The adolescent begins to resent all of the other people her mother associates with, feeling that they are becoming more important than she is. This is the time she needs her mother, to listen as she "expresses her doubts and confusion, her uncertainty about how to behave, her fears of failure, of not coming up to her own high expectations. As a sense of failure grows, so she feels increasingly 'empty,' worthless and unlovable" (Erichsen, 1986, p. 17).

Furthermore, not all fathers appear blameless in the etiology of eating disorders. Fathers who place unrealistic athletic or scholastic goals may cause the early manifestations of the disorder. Some of these men try to make their daughters into the sons they never had. In the eating-disordered adolescent this condition perpetuates the need for a slim, boyish figure. Fathers need to be aware of their potential role in the creation of eating disorders.

A typical reaction of the father of an eating-disordered daughter is to feel that she is trying to irritate him. In such cases he turns his back on her when she needs him the most because he fears that she may become a discredit to the family (Erichsen, 1986).

Since normal response during a crisis is to project blame on others, the parents of eating-disordered adolescents often focus blame on the adolescent. The adolescent, in turn, places the blame upon the parents (Squire, 1981). While this issue is not easily dealt with, it is one that must eventually be resolved by all family members if the eating-disordered adolescent is to recover.

PUTTING CHILDREN'S ANOREXIA AND BULIMIA IN PERSPECTIVE

Parents must be aware of the impact that manipulation can play in the lives of their eating-disordered children, who will do everything in their power to avoid eating. This includes lying and manipulation of parents, siblings, and therapists. Research indicates that divorce in eating-disordered families is often precipitated by their children's disorder. This may be caused by triangulation effects, which can side mother against father and daughter, father against mother and daughter, or mother and father against their daughter. Whatever combination develops also causes an internal family struggle for power over the situation. Some psychologists feel that an exertion of power on the part of both parents vis-a-vis their daughter will bring a quick end to their children's eating disorder. This will likely be a temporary cure, however, since none of the underlying psychological problems that precipitated the illness will have been resolved (Erichsen, 1986).

As eating disorders progress, adolescents will commonly use defense mechanisms to keep people at a distance. An adolescent uses defensive behavior to (a) protect self-esteem, (b) get attention, and (c) avoid stress and frustration. At this time parents need to stress three aspects of positive behavior to their children: (a) that they are unique and only need to live up to their own standards, not having to prove themselves or be understood all of the time; (b) that they have the right to make mistakes; and (c) that they control and choose their own behavior (Frey, 1985).

While it is necessary for the parents to support these positive behaviors, they often find it difficult, owing to their unwillingness, to allow their child to grow. Until parents can accept their child's disorder and resolve their own guilt feelings about it, they will be unable to aid in their child's recovery.

ALTERNATIVE ACTIONS

Therapeutic Approaches

There are currently 10 basic approaches used in the treatment of eating disorders. These approaches can be used singly or in combination, depending upon the individual involved.

Individual Therapy. Individual therapy has been found to be one of the most successful and useful approaches when working with individuals suffering from anorexia nervosa and bulimia (Garner & Garfinkel, 1985). Most eating-disordered clients usually do not come into therapy willingly; often they must be pressured by family members, a medical physician, or friends. Therefore, the first interview is very crucial for the psychologist. The need to build a caring, understanding, and trusting relationship with the client is paramount. People with eating disorders usually have withdrawn from their family and friends, and need to develop a firm relationship with someone they can trust (Piazza, 1978).

This type of therapy should be conducted on an outpatient basis unless the patient is at a life-threatening weight or medical complications are present. These factors would require a referral to an inpatient facility.

Before successful therapy can begin, the therapists must try to get clients to establish a weight that permits appropriate functioning. Once weight has become established and maintained, actual therapy can begin. Clients who suffer from eating disorders usually also suffer from intense chronic tension. Therefore, the therapist must encourage these clients to express their anxieties about eating and life. The therapist will also need to work with them on cognitive, behavioral, emotional, and perceptual issues (Garner & Garfinkel, 1985). The duration of therapy tends to vary, depending on the duration of the illness, the clients' receptiveness toward therapy, the extent of illness, and the views of the psychologist involved. Some therapists believe in short-term treatment of up to 6 months; many others feel that longer involvement, for up to 5 years, is needed (Franklin, 1985; Levenkron, 1982).

Family Therapy. The successful treatment of anorexia nervosa and bulimia can be enhanced by family therapy developed specifically for parents who have a difficult time accepting that their child has an eating disorder.

Often the best advice comes from those who have wondered if the nightmare would ever end.

> Never give up hope, and always have faith that it will end — and that your daughter will enter adulthood, and live the many years ahead of her with far more self-knowledge, genuine feelings, compassion, and strength that ever would have been possible had she remained that "perfect child." (Kinoy, 1984, p. 75).

Since this disorder affects the entire family, especially when younger siblings are involved, family therapy can be beneficial to help the family overcome denial of the disorder. It can also be used to enable family members to express their concerns as well as their needs and how they might be fulfilled (Garner & Garfinkel, 1985). Minuchin (1978) reported an effectiveness rate of 86% when a systems model of treatment was used. This model looks at individuals not in isolation from, but in the context of, their families.

Family approaches to therapy center around the recognition that abnormal behavior (in this context; the eating disorder) rarely arises simply from within the psyche of the person displaying the symptoms. Rather, the roots are often within the interaction of the family. The need to change these maladaptive patterns is paramount for positive treatment. From the family therapist's point of view, the display of such symptoms indirectly conveys specific needs and wants to other family members. Through improvement in family communication systems, positive results can be realized.

Hypnotherapy. General relaxation exercises, guided imagery, self-hypnosis, and meditation are now being used to aid eating-disordered clients in dealing with their high level of anxiety toward food and life in general. Hypnotherapy is practiced as a technique by which to comprehend the psychodynamics presented by the client. Self-hypnosis is seen as an effective tool in the treatment of the disorder. Self-hypnosis is beneficially being used by clients for relaxation, self-improvement, self-discovery, and symptom control. If practiced on a regular basis, these techniques of relaxation have been found to aid the anorexic and bulimic in combating the impact that stress can have upon an eating disorder. The client must believe that these techniques will work and must also want to recover, or the techniques will not be effective (ANAD, 1985).

Nutritional Counseling. Nutritional counseling is found to be effective if certain conditions are met, namely, if (a) the counseling is done by a qualified nutritionist; (b) food selection and eating patterns are taught, allowing the client to choose what specific foods are to be eaten; and (c) counseling is used in conjunction with psychotherapy (Squire, 1982).

By following nutritional guidelines the clients learn what foods need to be eaten and in what amounts, but they are also encouraged to be self-regulating in their diets. The counselor will ask clients to keep a food diary to make sure they are eating the proper amounts from each food group (Squire, 1982).

Many adolescents with these disorders are connoisseurs. They are preoccupied with food preparation, often preparing elaborate meals for their family. These adolescents are food experts, having a great deal of knowledge and information about food.

Bibliotherapy. Bibliotherapy consists of the therapists having their clients read specific articles or books dealing with eating disorders. This is done to help them understand the complexity of the disorder and what the possible consequences are if recovery is not achieved.

Drug Therapy. While medication is currently being used to treat anorexia nervosa and bulimia, it remains a controversial issue. Drugs are being used to correct hormone disorders and biochemical imbalances, to lift depression, and to serve as appetite stimulants (Bayer & Bayer, 1983; Marks, 1984). Although its effectiveness remains unproven, cyproheptadine is an appetite stimulant being used in the treatment of anorexia nervosa.

The outlook for the bulimic as to drug therapy is more promising than that of the anorexic. Two antidepressant drugs currently being used are phenelzine and imipramine (Marks, 1984). Extreme care must be taken by physicians in the dispensing of drugs to anorexic and bulimic patients because of their tendency toward drug addiction and suicide.

Couples Therapy. Couples therapy has been developed to work with the married client and spouse who have no children. The content of therapy deals with such issues as (a) the education of the spouse with regard to eating disorders; (b) the eating disordered client's feelings of frustration, guilt, and social isolation; (c) control issues; (d) family issues — coping with various relatives; (e) personality characteristics; and (f) sexual concerns (Leichner, Harper, & Johnson, 1985).

Before engaging in couples therapy, both individuals should be warned that this type of therapy may initially increase tension and conflict. However, it has been found to be useful when both are committed to the recovery of the eating-disordered individual (Leichner, Harper, & Johnson, 1985).

Inpatient Therapy. Hospitalization should occur once a client's weight drops below a level that is mandatory to maintain normal bodily functioning, to interrupt the binge purge cycle, or as soon as medical complications begin to develop. Hospitalization should also be advised for those clients who have not responded to other forms of therapy (Garner & Garfinkel, 1985).

Inpatient therapy differs by individual facility, but most tend to operate under the same basic principles. The four goals of an inpatient facility are to (a) improve eating, (b) allow patients to socialize with peers, (c) achieve a satisfactory initial weight gain, and (d) get the patient and family into therapy (Jacobson, 1985, p. 14).

The weight restoration phase consists of having patients gain a pound per week until they reach 90% of their ideal weight. The patients are permitted to manage their own food intake as long as they gain weight and do not indulge in any purging. Should this occur, a treatment team takes over the management of dietary intake. If patients still continue to eat insufficiently, tube feeding or intravenous feeding will become necessary. As food intake increases, caloric amounts must also increase in order to ensure gain in or maintainance of weight. The patients' eating is continually supervised by staff members who remain with them after meals to prevent excessive exercises or vomiting (Garner & Garfinkel, 1985).

Most facilities operate on a behavior modification approach, allowing the patients visitors, trips home, socialization time, exercise, and sometimes just leave to be out of bed as extra incentive for gaining weight. A hospital stay can range anywhere from several weeks to an extended period of time.

Group Therapy. Group therapy helps the eating-disordered client break down the walls of socialization, and can be used effectively when the right mixture of people are involved. A definite set of inclusion criteria should be involved when selecting members for group therapy, including (a) motivation to change, (b) absence of several denial, and (c) stated desire to meet and help others with eating disorders (Lenihan & Sanders, 1984, p. 252). It has also been found important to include clients who are well on the road to recovery, so that they might provide an incentive for others who see no end to their condition. Usually these groups meet on a time-limited basis of 12–14 weeks, but groups may be extended if all members of the group and therapist agree. The therapist must develop a warm,caring, trusting, and supporting atmosphere in order to put all group members at east. The therapist should try to avoid issues that would promote uneasiness within the group, especially at the very beginning (Lenihan & Sanders, 1984).

Support Groups. Self-help groups are seen as a growing influential factor for eating-disordered persons. Groups of people (eating-disordered as well as parents and loved ones) gather to share particular problems and to discuss those issues without the active involvement of a professional therapist. Parents tempted to explode at their children can find help by discussing the issue with others in the group, permitting an appropriate channel to vent frustration. Similarly, parents can confide their fears to other parents who have undergone the same stress. Self-help groups allow a forum for members to share feelings openly with others confronted with the same problem.

Eating Disorders and School Personnel

The school psychologist will be less involved in the diagnosis of bulimia than anorexia nervosa, since the age of onset of the former is usually the late teens, the twenties, and the early thirties (General Mills, 1981). School psychologists will become increasingly involved in the diagnosis of anorexia nervosa, since the age of onset is continually decreasing and it is known to appear in children as young as 10 years old (Anorexia Nervosa and Related Eating Disorders, 1985; Franklin, 1985).

Working with eating-disordered persons is a long-term treatment process that may be somewhat unrealistic for the school psychologist. However, the therapist is in a position to offer parents, students, and school staff awareness programs as a preventive measure.

Since most school personnel are unaware of the symptoms of eating disorders, it becomes the role of the school psychologist to provide in-service instruction to teachers and other school personnel. It is often very difficult for a teacher or staff member to identify the anorexic who hides under layers of clothing or the bulimic who is able to maintain a normal or nearly-normal weight. Teacher in-service programs need to include a presentation of the diagnostic criteria that are used for assessing an eating disorder, the symptoms that may or may not be present depending on the stage of disorder, the possible treatment options that are available, and an approved plan or action should they suspect a child has an eating disorder.

Anorexia nervosa can be detected by school personnel who are aware of the obvious signs of the disorder. These include rapid weight loss, moodiness, frequent absence from school, withdrawal into a private world, or, at the other end of the continuum, overinvolvement in school activities. Although bulimia tends to occur later in life, school personnel should be made aware of the obvious signs. These include frequent trips to the bathroom after lunch, enlarged neck glands, the consumption of large quantities of food with little or no apparent weight gain, discoloring of teeth, and frequent absence from school (Mallick, 1984).

Teachers should also be made aware of ways in which they may be unconsciously contributing to the increase of these disorders. This is especially true when dealing with physical education teachers and coaches who encourage students to be actively involved in physical fitness and weight control. For eating-disordered children this teacher becomes the positive reinforcement that enables them to continue to follow in a path leading toward eventual self-destruction (Romeo, 1984).

If well-informed, physical education instructors and coaches are in an excellent position to identify eating-disordered students. They can watch for a increase in physical activity, perfectionism, compulsive behavior, and spontaneous statements revealing image delusion. A program can also be developed by the school psychologist and physical education staff to include a preventive program in the school's health curriculum beginning at early adolescence (Romeo, 1984).

Being in a position to offer a program of weight monitoring, the school nurse is a valuable staff member and resource person for the school psychologist to work with in the prevention of eating disorders. A monitoring program would be an excellent way to detect weight losses or weight fluctuations before they get too far out of control. If a student fails to gain the proper amount of weight for age and bone structure, or loses an excessive amount of weight, anorexia nervosa should be suspected. Should a student's weight show continual fluctuations of 10 pounds or more, bulimia should be suspected (Mallick, 1984).

Eating disorders are not only physically, but also psychologically, dangerous and should not be taken lightly by psychologists, counselors, or teachers. School psychologists must be aware of the powerful impact they have on the prevention of eating disorders. In order to conduct a successful in-service program, they need to become knowledgeable about eating disorders. Through reading, dealing with recognized professionals who specialize in eating disorders, and attending quality continuing education programs, psychologists can become more knowledgeable. If they do not feel comfortable conducting the in-service training, a local expert can be invited in to conduct such a program (Hendrick, 1984).

A Parent-Awareness Model Program

The authors of this paper have developed a parent-awareness model program to supplement the school psychologist's traditional areas of involvement. While parents' awareness has been widely cited as an aspect of school psychologists' service to anorexic and bulimic students, no published parent-awareness programs have been identified by an exhaustive literature review.

The successful treatment of anorexia nervosa and bulimia can be enhanced by awareness programs developed specifically for parents who have a difficult time accepting that their child has an eating disorder. These parents include those whose children have never previously caused problems —the perfect child. Suddenly, their child refuses to eat, has restricted food intake to the minimum, or alternates between diets and binges. These parents need help in recognizing the importance of not rushing their child to recover; indeed, they need to "learn to live only one day or hour at a time" (Kinoy, 1984, p. 74).

The present authors' program complete with goals and specific objectives, can be inaugurated by school psychologists for the benefit of parents of eating-disordered adolescents. The program goals are (a) to increase parents' knowledge of anorexia nervosa and bulimia, (b) to increase their awareness of available treatments, (c) to facilitate their acceptance of their children's disorders, (d) to establish reasonable parental expectations for their children, and (e) to develop a sense of security and trust on the part of their children such that support network.

The model program consists of a minimum of 10 sessions, each one based on an essential theme related to eating disorders. They are as follows:

1. Confidentiality. The term *confidentiality* is defined, and the importance of developing a trusting atmosphere is discussed.
2. Education. The terms *anorexia nervosa* and *bulimia* are defined; diagnostic criteria, observable symptoms, physical problems, and possible causes are identified.
3. Treatments. Parents are made aware of all available treatments, suggested readings, and suggestions for finding a therapist.
4. Feelings. This includes identification of feelings toward their children and themselves, discussion of facing reality and accepting feelings, and encouragement of parents to listen to their children's feelings.
5. Defenses. Defense mechanism is defined, reasons for defensive behavior are explored, and aspects of positive behavior are discussed.
6. Parent–child relationships. Discussion topics include parents' relationships with their children, meeting the children's expectations, accepting limits as parents, and letting go.
7. Family. Roles played within the family, stress within the family, the importance of family support, and feelings of separation from children are demonstrated.
8. Guilt and manipulation. Parents are made aware of their guilt feelings (why they feel guilty, how they are allowing their children to manipulate them) and techniques that can be used to combat guilt and manipulation.
9. Communication. The importance of keeping an open line of communication, of not placing blame for the eating disorder on one person, and of setting realistic goals are discussed.
10. Nutrition. Areas of discussion include the caloric intake necessary to maintain a normal body weight, the importance of a variety of foods, the benefits of planning meals ahead, and the benefits of keeping a food diary (Irilli & Carty, submitted for publication).

Society places a great deal of pressure on its youth to excel and become the best individuals they can be. By our society's standards, children should excel both academically and athletically — and be thin and attractive. The media are continually portraying the thin, almost emaciated, look as the goal all young women must achieve. Given the effect and impact that television, movies, and magazines have on youth, the rate of anorexia nervosa and bulimia is skyrocketing. They tend to glamorize a dreary, miserable illness with an element of mystery and exciting danger. The irony is that the same magazines that warn today's youth of eating disorders also glorify the emaciated look and stress quick-weight-reduction diets. Today, being thin is equated with being competent and successful.

The female role patterns become identified with the models who grace the covers of leading fashion magazines as well as the actresses who light up the television and movie screens. Studies have shown that centerfold models and winners of the Miss America pageant have continued to get thinner in the last several years (News & World Report, 1982).

It becomes the obligation of parents and teachers to help students to overcome this illusion. Parents who suffer from their own body image distortions, whether overweight or underweight, are not setting a good example for their children. This is especially true of a mother who is constantly dieting and belittling other family members who are overweight.

Teachers must be aware of the strong impact they have on their students as role models. If they are not confident as to their own body image, they may pass their insecurities on to their students. They also have the opportunity to conduct lessons around the concept of body image and the stress that society places upon today's youth. This might be done quite effectively by the primary teacher who is confronted with an overweight child who may become the anorexic or bulimic of the future.

Until society can come to grips with the unrealistic pressures it is placing on its youth, it will be nearly impossible to prevent eating disorders from occurring. It will be left up to psychologists, educators, and parents to work together to help adolescents confront and overcome the pressures that are placed upon them.

One of the techniques discussed in the literature is promotion of an awareness of social–cultural issues concerning negative body images. Wooley and Wooley, of the University of Cincinnati, have used "such devices as showing educational films about the portrayal of women in the media, distributing feminist articles, and having patients rewrite advertising copy that capitalizes on stereotypes of women" (Garner & Garfinkel, 1985).

It becomes the role of the school psychologist to aid teachers and peers of an eating-disordered adolescent who is reintegrating into the classroom after hospitalization. The adolescent who is coming form an inpatient program is leaving a sheltered institutional environment for a normal, less protective environment. During the hospital stay, all food intake has been taken care of. Special precautions have been taken to shelter patients from the pressures that may have caused the disorder. Returning students are faced with a variety of anxiety-provoking situations the first few weeks after release from an inpatient program. They come face to face with teachers and peers who may be labeling them as having a mental disorder. The most uncomfortable situation for the eating-disordered victim is the lunchroom setting, where food choices must be made. Often, these students are placed in situations in which they feel as though everyone is watching to see what they eat.

Teachers need to be made aware of ways they can make the student's transition a comfortable one. This may consist of educating the other students about the danger of eating disorders and how they can aid in their fellow student's recovery process. Students also need to become more sensitive toward individual differences.

The best program of reintegration of eating-disordered students is a gradual one that begins with a school-based tutor. As these students become more comfortable with this arrangement, they may be gradually mainstreamed into the regular classroom. Tutoring should be gradually phased out at this time. The school psychologist should remain in close contact with the student's therapist throughout the reintegration process in order to avoid relapse (Mirkin, 1985). The issue of relapse is of highest concern during the first 2–6 months following treatment (Garner & Garfinkel, 1985). A supportive reintegration process may involve many months of close contact.

SUMMARY

Anorexia nervosa and bulimia are serious, life-threatening disorders with a wide range of physical and psychiatric components. It is estimated that there may be over a million young persons affected by the syndrome in the United States today. Victims can die from serious, vital-organ damage such as heart failure or rupture of the esophagus, or suffer long-term physical problems. No reliable national statistic concerning death rates are available, but it is estimated that 6–15% of victims of eating disorders will die. Early detection and treatment are vital in order to insure the greatest probability of cure. These disorders tend to be long-term illnesses and financial costs are high; they are highly destructive but, with professional treatment, they can be cured.

REFERENCES

American Psychiatric Association. (1980). *Diagnostic and statistical manual of mental disorders* (3rd ed.). Washington, DC: American Psychiatric Association.

Anderson, A. E., & Mickalide, A. D. (1983). Anorexia nervosa in the male: An underdiagnosed disorder. Psychosomatics, 24(12), 1066–1075.

Anorexia Nervosa and Associated Disorders. (1985). *Support groups: Basic Information and guidelines.* Highland Park, IL: ANAD.

Anorexia Nervosa and Related Eating Disorders. (1985). Anorexia nervosa and bulimia: Two serious eating disorders. In *Anorexia nervosa and bulimia.* Eugene, OR: ANRED.

Bayer, A. E., & Baker, D. H. (1983). *Adolescent eating disorders: Anorexia and bulimia.* Petersburg, VA: Virginia State University Press.

Erichsen, A. (1986). *Anorexia nervosa: The broken circle.* London: Faber and Faber.

Franklin, N. (1985). Starved for self-esteem. *Medical Self-Care,* pp. 41–46.

Frey, (1985, November). *Defensive behavior and what to do about it.* Paper presented at the School Psychology Series, Kent State University, Kent, Ohio.

Garner, D., & Garfinkel, P. (1985). *Handbook of psychotherapy for anorexia nervosa and bulimia.* New York: Guilford.

Golden, N., & Saker, I. M. (1984). An overview of the etiology, diagnosis, and management of anorexia nervosa. *Clinical Pediatrics, 23*(4), 209–214.

Halmi, K. A., & Falk, J. R. (1981). Common physiological changes in anorexia nervosa. *International Journal of Eating Disorders, 1*(1), 16–27.

Hendrick, S. S. (1984, May). The school counselor and anorexia nervosa. *School Counselor,* pp. 428–432.

Humphries, L. L., Wrobel, S., & Wiegert, H. T. (1982). Anorexia nervosa. *Academy of Family Physicians, 26*(5), 199–204.

Inbody, D. R., & Ellis, J. J. (1985). Group therapy with anorexic and bulimic patients: Implications for therapeutic intervention. *American Journal of Psychotherapy, 39*(3), 411–420.

Irilli, J. P., & Carty, C. J. (submitted for publication). The role of the school psychologist working with anorexia nervosa and bulimia.

Jacobson, B. (1985). *Anorexia nervosa and bulimia: Two severe eating disorders.* New York: Public Affairs Committee.

Kinoy, B. F. (1981). *When will we laugh again?* New York: Columbia University Press.

Leichner, P., Harper, D., & Johnson, D. (1985). Adjunctive group support for spouses of women with anorexia nervosa and/or bulimia. *International Journal of Eating Disorders, 4*(2), 227–235.

Lenihan, G. O., & Sanders, E. E. (1984, December). Guidelines for group therapy with eating-disorder victims. *Journal of Counseling and Development, 63,* 252–254.

Levenkron, S. (1982). *Treating and overcoming anorexia nervosa.* New York: Scribner's.

Lucas, A. R. (1981). Bulimia and vomiting syndrome. *Contemporary Nutrition, 6*(4).

Mallick, M. J. (1984). Anorexia nervosa and bulimia: Questions and answers for school personnel. *Journal of School Health, 54*(8), 299–301.

Marks, R. G. (1984, January). Anorexia and bulimia: Eating habits that can kill. *RN,* pp. 44–47.

Minuchin, S., Rosman, B., & Baker, L. (1978). *Psychosomatic families: Anorexia nervosa in context.* Cambridge, MA: Harvard University Press.

Mirkin, M. P. (1985). The Peter Pan syndrome: Inpatient treatment of adolescent anorexia nervosa. *International Journal of Family Therapy, 7*(3), 205–216.

Peters, C., Butterfield, P., Swassing, C. S., & McKay, G. (1984). Assessment and treatment of anorexia nervosa and bulimia in school-age children. *School Psychology Review, 13*(2), 183–191.

Piazza, E. V., & Piazza, N. (1978, June). Anorexia nervosa: A new treatment approach. *Female Patient,* pp. 43–47.

Romeo, F. (1984, March). *The physical educator and anorexia nervosa.*

Squire, S. (1981, October). Why thousands of women don't know how to eat. *Glamour,* pp. 245–246, 309–313, 315.

U. S. News and World Report. (1982, August). *Anorexia: The "starving disease" epidemic,* pp. 47-48.

Weiner, H. (1985). The physiology of eating disorders. *International Journal of Eating Disorders, 4*(4), 347–388.

BIBLIOGRAPHY: PROFESSIONALS

Boskind-White, M., & White, W. C. (1983). *Bulimarexia: The binge/purge cycle.* New York: Norton.
Describes the behavior, dangers, and consequences of bulimarexia. It includes a group therapy program that was developed by the authors after 7 years of applied research and treatment.

Garner, D. M., & Garfinkel, P. E. (1985). *Handbook of psychotherapy for anorexia nervosa and bulimia.* New York: Guilford.
Written specifically for the professional working with eating-disordered individuals, the handbook includes all phases of treatment from initial diagnosis through the maintenance of therapeutic gains. It describes the various approaches that are available to the professional, including psychoanalytic and cognitive–behavioral approaches, group psychotherapy, family therapy, in-patient programs, multicomponent programs, and supportive and educative methods.

Gross, M. (1982). *Anorexia nervosa.* Lexington: Collamore.
Focuses primarily upon the needs of the professional working with adolescents suffering from anorexia nervosa. Included in this book are the history of the disorder, the role of the physician, physiological changes that occur, treatment options, and the role of nutrition.

Irilli, J. P., & Carty, C. J. (submitted for publication) *The role of the school psychologist working with anorexia nervosa and bulimia. ERIC documents.*
This manuscript includes typical best practices for the diagnosis and treatment of anorexia nervosa and bulimia. The authors have developed a parent and adolescent awareness model program to supplement the school psychologist's traditional areas of involvement.

Levenkron, S. (1982). *Treatment and overcoming anorexia nervosa.* New York: Scribner's.
Especially written as a comprehensive treatment guide for psychologists and psychiatrists and a reference for educators and other professionals. It includes a description of the disease and the author's original program of nurturant–authoritative therapy. This type of therapy is based on regressive therapy, which allows the anorexic "to depend on and develop trust in another person."

Minuchin, S., Rosman, B., & Baker, L. (1978). *Psychosomatic families: Anorexia nervosa in context.* Cambridge, MA: Harvard University Press.
Places the emphasis on the role that the family plays in the etiology and maintenance of anorexia nervosa. It includes the therapist role, setting goals for change, and family challenges that must be overcome. Strategies for therapy are provided by various case studies presented.

BIBLIOGRAPHY: PARENTS

Bruch, H. (1978). *The golden cage: The enigma of anorexia nervosa.* Cambridge: Harvard University Press.
Written for parents, teachers, school counselors, and doctors so that they might be made aware of the importance of recognizing the initial signs of anorexia nervosa. It contains 70 case studies that outline the etiology, effects, and successful treatment of anorexia nervosa.

Erichsen, A. (1986). *Anorexia nervosa: The broken circle.* London: Faber and Faber.
Written by the mother of an eating-disordered adolescent, it includes her views as well as those of others on the symptoms, causes, mothers' and fathers' roles, family role, acceptance, and reality. According to the author, this book was written to "give mothers practical suggestions for coping with a distressing and difficult situation."

Kinoy, B. F. (1984). *When will we laugh again?* New York: Columbia University.
Especially written by and for the families of eating-disordered individuals with the help of eight professionals, the book includes a definition of the illness, available treatments, family roles, and the thoughts and feelings of the adolescents themselves.

Liu, A. (1979). *Solitaire: A young woman's triumph over anorexia nervosa.* New York: Harper and Row.
Tells the author's story of growing up and the anxieties that go along with being an adolescent. She suffered for an extended period of time before overcoming anorexia nervosa.

O'Neill, C. B. (1982). *Starving for attention.* New York: Continuum Books.
Describes the life of an adolescent girl growing up in a celebrity family. It explains how she became involved in a diet that got out of control and almost led her to self-destruction. The author includes the roles of her parents, family, therapist, and husband who led her down the road to recovery.

Children and Anxiety

Thomas J. Huberty
Indiana University

BACKGROUND

Anxiety is a familiar term, especially since almost every person reports experiencing anxiety at some time. The definition of anxiety is problematic, however, because it is a subjective term associated with many types of behavior patterns. A particular difficulty is differentiating children's anxieties and fears. Jersild (1954) distinguished anxiety from fear on the basis of the specificity of the stimuli and the consequent responses. Fear reactions were seen to occur in response to specific stimuli, which could be objects or abstract ideas. Conversely, anxiety was defined as a "painful uneasiness of mind concerning impending or anticipated ill" (p. 106). Anxiety was seen to be the result of worry and accompanied by a feeling of helplessness due to being unable to eliminate the problem.

He further suggested that worry is characterized by concerns about specific, objective problems, whereas anxiety is generalized and subjective. Since anxiety depends upon the ability to imagine events not present, both it and worry develop later than fear. Moreover, young children are not aware of the source of their anxiety, since is is more internalized. Anxiety reactions are considered to be more diffuse than fear reactions and have been referred to as "apprehension without apparent cause" (Johnson & Melamed, 1979). Thus, anxiety is likely to be more difficult to assess, since the stimuli and associated responses are difficult to delineate.

Barrios, Hartmann, and Shigetomi (1981) suggested that distinctions between fear and anxiety and between normal fears and phobias may be difficult to operationalize. Identifying a child or adolescent as being "fearful" or "anxious" does not allow for descriptions of behavioral patterns. Moreover, the responses of children so identified may be extremely variable. Furthermore, fears also can exist independently of an observable stimulus, such as when school avoidance is maintained or reinforced covertly or overtly by parents. Treatment programs for anxiety and fear may differ, depending upon whether anxiety is viewed as a specific target for intervention or as a correlate of other problems. Although defining anxiety is difficult because of its subjective nature and relationship to other terms and constructs, the following discussion nevertheless will present anxiety as a general pattern of apprehension and tension. The reader is referred to other chapters in this volume that discuss related concepts, such as fears and phobias and nervous habits.

Characteristics of Anxiety

Anxiety has been conceptualized as an unpleasant emotional state or condition, or as a stable personality characteristic of anxiety-proneness. Cattell (1966) and Cattell and Schier (1961, 1963) developed the concepts of state and trait anxiety. State anxiety is defined as anxiety shown in specific situations, such as test taking, and may or may not be associated with trait anxiety. Trait anxiety is the relatively stable tendency to show levels of anxiety across a variety of situations. Persons with high trait anxiety tend to perceive a wider range of situations as dangerous or threatening (Spielberger, 1983).

While the term *anxiety* often has a negative connotation, there also are positive aspects. Research data suggest that moderate amounts of anxiety may serve as stimuli to act and contribute to higher levels of motivation. A study by Sarason, Lighthall, Davidson, Waite, and Ruebush (1960) found that high-anxiety students did not perform as well as low-anxiety students in performing certain tasks. Two tasks requiring analytic skills under pressured (timed) and unpressured (untimed) conditions showed that high-anxiety children made fewer errors in untimed conditions, while low-anxiety children performed better in the timed condition. Thus, a high-anxiety student may be at a disadvantage when under pressure, but may perform better in unpressured situations, thus enhancing motivation and improved performance.

Most often, however, anxiety is seen as a negative factor that interferes with academic and personal–social functioning. Depending upon the severity, anxiety reactions in children and adolescents may be characterized oversensitivity to many normal environmental stimuli, fear of future outcomes, and concentration difficulties. Behavioral manifestations may include distractibility, impulsive acts, inattention to schoolwork, excessive movement, problems either in getting to sleep or staying asleep, "sweaty" hands and skin, heart palpitations, rapid breathing, nausea, headaches, stomach aches, and unusual fatigue. In extreme reactions, actual flight from the anxiety-producing situation or physical immobility might occur.

Anxiety Reactions and Disorders

Anxiety reactions may be distinguished from normal responses on the basis of their persistence, intensity or magnitude, and degree to which they contribute to maladaptive behaviors. They differ from normal reactions, which usually are relatively brief, do not reach such levels as to be considered a disorder, and do not cause significant, chronic interference with personal, social, or academic functioning. Indicators of the magnitude of an anxiety reaction might include degree of impairment and work- and school-related activity, results of psychological assessment, self-reports, and observation of overt behavior.

Anxiety reactions and disorders are difficult to identify and operationalize objectively, but some work of this kind has been done. The *Diagnostic and Statistical Manual of Mental Disorders – Third Edition* (DSM-III) (American Psychiatric Association, 1980) identifies three major types of child and adolescent anxiety disorders. A *separation anxiety disorder* occurs when separation from "major attachment figures" results in anxiety, perhaps to the point of panic. These children avoid being away from home or other familiar surroundings and tend to cling to parental figures. When separated, they often fear being abandoned or not being reunited with parents. Abnormal fears of death, of injury to self or parents, or of animals and/or monsters may occur, as well as sleeping problems, nightmares, and social withdrawal.

An *overanxious disorder* occurs when a child shows excessive worry and fearful behavior that is not the result of a specific objective event and is not in response to recent stressful occurrences. Worry about future events such as examinations, injury, meeting expectations of others, or ability to perform in a variety of areas may occur, as well as sensitivity to peer group attitudes, self-consciousness, tension, and somatic complaints. These children may be seen as being particularly mature because they frequently ask questions about the future. They also tend to show high levels of conformity to the expectations and standards of others, perfectionism, self-doubt, and nervous habits such as nail biting and hair pulling.

An *avoidant disorder* is manifested by significant avoidance of new persons, strangers, or events and a tendency to seek the comfort and security of familiar persons. They may cling to caretakers and be uncomfortable when asked to do tasks with strangers that are well within their capability. Initiative and interpersonal interaction tend to be low, and lack of normal levels of assertiveness may be seen.

DSM-III further describes the primary differences among the disorders for the purposes of differential diagnosis. Separation anxiety and overanxious disorders differ in that the former emphasizes maintaining close physical proximity to caretakers. There is not a particular aversion to strangers, as in the case of the overanxious disorder. Children showing an avoidant disorder have a desire for affection and acceptance from others, in contrast to schizoid disorders. These DSM-III categories, although perhaps helpful from a descriptive perspective, should be viewed with caution when one is attempting to make diagnoses. The data from studies that have attempted to establish the reliability of the anxiety reaction categories have shown variable results. The reader is referred to Werry, Methven, Fitzpatrick, and Dixon (1983) and to Spitzer, Forman, and Nee (1979) for further information.

Through empirical factor analysis methods, Quay and Werry (1979) have identified an anxiety–withdrawal disorder that is associated with maladaptive functioning of children and adolescents. While this disorder includes withdrawal as an accompaniment to anxiety, it is not inconsistent with the anxiety disorders identified in DSM-III, which also describe tendencies to withdraw from others. Quay and Werry (1979) list the results of several studies in which the following descriptors frequently have been found: anxious, fearful, tense, shy, timid, bashful, withdrawn, seclusive, friendless, depressed, sad, disturbed, hypersensitive, easily hurt, self-conscious, easily embarrassed, subject to feelings of inferiority, worthless, lacking in self-confidence, easily flustered, aloof, crying, secretive, and reticient. Anxious–withdrawn children and adolescents are less likely to be noticed by others than are more overt, acting-out children. A more typical pattern is withdrawal accompanied by tension. Behavioral paralysis, the inability to execute normal motor movements, might occur in extreme avoidance reactions.

Incidence

Quay and Werry (1979) summarized reports of incidence figures for anxiety disorders. In a sample of 1,600 normal children aged 6–12 years, 43% reported seven or more fears, the most frequent being fears of using others' drinking glasses or dishes, snakes, family illness, small cuts and bruises, and school grades. Fears and worries tend to decrease with age: boys report fewer fears than girls, younger children more than older ones, and black children more than white. Anxiety and chronic general fearfulness tend to decrease between 5 and 8 years of age in boys, but not in girls. Rutter, Tizard, and Whitmore (1970) conducted a study on the Isle of Wight and found anxiety states to be the most common in middle childhood. They constituted two-thirds of all emotional disorders, phobic and depressive disorders accounting for the majority of the remainder. Estimates of the frequency of anxiety disorders ranged from about 2.5% to twice that amount.

Anxiety does not seem to be related to social class, an equal number of boys and girls being represented. Family size is not a factor, although eldest children may be more prone to anxiety disorders. Only children seem more likely to show anxiety, possibly because they are more prone to parental overprotection. In boys showing the disorder, family disturbances tend to be more frequent, whereas the same pattern does not emerge for girls. With impending adolescence, girls tend to be at higher risk than boys for anxiety disorders, suggesting that perhaps personal–constitutional factors may be contributing variables.

While there is some evidence that anxiety disorders are rather distinct entitles (Quay & Werry, 1979), anxiety also may occur simultaneously with other behavior patterns such as low self-concept, depression, achievement problems, poor interpersonal relationships, and psychosis. These relationships indicate that anxiety as a factor in personal–social behavior can either be a primary cause of behavior or be a correlate of other patterns. In conceptualizing anxiety for purposes of establishing intervention programs, it must be determined if anxiety is to be the focus of treatment or if it is secondary to a more significant problem.

Relationship of Anxiety to Stress

Stress in children has received increased attention in recent years and is an example of how anxiety is a correlate of a behavior pattern. Stress is distinguished from anxiety in that it is associated with identifiable stimuli and has two components: a stressor and a person's subsequent response. "A stressor is an acute life event or a chronic environmental situation that causes disequilibrium in the individual. This disequilibrium is sufficient to cause the person to make an adjustment to the stressor. This adjustment is called a response. When both a stressor and a response to it occur, stress is present" (Blom, Cheney, & Snoddy, 1986). While stress often is perceived to be negative, pleasant events also can cause stress in children, such as performing in a school play. Coping responses to stress can be adaptive or maladaptive, either of which may have anxiety as an accompanying manifestation. Thus, stress is not synonymous with anxiety, but may be a significant factor to consider in children and adolescents experiencing anxiety. The reader is referred to the chapter "Children and Stress" in this volume for a more detailed explanation of the topic.

DEVELOPMENT

Definitive data on developmental trends and characteristics of anxiety are difficult to establish because of the overlap between anxiety and children's fears. Infants tend to show anxiety by generalized physical activity that becomes more specific with age. They show the most anxiety concerning falling, loud noises, and having physical needs met. At the age of about 7 months, most children go through a period of "stranger anxiety" in which they are very uncomfortable in the presence of strangers and show behaviors such as physical withdrawal, crying, and "clinging" to familiar persons. While such behavior may appear to be in response to a specific fear, the reactions tend to generalize to all strangers regardless of individual characteristics.

Another form of anxiety shown in most children is "separation anxiety," a normal developmental pattern occurring at about 9 months of age. The child may show significant resistance to being separated from a parent, despite the absence of any specific environmental event or trauma. Crying, temper tantrums, increased levels of activity, and resistance to baby-sitters may be common when a parent plans to separate from the child for a period of time. At this age, the child may fear the parent will not return and show evidence of general apprehension. Explanation and reasoning usually are not effective in reassuring the child that the parent will return. Separation anxiety normally decreases to low levels by the time the child enters school, although occasional episodes of the behavior may occur.

Anxiety in children tends to be rather diffuse with few specific referents at preschool ages. As children become older,anxiety tends to broaden and become less diffuse. Children also tend to show anxiety about more abstract concepts as they become older, such as forming friendships, peer acceptance, achievement, and personal appearance. They also may show increased anxiety about the stability of family relationships, death, and the future (Jersild, 1968).

Contributing Factors

Factors that can contribute to abnormal types and/or levels of anxiety in children include social skills, discipline practices of parents, child abuse, academic performance, situational variables such as family constellations, stress and pressure, perceived or real expectations by self and others, and degree of success in social and academic situations. Some observers see anxiety as a personality trait, as some children and adolescents may have a predisposition to anxiety. Others suggest that the specific situation is the major determinant of anxiety. Evidence by Endler and Hunt (1966, 1969) indicates that states such as anxiety and hostility are determined by the interaction of personal and situational variables rather than by either one alone. It is difficult, however, to determine the nature of the reciprocal causal relations between person and situation interactions, owing to limitations of present statistical techniques (Endler & Magnusson, 1976). Nevertheless, it is important to consider both the child and the situation in which anxiety is shown in order to determine contributing factors that may have implications for intervention.

Sex differences in anxiety have been shown by a number of researchers. Females tend to report more test-taking anxiety and higher levels of generalized anxiety (Maccoby & Jacklin, 1974; Oetzel, 1966). Stein and Bailey (1973) have suggested that females are more concerned about the possibility of failure in school situations, and show more anxiety about academic performance. While these relationships are not particularly strong, they do suggest that person variables may play a role in manifestations of anxiety. Since females tend to show higher levels of anxiety, it might be expected that they would show a lower self-concept. The available evidence is quite to the contrary, in that the reported self-concepts of male and females are similar from early school years throughout adulthood (Maccoby & Jacklin, 1974). Thus, one person's anxiety level may be an index of another's "healthy" adjustment. Although females tend to report higher levels of anxiety than males, they are equally able to adjust to environmental demands (Minton & Schneider, 1980).

PUTTING CHILDREN'S ANXIETY IN PERSPECTIVE

When considering a referral from a parent or teacher for a child experiencing anxiety, several points should be addressed:

1. Is the anxiety interfering with the child's personal–social and/or academic functioning?
2. Is anxiety pervasive across all areas of the child's functioning?
3. Is the anxiety a specific focus of concern and intervention or is it primarily a manifestation of a more pervasive or serious problem?
4. Is the anxiety a reflection of normal developmental levels or does it deviate from expectations in type or degree?
5. What are the relative contributions of personal and situational variables in the anxiety?
6. What resources are available to help teachers, parents, and the child cope with the problem?

Depending upon the answers to these questions, the intervenor will be able to determine the type and nature of the intervention plans appropriate for the child. A multimethod assessment approach will be necessary that should include obtaining information from school personnel, parent(s), and child. Developmental and family histories will be helpful, particularly if the anxiety appears to be of a chronic nature or if it is not attributable to specific environmental factors. The developmental history may come from teachers, parents, and other school personnel.

The child's academic performance can be determined by comparing the amount and type of work completed with other students' work and by looking at grades, gains made since the beginning of the school year, and whether the child is working to levels of capability. Performance on standardized tests is not likely to be extremely helpful in this regard, since children with anxiety disorders usually do not show consistent deficits. The nature of the child's social relationships can be determined by observation of the child in different social contexts and in interactions with other students. It is important to establish whether the child shows anxiety because of lack of ability or whether the ability exists but performance is inhibited. Behavioral observation and behavior rating scales also may be of assistance in determining if specific areas of functioning are impaired.

Pervasiveness of anxiety may be determined by observing the child's behavior in a variety of settings, by completing behavior rating scales, and by conducting interviews with teachers and parents may be helpful. Consistencies across settings and situations will give information about the types of environmental variables that are helping to maintain the behavior. If a high degree of consistency across situations is indicated, there is evidence that the anxiety may have a significant individual component, although it may be exacerbated by situational factors. If consistency and pervasiveness are not established, then one should investigate the nature of the situational variables, such as classroom demands, family relationships, and interpersonal relationship difficulties. Self-Report measures of anxiety, such as the Revised Children's Manifest Anxiety Scale (Reynolds & Richmond, 1978) may be helpful in establishing the type and degree of internalized aspects of anxiety. Other measures such as the Personality Inventory for Children (Wirt, Lachar, Klinedinst, & Seat, 1977) contain scales that may be helpful in determining the nature and extent of anxiety.

In some cases, it may be necessary to determine if anxiety is an accompaniment of a disorder,such as depression or obsessive–compulsive behavior. A psychological evaluation may be indicated if questions arise about the degree to which problems other than anxiety are suspected. In some situations, it may be necessary to make a referral for additional psychological or psychiatric evaluation. If such a condition exists, assessment and subsequent intervention may be focused upon the more significant disorder, and the anxiety treated as a secondary concern.

Determination of whether demonstrated anxiety is a function of normal developmental patterns is partially accomplished by comparing the child's behavior to that of others the same age. If the patterns differ in frequency, intensity, duration, pervasiveness, persistence, and maladaptiveness from that of normal children, then evidence exists for the presence of a condition that is not a developmental phenomenon. Conducting observations of other children, making comparisons with normal developmental patterns, and obtaining psychological testing data also may be helpful.

The relative contributions of personal and situational factors can be difficult to establish, since an interaction among them is likely.If the psychologist suspects that a child has a tendency to react with anxiety in many situations, information should be obtained as to the child's typical level of anxiety in these settings. The child's behavior, as well as the degree of consistency across situations, can then be compared with that of others. If the child has high levels of anxiety-associated behavior compared with others and shows consistency from setting to setting, then evidence exists of a significant individual component. If the child's typical level of anxiety is high,but shows variation across settings, then evidence is gleaned that a person–situation interaction exists.

In considering resources available to help the child, the nature and extent of the problem must be determined. If the anxiety is seen to be school-specific, then working with teachers and parents may be the appropriate approach. In making this determination, the school psychologist must evaluate the degree to which the persons having the most contact with the child are willing and able to assist in working with the problem. In situations in which enlisting the help of community agencies is important, the ongoing relationship among the agencies, school, and parents are important considerations.

ALTERNATIVE ACTIONS

If it has been determined that the anxiety shown by a child or adolescent should become the focus of treatment, there are various approaches to treatment that may be appropriate. Barrios et al. (1981) offer some points to consider when treating children's fears and phobias that can be applied to the treatment of anxiety disorders. Since children are not likely to refer themselves for treatment, the problem may be primarily in the perceptions of the referring adults. The child may be anxious, but resist treatment for a number of reasons. If the child's behavior is appropriate, but others' expectations are unreasonable, then the adults may be the appropriate clients.

Definition of how the behavior is a problem is appropriate consideration if it disrupts achievement of personal goals, adaptive ability, or comfort and satisfaction. In the case of a child, the impact of anxiety on individual, classroom, and family functioning is important, as well as the degree to which it interferes with development and learning. If anxiety is a reaction to other problems, such as learning difficulties, parenting behavior, physical illness, or psychotic behavior, the intervenor must determine where and how to begin treatment. The monetary costs of treatment, reactions of the child and others to treatment and subsequent behavior change, and logistical concerns such as changing schedules must be considered.

An important, yet seemingly paradoxical, concern is whether change on the part of the child would be beneficial to all persons involved. If the child's anxiety is intertwined with family behavioral patterns, for example, changes in the child's behavior might disrupt normal family functioning. While family patterns might not be ideal prior to treatment, they could become more dysfunctional as the child's behavior changes. Thus, when considering whether to change a child's anxiety behavior, many concerns must be addressed.

Case Study of Test Anxiety

Test anxiety, anxiety about taking tests and performing well on them, is one of the more common anxieties that students experience. The author once was asked to consult with school personnel about a 15-year-old girl who complained of test anxiety. Mary reported that she could study for the test and feel prepared to take it, but then would "freeze" when confronted with the actual task. Interviews with the teachers and her mother, a psychological assessment, and observations indicated that the test anxiety primarily reflected a fear of failure. Mary perceived that her mother expected high grades and would be disappointed if she did not achieve them. Mary also tended to be very dependent on her mother and had not yet accepted her mother's remarriage about a year earlier, which is about when the test anxiety had begun.

It was thus concluded that Mary did indeed experience anxiety about taking tests, but that a major reason for the anxiety was a fear of failure associated with possible parent disapproval. The anxiety was intensified by Mary's perception of competition for her mother's attention. In this situation, anxiety was a correlate of a more pervasive problem, i.e., the relationship between her and her mother. Treatment focused on providing a consultant to help Mary cope with test situations, as well as a referral for counseling to work on the relationship between her and her mother and stepfather.

Treatment Approaches

It is beyond the scope of this chapter to discuss in detail the various methods of treating anxiety in children. In the event that anxiety is part of a larger problem, such as family difficulties, then family therapy and involvement might be indicated. If a child is showing anxiety as a consequence of being in a classroom that is too competitive and is associated with failure, then consultation with the teacher may be an appropriate form of treatment. When the focus of treatment is primarily the child, behavioral techniques generally have shown the most success. More traditional forms of counseling and therapy may be helpful adjuncts, however, in formulating a treatment plan. In general, four methods of treating children's anxiety responses are most likely to be effective (Barrios et al., 1981): counterconditioning, modeling, operant, and self-control techniques.

Counterconditioning Techniques. If a child experiences anxiety, a counterconditioning approach would involve attempting to pair a positive stimulus with graded exposures to the anxiety-producing stimulus. The most familiar counterconditioning technique is systematic desensitization, in which a person is taught to maintain a relaxed state while being repeatedly exposed to the feared stimulus. While this technique has been used most often with specific fears, it could be helpful if the child is able to visualize an event that is anxiety-producing. This technique typically works best with older children who can create images of anxiety-producing situations. This technique may be helpful in treating test anxiety, as discussed above. If the student can be taught to relax by using desensitization procedures, the intervenor can develop a hierarchy of situations that gradually approximate actual test-taking. The lowest step on the hierarchy might be for the student to imagine opening textbooks to begin preparation for the test; the highest step might be for the student to imagine actually taking the test. These steps are presented to the student in a progressively more anxiety-producing situation while being relaxed by the desensitization procedure.

Modeling Techniques. Another technique used to treat anxiety responses is for the child to observe a model engaging in behavior that typically produces anxiety for the child. These techniques are most useful when the child experiences anxiety due to not knowing how to perform a function or if performance is inhibited by anxiety. This technique may be valuable in situations in which the child must interact or perform with others. A rather common problem occurs when students are very anxious about talking in front of a large group of people. Having the child observe someone else doing the task while being accompanied by a therapist is one method. In these situations, the therapist serves as a guide and facilitator, helping the student to notice the behaviors of the model that are successful in reducing anxiety.

Operant Techniques. Positive reinforcement techniques involving shaping, extinction, and fading have been used with children. Providing reinforcement for increasingly successful approximations of behavior that is incompatible with anxiety are appropriate goals. The use of punishment techniques is not likely to be effective in treating anxiety disorders and may well increase the experience of anxiety that is the focus of treatment. In the case of test anxiety, providing reinforcement as the student performs a series of tasks, such as opening books for study, entering a room where the testing is to occur, and taking the test may be helpful in gradually reducing anxiety.

Self-Control Strategies. Self-control strategies are used to help children manage their own anxiety responses by undertaking incompatible behaviors such as relaxation or self-talk. Techniques such as self-instruction, self-monitoring, stress inoculation training, and self-reinforcement may be helpful in reducing anxiety. The application and subsequent success of these techniques depends upon a child's willingness and ability to assume a large part of the responsibility for treatment. These techniques may be particularly helpful in cases of anxiety about tests or interpersonal relationships. If the child is capable of self-monitoring and is motivated to reduce anxiety, these techniques can be particularly valuable. The development of more direct personal control over anxiety can enhance the likelihood of more lasting effects of a treatment program and can reduce reliance upon teachers or parents in implementing a plan.

If these techniques or others do not prove to be successful, reevaluation is indicated to determine if other controlling variables are operating to maintain the anxiety. In these situations, the possibility exists that the anxiety is not an isolated problem but is a correlate of a more pervasive disorder. It also is possible that factors in the child's environment are interfering with treatment, such as child abuse or family problems. Referral for family therapy may be an appropriate consideration in these situations.

SUMMARY

Anxiety and related disorders are problems that children frequently experience in and out of school. While low orders of anxiety can have positive, facilitative effects on learning and performance, psychologists are more likely to become involved when problems develop with personal–social or academic functioning. Anxiety is distinguished from fears and phobias which occur in response to specific stimuli, and it differs from normal responses in persistence, intensity or magnitude, and maladaptiveness. While children and adolescents experiencing anxiety disorders may not be identified as often as those who "act out", evidence exists that these disorders are some of the most common.

In working with anxiety disorders, the intervenor must consider whether a child's anxiety is pervasive across all situations, how it affects personal–social and academic functioning, whether the pattern is abnormal from a developmental perspective, and to what extent it is an entity or is a correlate of other problems. If anxiety is identified as an individual focus of treatment, behavioral techniques are likely to be the most effective, although traditional counseling approaches may be helpful. Of particular concern will be in determining the degree to which person and situation variables contribute to the anxiety disorder. If a particular type of situation tends to create anxiety that is not evident elsewhere, then one type of treatment may be indicated. If the anxiety is more internalized in the person, then other types of treatment may be necessary. The psychologist must be knowledgeable and sensitive to the complexities of working with anxiety disorders of children and adolescents, and be appreciative of the multi-modal nature of assessment and intervention.

REFERENCES

American Psychiatric Association. (1980). *Diagnostic and statistical manual of mental disorders* (3rd ed.): Washington, D. C: Author.

Barrios, B. A., Hartmann, D. P., & Shigetomi, C. (1981). Fears and anxieties in children. In E. J. Mash & L. G. Terdal (Eds.), *Behavioral assessment of childhood disorders* (pp. 259–304. New York: Guilford.

Blom, G. E., Cheney, B. D., & Snoddy, J. E. (1986). *Stress in childhood.* New York: Teachers College Press.

Cattell, R. B. (1966). Patterns of change: Measurement in relation to state dimension, trait change, and process concepts. *Handbook of multivariate experimental psychology.* Chicago: Rand-McNally.

Cattell, R. B., & Schier, I. H. (1961). *The meaning and measurement of neuroticism and anxiety.* New York: Ronald.

Cattell, R. B., & Schier, I. H. (1963). *Handbook for the IPAT Anxiety Scale* (2nd ed.). Champaign, IL: Institute for Personality and Ability Testing.

Endler, N. S., & Hunt, J. (1966). Sources of behavioral variance as measured by the S-R Inventory of Anxiousness. *Psychological Bulletin, 65,* 336–346.

Endler, N. S., & Hunt, J. (1969). Generalizability of contributions from sources of variance in the S-R inventories of anxiousness. *Journal of Personality, 37,* 1–24.

Endler, N. S., & Magnusson, D. (1976). Toward an interactional psychology of personality. *Psychological Bulletin, 83,* 956–974.

Jersild, A. T. (1954). Emotional development. In L. Carmichael (Ed.), *Manual of child psychology* (2nd ed.) (pp. 833–917). New York: Wiley.

Jersild, A. T. (1968). *Child psychology* (6th ed.) Englewood Cliffs, NJ: Prentice-Hall.

Johnson, S. B., & Melamed, B. G. (1979). The assessment and treatment of children's fears. In B. B. Lahey & A. E. Kazdin (Eds.), *Advances in clinical child psychology* (Vol. 2). New York: Plenum.

Maccoby, E. E.l, & Jacklin, C. N. (1974). *The psychology of sex differences.* Stanford, CA: Stanford University Press.

Minton, H. L., & Schneider, F. W. (1980). *Differential psychology.* Prospect Heights, IL: Waveland.

Oetzel, R. M. (1966). Classified summary of research in sex differences. In E. E. Maccoby (Ed.), *The development of sex differences.* Stanford, CA: Stanford University Press.

Quay, H. C., & Werry, J. S. (Eds.) (1979). *Psychopathological disorders of childhood* (2nd ed.). New York: Wiley.

Reynolds, C. R., & Richmond, B. O. (1978). What I Think and Feel: A revised measure of children's manifest anxiety. *Journal of Abnormal Child Psychology, 6,* 271–280.

Rutter, M., Tizard, J., & Whitmore, K. (1970). *Education, health, and behavior.* New York: Wiley.

Sarason, S. B., Lighthall, F. F., Davidson, K. S., Waite, R. R., & Ruebush, B. K. (1960). *Anxiety in elementary school children.* New York: Wiley.

Spielberger, C. D. (1983). *State–Trait Anxiety Inventory. Manual.* Palo Alto, CA: Consulting Psychologists Press.

Spitzer, R. L., Forman, J. B. W., & Nee, J. (1979). DSM-III field trials: I. Initial interrater diagnostic reliability. *American Journal of Psychiatry, 136,* 815–820.

Stein, A. H., & Bailey, M. M. (1973). The socialization of achievement orientation in females. *Psychological Bulletin, 80,* 345–366.

Werry, J. S., Methven, R. J., Fitzpatrick, J., & Dixon, H. (1983). The interrater reliability of DSM-III in children. *Journal of Abnormal Child Psychology, 11,* 341–354.

Wirt, R. D., Lachar, D., Klinedinst, J. K., & Seat, P. D. (1977). *Personality Inventory for Children.* Los Angeles: Western Psychological Services.

BIBLIOGRAPHY: PROFESSIONALS

Gittelman, R. (Ed.). (1986). *Anxiety disorders of childhood.* New York: Guilford.
This book describes anxiety disorders from theoretical, assessment, developmental, and therapeutic perspectives.The volume describes a variety of approaches to understanding the nature of anxiety disorders in children as well as discussing the correlates of anxiety.

Morris, R. J., & Kratchowill, T. R. (Eds.). (1983). *The practice of child therapy.* New York: Pergamon.
This volume contains several chapters on the treatment of a variety of childhood disorders, including fears and phobias. Several behavioral treatment approaches are discussed that may be used directly or adapted for use with anxiety disorders. Many of the chapters describe disorders of which anxiety may be an accompaniment. Discussion is provided about etiology,incidence, and planning intervention programs.

Ross, A. O. (1981). *Child behavior therapy.* New York: Wiley.
This book describes various child disorders and proposes behavioral treatment approaches for them. Disorders that often accompany anxiety are discussed, such as isolation and withdrawal. A variety of treatment approaches are presented that address disorders such as fears and phobias, and include modeling, desensitization, forced exposure, and operant procedures.

Children and Assertiveness

Marie Boultinghause
Charlotte-Mecklenburg Schools, North Carolina

BACKGROUND

Assertiveness can be defined as "self-expression through which one stands up for his or her own human rights without violating the basic human rights of others" (Kelley, 1979, p. 2). Children who behave assertively are able to honestly and directly express their feelings and opinions while simultaneously showing respect for others and accepting responsibility for their own behavior. It is important that assertiveness not be confused with aggressiveness, which violates others' rights, and nonassertiveness, which allows one's own rights to be violated by others.

Although it is difficult to specifically assess the frequency of aggressive and nonassertive behavior, the school psychologist often receives referrals because of children's behavioral excesses and deficits. Parents and teachers often express concern about behavior by children that results in lack of peer acceptance, in name calling and peer ridicule, and in consequent emotional discomfort. Referrals may be made because of concern for extremely shy children who are afraid to speak up in class and unable to interact comfortably with peers. Children may be referred because of frequent conflict with authority figures. They may be unable to firmly say No without recanting, even when their personal well-being is at stake. Bright children may be referred because their inability to live up to perfectionist standards results in eventual failure to make academic effort; less able children may be referred because their expectations of future failure result in loss of motivation.

The school psychologist can play a critical role in helping children to learn alternative behaviors, accept responsibility for behavior, and learn respect for themselves as well as others. With the psychologist's help, children can acquire skills with which to appropriately adjust behavior when it results in pronounced conflict with authority figures, diminished self-esteem, poor interpersonal relationships, or inability to make decisions. Children do not automatically outgrow behavioral excesses and deficits. Fortunately, assertive behavior can be consistently taught, practiced, and generalized to real-life situations.

Verbal Components of Behavior

Assertive behavior involves expression of one's thoughts, feelings, and beliefs in direct, honest, and appropriate ways that do not violate the rights of others; the message does not humiliate, degrade, or dominate the recipient (Lange & Jakubowski, 1976). The child who behaves assertively expresses personal opinions but also respects differing opinions of peers.

Nonassertive behavior is a failure to honestly and directly express one's own thoughts and feelings that thus allows one's rights to be violated by others; the goal of appeasement suggests lack of respect for oneself and others (Lange & Jakubowski, 1976). Children who behave nonassertively do not defend themselves but assume the role of doormat in a vain attempt to be liked by others.

Aggressive behavior involves expression of one's thoughts, feelings, and beliefs in a manner that violates the rights of others; the goal is domination and winning regardless of the cost (Lange & Jakubowski, 1976). Aggressive behavior can be distinguished from assertive behavior by its violations of *others'* rights, inappropriateness, and lack of respect. Those who behave aggressively have no concern about the effect of their behavior on others.

Nonverbal Components of Behavior

Nonverbal components of assertive behavior are consistent with and emphasize the verbal message. Voice loudness is situation-appropriate, eye contact is firm but not staring, body gestures denote strength, and the speech pattern is fluent (Lange & Jakubowski, 1976). Assertiveness is best facilitated by systematic attention to nonverbal components of eye contact, body posture, gestures, facial expression, timing, and fluency as well as verbal content (Alberti & Emmons, in Alberti, 1977).

Nonverbal behaviors which typically accompany nonassertive expression include evasive eye contact, body gestures that convey anxiety and distract the listener from the verbal message, dysfluent speech, and bowed body posture; these behaviors convey weakness, anxiety, and self-effacement (Lange & Jakubowski, 1976). "Nervous" giggling and inappropriate laughter often accompany nonassertive behavior.

Nonverbal behaviors that accompany aggressive behavior tend to dominate or demean the recipient of the message. These include inappropriate voice volume, fixed eye contact, sarcastic or condescending voice tone, finger pointing (Lange & Jakubowski, 1976), physical proximity to the recipient that is "too close for comfort," and sometimes hands-on-the-hips posture.

DEVELOPMENT

Children begin to assert themselves at the moment of birth; thus begins a lifelong attempt to respond to and interact with their environment. As maturation continues and language is acquired and developed, children become increasingly able to express feelings, needs, desires, and responses. Styles of self-expression are heavily influenced by reinforcement and modeling, initially by parental figures and siblings, and eventually by school authority figures. Peer influence and modeling become increasingly more powerful as a child's chronological age increases.

Problems that are referred to the school psychologist frequently involve behavioral excesses and deficits that reflect failure to learn alternative behaviors. Once a particular behavior is learned, children may become stuck in behavioral ruts from which they are unable to extricate themselves without assistance. Poor peer relationships may be traced to children's bullying or failure to stand up for themselves. Continuing conflict with authority figures may reflect a "one-mode" pattern of responding or the reinforcement value of negative attention.

Other factors may also contribute to children's lack of assertiveness and consequent lack of self-esteem, anger toward themselves, and guilt. Extreme perfectionism may reflect a combination of children's own unrealistic expectations, misunderstanding (sometimes a correct understanding) of parents' and teachers' expectations, or inability to accept themselves as developing but imperfect human beings; self-statements may then result in failure to make reasonable academic or social efforts and produce what the children most fear —failure itself. Children's inability to say No when it is appropriate to do so may result from their inability to distinguish when it makes sense to do so, fear of the consequences of doing so, an overwhelming need for peer acceptance, or a lack of refusal skills.

Normal assertiveness is verbal/nonverbal behavior that is self-satisfying and does not result in intolerable conflict with peers and authority figures. This implies a personal assessment of comfort level and individual rights as well as development of an internal locus of control and lessening of need for control by others. Concepts of assertiveness also imply basic assumptions about human nature: (a) There is a close relationship between one's feelings and behavior; (b) behavior is learned; and (c) behavior can be changed (Percell, cited in Alberti, 1977).

The psychologist must be sensitive to the interaction of cultural, socioeconomic, and religious values that influence behavior. Galassi and Galassi stated that "Assertion occurs within a situation . . . that is embedded within a cultural context" (1977, p. 308). Grodner (1977) pointed out the necessity of thoroughly exploring the possibility that increased assertiveness might bring out cultural conflict and increase anxiety. Although there are a number of cross-cultural studies by Landau and Paulson, by Hwang, by Cheek, and by Grodner (reported in Alberti, 1977), that suggest the effectiveness of these procedures, it is important that careful consideration be given to the possibility that increased assertiveness might increase parent/child and home/school conflict. Certain religious groups disapprove of the direct expression of anger. An appropriate time to assess the impact of social/cultural/religious factors may be when the psychologist obtains parental permission to work with the child.

A number of studies have suggested that assertive procedures can be effectively used with child and adolescent populations. Thoft used assertive concepts with fourth, fifth, and sixth graders who lacked social skills and noted that the skills taught were transferred to the classroom and playground (Alberti, 1977). Waksman (1984) demonstrated improved self-concept and increased internal locus of control with 46 students in a middle school setting; positive changes were effected in less than 10 clock hours and without isolating those who had been identified as having interpersonal problems. McPhail successfully utilized assertive procedures with adolescents who suffered from feelings of powerlessness (Alberti, 1977). Garnett showed that behavior of juvenile delinquents became less aggressive as they acquired assertive skills (Alberti, 1977), suggesting that a child's aggressiveness may reflect lack of alternative responses.

Kuczen (1984) advocated the use of decision making, problem-solving skills, and systematic relaxation training to help parents and teachers reduce children's levels of stress. Dilberto (1983) outlined specific assertive procedures for use with elementary/middle school children to help them cope with peer pressure; a more comprehensive list of verbal assertive statements has been outlined by Smith (1975).

PUTTING CHILDREN AND ASSERTIVENESS IN PERSPECTIVE

The psychologist must be familiar with certain techniques in order to help a child learn and practice assertiveness skills. One of the most basic techniques is role playing in which the child recreates a situation verbally and acts out behavioral responses while a second person plays the role of another person in the interaction. Role reversal is a variation in which the second person assumes the child's role while the child assumes the second person's role (Rimm & Masters, 1974). Behavior rehearsal is practicing specific behaviors as if they were being performed in an in vivo situation and includes overt and covert elements; covert rehearsal is imagining the situation and mentally practicing an assertive response (Lange & Jakubowski, 1976). Lazarus (1977) gives many examples of the use of imagery in preplanning one's behavior.

The use of modeling is a "short-cut method for giving information about various assertive behaviors" (Lange & Jakubowski, 1976, p. 177). Modeling may be overt or covert, depending upon whether the child imagines someone else behaving assertively in a similar situation or actually observes and learns vicariously from another person who demonstrates assertive behavior (Lange & Jakubowski, 1976). The psychologist may note that the use of covert modeling offers potential advantages when overt modeling might be inappropriate or embarrassing to the child. The use of imagery may be enhanced by instructions to attend to sensory stimuli and to "tune in" to feelings aroused.

Cognitive restructuring is defined by Lange and Jakubowski (1976) as the "process by which individuals become aware of their thinking patterns which lead to ineffectual behaviors and change these thought processes to more productive ones" (p. 119); it includes the following steps: (a) identifying the specific situation in which a self-assertion challenge arises, determining appropriateness, and setting goals for that situation; (b) using cognitive–behavioral interventions; and (c) identifying one's personal rights (Lange & Jakubowski, 1976). This might include the A-B-C paradigm (Ellis & Harper, 1975) to aid in identifying irrational ideas and substituting rational ones and in identifying and coping with faulty internal dialogs, as explained by Meichenbaum (1975). Hopefully, the cognitive restructuring process will lead to reduction of the anxiety experienced in the specific situation, increase of one's repertoire of effective responses for that situation, development of a belief system that values the rights of oneself and others, and recognition of irrational assumptions and expectations in a specific situation (Lange & Jakubowski, 1976).

The psychologist can use coaching by making statements about general principles or specific behaviors. Feedback can be provided on the child's rehearsal of an alternative response and later role play can incorporate feedback. Feedback should (a) describe rather than label behavior, (b) be objective rather than evaluative, (c) be specific rather than general, and (d) request reaction from the receiver (Lange & Jakubowski, 1976). Feedback should be followed by praise for the child's attempts to practice an alternative, more desirable response. By use of the principal of successive approximation, the psychologist attends to desirable behavioral changes, thereby shaping the behaviors.

Anxiety can be lessened by the use of systematic relaxation training procedures that involve alternate tensing and relaxing of muscle groups, imagery, and deep breathing. For more comprehensive discussions of these processes, the reader may wish to refer to Lange and Jakubowski (1976), Jacobson (1938), Wolpe (1958), and Alberti (1977 p. 355).

Homework behavioral assignments, consisting of specific tasks similar to those practiced with the child, involve the "systematic planning and carrying out of specific cognitive, affective, and behavioral changes" outside the child–psychologist interaction, thus providing the opportunity for transition to real-life situations (Lange & Jakubowski, 1976, p. 172).

The psychologist must be sensitive to the wide variety of children's backgrounds and parental input into problematic situations in which the children become involved. For example, a child's getting into fights in school may be directly related to parents' admonition to "stand up for yourself," by which they may mean physical and verbal aggression rather than other means of refusing to allow oneself to be trampled upon. This type of behavior must be handled carefully so as not to alienate parents and further increase the child's difficulties; a desirable approach might be to ask parents about the potential consequences of their recommended approach to difficulties while adhering to the bottom line that all children and adults have the right not to be abused.

The psychologist must always take care not to attempt to impose personal preferences upon a child's behavior. It is unrealistic to label expected behavior during rough-and-tumble contact sports as "aggressive" so long as the players follow the game rules. In this type of situation, it is only when rules are not followed that behavior can be considered aggressive and violating the rights of others.

ALTERNATIVE ACTIONS

Enhancement of change can be fostered by encouraging a child to keep a journal of attempts at assertion, feelings about self, and alternatives for dealing with similar future situations. Nonhardening clay can be used to model one's feelings about the day's behaviors. Use of art techniques provides a change from typical verbal responses and can be used as a warm-up exercise for reticent children.

Modes of Delivery

The above procedures can be used in group as well as individual contacts with children. The group provides the opportunity for modeling and feedback by peers; it can also serve as a support group with opportunity for peer reinforcement of attempts at assertion.

Individual contact might be more effective with shy, withdrawn children who may at a future time choose to join the group. The psychologist might ask these children to list their rights as a human being, then to list the rights of their parents and other authority figures, and subsequently to list the rights of others. The psychologist might then briefly discuss the difference between human and role rights (see Kelley, 1979) and then proceed to practice acceptance of these human rights in simulations of a recent real-life events with which the children have been displeased with their own behavior. It is important to stress that the children must *not* accept responsibility for the behavior of others — only for their own.

Typical Real-Life Events

Name calling is one of the most destructive but common of children's behaviors. An adolescent described a recent name-calling incident to which he had responded with great anger; stuttering and articulation errors had increased when he became extremely upset which reinforced the protagonist's remarks. Author and student discussed the incident briefly and tried to determine the payoff for the name-caller. They then role-played a more assertive response with emphasis on (a) remaining calm, (b) maintaining eye contact, (c) using appropriate nonverbal behavior, and (d) using negative assertion (Smith, 1975): "Yes, and I've been thinking that I . . . ." The student was asked to observe the message's impact. Homework was assigned to rehearse in imagery or with a family member responses to future name-calling incidents; role reversal and journal entries were also used.

Behavioral deficits and excesses are common areas of difficulty. In either case, children should be encouraged to acknowledge their own rights and others', accept personal responsibility for behavior, express wishes and feelings in terms of "I" messages and personal responses to the situation. Attention should be directed to accompanying nonverbal behavior. The following might serve as an example: A student wishes to ask a girl for a date but is too shy. The psychologist has the student rehearse the scenario by, in turn, encouraging him to consider his rights as a human being, focus clearly on what he wants to do and how he wants to go about it, play the role of the girl in question while the psychologist plays the student's role, incorporate the modeled behavior with attention to nonverbal as well as verbal performance, and assess satisfaction with his *own* behavior — not the other's response! The psychologist may also teach the student systematic relaxation strategies, including deep breathing and imagery. As homework he can be assigned the task of rehearsing behavior in imagery, with a friend or family member, or while watching himself in the mirror, after which he must assess his behavior and plan an improved strategy.

Behavioral excesses often take the form of inappropriate expression of feelings that violate the rights of their target. A typical example in the school setting is the expression of anger by verbal or physical violence. The psychologist might help children to determine the real source of anger and how they wish to respond. Children might be asked to attempt a minirelaxation procedure before expressing negative feelings and to consider the message they wish to communicate. Then with the psychologist or another child they might practice communicating anger without violation of other people's rights and accepting responsibility for anger rather than blaming another person. For example, a child might be encouraged to say, with attention to nonverbal behaviors, "I feel angry when you continue to use my belongings without asking." If the adversary persists, the child might be encouraged to accelerate the situation by saying, "If you do not stop taking my things, I will ask Mrs. Jones to speak to you." The speaker is then obligated to carry through with action. Children could also be encouraged to keep records of their assertive attempts to deal with expression of anger, their feelings in handling the situations, and alterations of behavior over time in similar situations until they become satisfied with their own behavior.

It is important to note that one always has the right to choose not to be assertive but must accept responsibility for the choice made. The right to personally assess behavior and choose whether or not to change it necessarily involves one's acceptance of attendant consequences.

Saying No is a particularly important skill when one is faced with others' attempts to have one engage in an undesirable activity. This might run the gamut from refusing to lend toys, fending off sexual abuse by an adult, or declining to use drugs/alcohol, to graciously turning down a date. One technique that might be used is the "broken record" (Smith, 1975), which is effective in dealing with persistence, and should be accompanied by attention to nonverbal behavior, including eye contact. For example, the bold statement "No, I choose not to take a drink" is preferable to "I can't" or making excuses, which encourages coaxing. In the face of persistence, one can continue, "I realize you would like for me to . . . , but I won't," meanwhile remaining calm, maintaining eye contact, and being careful not to engage in incongruous nonverbal behavior such as irrelevant laughter. One might turn down a date by saying, "I appreciate your offer, but I don't want to go with you."

The psychologist may be asked for help in dealing with typical child behavior at home. A common source of parental frustration is a child's persistent avoidance of household tasks. An appropriate application of assertiveness principles might be: "I know that you're hungry; your dinner will be waiting after you take out the trash." When a child who has not yet completed assigned tasks pesters the parent to do something: "I know that you want to go to the party. I will be ready to take you as soon as you finish the dishes." If the child persists, the parent may continue, "I realize it may be difficult for you to understand, but I won't take you to the party until the dishes are finished." Thus, the parent rightfully accepts authoritarian role without being autocratic, as outlined by Silberman and Wheelan (1980), simultaneously enforcing the child's understanding of acceptance of responsibility and of the consequences of particular behavior as a counterpart of legitimate self-assertion.

SUMMARY

Assisting children in the development of assertiveness skills results in long-term benefits of increased self-esteem, improved interpersonal relationships, acceptance of responsibility for one's own behavior, and the ability to alter behavior when its consequences are undesirable. Systematic use of the cognitive–behavioral–affective/humanistic procedures described enables children to learn to maintain control of their input into a situation and accept concomitant responsibility for their behavior, thus developing an internal locus of control. By learning basic concepts of mutual respect, rights, and responsibility, children are able to simultaneously increase their level of assertiveness, decrease aggressive and nonassertive behaviors, decrease their levels of anxiety, and make decisions about when it is appropriate to be assertive. By learning to preplan and evaluate their own behavior and alter it when necessary, children increase their sense of mastery.

The effectiveness of the strategies described in dealing with both individuals and groups may be explained by the fact that, based on empirical research, they involve the whole person in a framework of concern for others, and give attention to nonverbal as well as verbal components of communication. As always, the psychologist must be sensitive to the impact of cultural–socio-economic–religious values that influence people's perceptions of appropriate behavior.

REFERENCES

Alberti, R. (1977). Issues in assertive behavior training. In R. Alberti (Ed.), *Assertiveness: Innovations, applications, issues.* San Luis Obispo, CA: Impact, pp. 353–364.

Alberti, R., & Emmons, M. (1977). Assertion training in marital counseling. In R. Alberti (Ed.), *Assertiveness: Innovations, applications, issues.* San Luis Obispo, CA: Impact, pp. 231–237.

Cheek, D. (1977). Assertive behavior and black lifestyles. In R. Alberti (Ed.), *Assertiveness: Innovations, applications, issues.* San Luis Obispo, CA: Impact, pp. 111–118.

DiLiberto, R., Jr. (January, 1983). Assertiveness training helps children learn to say "no:" Techniques for coping with peer pressure. *Early years: K/8, 13*(5), 52, 66.

Ellis, A., & Harper, R. (1975). *A new guide to rational living.* North Hollywood, CA: Wilshire.

Galassi, J. P., & Galassi, M. D. (1977). Assessment procedures for assertive behavior. In R. Alberti (Ed.), *Assertiveness: Innovations, applications, issues.* San Luis Obispo, CA: Impact, pp. 307–325.

Garnett, L. (1977). Assertion training with juvenile delinquents. In R. Alberti (Ed.), *Assertiveness: Innovations, applications, issues.* San Luis Obispo, CA: Impact, pp. 223–229.

Grodner, B. (1977). Assertiveness and anxiety: A cross-cultural and socio-economic perspective. In R. Alberti (Ed.), *Assertiveness: Innovations, applications, issues.* San Luis Obispo, CA: Impact, pp. 135–147.

Hwang, P. (1977). Assertion training for Asian-Americans. In R. Alberti (Ed.), *Assertiveness: Innovations, applications, issues.* San Luis Obispo, CA: Impact, pp. 129–134.

Jacobson, E. (1938).Progressive relaxation. Chicago: University of Chicago Press.

Kelley, C. (1979). *Assertion training: a facilitator's guide.* La Jolla, CA: University Associates.

Kuczen, B. (December, 1984). A.C.T. — A program for stress management. *Early Years: K/8, 15*(4), 26–27.

Landau, P., & Paulson, T. (1977). Group assertion training for Spanish speaking Mexican-American mothers. In R. Alberti (Ed.), *Assertiveness: Innovations, applications, issues.* San Luis Obispo, CA: Impact, pp. 119–128.

Lange, A., & Jakubowski, P. (1976). *Responsible assertive behavior.* Champaign,IL: Research Press.

Lazarus, A. (1977). *In the mind's eye.* New York: Rawson.

McPhail, G. (1977). Developing adolescent assertiveness. In R. Alberti (Ed.), *Assertiveness: Innovations, applications, issues.* San Luis Obispo, CA: Impact, pp. 215–222.

Meichenbaum, D. (1975). Self-instructional methods (how to do it). In A. Goldstein & F. Kanger (Eds.), *Helping people change: Methods and materials.* New York: Pergamon.

Percell, L. (1977). Assertive behavior training and the enhancement of self-esteem. In R. Alberti (Ed.), *Assertiveness: Innovations, applications, issues.* San Luis Obispo, CA: Impact, pp. 59–64.

Rimm, D., & Masters,J. (1974). *Behavior therapy: Techniques and empirical findings.* New York: Academic.

Silberman, M., & Wheelan, S. (1980). *How to discipline without feeling guilty.* New York: Hawthorn Books.

Smith, M. (1975). *When I say no, I feel guilty.* New York: Bantam Books.

Thoft, J. (1977). Developing assertiveness in children. In R. Alberti (Ed.), *Assertiveness: Innovations, applications, issues.* San Luis Obispo, CA: Impact, pp. 195–203.

Waksman, S. (Spring, 1984). Assertion training with adolescents. *Adolescence, 19*(73), 123–130.

Wolpe, J. (1958). *Psychotherapy by reciprocal inhibition.* Stanford: Stanford University Press.

BIBLIOGRAPHY: PROFESSIONALS

Alberti, R. (Ed.). (1977). *Assertiveness: Innovations, applications, issues.* San Luis Obispo, CA: Impact.
An excellent resource book that provides background data, addresses innovations in technique and assertiveness across cultures, and discusses special applications of assertiveness principles.

Alberti, R., & Emmons, M. (1974). *Your perfect right.* San Luis Obispo, CA: Impact.
Written for both laymen and professionals, this book includes material on human rights, assertive behavior, as well as using assertiveness to build relationships, distinguishing between anger and aggression, and being cautious about potential adverse reactions. Provides individual and group procedures, applications, and selected annotated bibliography.

Canter, L., & Canter, M. (1976). *Assertive discipline.* Los Angeles: Lee Canter and Associates.
With focus on power to the teacher, applies the use of assertive discipline skills to the classroom and the use of assertiveness skills for dealing with parents and school administrators. Provides practical guidelines in easy-to-read conversational style that may be helpful to both teachers and psychologists.

Lange, A., & Jakubowski, P. (1976). *Responsible assertive behavior.* Champaign, IL: Research Press.
An excellent overview of assertiveness philosophy and techniques; provides careful attention to verbal and nonverbal components of the three types of behaviors and their belief systems. Contains in-depth discussions of effective assertiveness techniques and provides structured exercises and specific application of assertiveness skills to practical real-life situations.

Silberman, M., & Wheelan, S. (1980). *How to discipline without feeling guilty: Assertive relationships with children.* New York: Hawthorn Books (division of Elsevier-Dutton).
An excellent, thoroughly practical volume written in conversational style, this resource book gives specific examples of the three kinds of behaviors and discusses parental rights, needs, and responsibility. It emphasizes the need for teachers and parents to accept rightful authority without being authoritarian and point out consequences of destructive ideals.

BIBLIOGRAPHY: PARENTS

Lutheran Social Services of Washington. (1982). *My very own book about me!* Spokane, WA: Author.
hildren's coloring/activity book prepared for collaborative use by parents or teachers and includes guidelines for its use. It uses an appealing format and assertiveness approach to help children protect themselves against sexual abuse.It provides a sensitive means of seeking to prevent sexual abuse of the young child.

Phelps, S., & Austin, N. (1975). *The assertive woman.* San Luis Obispo, CA: Impact.
Excellent, easily read resource for both males and females; contains a wealth of practical information despite its entertaining format. Divides behavior into four basic types with which we can easily identify. Provides practical examples by which one can choose and work toward behavioral changes.

Silberman, M., & Wheelan, S. See annotated bibliography for professionals.

Smith, M. (1975). *When I say no, I feel guilty.* New York: Bantam Books.
A popular book, this resource outlines specific types of assertions and provides guidance as to when each may be appropriately used. Gives examples of effective combinations of assertive statements.

Children and Biracial Identity

Andrew J. Adler
Metropolitan Public Schools, Tennessee

BACKGROUND

The biracial child is the issue of parents from separate racial groups. Sebring (1985) has termed these children as "first-generation interracial children." While the term *interracial* has been frequently used in the literature, *biracial* will be used here to denote the offspring of parents of different racial backgrounds in order to gain consistency with such terms as bicultural, bilingual, and biethnic.

Accurate figures on the number of biracial children in the United States are difficult to ascertain. Sources of information are census data and scattered investigations in the literature of anthropology, psychology, social work, and sociology. However, census data have not been found to be a reliable source of information since it is not possible to determine whether children born in a racially mixed union were actually born during that union. With a paucity in research studies, little integration of data has been attempted and a definitive work has not emerged.

Until June 1967, intermarriage in the United States was illegal in 16 states. At that time, the Supreme Court ruled antimiscegenation laws unconstitutional. In the early 1980s, interracial marriages made up only one-third of a percent of the 48.7 million married couples in the United States (Pope, 1986). Approximately 2,000 black–white marriages were taking place per year. Although Herr (1974) pointed out that the total number of black–white marriages increased by 26% from 1960 to 1970, Pope (1986) has noted a decline for the early 1980s. In 1980, the number of interracial marriages reached 167,000; a decline to 155,000 was reported by 1982.

By contrast, little attention has been devoted to intermarriage rates between U.S. citizens and Asian nationals. Schnepp and Yui (1955) noted that the years following World War II and the Korean War gave rise to approximately 15,000 "war bride" marriages; 10,000 of them between U.S. and Japanese citizens. It is not known whether the figures for the U.S. citizens considered blacks and whites in their study.

Kitano, Yeung, Chai, and Hatanaka (1984) reported interracial marriage rates for Korean-, Japanese-, and Chinese-Americans living in Los Angeles and Hawaii during the latter half of the 1970s. Of 661 recorded interracial marriages by Asian-Americans in Los Angeles, the Japanese-Americans had the highest rate of marriage to non-Asian-American spouses. They were followed by the Korean-Americans and Chinese-Americans. In Hawaii, Chinese-Americans and Korean-Americans were found to marry non-Asian-Americans in greater percentages than did Japanese-Americans.

Information extracted from several sources point to an incidence of black–white marriages that eclipses white–Asian-American marriages in the United States. It is highly likely that black–Asian-American marriages are the rarest.

The number of children produced by racially mixed marriages is also unclear. Golden (1954) cited a small number of children in a small sample of black–white marriages. Herr (1974) noted that information about the total number of children born to interracial couples was still inexact. He concluded that black–white marriages produced less offspring than homogenous black marriages. Although the exact number of biracial children in the United States is not known, it is likely, since intermarriage has generally increased, that we have an increasing, albeit small, number of first-generation biracial children.

DEVELOPMENT

Ethnicity is critical in identity formation (McGoldrick, Pearce, & Giordano, 1982). Throughout one's life, ethnic heritage, culture, and values reinforce membership within a group. According to Erikson's conception of ego development (1959), each child moves through a series of developmental phases, each phase having a specific crisis. Erikson hypothesized that identity versus role confusion was the psychosocial crisis of puberty and adolescence. How people perceive themselves, including their awareness of what others expect of them, is what is synthesized into a well-developed and integrated sense of identity. Identity can be weakened when one has not built a sense of self and also when the immediate milieu has not offered definite membership, support, and a meaningful place or role.

Erikson (1968) related the process of ego identity and development of a healthy self-esteem to racial identity. He posited that black children were at risk of developing "negative identities" because of the various disparaging, devaluing, and ambiguous messages encountered. In this conflict lies the crux of Erikson's identity crisis and confusion. Since Erikson wrote about "negative identities," television programming has incorporated increasing numbers of situations in which minority youths have been portrayed. Of these, shows such as Bill Cosby's "Fat Albert and the Cosby Kids" have stressed "positive identities." In the schools, values clarification and the development of understanding of self and others have been included more frequently as classroom activities. These activities have helped all children develop self-esteem.

The development of a healthy identity is often at risk for the biracial child. On a gradual basis, these children become aware of the distinctions between themselves, their families, and members of the majority group. Prejudicial feelings and racial awareness and preferences have been found to be present in children as young as 3 years old (Goodman, 1964; Porter, 1971). At this point, biracial children frequently begin to question themselves and their identity. Typical questions asked include the basic "Who am I?" and "Am I white or am I black (or Asian in the case of a white–Asian-American or black–Asian-American child)?" They may also question the meaning of minority group status in society and how they are different from other members of that group. These children often seek to qualify their biracialness by asking if it is better than being "all black" or "all Asian." Perhaps the most difficult conflict to resolve occurs when a biracial child perceives herself or himself to be a member of one group but is perceived by others to belong to another group, usually the minority group. The biracial child may feel pulled between two cultures.

Biracial children present a diverse set of characteristics. As Sebring (1985) has noted, the stresses of being the product of an interracial marriage can be severe and children's lives are affected by their parent's coping style, resources, and abilities. In particular, when parents have not reached a resolution of the conflict between their own self-concept and society's view of their marriage, children are at risk for many emotional and behavioral difficulties.

Biracial children also share a sense of duality in cultural orientation. This is especially characteristic of children from two-parent homes that maintain contact with the racial groups of the parents. The resulting broader base of experience can contribute to an enhanced sense of self and identity. Diversity of ethnic ties may allow for increased flexibility in interpersonal relations (D. Granberry, personal communication, January 12, 1986). This is less of a factor when divorce or separation has occurred and social contact has not been maintained with the racial group of the absent parent.

PUTTING CHILDREN AND BIRACIAL IDENTITY IN PERSPECTIVE

The prereferral activities of school psychology services for biracial children are not dramatically different from those of other children who might be brought to the attention of the school psychologist. The presenting problems are clarified in much the same way as in other cases whether the school psychologist is working alone or in conjunction with other school personnel. Prereferral consultation with parents and teachers often centers on the gathering of pertinent home, family, school, and community information. Ecological assessment is useful in understanding children's social and emotional development. In particular, Sue (1981) has cautioned that this process of information gathering must reflect the psychologist's sensitivity and understanding of how racial differences shape parenting roles and styles.

While parents and teachers of biracial children are valuable sources of information, extended family members can also be expected to give a wealth of information. The children's contacts and responses with extended family members can provide meaningful data about family strengths and cohesiveness (Faulkner & Kich, 1983). Since families are agents in protecting their children from society's prejudice and bigotry (Ladner, 1977), it is important to determine not only parenting styles and roles but also social support systems and contacts. Pertinent questions to ask parents include how the family transmits positive racial information to the child, especially family roots and heritage. Information about the parents' own prejudices, perceptions, and actions in respect to race in general, as well as their children's biracialness, should also be explored (Lyles, Yancey, Grace, & Carter, 1985; McRoy, Zurcher, Lauderdale, & Anderson, 1984).

Obviously one of the major hurdles faced by biracial children is the resolution of ambivalence over their ethnic identity (Sebring, 1985). Resolution of that quandary is a hallmark in the development of a positive racial identity that is tested when children are asked to classify themselves racially. When given a choice in racial self-classification, most biracial children classify themselves as biracial rather than identify with a single race (Arnold, 1984).

When confusion or denial of heritage is present, loneliness and isolation may result and the usual range of presenting problems for school psychologists may ensue. Chief among these is difficulty with peer interactions, academic difficulties that are not accounted for by other factors, and problems of attitude and self-esteem. However, Johnson and Nagoshi (1986) have noted that adjustment problems are speculative; they are less likely to be seen when there is community acceptance of interracial marriage. When the community is not hospitable or open to interracial marriages, problems are likely to be compounded. The social stresses to children and their families may have a cumulative cost.

While specific developmental issues affecting biracial children can be expected to be similar to those that characterize other children, racism in the U.S. society has varied effects on biracial students. Some students do not encounter as much racism in their lives, but others must contend with it daily. Whether rarely or repeatedly encountered, racism can be expected to have a very pronounced and profound effect on the biracial student. In the role of change agent, the school psychologist can have a marked influence in tempering the effects of racism on these students. Although integration and an increased emphasis on multicultural education in the school curriculum have been generative, these modifications alone cannot cure the social ills of racism in U.S. education today. Rohrer (1977) noted that schools cannot be expected to solve the problems caused by prejudice in our society. What schools can do is to provide for equality and opportunity for all children. Racial identity is to be encouraged and enhanced just as achievement is cultivated.

ALTERNATIVE ACTIONS

In many instances, the biracial student will come to the attention of the school psychologist for reasons that are seemingly unrelated to biracial identity. While a student's biracial background does not have to be an issue in the referral, it is prudent to probe for relevance. This probing is necessary as clarification of the referral reasons often point to secondary concerns that are sometimes unstated. If presenting problems relate to getting along with others, depression, family difficulties, or self-concept, it is especially crucial to explore the student's feelings, thoughts, and attitudes towards his or her biracial background and identity.

Concerns about biracial identity may be successfully addressed in the schools through counseling. Whatever the theoretical orientation of the school psychologist, three points are salient for counseling biracial children. First, it is imperative that the student be seen within a cultural context. Second, the psychologist must be perceived as knowledgeable about the child's cultural background. Third, the psychologist must examine her or his own attitudes, values, and perceptions on racism, interracial marriage, and biracial identity. Psychologists should be aware of their own feelings about these issues.

The most important goal in counseling biracial students and their families is to increase awareness of their heritage and to enhance the dignity and respect given that heritage. It is crucial to provide support and validation to family members as needed. Families can be encouraged to reinforce a biracial lifestyle and to emphasize role models from the racial groups that contribute to the family. To facilitate the development of positive self-identity in their children, parents must examine their own self-concept and self-esteem. Supporting their children's use of a biracial label can also facilitate the development of a healthy identity. School placements should be made into racially mixed schools where the school climate may be more accepting.

To be sure, there are many issues that demand consideration in counseling biracial children. In addition to the content of counseling, psychologists must be aware of process issues. In particular, transference and countertransference issues have been noted by Lyles et al. (1985) and by Pope (1986). The psychologist must be vigilant in recognizing both so as not to impede the therapeutic process. It is also essential to sort out what issues relate to biracial identity and what to psychoeducational concerns that affect all students.

Because of the small number of biracial students, it is likely that few school psychologists will encounter them in their practice. In urban areas with a culturally diverse population, however, more biracial students can be expected. In those settings, small-group counseling may be possible as well as individual counseling.

As consultants, school psychologists may contribute to curriculum planning and development in multicultural education. School psychologists could serve as useful resources in developing separate courses in the school curriculum or consulting on how multicultural education can be infused into a variety of courses that are already offered. A speaker's bureau could be organized that draws upon community members. School psychologists may be called upon to make presentations to subject area classes, parent–teacher organizations, and faculty groups.

SUMMARY

The issue of identity has an immeasurable effect upon the lives of children and adolescents, particularly biracial students. Biracialness, once hidden and denied, usually scorned, is receiving increased attention in respect to its social cost to children. While the exact number of biracial students in the United States remains unknown, educators have become more sensitized to cultural differences among the general student population. The inclusion of multicultural material in curricula has brought about an awareness of children who come from more than one cultural heritage. Biracial children, an overlooked minority group in our multicultural society, are perhaps best characterized as first-generation children of parents from separate racial backgrounds. The majority of biracial children are from black–white marriages, smaller numbers resulting from white–Asian-American or black–Asian-American marriages.

Ethnicity is critical in identity formation since cultural background, in many ways, defines who individuals are and what they are about. Biracial children bring their life experiences into the classroom, when there is often a "collision" between the child's cultural background and the set of expectancies that has become known as the culture of the school. A child from a biracial background is much more likely than a child from the majority culture or even single minority cultures to be an academic casualty and to develop problems related to self-concept and identity.

Although biracial children are a diverse population, they do have a common set of characteristics. Biracial children inherit from their parents and families the stresses of being different in a society that has marked racial distinctions. Often the object of scrutiny and curiosity, they experience the effects of racism at an early age. However, all biracial students also share a duality in cultural orientation, as a result of which it is typical for them to demonstrate an increased flexibility in personality functioning because of a broader experiential base.

The major problem in identity formation in the biracial child centers on ambivalence over ethnic identity. School psychologists can assist by providing individual, group, and family counseling. Effective services are predicted upon skilled counseling, collaboration with teachers and parents, and the psychologist's openness, awareness, and sensitivity.

The social needs of biracial children are coming into focus as the pressing concerns of an overlooked and unique group. This may be related to a recent emphasis on multicultural education, the emergence of bilingual school psychology as a subspecialty within school psychology, efforts to recruit more minority school psychologists, and an influx of small numbers of biracial children in refugee groups.

Few school psychologists will have the opportunity to work with biracial children. However, all school psychologists can work toward greater multicultural awareness and understanding. In this respect, school psychologists can be educational and community leaders in the teaching of positive self-regard, trust, tolerance, and respect for all individuals.

REFERENCES

Arnold, M. E. (1984). The effects of racial identity on self-concept in interracial children. (From *Dissertation Abstracts International, 45*(9), Abstract No. DA 8418608.

Erikson, E. (1959). Identity and the life cycle. *Psychological Issues, 1,* 102, 111.

Erikson, E. (1968). *Identity: Youth and crisis.* New York: Norton.

Faulkner, J., & Kich, G. K. (1983). Assessment and engagement stages in therapy with the interracial family. *Family Therapy Collections, 6,* 78–90.

Golden, J. (1954). Patterns of Negro–white intermarriage. *American Sociological Review, 19,* 144–147.

Goodman, M. E. (1964). *Race awareness in young children.* New York: Collier.

Herr, D. M. (1974). The prevalence of black–white marriage in the United States, 1960 and 1970. *Journal of Marriage and the Family, 36*(2), 246–258.

Johnson, R. C., & Nagoshi, C. T. (1986). The adjustment of offspring of within-group and interracial/intercultural marriages: A comparison of personality factor scores. *Journal of Marriage and the Family, 48,* 279–284.

Kitano, H. H., Yeung, W., Chai, L., & Hatanaka, H. (1984). Asian–American interracial marriage. *Journal of Marriage and the Family, 46*(1), 179–190.

Ladner, J. (1977). *Mixed families.* Garden City, NY: Anchor/-Doubleday.

Lyles, M. R., Yancey, A., Grace, C., & Carter, J. H. (1985). Racial identity and self-esteem: Problems peculiar to biracial children. *Journal of the American Academy of Child Psychiatry, 24*(2), 150–153.

McGoldrick, M., Pearce, J., & Giordano, J. (Eds.), (1982). *Ethnicity and family therapy.* New York: Guilford.

McRoy, R. G., Zurcher, L. A., Lauderdale, M. L., & Anderson, R. E. (1984). The identity of transracial adoptees. *Social Casework: The Journal of Contemporary Social Work, 65*(1), 34–39.

Pope, B. R. (1986). Black men in interracial relationships: Psychological and therapeutic issues. *Journal of Multicultural Counseling and Development, 14*(1), 10–16.

Porter, J. D. R. (1971). *Black child, white child: The development of racial attitudes.* Cambridge, MA: Harvard University Press.

Rohrer, G. K. (1977). Racial and ethnic identification and preference in young children. *Young Children, 32*(2), 24–33.

Schnepp, G. J., & Yui, A. M. (1955). Cultural and marital adjustment of Japanese war brides. *American Journal of Sociology, 61,* 48–50.

Sebring, D. L. (1985). Considerations in counseling interracial children. *Journal of Non-White Concerns in Personnel and Guidance, 13*(1), 3–9.

Sue, D. (1981). *Counseling the culturally different: Theory and practice.* New York: Wiley.

BIBLIOGRAPHY: PROFESSIONALS

Banks, J. A. (1984). *Teaching strategies for ethnic studies* (3rd ed.). Newton, MA: Allyn and Bacon.
This versatile book outlines key strategies, resources, and materials needed to teach ethnic studies and how to include them in the regular school curriculum. Various ethnic groups, including refugees, are discussed from a comparative standpoint.

Ladner, J. (1977). *Mixed families.* Garden City, NY: Anchor/Doubleday.
Traces issues through case studies, that impact on biracial children and transracially adopted children. Although the central issue is adoption, many of the dynamics that are present in the families are of interest to the school psychologist.

Verma, G. K., & Bagley, G. (Eds.). (1979). *Race, education, and identity.* New York: St. Martin's.
Through a series of essays, the editors look at race, education, and identity with a sociological perspective. Since the authors are mostly British, treatment of the topic is with reference to the United Kingdom.

Williams, J. E., & Morland, J. K. (1976). *Race, color, and the young child.* Chapel Hill: University of North Carolina Press.
Investigates the development of race and color concepts in young children. These are explored in the context of the implications that adult world phenomena have for children's learning.

BIBLIOGRAPHY: CHILDREN

Adoff, A. (1982). *All the colors of the race.* New York: Lothrop, Lee & Shepard Books.
An illustrated collection of poems of easy readability. The poems are written from the perspective of a child of a white father and a black mother. The poems are simple yet profound.

Friedman, I. R. (1984). *How my parents learned to eat.*
This engaging book for young readers explores the difficulty in learning to eat with knives, forks, and spoons and with chopsticks. The story is explained by a white–Asian-American girl with accompanying illustrations.

May, J. (1971). *Why people are different colors.* New York: Holiday.
Takes the position that to deny that racial groups exist would be futile. The colors of the people of the world are seen as adaptive changes. The book is heavily illustrated with examples and would appeal to middle school students with an interest in the life sciences.

Myles, B. (1976). *All it takes is practice.* New York: Knopf.
Relates the experiences of a would-be basketball player who befriends a new, biracial classmate. Their ordeal at the hands of some bullies forces them to confront bigotry and racial tension. Friendship is emphasized in this book for older middle school students.

RESOURCES FOR THE FAMILY

Biracial Family Network
P.O. Box 489
Chicago, IL 60637
(312) 667-5505

Biracial Family Resource Center
800 Riverside Dr., Suite 5G
New York, NY 10032
(212) 807-6284

Interracial Family Alliance
P.O. Box 16248
Houston, TX 77222
(713) 454-5018

Children and Birth Order

Albert F. Hodapp and Joan B. Hodapp
Northern Trails Area Education Agency, Clear Lake, Iowa

BACKGROUND

While 49.9% of all U.S. families in 1984 had no children, U.S. Census Bureau data also indicated that 20.7% were one-child families, 19% were two-child families, 7.2% were three-child families, and 3.2% were four-or more-child families. This meant that the average family size in 1984 was 3.24 persons (U.S. Census Bureau of the Census, 1985). Put another way, 80% of all U.S. and British children have siblings (Dunn, 1984). The importance of the sibling relationship can be seen by the finding that 4- to 6-year-old children spent twice as much time in each other's company as with their parents (Bank & Kahn, 1975). Dunn (1983) summarized the existing literature on sibling relationships as suggesting that "siblings may, by their behavior toward each other, create very different environments for each other within the family" (p. 787).

The first approach to sibling relationship study was Adler's pioneer work on birth order. Adler, emphasizing the psychological position of the child in the family constellation, believed birth order positions (firstborn, second, middle, youngest, only) established personality characteristics that had continuity between childhood and adulthood (Shulman & Mosak, 1977). Specific traits were felt to develop from the consistent problems or experiences unique to each birth order.

Adler's own childhood experiences may have had some impact upon his later theorizing about striving for social status in the family setting (Watson, 1963). Watson (1963) reported that Adler, a second-born male with rickets, described his older brother as a model child with athletic skills. Adler theorized that social interest, prompted by the fictional goal of a self-ideal, worked toward the creation of an idealized cooperative community (Ansbacher & Ansbacher, 1964).

Adler's theory generated numerous data-based studies contrasting birth order effects across a variety of academic and social variables. Birth order alone was considered predictive of differential outcomes in school achievement, career success, vulnerability to emotional distress, and the whole gamut of life experiences. The effects of birth order on intelligence received extensive attention. Zajonc (1976, 1983) and his colleagues (Zajonc & Markus, 1975) constructed the theory of confluence to explain the pattern of results. The confluence model established the absolute intellectual level in the family as the critical factor — that is, with each new child in the family, the average IQ of the family dropped until the new child developed his/her ability. The development of the child's mental ability is dependent upon the total mental ages of the child's family. Firstborns and those in the early ordinal positions had a decisive advantage over those born later. The firstborn also had the advantage of tutoring the younger sibling(s), which promoted achievement. But does the confluence model or birth order research adequately predict the social or educational levels of children in different ordinal positions?

H. Mosak's position (Shulman & Mosak, 1977) was that birth order research was often faulty because of lack of systematic control of key variables. Mosak placed importance on the variables of sex differences, age spacing, compensatory role demands due to death of a sibling, extrafamilial competitors such as cousins, and the impact of talented or handicapped siblings on normal siblings in the family.

Other important variables such as socioeconomic status (SES) and birth order distribution rates confounded earlier research sufficiently for Schooler (1972) to declare that birth order was unworthy of further research.

The most telling research of all, however, is that of Reimers & Keith (1986), which analyzed intelligence data for 10,976 high school seniors at both the group and the individual level for family size and birth order. The results suggest that SES and race have a significantly greater impact than birth order for which no clear pattern emerged.

While questions about birth order may serve as opening discussion points about the dynamics of child rearing, how much impact birth order really has upon particular individuals should be determined through interviews in the assessment procedures.

DEVELOPMENT

The Only Child

Perhaps among children of all birth order positions, the only child has the strongest negative stereotype. This stereotype may have been the decisive factor in parents' changing a child's status from only child to firstborn. Yet examples of successful adults who were an only child include Franklin D. Roosevelt (president), Martha Collins (governor of Kentucky), Ted Koppel (journalist), Marlene Shyer (writer), Cary Grant (actor), and Brooke Shields (model) (Lobsenz, 1986). Lobsenz (1986) has reported an increase in the percentage of married women expecting to have only one child. Falbo (1977b) reviewed studies on only child status in respect to intellectual ability, achievement, interpersonal orientation, and sex role development but found conclusive documentation only in the area of intellectual ability. Having the advantages of greater financial resources and an uninterrupted parent–child relationship, the only child's IQ is generally higher than that of the firstborn of four-child families. But the IQs of firstborns in two- and three-child families were generally higher than those of onlyborns.

The negative stereotype of the lonely, only child popularized in works such as *The Birth Order Book* (Leman, 1984) has been refuted. Falbo (1980) found that college students who were only children had made a number of close friends and had secured leadership positions in proportions comparable to levels for students from families with more than one child. In game situations, students from one-child families made cooperative moves sooner than students who had siblings; the relationship with trusting adults and the absence of sibling rivalry may have generated this effect. Polit & Falbo (1985) and Falbo (1980) concluded that only children were not put at a disadvantage by the absence of siblings when intelligence, achievement, motivation, peer popularity, self-esteem, educational attainment, behavior problems, loneliness, extroversion, and autonomy were evaluated. Only children actually had higher internal locus of control scores than children of first-, middle-, or last-born birth positions. Falbo (1980) suggested that only children, a potential control group for the study of sibling interaction effects, have been routinely grouped with firstborns by researchers. As a control group, only children could help researchers measure the effects of sibling tutoring in the family, a phenomenon that, in fact, has not been researched (Falbo, 1977a).

The Firstborn

The clinical literature stereotypes the firstborn child as having a high need for achievement, high responsibility scores, strong self-discipline, high need for approval by others, task orientation, and vulnerability to social pressure (Forer, 1976; Wilson & Edington, 1981). How does this compare to the results of data-based studies?

Pfouts (1980) studied 5- to 15-year-old males in two-child families. As a group, the firstborns were responsible, sensitive, serious, independent, and competitive, whereas secondborn males were social, athletic, easygoing, and imaginative. Three groups were studied. The first group consisted of brothers with equal IQs. They were recognized by both parents and teachers as being equally successful academically, but secondborn males were more athletic. The second group had secondborn males with higher IQs than their older brothers. In this situation, the firstborn males surprisingly maintained their status by developing their athletic skills. Competition between the brothers led to academic underachievement by the secondborn males. The third group of the Pfouts (1980) study was composed of firstborn males intellectually more capable than their younger brothers. This group of brothers performed in school as culturally expected, but were perceived as less socially adjusted and more self centered than their younger brothers, thereby supporting clinical personality stereotypes.

The cultural expectations for the firstborns are pervasive but also sex-specific. Noble (1981) found that mothers generally overestimated the mental and motor skills of their infants but mothers of male infants overestimated their sons' performance on the Bayley Scales of Infant Development (Bayley, 1969) for both Mental and Motor scales. Mothers of firstborns had higher expectations as measured by the Motor scale for their babies than did mothers of later born infants.

Gewirtz and Gewirtz (1965) found that mothers of only and of firstborn children spent twice as much time with their children as mothers spent with their later born children. For a while, not only has the first child a great deal of parental attention but that attention may be qualitatively different. Sears, Maccoby, and Levin (1957) noted that parents tended to interact more positively with their firstborn than later born children and to provide lower amounts of nurturing to each succeeding child. In findings consistent with this, Jacobs and Moss (1976) reported that mothers spent more quality time with their firstborn than with their secondborn children. Time spent in social, affectionate, and caretaking activities were more frequent for firstborn than secondborn children. However, the decrement in maternal treatment toward secondborn children was greatest for girls and notably smaller with boys. There was virtually no decrease in maternal treatment toward secondborn boys with older sisters. Knight (1982) noted that secondborn girls made more rivalry–superiority comments to peers than firstborn girls. In assessing birth order effects in cooperative--competitive social interactions for a sample of 105 children, Knight (1982) also found that firstborn and secondborn boys made approximately equal numbers of altruism/group enhancement choices.

Minnett, Vandell, and Santrock (1983) studied 7- to 8-year-olds in their interactions with their siblings. Birth order, age spacing, and sex of sibling were analyzed. Firstborns were more likely than secondborns to praise and teach their younger siblings; secondborns responded with more self-deprecating comments. More aggression was found between closely spaced siblings. Children spaced 3–4 years apart evidenced more frequent positive behavior and affection. Girls were more likely to praise and teach their siblings whereas boys were more likely to engage in neutral behavior, to work, or to play with their siblings. Cheating, aggression, and other negative behaviors were more typical of children in same-sex dyads than cross-sex dyads.

The one-child family represents a single-model situation, especially with consistency in discipline and values. Thus, the firstborn child orients himself/herself toward adults (Sutton-Smith, Roberts, & Rosenberg, 1964), and pays more attention to parents (Baskett, 1984). The two-child family represents a multiple-model situation, since both parents and the firstborn child interact with the younger child in a variety of teaching ways. In this situation, the parents may train the firstborn to assume the parent-surrogate role (Sutton-Smith et al., 1964) and to develop a task-oriented leadership style. With the birth of the second child, parental pressure for more mature behavior by firstborn children increases (Clausen, 1966), probably owing to the increase in family commitments. Baskett (1984) showed that firstborns, matched for age with later born children, received more negative feedback from parents and siblings than later born children. Using the data from the Fels longitudinal study, which controlled for family size, age, sex, and IQ assessments, McCall (1984) found that the IQ performance of the first child dropped 10 points during the 2 years following the birth of the younger sibling. After this 2-year period, the IQ of the firstborn increased. This supports the finding by Sears, Maccoby, and Levin (1957) that parental nurturance and interactions decrease with the birth of the second child.

The Secondborn

Authors such as Adler view the secondborn child as having the nearly insurmountable task of catching up with the pace-setting firstborn, who becomes the standard of comparison. The second child, looking for success and a family role, may be more inclined to follow a nonconformist role than the conservative firstborn (Wilson & Edington, 1981).

Actual studies have found that the dynamics of the two-child family may be more complicated than that, in that the composition of the sibling dyad impacts upon family functioning. Same-sex or cross-sex dyads may generate different types of interactions and demands for parents. The research data (Brim, 1958; Sutton-Smith & Rosenberg, 1965; Rosenberg & Sutton-Smith, 1964) revealed that secondborn children of cross-sex dyads were more imitative of their older sibling than secondborns of same-sex dyads. This imitative effect has also been strongly documented in males with older sisters. A contrast effect has also been documented in college males with older sisters who were found to have fewer feminine traits than males with brothers (Leventhal, 1965), suggesting that imitation occurs for some traits but a contrast effect happens for others.

Sears, Maccoby, and Levin (1957) stated that parental interactions with later born children seem to be influenced by the sex of the second child. For example, if the firstborn is a male, the parents might respond more positively to the birth of a girl than a boy. Hodapp and LaVoie (1976) found that secondborn children in cross-sex dyads imitated their older sibling more than adult male or female parent surrogate. The "novelty" of male–female dyads may ease some aspects of sibling rivalry.

Age spacing also impacts upon the family interaction. Parents exert greater influence in their interactions with their children than do siblings when age spacing reduces frequency, intensity, and duration of sibling contact (Koch, 1955). Miller and Zimbardo (1964) found that when 5 years or more separated the children, secondborns acted more like firstborns than secondborns close in age to their firstborns.

Middleborns

Firstborn and lastborn children being assigned unique roles in the family, middleborns have less-defined roles (Arnstein, 1978) and have a lifelong search for belonging (Wilson & Edington, 1981). With the firstborn as a guardian for tradition and the lastborn as the charmer, the middleborn may become more peer-oriented than family-oriented (Wilson & Edington, 1981). Clinical beliefs have some data-base support in the area of middleborns' self-esteem. As yet no studies have examined how the secondborn makes the transition to the role of middleborn.

Kidwell (1982) examined the self-esteem of over 2,200 10th grade males in a nationwide sample. Middleborns had significantly lower self-esteem than first- or lastborn males. Middleborns spaced 2 years apart from their adjacent siblings had significantly lower self-esteem than middleborns spaced 1, 3, or 4 years apart. Spacing effects were curvilinear in that there was a sharp drop in esteem from 1 to 2 years followed by an increase at 3- to 4-year spacing. Adolescent males with female siblings had higher self-esteem ratings than males with either all males or males and females as siblings.

In a study of 1,767 10th grade males Kidwell (1981) found that (a) when family size and spacing measures were controlled, birth order effects became nonsignificant; (b) having a larger number of siblings increased perceptions of parental punitiveness and decreased perceptions of parental use of reasoning and supportiveness; (c) as age spacing increased, adolescent males perceived more parental reasoning techniques; and (d) a U-shaped curve showed positive parent–child relationships at either 1 year sibling spacing or 4- to 5-year span.

Smith (1984) had 6th, 8th, and 10th graders complete a paper-and-pencil questionnaire on parental goals for them. Parents were interviewed. Data from 291 mother–child and 221 father–child dyads yielded the conclusions that firstborn and lastborn male adolescents were more accurate about paternal goals than middleborn males. Females with male siblings were more perceptive of maternal educational goals than other females, but small sample size leaves this finding suspect. The author concluded that parents who made their educational goals known to their children before adolescence were more successful than those parents who waited until adolescence.

Lastborn

Wilson & Edington (1981) state that the youngest children have a high need to accomplish significant successes, frequently question their ability, have personality traits of both the charmer and rebel, may be the recipient of much misinformation from peers, and may feel less parental pressure for standards. Research studies have often compared firstborn with laterborn children. (See previous discussion.)

PUTTING BIRTH ORDER IN PERSPECTIVE

Several studies have focused on birth order in relation to other salient variables. Olneck and Bills (1979) studied the effects of birth order and family size in a sample of 346 pairs of brothers. An initial finding that firstborn and lastborn men scored higher than middleborns, became nonsignificant when men were matched for age and number of siblings. Men from larger families tended to have lower test scores, less education, lower earnings, and lower occupational skills than men from smaller families. Olneck and Bills (1979) concluded that (a) there were no significant birth order effects on cognitive ability, educational attainment, or socioeconomic ranking; (b) family size data suggested that the economic factor took precedence over the psychological factor.

Nuttall, Nuttall, Polit, and Hunter (1976), in a study of 553 children from large and small families controlled for IQ, found that boys from two-child families had better grades than boys from large families of five or more children. Sibling spacing was significant for boys' achievement only when the researchers did not control for either IQ or family size. Firstborn girls also had higher achievement than later born girls until the authors controlled for IQ or family size, but with control for IQ and family size, birth order became a nonsignificant factor.

Steelman and Doby (1983) investigated the Wechsler Vocabulary and Block Design scores for 3,537 children 6–11 years of age. They reported the following findings: (a) Birth order is unrelated to verbal and nonverbal IQ for both white and black children; (b) family size is inversely related to verbal IQ scores of white and black children but not to the nonverbal IQ of either group of children; (c) the inverse impact of family size on verbal IQ does not differ by race; (d) the black only child surpassed the black children from two-child families on the vocabulary test because the black one-child family was more economically advantaged.

Hauser and Sewell (1985) examined birth order and educational attainment for 9,000 Wisconson high school graduates and for their siblings. Their findings were the following: (a) there was a negative effect of size of family on schooling; however, only children were not clearly advantaged or disadvantaged relative to other children from small families; (b) there were no birth order effects on educational attainment within families when other relevant factors had been controlled; (c) years of education appeared to increase with birth order when family size was controlled. In summary, Hauser and Sewell (1985) stated that there was no need for a theory to explain birth order, since there were no birth order effects on educational attainment.

Reimers and Keith (1986) tested the confluence model's accuracy for a sample of 10,976 high school seniors drawn from a nationwide representative sample of 58,270 students. The variables race, socioeconomic status (SES), family size, birth order, and ability were analyzed according to group and individual standings. In contradiction to the confluence theory, the lastborn child had the highest level of mental ability in the family size of four! The confluence model stated that family size and birth order have major impact on intelligence. Instead, the variables race and SES contributed significantly by explaining *17%* of the variance in ability, whereas family size and birth order together accounted for less than *1%* of the variance. Ability scores appeared to decline only when SES and race were not statistically controlled. The effects of family size and birth order were negligible, but SES and race were major factors influencing intelligence.

In summary, birth order had a negligible impact upon cognitive ability or educational attainment. In contrast, researchers have found that SES and race, and possibly family size, have a far greater impact upon the development of the individual's potential than birth order. The confluence model did not accurately predict outcomes. In fact, the lastborn child in a family of four was found to have the highest mental ability in that family constellation (Reimers and Keith, 1986). Since there were no birth order effects in these systematically controlled studies, the need for a theory doesn't exist.

ALTERNATIVE ACTIONS

Leman (1984) suggested the following strategies for parenting children of different ordinal positions. For firstborns, he recommended (a) reducing their perfectionistic tendencies by accepting reasonable quality, instead of the constantly pressing for improvement in the details; (b) adding responsibilities and privileges as they mature; (c) making sure that younger siblings have appropriate amounts of duties; (d) guaranteeing opportunities for them to spend time alone with their parents; (e) making sure they have a choice in the amount of babysitting they do. It is very significant that Essman and Deutsch (1979) found that 92% of high school students (grades 10–12) in a parent surrogate role who completed a questionnaire that covered nine problem situations involving younger siblings were found to use ineffective strategies in handling these situations. Commands, threats of physical punishment, and threats to inform parents were cited by the authors as common responses.

In parenting the middleborn Leman (1984) suggested these strategies: (a) Parents need to regularly listen to these children and, if necessary, schedule times to talk with them; (b) middleborn children need to have some special privileges that can be part of the family routine such as going to a certain restaurant; (c) even in economically disadvantaged homes, the use of hand-me-downs should not be an automatic practice that precludes occasional purchases of new items for the middle child; and (d) the photo album should contain a representative sample of middleborn child's developmental events.

Finally Leman (1984) suggested the following ideas for parents with their lastborn children: (a) Make sure the child has a fair share of household duties; (b) provide consistent parental discipline; and (c) provide strong positive response to the accomplishments of the youngest child.

Medeiros, Porter, and Welch (1983) suggested that parents establish a strategy of fostering compliments among siblings. They suggested that a box in which all family members contributed at least one thank you to each member each week might be a method of building appreciation awareness in the family.

SUMMARY

In the absence of substantive proof of any specific impact there is no need to generate a theory about the effects of birth order on children's development. In their practice, school psychologists should redirect parents to focus on individual differences so that children in any ordinal position have equal opportunity to develop their potential. Parents should consciously invest their emotional and financial resources equally among their children.

One issue in birth order research has been the amount of time parents spend with their children. Rogoff (1984) has stated that adults can calibrate the level of participation in a learning task so that learning proceeds at a comfortable but challenging pace. Parents need to be reminded that peer and/or sibling interactions are no substitute for quality time with each of their children. Strom (1981) found that when parents played with their preschoolers for as little as two 10-minute periods daily, behavior problems were decisively less. Parents must daily seek opportunities to express love to their children, even if the interaction takes less than a minute.

REFERENCES

Ansbacher, H., & Ansbacher, R. (1964). *Superiority and social interest. Alfred Adler: A collection of later writings.* Evanston, IL: Northwestern University Press.

Arnstein, H. (1978). *Brothers and sisters/Sisters and brothers.* New York: Dutton.

Bank, S., & Kahn, M. (1975). Sisterhood–brotherhood is powerful: Sibling subsystems and family therapy. *Family Process, 14*(3), 311–337.

Baskett, L. (1984). Ordinal position differences in children's family interactions. *Developmental Psychology, 20,* 1026–1031.

Bayley, N. (1969). *Bayley Scales of Infant Development.* New York: The Psychological Corporation.

Brim, O. (1958). Family structure and sex role learning by children: A further analysis of Helen Koch's data. *Sociometry, 21,* 1–16.

Clausen, J. (1966). Family structure socialization and personality. In L. Hoffman & M. Hoffman (Eds.), *Review of child development research,* Vol. 2. New York: Russell Sage Foundation.

Dunn, J. (1983). Sibling relationships in early childhood. *Child Development, 54,* 787–811.

Essman, C., & Deutsch, F. (1979). Siblings as babysitters: Responses of adolescents to younger siblings in problem situations. *Adolescence, 14,* 411–420.

Falbo, T. (1977a). Sibling tutoring and other explanations for intelligence: Discontinuities of only and last borns. (ERIC Document No. ED 149 243)

Falbo, T. (1977b) The only child: A review. *Journal of Individual Psychology, 33,* 47–61.

Falbo, T. (1980). *Only children, achievement, and interpersonal orientation.* Paper presented at the meeting of the American Psychological Association, Montreal.

Forer, L. (1976). *The birth order factor: How your personality is influenced by your place in the family.* New York: David McKay.

Gewirtz, J., & Gewirtz, H. (1965). Stimulus conditions, infant behaviors and social learning in four Israeli child-rearing environments: A preliminary report illustrating differences in environment and behavior between "only" and "youngest" child. In B. Foss (Ed.), *Determinants of infant behavior, III.* New York: Wiley.

Hauser, R., & Sewell, W. (1985). Birth order and educational attainment in full sibships. *American Educational Research Journal, 22,* 1–23.

Hodapp, A., & LaVoie, J. (1976). Imitation by second borns in adult–sibling dyads. *Genetic Psychology Monographs, 93,* 113–128.

Jacobs, B., & Moss, H. (1976). Birth order and sex of sibling as determinants of mother–infant interaction. *Child Development, 47,* 315–322.

Kidwell, J. (1981). Number of siblings, sibling spacing, sex, and birth order. Their effects on perceived parent–adolescent relationship. *Journal of Marriage and the Family, 43,* 315–332.

Kidwell, J. (1982). The neglected birth order: Middleborns. *Journal of Marriage and the Family, 44,* 225–235.

Knight, G. (1982). Cooperative–competitive social orientation: Interactions of birth order with sex and economic class. *Child Development, 53,* 664–667.

Koch, H. (1954). The relation of "primary mental abilities" in five- and six-year-olds to sex of child and characteristics of his abilities. *Child Development, 25,* 209–223.

Leman, K. (1984). *The birth order book: Why you are the way you are.* Old Tappan, NJ: Fleming H. Revell.

Leventhal, G. (1965). *Sex of sibling as a predictor of personality characteristics.* Paper presented at the annual meeting of the Southeastern Psychological Association, Atlanta.

Lobsenz, N. (1986, February 23). Sometimes it is good to be an only child, *Parade Magazine,* New York, NY.

McCall, R. (1984). Developmental changes in mental performance: The effects of the birth of a sibling. *Child Development, 55,* 1317–1321.

Medeiros, D., Porter, B., & Welch, I. (1983). *Children under stress; How to help with the everyday stresses of childhood.* Englewood Cliffs, NJ: Prentice Hall.

Miller, N., & Zimbardo, D. (1966). Motives for fear-induced affiliation: Emotional comparison or interpersonal similarity. *Journal of Personality, 341,* 481–503.

Minnett, A., Vandell, D., & Santrock, J. (1983). The effects of sibling status on sibling interaction: Influence of birth order, age spacing, sex of child, and sex of sibling. *Child Development, 54,* 1064–1072.

Noble, L. (1981). The impact of infant sex and birth order on the magnitude and direction of maternal expectation. *Dissertation Abstracts International, 41,* March, 3873A.

Nuttall, E., Nuttall, R., Polit, D., & Hunter, J. (1976). The effects of family size, birth order, sibling separation and crowding on the academic achievement of boys and girls. *American Educational Research Journal, 13,* 217–223.

Olneck, M., & Bills, D. (1979). Family configuration and achievement: Effects of birth order and family size in a sample of brothers. *Social Psychology Quarterly, 42,* 135–148.

Pfouts, J. (1980). Birth order, age-spacing, IQ differences and family relations. *Journal of Marriage and the Family, 42,* 517–531.

Polit, D., & Falbo, T. (1985). *Siblings and child development: Evidence from a meta-analysis of the literature on only children.* Paper presented at the Biennial Meeting of the Society for Research in Child Development, Toronto, Canada (ERIC document, No. ED 256 510).

Reimers, T., & Keith, T. (1986). Effects of family size and birth order on intelligence: Group and individual analyses of a national sample. Submitted for publication.

Rogoff, B. (1984). Adult assistance of children's learning. In T. E. Raphael (Ed.), *Contexts of school based literacy.* New York: Random House.

Rosenberg, B., & Sutton-Smith, B. (1964). Ordinal position and sex role identification. *Genetic Psychology Monographs, 70,* 297–328.

Schooler, C. (1972). Birth order effects: Not here, not now! *Psychological Bulletin, 78,* 161–175.

Sears, R., Maccoby, E., & Levin, H. (1957). *Patterns of childrearing.* Evanston, IL: Row, Peterson.

Shulman, B., & Mosak, H. (1977). Birth order and ordinal position: Two Adlerian views. *Journal of Individual Psychology, 33,* 114–121.

Smith, T. (1984). Sex and sibling structure: Interaction effects upon the accuracy of adolescent perceptions of parental orientation. *Journal of Marriage and the Family, 46,* 901–907.

Steelman, L., & Doby, J. (1983). Family size and birth order as factors in the IQ performance of black and white children. *Sociology of Education, 56,* 101–109.

Strom, R. (1981). *Growing through play: Readings for parents and teachers.* Monterey, CA: Brookes/Cole.

Sutton-Smith, B., Roberts, J., & Rosenberg, B. (1964). Sibling association and role investment. *Merrill-Palmer Quarterly, 10,* 25–38.

Sutton-Smith, B., & Rosenberg, B. (1965). Age changes in the effects of ordinal position on sex-role identification. *Journal of Genetic Psychology, 107,* 61–73.

U.S. Bureau of the Census (1985). *Statistical Abstract of the United States,* (106th ed.): Washington, DC: Government Printing Office.

Watson, R. (1963). *The great psychologists: Aristotle to Freud.* Philadelphia: Lippincott.

Wilson, B., & Edington, G. (1981). *First child, second child: Your birth order profile.* New York: McGraw-Hill.

Zajonc, R. (1976). Family configuration and intelligence. *Science, 192,* 227–236.

Zajonc,, R. (1983). Validating the confluence model. *Psychological Bulletin, 93,* 457–480.

Zajonc, R., & Markus, G. (1975). Birth order and intellectual development. *Psychological Bulletin, 82,* 74–88.

BIBLIOGRAPHY: CHILDREN

Shyer, M. (1985). *Here I am, an only child.* New York: Scribner.
A child's book that explores the advantages and disadvantages of being an only child.

Children and Cancer

Virginia L. Van de Water
Children's Hospital of The King's Daughters, Norfolk, Virginia

BACKGROUND

No one likes to think about a child having a potentially fatal illness, but cancer strikes 14 of every 10,000 children in the United States every year; leukemia is the most common childhood malignancy, with an incidence of 4 in 10,000. Cancer strikes primarily during the preschool years. The peak age for diagnosis of leukemia is 4 years, but the peak range is from 2 to 7 years. The incidence is slightly greater for males than females, by a 1.2:1 ratio. There are four types of leukemia, but acute lymphoblastic leukemia (ALL) is the most common and accounts for 75% of the leukemias. While it is the most frequent, ALL is also the most successfully treated, and long-term survivors are increasing in numbers. Primary brain tumors are the second most common form of childhood cancer and represent 20% of the total malig- Since they are the more common malignancies, this chapter will focus on ALL (Hanson & Mulvihill, 1982).

In the 1950s leukemia was always fatal, usually within 1 year from diagnosis. In the 1960s the length of survival improved owing to treatment with chemotherapy, but the disease was still ultimately fatal. In the 1970s after cranial radiation was added to chemotherapy, the first long-term survivors were seen. These treatments prevent the leukemia cells from finding a safe hiding place in the central nervous system, where they can multiply. Now, in the late 1980s, there is a 60% chance that an ALL patient will be alive and disease-free in 5 years. A realistic expectation is that many patients will survive to be healthy, functional adults. These treatments are recognized now to have neurotoxic effects that can be associated with learning disabilities, lower IQs, and perceptual difficulties. These are long-term side effects that may take years to be recognized, and the school may be the first to identify these toxicities and to deal with these effects.

Cancer is one of the most dreaded words in the language. When it is diagnosed in a child, there is a sudden and dramatic change in the family's lifestyle. All family members are affected, as is every aspect of their lives. The child is usually hospitalized the same day, and in the hospital he or she is introduced to dozens of caregivers (nurses, lab technicians, and physicians). The normal routine of home and school is replaced by painful procedures, a strange environment, medications that will cause nausea and/or baldness, and the hovering of anxious family members. The parents are usually absent from their jobs to be with the child through this ordeal. The siblings are left with babysitters and are often very confused by what has happened. The extended family may step in to help in a variety of ways or just to be supportive. Some families pull together, some pull apart. To cope with the stresses on the family, the hospital staff provides a variety of support mechanisms for the parents and the patient. For the parents there are chaplains, social workers, and parent support groups in addition to the physicians and trained nurses. For the child there are other cancer patients, the schoolteacher, and child life therapists, as well as the physicians and nurses. Whenever possible the child and parents are allowed to make choices to give them a sense of control in this new and confusing situation. The primary goal of the hospitalization is to stabilize the child, to begin the education of the child and family about the illness and treatment, and to begin to put the disease into remission. Usually a remission is achieved in 4–6 weeks. The child is usually hospitalized for 7–14 days. After discharge treatment is continued on an outpatient basis. Some of the medications can be taken at home, but some require clinic visits. Clinic visits are more common at first and then decline in frequency. Within weeks the child is ready to resume normal activities while continuing the required medical treatments. The treatment will continue for 2–3 years if there is no relapse. Careful monitoring is continued for years even after treatment ends. Families are encouraged to resume their normal lives as much as possible, but the disruption of lifestyle lasts for years.

The children who have solid tumors are likely to have had surgery in addition to the chemotherapy and radiation, which adds to the trauma. For brain tumor patients the recovery is likely to be much more complicated than for the leukemic because both the tumor and the surgery have done damage. It is very difficult to generalize about these patients because the sequelae depend on the size and location of the tumor as well as on the surgical effects. These children are likely to have permanent physical handicaps requiring long-term rehabilitative therapies. This is in marked contrast to the leukemia survivor, who has subtle neuropsychological sequelae. In addition, the survival rate for brain tumor patients is lower. Solid tumors in other body parts are often treated surgically, and the results range from nearly imperceptible as in removal of a kidney to a very visible amputation. These children are unlikely to demonstrate any neuropsychological sequelae but they may need some accommodation in the school situation depending upon the physical status.

DEVELOPMENT

There are many developmental issues related to the hospitalization and chronic illness aspects of cancer that are addressed in the chapters in this volume devoted to these two problem areas. Readers are referred to those chapters for more information regarding hospital adjustment, changes in body image, dependency, and cognitive level of awareness of disease at different ages.

In *The Private Worlds of Dying Children* (1974) Langner discusses the stages of information gathering that are characteristic of children regarding their affliction and the associated changes in self-image. Although the prognosis for cancer survival is constantly improving, some children will die, and even those who do not die proceed through some of the same steps. At first the patients are aware that "It" is serious; "It" is minimally understood, but everyone's reaction tells them that something is seriously wrong. Gradually the patients learn the names and side effects of the drugs used. They learn the purposes of the procedures and treatments. The disease is then recognized to entail a series of relapses and remissions without death, and ultimately in some cases relapses and remissions with death.

The self-concept is affected in a parallel fashion. At first children see themselves as well before the diagnosis. With the diagnosis of "It" comes the awareness of being seriously ill, but these children expect to get better. Depending on the course of the disease, the children may come to see themselves as always ill and never to get well. Finally in some cases the children comprehend that the disease has entered the terminal stage and that death is imminent.

In 1980 Spinetta and Deasy-Spinetta published a study describing some behavioral sequelae of school-aged children who had a variety of cancers and were in varying stages of treatment and remission. Age, sex, and type of cancer were nonsignificant variables in this study. The emotional changes were not pathological in degree but were believed to be real differences between cancer patients and their healthy peers. They reported that children in long-term remission were emotionally healthier than patients who were in relapse or in maintenance therapy. The cancer patients demonstrated greater inhibition in reaching out to others, and they were less likely to try new things or initiate activities. These patients were also less likely to express their feelings, whether positive or negative. In general, the cancer patients assumed a more self-protective posture, but the differences were subtle and not pathological. Some of the differences concerning school behavior in particular included a lower energy level that seemed to interfere with optimal performance, difficulty with concentration and completion of work, and a higher rate of learning disabilities. Cancer patients were found to attend school willingly but were required to be absent frequently for clinic visits and sometimes for malaise following treatment. Hence, although some patients may develop school phobia, it is a mistake to assume that their frequent absences represent a phobia. The study did not find the cancer patients to have significant problems with testing, social interactions, or increased vulnerability to injury.

PUTTING CHILDHOOD CANCER IN PERSPECTIVE

While children are hospitalized, teachers and classmates should maintain contact with them. Assignments should be forwarded to the hospital's schoolteacher so that the students stay current with class work. Children appreciate cards, letters, pictures, or cassette tapes made by their class. These are often prominently displayed in the patients' hospital rooms, and they reduce the sense of isolation from normal activities. Visitation by classmates will depend upon the hospital's regulations, and the teacher should consult with the family as to a good time for personal visits.

The parents will have several days of advance notice before discharge and will be counseled regarding the out-patient treatment regimen as well as the return to school. A conference with the parents, principal, teacher(s), and school psychologist is recommended to discuss the issues of mutual concern. These issues are explored in the next section; they include completion of missed work, frequency of absenteeism, whether the child wants to explain the disease and experience to the class, any restrictions or special privileges, and whether any siblings have special needs.

ALTERNATIVE ACTIONS

The Return to School

It is a shock to the school faculty and the student body to learn that a student has cancer, but there are several things that can be done to prepare the student and the faculty for the return to school. Reentry is an important milestone in treatment because it communicates optimism about the future. School can be the oasis of normality amidst all the disruption that has occurred in the child's life.

One of the first issues to confront is the faculty's concern for their responsibility regarding medical management. The family has been extensively educated regarding the disease and the treatment, and the responsibility for medication or other treatments will rest entirely with the family. At most, a teacher may be asked to make observations regarding the child's energy level. The hospital staff may include a person, usually a hematology/oncology nurse, who assists in the transition back to school. Depending upon the distance from the treatment center, this nurse may even be able to visit the school to discuss the particular student's needs. If the treatment center is remote, the nurse should still be available by telephone.

In preparation for the actual return classmates and faculty should be prepared for physical changes in the appearance of children afflicted by cancer. They may be bald; they may appear bloated or have lost weight. There may be a suntanned area at the radiation site. It is suggested that reentering patients return for a short visit before full-time attendance. A 1-hour visit on a Friday afternoon gives the student and classmates a chance to get reacquainted before the full-time return on Monday morning. Before they step into the classroom it should be decided whether these students wish to explain what has happened. Many patients want to explain it themselves and can put it in terms easily understood by classmates. The teacher may want to screen questions before they are addressed to a patient by having classmates put them in writing prior to the visit. It would be awkward for classmates to ask questions regarding death. While this is a legitimate issue and may be on the minds of classmates, another opportunity must be found. After the patient leaves, the class can discuss the visit and their feelings regarding the physical changes and their classmate's experience. By dealing with these issues this way the class can resume "business as usual" on Monday morning.

It is generally accepted that the disease should be dealt with openly and honestly, but some families wish to be secretive or at least selective in what is discussed with whom. These wishes should be respected by school personnel. Find out what terms the family is using, what the child has been told, and what can or cannot be discussed.

There may be some modifications or allowances made for cancer patients in the school routine. The most likely is a possible desire to hide baldness with a hat or wig. While a wig should create no problem for the school's rules, a hat may be a breech of the dress code. It is recommended that these children have permission to cover their baldness as long as the covering is not so outlandish as to be disruptive. They might be accorded the use of an elevator, if available, to conserve their energy. Another modification might be the use of a quiet place for some rest during the school day or even a shorter school day temporarily. One of the chemotherapy medications is associated with jaw pain that gum chewing relieves; some physicians may request permission for the patient to chew gum during school. All faculty should be informed of these special privileges to avoid an unpleasant or embarrassing confrontation between the patient and a staff member.

Leukemia patients should be able to resume all normal activities, including physical education upon return. Fatigue should be the only limiting factor, and these children should be encouraged to participate as much as possible. Overprotectiveness is to be avoided both at home and at school, but some families will persist in treating their children as more fragile than is necessary. This is not in the children's best interest, and a member of their medical treatment team should be contacted to clarify the need for restrictions.

Leukemia patients will be absent frequently for clinic visits, and the distance from the treatment center will influence how much time from school is lost. Some children can return to school after a treatment; some may choose to have a treatment in the afternoon in order to participate in a particular school activity in the morning. As much as possible the teachers should prepare for these scheduled absences by giving assignments ahead of time or allowing extra time for completion. It is common for children to bring their schoolwork with them to accomplish while at the clinic. Some children may be absent the day following treatment if nausea is severe. On some clinic visits patients will undergo such particularly unpleasant procedures as spinal taps or bone marrow aspirations. Some children become anxious and/or withdrawn in anticipation of these procedures. Others manifest their reaction the day after. Teachers may notice a pattern of declining school performance immediately before or after these procedures. Teachers are to be encouraged to be empathetic regarding these procedures. They may ask, "How did things go in clinic yesterday?" or "Are you doing okay today?." Teachers will want to change test schedules for students who become too nauseated to study in preparation, but it would be inappropriate to assume that patients could not take a test following a clinic procedure. Oversolicitousness may be well-intentioned but is not in the patient's best interest.

Academic and Behavioral Expectations

Once a cancer patient has returned to school on a full-time basis the issues of academic and behavioral expectations become important. Again, it should be emphasized that the return to school is a return to a life and to expectations that are normal for a child of his or her age with as few changes as possible.

Academically cancer patients can be expected to resume the curriculum and continue the way any child does who has been absent for a similar length of time. There may be some minor problems with incomplete work owing to fatigue or absences, but these should be manageable with more generous time allowances and good communication between home and school. Gradually, however, subtle changes may appear. These changes may be the long-term sequelae of the neurotoxic treatments. Some of the more frequent complaints of parents and teachers are a decline in the quality of handwriting, a gradual decline in grades, problems with new learning while old learning is intact, and decreased concentration.

Recently there have been studies to assess the neuropsychological sequelae of treatment for ALL. The research is complicated by the different chronological ages, the different stages of disease at diagnosis, the different lengths of remission, the number of relapses, the lack of premorbid test results, and the use of differing neuropsychological batteries. Nevertheless there are some consistent findings.

1. The younger the child is at diagnosis, the more likely he or she is to demonstrate neuropsychological deficits, including a lower IQ; usually IQs remain within the average range (Eiser, 1980; Jannoun, 1983; Lansky et al., 1984).
2. The combination of chemotherapy injected directly into the spine and cranial radiation is more neurotoxic than either alone.
3. The longer the treatment regimen, the greater the risk for deficits.
4. Mathematics and spatial skills are more often affected than verbal and reading skills (Copeland, 1985).
5. Memory, attention, and concentration skills are lower for leukemia patients who have had both chemotherapy and cranial radiation.
6. Functional deficits may be present even if the computerized tomography scan of the brain is within normal limits (Obetz, 1979).

There are some ambiguous research findings. Studies differ on whether it is the verbal or the performance IQ that is the more affected. This may depend upon the age at diagnosis and treatment. Verbal and reading skills may be affected, depending upon the measure used. One study found females to be more adversely affected than males (Robison, 1984).

Many studies suggest that the decrements in functioning may increase with the length of time since diagnosis. This is interpreted to mean that these are long-term sequelae and not that there is a progressive, degenerative condition.

Classroom teachers and school psychologists should observe cancer patients' academic performance with these findings in mind. These patients may demonstrate some of these changes and may need to be referred for formal evaluation. The standard criteria for special education placement, retention, and/or remedial services should be applied. The literature indicates that such patients are more likely than their healthy peers to be referred for such services.

Behaviorally, children in remission of cancer can be expected to be very similar to what they were before. Appropriate behavior in conformity with school rules is typical. As the Spinetta and Deasy-Spinetta study indicated, these children may be less outgoing or more cautious, but these changes should be minimal. If the premorbid personality of a patient, however, was manipulative, irresponsible, or opportunistic, then an exaggeration of these characteristics can be expected. Having cancer may be a unique opportunity for such a child to exploit. If behavior problems are observed, they should be discussed with the parents and medical personnel. The problem may be as simple as poor communication regarding expectations, or the behavior may indicate a significant adjustment problem that requires professional attention. Regardless of the reason for the behavior problem, standard discipline procedures should be implemented. If writing graffiti on the bathroom walls is a reason for suspension, then the cancer patient who does so should be suspended. This consistency sends the message that the child is expected to survive and function like everyone else. Documentation of behavioral changes, whether withdrawal or acting out, is important to the medical staff in their ongoing relationship with the child and family. Most physicians will appreciate being kept informed and will try to assist in resolution of any problems that arise. It is also comforting to the family if there is agreement between the school and medical professionals as to the courses of action.

Diagnosis in Preschool Years

A child who has had cancer and has been successfully treated as a preschooler poses for the schools no issues of reintegration or changes in learning and/or behavior. The parents may be aware, however, that the child is at greater risk for learning problems and request an evaluation or services before the school has a chance to observe the need for such services. This parental concern should be viewed as legitimate. Even if no specific concern can be voiced, it may be wise to do a baseline evaluation in order to monitor the child's future progress. A complete neuropsychological evaluation is seldom warranted; a standard psychoeducational evaluation including intelligence, perceptual, and academic measures should be adequate.

The focus of this material has been on the elementary situation because this is the level where the ALL diagnosis and its effects are most commonly found. Teenagers are more likely to be undergoing the long-term sequelae and to be concerned with the long-term consequences of their disease. They are often the most concerned about the physical changes of baldness and weight change; they are also coping with their own mortality more than the younger patients. Professional help is more likely to be needed for this age level.

Siblings of Cancer Patients

When a diagnosis of cancer is made, the family begins to focus its energies and concern on the patient, and every aspect of normal family life changes. At the hospital the medical staff provides education and support for the patient and parents, but the siblings left at home with neighbors, friends, and extended family undergo profound changes in their lifestyle, often without support. Some studies have focused on the siblings and have found that many have adjustment problems, including enuresis, headaches, decreased school performance, depression, anxiety, and psychosomatic complaints. In one study, half the families had at least one family member who needed psychiatric help (Binger, 1969).

In a study by Lavigne and Ryan (1979) siblings were found to be more withdrawn and irritable when there is a chronically ill child in the family. Siblings between 3 and 6 years of age are at greater risk for overall psychopathology; in this group the girls were having more adjustment problems than the boys. In the 7- to 13-year old age group male siblings had higher levels of psychopathology than females. The authors speculate that the age-specific differences may be related to traditional sex roles. Dependence in younger females is considered age-appropriate, and the patient usurps this role, whereas older girls often assume a greater responsibility for the care of younger siblings and household routines.

The siblings experience loss in several ways. The first is the loss of routine relationships with their parents and the afflicted sibling. This is greatest during the hospitalization, but it continues for years as treatment continues. Siblings also miss the family routine and typical family activities; they report feeling left out, abandoned, and isolated. A third loss is that of the relationship with the healthy child the patient formerly was; the patient is now physically different owing to baldness, markings for radiation, and weight changes. A final loss is the change in the environment. The home is often empty or in the charge of parent substitutes. At school and in the neighborhood friends may avoid them or ask them awkward questions.

A variety of emotional reactions have been identified repeatedly in the siblings. The first is anxiety. There is a great need for reassurance that the disease is not contagious and that the same thing is not going to happen to them. They may become very concerned about every physical complaint that they have as they empathize with the patient.

A second reaction is isolation from the parents and the sibling. The patient receives an inordinate amount of attention from parents and extended family. The patient also receives a larger share of the family finances. There are frequent complaints about the quantity and quality of presents given to the patient. Siblings see the patient as "the special person" as their own specialness disappears. They also report that they cannot talk to the patient as much as they would like or in the same way as they did before.

A third reaction is guilt. At some point in the sibling relationship the healthy child has probably wished that the now sick child would drop dead or had never been born, and this memory now haunts them as the reason for the child's illness. In a different way the siblings often feel responsible for each other; they guard secrets, and they protect each other from outsiders. The illness may be viewed as their failure to protect the sibling. They may feel guilt in recognizing their own jealousy over the attention, gifts, and privileges showered on the patient. Adults may unwittingly add to the sense of guilt by reminding the siblings that they should have no complaints because they are healthy and should be more understanding.

A fourth reaction is increased stress. The emotional tone of the home changes as the family focuses on the dreaded disease and the uncertain future. There is tension and stress as the many changes begin. It is difficult to cope with the expectations of parent substitutes, with the increased responsibilities, and with the uncertainty of what will happen next. It is also stressful to deal with questions from friends, neighbors, and classmates. The siblings are often very confused about how to answer and do not know how much to tell or whom to trust.

A final common reaction is fear. There is fear for their own well-being as well as for the sibling's. They may feel that there is a stigma associated with having cancer in the family and fear that it will spread to them. They are fearful of expressing any negative emotions, since this often results in criticism that they should be understanding and not add to the family's problems. They are also fearful when the adults engage in a "web of silence"; when the parents withdraw and do not discuss what is happening there is a tendency to fear the worst.

There are some suggestions that can be made to parents if the siblings demonstrate adjustment problems, many of which come from the siblings themselves (Iles, 1979). They want to be kept informed. Their age is important to consider so that the explanation is comprehensible and adequate; older children need and want more detail than younger children. They also need to understand that the patient's medical condition is variable, that some days or weeks will be better than others. Parents are advised to sometimes give priority to the healthy children. The patient should not be the constant focus of parental attention. The siblings want to be included in the hospital and clinical activities. It is a good idea to take them to a clinic to visit to see what goes on and to feel a part of what has become so routine for the patient and parent but from which they are usually excluded. Some hospitals have family programs and support groups for siblings that give them an opportunity to be participants. Patient and siblings should also be encouraged to talk honestly with each other. The sibling relationship is an intense one because so much is shared -the parents, the home, the routines and rituals, the extended family, and the many hours of companionship. When this is suddenly disrupted there is a profound effect on everyone, and talking openly is the best way to deal with the feelings and issues.

Teachers, counselors, and psychologists need to be aware of the emotional toll on these siblings. Some extra attention directed toward these siblings is suggested to help them maintain their emotional and academic equilibrium.

When Terminal

If the disease becomes terminal, it is a gradual process, and there should be no concern that a cancer patient will become very sick or die in the classroom. As the disease progresses, the child becomes weaker but may still wish to attend school on a part-time basis. This is desirable if possible. When the child is no longer able to attend school at all, teacher(s) and classmates are encouraged to maintain contact through cards, pictures and perhaps visits.

When a child dies a class discussion is appropriate. The class should be asked to think about other losses they have had such as a relative or pet — how they felt, and what they did. The school librarian may be able to suggest a book to be read to the class that deals with death at an appropriate level for that age group. It is not a good idea to explain death as a trip, sleep, or as going to the hospital since this may be misunderstood and lead to abnormal fears regarding trips, sleep, or going to the hospital. Drawing pictures of a memory that they have of their classmate is another form of expression. Not all children will want to talk about the death when it first occurs, so the teacher should be prepared for the topic to come up at a later time. Funeral attendance should be entirely optional, but the class or entire student body may want to plant a tree or plan some other type of memorial for their classmate as a positive expression of grief. (See the chapter on death in this volume for more ideas, information, and bibliography.)

SUMMARY

"The sick child can never approach normality in lifestyle unless he is in school and is productive in the role of the student" (Levine & Hersh, p. 376). This summarizes the importance of the school's role in a child's recovery. As the prognosis for cancer survival increases with the progress of health science, the schools will see increasing numbers of survivors preparing for their future. It is most important to treat these survivors as normally as possible by applying the standard academic and behavioral expectations. Not to do so sends the message that the child is not expected to do well. The most common malignancies, leukemia and brain tumors, are likely to involve neuropsychological defects of varying degrees; some of these deficits will be immediately apparent, but others will take years to be seen. The school psychologist is likely to be asked to do a psychoeducational assessment and to monitor the cancer patient's progress. When deficits are present the usual remedial efforts should be provided. Finally, the school psychologist can be a role model for other school personnel in expecting the school to provide the child with the greatest degree of normality in lifestyle.

REFERENCES

Binger, C. M., Ablin, A. R., Feuerstein, R. C., Kushner, J. H., Zoger, S., & Mikkelsen, C. (1969). Childhood leukemia: Emotional impact on patient and family. *New England Journal of Medicine, 280,* 414–418.

Copeland, D. R., Fletcher, J. M., Pfefferbaum-Levine, B., Jaffe, N., Ried, H., & Maor, M. (1985). Neuropsychological sequelae of childhood cancer in long-term survivors. *Pediatrics, 75,* 745–53.

Eiser, C. (1980). Effects of chronic illness on intellectual development. *Archives of Disease in Childhood, 55,* 766–770.

Hanson, M. R., & Mulvihill, J. J. (1982). Epidemiology of cancer in the young. In A. S. Levine (Ed.), *Cancer in the young.* New York: Masson.

Iles, J. P. (1979). Children with cancer: Healthy siblings' perceptions during the illness experience. *Cancer Nursing, 2,* 371–379.

Jannoun, L. (1983). Are cognitive and educational development affected by age at which prophylactic therapy is given in acute lymphoblastic leukemia? *Archives of Disease in Childhood, 58,* 953–958.

Langner, M. B. (1978). *The private lives of dying children.* Princeton: Princeton University Press.

Lansky, S. B., Cairns, N. U., Lansky, L. L., Cairns, G. F., Stephenson, L., & Garin, G. (1984). Central nervous system prophylaxis studies showing impairment in verbal skills and academic achievement. *The American Journal of Pediatric Hematology/Oncology, 6,* 183–190.

Lavigne, J. V., & Ryan, M. (1979). Psychologic adjustment of siblings of children with chronic illness. *Pediatrics, 63,* 616–624.

Levine, A. S., & Hersh, S. P. (1982). The psychosocial concomitants of cancer in young patients. In A. S. Levine (Ed.), *Cancer in the Young.* New York: Masson, pp. 367–387.

Obetz, S. W., Smithson, W. A., Groover, R. V., Houser, O. W., Klass, D. W., Ivnik, R. J., Colligan, R. C., Gilchrist, G. S., & Burgert, E. O. (1979). Neuropsychologic follow-up study of children with acute lymphocytic leukemia. *American Journal of Pediatric Hematology/Oncology, 1,* 207–213.

Robison, L. L., Nesbit, M. E., Sather, H. N., Meadows, A. T., Ortega, J. A., & Hammond, G. D. (1984). Factors associated with IQ scores in long-term survivors of childhood acute lymphoblastic leukemia. *American Journal of Pediatric Hematology/Oncology, 6,* 115–120.

Spinetta, J. J., & Deasy-Spinetta, P. (Eds.). (1981). *Living with childhood cancer.* St. Louis: Mosby.

BIBLIOGRAPHY: PROFESSIONALS

Binger, C. M., Ablin, A. R., Feuerstein, R. C., Kushner, Z. H., Zoger, S., & Mikkelsen, C. (1969). Childhood leukemia: Emotional impact on patient and family. *New England Journal of Medicine, 280,* 414–418.
A good review of the emotional impact of the diagnosis on family members based on interviews with families where a child had died.

Brunnquell, D., & Hall, M. D. (1982). Issues in the psychological care of pediatric oncology patients. *American Journal of Orthopsychiatry, 52,* 32–44.
A comprehensive review of issues such as: separation/loss, control/competence, mobility/isolation, treatment sequelae, and adjustment.

Levine, A. S., & Hersh, S. P. (1982). The psychosocial concomitants of cancer in young patients. In A. S. Levine (Ed.), *Cancer in the Young.* New York: Masson.
An excellent review of family dynamics and coping mechanisms. Includes a section on adolescent issues. Addresses some of the psychological issues for the physician as the caretaker.

The American Cancer Society and its local offices have materials specifically for the classroom teacher. One is "When You Have a Student with Cancer." Contact that office for additional titles.

BIBLIOGRAPHY: PARENTS

Adams, D. W., & Deveau, E. J. (1984). *Coping with childhood cancer: Where do we go from here?* Reston, VA: Reston.
A description of the cancer experience from the family's perspective, also with sections of interest to professionals.

Langner, M. B. (1978). *The private lives of dying children.* Princeton, Princeton University Press.
This book offers insights into the terminal phase of illness.

Pendleton, E. (1980). *Too old to cry, too young to die.* Nashville: Thomas Nelson.
Thirty-five teenagers discuss their disease, their concerns, and their coping. This would also be of interest to teenagers and professionals.

Spinetta, J. J., & Deasy-Spinetta, P. (Eds.). (1981). *Living with childhood cancer.* St. Louis: Mosby.
A description of the cancer experience from the family viewpoint. Some sections would be of interest to professionals.

The American Cancer Society and its local chapters have a variety of brochures and other materials that would be informative for parents.

The Candlelighters Childhood Cancer Foundation Quarterly Newsletter is an organization serving parents whose children have cancer. Membership is free. Their address is:
The Candlelighters Childhood Cancer Foundation
2025 Eye Street, N. W. Suite 1011
Washington, DC 20006
(202) 659-5136

BIBLIOGRAPHY: CHILDREN

What Happened to You Happened to Me", The American Cancer Society.
This 28-page booklet consists of drawings and quotations from cancer patients of various ages regarding their experience.

"Hospital Days — Treatment Ways", U. S. Dept. of Health and Human Services.
A coloring book of typical hospital scenes. It is available through:
OSU Comprehensive Cancer Center
357 McCampbell Hall
1580 Cannon Drive
The Ohio State University
Columbus, Ohio 43210

Hart, D. (1985). *Busy Days.* Omaha: Centering Corp.
This is appropriate for young children and siblings.

Rudolph, L. (1980). *When your brother or sister has cancer.* Available through the Candlelighters Childhood Cancer Foundation, 2025 Eye St., N. W., Washington, D. C., 20006. This is recommended for siblings.

Bach, A. (1980). *Waiting for Johnny Miracle.* New York: Harper & Row.
This is the story of a 17-year-old bone cancer patient. It is recommended for teenagers.

Osborne, M. (1982). *Run, run, as fast as you can.* New York: Scholastic.
This is the story of a teenage girl who struggles through her younger brother's malignancy and death. It is recommended for teenagers.

Children and Career Development

Edward M. Levinson
Indiana University of Pennsylvania

BACKGROUND

Work is an integral aspect of American life. Anderson (1982) has estimated that during the course of 45 working years, a person may spend as many as 94,000 hours on the job. The vast amount of time and energy invested in work has prompted writers to suggest that one's work may greatly influence one's social and personal development. Research has suggested that self-concept is intimately related to work performance and work satisfaction (Dore & Meachum, 1973; Greenhaus, 1971; Kalanidi & Deivasenapathy, 1980; Snyder & Ferguson, 1976; Super, 1957). Experiential validity for such research is found in the sheer frequency with which statements like "I am a(n) . . . (occupation)" are made. As Coles (1978) notes, people find it almost impossible to talk about themselves without reference to the kind of work they do.

How well an individual adjusts to work is frequently associated with that individual's general life adjustment. Adjustment to work has been conceptualized as consisting of two components: job satisfaction and job performance. Compared to satisfied workers, dissatisfied workers tend to experience a greater frequency of physical and mental health problems (Kornhauser, 1965; Portigal, 1976), an increased risk of heart disease and psychosomatic illnesses (O'Toole, 1973), and lower levels of overall life satisfaction (Bedian & Marbert, 1979; Haavio-Mannila, 1971; Iris & Barrett, 1972; Orphen, 1978; Schmitt & Mellon, 1980). They also tend to quit jobs more frequently than satisfied workers. Low-performance workers tend to be terminated from their jobs more frequently than high-performance workers. The economic cost to society of supporting such unemployed workers via welfare, unemployment, and other dependency programs should be apparent. The individual cost of unemployment and turnover is presented in a study by Sanborn, Sanborn and Cimbolic (1974), who found that individuals who are unemployed or frustrated in their work, or who have experienced a major change in their occupational status in the previous 12 months, are increasingly more likely to commit suicide than are individuals in more rewarding occupational situations. Thus, the adequacy of occupational choice has a tremendous effect on one's overall happiness and quality of life.

The foundation for effective career decision making is laid early in life and is rooted in self-awareness, occupational awareness, and knowledge of decision-making skills. As Seligman (1980) has suggested: "Finding a gratifying career may be compared to finding a suitable mate. It entails a process by which people seek a situation in which their needs will be fulfilled while their strengths and talents meet the needs of the career or spouse . . . A career change, like a divorce, is likely to be accompanied by [emotional upset] fear or failure and risk taking, perhaps precipitating a hasty and equally unrewarding 'second marriage' " (p. 6).

The school experience makes a critical contribution to the relative success youngsters have in making realistic and informed career decisions. Whereas in the mid-1960s school administrators did not believe that schools should provide job training and related career assistance to students, that belief has now reversed itself (McCleary & Thomson, 1979). In recent years, educators have come to accept vocational–career development as a major goal of public education (Goodlad, 1979; Marland, 1971). Although attempts to encourage such development are made at all levels of the educational system, different levels of the system encourage different aspects of development. As Hohenshil (1982) has suggested, self-awareness is typically encouraged at the elementary school level, occupational awareness is encouraged at the middle school or junior high school level, and decision making and preparation for entry level employment (or the next level of the educational system) is emphasized at the secondary school level.

Despite the attempts being made by schools to foster career development and adequate career decision-making skills, data suggests that such attempts have not adequately met the needs of students. Prediger, Roth, & Noeth (1973) studied 32,000 8th-, 9th-, and 11th-grade students in 200 schools in 33 states and found that help with career planning was their number one desire; yet half of the 11th graders reported that they received little or no career planning assistance. Biggers (1971) reported that high school seniors were as limited in their ability to use information in vocational decision making as they were in the fourth grade. More recent studies echo this same theme. Chapman and Katz (1983) found that most of the students whom they surveyed believed that their high school career planning resources were insufficient. Johnson, Baughman, and O'Malley (1982) found that two-thirds of the high school seniors they surveyed wanted more career planning assistance than they were currently receiving. Apparently their parents agree. A 1976 Gallup poll (Gallup, 1976) found that 80% of the adults surveyed believed that high schools should place greater emphasis on career planning, and 52% of those surveyed believed that more attention should be paid to career development in the elementary schools. Assisting students in effective career planning requires the in-

The author wishes to acknowledge Rene Fetchkan for her assistance in the preparation of this chapter.

volvement of parents, students, and school personnel and requires knowledge of the normal career development milestones thorough which children and adolescents typically progress. For the purpose of this chapter, the following definitions, taken from a panel of experts of the National Vocational Guidance Association (now the National Career Development Association) (Sears, 1982) will be used: *Work* is defined as conscious effort, other than having as its primary purpose either coping or relaxation, aimed at producing benefits for oneself and/or for oneself and others. *Career* means the totality of work one does in one's lifetime.

DEVELOPMENT

Career development has been defined as "the total constellation of psychological, sociological, educational, physical, economic, and chance factors that combine to shape the career of any individual over the life span" (Sears, 1982). A variety of career development theories have been postulated. It should be stated at the outset that even the most useful of these theories are either incomplete, not well substantiated by research, or still in the process of being developed and studied. The reader should be aware that no single theory has yet emerged as the one "right" or "best" theory of career development.

Most theories of career development assume that development is an orderly, predictable, and generally irreversible process, and is made up of definable and hierarchical stages. As is true with other aspects of development, the ages and rate at which individuals progress through these stages will vary. In particular, disadvantaged, minority, inner city, and handicapped youth tend to manifest slower than average rates of career development. The reasons for this slowed development include a lack of adequate role models, lack of work experience, and limited exposure to different kinds of occupations; all of these conditions characterize deprived environments.

The developmental theories of Ginzberg, Ginsburg, Axelrad, and Herma, (1951) and of Super (1957) will be combined and presented to provide the reader an overview of the typical career development stages through which individuals progress during the school years. Figure 1 summarizes these stages and lists specific developmental tasks that are appropriate to each stage. The growth stage, which extends from birth to age 14 years, includes the fantasy, interest, and capacity substages. During the fantasy substage (birth to 10 years), expressed choices are often unrealistic, are closely related to play life, and usually have little long-term significance. Careers such as cowboy, policeman, football player, movie star, or astronaut are typical examples. Earliest choices are often derived from parental roles, whereas later choices tend to be based on occupations of "heroes." The opportunity to role-play a variety of adult roles is valuable to children and should not be discouraged by adults. Adults should not be overly concerned with the inappropriateness of choices at this stage, for such choices are usually short-lived. Children at this stage have little understanding of the requirements and demands of various jobs, and are unaware of potential obstacles to attaining such jobs. As Isaacson (1985) notes, however, many adolescents and even adults do not advance beyond this stage. Their self-awareness or occupational awareness never sufficiently develops to allow more realistic career choices to be generated. Only as children become more aware of their interests (interest substage, ages 11–12) and abilities (capacity substage, ages 13–14) and begin to relate these to the world of work through exploration will more realistic career options be identified. Such exploration of the world of work generally occurs through contact with various workers, reading books, and watching television. During the interest substage, children begin to reject many of their earlier idealistic choices and focus upon activities and future goals that relate to present interests. During the capacity substage, young adolescents become more knowledgeable of their strengths and weaknesses and begin to realize that ability and aptitude must be considered along with interest in making career plans. This can have a disconcerting effect in that children begin to realize for the first time that they cannot be anything they want.

The exploration stage (ages 15–24) consists of three substages: tentative (ages 15–17), transition (ages 18–21), and trial (ages 22–24). During the tentative substage individuals, having explored a variety of occupational areas and having compared the requirements and demands of jobs in these areas to their abilities and interests, begin to narrow their occupational choices. Most young adolescents are able to express a tentative occupational preference and can explain the reasons for these preferences. However, it should be noted that occupational choices made during adolescence are often quite unstable. Although the field or occupational group that adolescents will eventually enter can be identified with some confidence, the specific occupation cannot. Once tentative choices are made, they are then explored further (often by means of part-time work experience, enrollment in certain courses, or training programs). During the transition substage (ages 18–21), these tentative choices are converted into a specific choice. It is during this stage that the individual makes the transition from school to work or from school to further education and training. During the trial substage (ages 22–24), a seemingly appropriate occupation has already been identified and a beginning job in the area is found and tried out as life's work. Commitment to the occupation is still limited,and many people make changes as a result of the experience encountered on the job or in training.

Many theorists believe that career choice is an implementation of one's self-concept and is influenced by a number of factors including role models, community resources, the level and quality of an individual's educational background, and the occupational structure, trends, and attitude of the community. Many theorists also believe that although each occupation requires a characteristic pattern of abilities, interests, and personality traits, there is enough diversity and overlap among these qualities that there are a variety of occupational areas that may be suitable for a particular individual (i.e.,

FIGURE 1

Developmental tasks by stage of career development and age.

STAGE	**GROWTH**			**EXPLORATION**		
Substage	**Fantasy**	**Interest (What do I like?)**	**Capacity (What am I good at?)**	**Tentative (What will I do ....**	**Transition ....)**	**Trial**
Estimated age range	**0–10**	**11–12**	**13–14**	**15–17**	**18–21**	**22–24**
Tasks	1. Gain awareness of personal qualities and develop a healthy self-concept. 2. Appreciate and consider the broad variety of careers and acquire knowledge of workers, their roles, and the value of work. 3. Develop a broad, flexible, and satisfying sex role identity. 4. Develop attitudes that are conducive to competence, cooperation, and achievement.		1. Gain awareness of aptitudes and values. 2. Develop decision-making, planning, and problem-solving skills. 3. Realize that different occupations have different requirements and provide different rewards. 4. Become aware of imminent academic choices and their relationship to post-high-school alternatives. 5. Assume responsibility for own career-related decisions.	1. Gain awareness of aspiration. 2. Develop tentative career goals and identify vocational options. 3. Explore tentative career goals and vocational options.	1. Specify a choice. 2. Acquire necessary skills for entry-level employment.	1. Implement vocational choice (acquire a job).

there is no single *right* occupational area or job for a person).

PUTTING CAREER DEVELOPMENT IN PERSPECTIVE

As individuals progress through the career development stages cited previously, they increase their career maturity. Seligman (1980) considers career maturity to be a lifelong *process* that, regardless of the stage or age involved, is characterized by increasing realism of career goals, increasing self-awareness, increasing congruence between self-image (abilities, interests, values, personality) and career goals, increasing competence for career planning and success, improving career-related attitudes, increasing knowledge of relevant options, and increasing productivity and satisfaction. Career-mature individuals are able to make realistic and informed career decisions and generally use a career-planning model similar to that described in Figure 2 on page 77.

The first step in the process is determining the type of decision to be made. For young children in career education programs the decision might be which occupational areas to study or which work settings in the community to visit. For junior high school or senior high school students, the decision might be which courses to take, or which vocational training programs to enroll in. For a young adult, the decision might be which job to take. Regardless of the decision to be made, the process is the same. Information about oneself is combined with information in the environment to generate appropriate and realistic options. The options are prioritized and a primary alternative is identified and implemented. Following implementation, the appropriateness and desirability of the primary alternative is evaluated, and a decision is made whether to continue to pursue that alternative, or to discard it and instead pursue another option. For example, students who have decided not to go to college and instead to pursue vocational training will consider their interests, aptitudes, and so forth, in combination with the information relative to the vocational training programs available, the requirements of the programs, the possibility of getting a job in the local community following such training, and will identify two or three desirable training programs. These will be prioritized and these students will enroll in the *most* desirable training program. After taking some courses in this program, they will evaluate their experience and decide to either continue on in the training program or decide to enroll in a different training program. A similar process would be used by a high school graduate who has gone on to college and must decide on a major.

What factors inhibit individuals from making realistic and informed career decisions? Specifically, inadequate self-awareness, inadequate occupational awareness, or inadequate decision making skills — or, simply put, lack of career maturity. To determine whether a student needs assistance in career planning, an assessment of the students' maturity in terms of these factors must be conducted. Vocational/career assessment allows such determinations to be made and provides both the student and helping professionals with information that can be used in the planning process (particularly in the exploration stage of the planning process).

Comprehensive vocational assessments include measures of mental ability, academic achievement, small- and large-motor coordination, personality, vocational interests, vocational aptitudes, vocational adaptive behavior (appropriateness of behavior in the work setting), and career maturity (Hohenshil, Levinson, & Buckland-Heer, 1985). A variety of techniques are used to complete such assessments including observation, interviews, performance tests, paper- and pencil-tests, work samples (specific job functions from a single occupation or a group of occupations are performed by a student under the observation of a trained examiner), and work experiences. As in any assessment, the specific components of the battery will depend on the referral question. Consequently, in many instances, it will not be necessary to complete an entire vocational assessment. For example, if a student faces an imminent decision (e.g., which vocational training program to enroll in), a professional, in order to determine if the student needs assistance may choose to assess that student's readiness to make that decision. Career maturity alone could be assessed, by interviewing techniques and paper-and-pencil tests such as the Career Maturity Inventory (Crites, 1973) or the Career Development Inventory (Super et al., 1979). If the student was found to have adequate self-knowledge, work-related knowledge (including knowledge of the vocational training programs available), and decision making skills, no further assessment or intervention would probably be necessary. If a deficiency of self-knowledge is discovered, a more comprehensive assessment of other areas would be necessary before determining an appropriate intervention strategy. If only limited knowledge of interests were found to exist, then only interest assessment would be necessary before planning could be initiated. Assessment of a student's readiness to make a career decision is often the first step in determining whether the student needs career planning assistance.

ALTERNATIVE ACTIONS

In addition to the goals of increasing self-awareness, increasing occupational awareness, and developing adequate decision-making skills, facilitating job readiness and placement are important areas of career-planning assistance to students. Career education programs operate in many schools and are designed to achieve all of the aforementioned goals. Such programs usually follow a model similar to that depicted in Figure 3, and are based on normal career development theory. The activities and experiences that make up career education programs are usually integrated into the regular education curriculum and are implemented by a variety of school personnel. The remainder of this section will describe actions designed to facilitate career planning, many of which are typically part of career education programs.

FIGURE 2

Career planning model.

Step 1 — *Determine Decision to be Made*
— Depends upon student's level of educational and psychological development

Step 2 — *Collect Appropriate Information*
— Internal Information
Interests
Aptitudes
Values
Aspirations
Achievement
Personality
Small/large motor coordination

— External Information
Types of occupations available
Personal requirements for entry
Educational requirements
Economic & social consequences
Relation of curriculum to various career options
Application process for entrance

Step 3 — *Generate Alternative Career Options*

Step 4 — *Select Primary Alternative & Specify Secondary Alternatives*

Step 5 — *Reality Testing in Sheltered Environment*
School courses
Co-op programs
Simulated work experience
Observation

Step 6 — *Evaluate Results of Reality Testing*

Step 7 — *Continue to Pursue Primary Alternative*

or

Return to Step 4 to consider secondary career alternatives

From *Best Practices in School Psychology* (p. 217) by T. H. Hohenshil, E. M. Levinson, and K. Buckland-Heer, 1985, Kent, OH: National Association of School Psychologists. Copyright 1985 by National Association of School Psychologists. Reprinted by permission.

TABLE 1

Common Misconceptions of Career Development

1. There is a single right occupation for everyone.
2. A person can do anything they want if they try hard enough.
3. Tests predict the specific occupation one will enter.
4. People should be encouraged to make career decisions as soon as possible.
5. People are unemployed because they lack skills (unemployment is due to a shortage of jobs).
6. One must choose between vocational and liberal arts education (the two can be combined).

Note: Compiled by Seligman, 1980.

FIGURE 3

Concepts of Career Education

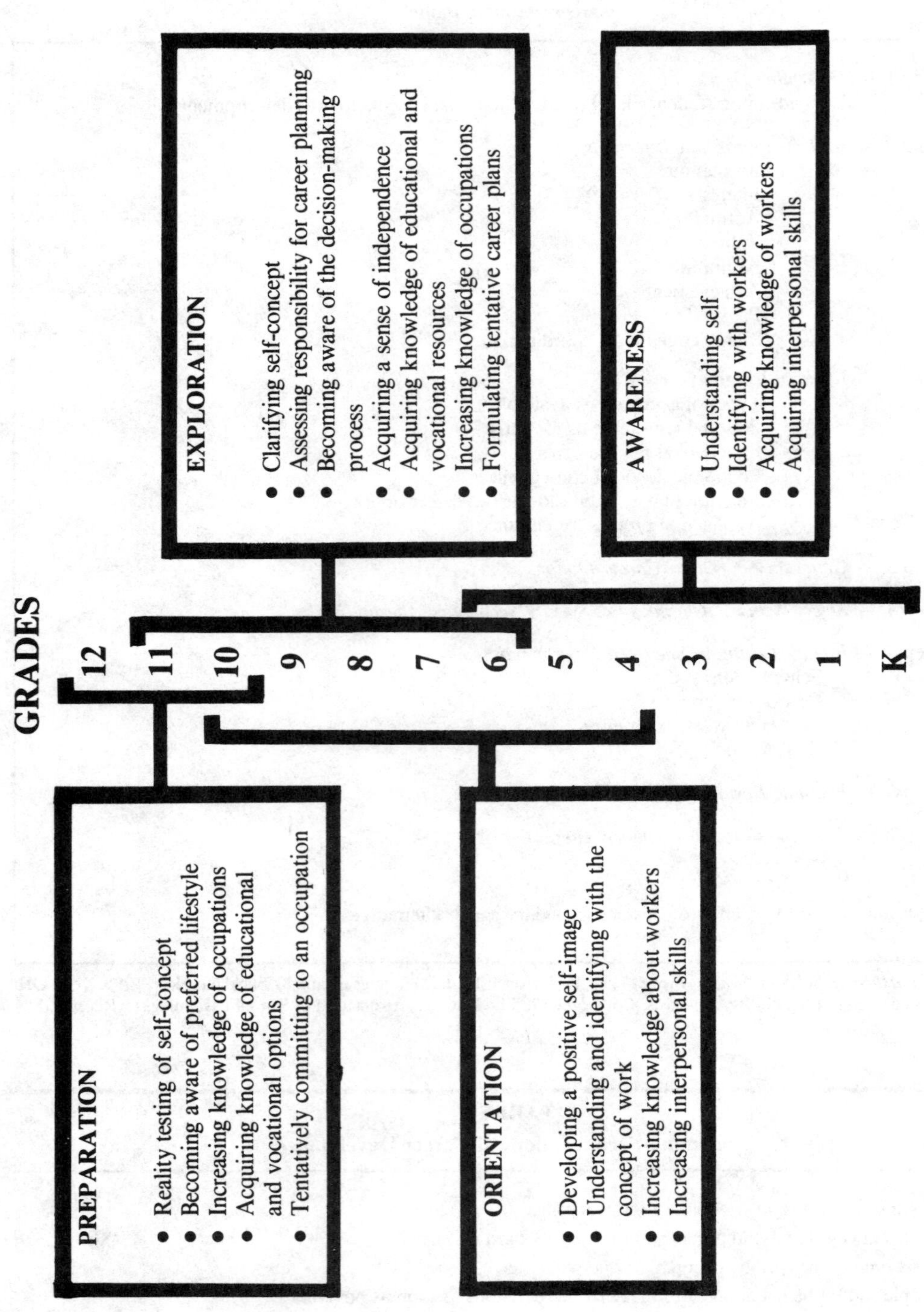

Increasing Self-Knowledge

Although, as discussed previously, vocational assessment is a method for determining the extent to which students need assistance with their career planning, it should also be thought of as a technique that can be used to increase a student's understanding of themselves. Many school systems have established vocational assessment programs; they are often dual-level programs and involve a variety of school personnel. Level 1 assessments typically include measures of mental ability, academic achievement, motor coordination, personality, vocational interests, vocational aptitudes, vocational adaptive behavior, and career maturity, and they utilize paper-and-pencil tests, performance tests, interviews, and observations. Level 2 evaluations may assess these same areas, but typically they emphasize vocational adaptive behavior, vocational interests, and vocational aptitudes and utilize more expensive and time-consuming techniques such as work samples and real and simulated work experiences. Given their expense, Level 2 evaluations should be recommended only for more severely handicapped individuals, or individuals for whom Level 1 assessment data proved inadequate for career planning. Should a Level 2 assessment be indicated for a student but not be available in a school system, the professional should consider making a referral to a nearby vocational rehabilitation center. Once assessment data have been gathered, it should be shared with the student in a counseling situation to increase the student's self-understanding.

A variety of commercial materials exist that can be used to promote self-awareness. Job Lab 1 (Houghton-Mifflin, Boston), Toward Affective Development (American Guidance Services, Circle Pines, MN), Developing Understanding of Self and Others (American Guidance Services), SRA Self Awareness Kits (Science Research Associates, Chicago), and Learning About Me: Developing Self Concept (Q-ED Productions, Coram, NY) are just a few of these materials. Self-understanding can also be promoted by assigning students classroom jobs, evaluating their performance, and providing the student with feedback. Discussions following job performance can focus on how well the student enjoyed the job, how well the student performed the job, and so on. Students can be asked to keep a diary or book to compile information that they learn about themselves as a result of these experiences. Classroom discussions focusing on topics like "What I Like About My Classmates" can also be helpful in developing self-awareness.

Increasing Occupational Awareness

A number of commercial materials, including filmstrips, books, and activity kits are available and can be used to promote occupational awareness. *The Dictionary of Occupational Titles* (U. S. Employment Service, 1981), and the *Occupational Outlook Handbook* (U. S. Department of Labor; 1982) are particularly valuable publications for use with junior or senior high school students. Local business and labor organizations are a particularly good source of printed occupational information. At the elementary level, units on "community helpers," field trips to local work establishments or vocational training facilities, or Career Days, which include guest lecturers in various occupational areas, will also aid in increasing occupational awareness. Weisgerber, Dahl, and Appleby (1981) have suggested initiating class discussion of a Job of the Week, and playing a game of "What's My Job" in quiz show format. Students can also involve themselves in the role playing of various workers, and can join job clubs (such as Future Farmers of America, Distributive Education Clubs of America, etc.), which exist in many schools. When selecting materials or techniques to increase occupational awareness, professionals should use their knowledge of the student to select materials that provide information about occupational areas that are realistic and appropriate for them.

Facilitating Adequate Decision Making

Because high school students frequently make decisions based upon limited information and knowledge, it is important to insure that they have adequate understanding of themselves and of the world of work before entering into the decision making process. Even with adequate information, however, inadequate decision making may still occur. Because decision making is such an anxiety-provoking task, young people frequently put it off for so long that their options become limited, or decisions occur by default. Group discussions designed to encourage the acceptance of such anxiety, yet stimulate an understanding of the necessity and importance of making timely decisions, can be helpful. If significant personal or emotional problems appear to be precluding decision making, individual counseling (either in a school or in a mental health facility) is recommended. Such problems should be addressed prior to encouraging decision making. Adolescents are often overly influenced by parents and peers when making decisions. Individual and group counseling are appropriate actions to consider in situations in which a student's decision is being overly influenced by peers. Family counseling sessions may be indicated when parents are dictating decisions. Professionals can encourage adequate decision making in students by setting up classes to specifically teach and model these skills. Activities can be initiated that require students to role-play actual decision making situations, allowing the students to improve these skills by practice (and feedback). A variety of commercial materials designed to promote decision making are also available, including Grow Power (Educational Activities, Coram, NY), and The Coping With Series (American Guidance Service, Circle Pines, MN).

Facilitating Job Readiness and Placement

Facilitating job readiness involves the development of positive job attitudes and work-related behaviors. Such attitudes and behaviors include such issues as punctuality, concern for quality workmanship, responding to criticism, relationships with co-workers, and so forth, and are best encouraged by modeling. In public schools, transforming a classroom into a simulated work situation (in which the teacher is a supervisor or employer and the students are employees) can help teach students positive job attitudes and behaviors. Such a program, developed for emotionally disturbed students, has been described by Levinson (1984). Vocational rehabilitation facilities frequently offer work adjustment training programs that can facilitate job readiness. Weisgerber, Dahl, & Appleby (1981) have suggested including such things as sign-in sheets, "tool licenses," competency checks, job evaluations, and Worker of the Week awards in classes to facilitate positive job attitudes and behaviors.

Kimeldorf and Tornow (1984) have described job clubs that can be established to facilitate both job readiness and job placement. Job clubs utilize a curriculum based upon "job search education" (Kimeldorf, 1984), peer support, and behavioral principles, and encourage the development of job-seeking skills and job acquisition. Students are taught to write application letters, complete applications, construct resumes, read employment ads, prepare for interviews, and make employer contacts. When attempting to encourage job placement, professionals should consult with local employment agencies and various business, industry, and labor organizations for assistance.

Roles for Parents and Professionals

Assisting students in career planning is a multidisciplinary endeavor and one that should involve a variety of school-based professionals. What roles various professionals assume in the process should be determined by their skills, competencies, and interests. The National Vocational Guidance Association (1985) has identified vocational and career competencies in the areas of assessment, counseling, provision of information, management and implementation, and these should be considered by professionals who are considering providing direct services to students or who are considering referring students to other professionals. Specific roles for teachers, principals, speech therapists, librarians, superintendents, counselors, and psychologists at the elementary, middle, and secondary school levels have been described by Smith (1983). A detailed description of the role of the school counselor has been described by the American School Counselor Association (1985). Roles for school psychologists in the vocational assessment process have been described by Hohenshil, Levinson, and Buckland-Heer (1985).

Parents have a tremendous influence on the career development of their children, and necessarily have to be involved in the career planning process. Roe (1957) proposed that the parent–child relationship and the emotional climate in the home are primarily responsible for occupational choice. She stated that children who experience rejection or neglect will gravitate toward occupations that are oriented away from people (for instance, technical or outdoor occupations, and jobs such as automobile mechanic or forest ranger), whereas children who experience an accepting home environment will gravitate toward occupations that are oriented toward people (for instance, social or business occupations, and jobs like counselor or banker). Parents also serve to influence their children's career development by acting as role models (i.e., children acquire many of their parents' personality characteristics and traits, which in turn influence the suitability of any given occupation). Parents' socioeconomic status is likely to influence the kinds of occupations to which children are exposed, and the living style preferences children develop. Research suggests that mothers have a greater influence over daughters' rather than sons' career development, and they especially influence daughters' aspiration level, and whether a traditional domestic or career-oriented path is chosen. Fathers' influence over sons' career development is especially strong during the later high school years and college years. Some occupations, like medicine and farming, are often "passed down" from fathers to sons. Probably the best thing parents can do is to model positive job attitudes and decision making skills for their children, and encourage discussion of interests, abilities, and values. Professionals interested in establishing a formal program for parents may wish to consider "Today's Youth and Tomorrows Careers," which is a seminar described by Otto (1984) designed to assist parents in helping their sons and daughters choose careers. Some of the materials used in this seminar are listed in the Annotated Bibliography for Parents.

SUMMARY

A necessary first step in assisting children and adolescents in the career development process is recognizing the influence that work has on the lives of people, and the responsibility that schools have to assist students in the process. To effectively assist a student in the career planning process, a professional must understand the normal developmental tasks that confront students at different ages and must understand the process by which realistic and informed career decisions are made. Professionals must know how to assess the degree to which students need assistance, and what kind of assistance is needed. In particular, they must be able to recommend activities designed to aid students in understanding themselves, in understanding the world of work, and in making sound, informed decisions. Since the career-planning process is a multidisciplinary effort, perhaps most importantly, professionals must involve parents and recognize and utilize the expertise of other school and community based professionals.

REFERENCES

American School Counselor Association. (1985). The role of the school counselor in career guidance: Expectations and responsibilities. *School Counselor, 32,* 164–168.

Anderson, W. T. (1982). *Job satisfaction among school psychologists.* Doctoral dissertation, Virginia Polytechnic Institute and State University, Blacksburg.

Bedeian, A. G., & Marbert, L. D. (1979). Individual differences in self perception and the job–life satisfaction relationship. *Journal of Social Psychology, 109,* 111–118.

Biggers, J. S. (1971). The use of information in vocational decision-making. *Vocational Guidance Quarterly, 19,* 171–176.

Chapman, W., & Katz, M. R. (1983, March). Career information systems in secondary schools: A survey and assessment. *Vocational Guidance Quarterly,* pp. 165–177.

Coles, R. (1978). Work and self-respect. In E. H. Erikson (Ed.); *Adulthood.* New York: Norton.

Crites, J. O. (1973). *Career Maturity Inventory.* Monterey, CA: CTB/McGraw-Hill.

Dore, R. & Meacham, M. (1983). Self-concept and interests related to job satisfaction of managers. *Personnel Psychology, 26,* 49–59.

Gallup, G. H. (1976, November 7), Eighth annual Gallup poll of the public's attitude toward public schools. *New York Teacher Magazine,* pp. 13–15.

Ginzberg, E., Ginsburg, S. W., Axelrad, S., & Herma, J. L. (1951). *Occupational choice: An approach to a general theory.* New York: Columbia University Press.

Goodlad, J. I. (1979). *What are schools for?* Los Angeles: University of California.

Greenhaus, J. H. (1971). Self-esteem as an influence on occupational choice and occupational satisfaction. *Journal of Vocational Behavior, 1,* 75–83.

Haavio-Mannila, E. (1971). Satisfaction with family, work, leisure, and life among men and women. *Human Relations, 24(6),* 585–601.

Hohenshil, T. H. (1982). School psychology + vocational counseling = vocational school psychology. *Personnel and Guidance Journal, 61,* 11–14.

Hohenshil, T. H., Levinson, E. M., & Buckland-Heer, K. (1985). Best practices in vocational assessment for handicapped students. In J. Grimes & A. Thomas (Eds.), *Best Practices in School Psychology.* Kent, OH: National Association of School Psychologists.

Holland, J. L. (1985). *Making vocational choices: A theory of vocational personalities and work environments.* Englewood Cliffs, NJ: Prentice-Hall.

Iris, B., & Barrett, G. V. (1972). Some relations between job and life satisfaction and job importance. *Journal of Applied Psychology, 56(4),* 301–307.

Isaacson, L. E. (1985). *Basics of career counseling.* Boston: Allyn & Bacon.

Johnson, L. D., Baughman, G. G., & O'Malley, P. M. (1982). *Monitoring the future.* Ann Arbor: University of Michigan Institute for Social Research, Survey Research Center.

Kalanidi, M. S. & Deivasenapathy, P. (1980). Self-concept and job satisfaction among the self-employed. *Psychological Studies, 25(1),* 39–41.

Kimeldorf, M. (1984). *Job search education.* New York: Education Design.

Kimeldorf, M., & Tornow, J. A. (1984). Job clubs: Getting into the hidden labor market. *Pointer, 28,* 29–32.

Kornhauser, A. W. (1965). *Mental health of the industrial worker.* New York: Wiley.

Levinson, E.M. (1984). A vocationally oriented secondary school program for the emotionally disturbed. *Vocational Guidance Quarterly, 33(1),* 76–81.

Marland, S. P. (1971). *Career education now* (Lesco Information Products (LIPCO 4523). Bethesda, MD: LIPCO. (ERIC Document Reproduction Service, No. ED 048 480).

McCleary, L. E., & Thomson, S. D. (1979). *The senior high school principalship: Vol. 3. The summary report.* Reston, VA: National Association of Secondary School Principals.

National Vocational Guidance Association. (1985). Vocational and career counseling competencies. *Vocational Guidance Quarterly, 34,* 131–134.

Orphen, C. (1978). Work and nonwork satisfaction: A causal–correlational analysis. *Journal of Applied Psychology, 63(4),* 530–532.

O'Toole, J. (Ed.), (1973). *Work in America: Report of a Special Task Force to the Secretary of Health, Education, and Welfare.* Cambridge, MA: MIT Press.

Otto, L. B. (1984, June). Bringing parents back in. *Journal of Career Education,* pp. 255–265.

Portigal, A. H. (1976). *Towards the measurement of work satisfaction.* Paris: Organization for Economic Cooperation and Development.

Prediger, D., Roth, J., & Noeth, R. (1973). A nationwide study of student career development: Summary of results. *ACT Research Report,* p. 61.

Roe, A. (1957). Early determinants of vocational choice. *Journal of Counseling Psychology, 4,* 212–221.

Sanborn, D. E., Sanborn, C. J., & Cimbolic, P. (1974). Occupation and suicide: A study of two counties in New Hampshire. *Diseases of the Nervous System, 35,* 7–12.

Schmitt, N., & Mellon, P. M. (1980). Life and job satisfaction: Is the job central? *Journal of Vocational Behavior, 16(1),* 51–58.

Sears, S. (1982). A definition of career guidance terms: A National Vocational Guidance Association perspective. *Vocational Guidance Quarterly, 31,* 137–143.

Seligman, L. (1980). *Assessment in developmental career counseling.* Cranston, RI: Carroll.

Smith, R. L. (1983). *The vocational counselor and guidance team.* Commerce, TX: Occupational Curriculum Laboratory.

Snyder, C. D.,& Ferguson, L. W. (1976). Self-concept and job satisfaction. *Psychological Reports, 38(2),* 603–610.

Super, D. (1957). *The psychology of careers.* New York: Harper & Row.

Super, D., Thompson, A., Lindeman, R. H., Jordan, J. P., and Meyer, R. A. (1979). *Career Development Inventory.* Palo Alto, CA: Consulting Psychologists Press.

U. S. Department of Labor. (1982). *The occupational outlook handbook.* Washington, DC: U. S. Government Printing Office.

U. S. Employment Service. (1981). *Dictionary of occupational titles.* Washington, DC: U. S. Government Printing Office.

Weisgerber, R. A., Dahl, P. R., & Appleby, J. A. (1981). *Training the handicapped for productive employment.* Rockville, MD: Aspen Systems.

BIBLIOGRAPHY: PROFESSIONALS

Hohenshil, T. H., Levinson, E. M., & Buckland-Heer, K. (1985). Best practices in vocational assessment of handicapped students. In J. Grimes & A. Thomas (Eds.), *Best practices in school psychology.* Washington, DC: National Association of School Psychologists.
Describes the various areas and techniques included in comprehensive vocational assessments, discusses assessment models, and describes roles for school psychologists in the process.

Kapes, J. T., & Mastie, M. M. (1983). *A counselor's guide to vocational guidance instruments.* Falls Church, VA: National Vocational Guidance Association.
Describes uses and technical characteristics of instruments designed to assess aptitudes, interests, work values, and career maturity. Sections on selecting tests, and instruments for special populations are included.

Osipow, S. H. (1968). *Theories of career development.* New York: Appleton-Century-Crofts.
Classic text that summarizes, compares, and contrasts the major theories of career development, including the theories of Ginzberg, et al., Super, and Roe.

Seligman, L. (1980). *Assessment in developmental career counseling.* Cranston, RI: Cranston Press.
Summarizes research on the career development of individuals at different stages of life and discusses appropriate assessment and counseling approaches that can be used at these different life stages. Case studies and descriptions of assessment tools are included.

BIBLIOGRAPHY: PARENTS[1]

Betterman, L. S. (1984, June). It's never too early: A career/college guide for students and parents. *Journal of Career Education,* pp. 234–240.
Provides parents and students with a step-by-step, grade-by-grade guide to career planning (Grades 8–12), and includes timelines for completing such things as interest and aptitude tests, college applications, PSATs, SATs, etc.

Hoyt, K. B. (1984, June). Helping parents understand career education. *Journal of Career Education,* pp. 216–224.
Describes how career education operates and discusses the parent's role in the process. Twelve practical suggestions for parents are included.

Meyer, R. S. (1984, June). Parents have a part in "Education with a Purpose." *Journal of Career Education,* pp. 241–247.
Provides 18 practical suggestions on how parents can be involved in the career education process.

Otto, L. B. (1984). *How to help your child choose a career.* New York: Evans.
Written specifically for parents of high school-aged children, this book discusses the influence parents have in the career-planning process and provides information on the world of work and educational and vocational career preparation options. A career explorations workbook and a bibliography are included.

BIBLIOGRAPHY: CHILDREN[1]

Career World. Highland Park, IL: General Learning Corporation.
This monthly magazine, appropriate for use with junior and senior high school students, provides information on general career planning issues, various occupational groups, and job acquisition. A teacher's guide is included with a yearly subscription.

Kimbrell, G., & Vineyard, B. S. (1978). *Entering the world of work.* Bloomington, IL: McKnight.
This textbook, appropriate for use with junior and senior high school students, is designed to teach positive job attitudes and job acquisition skills. It includes chapters on such topics as getting along with co-workers and employers and applying and interviewing for jobs.

Rettig, J. L. (1986). *Careers: Exploration and decision.* Belmont, CA: David S. Lake.
This book, appropriate for high school-aged students, guides students through the career decision making process. It includes practical discussions of career development theory, the world of work,and the decision making process.

FOOTNOTE

[1]These are materials which can be recommended by professionals to be used with children. It is most appropriate for children to use these materials under the supervision of parents, teachers, or other professionals.

Children and Cheating

James P. Murphy
Rider College

BACKGROUND

Cheating in school involves obtaining test scores or other recorded grades by dishonest or deceitful means through practicing fraud and trickery, which defeats the purposes of educational measurement. It constitutes a violation of accepted rules of academic integrity.

Cheating, which includes copying, permitting others to copy, plagiarizing, ghostwriting, and using crib sheets, endangers the validity of educational measurement, and thus causes inaccuracy in the assessment of students' abilities and performance (Bushway & Nash, 1977; Houser, 1978; Schab, 1980). Educators regard cheating as violating ethical principles and inhibiting the development of critical thinking, perhaps the major objective of formal education (Harp & Taietz, 1966). Thus, cheating has serious repercussions for the individual and the educational system.

Approximately 40–50% of students are reported to have engaged in some form of cheating at some period in their academic careers (Harp & Taietz, 1966; Houser, 1982; Schab, 1980). Conflicting conclusions have been reported in the literature concerning age and sex differences among students who cheat. The seminal studies of Hartshorne and May (1928) reported that older students cheated more often, but Black (1962) found no age differences.

The literature in general has supported the conclusion that males cheat somewhat more than females, who tend to have stricter attitudes against cheating, although the evidence is by no means conclusive (Anderson, 1957; Schab, 1980). Hartshorne and May (1928) and Black (1962) found no sex differences, whereas Feldman and Feldman (1967) reported that females cheated more in the earlier grades, but males surpassed them by the senior year in high school.

DEVELOPMENT

When cheating occurs in school, it is common for educators and parents to make generalizations about the personality and moral development of the person who engaged in cheating. Although some differences in personality variables, attitudes, and environmental contexts have a relationship with cheating, no single conclusion can be validly drawn concerning the character of a student who has cheated.

Students who engage in cheating have been described as more neurotic, more extroverted, more tense and irritable, and in more turmoil than noncheaters (Heatherington & Feldman, 1964; White, Zielonko, & Gaier, 1967). Preadolescents who described themselves as more trusting, tended to be more able to resist temptation (Doster & Chance, 1976). Students who had not experienced initial success, were fearful of failing, and who believed that present and future success was in jeopardy have been reported as risk for cheating (Bushway & Nash, 1977; Vitro & Schoen, 1972).

Other personality characteristics and behavior patterns have been empirically related to cheating. An external locus of control, for example, has been associated with cheating behavior (Johnson & Gormly, 1972). Increased cheating behavior also has been reported in students who were unaware of or indifferent to the immediate and long-range consequences of their behavior (Woods, 1957). Difficulty in controlling impulses and in attending to relevant environmental cues have been identified as behaviors more prevalent in students who have engaged in cheating (Blasi, 1980; Grim, Kohlberg, & White, 1968).

In addition to personal and behavioral characteristics, environmental variables have been found to have a great influence on whether students engage in cheating behavior. Children who perceived pressure from their home or school environment to obtain and maintain high grades were found to be at increased risk for cheating (Trabue, 1962; Woods, 1957). Hartshorne and May (1928) found that peer group affiliation was related to cheating. Students who associated with students who engaged in cheating were more likely to cheat than those who reported associating with noncheating students.

The moral climate of the school has been reported to influence the amount of cheating (Atkins & Atkins, 1936). Occurrence of cheating has been reported to have increased when students perceived the curriculum as lacking in meaning (Steininger, Johnson, & Kirts, 1964). In addition, increased cheating behavior has been reported in situations in which instruction was perceived as poor, assigned work was too easy or too difficult, and the teaching style was authoritarian (Bushway & Nash, 1977; Johnson & Klores, 1968).

Finally, classroom situations in which students have observed others successfully cheat and which minimize the possibility of detection have been linked to increased cheating behavior.

Thus, the factors that determine the presence and frequency of cheating are myriad and involve personal and environmental particularities. It is important for school psychologists to keep these factors in focus as they help clients cope with this emotionally charged issue.

PUTTING CHEATING IN PERSPECTIVE

When cheating has been discovered, there is often a tendency for teachers and parents to automatically interpret the behavior as reflecting character flaw in the student. Parents may become embarrassed and teachers frequently become angry and disappointed with the student. It is important that those involved in the evaluation of cheating situations and development of interventions to alleviate the problem be mindful of several issues associated with cheating. Cheating may involve moral judgment and reasoning, social learning, and/or societal conventions. Affective responses in children faced with the temptation to cheat also affect their decisions, as does the degree to which honesty is valued as part of their self-concept.

Moral Development

The majority of educators and students view cheating as morally wrong (Harp & Taietz, 1966), and a positive relationship has been reported between level of moral thinking and resistance to temptation. In recent years, moral behavior has been addressed in the literature primarily from two points of view. Grim, Kohlberg, and associates have stressed the development of moral reasoning in developmental stages. The cognitive aspects of moral development have been emphasized, moral action being viewed as mediated by cognitive processes such as moral beliefs, moral reasoning, and moral definition. In contrast, social learning theorists have considered behaviors such as cheating as objectively determined by external factors and have looked into learned action tendencies and their interactions in the process of making decisions concerning cheating (Blasi, 1980; Dienstbier, Hillman, Lehnoff, Hillman, & Valkenaar, 1975).

According to the cognitive approach, persons pass through stages in which moral reasoning undergoes structural developmental changes in a predictable sequence. Rules that form the basis for evaluation and decision making are formed through the moral reasoning process. Within this model cheating cannot be evaluated as to its morality unless a judgment was made prior to the act.

Various conclusions as to the presence and degree of relationship between moral judgment and moral action have been reported in the literature. Although moral reasoning has been viewed as an after-the-fact rationalization of behavior, Blasi (1980), in a comprehensive review of the literature, concluded that moral judgment and action are related. An important determinant of the degree of this relationship in individuals is the degree to which morality has been incorporated into the self-concept (Blasi, 1983).

According to the social learning approach, moral behavior is essentially erratic. Cognitive processes are used in this model to regulate relationships between situations and tendencies, and relationships between tendencies and behavior. In contrast to the moral reasoning approach, cognitive processes are not viewed as determining truth (Blasi, 1980). In evaluating cheating behavior, it is helpful for school psychologists to ascertain the degree to which the behavior has been generated from an internal system of rules. Also, an assessment of the interaction of previously learned and reinforced behaviors with the perceived demands of the situation in which the cheating has occurred will provide information from which to develop interventions.

Societal Conventions

It cannot be assumed that a behavior pattern will be interpreted by all concerned as a moral issue. It has been reported that cheating does not have the same moral meaning for everybody (Bem & Allen, 1974).

Decisions to cheat occasionally or to cheat in specific situations are often determined by nonmoral considerations (Blasi, 1980). Social conventions have been described as behavioral uniformities determined by the social systems in which they are formed (Nucci, 1984). In contrast, moral considerations derive from factors intrinsic to actions. Reasoning that concerns social conventions is assumed to represent a domain that is distinct from moral reasoning. Conventional rules involve behavioral regulations established to regulate the actions of members of a social system (Smetana, 1983). Merton (1937) has suggested that cheating may be an adaptive response developing from a general acceptance of the goals of institutions but not the sanctioned means to attaining the goals.

Responses of children to moral transgression have been found to differ from their responses to violations of social conventions. Their responses to moral transgressions focused on the *effects* of the acts on the victim, whereas responses to violations of convention focused on the *normative status* of the acts. That is, children's responses to violations of social conventions have focused on the governing rule as opposed to the victim (Turiel, 1983; Nucci & Nucci, 1982).

Emotional Arousal

Behavior associated with self-control in situations of temptation has been found to be strongly influenced by emotional states such as anxiety, fear, guilt, and/or shame (Dienstbier & Hunter, 1971). When a student encounters a potential cheating situation, emotional responses frequently occur that may deter cheating. When the emotional discomfort has been associated with the actual cheating, the probability of transgression has been found to be lower than when the emotional arousal has been linked to potential punishment. The individual must identify the discomfort as due to the transgression and its effect on the self-concept.

ALTERNATIVE ACTIONS

A three-level prevention model for prevention of cheating behavior has been described by Caplan (1964). Primary prevention interventions are designed to minimize the occurrence of an undesirable behavior primarily through a long-range educational approach. Secondary prevention involves directed activities with groups known to be at risk. Tertiary prevention involves working with those who have already exhibited the inappropriate behavior.

Primary and Secondary Prevention

Although the bulk of research in the area of cheating has been concerned with identifying the causes of cheating behavior, practitioners are primarily in need of strategies useful in the prevention and reduction of cheating in our schools. Primary prevention activities may begin at the school system level. Including the organization of the school as a whole in the encouragement of honest behavior provides children with the opportunity to directly experience attitudes and behaviors which are also being presented at more abstract levels in classroom instruction (Power & Reimer, 1978). A comprehensive approach to facilitating honest behavior in children, involving the education of secretaries, maintenance, and cafeteria employees as to how issues involving honesty are to be handled provides a living laboratory for children. A clearly written, institutionally accepted policy regarding cheating serves as a useful resource for teachers and others who encounter children in situations fraught with temptation (Sauer, 1983).

Within classrooms, educational programs that inform students about cheating and its effects on those who cheat and on other students facilitate the development of honest behavior.

The moral climate of the school influences the amount of cheating. Atkins and Atkins (1936) reported that cheating has been shown to be reduced by a nurturing emotional climate in the classroom, coupled with specific instructions to students about resisting the temptation to cheat prior to test taking, together with measures by the teacher that make cheating quite difficult.

Peer discussion groups have been suggested by many authors. Berkowitz, Gibbs, & Broughton (1980) concluded that teachers and counselors serve less as instruments for intervention than as agents for the facilitation of peer discussion leading to moral development. Although teachers and counselors do not directly advance the moral development of children as much as peers, their supervision and encouragement of meaningful peer discussion is valuable in the prevention of cheating.

Additional strategies for primary and secondary prevention of cheating include the development of educational materials that make it difficult for children to demonstrate competence through cheating. For example, teachers can be encouraged to design tasks to discourage or prevent cheating (Houser, 1982) and to provide regular progress checks on the development of papers. Retaining papers in their files, and using a wide variety of assignments over time have also been suggested as effective ways teachers can deter cheating. In short, reducing the opportunity for cheating behavior to occur serves to reduce cheating behavior.

Punishment conditions have been found to be equally as effective as nonpunishment conditions in deterring cheating on a short-term basis (Fischer, 1970). Coercive power, defined as including the use of threats that the assignment would have to be redone, or that those caught cheating would be sent to the principal, has been found to be an effective short-term deterrent to cheating (Houser, 1982).

However, while the use of punishment may yield desirable short-term results, it does not reduce the tendency to cheat on a long-term basis.

Initial emotional discomfort, when tied to punishment, becomes less effective as a deterrent over time, especially in situations where the opportunity to cheat without getting caught is present. Specific discussions of honesty and cheating, on topics such as test-taking behavior, copying homework, or permitting others to copy, as well as the feelings generated by these acts, will increase the association between emotional discomfort and cheating. This association is more likely to deter cheating on a long-term basis than the use of punishment.

Tertiary Prevention

While primary and secondary prevention intervention has long-range benefits in the deterrence of cheating, school psychologists most frequently intervene after cheating has been discovered. However, when useful strategies are developed at the tertiary prevention level, opportunities for primary and secondary prevention increase.

The following practices may be useful to psychologists when developing strategies specific to a particular situation involving cheating.

1. It is important for school personnel to avoid a purely personal, punitive response to the student. The situation can be used to encourage honest behavior in the future and to help children internalize appropriate responses.
2. Initially it is important to determine whether the cheating behavior has been viewed by the children as a moral issue or one of the social convention, through interviewing the student, and assessing the factors surrounding the cheating episodes.
3. Interventions generated from the student's point of view about the cheating behavior as a moral transgression or a breach of convention will have a higher probability of success. When the cheating has been viewed by the student as a moral issue, interventions involving the effects of the act on the student and others are most appropriate. When cheating has been viewed as a violation of social convention, interventions focusing on the behavior as deviant rather than immoral, are most appropriate (Nucci, 1984).
4. Interventions that make appropriate use of the confrontation situation and emotional arousal associated with cheating may serve to prevent future cheating. While emotional arousal in anticipation of punishment can lead to resistance to temptation, excessive punishment or reinforcement for honesty can draw more attention to the punishment or reinforcement than to the undesirable behavior. It is important for children who have engaged in cheating to dwell on the transgression itself and the behavioral standards that have been violated rather than on the threat that is inherent in the confrontation with authority. Withdrawal of a teacher's approval may eventually result in an act of repentance by the child. This approach is most effective in warm and accepting relationships. In dealing with copying, it is important for teachers to emphasize the rules, leave the door open to parental involvement, minimize anger, and reduce defensiveness in the student (Sauer, 1983).

SUMMARY

Cheating has been part of the educational process since the initiation of public education. It can have an erosive effect on the educational process owing to the resulting inaccuracies in the measurement of the progress of students. This in turn can lead to the setting of inappropriate goals for children. In addition, cheating, whether viewed as a moral issue or one of social convention, represents a violation of values that form the foundation of our society. Public education has become deeply involved in teaching societal norms and also in teaching decision making to children. These efforts are designed to help children develop positive mental health and character growth.

It is important that the issue of cheating be approached from the point of view of inculcating honest behavior. The literature has identified many determinants of cheating as well as strategies for dealing with transgression that reduce the probability of future occurrence. Educators who remember that not all transgressors view cheating as morally wrong, and that there are subtle and blatant reinforcers of cheating behavior in many areas of respectable society that muddy the issue for children, and those who can capitalize on the emotional arousal felt in those who cheat, will be more successful not only in deterring cheating in their classrooms but also in reducing the likelihood of cheating occurring in the future. As with most undesirable behavior, prevention approaches must address broad areas of child development. When attempting to deal with an undesirable behavior, it is always important to work within the framework of a warm, positive relationship that is characterized by honesty and respect. It is also important to stress the development of values and behaviors that facilitate the growth of the individual.The strengthening of these values and behaviors will automatically reduce the occurrence of undesirable behaviors such as cheating.

REFERENCES

Anderson, W. F., Jr. (1957). Attitudes of university students toward cheating. *Journal of Educational Research, 50,* 581–88.

Atkins, B. E., & Atkins, R. E. (1936). A study of the honesty of prospective teachers. *Elementary School Journal, 36,* 595–603.

Bem, D. J., & Allen, A. (1974). On predicting some people some of the time: The search for cross-situational consistencies in behavior. *Psychological Review, 81,* 506–520.

Berkowitz, M., Gibbs, J., & Broughton, J. (1980). The relation of moral judgment stage disparity to developmental effects of peer dialogues. *Merrill-Palmer Quarterly, 26,* 341–357.

Black, D. B. (1962). The falsification of reported examination marks in a senior university education course. *Journal of Educational Sociology, 35,* 346–54.

Blasi, A. (1980). Bridging moral cognition and moral action: A critical review of the literature. *Psychological Bulletin, 88,* 1–45.

Blasi, A. (1983). Moral cognition and moral action: A theoretical perspective. *Developmental Review, 3,* 178–210.

Bushway, A., & Nash, W. (1977). School cheating behavior. *Review of Educational Research, 47,* 623–632.

Caplan, G. (1964). *Principles of Preventive Psychiatry.* New York: Basic Books.

Dienstbier, R. A., Hillman, D., Lehnhoff, J., Hillman, J., & Valkenaar, M. C. (1975). An emotion–attribution approach to moral behavior interfacing cognitive and avoidance theories of moral development. *Psychological Review, 82,* 299–315.

Dienstbier, R. A., & Hunter, P. O. (1971). Cheating as a function of the labeling of natural arousal. *Journal of Personality and Social Psychology,17,* 208–213.

Doster, J. T., & Chance, J. (1976). Interpersonal trust and trustworthiness in preadolescents. *Journal of Psychology, 93,* 71–79.

Feldman, S. E., & Feldman, M. T. (1967). Transition of sex differences in cheating. *Psychological Reports, 20,* 957–58.

Fischer, C. T. (1970). Levels of cheating under conditions of informative appeal to honesty, public affirmation of value and threats of punishment. *Journal of Educational Research, 64,* 12–16.

Grim, P. F., Kohlberg, L., & White, S. H. (1968). Some relationships between conscience and attentional processes. *Journal of Personality and Social Psychology,8,* 239–252.

Harp, J., & Taietz, P.(1966). Academic integrity and social structure: A study of cheating among college students. *Social Problems, 13,* 365–373.

Hartshorne, H., & Mary, M. A. (1928). *Studies in deceit.* New York: Macmillan.

Heatherington, E. M., & Feldman, S. E. (1964). College cheating as a function of subject and situational variables. *Journal of Educational Psychology, 55,* 212–218.

Houser, B. B. (1978). Cheating among elementary grade level students: An examination. *Journal of Instructional Psychology, 5,* 2–5.

Houser, B. B. (1982). Student cheating and attitude: A function of classroom control technique. *Contemporary Educational Psychology, 7,* 113–123.

Johnson, C. D., & Gormly, J. (1972). Academic cheating: The contribution of sex, personality and situational variables. *Developmental Psychology, 6,* 320–325.

Johnson, R. E., & Klores, M. S. (1968). Attitudes toward cheating as a function of classroom dissatisfaction and peer norms. *Journal of Educational Research, 62,* 60–64.

Merton, R. K. (1957). *Social theory and social structure.* New York: Free Press of Glencoe.

Nucci, L. (1984). Evaluating teachers as social agents: Students' ratings of domain appropriate and domain inappropriate teacher responses to transgressions. *American Education Research, 21,* 367–378.

Nucci, L., & Nucci, M. (1982). Children's responses to moral and social conventional transgressions in free-play settings. *Child Development, 53,* 1337–1342.

Power, C., & Reimer, J. (1978). Moral atmosphere: An educational bridge between moral judgment and action. In W. Damon (Ed.), *New directions for child development: Moral development* (pp. 105–116). San Francisco: Jossey-Bass.

Sauer, R. (1983). Coping with copiers. *English Journal, 72,* 50–52.

Schab, F. (1980). Cheating in high school: Differences between the sexes (revisited). *Adolescence, 15,* 959–965.

Smetana, J. (1983). Social cognitive development: Domain distinctions and coordinations. *Developmental Reviews, 3,* 131–147.

Steininger, M., Johnson, R. E., & Kirts, D. K. (1964). Cheating on college examinations as a function of situationally aroused anxiety and hostility. *Journal of Educational Psychology, 55,* 317–324.

Trabue, A. (1962). Classroom cheating — An isolated phenomenon? *Educational Record, 43,* 309–316.

Turiel, E. (1983). *The development of social knowledge: Morality and convention.* Cambridge: Cambridge University Press.

Vitro, F. J., & Schoen, L. A. (1972). The effects of probability of test success, test importance, and risk of detection on the incidence of cheating. *Journal of School Psychology, 10,* 269–277.

White, W. F., Zielonko, A. W., & Gaier, L. (1967). Personality correlates of cheating among college women under stress of independent opportunistic behavior. *Journal of Educational Research, 61,* 68–70.

Woods, R. C. (1957). Factors affecting cheating and their control. *West Virginia Academy of Science Proceedings, 29,* 79–82.

BIBLIOGRAPHY: PROFESSIONALS

Blasi, A. (1980). Bridging moral cognition and moral action: A critical review of the literature. *Psychological Bulletin, 88,* 1–45.

Presents a comprehensive review of empirical research in the study of the relationship between moral reasoning and moral action. Specific aspects discussed include moral reasoning and honesty, and moral reasoning and delinquency. Divergent views of the relationship between moral cognition and moral action are described. The author draws conclusions based upon research evidence and suggests desirable directions for further investigation.

Bushway, A., & Nash, W. (1977). School cheating behavior. *Review of Educational Research, 47,* 623–632.

Reviews literature describing personal characteristics of those who engage in cheating. Contextual and situational factors affecting decisions to cheat are also discussed. Research investigating reasons for cheating is also reviewed in this concise and useful article.

Hartshorne, H., & May, M. A. (1928). *Studies in deceit.* New York: Macmillan.

The studies conducted by the authors are considered to be classic investigations of lying, cheating, and stealing. The authors included over 8,000 children in their national sample. The studies have had tremendous heuristic value and have generated considerable controversy and additional empirical research.

Children and Childcare

Mahlon B. Dalley and Susan M. Vess
University of Northern Colorado

BACKGROUND

Mothers in the United States often share childrearing with others. By 1982, 50% of women with children under 6 years of age were employed and 40% of single and 33% of married mothers of children under 1 year old work (Long, 1984). Burtman (1984) reported that the number of working mothers with children under 5 grew from 4.7 million to 6 million between 1977 and 1982. Two-thirds of working mothers live alone or with a partner who earns less than $10,000 annually. One-third of households headed by a single woman are below the poverty threshold (Long,1984).

For the majority of working couples, the second income allows the family to live above the poverty level for a family of four. In 60% of U.S. families, two adults work outside the home; another 20% are headed by a single parent who is usually employed (Long, 1984). Long also reported that two-fifths of households with at least one parent who is not working full time do not provide parental supervision of children in the afternoon. The norm of an employed father and an at-home mother is more myth than reality in the United States today.

According to Clarke-Stewart (1982), there were nearly 8 million preschool children whose mothers worked, and this number was expected to increase to 10.5 million in the next decade. With almost half of all mothers of preschoolers working, and the number of preschoolers increasing, childcare has become a major issue for the U.S. family.

Childcare is operationally defined as care given to children; however, more recently, the term has come to denote care given to a child by someone other than the mother. Terminology is rather confusing because the terms daycare, preschool, nursery school, family daycare homes, group daycare, in-home care, self-care, and childcare are used interchangeably. A helpful distinction is to use the term childcare to encompass all forms of other-than-mother care and daycare to designate out-of-home care. Other types of childcare are defined by function and structure.

There are multiple classifications for types of childcare. In most schemes, a distinction is made between in-home care and out-of-home care (Clarke-Stewart, 1982; Holland, 1985). Table 1 summarizes childcare alternatives as well as the characteristics, advantages, and disadvantages of each childcare option. In-home care, used by about 30% of working mothers, provides care within the family's residence by a sitter such as a relative, babysitter, or housekeeper (1982 Bureau of the Census, cited in Burtman, 1984). Out-of-home care is provided either at the caregiver's home or at a center. Family daycare, which is childcare provided in the caretaker's home, includes the children of approximately 40% of working mothers. Daycare centers or group care centers are located in large facilities such as remodeled homes and churches, or buildings designed specifically for childcare. Daycare centers offer structured activities, several caregivers, and extended business hours. Approximately 15% of working mothers use this daycare arrangement. Infant care, nursery school, school-age care, and self-care are other types of childcare (Mitchell, 1979).

Self-care is the system in which children under 14 years old care for themselves, and perhaps siblings, without adult supervision (Carter, 1985; Long, 1984). Latchkey is the designation applied to children who enter an empty house with their own keys (Garbarino, 1981). At least 5 million youngsters are currently latchkey children, and the number is expected to swell to almost 20 million by 1990 (Levine et al., 1982). After parent care, self-care is the second most common care arrangement for the school-age child in the United States (Long, 1984).

The forces of industrialization, urbanization, and compulsory education precipitated the development of out-of-home care for children; however, childcare has rarely been provided consistently. Legislation such as Mothers' Pension and aid to dependent children laws established the value of impoverished mothers remaining home to care for dependent children. Benefits accruing from the provision of childcare to low-income children include amelioration of the consequences of poverty; enhancement of children's cognitive, communicative, language, and social development; protective services in cases of child abuse and neglect; and the opportunity for young, single women to complete their education (Gordon, 1984). Hill and Bragg (1985) reported that secondary adult students with daycare for their children are more likely to complete high school or earn an equivalency diploma than those who do not.

Ambivalence in the United States about the role of women, maternal employment, and the value of children has led to a lack of public policy regarding childcare (Schiller, 1980). As a result, the government has been reluctant to enact legislation that facilitates the development of affordable, available, quality childcare. Among the negative results of this absence of policy are daycare providers who lack training in child development and experience working with young children, salaries that are inadequate to attract or keep quality personnel, frequent staff turnovers, and little opportunity for professional advancement of daycare workers (Schiller, 1980; Long, 1984; McNairy, 1984, Ainslie, 1984). Problems related to lack of quality private and public daycare are exacerbated by pressures to tighten eligibility criteria for economic assistance to the poor, by inadequacy of tax credits in covering the cost of daycare, and by the overall efforts to reduce government support of domestic programs.

DEVELOPMENT

Supervised Care

It is often believed that childcare is detrimental to children and contributes to the breakdown of the nuclear family and of society (White, 1981; Dail, 1982; Long, 1984; Schiller, 1980; Ainslie, 1984). However, many arguments against childcare are emotional or even misplaced.

Clarke-Stewart (1982) stated that intellectual development increases for daycare children over the first several years. However, this advantage is lost by middle-class children when home-reared children start school. Research findings indicate that children raised in quality daycare do not differ from home-reared children in intellectual growth (Belsky, 1984). Ramey, Dorval, and Baker-Ward (1983) studied socially disadvantaged children and found that daycare is an appropriate intervention strategy in the prevention of the intellectual declines that are often seen in these children.

Childcare's impact on bonding or attachment was studied extensively because care arrangements that deprive the children of continuous access to their mothers was considered detrimental to the children's emotional development (Belsky, 1984). Early research (Blehar, 1974) suggested that children in daycare were poorly attached to their mothers, as indicated by crying, reduced exploration and resistance behavior toward their mothers. More recent studies reported by Belsky (1984) fail to support these conclusions. He accounted for the discrepancy in research findings both by differences in the amount of time children were enrolled in daycare and by methodological inadequacies. There is general agreement that children exposed to unstable daycare arrangements, particularly in the first year of life, experience both short- and long-term emotional difficulties. However, there is little reason to believe that daycare adversely affects children's emotional development if childcare is of good quality and is stable (Belsky, 1984).

Daycare influences social development and relationships with both peers and adults. Daycare children are more outgoing, helpful, and cooperative and are less timid and fearful than children who are raised at home. However, children in daycare described by Clarke-Stewart (1982) are louder, and more boisterous, com-

TABLE 1

Childcare Options

Characteristics	Advantages	Disadvantages
1. In-home care		
Preferred for infants and toddlers Adult-oriented Familiar setting One-to-one adult-to-child ratio	Fewer morning "hassles" Fewer problems of illness Sitter often does housecleaning and cooking	Costly Some loss of privacy Hidden expenses (food and utilities) Less social contact with other children
2. Family daycare		
Home-like features Limit usually 5–6 children May or may not be licensed	Least costly of daycare options Exposure to other children Extended family, caring adult, homey feeling	Illness may be problem Taking child out in bad weather If unlicensed, parents are responsible for seeing that house is safe and not overcrowded
3. Relatives		
Half of working mothers use this arrangement In child's home or relative's home Generally not licensed	Familiar home setting Familiar adult May be least costly	Family disagreements may arise Disadvantages same as in-home care and family daycare
4. Daycare centers		
School-like setting Nursery schools usually included but part-time Adult-to-child ratios based upon state and federal standards Licensed	Usually trained staff Usually opened long hours Planned activities Educational materials Toys usually safe and age-appropriate Must meet safety standards	Nonhome, institutional environment Exposure to other's illnesses Limited provisions for illness High turnover in staff May not accept children under 2 years
5. Selfcare (latchkey)		
Children left alone because of economic restraints or when responsible	No cost May foster sense of responsibility	Child is alone without supervision

petitive, and aggressive than their peers. Clarke-Stewart stated that daycare children are more competent in social skills and are more self-reliant than are home-reared children. Belsky (1984) reported that exposure to daycare increases both positive and negative social interactions with peers.

Clarke-Stewart (1982) summarized the results of studies on childcare and physical development. For children from poor families, daycare advances motor development and activity, increases height and weight faster, and decreases the likelihood of pediatric problems. Both daycare centers and daycare homes provide these advantages for physical growth; the benefit for motor development occurs only in centers. There are no differences among children who come from families that already provide opportunities for physical development. Additionally, there is no difference between middle-class children in daycare and those receiving parent care in height, motor skills, or activity; but daycare children even in the best homes and in the best daycare centers catch flu, rashes, colds, and coughs more often than children cared for by their mothers.

Belsky (1984) found the most important considerations in the childcare experience to be group size, caregiver-to-child ratio, and caregiver training. Standards for caregiver to child ratios were established for federally funded daycare facilities by the Interagency Day Care Requirements, which base maximum ratios on the age of the child and the type of care given (Clarke-Stewart, 1982). Scarr (1984) asserted that the quality caregiver has training in child development or early childhood education and interacts more frequently and constructively with children than the untrained caregiver. Additionally, better-trained caregivers are more likely to praise, comfort, respond, question, and instruct children than caregivers with less training.

Among the disturbing features of out-of-home care is separation (Hock, 1984; Provence, Naylor, & Patterson, 1977). Separation can cause fear, worry, anger, and listlessness in the parent and the child. If the first separation of parent and infant or child is negotiated successfully, further separations are easier. Parental anxieties about leaving a child and the child's reaction complicate an already traumatic situation. A major outcome of parental distress is withdrawn, fretful, and negative children.

In general, research findings conclude that out-of-home care is not detrimental to children's development. Belsky's (1984, p. 16) answer to the question "Is daycare bad for children?" is, "it seems appropriate to conclude that it usually is not and certainly does not have to be, but that it can be."

Selfcare

Parents "fall" into self-care because of job demands, unavailability of daycare, and their children's resistance to participation in babyish care arrangements. Self-care usually evolves as parents allow their children to experiment with staying home alone for longer and longer time periods. According to Long (1984), self-care averages 2½ hours daily after parents are assured nothing bad happens and the child apparently copes. For other families, the necessity for self-care arises suddenly in response to a family crisis and continues until the crisis resolves or family relationships are realigned (Long, 1984).

Since children do not complain about it and the necessity for this arrangement persists, few parents express a desire to discontinue self-care. In fact 90–95% of parents claim self-care has advantages — especially development of responsibility, independence, and survival skills (Long, 1984; Garbarino, 1981). This optimistic view is tempered by parents' lingering concerns about leaving children unsupervised. Fears include accidents and death; tardiness and truancy; increased use of drugs and alcohol; too much television viewing; academic problems; poor nutrition leading to obesity; peer pressure for vandalism and delinquency; sexual acting out and victimization from peers, siblings, and other adults; and poor family relationships (Long, 1984; Garbarino, 1981; McNairy, 1984). Research has not demonstrated that these concerns are relevant to the majority of latchkey children. Successful self-care is more dependent on preexisting family relationships and the child's maturity (Long, 1984).

Although self-care is not harmful to most children, latchkey children do experience feelings of loneliness, fear, boredom, and resentment. Long (1984) has reported that half of former latchkey children resent their parents for leaving them alone, although this is not expressed until the children are grown. In a few children, the parameters of latchkey syndrome are emerging. Characteristics include fearfulness, sense of social isolation, negative self-concept, resentment of parents, and selection of a solitary career (Long, 1984).

PUTTING CHILDCARE IN PERSPECTIVE

Choosing Childcare

Many books and articles are filled with checklists and a myriad of suggestions for choosing childcare (Mitchell, 1979; Clarke-Stewart, 1982; *Parents' Guide,* 1981). A method for choosing childcare is presented in Figure 1, which is supplemented with Tables 1 and 2.

Step 1 in Figure 1 (and Table 2) assists parents in evaluating their needs and current situations. Step 2 lists childcare options and refers to Tables 1 and 2. Step 3 defines responsibilities that are frequently overlooked by parents, but are essential in maintaining quality childcare. Step 3 is represented as part of Step 2, since choosing a specific childcare arrangement entails defining responsibilities. Finding childcare is only part of the picture; maintaining quality care is just as important. Step 4 represents concerns that a parent may have about the childcare arrangement. The two arrows between Step 3 and Step 4 show that communication between parent and caregiver is vital in alleviating concerns or in correcting problems. If a problem arises and persists without resolution, the parent either moves to Step 5 and begins looking for another childcare arrangement or reevaluates the need for childcare. Table 2 can be used as a checklist to help parents make decisions about childcare. Table 2 lists in columns which correspond to steps 1, 2, 3, and 4 of Figure 1, the needs and circumstances parents may wish to consider in choosing childcare, aspects to investigate when choosing a childcare site, responsibilities of parents and caregiver, and situations that should alert the parent to potential difficulties.

Parents who use childcare successfully investigate all aspects of the childcare arrangement, visit the facilities occasionally without prior notification, identify a contact person for emergencies, and spend time at the facility with their children (Provence et al., 1977).

Financial Considerations

Childcare costs vary greatly depending upon the type of care, the number of children housed, and the age and developmental level of the child (*Parents' Guide,* 1981). Working parents pay an average of $53 a week for 40 hours of childcare. The average price for a family daycare home is $46 per week per child, and $103 per week for a private babysitter (Holland, 1985). The tax credit for childcare amounts to only about 20% of the total cost up to a maximum of $2,000 (Scarr, 1984). Families that qualify for local government assistance should be directed to city and county government offices for childcare information. Some local service clubs, religious groups, clergymen's associations, the YWCA, the Salvation Army, Lion's Clubs, Catholic Charities, United Jewish Appeal, United Way chapters, and other groups offer scholarships, sliding scales, and other assistance. Parents can also ask the childcare director for either a scholarship or the opportunity to volunteer their services in return for part of the fee (*Parents' Guide,* 1981).

Statistics indicate that many parents violate the law and/or standards of neglect out of economic necessity

FIGURE 1

Choosing and Maintaining Childcare: A Decision Making Model

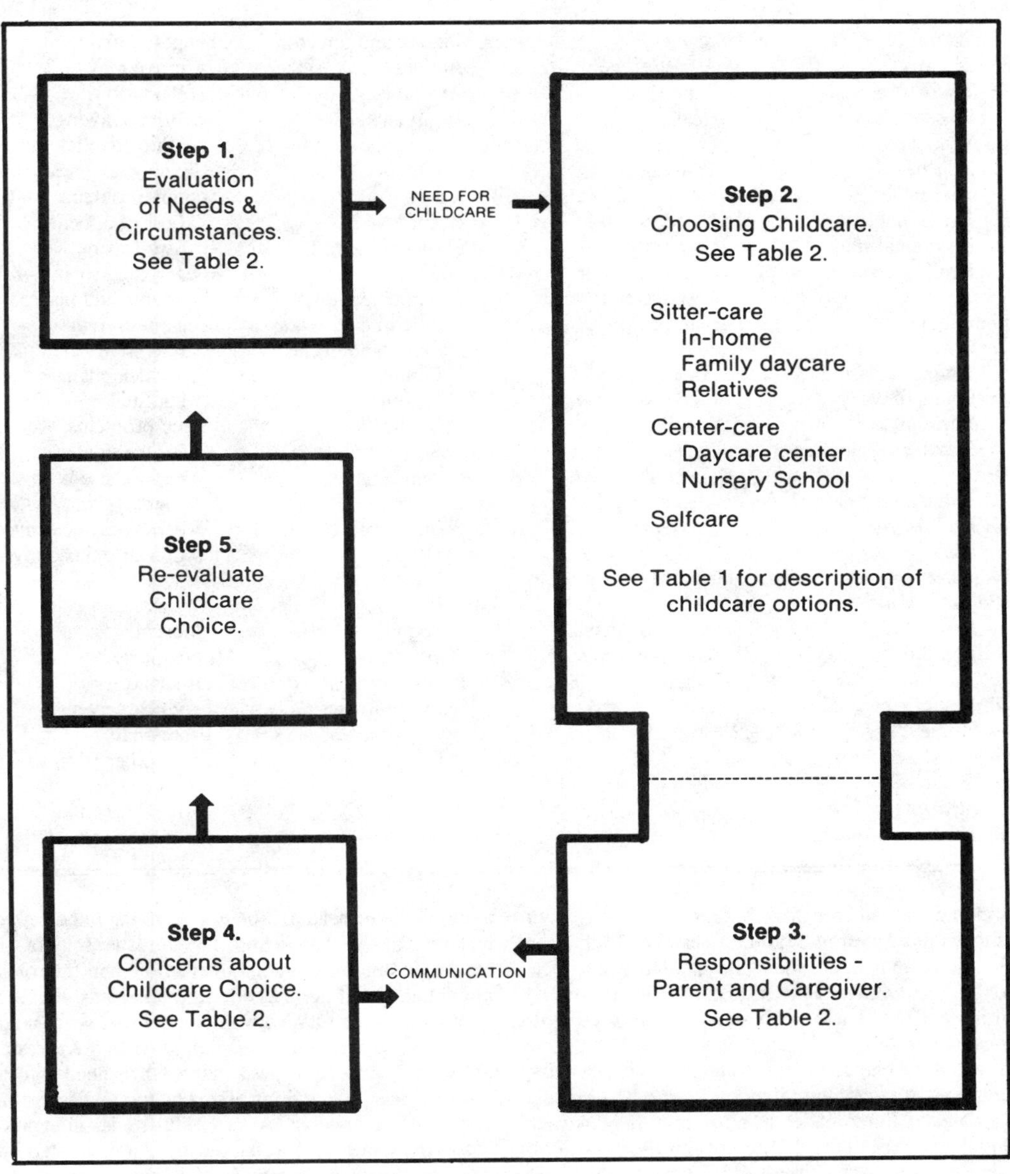

TABLE 2

Considerations in Choosing and Maintaining Childcare

Step 1. Needs and circumstances	Step 2. Aspects to consider in choosing childcare	Step 3. Responsibilities	Step 4. Concerns
Child's age	Caregiver	Caregiver and director	Changes in child
Infant	Attitude	Activities	Abusive play
Toddler	Experience	Availability	With dolls
Preschooler	Health	Clean and safe	With drawings
Schoolage	Philosophy	Communication	With friends
Child's needs	Training	Facilities	Clinging, excessive
Discipline	Director	Ratios	Eating problems
Eating habits	Attitude	Records	Loss of appetite
Emotional status	Commitment	Showing interest	Swallowing
Readiness skills	Philosophy	Parents	Fears, excessive
Social skills	Responsibility	Communication	People and places
Family needs	Eating area	Instructions	Separation fears
Costs of childcare	Facility	Dates and events	Excessive
Financial status	Look at it	Family	Sudden changes
Hours of work	Listen to it	Health	Unusual
Location of work	Smell it	Medication	Sleep problems
Number of children	Taste the food	Special foods	Bedwetting
Friends	Touch it	Monitoring	Fear of sleep
Health status	Play areas	On-time	Nightmares
Parents	Outdoor	Phone numbers	Withdrawal, excessive
Child	Indoor	Doctor	Closed-door philosophy
Neighbors	Sleep area	Friends	Discipline
Parent's work	Toileting area	Relatives	Physical
Flexibility	Toys and materials	Spouse	Unusual
Fulfillment	Age-approrpiate	Work	Morale of staff
Part-time	Clean	Routine established	Unusual stories
Philosophy of childcare	Safe	Showing interest	From caregiver
Homey	Wash area	Conferences	From child
One-to-one ratios		Parents' night	From other parents
School-like			
Structured			
Relatives			

by relying on self-care for children of all ages. For example, failure to provide adult supervision of children under 12 years is listed under the standards of neglect used by the Denver Department of Social Security (Cantwell, 1978). Under these standards, arrangements that constitute neglect of sufficient gravity to necessitate removal of the child from the home include (a) leaving infants and preschoolers at home alone, (b) leaving school-aged children under 12 alone after parents have been advised repeatedly that to do so is illegal, and (c) leaving children over 12 years old in charge of younger children for extended periods.

Handicapped Children

Spodek, Lee, and Saracho (1983) have indicated that issues touching upon preschool handicapped children are similar to those of their older handicapped peers: segregation, labels and stigma, and funding. Technical issues include social acceptance of young handicapped children by nonhandicapped peers, the role of the teacher in enhancing social interaction, and the role of nonhandicapped peers as educational agents. Research indicates that spontaneous interaction between handicapped and nonhandicapped children does not necessarily occur. Evidence suggests that teachers need to foster positive peer interactions. Teacher training issues are also a major concern. A successful social integration model for mainstreaming handicapped preschoolers into daycare centers is given by Stowitschek (1984).

Licensing

The purpose of licensing is to provide protection for consumers and to mandate the provision of positive services (Terpstra, 1984). However, a license for childcare services is not always obtained by childcare operators, particularly in the case of family daycare homes.

Parents need to take responsibility for determining if a facility is licensed, and if not, to decide if it is an acceptable option in spite of its unlicensed status. Childcare is regulated by each state. In the booklet *A Parents' Guide to Day Care,* the address of each state's childcare licensing agency is provided.

ALTERNATIVE ACTIONS

Supervised Care

Successful childcare is tied to resolution of separation anxieties of both parents and children. Factors that ease separation difficulties include healthy attachment, developmental status of the child, previous successful experiences with separations, and a daycare staff that is understanding and knowledgeable about separation (Provence et al., 1977). Additionally, parents should stay with their children for a brief period when the children begin daycare or have difficulty adjusting to the daycare program. Periodic unscheduled visits to the daycare center also assure children of their parents' love and reliability. Other suggestions for handling children with separation problems include briefly telling them that the parent is leaving, having a short goodbye ritual, promising to return later, and making a prompt departure. Hovering about insecure children, returning to them if they are unhappy or crying, attempting to distract them, and leaving when they are unaware contribute to future separation problems (Hock, 1984).

Provence et al. (1977) have suggested other ways to help a child adapt to daycare:

1. Tell the staff about the child's family and homelife so that the caregiver can talk to the child about home and neighborhood experiences.
2. Bring items such as a toy, a blanket, some possession of the mother or father, or a favorite game from home.
3. Post pictures of the family or of the parents with the child on his or her locker or cubbyhole.
4. Use puppet and doll play with themes of going to school and returning home.
5. Explain to the child why parents work and why the child is in daycare.

Self-care

For latchkey children, attention to the seeds of problems is the key to successful self-care. The negative effects of self-care can be minimized by attention to the following.

1. Nurturant parent–child relationship. The negative consequences of self-care are inseparable from problems with family dynamics. If parent and child are at odds, then self-care is no more successful than any other activity requiring their cooperation. Additionally, if parents are overtly worried about the consequences of self-care, the children may be frightened needlessly, causing self-care to fail. Latchkey children survive, and even thrive, when the parent–child relationship fosters cooperation and mutual confidence.
2. Age-appropriate self-care. Children who are insufficiently mature for the demands placed upon them often experience academic problems, develop social–emotional difficulties, resent their parents, and perceive adults as unresponsive to children's needs. Parents must arrange for supervised care for children who are young chronologically or socially.
3. Visibly safe home. Parents and children are realistically concerned about emergencies. When latchkey children get home, they need to feel that the house is safe to enter. Strong doors and windows, locks that keep the house safe from intrusion but are easily unlatched in case of emergency, large and/or yappy dogs, and fences or other barriers contribute to the feeling and the reality of safety. It isn't enough for parents to know that the wolf may huff and puff but not blow the house in. Children don't want the wolf to even approach the door.
4. Comfortable neighborhood. For self-care to succeed, it is important for both parent and child to be familiar with the neighborhood. One or more neighbors whom the child knows and trusts should be available for emergencies or questions.
5. Parental availability. If parents are unable to work close to home, children should have ready access to their parents by phone. Additionally, it is advantageous for children to have a phone friendship with a co-worker who can lend a comforting voice and ear. Parents and latchkey children should schedule a daily check-in time. This lets children regale or complain about school events when those happenings are fresh. Children are physically alone in self-care but need not be unsupervised or emotionally isolated.
6. Structured home time. Although an increased sense of responsibility is a benefit of self-care, latchkey children should not have more household obligations than their age-mates. Using housework to fill and account for time only fosters resentment in an already difficult situation.
7. Emergency measures. Even under optimum circumstances, children in self-care encounter strange, and even dangerous, situations. Latchkey children should be encouraged to role-play such experiences as calling the fire department, answering the door and phone, making snacks, and separating safe from dangerous physical symptoms (Long, 1984; McNairy, 1984; Mount & Smith, 1984).
8. Survival skills. A variety of programs have been designed to teach children about safety, emergency procedures, food preparation, weather, and health. Role playing and discussion of children's fears are integral parts of these programs. A good resource is Mount and Smith (1984).
9. School buildings. There are a variety of logistical problems associated with using schools as care centers, including staffing, funding, administration, liability insurance, janitorial services and scheduling of classrooms and cafeteria. Nevertheless, it can be arranged when one school responds to the needs of its neighborhood. Issues and suggestions for using schools as childcare centers are available in resources such as McCurdy (1985), Long (1984),and McNairy, 1984).

In summary, self-care can be a safe, successful

experience if it is conducted in the context of a loving and attentive family with a mature, informed, indirectly supervised child. Moreover, children in the same school and neighborhood form a logical grouping for providing for the safety, supervision, and companionship needs of latchkey children.

SUMMARY

Economic necessity and women's changing roles are the major reasons for the present increase in the number of children attending out-of-home care. The effect of daycare on the infant, toddler, and preschooler is more a function of the quality of the care than the actual placement. No consistent detrimental effects on children's development have been found with "quality" out-of-home care. The recent increase in the number of latchkey children is also attributable to economic necessity and role changes. Self-care does not necessarily produce unhealthy children if care, planning, and a wide range of resources are called upon to serve these children. A decision-making model takes into account the parents' and children's needs, childcare options with respect to their advantages and disadvantages, and various special responsibilities and concerns, and provides for reevaluation of choices.

REFERENCES

Ainslie, R. C. (Ed.). (1984). *The child and the day care setting: Qualitative variations and development.* New York: Praeger.

Belsky, J. (1984). Two waves of day care research: Developmental effects and conditions of quality. In R. C. Ainslie (Ed.), *The child and the day care setting: Qualitative variations and development* (pp. 1–34). New York: Praeger.

Blehar, M. C. (1974). Anxious attachment and defensive reactions associated with day care. *Child Development, 45,* 683–692.

Burtman, A. I. (1984). Who's minding the children? *Working Mother Digest, 2*(1), 88. (Available from Editor, *Working Mother Digest,* 230 Park Avenue, New York, NY 10169)

Cantwell, H. B. (1978). *Standards of child neglect.* Denver: Denver Department of Social Services.

Carter, D. (1985). The crisis in school-age child care: What you should know. . . . What you can do. *PTA Today, 10*(6), 4–8.

Clarke-Stewart, A. (1982). *Daycare.* Cambridge, MA: Harvard University Press.

Dail, P. W. (1982). Who will mind the child? A dilemma for many employed parents. *Journal of Home Economics, 74*(1), 22–23.

Garbarino, J. (1981). "Latchkey" children: How much of a problem? *Education Digest, 46*(6), 14–16.

Gordon, A. M. (1984). Adequacy of responses given by low-income and middle-income kindergarten children in structured adult–child conversations. *Developmental Psychology, 20*(5), 881–892.

Hill, A. M., & Bragg, D. D. (1985). *The impact of day-care services on the education of secondary and adult students in Ohio.* Columbus, OH: Ohio State University, National Center for Research in Vocational Education. (ERIC Document Reproduction Service No. ED 262229 CE 042641)

Hock, E. (1984). The transition to day care: Effects of maternal separation anxiety on infant adjustment. In R. C. Ainslie (Ed.), *The child and the day care setting: Qualitative variations and development* (pp. 183–205). New York: Praeger.

Holland, L. (1985, August). Choosing day care: A primer for parents. *Growing Parent, 13*(8), 1–8. (Available from Dunn & Hargitt, Inc., 22 N. Second St., Lafayette, IN 47902)

Levine, J. A., Seltzer, M. S., Gray, W., Baden, R. K., Genser, A., Pacquette, J., & Johnson, J. (1982). School-age child care. In E. F. Zigler & E. W. Gordon (Eds.), *Day care and social policy issues* (pp. 457–475). Boston: Auburn House.

Long, T. J. (1984). So who cares if I'm home. *Educational Horizons, 62*(2), 60–64.

McCurdy, J. (1985). Schools respond to latchkey children. *School Administrator, 42*(3), 16–18.

McNairy, M. R. (1984). School-age child care: Program and policy issues. *Educational Horizons, 62*(2), 64–67.

Mitchell, G. (1979). *The day care book: A guide for working parents to help them find the best possible day care for their children.* New York: Stein and Day.

Mount, R., & Smith, K. (1984). Kids on their own for the first time. *Educational Horizon, 62*(2), 63.

A parents' guide to day care. (1981). Mt. Ranier, MD: Gryphon House.

Provence, S., Naylor, A., & Patterson, J. (1977). *The challenge of daycare.* New Haven, CT: Yale University Press.

Ramey, C. T., Dorval, B., & Baker-Ward, L. (1983). Group day care and socially disadvantaged families: Effects on the child and the family. In S. Kilmer (Ed.), *Advances in early education and day care: A research annual* (pp. 69–106). Greenwich, CT: Jai.

Scarr, S. (1984). *Mother care/other care.* New York: Basic Books.

Schiller, J. D. (1980). *Child care alternative and emotional well being.* New York: Praeger.

Spodek, G., Lee, R. C., & Saracho, O. N. (1983). Mainstreaming handicapped children in the preschool. In S. Kilmer (Ed.), *Advances in early education and day care: A research annual* (pp. 107–131). Greenwich, CT: Jai.

Stowitschek, J. J. (1984). *A social integration model for young handicapped children. Final report, August 1, 1981–August 31, 1984.* Logan, UT: Utah State University, Exceptional Child Center. (ERIC Document Reproduction Service No. ED 254021 ED 171730)

Terpstra, J. (1984). *Licensing of children's services.* Washington, DC: Children's Bureau (DHHS/OHS). (ERIC Document Reproduction Service No. ED 255304 PS 015011)

White, B. L. (1981). Viewpoint. Should you stay home with your baby? *Young Children, 37*(1), 11–17.

BIBLIOGRAPHY: PROFESSIONALS

Ainslie, R. C. (Ed.). (1984). *The child and the day care setting: Qualitative variations and development.* New York: Praeger.
Contains seven chapters written by well-known authors in the field of early childhood. Each chapter summarizes the major concepts and research of a particular area. In a comprehensive treatment of the research that has been conducted on the effect of daycare, Belsky's chapter summarizes the findings over the past 20 years.

Kilmer, S. (Ed.). (1981). *Advances in early education and day care: A research annual* (Volume 2). Greenwich, CT: Jai.
The second book in a series that was developed as a forum for communication among those engaged in research and conceptualization of childcare. The eight chapters are built around the roles of parents and teachers and the preparation of personnel.

Kilmer, S. (Ed.). (1983). *Advances in early education and day care: A research annual* (Volume 3). Greenwich, CT: Jai.
The third volume in this series presents several major day care research projects and issues. Of particular note are Ramey, Dorval, and Baker-Ward's chapter on the effect of daycare with socially disadvantaged families and Spodek, Lee, and Saracho's chapter on mainstreaming handicapped children into preschool programs.

Schiller, J. D. (1980). *Child-care alternatives and emotional well-being.* New York: Praeger.
The research presented by Schiller focuses on questions such as Does age of entry into care affect the child, Does stability in the care arrangement affect the child's social/emotional adjustment, and Does the amount of time in childcare affect development? Her chapter on the history and background of childcare is most informative for those interested in historical perspectives.

Zigler, E. F., & Gordon, E. W. (Eds.). (1982). *Day care: Scientific and social policy issues.* Boston: Auburn House.
A comprehensive book of collected articles, essays, research projects, and research findings. This book is valuable as an introduction to defining childcare issues, identifying research questions, and discussing the future of daycare. A particularly important chapter for those interested in the latchkey child is that by James A. Levine and colleagues.

BIBLIOGRAPHY: PARENTS

Clarke-Stewart, A. (1982). *Daycare.* Cambridge, MA: Harvard University Press.
An easily read book that puts research findings into perspective for practitioners and parents and presents an overview of the history and changing values and needs of working mothers. This book has a bias in presenting mostly positive aspects of daycare.

Holland, L. (1985, August). Choosing day care: A primer for parents. *Growing Parent, 13*(8), 1–8. (Available from Dunn & Hargitt, Inc., 22 N. Second St., Lafayette, IN 47902)
An excellent, easily read six-page article in which the parent is given advice on how to choose daycare, what options are available, and preventing abuse in care situations.

Mitchell, G. (1979). *The day care book: A guide for working parents to help them find the best possible day care for their children.* New York: Stein and Day.
A single mother searching for daycare for her two children is described in the first part of the book. Her decision-making process is analyzed. Grace Mitchell not only provides sound advice in choosing childcare with her look, listen, smell, touch, and taste methods, but also presents a realistic picture of what a parent goes through in selecting daycare.

A parents' guide to day care. (1981). Mt. Rainier, MD: Gryphon House.
This 62-page pamphlet prepared originally by the United States Printing Office for parents who are in the process of deciding upon childcare presents helpful checklists and guidelines for selecting childcare. The addresses of state daycare agencies are given at the back of the book.

Provence, S., Naylor, A., & Patterson, J. (1977). *The challenge of daycare.* New Haven, CT: Yale University Press.
Written for literate parents and practitioners who want to expand their knowledge in childcare. Individual cases that help illustrate the issues in daycare and the complexities involved are presented. The chapter on the problem of separation helps professionals and parents better understand this emotional difficulty.

BIBLIOGRAPHY: CHILDREN

Rogers, F. R. (1985). *Going to day care.* New York: Putnam.
Mr. Rogers puts together this children's book that provides the preschooler with a good description of both a daycare center and a family daycare facility. Colorful photographs depicting childcare facilities and an age-appropriate script makes this book one that parents and children alike can enjoy together while talking about the experience of daycare.

Hammond, L. (1982). *Dog goes to nursery school.* New York: Golden Press, Western Publishing.
This story about Dog's first day of nursery school is part of the Little Golden Book series. This fun book helps the child identify with a cartoon character who is going through many of the fears that children experience. Additionally, Dog discovers that he enjoys some of his favorite home activities at school.

Children and Chronic Illness

Margaret L. Potter
Northern Trails Area Education Agency, Clear Lake, Iowa

BACKGROUND

It is estimated that 10–20% of all children have a chronic medical disorder (Gortmaker & Sappenfield, 1984). Two percent of all children suffer from a severe chronic illness that regularly interferes with daily activities (Perrin, 1986). According to these estimates, then, in a school of 1,000 pupils, at any given time perhaps 20 students are contending with a significant medical disorder, and another 100–200 students have chronic medical concerns of a less significant nature. Thus, chronic illness in children, while not receiving a great deal of attention in the professional literature, is something educators must deal with on a regular basis. And as medical advances lead to increased survival rates, more children who once would have died are now living. In fact, although rates of occurrence of various chronic disorders generally have remained stable, estimations of actual numbers of children with a chronic health impairment doubled between 1966 and 1980. This increase may be due to part in changes in survey techniques, but a large part of the increase can be attributed to an increase in survival rates (Gortmaker & Sappenfield, 1984; Perrin, 1986).

Definition

Chronic illness can be considered to be any medically managed illness with a treatment course considered to continue over a period of years. Falling under this category would be such conditions as cancer, diabetes, epilepsy, cystic fibrosis, spina bifida, asthma, cardiac disorders, juvenile rheumatoid arthritis, phenylketonuria (PKU), hemophilia, and kidney disorders. This list is by no means exhaustive and the material in this chapter should not be considered restricted to cases involving just these disorders. The material is also relevant to students with a myriad of other disorders such as those who have suffered from severe burns, disfigurement, amputation, or paralysis due to accidents. In other words, the focus of this chapter will be on medically labeled disabilities that generally have an indirect rather than direct influence on school performance.

There is more variety than unity among chronic illnesses. Not only do the medical specifics of each condition vary, but circumstances also vary. For some, the illness may have been diagnosed at, or soon after, birth. For others, onset and/or diagnosis may not have occurred until they were preschoolers, grade school students, or even adolescents. In these cases, onset may have been gradual, as in the case of a tumor affecting motor skills, or sudden, as in the case of a grand mal seizure. Signs of the illness are readily observable in some cases; in others few persons outside the family may know of the illness. With proper medical control, conditions such as epilepsy, diabetes, and asthma are generally not considered to be fatal illnesses. While many kinds of cancer are no longer considered to be incurable, those children with cystic fibrosis or sickle cell anemia know that their chances of living past young adulthood are slim, and those with cancer and other diseases may feel that their future is, at best, uncertain.

The Role of the School

The school plays an important role in any child's life, for as Kirten and Liverman (1977) put it, "School is the occupation of the child." School attendance may be especially important for the student with a chronic illness. School is a symbol of normality and may be one of the only places where those with chronic illnesses are not viewed chiefly in terms of their illness (Eiser, 1980). In a life governed by medical rules and regimens, school may be the one place where a child or adolescent can feel some sense of control and accomplishment (Kagan-Goodheart, 1977). The school also plays a major role in social and emotional development. This aspect of a student's education is especially important in that emotional health may have a significant influence on physical health (Toch, 1972).

When a child or adolescent has a chronic illness, the main goal of intervention on the part of school personnel is to facilitate coping with the illness, its demands, and its limitations. Because the illness impacts on many people other than the ill student, interventions must address not only the needs of the student, but also the needs of these other people, both for the student's sake and for their own sake.

In working with a chronically ill student, professionals need to take into account the student's developmental ability to cope with the illness intellectually and emotionally. In working with families and friends, it helps to understand some of the wide variety of emotional reactions to chronic illness. This understanding can provide a basis of the creative problem solving that may be necessary in dealing with the specific needs and situations that may arise.

Because individual situations vary so much and because of the lack of research findings to give guidance as to what or what not to do in a given situation, the following discussion primarily is intended to serve as general background information. For more detailed information about specific health impairments and related issues see other chapters in this volume or refer to sources listed at the end of this chapter.

DEVELOPMENT

A young person with a chronic disease or disability should be seen as first of all a young person, then as someone with a disease or disability. One must continually beware of submerging the person in the disease/

disability. As van Eys (1977) put it when discussing children with cancer:

> The child with cancer is just that, nothing more or less. He is not a normal child who has a cancer that can be removed without any trace, nor is he a child who labors under a burden that should be constantly lifted from him as the overwhelming focus of his care. The child should be accepted for what he is, a child with cancer, who would be a different person if the cancer suddenly did not exist or if the memory were suddenly erased. (p.165)

Emphasis on Normality

Since it can be easy for medical professionals to lose sight of the person in their concern over the physiological disorder, it is all the more important for the school to focus on the person behind the disability. General consensus indicates that the child with a disability should be treated as normally as possible (Cyphert, 1973; Fithian, 1984). This aim for normality extends to even the terminally ill. Keeping up with schoolwork can provide concrete goals for the student to work toward and incentive for carrying out treatments and for living life to the fullest (Wilmott, Burroughs, & Beele, 1984). Fithian (1984) points out that often terminally ill children must put forth much energy and courage just to attend school. "To have their teachers regard their presence as meaningless is insulting . . . . It is analogous to taking meaningful work away from an adult with a serious illness but leaving him or her with a desk" (p. 7).

Educational Needs

Treatment Effects. For the most part, chronic illnesses do not directly affect a student's cognitive abilities. However, academic progress can be negatively affected by chronic illness (Stehbens, Kisker, & Wilson, 1983). Merely the frequent absences necessitated by some medical conditions may slow a student's progress. The long-term effects of the intensive treatment regimens now used in battling illnesses are as yet unclear, but there is some evidence that chemotherapy and radiation treatments directed toward the brain may negatively affect cognitive as well as academic abilities (Van de Water, 1986). Also, the side effects of some medications can influence attention, concentration, mood, and energy.

Emotional States. Students who are depressed because their health is not good, are anxious about an imminent hospitalization, or whose families are in turmoil likely will not be doing the best schoolwork possible. But care must be taken not to automatically attribute all academic problems to the illness. Academic difficulties may be due to factors unrelated to the illness such as general ability, learning disabilities, or a behavioral disorder. If a student is having academic difficulties, all possible causes should be explored.

Stamina. Because of the effect of the illness or of treatment, the chronically ill student may not be able to move at the same pace as other students. Some students may be able to tolerate intense activity over a short period of time; others may be able to handle a more moderate level of activity over a longer period of time. Advance notice and planning may be necessary in some cases so that adjustments can be made in medications and scheduling to allow the fullest possible level of participation in regular and special school activities.

School Phobias. In some cases, frequent absences may be due not to the illness itself, but to avoidance of perceived or actual school stresses. (McCollum, 1981). Social acceptance is a major concern of almost every child or adolescent and every time a student has to return to school after an extended absence or has to start a new school, that social acceptance is tested. There also may be the fear of academic failure, especially for students whose school experience has not previously been successful or for students who fear that their illness will affect their ability to keep up academically. Parents may indirectly add to a student's anxiety about attending school especially if the child's health is fragile. Extra sensitivity and good communication between school personnel and such students' parents and/or physicians may be needed to determine whether absences are due to illness or to a school phobia.

Understanding of Illness

Children's understanding of their illness and its implications will change as they grow older. This developmental change in understanding has been looked at from a number of perspectives, such as Piagetian, Ericksonian, and Kohlbergian (Cerrato, 1986; McCollum, 1981; Perrin & Gerrity, 1984). The following is a summary of levels of understanding from infancy through adolescence.

Infancy (Birth to 18 Months). Infants have no conception of illness because they only know what they experience themselves. They do not understand that illness and its possibly painful treatment are not a part of normal life. Necessary separation from family can be especially painful to a child who has not yet developed a sense of object permanence. Since much of an infant's development of cognitive, social, and motor skills depends on interaction with the environment, restriction of movement or experience may delay or distort the normal developmental process (Perrin & Gerrity, 1984).

Toddlerhood (18–36 Months). The toddler is beginning to have mental representations of the world. Toddlers understand their illness only as something that interferes with their world and only as it affects them. They have magical and egocentric views of causality. They tend to believe that something they want to happen will happen. Conversely, they may interpret illness as something they caused to happen. Toddlers are developing an increasing sense of autonomy and a need to have some control over their world. This may be more difficult because of restrictions imposed by illness and a reluctance on the part of parents to relinquish to the child some of the total care responsibilities they had to provide the infant.

Preschoolers (4–7 Years). As with younger children, preschoolers' understanding of illness tends to be magical and egocentric. They are beginning to have some idea of cause and effect, but their idea of causal relationships is tenuous and relies heavily on contiguity of events in terms of time or location. Their understanding of cause is still superficial without benefit of an understanding of the interrelationship of events or the rules and principals that guide events. They are "perception bound" and define illness by external signs. They may have an anthropomorphic view of parts of their bodies and still tend to believe that bad things, such as illness, happen as a result of wrongdoing or outside agents. Since their thought is not completely logical yet, they may construct contradictory theories about their illness.

Midchildhood (7–12 Years). Although school-age children are rapidly developing logical thought, generally they still understand only information that is related to their own bodily functions that they can feel or observe. Since they are beginning to understand the interrelationships among events, at the age of about 9 or 10 years children start to understand some of the active processes and transformations occurring in their bodies. Rules and an understanding of the sequence of events replace a reliance on the perceptual features of an event, but these rules may be viewed in a very rigid sense. School-age children typically believe firmly that it is germs that cause illness.Only as they get to be 11 or 12 years old do they start to understand the body's own healing powers and the role they can play in preventive care.

Adolescence. Adolescents are increasingly capable of understanding abstract concepts and complex interrelationships. This increased ability may help or hinder the adolescent in coping with illness. While younger adolescents may understand the interrelationships of body parts, they still may not grasp the actual mechanisms by which body parts function. As a way of trying to feel some control, teenagers may take an intellectual view of their illness and try to learn as much as possible about it. Sometimes, however, intellectual understanding may surpass emotional ability to cope, so it is important to let young people set their own pace in seeking information. This intellectualization may also lead adults to think adolescents can be rational about their illness. This is rarely the case, and even intelligent teenagers will construct their own personal theories about illness. These theories may blend emotion, fact, and fantasy, as well as a component of self-blame (McCollum, 1981).

Coping and Adjustment

The manner in which a person copes with chronic illness depends on a myriad of factors such as age, sex, temperament, characteristics of the disease and its treatment, reactions of others, family structure and coping style, and sociocultural factors such as economic status, religious beliefs, cultural background, and community involvement.

Coping strategies may involve the use of defense mechanisms such as denial, projection, introjection, suppression of feelings, acting-out behavior, and regression (Waechter, 1979). While maladaptive reliance on any of these defense mechanisms may lead to behavioral or academic problems, these means of defense can be very adaptive in coping with the sometimes overwhelming pressures of chronic illness. For example, Ross (1978) notes that remission in cancer patients is often characterized by a healthy denial of illness. "Healthy denial" means that while the existence of the disease may be essentially denied,the patient still keeps appointments for checkups and treatments. A pathological denial, on the other hand, would be characterized by such things as refusing treatment in the face of overt signs of illness, lack of judgment in regard to treatment, and inability to detect the worsening of one's condition. Healthy denial can help one to function even in the face of a very uncertain future (Zeltzer, Kellerman, Ellenberg, Dash, & Rigler, 1980).

The results of studies examining the coping skills and adjustment of the chronically ill vary. While some problems have been noted, the overall impression of these studies is positive — chronic illness does not necessarily bring psychological problems with it (Tavormina, Kastner, Slater, & Watt, 1976; Zeltzer, et al., 1980).

However, studies of young adults with chronic illness are relatively rare, especially studies that include illnesses like cystic fibrosis where only in recent years have there been young adult survivors (Pless & Pinkerton, 1975). Because of this paucity of studies, little is known about the long-term adjustment of persons suffering from various childhood chronic illnesses. Pless and Pinkerton concluded from the studies they reviewed that while there may be cases in which children with severely disabling disorders learn to function very well as adults, there are many cases in which failure to cope and adapt successfully in childhood carries over to adulthood.

PUTTING CHRONIC ILLNESS IN PERSPECTIVE

The Family

In many ways, chronic illness in a young person belongs not just to the patient but to the entire family. Until children are old enough to take on the responsibility of their own health care, that responsibility rests with parents and/or other older family members. The demands of the disease in terms of time and emotional and financial commitments may become the central focus of family life on a sporadic or continuous basis. Most importantly, the reaction of the family to these children and their illness will be a major influence on their perception of themselves and their illness. If they feel accepted by their family they can withstand the adverse reactions of others (Ross, 1978). "In terms of psychological issues, *the patient is the family,* not only the sick child" (Sourkes, 1977, p. 66).

Parents. The stages of adjustment that parents of a chronically ill child go through have been compared to the stages in the grief process as outlined by Elizabeth

Kubler-Ross and others (Capell & Bensman, 1979). Elbert (1982) summarizes these stages as shock and denial, anger and rage, disorganization and despair, and finally acceptance and hope. The proposed structure of McCollum and Gibson (1970) is more dependent on the chronology of chronic illness and includes four stages: prediagnostic, confrontational, long-term adaptive, and terminal.

Parents' initial reaction to a diagnosis of serious illness in a child is generally one of shock and disbelief. Because of this state of shock, parents may be able to remember little or nothing of what the doctor may have told them (Capell & Bensman, 1979; McCollum, 1981; McCollum & Gibson, 1970).

Grief may occur not only at the point of diagnosis and at the time of death, if the child does die, but intermittently throughout the course of the illness. It may crop up unexpectedly, especially at points of change in a child's life when limitations of the disease are emphasized anew. It may be during remission that the parents temporarily fall apart because it is "safer" than to let all the fears and anxieties show (Ross, 1978).

Guilt is another common reaction. Parents feel a responsibility to keep their children safe. When something happens to a child, parents often feel as though they were at fault — it was something they did or did not do that caused the child's ill health (McCollum, 1981; Sourkes, 1977). Parents also may feel guilty about resenting the disruptions the illness has caused in their lives (Sourkes, 1977) or guilt about the natural feelings of impatience and annoyance that parents occasionally have when dealing with their children (McCollum, 1981).

Anger often is the result of a feeling of helplessness, of not being able to fight this thing that is endangering their child, or not being able to control the events that now dominate their lives. While anger may be used as a means of defense — an emotional reaction to an overwhelming situation — it should not be dismissed lightly. Often parents do have something concrete to be angry about; mistakes are made and parents have a right to expect that serious efforts will be made to rectify those mistakes when possible (Capell & Bensman, 1979).

Anxiety may be reflected by parents in their concern about whether their reactions to their child's illness are "normal." They may be deeply concerned about whether they will be able to emotionally, physically, and financially handle all of the demands of the illness.

As with the patients themselves, denial by parents can be adaptive. As long as denial does not lead to irrational decisions or abandonment of necessary treatment, it can help parents avoid being overwhelmed by the disease.

It must also be recognized that a child's chronic illness is not the only stress with which the parents must deal. There may also be financial problems, marital problems, concerns about other children or family members, and stress related to jobs.

Siblings. It is easy for siblings to become the forgotten partners in a family's dealings with chronic illness. Yet chronic illness is a major disruptive force within the family, often drastically altering roles, expectations, and lifestyle. Sibling relationships may vary widely, but they are generally relationships that last a lifetime and are very special. The siblings of a chronically ill person thus have a definite stake in what is going on, but their ability to cope may be affected by a multitude of factors such as age, maturity, ability to comprehend the situation, their own place and adjustment within the family, and the honesty and the appropriateness with which the parents communicate with them about the illness and its ramifications (Craft, 1979).

On the basis of her review of research on siblings of chronically ill children, McKeever (1983) concluded that these siblings are at risk for emotional and behavioral problems that they might not otherwise experience. Siblings are often uninformed about the chronic illness because parents feel uncomfortable or unable to talk with them about it. This may be because they serve in the role of "public informer"; therefore information to them is controlled in order to control what is known outside the family. The siblings may not want to ask for information, to spare the parents the pain of having to talk about the situation. Also, the timing perceived as appropriate for communicating information may not match a sibling's ability to understand it (by the time a child is old enough to understand why an older brother must have daily insulin shots, the treatment may be so routine that no one thinks to explain it). Lack of information, communication, and understanding can lead to reactions such as anger, resentment, attention-getting behavior, feelings of guilt and self-blame, feelings of isolation, and fear of being similarly affected.

McKeever (1983) urged that siblings be helped to develop their own identities and to understand the similarities and differences between themselves and their ill brother or sister, that they be provided realistic, age-appropriate information about the illness and its treatment, that they be kept updated, and that the needs and adjustment of siblings be an active consideration by parents and professionals when making decisions related to the illness.

Classmates

Having a close friend who is faced with a debilitating, or even potentially terminal, disease or a permanent disability due to injury may be almost as traumatic as actually having the disability. Teachers and other adults need to be open to the questions of peers and sensitive to their search for answers. There is also the danger of underestimating the understanding and coping abilities of a child or a teen — care must be taken by adults who really want to spare their own feelings not to gloss over the truth ostensibly to "protect" young persons (Cyphert, 1973).

In some cases, peers may automatically rally around their disabled friend; in other cases modeling of acceptance and encouragement of active support, such as visiting or writing letters to a hospitalized classmate, may be necessary. As with adults, discomfort and lack of understanding are often due to lack of knowledge. Providing accurate information to classmates minimizes misinformation that may circulate and increases the likelihood of normal peer interactions.

School Staff

When teachers learn of a serious illness or disabling injury in a student, they may go through much the same process as a parent, that is, shock, disbelief, anger, and grief (Cahners, 1979; Isaacs & McElroy, 1980; Martin, 1974). As significant people in the student's life, teachers' abilities to cope with this new and unknown situation may, through verbal and nonverbal communication, have an important effect on the student's self-esteem and ability to cope.

The teacher's reactions to illness in relation to the teacher's own mental health should not be ignored. Potentially terminal illnesses or severe permanent injury may induce teachers to start questioning the value of their lives or may trigger the perception of symptoms of the disease in themselves or in loved ones (Cyphert, 1973). It is generally agreed that in order to work successfully with a chronically ill student, especially one with a potentially terminal illness, their teachers must come to terms with their own personal feelings in relation to the disease and its consequences (Cahners, 1979; Kirten & Liverman, 1977; Martin, 1974).

A major contribution to successful coping with chronic illness comes from having a sense of control; an important component of a sense of control is knowledge of what one is dealing with. Full knowledge and understanding of the situation is often what school staff lack. This can lead to withdrawal, anxiety, solicitude, and even hostility at having to deal with a student with special needs (Isaacs & McElroy, 1980).

ALTERNATIVE ACTIONS

A close partnership between the school and the health care professionals serving a student afflicted by chronic illness can only be of benefit to all involved. Each group of professionals has unique contributions to make to the other without which neither can be totally effective in serving the disabled student. Those in charge of medical care often have met the child or adolescent only *after* the onset of the illness or occurrence of the injury; thus they lack a good baseline with which to judge the young person's adaptation to the illness/injury. The school staff not only will have known the student before the illness/injury in many cases, but will be able to monitor the student after discharge from the hospital.

With consultative help from the health care professionals familiar with the specific disease or injury involved, the school can provide an extensive, readily available and free network of support services to the student and his or her family. This can include services from social workers, psychologists, counselors, special educators, adaptive physical education teachers, vocational education people, nurses, speech clinicians and physical and occupation therapists, along with all of the teachers in the various disciplines represented in the typical school. Support services such as these and reintegration into the social milieu of the school may be a major influence on the ultimate effectiveness of any medical treatment.

Assessment Issues

Assessment of Adjustment. It seems logical that in view of the inherent stresses of a long-term, possibly life-threatening illness the chronically ill student is at risk for psychological and general adjustment problems. This may well be the case; however, the concept of adjustment is something that is very hard to define and even more difficult to assess (Pless & Pinkerton, 1975). A key question is whether the same standards of "adjustment" apply to ill or disabled persons or whether behavior that may be considered "less adaptive" in a healthy student is actually adaptive for a student who must deal with a chronic illness. For example, as mentioned earlier, denial may be a very useful and healthy means of coping with illness at some points. Likewise, a certain degree of dependency may be a necessary result of the demands of the illness.

Pless and Pinkerton (1975) reviewed the use of standard subjective and objective measures of adjustment with chronically ill children. Key problems with these measures arise as to their technical adequacy, the applicability of norms, and their reliability when applied to the chronically ill. It seems that perhaps the best use of these measures of adjustment is not in a normative manner. Rather, they can be used as a means of gathering qualitative data — information that can be used in conjunction with other available information to aid in the development of interventions aimed at improving the student's coping skills and addressing present problems.

Assessment of Cognitive and Academic Skills. A chronically ill preschooler may be referred for evaluation because of concern about general developmental skills. A school-aged child may be referred because of concern about general cognitive, academic, or behavioral skills. Obtaining an accurate assessment of abilities and skills can be difficult in these cases. Normal development in the preschooler is heavily dependent upon experiences and interactions with people, objects, and events in the world. The preschooler who has spent much of his life in the hospital or who is relatively immobile has not had the same developmental opportunities as others of the same age. Care must be taken when making any normative comparisons in these cases. A more useful approach may be to take a qualitative look at skills that have been mastered and skills the child may need assistance in mastering.

For school-aged children, academic deficits due to frequent absences may complicate the determination of whether there may also be a mental, behavioral, or learning disability present. Again, norm-referenced tests may be of questionable validity, since the student's life experiences may be very different from those of the norm group. Also,medication may affect a student's test performance as might mood, attitude, and physical discomfort. In these cases, gathering information on past performance for comparison with present performance and initiating curriculum-based assessment and diagnostic teaching techniques may be more useful than standardized testing.

Legal Requirements

Under PL 94-142, the Educational for All Handicapped Children Act of 1975, chronically ill students are eligible for special education services in all states under the provisions for "other health impaired" if the health problems adversely affect the child's educational performance (Walker, 1984). The most frequent type of special education services that might be needed are related support services such as occupational and physical therapy, adaptive physical education, special transportation, school health services, and counseling and psychological services. Occasionally, students may need to be served in a more restrictive instructional setting, but for the most part provision of support services is all that is needed to allow them to be served within the regular education setting. Often children who receive only district-provided support services such as counseling, administration of medication, or schedule modifications are not officially labeled as special education students. This avoids the necessity of labeling and is acceptable as long as they are receiving the needed services. If needed services are not being provided, the provisions of PL 94-142 may need to be invoked to assure that these students do receive a free and appropriate education (Walker, 1984).

Coordination of Services

Monitoring of ongoing needs of a student with a chronic illness and the others affected by the illness is perhaps most easily accomplished by having one person within the school designated case manager. Since the student will change classroom teachers from year to year, this person may logically be the school nurse, school psychologist, social worker, counselor, special education teacher, or even principal or assistant principal. This person can make a specific effort to be aware of how things are going for the student and can serve as a central point for fielding concerns of others who deal with the student. If problems arise, the case manager may opt either to deal with them directly or to consult with and possibly refer the student to other support personnel within or outside the school.

The case manager can also serve as the school's main contact person with the family, maintaining awareness of the family situation and how it may be affecting the school performance of the health-impaired student and school-age siblings. Depending on the individual situation, the case manager may have minimal contact with the student and family, or there may be a great deal of contact necessary. The need for involvement may also vary as the course of the illness varies. To make this sort of system most effective, all school staff, as well as the parents and medical personnel, should know who the case manager is and what sort of information should be brought to this person's attention.

Intervention Options

Relatively little has been published in regard to the effectiveness of specific interventions with chronically ill students, their families, classmates, and school staff. Since the interventions that have been reported are often specific to one population, it is difficult to evaluate their merits as applied to other populations. What follows, therefore, are only a few suggestions. The value of the interventions will depend on the specific needs of the targets of intervention and on how well the intervention is adapted to those needs.

1. Work directly with the student, teachers, and parents to develop a written plan of how to deal with make-up work, schedule modifications, emergency situations, and so on.
2. Consider arranging volunteer or paid tutoring for students with short, but frequent, absences.
3. Whenever possible, have peers or older students, rather than adults, provide any assistance the student may need.
4. Use behavioral techniques to deal with treatment noncompliance or behavioral concerns (Creer and Christian, 1976).
5. Arrange support networks for students, parents, and siblings either through support groups or on an individual basis.
6. Provide reading resources for children, parents, and professionals; See bibliographies at the end of this chapter.
7. Have the chronically ill student or siblings be the "expert" on their illness during a Handicap Awareness unit.
8. Arrange in-services for staff. When appropriate, include students as presenters.
9. Be a good listener.

Above all, be creative and flexible. For further suggestions see Potter (1985).

SUMMARY

Two percent of all children and adolescents have a chronic illness that significantly interferes with daily activities. Many other young people have health impairments that may occasionally interfere with their activities at home and at school.

Research indicates that the presence of a chronic illness does not necessarily result in psychological or educational problems. However, common sense and experience indicate these young people are at risk and may need special consideration in order to cope effectively with the demands of everyday life inside and outside of the school. Likewise, attention may need to be paid to the emotional needs of those close to the student, such as parents, siblings, classmates, and teachers, both for the student's sake and for their own sake.

There is a tremendously wide range of disabilities, circumstances, personalities, and resources that may be involved when working with people affected by a chronic illness. To state that a student has a chronic illness does not immediately suggest specific interventions. Each case must be considered on an individual basis, and involvement of school staff will range from basic awareness of the existence of the illness to the provision of extensive support services.

Although specific services must be individualized, ideally every school should have a general plan for serving chronically ill students. This plan would include provisions for a case manager, for dissemination of information to students, staff, and parents, and for the development of flexible and individualized services as needed.

As services relating to a particular child or adolescent are considered, there are some key factors that should be kept in mind:

1. Always be aware of the developmental nature of a child's understanding of illness and the relative change in importance of issues related to the illness as the young person matures physically and emotionally.
2. Accurate information needs to be available to all involved and presented in a timely and understandable manner.
3. Easy communication among *all* — students, parents, professionals — is vital.
4. Expectations must be individualized; it can be very misleading to compare the cognitive and emotional development of the chronically ill child to that of "average" children who have had entirely different life experiences.
5. Above all, be flexible and innovative in approaching issues that arise, the goal in mind always being to help the chronically ill young person to live as normal a life as is possible.

Working with a chronically ill child or adolescent can require much sensitivity, creativity, and emotional commitment, especially when the illness is considered to be terminal. The best service can be provided when all people involved, including the ill child, can work together as a team. This may take some effort and negotiation — medical, social service, and educational personnel can all be very protective of their own turf. But the goal of all involved is to help the young person who is the one who ultimately must deal with the illness, its uncertainties, and its long-term implications.

REFERENCES

Cahners, S. (1979). A strong hospital–school liaison: A necessity for disfigured children. *Scandinavian Journal of Plastic and Reconstructive Surgery, 13,* 167–168.

Capell, J., & Bensman, A. (1979, May).Behavioral adaptations that may be problems in the management of children with handicaps. Paper presented at the workshop Coping With Chronic Disability, Minneapolis.

Cerrato, M. C. (1986). Developmental issues in chronic illness: Implications and applications. *Topics in Early Childhood Special Education, 5,* 23–35.

Craft, M. (1979). Help for the family's "other" child. *American Journal of Maternal Child Nursing, 4,* 297–300.

Creer, T. L., & Christian, W. P. (1976). *Chronically ill and handicapped children: Their management and rehabilitation.* Champaign, IL: Research Press.

Cyphert, F. R. (1973). Back to school for the child with cancer. *Journal of School Health, 43,* 215–217.

Eiser, C. (1980). How leukemia affects a child's schooling. *British Journal of Social and Clinical Psychology, 19,* 365–368.

Elbert, A. (1982). The forgotten ones: Helping children and adolescents cope with death. In J. Grimes (Ed.), *Psychological approaches to problems of children and adolescents.* Des Moines, IA: Iowa Department of Public Instruction. (ERIC Document Reproduction Service No. ED232082)

Fithian J. (1984). General overview. In J. Fithian (Ed.), *Understanding the child with a chronic illness in the classroom.* Phoenix, AZ: Oryx.

Gortmaker, S. L., & Sappenfield, W. (1984). Chronic childhood disorders: Prevalence and impact. *Pediatric Clinics of North America, 31,* 3–18.

Isaacs, J., & McElroy, M. (1980). Psychosocial aspects of chronic illness in children. *Journal of School Health, 50,* 318–321.

Kagen-Goodheart, L. (1977). Reentry: Living with childhood cancer. *American Journal of Orthopsychiatry, 47,* 651–658.

Kirten, C., & Liverman, M. (1977). Special education needs of the child with cancer. *Journal of School Health, 47,* 170–173.

Martin, J. (1974).Attitudes toward epileptic students in a city high school system. *Journal of School Health, 44,* 144–146.

McCollum, A. (1981). *The chronically ill child.* New Haven, CT: Yale University Press.

McCollum, A., & Gibson, L. (1970). Family adaptation to the child with cystic fibrosis. *Journal of Pediatrics, 77,* 571–578.

McKeever, P. (1983). Siblings of chronically ill children: A literature review with implications for research and practice. *American Journal of Orthopsychiatry, 53,* 209–218.

Perrin, E. C., & Gerrity, S. (1984). Development of children with chronic illness. *Pediatric Clinics of North America, 31,* 19–31.

Perrin, J. M. (1986). Chronically ill children: An overview. *Topics in Early Childhood Special Education, 5,* 1–11.

Pless, I. B., & Pinkerton, P. (1975). *Chronic childhood disorders: Promoting patterns of adjustment.* London: Henry Klimpton.

Potter, M. L. (1985). Chronic illness in childhood and adolescence: Considerations for school personnel. In J. Grimes & A. Thomas (Eds.), *Psychological approaches to problems of children and adolescents, (Vol. 2).* Des Moines: Iowa Department of Public Instruction.

Ross, J. (1978).Social work intervention with families of children with cancer: The changing critical phases. *Social Work in Health Care, 3,* 257–272.

Sourkes, B. (1977). Facilitating family coping with childhood cancer. *Journal of Pediatric Psychology, 2,* 65–67.

Stehbens, J., Kisker, C. T., & Wilson, B. (1983). School behavior and attendance during the first year of treatment of childhood cancer. *Psychology in the Schools, 20,* 223–228.

Tavormina, J. B., Kastner, L. S., Slater, P. M., & Watt, S. L. (1976). Chronically ill children: A psychologically and emotionally deviant population? *Journal of Abnormal Child Psychology, 4,* 99–110.

Toch, R. (1972). Too young to die. In B. Schoenbert, A. Carr, D. Peretz & A. Kutscher (Eds.), *Psychosocial aspects of terminal care.* New York: Columbia University Press.

van Eys, J. (1977). The outlook for the child with cancer. *Journal of School Health, 47,* 165–169.

Van de Water, V. (1986). Cancer survivors in your district [summary]. In *Proceedings of the 18th Annual Convention of the National Association of School Psychologists* (pp. 172–173). Hollywood, FL: NASP.

Waechter, E. H. (1979). The adolescent with a handicapping, chronic, or life-threatening illness. In R. Mercer (Ed.), *Perspectives on adolescent health care* (pp. 186–209).

Walker, D. K. (1984). Care of chronically ill children in schools. *Pediatric Clinics of North America, 31,* 221–233.

Wilmott, R., Burroughs, B. R., & Beele, D. (1984). Cystic fibrosis. In J. Fithian (Ed.), *Understanding the child with a chronic illness in the classroom.* Phoenix, AZ: Oryx.

Zeltzer, L., Kellerman, J.,Ellenberg, L., Dash, J., & Rigler, D. (1980). Psychologic effects of illness in adolescence: II. Impact of illness in adolescents — Crucial issues and coping styles. *Journal of Pediatrics, 97,* 132–138.

BIBLIOGRAPHY: PROFESSIONALS

Fithian, J. (Ed.). (1984). *Understanding the child with a chronic illness in the classroom.* Phoenix, AZ: Oryx.
Each of 14 chapters deals with a specific childhood chronic illness. Along with information about the illnesses, the authors offer practical information on how each illness might, or might not, affect the young person's ability to function in school.

Garwood S. G. (Ed.). (1986). Chronically ill children. *Topics in Early Childhood Special Education, 5(4).*
Topics of articles in this issue include developmental issues, financial issues, resources available to teachers, professional attitudes, and communication between health care providers and educators. Although the focus is on young children, most of the information is also applicable to older students.

Hobbs, N., & Perrin, J. M. (Eds.). (1985). *Issues in the care of children with chronic illness: A sourcebook on problems, services, and policies.* San Francisco: Jossey-Bass.
The 42 chapters of this book were commissioned for the Vanderbilt University study of chronically ill children. Included are chapters on cognitive and social development, educational programming, health care financing, social services, and professional training.

Potter, M. L. (1985). Chronic illness in childhood and adolescence: Considerations for school personnel. In J. Grimes & A. Thomas (Eds.), *Psychological approaches to problems of children and adolescents.* Des Moines, IA: Iowa Department of Public Instruction.
This chapter is an expanded version of the present article. More in-depth information is provided, especially in regard to developmental issues, research relating to adjustment, and assessment and monitoring considerations. Thirty-nine intervention suggestions are provided for use with students, parents, siblings, classmates, and teachers.

BIBLIOGRAPHY: PARENTS

The Exceptional Parent, Subscription address: 296 Boylston Street, Third Floor, Boston, MA 02116.
This monthly magazine provides practical information and articles for parents, teachers, and community agencies serving children with special needs. An interesting feature is the Letters to the Editor section, in which readers with children with rare diseases can make contact with others in a similar situation.

McCollum, A. (1981). *The chronically ill child: A guide for parents and professionals.* New Haven, CT: Yale University Press.
McCollum takes a comprehensive look at developmental issues with which families of chronically ill children need to deal from birth to young adulthood. Also included are chapters on facing the diagnosis, safeguarding family relationships, questions of another baby, genetics, financial and emotional resources, and crucial questions. An excellent reference and resource book.

Encyclopedia of Organizations (1986). Detroit: Research Co.
The current edition of this reference book is generally available through public libraries. It is the best source for current addresses of organizations serving people with chronic illnesses or low-incidence handicaps. *Closer Look,* National Information Center for the Handicapped, Box 1492, Washington, D. C. 20013 is also a good source of information.

BIBLIOGRAPHY: CHILDREN

Baskin, B., & Harris, K. (1977). *Notes from a different drummer: A guide to juvenile fiction portraying the handicapped.* New York: Bowker.

Baskin, B., & Harris, K. (1984). *More notes from a different drummer (2nd ed).* New York: Bowker.

Dreyer, S. S. (1977, 1981). *The Bookfinder: A guide to children's literature about the needs and problems of youth aged 2-15* (Vols. 1, 2). Circle Pines, MN: American Guidance Service.

These reference books provide annotated bibliographies of children's literature indexed by topic.

Children and Communicable Diseases

Robert G. Harrington
University of Kansas

BACKGROUND

Germ infection and the dysfunction of the body's natural immune system are the root causes of childhood diseases (Hoeprich, 1983). In a study of emergency room visits in 1977 during hours that physicians' offices were closed, patients less than 18 years old accounted for 58% of the 858 visits, which were randomly selected from all seasons of the year. The most frequent diagnoses made were related to some sort of infectious childhood disease (Moffett, 1985). Follow-up research suggests that the frequency of infectious diseases in children remains high even in the 1980s in the United States. For example, the "flu," the "common cold," or "sore throat" are the most common illnesses in humans. All of these infectious diseases are also communicable. In fact, viral respiratory infections of these types accounted for 60% of all illnesses experienced by a group of families (Youmans et al., 1975).

Many childhood infectious diseases are not contagious (e.g., urinary tract infections and osteomyelitis). Noncontagious diseases are not disappearing and some are becoming more frequent because greater numbers of patients with host defects are surviving. In contrast, most of the childhood communicable diseases are decreasing in frequency, but the frequency of sexually transmitted diseases is increasing. For example, the number of reported infections from three childhood communicable diseases in 1955 were the following: diphtheria, 1,984; whooping cough, 62,786; paralytic polio, 13,850. In 1979 these same diseases were much less numerous: diphtheria, 59; whooping cough, 1,623; paralytic polio, 13 (Moffett, 1985). In contrast, the increase in sexually transmitted communicable diseases has been rather dramatic. For example, in 1955 there were 236,197 reported cases of gonorrhea; in 1979 there were 1,003,938 cases. Since a significant percentage of gonorrhea infections are never reported and because a large number of these infections remain asymptomatic and unrecognized, the official number of reported cases is surely a gross underestimate of the actual cases (Krugman & Katz, 1981).

Several frequency trends can be observed for childhood communicable diseases (Moffett, 1985). Some contagious diseases, such as diphtheria, polio, and measles, have followed a curve showing a rapid decrease followed by a persistent low frequency. Failure to eradicate these contagious diseases may be attributed to small groups of susceptible individuals, usually infants, who have not been immunized or to ethnic or cultural subgroups that do not obtain preventive medical care. Other communicable diseases, such as salmonellosis and hepatitis, have shown an upward curve, indicating a gradually increasing frequency equal to or greater than the increase in population. These diseases have persisted because of poor personal hygiene, lack of good sanitation, and in the case of hepatitis B the increased use of illegal drugs. Finally certain communicable diseases such as meningococcemia and syphilis have shown a steady or cyclic type of curve. This pattern may be due to lack of health education and the insidious and chronic nature of the diseases. The explosive increase in gonorrhea is an epidemic that stands alone but it has been reported that the incidence of gonorrhea may have leveled off in the 1980s.

Table 1 summarizes the characteristics of the major childhood communicable diseases, including the identifying symptomatology, prevalence of the disease, mode of transmission, and recommended methods for prevention.

DEVELOPMENT

Medical Aspects of Childhood Communicable Diseases

There are several reasons why children are highly susceptible to developing more severe responses to infectious communicable diseases than adults (Mandell, 1985). A first exposure to an infection during early childhood often produces a fever and rather severe illness. A reexposure, such as may occur in an older child or an adult, is more likely to produce a mild illness because of the antibodies produced from the first infection. Young children are also less likely to have the benefits of cross-reacting antibodies from a previous infection with a similar but different organism. Furthermore, the small air passages of children are more easily obstructed by edema or secretions, exacerbating the symptoms. Finally, there is considerable evidence to show that the rapid growth rate of cells, such as occurs in fetal tissue, makes them more readily infected by most viral agents than are adult cells.

What all communicable diseases have in common is that they are all caused by viruses or bacteria. There are five main ways by which viral or bacterial infections are spread. These infectious diseases can be transmitted through the water supply, contaminated food, animal vectors, the air we breath, and personal contact with a carrier of the virus (Gratz & Piliavin, 1984).

The medical treatment of an established viral or bacterial infection usually is restricted to symptomatic relief to make the patient as comfortable as possible. For example, fluid therapy may be used to control dehydration, and aspirin may be given to relieve aches and to reduce fever. There are few drugs that can be directly used to combat an infecting virus. Viral diseases are resistant to the usual forms of drug therapy now available, such as penicillin and the other antibiotics (Marks, 1985). This is because viruses use the machinery of living cells for replication. Consequently, drugs that

TABLE 1[a]

Characteristics of Communicable Diseases in Childhood

Identification	Prevalence	Transmission	Prevention
AIDS: Onset includes anorexia, diarrhea, weight loss, fever, and fatigue progressing until an opportunistic disease develops. Case fatality rate is about 46% in reported cases.	Homosexual or bisexual males represent 72% of cases, drug abusers 17%, Haitians 4%, Hemophiliacs 1%.	Predominantly homosexual intercourse, unclean hypodermic needles, transfusion of blood or blood products.	Avoidance of unprotected sexual contact with AIDS carriers and sharing of drug paraphernalia.
Chickenpox: Onset includes slight fever, aches, and skin eruptions. Neonatal mortality rate is 30%. Chickenpox is an antecedent of Reye syndrome.	Worldwide. In metropolitan communities 75% of the population has had chickenpox by age 15 and over 90% by adulthood.	From person to person by direct contact, or airborne spread of secretions, and indirectly through contaminated articles.	Protection from exposure; immunization.
Diphtheria: Acute bacterial disease of tonsils, pharynx, larynx, nose, other mucous membranes, and sometimes the conjunctiva or genitalia. An average of four cases is reported annually.	Occurs in colder months in temperate zones primarily in unimmunized children below 15 years old.	Contact with a carrier; more rarely with soiled articles. Raw milk may serve as a vehicle.	Active immunization with diphtheria toxoid and follow-up immunizations.
Gonorrhea: A sexually transmitted bacterial disease of the genital and rectal areas with discharge from the urethra or cervix.	Common worldwide, affects both sexes, and all ages. Grossly underreported.	By direct sexual contact or molestation.	Avoidance of contacts with infected carriers.
Hepatitis: Onset is abrupt, with fever, malaise, anorexia, nausea, abdominal discomfort. Varies from a mild illness lasting 1–2 weeks rarely to a severely disabling disease. Most cases are mild in children.	Worldwide, sporadic, and epidemic with cyclic recurrences. Outbreaks may occur in daycare centers.	Person-to-person contacts by fecal–oral route, or may be transmitted by contaminated water and food, including milk, sliced meats, salads.	Education about good sanitation and personal hygiene; daycare center teachers must wash hands after every diaper change and before serving food.
Hepatitis B: Onset with vomiting, rash, and often jaundice. Case mortality rate is <1%.	Worldwide infection is most common in young adults.	Only blood, saliva, and vaginal fluids are infectious. Exposure occurs through needle stick accidents or sexual exposure.	Vaccination.
Measles: An acute, highly communicable viral disease with fever, conjunctivitis, cough, and red rash. Most severe in the very young and in malnourished children with a case fatality of 5–10%.	With childhood immunization, cases have dropped by 99% and are limited to preschoolers and adolescents and those refusing vaccination.	By droplet spread, or direct contact with nasal or throat secretions of infected person. Measles is one of the most readily transmitted communicable diseases.	Vaccination at 15 months or as soon as possible thereafter.
Mumps: An acute viral disease with fever, swelling, and tenderness of the salivary glands. The CNS is frequently involved as aseptic meningitis. Death is a rare outcome. Due to vaccine programs the risk of infection is greatest in older children	Occurs less frequently than other common childhood diseases. Winter and spring are seasons of greatest prevalence.	By droplet spread and by direct contact with saliva of an infected person.	Vaccination administered after 1 year of age; 95% of recipients develop a long-lasting immunity.

(Table 1 continued)

Identification	Prevalence	Transmission	Prevention
Pertussis (whooping cough): An acute bacterial disease involving the respiratory tract. Symptoms include violent coughs followed by a high-pitched whoop. Fatality is low.	Disease is common regardless of race, climate, or georgraphic location. During 1979–1983 an average of 1753 cases were reported per year in the USA.	Primarily with direct contact of discharges from respiratory mucous membranes of infected persons. Frequently brought home by an older sibling.	Active immunization. Education of the public to the dangers of whooping cough and to the importance of maintianing an immunization schedule.
Paralytic polio: An acute viral infection ranging from inapparent infection to aseptic meningitis to paralytic disease and death. Symptoms include fever, malaise, headache, nausea, vomiting, excruciating muscle pain, and spasms, and stiffness of the neck or back, with or without flaccid paralysis, the hallmark of the disease.	Worldwide; most common in summer and early autumn in temperate climates. From 1967–1983 an annual average of 12 cases was reported in the United States.	Direct contact through close association.	Injected or oral vaccine.
Rubella: A mild infectious disease. Children may present few or no constitutional symptoms.	Worldwide. Prevalent in winter and spring. When When children are well immunized, infections in adolescents and young adults are most important.	Infection is by direct contact with carriers or with articles soiled from discharges from nose and throat.	Vaccination.
Salmonellosis: A bacterial disease commonly manifested by sudden headache, abdominal pain, diarrhea, nausea, and sometimes vomiting. Dehydration among infants may be severe. Fever is almost always present. Mortality is rare except in the very young.	Worldwide. As few as 1% of clinical caes are reported. Incidence is highest for infants and young children.	Usually traced to foods such as commercially processed meats, inadequately cooked poultry, raw sausages, foods with uncooked eggs, unpasteurized milk or dairy products, and foods contaminated by a rodent or infected foodhandler.	Thorough cooking of all food stuffs. Education of food handlers in the importance of hand-washing, refrigerating food, and maintaining sanitary kitchens.
Syphilis: Characterized by a primary lesion, and late lesions of skin, bone, viscera, the CNS and the cardiovascular system. Late manifestations shorten life, impair health, and limit occupational efficiency.	Involves young people primarily 15–30 years old. More prevalent in urban than in rural areas and in in males than in females. High prevalence among male homosexuals.	By direct contact with infectious body fluids (saliva, semen, blood, vaginal discharges).	General health promotion measures, sex education.
Tuberculosis: Initial infection usually goes unnoticed but tuberculin sensitivity appears in a few weeks.	Worldwide; in 1983, the incidence rate was 10/100,000. Mortality and morbidity increase with age, are higher among the poor, are higher in cities.	Exposure to airborne droplets or prolonged exposure to a carrier.	Reduction of overcrowded living conditions. Education of the public in mode of spread and methods of control.

[a]The contents of Table 1 have been adapted from: Benenson, A.S. (Ed.). (1985). *Control of communicable diseases in man.* Washington, DC: American Public Health Association.

inhibit viral development also inhibit the functions of the host cell. Despite this fact, it is not uncommon for parents to try to seek penicillin or other antibiotic treatment for their children suffering from viruses. Nonetheless, a small number of antiviral drugs are available for specific infections.

The most successful controls over communicable diseases have been eipdemiological. Worldwide immunization is credited with the eradication of smallpox, once one of the most feared viral diseases. Nationwide surveys have shown that as many as 1 in 3 children lack protection against one of the major childhood diseases (Hickson & Hinman, 1983). This situation has existed despite the availability of safe, effective, and frequently free, vaccines. As a result, epidemics of childhood diseases still occur among children of all ages.

School officials may require students to be vaccinated or immunized and to undergo physical examinations as prerequisites to school attendance. In addition, students may be restricted or barred from attending school if they are suffering from a contagious or infectious disease or if they are so physically unclean as to threaten the health of other students. Boards of education may also, in extreme cases such as widespread epidemics, authorize the closing of schools. In fact, boards of education hold the power and authority to adopt any reasonable regulation designed to safeguard the health and safety of students attending the public schools. This right, which is not always detailed in state constitutional or statutory provisions, is legitimized through the police power of the state.

The school's right to demand vaccination or immunization as a condition of attendance has been attacked on several grounds, including the violation of such constitutionally protected rights as religion, personal liberty, and the right to due process and equal protection of the laws. In all cases where statutory enactments have required or authorized the local board of education to require vaccination as a condition of school attendance, courts have upheld the action of the school board. Court cases challenging schoolboard authority in regard to required immunizations prior to school attendance are now relatively rare. Of course, the major exception to this situation is the current AIDS controversy. Whether child victims of the AIDS virus should be excluded from attending school has been controversial because of the dispute about how the virus is communicated. Only recently was a 14-year-old boy from Indiana, Ryan White, granted permission to return to his school as the result of a court decision overruling the board of education's action to exclude him on the grounds that his presence represented a health hazard to other students.

Social Psychological Aspects of Communicable Diseases

Often a feeling of malaise is one of the earliest manifestations of an infectious disease. Among the behaviors that may be observed are the following: listlessness, inability to concentrate, lack of drive, uneasiness, light-headedness, weakness, headache, and anorexia (Hoeprich, 1983). When an infectious disease becomes a chronic condition, it may be termed a physical or health disability. Physical and health disabilities have been described as medical conditions that so limit the alertness, vitality, or strength of the child that his or her educational performance is adversely affected (Willis, Culbertson, & Mertens, 1984). These children may evidence characteristics similar to learning-disabled children or behaviorally disordered children. When the medical condition is severe their social and emotional status may also be affected. For example, what children believe about the causal factors of illness may affect not only the self-esteem of an afflicted child but also the attitudes of her or his healthy peers.

Blaming oneself for illness seems to decrease whereas blame attributed to external sources seems to increase with chronological age. According to Piagetian cognitive development theory (Brewster, 1982) children's understanding of illness causation progresses through three stages. During the preoperational stage of cognitive development young children perceive disease as being caused by some personal wrongdoing. In the concrete operational stage children begin to understand the physical causal of disease through the transmission of germs. In the final, formal operational stage, children acknowledge multiple causation of disease, such as physical weakness, susceptibility, and personal actions.

The misinformation of peers may also have a social psychological impact. Price, Desmond, & Kukula (1985) found that students with the highest level of knowledge about AIDS correctly answered only 47% of the questions on a survey about the topic. Less than one third of the 250 adolescents they sampled reported that they had received any information on AIDS from their schools. Not only may afflicted children and school-age peers misunderstand communicable diseases, but parents and even educational staff may harbor prejudices and stereotypes about children affected by infectious diseases. For example, during the polio epidemics of the 1940s and 1950s towns were sprayed with DDT in an effort to kill flies that might be infected even though there was no evidence that the virus might be carried by insects. Because the popular belief was that polio was a "summer" disease, many schools delayed school openings. Milwaukee called a citywide quarantine preventing children from leaving their own backyards (Leerhsen, Murr, & Witherspoon, 1985). Occasionally the outbreak of a communicable disease has resulted in a major scientific breakthrough such as the concept of vaccination, but just as often adults as well as children have become overly suspicious and have sought out human scapegoats.

PUTTING CHILDREN'S COMMUNICABLE DISEASES IN PERSPECTIVE

Because school psychologists have a unique view of the social psychological aspects of children's health, their knowledge of schools as organizational systems, and their understanding of ecological psychology and family systems theory, they have several roles in cases of communicable disease. Their viewpoint is valuable to primary health providers, such as physicians and school nurses, since children spend the major parts of their days at school.

Dealing with communicable diseases in the public schools can be divided into three main strategies: (a) communicable disease prevention, (b) health promotion, and (c) intervention in cases of communicable disease.

The school psychologist supports communicable disease prevention through programs designed to encourage students to reduce or eliminate unhealthy behaviors. But health promotion is complementary to disease prevention. Health promotion in the schools involves strengthening and reinforcing behaviors by the students that actively improve health. That is, promoting healthful behavior should not be seen merely as the residual outcome of reducing health-compromising behavior. Finally, when a child is diagnosed by some health professional as having a communicable disease, or when a communicable disease has spread to epidemic proportions, the school psychologist is then invested with an intervention role involving information dissemination and consultation on the psychological aspects of the illness. Whichever roles are adopted, the steps taken should complement the activities of other professionals concerned with school health problems, working as interdisciplinary team members to bring the communicable disease under control.

ALTERNATIVE ACTIONS

Communicable Disease Prevention

Specifically, what are the responsibilities of school psychologists in dealing with vaccine-preventable diseases? Dissemination of knowledge is probably their most important contribution. Schools have a primary role in disease prevention and control in communication. The spread of communicable diseases is greatest in the public school classrooms, but throughout the school-age years, from kindergarten through high school, the greatest numbers of children can be most easily tracked for disease protection through school records. School officials should be committed to making sure that students are properly immunized. Furthermore, unlike most health professionals school teachers, school administrators, and school psychologists have the greatest opportunity to observe children daily. Suspect skin rashes or other signs of impending diseases often are first noticed in school and should be reported to the school nurse. To avoid the threat of potential epidemics in schools, school psychologists working as members of a school health team might consider the following steps.

The immunization records of students should be reviewed regularly classroom by classroom. The records of older students should be reviewed first, followed gradually by the records of earlier grades. All age groups, not just children first entering school, should be reviewed.

The goal should be 100% immunization, with exemptions for children only when absolutely necessary, such as religious reasons. When new or transfer students' immunization records are missing or incomplete, they should be referred, with the permission of their parents, to local health care providers for inoculations. Students should be enrolled only after they have presented proof of adequate immunization; the exclusion procedure should be enforced by screening of all students at the beginning of each school term. The same standardized immunization information should be kept for all students. This record should include at least the student's name, birthdate, sex, date of immunization, names of persons administering immunizations, specific types of vaccines received, exemption status, and miscellaneous medical notes (Hickson & Hinman, 1983).

Community support should be enlisted to strengthen and enforce school immunization laws. Some states still do not have comprehensive laws requiring proper immunization for school entrance. It is suggested that members of the school health teams mobilize a concerted action to improve the laws if required immunizations for school attendance do not cover all the major childhood diseases or if they do not contain a provision excluding enrollment of unimmunized students. These legislative mandates will be necessary if schools are to realize a disease-free school population.

Any cases of disease that are suspected to be communicable should be reported to the local health department for follow-up and investigation. Furthermore, the school health team should implement the recommendations of the local health board if there is an outbreak of a communicable disease in the school community. When the disease poses an imminent threat to the health of the rest of the students in a school building, it may be necessary occasionally to identify and send home immunization-exempted students and to warn their families of the potential danger their children face during the outbreak.

School personnel should collaborate with the health department on public awareness programs to alert parents to immunize their children before they enter school. The school health team should send home to parents regular reminders of immunization schedules in school newsletters or other direct correspondence with parents. Lessons on preventing communicable diseases should be included in the health curriculum at every grade level, and teachers should be told about the importance of promptly reporting any skin rashes or other signs of illness they observe in their children.

School Health Promotion

Health promotion has been defined as the implementation of efforts to foster improved health and well-being in all physical health, social health, psychological health, and personal health (Perry, 1984).

Student health promotion includes three types of roles for the school psychologist: health behavior campaigns, educational activities, and community organization programs (Shellenberger & Couch, 1984). All three of the approaches involve the school psychologist directly and will be described briefly.

Health behavior campaigns focus on changes at the

larger, impersonal, environmental level. These efforts emphasize awareness, knowledge, motivation, and the larger environmental changes. Health behavior campaigns are usually conducted at the classroom level or school organizational level. Health behavior campaigns in the classroom can take many forms such as class discussions or specific presentations about how to avoid sickness. Curricular materials appropriate for different grade levels are available to help in the development of these classroom health campaigns (Rothman & Byrne, 1981). In addition, teachers might prepare their own minicourses on various health-related skills. Parents might be encouraged to participate in these classroom health behavior campaigns by attending school-sponsored cross-generational activities; they might also be instructed in how to provide opportunities for their children to practice their new skills at home.

At the school organizational level health behavior campaigns can take the form of posters, newsletters, and campaigns by student-elected officers to improve student health habits schoolwide and to reduce health-compromising habits. Students could brainstorm ways to reconstruct their own environments to be more health-promoting. Such a comprehensive approach to organizational change would provide greater numbers of health promotional events and would increase the probability of behavior change.

In general, the role of the school psychologist in health behavior campaigns in the classroom and at school organizational level is that of a change initiator providing information, correcting normative expectations, encouraging the adoption of new programs for students, and providing the tools to enact these programs.

Involvement in educational activities is a second function for the school psychologist involved in health promotion. Their focus is on the immediate personal environments of individual students in the school. Behavioral screenings might be conducted to screen for specific health-promoting behavior. Special classes might be established to promote specific healthful behaviors. For example, small groups might be facilitated by the school psychologist to discuss eating habits, their relationship to eating disorders, and their contribution to the resistance of infectious diseases. In one study a positive reinforcement program was effective in increasing two learning-disabled students' ability to maintain clean hands, face, and teeth (Salend & Mahoney, 1982).

Community-based programming, the third health promotion role for the school psychologist, focuses on changes in the social environment of the community through the identification and education of key community leaders and the organization of task forces relevant to overall community health promotion programs and specific community-initiated projects. A secondary goal of this community-based programming is to integrate the school, the family, and the community into health-promoting activities. Health resources across the community need to be catalogued and shared with these groups. The local mass media might be engaged also in publishing the health-enhancing choices students are making, especially those choices that they learned in school.

Intervention in Cases of Communicable Diseases

When there is an outbreak of a communicable disease in a school building the school psychologist comes into an intervention role. At an initial stage, the school psychologist might become involved in health behavior assessments, the purpose of which is to identify students most at risk for contracting the communicable disease because of such variables as their lifestyle, eating habits, previous health history or a lack of good personal hygiene. The Aggregate Neurobehavioral Student Health and Educational Review (the ANSER System) (Levine, 1980) might be used informally to add a degree of structure to the health behavior assessments. The ANSER System was designed to assist in the collection, comparison, and interpretation of data from parents, school personnel, and students in regard to the impact of students' health problems on their educational achievement. In addition, in the context of health behavior assessments it is important to assess the amount of control students think they have over their own health behavior. The results of health behavior assessments can be used in several ways. They can be used to locate subgroups of students with particular problems and describe the health patterns that are most characteristic of problematic students. They can serve as personalized feedback to the teachers, students, and administrators in schools to identify areas in which health promotion activities are most needed. The information can also provide an impetus for parent–teacher consultation on treatment of these problems.

A second stage of intervention in the context of an outbreak of a communicable disease would involve the school psychologist in designing and initiating activities addressed to the disease in question. Interventions with individual students might involve discussion regarding relevant health habits, encouragement to adopt specific regular health-enhancing behaviors, individual or group counseling to reduce existing health-compromising habits, and minicourses designed to inform and revise students' and/or parents' misconceptions about the particular communicable disease afflicting the school. For example, a 90-minute course on the AIDS virus was conducted at the 110 high schools in Manhattan to teach specific information about how the AIDS virus spreads, the risk groups for the disease, the symptoms, the civil liberties issues involved in testing for the AIDS virus, and how the disease can best be avoided (Lawrence Journal World, 1986).

It is the goal of school-based interventions to redirect the student toward activities promoting physical, social, psychological, or personal well-being, and activities that will hopefully displace the purposes and functions that were served by other, health-compromising behaviors.

SUMMARY

In recent years the number of cases of childhood communicable diseases has declined significantly, aside from sporadic outbreaks. For example, in 1982 there were fewer than 2,000 cases of measles reported across the entire United States. On the other hand, in 1977 more than 57,000 cases of measles were reported. In 1982, the total number of reported cases of the seven major childhood diseases was less than 10,000. In the 1950s that many cases of polio alone were diagnosed each year in the United States.

With all of this success in prevention one might wonder why schools should develop time-consuming and seemingly unnecessary school health teams, with the school psychologist as a member. It is, however, the time and effort invested in these communicable disease prevention and health promotion efforts that reduce the need for intervention later on. Beyond its human significance, communicable disease prevention and health promotion also have financial value. Experts estimate that for every dollar invested in the measles vaccine there is a return of more than $14 in direct and indirect savings, including the costs of physicians' visits, extended care, medicines, and so on. The cost-effectiveness ratio is as high for other diseases as well (Perry, 1984; Shellenberger & Couch, 1984).

Disease control and health promotion have become salient topics in U.S. schools in the 1980s. There is also substantial evidence that interventions with children and adolescents can positively affect their health-related behavior (Rothman & Byrne, 1981). The distinguishing feature of school programs for communicable disease prevention, health promotion and intervention is the added benefit that many students are involved simultaneously, thus creating new normative standards and student expectations about what is to be considered healthful behavior.

REFERENCES

Associated Press. (September 2, 1986). Public schools combat AIDS. *Lawrence Journal World,* p. 38.

Benenson, A. S. (Ed.). (1985). *Control of communicable diseases in man.* Washington, DC: American Public Health Association.

Brewster, A. B. (1982). Chronically ill hospitalized children's concepts of their illness. *Pediatrics, 69,* 355–362.

Gee, E. G., & Sperry, D. J. (1978). *Education, law and the public schools: A compendium.* Boston: Allyn & Bacon.

Gratz, R. R., & Piliavin, J. A. (1984). What makes kids sick: Children's beliefs about the causative factors of illness. *Children's Health, 12,* 155–160.

Hickson, M. A., & Hinman, A. R. (1983, September). Here's how you can carry on the fight against epidemics in your school. *American School Board Journal,* pp. 40–41.

Hoeprich, P. D. (1983). *Infectious diseases: A modern treatise of infectious processes.* Philadelphia: Lippincott.

Krugman, S., & Katz, S. (1981). *Infectious diseases of children.* St. Louis: Mosby.

Leershen, C., Murr, A., & Witherspoon, D. (September 23, 1985). Epidemics: A paralyzing effect. *Newsweek,* p. 23.

Levine, M. D. (1980). *The ANSER system: Aggregate neurobehavioral student health and educational review.* Cambridge, MA: Educators' Publishing Service, Inc.

Locke, D. (1978). *Virus diseases.* New York: Crown.

Mandell, L. A. (Ed.). (1985). *Essentials of infectious diseases.* Boston: Blackwell.

Marks, M. I. (1985). *Pediatric infectious diseases for the practitioner.* St. Louis: C. V. Mosby Company.

McKeown, T. (1976). *The modern rise of population.* New York: Academic.

Moffett, H. L. (1985). *Pediatric infectious diseases: A problem-oriented approach.* Philadelphia: Lippincott.

Perry, C. L. (1984). Health promotion at school: Expanding the potential for prevention. *School Psychology Review, 13,* 141–149.

Potts, E., & Morra, M. (1986). *Understanding your immune system.* New York: Avon Books.

Price, J. H., Desmond, S., & Kukula, G. (1985). High school students' perceptions and misperceptions of AIDS. *Journal of School Health, 55,* 107–109.

Reutter, E. E. (1970). *Schools and the law.* Dobbs Ferry, NY: Ferry, NY: Oceana.

Rothman, A. I., & Byrne, N. (1981). Health education for children and adolescents. *Review of Educational Research, 51,* 85–100.

Salend, S. J., & Mahoney, S. (1982). Teaching proper health habits to mainstreamed students through positive reinforcement. *Journal of School Health, 13,* 539–542.

Shellenberger & Couch. (1984). The school psychologist's role in promoting the health and well-being of children. *School Psychology Review, 13,* 211–215.

Willis, D. J., Culbertson, J. L., & Mertens, R. A. (1984). Considerations in physical and health-related disorders. In S. J. Weaver, (Ed.), *Testing children* (pp. 185–196). Kansas City, MO: Test Corporation of America.

Youmans, G. P., Paterson, P. Y., & Sommers, H. M. (1975). *The biological and clinical basis of infectious diseases.* Philadelphia: Saunders.

BIBLIOGRAPHY: PROFESSIONALS

Benenson, A. S. (1985). *Control of communicable diseases in man.* Washington, DC: American Public Health Association. Intended as a ready resource of information on how to recognize the major communicable diseases that afflict children and their major physical effects on the developing child. It also serves as a reference on how to prevent and control each of the communicable diseases described.

Krugman, S., Katz, S. L., Gershan, A. A., & Wilfert, C. (1985). *Infectious diseases of children.* St. Louis: Mosby.
Serves as an excellent reference regarding the most common infectious diseases of children. For the reader who is interested in a comprehensive understanding of the development and prognosis of a specific communicable disease this is a well-written resource.

Nichols, S. E., & Ostrow, D. G. (Eds.). (1984). *Psychiatric implications of acquired immune deficiency syndrome.* Washington, DC: American Psychiatric Press.
Provides advice and guidance for mental health workers called upon to counsel persons who have or who are concerned about AIDS. Furthermore, the book has heuristic value in helping the professional to understand the psychological dynamics of other individuals with severe communicable diseases.

Perry, C. (1982). *Adolescent health: An education-ecological perspective.* In T. Coates, A. Peterson, & C. Perry (Eds.), *Promoting adolescent health: A dialog on research and practice.* New York:Academic, pp. 73–86.
The purpose of this chapter is to describe techniques that educators can employ to enhance the health and well-being of adolescent students through prevention and control of health-threatening factors in the school as well as in the broader ecology of the adolescent.

Willis, D. J., Culbertson, J. L., & Mertens, R. A. (1984). Considerations in physical and health-related disorders. In S. J. Weaver, (Ed.), *Testing children* (pp. 185–196). Kansas City, MO: Test Corporation of America.
This chapter discusses representative physical and health-related disorders that could result from one of the childhood communicable diseases. The psychologist is instructed in the ways of assessing children who present with these problems, on the integration and interpretation of test data, and on the communication of results to the family, school, and other professionals.

BIBLIOGRAPHY: PARENTS

Kassler, J. *Gay men's health: A guide to the AIDS syndrome and other sexually transmitted diseases.* New York, NY: Harper & Row.
AIDS and other sexually transmitted diseases are often misunderstood illnesses. This guide explains these diseases in simple terms, and describes the impact these diseases have on health. This book is a valuable resource for those who want to know the facts about the origins of sexually transmitted diseases.

Potts, E., & Morra, M. (1986). *Understanding your immune system.* New York: Avon Books.
This paperback book is written in a very popular style on the immunological system. The book is designed to help parents understand the immune system, where problems may arise, how to strengthen immunity, and why viruses and bacteria invade the body to cause communicable disease. There is also an easy-to-read introduction on childhood communicable diseases. This book could be used in bibliotherapy with parents of children with communicable diseases.

Rios, E. T. (1982). *Communicable diseases, teacher's manual, level 1, grades 1–3.* New York: Educational Factors.
Serves as an early elementary school teacher's guide to discussing communicable diseases with the class. Activities appropriate to this grade level are suggested. The teacher's role in preventing childhood communicable diseases is also explained.

Rios, E. T. (1982). *Communicable diseases, teacher's manual, level 2, grades 4–6.* New York: Educational Factors.
Topics for discussion as well as classroom activities appropriate to grades 4–6 are presented for the classroom teacher's use. This is an excellent resource for the teacher who wants to begin a module on the sometimes delicate topic of communicable disease.

Spock, B., & Rothenberg, M. (1985). *Dr. Spock's baby and child care.* New York: Dutton.
Dr. Spock's book is a classic on healthful child-rearing tips for the parent of an infant or young child. The book contains useful ideas on how to manage certain childhood diseases until proper medical care is provided. In addition, Dr. Spock shares some of his clinical wisdom about how parents can cope with their own anxieties when their children are sick.

BIBLIOGRAPHY: CHILDREN

Donahue, P., & Capellaro, H. (1975). *Germs make me sick: A health handbook for kids.* New York: Knopf.
Probably best used as a focus for a classroom discussion on how germs affect health. The book is written at a reading level that most early elementary school children should understand. Otherwise, this book could be used for the purposes of bibliotherapy under professional supervision in cases where children have been identified as at risk because of poor personal hygiene.

Rios, E. T. (1982). *Communicable diseases, student's manual, level 1, grades 1–3.* New York: Educational Factors.
This student manual is intended to complement the associated teacher's manual so that classroom discussion and related activities regarding how diseases are communicated from child to child can occur. There is also a Spanish version of the manual.

Rios, E. T. (1982). *Communicable diseases, student's manual, level 2, grades 4–6.* New York: Educational Factors.
This student's manual is intended to extend and reinforce the ideas about student health promotion and communicable disease prevention described in the level 1, grades 1–3 version of this teaching tool. Discussion topics and class activities appropriate for later elementary school children are presented. There is also a Spanish version of this manual.

Children and Competition

Doris J. Benson
Louisiana State University-Shreveport

BACKGROUND

Winning isn't the only thing, it is everything. This motto has become a dominant theme in our society. It reflects the degree to which competition has permeated every segment of the U.S. culture. Competition, which can be described as a striving against another person or persons, or against a standard, to gain some object, or superiority, has engulfed children as young as 3 years of age and adults in their eighth decade of life or later, as witnessed by the proliferation of contests and competitive activities in every area of life. Although it doesn't exist in every society, children in our culture acquire competitiveness naturally.

Directly related to the social structure of a society, competition is found in primitive as well as highly evolved cultures. Societies that stress competition over cooperation are characterized by strong ego development of individuals, a will to power over fellow beings, a valuation of property for individual versus group ends, a social structure that depends upon the initiative of the individual, and a single scale of success. Individual achievement is measured against that of others, and the sense of individual security is undermined. Cooperative societies, in contrast do not depend on individual exercise of power over another, nor on the initiative of individuals. Emphasis is placed upon working together to a common end and for the benefit of the group. Rising in status above one's peers is discouraged. The individual's sense of security is strong in these societies (Mead, 1976). Still other societies are highly competitive, but not individual-oriented. Examples of modern-day societies of this kind include Japan and Russia. They stress the importance of and reliance upon family, occupation, or community instead of the individual (Munroe & Munroe, 1975).

Because of the central role that competition plays in our society, it will affect the development of all children. The effects can be positive. Skill development can be facilitated, self-discipline encouraged, social relationships enhanced, and mental and physical growth aided by competition. It can affect children negatively: competition can cause stress, burnout, and psychological and physical trauma and injury, and it can undermine self-esteem (Berlage, 1983; Burke & Kleiber, 1976; Crawford, 1983; Elkind, 1981; Thomas, 1978; and Tutko & Bruns, 1976). Ultimately, its impact will depend upon the social context within which it occurs, the personality and familial dynamics of the individuals involved, and the manner in which the competitive situations are structured.

There are many vehicles in our society, formal and informal, through which competition is expressed, including schools, families, professional and social institutions, recreation, and organized sports. If we are to insure that children are not adversely affected by competition, we must understand its nature and development and the factors that mediate its impact, as well as acquire knowledge as to how we can minimize its negative effects while encouraging its positive impact.

DEVELOPMENT

Sociocultural Differences

Born with an instinct to survive, children also seem to inherit an impulse to purposeful and seemingly aggressive activities. They can learn to channel these tendencies into cooperative or competitive ends. The degree of competitiveness varies from society to society and within cultures. Knight and Kagan (1977) found that Anglo-American children exhibit more competitive behaviors than Mexican children. These differences increase with age, from 5 to 9 years, Mexicans becoming slightly more prosocial and Anglos more competitive. The differences remain constant after age 9. Latvian-American children, however, were found to be slightly more competitive than Anglo-American children (Galejs & Stockdale, 1980). Though family size and birth order of children have a negligible effect on competitiveness, parental rearing styles and socioeconomic levels have a greater impact. Anglo-American children in lower socioeconomic level homes display more frequent prosocial behavior (Knight & Kagan, 1977). Overall, males tend to be more competitive than females, but the trend is not universal, and differences exist within cultures. One investigator found a positive relationship between parental strictness and competitiveness among primary-school-age boys; and, in contrast a positive relationship between competitive as well as cooperative attitudes and parental strictness for girls. These findings suggest parents may promote a double standard with regard to competition based on sex (Arap-Maritim, 1984).

Developmental Trends

Competitive behavior tends to develop in a predictable sequence. Preschoolers aged 3–5 years, who are characterized by an egocentric world view, do engage in selfish behaviors. They often strive to obtain a desired object from or position over a peer or peers. But they seem motivated primarily by a yearning to attain the object or goal and less by a need to "best" or shine against their peers. Consequently, they do not judge the outcome in status terms, or decide if their behavior was better or worse than that of peers. When U.S. preschoolers were compared with Chinese preschoolers (Galejs & Huang, 1983), no differences were found, though the Chinese culture is the less competitive. Apparently, older children, aged 6–10 years, begin to exhibit a sense of superiority as a social value when engaging in competitive behavior, make social comparisons more often, and consciously attempt to outperform their peers. The outcomes have important consequences and implications for the self-evaluation that children begin to make at this stage.

Adult Structured Versus Children's Spontaneous Competition

Developmentally, primary and early secondary school-age children are at the formative stages of self-identity. They spontaneously engage in certain types of competitive behavior that tend to facilitate this process. When engaging in contests, children do formulate rules, provide structure, and allow for a winner. In contrast to adult-controlled children's contests, children-controlled ones are characterized by shared decision making and shared power, participation by everyone, and no fear of loss of love due to failure to win. Consequently, negative self-evaluations tend to be limited and children are able to acquire skills, receive feedback, and develop self-confidence in a safe, nonjudgmental context. Acceptance within this structure is based upon what each child contributes to the group. Mutuality and interdependence are promoted, and winning is less important than belonging and participation (Tutko & Bruns, 1976; Berlage, 1983).

The following information from sports competition underscores this phenomenon. When surveyed about the importance of winning, 72% of children in youth football indicated they would rather play regularly on a losing team than sit on the bench of a winning team (Thomas, 1978). Children naturally seek out competitors at their own level or similar level of ability, whereas adults often use chronological age to determine matches. This tends to result in vast discrepancies because of uneven physical, intellectual, and social development during childhood and adolescence.

Social Contexts

Organized children's sports such as Little League baseball and Pop Warner Football epitomize the kind of competition that can be psychologically and physically damaging to children. When managed inappropriately, children may suffer early burnout and withdrawal as a result of excessive pressures. Those with minimal skills may be dissuaded from later participation in what could be pleasurable lifetime activities.

The damage is not restricted to poor competitors or the losers; successful competitors suffer as well. The emphasis on external rewards may undermine intrinsic motivation, which can cause many children to avoid worthwhile activities. The stars and superstars often feel cheated out of childhood because their preoccupation with a lone activity leads them to neglect other important areas of development. They may have limited social skills, and are often lonely. Many become narcissistic and develop generalized feelings of superiority and thus a distorted perspective. Their self-worth becomes inextricably confused with their talent and the number of contests won.

Furthermore, in organized children's sports physical hazards are a particular concern. One of three children under the age of 15, or 17 million children, sustain injuries serious enough to require a physician (McEwin, 1981). Extreme stress on immature physical systems makes the risk of permanent bone and joint damage extremely great. This is especially crucial because the damage may not be detected until later in life.

Another damage is the development of coronary heart disease later in life. Type A behavior, including excessive competition, is related to the disease. Such behavior usually begins in childhood as a direct result of excessive social pressures (Matthews & Angulo, 1980).

Ames (1984) found that children in competitive, in contrast to individualistic, learning situations focus on how smart they are instead of thinking about how to improve their efforts. Such a focus can contribute to learned helplessness, and impair the self-image.

On the other hand, individual competitive reward structures that lead to competitive behavior have been associated in academic settings with greater performance and achievement than cooperative reward structures (Slavin, 1977). However, this is restricted to situations in which students are similar in abilities, or perceive that there are not vast ability discrepancies, and in which rewards are allocated on the basis of individual effort. In such instances, competition can stimulate individual effort and productivity, promote higher standards and aspirations, enhance interest in learning activities, and decrease the monotony of routine daily tasks (Clifford, 1972). However, academic settings that promote cooperative reward structures and increase cooperative behavior among students are associated with greater social behavior and feelings of belonging (Slavin, 1977).

Apparently, the most beneficial situations for optimal learning are those that combine individual competition with group cooperation so as to foster both achievement, performance, and prosocial behavior. Such situations lessen ability discrepancies and promote involvement and willingness to participate on the part of less able students.

Negative Competition

It seems that competition is a manifestation of self-orientation and in part an outgrowth of social comparison in our society. It does develop naturally in our culture and can serve positive ends by contributing to psychological growth and development. This natural development can be interfered with, however, by parents, educators, coaches, and other adults — most of whom are motivated by a belief that competition is essential for development and achievement in our society. But others force children to compete for selfish reasons: They glory in their children's accomplishments or use them to help them gain social advantage. The potential harm to children is escalated when competition is highly structured by adults, and children are unevenly matched in abilities, skills, or development. When winning is the ultimate purpose, undue pressure is exerted, and the children are not involved in the decision making on competitive events, the consequences may be negative. When children with lesser skills and abilities are excluded from participation in such events, power on one hand, and failure on another, are concentrated on a few and interdependence is undermined. The risks undoubtedly arise when the activities are no longer fun for the participants. Many youths may turn to drugs and involvement in antisocial behavior as a defense against too much competition.

PUTTING CHILDREN AND COMPETITION IN PERSPECTIVE

At-Risk Children

Though excessive competition can be detrimental to all children, the effects are more damaging in particular instances. The impact seems to be mediated by personality characteristics, emotional makeup, family dynamics, and social/situational contexts. Children most at risk are those with low self-esteem and low self-confidence. Emotional trauma and stress may occur when they find themselves involved in competitive interactions. Low achievement may result for children with an external locus of control. Where competition is preeminent, children with an internal locus of control tend to achieve more than the former. For children who have learned helplessness, competition seems to prevent their effective appraisal of outcomes to such an extent that they are unable to improve their strategies. Other children have adequate self-esteem but are especially prone to suffer from competitive state or trait anxiety. The stress such children undergo often results precisely in the feared outcome.

Highly anxious students worry more than peers about playing poorly and losing, and about the evaluations of parents, coaches, and teammates (Passer, 1983). In consequence, in competitive sports events highly anxious students have been found to perform less well than low-anxiety peers of comparable ability despite their self-perceived and coach-rated equality of competence.

Competition is such an integral part of our society that it is unnatural for a child to refuse to compete in all or most social and academic activities. Yet there are some children who demonstrate a fear or strong disinclination to compete. (Excluding those who are motivated by culture or religion.) Such children avoid situations where there is overt social comparison (Pepitone, 1972). For some, low ability may be the source of their reluctance. Others may be competent or skillful, butdecline to stand above their peers for fear of offending or alienating them. They are often shy and lack assertiveness. Given the essential role that social comparison plays as feedback for realistic appraisal, avoidance of it may cause such children to have distorted self perceptions and thus be at risk for social maladjustment. An effective intervention seems to be involvement of such children in interdependent group competition in which ability discrepancies are minimized and social rewards and peer support exist (Slavin, 1977). Group competition has been shown to increase cohesiveness and greater mutual attraction and to increase self-esteem and self-ratings, as well as decrease anxiety (Michaels, 1977).

Competition in the Family

Attitudes towards competition and competitive style are first learned by children in the home. Parents model behaviors that children learn to imitate. Sibling competition is related to parental behavior and the status of the children within the family. Where parents display fierce competitiveness, focus on winning at all costs, and allow competition to become pervasive within the family to the extent that all activities, such as chores, recreation, problem solving, and even style of dressing, become contests, children are adversely affected. In homes in which winners occupy an inordinately high status, losers are unduly teased or taunted, and excessive pressures replace fun and relaxed interactions, children tend to develop negative competitive attitudes at best and may suffer emotional damage at worst.

Sibling rivalry is a unique kind of competition. Though highly complex, sibling interactions and relations are related to situational as well as developmental factors. Birth order, age of siblings, age spacing, sex, and parental behavior are a few variables that will impact upon the nature and amount of sibling competition. Competition between siblings has been found to exist in the form of antagonistic and aggressive behavior. In U.S. homes such rivalry is typical. In families in which siblings aged 3–17 years lived, 82% were found to have taken violent action against a sibling in the previous year (Straus, Gelles, & Steinmetz, 1980). This rivalry tends to decrease with age from 90% among preschoolers to 64% among teenagers.

In preschool children, competition of an aggressive nature is found more in mixed-sex dyads, whereas the reverse is true in school-age children. Also with older, school aged children, the more widely spaced (two or more years), the more competitive the siblings (Minnett, Vandell, & Santrock, 1983).

Parents can minimize sibling rivalry by avoiding the appearance of favoritism or inequitable discipline, structuring cooperative and interdependent activities, and easing the transition of a new baby into the household by discussion of the infant's care and needs and sharing childcare responsibilities, where possible, among siblings.

Competitive though familial interactions may be, they can serve as a source of positive growth and experience. Siblings can learn to negotiate, accommodate one another, and gain valuable social experience in a familiar and relatively protected environment.

Assessment Methods

Children who are at risk for competitive stress can be identified in a number of ways. They can be assessed by one of the standardized instruments, such as the Competitive Anxiety Inventory, the Social Behavior Inventory or the State/Trait Anxiety Scale, and by various self-esteem and locus of control measures. However, adults can ultimately find indicators for all children in their reactions towards competitive activities. When situations become too stressful, children may find it difficult to concentrate or show diminished enthusiasm, may refuse to practice or even to participate, and may feign illness, easily sustain injury, or develop psychosomatic ailments. In extreme instances, particularly with at-risk children, nervous mannerisms, regression, nightmares, and maladaptive behavior may surface. Though highly talented or successful competitors show less state anxiety, psychological stress may be manifested by an excessive preoccupation with competition, denial of failure, inability to accept responsibility, development of an excessively inflated ego, and loss of perspective.

ALTERNATIVE ACTIONS

There is considerable evidence that cooperative interaction yields greater benefits and fewer dangers for individuals and society than competitive interactions. Some of the benefits include greater achievement as well as mutual friendships and interdependence, fulfillment of affiliation needs, strengthening of cross-ethnic relationships, reduction of cliques, greater participation of more individuals, and less psychological harm. Competition, however, will likely remain an important part of our culture. It seems instructive, therefore, to try to promote its positive impact. Parents and educators can help by acknowledging and reinforcing cooperation as a primary purpose in children's interpersonal activities. However, group competition may be the most effective means of achieving this end.

Structure of Positive Competition

When children are allowed as much as possible to structure their own activities, and are involved in the decision-making process, they learn interdependence and valuable social skills. Adults can reduce stress in competitive situations if, when giving children feedback about their performance, they communicate affection and acceptance for participation, reward effort, and place less emphasis on outcome. Greater benefits accrue when activities are structured to allow all children to participate in some way. When emphasis is placed on enjoyment instead of winning, the potential for harm is minimized. Children seem to profit from competitive situations in which their well-being takes precedence over the events, and events are structured as outlined above.

With regard to formal competition or organized sports, adults can ensure that children have the right to determine when to participate or quit without fear of pressure or humiliation. Psychological growth and physical well-being are protected when children who participate regularly are instructed by a qualified person who is knowledgeable about child development. Treating children in a manner consistent with their emotional and physical maturity, and with patience and support, is crucial. Proper medical supervision is essential, and children should be encouraged to report any pain without fear of ridicule or loss of esteem. Children benefit and learn when they are permitted to ask questions and to understand the reasons for particular instructions and rules.

Coping With Loss in Competitions

It is natural for children to react negatively to losing a competitive event. They may cry or become sullen or depressed. Parents can provide emotional support at this time. Empathy and encouragement are needed, whereas assigning blame or punishment are to be avoided. Ignoring them or remaining silent at such times may be perceived as implicit blame and can cause them to feel guilt. Forbidding children to fret about losses does not appear to be a good recourse either. Parents can be most effective by helping the child understand and adjust to failure, and use it as feedback. Emotional adjustment and maturity are fostered when children are helped to regard the loss as an inevitable part of life, particularly in a highly individualistic culture such as ours. When parents emphasize what can be learned from the loss and what significance it holds instead of reflecting their own perceptions and needs, children can better put the loss in proper perspective. The more pervasive and lasting the effects of loss, the more care parents need to exercise. If reactions are to a marked degree, temporary withdrawal from the precipitating activity may be warranted. In other instances, professional consultation may be advisable.

Another source of concern for parents and professionals is the child who is having peer group trouble because of her or his performance. The child may be teased or ridiculed. Parents can investigate the situation to determine if the child behaves so as to contribute to the reactions of the other children. The child may cry unnecessarily, taunt others, or refuse to accept responsibility for mistakes. Parents can help by providing an atmosphere that permits the child to openly express feelings. Parents of children who want to withdraw from competition might assist them in exploring the reasons. Even if they are highly talented, they should ultimately be the ones to decide about continued participation since the reasons have been clearly set forth. Children who are blamed or criticized even if they are eventually allowed to quit often suffer lasting guilt feelings. In such instances of peer group difficulties, an indirect approach may be needed such as helping them with social skills. The problem may be a result of inadequately structured activities or too much social pressure. Sometimes all that is required is for such children to be afforded the structured interaction in cooperative situations that is lacking.

SUMMARY

Competition is as American as apple pie, and it will likely be with us for quite some time. Children will naturally learn to be competitive within our major institutions, from the family to the workplace, as they strive to secure or maintain a desired object or position. When properly structured, competition can serve positive ends. However, parents, educators, and community leaders, in their efforts to give children a competitive edge, or to satisfy personal needs, may contribute to the almost unbridled expression of competition that characterizes our society. The dangers of this phenomenon are that it can result in unreasonable expectations and cause inordinate pressure to be placed upon children. Consequently, the very existence of childhood as a period in which one is permitted to grow at one's own pace in a protected environment can be threatened; it may even become impossible for highly pressured children to reach maturity emotionally unscathed. Though some children are more at risk of sustaining damaging consequences than others, all seem to benefit more from cooperative than competitive interactions. Cooperation impacts positively on socialization, cognitive and physical development, psychological growth, and achievement.

Yet, since competition develops naturally in our culture, its absence is more suspect than its presence. When appropriately structured, it can stimulate motivation, foster self-awareness and knowledge and understanding of others, and lead to empathy and altruism. In our society, learning to successfully handle competition is a social prerequisite that can be used as an index of adjustment. When competitive energies are utilized in a cooperative manner, individuals and society benefit.

School psychologists can play an important role in minimizing the impact of inappropriate competition upon our children and youths by proactive involvement. Adults within our institutions can be brought to understand the importance of natural competition and cooperative experiences and the importance of group competition; they can be guided as to how to adequately promote and structure them. As early as preschool, children must be helped to channel aggressive energies into positive and cooperative behaviors that receive reinforcement. School-aged children can be allowed to control many competitive activities and can be instructed in cooperative activities. Competition that results in fun for participants, positive learning experiences, fulfillment of affiliation needs, and positive socialization should be encouraged. Parents and educators can be challenged to insure that competition is not allowed to subordinate school children's health and well-being, and their sense of security.

The following questions can be used to gauge the appropriateness of children's reactions to competition.

Does the child exhibit a fear of social comparison or normal competitive situations?

Is competition used excessively, i.e., as an extrinsic motivator for normally intrinsic behaviors, such as school learning?

Does the child show an overreaction to loss or does the reaction last for more than a few days?

Does the child exhibit somatic complaints or anxiety prior to or after competitive events?

Is the child highly competent, but an underachiever?

Is the child highly susceptible to group pressure or does the child lack assertiveness?

Can the child function appropriately as a member of a competitive team?

Does the child exhibit a fierce win-at-all-costs attitude?

Do competitive behaviors generalize into dislike or aggression towards rivals?

Is the child becoming increasingly or markedly more competitive and antagonistic with siblings as she or he gets older?

Is the child socially competitive to the degree that he or she is avoided by peers and friendships are undermined?

These are just a few of the questions that, answered affirmatively, can suggest the need for parents and educators to intervene or seek professional consultation.

REFERENCES

Ames, C. (1984). Achievement attributions and self-instructions under competitiveness and individualistic goal structures. *Journal of Educational Psychology, 76,* 478–487.

Arap-Maritim, E. K. (1984). Relation of parental strictness to competitive and cooperative attitudes of primary school children. *Psychological Reports, 54,* 864–866.

Berlage, G. I. (1983, November). *Middle-class childhood: Building a competitive advantage or early burnout.* Paper presented at the annual meeting of the Pennsylvania Sociological Society, Villanova, PA.

Bowman, R. P., & Rotter, J. C. (1983). Computer games: Friend or foe? *Elementary School Guidance and Counseling, 18,* 25–34.

Brady, J. E., Newcomb, A. F., & Hartup, W. W. (1983). Context and companion's behavior as determinants of cooperation and competition in school-age children. *Journal of Experimental Child Psychology, 36,* 396–412.

Burke, E., & Kleiber, D. (1976). Psychological and physical implications of highly competitive sports. *Physical Educator, 33,* 63–70.

Bunker, L. K. (1981). Elementary physical education and youth sport. *Journal of Physical Education and Recreation, 52,* 26–28.

Clifford, M. M. (1972). Effects of competitions as a motivational technique in the classroom. *American Educational Research Journal, 9*(1), 123–137.

Christie, I. (1984). Children in competitive swimming — Effects of hard physical training. *Physical Educator, 41,* 121–129.

Crawford, M. (1983). Competitive sports for the multi-handicapped: A model for development. *Physical Educator, 40,* 105–110.

Elkind,, D. (1981). *The hurried child.* Reading, MA: Addison-Wesley.

Foster, W. K. (1984). Cooperation in the game and sport structure of children: One dimension of psychosocial development. *Education, 105,* 201–205.

Galejs, I., & Huang, V. (1983). Competitive behaviors of American and Chinese children working individually and working together: A comparative study. *Journal of Multilingual and Multicultural Development, 4,* 339–348.

Galejs, I., & Stockdale, D. F. (1980). Cooperative and competitive preferences and locus of control in Anglo-American and Latvian-American school-age children. *Journal of Multilingual and Multicultural Development, 1,* 49–56.

Hoffman, S., & Wundram, B. (1984). Sharing is . . . Views from 3-year-olds and thoughts for teachers. *Childhood Education, 60,* 261–265.

Johnson, D. W. (1984). Cross-ethnic relationships: The impact of intergroup cooperation and intergroup competition. *Journal of Educational Research, 78,* 75–79.

Johnson, D. W., & Johnson, R. T. (1983). The socialization and achievement crisis: Are cooperative learning experiences the solution? *Applied Social Psychology Annual, 4,* 119–164.

Knight, G. P., Dubro, A. F., & Chao, C. (1985). Information processing and the development of cooperative, competitive, and individualistic social values. *Development Psychology, 2,* 37–45.

Knight, G. P., & Kagan, S. (1977). Development of prosocial and competitive behaviors in Anglo-American and Mexican children. *Child Development, 48,* 1385–1394.

Kulewicz, S. (1981). The Children, not the games. *Journal of Physical Education and Recreation, 52,* 67–69.

Matthews, K. A., & Angulo, J. (1980). Measurement of the type A behavior pattern in children: Assessment of children's competitiveness, impatience–anger, and aggression. *Child Development, 51,* 466–475.

McEwin, K. C. (1981). *Focus on interscholastic sports and the middle school.* East Lansing: Michigan State University, Michigan Association of Middle School Educators.

Mead, M. (1976). *Cooperation and competition among primitive peoples* (rev. ed.). Glouchester, MA: Peter Smith.

Michaels, J. W. (1977). Classroom reward structures and academic performance. *Review of Educational Research, 47*(1), 87–98.

Minnett, A. M., Vandell, D. L., & Santrock, J. W. (1983). The effects of sibling status on sibling interaction: Influence of birth order, age spacing, sex of child, sex of sibling. *Child Development, 54,* 1064–1072.

Munroe, R. L., & Munroe, R. N. (1975). Cross-cultural human development. Monterey, CA: Brooks/Cole.

Nowicki, S., Jr. (1982). Competition–cooperation as a mediator of locus of control and achievement. *Journal of Research in Personality, 16,* 157–164.

Passer, M. W. (1983). Fear of failure, fear of evaluation, perceived competence, and self-esteem in competitive-trait-anxious children. *Journal of Sport Psychology, 5,* 172–188.

Pepitone, E. (1972). Comparison behavior in elementary school children. *American Educational Research Journal, 9*(1), 54–63.

Scanlan, T. K., & Lewthwaite, R. (1984). Social psychological aspects of competition for male youth sport participants: I. Predictors of competitive stress. *Journal of Sport Psychology, 6,* 208–226.

Scanlan, T. K., & Passer, M. (1981). Competitive stress and the youth sport experience. *Physical Educator, 38,* 144–151.

Slavin, R. E. (1977). Classroom reward structure: An analytical and practical review. *Review of Educational Research, 47*(4), 633–650.

Smith, T. (1983). Competition trait anxiety in youth sport; differences according to age, sex, race and playing status. *Perceptual Motor Skills, 57,* 1235–1238.

Stockdale, D. F., Galejs, I., & Wolins, L. (1983). Cooperative–competitive preferences and behavioral correlates as a function of sex and age children. *Psychological Reports, 53,* 739–750.

Straus, M. A., Gelles, R. J., & Steinmetz, S. K. (1980). Behind closed doors: Violence in the American family. New York: Anchor Books.

Strube, M. J. (1981). Meta-analysis and cross-cultural comparison: Sex differences in child competitiveness. *Journal of Cross-Cultural Psychology, 12,* 3–20.

Thomas, J. R. (1978). Is winning essential in youth sports contests? *Education Digest, 43*(9), 53–55.

Tutko, T. A., & Bruns, W. (1976). *Winning is everything and other American myths.* New York: Macmillan.

Weinberg, R. S. (1981). Why kids play or do not play organized sports. *Physical Educator, 38,* 71–76.

BIBLIOGRAPHY: PROFESSIONALS

Bowman, R. P., & Rotter, J. C. (1983). Computer games: Friend or foe? *Elementary School Guidance and Counseling, 18,* 25–34.
Discusses concerns about computer games, such as violence, competition, and becoming "hooked." A list of useful games is provided including those that can be used in counseling. New games can enhance cooperation, allow a child to create, and present programs for social and emotional learning.

Johnson, D. W., & Johnson, R. T. (1983). The socialization and achievement crisis: Are cooperative learning experiences the solution? *Applied Social Psychology Annual, 4,* 119–164.
Reviews theory and research into the impact of cooperative, competitive, and individualistic learning experiences on socialization, on cognitive and social development, and on achievement and related attitudes. The impact of peer relationships on children's and adolescents' values, attitudes, perspectives, prosocial and emotional behaviors, perspective-taking ability, and psychological health.

Tutko, T. A., & Bruns, W. (1976). *Winning is everything and other American myths.* New York: Macmillan.
Provides a comprehensive picture of organized sports and its effects on all those who are involved. Gives the reader a good perspective on the pros and cons of competition, with practical suggestions.

BIBLIOGRAPHY: PARENTS

Elkind, D. (1981). *The hurried child.* Reading, MA: Addison-Wesley.
Focuses on children and stress. Gives a poignant portrayal of how our society forces children to relinquish their childhood in favor of early adulthood and its pressures, but with few of the accompanying rights or advantages. Sets forth the dangers inherent in this phenomenon and gives practical suggestions for reversing the trend.

McEwin, K. C. (1981). *Focus on interscholastic sports and the middle school.* East Lansing: Michigan State University, Michigan Association of Middle School Educators.
Gives the parent a clear presentation of the controversy surrounding interscholastic sports below the high school level. Sets forth the express advantages and disadvantages.

Children and Computer Learning

C. Rick Ellis
Virginia Beach Public Schools, Virginia

BACKGROUND

"Le mariage du siecle," or the marriage of the century, is how the French Minister of Education referred to the use of computer technology in education (cited in Hawkridge, 1983). When and how will this marriage take place, will it be a long partnership, or will it end in a quick divorce? These questions are being considered by an ever increasing number of professionals, researchers, and lay people alike. The answers are not only likely to have a profound effect on the classroom environment, but also on our society as a whole. Preliminary research indicates that computer use can substantially increase the achievement level of the disadvantaged and those considered as having low aptitude. Could it not then raise the overall level of opportunity and social standing of this group, which is composed in a high proportion of minority students? The prospects are easy to consider, but if our hopes are to come to fruition, careful planning and evaluation is imperative.

Moursund (1984) noted that we are rapidly approaching the point where there will be one computer for every 30 students and that the numbers of computers in the classroom will continue to increase. A study conducted by the research firm Market Data Retrieval (1985), found that 570,000 microcomputers were being used for instruction in this country in 1984, an increase of 75% over the previous year. Most experts in the field such as Papert (1980) view the computerization of the classroom with great optimism and feel that many of its promises will come to fruition. The highly optimistic believe that the computer will be able to act as an individual tutor possessing all the positive qualities of Einstein, Plato, and Ghandi.

Not all experts feel that the computer will fulfill its promises to the field of education. Some use such terms as "fast rule-following idiot machine" (Jarrett, 1980) to describe it and view it as another attempt at a "quick fix" for our questionable educational system. Skeptics believe computer technology will fall far short of its potential to improve the quality of childrens' learning experiences.

Predictions that the latest advances in technology will revolutionize instruction are not new in the field of education. With each new development in the audiovisual field, claims have been made that the missing ingredient for the optimum instructional program has arrived. Televisions, teaching machines, and movie projectors were all felt to be the technology to revolutionize the field. With education's long history of unfulfilled promises that new technology will solve all its ills, skeptics have good reason to view computers with less than complete optimism. Despite educators' concerns about its effectiveness, manufacturers have already developed comprehensive computer curriculum systems for district wide implementation with the capacity to put a computer on every desk (Computer Curriculum Corporation, 1986). Using a Local Area Network (LAN), such systems will connect each student's computer to their teacher's computer, which in turn will be connected to a computer at the building's office. All of the building-level computers will be connected to one in the central administration office. The cost of such systems is beyond the resources of most school districts, but it is anticipated that the price of the current generation of computers will continue to decline at a rate of approximately 20% per year, making the economic factors related to such systems much more favorable.

As authors such as Naisbitt (1984) and Toffler (1980) indicate, our society is moving from an industrial-based economy to an information-based economy. This shift has been swifter than this country's transition from an agrarian to an industrialized society many decades ago. High-growth industries such as robotics and satellite communications are based on computer technology and will require personnel well trained in computers. In 1984 over 11 million computers were sold in this country (U.S. Department of Commerce, 1985); by virtue of these numbers alone, a definite need is established to make computers a part of our educational system in order to prepare students for the job market of the future. However, the mere fact that computer skills will be important for employment does not mean that the education of our children should be turned over to these relatively untried machines.

Maddux (1986) noted that caution should be used before wholeheartedly accepting the virtues of computer technology as applied to the educational process. He feels that erroneous assumptions are often made that computers are an end in themselves and that they can fulfill the most optimistic of expectations. Roblyer (1985) noted that it is often assumed without supporting evidence that computers can (a) replace or supplement current educational practices and increase students' achievement; (b) increase class size and learning while being more cost-effective than other methods of instruction; (c) increase students' retention of material and reduce learning time; (d) achieve these gains equally across content areas and grade levels; and (e) improve problem-solving skills and students' attitudes toward learning. Even though the effectiveness of other educational practices are coming under closer scrutiny, educational computing has continued to grow with little consideration of its effectiveness.

In evaluating any aspect of the computer field it is necessary to keep in mind that it is changing very rapidly and the state of the art today may be obsolete within a short time. For example, the memory, graphics, and voice capability of the hardware continue to expand and software programs are continually being refined to take advantage of these superior systems. This changing technology presents a significant challenge to researchers in the field. Because of the speed at which the field is changing it is difficult to conduct studies and provide educational decision makers with direction in a timely fashion. By the time an evaluation of a particular system is published, it may well have been replaced by one that is far superior.

The growth of computerized methods in education provides an excellent opportunity for support specialists such as school psychologists to become more involved in both the special and the regular education process. As experts in learning, memory, motivation, reward structures, and cognitive styles we can expand our sphere of influence through involvement with computers. Involvement can begin by serving on committees or offering to review software for a particular population. In any event computerized learning will continue to become an increasingly more important aspect of education in the future and school psychologists should make it a priority to be a part of its growth.

DEVELOPMENT

Computer Readiness

Once computers are accepted as a part of our cultural and educational context, the question arises as to the appropriate age for students to start with these machines. Opinions vary greatly, some believing the earlier the better, others feeling that children need well-developed conceptual skills before being exposed to the symbolic world of computers. Advocates of both positions present good arguments justifying their positions, but little evidence is available to support their claims.

Those advocating the early introduction of computers view them much the same as a foreign language; the earlier the exposure, the greater the learning, retention, and future application. Advocates of this position, such as Bitter and Watson (1983), believe that children must be provided with early computer experience in order to develop positive attitudes and not view them as "frightening beings." Pogrow (1985) found that when information is presented in electronic graphic form to young children, learning and retention are greater than when presented orally. Viewing the issue from a functional perspective, looking at a "picture book" is not much different for a child from viewing the same images on one of the latest generation of personal computers. The motor skills are minimized. The child only has to push a button on the mouse to present the next image. In respect to color and screen resolution the image on the computer is similar to that of a printed children's book and the computer can also produce speech to supplement the pictures. Those favoring early introduction of computers to children present a valid argument when evaluating only the sensory quality of the child–computer interaction or when considering the future need for computer literacy.

Those advocating a more cautious position on the introduction of computers to children would view the above analysis from a different perspective. In their analysis of the child–computer interaction they would include factors beyond the sensory input/output level. One overlooked aspect in the "picture book" example is the affective component. Children often form attachments to objects even when in pictorial form. It is difficult to imagine a child hugging or kissing a computer screen when a particularly appealing image appears, or a child carrying around a diskette which contains a favorite story. This is only one aspect of the complex nature of early learning that can be easily overlooked when focusing on only the sensory qualities.

In order to evaluate the potential benefits of computers in the early years, it is helpful to determine which principles of early childhood education can be facilitated by the computer and which cannot. Categorizing some of the generally accepted principles noted by Clements (1985), constructive teaching characteristics can be facilitated by computer include generating positive self-image; enhancing intrinsic motivation; affording responsiveness to the child; involving children in active participation in learning; setting goals while predicting and confirming events; providing many opportunities for learning without pressure for mastery; using techniques to ease the learning of complex material; instructing students on general rules about regularities; teaching application of rules to a variety of tasks; and allowing for the adjustment of learning for children of different abilities, interests, and cognitive styles. Practices that are difficult or impossible for the computer at the present time are encouraging autonomy and exploration; providing feedback that is a natural consequence of the child's behavior; exploring problems that involve real situations and concrete materials; encouraging multiple solution and alternative routes; transferring learning through self-discovery of principles; affording opportunities for free and creative expression; and developing aesthetic interests, skills, and values. As innovative and creative software becomes the rule rather than the exception, computers will be able to better facilitate the more difficult early learning goals while making the interaction process more natural and friendly.

Developmental Factors

Either intentionally or by default, all software makes important assumptions about the type of children who will be using the program. Popular software packages for children list only the age range for the potential user but are often unable to provide activities appropriate to all children within the range, especially those at the extremes. The ability of authors to take into account the factors that promote a close "fit" between the program and the child, such as developmental level, determines the "success" of the programs.

Consideration of developmental levels sets the main focus of learning on those activities that contribute most effectively to cognitive, social, and emotional growth. Developmental psychology provides some guidelines to use when considering when and how to involve children with computers.

Extensive computer involvement before children reach the intuitive phase (ages 4–7) of the preoperational thought period (Piaget & Inhelder, 1969) should be viewed with caution. Before this time children are egocentric, unable to take alternative viewpoints, able to classify only by single salient features, and still acquiring the basic principles of symbolic language. Children at the intuitive stage, beginning at about age 4 years, are able to think in terms of classes, see relationships, handle number concepts, and begin to develop the notion of conservation. Although they are not yet prepared for advanced applications, they may benefit from reinforcement of basic concepts acquired through traditional methods. One innovative application of computer technology for children at this level is Texas Instruments' *Touch and Tell.* When the child touches the object represented in pictorial form the "toy" says the name, color, or shape of the object, much the same as a parent would when interacting with the child about the materials. Knowledge of which buttons to press, and beginning familiarity with the computer, are the most important skills necessary for a preschool child. Simple games that teach keyboard use and how to interpret the screen display are available for children at this age. The major objective of introducing children to computers at this level should be to establish a positive relationship and to ensure that the experience is fun.

As children's capacity to learn, read, and form symbolic relationships increases, their ability to benefit from this new technology increases also. Most beginning computer applications are directed toward the child functioning at the concrete operations stage (ages 7–11). Here, according to Piaget, the child is able to use logical operations such as reversibility, classification, and seriation. Roblyer (1985) indicates that this is the level at which children can most benefit from computer-assisted instruction (CAI). The positive effects of CAI at this level may be due to students' ability to profit from a highly structured situation that provides immediate feedback (Kulik, Bangert, & Williams, 1983). When evaluating computer systems, developmental levels should be used as an index of learning at given ages, but should not place limits on experiences that are available to children.

Computer Literacy

Computer literacy is the ability to understand the capabilities, application, and implications of computer technology. The methods used to introduce children to computers and the type of literacy activities in which they should engage during their early years require close scrutiny. Hyson and Morris (1985) found that despite our computer-dominated environment, children's ideas about computers, even when provided a school literacy program, can often be vague or distorted. It cannot be assumed that children will learn and understand about computers on their own, or through brief exposure in school.

Computer literacy can range from knowledge of the names of the hardware components to advanced electronics and assembler language programming. Computer literacy usually begins when a child attains keyboard literacy. Some software programs that address the preschooler require only that the child press any key on the keyboard in order to indicate a choice when given two or more options. Instruction should provide the opportunity for the child to interact through different methods, facilitate skills necessary for future use, and provide the opportunity for mastery and enjoyment allowing the child–computer relationship to include positive affective components. Early learning on computers should include the objectively defined curriculum objectives along with the subjectively defined goals of mastery and efficacy. Hyson (1985) found that young children's affective responses are related to the degree of personal control the program allows. The learning tasks at this level should require little planning, integration, or use of symbols. As a child's knowledge of the computer expands, more direct assistance is necessary in order to gain understanding of the more symbolic and abstract aspects of the computer's operation. If instruction is organized properly, a child can move through the various stages of knowledge at a pace that provides optimum challenge and enjoyment according to appropriate developmental sequences.

The development of programming skills, or knowledge of a particular language such as BASIC or COBOL, is not necessary for a child to benefit from computers. Through the use of already published programs, word processors, electronic spreadsheets, data base managers, and a host of other applications programs, the needs of most computer users can be achieved. For users who would like to develop unique applications for computers, a variety of secondary languages are available that closely resemble the English language and provide the user a great deal of application flexibility. At the beginning level, LOGO is the most popular; it has been used with great success to introduce beginning computer concepts and elementary graphics to early elementary and preschool children.

At the upper end of the computer literacy spectrum, school systems will begin to develop computer high schools, or technology centers much like present schools for the arts or Cleveland Ohio's Aviation High School. The level of knowledge that the graduates of such programs will possess is difficult to imagine, since we have not yet experienced an entire graduating class of students who have been computer-literate since the beginning of their formal education.

PUTTING COMPUTER LEARNING IN PERSPECTIVE

The perspective taken toward computers will determine what types of applications are emphasized for children and the methods by which their effectiveness is evaluated. There are a number of possible applications for computers, all with differing goals. If fantasy games are used as enrichment activities or to facilitate computer literacy, it would be inappropriate to evaluate academic levels in comparison to the amount of computer use. If computers are highly visible in a school building, the assumption would be that the school is innovative and the students are being provided quality instruction. This is not necessarily the case.

Before evaluating educational computing, the areas of potential application must be determined. Clements (1985) provides three perspectives on how the computer can be viewed in the educational environment. It can act as an individual tutor, a tool to aid in the performance of other tasks, or as a specific course of study. Another application of computers in the school is computer-managed instruction, but its cost effectiveness is yet to be established. Table 1 lists the various perspectives on educational computing.

Computer as Tutor

The most widely used application of computer technology for children is that of tutor. The electronic tutor can take three basic forms. The first application is to provide reinforcement of curriculum material presented by the teacher. The most common form of this application is supplemental drill-and-practice activities in which the computer acts as electronic flash cards or ditto sheets of previously introduced material. Second, the computer can take responsibility for the entire presentation, instruction, and evaluation of a specific set of academic goals, while providing remedial activities for areas of deficit. Although widely used by the military and businesses in conjunction with video disk technology, this application has not been used to a great extent in school systems. Finally, the computer can be utilized to enrich and expand upon children's present knowledge by providing activities that call for synthesis and application of previously presented material. Simulation activities are the most common form of this application.

Regardless of the application, it is the computer program that controls the presentation of material to the student. In essence, what the program does is provide a stimulus to the child such as "2 × 3 = ?" What happens after the child responds depends upon the sophistication of the program. If the child answers incorrectly by entering "5," the program may perform an "error analysis" and remind the child that the operation is multiplication and then ask the child to try again. Information can be presented at different speeds and at varying levels of difficulty. By using branching techniques the program can pinpoint where in the skill sequence a child's problem-solving capability is deficient and provide instruction in the area of deficit until mastery is achieved. Once the basic concepts are acquired, drill-and-practice is provided to give the child an opportunity to apply these skills. Enrichment activities often include simulation exercises in which it is necessary to apply the skills to real-life examples.

Effectiveness of Computers

After observing the quality of some of the latest software, the assumption would be that computers can easily fulfill the most optimistic of promises. But this is not the case. In an extensive analysis of the effectiveness of computer applications in the classroom, Roblyer (1985) condensed the meta-analysis of over 600 studies. The results indicate that computerized instruction has the most beneficial effects at the elementary level, less at the secondary, and the least at college level; that is, overall, computer use resulted in decreased effects as grade level increased. Gains from computer involvement were found to be greater for students of low aptitude and for those considered to be disadvantaged. Supplemental CAI was found to be more effective than substitute CAI, indicating that it cannot replace teachers but can add significantly to learning and retention. Gains in achievement were often greater in the area of math than in reading and language arts, except at the college level, where the reverse effect was found. Findings indicate that computerized instruction can significantly reduce instructional time, particularly at the higher grade levels. In those studies that addressed attitudes, students who received CAI developed more favorable attitudes toward computers and learning than control subjects. More recent studies found more significant results, thus supporting the assumption that as the field matures, more substantial benefits will be derived from computer applications. In Roblyer's analysis of the results of CAI to improve problem solving, critical thinking, and other higher-order skills, he concluded that despite its current popularity, the area is still in its infancy and that further study is necessary before conclusions can be drawn about its effectiveness.

Many of the computer programs used in early studies were only initial efforts at formalizing the complex process of learning. As the field continues to integrate the knowledge of related fields such as developmental psychology, educational psychology, human factors engineering, tests and measurement, computer science, and education, higher-quality systems will be developed along with appropriate methodologies to evaluate their effectiveness.

Our present knowledge base does give guidelines by which to evaluate CAI. Scarola (1984) noted that the software that provides the best opportunity for learning

TABLE 1

Computer Applications in Education

Perspective	Purpose
Computer as:	
Instructional manager	Document and organize the educational progress of each child as goals and objectives are achieved.
Subject matter	To develop expertise in the field of computer science. Usual applications involve the mastery of languages such as BASIC and COBOL.
Learning tool	Through the use of software such as word processors, communication packages, or electronic spreadsheets, students improve writing skills, obtain resource material, or develop their own math applications.
Tutor	To facilitate learning goals, material is presented by computer.
A. Supplemental drill-and-practice	To reinforce previously introduced material for the facilitation of skill development.
B. Instructor	To present information, explain concepts, and evaluate skill level. Computer assumes responsibility for entire learning program.
C. Enrichment	To expand upon current knowledge level and provide activities that require synthesis and application.

crosses and merges disciplines so as to help children learn (a) by engaging them in accurate simulations of real-life phenomena; (b) by providing age-appropriate problems and guiding them through the steps necessary for their solutions; (c) by allowing practice of acquired skills in new ways to facilitate overlearning; and (d) by providing an individualized tool that will allow for user-controlled activities.

Characteristics of Children to Be Considered

If computer systems are evaluated only on their ability to take children through appropriate educational goals and objectives, a narrow view is created of this potentially powerful learning tool. Visitors to video arcades are quick to observe that computerized activities provide participants with a highly reinforcing involvement. In an examination of the motivational aspects of software for children, Lepper (1985) finds three major theoretical orientations that should be considered. One orientation focuses on the individual as a seeker of challenge, with a need for accomplishment, thus making the goal structure, difficulty levels, and the goal relevance the central focus of software design. The second group attempts to find the optimum level of surprise, incongruity, complexity, or discrepancy as the critical variables for increased motivation. The third focuses on perceived control and mastery over the external environment, thus making the contingencies between actions and outcomes its central focus. Another powerful solicitor of intrinsic motivation is fantasy involvement, whose potential is only now being realized through the medium of computer technology. Although not associated with any traditional theory of motivation, the popularity of programs that contain this element substantiate its ability to elicit motivation in children.

Motivational factors and the appropriateness of curriculum are not the only considerations appropriate to the evaluation of the child–computer interaction. Children differ in the ways they approach tasks, process information, and respond to stimuli. Important elements that should be considered regarding cognitive styles include field independence–dependence, scanning–focusing, cognitive complexity–simplicity, and reflectivity–impulsivity. In order to develop systems that are truly functional, how children perceive and organize material presented by the computer must be determined. Just as intellectual strengths and weaknesses influence the ways in which children approach traditional academic tasks, they will also influence performance on computerized tasks. If computers are going to be successfully used in education these various factors must be considered.

Difficulties With Implementation

Given that motivational factors, intellectual level, and cognitive styles all have an influence on the success of computerized learning, why has the field been unable to incorporate this knowledge to produce programs of superior quality? The difficulty in applying such knowledge is similar to the general difficulty of turning sound educational theory into practice. Even if it were possible to bring together enough experts to develop the ultimate curriculum, special problems arise because of the numerous complexities and unique difficulties specific to computers. The obstacles to the development of software that will create the optimum learning environment include the need for cross-discipline experts, the long duration between the decision to develop a program and its realization, and the increasingly competitive nature of the industry, which sometimes places more emphasis on the cartoon character used in their program than on research.

Hopes for the Future

If the obstacles to computerizing learning tasks are so great and any advantage as to the cost–benefit ratio of computers versus other methods of instructional support has yet to be established, then what is the justification for placing such emphasis on this relatively untried technology? One answer is the *potential* richness of the child–computer relationship. This interaction varies according to the sophistication of the software program, which is capable of determining whether a child has mastered the prerequisite skills, outlining the task requirements, presenting the problem, prompting the child, interpreting the child's input, providing feedback based on the quality of that input, and adapting new lessons to the child's individual needs.

As equipment costs continue to decline, the way in which children interact with computers will change. The present mode of interaction usually involves only a keyboard and screen. The technology is available to communicate via a variety of input devices, including key press, mouse, light pen, joystick, touchpad, optic scanner, and the voice recognition device. The computer can respond through the production of text, graphics, synthesized speech, or a growing number of other peripheral devices. With such potentially rich modes of interaction through these various devices, theoretically sound software programs can be greatly enhanced and many of our hopes for the future will come to fruition.

ALTERNATIVE ACTIONS

Because of the rate at which the application of computer technology in education is growing there is the definite potential for negative consequences. The longer it takes to address the problems the more difficult it will be to change how computers are being utilized. One of the pioneers in the field, Joseph Weizenbaum, the developer of the popular program ELIZA, voiced his concern over a decade ago when he wrote "until recently society could always meet the unwanted and dangerous effects of its new inventions by, in a sense, reorganizing itself to undo or to minimize the effects" (Weizenbaum, 1976, p. 272). The areas of concern in reference to children's learning are the general overapplication and misapplication of computers in the educational process; the overall emphasis on computers, logic, and the systematic method of thinking as opposed to emotions, intuition, and creative thought; the lack of ethics in computer use; equity issues as related to race and gender; and computer availability for the handicapped.

Areas and Methods of Implementation

The literature does provide some initial direction so that decisions on computer applications can be based on empirical foundations. Roblyer (1985) has recommended that CAI be evaluated in terms of its cost effectiveness in improving instruction. He noted that a strong case can be made, economically, for the application of computer technology for the disadvantaged, those in need of remediation, and students at the elementary level. CAI should be viewed in relation to other methods available to assist in improving achievement. When considering expenditure per pupil, methods of instructional support such as educational television may achieve results equal to or better than CAI. School systems should examine the effects of alternative programs before committing to the adoption of CAI. An examination of the present instructional system is absolutely necessary before computerized methods are adopted in order to measure the effectiveness of the curriculum and to determine in what areas supplemental CAI is indicated. The initial efforts of those advocating the adoption of computer technology may cause a great deal of time to be spent in noncomputer areas of the educational system.

Once computer applications are determined to be a priority for school systems, methods to introduce this new technology to children must be established. Despite common assumptions that children have unconditional positive regard for computers, some evidence exists that they do not always view them favorably. Pulos and Fisher (1986) found that most children who had taken part in a typical computer literacy program were *not* interested in computers, did not intend to use them as adults, and had many misconceptions about their operation. They also found that typical stereotypes about computer users were prevalent. When asked what type of kids liked computers, the children surveyed singled out unusually bright or asocial children. This study indicates the need for quality programs of computer literacy that create an interest in the area, expose children to meaningful ways they can use the computer, and provide realistic information about the subject. Methods of achieving these goals have often been neglected by educators.

Once the appropriateness of computer education has been established and programs developed for literacy, who will provide the instruction? Currently, the credentials required for instructors in this area vary greatly from state to state. There is a definite lack of knowledgeable personnel because of the speed at which school systems have attempted to implement computer training programs. In no other area of education would a learning environment be permitted in which students can quickly become more knowledgeable than the teacher.

The Human Touch

Naisbitt (1984) cautions that in order for "high tech" to be successful there also must be a counterbalancing human response, or "high touch." Training programs must take into account the fact that some students are "computer phobic" and they should be introduced in as sensitive and supportive an environment as possible. Once they are in place, students should not be required to spend extensive periods of time working at computers; opportunities for human interaction should also be provided. Caution should likewise be used in emphasizing computer versions of academic lessons in contrast to "real" ones. Although children enjoy computer-simulated activities, the act of examining the physical properties of materials, planning the activities, and observing the consequences of mistakes are all important parts of learning and should not be compromised because a program "demonstrates the principle graphically."

Ethical Concerns

While computers can provide vast potential for the enrichment of our lives, they also create the opportunity for users to abuse their power. The issue of computer ethics has been given little attention with the exception of software piracy, which causes great concern for software publishers. When their crime is against a multinational bank or the federal government, the media portray computer criminals as Robin Hood characters. When caught, these thieves are sometimes allowed to make restitution by aiding the organization in developing better security systems for their computer. One such criminal turned his capture into a highly lucrative consulting business.

While students may agree in the abstract that ethical standards are important, they often compromise personal integrity in order to expediently reach their goals. Resistance will be encountered if attempts are made to provide formal instruction in the area of ethics. Ethics should be taught, but not necessarily by instruction. While the most effective way teachers impart ethics is through their status role models, discussion of "professional problems" at higher levels is recommended.

Hannah and Matus (1984) advocate the formal instruction of computer ethics through the use of critical incidents or dilemmas. By providing students with a brief story about children faced with an ethical decision teachers can encourage students to examine their beliefs and consider possible consequences of their actions. The teacher's goal is to facilitate the development of personal responsibility without forcing socially acceptable standards upon the students.

Equity Issues

As computers become more useful for instructional purposes and computer literacy becomes an important skill for the job market, concern about equity issues will grow. The results of the Market Data Retrieval (1985) study found that the average number of computers per public school building was 8.2. For affluent schools the number was 10.6, and for schools with a large percentage of poor students, which often contain a high proportion of minority students, there were 6.8. The number of computers per school not only reflect inequality, but the use of the computers also reflects differential treatment. Since computers in poorer districts are usually paid for with Chapter I funds, they must be used only for remediation (Microgram, 1984). Therefore they cannot be used to provide children with the opportunity for advanced applications, for the development of higher-order thinking skills, or for creative activities. Studies of computer inequality are prominent in the literature and indicate that the gap between the rich and the poor is widening (Lipkin, 1984). Although support from the national level is doubtful, Lipkin (1984) is hopeful that state-level computer equity programs promoting equal access for the disadvantaged will continue to grow in numbers and gain emphasis nationwide. If diverse cultural groups who suffer from inequality and educational discrimination are provided with equal access to high-quality instructional technology, these injustices may be reduced (Dede, 1981).

Innovative programs at the local level are providing some large-scale solutions to computer inequity. Houston Independent School District has almost 20 projects designed to promote equal computer access. The numerous programs include disadvantaged parent/child after-school computer training, sales of discounted computers, a software lending library, an English-as-a-second-language computer project, computer camps, and business–school partnerships. In order to bring computers to children who might never have the opportunity to work with the machines, Playing to Win was established in New York City's Spanish Harlem. This nonprofit foundation is funded by private donations and gives over 700 children per week the opportunity to work with computers under direct supervision (Reinhold, 1985).

Gender Issues

Equity is not only an issue in relation to economic and racial concerns. Even when computers are available in their schools, girls suffer from the same level of inequality as the disadvantaged, but for different reasons. Fisher (1984) noted three reasons why girls are less inclined and less willing than boys to become involved with computers: software bias in the form of male-oriented themes; social bias on the part of parents, teachers, and peers that computer use is a male activity; and the content and structure of male biased programming languages that are used in introductory computer classes. Attempts have been made to develop female-oriented software, but Brady and Slesnick (1985) find that "fluffware" does little to improve the attraction for girls and in some cases reinforces sexual stereotypes. The authors recommend sex-neutral software that provides girls the opportunity to explore different modules that may be of particular interest. In order to address the social biases against girls taking part in computer activities, exposure to successful female role models and career information can increase motivation in this nontraditional area. In order to address girls' negative reaction to traditional programming languages such as BASIC and COBOL, Fisher, (1984) recommends the use of secondary languages that create a high level of interest by means of well-developed graphics (LOGO) and language capability (PILOT). It would be counterproductive to make computers more feminine, but through equal access and exposure to the potential benefits increased involvement can be facilitated.

Resources for the Handicapped

The students who will ultimately gain the most from the computer explosion are the handicapped. Computers can enhance handicapped children's sense of control while promoting their autonomous interaction with people and things that make up the world. If a child is only able to blink an eye, computer controls to achieve functional and communication goals are possible that would never be achieved through traditional means. One particularly innovative application of computer technology is the development of a system that provides an entire scope and sequence of geometry curriculum for the blind (Schweikhardt, 1985). By providing a tactile "screen" composed of thousands of pins, the child can feel the material that is normally provided visually. Computers have provided the means for parapalegics to "walk," by using computer-controlled muscle-stimulating devices; or the deaf to "hear," by digitizing sound and converting it to text on the computer screen; and for learning-disabled students to learn "regular" curriculum through alternative methods of instruction.

Since school systems rarely have the resources necessary to find, purchase, and implement computer systems for handicapped children, many of the state-of-the-art systems are never provided to those children who could most benefit. Even when economic resources are provided, appropriate personnel are often unable to keep abreast of the numerous developments in the field necessary to obtain the most appropriate system for a child in need. An extensive project has been sponsored by the U.S. Department of Education to provide interested educators and software developers with a forum to support both groups. LINC Resources and the Special Education Software Center provide persons in the field with a source of computer products that can be obtained through an 800 number service, in published form, or via a nationwide computer database. Developers are provided feedback about their products and are given marketing advice (LINC Notes, 1986).

SUMMARY

The many facets of computers and children's learning have just begun to be evaluated in a systematic manner. In order to provide direction for future applications, continued evaluation must be a priority. Assumptions about the effectiveness of computers have yet to be proven, but preliminary results indicate that computers can be the means of providing for students who have not responded to traditional instruction methods. At the elementary level children can benefit substantially from CAI. Although positive effects in the areas of reading and language arts are marginal at the present level of technological development, as the field evolves out of its infancy, the number of substantiated areas of benefit will continue to rise.

Research on motivational variables, cognitive styles, and developmental levels has not provided the direction necessary to develop quality software on a large scale. In order to create systems that have utility in education, software houses cannot function in isolation from those who use their software. The potential exists for the programs to measure their own effectiveness. To achieve such an end the various noncurricular factors can be operationalized and then systematically varied to assess the influence of each in relation to learning rate, recall, and application. The major obstacle to such applied research is determining how to transfer a specific theoretical orientation into specific computer activities. This provides a significant challenge to developers because of the complex nature of factors such as motivation. By pursuing this method our ability to control such factors should improve considerably (Lepper, 1985).

Unsubstantiated claims that the computer will invade our privacy and reduce the "personal touch" from our relationships are countered by those who note all the benefits that can be gained through computer technology. Higher productivity, extended leisure time, and the reduction of mundane and clerical tasks have all been noted as potential benefits of computers. New computer technology, such as video disk systems, will be available for application in educational settings and will greatly expand the scope of educational activities for children. While this "revolutionary" equipment is being tested in the classroom, our present form of technology will be expanded in areas of proven effectiveness based on proven methods of implementation. The cycle will surely continue through generations of technological developments.

The computer is an excellent tool that can be utilized to maximize the potential of every human being. If viewed through the eyes of science fiction writers, the beginning of the computer age is the preface to the decline of mankind. Much of the attraction toward these tales derives from the naivete of the public. Weizenbaum (1976) indicated that we attribute far too much power to the computer and that it does not deserve its esteem and reverence. The only way to demystify this powerful force is through greater understanding of its true strengths and weaknesses, and schools should be at the forefront of this enlightenment effort.

Computers will not cure all of the ills of our society or the educational system. In fact, it has the potential to produce negative consequences. If the promise of computers to education is to be realized, a number of critical issues must be addressed: (a) School programs must be based on research that demonstrates their effectiveness in application; (b) awareness of ethical and moral issues should be a priority for computer educators; (c) involvement of disadvantaged students with computers must be prioritized; (d) efforts must be made to develop programs to facilitate the involvement of girls with computers; and (e) resources and personnel to implement computer applications for the handicapped must be made available to all educators.

REFERENCES

Bitter, G., & Watson, N. R. (1983). *The apple logo primer.* Reston, VA: Reston.

Brady, H., & Slesnick, T. (1985). Girls don't like fluffware either, *Classroom Computer Learning, 5*(8), 22–26.

Clements, D. H. (1985). *Computers in early and primary education.* Englewood Cliffs, NJ: Prentice-Hall.

CCC MICROHOST Instructional System. [Computer program]. Palo Alto: Computer Curriculum Corporation. (1986). Author.

Dede, C. (1981). Educational, social and ethical implications of technological innovations. *Programmed Training and Educational Technology, 18*(4), 211.

Fisher, G. (1984). Access to computers. *The Computing Teacher, 11*(8), 24–27.

Hannah, L. S., & Matus, C. B. (1984). A question of ethics. *The Computing Teacher, 12*(1), 11-14.

Hawkridge, D. (1983). *New information technology in education.* Baltimore: John Hopkins University Press.

Hyson, M. C. (1985). The computer as an elicitor of emotion in young children. In K. Duncan and D. Harris (Eds.), *Proceedings of the World Conference on Computers in Education* (p. 105). North-Holland: Elsevier Science Publishers B.V.

Hyson, M. C., & Morris, S. K. (1985, July 19). *The effects of direct experience on children's concepts and attitudes concerning computers.* Paper presented at the World Conference on Computers in Education, Norfolk, VA.

Jarrett, D. (1980). *The good computing book for children.* London: EEC Publications.

Kulik, J. A., Bangert, R. L., & Williams, G. W. (1983). Effects of computer-based teaching on secondary school students. *Journal of Educational Psychology, 75*(1), 19–26.

Lepper, M. R. (1985). Microcomputers in education: Motivational and social issues. *American Psychologist, 40*(1), 1–18.

LINC Notes. (1986). Columbus, OH: LINC Resources.

Lipkin, J. (1984). Computer equity and computer educators (you). *The Computing Teacher, 11*(8), 19–21.

Maddux, C. D. (1986). Microcomputers in education and counseling: Problems and cautions. *Techniques: A Journal for Remedial Education and Counseling, 2*(1), 9–14.

Malone, T. (1980). What makes things fun to learn? A study of intrinsically motivating computer games. Palo Alto, CA: Xerox Palo Alto Research Center.

Moursund, D. (1984). The two percent solution. *The Computing Teacher, 11*(7), 3–5.

Naisbitt, J. (1984). *Megatrends: Ten directions transforming our lives.* New York: Warner Books.

Papert, S. (1980). *Mindstorms: Children, computers, and powerful ideas.* New York: Basic Books.

Piaget, J., & Inhelder, B. (1969). *The psychology of the child.* New York: Basic Books.

Pogrow, S. (1986, January). Getting the most from computers. *Principal,* pp. 14–19.

Pulos, S., & Fisher, S. (1986, January). Why kids aren't crazy about computers. *Principal,* pp. 26–27.

Raising the stakes for educational opportunity. (1984, August–September). *Microgram Newsletter,* pp. 1–2. Walter Mill, NY: Educational Products Information Exchange.

Reinhold, F. (1985). Sorting out the equity issues. *Electronic Learning, 4*(5), 33–37.

Roblyer, M. D. (1985). *Measuring the impact of computers on instruction: A nontechnical review of research for educators.* Washington, DC: Association for Educational Data Systems.

Scarola, R. (1984). Learning software. In S. Brand (Ed.), *The whole earth software catalog,* 174–191. Garden City, NY: Quantum.

Schweikhardt, W. (1985, July 20). *Teaching the blind to read tactile graphics.* Paper presented at the World Conference on Computers in Education, Norfolk, VA.

Toffler, A. (1980). *The third wave.* New York: Bantam.

U.S. Department of Commerce. (1985). *1985 U.S. Industrial Outlook* (26th ed.). Washington, DC: U.S. Government Printing Office.

Update on the school market for microcomputers. (1985). Westport, CT: Market Data Retrieval, Inc.

Weiss, D. J. (1985). Adaptive testing by computer. *Journal of Consulting and Clinical Psychology, 53,* 774–789.

Weizenbaum, J. (1976). *Computer power and human reason: From judgement to calculation.* San Francisco: Freeman.

BIBLIOGRAPHY: PROFESSIONALS

Budoff, M., Thormann, J., & Gras, A. (1984). *Microcomputers in special education.* Cambridge: Brookline.
Provides an in-depth introduction to computers for the educator who has already developed some understanding of basic concepts. Comprehensive descriptions of the internal processing of the computer are given along with comparisons of widely used languages, but always at a level the novice can comprehend.

Callison, W. L. (1985). *Using computers in the classroom.* Englewood Cliffs, NJ: Prentice-Hall.
Provides an excellent overview to the area of educational computing and computers in general. Written for the teacher and administrator, Callison covers all the major areas of computer use for schoolchildren, including the handicapped, along with discussion of administrative applications. An extensive list of resources is provided for the various applications.

Clements, D. H. (1985). *Computers in early and primary education.* Englewood Cliffs, NJ: Prentice-Hall.
Provides a practical approach to computers for those concerned with the education of children from preschool through third grade. Through the use of examples, photos, and computer-generated figures the reader is able to get a good feel for what actually happens between a young child and a computer. LOGO and other popular early learning programs are covered in detail.

International Council for Computers in Education. *Computing Teacher Journal,* University of Oregon, Eugene, OR 97402.
Published nine times annually. Authoritative source for information on the instructional use of computes at the precollege level. Provides overview articles and reviews of current research on computer-related topics and provides practical ideas for the implementation of computer programs.

LINC Resources, Inc., 3857 North High St., Columbus, OH 43219. The Special Education Software Center, Building B. Room S312, 333 Ravenswood Av., Menlo Park, CA 94025. Free search service: Voice, 800-327-5892; Online, 800-435-7639 (Type "HELP").
Provides free assistance to the educator attempting to find computer materials for the handicapped. Also acts as a free consultant to software developers to assist in product design and marketing efforts.

BIBLIOGRAPHY: PARENTS

Brand, S. (Ed.). (1986). *Whole earth software catalog.* Garden City, NY: Quantum.
Updated regularly. An invaluable source of information on the variety of possible applications of computers. Domain editors give down-to-earth, and sometimes multiple perspectives on software. Emphasis is placed on providing sample screen displays, many of which are in color. Domain headings range from "Playing" to "Managing" and almost everything in between. This publication gives the reader the feeling of being an industry "insider." Excellent money-savings tips are provided for those interested in hardware or software.

Popular computing, P.O. Box 307, Martinsville, NJ 08836.
Twelve issues per year. Generally accepted as one of the best general computer magazines. Covers a wide range of computer applications for both home and business. A good source for beginners to become familiar with the various products and applications.

Family computing. Scholastic, Inc., P.O. Box 2512, Boulder, CO.
Twelve issues per year. Once a computer is purchased for home use it is difficult to determine what to do with it. This magazine provides numerous activities for home application such as games, cooking, finance, and correspondence.

Children and Corporal Punishment

Ron Edwards
University of Southern Mississippi

Jean Edwards
Mississippi State Department of Education

BACKGROUND

> Fear of punishment has always been the great weapon of the teacher . . . The subject is so familiar that nothing more need be said about it.
>
> William James, 1892

Despite the conclusion reached by James, issues involving the ethics, morality, legality, and efficacy of corporal punishment (CP) remain controversial. While these issues are debated, children across the nation are subjected to CP in various forms and degrees of severity. Estimates from various sources suggest that there are 2 million to 3 million incidents of CP annually in U.S. homes and schools involving hundreds of thousands of nonhandicapped and handicapped children.

Inherent in any discussion of CP is the need for a clear definition. In the absence of a widely recognized definition, reference to CP in the following discussion will mean *the intentional infliction of physical pain by parents or school personnel as punishment for children.*

Historically, CP in the United States was practiced well before the founding of the nation, dating back to the colonial period, during which children were viewed as "young vipers" who must have the devil beaten out of them. As early as 1645, rules were established to extend parental "rod-enforced training" of children in the home to the schools "in loco parentis" (Piele, 1979). Three centuries later, the United States Supreme Court legally sanctioned the use of CP, singling out schools as the only public institution allowed to administer it (*Ingraham v. Wright,* 1977).

Currently, 29 states authorize CP in the schools, including two states that disallow individual school boards from prohibiting the practice of CP. Only eight states have eliminated the use of CP in the schools, and the remaining 13 states do not address the issue. Internationally, the United States and Great Britain are the only developed, English-speaking countries sanctioning CP (Lodholz, Hyman, Knoff, Townsend, & Zins, 1986).

National surveys and Gallup polls have consistently found that over 50% of all teachers, parents, and administrators favor the reasonable use of CP (Bryant, 1978). However, *reasonable* is subject to different interpretations. There is evidence to suggest that CP is often administered in a haphazard and discriminatory fashion (Hyman & McDowell, 1977). Clark, Erdlin, and Hyman (1984) found that specific guidelines for the use of CP are seldom followed and that punishment is frequently disproportionate to the severity of the infraction.

The most frequent recipients of CP are students with emotional or behavioral problems, as well as black, Hispanic, and lower socioeconomic status (SES) white students (Hyman & McDowell, 1977). Check (1979) found that CP is used more frequently (a) in public schools, (b) by teachers with less education and experience, (c) by middle school teachers, (d) by male teachers, and (e) by teachers in schools with high percentages of lower SES and/or black students.

There is also evidence to suggest that users of CP display negative personality characteristics. Rust and Kinnard (1983) correlated educators' personality variables with their use of CP and found that heavy users of CP tended to be relatively inexperienced, closed-minded, neurotic, and impulsive compared to teachers who did not use CP. Farley (1983) reported that the use of CP often reflects symptoms of frustration, lack of knowledge about effective alternatives, and a generally punitive atmosphere.

Given the lack of evidence for the effectiveness of CP and the numerous problems believed to be associated with its use, why does CP continue to be such a popular method of classroom discipline? CP is attractive to school personnel because it is easy to use, requires little training and no expensive equipment, and can be applied by anyone in any setting (Bongiovanni, 1979; Smith, Polloway, & West, 1979).

Users of CP may find themselves trapped in the CP cycle. The administration of CP is likely to be followed by reduction of emotional tension in the punisher; the immediate, though temporary, cessation of the punished behavior; and the approval of colleagues (Rose, 1981; Sulzer-Azaroff & Mayer, 1986). These sources of reinforcement maintain the use of CP and decrease the likelihood that alternative methods of discipline will be considered.

Attitudes of school personnel, parents, and students regarding the use of CP also help to maintain its use. CP is steeped in religious connotations as reflected in the biblical admonition that "to spare the rod is to spoil the child." Proponents of CP believe that it is the only form of discipline that some children understand (Bongiovanni, 1979). Clarizio (1975) identified three myths surrounding the use of CP, namely that (a) physical punishment helps to develop in a child a sense of personal responsibility, thrift, learning, self-discipline, and character; (b) occasional paddling contributes substantially to the child's socialization; and (c) corporal punishment is the only resource for maintaining order. School personnel suggest that the threat of CP offers teachers a necessary means of self-protection and that CP is used only as a last resort justified within the concept of in loco parentis (Hyman, Bongiovanni, Friedman, & McDowell, 1977). The National Education Association (1972) reported that students prefer CP because (a) it is an easy way out, (b) it does not require much time or any real change in behavior, (c) it presents opportunities to demonstrate toughness and endurance, and (d) it provides relief for students who feel guilty about their offenses.

Despite the popularity of CP among many children, parents, and school personnel, opposition to its use is increasing. Opponents of CP argue that it is ineffective, has undesirable side effects, and is inhumane, and that better alternatives are available. Ideally, support or opposition to the use of CP should be based on scientific evidence. Unfortunately, sound empirical evidence of the effects of CP is not available. In the absence of such evidence, positions regarding the use of CP must be based on theoretical considerations and generalizations from related areas.

Many opponents indicate that CP is associated with a variety of negative side effects on children and schooling. Among these are (a) failure to decrease punished behaviors, (b) unintentional punishment of appropriate behaviors, (c) failure to teach appropriate behaviors, (d) promotion of retaliatory aggressive reactions, (e) reinforcement of avoidance behaviors such as truancy, dropping out, and withdrawal, (f) modeling of ineffective problem-solving strategies, (g) promotion of behaviors inconsistent with the values of schools and society, (h) elevation of teacher and student anxiety, (i) discouragement of attempts to develop more positive forms of discipline, and (j) in general, creation of a punitive learning environment for teachers and students (Bellak & Antell, 1979; Bongiovanni, 1979; Farley, 1983; Hyman & McDowell, 1977; Hyman & Wise, 1979). For these reasons, numerous advocacy, professional, and legal groups have adopted resolutions opposing CP.

DEVELOPMENT

As with other aspects of CP, developmental considerations must be largely speculative owing to the absence of empirical information. There is some evidence that CP is used more frequently with younger children and that its use in the schools peaks in the middle school years and decreases thereafter. The effectiveness of CP and its presumed side effects may be positively related to the aversiveness of the act and negatively related to age. Because the physical pain associated with CP is likely to be much greater for younger children, it should suppress behavior more effectively. At the same time, the increased aversiveness would be expected to result in stronger and more frequent occurrences of negative side effects. As children reach middle school age, their desire to please adults and to avoid their disapproval begins to be replaced by a desire to please their peers. For many older children evidence of defiance of parental or school authority and demonstrations of their ability to experience CP without crying are sources of peer approval. Such peer reinforcement would be expected to reduce the aversiveness of CP and result in decreased effectiveness as well as decreased side effects.

PUTTING CORPORAL PUNISHMENT IN PERSPECTIVE

In behavior theory, *punishment* is defined in terms of its observed effects on behavior (Azrin & Holz, 1966; Bongiovanni, 1979; Kazdin, 1980). When any behavior is followed by events that result in subsequent reduction in the frequency of such behavior, punishment is said to have occurred. When any behavior is followed by events that fail to reduce the frequency of such behavior, punishment has not occurred. It is important to emphasize that punishment is defined solely in terms of its behavioral effects. Whether an event is thought to be punishing or intended to be punishing by the persons controlling the event is irrelevant.

Most often the term punishment is used to refer to the introduction of an aversive event following the occurrence of some undesirable behavior (Azrin & Holz, 1966). CP would normally be included in this category, as paddling is generally considered to be an aversive event. How can one know whether an event is really aversive? One must observe the effects of the event on behavior. If CP is introduced following some behavior and a decrease in the frequency of that behavior is observed, then CP can be judged to have been an aversive event and the procedure a punishment.

Must the consequences of a given behavior then be administered blindly in a trial-and-error fashion? The answer must be yes and no. Certainly an educated guess can be made as to the probable punishing nature of a consequence and many times be correct. On the other hand, the effects of an attempted punishment must be expected to vary across different children and even across time and situations for the same individual. So, although consequences can be selected based on expectations of their effects, final categorization as punishers must follow observation of the effects on individual children at a particular time and in a particular situation and such effects must be continually monitored to detect changes in their effects with the passage of time and as the situation changes. Whether CP meets the psychological criterion of punishment thus depends on empirical observation of its behavioral effects. As discussed previously, such empirical evidence of the effects of CP does not exist. Behavioral theory may still influence predictions of the effectiveness of CP by identifying variables that have been found in laboratory investigations to influence the effects of punishment.

One important variable influencing punishment effectiveness is the intensity of the punishing event: In general, effectiveness increases as the intensity or severity of the punishing event increases (Johnston, 1972). In fact, in some situations, mild punishment has been shown to be less effective than no punishment at all. How severe or intense is paddling? Obviously, the severity of paddling will vary by punisher. Some school personnel will deliver more severe paddlings than will others. Most school personnel, thankfully, will be oriented toward minimizing rather than maximizing the severity of punishment because of concerns related to the long-term effects on the child and to possible legal consequences if punishment is too severe. Perhaps more importantly, the severity of punishment will vary across individual children.

The novelty of attempted punishment also will influence its effectiveness. CP is likely to be more effective with children who have rarely experienced it; its effectiveness can be expected to decrease with repeated use. As noted earlier, certain children tend to repeatedly receive CP both at home and in school; especially for such children its effectiveness can be expected to decrease over time. By the same token CP can be expected to be most effective with children who are rarely spanked at home or at school, but such children are the least likely to receive CP.

A third factor influencing the effectiveness of a proposed punishment is its immediacy following undesirable behavior. The less time that elapses between the occurrence of an undesirable behavior and the administration of punishment, the more effective punishment will be (Krumboltz & Krumboltz, 1972). But it is nearly impossible in the school situation to deliver CP soon after the undesirable behavior. Considerations such as minimizing instructional interruptions and ensuring due process procedures result in inevitable delays in the administration of CP.

A fourth factor influencing the effectiveness of a possible punishment is the availability of alternative behaviors that bring about reinforcing consequences that are similar to those associated with the punished behavior (Rose, 1981). While not all are known, several likely sources of reinforcement of undesirable behavior in children can be identified. Among the most likely are teacher attention, peer attention, and relief of frustration associated with academic failure. Unfortunately, children who are frequent recipients of CP often are children who have learned to obtain reinforcement from inappropriate behaviors rather than from acceptable alternative behaviors.

Consistency in the occurrence of punishment following specific behaviors tends to increase the effectiveness of punishment (Azrin, Holz, & Hake, 1963). To ensure such consistency in a school would require continuous surveillance of children's behavior and certainly detract from instruction. Even if a school tried to accomplish this objective it is highly unlikely that every instance of a specific undesirable behavior could be detected. Additionally, there are few behaviors which school personnel would agree should always be followed by punishment. In most cases, punishment depends on extreme examples, or on repeated occurrences, of certain behaviors. The result is that many instances of specific behaviors and many occurrences of highly similar behaviors go unpunished.

The presence or absence of stimuli reliably associated with the occurrence of punishment is a sixth factor influencing its effectiveness. With respect to CP in the schools, reliable associations between antecedent stimuli and the administration of CP are generally lacking. Whether a given behavior will be followed by CP may depend on whether the principal is present on a given day, whether the principal is involved in other activities, whether the teacher is feeling well, whether the rest of the class is well-behaved or disruptive, and many other unpredictable circumstances.

ALTERNATIVE ACTIONS

Many alternatives that are more constructive than CP are available to reduce undesirable behavior in children (Sulzer-Azaroff & Mayer, 1986). Child advocates need to encourage more frequent use of constructive methods of discipline as alternatives to CP. School personnel should be in the forefront of this effort and should direct their attention to four avenues of influence each of which should be addressed at a national level by groups of parents, educators, and psychologists and at a local level by individuals.

First, a clear position encouraging the use of alternatives to CP needs to be taken. Child advocate groups need to work collectively to promote laws and regulations at both the federal and state levels restricting or eliminating the use of CP in our schools. Individuals should take advantage of every opportunity they have to make their personal and professional opinions known to the parents and school personnel with whom they work. If every individual were able to persuade two or three parents, teachers, or principals to join in opposition to CP, the collective effect would be tremendous.

A second avenue of influence is the promotion of critically needed research on the effects of CP. Professional educational and psychological associations can advocate and provide financial support for research on CP. Individuals can promote the collection of data in their local systems relative to the incidence of CP and the frequency of behaviors that CP is intended to reduce. Such data, when assessed by quasi-experimental techniques, can yield valuable information. Additionally, individuals can advocate experimental studies of the effects of CP at the local level.

Educational efforts represent a third avenue of influence that can be pursued collectively and individually. National actions might include media presentations, papers at national meetings of educational associations and PTAs, and articles in the popular media. At the local level, in-service programs for parents, teachers, and principals can be offered and when opportunities arise to appear on local TV and radio shows or to submit or contribute to articles in local newspapers, they should be actively pursued.

The final, and perhaps most important, avenue of influence is the promotion of more acceptable forms of behavior control in homes and schools. The alternative disciplinary techniques to be considered can be grouped into two broad categories: (a) alternative punishment techniques (e.g., response cost, overcorrection, timeout, etc.), and (b) techniques based on positive reinforcement for appropriate behaviors (e.g., reinforcement of incompatible alternative behaviors, differential reinforcement of lower rates of maladaptive behaviors, differential reinforcement of the omission of behaviors, etc.). Description of such constructive alternatives to CP is beyond the scope of this chapter; further information can be obtained from the sources presented in the annotated bibliography. At the national level, such promotion would again take the form of educational efforts by promoting the widespread distribution, in both professional and popular media, of information pertaining to more acceptable forms of discipline. Individuals, in addition to local educational efforts, can become involved in direct service activities in which alternative means of behavior control are substituted for CP. Programs for individual children, classrooms, and entire schools can be designed, implemented and evaluated.

SUMMARY

Considering the frequency with which CP is used in our nation's homes and schools, parents and educators are certain to be presented with opportunities to influence its use. A responsible position regarding the use of CP must involve educating parents, school personnel, and the general public with respect to (a) the absence of empirical information supporting the effectiveness of CP, (b) the potentially damaging side effects of CP, and (c) the availability of more desirable methods for disciplining children. Concerted efforts by parents and school personnel, individually and collectively, to discourage the use of CP and promote more positive behavioral control procedures may eventually result in the disappearance of physical punishment from our homes and schools.

REFERENCES

Azrin, N. H., & Holz, W. C. (1966). Punishment. In W. A. Honig (Ed.), *Operant behavior: Areas of research and application* (pp. 380–447). New York: Appleton.

Azrin, N. H., Holz, W. C., & Hake, D. F. (1963). Fixed-ratio punishment. *Journal of Experimental Analysis of Behavior, 6,* 141–148.

Bellak, L., & Antell, M. (1979). An intercultural study of aggressive behaviors on children's playgrounds. In I. Hyman & J. Wise (Eds.), *Corporal punishment in American education* (pp. 143–153). Philadelphia: Temple University Press.

Bongiovanni, A. F. (1979). An analysis of research on punishment and its relation to the use of corporal punishment in the schools. In I. A. Hyman & J. H. Wise (Eds.), *Corporal punishment in American education* (pp. 351–372). Philadelphia: Temple University Press.

Bryant, J. A. (1978). An analysis of the perceived attitudes and behavioral responses of disciplinarians and their use of selected punishing stimulus (Doctoral dissertation, Georgia State University, 1977). *Dissertation Abstracts International, 38,* 6424A–6425A. (University Microfilms No. 78-4944, 174.

Check, J. F. (1979). Classroom discipline — Where are we now? *Education, 100*(2), 134–137.

Clarizio, H. (1975). *Some myths regarding the use of corporal punishment in the schools.* Paper presented at the annual meeting of the American Educational Research Association.

Clark, J., Erdlin, R. J., Jr., & Hyman, I. (1984, April). *Analysis of recent corporal punishment cases reported in national newspapers.* Paper presented at the annual meeting of the National Association of School Psychologists, Philadelphia.

Farley, A. (1983). National survey of the use and non-use of corporal punishment as a disciplinary technique with the United States public schools (Doctoral dissertation, Temple University, 1983). *Dissertation Abstracts International, 44,* 1385A.

Hyman, I. A., Bongiovanni, A., Friedman, R. H., & McDowell, E. (1977). Paddling, punishing, and force: Where do we go from here? *Children Today, 6,* 17–23.

Hyman, I., & McDowell, E. (1977, March). *The social costs of the maltreatment of children in the schools: Mental health considerations.* Paper presented at the conference on the Social Costs of Maltreatment of Children sponsored by the Protective Service Resource Institute, Rutgers Medical School, New Brunswick, NJ.

Hyman, I., & Wise, J. (Eds.). (1979). *Corporal punishment in American education: Readings in history and practice.* Philadelphia: Temple University Press.

Ingraham v. Wright, 430 U.S. 651 (1977).

Johnston, J. M. (1972). Punishment of human behavior. *American Psychologist, 27,* 1033–1054.

Kazdin, A. E. (1980). *Behavior modification in applied settings* (2nd ed.). Homewood, IL: Dorsey.

Krumboltz, J. D., & Krumboltz, H. B. (1972). *Changing children's behavior.* Englewood Cliffs, NJ: Prentice-Hall.

Lodholz, K., Hyman, I., Knoff, H., Townsend, R., & Zins, J. (1986, April). *Supporting paper of corporal punishment position statement.* Paper presented at the Delegate Assembly of the National Association of School Psychologists, Hollywood, FL.

National Education Association. (1972). *Report on the task force on corporal punishment* Washington, DC: Author. (ERIC Document Reproduction Service No. ED 070 173)

Piele, P. K. (1979). Neither corporal punishment cruel nor due process due: The United States Supreme Court's decision in Ingraham v. Wright. In I. A. Hyman & J. H. Wise (Eds.), *Corporal punishment in American education* (pp. 91–106). Philadelphia: Temple University Press.

Rose, T. L. (1981). The corporal punishment cycle: A behavioral analysis of the maintenance of corporal punishment in the schools. *Education and Treatment of Children, 4,* 157–169.

Rust, O. J., & Kinnard, K. Q. (1983). Personality characteristics of the users of corporal punishment in the schools. *Journal of School Psychology, 21,* 91–105.

Smith, J. D., Polloway, E. A., & West, G. K. (1979). Corporal punishment and its implications for exceptional children. *Exceptional Children, 45,* 264–268.

Sulzer-Azaroff, B., & Mayer, G. R. (1986). *Achieving educational excellence using behavioral strategies.* New York: Holt, Rinehart, and Winston.

BIBLIOGRAPHY: PROFESSIONALS

Collins, M., & Fontenelle, D. (1982). *Changing student behaviors: A positive approach.* Cambridge, MA: Schenkman.
Provides teachers with a framework that will ensure them the right to teach and students their right to learn. Presents positive approaches to applying learning principles in the classroom so that students will learn appropriate social behaviors and academic skills.

Hyman, I., Flannagan, D., & Smith, K. (1982). *Discipline in the schools.* In C. R. Reynolds and T. B. Gutkin (Eds.), *The handbook of school psychology* (pp. 454–480). New York: Wiley.
Presents a broad overview of the major historical and contemporary issues involving discipline. Topics in the chapter range from theoretical considerations to practical applications.

Rose, T. L. (1984). Current uses of corporal punishment in American public schools. *Journal of Educational Psychology, 76,* 427–441.
Describes the uses of corporal punishment across demographic, administrative/procedural, and administrative opinion variables in U.S. public schools. Discusses research directions and instructional implications.

Sulzer-Azaroff, B., & Mayer, G. R. (1986). *Achieving educational excellence using behavioral strategies.* New York: Holt, Rinehart and Winston.
Basic learning concepts and explanations of their use are presented in terms of typical classroom and childhood situations. Rationale for using certain procedures and detailed tables provide guidelines for choosing which procedures to use for a given problem.

Walker, H. M. (1979). *The acting out child: Coping with classroom disruption.* Boston: Allyn & Bacon.
Provides materials to build skills necessary to successful application of techniques for decreasing acting-out behavior and managing the general classroom environment more effectively. The text is valuable to school administrators and professionals who serve teachers in consultative roles.

Children and Courts

Gary T. Kittrell
Lamar County Schools, Georgia

BACKGROUND

Recent years have witnessed an increase in the involvement of children in our system of law courts which have begun to provide an initial setting from which to start a plan for the remediation of several social problems involving children. These problems have included divorce and child custody issues, child neglect and abuse, and violations of juvenile law. At present, well over 1 million children are becoming involved in this legal process each year.

Divorce and Custody

Since the maintenance of divorce statistics began in 1890, there has been an increasingly accelerated number of divorces recorded in this country. The divorce rate increased more than 300% between 1890 and 1970, declining during depression years and rising higher after

World War II. In 1963, according to the U. S. Bureau of the Census statistics, 562,000 children under the age of 18 years were involved in marital breakups. And since 1970, the rate has risen significantly (Napier & Whitaker, 1978). It is currently estimated that as many as 40% of all marriages will end in divorce (Ware, 1984).

Court involvement of children during divorce proceedings frequently occurs when custody arrangements cannot be satisfactorily made between parents and attorneys. This occurs in approximately 10% of divorce cases. This type of court involvement and subsequent custodial arrangements are significantly disrupting to the children involved (Ware, 1984).

Child Abuse and Neglect

Thousands of children each year become directly involved in the court process as victims of abuse and/or neglect. This includes stressful involvement in adult criminal proceedings against perpetrators of antisocial acts, who may be their own family members. These cases frequently involve disruptive out-of-home placement for children as part of the legal protective response.

The legal concept of child abuse and neglect is wide in scope, including physical, emotional, and sexual abuse and physical and emotional neglect. These situations affect children of all ages, infants through adolescents.

Reported physical abuse cases are on an increase and are a very serious problem in that this form of abuse causes extreme emotional trauma and even life-threatening situations. Legal definitions of physical abuse are vague and vary from frequent spankings to altercations requiring hospitalization. Definitional vagueness and the fact that incidence figures are based only on legally reported incidents, which may only be a fraction of the true total, indicate that child abuse may be a more serious problem than the numbers show us. According to researchers, in 1975 there were approximately 2 million children in the United States who had encountered some sort of physical violence from members of their own family (Gelles, 1979). According to the National Center for Missing and Exploited Children, presently, 2,000–3,000 children every year are murdered and buried in "John and Jane Doe" graves; 25,000 are abducted, molested, and released; one in four females and one in ten males will be sexually exploited before they reach the age of 21 (cited in Georgia Council for Children, 1985).

Juvenile Law Violations

By far the largest direct exposure of children to the court and juvenile justice system occurs through reported violations of juvenile law. Research has shown that the numbers of children involved in law violations is significant. Surveys of high school students have shown that 95% of those questioned admitted to at least one delinquent act. Most minor and infrequent violators go unnoticed by the juvenile court. However, over 1 million children in this country are referred to juvenile courts each year (Brown, 1983).

Juvenile law violations consist of delinquent and status offenses. A delinquent act involves violations of state and federal laws and local ordinances, that if committed by an adult, would be considered a crime. A status offense involves the commission of an act, legally prohibited to juveniles, that would not be a crime if committed by an adult. Examples of status offense are running away from home, violations of probationary rules, and truancy (National Juvenile Justice Clearing House, 1982).

The legal treatment of juvenile law violators has not been consistent across states or even across counties and municipalities within the states. This has been partly due to factors such as differences in age criteria regarding the categorization of juveniles and offenses, and differences in local court procedures regarding juvenile affairs. Other factors have included the levels of training and expertise regarding juvenile law on the part of superior court judges. Many of these judges reluctantly handle juvenile cases on a part-time basis and do not always have an adequate background in children's issues.

Court Referral Process

Most states are currently reporting increases in yearly referral rates. Over 80% of all referrals involve the police. Other sources include the school systems, parents, and private citizens. Approximately 50% of all referrals are handled formally, with mandatory appearances before a judge or other court official and subsequent involvement in treatment and rehabilitation programs (Brown, 1983). Children of preschool and early elementary school age are more likely to be referred to court for issues of abuse and/or neglect. Children are usually 12 years old or older when initially involved with the court as law violators, the average age range being 13–15 years (Pabon, 1980).

The Court Process

Once a referral has been made to an initial intake officer at the court, a child may be released to parents or guardians, turned over to social service agencies, or held in detention for official court hearings, depending on case-specific information. Juveniles who require official hearings appear before a judge in the fact finding or adjudicatory stage of the court's proceeding. During hearings, children have the right to be accompanied by legal counsel, just as in adult court proceedings. Once judgments have been made, the court has a number of options. The most widely exercised option is probation. This option allows children to stay at home, to attend school, and to participate in treatment programs on an outpatient basis, in their community under the supervision of a probation officer. However, children who commit serious offenses or who are in need of more structure and attention may be sent to juvenile correctional centers, residential treatment centers, or inpatient hospitals. This amounts to approximately 5% of all referrals (Brown, 1983). The purpose of residential programs is to provide supervision 24 hours a day and treatment for serious cases. When it is deemed appropriate by program staff and the court, these children are released to a program of supervised aftercare in their local communities (Judge M. Glaze, personal communication, April 3, 1986). Additional information regarding the court process as it pertains to juvenile law violations is shown in Figure 1.

DEVELOPMENT

The numbers of children involved in our court systems and subsequent court-ordered treatment programs constitute a significant consideration for school psychologists and school personnel in general. It is important to understand the developmental dynamics associated with court involvement since school psychologists frequently come into contact with this population in special education programs and through consultations in the schools.

Unfortunately, there is no clear-cut system for categorizing characteristics of court-involved children. Very little research has been done that adequately covers this wide spectrum of behavioral considerations. However, there are a number of studies that help us identify some of the more general characteristics of this diverse population in terms of demographic variables and emotional–behavioral responses to court situations.

Demographic Variables

Numerous studies have examined the relationship between familial demographic variables, such as sex, socioeconomic status, education, and occupation, as they relate to contact with the juvenile justice system. Many of these studies are conflicting and some seen inconclusive in general. A majority of studies supported the contention that at least four times as many males as females are referred to the court. The type of referral reasons differed, males being referred for more serious law violations, such as burglary and theft, and girls being gradually referred more often for incorrigible behavior, such as running away from home, and for being victims of abuse (President's Commission, 1975). The commission reported that children brought to the court typically came from families in urban areas at the lower socioeconomic levels and families in which there is a single parent. In addition, in many of the demographic studies, family structure is reported to be one of the most critical variables in the problems presented to the court system. In particular, these studies found that a very high percentage of children came from families in which the parents were divorced. Monahan (1972) proposed that instead of supporting blanket indictments of such families, further investigation of familial characteristics was necessary. Further research indicated that divorce itself did not necessarily lead to children's problems; rather, the more critical factor is the manner in which families deal with the divorce and subsequent disrupting factors (Ferdinand, 1975).

Emotional–Behavioral Considerations

Children of early elementary school-age (6–8 years) are frequently brought to court because of custody hearings or as part of abuse and neglect cases. These children, who are deprived of one of their parents or who are experiencing other significant family dysfunction, may suffer from generalized lags in ego development, which may lead to inadequate socialization skills and interpersonal relationships later on. They may also experience significant levels of depression and have feelings of helplessness (Ware, 1984). Many children in this age group experience feelings of guilt associated with their parents' separation. Frequently, children experience significantly elevated levels of guilt and generalized anxiety when they are called on to testify against family members in the court setting.

Abused and/or neglected children in this age range frequently have significant feelings of guilt associated with the experience of being abused. They seem to feel that they are at fault for their own abuse (Jewett, 1982). Severe physical trauma and emotional trauma have been correlated with a high risk of cognitive impairment and have even been considered to be precipitating factors in the emergence of multiple personality disorders that are usually diagnosed later in life (Allison & Schwarz, 1980).

As to the behavior of abused and/or neglected children in the school, it is well to remember children of more typical experience, to a large extent, participate in learning tasks in order to please and be pleased by their "parentified" teachers (Rinsley, 1980). According to Erickson (1963), normally adjusted children are able to utilize parental relationships for the displacement of primitive wishes, fears, fantasies, and idealizations in an environment of basic trust without undue fear of rejection or punitive retaliation. These children are able to displace these projections onto teachers and other authority figures who are parent symbols away from the home. In contrast, many court-involved children have experienced a break-up in this process of establishing trust and fail to extend this outside their nuclear family, cannot appropriately parentify their teachers, and remain inflexible and excessively egocentric (Rinsley, 1980). This situation may lead to an emotional inability to attain success in school and can lead to the development of problems such as school phobia and oppositional disorders. Other behaviors in the school that are characteristic of this age group include excessive withdrawal, poor impulse control, hyperactivity, poor anger control, and difficulty in forming and maintaining appropriate interpersonal relationships.

Court-involved preadolescent children (9–12 years old) can be expected to exhibit emotional and behavioral responses that overlap with the younger age groups. However, preadolescents tend to be much more guarded in expressing feelings and disclosing emotional problems openly to others. They tend to cover up their feelings of loneliness, fear, depression, and despair because of the discomfort and embarrassment involved in self-disclosure to peers and adults, who are frequently perceived as untrustworthy. Court involvement seems to exacerbate these feelings of distrust, since openness and trust sometimes means more extensive involvement with the court system. These children frequently feel very isolated and fearful of their environment even though they attempt to cover up by "being cool."

FIGURE 1

The Juvenile Law Court Process

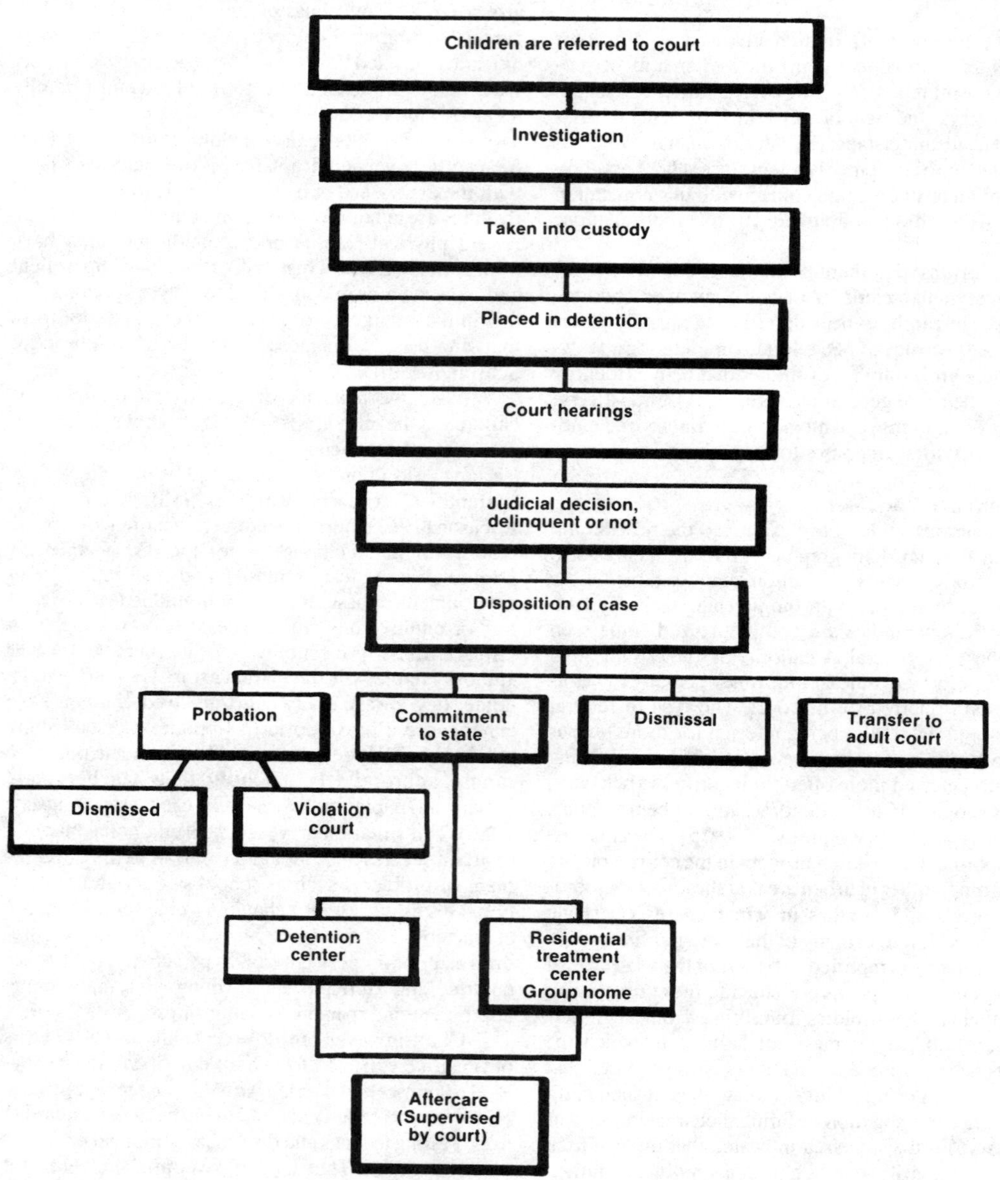

Preadolescents may feel very academically frustrated, since many of them have lacked success in school over an extended time for various reasons. These children tend to care more for the social than the academic aspects of school. However, they frequently have significant difficulty in maintaining appropriate relationships with other children and school personnel (Pogrebin, Poole & Regali, 1984).

Adolescent court-involved youths are considered to have more negative behavior characteristics than the other two groups combined. They have to deal not only with various particular emotional problems, but also with the normal turmoil experienced by adolescents going through rapid physical and emotional changes. Research indicates that adolescents with poor support systems who have previously been involved in the court system as victims of divorce, neglect, or abuse and at a high risk for continued involvement in the court system by virtue of involvement in delinquent behavior (Rinsley, 1980).

Normal adolescents experience a great deal of life stress through the developmental process. Insecurity and generalized self-doubts are frequent problems and self-esteem is very much at stake. Court involvement, frequently, does nothing to elevate self-esteem and can add to the adolescent's low self-appraisal and generalized feelings of anxiety and isolation.

Court-involved adolescents can be expected to exhibit behavior in the school that reflects an excessive level of insecurity and negativity regarding academics and interpersonal relationships with peers and teachers. Delinquent adolescents frequently have below average academic achievement levels even though many possess normal or above average ability (Millman, Shaefer & Cohen, 1982). Many court-involved adolescents are also diagnosed as learning-disabled and behavior-disordered (Fahey, 1984).

Like the preadolescent group, these youths tend to be very guarded in expressing feelings and to avoid self-disclosure. These factors, combined with low self-esteem, can cause deficits in assertiveness and other social skills. These youngsters tend to settle into negative peer groups where they are frequently more easily accepted than in the higher-achieving groups in the school. They tend to adhere to group pressure even to the extent of violating laws. It should be of interest to school psychologists that this group of court-involved youths, especially those involved in court-ordered treatment programs, tend to be very manipulative and proficient at fragmenting treatment efforts in their attempt to avoid self-disclosure (Rinsley, 1980).

In summary, as a result of dysfunctional situations in children's lives and the added stress of legal embroilment, court-involved children may suffer substantial deficits in the developmental support systems. Frequently these children do not receive the emotional support needed for them to proceed through normal psychosocial development. This frequently precipitates high levels of emotional distress and subsequent inappropriate behavior (Jewett, 1982). The court process itself may initially exacerbate this problem through the negative aspects of the labeling process and stressors involved in court-mandated changes for children. School psychologists need to be aware of these dynamics when planning intervention strategies.

PUTTING CHILDREN AND THE COURTS IN PERSPECTIVE

In order to plan for effective intervention with court-involved children, school psychologists would do well to remember that they are not dealing with a problem relating solely to the school. Court-involved children have complex systematic problems that encompass difficulties at home, at school, and in the community as well.

It is also important to realize that many of these children are already involved in mandated treatment programs involving various modalities and differing degrees of restrictive supervision. In order for psychologists to enter into a plan aimed at altering a child's maladaptive transactional patterns in the school, it is important to adopt a comprehensive perspective regarding the functional analysis of the child's social and treatment environment. Unless this is done, the psychologist may only provide a fragmented service with minimal positive results and may possibly contradict already existing services being delivered in the child's court-ordered plan of treatment and rehabilitation.

There are many important, specific considerations for school psychologists who work with this population of children. One of the most pervasive problems relating directly to the school setting is the issue of preconceived attitudes on the part of school system personnel towards working with court-involved students. As mentioned earlier, these children bring with them into school a varied assortment of academic disabilities, developmental gaps in socialization, and other negative personality characteristics. Teachers and school administrators must deal with these problems on a daily basis, many times without adequate information regarding individual cases. Certain attitudes on the part of school personnel towards court-involved and handicapped children have become generalized. Emotionally disturbed or behaviorally disordered children are seen as unmotivated to learn, unfriendly, impolite, dishonest, unhappy, aggressive, and in great need of professional help (Hannah & Pilner, 1983). Many court-involved children have specific learning disabilities and generalized cognitive deficits. The literature also reveals that teachers view these children as extremely dependent, disruptive, socially distant, academically frustrated, angry, and hostile. Strong conceptions such as these on the part of school personnel, coupled with the tendency of court-involved children to have low self-esteem and distrust of adults in positions of authority, can cause serious communications difficulty regarding educational and treatment efforts.

TABLE 1

Preferred Intervention Methods

Techniques	Delivery format	Key concepts
Behavior therapy	Individual or group	Stresses "present" behavior and learning theory; deviant behavior is seen as the result of faulty learning; focuses on overt behavior, specific treatment plans for specific behavior change, and objective evaluation of therapeutic results.
Rational–emotive therapy	Individual, group, or family counseling	An irrational belief system is regarded as the cause of emotional dysfunction; clients are "challenged" to examine the validity of their irrational beliefs; past experiences are noted, but emphasis is placed on present behavior; a very directive approach that requires normally intelligent clients.
Reality therapy	Individual or group	Helps clients determine whether they have "success" or "failure" identities; people are understood to create their feelings by their choices and behavior; clients accept responsibility for their actions; emphasis is on behavior controlling our perceptions.
Transactional analysis	Individual or family counseling	Personality is perceived to be made up of parent, adult, and child ego states; focus is on client's learning the "games" they are playing so that they can engage with others on a more intimate level; adolescents are taught to recognize ego states so that they can utilize the adult state; emphasis is on the past, and revised games, rackets, injunctions, scripting are key concepts.

ALTERNATIVE ACTIONS

Treatment issues regarding court involved children have for many years posed a complex and difficult problem, not only for school psychologists, but for the entire treatment community as well. Practitioners and researchers have confronted and frequently overwhelmed these youngsters by the various modalities used to treat, rehabilitate, remodel, "remake," or otherwise "recycle" them into normally functioning individuals. The majority of research seems to have centered on a few theoretical models that are favored over others in the treatment of this population of children.

Treatment Techniques

Preferred treatment modalities include many behavioral approaches such as token economics, response-cost contingency programs, and assertiveness training. Also included are cognitive–behavioral methods such as rational-emotive therapy and reality therapy. Transactional analysis is one of the few strictly insight-oriented approaches recommended for this population. Research has shown that client-centered approaches in general are much less effective than the more behavior-oriented and directive approaches (Corey, 1985). For more information regarding intervention strategies and their treatment goals, see Table 1. The above-mentioned intervention strategies were selected for presentation because of their demonstrated effectiveness in treating court-involved children. However, the list is not meant to be all-inclusive. It is also recommended that the reader refer to a reference source such as Gerald Corey's *Theory and Practice of Counseling and Psychotherapy* for a more comprehensive review of current treatment modalities.

Service Provision Model

Whether school psychologists are interested in becoming involved in primary prevention efforts with very young children and their families, secondary prevention involving interventions in the schools, or tertiary treatment efforts through outside referral sources, they must consider the selection of a model for the "effective" provision of treatment services. This consideration is probably more important than the selection of a treatment technique in the long run. This population of children is usually involved with many different agencies, each with its own treatment plans and individual goals. The chances of duplicating efforts or applying contradicting methods of treatment are very great.

It is clear that inconsistent, fragmented efforts on the part of several different agencies has not been a realistic or effective approach to the overall treatment of court-involved children. An alternative to this fragmented service orientation is the multiagency treatment team. This model for providing services has been adopted on a national level and implemented in most states through the state departments of human resources, youth services, and mental health, and/or family and children's services (D. Wilkinson, personal communication, April 11, 1986). It has been recommended that treatment teams be established on behalf of troubled children in each community. These teams or committees can be single- or multicounty committees, depending upon the size of the community and the geographic availability of resources. The underlying purpose for the development of such teams is to improve and to facilitate the coordination of services to troubled children and their families. Many school systems across the nation are currently actively involved in these committees. According to some administrators, school psychologists are in a good position to greatly benefit from involvement with these teams depending on their level of training and expertise in networking (J. McGavin, personal communication, April 11, 1986).

There are many different ways treatment teams can set out to achieve their basic goals. Teams are encouraged to adapt their structure so as to address the needs of their own community. See Table 2 for a list of the types of problems handled by multiagency treatment teams. As official representatives of their local agencies, team members can develop guidelines or policy on issues such as release of information, service delivery responsibilities to mutual clients, written agreements on referrals, and criteria for referral of cases to state funding sources for the purchase of outside treatment services. A major advantage to bringing staff from different agencies together is the increase in knowledge of community resources and how to use them effectively.

TABLE 2

Types of Problems Addressed in Multiagency Treatment Teams

Subject areas
Court-involved cases
Crisis intervention cases
Physical problems such as major surgery
Child abuse and neglect
Mentally handicapped issues
Vocational issues for adolescents
Alcohol and drug problems
Issues posed by runaways
Emergency shelter care
Problems of socially maladjusted children
Problems of severely emotionally disturbed children
Custody cases
Truancy
Academic assistance
School discipline
Suicide prevention
Behavior disorders
Autism
Multiproblem families

A good example of the multiagency treatment team in action was found in Clayton County, Georgia. This team incorporates the resources of the juvenile court, school system, psychoeducational center, and mental health center and hospital as well as the state division of youth services, the department of family and children's services, and other state services in an effectively combined effort at working with difficult court-involved cases (M. McDonald, personal communication, April 12, 1986).

Treatment teams take on the role of advocates on behalf of troubled children. Of course, such advocacy can and must take place in several different arenas. Local teams may need to advocate for troubled children in their communities, with their state-level counterparts, within their local, state, and national legislators and with the general public.

A substantial component of a policy of advocacy involves educating the public about the needs of court-involved children. Local teams may wish to sponsor workshops and symposiums, develop newspaper articles, and issue public service announcements.

Research indicates that successful multidisciplinary teams have mastered the art of effectively sharing information regarding clients in a format that allows for comprehensive and effective joint treatment planning and follow-up procedures (Pogrebin et al., 1984). An expansion of the roles of school psychologists to include active involvement in treatment teams might add a useful and more effective dimension to consultation services and clinical intervention with court-involved children. It is recommended that psychologists contact their local special education directors, mental health center, or department of family and children's services for more information on this topic.

SUMMARY

Children who become involved with our system of courts pose a unique and complex challenge for school psychologists on a national level. Most court-involved cases come as a result of community intervention into issues such as divorce and custody decisions, child abuse or neglect, and violations of juvenile law. Research has reflected a rapid acceleration in the numbers of these cases.

The characteristics shared by this population of children include a wide spectrum of emotional and behavioral dysfunction. These children have significant academic difficulty and frequently have difficulty forming and maintaining adequate interpersonal relationships with peers and adults as well.

In attempting to effectively deal with the problems associated with this population, school psychologists must adopt a comprehensive orientation regarding the court-involved child's emotional, social, and treatment environment.

A networking format involving the effective utilization of all parts of the treatment community has been shown to be the most effective means of organizing treatment interventions with court-involved children. This model tends to reduce the negative impact of fragmented or contradictory services and expands the role of the school psychologist in the area of treatment services in general.

REFERENCES

Allison, R., & Schwarz, T. (1980). *Minds in many pieces.* New York: Rawson & Wade.

Brown, W. (1983). *What parents should know about juvenile delinquency and juvenile justice.* York, PA: William Gladden Foundation.

Corey, G. (1985). *Theory and practice of counseling and psychotherapy.* Monterey, CA: Brooks/Cole.

Erickson, E. (1963). *Childhood and society.* New York: Norton.

Fahey, D. (1984). School counselors and psychological aspects of learning disabilities. *School Counselor, 31,* 433–440.

Ferdinand, T. (1975). Patterns and family structure of urban, village and rural delinquents. In C. Bersani. (1975). *Crimes and delinquency.* New York: Macmillan.

Gelles, R. (1979). Violence toward children in the United States. In R. Bourne & E. Newberger (Eds.), *Critical perspectives on child abuse* (pp. 53–68). Lexington, MA: Lexington Books.

Hannah, E., & Pilner, S. (1983). Teacher attitudes toward handicapped children. *School Psychology Review, 12,* 12–23.

Jewett, J. (1982). *Helping children cope with separation and loss.* Harvard, MA: Howard Common.

Millman, H., Schaefer, C., & Cohen, J. (1982). *Therapies for school behavioral problems.* San Francisco: Jossey-Bass.

Monahan, T. (1972). Family status and the delinquent child: A reappraisal and some new findings. In R. Giallombardo (Eds.), *Juvenile Delinquency: A book of readings.* New York: Wiley.

Napier, A., & Whitaker, C. (1978). *The family crucible.* New York: Harper and Row.

Pabon, E. (1980). Mental health services in the juvenile court: An overview. *Juvenile and Family Court Journal, 31,* 23–34.

Pogrebin, M., Poole, E., & Regali, R. (1984). Constructing and implementing a model juvenile diversion program. *Youth and Society, 15,* 305–324.

President's Commission on Law Enforcement and Administration of Justice. (1975). In C. Bersani (Ed.), *Crime and delinquency.* New York: Macmillan.

Rinsley, D. (1980). *Treatment of the severely disturbed adolescent.* New York: Jason Aranson.

Georgia Council for Children. (1985). Missing children discussed at annual meeting. *Newsletter of the Georgia Council of Children,* p. 2.

U. S. Bureau of the Census. (1980). *Marital Status and Living Arrangements,* Vol. 365, p. 20.

Ware, C. (1984). *Sharing parenthood after divorce: An enlightened custody guide for mothers, fathers and kids.* New York: Bantam Books.

BIBLIOGRAPHY: PROFESSIONALS

Apter, S. (1982). *Troubled children/Troubled systems.* New York: Pergamon.
System, or organizational, difficulties are examined from an ecological perspective, which views emotional disturbance as a mismatch between a child's abilities and the demands of her or his environment and not as some deficit residing in the child alone. Apter uses the ecological perspective as an organizing concept for a discussion of current problems including programming, mainstreaming, and prevention procedures employed with emotionally disturbed students.

Kanfer, F., & Goldstein, A. (1980) *Helping people change: A textbook of methods.* New York: Paragon.
Includes most of the therapeutic techniques currently in use with normal to moderately disturbed clients. A very broad range of theories and modalities are covered with very well organized and useful case examples along with practical explanations of specific intervention strategies.

Lamson, A. (1983). *Psychology of juvenile crime.* New York: Human Sciences.
Examines the causes, characteristics, and treatment of juvenile delinquency based on clinical observation, insight, and professional opinion.

Millman, H., Schaefer, C., & Cohen, J. (1982). *Therapies for school behavior problems: A handbook of practical interventions.* San Francisco: Jossey-Bass.
Offers a broad range of interventions aimed at the behavioral difficulties of school children in the school. Issues covered include truancy, disruptiveness, impulsivity, dishonesty, procrastination, prejudice, anxiety, substance abuse and others.

Rinsley, D. (1980). *Treatment of the severely disturbed adolescent.* New York: Jason Aranson.
Offers a thorough discussion of the etiology and treatment of emotional disturbance in adolescents from a psychoanalytic perspective. A very good explanation of adolescents' resistance characteristics and attempts at treatment intervention is given.

BIBLIOGRAPHY: PARENTS

Brown, W. (1983). *What parents should know about juvenile delinquency and juvenile justice.* York, PA: William Gladden Foundation.
Offers a brief, but very well organized overview of delinquency and the juvenile justice system. There is also a section of questions and answers that is very enlightening.

Francke, L. (1983). *Growing up divorced: How to help your child cope with every stage — from infancy through the teens.* New York: Fawcett Crest.
Offers a complete description of the crises facing children of divorce and focuses on relieving distress before it becomes damage. Guides the parent through the many trying stages of a child's life, from the age of helplessness through the age of false maturity.

Napier, A., & Whitaker, C. (1978). *The family crucible.* New York: Harper & Row.
An excellent presentation of family systems theory in action. It is recommended especially for those parents who are about to enter into family counseling, since it offers explanations of what underlies therapeutic encounters in a very understandable and entertaining format.

Children and Creativity

Jack H. Presbury and A. Jerry Benson
James Madison University

E. Paul Torrance
University of Georgia

BACKGROUND

What Is Creativity?

Lefrancois (1982) stated that "just as very low intelligence is stupidity, so very low creativity is ordinariness" (p. 264). This statement defines creativity about as well as any. Because there are as many definitions of creativity as there are authors who deal with the topic, the reader is referred to the following sources for more views on creativity: Gowan (1981), Guilford (1960), Koestler (1964), Kubie (1985), Osborn (1963), Torrance (1962a), Wallas (1926), Watson (1928), and Wertheimer (1945).

While most definitions focus on some internal process taking place within the creative individual (process definition), the nature of the creative product is really all we have to go on in recognizing creativity. A product or response is considered creative to the extent that appropriate observers independently agree that it is creative (Amabile, 1983, p. 31). This consensual definition of creativity (product definition) is helpful when judging a work of art, an invention, or some tangible result of the creative process. The problem, however, is that most creativity is of a more pedestrian form, small "bright ideas" that we all have and that may never result directly in a product. For this reason, highly creative individuals often go unrecognized.

If a child creates a product that surprises and delights us, then the product definition of creativity is useful. If, on the other hand, we are able to see only indications of creative ability, or the behaviors associated with thwarted creative urges, then it is necessary to rely on a process definition to understand creativity. Such a definition would attempt to explain the thinking behind creative production.

How Does Creativity Work?

The process of creative thinking is covert. We can only infer what dynamics of mind are at work during this process. One has simply to read the literature on creative behavior to discover that, regardless of the medium in which they work, people who produce creative ideas all identify an irrational component in the creative process that seems beyond their control. Ideas seem to dawn on them, to "come out of the blue." They report "just knowing" the truth and correctness of a solution. For this reason, some authors have emphasized the mysterious aspects of creativity and have suggested that only those who possess a special talent or genius will be creative (Gowan, 1981).

Other writers have suggested that creativity operates as an attendant quality of intelligence; the brighter a person is, the more creative the person is likely to be. In a classic study, Getzels and Jackson (1962) found that highly creative students were not the most "intelligent" students as measured by I.Q. tests. New research into intelligence has shown that what current tests of intelligence measure may be only a small portion of intelligence, and that many aspects have been left out, such as "tacit" intelligence (Sternberg, 1985), "metaphorical" intelligence (Gardner, 1983), and divergent thinking (Guilford, 1959). Since metaphorical and tacit intelligence, together with divergent thinking, are integral components of creative thinking, one possible explanation of the Getzels and Jackson results would be that current intelligence tests do not assess creative intelligence, but rather only conventional or academic intelligence, which is necessary but not sufficient for creative thinking.

Rather than considering the creative process to be solely an unconscious, mysterious dynamic out of the creator's control or a willful application of intelligence, it seems clear that creativity is a thought process that, depending on its goal, may employ all known aspects of intelligence. In other words, creative thinking may be a more comprehensive construct than intelligence.

The creative process begins with novel or original thinking that is *tacit* or implicit. It is unconventional and often only partially conscious, and the ideas frequently take the form of a concrete metaphor or prototype. The creative act is not complete, however, until the thinking brings about some sort of communicable product. The end phase of creativity involves more conventional, deliberate, explicit, and critical thinking, the type of intelligence labeled *convergent* by Guilford (1959).

Divergent thinking produces many ideas and varied solutions to a problem. Creative people maintain the flexibility to move between divergent and convergent thinking. Coleman (1976) calls this the fertile tension between discipline and impulse. It is the internal negotiation between what is intuitively correct and the constraint of tradition, criticism, and the intellectual marketplace. Coleman (1976) suggests that those who score higher on IQ tests than on open-ended tests are *convergers;* those who do better on open-ended tests are *divergers.* In the middle are the *all-arounders,* who can do both types of thinking. People who display high levels of creative production are probably all-arounders.

DEVELOPMENT

In the early stages of life, before children are able to frame their experiences in cause-and-effect scientific thinking, they have little trouble accepting their fantastic and fictional ideas. Fact and fantasy, dreaming and waking, wish and reality, a lie and the truth, all are without clear distinctions in the mind of a child at this stage (Werner, 1948). Children are very good at producing metaphors (Gardner, 1982). Mother's saucepan can become a hat, a hammer, or a flying object, depending on what is needed in a moment of play.

Picasso reported that when he painted, he did so with the mind of a child. It is often said that in order to begin to think creatively, one must "suspend disbelief." Children do this easily. What happens, then, to children who grow into uncreative adults?

The answer to this seems to be that as children develop, they begin to value other forms of thinking and knowing and lose touch with childlike processes. They tend to become conventional. They develop a "set" as to what things are and a "functional-fixedness" as to how things are to be used. In this process they lose the metaphorical possibilities and associations that can create new relationships. Mother's saucepan is then for cooking only.

A small child who creates charming and startling metaphors, but who does so in an attempt to describe experience, cannot rightfully be called creative. The child is unaware of the significance of such communication. Gardner (1982) has found that while young children regularly produce metaphoric speech, they cannot understand metaphors that are presented to them by others. Thus, a child who, in unconscious metaphors, describes a bald man as having a "barefoot head," or the ocean waves making ridges on the sand as "like a little girl's hair being combed" (Gardner, 1982), is likely to protest as "silly" an adult describing someone as "green with envy" or "full of himself."

During the sensorimotor stage of the years 0–2, little encouragement of an instructional nature is needed (Gardner, 1982). "The child is viewed as a seed, which though small and fragile, contains within its husk all the necessary 'germs' for eventual artistic virtuosity" (p. 208). The child will discover what is necessary for expression of her or his creative gift. According to Gardner, what is needed is love, a rich environment, and encouragement to explore. The developing child needs only to be shielded "from pernicious forces in the society so that his inborn talents can flower" (p. 208). However, recently in our culture, there has been a movement toward early instruction of children. Increasingly, parents are enrolling their preschool children and infants in these stimulation programs in order to give them competitive advantage. One developmentalist has suggested that these children develop a "robot virtuosity with little understanding and no lasting gain" (Bowen, 1986, p. 16). A major danger is the development of "conditions of worth" (Rogers, 1951) in which children come to view themselves as valuable only for what they can achieve.

Piaget (1950) described the period between 2 and 7 years as an intuitive time during which children explore various symbols and images of the world that are unsystematic and prelogical. Gardner (1982) stated that during this period specific instruction has little effect on creative production and may be counterproductive. This is a delicate time for children because, along with this natural creative tendency for exploration and experimentation, there also emerges a literal phase. One has only to watch youngsters in the first or second grade who are given the task of drawing to appreciate this. If the children are sitting together at a table, they are likely to produce drawings that are replicas of the first drawing that happens to be completed. The beginnings of an impulse toward conventional are manifested. Children tend to conform to their peers; they are strongly disposed to follow the rules exactly and tolerate no deviation. Their experimentation and novelty decrease and their drawings tend to be limited to copying forms around them (Gardner, 1982). Convention begins to eclipse invention.

Literalism is the beginning of a form of thinking that leads to science. As this type of thinking grows more mature, it eventually makes the child a better critical thinker who deals with the world in more precise ways. Before this event, however, the child remains an "incipient artist" who possesses what could be called a "first draft" notion of how symbolic representation of experience works (Gardner, 1982). At this time, a child requires more in-depth experience with any medium of expression. In the latter phases of this stage, as children give up the spontaneous production of metaphors and develop a desire to reproduce the world around them factually, direct instruction becomes useful in their strivings toward mastery. Instruction should not emphasize technique over expression, lest the need to conform become paramount.

During the next period of development, which Piaget called concrete–operational, the crisis point is reached. Between the ages of 7 and 12, the literal phase is intensified and the invitation to conform is enormous. Torrance (1967) identified what is called the "fourth-grade slump." At about this stage of education, an alarming number of children display a marked decline in their creative production. It is then that male and female roles become important, peers become significant evaluators, children are expected to behave in more adult-like ways, and the school curriculum changes.

> Curriculum content begins to emphasize the realistic and the factual. Lessons become more formal and organized. Students are invited to be critical of other people's ideas; guessing and hazarding uncommon responses are discouraged. Credit is given only for what is written down, and marks become an indicator of acceptability. . . . Children, it is thought, need to learn that the world isn't all roses, that animals don't talk, that competition is keen, and that the rewards of life go to persons who are alert, practical and realistic. (Strom & Bernard, 1982, p. 309)

Compulsive conformity is the antithesis of creative thinking. Imagination, the precondition for original thought, is often given up as a liability at this stage (Collangelo & Ziffran, 1979). Whether a child enters adolescence equipped to preserve creative thinking or experiences the virtual extinction of creativity depends on what happens in this phase.

After age 12, children move into formal operational thinking, and critical reasoning skills advance to a new level. Every parent and teacher of children this age can report that these children hate their hair, think their nose is shaped wrong, and wish they were taller, shorter, thinner, or heavier. This self-critical attitude is also applied to their creative production. Therefore, during the concrete–operational stage children should be "encouraged, gently but definitely, to take a somewhat more critical stance toward [their] work" (Gardner, 1982, p. 216). If presented with problems and various solutions and given the opportunity to practice self-evaluation and self-improvement, the child will gain "familiarity with the practice of criticism. . . . By the time he enters adolescence, criticism is already a familiar tool that he can now apply to himself as well as accept graciously" (p. 216).

At all levels of development, the locus of control and evaluation should rest with the child. To impose conventional standards upon children runs the risk of inviting them to work for the approval of others before they have learned to approve of themselves. Creative thinking proceeds from intuition to convention; it is an inside to outside process. If children are constantly adapting or accommodating to external pressures, their creative energies are used up in the task of survival.

PUTTING CHILDREN'S CREATIVITY IN PERSPECTIVE

Measurement

The empirical approaches to measurement are as varied as the definitions of the constructs that underlie them. However, a review of these definitions suggests three categories into which measurement approaches can be classified: personal characteristics; product; and process (Amabile, 1983).

Measures of *personal characteristics,* based upon the assumption that creative individuals will demonstrate similar personality traits, typically involve personality inventories or biographical inventories/case studies. Amabile (1983) noted the following techniques:

1. Creativity scales derived from personality inventories. For example — Helson's (1965) adaptation of the California Psychological Inventory, Cattell and Butcher's (1968) adaptation of the Sixteen Personality Factor Questionnaire.
2. Personality tests specifically designed to assess traits characteristic of creative individuals. For example — the How Do You Think? test (Davis & Subkoviak, 1975); the What Kind of Person Are You? test (Torrance & Khatena, 1970).
3. Biographical inventories. For example — the Alpha Biographical Inventory (Institute for Behavioral Research in Creativity, 1968); and the Biographical Inventory: Creativity (Schaefer, 1969).

The second category of measurement techniques involves analysis of the *product.* Jackson and Messick (1965), in approaching the question of exactly what judges mean when they call something "creative," suggested that judgments of creativity are composed of four aesthetic responses occurring together (Amabile, 1983): (a) Surprise is the aesthetic response to unusualness in a product, judged against norms for such products; (b) satisfaction is the response to appropriateness in a product, judged within the context of the work; (c) stimulation is the response to transformation in the product, evidence that the product breaks away from the constraints of the situation as typically conceived; and (d) savoring is the response to condensation in a product, the judged summary power or ability of the product to condense a great deal of intellectual or emotional meaning in a concise and elegant way.

The final category of measurement focuses upon the creative *process.* Behavioral assessments of the creative process might include the Unusual Use Test (Guilford, 1971), the Torrance Tests of Creative Thinking (Torrance, 1974), the Modes of Thinking in Young Children Analysis (Wallach & Kogan, 1965), and the Remote Associates Test (Mednick, 1967).

As Torrance (1979) noted, failure to accept the multivariate nature of creativity has produced needless confusion in attempts to measure the construct. We must combine tests and observations, looking for the creative nature of the process rather than the rightness or wrongness of the answer or specific traits or characteristics. For example, Hunt (1982) cites research utilizing protocol analysis of creative tasks in trying to delineate the steps of information processing involved.

Besides the formal instruments that measure creativity, many informal methods exist. Most important, however, is the attitude of the psychologist and educator, who must remain open to the possibility that any "problem" child under consideration may be suffering from lack of conventionality and that the symptoms displayed may be secondary to a divergent thinking style. A content analysis of traits listed by parents who were describing their creatively gifted children revealed the following thematic behaviors: overactive physically and/or mentally; annoying curiosity; forgetful and absent-minded; does not participate well in class; mind wanders; likes to work alone; enjoys pretending; sensitive; uncommunicative; feels left out; good in one subject, poor in others (Torrance, 1981).

Recognizing the Needs

All children have the potential for creative thinking. When they do not behave in creative ways, it is usually because they have lost touch with, or fail to honor, their intuitive and metaphorical ways of thinking. As they become more skilled at critical and conventional thought, they may grow more factual and literal in their orientation. If this shift involves a rejection of their less precise and partially formed ideas, they will have lost the wellspring of creativity.

Some children, despite enormous pressures to do otherwise, retain their creative gift and continue to be unconventional thinkers. This often puts them at odds with the belief system in which they live.

Since creative children tend to be introspective, they often fail to learn the social system in which they function. Creative children are sometimes candid to the point of lacking tact. Adults often find their behaviors to be obnoxious. These children find humor in topics generally regarded as sacrosanct and are, therefore, thought to be mocking and irreverent. They "toy" with ideas, they break rules that make no sense to them, and they challenge authority. They often become outcasts. Wellborn (1980) found that depression, delinquency, withdrawal and suicide were relatively high in creatively gifted students who were scorned and ridiculed in school. Of all school dropouts, 17% are creatively gifted (Strom & Bernard, 1982).

Examining the personality traits that creative people seem to share makes it obvious that the creative thinking process and the design of school often do not mix well. Arieti (1976) identified several characteristics of creative thinking that are problematic: (a) *Aloneness.* Creative children need to spend a great deal of time alone; our cultural emphasis on "togetherness" makes this difficult. (b) *Inactivity.* The creative process requires that one not "just do something," but rather, wait for ideas to form; inactivity is often considered laziness. (c) *Daydreaming.* Reverie or hypnogogic states seem crucial to original thinking; this is usually seen as a wasteful or unrealistic use of cognition. (d) *Free thinking.* Allowing one's mind to deal with any ideas that come to it or to go off on tangents is frowned upon as undisciplined thought; it is essential, however, for achieving new associations and combinations of elements. (e) *Gullibility.* Creative children tend to get excited about new ideas and may not initially see the drawbacks or flaws in them; this allows the ideas to develop in safety before they are criticized. Our culture tends to consider a gullible person a fool, and favors a disposition of skepticism and a critical attitude.

Because of their thinking and learning styles, creative children may be considered behavior problems by parents and teachers. Their thinking may be viewed as so strange and "spacey" as to cause concern about their emotional stability. Torrance (1963) studied teachers from several countries regarding their attitudes toward creative behaviors in their students. He found that, of 62 student behaviors listed, conforming behaviors (being courteous and obedient, handing work in on time, accepting the judgment of authorities, etc.) were most prized and creative behaviors were consistently listed as least desirable. This lack of understanding of creative thinking by teachers, plus the likelihood that they are abrasive in class, will often result in the referral of these children to a school psychologist, counselor, or other mental health specialist. At this point, it becomes crucial that these professionals be able to recognize creative children as distinct from other categories, such as learning-disabled, emotionally disturbed, lazy, and personality disordered.

ALTERNATIVE ACTIONS

Encouraging the Creative Process

It is generally believed that the creative process proceeds through the phases of *saturation, incubation, illumination,* and *verification.* For this creative process to become activated, the creative person must first experience a sense of disequilibrium. If the environment does not provide this disquieting sensation, the person will. This is why so many creative children get into trouble. Some would say they are bored. It would be more accurate to say that they are seeking creative expression. If they were merely bored, then some event that could distract or entertain them would make this sensation disappear. When the creative spark hits, it is what Hofstadter (1985) referred to as the activation of a "rut detector." In computer parlance, "the possession of this ability to *break out of loops of all sorts* seems the antithesis of the mechanical" (p. 532; emphasis in original).

Children, especially once the creative process has begun, may be "possessed" by a new idea and the need to pursue it to a conclusion. They may become so preoccupied that those around them will be worried. They may be admonished to "snap out of it," or to get their mind on the task at hand. Unfortunately, the creative preoccupation may often have nothing to do with the task at hand. This phase is known as *saturation.* The creative person is compelled by the idea and focuses total energy on it.

The next phase, *incubation,* comes when the creative thinker has exhausted all rational routes to the solution of a problem. Incubation is the unconscious process of "cooking" the ideas into a suprarational stew. During this phase, children may withdraw or appear to daydream. If they experience love and respect from others during this incubation phase of creativity, they will come to welcome such experiences. If not, this uncomfortable time will come to be regarded as an inappropriate bad mood to be gotten over as soon as possible.

Illumination can come as an instant "aha!" It can also insidiously crystallize, almost without its creator realizing it. Either way, this is the creative high — the joyful time to be savored. For many children, the creative process is short-circuited at this point. With the release of tension and the achievement of a tentative answer, many children will feel satisfied and may not have the motivation to work further on the idea. In order for creative illumination to result in creative production, children must be nudged past this sticking point and encouraged to elaborate the idea. This is where careful and skilled listening is important. It is important to encourage some form of expression of the idea. This is another crisis point in the creative process.

Most children will wish to intensify the joy of illumination by sharing the experience with others. Unfortunately, their attempts to communicate the experience are often received as less than exciting by other people (Strom & Bernard, 1982). We have all had the experience of trying to share one of those "you-had-to-be-there" happenings with others and being disappointed that they didn't get it. The listener must display genuine interest and somehow convey to the child that all new ideas are exciting, even if they are only "half-baked." The listener at this stage must be nonjudgmental.

It may be that an idea will be expressed metaphorically through an artistic presentation, instead of a logical explanation. A poem, a drawing, or a dance may be a more fitting medium for expression of the idea. Children should be encouraged to work toward mastery of their favored medium of expression. This may take some exposure to various art forms before a parent, for example, can tell whether dance, poetry, graphic art, prose, or other medium is the favored mode of expression.

Later, as a child begins to master the techniques of the medium, then the process of *verification* of the creative product expressed through the medium can begin. The child can begin to self-criticize without becoming discouraged. It is important to remember that technical mastery of the medium is not necessary for the development of the creative process. Mark Twain couldn't spell, Bob Dylan couldn't sing, and Albert Einstein couldn't do sums.

Suggestions

It cannot be said too often that the most important service aspect of the helping professions is the ability to reframe, or to see alternatives, when presented with problem children. One can approach children with a pathology-seeking attitude and thus find many pathological children; or one can adopt the presumption of health. Armed with the presumption of health, the helping professional will easily see, when others fail to see, that many problem behaviors in children are associated with creative thinking.

When the helping professional reframes the situation in this manner, it then becomes possible to relabel behaviors. For example, Lenba (1985) contended that lying is the first clear indicator of intellectual creativity. Viewed in this perspective, one can easily see that children's imaginations are rich with fiction and the reporting of their fantasies is, by harsh definition, a lie. But the expression of fantasy is not an intent to deceive. No one would ask the child to quit imagining since this is where creative ideas begin.

In addition to reframing and relabeling behaviors, the helping professional can work toward creating a better environment for children to entertain their creative energies by the following:

1. Provide a refuge somewhere in the system. Torrance (1979) noted that the very fact of producing an original idea or product automatically places one in the minority, at least for a time, and is thus stressful. Almost inescapably, the creative child will come into conflict with the "authorities" in the system and must have a source of encouragement and support.

2. Accord children the right to fail. It is incumbent upon families to support the child and encourage risk taking. Educators must remind themselves of the importance of risk taking and trying rather than the rightness of the response.

3. Provide sponsors and patrons.

4. Help creative people understand their creativity. Torrance (1979) noted that creative persons are likely to experience social demands as more restrictive than do their peers and may engage in active behavior to change the situation. "The creative person needs help in recognizing that his actions aggravate rather than relieve his actual state of helplessness" (p. 369).

5. Make resources available. A teacher who does not possess the skills or concepts to help in furthering a particular child's quest, needs to acknowledge this and help find someone who can help the child. Schools need to tap into both financial resources and potential content areas of local businesses and industry. Opportunities for experimentation and production through clubs (e.g., a creative writing club, a drama club, etc.), various school courses/activities, and family-supported or community activities should be pursued.

In consultation with parents, it may be helpful to give them a list that will guide them as they deal with their creative children. Many authors (Brunswick, 1971; Glover, et al., 1982; Klausmeier, 1985; Strom & Bernard, 1982; Torrance, 1962b) have suggested ways in which parents and teachers can encourage the development of the creative process in children. Besides encouragement that refines creativity, other rules of thumb designed to preserve this gift in children as they pass through the literal and critical phases of their development include the following:

1. Respect the way each child thinks. Do not be quick to dismiss answers as wrong or inappropriate.

2. Provide toys and activities that develop imagination. Do not be quick to dismiss ideas as unrealistic or useless.

3. Permit time for thinking or daydreaming. Do not demand production excessively.

4. Accept children's tendency to look at things differently. Do not dismiss unusual perspectives as weird.

5. Prize individuality. Be careful about asking for too much conformity.

6. Edit, criticize, and question children's ideas with great caution. Do not teach them that their ideas are without merit.

7. Encourage children to "mess around" with words, drawings, rules to games, etc. Do not teach them that dictionaries, art standards, or rules are sacrosanct and unchangeable.

8. Foster productivity. Ask children to produce their ideas in a communicable form.

9. Encourage children not to accept facts and ideas solely on the basis of authority.

10. Encourage children to guess and follow up on their hunches. Minimize their belief in "right" answers.

11. Honor your own "crazy" ideas, curiosity and divergent thoughts. Be a role model.

12. Be a mentor to a child. This means taking delight in the child's development and lovingly guiding the progress of the child's creative gift.

SUMMARY

Creative behavior is, by definition, unusual and unconventional. Normal is ordinary, and ordinary is the antithesis of creative. Parents and educators must try to understand the creative experience and to encourage its development.

The Danish philosopher Soren Kierkegaard was

fond of telling a story about how a man who was fascinated by wild ducks came to a pond to feed them and watch them fly south each year. After several seasons, because he fed them, the ducks no longer bothered to fly south. In a few more years they even lost the knack of flying and spent their lives swimming around in the same pond. Kierkegaard's point: You can tame wild ducks, but you can never make tame ducks wild again (Theobald & White, 1974). The world needs "wild ducks," those people who are innovative and outside the clutches of compulsive conformity. The creative potential of children is a wildness that manifests itself as curiosity, energy, ingenuity, and originality. It is the "wild ducks" who should be our top priority (Rekdal, 1977).

REFERENCES

Amabile, T. M. (1983). *The social psychology of creativity.* New York: Springer-Verlag.

Arieti, S. (1976). *Creativity: The magic synthesis.* New York: Basic Books.

Bowen, E. (1986, April 7). Trying to jump-start toddlers. *Time,* p.66.

Brunswick, J. (1971). Ten ways of helping young children gifted in creative writing and speech. *Gifted Child Quarterly, 6,* 3.

Cattell, R. B., & Butcher, H. J. (1968). *The prediction of achievement and creativity.* New York: Bobbs-Merrill.

Coleman, D. (1976, October). The fertile tension between discipline and impulse. *Psychology Today,* pp. 53–57.

Collangelo, N., & Ziffran, R. (1979). *New voices in counseling the gifted.* Dubuque, IA: Kendall/Hunt.

Davis, G. A., & Subkoviak, M. J. (1975). Multidimensional analysis of a personality-based test of creative potential. *Journal of Educational Measurement, 12,* 37–43.

Gardner, H. (1982). *Art, mind and brain: A cognitive approach to creativity.* New York: Basic Books.

Gardner, H. (1983). *Frames of mind: The theory of multiple intelligences.* New York: Basic Books.

Getzels, J. W., & Jackson, P. W. (1962). *Creativity and intelligence.* New York: Wiley.

Glover, J. A., Bruning, R. H., & Filbeck, R. W. (1983). *Educational psychology: Principles and applications.* Boston: Little, Brown.

Gowan, J. C. (1981). Creative inspiration in composers. In J. C. Gowan, J. Khatena, and E. P. Torrance (Eds.), *Creativity: Its educational implications.* Dubuque, IA: Kendall/Hunt.

Guilford, J. P. (1959). Three faces of intellect. *American Psychologist, 14,* 469–479.

Guilford, J. P. (1960). The psychology of creativity. *Creative Crafts, 1,* 5–8.

Guilford, J. P. (1971). *Creativity tests for children: A manual of interpretation.* Orange, CA: Sheridan Psychological Services.

Helson, R. (1965). Childhood interest clusters related to creativity in women. *Journal of Consulting Psychology, 29,* 352–361.

Hofstader,, D. R. (1985). *Metamagical themas: Questing for the essence of mind and pattern.* New York: Basic Books.

Hunt, M. (1982). *The universe within: A new science explores the human mind.* New York: Simon and Schuster.

Institute for Behavioral Research in Creativity. (1968). *Alpha Biographical Inventory.* Greensboro, NC: Prediction Press.

Jackson, P., & Messick, S. (1965). The person, the product and the response: Conceptual problems in the assessment of creativity. *Journal of Personality, 33,* 309–329.

Klausmeier, H. J. (1985). *Educational psychology* (5th ed.). New York: Harper and Row.

Koestler, A. (1964). *The act of creation.* New York: Dell.

Kubie, L. S. (1985). *Neurotic distortion in the creative process.* Lawrence, KS: University of Kansas Press.

Lefrancois, G. R. (1982). *Psychology for teaching: A bear rarely faces the front.* Belmont, CA: Wadsworth.

Lenba, C. A. (1985). New look at curiosity and creativity. *Journal of Higher Education, 29,* 132–140.

Mednick, S. A. (1967). *The remote associates test.* Boston: Houghton Mifflin.

Osborn, A. F. (1963). *Applied imagination* (3rd ed.). New York: Scribner's.

Piaget, J. (1950). *The psychology of intelligence.* New York: Harcourt, Brace & World.

Rekdal, C. K. (1977). Personality inventories as tests of creative potential and their use as measurements in programs for the gifted. *Gifted Child Quarterly, 21,* 4.

Rogers, C. R. (1951). *Client-centered therapy: Its current practice, implications, and theory.* Boston: Houghton Mifflin.

Schaefer, C. E. (1969). The prediction of creative achievement from a biographical inventory. *Educational and Psychological Measurement, 29,* 431–437.

Sternberg, R. J. (1985). *Beyond I.Q.: A triarchic theory of human intelligence.* Cambridge: Cambridge University Press.

Strom, R. D., & Bernard, H. W. (1982). *Educational psychology.* Monterey, CA: Brooks/Cole.

Theobald, T., & White, K. (1974). How to unstuff a wild duck. *Journal of Creative Behavior, 8,* 78–80.

Torrance, E. P. (1962a). *Guiding creative talent.* Englewood Cliffs, NJ: Prentice-Hall.

Torrance, E. P. (1962b). Ten ways of helping young children gifted in creative writing and speech. *Gifted Child Quarterly, 6,* 3.

Torrance, E. P. (1963). The creative personality and the ideal pupil. *Teachers College Record, 65,* 220–226.

Torrance, E. P. (1967). *Understanding the fourth-grade slump in creative thinking* (Final report). Washington, DC: U.S. Office of Education.

Torrance, E. P. (1974). *Torrance tests of creative thinking: Norms–technical manual.* Bensenville, IL: Scholastic Testing Service.

Torrance, E. P. (1979). Unique needs of the creative child and adult. In National Society for the Study of Education, *The gifted and the talented: Their education and development* (pp. 352–371). Chicago: University of Chicago Press.

Torrance, E. P. (1981). Non-test ways of identifying the creatively gifted. In J. D. Gowan, J. Khatena, & E. P. Torrance (Eds.), *Creativity: Its educational implications* (second edition). Dubuque, IA: Kendall/Hunt.

Torrance, e. P., & Khatena, J. (1970). What kind of person are you? *Gifted Child Quarterly, 14,* 71–75.

Wallach, M. A., & Kogan, N. (1965). *Modes of thinking in young children.* New York: Holt, Rinehart & Winston.

Wallas, G. (1926). *The art of thought.* London: Watts.

Watson, J. (1928). *Behaviorism.* London: K. Paul.

Wellborn, S. N. (1980, December 15). The gifted child: Big challenge for colleges. *U.S. News and World Report,* p.66.

Werner, H. (1948). *Comparative psychology of mental development.* New York: International Universities Press.

Wertheimer, M. (1945). *Productive thinking.* New York: Harper & Row.

BIBLIOGRAPHY: PROFESSIONALS

Gardner, H. (1982). *Art, mind, and brain: A cognitive approach to creativity.* New York: Basic Books.
A compilation of articles written by Gardner and others involved in Project Zero, a group at Harvard University who studied creativity. The book is extremely readable yet faithful to the research. Fascinating chapters on such topics as artistic development in children, child prodigies, television's effect on children, and brain damage and art will help the reader establish a broad understanding of the field. From this research, Gardner began to develop his ideas about intelligence that led to the popular book *Frames of Mind,* which we also recommend.

Parnes, S. J., Noller, R. B., & Biondi, A. M. (1977). *Guide to creative action* and *Creative actionbook.* New York: Scribner's.
This two-volume set is the result of many years of curriculum development at the State University of New York at Buffalo and the Creative Education Foundation. It is both a book of readings and a curriculum guide that contains explanations for exercises in creative problem solving, lists of films and books on creativity, and questions and topics for research. The Creative Education Foundation also publishes the *Journal of Creative Behavior* and hosts a yearly convention known as the Creative Problem Solving Institute (CPSI) in Buffalo.

Torrance, E. P. (1979). *The search for sartori and creativity* (soon to be published under the title: *Beyond A-ha!*). Great Neck, NY: Creative Education Foundation, and Creative Synergetic Association.
Explores the research that led to the development of the Torrance Tests of Creative Thinking. Each chapter discusses a factor that is a component in creative thinking. Both norm-referenced and criterion-referenced factors are discussed. Such thinking characteristics as originality, elaboration, openness, humor, and fantasy are explored and their contribution to the creative process is established. Reading this book is a good way to become familiar with the research and to understand the rationale behind the construction of the TTCT.

BIBLIOGRAPHY: PARENTS

G/C/T: The world's most popular magazine for parents and teachers of gifted, creative, and talented children. G./C./T. Publishing Co., P.O. Box 6448, Mobile, AL 336660-0448.
In case you have noticed that most programs in schools for children with special abilities are labeled with the terms "talented" and/or "gifted," here is a magazine that gives equal attention to creative children. The articles are readable and interesting. Included are exercises in problem solving, poetry, and cartoons.

Davis, G. A. (1981). *Creativity is forever.* Cross Plains, WI: Badges Press.
An easy-to-understand book that uses everyday examples to explain the creative process. Sterile academic treatment of the subject is avoided and is replaced by humorous and imaginative comments on the subject of creativity.

Samples, B. (1976). *The metaphoric mind: A celebration of creative consciousness.* Reading, MA: Addison-Wesley.
In this interesting book, the author makes a plea to educators to tame technocracy and to honor metaphorical forms of thought. This is a good treatment of the differences between the binary, logical type of thinking that currently leads to academic success and metaphorical thinking, which is the starting point of creativity.

Children and Delinquency

Rick Jay Short
University of Nebraska - Omaha

BACKGROUND

Delinquency in the United States is a serious and worsening problem (U. S. Department of Commerce, 1983). In 1981, juveniles under the age of 18 represented 16% of the population. They were responsible for almost 50% of all property crime and for 20% of all arrests for crimes in the United States. Juveniles accounted for over 33% of felonies committed in that year. From 1973 to 1977, 23% of all violent crimes committed against persons were committed by juveniles. Since 1969, juvenile arrests for violent crime have increased by 246%, over double the increase for adults. Also, juvenile courts saw almost 5% of the juvenile population in 1979, an increase from 2% in 1960 (U. S. Department of Commerce, 1983).

Although delinquent boys have traditionally outnumbered delinquent girls by at least 6 to 1, the gap between sexes seems to be narrowing. Since 1970 juvenile arrests and violent crimes by females under 18 have increased by over 16% (Burquest, 1981). From 1965 to 1981, delinquent offenses involving females increased 78%, almost twice the rate of increase for males (Knopf, 1984).

Delinquency is essentially a sociolegal entity. Adolescents are not technically delinquent until they have been adjudicated delinquent by a juvenile court. Not all — indeed, not even very many — adolescents who engage in norm-violating behavior are ever adjudicated to be delinquent. Most instances of adolescent norm-violating behavior go unapprehended by authorities. Society regards some illegal behaviors, such as Halloween pranks, as developmentally appropriate expressions of middle-class adolescence. In fact, 90% of the U.S. population report committing delinquent acts at some time during adolescence (Hindelang, Hirschi, & Weis, 1981). However, police actually apprehend only a small percentage of adolescents who engage in delinquent behavior. Of the relatively few cases of such behavior that go to juvenile court, only about 2–3% result in actual determination of delinquency. Although evidence is somewhat conflicting, data suggest that minority and lower socioeconomic status (SES) adolescents may be overrepresented in this group.

Formally, delinquency refers to any illegal act committed by a juvenile. This definition includes several classes of behavior, called status offenses, that are crimes for juveniles but not for adults. These behaviors include truancy, associating with immoral persons, breaking curfew, and incorrigibility (Lewis, 1985). An adolescent is therefore potentially more at risk of breaking the law than an adult; there are more applicable laws for an adolescent to break.

Delinquency is not a univariate construct; delinquents as a group may have few common characteristics. Delinquents do, however, vary reliably on several dimensions that are well substantiated in the literature (Quay, 1964; Quay & Peterson, 1979, 1983). A dimensional system based on the factor analysis work of Quay and his associates has seen widespread use within juvenile delinquency institutions. Writers in the school psychology literature have recently applied Quay's work to school populations (Knoff, 1985; Lahey & Piacentini, 1985). These applications have often focused on the classification of behavior disorders rather than on dimensions and treatment of delinquents. Quay's work may most effectively and succinctly describe delinquent behavior, regardless of the setting. Quay's dimensions of delinquency include the following: unsocialized–psychopathic delinquency, disturbed–neurotic delinquency, subcultural delinquency, and inadequate–immature delinquency.

Unsocialized–Psychopathic Delinquents

Unsocialized–psychopathic delinquents fit most closely the DSM III diagnosis of Conduct Disorder, Undersocialized Aggressive type. Unsocialized–psychopathic delinquents appear to be alienated from and distrustful of others and are frequently aggressive or abusive. They are often defiant, irritable loners who seem to seek out rather than to avoid trouble. These delinquents tend to perceive themselves as victims of their environment and fail to perceive their responsibility for the consequences of their behavior. Thus, psychopathic delinquents often interpret as injustices treatment strategies that involve behavioral consequences for their behavior. They respond to such programs with (in their view) justifiable anger and/or manipulation. Most children perceive disciplinary contingencies as deserved or expected consequences for their behavior. Unsocialized–psychopathic delinquents perceive these contingencies as either attacks form a hostile environment or as manipulative attempts to co-opt them.

Socialized–Subcultural Delinquents

Socialized–subcultural delinquents may also exhibit aggressive, acting-out behavior. However, these delinquents bond themselves to a subculture — often a gang — that exhibits antisocial norms, resulting in group-oriented law-breaking. Socialized–subcultural delinquents are highly susceptible to peer influence, particularly when that influence involves a rejection of authority and societal standards. Socialized–subcultural delinquents are often of low socioeconomic status and show little evidence of psychopathology. Delinquent peer pressure molds their perceptions and behavior. A relatively parallel DSM III diagnosis for socialized–subcultural delinquency is Conduct Disorder, Socialized Aggressive type.

Inadequate–Immature Delinquents

Inadequate–immature delinquents have poor social awareness and skills. They seem to have difficulty in coming to grips with school and home demands. Their delinquent behavior is related to frustration and impulsivity rather than anger, pathology, or peer pressure. Adolescent peers often ostracize and taunt inadequate-immature delinquents because of their social ineptitude. Quay suggests that inadequate–immature delinquents often fit the DSM III diagnosis of Attention Deficit Disorder.

Disturbed–Neurotic Delinquents

The final type of delinquency identified by Quay is the disturbed–neurotic delinquent. Disturbed–neurotic delinquents are characterized by feelings of guilt, anxiety, and inferiority. They exhibit a fear of failure and are often depressed. These delinquents frequently express physical concerns. Although they have broken the law, their behavior is often secondary to emotional concerns. Therefore, disturbed–neurotic delinquents are less likely to engage in repeat offenses and aggressive behavior than are other types of delinquents.

While these dimensions outline the psychological nature of different types of delinquents, they do not show that delinquents differ markedly from other adolescents. In fact, at least one writer (Bernstein, 1981) has suggested that attempted differentiation of delinquents from nondelinquents has proven evasive and possibly unproductive in treatment. However, psychopathic delinquents do differ appreciably from other types of delinquents and from nondelinquents. These differences occur in areas of moral development (Jurkovic & Prentice, 1977), ability to see other's perspective (Chandler, 1973), aggressiveness (Short & Moore, 1986), stimulus seeking (Skrzypek, 1969), and attribution of hostility to others (Nasby, Hayden, & DePaulo, 1980).

DEVELOPMENT

The antecedents of delinquency may lie in early childhood. At least three lines of inquiry into these antecedents have occurred, each of which may explain in part how delinquent behavior develops. These lines are aggression, family characteristics, and biosocial factors.

Aggression

Aggression, like delinquency, is difficult to define. Aggression often refers to unpredictable acts intended to produce pain in a victim or to get something from a victim. In most children, these acts decline in frequency and intensity from early childhood to adolescence.

Aggressive behavior is quite common in early childhood. Young children often hit or push other children in frustration or to get toys they want. Disruptive/aggressive acts account for almost 50% of social interactions among 12- to 18-month-olds. However, they constitute only about 20% of such interactions of 2½-year olds (Holmberg, 1977). This decline continues into preschool children, during which aggressive behavior is much less likely to occur. Aggressive behavior during the preschool years is more hostile, but more verbal, than in earlier years (Hartup, 1974). This developmental trend suggests that physical aggression declines as the potential for actually inflicting damage increases.

During early childhood, males and females are equally aggressive. Sex differences in aggressive behavior become clear in preschool years, males showing a greater tendency to such behavior than females. By middle childhood, unprovoked physical attacks are uncommon, and most are instigated by males (Patterson & Cobb, 1971; Kagan & Moss, 1962).

Adolescents as a group rarely engage in physical assault. Adolescents express aggression through taunting, name calling, or cursing; they rarely inflict physical damage (Holmberg, 1977; Maccoby and Jacklin, 1973). However, the rate of arrests of teenage males for physical assault is higher than for any other age group. While adolescent physical assault is rare, its occurrence is socially significant because of the adolescent's ability to inflict damage on a victim.

Thus, violent adolescents may lag behind their peers in this developmental sequence in respect to aggressive behavior. While other children outgrow their physically aggressive tendencies, violent delinquents remain physically aggressive until well into adulthood.

Family Characteristics

The family exerts a significant influence on the development of delinquency. Harsh punishment and inconsistent, neglectful parental discipline correlate with delinquency, as do poor identification with parents and lack of parental support and nurturance. Parental modeling of antisocial and criminal behavior has also been associated with delinquency. Overall, delinquency seems to relate more to family disorganization and lack of communication than to other commonly mentioned factors, including broken families, low SES, and minority status (Schumer, 1983).

Biosocial Factors

Evidence suggests that biosocial factors also play an important, if poorly understood, role in the development of delinquency. Hardcore delinquents may respond to punishment in a different manner than normal adolescents (Mednick & Christiansen, 1977). Mednick and Christiansen demonstrated that hardcore delinquents evidence a lower autonomic responsiveness — a higher tolerance for and a quicker recovery rate from pain and aversive stimuli — than normal subjects. Delinquents may have difficulty in learning to avoid the noxious consequences of negative behavior that teach normals to avoid such behavior. Psychopathic delinquents also evidence a chronically low level of cortical arousal and may therefore be understimulated. (Whitehill, DeMyer-Gapin, & Scott, 1976). This understimulation results in a tendency to seek out physiological arousal, often in illegal activities. These findings provide empirical support for the illegal thrill-seeking characteristic of the criminal personality (Yochelson and Samenow, 1976; Agee, 1979).

PUTTING DELINQUENCY INTO PERSPECTIVE

Within the above framework, several key points may aid the school psychologist in dealing with delinquency in the school setting.

1. Juvenile delinquent treatment facilities have used distinctive treatment strategies for delinquents based on distinguishing dimensional considerations for many years (Agee, 1979). These strategies have apparently received little attention outside of delinquent facilities. According to Quay (1964), each delinquent type has distinctive characteristics that may require distinctive treatment/intervention strategies. Diagnosis of delinquent type, followed by interventions based on the diagnosis, should be effective treatment tools in the schools as well as in delinquent facilities.

2. Delinquents often first evidence antisocial behavior during the preschool or early school years. Because of increased ability to inflict damage as size and strength increase, such behavior becomes more problematic with age. Early antisocial behavior appears to be the best predictor of adolescent and adult violent behavior (Marohn, 1982). The best chance to identify and alter delinquent potential may lie in early childhood prevention efforts.

3. Without appropriate intervention, adolescent delinquency seems to be exacerbated by participation in the public schools. Delinquents who drop out of school show a marked decrease in norm-violating behavior following their departure from school (Polk & Schafer, 1972). Delinquents are characteristically academically deficient and negative toward school. Decreased rates of delinquent behavior following dropping out may therefore result from decreased pressure and alienation caused by academic failure (Kvaraceus, 1971).

4. While most adolescents self-report having engaged in illegal acts, most of these infractions are relatively minor and infrequent. Adolescents who are adjudicated delinquent tend to engage in more serious and more chronic criminal behavior than their nondelinquent peers. Contrary to widely held belief, race and SES factors seem to be only moderately related to formal delinquent status (Hindelang, Hirschi, & Weis, 1981).

5. Family factors seem to play a major role in the development and maintenance of delinquent behavior, particularly during early formative years. Family factors, however, are insufficient explanations for all delinquent behavior; some children experience extremely negative family situations without engaging in corresponding delinquent behavior. Others are products of apparently adaptive home environments, yet are chronic delinquents. Practitioners should be aware of and investigate family factors in delinquency, but they should avoid inflexible blaming of such factors for delinquent patterns.

6. Cognitive factors may relate to chronic delinquent behavior patterns. Chronic, severe delinquents appear to maintain characteristic misperceptions of their environment (Yochelson & Samenow, 1976; Agee, 1979). These misperceptions may include the belief that they are actually victims of their upbringing, their past, their family, or society in general rather than perpetrators of crimes. Chronic delinquents often feel no responsibility for damage that they inflict, even blaming their victims for causing their criminal behavior. Another faulty cognition is the idea that everyone is a criminal, but some are unlucky enough to get caught. These faulty cognitions interfere with normal functioning and response to social contingencies and limit adaptive insights and behavioral responses, even within a supportive environment.

ALTERNATIVE ACTIONS

Prevention of delinquency occurs at three levels: primary, secondary, and tertiary prevention (Kvaraceus, 1971; Sabatino & Mauser, 1978). The goal of primary prevention is the early identification and treatment of potential delinquents. Secondary prevention involves devising and carrying out a program to prevent an identified problem from becoming any more severe; secondary prevention is the level of intervention most familiar to school psychologists. Tertiary prevention consists of providing rehabilitative services.

Primary prevention seems to be the most efficient and effective means of dealing with delinquency (Cowen & Lorion, 1976). Also, the public school is the most logical setting for primary prevention efforts. The public school is the only public institution with consistent and universal access to young children, the age group most likely to benefit from preventive programs; therefore, primary prevention programming in the public schools may be the best strategy for dealing with delinquency. And the school psychologist, with training in human learning, development, and behavior, seems to be the ideal professional to work with such programs. However, primary prevention of delinquency in the schools has been problematic for several reasons: (a) The tendency to label children on the basis of their placement or program causes school and parental concern. Labels create expectations for behavior that bias observers in the direction of the label. Few parents want their child labeled predelinquent or at risk of delinquency, especially when the basis for that label is nothing more than the probability of future problems. (b) Decision makers are reluctant to allocate resources for potential, rather than immediate, problems. Most funding sources and administrators require a demonstration of need before a program will receive priority. (c) Professionals may disagree as to what constitutes an appropriate prevention program. Such disagreement is particularly evident in controversial and complex entities such as delinquency.

Psychologists and educators have implemented several effective primary prevention programs in the schools. Many of these programs build social problem-solving and/or social cognitive skills, based on findings that delinquents are often deficient in such skills (Chandler, Greenspan, & Barenboim, 1974; Short & Simeonsson, 1986; Shure & Spivack, 1972). An early prevention program developed by Ojemann (1967) encourages awareness of the dynamics of human behavior and understanding of others' perspective. The focus of Ojemann's program is to develop life skills in problem solving and communication. Project AWARE (Elardo & Caldwell, 1979) incorporates the social problem-solving emphasis of Shure and Spivack (1972) with training in perspective-taking skills. Chandler (1973) demonstrated the importance of perspective-taking skills in understanding delinquency and antisocial behavior. Project AWARE uses guided classroom discussions to teach understanding of others and consequences of problem solutions. These programs can provide systematic and effective resources to the school professional in carrying out primary prevention efforts.

Secondary and tertiary prevention have traditionally been the province of the courts and training schools. Recent class-action lawsuits have forced greater emphasis to be placed on community- and school-based services for delinquents. However, schools often have limited resources and expertise in dealing with delinquents. Therefore, delinquents returning to school perform poorly and often ultimately disrupt classes or drop out of school.

Alternative schools or classrooms are one school-based strategy for serving delinquents (Sabatino & Mauser, 1978). At a basic level, these programs apply learning and behavioral principles to improve academic achievement, attitude toward school, and vocational skills. Alternative schools or classrooms use individualized instructional planning and consistent behavioral contingencies to increase achievement and to improve behavior. In addition, commitment building through teacher contact and peer meetings improves attitude toward school. Vocational activities often include teaching basic job-seeking and job-maintenance skills, along with counseling and interpersonal social skills-building activities (Sabatino & Mauser, 1978).

As stated above, services may be most effectively provided when the characteristics of delinquent types and strategies that have proven effective with them are taken into consideration (Agee, 1979). With this information, the school professional can better assess the significance of particular behaviors relative to overall cognitive and behavior patterns.

Because the unsocialized–psychopathic delinquent is assaultive, mistrustful, and egocentric, and has few real relationships, intervention often involves establishment of control over behavior. Clear, consistent behavior contingencies are important for behavior control and behavior change. Such contingencies are difficult to carry out because psychopathic delinquents often actively and aggressively resist attempts to enforce such contingencies. These delinquents seldom benefit from traditional affective or insight-oriented counseling. Effective programming efforts with these delinquents consist of stressing the relationship between behavior and consequences. An important characteristic of the intervenor in this case is the ability to avoid being manipulated into lowering standards or falling to apply consequences.

Socialized–subcultural delinquents, heavily influenced by peers and embracing an antisocial value system, present a different challenge to school psychologists. Effective interventions minimize maladaptive peer influence, encourage independence in decision making, and work toward redirection of antisocial values. Teaching of adaptive social skills, such as might happen in athletic teams and shop classes, is also important in redirecting form an antisocial orientation. Important characteristics of intervenors with socialized–subcultural delinquents are genuine respect for the perspective of the delinquent and comfortable awareness of their own values.

Disturbed–neurotic delinquents, whose norm-violating behavior is often the result of fears and perceived inadequacies, may benefit most from traditional affective and insight-oriented counseling. Training in alternative methods of dealing with unpleasant emotions may lead to decreased occurrence of maladaptive behavior. Effective intervenors with disturbed–neurotic delinquents are willing to become personally involved with them, allowing them to share and explore difficult emotions and modeling their appropriate expression.

Inadequate–immature delinquents, impulsive, dependent, and distractible as they are, often require patient structuring of their environment to minimize opportunities for maladaptive behavior. Behavioral contingencies and cognitive–behavioral interventions to deal with impulsivity are frequently effective strategies. These delinquents require a great deal of attention and get it through immature acting-out behaviors. Intervenors should be patient and willing to repeat strategies a number of times. Progress with the inadequate–immature delinquent is often very slow.

SUMMARY

With the growth of female delinquency and violent delinquent crimes, the problem of delinquency seems to be increasing. The schools will bear more responsibility for these adolescents because of the national trend toward deinstitutionalization. Given these facts, the school psychologist's role in intervening with delinquency may be pivotal in controlling it. The school psychologist may best be able to deal with delinquency at the primary prevention level; however, funding and staffing problems may make primary prevention unfeasible. As an alternative, the school psychologist should be aware of research in the field of juvenile delinquency, particularly as it relates to assessing and treating dimensions of delinquency.

REFERENCES

Agee, V. L. (1979). *Treatment of the violent incorrigible adolescent.* Lexington, MA: Lexington Books.

Bernstein, R. M. (1981). The relationship between dimensions of delinquency and the development of self and peer perception. *Adolescence, 16,* 543–556.

Burquest, B. (1981). The violent girl. *Adolescence, 16,* 749–764.

Chandler, M. J. (1973). Egocentrism and antisocial behavior: The assessment and training of social perspective-taking skills. *Developmental Psychology, 9,* 326–332.

Chandler, M. J., Greenspan, S., & Barenboim, C. (1974). Assessment and training of role-taking and referential communication skills in institutionalized and emotionally disturbed children. *Developmental Psychology, 10,* 546–553.

Cowen, E. L., & lorion, R. P. (1976). Changing roles for the school mental health professional. *Journal of School Psychology, 14*(2), 131–138.

Elardo, P. T., & Caldwell, B. M. (1979). The effects of an experimental social development program on children in the middle childhood period. *Psychology in the Schools, 16,* 93–100.

Hartup, W. (1974). Aggression in childhood: Developmental perspectives. *American Psychologist,29,* 336–341.

Hindelang, M. J., Hirschi, T., & Weis, J. G. (1981). *Measuring delinquency.* Beverly Hills: Sage.

Holmberg, M. C. (1977). *The development of social interchange patterns from 12 to 42 months: Cross-sectional and short-term longitudinal analyses.* Unpublished doctoral dissertation, University of North Carolina at Chapel Hill.

Jurkovic, G. J., & Prentice, N.M. (1977). Relation of moral and cognitive development to dimensions of juvenile delinquency. *Journal of Abnormal Psychology, 86,* 414–420.

Kagan, J., & Moss, H. A. (1962). *Birth to maturity: A study in psychological development.* New York: Wiley.

Knoff, H. (1985). Best practices in dealing with discipline referrals. In J. Grimes & A. Thomas (Eds.), *Best practices in school psychology* (pp. 251–262). Kent, OH: National Association of School Psychologists.

Knopf, I. J. (1984). *Childhood psychopathology.* Englewood Cliffs, NJ: Prentice-Hall.

Kvaraceus, W. C. (1971). *Prevention and control of delinquency: The school counselor's role.* Boston: Houghton Mifflin.

Lahey, B. B., & Piacentini, J. C. (1985). An evaluation of the Quay-Peterson Revised Behavior Problem Checklist. *Journal of School Psychology, 23,* 285–289.

Lewis, D. O. (1985). Juvenile delinquency. In D. Schaffer, A. A. Erhardt, & L. L. Greenhill (Eds.), *The clinical guide to child psychiatry.* New York: Free Press.

Marohn, R. C. (1982). Adolescent violence: Causes and treatment. *Journal of the American Academy of Child Psychiatry, 21,* 354–360.

Mednick, S. A., & Christiansen, K. O. (1977). *Biosocial bases of criminal behavior.* New York: Gardner.

Nasby, W., Hayden, B., & DePaulo, B. M. (1980). Attributional bias among aggressive boys to interpret unambiguous social stimuli on displays of hostility. *Journal of Abnormal Psychology, 89,* 459–468.

Ojemann, R. (1967). Incorporating psychological concepts in the school curriculum. *Journal of School Psychology,k 5,* 195–204.

Patterson, G. R., & Cobb, J. A. (1971). A dyadic analysis of "aggressive" behaviors. In J. P. Hill (Ed.), *Minnesota Symposium on Child Psychology (Vol. 5) (pp. 72–129).* Minneapolis: University of Minnesota Press.

Polk, K., & Schafer, W. E. (1972). *Schools and delinquency.* Englewood Cliffs, NJ: Prentice-Hall.

Quay, H. C. (1964). Dimensions of personality in delinquent boys as inferred from factor analysis of case history data. *Child Development, 35,* 479–484.

Quay, H. C., & Peterson, D. R. (1979). *Manual of the Behavior Problem Checklist.* Privately printed: University of Miami, Miami, FL.

Quay, H. C., & Peterson,D. R. (1983). *Interim manual for the Revised Behavior Problem Checklist.* Privately printed: University of Miami, Miami, FL.

Sabatino, D. A., & Mauser, A. J. (1978). *Specialized education in today's secondary schools.* Boston: Allyn and Bacon.

Schumer, F. (1983). *Abnormal psychology.* Lexington, MA: Heath.

Short, R. J., & Moore, C. C. (1986). *Correlates of peer perception in delinquent males.* Unpublished manuscript.

Short, R. J., & Simeonsson, R. J. (1986). Social cognition and aggression in delinquent adolescent males. *Adolescence, 21,* 159–176.

Shure, M., & Spivack, G. (1972). Means–end thinking, adjustment, and social class among elementary school-aged children. *Journal of Consulting and Clinical Psychology, 38,* 348–353.

Skrzypek, G. J. (1969). Effects of perceptual isolation and arousal on anxiety, complexity preference, and novelty preference in psychopathic and neurotic delinquents. *Journal of Abnormal Psychology, 74,* 221–229.

United States Department of Commerce. (1983). *Statistical abstracts of the United States (1982–1983).* Washington, DC: Author.

Whitehill, M. DeMyer-Gapin, S., & Scott, T. J. (1976). Stimulation seeking in antisocial preadolescent children. *Journal of Abnormal Psychology, 85,* 101–104.

Yochelson, S., & Samenow, S. E. (1976). *The criminal personality.* New York: Jacob Aronson.

BIBLIOGRAPHY: PROFESSIONALS

Clarizio, H. F., & McCoy, G. F. (1983). Juvenile delinquency. In H. F. Clarizio & G. F. McCoy (Eds.), *Behavior disorders in children* (pp. 281–332). New York: Harper and Row.

The chapter on juvenile delinquency in this standard text provides a short, school-oriented review of the field with a section on the Quay dimensional system.

Kvaraceus, W. C. (1971). *Prevention and control of delinquency: The school counselor's role.* Boston: Houghton Mifflin.
Although not a recent work, this book provides recommendations for working with the delinquent in the school and community. The book outlines the relationship of the delinquent and the school.

Redner, R., Snellman, L., & Davidson, W. S. (1983). Juvenile delinquency. In R. J. Morris & T. R. Kratochwill (Eds.), *The practice of child therapy* (pp. 186–213). New York: Pergamon.
A behavioral orientation toward definition and treatment of delinquency. An excellent resource for the school practitioner.

Rutter, M., & Giller, H. (1984). *Juvenile delinquency: Trends and perspectives.* New York: Guilford.
This book provides comprehensive and detailed information about theories, approaches, and characteristics of delinquency. Probably the most thorough current treatment of the subject.

Sabatino, D. A., & Mauser, A. J. (1978). *Specialized education in today's secondary schools.* Boston: Allyn and Bacon.
Sabatino and Mauser integrate much of the findings and theories concerning norm-violating youth with practical insights about their education, including assessment. This work is recommended for the school psychologist working with delinquents and almost-delinquents.

BIBLIOGRAPHY: PARENTS

York, D., & York, P. (1984). *The TOUGHLOVE parent's manual.* TOUGHLOVE, P. O. Box 1069, Doylestown, PA, 18901.
This manual provides concrete suggestions to parents for giving structure for difficult adolescents. Suggestions are practical and based on approaches developed and implemented by these parents of difficult adolescents. Information about workshops and support groups is also available.

Children and Dependency

Charles K. McBride and Max A. McFarland
Nebraska Department of Education

BACKGROUND

The cluster of behaviors typically thought to constitute childhood dependency has been and continues to be of concern to the practicing psychologist. Psychologists and educators face on a daily basis those children who at least intuitively seem too dependent upon their environment and lack independent decision-making skills. These concerns frequently are considered to be of secondary importance because they do not constitute the primary reason for referral. However, such issues also receive minimal attention simply by virtue of the absence of definitive conclusions (in the professional literature and practice) as to definitions, ramifications, and treatments. While such behaviors are usually observed and addressed on an informal basis, rarely is dependency formally assessed, its manifestations thoroughly understood, and primary treatment implemented.

Dependency is a cluster of behaviors subsumed within other factors considered to reflect internalizing disorders. For example, behavioral traits such as clinging to adults, preferring young children, being withdrawn, feeling worthless, fearing mistakes, and having poor peer relations (Achenbach & Edelbrock, 1978), all express dependency. As such, incidence is difficult to determine. All children, at some point in their development, display behavior reflecting dependency. In fact, such dependent-behavior patterns during infancy are felt to be crucial to normal adjustment later on in life (Ainsworth, 1979). Consequently, it is quite difficult to accurately determine which symptoms are significant and it is even more difficult to view these symptoms from a normative perspective.

Definitions of *dependency* in the literature are as varied as the application of the term itself. Applied to an adult it traditionally has been considered to mean passively allowing others to assume responsibility for areas of one's life because of lack of self-confidence and an inability to function independently (American Psychiatric Association, 1980); such difficulties are not recognized within the literature as a specific childhood disorder. This does not imply, however, that these issues are unimportant. Behavioral descriptors that appear in many teacher referrals made for diagnostic service frequently include characteristics typically associated with adult dependency and are consistent with a consensus found in the literature (Ainsworth, 1969; Gewirtz, 1972; Schaefer & Millman, 1981). Characteristics such as a lack of self-confidence, poor independent work habits, anxiety, and impaired social relationships are not uncommon. Additionally, these characteristics are observed to coincide with a student's having difficulties making independent decisions, demanding attention, acting immaturely, requiring constant direction, relying upon others, and distrusting their abilities. Consequently, these associated behaviors of a dependency problem are seen to be rather common characteristics of children referred because of various psychological and/or educational problems.

In order to provide effective treatment strategies, it is imperative to identify these symptomatic behaviors and to understand their implications. In addition to the previously discussed intrapersonal and interpersonal problems, dependency can be associated with deficits in cognitive problem-solving skills and in social skill development. While dependency is typically thought of as an overt behavioral problem in need of modification, underlying skill deficits are also associated with the perpetuation of dependency if not its origin. For example, dependent children frequently have difficulty starting academic tasks, are unable to perform such tasks in a logically organized manner, and are unable or unwilling to do so independently. It is difficult to ascertain whether such cognitive skill deficits occur as a result of a history of dependent behavior interactions (reliance upon others, lack of self-trust, etc.), or whether dependency develops as a function of such cognitive deficits. However, it does appear that such factors coexist. Similarly, these children also frequently exhibit social interaction skill deficits — such as preferring to interact with younger children, withdrawing from peer group activities, and choosing not to initiate interaction — that interfere with interpersonal relationships. Therefore, in addition to being a behavioral concern, dependency may indicate cognitive and/or social skill deficits. The recognition of these deficits is of critical importance in that they have consistently been found to be associated with critical adjustment problems in adolescence and adulthood (Camp, 1977; Cowen, Pederson, Babigian, Izzo, & Trost, 1973).

In addition to social, emotional and academic ramifications, the dependency factor(s) can diminish a child's self-initiated motivation and result in avoidance and/or manipulative behavior. For example, some children who can cope adequately with the expectations of their environment choose instead to control others and avoid risk taking through manipulative behavior. Such behavior may be the result of cognitive or social skills deficits and may serve, by virtue of being self-reinforcing, to perpetuate dependency. This can be an interaction between a parent or other adult and a child that generates an initial situation of dependency, which then evolves into a "learned helplessness" (Diener & Dweck, 1980) interaction pattern exhibited by the child within the home or school.

While dependency has several identifying characteristics, which have previously been addressed, it is necessary to attach a more concise definition of the phrase *learned helplessness.* Although learned helplessness is a component of dependency, it should not be used as synonymous when dependency is being considered in a global sense. For the child who suffers from learned helplessness, self-expectations are unrealistic and outcomes of various situations are viewed as uncontrollable (Dweck & Reppucci, 1973). Consequently, no matter how hard such students try, the results are perceived as failure even though they may have been successful. This type of cognitive distortion is an identifying characteristic of learned helplessness. The victim of learned helplessness overestimates failure and underestimates success, which may further contribute to the lowering of self-concept and add to a growing feeling of inadequacy and inferiority involving self-comparison with peers. When evaluating their own progress, children often compare themselves with students possessing a much higher level of ability than their own. Children characterized by learned helplessness accept failure as defeat, whereas "normal," mastery-oriented children evaluate failure and cognitively plan a strategy for future success (Butkowsky & Willows, 1980; Diener & Dweck, 1980).

It is important to note that the display of learned helplessness may be situation-, subject-, or person-specific. This is to say that a child may exhibit learned helpless behavior only in reading class, for example, or solely with the mother at home (Dweck & Reppucci, 1973). It is the breadth of learned helplessness exhibited, such as being displayed across all settings/persons versus only one, that helps to determine the severity of a problem and the treatment that will be necessary.

Thus, dependency may be not only a pervasive problem but also at least partially a subtle or covert problem. Few children are actually referred for school psychology attention primarily because of interfering dependency. Instead, these referrals are typically precipitated by the suspicions of more obvious learning disorders such as cognitive dysfunction, specific learning disabilities, severe behavioral impairment. However, while frequently a problem that is masked by more obvious referral complaints, the dependency relationships may actually constitute the most critical concern — that being interference with the child's cognitive and social adjustment.

DEVELOPMENT

It is apparent that most, if not all, of the previously described symptomatic characteristics of the dependent child are observed in the normal development of most children. Research shows that secure attachment as an infant is a good predictor of future autonomous functioning (Erickson, Sroufe, & Egeland, 1985). If children are to develop trust, both within themselves and toward others in later years, a secure attachment is a prerequisite. For example, at age 22 months, securely attached infants are more cooperative with the mother and other adults. At age 2 years, such children exhibit more enthusiasm, persistence, and compliance in problem solving, and tend to be more active learners. They are more socially competent with peers at age 3½ years and more ego-resilient at age 5 years (Erickson, et al., 1985).

Relationships develop over time, and as a result of interactions between children and various elements in their environment, such as parents, siblings,and peers. Dependency, then as well as many other such intrafamily relationships, may develop as a function of the bidirectional relationship between child and environment factors (Bell & Harper, 1977). As such, it is unlikely that pinpointing causative factors will be possible.

More specifically, dependency in children may develop within their home in part because siblings provide unneeded assistance when difficulty is experienced.

The parents may also take an active role in the development of dependency by being overprotective, thus decreasing the opportunity for "normal" social, behavioral, and/or cognitive growth. In this type of environment children let others provide for them and have difficulty making their own decisions (Gardner, 1979). A "smother love" situation is created in which such children do little for themselves and thus become increasingly more dependent upon others (Schaefer & Millman, 1981). Parents and siblings who through their own actions and verbalizing preemptively meet the needs of younger children by tying their shoes, feeding them, talking for them, etc., may develop and perpetuate a cycle in which such children's lack of independence is inadvertently reinforced and the parent and siblings also are reinforced in their overprotective and intrusive behavior. Such children's total reliance upon their parents can be reinforcing by fulfilling a "need to be needed." Furthermore, the children's dependency can be reinforced through anxiety reduction, increased ability to control (manipulate) adults, and by a reduced need to initiate self-care. Again, while such interactions frequently occur in normal development, it is when such a cycle prevents children from becoming increasingly capable of secure detachment and independent decision making that dependency becomes problematic.

Dependency, which may in part be generated and nurtured through "smother love," in the home, can then be transferred into the educational environment with the development of learned helplessness (Diener & Dweck, 1980). "Learned helpless" children lack persistence, positive affect, problem-solving skills, decision-making strategies, and the ability to use self-monitoring and self-instructing techniques appropriately. They put little trust in their judgment because of past perceived failures and are therefore extremely cautious about any risk taking. Children subject to learned helplessness are intellectually reliant and unable to independently resolve problems necessary to master academic skills. It can then be assumed that these dependent children may develop peer reliance and strive to gain direction and reinforcement from others when an adult is not available. Consequently, in addition to parents, siblings,and the affected children, peers are frequently involved in this self-perpetuating cycle of developing dependence.

It is important to note that other specific situations, considered to be normal occurrences, may increase dependency. For example, chronic or acute health factors or handicapping conditions may function initially as catalysts, thereby starting the development of such a dependency cycle. Even when the health factors are remediated, the cyclical interactions may continue. Such a cycle is extremely difficult to reverse simply because all factors involved (those associated with both the environment and the child) are perpetually being reinforced. Additionally, the original causal factors may be quite different from the interactions that subsequently serve to maintain the dependent relationships.

PUTTING CHILDHOOD DEPENDENCY IN PERSPECTIVE

To more fully understand childhood dependency, the extent to which the dependency is problematic, and to delineate effective intervention strategies, comprehensive assessment is necessary. As is the case with many types of behavioral disorders, a multimethod (Ollendick & Hersen, 1984) or ecological (McFarland & Johnson, 1986) approach to assessment becomes necessary. The decision-making process through which a multidisciplinary assessment team (MDT) moves is of critical importance; it must utilize various assessment instruments and techniques in order to gather data necessary for enhanced understanding. The following series of evaluative questions may serve to guide the MDT in the decision-making process. The specific type of assessment instruments and techniques used are of minor importance.

1. Does the dependency problem result from a skills deficit or a performance deficit? Does the child possess the cognitive and/or social-problem-solving skills, learning aptitudes, etc. to make independent decisions? Do the results of intellectual assessment indicate the necessary problem-solving skills? Can the child self-instruct? Does the child display appropriate social skills in some settings and not others? If so, then behavioral issues take on priority importance. If not, then cognitive and/or social skills building may be necessary. To address these questions, several assessment methods must be employed including intellectual/achievement testing, systematic observation, social skills checklist, behavior checklists (parents and teachers), curriculum evaluations, and adaptive behavior.
2. Is the dependency displayed in a specific setting (reading class or math class, home or school, playground or classroom) or with a specific person (male or female, adult or peer) or is it displayed in a more pervasive manner? Setting analysis, behavior rating scales (parents and teachers), and anecdotal reports are necessary to investigate setting- and person-specific factors.
3. Do the dependent behaviors reflect a manipulative coping pattern through which the child maintains control over the environment? Do they reflect more of a withdrawal pattern, stemming from an insecure, fearful, anxious childhood? Are both patterns involved? Systematic observations of interactions with adults and peers, behavior rating scales (parents and teachers), interviews, and anxiety measures would be useful.
4. Is cognitive distortion present, and to what extent? Are such statements about the self congruent with overt behavioral patterns? What are the child's attitudes and perceptions about the self and the environment? Assessment methods to be utilized include self-reports, observations, projective testing, and interviews.
5. Is the family unit or individuals within the family caught up in the dependency-perpetuating cycle? What are the reinforcement contingencies and roles in the family interactions? What are the adult perceptions? These data are difficult to obtain and require the common measure of: parental/family interviews, self-

FIGURE 1

MDT Decision-Making Process Resulting in Alternative Actions

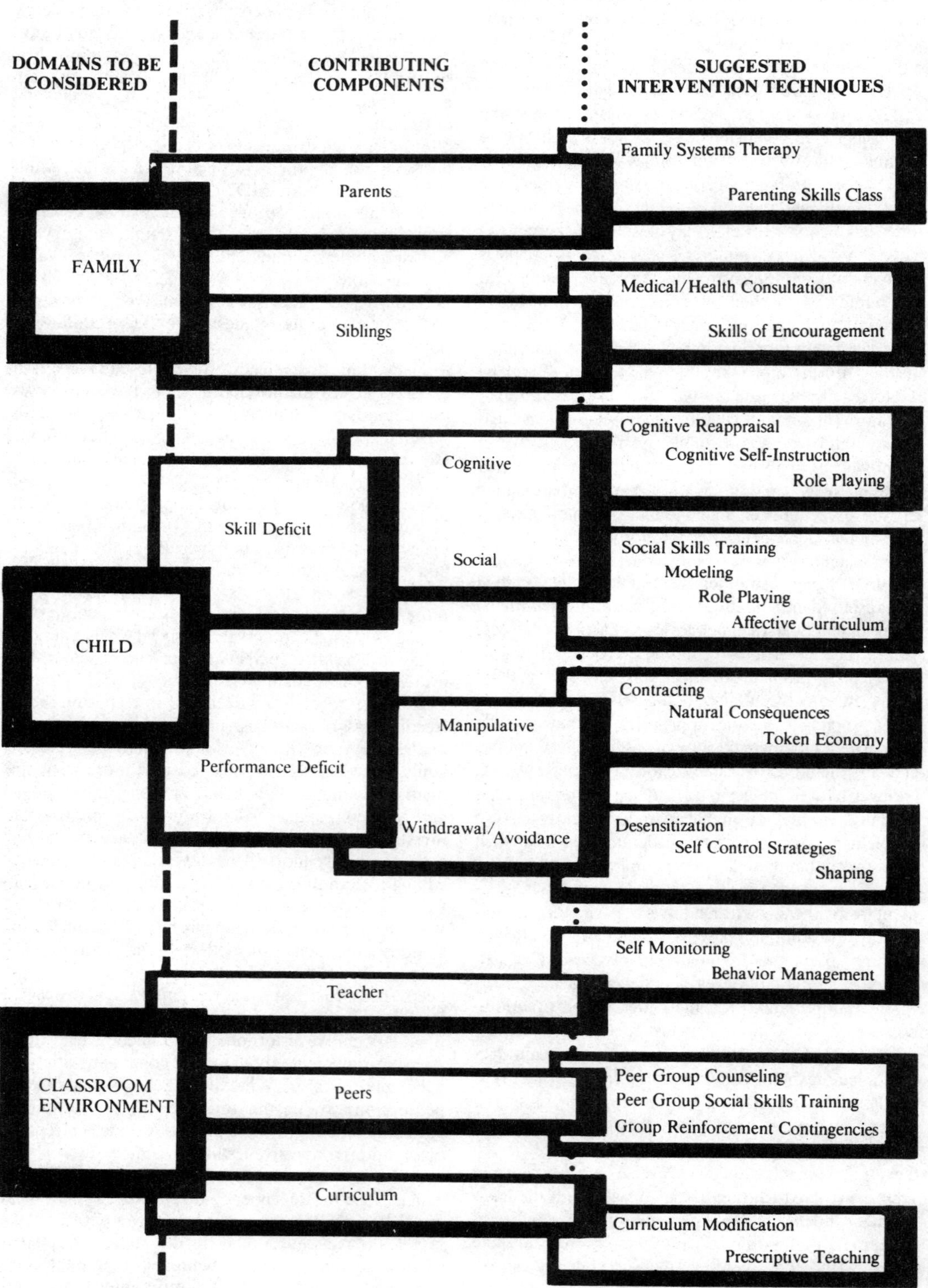

reports, behavior rating scales (parents), and adaptive behavior assessments. Such information can also be supplemented by systematic observation of family interaction (in home or analogue), projective testing, and completion of family interaction inventory.

6. To what extent does the classroom environment tend to perpetuate the cycle? What are the teacher's perceptions? Does the child's aptitude and achievement match the curriculum and adults' expectations? What is the status of the child's peer relationships? In order to answer these questions the following methods are useful: classroom observations (coding child–teacher interaction and collecting normative peer data), behavior-rating scales (teachers), observations of peer interaction (in classroom and on playground), interviews, sociometric evaluations, social skills checklists, curriculum evaluations.

7. To what extent does the child's history bear upon current behavioral patterns? Has there been or are there still health concerns regarding child, siblings, parents; is there a handicapped sibling; is there past trauma, etc.? This requires a detailed family medical history to be obtained.

By addressing these questions, an MDT is forced to evaluate many characteristics of the child and the social ecosystem(s). A wide variety of instruments and techniques can be used effectively so long as the MDT does not circumvent the comprehension decision-making process.

ALTERNATIVE ACTIONS

The outcome of the previously described comprehensive process is an effective and complete intervention plan. The breadth of the intervention plan will depend on the data collected. Alternative strategies are chosen and presented as a function of the ecological assessment. The flow chart in Figure 1 displays domains assessed, specific factors considered, and examples of suggested intervention.

To clarify the use of the flow chart, two examples are offered.

Example 1: A child with a skill deficit in reading, who exhibits a specific dependency in the classroom with constant attention-getting techniques such as frequent hand raising and failure to begin tasks independently. The child then becomes reliant on peers for directions and even responses. In the home, parents and siblings are eager to ease the frustration by reading signs, ice cream flavors, and movie titles. Consequently, the dependent child learns to be helpless and more dependent on adults and others in the social ecological system.

Example 2. In using the flow chart, specific strategies may be chosen and implemented to not only fit the needs of the child, but also to take into account the entire system(s) within which that dependent child is expected to function. A child and family unit have developed disruptive overprotective interaction patterns throughout the child's early development that have been precipitated by early chronic health problems experienced by the child. The child has not been given the opportunity to develop age-appropriate cognitive problem-solving and decision-making or interpersonal relationship skills. Thus, when faced with a cognitive dilemma or a novel social situation, the child exhibits dependent behaviors such as total reliance upon others, learned helplessness in school, lack of self-trust and is fearful of, withdraws to avoid, the overwhelming situation. It becomes obvious that all three of the major domains of family, child, and classroom must be considered in the intervention plan. Even though the child manipulates to avoid difficult situations, it appears that the child does not have the cognitive/social skills to successfully change such behaviors in school, at home or with peers. Therefore, cognitive problem solving, self-instruction, social skills training, and an affective curriculum might be helpful. The family must be involved in that the child's avoidance is being reinforced and new interaction skills (encouragement, appropriate reinforcement) need be developed with consistent follow-through by parents, teachers, and siblings. Medical consultation is necessary to rule out or correct any health-related factors. Peers need be involved in small-group social skills training and modeling. If the child's apprehensiveness is great enough, perhaps desensitization or other therapeutic support will be needed.

SUMMARY

It has been shown that dependency in childhood is a multifaceted dilemma. Even though it is typically considered to be solely an overt behavior problem, there may be other critical factors involved. Cognitive problem-solving deficits, social skills deficits, and/or behavior problems related to dependency patterns may seriously jeopardize children's future adjustment. Dependency is rarely perceived as a primary referral concern, even though these inter-related problems should be considered to be of paramount importance in regard to a child's development.

Dependency in children develops over time as the result of reciprocal transaction patterns between them and various aspects of their environments. Consequently, determining causation is rarely possible, and in most cases any attempt is futile. Rarely, if ever, should a single person or event receive the blame for developing a dependent relationship. However, many, if not all, characteristics of the child and the environment may need be involved in the intervention plan.

A comprehensive ecological approach to assessment is needed initially, and must be ongoing. The assessment should involve formal and informal instruments and techniques, and it should incorporate current practices. The key to comprehensive assessment is a decision-making process on the part of an MDT that produces intervention targets and methods that are a direct outgrowth of the assessment data.

REFERENCES

Achenbach, T. M., & Edelbrock, C. S. (1978). The classification of child psychopathology: A review and analysis of empirical efforts. *Psychological Bulletin, 85,* 1275–1301.

Ainsworth, M. D. S. (1969). Object relations, dependency, and attachment: A theoretical review of the infant–mother relationship. *Child Development, 40,* 969–1025.

Ainsworth, M. D. S. (1979). Infant–Mother Attachment. *American Psychologist, 34,* 932–937.

American Psychiatric Association. (1980). *Diagnostic and statistical manual of mental disorders* (3rd ed.). Washington, DC: Author.

Bell, R., & Harper, L. (1977). *Child effect on adults.* Hillsdale, NJ: Erlbaum.

Butkowski, I. S., & Willows, D. M. (1980). Cognitive-motivational characteristics of children varying in reading ability: Evidence for learned helplessness in poor readers. *Journal of Educational Psychology, 72,* 408–422.

Camp, B. W. (1977). Verbal mediation in young aggressive boys. *Journal of Abnormal Psychology, 86,* 145–153.

Cowen, E., Pederson, A., Babigian, M. Izzo, L., & Trost, M. (1973). Long-term follow-up of early detected vulnerable children. *Journal of Consulting and Clinical Psychology, 41,* 438–446.

Diener, C. I., & Dweck, C. S. (1980). An analysis of learned helplessness: II. The processing of success. *Journal of Personality and Social Psychology, 39,* 940–952.

Dweck, C. S., & Reppucci, N. D. (1973). Learned helplessness and reinforcement responsibility in children. *Journal of Personality and Social Psychology, 25,* 109–116.

Erickson, M. F., Sroufe, L. A., & Egeland, B. (1985). The relationship between quality of attachment and behavior problems in preschool in a high risk sample. *Monographs of the Society for Research in Child Development, 52*(1–2).

Gardner, W. I. (1979). *Children With Learning and Behavior Problems* (2nd ed.). Boston: Allyn and Bacon.

McFarland, M. A., & Johnson, H. S. (1986). *Utilizing ecological identification information in the assessment of student progress.* Paper presented at the annual meeting of the Midwest Symposium for Leadership in Behavioral Disorders, Kansas City.

Ollendick, T. H., & Hersen, M. (Eds.). (1984). *Child behavioral assessment.* New York: Pergamon.

Richman, L. C., & Lindgren, S. D. (1981). Verbal mediation deficits: Relation to behavior and achievement in children. *Journal of Abnormal Psychology, 90,* 99–104.

Schaefer, C. E., & Millman, H. L. (1981). *How to help children with common problems.* New York: Van Nostrand Reinhold.

BIBLIOGRAPHY: PROFESSIONALS

Camp, B. W., & Bash, M. A. (1985). *Think aloud.* Champaign, IL: Research Press.
Each volume in this series provides structured lessons helping elementary students to make full use of their cognitive skills in social behavior and coping with everyday situations. As students advance through the program, they are taught self-monitoring and self-evaluation.

Mann, P. H., Suiter, P. A., & McClung, R. M. (1979). *Handbook in diagnostic-prescriptive teaching* (2nd ed.). Boston: Allyn and Bacon.
Presents a frame of reference for examining learning processes and provides a rationale of children's failure. Diagnostic procedures and specific assessment devices are discussed, learning difficulties as well as behavioral concerns being addressed. Specific strategies are listed.

McGinnis, E., & Goldstein, A. P. (1984). *Skillstreaming the Elementary School Child.* Champaign, IL: Research Press.
Serves as a guide for teaching prosocial skills through a structured approach. The book provides both a teacher and a student checklist, a progress summary sheet, and a student mastery record. It stresses four key components during instruction: (1) modeling, (2) role playing, (3) performance feedback, and (4) transfer of training.

Swift, M. S., & Spivack, G. (1978). *Alternative teaching strategies.* Champaign, IL: Research Press.
Provides teachers, psychologists, and counselors with strategies that encourage classroom behaviors that enhance learning and redirect behaviors that interfere with learning. It also discusses common elements among teaching strategies and provides guidance in structuring classroom environments.

BIBLIOGRAPHY: PARENTS

Dinkmeyer, D., & McKay, G. D. (1976). *Systematic training for effective parenting.* Coral Springs, FL: CMTI.
Explains the STEP program in detail utilizing a practical approach and covers a complete sequence of parenting skills, from discovering the goals of misbehavior to holding family meetings.

McKay, G. D. (1976). *The basics of encouragement.* Coral Springs, FL: CMTI.
This booklet stresses encouragement and accepting children as they are. The author addresses the importance of evaluating the behaviors and not the person. There is also focus on the positive, emphasizing effort and improvement, and on assets and strengths. The crucial differences between praise and encouragement are discussed.

Children and Depression

D. H. Saklofske
University of Saskatchewan, Canada

H. L. Janzen
University of Alberta, Canada

BACKGROUND

Knowledge about adult depression at the theoretical, research, and clinical levels has steadily accumulated during this century. By comparison, the recognition that depression may occur during childhood and into early adolescence is a much more recent occurrence. Although earlier references to childhood depression (CHD) can be cited, including the well-known writings of Spitz (1946) on anaclitic depression and Bowlby (1971) on maternal separation, support for the concept of CHD is quite recent.

There is general agreement that depression can and does occur during childhood and adolescence. The *Diagnostic and Statistical Manual of Mental Disorders,* or DSM III (American Psychiatric Association, 1980), states that major depression may begin in infancy. PL 94-142 also specifies a marked degree of depression or unhappy mood over time as one characteristic in the identification of behavioral disturbance in children. Dysphoric mood is a universal part of human experience (Cantwell & Carlson, 1979) precipated by, for example, loss. Depressive symptoms can arise as part of some other affective or physical condition and such symptoms may be fairly wide-ranging in children. Feeling sad or "blue" is not infrequent but most children do recover from this transient and nonpathological mood state. For others, the depression can be more severe and chronic and can interfere with all aspects of daily life.

Depression in adults and adolescents is seen as relatively similar (Hudgens, 1974) but Inamdar et al. (1979) point to the "many differences, at least in early and mid-adolescence, which warrant more cautious comparison and further study" (p. 159). The DSM III manual states that "although the essential features of a major depressive episode are similar in infants, children, adolescents and adults, there are differences in the associated features" (p. 211). Gittleman-Klein (1971) concluded that there is not "a well-defined clinical picture common to children said to suffer from depression, there is as yet no single substantiated syndromal description of childhood depression" (p. 71).

Incidence

The lack of consensus about diagnostic criteria, the symptom–syndrome controversy, and varying assessment methods have yielded divergent estimates of CHD. Incidence figures vary with the age of subjects studied and kind of samples studied. Thus, we may hear that CHD is more common than first thought (e.g., Carlson & Cantwell, 1980; Kovacs & Beck, 1977) or that "the syndrome, if it exists, is very rare" (Costello, 1984, p. 309) or seldom occurs before adolescence (Cytryn et al., 1980).

Kashani et al. (1981) reviewed 11 studies that described the incidence of CHD at 0.14–59%, but Teuting, Koslow, and Hirschfeld (1982) summarized the incidence of moderate to severe childhood depression at less than 1–33%. Within the general population, estimates of CHD tend to be less than 10% depending on the diagnostic method employed (Kashani & Simmonds, 1979; Kashani et al., 1983; Lefkowitz & Tesiny, 1985; Paananen & Janzen, 1986).

Paananen and Janzen (1986) suggest that the male:female ratio for depression is 1:2, whereas Lefkowitz and Tesiny state that "prior to puberty, sex is not yet a risk factor for depression" (p. 654). For adolescents, the incidence of self-reported depressed mood is estimated at 18% (Kandel & Davies, 1982).

Prevalence figures of depression are much higher for various groups of referred and clinical samples of children. Depressive symptoms are reported in 57–62% of children referred to an educational diagnostic center (Brumback, Jackoway & Weinberg, 1980). Depression in psychiatric groups ranges from 54% to 10% for children and 23% for adolescents with twice as many preadolescent boys as girls being depressed but reversing during adolescence (Colbert et al., 1982). Carlson and Cantwell (1980) studied children and adolescents receiving psychiatric treatment and found that 60% had depressive symptoms, 49% had depressive syndromes, and 27% were diagnosed as depressive disorder. Depression was twice as frequent among inpatients (36%) as outpatients (16%). Children receiving medical treatment manifest high rates of depressive symptoms and a diagnosis of depression has been estimated at 7–17% (Kashani & Hakami, 1982).

These figures may be cast against a lifetime estimate of 5.3% for major depression (Robins et al., 1984), although the DSM III manual suggests a higher incidence of major depressive episodes in adults. It would seem that depressive symptoms occurring as a reaction to stress, as a symptom of some other disorder, or even as an early manifestation of depression are not uncommon in preadult groups. However, the incidence of severe depression (i.e., a major depressive episode) is generally low but increases for children and adolescents experiencing personal, educational, and medical problems.

Symptoms of Depression

Cytryn et al. (1980) compared the CHD diagnostic criteria of Cytryn and McKnew (1972), Weinberg et al.

(1973), the Childhood Depression Index (CDI) of Kovacs and Beck (1977), and DSM III and found considerable overlap. Variations, especially in associated features, tend to reflect differences in age or developmental level, the type of population under consideration, and the importance assigned to each symptom. The following symptoms are most often mentioned, although not by all "experts", and differing opinions are not uncommon.

Changes in mood and affect are the most obvious features of CHD. These children may look, or describe themselves as, sad and miserable, seldom smiling and not seeming to have fun or to enjoy themselves ("he is such an unhappy little boy"). While increased emotionality can cause some depressed children to become oversensitive and cry more frequently ("she cries at the drop of a hat"), others may become irritable, moody, and negativistic. This may be extended to include hostility, anger, and aggressive or antisocial behavior. Depressed children appear to be "down on themselves" and may describe themselves as being "a loser . . . no good . . . bad . . . stupid." This manifestation of helplessness, low self-esteem and self-deprecation can include guilt ("I don't deserve presents") and suicidal thoughts ("I wish I was dead . . . I would be better off dead") or even suicide attempts, especially upon entering adolescence.

Depressed children tend to be uninterested in most activities, losing interest in favorite hobbies, sports, and pastimes. When invited to participate in some activity, the depressed child may respond in a flat tone with "I don't care . . . it doesn't matter," shrugging the shoulders and shaking the head or not responding at all. Decreased interaction with family and friends and lessened participation in previously shared or social activities may occur ("he never plays with his friends anymore . . . she has dropped out of all her clubs and sports"). This can range from apathy to withdrawal ("he spends most of his time just sitting in his room") to angry demands to be left alone ("get off my back . . . go away, leave me alone") and open disrespect and aggression towards loved ones ("I hate you, I hate you all").

Various physical complaints may arise including headaches, abdominal discomfort, and constipation. Eating disturbances include loss of appetite and weight loss, although weight gains can occur in some instances. Sleep is affected to the extent that the child may experience insomnia, restless sleep, or nightmares. Some children experience difficulty waking up in the morning and then appear tired throughout the day, whereas a few others may have trouble getting back to sleep after waking early. Depressed children seem to lack energy and to "drag about"; others become agitated and restless ("he's so fidgety and tense"). Depressed children may also be slow to respond to questions and everyday situations. Cognitive processes, including thinking, problem solving, and planning activities seem slower than usual ("she just plods along in school"). Attention, concentration, and memory can be negatively affected ("he can't stick to the task"). This may be linked to the not infrequent observation of school difficulties ("his memory is terrible . . . he can't focus on his work") and decreased effort and motivation ("she doesn't make any effort . . . sits and does nothing"). The depressed child may complain "I don't like school, I don't want to go to school."

Diagnostic Classification

The above list of symptoms is not sufficient to discriminate between the essential and associated features of CHD, to argue for the existence of a syndrome or disorder, or to permit a differential diagnosis. However, there is some consensus that the basic affective, cognitive, and other components of depression are similar for adults and children, and the assumption that CHD may be diagnosed by employing modified adult criteria is reflected in several clinical descriptions. Weinberg et al. (1973) modified adult depression criteria and suggested that a symptom was present if there was a change in or concern about one or more of their listed behaviors. For a diagnosis of depression, the child must show the presence, for *more than a month,* of both dysphoric mood and self-deprecation as well as *two* of the following eight symptoms: aggressive behavior, sleep disturbance, change in school performance, change in attitude toward school, decreased socialization, somatic complaints, loss of usual energy, and change in appetite or weight.

The DSM III is intended to provide "clear descriptions of diagnostic categories in order to enable clinicians and investigators to diagnose, communicate about, study and treat various mental disorders" (p. 12). It is assumed that depression may occur at any age and that the essential features of depression are similar across age groups, allowing for some developmental differences in associated features. CHD is described under "Affective Disorders" rather than "Disorders Usually First Evident in Infancy, Childhood or Adolescence."

Depression can range from the severity of a Major Depressive Disorder to less severe or briefer mood disturbances. Depressive symptoms may occur together with other affective and organic disorders. Major Depressive Episode is diagnosed when dysphoric mood or loss of interest or pleasure in most activities is prominent and relatively persistent. Other associated symptoms include "appetite disturbance, change in weight, sleep disturbance, psychomotor agitation or retardation, decreased energy, feelings of worthlessness or guilt, difficulty concentrating or thinking, and thoughts of death or suicide or suicidal attempts" (p. 210).

Harrington (1984) suggested that DSM III "should be considered a work in progress" (p. 133), but Cytryn et al. (1980) concluded that DSM III is a valid system for the diagnosis of affective disorders in children and adults. However, Izard and Schwartz (1986) contend that "most clinicians and researchers who apply DSM III criteria to children of varying ages draw upon their knowledge of normal development and of the histories of the children being diagnosed in order to adapt and to adjust the criteria to the particular developmental levels of the children" (p. 73).

Revisions to DSM III are under way. The proposed revised criteria for CHD require the presence of *five* or more of these primary symptoms: dysphoric mood, anhedonia, self-deprecating ideation, tearfulness, low sense of self-esteem or self-worth, social withdrawal, impairment of school work, psychomotor retardation, difficulty with biological functions including eating and sleeping, and morbid ideation or suicide attempts (Wallbrown et al.,1986).

DEVELOPMENT

Various explanations and theories have been put forward to describe the causes and effects of depression in children and adolescents. Several of the more prominent positions from the biological and psychological literature are described here.

Psychoanalytic Theories

Freud's psychoanalytic theories dominated the mental health field for most of the first half of this century. The trauma of loss or rejection by a parent or loved on that can occur following separation, divorce, death, or even the introduction of a new sibling may lead to later depression if the basic conflict proves not to be resolvable. Klein (1948) pointed to disturbances in early mother–child relationships as the basis for later depression. The turning of aggression back on to the self, in which the superego is the instrument of punishment, was an important theme in descriptions of depression. A well-developed personality structure including the ego and superego was deemed necessary to experience loss of self-esteem, blame, censure, guilt, and to internalize aggression. Thus Rie (1966) argued that depression was psychodynamically impossible during childhood.

Learning Theories

A basic premise here is that depression results from a decrease in response-contingent reinforcement (Ferster, 1973) or the loss of reinforcer effectiveness (Costello, 1972). Ferster hypothesized that the decreased activity and the increased passivity and avoidance behavior associated with depression is linked to various aversive experiences. As well, inadequate or inappropriate reinforcement may result in the failure to learn appropriate behaviors to potentially positive reinforcers.

Lewinsohn suggested that depression resulted from a low rate of response-contingent positive reinforcement and from too much punishment (Lewinsohn & Hoberman, 1982; Lewinsohn & Shaw, 1969). In particular, the low rate of positive reinforcement that elicits depressive symptoms is associated with deficiency of social skills. Although some individual may provide positive reinforcement to compensate depressive symptoms, others avoid depressed persons, which further reduces the sources and amount of positive reinforcement available to them. This serves to maintain or increase depressive behavior.

Cognitive Theories

In recent years, cognition has been considered to play a major role in the etiology and maintenance of depression (Beck, 1967; Ellis & Bernard, 1983; Kovacs & Beck 1977; Meichenbaum & Burland, 1979; Rehm, 1977; Seligman, 1975). Beck stated that mood is determined by the way experience is structured. Depression is distorted thinking in which individuals hold a negative view of themselves,their world, and their future. Incoming information and experiences are distorted in a negative way to fit with existing schemata. Cognitive errors result in negative conclusions not supported by facts or evidence, a focus on detail out of context, overgeneralization, inaccurate labeling of events, and a tendency to exaggerate or minimize the significance of events. Beck suggested that these distorted cognitions arise from early traumatic experiences that have sensitized the individual to react negatively to certain events.

Seligman's (1975) theory of learned helplessness suggests that inescapable and uncontrollable aversive situations lead to a sense of hopelessness and helplessness that can generalize to future events. One's behavior and the probability of rewards are believed to be separate and independent. This loss of control over environmental reinforcers and the perceived inability to change this situation results in depression. Seligman and Peterson (1986) have applied an attributional reformulation of this model to childhood depression.

Biological Theories

The biological correlates of adult depression reflected in pharmacological treatment studies employing, for example, monamine oxidase (MAO) inhibitors and tricyclic antidepressants and in biochemical and neurophysiological laborabory studies, prompted the suggestion that a biochemical classification of depression was possible (Cantwell & Carlson, 1979; Maas, 1975). The implication of the biogenic amines norepinephrine, dopamine, and serotonin in adult affective disorder has resulted in the catecholamine and indoleamine hypotheses of depression (Arieti & Bemporad, 1978).

While some preliminary research with children has been reported (Cantwell & Carlson, 1979), the results are not clear. Puig-Antich's (1986) review of such biological markers as sleep EEG, neuroendocrine markers (e.g., cortisol secretion), growth hormone secretion, and neurotransmitters indicated that "age and puberty have major effects in most psychobiological markers of depression" (p. 368). Considerable gains in our knowledge of state and trait biochemical markers of childhood depression may be a expected in the foreseeable future.

Genetic and Family Theories

There is quite strong evidence of a role of genetic or inheritance factors in the transmission of affective disorders based on studies of identical twins (Gershon et al., 1976) and of the natural and adopted children of affectively ill parents (Cadoret, 1978; Cytryn et al., 1986; Weintraub et al., 1986). The risk of affective disorders in children increases when both parents are affectively ill (Gershon et al., 1982); the morbidity rate is two times greater for children with one versus no affected parents and increases to four times for "the offspring of dually affected parental matings" (Puig-Antich, 1986, p. 346). There is growing evidence of a genetic predisposition for depression (Cytryn et al., 1982; Gershon et al., 1983;

McKnew et al., 1979). The recent Fourth World Congress on Biological Psychiatry heard a report that children of seriously depressed mothers are nearly three times more likely to develop major depression than those whose mothers have never been depressed. Rutter (1986a) stresses that parental depression constitutes an environmental and a genetic risk for their children.

Integrated Views

The genetic models are incapable of perfect prediction and the mechanism of transmission of affective illness has eluded researchers to date. Neither is there overwhelming evidence for any one "psychological" explanation. While other orientations may be a cited, such as the life events model (Paykel, 1979), there is an increased recognition of the multidimensional nature of depression. Genetic factors, physiological and psychological stress, and developmental events are all potential pathways to depression (Akiskal & McKinney, 1975). Arieti and Bemporad (1978) held that depression may be "the final common pathway for various processes that alter the psychological equilibrium in different patients" (p. 56). Izard and Schwartz (1986) have concluded that "the etiology of depression can be generally understood in terms of defective or missing links between the biochemical, emotion, cognitive, motor, and social systems, and the sources of the breakdowns in intersystem interaction and integration lie in the various biological and social processes of human development" (p. 66).

Developmental Considerations

Depressive manifestations and vulnerabilities vary as a function of age and developmental stage (e.g., Carlson & Garber, 1986; Cicchetti & Schneider-Rosen, 1986; Rutter, 1986b). Emde et al. (1986) distinguish four periods of childhood (i.e., infant, preschool, school age, and adolescence) and describe the changing meaning of depressive feelings at each period. Izard and Schwartz (1986) document various developmental changes in patterns of emotions in CHD. Rutter's (1986b) discussion of developmental changes in relation to depressive feelings and depressive disorder focuses on "three phases of transition" (p. 20). The first phase is observed at about 6 months when infants first exhibit the "protest-despair-detachment sequence" after institutional placement (e.g., in a hospital). After age 4 to 5 years, this reaction is lessened, possibly because children now have the cognitive skills needed to better understand such occurrences. The third phase is observed at puberty. An increase in depressive feelings, especially among girls, and in suicide occur during adolescence. Suicide and parasuicide, which can often be linked with depression, are quite rare prior to puberty. Rutter further observes that grief reactions following bereavement are much more intense in adolescents than younger children. It is also suggested that depression and other affective problems in childhood may be "a precursor of significant psychopathology in adolescence" (Cytryn et al., 1986, p.173).

PUTTING CHILDHOOD DEPRESSION IN PERSPECTIVE

The School Psychologist's Initial Role in the Diagnosis of Depression

The identification and diagnosis of depression in childhood remains extremely complex. Awareness of the variety of symptoms described earlier is certainly necessary as an initial indicator. However, school psychologists may find that a referral for assessment may be requested for other reasons — reasons that may well be *correlates* of depression. For example, school phobia is often found in the active or initial phase of depression. Additionally, more than one third of the referrals for diagnosis of various behavioral and learning disorders eventually have revealed depression as a major correlate. The results of psychometric testing did not explain the failure to learn as due to specific learning disabilities. School psychologists, therefore, must be aware of the behaviors that are frequently associated with depression. Depressed children show significantly more conduct problems, anxiety, impulsivity, hyperactivity, muscular tension, inattention, passivity, low self-esteem, and attention-demanding or antisocial (stealing, lying, aggression) behaviors than nondepressed children. About two thirds of children referred for these problems are found in the regular classroom. The initial tasks required of the school psychologist are (a) to interview the teachers, parents, and the referred child; (b) to observe the child in a natural or classroom setting; (c) to use psychometric tests to determine the child's strengths and weaknesses so as to aid in treatment planning; and (d) to administer one or several children's depression measures to verify the observations and the child's own subjective expressions of feelings, perceptions, and cognitions.

If the child's own perceptions, as indicated by responses to the depression measures, verify the observed and reported symptoms, a diagnosis of depression can be made. However, to avoid possible overidentification or misidentification, a multistage, multiscreening model as proposed by Reynolds (1986) can be used. All major depression measures and interview schedules are briefly described within the context of this model.

Multistage Screening and Diagnosis

The following model is described in detail elsewhere (Reynolds, 1986) and will only be discussed in short form here. Tested over a 3-year period in several school districts, the multistage model has proven to be effective in several respects. First, it limits the school psychologist's involvement primarily to clinical interviewing. Second, it draws on the available sources of assistance and information from schoolteachers, counsellors, and parents. Third, if the plan is accepted at board level, it allows for early identification and subsequent treatment. Thus, school psychologists require appropriate training in the assessment of depression.

Stage 1 of the model involves group assessment (screening) at all age levels (grade 3 and above) with one or several self-report depression measures. This screening is to be carried out by classroom teachers who have been trained in the administration and scoring of the questionnaires. A brief in-service may be required beforehand. To reduce the high rate of false-positives at this stage, administration of more than one measure is suggested. Teachers may need to read the questionnaires to younger children and adolescents with reading difficulties. Possible choices of child depression measures include (a) Children's Depression Inventory (CDI; Kovacs, 1981); (b) Children's Depression Scale (CDS; Lang & Tischer, 1978); and (c) Child Depression Scale (CDS; Reynolds, in press).

Although other measures are available, these three are brief, the Lang and Tischer scale being the longest. The measures can be administered to individuals or groups in 30 minutes. A number of reviews have documented the adequate validity and reliability of these scales (Reynolds, 1986; Costello, 1984; Paananen & Janzen, 1986).

Some appropriate adolescent depression measures are the Reynolds Adolescent Depression Scale (RADS; Reynolds, in press), the Beck Depression Inventory (BDI), modified for use with adolescents by Chiles, Miller, and Cox (1980), and the Hamilton Depression Rating Scale (Hamilton, 1960).

With utilization of scoring keys and predetermined cutoff scores as suggested by the test authors, the process of scoring and identification at Stage 1 can be undertaken by clerical staff, aides, schoolteachers, or counsellors. Computer scoring would minimize administrative time. Students who are identified are then included in the second stage of screening.

At an interval of 3–6 weeks following Stage 1 screening, all students thus identified should be reassessed with the same measures as used in Stage 1. This may be done by teachers, or by the school psychologist with small groups or individuals, at recess or other convenient times. Reynolds also advises that a few non-depressed children be included in this stage of assessment to provide for variability in the grouping of children and to reduce potential negative reactions to a second screening.

Those students for whom a high score may reflect a temporary dysphoric mood on Stage 1 screening may not score in the depressed range at Stage2. These students may also be faking. Students who score in the nondepressed range at Stage 2 should be considered nondepressed but be identified for further evaluation for other presenting problems or for depression at a later time. Students identified at Stage 1 and Stage 2 as depressed are then individually evaluated at Stage 3.

Stage 3 involves individual clinical interviews with all students identified as depressed at *both* Stage 1 and 2. This work must be done only by a clinically trained school psychologist or another trained psychologist called in for school consultation purposes. Clinical interviews provide additional sources of both data and method variance in the assessment, thus increasing the validity of the diagnostic procedure. The interview schedules suggested below can be used to obtain more refined information, or to assist in delineating areas of concern associated with certain depressive symptoms. A carefully structured clinical interview is essential not only for proper and differential diagnosis but also for planning therapeutic interventions.

Suggested interview schedules include the Schedule for Affective Disorders and Schizophrenia for School-Age Children (K-SADS; Puig-Antich & Chambers, 1978), the Children's Depression Rating Scale (CDRS; Poznanski et al., 1979), the Interview Schedule for Children (ISC; Kovacs, 1983), the Diagnostic Interview for Children and Adolescents (DICA; Herjanic, & Reich, 1982), and the Diagnostic Interview Schedule for Children (DISC; National Institute of Mental Health, in preparation).

In terms of time, the CDRS is recommended by Reynolds (30–40 minutes) over the K-SADS (90 minutes). However, the K-SADS provides a more formal DSM III classification and further diagnosis for conduct disorder. The CDRS may be sufficient for school use, since it may not be critical for a DSM III classification to be made if treatment is effected in the school. The CDRS also provides for a cutoff score to identify major depression in children and adolescents.

From Diagnosis to Plans of Action

Awareness and knowledge of the depression scales and interview schedules is an important step in the recognition and subsequent treatment of depression in referred students. School psychologists may need to seek out training workshops in the clinically based interview schedules and obtain a background in clinical disorders. Rarely will the school psychologist be faced with a single diagnosis of major depression. When it is deemed to be present, it may be necessary, as an initial step, to *refer* the child to other professionals for additional assessment and treatment. However, it is more likely that a coordinated program of assessment and treatment will be needed. For example, referral to an outside mental health agency for psychiatric evaluation may coincide with an in-school treatment plan involving the school psychologist, counsellor, teacher, and parents. Whereas the psychiatrist may focus on the depression per se, the in-school plan could include (a) specific classroom reinforcement schedules; (b) development of an individual educational plan (IEP) for remediation of learning difficulties; (c) suggestions to the parents to modify symptoms of home-related problems (e.g. lying, stealing, sibling rivalry, home-study skills); and (d) other specific interventions aimed at the *correlates* of depression specific to the classroom or school environment.Coordination from diagnosis to a plan of action may be the key role for the school psychologist. The following section describes other alternative actions, should the school psychologist decide to become involved directly in the treatment process.

ALTERNATIVE ACTIONS

Although much has been written about the treatment of adult depression, very little empirical evidence is available about the treatment of childhood depression.

This limited evidence does indicate "treatment of childhood and adolescent depression can be implemented successfully in a school setting" (Clarizio, 1985, p.319). Studies of direct treatment by school psychologists and indirect teacher-mediated intervention have shown a modicum of success. The starting point, however, is for the school psychologist to resolve certain issues, which may include (a) whether depression is a symptom, a syndrome, a disorder, or a disease; (b) whether to alter behaviors or cognitions or both; (c) whether to refute the irrational beliefs; and (d) whether to focus on the mood state or the lack of social skills. In the absence of solid, empirically based answers to aid in the choice of intervention strategies, school psychologists will need to rely on rational evaluation of a variety of treatment modes in respect to therapeutic effectiveness, cost efficiency, time, and availability of external human and social resources. The following samples will familiarize the school psychologist with some current techniques. For a detailed account of treatment models the reader is referred To Beckham and Leber (1985), Perry, Frances, and Charkin (1985), and Clarisio's (1985) description of cognitive–behavioral treatments of CHD.

Samples of Some Successful Treatment Techniques

Whereas the treatment of CHD is generally a long-term consistent application of a system or model, the examples of techniques that follow have shown positive results in the short term. Following Freden (1982), all techniques, at some point in therapy, provide for at least three levels of amelioration, all influencing one another: Level 1, primary groups (family, friends, school); Level 2, external life (what children do or do not do); Level 3, inner life (feelings, perceptions, cognitions).

Successful treatment, then, will require investigation of possible intervention at more than one of these levels. The clinical interview will be the main source of information to determine which level to apply first. The school psychologist should also consider such factors as age, sex, family support, level of cognitive skills, social skills, peer support, and availability of external resources in beginning treatment.

The Crystal Ball Technique. de Shazer (1985) described this brief therapy technique in the treatment of a patient who had depressive thoughts about the future. The technique does not involve a formal trance. Clients are asked to visualize several different crystal balls. In the first one, they visualize an early pleasant memory and describe it fully, paying attention to their own and other people's behavior. The second crystal ball involves recall of a surprisingly forgotten event; some success in life that is an exception to the current problems. The third ball is oriented to the future, with visualization of successful resolution of the problem. The fourth crystal ball is used to have the client remember the manner in which the problem(s) has been solved. The standard theme throughout is to ask the client "What will things be like for you and others when the problem is solved?" (de Shazer, 1985, p. 83).

Write, Read, and Burn. This technique can easily be applied to children and adolescents who complain of obsessive–depressive thoughts. Quite simply, clients write all their good and bad memories on odd-numbered days, read the previous day's notes on even-numbered days, and burn (or shred) them. If unwanted negative thoughts come to them at unscheduled times they are to say to themselves "I have other things to think about now; I'll think about this at my regular time" (de Shazer, 1985, p. 120). de Shazer reported success with this technique within a week, since it quickly objectifies the concerns, and the troubles symbolically and substantively "go up in smoke."

Doing Something Different. This brief therapy technique has been applied by behavioral and cognitive therapists as well as by parents and teachers. The therapist must fully understand the daily behaviors first before suggesting that the expected routine be changed. However, the therapist does not need to make a direct suggestion. It is best for the client's parents or significant others involved in the treatment to suggest the change in behavior or task. A successful application of this technique is described by de Shazer (1985).

Coverant Control Technique. Johnson (1971) described a coverant control procedure for depressive thoughts in adolescents. In spite of major behavior improvements, an adolescent client still reported persistent depressive feelings. The coverant intervention used positive self-statements by requiring them to be paired with a high-probability behavior. In the case cited by Johnson, the 17-year-old was required to carry a set of index cards in his pockets with a description of a positive change he had made. This young man read the cards to himself each time he was about to urinate. A rather unorthodox procedure; nevertheless, the depressed thoughts ceased after 2 weeks on this task, and were replaced by spontaneous positive thoughts. The theoretical rationale for the procedure is well grounded, although other high-probability behaviors may have more appeal.

Reward, Punishment, and Impersonal Distractions. Cantanese, Rosenthal, and Kelly (1979) described a combination strategy to reduce depression significantly. The treatment involved choosing any one of the following: (a) visualizing pleasant scenes; (b) doing some brief, pleasant task; (c) mentally scolding oneself when feeling "blue"; (d) performing a mildly aversive task; and (e) thinking about something *not* related to the problem.The authors reported good maintenance of reduced depressive feelings over a 2-year period.

The key to these strategies is to "distract" and "assert" oneself in doing something different. Consequently, they border on the brief therapy technique described by de Shazer (1985).

Characteristics of Therapy

Depression may be a separate problem of mild to serious proportions or just one of the various factors in another syndrome. Appropriate therapy approaches are many. Treatment may be broadly directed or narrowly focused on bothersome symptoms. The goals of therapy, however, would usually include (a) improved self-directed activity, (b) realistic appraisal of one's situation, (c) more satisfactory social relationships, and (d) increased positive feelings and self-statements. Posttherapy evaluation is always recommended to determine if treatment has been successful.

School psychologists may well be familiar with a number of cognitive, behavioral, or other models of treatment. All are reported to have had some success, but as Clarizio (1985) pointed out, selection of treatments should be focused on what has been found to be successful with children in school settings. For example, Beck and Young (1985) claim that cognitive strategies are *less* effective for patients with severe endogenous depression, borderline personality disorders, impaired memory functions, and the schizoaffective disorders. On the other hand, cognitive techniques are recommended if the client is introspective, has close relationships with others, is a good organizer and planner, is conscientious about responsibilities, and can reason abstractly.

Any form of therapy involves a reciprocal and collaborative relationship between client and practitioner. Needless to say, much could be written about "therapist characteristics" including the desirable personal qualities of warmth, accurate empathy, and genuineness. Without this, no technique will be of much value.

Psychotherapy and Pharmacotherapy

In a detailed review comparing a variety of therapies with medication, Beckham and Leber (1985) conclude that "there is currently no evidence to support strict adherence to either a psychotherapeutic or pharmacological model of treating outpatient depression" (p. 328). Although medication may well be the treatment of choice for endogenous depression, not all depressions involve disturbances of neurochemical functioning. School psychologists must recognize that even depressions that are biological in origin will cause disruptions in the client's personality and social functioning and require adaptive counselling. Although group psychotherapy approaches have not been found to be as effective as individual strategies, purely psychological interventions may not be sufficient in some cases. There is a need, therefore, for close collaboration among mental health professionals in providing quality care for depressed children and adolescents. Beckham and Leber (1985) suggest that a combination or multimodal treatment may well be more effective, since neither medication nor psychological approaches alone have any clear superiority.

SUMMARY

The underlying theme in this chapter has been that although childhood depression may mean different things to different people, it is generally defined as a disorder of considerable length with specific symptoms and signs that substantially interfere with a child's functioning or cause great personal distress. As such, it differs from everyday sadness or situationally based "blues." The evidence currently available supports the validity of the *concept* of childhood depression, from major depression to its milder forms, even if the incidence figures vary from study to study and setting to setting. Regardless of the variety of explanations of the etiology of such depression, it has been associated with a number of psychological, social, and educational problems. For this reason, it is imperative for school psychologists to be aware of its correlates and developmental factors.

Depression that is real and severe may also be associated with a variety of medical illnesses. Although biological conditions alone may not predispose a person to depression, certain biological conditions may affect a child's ability to cope, not only with the illness, but also with other environmental demands and stressors. It is essential, therefore, that school psychologists seek *collaboration* with medical and psychiatric professionals.

Recognition and diagnosis are the crucial first steps to recovery. Difficulty lies not so much with the *use* of diagnostic criteria, nor in the instruments, but in the *differential process* of assessment. A wealth of information is now available as to possible causes, explanations for causes, developmental factors, and physical conditions affecting the expression of depression. The task of the school psychologist is to determine which factors require attention and deserve immediate action and who is to be involved in the subsequent treatment.It is our view that *consultation* and *collaboration* with other professionals and agencies outside the school will be needed when a diagnosis of major depression is made.

Today's children and youth are facing increased pressure and demands at home and school. The risk of depression is aggravated by higher rates of disrupted families, poverty, frequent moves by parents, and higher expectations of academic performance, to name a few factors. As child advocates, school psychologists must strive for a society that promotes mental health. Hence, their future role may be increasingly that of consultant to parents and teachers, so as to prevent or at least reduce the risk of depression. However, although commitment to *prevention* will be a continuing and ever expanding function of the school psychologist, for now, the school psychologist's main purpose at the diagnostic stage should be to try to pinpoint the level at which the fundamental problem is to be found, and then to collaborate in its treatment.

REFERENCES

Akiskal, H. S., & McKinney, W. T. (1975). Overview of recent research in depression: Integration of ten conceptual models into a comprehensive clinical frame. *Archives of General Psychiatry, 32,* 285–305.

American Psychiatric Association. (1980). *Diagnostic and statistical manual of mental disorders* (3rd ed.). Washington, D. C.: APA.

Arieti, S., & Bemporad, J. (1978). *Severe and mild depression.* New York: Basic Books.

Beck, A. T. (1967). *Depression: Clinical, experimental and theoretical aspects.* New York: Harper & Row.

Beck, A. T., & Young, J. E. (1985). Depression. In D. H. Barlow (Ed.), *Clinical handbook of psychological disorders: A step-by-step treatment manual* (pp. 206–244). New York: Guilford.

Beckham, E. E., & Leber, W. R. (Eds.). (1985). *Handbook of depression: Treatment, assessment and research.* Homewood, IL: Dorsey.

Bowlby, J. (1971). *Separation.* New York: Basic Books.

Brumback, R. A., Jackoway, M. K., & Weinberg, W. A. (1980). Relation of intelligence to childhood depression in children referred to an educational diagnostic center. *Perceptual and Motor Skills, 50,* 11–17.

Cadoret, R. J. (1978). Evidence for genetic inheritance of primary affective disorder. *American Journal of Psychiatry, 135,* 463–466.

Cantwell, D. P., & Carlson, G. A. (1979). Problems and prospects in the study of childhood depression. *Journal of Nervous and Mental Disease, 167,* 522–529.

Carlson, G. A., & Cantwell, D. P. (1980). Unmasking masked depression in children and adolescents. *American Journal of Psychiatry, 137,* 445–449.

Carlson, G. A., & Garber, J. (1986). Developmental issues in the classification of depressed children. In M. Rutter, C. E. Izard, & P. B. Read (Eds.), *Depression in young people: Developmental and clinical perspectives* (pp. 399–434). New York: Guilford.

Catanese, R. A., Rosenthal, T. L., & Kelly, J. E. (1979). Strange bedfellows: Reward, punishment and impersonal distraction strategies in treating dysphoria. *Cognitive Therapy and Research, 3,* 299–305.

Chiles, J. A., Miller, M. L., & Cox, G. B. (1980). Depression in an adolescent delinquent population. *Archives of General Psychiatry, 87,* 1179–1184.

Cicchetti, D., & Schneider-Rosen, K. (1986). An organizational approach to childhood depression. In M. Rutter, C. E. Izard, & P. B. Read (Eds.), *Depression in young people: Developmental and clinical perspectives* (pp. 71–134). New York: Guilford.

Clarizio, H. F. (1985). Cognitive–behavioral treatment of childhood depression. *Psychology in the Schools, 22,* 308–327.

Colbert, P., Newman, B., Ney, P., & Young, J. (1982). Learning disabilities as a symptom of depression in children. *Journal of Learning Disabilities, 15,* 333–336.

Costello, C. G. (1972). Depression: Loss of reinforcers or loss of reinforcer effectiveness. *Behavior Therapy, 3,* 240–247.

Costello, C. G. (1984). Childhood depression. In J. Mash & L. Terdal (Eds.), *Behavioral assessment of childhood disorders* (pp. 305–346). New York: Guilford.

Cytryn, L., & McKnew, D. H. (1972). Proposed classification of childhood depression. *American Journal of Psychiatry, 129,* 149–155.

Cytryn, L., McKnew, D. H., Bartko, J. J., Lamour, M., & Hamovit, J. (1982). Offspring of patients with affective disorders II. *Journal of American Academy of Child Psychiatry, 21,* 389–391.

Cytryn, L., McKnew, D. H., & Bunney, W. E. (1980). Diagnosis of depression in children: A reassessment. *American Journal of Psychiatry, 137,* 22–25.

Cytryn, L., & McKnew, D. H., Zahn-Waxler, C., & Gershon, E. S. (1986). Developmental issues in risk research: The offspring of affectively ill patients. In M. Rutter, C. E. Izard, & P. B. Read (Eds.), *Depression in young people: Developmental and clinical perspectives* (pp. 163–188). New York: Guilford.

de Shazer, S. 1985). *Keys to solution in brief therapy.* New York: W. W. Norton.

Ellis, A., & Bernard, M. (1983). Rational–emotive approaches to the problems of childhood. New York: Plenum.

Emde, R. N., Harmon, R. J., & Good, W. V. (1986). Depressive feelings in children: A transitional model for research. In M. Rutter, C. E. Izard, & P. B. Read (Eds.), *Depression in young people: Developmental and clinical perspectives* (pp. 135–160). New York: Guilford.

Ferster, C. B. (1973). A functional analysis of depression. *American Psychologist, 28,* 857–870.

Freden, L. (1982). *Psychological aspects of depression: No way out?* New York: Wiley.

Gershon, E. S., Bunney, W. E., Leckman, J. F., Van Eerdewegh, M., & Debauche, B.A. (1976). The inheritance of affective disorders: A review of data of hypotheses. *Behavior Genetics, 6,* 227–261.

Gershon, E. S., Hamovit, J., Guroff, J. J., Dibble, E., Leckman, J., Sceery, W., Targum, S., Nurnberger, J., Goldin, L., Bunney, W. (1982). A family study of schizoaffective, bipolar I, bipolar II, unipolar, and normal control probands. *Archives of General Psychiatry, 39,* 1157–1167.

Gershon, E. S., Nurnberger, J., Nadi, N. S., Berrettini, W.H., & Goldin, L. R. (1983). *The origins of depression: Current concepts and approaches.* New York: Springer-Verlag.

Gittleman-Klein, R. (1977). Definitional and methodological issues concerning depressive illness in children. In J. G. Schulterbrandt & A. Rasksin (Eds.), *Depression in childhood: Diagnosis, treatment and conceptual models* (pp. 69–80). New York: Raven.

Hamilton, M. (1960). A rating scale for depression. *Journal of Neurology, Neurosurgery and Psychiatry, 23,* 56–62.

Harrington, R. G. (1984). Assessing childhood anxiety and depressive disorders. In S. Weaver (Ed.), *Testing children: A reference guide for effective clinical and psychological assessment* (pp. 161–184). Kansas City: Test Corporation of America.

Herjanic, B., & Reich, W. (1982). Development of a structured psychiatric interview for children: Agreement between child and parent on individual symptoms. *Journal of Abnormal Child Psychology, 10,* 307–324.

Hudgens, R. W. (1974). *Psychiatric disorders in adolescents.* Baltimore: Williams & Wilkins.

Inamdar, S. C., Siomopoulis, G., Osborn, M., & Bianchi, E. C. (1979). Phenomenology associated with depressed moods in adolescents. *American Journal of Psychiatry, 136,* 156–159.

Izard, C.E., & Schwartz, G. M. (1986). Patterns of emotion in depression. In M. Rutter, C. E. Izard, & P. B. Read (Eds.), *Depression in young people: Developmental and clinical perspectives* (pp. 33–70). New York: Guilford.

Johnson, W. G. (1971). Some applications of Homme's covert-ant control therapy: Two case reports. *Behavior Therapy, 2,* 240--248.

Kandel, D. B., & Davies, M. (1982). Epidemiology of depressive mood in adolescents. *Archives of General Psychiatry, 39,* 1205–1212.

Kashani, J. H., & Hakami, N. (1982). Depression in children and adolescents with malignancy. *Canadian Journal of Psychiatry, 27,* 474–476.

Kashani, J. H., Husain, A., Shekim, W. D., Hodges, K. K.,Cytryn, L., & McKnew, D. H. (1981). Current perspectives on childhood depression: An overview. *American Journal of Psychiatry, 138,* 143–153.

Kashani, J. H., McGee, R. O., Clarkson, S. E., Anderson, J. C., Walton, L. A., Williams, S., Silva, P. A., Robins, A. J., Cytryn, L., & McKnew, D. H. (1983). Depression in a sample of 9 year old children. *Archives of General Psychiatry, 40,* 1217–1223.

Kashani, J. H., & Simmonds, J. F. (1979). The incidence of depression in children. *American Journel of Psychiatry, 136,* 1203–1205.

Klein, M. (1948). Mourning and its relation to manic–depressive states. In M. Klein (Ed.), *Contributions to psychoanalysis, 1921–1945.* London: Hogarth.

Kovacs, M. (1981). Rating scales to assess depression in school-age children. *Acta Paedopsychiatrica, 46,* 305–315.

Kovacs, M. (1983). *The Interview Schedule for Children (ISC): Interrater and parent-child agreement.* Unpublished manuscript.

Kovacs, M., & Beck, A. T. (1977). An empirical-clinical approach toward a definition of childhood depression. In J. G. Schulterbrandt & A. Raskin (Eds.), *Depression in childhood: Diagnosis, treatment and conceptual models* (pp. 1–25). New York: Raven.

Lang, M., & Tischer, M. (1978). *Children's Depression Scale.* Victoria: The Australian Council for Educational Research.

Lefkowitz, M. M., & Tesiny, E. P. (1985). Depression in children: Prevalence and correlates. *Journal of Consulting and Clinical Psychology, 53,* 647–656.

Lewinsohn, P., & Hoberman, H. (1982). Depression. In A. Bellack, M. Hersen, & A. Kazdin (Eds.), *International handbook of behavior modification and therapy* (pp. 397–431). New York: Plenum.

Lewinsohn, P., & Shaw, D. (1969). Feedback about interpersonal behavior as an agent of behavior change: A case study in the treatment of depression. *Psychotherapy and Psychosomatics, 17,* 82–88.

Mass, J. W. (1975). Biogenic amines and depression. *Archives of General Psychiatry,32,* 1357–1361.

McKnew, D. H., Cytryn, L., Efron, A. M., Gershon, E. S., & Bunney, W. E. (1979). Offspring of manic–depressive patients. *British Journal of Psychiatry, 134,* 148–152.

Meichenbaum, D., & Burland, S. (1979). Cognitive behavior modification with children. *School Psychology Digest, 8,* 426–433.

Paananen, N., & Janzen, H. L. (1986). Incidence and characteristics of depression in elementary school children. *Canadian Journal of School Psychlogy, 2,* 7–19.

Paykel, E. S. (1979). Recent life events in the development of depressive disorders. In R. A. Depue (Ed.), *The psychobiology of the depressive disorders* (pp. 245–262). New York: Academic.

Perry, S., Frances, A., & Clarkin, J. (1985). *A DSM-III casebook of differential therapeutics: A clinical guide to treatment selection.* New York: Brunner/Mazel.

Poznanski, E. O., Cook, S. C., & Carroll, B. J. (1979). A depression rating scale for children. *Pediatrics, 64,* 442–450.

Puig-Antich, J. (1986). Psychobiological markers: Effects of age and puberty. In M. Rutter, C. E. Izard, & P. B. Read (Eds.), *Depression in young people: Developmental and clinical perspectives* (pp. 341–381). New York: Guilford.

Puig-Antich, J., & chambers, W. J. (1978). *Schedule for Affective Disorders and Schizophrenia for School Age Children (6–16 years) Kiddie — SADS.* Unpublished manuscript. New York: New York State Psychiatric Institute.

Rehm, L. (1977). A self-control model of depression. *Behavior Therapy, 8,* 787–804.

Reynolds, W. M. (1986). A model for the screening and identification of depressed children and adolescents in school settings. *Professional School Psychology, 1,* 117–129.

Reynolds, W. M. (in press). *Reynolds Adolescent Depression Scale.* Odessa, FL: Psychological Assessment Resources.

Rie, H. E. (1966). Depression in childhood: A survey of some pertinent contributions. *Journal of the American Academy of Child Psychiatry, 5,* 653–685.

Robins, L. N., Helzer, J. E., Weissman, M. M., Orvaschel, H., Gruenberg, E., Burke, J. D., & Regier, D. A. (1984). Lifetime prevalence of specific psychiatric disorders in three sites. *Archives of General Psychiatry, 41,* 949–958.

Rutter, M. (1986a). Depressive feelings, cognitions and disorders: A research postscript. In M. Rutter, C. E. Izard, & P. B. Read (Eds.), *Depression in young people: Developmental and clinical perspectives* (pp. 491–519). New York: Guilford.

Rutter, M. (1986b). The developmental psychopathology of depression: Issues and perspectives. In M. Rutter, C. E. Izard, & P. B. Read (Eds.), *Depression in young people: Developmental and clinical perspectives* (pp. 3–30). New York: Guilford.

Rutter, M., Izard, C. E., & Read, P. B. (1986). *Depression in young people: Developmental and clinical perspectives.* New York: Guilford.

Seligman, M. (1975). *Helplessness: On depression, development and death.* San Francisco: Freeman.

Seligman, M. E. P., & Peterson, C. (1986). A learned helplessness perspective in childhood depression: Theory and research. In M. Rutter, C. E. Izard, & P. B. Read (Eds.), *Depression in young people: Developmental and clinical perspective* (pp. 223–249). New York: Guilford.

Spitz, R. (1946). Anaclitic depression. *Psychoanalytic Study of the Child, 2,* 113–117.

Teuting, P., Koslow, S. H., & Hirschfeld, R. M. (1982). *Special report on depression research* (DHHS Publication No. ADM-1085, National Institute of Mental Health). Washington, DC: U. S. Government Printing Office.

Wallbrown, F., Merydith, S., Chiarella, D., Guy, D., & Engin, A. (1986). *Childhood depression: Diagnosis and treatment.* Paper presented at the annual meeting of the National Association of School Psychologists, Hollywood, FL.

Weinberg, W. A., Rutman, J., Sullivan, L., Penick, E. C., & Dietz, S. G. (1973). Depression in children referred to an education diagnostic center: Diagnosis and treatment. *Journal of Pediatrics, 83,* 1065–1072.

Weintraub, S., Winters, K. C., & Neale, J. M. (1986). Competence and vulnerability in children with an affectively disordered parent. In M. Rutter, C. E. Izard, & P. B. Read (Eds.), *Depression in young people: Developmental and clinical perspectives* (pp. 205–220). New York: Guilford.

BIBLIOGRAPHY: PROFESSIONALS

Bellack, A. S., Elkin, I., Rush, A. J., & Spitzer, R. L. (Eds.). (1985). *Handbook of depression, treatment, assessment, and research.* Homewood, IL: Dorsey.
This handbook of depression contains 27 chapters from 53 distinguished contributors. Comprehensive coverage is given to various treatment strategies and diagnostic and assessment methods. A number of basic research and special topics are included, one of which is depression in children and adolescents, by K. Hodges and L. Siegel.

Clarizio, H. F. (1985). Cognitive–behavioral treatment of childhood depression. *Psychology in the Schools, 22,* 308–322.
Behavioral and social skills approaches and the cognitive views of Beck, Seligman, Ellis, and Rehm are succinctly reviewed as they relate to the treatment of childhood depression. Some consideration is given to the implications of these treatment approaches for school psychologists.

Mash, E. J., & Terdal, L. G. (Eds.). (1984). *Behavioral assessment of childhood disorders.* New York: Guilford.
Although only one of its 16 chapters (C. G. Costello) focuses directly on the assessment of childhood depression, those on behavioral assessment strategies and on topics such as conduct disorders, social skills deficits, fears and anxieties, chronic illness, and sleep disturbance are relevant to professionals working with the full spectrum of childhood disorders.

Reynolds, W. M. (1986). A model for the screening and identification of depressed children and adolescents in school settings. *Professional School Psychology, 1,* 117–129.
This article describes multistage and multimethod assessment procedures for the identification of depression in school children and adolescents. The three screening stages are presented as they might be employed in the school setting.

Rutter, M., Izard, C. E., & Read, P. B. (Eds.). (1986). *Depression in young people, developmental and clinical perspectives.* New York: Guilford.
This most recent book on childhood depression includes 18 chapters written by well-known experts from various branches of psychiatry and psychology. The chapters deal with developmental issues and perspectives, parental depression and other risk indices, methods and measurement, and directions for future research.

BIBLIOGRAPHY: PARENTS

Butler, L. F., & Miezitis, S. (1980). *Releasing children from depression: A handbook for elementary teachers and consultants.* Toronto: The Ontario Institute for Studies in Education.
A number of practical suggestions and strategies "that have proved successful" with depressed children are clearly illustrated in this manual. Teachers and parents may find useful suggestions for dealing with low self-esteem, withdrawn behavior, aloofness, self-deprecating remarks, sadness, tearfulness, and other depressive behaviors.

Greist, J. H., & Jefferson, J. W. (1984). *Depression and its treatment.* New York: Warner.
This easily readable paperback book is intended to provide information about depression to the general public as well as mental health professionals. Topics deal with various questions about depression and different treatments, and a list of nontechnical readings is included.

Children and Different Cultural Backgrounds

Keren Chansky Suberri
Temple University

BACKGROUND

The United States is a nation of ever increasing ethnic diversity: The nonwhite percentage of the total population increased from 17.0% in 1970 to 23.3% in 1980 (de Anda, 1984). In 1980, there were roughly 313,000 Native American (American Indian, Eskimo, and Aleut) school-age children in the United States, 809,000 school-age children of Asian or Pacific Island descent (Japanese, Chinese, Filipino, Korean, Indian, Vietnamese and others), close to 4,000,000 school-age Hispanic children (Chicanos, Puerto Rican, Cuban, and others) and 7,400,000 children of Afro-American descent (Bureau of Census, 1980). In addition, each year thousands of refugees from Southeast Asia and many other countries have flocked to the United States, 28% of these being school-age children (U.S. Department of Health and Human Services, 1985).

Culture

What is culture? Culture refers to the habitual patterns of behavior that characterize a given group of people (Henderson, 1982). Cultures differ in a number of ways, some more obvious than others. Language is one way with which all are familiar. Another obvious cultural difference is dress. Other ways in which cultures differ include religious practices (often dress is one manifestation of religious practices), social values, family roles, education, social interactions, gestural communication or body language, music, dance, and cuisine. Some differences among cultures are more subtle than others.

Many patterns of behavior that are thought of as natural or normal in one culture are not necessarily thought to be so by other cultures. For instance, in mainstream U. S. culture it is commonplace for a young man and a young woman to go out together, for example, to a movie, on a date. In some cultures, however, a young woman is not permitted to date unless she is accompanied by a family escort. In other cultures dating among teenagers and young adults is not permitted under any circumstances, a limitation that seems extraordinary to our youth. Similarly, there are cultural practices of the mainstream U. S. culture that may seem arbitrary to persons of another culture. For example, in the mainstream U. S. culture it is acceptable for a woman to carry a handbag with her personal effects, whereas a man must keep his personal effects in his pockets or a briefcase or carry these articles in his hands.

Cultural awareness and sensitivity represent a continuum defined at one end of the spectrum by obliviousness and the other end by stereotyping. Sensitivity to the particularities of other cultures requires considerable cognizance of the ways in which our own cultural conditioning influences our day-to-day lives. Only a fine line distinguishes cultural sensitivity from cultural stereotyping. When differences in cultures have been emphasized, while both the commonalities among cultures and the heterogeneity of behaviors within cultures have been ignored, the result has been a distorted perception of ethnic groups. This has led to cultural stereotyping. It is important to recognize that while a cultural group is defined by its similarities of behavior, there are also considerable differences within any one group.

While the cultural practices of one group may seem unusual, strange, or even unacceptable, one must not lose sight of the fact that no culture can validly be held to be superior to another. For the most part, the behavioral practices of each cultural group have evolved as adaptive behaviors to a given set of circumstances. Subsequently, these practices have become a deeply ingrained way of life, even though the original set of circumstances that led to their development may no longer exist.

There exist large bodies of literature that describe the familial characteristics, cognitive style, and motivational patterns of many of the ethnic minority groups in the United States. Researchers in this area have disagreed not only in their descriptions of given ethnic groups with regard to these factors (Staples & Mirande, 1980), but also in their conclusions with regard to the effects of these factors on the functioning of individual group members (Henderson, 1982). Studies that claim to have found a link between a particular characteristic of a particular ethnic group and that group's success or failure in U. S. society can be countered by other studies that provide empirical evidence that refute these claims.

Expectations for Children of Different Cultural Backgrounds

A person's expectations about individuals of different cultural backgrounds are molded to some extent by personal biases. One common bias in modern U. S. society has arisen from the concept of the "melting pot." The goal of the melting pot was the creation of a unique culture in which all individuals were to be treated identically, for they were to share one history, heritage, and language of one United States. On the surface, this appears to be a noble goal. However, in reality the melting pot ideal encouraged individuals to abandon their native cultures and replace it with mainstream culture. In short, the concept of the melting pot was an attempt at cultural homogenization. Modern-day social scientists agree that it was a misguided ideal that was never realized.

The effect of the melting pot philosophy on most U.S. school children has been to force them to make a choice of great magnitude, a choice of values. At a time in their lives when values are not consciously articulable, children have been forced to choose between the values and culture of their home and the values and culture of their school (Ramirez & Castaneda, 1974).

While it is unrealistic and undesirable to expect children to completely abandon their native culture and replace it with mainstream culture, it is equally unrealistic and undesirable to anticipate a separatist way of life in which each cultural group sets up its own community and has little or no contact with other communities. What is desirable for children of culturally different backgrounds is a bicultural way of life in which they are able to function effectively in both their native cultural world and in the mainstream cultural world. The following description of the bicultural/multicultural individual is offered by Ramirez (1984):

> A bicultural–multicultural person has had extensive socialization and life experiences in two or more cultures and participates actively in these cultures. That is, his or her day-to-day behaviors show active participation in two or more cultures and extensive interaction with members of those socio-cultural groups. (p. 82)

Thus, biculturalism is the goal to be strived for with regard to children of different cultural backgrounds. We should encourage them to be proud of and to be active participants in their native culture, but at the same time help them to prepare to be active participants as well in mainstream U. S. culture.

The purpose of this chapter is not to provide panaceas for each of the different problem situations faced by children of different cultural backgrounds and by those who care and provide educational programs for them. This would be impossible, given the unique circumstances of each child, from a particular family and cultural group, in a particular setting. Rather, the goal is to heighten the awareness of mental health professionals so as to enable them to make enlightened and appropriate decisions in handling the various situations that may present themselves in their work with children and families of different cultural backgrounds and with the school personnel who provide programs for these children and their families.

DEVELOPMENT

An individual's adjustment to a new cultural context is accompanied by stress that is attributable to several factors: (a) difficulties in communication, (b) the presence of unfamiliar norms of behavior in the new culture, (c) differences in role expectations between the culture of origin and the new culture, (d) differences in the value systems of the two cultures, (e) a sense of loss from being uprooted from one's original surroundings, and (f) feelings of impotence in dealing with a new environment (Padilla, 1985). Stress is increased because persons undergoing this experience often feel as if they do not belong to either the new culture or to their native culture. In addition, they are torn between adopting the mainstream culture's values and retaining their own cultural identity (Huang, 1977; Sluzki, 1979).

The factors that affect the degree of stress people experience in this transition include the following: (a) their psychosocial age or developmental stage, (b) their self-esteem, (c) their generational status as the process of adjustment to a new culture persists across several generations, (d) their facility in the mainstream language, (e) the degree of differences in the two cultures, and (f) the pressure exerted on them to conform to mainstream culture (Berry, 1980; Padilla, 1985; Szapocznik & Kurtines, 1980).

Little research has been conducted exclusively on the adjustment of children to new cultures. Typically, what is reported in the literature is the adjustment proccess of adults. It is important to understand the adjustment patterns of adults, because parents, by their actions, communicate to their children how much and which types of interaction with mainstream culture are acceptable to them.

Four adjustment patterns have been identified: (a) abandoning the native culture and replacing it with the new culture (assimilation), (b) holding on tightly to the native culture and having only limited contact with the mainstream culture (traditionalism), (c) maintaining neither a strong identification with their native culture nor a strong identification with mainstream culture (transitional/marginal), and (d) retaining a fair degree of what is distinctive in the native cultural tradition, but at the same time integrating the cultural traditions of the new culture (biculturalism). For further discussion of this topic the reader is referred to English (1984).

There is empirical research that suggests that children and adults who adopt a bicultural way of life, those who remain strongly identified with their native culture while participating in mainstream culture, are better adjusted psychologically than ethnic minority individuals who are not bicultural (Ramirez, 1969, 1977, 1980; Szapocznik, Scopetta, Kurtines, & Arnalde, 1978).

It should be pointed out that although biculturalism may be the healthiest variant from a mental health standpoint, it is not attained with ease. Becoming bicultural is a *process* that necessitates constant decision making on the part of the individual — which aspects of the native culture to retain, which aspects of the mainstream culture to adopt? This evolutionary nature of biculturalism/multiculturalism has been articulated in the following description of the multicultural individual:

> The multicultural person . . . is not simply the person who is sensitive to many cultures. Rather, he is a person who is always in the process of becoming *a part* of and *apart from* a given cultural context. He is very much a formative being, resilient, changing and evolutionary. He has no permanent cultural character but neither is he free from the influences of culture (Adler, 1977, p. 31)

This process of constant decision making is in and of itself a stressful one, for it is only on rare occasions that an individual has clear-cut guidelines to utilize in making these decisions. If the individual is fortunate to have a social group (religious or other) with which to identify, the process is easier.

It is not uncommon for a person's adjustment pattern to change or be significantly altered over time. Some factors that affect the formation or change in an individual's adjustment pattern or world view are the following: (a) the amount of contact with mainstream culture, (b) the type of interaction the individual has with mainstream culture, either pleasant or aversive, (c) the receptiveness of the environment to nonmainstream cultures, and (d) the availability of formal and informal support systems, in which there are individuals who can provide empathic emotional support, serve as role models, facilitate understanding of the values and perceptions of the mainstream culture, and suggest ways to meet the new behavioral demands without compromising ethnic values and norms (de Anda, 1984).

PUTTING CHILDREN AND DIFFERENT CULTURAL BACKGROUNDS IN PERSPECTIVE

The major factors that the mental health professional needs to consider in formulating any plan of action or advice pertaining to the adjustment of an ethnic minority child can be conceptualized as a group of three interrelated factors: (a) individual factors, (b) family factors, and (c) ecological factors.

Individual Factors

Present Direction of Child's Adjustment Pattern. It is important to keep in mind two factors in determining the present direction of a child's cultural adjustment pattern: (a) the adjustment pattern is given to change and (b) it is greatly affected by the parents' adjustment patterns. If, for example, the parents feel strongly that the native culture must be maintained and they allow or encourage only minimal contact with mainstream culture, this will directly impact on the child's adjustment. Some children react to this type of situation by withdrawing socially; they maintain only minimal social contact with children of mainstream culture. Other children may react to this situation by rejecting their native culture and by trying to assimilate or adopt the mainstream culture in all its facets, at the expense of losing ties to their native culture.

Child's Developmental Stage. Age has been shown to be a factor in adjustment to a new culture. One study revealed that students who immigrated after the age of 14 experience greater stress than those who immigrated before age 14 (Padilla, Alvarez, & Lindholm, 1985). The explanation offered by these researchers is that the older the child, the deeper the sense of ethnic identity already developed, and therefore the more difficult the adjustment.

While young children may be aware of some ways in which their native culture differs from mainstream culture, many differences may not be consciously articulable. Unlike adults, young children are not capable of participating in the sophisticated decision-making process inherent to attaining biculturalism. They will become bicultural provided they are afforded socialization opportunities in both cultures. Biculturalism is facilitated when agents of the mainstream culture (e.g., teachers, classmates, neighbors) demonstrate respect for a child's native culture and when agents of the native culture (e.g., immediate and extended family) accept the mainstream culture.

Self-esteem. Self-esteem has been shown to be a factor in a individual's adjustment to a new culture. Several studies show that persons with high self-esteem experience less stress in adjusting to a new cultural identity (Chan, 1977; Padilla, 1985; Padilla, Alvarez, & Lindholm, 1985; Pearlin & Schooler, 1978). Ethnic identity is an important part of an individual's self-concept. When children feel proud of their ethnic or cultural background, this enhances their self-esteem.

Language. Children's communicative abilities are influenced by individual and social factors. Their facility in English affects their academic progress as well as the degree to which they can participate in and benefit from participation in social activities of the mainstream culture. Similarly, their facility in their native language often moderates the degree to which they will participate in and benefit from social activities of the native culture. Children's facility in the language of their native culture also moderates the degree of strength of family ties. Often parents and grandparents speak only the language of the culture of origin and children speak only English, thus rendering their communication difficult. Therefore, it is important to encourage bilingualism in ethnic minority children.

Family Factors

Present Direction of Parents' Adjustment Pattern. As previously discussed, the direction of the parents' adjustment pattern has an effect on the direction of the child's adjustment pattern. Parents experience stress in adjusting to a new culture. Some parents react to this stress by holding on tightly to their native culture ways and familiar roles. Often parents adopt this mode of adjustment because they fear they are becoming alienated from their children as their children become more and more assimilated to mainstream culture.

Other parents have a different reaction. Out of fear that their children will suffer from prejudice, discrimination, and limited opportunities in the mainstream culture, they encourage their children to assimilate, that is, to adopt mainstream culture values and lifestyles at the expense of relinquishing their native culture. As Ramirez and Cox (1980) point out, these parents do not deny their native culture because they see the dominant culture as better, but rather because they mistakenly see assimilation as a necessary prerequisite to successful functioning in the U. S. society.

Bicultural parents retain strong ties with their native culture yet still have comfortable interactions with mainstream culture, in addition to or outside of their work situations. Bicultural parents can provide positive role models for their children in their efforts to develop bicultural identifies. Mental health professionals can help parents provide a bicultural role model for their children.

Migration Status. It is important to recognize that the adjustment period for immigrants persists over several generations. That is, United States-individuals whose parents or grandparents were immigrants continue to experience some stress in adjustment to mainstream culture (Padilla et al., 1985). In addition, the circumstances of migration may moderate the individual's adjustment to mainstream culture. Examples of different circumstances of migration include involuntary servitude, as in the case of Afro-Americans, escape from political oppression, escape from economic oppression, a desire for better employment opportunities, and a desire for better educational opportunities.

Parents' Facility in English. Parents' facility in English is an important variable. It is an indicator of the degree to which parents can interact comfortably with mainstream society and hence serve as bicultural role models for their children. Also, as mentioned previously, when children's dominant language is English and their parents' dominant language is their native tongue, parents and children often experience marked communication difficulties, which increases stress in adjustment for both parent and child.

Role of Extended Family. Preserving strong family ties with the extended family represents an important social support system for ethnic minority individuals. Research has shown that the maintenance of strong ties with extended family is one of several factors that significantly contribute to the development of the bicultural functioning of minority group members.

Ecological Factors

Receptiveness of Environment. The results of research dealing with the effect of discrimination and prejudice on an individual's adjustment point to the heterogeneity of adjustment responses of immigrants. Some researchers have found that perceived discrimination is a major factor contributing to the maintenance of native ethnic identity. "Individuals insulate themselves from the majority society by maintaining close friendship ties with members of their ethnic group, thereby buffering discriminatory practices of members of the dominant group against them" (Padilla, 1985, p. 52). In contrast, other researchers have found that where ethnic minority individuals were subject to considerable discrimination, they were more likely to favor assimilation, incorporating the values of the mainstream culture while rejecting their own ethnic identity (Ramirez & Castaneda, 1974).

When school environments provide children with the educational experiences necessary to function in both the native and the mainstream cultures, their bicultural identity is facilitated. Such an environment allows persons to "remain identified with the lifestyles and values of his home and neighborhood while he becomes familiar with the lifestyle and value system of the mainstream American middle class" (Ramirez & Castaneda, 1974, p. 35).

Interaction With Mainstream and Native Cultures. Development of a bicultural identity is contingent upon extensive contact and socialization with both the mainstream and the native cultures. The extent of interaction that children have with both mainstream and native cultures can be determined by examining a number of factors: the ethnic composition of the neighborhood where they live, the ethnic makeup of the people with whom they and their parents interact socially, the affiliation of the children and their families to religious organizations and the ethnic makeup of these groups, the ethnic makeup of clubs or community organizations to which they and their families belong, the strength of the extended family ties and the ethnic makeup of the school and of the parents' places of work. For further information the reader is referred to the *Biculturalism/Multiculturalism Experience Inventory* in Ramirez, 1983.

ALTERNATIVE ACTIONS

There are a number of actions that the mental health professional can take to facilitate the adjustment of ethnic minority children and encourage their development of a bicultural identity. These measures can be appropriately implemented at the level of the individual child, the parents, the school, and the community.

Level 1: The Child

Provision of individual counseling for ethnic minority children adjusting to mainstream culture can prove beneficial. Through counseling they can begin to see that migration is a stressful experience for nearly everyone. They can begin to see that it is normal, albeit painful, to feel pulled by one's ties to two different cultures. The mental health professional can help these children adopt a bicultural adjustment pattern, in which they feel high commitment and identification with both cultures. The mental health professional can help them identify behaviors that can increase contact with mainstream culture in nonaversive ways, such as socialization with children of mainstream culture. It is important to help ethnic minority children see that interaction with mainstream children does not have to come at the expense of their ties with the native country.

Level 2: The Parents

Often parents need to be helped to recognize that the process of migration is naturally stressful. They experience stress, but may not feel that the emotional upset is legitimate, especially parents who feel that their standard of living has been improved by immigration to the United States. Once parents recognize their stress and emotional strain, they are in a position to reduce it by adopting a bicultural adjustment pattern for themselves and by encouraging biculturalism in their children. Some important means by which parents can promote biculturalism in their families are by continuing their own strong ethnic identification, encouraging bilingualism, being accepting of their children's mainstream culture friends as well as their native culture friends, and strengthening extended family ties through visitation, letters, and phone calls, and through communication of oral family histories about grandparents and great-grandparents (Ramirez & Cox, 1980). Other ways to promote biculturalism include affiliation with religious organizations, community organizations, and subscriptions to newspapers and magazines of both the native culture and mainstream culture.

Level 3: School Personnel

The mental health professional can facilitate the adjustment of ethnic minority children by creating a school environment that is receptive to the cultural diversity of its students. The first step to creating this environment is for school personnel to develop a sense of their own ethnic and personal identity and be accepting of their own group affiliation. Next, school personnel need to increase their sensitivity to cultural differences. It is also important for school personnel to increase their knowledge about the heritage, history, traditions, customs, and language of the many ethnic groups in modern U. S. society. In increasing one's sensitivity to cultural differences, the role of teachers' expectations with regard to minority children can be presented. Henderson (1982) has presented a set of exercises intended for this purpose. School consultation and in-service training may both be effective to this end.

Once the teachers have developed a sensitivity to cultural differences and similarities, this quality can be imparted to the children in their classrooms by means of a curriculum of multiethnic education. The goal of multiethnic education is to develop an acceptance and appreciation of the rich cultural diversity in the United States. An example of this type of curriculum can be found in King (1980), in which a set of methods and materials is presented that is appropriate for teaching ethnic awareness to children of elementary school age.

Level 4: The Community

One of the most important variables that affect the extent to which an individual is able to retain characteristics of his or her native culture is the degree and availability of community support for the native culture (Szapocznik & Kurtines, 1980). The mental health professional can benefit ethnic minority families by helping them link up with existing support systems, by helping bicultural families to organize their own support systems, and by increasing the cultural sensitivity of the community as a whole.

SUMMARY

The United States is a country of increasing ethnic diversity. If mental health practices in the schools are to be relevant and effective for minorities, they must take into consideration the students' ethnic heritage and culture. The adjustment of the ethnic minority individual to mainstream culture involves a reorganization of ethnic identities. This adjustment is typically accompanied by stress. Little research has been conducted exclusively on the adjustment of children to new cultures. Typically, what is reported in the literature is the adjustment process of adults. It is important to understand the adjustment patterns of adults because parents, by their actions, communicate to their children how much and which types of interaction with mainstream culture is acceptable to them. Four adjustment patterns have been identified: (a) abandoning the native culture and replacing it with the new culture (assimilation), (b) holding on tightly to the native culture and having only limited contact with the mainstream culture (traditionalism), (c) maintaining neither a strong identification with the native culture nor a strong identification with mainstream culture (transitional/marginal), and (d) retaining a fair degree of what is distinctive in the native cultural tradition, but at the same time integrating the cultural traditions of the new culture (biculturalism). While it is unrealistic and undesirable to expect children to completely abandon their native culture and replace it with mainstream culture, it is equally unrealistic and undesirable to anticipate a separatist way of life in which each cultural group sets up its own community and has little or no contact with other communities. What is desirable for children of culturally different backgrounds is a bicultural way of life in which they are able to function effectively both in their native cultural world and in the mainstream cultural world. Empirical research suggests that bicultural individuals enjoy better mental health than ethnic minority individuals who are not bicultural.

In formulating a plan of action or advice pertaining to the adjustment of an ethnic minority child a number of individual, family, and ecological factors should be considered. The mental health professional can facilitate the adjustment of ethnic minority children by helping them and their parents adopt a bicultural mode of functioning, by helping to create an environment of cultural pluralism in the school, and by developing the availability of community support for minority cultures.

REFERENCES

Adler, P. S. (1977). Beyond cultural identity: Reflections on cultural and multicultural man. In R. Brislin (Ed.), Topics in culture learning. (Vol. 2). Honolulu: University of Hawaii, East–West Culture Learning Institute.

Berry, J. W. (1980). Acculturation as varieties of adaptation. In A. M. Padilla (Ed.), *Acculturation. Theory, models and some new findings* (pp. 7–26). Boulder, CO: Westview.

Bureau of the Census. (1983). *1980 Census of Population. General Social and Economic Characteristics.* Washington, DC: U. S. Department of Commerce.

Chan, K. B. (1977). Individual differences in reactions to stress and their personality and situational determinants: Some implications for community mental health. *Social Science and Medicine, 11,* 89–103.

de Anda, D. (1984). Bicultural socialization: Factors affecting the minority experience. *Social Work, 29*(2), 101–107.

English, R. A. (1984). *The challenge for mental health: Minorities and their world views.* The Second Annual Robert C. Sutherland Lecture. Austin: University of Texas. (ERIC Document Reproduction Service No. ED 255 796)

Henderson, R. W. (1982). Teacher relations with minority students and their families. Washington, DC: Office of Special Education and Rehabilitative Services. (ERIC Document Reproduction Service No. ED 249 213)

Huang, K. (1977). Campus mental health: The foreigner at your desk. *Journal of American College Health Association, 25,* 216–219.

King, E. W. (1980). *Teaching ethnics awareness: Methods and materials for the elementary school.* Santa Monica, CA: Goodyear.

Padilla, A. M. (1985). Acculturation and stress among immigrants and later-generation individuals (Occasional Paper No. 20) (pp. 38–69). Los Angeles: University of California, Spanish Speaking Mental Health Research Center.

Padilla, A. M., Alvarez, M., & Lindholm, K. J. (1985). *Generational status and personality factors as predictors of stress in students* (Occasional Paper No. 20) (pp. 1–14). Los Angeles: University of California, Spanish Speaking Mental Health Research Center.

Padilla, A. M., Wagatsuma, Y., & Lindholm, K. J. (1985). *Generational differences in acculturative stress and personality among Mexican and Japanese Americans* (Occasional Paper No. 20) (pp. 18–34). Los Angeles: University of California, Spanish Speaking Mental Health Research Center.

Pearlin, L., & Schooler, C. (1978). The structure of coping. *Journal of Health and Social Behavior, 19,* 2–21.

Ramirez, M. (1969). Identification with Mexican-American values and psychological adjustment in Mexican-American adolescents. *International Journal of Social Psychiatry, 11,* 151–156.

Ramirez, M. (1977). Recognizing and understanding diversity: Multiculturalism and the Chicano movement in psychology. In J. L. Martinez (Ed.), Chicano psychology. New York: Academic.

Ramirez, M. (1983). *Psychology of the Americas. Mestizo perspectives on personality and mental health.* New York: Pergamon.

Ramirez, M. (1984). Assessing and understanding biculturalism–multiculturalism in Mexican-American adults. In J. L. Martinez (Ed.). *Chicano psychology* (2nd ed.). New York: Academic.

Ramirez, M., & Castaneda, A. (1974). *Cultural democracy, bicognitive development and education.* New York: Academic.

Ramirez, M., & Cox, B. G. (1980). Parenting for multiculturalism: A Mexican-American model. In M. D. Fantini & R. Cardenas (Eds.), *Parenting in a multicultural society* (pp. 54–62). New York: Longman.

Sluzki, C. E. (1979). Migration and family conflict. *Family Process, 18,* 379–390.

Staples, R., & Mirande, A. (1980). Racial and cultural variations among American families. *Journal of Marriage and the Family, 42,* 887–903

Szapocznik, J., & Kurtines, W. (1980). Acculturation, biculturalism and adjustment among Cuban Americans. In A. M. Padilla (Ed.), *Acculturation. Theory, models and some new findings* (pp. 139–159). Boulder, CO: Westview.

Szapocznik, J., Scopetta, M. A., Kurtines, W., & Arnalde, M. A. (1978). Theory and measurement of acculturation. *Interamerican Journal of Psychology, 12,* 113–130.

U. S. Department of Health and Human Services. (1985). *Report to the Congress: Resettlement program.* Washington, DC: Social Security Administration, Office of Refugee Resettlement.

BIBLIOGRAPHY: PROFESSIONALS

Fantini, M. D., & Cardenas, R. (1980). *Parenting in a multicultural society.* New York: Longman.
An anthology of papers dealing with the many facets of the current debate over parenting. A unifying theme of this anthology is found in the concept of cultural pluralism. Contributors are leading researchers and professionals in the fields of parent education, child psychology, human development, and public education.

Henderson, R. W. (1982). *Teacher relations with minority students and their families.* Washington, DC: Office of Special Education and Rehabilitative Services. (ERIC Document Reproduction Service No. ED 249 213)
Discusses the topics of cultural diversity, ethnic stereotyping, characteristics of minority children and their families, and teacher expectations and student performance. This is one of a series of 24 modules on how stereotyped conceptions of minority children and their families may influence teacher expectations and affect student performance. This module includes useful self-assessment items. It is directed toward teacher–trainers.

Ramirez, M. (1983). *Psychology of the Americas. Mestizo perspectives on personality and mental health.* New York: Pergamon.
Presents new models for understanding the individual development of pluralistic identities, the mental health of families coping with acculturation stress, the person–environment fit of immigrants, and intergroup and international relations in situations of conflict. The *Biculturalism/Multiculturalism Experience Inventory,* a comprehensive questionnaire that can be used to determine the degree of biculturalism/multiculturalism an individual has attained, is reproduced in full in this volume.

Staples, R., & Mirande, A. (1980). Racial and cultural variations among American families: A decenniel review of the literature on minority families. *Journal of Marriage and the Family,* 887–903.
Provides an extensive review of the literature on Asian-American, black, Chicano, and Native American families. They report that the negative stereotypes of minority families presented in the literature have not been supported empirically.

Children and Divorce

Howard M. Knoff
University of South Florida

Of all the sources of mental health problems related to children's development in family, school, and community, divorce is perhaps the most prevalent yet the least researched and understood. To date, there have been only four major longitudinal studies on the effects of divorce on school-aged children (Guidubaldi, Cleminshaw, Perry, & McLoughlin, 1983; Guidubaldi & Perry, 1985; Hetherington, 1979; Hetherington, Cox, & Cox, 1978; Kurdek, 1983; Kurdek, Blisk, & Siesky, 1981; Wallerstein, 1984; Wallerstein & Kelly, 1976). While some of these have been criticized for methodological shortcomings, tentative conclusions can now be drawn concerning both the effects of divorce on children and ways to understand why some children of divorce cope better than others. This chapter will review these four longitudinal (and other) studies, suggesting pragmatic conclusions and directions for school psychologists. It must be emphasized from the onset, however, that far more research remains to be done and that future studies may contradict these conclusions and suggestions. Clearly, school psychologists need to monitor and critically analyze the research literature, changing and broadening their views when influenced by methodologically sound data and research.

BACKGROUND

From the perspective of simple incidence the number of children affected by divorce is staggering. The divorce rate has more than tripled since 1960 and doubled between 1970 and 1981. In 1970, 11.9% of all children in the United States were living in single-parent homes, partly owing to divorce; this percentage increased to 20.1% of all children in 1981, and 22.5% in 1983. Census and other data now suggest that approximately 40% of all current marriages will end in divorce (1,179,000 divorces were granted in the United States in 1983 alone), and that 40–50% of all children born during the past decade will spend some time living in a single-parent family (Hetherington, 1979; National Center for Health Statistics, 1984; U.S. Bureau of the Census, 1982a, 1982b). Significantly, some of these percentages actually are underestimates, since children living in remarried households have not been included.

From a psychological perspective, these divorce experiences do have long-term impact on children's —especially boys' — development and adjustment, and the impact is evident in all settings and environments. In schools, for example, divorce has been related to increased anxiety, aggressiveness, and other emotional reactions; to poorer social and academic competence ratings and scores; and to increased likelihood of grade retentions and referrals to school psychologists. In the home, divorce has been related to poor general family health, lower ratings of children's social competence, significant changes in parents' personal functioning and interactions with their children, and decreased financial stability for the custodial parent (often the mother). Some observers have suggested that many of these social–emotional reactions to divorce first occur outside of the home, often in schools, because the familial atmosphere is not conducive to their expression. In any case, the interdependent psychological effects of divorce across both home and school settings are apparent. For the practitioner, the possible or likely impacts of divorce on children of all ages must be understood. Furthermore, proactive intervention programs to prevent and minimize these impacts must be developed.

DEVELOPMENT

For both the parents and the children, divorce should be conceptualized as a long-term multistage process the repercussions of which are dependent on (a) the age of the children at the time of the divorce; (b) their sex; (c) the length of time since the divorce; (d) financial, custodial,and other changes after the divorce, including the availability of support systems to cushion the effects of the divorce; and (e) familial conditions and preparations prior to divorce (Kurdek, 1981; Guidubaldi, Perry, & Nastasi, in press). As noted above, four major longitudinal studies have been done, each contributing to this conclusion. In 1971, Wallerstein and Kelly began to investigate the effects of divorce on a sample of 131 children between the ages of 2½ and 18 years from 60 divorced families of Marin County, California. Utilizing interviews and questionnaires with the children and their parents, this sample was evaluated just after the parental separation, and then 1, 5, and 10 years following the divorce.

Hetherington, Cox, and Cox (1978) collected data on a sample of 48 divorced and 48 intact middle-class families and their preschool children from Virginia over a 2-year period. Employing a more controlled experimental design than Wallerstein and Kelly, these researchers matched their divorced and intact families by age, sex, birth order, and nursery school attendance of the child, and by the parents' age, education, and length of marriage. They also collected more reliable, multivariate data through the use of structured diary records; behavioral observations of parent–child, teacher–child, and peer–child interactions; behavior and checklist ratings by parents and teachers; and assessments of personality, cognitive, and social development.

Kurdek, Blisk, and Siesky (1981), meanwhile, investigated 74 white, divorced, middle-class families from Dayton, Ohio (60 mothers and 14 fathers); 33 of these single parents were members of the local chapter of Parents Without Partners and 41 were friends of these members. In total, these families accounted for 132 children ranging in age from 5 to 19 (mean = 12.56) years. Using measures evaluating the children's social and interpersonal relations skills and locus of control and their parents' postdivorce adjustments, these authors addressed the factors that helped to mediate the divorce experience. The longitudinal study ultimately involved 58 children ranging in age from 8 to 17 (mean = 13.09) years whose parents had been separated 1–14 years (mean separation = 14.54 years) for the Time 1 assessment. The Time 2 assessment, which occurred 2 years later, involved 24 of the original group (mean age = 13.32 years) and 14 siblings (mean age = 13.53 years) as a supplemental group. No significant differences or biases were evident statistically between the Time 1 and the Time 2 groups.

Finally, Guidubaldi, Cleminshaw, Perry, and McLoughlin (1983) completed a nationwide study (representing 38 states) of 699 children in grades 1, 3, or 5 from divorced and intact families during the 1981-1982 school year in an attempt to overcome the methodological limitations of past research, namely (a) small, biased samples, (b) inadequate or nonexistent control groups, (c) poor control or absence of control of socioeconomic status and other potentially confounding variables, and (d) lack of multisetting, multimethod, and multifactored assessments. These researchers utilized 144 school psychologists who collected demographic, family and school, social–emotional, academic–intellectual, and mental and physical health data from the randomly sampled children. This project represents the most methodologically sound research to date, and already a 2-year follow-up study has been completed with plans to identify and analyze a 3-year cohort.

Reactions by Age of the Child

While the limitations of the longitudinal studies should be kept in mind, differential effects on children's reactions to divorce that are due to age have been identified. In general, children from divorced homes seem to be at greater social–emotional and academic–intellectual risk than those from intact families although the child's developmental status and sex appear to be mediating variables. These variables aside, Kurdek (1981) and Wallerstein and Kelly (1976, 1980) summarize these age-related effects as follows.

Infants' reactions to divorce are closely related to their primary caretakers' emotional status and adjustment. Given research suggesting that adults' adjustments to divorce may take 2 years or longer (Hetherington, Cox, & Cox, 1978), infants are clearly at developmental risk. For example, while the physical development of the infant is also at stake, the child's emotional development is often dependent on the parent–child bonding, nurturing, and identification processes that begin early in life. These processes have been related to infants' positive physical and emotional development, and they occur whether the primary caretaker is married or divorced. In a single-parent environment, the primary caretaker will need to take special care to protect the infant from negative interactions resulting from divorce-related stress responses. The absence of research specifically with divorced parents and their infants should not diminish practitioners' concern about the effects of divorce at this age level. Clearly, however, future research is necessary here to validate what the existing literature currently predicts.

Preschoolers have sometimes reacted to their parents' divorce with diverse emotional manifestations: anxiety, nightmares, depressed play, eating disturbances, bed wetting, sexual identity difficulties, irritability, aggressiveness, bewilderment, self-blame, and guilt. Much concern has been expressed for preschoolers experiencing divorce, because their level of cognitive development may cause them to misunderstand or misinterpret why their parents have separated. While more definitive research on this theoretical concern is needed, the behavioral and emotional reactions are indeed real. Intervention for preschool children in single-parent settings, therefore, must be made available if needed; school psychologists with their knowledge of child development should take the lead in helping others to discriminate between typical developmental patterns and those specific to divorce at this, and other, age levels.

School-aged children commonly react to their parents' divorce with depression, withdrawal, grieving, fear, fantasies of responsibility and reconciliation, anger, decreased academic and other school performance, sense of loss or rejection, requests for explanations, shame, and conflicts over which parent to express loyalty to. Guidubaldi, Cleminshaw, Perry, and McLoughlin (1983), controlling for IQ differences across their divorced and intact child samples, found that first-, third-, and fifth-grade children in homes touched by divorce scored more poorly on the following scales of the Hahnemann Elementary School Behavior Rating Scale (HESBRS): Originality, Independent Learning, Involvement, Productive with Peers, Intellectual Dependency, Failure Anxiety, Unreflectiveness, Irrelevant Talk, Social (Over)Involvement, Negative Feelings, Holding Back/Withdrawn, Critical/Competitive, Blaming, and Inattention. In addition, teachers' ratings of competence in communication and social interaction, teacher and parent ratings of the child's popularity, and Wide Range Achievement Test (WRAT) reading and spelling scores were negatively affected. These children from divorced homes also had more school absences and poorer school grades in reading and math and were more likely to have been retained. Controlling for socioeconomic status (SES), children from divorced homes scored poorer on all of the HESBRS scales noted above except the Originality and Productive with Peers scales. These results indicate that, with the differences across the two samples due to IQ and SES partialed out, children from this national sample of divorced families were at greater social and academic risk than their peers in families unaffected by divorce.

Across the three age ranges within the Guidubaldi et al. (1983) study, another significant finding resulted. While others (e.g., Kurdek, Blisk, & Siesky, 1981) had found that older children generally exhibited relatively more positive levels of adjustment to divorce, Guidubaldi et al. reported that first graders showed significantly fewer negative effects from the divorce experience than fifth graders. For example, first graders showed better adjustment than the older children on five of the HESBRS scales (Productive with Peers, Failure Anxiety, Negative Feelings, Critical/Competitive, and Blaming), on three of the Vineland Scale domains (Communication, Socialization, Motor), on the WRAT math scores, and on the Regular class versus Special class placement measure. The fifth graders showed better adjustment on the Vineland's Daily Living domain, the optimism and locus of control measures, and on the parent ratings of number of current adjustment problems. The age measure in the Guidubaldi study, however, was often significantly confounded with the sex variable. Briefly, divorce more seriously affected boys than girls, and *older* boys manifested more significant adjustment problems than younger boys. Yet, while first-grade girls also manifested significant divorce-related problems, these problems were not more seriously represented in the fifth-grade female sample.

Finally, *adolescents* reportedly react to their parents' divorce with interpersonal relationship, self-identity, and independence problems and signs of sadness, shame, embarrassment, anxiety about the future and their own potential marriages, and withdrawal. While some believe that adolescents should more easily adjust to their parents' divorce because they can cognitively understand the separation and process, others feel that the adjustment is more likely to be difficult because the adolescents have experienced more exposure to the parental conflicts. This remains an empirical question, one that may have other intervening variables that may confuse any seemingly clear results.

Reactions by Sex of the Child

As alluded to above, there is consistent, significant evidence that boys experience far more problems from divorce than girls across the areas of general social–emotional and academic–intellectual development, that these problems get more serious from grades 1–5, and that they persist through grade 7 (Guidubaldi & Perry, 1985; Kurdek, 1981; Wallerstein & Kelly, 1980). Boys from the divorce-affected sample of Guidubaldi et al. (1983) manifested significantly poorer adjustment than girls from the same sample on 10 HESBRS scales (Independent Learning, Productive with Peers, Unreflectiveness, Irrelevant Talk, Social (Over) Involvement, Negative Feelings, Holding Back/Withdrawn, Critical/Competitive, Approach to Teacher, and Inattention) on the Vineland Daily Living domain, on measures of peer popularity and optimism, on reading, math, and classroom conduct grades, and on WRAT reading, spelling, and math scores.

While girls from the divorced sample were statistically indistinguishable from the intact-family sample of girls as they got older, boys from homes of divorce maintained their poorer adjustment than intact-family boys over time. For example, in their original study (Guidubaldi et al., 1983) fifth-grade divorced-family boys scored more poorly than fifth-grade intact-family boys on 11 of the 16 HESBRS Scales (all except the Originality, Involvement, Productive with Peers, Intellectual Dependency, and Approach to Teacher scales), the Vineland Social domain, a peer rejection measure, and grades in mathematics. Two years later (Guidubaldi & Perry, 1985), these divorced-family boys still manifested more problems than their intact-family peers; higher frequencies of maladaptive symptoms on the Achenbach Parent and Teacher Rating Scale; lower ratings for appropriateness of behavior, work effort, and happiness; and lower scores on an internal locus of control measure.

With respect to relations in the divorced family, sex differences favoring girls persisted. For example, boys exhibited poorer adjustments to parents' authoritarian child-rearing styles (results for girls were mixed) *and* permissive parenting styles (girls responded positively to this style). However, boys seemed to exhibit better adjustment than girls when the custodial parent was satisfied with the ex-spouse's parenting support.

While there are many hypotheses to explain these sex differences within samples of divorced children (see Guidubaldi, Cleminshaw, Perry, & McLoughlin, 1983, and Kurdek, 1981 for reviews), only future research will provide a full understanding. At this point, practitioners should be aware that there are differential adjustment differences across the sexes, and that interventions may need to be individualized across this variable for greatest success.

Length of Time Since Divorce

Aside from the interaction of time and sex discussed above, it appears that some children are able to adjust and decrease their emotional reactions to the experience of divorce, but a significant proportion continue to exhibit troublesome behavioral and academic patterns for a period of years. For example, in the 1-year follow-up study of Wallerstein and Kelly (1976, 1980), it was estimated that 44% of preschool children, 23% of younger latency-aged children, and 50% of older latency-aged children continued to have similar or worse levels of adjustment problems. These problems persisted at a 5-year follow-up, in which more than one third of the original sample was deemed to be at moderate to severe levels of depression, and at a 10-year follow-up, in which preliminary data indicated some emotional traces of sorrow and anger (Wallerstein, 1984).

Kurdek, Blisk, and Siesky (1981), reporting on a 2-year follow-up of a previous Dayton, Ohio sample, found that children whose parents had been separated for about 4 years were not experiencing severe adjustment problems related to the divorce as measured by a 14-item open-ended parent questionnaire, a 13-item open-ended child questionnaire assessing the children's understanding of the divorce, and a 34-item structured child questionnaire assessing children's feelings about the divorce. Nonetheless, these children still expressed primarily negative feelings toward the divorce experience, and their parents felt that their children's adjustment was related to their feelings and *not* their understanding of the divorce. Assessments of the children in the sample 2 years later generally revealed no severe problems related to the divorce experience. Differentially, the more well-adjusted children were older, had parents who had been divorced for a longer period of time, and were characterized by an internal locus of control and high levels of interpersonal functioning and reasoning.

Guidubaldi, Perry, and Nastasi (in press) reported the comprehensive results of their 2-year follow-up of the 1983 national sample of elementary school children. Their results indicated that children of divorce (average length of time since divorce = 6.41 years) continued to demonstrate poorer mental health, social competence, and overall adjustment *and* a broad range of deviant behavior as measured on the HESBRS and the Achenbach parent and teacher rating scales. Specifically, the children from divorced homes were rated more poorly (a) by parents on indices of hostility to adults, peer popularity, nightmares, and anxiety and (b) by teachers on indices of school-related behavior, dependency, anxiety, aggression, withdrawal, inattention, peer popularity, locus of control, and maladaptiveness. Furthermore, they scored more poorly on (a) WISC-R IQ scores, (b) WRAT reading, spelling, and math scores, (c) Vineland Teacher Rating scores in the daily living, social skills, and communication domains, (d) classroom reading and math grades, and (e) physical health ratings. The children of divorce also were more likely to repeat a grade and be referred to the school psychologist.

Guidubaldi's findings were consistent with those of Hetherington, Cox, and Cox (1979) and Wallerstein (1984). Therefore, the discrepancies found by Kurdek might have been the result of his methodology and sampling procedures, the assessment tools used, or some idiosyncrasy of the specific sample. In general, however, it does appear that children can adjust to divorce over a period of years.

Changes After Divorce and Availability of Support Systems

Many longitudinal studies have investigated mediating variables or factors that facilitate children's long-term adjustment to the divorce experience. Summarized by Guidubaldi, Perry, and Nastasi (in press) and by Kurdek (1981), these factors include (a) a relatively limited financial loss or impact to the custodial parent, the family, and its predivorce routine and standard of living; (b) the ability of the child to find and use support systems and personal coping skills; (c) low interparent conflict and hostility preceding and following the divorce; (d) postdivorce consistency between the parents with respect to child rearing and disciplinary practices; (e) approval, love, and positive relationships with both parents; (f) authoritative (as opposed to authoritarian) discipline approaches from the custodial parent; (g) an emotional climate that permits child and family discussions of divorce-related issues and concerns; (h) more frequent and reliable visitations with the noncustodial parent; (i) specific school characteristics such as smaller school populations, environments emphasizing structure and orderliness, traditional rather than open classroom structures, and proximity of school to the home (i.e., shorter distances requiring less busing); and (j) family support factors such as the availability of and interaction with helpful relatives (especially relatives of the noncustodial parent), friends, child-care assistance (e.g., nursery schools), and involvement by the custodial parent in social/recreational groups and experiences.

The parents' own emotional stability has been clearly related to their children's divorce adjustment. In general, the research (reviewed in Kurdek, 1981) currently suggests that many divorced parents may need up to 2 years to overcome the emotional effects of divorce. During the first year, these parents are characterized as (a) less able to accomplish their parenting tasks, (b) less likely to make maturity demands on their children, (c) more inconsistent in disciplinary approaches and parent–child communication processes, and (d) as less interactive and affectionate with the children. Mother–son interactions also were observed to be particularly tense during this period with increased acts of aggression by boys, increased attempts to be authoritarian by mothers, and increased feelings of incompetence and helplessness in parenting by mothers. By the end of the second postdivorce year, significant decreases in poor parenting practices, conflictual parent–child relationships, and poor parental social–emotional adjustment were noted.

Expanding on parental disciplinary styles in respect to children's divorce adjustment, Guidubaldi evaluated Baumrind's (1968) three patterns of child rearing in his longitudinal study: the *Authoritarian* parent who often uses punishment, force, and rejection to control; the *permissive* parent who allows the child to set his or her own controls; and the *authoritative* parent who directs the child using reason, problem-solving, yet firm structure. Overall, boys from divorced homes were found to have exhibited poorer adjustment to both the authoritarian and permissive styles. Girls, however, demonstrated mixed adjustment patterns with authorit arian parents and positive adjustment with permissive parents. No clear results occurred for authoritative parents with children of either sex. Hetherington, Cox, and Cox (1978) reported that custodial mothers in their longitudinal sample often became more controlling and restrictive (authoritarian) with their children after the divorce, whereas noncustodial fathers became more permissive and indulgent. Thus, utilizing Guidubaldi's results, Hetherington's divorced parents appeared to be using those styles that are least helpful in their children's long-term adjustment.

To summarize, the research suggests (a) that divorced parents may be best off using the same disciplinary approaches and styles with their children, (b) that they need to communicate about and support each other's disciplinary decisions, and (c) that they should maintain overt expectations for their children's appropriate behavior and continued social maturation. The research also tentatively suggests avoiding authoritarian and permissive disciplinary styles for boys. While the permissive disciplinary style was related to girls' positive adjustment, more research is needed. Finally, divorced parents need to receive clear information on the different parenting styles of Baumrind's (1968) and other observers and their possible effects on their children's overall divorce-related adjustment.

Familial Conditions and Preparations Prior to Divorce

Through interpolation from the longitudinal and other studies, a number of predivorce family conditions may be found that will help children's postdivorce adjustment and development. These "preparations" prior to the divorce may be considered preventive, however, it is likely that children who are living in environments fraught with interparental conflict, threats of divorce, or parental separation are already experiencing social–emotional reactions to significant stresses (Emery, 1982; Yamamoto, 1979).

The Child's Perspective. Children need to receive information, appropriate to their chronological, developmental, and social–emotional age levels, about an upcoming separation or divorce and the broad implications of those actions. This communication hopefully emanates from both parents in a joint discussion, but it also can occur during sessions coordinated by a private psychologist or marriage and family therapist. With the parents' permission, discussions with a school psychologist, individually or in divorce or separation counseling groups, could further support these children — even before the divorce is final. Among the important themes that can be expressed continually to children of a future divorce are that (a) their parents still love them; (b) they are not responsible for the divorce, that it is a problem between their parents independent of themselves; (c) their physical, social–emotional, and other needs will be taken care of as much as possible; (d) their parents will be available as much as possible to talk with them about their concerns or fears; (e) everyone will try to work together to make the situation as comfortable as possible, but they themselves are still expected to perform their responsibilities with respect to home and school; and that (f) it's alright to feel bad about the situation, but there are people who do care and can help them through these bad feelings.

The Parents' Perspective. For parents, the predivorce period also should include preparations for the broad implications of the divorce. As noted by Guidubaldi, Perry, and Nastasi (in press), family and community support factors (e.g., the availability of relatives, friends, community education, and recreation resources) are important to divorced children's adjustment. Clearly, they are also important to the parents' adjustment. During the predivorce or marital separation period, it is important for people facing divorce to receive some guidance or personally to explore their supportive resources. While close relatives or friends often provide the most support, the availability of legal, mental health, community-oriented, educational/vocational, and religious support systems should also be investigated. More specifically, predivorce preparations should address the financial stability of the custodial parent (usually the mother), the custody and visitation arrangements themselves, and the development of predivorce joint parenting agreements.

The relationship between the custodial parent's (and family's) financial stability and children's postdivorce adjustment has been well-documented (see above). If the importance of this issue is known by the divorcing parents, attending lawyers, divorce judges, and state and Federal legislators, perhaps more binding and equitable predivorce agreements protecting children's financial interests can be reached. Federally, the Child Support Enforcement Act was developed to ensure that a divorce's financial stipulations are met. However, this act has been inconsistently implemented state by state, resulting nationally in significant amounts of unpaid child support (Guidubaldi, Perry, & Nastasi, in press). On a more personal level, perhaps the message that custody payments may facilitate children's overall divorce adjustment will diffuse some of the resistance that often occurs when noncustodial parents are forced to support, but not participate in, a household responsible for rearing their biological children. This message would emphasize the noncustodial parents' continuing role as a parent while de-emphasizing the notion that alimony is provided for the ex-spouse's personal use.

Custody arrangements, visitation decisions, and joint parenting agreements prior to a divorce also can significantly affect children's postdivorce adjustment. In this respect also, parents and others initially need to understand the research that correlates these variables with children's adjustment over time. Briefly, it appears that joint custody arrangements may have the greatest potential to positively affect children's long-term adjustment so long as the respective parents can agree to and use consistent parenting styles. An increase in joint custody decisions, however, will necessitate radical changes in divorce courts' conceptualizations of divorce settlements and divorcing parents' pleas for child custody. Indeed, mothers alone continue to receive custody of their children in the vast majority (90%) of custody cases (Guidubaldi, Perry, & Nastasi, in press).

Predivorce agreements encouraging consistent, ongoing, and important amounts of visitation by the noncustodial parent are extremely important to the adjustment of the children. Such agreements hopefully can minimize the effects of postdivorce difficulties in this area, thus decreasing future parental conflict, another variable related to children's postdivorce adjustment. Visitation agreements should particularly target male children who have the more severe and long-lasting postdivorce adjustment difficulties. Longitudinal research emphasizes that divorced boys' relationships with their fathers and postdivorce father–son interactions (often during visitation, given the custody statistics noted above) significantly predict their general adjustment. The overall implications, then, are clear: (a) Divorcing parents need to understand the reasons for and develop a "parenting package" that describes the practices that they agree to use consistently with their children after the divorce; and (b) significant amounts of tension-free, noncustodial visitation after the divorce (especially with any sons involved) should be part of this parenting package.

Discipline is another important issue that parents should agree upon as part of the parenting package. Differential discipline styles, both before and after a divorce, are often a source of considerable tension, and predivorce agreements may decrease this tension and result in more positive parent–child interactions. From a preventive perspective, predivorce agreements in this and other parenting areas can open a needed communication process that must continue after the divorce; this process should focus away from parents' personal divorce traumas and onto the reality that their children still need support, guidance, and joint parenting efforts. Emery (1982) has suggested that many children's adjustment problems are related not to the divorce but to continuing interparental conflict after the divorce. If true, then the agreements within the parenting package may decrease subsequent parental conflicts, thereby increasing the probability of children's more positive adjustment.

Obviously, the sensitivity of the above issues, and the possibility that they actually precipitated the divorce, sometimes make them difficult to resolve. However, as their psychological importance to the adjustment of the children of divorce is clear, school psychologists need to emphasize these issues while advocating respect for the children and their psychological rights. Over the past 5 years, the process of divorce mediation has been advanced as an especially effective way of resolving many of these important issues. From a research perspective, we need to fully explore the efficacy of mediation (and other procedures) as an advocacy technique for children of divorce. From a practitioner perspective, the social–emotional and academic–intellectual effects of divorce on children need to be publicized so that parents and community systems (legislative, judicial, mental health) can consider the entire family system when making decisions that at first glance appear only to involve a divorcing husband and wife.

PUTTING DIVORCE IN PERSPECTIVE

Because divorce is a phenomenon of the family or home, its effects in the school system or classroom are indirect. Thus, for school psychologists and other school support staff, interventions addressing the effects of divorce must occur with the full knowledge and support of the divorced parents (or of the custodial parent if the noncustodial parent abdicates responsibility) and often should be coordinated with other, nonschool interventions such as private counseling or community-based support. Once parental consent has been received, however, these interventions should focus particularly on ways to minimize the *school-related* social–emotional, and academic–intellectual effects of the divorce. That is, the more pervasive issues and family-related effects of divorce should remain the responsibility of community or private mental health services if they are called on by the parents. Without parental consent, the school system is limited to interventions that are available to all children and that do not unduly target the children of divorce.

In developing supportive interventions at school for children of divorce, both general and divorce-specific information is needed. The general information should include baselines of the child's predivorce and preseparation social–emotional and academic–intellectual development for comparative purposes. This information should include results from previous standardized and individual tests, academic grades and teacher ratings or comments on classroom conduct and effort, referrals or records for behavioral or learning problems or services, and documentation of psychological or other supportive intervention. The divorce-specific information should provide school staff with an understanding of the divorce situation and the current home/divorce environment, and it should be related to those variables that the research literature has identified as important to children's divorce adjustment. This information, ideally collected from both parents' perspectives, should include an understanding (a) of the parents' desired involvement with the school and the specific interactions they want from the school (e.g., does the noncustodial parent wish to receive report cards and other communications from the teacher or principal?); (b) of the custodial arrangements chosen (e.g., have any siblings been separated between the parents; is a joint custody arrangement in force?); (c) of the parents' disciplinary styles and ability to maintain consistency; (d) of other mental health and community support services being used by the parents or child (e.g., counseling, a big brother or sister); and (e) of any other pertinent variables noted from the longitudinal studies above. In collecting all of this information, school psychologists must limit themselves to questions and information relevant to the school and any school-based interventions; care should be taken to avoid irrelevant and unnecessarily personal (voyeuristic) questions and to maintain the child's, parents', and family's right to confidentiality.

Two other factors are important to any potential intervention process: the actual need for intervention and the coordination and cooperation of school support staff and teachers. In considering the first factor, school psychologists cannot automatically assume from the longitudinal studies that all children of divorce will have adjustment difficulties and require intervention services. Some children, in the case of an acrimonious predivorce home environment, may actually demonstrate better psychological development and overall adjustment after the divorce, whereas others may possess individual coping skills or already existing emotional support systems that minimize any negative reactions. School psychologists must ensure that behavior motivating referral of these children is significant in frequency, duration, and intensity, and must determine whether these difficulties are related, to some degree, to the divorce experience or to some other coincidental issue or condition.

As with almost any comprehensive school intervention initiative, the coordination and cooperation of school support staff and teachers is critical (see Maher & Pfeiffer, 1983, for reviews). This is especially true given the sensitive nature of divorce for both the parents and children experiencing it. School staffs must organize themselves such that everyone clearly understands which procedures are used with children experiencing divorce difficulties and what intervention programs and techniques are available for use within the district. Part of these procedures may involve a "case manager" approach, in which one individual is chosen as the primary contact between the home and school so that confusing, multiple intervention messages are avoided. Other procedures should ensure periodic review and evaluation of all district policies and processes related to divorce and divorce interventions. Clearly, this coordination is most easily accomplished when the school district uses a mental health/child study team approach at either the district or individual-building level that meets regularly to plan and consider all identified child problems. However, if the need existed, a district could form a special districtwide mental health team to specifically address the needs of children of divorce.

ALTERNATIVE ACTIONS

From a school psychologist's perspective, intervention programs addressing the impact of divorce can focus on primary, secondary, or tertiary prevention. While most school psychological interventions occur in schools with specific children, divorce-related preventive intervention may also involve family or community programs. For example, parent or family support groups around divorce issues have been especially highlighted in the intervention literature, and comprehensive community education and in-service programs are also important considerations.

In the Schools

There are three ways, minimally, that schools can prepare children for the effects of a divorce. They can (a) serve children who have actually experienced a divorce by maintaining school conditions and programs that correlate with their postdivorce social and academic adjustment (tertiary prevention); (b) develop preventive programs for children who are likely to experience a divorce *before* it occurs (secondary prevention); and (c) develop programs for *all* school children in a particular school district to help them understand and deal with divorce as a common life crisis (primary prevention). Across all three levels of prevention, school psychologists first must convince school personnel that divorce is a significant problem in the community and that its effects do cross into and affect the school environment and everyday classroom experience. This process involves in-service programs to educate and inform all administrators, teachers, and support and other staff (a) on the possible effects of divorce on children at various age levels, (b) on ways to identify divorce-related maladjustment, and (c) on what support staff to contact for a coordination of services and interventions. Once a staff understands the potential impact of divorce and is committed to supporting children in this area, specific, child-focused programs can be developed and implemented.

From a tertiary prevention perspective, five school climate dimensions were identified by Guidubaldi et al. (1983) as affecting students' adjustment to divorce: a safe and orderly environment, continued high expectations for these students, maintaining the level of time a student remains on task and exposed to the opportunity to learn, frequent monitoring of student progress, and reinforcement practices. In developing or maintaining these positive conditions, teachers and other school officials should attempt to involve *both* parents in the education of their children (unless, of course, the project is rejected by one of the parents or prohibited by a court decision or ruling). This may involve duplicate report cards or progress reports for both parents, separate conference invitations, or two phone calls to communicate positive or negative classroom information. By involving both parents, children of divorce will realize that they are still accountable to both parents and, significantly, that both parents care for them and feel that their academic development is important.

From a secondary and tertiary program perspective, Drake and Shellenberger (1981) provide a good review of programs for children of separation or divorce, including (a) counseling groups for children from homes headed by a single, previously divorced, or separated parent; (b) programs that integrate stories or books about other children's divorce experiences and feelings that then stimulate the program participants to discussion and expression of personal experiences and feelings; (c) programs that coordinate crisis intervention, coping, and social skills training for children; and (d) programs emphasizing brief psychotherapeutic intervention (see also Kelly & Wallerstein, 1977, and Stuart & Abt, 1981). Generally, these intervention programs and ideas are only described in the literature; very few studies have completed program evaluations or have collected data demonstrating program efficacy with respect to children's social or academic changes. While this should not discourage school psychologists from using these therapeutic approaches, hopefully some can be implemented with evaluation methodologies that demonstrate their reliability, validity, and clinical utility.

From a primary prevention perspective, divorce education programs should be developed to systematically include all children in a specific school district. Such programs could help children, at their various individual age and developmental levels, (a) to understand the broad implications of divorce, (b) to relate more effectively with peers who have gone or are going through that experience, (c) to cope with their own natural fears that *their* parents also might get divorced, and (d) to be better prepared if they themselves face divorce at some time in the future. Similar to the drug education and other preventive programs of the past two decades, these divorce programs should address divorced and nondivorced children's social and academic problems by preparing children's families, schools, and communities with positive approaches and responses to the experience of divorce and its multifaceted effects.

In the Community

Within the community setting, school psychologists can (a) help to develop support services for children of divorce, for example, big brother/big sister programs (tertiary prevention); (b) participate in parent or family support groups addressing divorce or separation issues (tertiary or secondary prevention); (c) sponsor comprehensive community education programs or open houses to acquaint the public with the effects of divorce and with the programs that are available in the schools or community (at all prevention levels); and (d) develop a school–community coordinating board or system organizing all mental health and supportive service agencies toward a more unified approach to divorce services and interventions (primary prevention). As one example of a community-based preventive program, Stolberg and Cullen (1983) developed a Divorce Adjustment Project (DAP) that targeted families of divorce and their adjustment and other difficulties during the first 2 years after a divorce. The DAP has three primary components, a children's support group, a discussion sequence focused on the planning process beyond the divorce, and a parents' group that provides "parenting alone" suggestions and supports. Collectively, the program attempts (a) to provide a supportive environment among a group of people all experiencing the same life crisis; (b) to identify problem behavior and maladjustment patterns related to the divorce experience and the processes that influence those patterns; (c) to teach both parents and children specific coping skills and procedures that can enhance their adaptive responses to the divorce; and (d) to replace social support systems that are lost when the divorce occurred. While a 3-year evaluation of the program is pending, the initial results indicate that the DAP shows promise as an integrated, preventive response to divorce for parents and their children.

SUMMARY

The rate of divorce continues at a staggering pace and its social and academic effects on children constitute a major mental health and educational problem for schools and communities. School psychologists need to understand that children appear to react differently to the divorce experience depending on their age, developmental maturity, sex, the length of time since the divorce, and the support systems available. These children's reactions, however, must be analyzed and considered within the contexts of their school and family environments. Clearly, some children of divorce are able to weather the experience with minimal discomfort, but others appear to require specific emotional and other supports in order to adapt. Thus, analyzing each child as an individual and each child's individual school and home ecologies is of paramount importance.

From an intervention standpoint, primary, secondary, and tertiary prevention programming is necessary to comprehensively address both children's *and* parents' divorce adjustments and adaptations. School psychologists should increase in school staff and the community at large an understanding of and sensitivity to the problems and issues of divorce, and should coordinate programs for children of divorce (and their parents), children at risk of divorce, and all other children — as it is inevitable that they will interact with divorced children and, perhaps feel the emotionality of this life event. Furthermore, school psychologists should become involved in practical research that identifies the variables and intervention programs or strategies that most effectively affect children's social and academic adjustments.

In a sense, *every* child in today's society is at risk for divorce. Divorce appears relatively indiscriminate in its incidence in respect to social positions. It must be viewed as a public and mental health epidemic. School psychologists must utilize their special training and skills in dealing with human behavior and mental health development and begin to address the special problems of children of divorce. We also must assume leadership positions in the schools and community to encourage comprehensive, coordinated, and communitywide responses. Given that 40–50% of all children born during the past decade will spend some time living in a single-parent family, the problems associated with divorce clearly will not go quietly away. We must acknowledge these problems and begin to develop sound solutions.

REFERENCES

Baumrind, D. (1968). Authoritarian vs. authoritative parental control. *Adolescence, 3,* 255–272.

Drake, E. A., & Shellenberger, S. (1981). Children of separation and divorce: A review of school programs and implications for the psychologist. *School Psychology Review, 10,* 54–61.

Emery, R. E. (1982). Interparental conflict and the children of discord and divorce. *Psychological Bulletin, 92,* 310–330.

Guidubaldi, J., Cleminshaw, H. K., Perry, J. D., McLoughlin, C. S. (1983). The impact of parental divorce on children: Report of the nationwide NASP study. *School Psychology Review, 12,* 300–323.

Guidubaldi, J., & Perry, J. D. (1985). Divorce and mental health sequelae for children: A two-year follow-up of a nationwide sample. *Journal of the American Academy of Child Psychiatry, 24,* 531–537.

Guidubaldi, J., Perry, J. D., & Nastasi, B. K. (in press). Growing up in a divorced family: Initial and long-term perspectives on children's adjustment. In S. Oskamp (Ed.), *Annual review of applied social psychology.* New York: Sage.

Hetherington, E. M. (1979). Divorce: A child's perspective. *American Psychologist, 34,* 851–858.

Hetherington, E. M., Cox, M., & Cox, R. (1978). Effects of divorce on parents and children. In M. E. Lamb (Ed.), *Nontraditional families: Parenting and child development* (pp. 233–288). New Jersey: Erlbaum.

Kelly, J. B., & Wallerstein, J. S. (1977). Brief interventions with children in divorcing families. *American Journal of Orthopsychiatry, 47,* 23–36.

Kurdek, L. A. (1981). An integrative perspective on children's divorce adjustment. *American Psychologist, 36,* 856–866.

Kurdek, L. A. (Ed.). (1983). *Children and divorce.* San Francisco: Jossey Bass.

Kurdek, L. A., Blisk, D., & Siesky, A. E. (1981). Correlates of children's long-term adjustment to their parents' divorce. *Developmental Psychology, 17,* 565–579.

Maher, C. A., & Pfeiffer, S. I. (Eds.). (1983). Multidisciplinary teams in the schools: Perspectives, practices, and possibilities [Special issue]. *School Psychology Review, 12*(2).

National Center for Health Statistics. (1984). Births, marriages, divorces, and deaths for 1983. *Monthly Vital Statistics.* Rep. 23, PHS–84–1120.

Stolberg, A. L., & Cullen, P. M. (1983). Preventive interventions for families of divorce: The Divorce Adjustment Project. *New Directions for Child Development, 19,* 71–81.

Stuart, I. R., & Abt, L. E. (Eds.). (1981). *Children of separation and divorce: Management and treatment.* New York: Van Nostrand Reinhold.

U.S. Bureau of Census. (1982a). *Household and family characteristics: March 1981.* (Current Population Report Series P-20, No. 371.) Washington, DC: U.S. Government Printing Office.

U.S. Bureau of Census. (1982b). *Household and family characteristics: March 1981.* (Current Population Report Series P-20, No. 372.) Washington, DC: U.S. Government Printing Office.

Wallerstein, J. S. (1984). Children of divorce: Preliminary report of a ten-year follow-up of young children. *American Journal of Orthopsychiatry, 54,* 444–458.

Wallerstein, J. S., & Kelly, J. B. (1976). The effects of parental divorce experiences of the child in later latency. *American Journal of Orthopsychiatry, 46,* 256–267.

Wallerstein, J. S., & Kelly, J. B. (1980). *Surviving the breakup: How children and parents cope with divorce.* New York: Basic Books.

Yamamoto, K. (1979). Children's ratings of the stressfulness of experiences. *Developmental Psychology, 15,* 581–582.

BIBLIOGRAPHY: PROFESSIONALS

Guidubaldi, J., Cleminshaw, H. K., Perry, J. D., McLoughlin, C. S. (1983). The impact of parental divorce on children: Report of the nationwide NASP study. *School Psychology Review, 12,* 300–323.
Provides a critical description of the various longitudinal studies to date investigating the effects of divorce on children and adolescents. Describes the nationwide NASP/Kent State University study with its various results and their implications.

Hetherington, E. M., Cox, M., & Cox, R. (1985). Long-term effects of divorce and remarriage on the adjustment of children. *Journal of the American Academy of Child Psychiatry, 24,* 518–530.
This article discusses the results of a 6-year longitudinal study of the effects of divorce on parents and children from Virginia. Presenting a great deal of statistical data and interpretation, this study also provides information about various tools that help to analyze parents' and children's reactions to divorce.

Kurdek, L. A. (Ed.). (1983). *Children and divorce.* San Francisco: Jossey-Bass.
Provides a summarization of the results of Kurdek's longitudinal study in Dayton, Ohio, investigating divorced children's social and interpersonal relations skills and their parents' post-divorce adjustments. Also analyzes the difficulties of research in the area of divorce, and the divorce experience from an ecological perspective.

Stuart, I. R., & Abt, L. E. (Eds.). (1981). *Children of separation and divorce: Management and treatment.* New York: Van Nostrand Reinhold.
An edited book analyzing children of separation and divorce and ways to intervene and address their adjustment difficulties. One chapter by Drake specifically focuses on the role of the school in helping children to cope with divorce. Additional chapters look at other resources in the management and treatment process.

Wallerstein, J. S., & Kelly, J. B. (1980). *Surviving the breakup: How children and parents cope with divorce.* New York: Basic Books.
An excellent resource that provides practical descriptions and suggestions on how children and parents deal with the divorce experience. Based on the authors' experiences with their longitudinal study in California, this book is recommended for both the professional and parents.

BIBLIOGRAPHY: PARENTS

The following books provide unique, personal perspectives on divorce in an attempt to help parents to understand their reactions to the experience and those of their children:

Gardner, R. (1977). *The parents book about divorce.* New York: Doubleday.

Glass, S. M. (1980). *A divorce dictionary: A book for you and your children.* Boston: Little, Brown.

Stein, S. B. (1979). *On divorce: An open family book for parents and children together.* New York: Walker.

Salk, L. (1978). *What every child would like parents to know about divorce.* New York: Harper and Row.

BIBLIOGRAPHY: CHILDREN

Martin, M., Martin, D., & Porter, J. (1983). Bibliotherapy: Children of divorce. *School Counselor, 30,* 312–315.
An annotated bibliography of books about divorce that are appropriate for children and adolescents. An important feature of this bibliography is that it describes each book and designates the grades of the children it is appropriate for.

Craver, K. (1983). Breaking up is hard to do. *School Counselor, 30,* 315–319.
Another annotated bibliography of books about divorce that are appropriate for children and adolescents. This bibliography separates the books into fiction and nonfiction and also describes each book and designates the grades of the children it is appropriate for.

Children and Drug Abuse

Susan G. Forman and Mickey K. Randolph
University of South Carolina

BACKGROUND

Each year a large number of adolescents begin experimenting with alcohol and/or drugs, and a significant percentage will remain users. A number of recent surveys have revealed that substance use has reached epidemic proportions among youths and that initiation of substance use is occurring at an earlier age than ever before.

Prevalence

Alcohol is the most commonly abused substance among U.S. adults and adolescents. In a national survey, Johnston, Bachman and O'Malley (1982) found that 56% of junior high school students and 93% of high school seniors had used alcohol. Furthermore, 5.7% reported using alcohol on a daily basis. An alarming 41% of the high school seniors surveyed reported at least one occasion during the 2 weeks prior to the survey when they had had five or more consecutive drinks.

This survey also indicated that marijuana, more than any other substance, is used on a daily basis and is the most widely used illicit substance. Some 60% of high school seniors had tried it, 29% reported current use (once or more during the previous 30 days), and 6.3% reported daily use. Other drugs frequently used by these adolescents included stimulants (28% of respondents), inhalants (18%), cocaine (16%), sedatives (15%), hallucinogens (15%), heroin (1.2%), and other opiates (10%). Table 1 lists these commonly abused substances and their effects.

Use versus Abuse

Researchers and writers in the field of substance abuse have defined substance abuse in a variety of ways. Millman and Botvin (1983) pointed out that a large number of adolescents experiment with drugs and do not repeat the experience. Some use drugs occasionally without suffering any negative consequences. However, others engage in compulsive and constant use and experience physical and psychosocial deterioration. Hence these authors define substance abuse in terms of deviation from accepted patterns of use in a given society. Alternatively, the National Institute on Drug Abuse (1981) defined substance abuse as the use of a chemical substance that causes physical, mental, emotional, or social harm to an individual or those close to him or her. There is no definite boundary that separates use from abuse; however, frequency, quantity, and negative consequences such as health problems, injuries, arrests, and school discipline or academic problems are usually considered.

Some writers in the area believe that any substance use by adolescents is abuse; however, others believe that use is responsible if it does not interfere with one's ability to accomplish life tasks. Examples of responsible use would include delaying the first use of the substance, limiting the amount of the substance used per occasion, limiting the number of occasions of use, and avoiding risk situations (e.g., driving) (Hawk, 1985).

Newton (1981) described five stages of adolescent drug use: (0) exposure to drugs, (1) learning the mood swing, (2) seeking the mood swing, (3) preoccupation with the mood swing, and (4) using drugs to feel normal. Adolescents are exposed to drugs through peers, media, and family influences. Stage 1, learning the mood swing, involves introduction to a drug that makes the user feel good; this typically happens with peers. During stage 2, seeking the mood swing, usage progresses from occasional, to regular weekend use, to occasional weekday and finally to regular weekday use. By stage 2, considerable time is spent obtaining drugs. During stage 3, preoccupation with the mood swing, most of the adolescent's time is devoted to getting high. Solitary, as opposed to social use of drugs, and dealing of drugs frequently occur. During stage 4, using drugs to feel normal, drugs are used continuously to get through the day.

Negative Consequences

The negative consequences of even the most frequently abused substances, alcohol and marijuana, have been established. Excessive use of alcohol by adolescents has been related to belligerence, accident proneness, impaired school performance, and problems involving the law (Cohen, 1981). Among teenagers 45% of fatal automobile accidents (Mayer, 1983) and over 40% of adolescent suicides (Forrest, 1983) involve alcohol. Marijuana can result in impaired psychomotor performance and impaired immediate recall as well as passivity and loss of motivation (Cohen, 1981). Also, decreased pulmonary function, bronchitis, and sinusitis have been reported among adolescents who frequently smoke marijuana (Millman & Botvin, 1983).

Thus, serious negative consequences of even relatively short-term use of various chemical substances by adolescents has been found. Long-term continued use into adulthood leads to more significant health, psychological, and behavioral effects.

DEVELOPMENT

Adolescents seem to progress along what has been called a substance use hierarchy. Initial experimentation usually begins with tobacco, beer, wine and hard liquor. Marijuana use usually starts later. Some adolescents go on to experiment with depressants, stimulants, and psychedelics. Opiates are usually the last substance tried (Millman & Botvin, 1983). Most initial use takes place in social situations, and at particular points in the substance use hierarchy, most adolescents make a conscious decision to explore no further.

TABLE 1

Commonly Used/Abused Drugs and Their Effects

Drug and Prescription Name	Effects	Overdose effects
Depressants		
Alcohol Diazepam (Valium) Chlordiazepoxide (Librium) Pentobarbital (Nembutal) Secobarbital (Seconal) Methaqualone (Quaalude) Amitriptyline (Elavil)	Depressed central nervous system, decreased activity, drowsiness, impairment of visual–motor coordination, confusion, disorientation, slurred speech	Mental confusion, coma, possible death
Stimulants		
Amphetamine (Benzedrine) Dextroamphetamine (Dexedrine) Methylphenidate (Ritalin) Phenmetrazine (Preludin) Cocaine	Stimulated central nervous system, feelings of well-being, euphoria, dilated pupils, increased energy; abuse results in nervousness, irritability, tremors, fatigue, insomnia, dizziness, confusion	Agitation, increase in body temperature, hallucinations, convulsions, possible death
Opiates		
Heroin Opium Morphine Codeine Hydromorphone (Dilaudid) Oxycodene (Percodan) Methadone Meperidine (Demorol)	Depressed central nervous system, depressed cardiac and respiratory activity, drowsiness, mood changes, euphoria, nausea, constricted pupils	Slow, shallow breathing, clammy skin, convulsions, coma, possible death
Cannabis		
Marijuana Hashish	Drowsiness, relaxed inhibitions, euphoria, increased appetite, reddened eyes, altered time perception, social withdrawal, impairment of motor performance and reaction time	Insomnia, hyperactivity, decreased appetite in some individuals
Psychedelic drugs		
Lysergic acid diethylamide (LSD) Psilocybin Mescaline 2, 5-Dimethoxy-4-methyl-amphetamine (STP) Dimethyltryptamine (DMT) Phencyclidine (PCP)	Feelings of enhanced mental ability, increased awareness of sensory input, alterations in perceptions, thoughts, feelings and behavior, altered body image and inability to differentiate self from surroundings, rambling speech, dilated pupils	Unpredictable "trip" episodes, psychosis, possible death
Inhalants		
Glues Cleaning solution Nailpolish remover Lighter fluids Paints Paint thinners Aerosols Petroleum products Amyl and butyl nitrate	Brief euphoria, dizziness, rapid heart rate, confusion, slurred speech, poor coordination, drunken behavior	Unconsciousness, coma, possible sudden death

Studies indicate that the modal grade for first use of alcohol is grade 9, 56% of high school seniors reporting initial use before high school. Most marijuana use also seems to start during middle school and early high school. However, 3.6% of high school seniors report that they had tried an illicit substance before they entered sixth grade. With the exception of alcohol, inhalants, and marijuana, more than one-half of initial use occurs after completion of the ninth grade (Johnston et al., 1982).

PUTTING CHILDREN'S DRUG ABUSE IN PERSPECTIVE

Determinants of Substance Use

A wide variety of social, psychological, behavioral, and developmental factors have been found to be associated with substance use and abuse in adolescents (Jessor & Jessor, 1977).

Social factors include the influence of parents, siblings, and friends who use these substances. Adolescents from families in which parents or older siblings take drugs tend to use drugs. In addition, family instability and family problems are related to adolescents' drug abuse. Adolescents from lower socioeconomic groups are also more likely to become abusers. Because the peer group is of major importance to adolescents and they are very responsive to pressures to conform, peer influence is a major factor associated with adolescent substance abuse. Many studies have found a strong relationship between adolescents' substance use and that of their friends (Millman & Botvin, 1983).

A range of psychological factors have been related to substance abuse by adolescents although causality has not been established. Abusers have been found to have an external locus of control, lower self-esteem, high degree of dissatisfaction and pessimism, high need for social approval, low social confidence, high anxiety, low assertiveness, and a tendency to impulsivity and rebelliousness (Flay, d'Avernas, Best, Hersell, & Ryan, 1983).

A number of behavioral factors have also been found to differentiate substance abusers and nonusers. Substance abusers tend to get lower grades, do not participate in extracurricular activities, and are likely to be involved in school disciplinary incidents (Millman & Botvin, 1983).

ALTERNATIVE ACTIONS

Prevention

Research indicates that the most effective substance abuse prevention programs have been school programs that focus on helping students develop specific personal and social coping skills in an attempt to counter one or more variables related to substance abuse. The programs are based on social learning theory (Bandura, 1977) and problem behavior theory (Jessor & Jessor, 1977), which view the use of substances as a socially learned, purposive, functional behavior that is the result of both personal and social/environmental factors.

Most coping skills programs were initially developed to prevent cigarette smoking; however, more recently they have been evaluated with respect to prevention of alcohol and drug use. This is partially a result of the fact that researchers in the field of substance abuse have found that there is an association between the factors that underlie various types of substance use.

Two major types of coping skills programs can be identified in the literature on substance abuse prevention. The first of these teaches adolescents skills that can be used to deal with social influence and pressure. These have been called "Saying No" programs. The second type of coping skills program provides training in a range of personal and social skills that can be used to deal with the wide variety of factors, both social/environmental and personal, that may influence substance use.

Social Influence Programs. Social influence programs are based on the work of Evans (1976), who used the principle of social inoculation in a smoking prevention program. Assuming that social variables are of major importance in the decision to use substances, it is thought that resistance to social pressures for substance use will be greater if the individual has been given experience dealing with social pressure, in a controlled setting.

Most social influences, or Saying No, programs have three components: (a) information about drugs, their immediate and long-term effects, and how *social* influences, especially peer pressure, are related to their use; (b) skills training in resisting social pressures; (c) training in decision-making skills. Social influences programs that have shown evidence of effectiveness include the Counseling Leadership Against Smoking Project (project CLASP) (McAlister, Perry, Killen, Slinkard, & Maccoby, 1980), the Robbinsdale Antismoking Project (RASP) (Hurd, Johnson, Pechacek, Bast, Jacobs, & Luepker, 1980), and the prevention of Cigarette Smoking in Children Project (PCSC) (Murray, Johnson, Luepker, Pechacek, & Jacobs, 1980).

The Waterloo Smoking Prevention Program (Flay, d'Avernas, Best, Hersell, & Ryan, 1983) provides one of the best examples of a Saying No program that produced positive results. The program consisted of six 1-hour weekly sessions delivered to sixth graders at the beginning of the school year by health educators. In addition, two booster sessions at the end of grade 6, two booster sessions at the beginning of grade 7, and one booster session at the beginning of grade 8 were provided. The program had three major components.

The first consisted of information about the consequences of smoking and the reasons for smoking, through activities that elicited the information from the students. The information was repeated through videotapes, poster making, role playing, and class discussion.

The second component focused on social influences, including family, peer, and media influences. Skills to resist these pressures, such as refusal skills, were taught, role-played, and practiced.

The third component focused on decision making and public commitment. The decisional balance sheet (Janis & Mann, 1977) was used as a structure for the decision-making process. Students listed (a) injuries to themselves if they smoke; (b) injuries to others; (c) benefits to themselves; (d) benefits to others; (e) those who will disapprove; and (f) those who will approve. In the public commitment procedure, students announced their decisions and reasons to their classmates. Their announcements were taped, supposedly to be shown to future sixth grade students.

An evaluation of this program indicated reduced onset of smoking, as well as increases in the number of smokers who quit. The program seemed to have the greatest effect on students who were at risk for becoming smokers.

Broad-Spectrum Programs. Broad-spectrum coping skills programs teach students general coping skills as well as skills and knowledge specifically related to substance abuse. Cognitive–Behavioral Skills Training (Schinke, 1982) and Life Skills Training (Botvin, 1983) are broad-spectrum coping skills programs that have received empirical support in the research literature. Cognitive–Behavioral Skills Training focuses on smoking prevention. Life Skills Training is the broad-spectrum program having the most research support with respect to prevention of both smoking and drug and alcohol use.

Life Skills Training is typically conducted in 10 weekly classroom sessions. The program has five major components: (a) cognitive, (b) decision making, (c) anxiety management, (d) social skills training,and (e) self-improvement.

The cognitive component involves presentation of information on the short and long-term consequences of substance use, prevalence, social acceptability, and the process of becoming dependent on tobacco, alcohol, or marijuana. The decision-making component addresses the decision-making process, how to resist persuasive tactics, and independent thinking. Special attention is given to resisting advertising techniques. The anxiety management component provides students with techniques such as physical relaxation and imagery that can be used to cope with anxiety. The social skills training component addresses communication skills, including verbal and nonverbal communication, as well as techniques for avoiding misunderstandings. Initiating social contacts, basic conversational skills, and boy–girl social interactions are also explored. In addition, students are taught assertiveness techniques and how they can be used to resist peer pressure to smoke, drink, or use drugs. The self-improvement component provides information on self-image and how it is formed, and the relationship between self-image and behavior. Students are taught behavioral self-management techniques and carry out a self-improvement project.

Life Skills Training has been shown to be effective in prevention of cigarette smoking (Botvin & Eng, 1982; Botvin, Eng, & Williams, 1980; Botvin, Renick, & Baker, 1983) as well as prevention of drug and alcohol use (Botvin, Baker, Renick, Filazzola, & Botvin, 1984) in middle and high school students. This type of training has been conducted by teachers and peer leaders, as well as specially trained staff.

Early Intervention

Early intervention programs are targeted at students who have begun experimenting with drugs and/or alcohol or at those who are most at risk, such as children of substance abusers or students with behavioral problems. The Student Assistance Program is an example of a relatively successful early intervention program (Morehouse, 1982). This program uses professional counselors to provide individual and group counseling for high-risk students. Counseling goals, for those who have begun to use drugs and/or alcohol, are to help reduce alcohol or drug use, to improve self-esteem, and to improve ability to function in school, with peers and with family members. In addition, the counselors also conduct preventive groups for those with at-risk characteristics, such as children of alcoholics.

Project SCCOPE, the South Carolina Coping Skills Project (Forman & Neal, in press) is an additional early intervention approach that is currently being evaluated. Project SCCOPE has adapted Life Skills Training (Botvin, 1983) for use with high-risk adolescents in a small-group training format. In addition, in order to enhance the effects of the coping skills training, school staff and parents are trained to model, cue, and reinforce the coping skills in the school and home environments.

Treatment

Targeting adolescents who abuse alcohol and/or drugs is not a simple task, even for individuals in close daily contact. Cornacchia, Smith, and Bentel (1978) reviewed the primary resources for determining those adolescents in need of treatment. They indicated that the most effective methods for locating substance abusers are self-referral, clinical tests, such as blood or urine analysis, and peer identification. However, because these procedures either require the adolescent to recognize and report the problem or in some situations may be illegal, they have not produced a substantial number of treatment referrals. As an alternative, Baron (1981) and Milgram (1983) have recommended the use of observation by an individual (parents or school official) who is familiar with the behavioral and personality effects and symptoms of drug and alcohol abuse.

A variety of behaviors have been associated with adolescent substance abuse. Table 2 lists behaviors that identify potential substance abusers. The personality characteristics of substance users reviewed above should also be considered.

Once an adolescent is suspected of substance abuse, or has been identified as an abuser, parents should be notified immediately. The school staff member who identifies a potential problem should help the parent and adolescent locate services.

A variety of treatment approaches exist for the adolescent substance abuser. Outpatient facilities and residential centers are the primary treatment modalities offered and involve crisis intervention, detoxification, traditional psychotherapy, and behavioral approaches in the form of family, group, and individual therapy.

TABLE 2

Symptoms of Alcohol and Drug Abuse

Decrease in school attendance
Decrease in academic performance
Displays of unusual degrees of activity or inactivity
Deterioration of personal appearance
Changes in appetite or sleeping habits (increase or decrease)
Speech problems (slurred, rambling, incoherent)
Motor incoordination
Unpredictable displays of temper
Wearing sunglasses at inappropriate times
A pattern of spending most of the time at home alone in room
Borrowing or stealing money (to support habit)
Wearing long-sleeved shirts (to hide needle marks)
Getting into trouble with legal authorities
Radical change in peer groups
Withdrawing from activities (e.g., church, school, community)
Association with known substance users
Appearance of intoxification with or without a smell of alcohol
Physical changes such as red, watery eyes, runny nose, shortness of breath
Possession of unexplained expensive articles or large sums of money
Possession of drug paraphernalia (e.g., incense, pipes, eye droppers)

Some programs focus on complete abstinence, but others stress controlled use. Some treatment programs stress voluntary participation; others serve individuals who have been required by school or legal officials or parents to seek treatment. One characteristic most programs share is an emphasis on assessment of the adolescent's problem and a comprehensive treatment approach designed to address problems other than substance abuse.

A crisis intervention approach from a medical facility will initially be needed if the use of substances has resulted in an overdose or a comatose state. Additionally, some adolescents may need to be served by a detoxification facility before progressing to other types of treatment. However, with the exception of these medically oriented approaches, the majority of treatment programs focus on traditional psychotherapy or behavioral approaches.

Residential programs are recommended for those who need complete supervision in order to abstain from alcohol and/or drugs or who may pose a danger to themselves. Outpatient programs may be best for those who require more limited help to refrain from alcohol or drug use (Cornacchia et al., 1978). Most of the programs, whether residential or outpatient, employ a multimodal approach to treatment, emphasizing the physical, psychological, and social well-being of the individual.

Behavioral methods are common treatment strategies used in residential and outpatient facilities. Behavioral contracting is a frequently used technique to reduce or eliminate the use of alcohol and/or drugs and to increase more desirable behaviors. Contracting has been used extensively with individuals, families, and groups; it appears to be a successful method for motivated substance abusers and their families (Bratter, 1972; Cassady, 1975; Controneo & Krasner, 1976; Frederiksen, Jenkins, & Carr, 1976). In addition to contracts, many researchers have found beneficial results in training adolescents in specific coping skills, such as assertiveness, relaxation, problem-solving, and desensitization (Bratter, 1972; Ross, 1976). Families typically receive instructions in parenting and communication skills (Teicher, Sinay, & Stumphauzer, 1976).

Therapists advocating a psychoanalytic approach work with individuals and families to solve not only the substance abuse problem, but general problems in living. Sheldon, Davis, and Kohorn (1978) have stressed the importance of developing good relationships with their adolescent clients and recommended an approach that focuses on accepting responsibility and dealing with feelings of anxiety, inferiority, depression, and self-destruction. There is typically an emphasis on having these adolescents gain some insight into their problems.

In summary, treatment programs targeted for the adolescent substance abuser typically focus on a variety of problems encountered by the adolescent as well as the abusive behavior. Both public and private agencies administer these programs. Individuals working with schools, adolescents, and families should become familiar with the various private psychotherapists, private physicians, public and private hospitals, hot lines, outpatient clinics, mental health centers, city and county agencies, and religious organizations designed to provide services for the adolescent substance abuser and the family. Each state has an agency that is responsible for coordinating services for substance abusers. These state agencies can be helpful in providing information about specific local resources (Cornacchia et al., 1978).

SUMMARY

Alcohol and drug abuse have been identified as one of the most serious problems facing youth today. Because of their educational background and professional skills, school psychologists can play a major role in the development and implementation of school-based substance abuse programs. Comprehensive school-based services would include (a) educational programs for school staff and parents regarding definition, identification, and treatment of the problem, (b) prevention and intervention programs for students, (c) liaison with and referral to community services related to treatment of substance abuse, and (d) school policies that discourage substance use. School psychologists can assist in these areas through providing in-service training for school staff, parent training, consultation to teachers and administrators, group and individual counseling for students, and communication with community services.

REFERENCES

Bandura, A. (1977). *Social learning theory.* Englewood, Cliffs, NJ: Prentice-hall.

Baron, J. D. (1981). *The parent handbook of drug abuse.* Pasadena, TX: Drug Abuse Program of America, Inc.

Botvin, G. J. (1983). *Life skills training: A self-improvement approach to substance abuse training.* New York: Smithfield.

Botvin, G. J., Baker, E., Renick, N., Filazzola, A. D., & Botvin, E. M. (1984). A cognitive–behavioral approach to substance abuse prevention. *Addictive Behaviors, 9,* 137–147.

Botvin, G., & Eng, A. (1982). The efficacy of a multicomponent approach to the prevention of cigarette smoking. *Preventive Medicine, 11,* 199–211.

Botvin, G., Eng, A., & Williams, C. (1980). Preventing the onset of smoking through life skills training. *Preventive Medicine, 9,* 135–143.

Botvin, G., Renick, N., & Baker, E. (1983, November). *Life skill training and smoking prevention: A one-year followup.* Paper presented at American Public Health Association meetings, Los Angeles.

Bratter, T. E. (1973). Treating alienated, unmotivated, drug-abusing adolescents. *American Journal of Psychotherapy, 27,* 585–598.

Cassady, J. L. (1975, September). *The use of parents and contract therapy in rehabilitating adolescents involved in drug and alcohol abuse.* Paper presented at meeting of the Alcohol and Drug Problems Association of North America, Chicago.

Cohen, S. (1981). *The substance abuse problem.* New York: Haworth.

Controneo, M., & Krasner, B. R. (1976). Addiction, alienation and parenting. *Nursing Clinics of North America, 11,* 517–525.

Cornacchia, H. J., Smith, D. E., & Bentel, D. J. (1978). *Drugs in the classroom: A conceptual model for school programs.* Saint Louis: Mosby.

Evans, R. I. (1976). Smoking in children: Developing a social psychological strategy of deterrence. *Journal of Preventive Medicine, 5,* 122–127.

Flay, B. R., d'Avernas, J. R., Best, J. A., Kersell, M. W., & Ryan, K. B. (1983). Cigarette smoking: Why young people do it and ways of preventing it. In P. J. McGrath & P. Firestone (Eds.), *Pediatric and adolescent behavioral medicine,* (pp. 132–183). New York: Springer.

Forman, S. G., & Neal, J. A. (in press). School-based substance abuse prevention programs. *Special Services in the Schools.*

Forrest, G. G. (1983). *How to cope with a teenage drinker.* New York: Atheneum.

Frederiksen, L. W., Jenkins, J. O., & Carr, C. R. (1976). Indirect modification of adolescent drug abuse using contingency contracting. *Journal of Behavior Therapy and Experimental Psychiatry, 7,* 377–378.

Hawk, D. E. (1985). Substance abuse prevention: Components of program planning. In J. E. Zins, D. I. Wagner, & C. A. Maher (Eds.), *Health promotion in the schools* (pp. 99–112). New York: Haworth.

Hurd, P. D., Johnson, C. A., Pechacek, T., Bast, L. P., Jacobs, D. R., & Luepker, R. V. (1980). Prevention of cigarette smoking in seventh grade students. *Journal of Behavioral Medicine, 3,* 15–28.

Janis, I. L., & Mann, L. (1977). *Decision-making: A psychological analysis of conflict, choice and commitment.* New York: Free Press.

Jessor, R., & Jessor, S. L. (1977). *Problem behavior and psycho-social development: A longitudinal study of youth.* New York: Academic.

Johnston, L. D., Bachman, J. G., & O'Malley, P. M. (1982). *Highlights from student drug use in America, 1975–1981.* Washington, DC: U.S. Department of Health, Education and Welfare.

Mayer, W. (1983). Alcohol abuse and alcoholism: The psychologist's role in prevention, research, and treatment. *American Psychologist, 38,* 1116–1121.

McAlister, A., Perry, C. L., Killen, J., Slinkard, L. A., & Maccoby, N. (1980). Pilot study of smoking, alcohol, and drug abuse prevention. *American Journal of Public Health, 70,* 719–721.

Milgram, G. G. (1983). *What, when and how to talk to children about alcohol and other drugs: A guide for parents.* Center City, MN: Hazelden.

Millman, R. B., & Botvin, G. J. (1983). Substance use, abuse and dependence. In M. D. Levine, W. B. Carey, A. C. Crocker, & R. T. Gross (Eds.), *Developmental behavioral pediatrics* (pp. 683–708). New York: Saunders.

Morehouse, E. R. (1982). The student assistance program: An alcohol and drug abuse prevention model. In E. Aronowitz (Ed.), *Prevention strategies for mental health* (pp. 113–125). New York: PRODIST.

Murray, D. M., Johnson, C. A., Luepker, R. V., Pechacek, T. F., & Jacobs, D. R. (1980). *Issues in smoking prevention research.* Paper presented at the annual conference of the American Psychological Association, Montreal.

National Institute on Drug Abuse. (1981). *Adolescent peer pressure: Theory, correlates, and program implication for drug and abuse prevention* (DHHS Publication No. ADM 81-1152). Washington, DC: U.S. Government Printing Office.

Newton, M. (1981). *Gone way down: Teenage drug use is a disease.* Tampa. American Studies Press.

Ross, S. M. (1974). Behavior group therapy with alcohol abusers. In J. C. Cull & R. E. Hardy (Eds.), *Alcohol abuse and rehabilitation approaches* (pp. 113–136). Springfield, IL: Thomas.

Sheldon, R. B., Davis, H. G., & Kohorn, R. L. (1974). Individual counseling and therapy with the alcohol abuser. In J. G. Cull & R. E. Hardy (Eds.), *Alcohol abuse and rehabilitation approaches* (pp. 137–154). Springfield, IL: Thomas.

Teicher, J. D., Sinay, R. D., & Stumphauzer, J. S. (1976). Training community-based paraprofessionals as behavior therapists with families of alcohol abusing adolescents. *American Journal of Psychiatry, 133,* 847–850.

BIBLIOGRAPHY: PROFESSIONALS

Austin, G. A., & Prendergast, M. L. (1984). *Drug Use and Abuse: A guide to research findings: Vol. 2. Adolescents.* Denver: ABC–Clio Information Services.
A resource guide that provides a comprehensive review of existing literature in the area of adolescent substance use. A variety of substances are included as well as a wide range of research findings, including use, incidence, prevention and treatment.

Cornacchia, H. J., Smith, D. E., & Bentel, D. J. (1978). *Drugs in the classroom: A conceptual model for school programs.* Saint Louis: Mosby.
An excellent resource for professionals working in or with the school system. It provides a detailed model for establishing drug/alcohol prevention and intervention programs within a school. Additionally, this text presents an overview of the substance abuse problem in adolescents.

Glynn, T. J., Leukefeld, C. G., & Ludford, J. P. (1983). *Preventing adolescent drug abuse: Intervention strategies.* Rockville, MD: National Institute of Drug Abuse.
Provides an excellent review of a range of approaches to substance abuse prevention; reviews media, social–psychological, health promotion, coping skills, community, family, values and social skills interventions.

Severson, H. H. (1984). Adolescent social drug use: School prevention program. *School Psychology Review, 13,* 150–161.
Reviews social drug use by adolescents, focusing on alcohol, cigarettes, marijuana, and chewing tobacco. Also provides information on school-based prevention programs and the role of the school psychologist.

Tessler, D. J. (1980). *Drugs, kids and schools: Strategies for educators and other concerned adults.* Santa Monica, CA: Goodyear Publishing Company.
Reviews the types of drugs used by adolescents and why they use them. An unusual section describes the substance use patterns of minorities. Finally, sections are included concerning the impact of family and school on substance use and prevention with discussion exercises to use with adolescents.

BIBLIOGRAPHY: PARENTS

Baron, J. D. (1981). *The parent handbook of drug abuse.* Pasadena, TX: Drug Abuse Program of America.
Provides a detailed discussion on the most commonly used drugs by adolescents, including marijuana, alcohol, depressants, stimulants, and hallucinogens. The physical symptoms of substance use as well as the social–emotional changes are discussed. Included are specific preventive techniques that parents can use to decrease the possibility of adolescent drug use and treatment recommendations.

Cretcher, D. (1982). *Steering clear: Helping your child through the high risk drug years.* Minneapolis: Winston.
Describes the substance abuse problem of adolescents and provides guidelines for parents to prevent substance abuse in their families.

Dupont, R. L. (1985). *Getting tough on gateway drugs. A guide for the family.* Washington, DC: American Psychiatric Press.
Alcohol, marijuana and cocaine are introduced as "gateway" drugs, which open the door for more extensive drug use and behavior problems in adolescents. The author discusses the role that families can have in stopping or preventing drug use. He focuses on setting limits and a tough love approach.

Meyer, R. (1984). *The parent connection: How to communicate with your children about alcohol and other drugs.* New York: Franklin Watts.
Provides detailed information on alcohol and drugs and how parents can determine if their child is abusing these substances. There is a strong emphasis on communication skills and resolving attitudinal differences between parents and their children. The author explores how substance abuse can operate within the family.

Milgram, G. G. (1983). *What, when and how to talk to children about alcohol and other drugs: A guide for parents.* Center City, MN: Hazelden.
Provides information on societal influences on drug and alcohol use as well as family and peer influences. The author emphasizes the use of communication skills, discussion exercises, and values clarification exercises to help parents talk with their children. Finally, suggestions are offered to parents on how to identify alcohol and drug problems in their children and ways to find help for the problem.

BIBLIOGRAPHY: CHILDREN

Butterworth, W. E. (1979). *Under the influence.* New York: Four Winds Press.
A nonfiction account of possible life stressors that influence adolescents to use substances and some of the possible consequences of that choice.

Donlan, J. (1977). *I never saw the sun rise.* Minneapolis: CompCare.
A realistic account of a chemically dependent teenager presented in a diary format. The adolescent provides a detailed description of her entry into the drug world, the drug years, and her eventual recovery.

Due, L. A. (1980). *High and outside.* New York: Harper & Row.
A realistic account of a teenage alcoholic and the problems drinking can lead to at home, at school, and with friendships. The risk of suicide is included as well as discussion of possible treatment options.

Greene, S. M. (1979). *The boy who drank too much.* New York: Viking.
A boy must deal with his drinking problem, his father's drinking, and physical abuse in addition to problems at school and with friends. A rehabilitation program provides a solution.

Wrenn, C. G., & Schwarzrock, S. (1971). *The mind benders.* New York: American Guidance Services.
A true account of drug use is presented by an ex-drug abuser. Included are reasons why adolescents begin using drugs and the consequences (both physical and legal).

Wrenn, C. G., & Schwarzrock, S. (1971). *Facts and fantasies about drugs.* New York: American Guidance Services.
Identifies the major drugs used by adolescents today, why they use them, and their consequences. Consequences are discussed from several perspectives, including physical, personal, and legal ramifications.

Children and Encopresis

Dale T. Simonson
Mississippi Bend Area Education Agency, Bettendorf, Iowa

BACKGROUND

Definition

Encopresis is repeated defecation in clothing, or other inappropriate places, after the age when bowel control is typically achieved. Definitions of encopresis either include both voluntary and involuntary defecation (American Psychiatric Association, 1980; Wright, 1973), or limit the application of the term to involuntary defecation only (Pierce, 1985; Schaefer, 1979). In either case, a diagnosis of encopresis is not appropriate until after the age of 4 years (Levine, 1982; Schaefer, 1979).

Encopretic children may soil themselves once or many times each day or only several times per month (Schaefer, 1979; Schmitt, 1984). The soiling episodes occur most frequently during the late afternoon or early evening and less frequently during the school day (Levine, 1975; Schaefer, 1979). Nocturnal encopresis is relatively rare (Levine, 1982). The consistency of the feces being passed can be formed, semiformed, or liquid (Levine, 1975).

Incidence

Among 7- to 8-year-old children, the incidence of encopresis is 1.5%, encopretic boys outnumbering encopretic girls by a ratio of between 3.5 and 6 to 1 (Levine, 1982; Pierce, 1985; Schaefer, 1979). The incidence of encopresis declines throughout childhood, and by age 16, encopresis is virtually absent. Encopresis occurs at all levels of intelligence (Sluckin, 1981) and within all social brackets (Pierce, 1985).

Subtypes

Children who have never been fully toilet-trained exhibit primary, or continuous, encopresis. In contrast, children who have been completely toilet-trained and have regressed to bowel incontinence suffer from secondary, or discontinuous, encopresis (Levine, 1982). An additional distinction between retentive and nonretentive encopresis may have direct implications for treatment. Children with retentive encopresis withhold feces, often becoming impacted. On the other hand, children with nonretentive encopresis pass normal bowel movements. As many as 80–95% of all cases of encopresis are of the retentive type (Fitzgerald, 1975; Levine, 1975).

Etiology

The etiology of encopresis appears to be multidimensional and involves a complex interaction between a child's personality, familial characteristics and experiences, as well as physiological predisposing factors (Bemporad, Kresch, Asnes, & Wilson, 1978). One multifactorial etiological model (Levine, 1982) identifies possible potentiators of risk for encopresis at consecutive age levels. During the infancy and toddler years, early colonic inertia and simple constipation, congenital anorectal problems, parental overreaction, and coercive medical interventions place a child at risk. During the ages 2–5 years, possible potentiators include coercive or extremely permissive training, idiosyncractic toilet fears, and painful or difficult defecation. During the early school years, avoidance of school restrooms with limited privacy, task impersistence, frenzied lifestyles, and psychosocial stresses are possible contributing factors.

Some authors (Bemporad, Kresch, Asnes, & Wilson, 1978; Bemporad, Pfeifer, Gibbs, Cortner, & Bloom, 1971) have reported a connection between coercive toilet training and encopresis. Others (Hoag, Norriss, Himeno, & Jacobs, 1971; Wolters & Wauters, 1975) have questioned this relationship.

DEVELOPMENT

Normal Bowel Control

Children generally do not reach the levels of physical and psychological maturity to face the complex tasks of sphincter control and toilet training until the age of 15–18 months or later (Brazelton, 1962). The actual conditions necessary for children to cooperate in their own toilet training include the ability to control the sphincter muscles, the ability to postpone the urge to defecate, and the ability to give a signal to be taken to the bathroom or to go there independently (Fraiberg, 1959). An understanding of the social implications of defecation may also be a necessary criterion for determining readiness for toilet training (Schaefer, 1979).

The majority of children achieve bowel control by 3 years of age, although girls tend to be slightly ahead of boys (Largo & Stutzle, 1977; Stein & Susser, 1967). The actual amount of time needed to accomplish bowel control tends to be less the later that training is initiated (Schaefer, 1979).

Psychogenic Megacolon

Since a majority of encopretic children are of the retentive type, a thorough understanding of the development of this condition is crucial. Rather than failing to retain their feces, children with retentive encopresis actually retain their feces too well. What begins as simple constipation and voluntary retention may eventually lead to an abnormal defecation pattern and an impacted and distended bowel (Wright, 1973). As the retention becomes chronic, loss of bowel tone and psychogenic megacolon, a dilation of the rectum and/or colon by retained feces, can develop. In severe cases, sensory feedback from the bowel becomes impaired. As a result, children may not be aware that they have soiled (Levine, 1975). In addition, with increased water absorption from the retained fecal material, harder and harder feces develop. The painful defecation that results can then lead to further avoidance of defecation (Levine, 1982).

The pressure of the impaction can make the sphincter muscles incompetent, resulting in the seepage of new liquid fecal material around the impaction and leakage out into underclothing. This soiling is often called overflow or paradoxical diarrhea (Schmitt, 1984). Children with retentive encopresis may periodically pass large feces, even large enough to block the toilet. A temporary resolution of the symptoms may follow, before the cycle repeats (Johns, 1985).

As a point of clarification, megacolon can also result from actual physical conditions. For example, Hirschsprung disease, an organic disorder causing megacolon, results from an absence of nerve fibers in the walls of the rectum or large intestine (Wright, 1973). In this condition, the colon is unable to respond to the pressure created by normal amounts of fecal material with a defecation reflex. The incidence of psychogenic megacolon is approximately 20 times that resulting from Hirschsprung disease.

PUTTING ENCOPRESIS IN PERSPECTIVE

Encopresis can have a significant negative impact on affected children and their families. Parents may try a variety of methods to alleviate the problem and may experience anger and frustration from their lack of success in teaching their children bowel control. Their repeated failures may evoke feelings of helplessness and guilt as well (Halpern, 1977). They may restrict family activities in order to avoid public embarrassment. Parents may even be reluctant to seek professional treatment owing to their lack of knowledge regarding the frequency of the problem (Levine, 1982).

As for the children themselves, their symptoms may interfere with many aspects of their functioning. They may live in constant fear of discovery and exposure and face ruthless peer ridicule and cruel nicknames (Levine, 1982). They may isolate themselves and display excessive dependency. Their self-esteem may suffer, and depression may result. Their fears of being unable to have appropriate bowel movements may, in fact, increase their anxiety and exacerbate their problems (Bornstein, Sturm, Retzlaff, Kirby, & Chong, 1981).

ALTERNATIVE ACTIONS

The literature regarding the treatment of encopresis has consisted mainly of case study reports, although some studies have used reversal designs or techniques involving multiple baselines across subjects. Successful treatment approaches have ranged from simple reinforcement procedures to comprehensive, multifaceted interventions.

Before beginning any treatment program, a family physician should examine the encopretic child to determine whether any medical problems, including impaction, are present. Consultation with a specialist may be indicated in the most severe, chronic cases.

Positive Reinforcement Techniques

Young and Goldsmith (1972) reported the treatment of an 8-year-old encopretic boy who received a toy car immediately after each appropriate defecation. If soiling occurred, he cleaned himself and his underwear. After 2 weeks the frequency of encopresis had decreased significantly. For the next 2 weeks the boy received a toy car only at the end of each day regardless of the number of appropriate defecations. Later, the boy earned stamps that could be exchanged for preselected gifts.

In another study (Pedrini & Pedrini, 1971), an 11-year-old boy received one book coupon for each of eight daily class periods when no soiling occurred. Each successive book required an increasingly greater number of coupons than the first. By Week 6 of the treatment, no soiling occurred, and in the following school year only one soiling incident occurred despite the absence of specific reinforcers.

Bach and Moylan (1975) used positive reinforcement techniques with a 6-year-old boy with retentive encopresis as well as enuresis. The boy received 25 cents for every bowel movement in the toilet, 10 cents for every urination in the toilet, and 10 cents for every morning his bed was dry. He also received praise immediately after the desired behavior. The parents ignored inappropriate bowel and bladder movements, and the boy changed his clothes as perfunctorily as possible. Although the enuresis was responding satisfactorily after 12 weeks, a marked improvement in the encopretic problem was noted only after adding the component of a verbal prompt, 5 cents, and praise for just attempting to have a bowel movement in the toilet.

In the treatment of a 10-year-old boy using a variable-ratio schedule of reinforcement (Bornstein et al., 1983), the therapist told the boy that they would be playing a game employing two identical cards. On one card the parents recorded daily soiling in one column and appropriate toileting incidents in a second column. On the other card the therapist randomly placed a series of stars. On those days where stars appeared, the boy earned financial rewards. The boy received praise when he had not soiled and when he passed appropriate bowel movements. During the first phase of treatment, stars appeared on a variable-ratio schedule of one star every two days for both the soiling and bowel movements columns. The parents gradually phased out reinforcement.

Lyon (1984) used a decelerating ratio of reinforcement in the treatment of an 8-year-old mildly mentally retarded boy in a school setting. In the first phase of treatment, the boy received a sticker and verbal praise if he had not soiled when checked at morning recess, at lunchtime, at afternoon recess, and at the end of the academic day. He also received one sticker in both the morning and afternoon if he appropriately requested to use the restroom. Three stickers earned 20 minutes of free time with the teacher. When he was continent for seven consecutive days, he earned an ice cream cone. If he soiled, he cleaned himself and his clothing in the faculty washroom and changed into clean clothing. In the second phase, the checks occurred only at lunchtime and at the end of the day, and requests to use the restroom earned verbal reinforcement only. Four stickers were needed to earn free time with the teacher. In the third phase, the checks took place at the end of the day only, and five stickers earned free time. The boy was completely continent by the third phase and remained so at a 5-month follow-up.

In the treatment of a 6-year-old encopretic boy (Plachetta, 1976), the parents ignored the unpleasant aspects of his soiling. The boy washed out soiled clothing, not as punishment but as a step in accepting responsibility. In the morning, at noon, after school, and before bed, the boy attempted to defecate, earning a penny for each 10-minute attempt and a nickel for each success. The parents also praised his efforts. In addition, the boy put a star on a chart each day when no soiling occurred. After 8 weeks, the soiling ceased, with no additional soiling in the next 2 years. Ayllon, Simon, and Wildman (1975) also used a star chart to reinforce a 7-year-old boy for days without soiling. Seven stars earned a special outing.

Aversion Techniques

Edelman (1971) reported the case of a 12-year-old girl who was required to indicate when and under what conditions she soiled and the consequences she received. In the evening she stayed in her room for 30 minutes if she had soiled during the day. Although the mean number of soiling incidents decreased, a further decrease resulted when she could avoid the aversive task of dishwashing if evidence of soiling was lacking when she was checked by her mother in the evening. A 3-month follow-up saw complete suppression of soiling.

Ferinden and Van Handel (1970) used aversive techniques in the treatment of a 7-year-old boy. The boy brought a change of clothing to school and washed himself and his soiled clothing, with strong soap and water below room temperature, when soiling occurred. After school, he made up the time lost from the classroom. During treatment, the school psychologist discussed the social implications of soiling with the boy. No soiling had occurred at a 6-month follow-up.

Overcorrection Procedures

Rolider and Van Houten (1975) wrote that since sitting on the toilet for a long period of time resembles time out, it can function as a negative reinforcer for appropriate defecation. During summer vacation, the mother of a 12-year-old girl checked her underwear 10 times per day on an hourly basis ending at bedtime. In a differential reinforcement of other behavior (DRO) condition alone, the girl received candy or a coupon for clean underwear during the hourly checks. Every five coupons earned a surprise gift. In a subsequent DRO plus overcorrection condition, the girl washed her soiled underwear and five other articles of underwear when soiling occurred. She also approached the bathroom from several points in the house and sat on the toilet for a few seconds. During the negative reinforcement condition, the girl sat on the toilet for 20 minutes, or until she defecated, immediately after waking. If she did not defecate, she sat on the toilet for 40 minutes, or until she defecated, at 1:00 p.m. If she did not defecate, she sat on the toilet for 90 minutes, or until she defecated, at 7:30 p.m. The frequency of soiling was least during the negative reinforcement condition.

Crowley and Armstrong (1977) treated three boys by giving them the primary responsibility for recording the times and places of both soiling incidents and appropriate bowel movements. The parents numbered seven pairs of underwear and handed them out daily in order to confirm accidents. They checked for soiled pants before breakfast, lunch, dinner, and bedtime and after school. When accidents occurred, the children bathed and washed their clothes and other items for a period of time not to exceed one-half hour. Positive practice followed for about one hour. After sitting quietly for 10 minutes, the children went to the bathroom and tried to have a bowel movement for 10 minutes. During one of the rest periods, one parent role-played what the child should have done in the situation in which the accident occurred and requested that the child explain the reasons for not soiling. Through behavior rehearsal, parents learned how to respond verbally to soiling incidents and appropriate bowel movements.

Grimes (1983) reported the successful treatment of a 9-year-old boy by means of a self-regulatory model incorporating a program similar to that used by Crowley and Armstrong (1977). The boy made the primary decisions regarding the contents of a contingency contract that specified the goals of treatment and the reinforcement contingencies. The boy was involved in designing the overcorrection procedures also. Through visual imagery techniques, the boy learned how to recognize the rectal sensations that signal the need to defecate and how to excuse himself from the playground and classroom when he had to use the restroom. Grimes (1983) attributed the success of this program to the child's being more actively involved in the planning of the program.

Doleys, McWhorter, Williams, and Gentry (1977) used periodic pants checks, full cleanliness training (FCT) contingent upon soiling, and positive reinforcement for appropriate toileting behavior in the treatment of three encopretic males. The parents checked their children's pants every hour at the beginning of treatment and less frequently as soiling decreased. As part of the FCT procedure, with each soiling episode the parents expressed their displeasure. The children scrubbed their soiled clothes for 20 minutes and bathed in cool or cold water for 20 minutes. The children received a token or point on a chart in the bathroom for each appropriate defecation. They exchanged a specified number of points or tokens for selected reinforcers, the criterion being increased gradually.

Comprehensive Approaches

Other successful treatment approaches have included reinforcement contingencies as well as direct physical interventions. The success of these programs has been due, in part, to their addressing the irregular defecation patterns of many encopretic children.

Wright (1973, 1975) described a program that combined behavior modification procedures and the use of laxatives. After being convinced that the program would be successful and being told of the importance of compulsory adherence to the program, the parents identified reinforcers that could be given for each appropriate defecation and for entire days without soiling. The parents also specified negative consequences, such as 30 minutes in the bathtub or restricted privileges, that could be used whenever soiling occurred. To insure regular defecation, to avoid impaction, and to permit the colon to regain its normal size and tone, the children tried to defecate upon arising in the morning. If they could not, nonprescription glycerin suppositories were given. If defecation had not occurred by the time breakfast ended, they were given Fleet enemas before leaving for school. After 2 weeks with regular bowel movements and no soiling, the external aids to defecation were discontinued for one day. After another successful week, aids were discontinued for an additional day of the week. Thus, the aids were gradually eliminated totally. Following each soiling episode during the weaning process, aids were added for one day of the week until the children were receiving aids every day or until they again went a week without soiling. Generally, encopresis was alleviated in 15–20 weeks. Wright (1975) stated that in cases of nonretentive encopresis, less emphasis needs to be placed on the use of the laxatives.

Levine (1982) reported an eclectic treatment program that had been used successfully with over 100 children. Following a thorough physical examination and history, an education and demystification process took place. In a positive and nonaccusatory environment, parents and children received extensive information regarding normal bowel functioning and the development and treatment of encopresis. An initial cleansing procedure consisting of four 3-day cycles of Fleet enemas, Dulcolax suppositories and Dulcolax tables followed. In the training phase, the children made 10-minute, twice daily visits to the toilet at the same times each day. To facilitate defecation, light mineral oil served as a stool softener. The program also included the use of kitchen timers, reinforcement charts, oral laxatives, and increased dietary fiber when needed. Children washed themselves, but not their soiled clothing, when soiling episodes occurred. The program continued for long periods of time, at least 6 months. Levine (1982) suggested that in school, encopretic children may need to be allowed to use a private restroom, to go to the toilet whenever they request, to have extra clothing available, and to be excused from gym class or showers in order to avoid public embarrassment.

SUMMARY

Treatment approaches to encopresis form a continuum ranging from simple reinforcement strategies to comprehensive programs involving conditioning and cathartics. The choice of a positive reinforcement technique rather than a more intrusive, aversive technique helps to make corrective bowel training a less stressful task. In addition, successful approaches reinforce appropriate defecation as well as nonsoiling, in order to avoid overemphasis on retention of feces and possible exacerbation of the symptoms.

Treatment of encopresis consists of education and training, the main goals of which are the establishment of regular patterns of elimination and the improvement of children's autonomy in the area of eliminative functioning. Whether treatment takes place at home, at school, or in a coordinated effort, treatment may require weeks, if not months, of compulsory adherence. In the case of retentive encopresis especially, the frequency of soiling itself may decrease dramatically and quickly with treatment, although the increased frequency of appropriate, unaided bowel movements may be more difficult to achieve.

The development of individualized treatment plans presents opportunities for joint efforts among parents, teachers, medical personnel, school psychologists, and the encopretic children themselves. Although many professionals need to overcome initial repulsion by the symptoms of encopresis, sensitive and prompt treatment is imperative. Successful intervention can prevent the development of serious secondary emotional problems and enhance self-esteem and interpersonal relationships.

REFERENCES

American Psychiatric Association. (1980). *Diagnostic and statistical manual of mental disorders* (3rd ed.). Washington, DC: Author.

Ayllon, T., Simon, S. J., & Wildman, R. W. (1975). Instructions and reinforcement in the elimination of encopresis: A case study. *Journal of Behavior Therapy and Experimental Psychiatry, 6,* 235–238.

Bach, R., & Moylan, J. J. (1975). Parents administer behavior therapy for inappropriate urination and encopresis: A case study. *Journal of Behavior Therapy and Experimental Psychiatry, 6,* 239–241.

Bemporad, J. R., Kresch, R. A., Asnes, R., & Wilson, A. (1978). Chronic neurotic encopresis as a paradigm of a multifactorial psychiatric disorder. *Journal of Nervous and Mental Disease, 166,* 472–479.

Bemporad, J. R., Pfeifer, C. M., Gibbs, L., Cortner, R. H., & Bloom, W. (1971). Characteristics of encopretic patients and their families. *Journal of the American Academy of Child Psychiatry, 10,* 272–292.

Bornstein, P. H., Balleweg, B. J., McLellarn, R. W., Wilson, G. L., Sturm, C. A., Andre, J. C., & Van Den Pol, R. A. (1983). The "bathroom game": A systematic program for the elimination of encopretic behavior. *Journal of Behavior Therapy and Experimental Psychiatry, 14,* 67–71.

Bornstein, P. H., Sturm, C. A., Retzlaff, P. D., Kirby, K. L., & Chong, H. (1981). Paradoxical instruction in the treatment of encopresis and chronic constipation: An experimental analysis. *Journal of Behavior Therapy and Experimental Psychiatry, 12,* 167–170.

Brazelton, T. B. (1962). A child-oriented approach to toilet training. *Pediatrics, 29,* 121–128.

Crowley, C. P., & Armstrong, P. M. (1977). Positive practice, overcorrection and behavior rehearsal in the treatment of three cases of encopresis. *Journal of Behavior Therapy and Experimental Psychiatry, 8,* 411–416.

Doleys, D. M., McWhorter, A. Q., Williams, S. C., & Gentry, W. R. (1977). Encopresis: Its treatment and relation to nocturnal enuresis. *Behavior Therapy, 8,* 77–82.

Edelman, R. I. (1971). Operant conditioning treatment of encopresis. *Journal of Behavior Therapy and Experimental Psychiatry, 2,* 71–73.

Ferinden, W., Jr., & Van Handel, D. (1970). Elimination of soiling behavior in an elementary school child through the application of aversive techniques. *Journal of School Psychology, 8,* 267–269.

Fitzgerald, J. F. (1975). Encopresis, soiling, constipation: What's to be done? *Pediatrics, 56,* 348–349.

Fraiberg, S. H. (1959). *The magic years: Understanding and handling the problems of early childhood.* New York: Scribner.

Grimes, L. (1983). Application of the self-regulatory model in dealing with encopresis. *School Psychology Review, 12,* 82–87.

Halpern, W. I. (1977). The treatment of encopretic children. *Journal of the American Academy of Child Psychiatry, 16,* 478–499.

Hoag, J. M., Norriss, N. G., Himeno, E. T., & Jacobs, J. (1971). The encopretic child and his family. *Journal of the American Academy of Child Psychiatry, 10,* 242–256.

Johns, C. (1985). Encopresis. *American Journal of Nursing, 85,* 153–156.

Largo, R. H., & Stutzle, W. (1977). Longitudinal study of bowel and bladder control by day and night in the first six years of life. *Developmental Medicine and Child Neurology, 19,* 598–606.

Levine, M. D. (1975). Children with encopresis: A descriptive analysis. *Pediatrics, 56,* 412–416.

Levine, M. D. (1982). Encopresis: Its potentiation, evaluation, and alleviation. *Pediatric Clinics of North America, 29,* 315–330.

Lyon, M. A. (1984). Positive reinforcement and logical consequences in the treatment of classroom encopresis. *School Psychology Review, 13,* 238–243.

Pedrini, B. C., & Pedrini, D. T. (1971). Reinforcement procedures in the control of encopresis: A case study. *Psychological Reports, 28,* 937–938.

Pierce, C. M. (1985). Encopresis. In J. I. Kaplan & B. J. Sadock (Eds.), *Comprehensive textbook of psychiatry* (4th ed.) (pp. 1847–1849). Baltimore, MD: Williams & Wilkins.

Plachetta, K. E. (1976). Encopresis: A case study utilizing contracting, scheduling and self-charting. *Journal of Behavior Therapy and Experimental Psychiatry, 7,* 195–196.

Rolider, A., & Van Houten, R. (1985). Treatment of constipation-caused encopresis by a negative reinforcement procedure. *Journal of Behavior Therapy and Experimental Psychiatry, 16,* 67–70.

Schaefer, C. E. (1979). *Childhood encopresis and enuresis.* New York: Van Nostrand Reinhold.

Schmitt, B. D. (1984). Encopresis. *Primary Care, 11,* 497–511.

Sluckin, A. (1981). Behavioral social work with encopretic children, their families and the school. *Child: Care, Health and Development, 7,* 67–80.

Stein, Z., & Susser, M. (1967). Social factors in the development of sphincter control. *Developmental Medicine and Child Neurology, 9,* 692–706.

Wolters, W. H., & Wauters, E. A. (1975). A study of somatopsychic vulnerability in encopretic children. *Psychotherapy and Psychosomatics, 26,* 27–34.

Wright, L. (1973). Handling the encopretic child. *Professional Psychology, 4,* 137–144.

Wright, L. (1975). Outcome of a standardized program for treating psychogenic encopresis. *Professional Psychology, 6,* 453–456.

Young, I. L., & Goldsmith, A. O. (1972). Treatment of encopresis in a day treatment program. *Psychotherapy: Theory, Research and Practice, 9,* 231–235.

BIBLIOGRAPHY: PROFESSIONALS

Crowley, C. P., & Armstrong, P. M. (1977). Positive practice, overcorrection and behavior rehearsal in the treatment of three cases of encopresis. *Journal of Behavior Therapy and Experimental Psychiatry, 8,* 411-416.
This article describes a treatment program that incorporates a variety of behavioral techniques, which could be used in total or in part. The treatment take into consideration the multidimensional nature of encopresis.

Grimes, L. (1983). Application of the self-regulatory model in dealing with encopresis. *School Psychology Review, 12,* 82–87.
This self-regulatory model provides a format for assisting the encopretic child to accept more responsibility for treatment. Also included are examples of a visual imagery script and a written contract that can be used along with an overcorrection procedure.

Levine, M. D. (1982). Encopresis: Its potentiation, evaluation, and alleviation. *Pediatric Clinics of North America, 29,* 315–330.
Besides providing details of Levine's eclectic treatment approach, this article provides an excellent overview of the many factors that contribute to the development of encopresis. This article also provides a description of the clinical picture of encopresis and its impact on a child's lifestyle and affect.

Lyon, M. A. (1984). Positive reinforcement and logical consequences in the treatment of classroom encopresis. *School Psychology Review, 13,* 238–243.
This article provides an example of the type of reinforcement program that can be used in the school. A decelerating rate of reinforcement procedure shows the practitioner how to accomplish the sometimes difficult task of fading out reinforcers.

Schaefer, C. E. (1979). *Childhood encopresis and enuresis.* New York: Van Nostrand Reinhold.
This book is the best individual resource available to the professional. The chapters provide thorough coverage of the definition, diagnosis, etiology, and treatment of encopresis. The information provided regarding normal bowel physiology and toilet training practices provides excellent background information.

Children and Enuresis

Arthur C. Houts
Memphis State University

BACKGROUND

Researchers and health care professionals refer to any accidental or uncontrolled wetting as *enuresis.* In general, enuresis is diagnosed when a child wets without control after age 3½ years, the approximate age that most children achieve bladder control. Most children achieve daytime control by age 3, and nighttime control follows shortly thereafter. Failure to learn daytime control is called *diurnal* enuresis; failure to learn nighttime control is called *nocturnal* enuresis or bedwetting. Diurnal enuresis can occur with or without bedwetting. The child who has daytime wetting problems, regardless of the presence or absence of nighttime wetting, should be given a thorough medical evaluation because the incidence of significant medical problems among these children is considerably higher than among children who show only nighttime wetting (Arnold & Ginsberg, 1973).

A further important distinction in classification is based on whether the child has ever had an extended period of dryness. *Primary nocturnal enuresis* is the term used to describe cases of simple bedwetting in which a child has never had at least a 2-month period of consecutive dry nights. Primary nocturnal enuresis accounts for about 80% of all bedwetting. *Secondary nocturnal enuresis* is the diagnosis given to cases in which children resumed wetting after being dry for 2 months or more. Secondary nocturnal enuresis often results from more complex or serious medical or emotional problems. About 20% of children identified as bedwetters are secondary enuretics. The average age of onset for secondary enuresis is usually between 5 and 8 years.

All children with enuresis should receive a routine pediatric physical examination that includes a urinalysis, but children with diurnal or secondary enuresis require more extensive medical assessment to rule out organic causes of the enuresis. Because the vast majority of children with voiding problems fall into the category of primary nocturnal enuresis or simple bedwetting, this chapter concentrates on the development and treatment of that problem. When the school psychologist is consulted about a child with voiding problems and the symptoms include daytime wetting or the history indicates secondary enuresis, the child should be referred for medical assessment and treatment.

The diagnosis of primary nocturnal enuresis does not depend on a particular frequency of bedwetting. One child may wet his bed twice a month for years, and another may wet the bed twice a week. Low frequencies, though, are rare. The majority of primary nocturnal enuretics wet the bed five to seven nights per week, and many wet more than once a night. Secondary enuretics show a more sporadic pattern of wetting and generally a lower frequency. From the standpoint of psychosocial adjustment, even occasional bedwetting beyond the age of five is likely to be a problem for children and parents, leading to embarrassment and frustration.

DEVELOPMENT

Bedwetting and Age

Figure 1 shows the percentage of children who were reported to have wet the bed at least once per month from ages 4–12 years. It is based on the averages of nine studies conducted in the United States, Western Europe, Australia,and Israel. A majority of these children were found to wet the bed every night of the week. Good estimates of the incidence of bedwetting among adolescents and adults are simply not available, probably because the problem is kept more of a secret with older children. But several studies of military recruits show that some 1–3% of 18-year-olds still wet the bed.

Gender Differences, Family History, and Motivational Factors

Overall, 66–75% of children who wet the bed are boys. The sex difference is greater at the younger ages. From age 11, the ratio of boys to girls is about equal.

Bedwetting tends to run in families and may be partly hereditary. But family history is only part of the story. Many children whose mother, father, or older brother wet the bed do not become bedwetters. Many other children with no such family history do become bedwetters. There is no consistent evidence regarding the relationship between enuresis and toilet training. Some very young children who have diurnal enuresis alone may have simply failed to be toilet trained. However, most children who have nocturnal enuresis have been successfully toilet trained and do not have problems of control during the day.

The most important thing for parents and professionals to understand is that bedwetting does not mean that a child is lazy or lacks willpower. Parents need to be told that their child is just not able to control his or her bladder functioning during sleep. Bedwetting is not the child's fault. Therefore, it is especially important to caution parents against using punishment to deal with bedwetting.

Do Bedwetters Outgrow Bedwetting?

This question is often asked by parents, and the answer is important in helping them make a decision about what to do. Figure 1 suggests that the older a bedwetting child is, the less likely it is that he or she will continue wetting the bed. Of children who wet the bed at age 4, as many as three out of four will probably have outgrown their bedwetting by age 12. However, up to 8 years can be a long time to wait!

An important study by Forsythe and Redmond (1974) provides a good answer to the question, how soon will a child just outgrow bedwetting? These investigators identified almost 1,200 bedwetters between the ages of 5 and 19 and followed them up over 15 years to see how long it took for children to become dry on their own. Children who received treatment during the follow-up period were excluded from the analysis. For children between the ages of 5 and 9, the average yearly rate of spontaneous "cure" was 14%. For the age groups 10–14 and 15–19, the average annual spontaneous remission rate was 16%. This means that 1 of every 7 or 8 children who wets the bed will be dry a year later if nothing is done and that on the average it will take more than 3 years for bedwetting to stop spontaneously. Also of interest is the implication that annual rates of spontaneous remission do not appear to increase with age. Older children who wet the bed do not have a much better chance of just outgrowing it in the next 12 months than do younger children.

The decision simply to wait for a child to stop wetting should be weighed against the costs and risks. Some families will manage the inconveniences of bedwetting and associated family tensions better than others. Children, however, rarely avoid the experience of being embarrassed and restricted in their social relationships. These negative effects for the child become even more important as the child gets older. The strategy of waiting for a child to outgrow the problem is not usually productive, and effective treatments for bedwetting are now available. Therefore, it is not advisable for parents of school-age children to just wait for the problem to go away.

PUTTING ENURESIS IN PERSPECTIVE

This question Why does my child wet the bed? is usually the first one that parents ask. Today, we know there is no simple answer. For any particular child bedwetting may be caused by several factors.

Physical Factors

The two physical health factors that can cause bedwetting are: (a) infection and chronic disease and (b) physical defects, specifically in the bladder and kidneys.

Urinary tract infections are found in about 5% of boys and 10% of girls who wet the bed (Stansfeld, 1973). Urinary tract infections usually produce painful symptoms such as burning sensations upon urination that signal parents to get appropriate medical examination and treatment. However, since a child can have a urinary tract infection without obvious symptoms, a basic medical exam is very important. The basic screening test for urinary tract infection is a urinalysis, typically performed in a pediatrician's office. If the urinalysis suggests that there may be infection, it can be followed by a culture and sensitivity test. This procedure is used to determine what type of bacteria are present (culture) and what medications can be used to cure the infection (sensitivity). Most urinary tract infections are effectively treated with antibiotics (Margileth, Pedreira, Hirschman, & Coleman, 1976).

Some children with urinary tract infections will stop bedwetting when their infections are cured; for others, the bedwetting may persist. In general, roughly 40% of the bedwetting children successfully treated for urinary tract infection stop wetting the bed when the infection is cleared (Schmitt, 1982). Thus, for the majority of these children, the bedwetting will still have to be dealt with after the infection has been medically treated.

Diseases other than urinary tract infection can lead to poor bladder control that results in both daytime and nighttime wetting. These include disorders of the kidneys such as nephritis and disorders of the endocrine glands such as diabetes. Such diseases cause incomplete processing of urine, resulting in large amounts of fluid that the body must process.

At one time physical defects were thought to be a major cause of simple bedwetting, and therefore internal examinations were common. Because the diagnostic yield from such exams has been consistently low (2%–5%), many medical researchers have concluded

FIGURE 1

The percentage of children in the general population who wet the bed from age 4 to age 12. Based on data collected in the United States, Western Europe, Australia, and Israel.

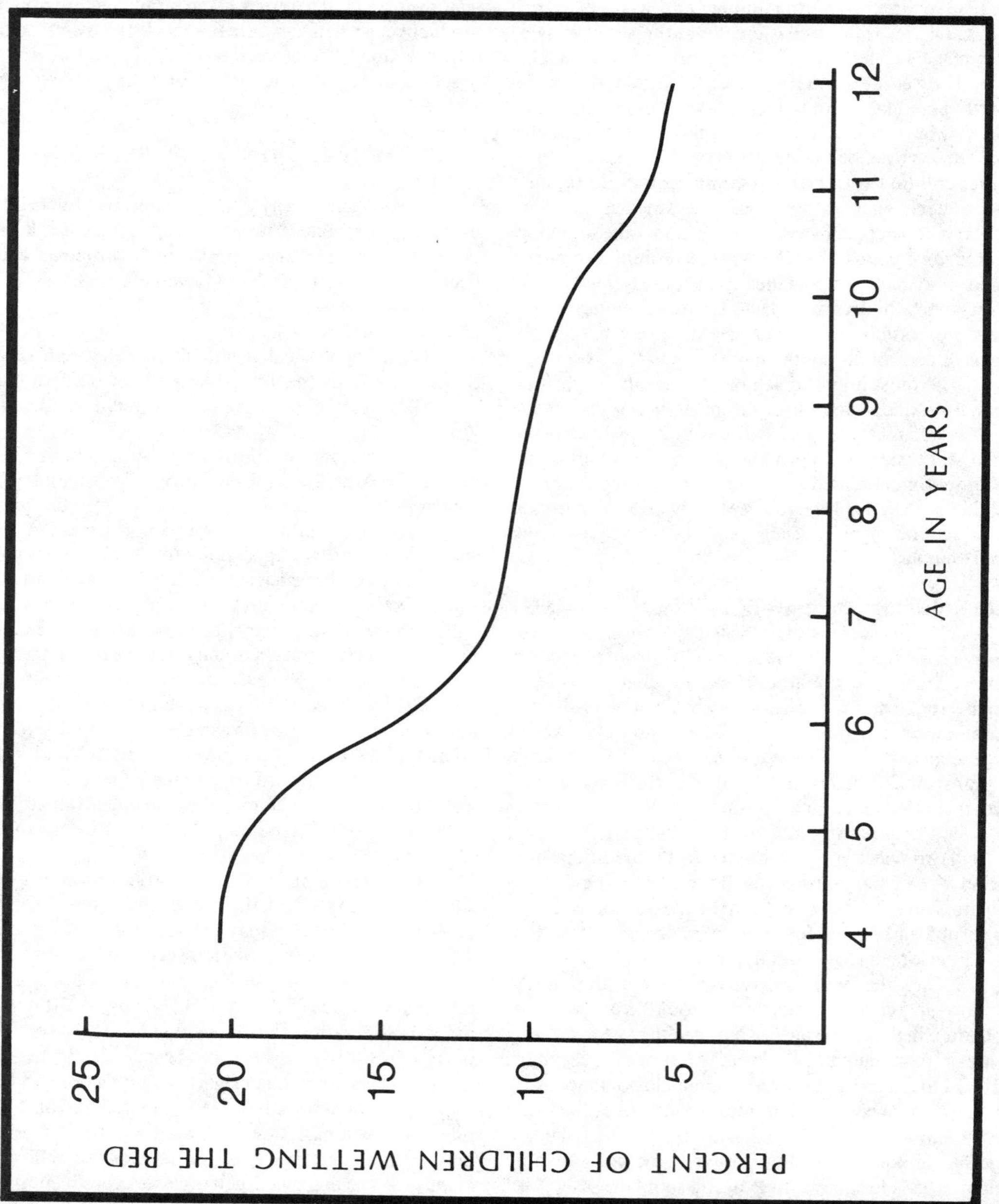

Note: From *Bedwetting: A guide for Parents and Children* by A. C. Houts and R. M. Liebert, 1984, Springfield, IL: Thomas.

that the routine use of these costly examinations for simple bedwetting should be stopped. In the absence of significant warning signs such as a history of disease, daytime wetting, or any current signs of infection, medical authorities now agree that bedwetting alone does not warrant the routine use of these invasive internal examinations (American Academy of Pediatrics: Committee on Radiology, 1980; Shaffer, 1977). Nonetheless, some instances of bedwetting are the result of physical defects, and when there is reason to suspect such a defect, complete urological examinations need to be conducted.

Emotional Factors

The notion that bedwetting is caused by emotional problems was proposed by Freud. It is a popular idea with parents and with many psychologists and psychiatrists. Some 36% of parents surveyed in a study of 1,379 parents attending pediatric clinics said that they thought bedwetting was caused by emotional problems. Among parents of bedwetting children, emotional problems were ranked second only to deep sleep as the believed cause of bedwetting. Parents of nonbedwetting children ranked emotional problems as the leading cause of bedwetting (Haque et al., 1981). Clearly, many people believe this theory.

One result of accepting the emotional problems theory is the further conviction that elimination of bedwetting without other emotional relief will result in "symptom substitution." Some evidence does show that a small percentage of children who wet the bed also have clear emotional problems. These children are more likely to be girls than boys. Also, serious emotional problems are more common in secondary enuretics and children who are both day and night wetters. Even in this minority, though, it is not clear whether emotional problems are the cause or the result of bedwetting (Shaffer, 1977).

The results of a study done at Yale some years ago suggest that bedwetting is more likely to be a cause of emotional problems rather than a result of them. The study found that the children who stopped wetting the bed showed little evidence of new problems (Baker, 1969). Bedwetting is most often *not* a symptom of some deep-seated and hidden psychological problem.

Deep Sleep and Sleep Disturbance

It is very common for parents and professionals to say that children wet the bed because they are "deep sleepers." This idea is especially appealing because most of the children who wet the bed are capable of controlling their bladders during waking hours, and many of them sleep through the night, never being aroused by the uncomfortable sensations of a wet bed. However, research indicates that bedwetters are *not* more difficult to arouse (Boyd, 1960). Perhaps parents of bedwetters just don't know how difficult it can be to wake up a typical child during the night. At some point they try to wake a bedwetting child in the hope that this will prevent bedwetting, and find it difficult. However, they have little occasion to wake a brother or sister who does not wet the bed, but who would probably be just as difficult to awaken (Graham, 1973). This lack of systematic comparison plus the common sense appeal of the deep sleep theory may account for the popularity of this belief. Interestingly, the belief that enuresis is associated with or even caused by depth of sleep persists despite the fact that researchers have long since abandoned this notion, as the data failed to support it. In addition, physiological studies of the sleep cycle are equivocal, indicating that bedwetting does not reliably occur in any one of the stages of sleep (Mikkelsen et al., 1980). On the whole, depth of sleep does not appear to be a plausible cause of bedwetting.

Learning

For most simple bedwetting physical health, emotional problems, and similar disturbances do not answer the question about etiology. There is another, different type of answer to this question, and it is the one that psychologists who treat bedwetting generally accept: Simple bedwetting often occurs because the child has failed to learn to attend and respond to his or her need to urinate while asleep.

For most children this learning occurs without special training, but many others must be trained to keep dry at night by learning to attend to their own bodily needs. This explanation of simple bedwetting leads to a very different type of treatment than "deep psychological" or other explanations.

ALTERNATIVE ACTIONS

Treatments for bedwetting can be broadly classified as either drug treatment or psychological treatment. The following discussion of treatments is confined to drug therapy and behavior therapy. The emphasis on behavior therapy is based on treatment outcome literature that shows that other psychological treatments such as psychoanalysis, hypnosis, family systems therapy, and supportive counseling have either not been adequately evaluated or they have been evaluated and found ineffective (Houts & Liebert, 1984).

Drug Treatment

The use of drugs and compounds to treat simple bedwetting has a long history of failure. For example, in 1550 B.C. Egyptian doctors prescribed compounds made from juniper berries, cyprus, and beer. A thousand years later Thomas Phaer, "The Father of English Pediatrics," recommended a powder made from the dried trachea of a rooster (Glicklich, 1951).

Today, if a prescription is given for simple bedwetting, the medication is likely to be Tofranil®, which is a brandname for *imipramine hydrochloride.* A typical dose of Tofranil is 25–75 mg, depending on the child's weight, and the medication is usually given during the hour before bedtime. Tofranil was used in larger doses to treat depression in adults long before it was introduced as a drug treatment for bedwetting in children. The use of Tofranil to treat bedwetting was an accidental discovery based on the observation that adult incontinent psychiatric patients treated for depression often became dry as a side effect of the medication (MacLean, 1960).

An important distinction must be made between a treatment's ability to stop bedwetting (initial arrest) and its ability to prevent bedwetting permanently (lasting cure). For example, research shows that about 50% of children treated with Tofranil will become dry during treatment. However, of these children who have an initial arrest of bedwetting, almost all will be regularly wetting their bed again a year later. Thus, the lasting cure rate of Tofranil for bedwetting is 5–15% (Blackwell & Currah, 1973). This lasting cure rate is about equal to the average annual spontaneous remission rate. What Tofranil in fact does, then, is temporarily reduce bedwetting in many children, but permanently eliminate it in very few.

An additional problem with Tofranil is that it produces many effects. Among its physical effects are increased heart rate (sometimes accompanied by irregular heartbeat), muscle tremor, profuse sweating, increased blood pressure, loss of appetite, and retention of urine. In general, these broad effects are thought to be due to the stimulant action of the drug on the central nervous system. If Tofranil is used, it must be given carefully. The drug is supplied in small tablets that are easy for a child to swallow in large quantities. In addition, children and parents, impressed by an immediate reduction in wetting, may think that more of the drug will result in a cure. Such magical thinking is dangerous. Several cases of Tofranil poisoning have been reported (Herson, Schmitt, & Rumack, 1979; Parkin & Fraser, 1972).

Some physicians have been experimenting with another drug, Ditropan® to treat simple bedwetting (Buttarazzi, 1977). This drug has been shown to reduce spasms of the bladder and to increase bladder capacity (Thompson & Lauvetz, 1976). It is thought to act directly on the bladder muscle and does not have the negative side effects and dangers of Tofranil. However, the effectiveness of Ditropan for bedwetting has not been established, since there are currently no controlled clinical trials reported in the literature.

Behavioral Treatment

Behavior therapy involves the elimination of bedwetting by direct methods of training. The training itself is carried out at home by parents and child. Preparing and motivating a parent and child to carry out behavioral training procedures is a major component of behavior therapy approaches. The effectiveness of the training depends on the willingness and ability of parents and children to follow the procedures through correctly to a conclusion.

Four types of behavior therapy have been used to treat bedwetting: (a) bell and pad training, (b) retention control training, (c) dry-bed training, and (d) full spectrum home training. All four have received rather extensive evaluation, and it is possible to draw conclusions about their overall effectiveness as well as their practical feasibility. Moreover, comparison of the lasting cure rates of drug and behavior therapy treatments reveals clearly that for simple bedwetting behavior therapy is superior (Houts & Liebert, 1984).

Bell and Pad Training. This is the oldest form of behavior therapy and was developed by Mowrer and Mowrer (1938). The treatment relies on a urine alarm device that consists of a pad and a battery-operated alarm. Such devices are commercially available from Sears and other suppliers (see Parents' Bibliography). When the child wets the bed, the alarm sounds, and a caregiver must wake the child. Since it was first developed almost 50 years ago, bell and pad training has been extensively used and researched. Several hundred controlled scientific investigations have been conducted. For simple bedwetting bell and pad training is very effective. About 75% of children treated with the bell and pad for an 8- to 14-week period achieve an initial arrest of bedwetting, but by 1 year follow-up approximately one third experience a relapse (Doleys, 1977). The most common cause of failure to achieve an initial arrest with this treatment is not following the procedures completely and correctly. The procedures are demanding on the family, and single parents who have psychological problems of their own as well as couples with marital problems have been less successful than families without such problems (Dische, Yule, Corbett, & Hand, 1983).

The most common specific cause of failure is that parents do not wake the child every time the alarm sounds (Lovibond, 1964). If the child is permitted to sleep through the alarm, as many children have a tendency to do at first, the child never develops the sensitivity to wake up to the alarm by himself. A second common cause of failure is that parents permit the child to get up, turn off the alarm, and return to bed without becoming fully awake or going to the bathroom. A third cause of failure is not continuing long enough. About 10 weeks is typically required, and for some children as many as 16 weeks may be needed. Families may abandon the training prematurely. Several studies show that parents who are intolerant of a child's bedwetting and find it difficult to carry out detailed instructions tend to drop out of this training before its beneficial effects are realized (James & Foreman, 1973; Morgan & Young, 1975).

If children become dry as a result of bell and pad training and then experience a relapse, they usually do so within the first 6 months after the training is completed. Fortunately, most children who relapse after bell and pad training can be successfully retrained with a 2- to 4-week reapplication of the bell and pad regimen (Doleys, 1977). It is still unclear why some children relapse and others remain dry. Family problems have been associated with relapse (Dische et al., 1985), and in our own research we have found that children who were previously treated with Tofranil had a stronger tendency to relapse than children who had not previously received drug therapy (Houts, Peterson, & Liebert, 1984).

Researchers have devised a powerful method for preventing relapse from the outset. *Overlearning,* as the method is called, requires the child to drink a large quantity of fluid during the hour before bedtime. Overlearning is usually started after the child has been dry for two consecutive weeks. It is continued with the bell and pad in place until the child is dry for another two consecutive weeks. The overlearning procedure has been shown to cut the chance of relapse in half (Young & Morgan, 1972). With the addition of overlearning, the lasting cure rate of bell and pad training for simple bedwetting is more than 60%.

Retention Control Training. Studies show that bedwetting children have smaller bladder capacities than nonbedwetting children (Starfield, 1967; Zaleski, Gerrard, & Shokier, 1973). The goal of retention control training is to increase the child's bladder capacity, defined as how much urine the child produces after holding for as long as he can. The training itself is rather simple. Once a day the parent and child do prescribed exercises for a 2– to 3–hour period. The child drinks a large quantity of fluid (16–32 ounces) and then practices holding for as long as possible after he feels the need to urinate. The child is usually given rewards for holding for longer and longer periods of time, up to 45 minutes. After each training session, the child urinates into a measuring cup, and the parent records the amount of urine the child has produced.

Retention control training produces a lasting cure in less than 30% of children with simple bedwetting (Houts & Liebert, 1984). As a single treatment for bedwetting, this approach is not as effective as bell and pad training, though there is some evidence that it may be a useful adjunct to standard bell and pad training, especially when attempting to treat children with concomitant, nonorganic daytime wetting (Fielding, 1980).

Dry-Bed Training. Dry-bed training is a behavior therapy program developed by Azrin and his colleagues (Azrin, Sneed, & Fox, 1974). The program has been described in detail in a self-help book (Azrin & Besalel, 1979). Dry-bed training consists of four procedures. The nightly waking schedule requires that children in treatment be awakened every hour during the first night of training. At each waking, they are taken to the bathroom and asked to urinate; they are then encouraged to withhold urinating for the next hour. They are given fluids to drink throughout the night. On the second night they are awakened 3 hours after going to bed. If they are dry, then the next night they are awakened 2½ hours after going to bed. The waking time is moved ahead by half an hour each night following a dry bed and is stopped when waking is scheduled 1 hour after bedtime. If the children wet twice in 1 week, the cycle of the nightly waking schedule starts over, with waking scheduled 3 hours after bedtime.

In the second procedure, called positive practice, the children under treatment must lie down in bed and count to 50, then get up and go to the bathroom and try to urinate. As with other behavior therapy procedures, they are praised for success. The process of lying down, counting, and going to the bathroom is repeated 20 times. The 20 trials of positive practice are also done in the middle of the night immediately after the bed is wet and also before bedtime the next night after accidents have occurred.

The third procedure of dry-bed training is the bell and pad, used as described earlier. The bell and pad is put on the children's beds after the first night of hourly waking. If the bell and pad signals that the children have an accident in the night, they are awakened and reprimanded for wetting the bed. They are then required to do the fourth procedure, which is called cleanliness training. This is done immediately after bedwetting; the children are required to change wet clothes and bed linens. They place all wet linens in the laundry and remake the bed with clean sheets. After 20 trials of positive practice are completed, the bell and pad is reactivated and the children go back to sleep.

In their original report on dry-bed training, Azrin and his colleagues recommend the use of the bell and pad until children have achieved seven dry nights in a row. After that goal was reached, the bell and pad was taken off the bed and not put back on unless wetting occurred two nights in any subsequent week. Also, in their original report the dry-bed training procedures were started by a professional trainer who visited the home and carried out the first night of training, which involved waking every hour (Azrin, Sneed, & Foxx, 1974). Parents administered the training every night after that. In their later uses of dry-bed training, Azrin and his associates eliminated the bell and pad from dry-bed training (Azrin & Thienes, 1978) and taught parents to administer the treatment completely on their own without a professional trainer (Azrin, Thienes-Hontos, & Besalel-Azrin, 1979).

These changes — the elimination of the bell and pad and the elimination of the trainer — are very important in understanding the effectiveness of dry-bed training where research has produced two important conclusions. First, the inclusion of bell and pad training in this treatment package should not be considered optional. The overall effectiveness of dry-bed training is reduced substantially if bell and pad training is left out. Second, there does not appear to be any appreciable gain in treatment effectiveness when a professional trainer conducts the first night of treatment than when parents do it (Houts & Liebert, 1984).

Relapse after dry-bed training (39%) is virtually identical to that following simple bell and pad training (41%) (Bollard, 1982). In addition, dry-bed training is more difficult to carry out than simple bell and pad training. The requirements of the nightly waking schedule and the demands of positive practice are rather severe.

Full-Spectrum Home Training. This is the name Houts and Liebert (1984) gave their home-implemented behavior therapy program for simple bedwetting. The program was designed to provide parents and children with an inexpensive, easy-to-use, and effective combination package treatment for simple bedwetting. Their goal was to develop the strongest possible combination of behavioral procedures, and they created a full set of support materials for the package that would facilitate its home use. The treatment program is described in detail in a self-help book for parents and teachers (Houts & Liebert, 1984).

Full-spectrum home training includes bell and pad training, cleanliness training, retention control training and overlearning, as well as several additional features designed to enhance its effectiveness and simplify its use. In the initial evaluation of this treatment package, the training was done in a single session, in groups, to minimize the financial cost to families. Parents and children filled out an explicit behavioral contract together as a trainer modeled each of the procedures point by point. A manual containing explanations and support materials was provided to parents, and a wall chart ("Daily Steps to a Dry Bed") was given to the child. The first outcome evaluation of the program included 60 families, and 81% of the children achieved an initial arrest of bedwetting defined as 14 consecutive dry nights. Most did so within an 8-week training period. Of those families who failed to reach the goal of a dry bed, 4 of 5 had prematurely terminated their child's training. At 1-year follow-up, 24% of the children had relapsed, a rate that is approximately half that reported by studies using the bell and pad method alone. A permanent solution to the bedwetting problems was obtained for 61% of the children who participated (Houts, Liebert, & Padawer, 1983).

Subsequent research on full-spectrum home training has determined that the inclusion of the overlearning component in this treatment package is the crucial ingredient for reducing the rate of relapse found with bell and pad treatment (Houts, Peterson, & Whelan, in press). Also, the positive results of the initial outcome evaluation have been replicated in a subsequent clinical trial (Houts & Whelan, 1985).

SUMMARY

When a school psychologist is consulted about a child who has enuresis, it is important to do a careful assessment to determine the type of enuresis. Children who have daytime wetting and those whose nighttime wetting has resumed after a period of 2 months or more of consecutive dry nights may require rather extensive medical examination and treatment. All children, even those who are simple bedwetters without apparent complications, should first be referred to their pediatrician for a physical examination and urinalysis. If the problem is simple bedwetting, or primary nocturnal enuresis without medical complications, the school psychologist can assist the parents in helping their child to overcome the problem through home-implemented behavioral treatment.

Full-spectrum home training is the treatment of choice in most cases. If the family is an intact one and the parents are generally supportive and understanding of the child, this program can be carried out by having the parents follow the detailed instructions provided in the self-help book of Houts & Liebert (1984). For such families, weekly consultation may not be necessary, though the professional should provide some support and follow-up even if only by telephone. For other families, weekly consultation with the school psychologist will be necessary to keep the family motivated and to insure that the procedures are followed carefully. Most cases of simple bedwetting can be successfully treated by these methods.

While medication treatment is not generally a permanent solution to enuresis, it may be the best alternative for some children, especially those for whom the enuresis has become a major barrier to social development and self-esteem and whose families are unable to implement a program of behavior therapy. In such cases, Tofranil or Ditropan may provide the child with some temporary control over the problem and enable the child to participate in activities that require sleeping over, such as camping trips or summer camp. Because prolonged, uncontrolled wetting can result in damage to self-esteem, it is important to seek a permanent solution to the problem. Thus, a course of family therapy to prepare the family for conducting behavioral treatment is desirable.

In dealing with a child who wets, there is no substitute for a caring and concerned family, particularly one that understands that children rarely choose to be enuretic. In the United States there are some 5–7 million school-aged children who exhibit enuresis, and given the availability of effective psychological treatments for simple bedwetting, it is possible that school psychologists can become major providers of service to deal with this age-old problem of childhood.

REFERENCES

American Academy of Pediatrics: Committee on Radiology (1980). Excretory urography for evaluation of enuresis. *Pediatrics, 65,* 644–645.

Arnold, S. J., & Ginsberg, A. (1973). Enuresis, incidence and pertinence of genitourinary disease in healthy enuretic children. *Urology, 2,* 437–443.

Azrin, N. H., & Besalel, V. A. (1979). *A parent's guide to bedwetting control.* New York: Simon and Schuster.

Azrin, N. H., Sneed, T. J., & Foxx, R. M. (1974). Dry-bed training: Rapid elimination of childhood enuresis. *Behavior Research and Therapy, 12,* 147–156.

Azrin, N. H., & Thienes, P. M. (1978). Rapid elimination of enuresis by intensive learning without a conditioning apparatus. *Behavior Therapy, 9,* 342–354.

Azrin, N. H., Thienes-Hontos, P., & Besalel-Azrin, V. (1979). Elimination of enuresis without a conditioning apparatus: An extension by office instruction of the child and parents. *Behavior Therapy, 10,* 14–19.

Baker, B. L. (1969). Symptom treatment and symptom substitution in enuresis. *Journal of Abnormal Psychology, 74,* 42–49.

Blackwell, B., & Currah, J. (1973). The psychopharmacology of nocturnal enuresis. In I. Kolvin, R. C. MacKeith, & S. R. Meadow (Eds.), *Bladder control and enuresis* (pp. 231–257). London: William Heinemann.

Bollard, J. (1982). A 2-year follow-up of bedwetters treated with dry-bed training and standard conditioning. *Behavior Research & Therapy, 20.* 571–580.

Boyd, M. M. (1960). The depth of sleep in enuretic school children and in non-enuretic controls. *Journal of Psychosomatic Research, 4,* 274–281.

Buttarazzi, P. J. (1977). Oxybutynin chloride (Ditropan) in enuresis. *Journal of Urology, 118,* 46.

Dische, S., Yule, W., Corbett, J., & Hand, D. 91983). Childhood nocturnal enuresis: Factors associated with outcome of treatment with an enuresis alarm. *Development Medicine and Child Neurology, 25,* 67–80.

Doleys, D. M. (1977). Behavioral treatments for nocturnal enuresis in children: A review of the recent literature. *Psychological Bulletin, 84,* 30–54.

Fielding, D. (1980). The response of day and night wetting children and children who wet only at night to retention control training and the enuresis alarm. *Behaviour Research & Therapy, 138,* 305–317.

Forsythe, W. I., & Redmond, A. (1974). Enuresis and spontaneous cure rate: Study of 1129 enuretics. *Archives of Disease in Childhood, 49,* 259–263.

Glicklich, L. B. (1951). An historical account of enuresis. *Pediatrics, 8,* 859–876.

Graham, P. (1973). Depth of sleep and enuresis: A critical review. In I. Kolvin, R. C. MacKeith, & S. R. Meadow (Eds.), *Bladder control and enuresis* (pp. 78–83). London: William Heinemann.

Haque, M., Ellerstein, N. S., Gundy, J. H., Shelov, S. P., Weiss, J. C., McIntire, M. S., Olness, K. N., Jones, D. J., Heagarty, M. C., & Starfield, B. H. (1981). Parental perceptions of enuresis: A collaborative study. *American Journal of Diseases of Childhood, 135,* 809–811.

Herson, V. C., Schmitt, B. D., & Rumack, B. H. (1979). Magical thinking and imipramine poisoning in two school-aged children. *Journal of American Medical Association, 241,* 1926–1927.

Houts, A. C., & Liebert, R. M. (1984). *Bedwetting: A guide for parents and children.* Springfield, IL: Thomas.

Houts, A. C., Liebert, R. M., & Padawer, W. (1983). A delivery system for the treatment of primary enuresis. *Journal of Abnormal Child Psychology, 11,* 513–519.

Houts, A. C., Peterson, J. K., & Liebert, R. M. (1984). Effect of prior imipramine treatment on the results of conditioning therapy in children with enuresis. *Journal of Pediatric Psychology, 9,* 505–509.

Houts, A. C., Peterson, J. K., & Whelan, J. P. (in press). Prevention of relapse in home-implemented treatment for primary enuresis: A components analysis. *Behavior Therapy.*

Houts, A. C., & Whelan, J. P. (1985, November). *Filmed vs. live delivery of Full Spectrum Home Training for primary enuresis.* Paper presented at the 19th Annual Convention of the Association for the Advancement of Behavior Therapy, Houston.

James, L. E., & Foreman, M. E. (1973). A-B status of behavior therapy technicians as related to success of Mowrer's conditioning treatment for enuresis. *Journal of Consulting and Clinical Psychology, 41,* 224–229.

Kimmel, H. D., & Kimmel, E. (1970). An instrumental conditioning method for the treatment of enuresis. *Journal of Behavior Therapy and Experimental Psychiatry, 1,* 121–123.

Lovibond, S. H. (1964). *Conditioning and enuresis.* Oxford: Pergamon.

MacLean, R. E. G. (1960). Imipramine hydrochloride (Tofranil) and enuresis. *American Journal of Psychiatry, 117,* 551.

Margileth, A. M., Pedreira, F. A., Hirschman, G. H., & Coleman, T. H. (1976). Urinary tract bacterial infections: Office diagnosis and management. *Pediatric Clinics of North America, 23,* 721–734.

Mikkelsen, E. J., Rapoport, J. L., Nee, L., Gruneau, C., Mendelson, W., & Gillin, J. C. (1980). Childhood enuresis. I: Sleep patterns and psychopathology. *Archives of General Psychiatry, 37,* 1139–1144.

Morgan, R. T. T., & Young, G. C. (1975). Parental attitudes and the conditioning treatment of childhood enuresis. *Behavior Research & Therapy, 13,* 197–199.

Mowrer, O. H., & Mowrer, W. M. (1938). Enuresis — a method for its study and treatment. *American Journal of Orthopsychiatry, 8,* 436–459.

Parkin, J. M., & Fraser, M. S. (1972). Poisoning as a complication of enuresis. *Developmental Medicine and Child Neurology, 44,* 727–730.

Schmitt, B. D. (1982). Nocturnal enuresis: An update on treatment. *Pediatric Clinics of North America, 29,* 21–37.

Shaffer, D. (1977). Enuresis. In M. Rutter, & L. Hersov (Eds.), *Child psychiatry: Modern approaches.* Oxford: Blackwell.

Stansfeld, J. M. (1973). Enuresis and urinary tract infection. In I. Kolvin, R. C. MacKeith, & S. R. Meadow (Eds.), *Bladder control and enuresis* (pp. 102–103). London: William Heinemann.

Starfield, B. (1967). Functional bladder capacity in enuretic and nonenuretic children. *Journal of Pediatrics, 70,* 777–781.

Thompson, I. M., & Lauvetz, R. (1976). Oxybutinin in bladder spasm, neurogenic bladder, and enuresis. *Urology, 8,* 452–454.

Werry, J. S., Dowrick, P. W., Lampen, E. L., & Vamos, M. J. (1975). Imipramine in enuresis: Psychological and physiological effects. *Journal of Child Psychology and Psychiatry, 16,* 289–299.

Young, G. C., & Morgan, R. T. T. (1972). Overlearning in the conditioning treatment of enuresis: A long-term follow-up study. *Behaviour Research & Therapy, 10,* 419–420.

Zaleski, A., Gerrard, J. W., & Shokeir, M. K. K. (1973). Nocturnal enuresis: The importance of a small bladder capacity. In I. Kolvin, R. C. MacKeith, and S. R. Meadow (Eds.), *Bladder control and enuresis* (pp. 95–101). London: William Heinemann.

BIBLIOGRAPHY: PROFESSIONALS

Physiology of Micturition and Medical Treatment

Cohen, M. W. (1975). Enuresis: *Pediatric Clinics of North America, 22,* 545–560.
Provides a review of the medical treatment literature.

Schmitt, B. D. (1982). Daytime wetting (diurnal enuresis). *Pediatric Clinics of North America, 29,* 9–20.
Discusses the problem of daytime wetting and provides a review of the medical complications found in this type of enuresis.

Turner-Warwick, R., & Whiteside, C. G. (Eds.) (1979). *The urologic clinics of North America:* Vol. 6. *Clinical urodynamics.* Philadelphia: Saunders.
An edited volume that describes the basic physiology of micturition as well as current medical assessment procedures.

Psychological Approaches

Doleys, D. M. (1977). Behavioral treatments for nocturnal enuresis in children: A review of the recent literature. *Psychological Bulletin, 84,* 30–54.
Provides good review of behavioral treatment to 1977.

Houts, A. C., & Liebert, R. M. (1984). *Bedwetting: A guide for parents and children.* Springfield, IL: Thomas.
Chapter 3 provides an updated review of behavioral treatment approaches and also discusses the effectiveness of other treatments.

Kolvin, I., MacKeith, R. C., & Meadow, S. R. (Eds.) (1973). *Bladder control and enuresis.* London: William Heinemann.
Provides good coverage of epidemiology and a somewhat dated overview of the problem.

BIBLIOGRAPHY: PARENTS

Self-Help Books

Azrin, N. H., & Besalel, V. A. (1979). *A parent's guide to bedwetting control.* New York: Simon and Schuster.
A self-help book for parents who want to implement the dry-bed training program. The authors state that the use of the bell and pad device is optional, but research conducted after the publication of this book suggests that the bell and pad should be included in this program.

Houts, A. C., & Liebert, R. M. (1984). *Bedwetting: A guide for parents and children.* Springfield IL: Thomas.
A self-help book for parents. Provides information and support materials needed to implement Full Spectrum Home Training.

Urine Alarm Devices

Wee Alert. This urine alarm is marketed through Sears Roebuck and Company and can be purchased as a catalogue-ordered item. Similar devices are sold by J. C. Penney and Jefferson Ward under different brand names. This alarm uses the conventional bed-pad to detect wetting and is the one most often described in the self-help books mentioned above.

Wet-Stop. This alarm is available from Palco Labs, 5026 Scotts Valley Dr., Scotts Valley, CA 95066. This device is very reliable and replaces the bed pad with a small absorbent strip that is placed inside the child's underwear. Instructions for using the alarm are adequate and can be adapted for use with the above self-help books.

Nytone. This alarm is available from Nytone Medical Products, 2424 South 900 West, Salt Lake City, UT 84119. The alarm device is worn on the wrist and relies on an underwear insert as opposed to the bed pad.

Children and Family Size

Patrick H. Tolan
DePaul University

Dennis McGuire
Institute for Juvenile Research, Chicago

BACKGROUND

The average family size has decreased steadily since 1900 from 4.8 persons in 1900 to 2.8 in 1980 (Current Populations Reports, 1985). This trend implies an increasing homogeneity in size, an end to large families, and consequently a decreasing influence by family size on the psychological and educational functioning of children. However, much of this average diminishment is due to the rapid rise in the number of single-person and childless households, which constituted 39.7% of households in 1950 as compared to 53.8% today (McCubbin & Dahl, 1985). In addition, approximately 10% of households today are single-child families (Wagner, Schubert, & Schubert, 1979). Large families (more than four children), although diminishing from 20% of the population in 1950 to 13.8% of the population in 1980 continue to constitute a significant portion of the population (McCubbin & Dahl, 1984). Evidently, family size still varies substantially and is influential on academic and psychological functioning. How it effects psychosocial functioning and how to use information about the effects are the focus of this chapter.

Research to date has generally taken a "direct

effects" approach to understanding the influence of family size, concluding that increasing family size has a direct negative effect on the intellectual/academic functioning and behavioral/emotional adjustment of its members. However, such an interpretation cannot adequately account for the variations in results across research studies, and it also provides little information that practitioners can apply to individual cases beyond counseling birth control. One alternative approach that is comprehensive and useful in understanding these results is a systemic view (Koestler, 1979; Minuchin & Fishman, 1981).

Family Size and Intellectual/Academic Functioning

An extensive literature exists on the effect of family size on intelligence and academic achievement. Early statistical studies indicated that children from large families performed more poorly on academic tests than their small-family counterparts (Schooler, 1972). These differences were attributed to a lower family mental ability among larger families and the explanation was labeled *confluence theory* (Zajonc, 1976). According to this theory, individual intelligence is affected by the intellectual stimulation of the growing child's immediate social environment, most directly the family, in the following manner. Because the level of knowledge and skills possessed by adults is usually greater than that of children, the proportion of adults to children in the family directly determines the "mental ability" of the family and, in turn, the development of intellect in the individual members. Therefore, children from large families are hindered in their intellectual development (Zajonc, 1976). According to this theory, single children, representing the other extreme, would show the highest intellectual abilities. Early large-scale studies of general populations seemed to bear out this theory (Wagner, Wagner, & Schubert, 1979, 1985).

However, later more sophisticated and specific studies showed that the results used to build confluence theory were confounded by socioeconomic status (SES) and birth order differences between the large- and small-family samples used (Belmont & Marolla, 1973; Lancer & Rim, 1984). For example, Page and Grandon (1979) found that the relationship between family size and intellectual ability was substantial only for children from the lower 25% of the SES strata.

A more recent explanation, called *admixture theory,* emphasizes the interactive effect of many variables on intellectual ability. This remains the prominent "direct effects" theory today. This arose out of studies that have found either no relation between family size and intellectual performance (Mednick, Baker, & Hocevar, 1985), or have found that its influence is heavily dependent on other variables such as socioeconomic status, birth order, and spacing of sibling births (Belmont & Marolla, 1973; Wagner, et al., 1985).

Although more theoretically capable than confluence theory, admixture theory still leaves most of the variation in abilities among children in similar sized families unexplained. Also, admixture theory has difficulty explaining how family size should be considered in planning interventions with children of families of differing sizes. By considering how family size influences the systemic functioning of the family and thus influences attitude and capabilities related to academic and intellectual performance, a clearer and more useful formulation of its impact for a specific child can be developed.

Family Size and Behavioral/Emotional Adjustment

Although less extensive than research on intellectual and academic performance, studies of the effects of family size on behavioral and emotional adjustment indicate similar trends. Overall, the studies suggest that impairment increases as family size increases. Family size has been related to differences in rates of psychological and behavioral problems, types of problems, and severity of problems (Tuckman & Regan, 1967; Wagner et al., 1985).

Types of Problems. A large number of psychological problems have been reported as more common among members of large families than smaller families. Among these are family tension (Moore & Holtzman, 1965), neurosis (Rutter & Graham, 1976), antisocial and delinquent behavior (Rutter & Graham, 1976), suicide (Chen & Cobb, 1960), childhood schizophrenia (Mintz, 1967), and alcoholism (Riess & Safer, 1973). However, like the studies of intellectual abilities many of these studies did not consider the relative impact of family size compared to other familial and extrafamilial influences. Studies that did consider other variables' impact do not support a direct relationship between family size and behavioral/emotional adjustment. Mednick et al. (1985) surveyed a Danish cohort on a large variety of psychosocial indicators and found no differences related to family size on any of these. Similarly, Touliatos and Lindholm found that family size had little effect on general adjustment of children (Touliatos & Lindholm, 1980a), school adjustment according to teacher ratings (Lindholm, Touliatos, & Rich, 1977), or level or type of behavior problems (Touliatos & Lindholm, 1980b). Tolan and Lorion (1986) found that family size did not correlate with extent or seriousness of delinquency. Similarly, single children do not differ in risk for psychological problems from the general population, although there is some evidence that they are underrepresented among clinical populations (Howe & Madgett, 1975). Apparently, family size does not directly affect the likelihood of psychological problems or the seriousness of those problems.

There is some evidence that children from large families will differ in the types of problems for which they are referred. Searcy-Miller, Cowen, and Terrell (1977) reported that, compared to children from families with two or fewer siblings, children from large families referred to a prevention program were more likely to have learning problems and social inhibition problems. Children from smaller families, on the other hand, were more likely to have aggression problems and to be rated as more maladjusted overall. Similarly, Boone and Montare (1979) reported that problems with aggressiveness decreased as family size increased. However, when only aggressive children were compared, those from large families were rated more poorly than their small-family counterparts (Murrell, 1974; Wadsworth, 1979).

Personality Style. Studies of differences in personality style by family size have suggested that children from large families may have poorer self-concepts than single-child and medium-sized family members (Falbo, 1984; Wagner et al., 1979). They are likely to be less extroverted (Eysenck & Carlson, 1970), feel more alienated from their parents (Nye, Carlson, & Garrett, 1970), will take more risks (Jamieson, 1969), and are less emotionally expressive (Wagner et al., 1979). On the positive side, children from large families are likely to be more cooperative, altruistic, responsible to others, and creative (Bossard & Boll, 1956; Wagner et al., 1979). Children from single-child families tend to be less affiliative, more self-centered, and more socially isolated than children from larger families (Falbo, 1981; Kaplan, 1970). Miller and Maruyama (1976) reported that single children were less frequently chosen as playmates by peers than children from larger families. As adults, single children, although more successful occupationally, are less socially oriented (Falbo, 1984).

As these brief reviews show, more sophisticated and specific studies have indicated that the effects of family size in each area of psychosocial functioning are mediated by several other factors. Perhaps most importantly, family systemic characteristics such as organization, values, and orientation towards family, school, and peers can differ as a function of family size (Bossard & Boll, 1956; Falbo, 1984; McGuire & Tolan, in press; Nye et al., 1970). This emphasis can be the most productive focus for understanding family size effects in planning assessment and intervention.

The systemic approach focuses on the patterns of interaction existing among the individuals in a context of major systems that organize as well as maintain behaviors by the individuals. A child's major systems are the home, school, and peer network. While it can be said that each of these systems determines the behaviors exhibited within it, it is also true that the child must balance the different roles, interests, and obligations of each system to function adaptively and successfully (Koestler, 1979; Minuchin & Fishman, 1981). According to this view, problems develop when children are unable to balance the different systems' interests and their roles in each. For example, if the family system requires that a child take on a great deal of the parenting functions for an indisposed parent, he or she may have little time or energy left for peer relationships or school work. Applying this model to evaluate the influence of family size, it can be seen that the family's size may have a significant effect on the child's ability to negotiate a balance between the different systems' demands.

Family sizes can be grouped into three categories: the single-child family, medium-sized families (2–3 children), and large families (4 or more children). Each size results in different systemic organization; therefore, each requires different considerations and approaches in assessment and interventions. In the following section we examine typical systemic effects of different-sized groupings, focusing on single-child and large families and addressing normal development and the typical problems of each, as well as advising assessment and intervention approaches.

DEVELOPMENT

The Single-Child Family

Two distinguishing characteristics of the single-child family are the lack of a sibling subsystem and the prominence of the marital subsystem (Bank & Kahn, 1975; Falbo, 1984). This creates a less complex family organization, and keeps the child closely in touch with the marital relationship. Parents with one child tend to have fewer demands on their time and finances than parents in larger families. Thus, their marital relationship maintains centrality, whereas in larger families, the parenting relationship often overshadows these concerns. As a by-product of this organization, single children are more often included in marital and parental decisions (Hawke & Knox, 1978). A less desirable by-product is that the family can be overly invested in the child's academic achievement and the child may be under greater than usual parental scrutiny (Falbo, 1984). Also, there is the lack of opportunity to engage in and learn about sibling relationships, which is a critical training ground for developing social skills and peer relations. The sibling relationship also serves to buffer "spillover" of marital issues into parent–child relations. The single child lacks this benefit.

The relationships among the school, family, and peer systems of single children may be attenuated. They may have more difficulty adapting to being one of a group at school and can appear unable to cooperate with peers in accomplishing school tasks (Falbo, 1976). Also, these children may have limited skills for competing with classmates for teachers' attention.

Problems associates with the status of a single-child family are primarily related to the child's "overinvolvement" with or proximity to the marital relationship and the exaggerated centrality of the marital system in the family. Because these children are often directly subject to parental conflicts and concerns without the buffer of siblings, they may become preoccupied with marital concerns such as disharmony or financial strains (whether real or imagined). Thus, they may have little energy left for or interest in school or peer system demands. During contacts with school parents of single children may focus on their personal disappointments and desires in regard to their children's academic performance. They can sound as though their children are seen as merely extensions of themselves or as an index of the success of their marriage. This can easily generate misunderstanding and antagonism between parents and the school, the child feeling caught between the two systems (McGuire & Lyons, 1985).

In the peer system, problems most likely will develop because of inexperience with peers. Single children are often more experienced and comfortable with adult company. They may simply lack social skills necessary to develop peer relationships and to resolve arising conflicts. Also, they may not understand the necessity of sharing adult attention with other children. Depending on which of these issues apply to a given child, conflicted peer interactions or social isolation can occur.

It should be noted that most single children make adequate adjustments to these systemic demands. As Falbo (1984) discussed, parental attention may develop self-esteem and self-reliance rather than self-indulgence in the single child. Similarly, a lack of opportunity for sibling interaction may encourage the child to engage in peer relations early.

To deal effectively with a single child's problems, the psychologist may need to educate or counsel the child's parents to distinguish parental from marital roles and determine what should and should not be shared with the child about these ares of family life. Also, some parents may need help to differentiate child performance from personal and marital esteem. Additionally, opportunities for peer relations may need to be provided.

The Large Family

Large families can be produced in several ways. The most obvious is the birth of a large number of children to the same two parents, which we refer to as a biologically large family. A second way a large family may be formed is multigenerational, the common functioning of more than one generation as one family. With the increasing divorce rates and remarriages, many large families are now formed by the blending of two families. Each type of large family system differs in important ways and brings specific systemic issues into primacy. Thus, consideration of how the family was formed is important. Nevertheless, large-family systems have several common characteristics.

The organization of large families tends to be more complex than in smaller families. Along with the marital, parental, and sibling subsystems that constitute other families, several sibling subsystems may exist. Often these are broken down into groups of two or three based on age, gender, or other characteristics. Each subsystem is usually "responsible" for addressing certain concerns of the whole family. The closeness or alliance between siblings shifts, depending on which subsystem distinctions are functioning at the time. Thus the relative prestige and influence of each sibling shifts frequently. Also, because one is always part of a subsystem, individual attributes are less influential than one's subsystem alliances.

Often the sibling subsystem will be most central and have the most power for transmitting and blocking information flow. Older siblings are usually required to take on many parental responsibilities. In a sense, the parents rear the older children and the older children rear the younger children. In a study by Bossard & Boll (1956) 82% of siblings from large families reported that care of siblings was a major family role for them; notably 69% were satisfied with these responsibilities. Younger siblings are less likely to have parental duties and so may have a relatively underdeveloped sense of responsibility, which can conflict with the other members' strong value of family duty. Also, they can be "out of synch" with the rest of the family developmentally, because families often advance through life stages in accordance with the oldest children's ages. This leaves younger children to negotiate developmental tasks on their own (McCubbin & Dahl, 1985; McGuire & Tolan, in press). In some cases, younger siblings will be burdened with the additional role of "monitoring" the marital relationship of the parents, which impairs normal preparation to leave home (Haley, 1981).

The marital subsystem will often be least prominent, the husband and wife relating to each other almost entirely as parents and managers of the group (Nye et al., 1970). The parenting period is quite extended, and, in some cases, parenting serves to maintain a tenuous marital relationship by allowing avoidance of a focus on marital problems (Haley, 1981).

Members of large families are likely to feel more bound to their family than those of smaller families (Bossard & Boll, 1956; Nye et al., 1970); larger families tend to instill less of an individualistic orientation and emphasize instead the commitment to the group. Individual members define their self-esteem less by their own accomplishments and more by doing their part as one of many. Attitudes towards socializing, use of leisure time, and basic identity are all more family-centered. This value may clash with the individualistic values held by peers and schools. Thus, large-family members may be less explorative outside the family and have less invested in peer and academic areas (McGuire & Tolan, in press).

Just as individual members' identity is more intimately tied to others in a large family, the sense of property is also modified. Ownership is often transient, material goods being handed down to younger siblings. Economic resources can be sparse, or must be spread further, so that personal possession often becomes a luxury (Espenshade, Kamenske, & Turchi, 1983); sharing is strongly emphasized. Similarly, privacy is emphasized less in large families. Bedrooms are shared, and use of the central living spaces usually requires being with others (Bossard & Boll, 1956; Espenshade et al., 1983).

In general large families are more rule-governed than smaller families (Wagner et al., 1985). Privileges, responsibilities, and discipline may all be determined more by rule than by individual accommodation. The individual relationship between parents and a given child will be less central to decision making (Hurley & Horn, 1971). In part this is due to the number of children, which limits the parents' direct attitude to each child (Nye et al., 1970), and in part it promotes the family values of fairness and equal treatment (Bossard & Boll, 1956). As a by-product of the rule-oriented family organization, discipline will be communicated less by verbal reasoning and more by expectations for compliance (Elder & Bowerman, 1963). Children may feel less approved of by parents because of this (Nye et al., 1970).

Given these systemic characteristics, the large family tends to instill strong affiliation to the family, which can serve as a source of esteem and aid family members' development of adaptive skills for extrafamilial social relations. However, they may emphasize the distinction of the family from the rest of the world too strongly and cause the family's interests to eclipse the individual's. Moreover, when there is a strong distinction of "inside the family" from "outside the family," and the family defines itself as different or antagonistic to the extrafamilial systems, loyalty to the family may limit a child's engaging peers and/or investing in school activities.

Because of the complexity of large-family systems and the delegation of parental responsibilities to siblings, in contacts with these parents professionals can sustain the impression of parental disinterest or lack of sensitivity to the child's needs as a student. Additionally, parents may simply be less accessible to school personnel, because of time demands of other children and/or employment. In fact, an older sibling may be sent to represent the family at a school meeting. An assessment must be made of each case, but often this member is well versed in the matters at hand and can represent the parents reliably.

Despite a strong investment in siblings as a peer group, large-family members tend to have very adequate social skills and can apply them readily to the peer system. Because they have been a member of a "group" since birth and are comfortable with interdependence, they tend to have tolerant and caring interpersonal attitudes. They are likely to value cooperation more than peers from smaller families and are able to listen as well as speak for themselves in a group. Self-control is often less difficult for members of large families, as it is instilled early. Problems in peer relations may reflect an overdeveloped interest in family functions, excluding peers in order to stay engaged with siblings.

In addition to these general characteristics of children from large families, the ordinal position of the children can effect risk for several types of problems in peer and school interests (see chapter on birth order in this volume). Older children may have difficulty finding time for outside peer and school interests because they are often delegated extensive parenting responsibilities for younger siblings. Although this sharing of parenting is inevitable, a more equitable sharing of these responsibilities may be needed to promote an adaptive balance between home, school, and peer interests.

The last-born siblings in large families are most likely to develop problems. The parents are often exhausted by the time the younger children are born. The parents' marital relationship may be developmentally pushing toward the "postparental" stage (McCubbin & Dahl, 1985). On the other hand, the length of the parenting stage is so extended that parents may feel unable to rekindle and therefore renegotiate marital intimacy. Moreover, some parents may have difficulty facing the impending loss and solitude of the "empty nest" that accompanies the postparental stage of marriage. In addition, the caretaking roles learned by older children and useful in developing their own independence and preparing them to leave home are not passed onto the younger siblings. Therefore, these children may not possess skills necessary for independent action in the school and peer systems. All of these factors increase the risk to siblings in these birth-order positions of psychological problems. They may need direct intervention to develop independence-oriented skills; or consultation with parents may be needed to lessen the children's role as monitor of marital issues.

PUTTING FAMILY SIZE IN PERSPECTIVE

In addition to the information provided above, several other factors need to be considered when evaluating family size effects. First, are the consistent interaction effects noted between socioeconomic status and large family size (Mednick et al., 1985; Wagner et al., 1985), as well as the effects of sibling birth order (Kidwell, 1981). Also, the gender of siblings and spacing of births can also be influential. For example, large families with mostly male siblings may be more authoritarian than those with more females (Kidwell, 1981). Those with little spacing between siblings may be overwhelmed by recurring intense developmental crises, whereas those with too great a spacing can function as two separate families and must try to cope with many varied family developmental tasks simultaneously (McCubbin & Dahl, 1985). Furthermore, the manner in which a large family was formed (biological vs. "blended" vs. multigenerational family) can be critical in determining both what problems present and how to intervene. Consulting chapters on these types of families and the issues they face in this volume and other sources is suggested.

If a family differs in socioeconomic status or ethnicity from that of most of the school population and school personnel, differences in values can be mistaken for maladaptive behavior. This may cause single-child families to be seen as inconsiderate of the needs of other students or large families to appear uninterested in school achievement. Without adequate consideration of these system–relation issues essential communication can be blocked. Finally, it is important to be aware of the school's limitations and capabilities to acknowledge and accommodate value differences (McGuire & Cimmarusti, 1986).

We also want to caution against overemphasizing family size in evaluating family effects on the behavior of children. Family size may be so simply one of several family effects on the child, and in some cases, it may not be contributing to the cause of a problem observed (McCubbin & Dahl, 1985; Minuchin & Fishman, 1981). In a sentence, it is important to consider family size, especially when working with large family members, but it is also important *not* to overemphasize it.

ALTERNATIVE ACTIONS

In evaluating the impact of family size and planning intervention, it is important to consider all aspects of family–school–peer systems relationships with an emphasis on how a child is able to balance interest in all three areas. Thus, a first step is to assess the relative balance across systems and determine which seem over-demanding of the child's time and interest and which seem underdemanding. Specific to family size, if the child is from a single-child family, then evaluation of peer relations skills and their involvement in marital matters needs to be done. If the child is from a large family, assessment of the family's relation to the outside community, particularly the school is in order. Also, the sibling subsystem organization may need attention, with birth order of particular interest. As sibling subsystems are often the best focus for intervention in large families adequate knowledge of their organization is important (Banks & Kahn, 1975; McGuire & Tolan, in press). Finally, it is important to assess the extent to which consultation, education, or direct intervention is necessary to remedy the problem.

Some families may merely need education about family-size effects related to children's academic and behavioral problems. For example, as single children do not have exposure to siblings and therefore are likely to be more comfortable relating to adults than peers, their parents may need to be given this information and encouraged to seek out avenues for peer interaction. An example of this type of intervention for large families would be to make the family aware that the older children's parenting responsibilities can interfere with school and peer relations and to suggest sharing of these responsibilities among siblings is necessary.

In some cases brief intervention with a child to aid development of social skills or adapt to the demands of the school setting can be adequate. Thus single children may need social skills training to develop peer relations, whereas children from large families may need support to develop adequate self-interest. Another type of action might be brief intervention with the parents to attenuate intrafamily problems that are "spilling over" into school, causing an imbalance between the three systems. In single-child families, work with the parents to block the overinvolvement of the child in marital concerns can be effective. Parents in large families may need aid to renegotiate marital intimacy or otherwise remove the youngest child from their marital concerns and allow him or her to develop appropriate independence interests.

A further step that may be needed is brief or extensive family therapy oriented toward mediating difficulties within the family that are affecting home–school relations or difficulties in the home–school system relationships. One method is to convene a meeting of family members and school personnel to mediate the cross-system difficulties. A step-by-step explanation of how to do this is available in McGuire and Lyons (1985). A single-child family–school meeting may focus on bringing parents and teachers together to promote a more healthy balance between academic achievement and social interests. In a large family, such a meeting may focus on a plan between school and parents to allow an oldest child to meet family responsibilities as well as school requirements and peer interests.

Finally, family therapy by a professional in or outside the school system may be needed to highlight family-size effects and modify family organization and/or realign the family–school–peer interests of the child. For example, a single-child family system that exhibits more severe marital disharmony or one that is not reactive to less extensive interventions may need such family therapy to extricate the child from the marital system. Similarly, a large family that is unable to independently reorganize the sibling subsystem to better distribute family responsibilities may need such work (McGuire & Tolan, in press).

SUMMARY

Family size can be an important variable to consider in evaluating and intervening with school children and their families. Although an overall trend in research has been to suggest that as family size increases, academic and behavioral impairments are more likely, a "direct effect" model is not an adequate explanation of family-size effects and is difficult to apply in daily practice. An alternative view is a systemic approach, which focuses on the relations between individual children and the three major systems (family, school, peers) that make up their "developmental context." Problems in functioning are seen as the result of an inability to balance the demands of these three systems. The two most distinct types of family systems in relation to size are large families (more than four siblings) and single-child families. Each of these tends to have a distinct systemic organization, which affects the child in predictable ways. Single-child families tend to focus more on the marital subsystem than other families. Also, these children do not have the opportunity for sibling interaction. These characteristics can subject the single child directly to parental marital concerns. Also, the child may lack interest or skills in developing peer relations. Large families tend to focus on the sibling subsystem, the marital concerns being eclipsed by the parental relationship. Also the complexity and size of the system makes extensive demands on family members, especially older siblings, to aid in parenting functions. Little time or energy may be left for school and peers. Youngest siblings in these families are at risk for problems due to underdevelopment of self-interest and the difficulties related to parental renegotiation of marital intimacy that mark the postparental family developmental stage.

Assessment and intervention require understanding family size effects on the family system and should be oriented towards balancing interests of that system with those of the school and peers. Education, consultation, and direct interventions may be needed at times to remediate the difficulties resulting from systems imbalance. Also, the relative impact of family size compared to other influences on the child and family needs to be considered. Family size effects should not be overemphasized just as they should not be dismissed as trivial.

REFERENCES

Bank, S., & Kahn, M. D. (1975). Sisterhood–brotherhood is powerful: Sibling sub-systems and family therapy. *Family Process, 14,* 311–337.

Belmont, L., & Marolla, F. A. (1973). Birth order, family size, and intelligence. *Science, 182,* 1096–1101.

Boone, S. L., & Montare, A. (1979). Aggression and family size. *Journal of Psychology, 103,* 67–70.

Bossard, J. H. S., & Boll, E. S. (1956). *The large family system.* Philadelphia: University of Pennsylvania Press.

Chen, E., & Cobb, S. (1960). Family structure in relation to health and disease. *Journal of Chronic Diseases, 12,* 544–567.

Current Population Reports. (1985). *Household and family characteristics* (Series P–20, No. 371, March).

Elder, G. H., & Bowerman, C. E. (1963). Family structure and child rearing patterns: The effect of family size and sex composition. *American Sociological Review, 28,* 891–905.

Espenshade, T. J., Kamenske, G., & Turchi, B. A. (1983). Family size and economic welfare. *Family Planning Perspective, 15,* 289–294.

Eysenck, H. J., & Carlson, D. (1970). Personality in primary school children, III. Family background. *British Journal of Educational Psychology, 40,* 117–131.

Falbo, T. (1977). The only child: A review. *Journal of Individual Psychology, 30,* 216–220.

Falbo, T. (1981). Relationships between birth category, achievement, and interpersonal orientation. *Journal of Personality and Social Psychology, 41,* 121–131.

Falbo, T. (1984). *The single-child family.* New York: Guilford.

Haley, J. (1981). *Leaving home: The therapy of disturbed young people.* New York: McGraw-Hill.

Hawke, S., & Knox, D. (1978). The one child family: A new lifestyle. *Family Coordinator, 27,* 215–219.

Howe, M. C., & Madgett, M. E. (1975). Mental health problems associated with the only child. *Canadian Psychiatric Association Journal, 20,* 189–194.

Hurley, J. R., & Horn, R. L. (1971). Shifts in child-rearing attitudes linked with parenthood and occupation. *Developmental Psychology, 4,* 324–328.

Jamieson, B. D. (1969). The influences of birth order, family size, and sex differences on risk taking behavior. *British Journal of Social and Clinical Psychology, 8,* 1–8.

Kaplan, H. B. (1970). Self-derogation and childhood family structure. *Journal of Nervous and Mental Disease, 151,* 13–23.

Kidwell, J. S. (1981). Number of siblings, sibling spacing, sex, and birth order: Their effects on perceived parent–adolescent relationships. *Journal of Marriage and the Family, 43,* 315–332.

Koestler, A. (1979). *Janus: A summing up.* New York: Vintage Books.

Lancer, I., & Rim, Y. (1984). Intelligence, family size, and sibling age spacing. *Personality and Individual Differences, 5,* 151–157.

Lindholm, B. W., Touliatos, J., & Rich, A. (1977). Influence of family structure and school variables on behavior disorders of children. *Psychology in the Schools, 14,* 99–104.

McCubbin, H., & Dahl, B. B. (1985). *Marriage and family: Individuals and life cycles.* New York: Wiley.

McGuire, D., & Cimmarusti, R. (1986). *School problems: An intercontextual typology.* Manuscript submitted for publication.

McGuire, D., & Lyons, J. (1985). A transcontextual model for underachievement school problems. *American Journal of Family Therapy, 13,* 37–45.

McGuire, D., & Tolan, P. H. (in press). Large family siblings in therapy. In M. Kahn & K. G. Lewis (Eds.), *Siblings in therapy.* New York: Norton.

Mednick, B. R., Baker, R. L., & Hocevar, D. (1985). Family size and birth order correlates of intellectual, psychosocial, and physical growth. *Merrill-Palmer Quarterly, 31,* 67–83.

Miller, N., & Maruyama, G. (1976). Ordinal position and peer popularity. *Journal of Personality and Social Psychology, 33,* 123–131.

Minuchin, S., & Fishman, H. C. (1981). *Family therapy techniques.* Cambridge, MA: Harvard University Press.

Mintz, S. B. (1967). Childhood schizophrenia: The factors of maternal identification, projection, and vicarious acting out as related to birth order, sibling spacing, and size of family. *Dissertation Abstracts International, 27,* 4654B. (University Microfilms No. 65–14433)

Moore, B., & Holtzman, W. H. (1965). *Tomorrow's parents: A study of youth and their families.* Austin: University of Texas Press.

Murrell, S. A. (1974). Relationships of ordinal positions and family size to psychosocial measures of delinquents. *Journal of Abnormal Child Psychology, 2,* 39–46.

Nye, F. I., Carlson, J., & Garrett, G. (1970). Family interaction, affect, and stress. *Journal of Marriage and the Family, 216,* 216–226.

Page, E. B., & Grandon, G. M. (1979). Family configuration and mental ability: Two theories contrasted with U.S. data. *American Educational Research Journal, 16,* 257–272.

Riess, B. F., & Safer, J. (1973). Birth order and related variables in a large outpatient population. *Journal of Psychology, 85,* 61–68.

Rutter, M., & Graham, P. (1976). Social circumstances of children with psychiatric disorders. In M. Rutter, J. Tizard, & K. Whitmore (Eds.), *Education, health, and behaviour: Psychological and medical study of childhood development.* 121–150. New York: Wiley.

Schooler, C. (1972). Childhood family structure and adult characteristics. *Sociometry, 35,* 255–268.

Searcy-Miller, M. L., Cowen, E. L., & Terrell, D. L. (1977). School adjustment problems of children from small vs. large families. *Journal of Community Psychology, 5,* 319–324.

Tolan, P. H. (in press). Implications of age of onset for delinquency risk identification. *Journal of Abnormal Child Psychology.*

Touliatos, J., & Lindholm, B. W. (1980a). Birth order, family size, and children's mental health. *Psychological Reports, 46,* 1097–1098.

Touliatos, J., & Lindholm, B. W. (1980b). Birth order, family size, and behavior problems in children. *Child Psychiatry Quarterly, 13,* 1–8.

Tuckman, J., & Regan, R. A. (1967). Size of family and behavior problems. *Journal of Genetic Psychology, 111,* 151–160.

Wadsworth, M. (1979). *Roots of delinquency.* Oxford: Robertson.

Wagner, M. E., Schubert, H. J. P., & Schubert, D. S. P. (1979). Sibship–constellation effects on psychosocial development, creativity, and health. *Advances in Child Development and Behavior, 14,* 58–155.

Wagner, M. E., Schubert, H. J. P., & Schubert, D. S. P. (1985). Family size effects: A review. *Journal of Genetic Psychology, 146,* 65–78.

Zajonc, R. (1976). Family configuration and intelligence. *Science, 192,* 227–236.

BIBLIOGRAPHY: PROFESSIONALS

Bossard, J. H. S., & Boll, E. S. (1956). *The large family system.* Philadelphia: University of Pennsylvania Press.
A dated but still useful report of the characteristics common to large-family systems. It does not provide practical information for intervention, but rather is useful for background reading. The focus on the siblings is particularly useful.

Falbo, T. (1984). *The single-child family.* New York: Guilford.
The only volume focused on research on the single-child family. Also includes some chapters addressing clinical issues. Serves best as background reading.

McGuire, D., & Tolan, P. H. (in press). Large-family siblings in therapy. In M. Kahn & K. G. Lewis (Eds.), *Siblings in therapy.* New York: Norton.
A presentation of the large-family characteristics relevant to family therapy and evaluation. Provides a theoretical overview as well as specific practical techniques for interventions. Primary focus is on the sibling subsystems.

Wagner, M. E.,Schubert, H. J. P., & Schubert, D. S. P. (1979). Sibship-constellation effects on psychosocial development, creativity, and health. *Advances in Child Development and Behavior, 14,* 58–155.
Provides fairly current summary of research on family size related to intellectual, academic, and behavioral adjustment. This is less a critical review with details of research than a brief tallying of accumulated research.

Children and Fear of Nuclear Threat

Luella B. Chatters
Adrian College

BACKGROUND

Introduction

Human beings have always lived with the possibility of catastrophes that were beyond their control. Natural dangers such as earthquakes, storms, volcanoes, and glaciers endangered the lives of our primitive ancestors and, to some extent, still threaten the lives of many people in modern societies. Certain uncontrollable threats exist that individuals must accept as dangers of living.

Today other dangers have been added to the list of pervasive forces that threaten human life. Chemical food additives, environmental pollution, and nuclear contamination are all sources of imminent or long-term danger. The issue of nuclear threat poses the ultimate in the list of dangers that threaten life on our planet.

Nuclear technology affects people's lives intensely but often in ways that they cannot fully understand. The future of the human race is bound up with the use or nonuse of nuclear weapons (Beardslee & Mack, 1982). Yet people live with the looming threat that nuclear power may suddenly be unleashed, purposefully or accidentally, in a disaster of unimaginable proportions. For those who grow up in a world of nuclear weapons the threat of the possible end of humanity's existence may be an issue that obscures all other concerns. The biological sense of an endless chain of life is threatened. Mack (1982) stated that nuclear weapons have created psychiatric and psychological issues that are just beginning to be fathomed.

Although all people live under the threat of nuclear war, today's children have never lived in a world where that threat did not exist. Television has depicted the tragic events of Hiroshima and Nagasaki to most children. Young people have learned that, at the touch of a button, all they have known and valued may be destroyed. What impact does this knowledge have upon a child's development?

School psychologists are in a position to study this impact and to assist schools and parents in dealing with this issue. Educational institutions have tended to avoid issues that stimulate questions about the basic assumptions of our society or that cause young people to ask hard questions that adults are not prepared to answer (Mack, 1984b). School psychologists have frequently been called upon to provide guidance to schools in dealing with controversial, problematic, or values-laden issues. Educational inquiry into previously forbidden areas such as sex, death, divorce, and abuse of controlled substances is now often dealt with comfortably by professionals and accepted by parents and communities as an appropriate province of educators. Yet nuclear threat represents a current issue that is avoided in school programming.

Mack (1984b) stated that resistance to nuclear education is an expression of a conscious and unconscious desire not to know about a danger that shakes our most basic security. Well-intentioned adults do not wish to frighten children by dealing with an issue that they themselves fear to consider. Yet psychologists are often in an ideal position to assess children's fears and concerns, to counsel with them, and to educate parents and professionals in ways to deal with this sensitive issue.

Research

There has been little continuous research conducted to determine what children and adolescents think about nuclear threat. Although there are methodological limitations to many of the studies that have been conducted, the findings do raise serious concerns about the impact of nuclear threat on children's lives. The first questionnaire studies were conducted by psychologists Escalona and Schwebel in the early 1960s as a response to the Cuban missile crisis. Escalona (1965) examined 311 children from widely different socioeconomic groups who ranged in age from 10 to 17 years. Schwebel (1965) surveyed 3,000 junior and senior high school students of various socioeconomic backgrounds. Both researchers found a greater degree of fear of war than they had expected; it ranged from 42–45% in Schwebel's study to 70% in Escalona's study. Since this figure decreased after the Cuban missile crisis was settled, these researchers concluded that situational crises correlate with children's fears.

In 1983 Bachman conducted what may be the best study from a methodological viewpoint (Bachman, 1983; Tizard, 1984). He and his colleagues at the University of Michigan Institute of Social Research administered questionnaires to 16,000–19,000 high school seniors from 1975 through 1982. These students were drawn from public and private schools throughout the United States. To the question "Of all the problems facing the nation today, how often do you worry about the chance of nuclear war?" Bachman found a fourfold increase (from 8% to 30%) from 1975 to 1982 of those who worry "often." He also found a 61% increase (from 22% to 36%) during that period of those who agreed or mostly agreed with the statement "Nuclear or biological annihilation will probably be the fate of all mankind within my lifetime."

A 1983 study based upon Schwebel's questions was conducted just after the Soviet downing of a Korean airliner. The researchers surveyed 256 ninth graders from three cities in California and one in Maine; these students represented a wide range of socioeconomic backgrounds and intellectual achievement. In response to the question "Is there going to be a nuclear war?" 64% answered "yes" (Gould, Berger, Gould, & Eden, 1984).

In 1977 the American Psychiatric Association appointed a task force to study the psychological impact of nuclear advances. Among the subjects to be studied was the impact of nuclear developments on children and adolescents. Beardslee and Mack (1982) reported on a study that involved 4,000 children in the Boston area. Approximately 40% of the group reported that they were aware of nuclear developments before the age of 12. The authors suggested that the threat of nuclear annihilation has penetrated deeply into the consciousness of U.S. children and has produced anxiety and fear of the future.

In the last 3 years additional questionnaire studies have been conducted and each has suggested that the majority of respondents were concerned about the nuclear threat (Mack, 1983a). Researchers in other countries (Sweden, Finland, Canada, U.S.S.R.) have generally found that young people surveyed express a greater concern than their U.S. counterparts. Mack (1983b) supported these findings and stated that Soviet children have been exposed to detailed information about the effects of nuclear explosions through classroom instruction and media information and may be better able to imagine the consequences of nuclear war because of the millions of deaths their country suffered in World War II.

Coles (1985) recently reported on his 6-year clinical study with children. His conclusions suggested that economic class plays a primary role in children's awareness and concerns about nuclear threat. Poor children, he concluded, are concerned with the more immediate dangers in their experience and with having basic needs for hunger, shelter, and nurturance met. They do not have the leisure to worry about the nuclear bomb. The children of well-to-do, educated, politically active parents appeared to have serious concerns about nuclear issues.

In summary, research into the effects of the nuclear threat did not begin until the 1960s, developed slowly, and has shown a recent increase in this decade. The results of reported studies suggest that the majority of school-age children are aware of the nuclear threat and fearful of the possibility of nuclear war within their lifetimes. Children's awareness, their developmental needs, and current situational events all appear to play a part in the extent of children's concerns about nuclear issues.

DEVELOPMENT

Facing the Issue

Living with the nuclear threat is frightening for both children and adults. Lifton (1982) pointed to the absurdity of dealing with the sense that everything we have known or loved may be annihilated in a moment and, at the same time, carrying on our daily lives as though that fact did not exist.

In order to deal with this emotional issue, persons use the defense mechanisms of denial, suppression, and avoidance (Schwebel, 1982). This method may be effective in temporarily helping the individual to avoid stress, but movies, television, newspaper articles, and discussions may periodically bring the issue into one's consciousness. From a psychological point of view, persons tend to resist the anxiety that confronts them when dealing with the possibility of a nuclear disaster. They turn away and address themselves to problems of a more manageable scale. Mack (1983a) also described the collective resistance that exists in our society to knowledge of the nuclear threat. Persons tend to deny data because to accept it is too great a threat to our collective security and our sense of nationalism. To challenge national authority, political values,and economic purposes creates extreme anxiety.

If adults are faced with difficulty in dealing with the issue of the nuclear threat, how then can they justify presenting the issue to children? The fear and despair involved with facing this issue have tended to make it a taboo subject that is not discussed with children (Engel, 1984).

It is generally accepted that one must deal with both facts and feelings in order to cope with problems. Facing the facts regarding the nuclear threat and exploring adults' and children's feelings about this subject appear to be essential if we are to reduce children's fears.

Effects on the Development of Personality, Values, and Goals

Do children pay attention in their contemplation of the future to the nuclear threat and, if so, what are the consequences to their present and future lives? Reifel (1984) stated that most children have learned about nuclear weapons from television and/or the classroom. Few children reported having discussed this issue with their parents. Their awareness was not reported in terms of facts but in terms of fear and horror. Films such as "The Day After" had generated awareness of nuclear danger and expression of personal fear.

Children's conception of war and peace is influenced by their developmental level (Taipale, 1984). Children aged 6–9 years are frequently concerned with issues of separation, loss, change, deterioration, and death (Kastenbaum, 1979). Their understanding of war is limited by their concrete thinking ability, and their fears tend to relate to being left alone or without the support of a loved one. Young children have active imaginations and limited ability to form mental barriers; thus, they are often poorly informed but more worried than older children. Their awareness may often be revealed in play and stories (Eisenbud, VanHoorn, & Gould, 1985).

A developmental task of later childhood and preadolescence is to get through the painful process of learning about death. Nuclear threat may increase the fears and worries children experience as they struggle with this issue. At this stage of concrete thinking children become more capable of verbalizing their fears about nuclear disaster.

Adolescents have arrived at the highest level of mental activity and are thus able to comprehend the realities of nuclear issues. Mack (1981) reported that the nuclear threat rated high on the list of concerns expressed by surveyed adolescents and that their reactions to this threat ranged from fear, sadness, and helplessness to cynicism, anger, and rage. Many indicated uncertainty about their personal future, doubt about raising families, and inability to make longterm plans. College-age students reported thinking less about nuclear war and considering it less likely than did high school students. Escalona (1982) suggested that the reaction of this group is likely related to the difficulty of simultaneously planning for the future and contemplating the nuclear threat to the future.

Psychological and cognitive effects of nuclear threat are related to developmental stages. Erickson (1963) asserts that a major task of adolescence is the healthy establishment of personal identity and related ideas about future roles. Concerns about nuclear disaster may weaken and impede the realization of these tasks. In such an insecure psychological climate children may come to believe that one can depend on nothing. Not perceiving life as stable and enduring affects the development of a healthy ego. The sense of futurelessness may contribute to some of the behavioral ills of today's younger generation (Mack, 1984b). Goodman et al. (1983) stated that nuclear threat contributes to the tendency of teenagers to be impulsive and to seek immediate gratification in personal relations and behavior. Rogers (1982) suggested that the fatalism and futility of youth today may relate to nuclear threat. Lifton and Olsen (1974) discussed "nuclear numbing," a reaction to nuclear threat that may be seen in impaired ability to form lasting human relationships. The sense that all human associations are pointless because they are subject to sudden irrational termination may make individuals avoid meaningful interpersonal relationships.

PUTTING FEAR OF NUCLEAR THREAT IN PERSPECTIVE

Research studies have suggested that many children are deeply affected by fear of the nuclear threat; however, not all children appear to be equally anxious about the issue. Personal or family concerns may present a more immediate threat for many children. Family, social, economic, and educational status as well as the concern of parents about nuclear issues appear to influence children's awareness and fears (Coles, 1986). "Some of us have the leisure to worry about some issues that others ignore, because they are overwhelmed by different issues" (p. 280).

Psychologists need to assess young people's concerns in the context of normal developmental needs and anxieties. The result of one study of adolescents found that the fear of nuclear war was rated third behind the fear of a parent dying and the fear of getting bad grades (Beardslee & Mack, 1982).

Before adults can assess the effect of this issue on children, they must explore their own reactions to the nuclear threat. Becoming informed about nuclear facts, talking to others about one's own fears and defenses, exploring appropriate materials to share with children, and determining action-related responses may provide a starting point for adults who wish to help children cope with this problem.

Most children who have been surveyed about this issue have suggested that they feel that there is no one with whom they may discuss the nuclear problem. Hence, it is important to create opportunities for children to be able to talk about their concerns. Articulating their thoughts and emotions about the nuclear threat may help both children and adults to overcome some of the anxiety and feelings of helplessness. In addition children will have the opportunity to see adults as role models for facing difficult issues, sharing confidences, and seeking solutions to problems.

ALTERNATIVE ACTIONS

Dealing with children's concerns about nuclear threat requires choosing from many possible assessment, educational, and therapeutic methods. Psychologists who wish to choose appropriate approaches will first need to consider the following points:

1. Determine the developmental level of the children under consideration. The expression of their concerns regarding the nuclear threat will relate to developmental stages and tasks and what they are able to understand. For instance, young children aged 3–7 years are by nature egocentric and perceive the world as revolving around them. They are also limited by their concrete thinking ability and can perceive the world and concepts such as time only in terms of their own experience. Their understanding of nuclear war will also be impeded by their narrow experience and limited ability, because of the concreteness of their thinking, to put information into some sort of meaningful framework. Older children can begin to think abstractly and understand educational materials related to this subject.
2. Consider how effectively the children's basic needs are being met. Maslow (1954) suggested that higher-level needs cannot be met until basic needs are satisfied. Thus hunger, nurturance, and security issues will have priority over the nuclear threat for some children.
3. Consider the children's socioeconomic environment and their exposure to information about the nuclear threat. Families differ significantly in their awareness of nuclear issues and their openness in discussing related concerns. Parents who worry a lot tend to have children who worry a lot.
4. Be aware of current media presentations that may increase children's fears. Television appears to be the major source of nuclear information for most children. Discussions of TV programs may reduce the fearful effects of the material.
5. Create opportunities for children to talk about nuclear fear. Many young people feel they have no one with whom to discuss this problem and need to be assured that some adults are open to sharing this issue and will not minimize their concerns. It is essential that adults break the silence surrounding nuclear issues if they are to help children cope.
6. Assess the concerns of children by observing their creative play, artwork, and behavior. Psychologists are trained to be skilled observers and need to use those skills to assess the child's non-verbal messages.

If the nuclear threat is problematic for children, what can professionals do? A number of educational and therapeutic techniques can be implemented after the children's concerns and needs are assessed.

1. "Educational programs are needed which provide accurate information about nuclear science and technology and the political, historical, and cultural realities of the arms competition" (Mack, 1984a, p. 3). Suggestions for educational and curricular materials are noted at the end of this chapter.
2. Bibliotherapy and film therapy may serve to open discussion and provide a supportive environment in which children can discuss their fear of the nuclear threat.
3. Provide counseling for clients who display fear, anxiety, doubt, and/or uncertainty about nuclear threat. Ellis (1984) stated that the main purpose of counseling is to help people survive and be happy; then it is the responsibility of the psychologist to help clients to cope with external threat.
4. Serve as a resource person to parents and school personnel regarding the impact of the nuclear threat upon children and their responsibility for helping children to understand and cope with this source of disquiet.
5. Confront attitudes and prejudices that interfere with thinking. Since distrust, fear, and ideological polarization appear to have contributed to the present nuclear threat, it is important for persons to have opportunities to reexamine methods of achieving conflict resolution and cooperation. Suggesting that nuclear weapons can be controlled through peaceful negotiations may provide children with hope and alleviate a sense of helplessness. Stress the democratic process as a means of decision making.
6. Children's behavior needs to be addressed in light of psychological reactions to the nuclear threat. As psychologists look for the causes of lack of motivation, controlled substance abuse, depression, resistance to authority, and suicide, they need to consider whether these serious problems are related to the child's response to living with uncertainty about the future. Children must become aware of what is being denied by themselves and others if they are to reduce nuclear fear and choose self-actualizing behaviors.
7. Psychologists may wish to participate with other professionals in studying the effects of the nuclear threat on our society. Primary prevention requires professional involvement in controversial areas of values and may imply political overtones (Schwebel, 1984). A rationale for that involvement has been provided by Gearhart (1984) and recommended by professional organizations such as Psychologists for Social Responsibility, the National Educational Association, and the Physicians for the Prevention of Nuclear War. Awareness and involvement appear to reassure children that adults are doing something, that change can occur, and that individuals can make a difference. Meaningful activity dissipates fear (Jacobsen, 1984) and encourages the belief that persons can prevent nuclear catastrophe.

SUMMARY

The consequences of children's experience of growing up under the influence of nuclear crisis have direct implications for professionals (Schwebel, 1984) and suggest the need for case study, research, and primary prevention. School psychologists are in a position to provide leadership to schools and parents in facing this controversial and troublesome issue. They can also provide needed support to children as they attempt to grasp and cope with the challenge of living in a nuclear world. Snow and Goodman (1984) suggested that the task of professionals is to help children to become comfortable in an age of ambiguities, to make informed decisions, and to act upon them. Other important goals include encouraging critical thinking and developing problem-solving and conflict resolution skills.

Thomas (1984) suggested that humans are designed biologically as an intensely social species and have a genetically determined tendency toward affection. School psychologists may be able to help children to develop more satisfactory relationships with others through cooperation and a sense of social concern and responsibility that extends from personal to global areas.

It is important for school psychologists to make a personal and professional commitment to help children to deal with the nuclear threat through counseling and education. Creating peaceful resolution of problems is an active process for both adults and children and bridges emotional and cognitive areas.

REFERENCES

Bachman, G. (1983). American high school seniors view the military: 1976–1982. *Armed Forces and Society 10*(1), 86–104.

Beardslee, W., & Mack, J. (1982). The impact on children and adolescents of nuclear developments. *Psychological Aspects of Nuclear Development* (Task Force on Psychological Aspects of Nuclear Developments, Report 20). Washington, DC: American Psychiatric Association.

Coles, R. (1985, December 8). Children and the bomb. *New York Times Magazine,* pp. 44–62.

Coles, R. (1986). *The moral life of children.* Boston: Atlantic Monthly Press.

Eisenbud, M., Van Hoorn, J., & Gould, B. (1985). *Children, adolescents, and the threat of nuclear war: An international perspective.* Reprints available from Monika M. Eisenbud, M.D., 440 Lexington St., Newton, MA 02166.

Ellis, A. (1984). The responsibility of counselors and psychologists in preventing nuclear war. *Journal of Counseling and Development, 63*(2), 75–76.

Engel, B. (1984). Between feeling and fact: Listing to children. *Harvard Educational Review, 54*(3), 304–314.

Erickson, E. (1963). *Childhood and society* (2nd ed.). New York: Norton.

Escalona, S. (1965). Children and the threat of nuclear war. In M. Schwebel (Ed.), *Behavioral Science and Human Survival.* Palo Alto, CA: Science and Behavior Books, Inc., 201–209.

Escalona, S. (1982). Growing up with the threat of nuclear war: Some indirect effects on personality development. *American Journal of Orthopsychiatry, 52,* 600–607.

Gearhart, J. (1984). The counselor in a nuclear world: A rationale for awareness and action. *Journal of Counseling and Development, 63,* 67–72.

Goodman, L., Mack, J., Beardslee, W., & Snow, R. (1983). The threat of nuclear war and the nuclear arms race: Adolescent experience and perception. *Political Psychology, 4*(3), 501–530.

Gould, J., Berger, B., Gould, B., & Eden, E. (December, 1984). The threat of war in the minds of junior high school students in the U.S.A. Paper presented at the symposium *The psychological effect of the nuclear threat on children: Strategies for action.* Symposium conducted at University of California, Berkeley.

Jacobson, J. (1984). Beginnings. *Harvard Educational Review, 54*(3), 337–341.

Kastenbaum, R. (1979). *Humans developing — A lifespan perspective.* Boston: Allyn & Bacon.

Lifton, R. (1982). Beyond psychic numbing: A call to awareness. *American Journal of Orthopsychiatry, 52,* 619–629.

Lifton, R., & Olsen, E. (1974). *Living and dying.* New York: Praeger.

Mack, J. (1982). The perception of U.S.–Soviet intentions and other dimensions of the nuclear arms race. *American Journal of Orthopsychiatry, 52,* 590–599.

Mack, J. (1983a, September 20). *The psychological impact of the nuclear arms competition on children and adolescents.* Testimony to Select Committee on Children, Youth, and Families, United States House of Representatives.

Mack, J. (1983b, October 19). What Russian children are thinking about nuke weapons. *New Haven Register.*

Mack, J. (1984a). Research on the impact of the nuclear arms race on children in the U.S.A. *Children and Nuclear War.* Reprinted from International Physicians for the Prevention of Nuclear War Report, Vol. 2, No. 7, pp. 1–3.

Mack, J. (1984b). Resistances to knowing in the nuclear age. *Harvard Educational Review, 54*(3), 260–270.

Maslow, A. (1954). *Motivation and personality.* New York: Harper and Row.

Reifel, S. (1984). Children living with nuclear threat. *Young Children, 39,* 74–80.

Rogers, C. R. (1982). A psychologist looks at nuclear war: Its threat, its possible prevention. *Journal of Humanistic Psychology, 22*(4), 9–20.

Schwebel, M. (1965). Nuclear cold war: student opinion and professional responsibility. In M. Schwebel (Ed.), *Behavioral Science and Human Survival.* Palo Alto, CA: Science and Behavior Books, Ins., 210–223.

Schwebel, M. (1984). Growing up with the bomb: Professional roles. *Journal of Counseling and Development, 63,* 73–74.

Snow, R., & Goodman, L. (1984). Decision making in a nuclear age. *Journal of Education, 166*(1), 103–107.

Taipale, V. (1984). European research on children and war. *Children and Nuclear War.* Reprinted from International Physicians for the Prevention of Nuclear War Report, Vol. 2, No. 1, pp. 7–8.

Thomas, L. (1984). Lewis Thomas discusses the threat of nuclear war. *Harvard Educational Review, 54*(3), 251–259.

Tizard, B. (1984). Problematic aspects of nuclear education. *Harvard Educational Review, 54*(3), 271–281.

BIBLIOGRAPHY: PROFESSIONALS

Educators for Social Responsibility. (1982). *Dialogue: A teaching guide to nuclear issues.* Cambridge, MA: Educators for Social Responsibility.
Adopts the premise that the issue of nuclear war can be dealt with only by older students, those in grades 7–12. Although sections are provided for elementary school students, they cover themes like cooperation, sharing "scary things," and peace.

French, D., Greeley, K., & Markowitz, S. (1983). *Crossroads: Quality of life in a nuclear world: A high school social studies curriculum.* Boston: Jobs With Peace.

French, D., Greeley, K., Markowitz, S., & Zane, R. (1983). *Crossroads: Quality of life in a nuclear world: A high school English curriculum.* Boston: Jobs With Peace.

French, D., & Phillips, C. (1983). *Crossroads: Quality of life in a nuclear world: A high school science curriculum.* Boston: Jobs With Peace.
These three curricula accomplish a great deal by breaking the silence that most commercial texts have maintained about the threat of nuclear war. Shortcomings include some adults moralizing, vagueness, and over simplification.

Children and Fears and Phobias

Thomas R. Kratochwill, Cynthia Sanders, and Stacy Wiemer
University of Wisconsin-Madison

Richard J. Morris
University of Arizona

BACKGROUND

Psychologists and educators regard fear as a normal part of the child's development. The expression of fear is regarded as a positive feature in that normal fears help children cope with the challenges they face. In this regard fears are a normal way for children to adapt to their environment and deal with various stressors in daily life.

In recent years there has been increased concern about understanding how fears develop and the relation between normal fears and the development of more severe fears called "clinical fears" or "phobias." This chapter provides an overview of some definitional issues in children's fears and phobias, reviews some of the common fears and phobias that children and adolescents are likely to experience, discusses some theories related to the development of more severe phobias or debilitating fears, and reviews some common psychological intervention strategies that are often employed by mental health professionals to treat children's fears and phobic disorders.

Fear vs. Phobia: Definitional Issues

Professionals have struggled with developing adequate definitions of fears, phobias, and related emotional states for many years. In fact, in the professional literature a great deal of confusion regarding definitions and criteria for definition is apparent. What one finds is a great deal of interchanging and mixing of terms such as fear, phobia, anxiety, stress, and worry. However, some authors have made distinctions between fears and phobias. For example, Marks (1969) noted that there are four criteria that distinguish a phobia from a fear. Specifically, he argued that a phobia is a special form of fear that (a) is out of proportion to the demands of a situation, (b) cannot be explained or reasoned away, (c) is beyond voluntary control, and (d) leads to avoidance of the feared situation (Marks, 1969, p. 3). Subsequently, Miller, Barrett, and Hampe (1974) proposed additional criteria, noting that phobia persists over an extended period of time, is unadaptive, and is not age- or stage-specific. Graziano, DeGiovanni, and Garcia (1979) used the term *clinical fear* to describe those with a duration of over 2 years, or an intensity that is debilitating to the client's life routine (p. 805).

An example of a childhood fear that would meet the phobia criteria described above was a case presented to one of the authors several years ago in a school setting:

> When Paul was approximately 5 years old, he had a rather bad experience in the family bathroom. Apparently one day when sitting on the stool a bookshelf mounted above the toilet fell down on him and caused him to be lodged into the toilet. Fortunately, the parents were present and were able to assist him. Although he demonstrated an immediate fear of going back into the bathroom and using the stool, his parents were able to overcome this fear relatively quickly. In the meantime,

his father had again mounted the bookshelf on the bathroom wall. Unfortunately, some time later the exact same incident occurred again. To make matters worse, the second time his parents were not readily available to assist him. He apparently was lodged in the toilet for an extended period of time and became extremely terrified. After this experience Paul would not enter the bathroom. To accommodate this fear his parents placed a small portable potty in the kitchen for Paul to use.

In addition to being afraid to use the bathroom after these two experiences, Paul also developed a more severe phobic reaction to other toilets, including those in public places and in his half-day kindergarten school. In order to avoid the bathroom at school, he was able to go to the bathroom at home in the morning and then once he arrived home at noon. In general, he was able to avoid using public bathrooms. Unfortunately, there were accidents when he was required to use a bathroom, but owing to his rather severe phobic reaction, he did not. At the time the case was brought to the attention of the school psychologist, school staff were considering retaining Paul for another year in kindergarten. In this way, the school psychologist fortunately became involved in the case and the parents received the professional assistance they needed to help Paul overcome his phobia.

This case demonstrates that a particular kind of fear might develop as a consequence of certain specific negative emotional experiences. In fact, most children recover from these aversive experiences if they are not too intense and do not occur very often. However, in Paul's case it was obvious that the two experiences were intense enough for him to develop a rather severe clinical fear, or phobia.

Another term that is commonly used to describe children's fears, phobias, and related states is *anxiety*. Traditionally, anxiety is used in an explanatory role. For example, children are said to be disruptive because they are anxious. Or children are described as dispositionally anxious. An alternative to this traditional notion of anxiety is the conceptualization, that we find useful, presented by Nietzel and Bernstein (1981), that involves four aspects of anxiety within a social learning context: In this conceptualization it is proposed that (a) anxiety is not a trait or personality characteristic that is internal to the individual; (b) it can be acquired through different learning mechanisms; (c) it consists of several response components; and (d) anxiety response channels are not highly correlated (pp. 16–19).

The latter two dimensions of anxiety need to be elaborated, since they form the basis of how fears, phobias, anxiety, and related terms might be defined in terms of children's actual reactions. To begin with, anxiety (or fears and phobias) can be conceptualized in terms of three response systems or channels (Lang, 1978a, 1978b) — motor, cognitive, and physiological. The cognitive is a subjective system in which the child self-reports cognitions, feelings, and emotions associated with the fear. For example, a child might report being afraid of dogs at either the approach or even the thought of dogs. This kind of self-report suggests both a cognitive and a motor element associated with the fear.

The physiological channel or system involves reactions of the sympathetic portion of the autonomic nervous system. For example, a child might show basic physiological reactions such as elevated blood pressure, heart rate, or respiration rate as well as a galvanic skin response in anticipation of some feared event. Finally, a motor system or channel involves overt behavior avoidance responses in the presence of certain stimuli.

It is very useful to define children's fears, phobias and anxiety in the context of the three systems or channels. Thus, evidence of fear, phobia, or anxiety can be obtained from any one or any combination of the three systems. Interestingly, research has indicated that the three systems do not necessarily correlate highly when all three are assessed simultaneously and subjects are presented with a stimulus that is purportedly fearful.

DEVELOPMENT

Number of Fears

Fears and phobias are found in children from infancy through adolescence and into the adult years. The number of fears exhibited in children does appear to vary according to the age of the child. Jersild and Holmes (1935) concluded that four to five fears were exhibited by 2- through 6-year-olds as reported by their mothers and teachers. Eme and Schmidt (1978) also reported that four to five fears appeared in their sample of 9-year-old children. In addition, a specific fear was reported at least once for 90% of the 2- to 14-year-olds sampled by MacFarlane, Allen, and Hozik (1954). Of the 482 mothers interviewed by Lapouse and Monk (1959), 43% reported greater than seven fears in the 6-through 12-year-old group. More recently, Ollendick (1983) concluded that 8- through 12-year-olds averaged from 9 to 13 fears as reported by 217 mothers.

Of the 612 mothers who completed a fear inventory in an investigation by Stanley and O'Donnell (1984) 10–20% reported that their 6- through 16-year-old children had greater than seven fears of an intense severity. However, at each age level, 40–58% of the males sampled had fewer than five reported fears, as did 26–36% of the female sample.

Some investigators have noted a decrease in the number of fears as age increases (Bauer, 1976; MacFarlane et al., 1954). Yet, other investigators have found no such developmental differences; for example, MacFarlane et al. (1954), Jersild and Holmes (1935), and Lapouse and Monk (1959) found that the number of fears reported in their samples decreased until age 11, where the number peaks and then declines once again at age 12.

Thus, the number of fears do tend to fluctuate from four to more than seven in various studies that have examined this question. Also, it has been found that severe fears tend to be experienced by a fairly large proportion of children and adolescents.

Types of Fears of Children at Different Ages

An important focus of normative investigation on children's fears has been on the unique fears that children experience at different age levels.

Fears Exhibited in 2- Through 6-year-old Children. Children from the ages 2 through 6 years appear to have less "reality-based" fears than those of other age groups. One study reported that 74% of the 19 kindergarten students interviewed feared ghosts and monsters (Bauer, 1976). Conversely, only 5% of the 20 sixth graders sampled acknowledged such fears. Maurer (1965) asked children aged 5–6 what things they were afraid of. Their responses included ghosts and monsters as well. Jersild and Holmes (1935) reported similar findings. These authors as well as others (Lapouse & Monk, 1959; Maurer, 1965; Bauer, 1976) reported that children say that the dark, animals, dogs, and bugs are common fears. Generally, it appears that children aged 2–6 years have more global and, from an adult perspective, irrational fears.

Fears Exhibited in 7- Through 12-year-old Children. Children between the ages of 7 and 12 years appear to exhibit fears reflecting threatening situations, the consequences of which are more readily identifiable. These children appear to be concerned primarily over bodily injury, physical damage, and various natural events (Bauer, 1976; Eme & Schmidt, 1978; Ollendick, 1983; Stanley & O'Donnell, 1984; Miller et al., 1974; Moracco & Camilleri, 1983). It also appears that various school-related fears develop at this time, including such matters as fear of failing a test (Orton, 1982) and fear of getting poor grades (Moracco & Camilleri, 1983).

Although physical injury and school-related fears are reported in much of the incidence research, there is some diversity in the kinds of fears reported by students. For example, Croake and Knox (1971) asked 968 third- and sixth-grade students to rate items on a fear survey schedule. They found that political fears emerged as the most prevalent, whereas these children "hardly ever" worried about animals.

Angelino et al. (1956) reported children aged 9–12 years listed social fears as well as scool-related fears as a primary concern. Lapouse and Monk (1959) found similar results in light of their sample of 482 6- through 12-year-olds. In an investigation by Moracco and Camilleri (1983), 121 third-grade students completed a fear survey schedule that indicated that the most common worry was "afraid something will happen to mother or father."

Thus, research has indicated that bodily dangers, natural events, and school-related fears seem to be the most prevalent for children aged 7–12, although there are additional fears that do appear in some studies. Generally, the fears are reality-based and perceptually threatening.

Fears Exhibited in 13- Through 18-year-olds. Few investigations have focused on the fears of adolescence compared with studies of younger children. Croake and Knox (1971) reported political fears to be the most prevalent in 212 ninth-grade students who completed a fear survey schedule. Worries about personal social relations as well as physical injury have also been reported. Bamber (1974) asked Irish-American adolescents (1,112 students) to complete a fear survey schedule and found that social rejection, social isolation, and fear of tissue damage were the primary concerns.

Thus, it appears that fear of physical danger persists from late childhood into adolescence. Fears about social relations also become more apparent during this developmental period. Unfortunately, we know less about the fears in this particular group of children than in younger children.

PUTTING CHILDREN'S FEARS AND PHOBIAS IN PERSPECTIVE

How fears and phobias develop in children can be understood through looking at the many various theories that have been advanced to explain these phenomena. Basically four different theoretical perspectives have been advanced in behavioral psychology to conceptualize the development of fears and phobias, including the positions of Pavlov (1927), Skinner (1938, 1953); Hull (1943), Mower (1960), and Bandura (1969, 1977a, b).

One of the oldest fear development studies in behavioral psychology was presented by Watson and Rayner (1920); it involved an 11-month-old child named Albert. These investigators reported that through a classical conditioning procedure they had been able to teach the child to become afraid of a white rat, and to generalize this conditioned fear to other animals and objects. It was reported that the rat did not elicit any fear reaction from the child until after its presence had been paired with a loud noise.

Although this particular investigation spawned a large number of further empirical investigations into the development of fears, most observers regard the original Watson and Rayner (1920) study as hopelessly confounded (Harris, 1979). A major problem with the investigation was establishing whether a classical conditioning really ever occurred.

Another theoretical framework that integrates both classical and instrumental conditioning was presented by Mower (1960) and labeled a two-factor learning theory. Mower combined classical conditioning with Hull's instrumental learning to account for the conditioning and maintenance of fears. For example, he noted that fear was a classically conditioned response (CR) that came about by pairing an aversive unconditioned stimulus (UCS) with a previously neutral stimulus (CS). The conditioned fear response (CR) was said to motivate avoidance behavior whenever the CS was present. This avoidance behavior reduced the CR, which in turn, reinforced the organism to engage in the avoidance behavior.

Mower's initial work facilitated Wolpe's (1958) conceptualization of systematic desensitization in treatment of fears, phobias, and anxiety. Wolpe noted that neurotic behavior (such as a severe fear) was a persistent and unadaptive habit that was something individuals had learned and therefore could unlearn. He argued that these types of behavior patterns were learned through temporal contiguity of the stimulus and response (classical conditioning) and maintained by drive reduction (Hullian instrumental learning).

Another behavioral theory that accounts for the development of fears is based on the operant conditioning model (Skinner, 1938, 1953). In this theoretical model the avoidance response, or motor behavior, is said to be reinforced through various conditions. For example, parents or teachers might reinforce a child's avoidance of certain situations or objects. This, in turn, strengthens the actual fear and leads to future motor avoidance of the stimulus. Basically, the operant framework assumes that fear responses are learned and aspects of the environment are responsible for this learning and for maintenance of the behavior. In this regard, classical conditioning is not considered necessary for fear responses to occur.

A final behavioral model involves social learning theory (Bandura, 1969, 1977a). In this theoretical model vicarious learning conditions fears. In this case the individual acquires a fear by directly observing exposure of a model to a traumatic or aversive event. Social learning theory assumes that psychological functioning involves "a reciprocal interaction" between the subject and the environment. This theoretical model also accommodates the belief that a great deal of self-directed behavior is involved in human performance.

Both the operant and the social learning models have a great deal of empirical support compared with the other models presented. However, neither model has done particularly well in accounting for a broad range of children's fears and phobias. Nor have investigators done extensive research work with children and adolescents.

ALTERNATIVE ACTIONS

A variety of psychological intervention procedures have been used for children experiencing a broad range of fears and phobias. A number of major books have been published dealing with treatment of childhood and adolescent fears, phobias, and anxiety (Kellerman, 1981; Morris & Kratochwill, 1983; — see also the annotated bibliography). Much of the published empirical literature suggests that behavior therapy procedures can be used effectively to reduce various fears and phobias in children and adolescents. We will review below some major behavior therapy methods that can be used to intervene with children experiencing these difficulties as well as outline some strategies that need to be taken into account in selecting a treatment procedure. These strategies will be useful to professionals and parents in deciding whether a formal intervention program should be developed and in preventing the development of a severe disorder.

There are four major behavior therapy methods that are used to treat children experiencing fears and phobias: desensitization (with variations), contingency management procedures, modeling procedures, and cognitive behavioral methods. Flooding therapies are sometimes considered a part of the major behavior therapies, but we do not recommend these procedures and they will not be discussed here.

Systematic Desensitization

Systematic desensitization was developed in the early 1950s by Wolpe (1958). In this form of intervention it is assumed that a fear or anxiety response is learned and that it can be inhibited by substituting an activity that is antagonistic to this response. Usually relaxation or some type of induced state of calmness is used to inhibit the anxiety response during treatment. Thus, the desensitization procedure will involve exposing children in small graduated steps to some fear stimulus while they are performing the actual activity antagonistic to the feelings of tension or arousal. The graduated exposure to the fear or anxiety event can take place in real life or in an imaginary context.

Systematic desensitization has three major components: relaxation training, development of an anxiety hierarchy, and the actual systematic desensitization treatment procedure. In the relaxation phase the student is taught methods to relax, essentially through relaxing and tensing various muscle groups. In anxiety hierarchy development a therapist designs, with the client's assistance, a hierarchy of various situations or events from the least to the most anxiety-provoking. The hierarchies usually differ in respect to the number of people present, particular settings in which fears occur, and the number of items in the hierarchy. During systematic desensitization proper the therapist actually pairs relaxation training with the components of the hierarchy. The client is asked to imagine each scene as vividly as possible while maintaining a relaxed condition. The hierarchy elements developed during the previous phase are then presented in ascending order while relaxation is paired with the condition.

There are a number of variations of systematic desensitization. For example, children can often participate in systematic desensitization in a group format. In this case students participate at the pace of the slowest member in the group. *In vivo desensitization* involves exposing students to actual situations in the hierarchy rather than relying on the imagination. Such procedures would have obvious benefits for children who are unable to imagine or whose treatment might be better focused on real as opposed to symbolic representations of the problem area. Another variation is called *emotive imaginary;* it involves having children listen to the therapist describe particular anxiety-arousing scenes or scenarios that concern their favorite hero, such as He-Man or Superman. Then they are requested to imagine a favorite hero successfully overcoming the anxiety or fear during a particular scene. Other variations of systematic desensitization involve contact desensitization and self-control desensitization (see Morris & Kratochwill, 1983).

Contingency Management

Contingency management procedures are associated with the operant or applied behavior analysis model of treatment. As noted above, this particular model focuses on the environmental consequences for learning and unlearning of fear-related responses. A most common therapeutic procedure used within contingency management is positive reinforcement. This procedure has been used alone and in combination with other behavioral procedures to facilitate children's adaptation to settings that had previously been deemed fearful. For example, in one project Vaal (1973) used a contingency contracting system for a 13-year-old-boy who had previously been afraid to attend school and the contingency management program was set up to gradually get the child back to school. He was permitted various privileges, such as going bowling, attending a basketball game, that were contingent on meeting certain criteria for school attendance. The treatment program, that lasted approximately 6 weeks, was generally successful. A variety of other behavioral procedures have also been used within the contingency management or operant approach to treatment. These procedures are outlined in great detail in many child therapy textbooks (see Morris & Kratochwill, 1984; Ollendick & Cerny, 1984).

Modeling Interventions

Modeling treatment approaches are associated with the social learning theory of Bandura and his coworkers. The modeling procedures generally consist of having the model, that can be a therapist, teacher, or parent, model or demonstrate certain positive responses for the client observer. The model engages in certain behaviors that are fear-provoking, or result in anxiety for the client. The following requirements must be met in order for modeling to be successful: Clients must (a) attend to certain aspects of the modeling situation, (b) retain what has been learned in the modeling situation, (c) reproduce or match what has been observed, and (d) be motivated to carry out the observed behavior (Bandura, 1977a). The therapist must also be able to guarantee that the model does not experience any perceived or unsafe consequences in the fear or anxiety situation. Moreover, the model is typically instructed to approach the target situation gradually and with caution so as to enhance the modeling effect.

Modeling can occur in either a live or symbolic mode. For example, in live modeling clients view children participating successfully in various activities such as going to school without any fear. Symbolic modeling, a more common strategy, involves having children view a tape of individuals like themselves participating in a fear-laden experience. For example, Melamed and Siegel (1975) examined the relative effectiveness of symbolic modeling in reducing the anxiety level of children who were facing hospitalization and surgery. The children ranged in age from 4 to 12 years and were all being hospitalized for the first time and scheduled for elective surgery. The 30 children arrived at the hospital 1 hour prior to admission time and viewed a 16-minute film, *Ethan Has an Operation.* The authors described the film in the following manner:

> [The film] depicts a 7-year-old white male who has been hospitalized for a hernia operation . . . [it] consists of 15 scenes showing various events that most children encounter when hospitalized for elective surgery from the time of admission to the time of discharge including the child's orientation to the hospital ward and medical personnel such as the surgeon and anesthesiologist; having a blood test and exposure to standard hospital equipment; separation from the mother; and scenes in the operating and recovery rooms. In addition to explanations of the hospital procedures provided by the medical staff, various scenes are narrated by the child, who describes his feelings and concerns . . . at each stage of the hospital experience. Both the child's behavior and verbal remarks exemplify anxiety and apprehension; he is able to overcome his initial fears [coping model] and complete each event in a successful and nonanxious manner. (Melamed & Siegel, 1975, p. 514)

The results of this investigation showed that the film modeling condition significantly reduced measures of situational anxiety in children compared with measures in a control condition, and that these significant differences were maintained at the follow-up period.

Thus, modeling treatments can be very helpful in working with children. Unfortunately, while modeling procedures have been used extensively with children's non-school-related fears and anxieties, relatively little work has been published on school-related fears and anxieties other than the work on the treatment of social withdrawal/social isolation (Morris & Kratochwill, 1985).

Self-control Methods

Self-control methods of treatment are typically associated with cognitive behavior modification procedures (Meichenbaum & Genest, 1980). There are relatively few treatment studies focused on the school-related fears and anxieties of children and adolescents (Ramirez, Kratochwill, & Morris, in press). The underlying approach in self-control therapies is the view that cognitive processes contribute substantially to any behavior change program that is established, and that children and adolescents can regulate their own behavior. Also, therapists serve the role of instigator or motivator, but the individual child is primarily responsible for carrying out the intervention program.

Self-control procedures involve the following major components of the therapeutic approach: (a) becoming aware of negative thinking styles that impede performance and lead to an emotional upset and inadequate performance, (b) generating in collaboration with the trainer, a set of incompatible self-statements, rules, and strategies that the student can employ, and (c) learning specific adaptive cognitive behavioral skills (Meichenbaum & Genest, 1980, p. 403). Clients must be aware of their anxiety reactions, possibly across the three response channels, in order for the program to be effective. An intervention reported by Craddock, Colter, and Jason (1978) illustrates the use of a cognitive self-control program. These authors studied the relative effectiveness of cognitive behavior rehearsal and a systematic desensitization program on reduction of speech anxiety in highschool freshman girls. In the cognitive intervention treatment the students were provided a treatment rationale and the necessary steps that they needed to take into account in preparation and delivery of a speech. The students were also guided through imaginary exercises. Subsequently, treatment sessions consisted of learning 18 hierarchical steps in preparing and giving a speech as well as studying potential coping strategies that could be employed prior to and during the speech. For example, a girl might say to herself, "I can handle this step by taking a deep breath and remaining calm." Items in the hierarchy were presented for 1 minute, and then the students were requested to imagine themselves using a coping strategy at each step. When these results were compared to a more conventional systematic desensitization procedure, the cognitive rehearsal group demonstrated a significant reduction relative to a delayed treatment control group in scores on a speech anxiety measure. However, on motor measures such as stammering and hand tremors, no differences were found in this study.

SUMMARY

Relatively few guidelines have been established for selecting a specific intervention program to work with children experiencing fears, phobias, or anxiety. However, Barrios, Hartmann, and Shigetomi (1981) have raised some important issues related to making the decision whether treatment is indicated or not, as well as some guidelines for selecting specific procedures. First of all, taking a developmental perspective on children's fears, phobias, and anxiety reactions provides some helpful information for deciding whether intervention should be scheduled, given that much of the available evidence suggests that many common fears are part of normal development and are not a cause for alarm (Harris & Ferrari, 1983). Some specific questions raised by Barrios et al. (1981) can help in making these decisions. The first issue that needs to be addressed is who is actually complaining? Since most children are not self-referred to treatment, but rather are brought to mental health professionals by parents, teachers, or others, it is important to emphasize that the perceptions of the adult are very important. Therapists also need to consider that a child may not necessarily be motivated to participate in treatment. Under these conditions it may be possible that the adult demands or specific expectations of fearless behavior by the child are unreasonable. Thus, the focus of intervention may be on the parent or the adult careprovider rather than the child.

A second issue is whether the actual fear behavior can be considered a problem. As implied above, in defining a clinical fear or phobia, a problem is found to exist when the behavior disrupts the person's overall functioning, ability to adjust to the environment, and sense of comfort, satisfaction, and freedom, as well as the pursuit of various personal goals (Karoly, 1975). Thus, it is important to take a family systems perspective when making a decision to treat. Also, one must be concerned with how fears are related to other areas of functioning. It may be that another major problem should be the central focus for an intervention program. Thus, a child's fears or anxieties may be a reaction to other kinds of difficulties. Moreover, the child's fear may be linked to certain family dysfunctions or even child abuse.

When developing an intervention program for a child experiencing a severe fear, it is necessary to consider the cost of the treatment and whether there is any demonstrated effectiveness of the procedure. A great deal of time, money, and effort often goes into treating a problem that is rather isolated and may become nonproblematic as the client gets older. Finally, an important question is what should be different for the child in the absence of the problem? Basically, the mental health professional must consider short- and long-term consequences for a child when a decision is made to treat or not to treat. Answers to the aforementioned questions will determine whether more serious emotional problems for the child can be prevented, or whether immediate intervention for more specific types of fears is necessary.

When selecting an intervention program for a child experiencing fear, phobia, anxiety, it is also necessary to consider a series of questions that relate to conducting a carefully developed functional analysis of the problem. We have found the guidelines presented by Kanfer and Saslow (1969) to be useful in this process. Specifically, one question that needs to be addressed is what is the target response? As noted above, anxiety or fear can occur within physiological, cognitive, or motor response domains. Within the cognitive fear domains various images, thoughts, and feelings may be an important focus of the intervention. In addition, the child may demonstrate problematic motor responses that involve escape or avoidance of various situations, such as school. In this regard, it is important to keep in mind that the various fear behaviors the child is demonstrating may be appropriate in a harmful, dangerous, or aversive environment. The child may also display social skills deficits or inability to perform various academic skills. Thus, the appropriate focus of intervention may actually be on teaching social skills or various areas of the academic curriculum.

A second question is under what conditions does the problem response occur? A careful functional analysis of the environment can further help the clinician to determine whether there are basic skills deficits involved or whether there is a conditioned or learned emotional reaction to some anxiety-provoking stimulus.

Related to this issue are the characteristics of the individual child that should be considered prior to the selection of treatment. The more common ones include, treatments that involve self-control or desensitization, or the child's skills in language and imagery. Generally, the child's ability to participate in a self-management program should be assessed before this type of intervention is established.

Various aspects of the child's environment must be assessed when the treatment program is selected. This will often include a comprehensive assessment of the behavior, skills, and motivations of any adults involved, as they might contribute to the problem. In addition, characteristics of siblings, teachers, or others who are related to the child in the social environment would need to be assessed.

REFERENCES

Angelino, J., Dollins, J., & Mech, E. (1956). Trends in the "fears and worries" of school children as related to socioeconomic status and age. *Journal of Genetic Psychology, 89,* 263–276.

Bamber, J. H. (1974). The fears of adolescents. *Journal of Genetic Psychology, 125,* 127–140.

Bandura, A. (1969). *Principles of behavior modification.* New York: Holt, Rinehart, & Winston.

Bandura, A. (1977a). *Social learning theory.* Englewood Cliffs, NJ: Prentice-Hall.

Bandura, A. (1977b). Self-efficacy: Toward a unifying theory of behavior change. *Psychological Review, 84,* 191–215.

Barrios, B. A., Hartmann, D. P., & Shigetomi, C. (1981). Fears and anxieties in children. In J. E. Mash & L. G. Terdal (Eds.), *Behavioral assessment of childhood disorders* (pp. 259–304). New York: Guilford.

Bauer, D. (1976). An exploratory study of developmental changes in children's fears. *Journal of Child Psychology and Psychiatry, 17,* 69–74.

Craddock, C., Cotler, S., & Jason, L. A. (1978). Primary prevention: Immunization of children for speech anxiety. *Cognitive Therapy and Research, 2,* 389–396.

Croake, J. W., & Knox, F. H. (1971). A second look at adolescent fears. *Adolescence, 6,* 279–284.

Croake, J. W., & Knox, F. H. (1973). The changing nature of children's fears. *Child Study Journal, 3,* 91–105.

Eme, R., & Schmidt, D. (1978). The stability of children's fears. *Child Development, 49,* 1277–1279.

Graziano, A. M., DeGiovanni, I. S., & Garcia, K. A. (1979). Behavioral treatments of children's fears: A review. *Psychological Bulletin, 86,* 804–830.

Harris, B. (1979). Whatever happened to Little Albert? *American Psychologist, 34,* 151–160.

Harris, S. L., & Ferrari, M. (1983). The development factor in child behavior therapy. *Behavior Therapy, 14,* 54–72.

Hull, C. (1943). *Principles of behavior.* New York: Appleton-Century-Crofts.

Jersild, A. T., & Holmes, F. B. (1935). Methods of overcoming children's fears. *Journal of Psychology, 1,* 75–104.

Kanfer, F. H., & Saslow, G. (1969). Behavioral diagnosis. In C. M. Franks (Eds.), *Behavior therapy: Appraisal and status.* New York: McGraw-Hill.

Karoly, P. (1975). Operant methods. In F. H. Kanfer & A. P. Goldstein (Eds.), *Helping people change.* New York: Pergamon.

Kellerman, J. (1981). *Helping the fearful child.* New York: Norton.

Lang, P. J. (1978a). Anxiety: Towards a psychological definition. In H. S. Akiskal & W. L. Webb (Eds.), *Psychiatric diagnosis: Exploration of biological criteria.* New York: Spectrum.

Lang, P. J. (1978b). Self-efficacy theory: Thoughts on cognition and unification. In S. Rachman (Ed.), *Advances in Behavior Research and Therapy, 1,* 187–192.

Lapouse, R., & Monk, M. A. (1959). Fears and worries in a representative sample of children. *American Journal of Orthopsychiatry, 29,* 803–818.

MacFarlane, J. W., Allen, L., & Hozik, M. P. (1954). *A developmental study of the behavior problems of normal children between twenty-one months and fourteen years.* Berkeley, CA: University of California Press.

Marks, I. M. (1969). *Fears and phobias.* New York: Academic.

Maurer, A. (1965). What children fear. *Journal of Genetic Psychology, 106,* 265–277.

Meichenbaum, D., & Genest, M. (1980). Cognitive behavior modification: An integration of cognitive and behavioral methods. In F. H. Kanfer & A. P. Goldstein (Eds.), *Helping people change* (2nd ed.) (pp. 390–422). Elmsford, NY: Pergamon.

Melamed, B., & Siegel, L. (1975). Reduction of anxiety in children facing hospitalization and surgery by use of filmed modeling. *Journal of Consulting and Clinical Psychology, 43,* 511–521.

Miller, L. C., Barrett, C. L., & Hampe, E. (1974). Phobias of childhood in a prescientific era. In A. Davids (Eds.), *Child personality and psychopathology: Current topics* (pp. 89–134). New York: Wiley.

Moracco, J., & Camilleri, J. (1983). A study of fears in elementary school children. *Elementary School Guidance & Counseling,* 82–87.

Morris, R. J., & Kratochwill, T. R. (1983). *Treating children's fears and phobias: A behavioral approach.* Elmsford, NY: Pergamon.

Morris, R. J., & Kratochwill, T. R. (1984). *The practice of child therapy.* New York: Pergamon.

Morris, R. J., & Kratochwill, T. R. (1985). Behavioral treatment of children's fears and phobias: A review. *School Psychology Review, 14,* 84–93.

Mower, O. H. (1960). *Learning theory and behavior.* New York: Wiley.

Nietzel, M. T., & Bernstein, D. A. (1981). Assessment of anxiety and fear. In M. Hersen & A. S. Bellack (Eds.), *Behavioral assessment: A practical handbook* (2nd ed.) (pp. 215–245). New York: Pergamon.

Ollendick, T. H. (1983). Reliability and validity of the revised fear survey schedule for children (FSSC-R). *Behavior Research and Therapy, 21,* 685–692.

Ollendick, T. H., & Cerny, J. A. (1984). *Clinical behavior therapy with children.* New York: Plenum.

Orton, G. (1982). A comparative study of children's worries. *Journal of Psychology, 110,* 153–162.

Pavlov, I. P. (1927). *Conditioned reflexes* (translated by G. V. Anrep). London: Oxford University Press.

Ramirez, S. Z., Kratochwill, T. R., & Morris, R. J. (in press). Cognitive behavioral treatment of childhood anxiety disorders. In L. Michelson & M. Asher (Eds.), *Cognitive–behavioral assessment and treatment of anxiety disorders.* New York: Guilford.

Skinner, B. F. (1938). *The behavior of organisms.* New York: Appleton-Century-Crofts.

Skinner, B. F. (1953). *Science and human behavior.* New York: MacMillan.

Stanley, A., & O'Donnell, J. (1984). A developmental analysis of mother's reports of normal children's fears. *Journal of Genetic Psychology, 144,* 165–178.

Vaal, J. J. (1973). Applying contingency contracting to a school phobic: A case study. *Journal of Behavior Therapy and Experimental Psychiatry, 4,* 371–373.

Watson, J. B., & Rayner, P. (1920). Conditioned emotional reactions. *Journal of Experimental Psychology, 3,* 1–14.

Wolpe, J. (1958). *Reciprocal inhibition therapy.* Stanford, CA: Stanford University Press.

BIBLIOGRAPHY: PROFESSIONALS

Kahn, J. H., Nursten, J. P., & Carroll, H. C. (1981). *Unwillingly to school: School phobia or school refusal: A psycho-social problem* (3rd ed.). Oxford: Pergamon.

This is a dynamically oriented text that deals with a wide range of issues surrounding school phobia and refusal to attend school. Included are chapters dealing with an overview of the problem, facilities for the treatment of school refusal, and various professional approaches to dealing with the issues of treatment.

Morris, R. J., & Kratochwill, T. R. (1983). *Treating children's fears and phobias: A behavioral approach.* Elmsford, NY: Pergamon.

This is a behavioral theory-oriented professional resource book that includes a comprehensive review of research in the field. The book includes chapters on diagnosis, incidence, and assessment. Also included are chapters reviewing systematic desensitization, flooding therapies, contingency management, modeling therapies, and self-control cognitive therapies. A comprehensive review of methodological and conceptual aspects of research is also presented.

BIBLIOGRAPHY: PARENTS

Wolman, B. B. (1978). *Children's fears: Help your child overcome the tyranny of anxieties, phobias, and fears.* New York: Signet.

This paperback book provides a traditional approach to understanding children's fears. The book includes an overview of the psychology of children's fears including, for example, a discussion of do's and don'ts for parents. Thereafter, the book includes a discussion of 53 specific fears.

BIBLIOGRAPHY: CHILDREN

There are relatively few books dealing with fears and phobias written specifically for children. However, there are some children's books that deal with fears or fear-related issues in content. These include:

Goins, E. H. (1971). *She was scared silly.* Austin, TX: Steck-Vaughn.

Leaf, M. (1948). *Boo: Who used to be scared of the dark.* New York: Random House.

The Leaf book is potentially useful because it relates the story of Boo, who is afraid of many things but is able to overcome his fears. The books are at a lower to middle elementary reading level, but can be read to the child as well as discussed by the parent.

Children and Firesetting

Melissa Gordon
Village Community School, New York, New York

BACKGROUND

For the school psychologist the problem of identifying, understanding, and responding to the juvenile firesetter is of critical concern, as reported incidence levels are quickly escalating. A recent report by the National Firehawk Foundation indicates that if children play with matches one time a fire will result in 33% of the incidents. Fires will result in 81% of all instances in which children play with matches more than once (Fahy, 1986). As scientific findings replace or at times reaffirm earlier common sense notions and casual observations about juvenile firesetting, research indicates that interest in fire is a normal phase of development, that certain factors seem to promote or limit the development of the impulse to set fires, that by addressing certain questions one can gain a clearer understanding of the act, and that there are in fact ways to effectively intervene diminish the frequency of firesetting.

During the 1970s startling facts and trends began to emerge about firesetting. Arson had increased by 325% over the past 10 years (Fisher, 1984). Firesetting seemed to be an intractable problem, increasingly a crime of the young (Sandrick, 1982). Although to date there is no sufficient centralized, nationwide data-gathering system or information dissemination network to deal with juvenile arson, certain cold, stark facts are coming to public attention: (a) The United States has the highest rate of arson in the world (Collins, 1984); (b) Children under 18 years of age are responsible for 40–70% of documented, intentionally set fires (Baizerman & Emshoff, 1984); (c) School fire statistics rose 18.5% in 1984 according to a government fire loss report (National Firehawk Foundation, 1986); (d) Fire is the second leading cause of death in childhood (Abston, cited in Fineman, 1980); (e) Setting of fires seems to rank among the nation's fastest growing crimes (Wooden, 1985).

Despite the growing evidence that the problem of juvenile arson may reach epidemic proportions, researchers are still not in full agreement about a basic fact, what constitutes a "problem" firesetter and how do these children differ from children who play with fire without the authorization or supervision of adults, but as part of a normal developmental phenomenon (Kafry, 1980). Juvenile firesetting as it exists today may be examined from a number of different perspectives: (a) the act and its consequences, (b) the motives of the firesetter, (c) the personality profile of the firesetter, and (d) the sociopsychological types of firesetters.

The Act of Firesetting

The reason for setting fire and its consequences are of primary importance to insurance companies trying to assess damage, to arson investigators and people working within the legal system who are trying to determine the effect on property and persons, and to clinicians who must try to incorporate specific knowledge about the act itself to devise a successful intervention. A child who unintentionally sets the livingroom curtains on fire with few if any repercussions for example, would receive a very different type of intervention than a child who accidentally sets the livingroom curtains on fire, inadvertently killing a sibling and burning the house down. Thus the level of emotional trauma is often independent of the motive but directly related to the consequences of the act. In addition researchers trying to operationally define firesetting consider the seriousness of the act (Jacobson, 1985), and whether it recurs (Gaynor, McLaughlin, & Hatcher, 1983) in making distinctions such as which children to include in a study and which children may be at risk for setting future fires. Finally, clinicians often monitor the behavior of a firesetting child to observe whether the act recurs as a signal of success or failure of a specific intervention (Awad & Harrison, 1955; Denholtz, 1972; Eisler, 1972).

Motivations of the Juvenile Firesetter

Specific reasons why children set fires have been described in the literature: (a) excitement, (b) enjoyment, (c) accident proneness in children who play with matches, (d) catharsis, and (e) expression of anger (Lowenstein, 1979). The "vengeful" firesetter preoccupied with fantasies of destroying others may set fire to destroy or hurt a family member who seems cold or rejecting or to get rid of a rival for attention and love (Yarnell, 1940). Some children set fires as a cry for help (Wooden & Berkey, 1984) much like the child suicide. Sometimes self-immolation fantasies are present. In recent studies of juvenile firesetters in Houston and in New York City, spite and revenge and mischief or vandalism respectively were reported as strong motives (McKinney & Corral, 1985). This suggests that besides intrapsychic conflicts, cultural milieu may have an impact on motive. The distinction between the "curiosity" versus the "pathological" firesetter (Fineman, 1980) is based on the motives of the former as exploratory and of the latter as a symptom of a deeper disturbance. This has import for the school psychologist because of strong implications for intervention. The "curiosity" firesetter in most instances benefits from a short-lived educative/therapeutic intervention plan suitable for a school-based intervention. The "pathological" firesetter in most cases needs a more thorough, prolonged, educative/psychotherapeutic intervention that may be best accomplished by outside referral.

Personality Profile of the Juvenile Firesetter

Personality profile classification is based on the assumption that there is a certain set of personality traits that distinguishes firesetters from their nonfiresetting counterparts. One of the best examples of this typing approach is exemplified in the American Psychiatric Association's *Diagnostic And Statistical Manual III,* in which firesetting is classified as "socialized nonaggressive conduct disorder," "undersocialized aggressive conduct disorder," and "pyromania," a disorder of impulse. While the first two categories may be useful for the school psychologist, the third, "pyromania" is of least relevance, since it is so rare as to be almost nonexistent in children and represents a more crystallized pattern of pathology often found in later developmental phases (Fineman, 1980). Some personality traits most frequently found in descriptions of firesetters are aggressive (Kolko, Kazdin, & Meyer, 1985; Lowenstein, 1949; Yarnell, 1940), impulsive (Rothstein, 1963; Sakheim, Vigdor, Gordon, & Helprin, 1985; Vandersall & Weiner, 1970), and deviant sexuality (Fineman, 1980; Macht & Mack, 1968; Mavromatis & Lion, 1977).

Types of Juvenile Firesetters

An alternative approach to categorization of firesetters uses a sociopsychological framework, taking into consideration interactive factors of age, motive, and personality traits. On the basis of a sample of 104 juvenile firesetters, four different types of firesetters have been isolated: (a) youngsters under age 10 who set fires by accident, (b) the largest group, older children who set fires as a call for help and have many other problems, (c) delinquents who act out against restraints in society by setting fires, and (d) the least prevalent, severely emotionally disturbed firesetters (Wooden & Berkey, 1984). A different typology based on personality traits distinguishes among 20 juvenile firesetters on the basis of (a) the "infantile," "impulsive," "regressive" type, (b) the "controlled," "constricted," and "compulsive" type, and (c) the "independent," "assertive," "pseudoimmature" type (Vandersall & Weiner, 1970).

A third typology, developed by a researcher at the U.S. Fire Administration, provides a classification of juvenile firesetters by risk factors: (a) "low risk" curiosity firesetters representing 60% of cases reported; (b) "definite risk" juvenile firesetters, representing 37% of cases reported, and (c) "extreme risk," representing 3.2% of cases reported (Fineman, cited in Fisher, 1984).

These four conceptual approaches to firesetting both highlight the complexity of the problem and suggest the possibility that firesetting does not exist as a sole symptom, but rather in constellation with other symptomatology. In this context Macht and Mack (1968) referred to firesetting as a syndrome, a term used in medical discourse to indicate a concurrence of symptoms that suggest a distinct disorder. Research demonstrates that firesetting usually does appear in concert with other symptoms. Correlational studies list at least 80 such variables. Some behavioral correlates frequently mentioned are (a) family problems such as abuse, neglect, and parental absence (Fine & Louie, 1979; Jacobson, 1985; Nurcombe, 1964); (b) school problems such as truancy and/or learning disabilities (Gruber, Heck, & Mintzer, 1981; Rothstein, 1963; Yarnell, 1940); and (c) interpersonal problems (Justice, Justice, & Kraft, 1974; Kolko et al., 1985; McGrath, Marshall, & Prior, 1979).

As more data are accumulated on juvenile firesetters, the findings indicate that it is not yet possible to accurately identify a prospective firesetter solely on the basis of any of these categorizations. What has been established is the unsettling fact that there are probably children in every school who set fires at least in play. Unless the fire is very serious, these children rarely come to the attention of the school psychologist. Although often present, firesetting is rarely *the* presenting problem. In fact it often is hidden and only materializes in specific response to the questions, "Does your child play with matches or lighters?" or "How many fires has your child set?" Most often when a child sets a fire parents extinguish it and mete out some punishment. It often goes unreported and the child goes untreated. People apparently do not fully understand the dangers of juvenile firesetting. Even when firesetting is an identified symptom, research indicates that only about one third of adults would refer a firesetting child to a mental health professional (Winget & Whitman, 1973). Yet, in the words of one expert, "America is burning and in many instances American children are igniting the torches" (Wooden, 1985, p. 23).

DEVELOPMENT

The question of how children with a natural curiosity about fire develop into recidivist firesetters is still unclear. While firesetting seems to transcend demographic boundaries (McKinney, 1985), age seems to be a determining factor that both shapes the act of firesetting and affects the way we interpret the behavior. Gender may also be a yet unexplored mediating factor in the development of firesetting.

There is no single developmental theory that can adequately explain why at one age some children are merely curious about fire, others play with fire, and some deliberately and repeatedly set fires. The first attempts at research in this area were done by psychoanalysts who proposed firesetting as a disorder reflecting the phallic–urethral phase of development (Freud, 1932; Klein, 1975; Stekel, 1924). Firesetting was equated with masturbation, and enuresis was a key symptom thought to coexist with the setting of fires. This research led to a dead end as the notion that enuresis occurs with statistically significant frequency in firesetters has not been demonstrated (Chess & Hassibi, 1978).

Other classical psychoanalytic theorists placed firesetting as a disorder reflecting problems in the oral phase of development (Arlow, 1955; Kaufman, Heins, & Reiser, 1961; Stone, cited in Fineman, 1980). They saw firesetting as a fusion of aggressive and erotic drives, i.e., setting a fire combined components of anger and sexual excitement.

The recent trend in psychoanalytic developmental theory, which deemphasizes the classic drive/discharge model and stresses the importance of the effects of the "facilitating environment" and the influence of the family in general on symptom formation, has implications for the development of the juvenile firesetter. Aggressive and erotic drives are no longer viewed as critical; instead faulty childcare and, alternatively, the absence of "good enough mothering" are implicated in the development of childhood pathology. While firesetting per se has not been studied in specific detail, it follows that an "object relations" theory of the development of the juvenile firesetter may lead to a better understanding of the problem.

In a somewhat similar vein, Fineman (1980) has adapted a social learning perspective in which he looks at firesetting as it develops over time. A normal curiosity in the young child may in some cases be reinforced by social factors (such as negative attention and power gains) surrounding the child's first experience with fire. The symptom of firesetting may then develop into a pathological, repetitive coping mechanism.

Although trying to identify firesetters on the basis of conflicts specific to developmental phase or on the basis of developmental arrests has not succeeded, there are still strong developmental considerations that should be kept in mind for work with juvenile firesetters. Around 9 or 10 years of age is the critical time when a child is no longer classified as a "curiosity" firesetter (Fineman, 1980; Wooden & Berkey, 1984). After this age any intense interest in fire play is seldom mere curiosity; it is almost invariably a clear sign of more serious underlying problems. This of course does not preclude the possibility that pathological firesetters may be found at earlier ages.

Although there are cases of very young children starting fires, children usually do not begin to set fires before the developmental age of 4 years, when most have the dexterity and cognitive ability to coordinate the act (Carter, cited in Sensor, 1978). Recent research indicates that one third of the children killed in fires in the United States started the fires themselves by playing with incendiary materials. Of those aged two and younger 14% apparently started the very fires that ended their own lives (Fahy, 1986).

Fire play seems to develop out of a normal curiosity about and attraction to fire that is most noticeable in 2 to 7-year-olds (Federal Emergency and Management Agency, U.S. Fire Administration, 1980). Although only 45% of elementary school children studied were found to play with fire, children's interest in fire is almost "universal" (Kafry, 1980). Most of this early interest should dissipate after fourth or fifth grade. Even if a child does play with fire at an early age there is no convincing evidence that it predisposes her or him to pyromania in adulthood. Some research even suggests the opposite result, that child firesetters may neutralize this desire by working in fire-related fields as adults (Wooden, 1985).

The younger children who set fires are more likely to do it by themselves in or near their own home. Older children often set fires in an interpersonal context outside or away from home (Sensor, cited in Grimes & Thomas, 1985). For a number of reasons schools are often the target. They represent a surrogate home, are an institution of authority in society to some, and a symbol of learning problems to others. The peer group often uses the school as an object of a dare. Adolescent firesetters seem to use firesetting specifically for purposes of excitement, acting in pairs with an active and a passive member (Yarnell, 1940). Firesetting arises mostly out of aggression or revenge; in adolescents it often takes on a stronger sexual connotation (Bender, cited in Shaw, 1966).

An ex post facto study of case material of known firesetters revealed that they had participated in less serious behavioral problems early in their developmental history. The behaviors seemed to escalate on a continuum from high-frequency, low-intensity acts to low-frequency, high-intensity acts (Patterson, 1982). For example, a child who lies and is disobedient (high-frequency, low-intensity acts) may be more likely to develop into a firesetter (low-frequency, high-intensity act) in later years. One of the tasks of the school psychologist is to halt this progression by seriously attending to the high-frequency, low-intensity behavioral problems in children.

It is possible that children who at a certain developmental phase set fires in response to phase-related conflicts may again set fires if they later regress to a behavior pattern reminiscent of the earlier phase or encounter similar conflicts. For example, a toddler who sets fires as an angry expression of thwarted strivings for autonomy may meet similar authority-related conflicts at adolescence and may revert to firesetting behavior even though it has been absent during intervening phases.

Although the nature of the precipitating conflicts at different ages may be similar, firesetting often takes on different meanings at different developmental levels. Similarly the act may have different meaning for a boy than for a girl. The fact that incidence levels are significantly higher for boys (Nurcombe, 1964; Vandersall & Weiner, 1970; Yarnell, 1940) and the fact that a small body of research notes that adolescent females set fires for specific reasons such as needs relating to acquisition of clothes and furnishings, and desire for masculine attention (Lewis & Yarnell, 1951) hint at differences between males and females in motivation. In addition, current research pointing to gender differences in the raising of children (e.g., instances in which the mother sees daughters as extensions of herself and sons as separate and different (Chodorow, 1978; and Gilligan, 1982) lends support to the notion that in setting fires girls may be trying to recapture past relationships with their mothers motivated by needs of purification and reunion. Boy firesetters, on the other hand, may harbor fantasies of destruction and separation.

PUTTING CHILDREN'S FIRESETTING IN PERSPECTIVE

Since this is an age of latchkey children, most have access to matches and lighters and few have adequate supervision and training in fire safety — a deadly combination. School psychologists' efforts must be both preventive and responsive. Before school psychologists may become fully cognizant of some of the reasons why children set fires, they must at a minimum familiarize themselves with specific, contextual factors that increase as well as those that lessen the probability of the behavior. Preventive measures such as educating children on fire safety, and encouraging parents to keep incendiary materials inaccessible and to supervise their children, may be beyond the bailiwick of the school psychologist. Regardless, psychologists who adopt a consultative role with other school personnel can certainly press for these precautions to be addressed by schools and for fire safety to be incorporated into the elementary school curriculum.

While the reasons for setting fires are obviously overdetermined, there are certain specific psychological factors that may predispose a child to set more fires or may inhibit further firesetting. The usual means of identifying these factors is a test or an interview. One test designed specifically to assess juvenile firesetters, the Lowenstein Fire-Raising Diagnostic Test (1979), consists of 12 questions based on a simple true/false format. The advantages of the Lowenstein test are speed of administration and ease in scoring and interpretation. The disadvantages are major, however; no normative data are available and information about predictive validity is vague and inconclusive.

In an exploratory research study comparing the psychological test profiles of known juvenile firesetters in residential treatment with a control group of juveniles in residential treatment, the firesetters displayed the following distinguishing characteristics: (a) less ego and superego control, (b) more reactivity than reflectivity, (c) less obsessive binding of tension and anxiety (as seen by a lack of overt anxiety), (d) less empathic understanding of others, (e) greater difficulty in expressing anger, (f) poorer social relationships, and (g) more frequent authority conflicts (Sakheim et al., 1985). These same authors also correlated factors mentioned prominently in the theoretical and clinical literature on firesetting with the actual psychological test data of known juvenile firesetters. For example, rejecting parents has been mentioned as a salient feature of firesetting (Macht & Mack, 1968; Yarnell, 1940). This factor should then appear in test results with prevalent themes of parental rejection in TAT stories or in Rorschach responses. Firesetters were in fact distinguished from nonfiresetters by stronger levels of sexual excitement, and by feelings of maternal rejection coupled with less oral aggression and fewer raging responses to insults (Sakheim et al., 1985).

The Federal Management Administration (1984) has designed manuals to be used if there is no time to combine a test battery with an in-depth interview. One is for personnel who work with juvenile firesetters (7–14 years), and a second is for younger children. These can be used by school psychologists who want a quick, formulaic method of questioning a child and family to determine if an incident under investigation is of "little concern," "definite concern," or "extreme concern." Family interview forms and a behavior category profile sheet are included.

When conducting an interview two points are of the essence: speed and rigor. The main goal is to find out why the child in question set the fire and to institute changes in his or her life that will halt the behavior. There are also legal considerations that differ from state to state to protect the rights of the child firesetter as well as the community. A city attorney or juvenile court judge would probably know the necessary legal implications (Federal Emergency Management Agency, 1984) of how arson is viewed in your state in respect to age of offender and to the legal definition of *firesetter.*

If the school psychologist cannot begin an assessment of the situation quickly, an outside referral should be strongly considered. If the evaluation is done in school, the clinician should try, in addition to collecting historical and antecedent information from child and family, to ascertain the specific incendiary devise used, its continued accessibility to the child, and the feelings the child experienced prior to, during, and after the fire (see Bumpas, 1983 for a method of graphing the act). It is also important to have the child relate in his or her own words whatever actions were taken in trying to escape from or put out the fire. The child's awareness level of the consequences of the act should also be considered. Similarly, it is necessary to assess the appropriateness of the parents' response. Underreaction may be a sign of denial of the importance of the act, of guilt, or of a true misunderstanding of the import of the event. Overreaction *may* signal that the home environment is noxious or punitive, or that fire has a high symbolic valence in this family and may come to be used as a weapon. find out what the child's previous exposure to fire has been and if the child has been taught to light matches. Is there a parent working in a fire-related field? Have parents unconsciously fueled the symptom by vicariously sharing their own firesetting escapades with children, watched fires with the child in a pleasureable way, or given match-lighting a favorable connotation by having the child light adults' cigarettes.

In closing the interview, explore the child's reaction to the fire. Specifically, ask if the child has a hidden cache of matches or lighters or any future plans to set fires? Dreams and fantasies may also be solicited to help uncover the symbolic meaning of fire for that particular child. Answers to these questions plus available test data should help to distinguish between the positive and negative prognostic indicators and the "curiosity" and the "pathological" firesetter.

Most importantly each incident of firesetting should always be considered serious, as should each suggestion of a future act. Although the target of the underlying problem may change, the psychological motives that precipitated the act will most likely not dissipate with time. Proper early intervention can result in prevention.

ALTERNATIVE ACTIONS

Treatment considerations for the juvenile firesetter are based on the emotional state of the child, the stability of the home situation, the seriousness of the firesetting incident, and the likelihood of its recurrence. For the less serious incidents, one-time "curiosity" firesetting, a school-based intervention is usually ameliorative. For more serious incidents of "high risk" or "pathological" firesetting referral to a mental health facility is almost always indicated and should be initiated as soon as possible. In situations in which the act seems limited to a specific location (e.g., the child only sets fires in the home and/or where there is a noxious home environment), temporary residential treatment should be explored. There is some evidence that indicates that in situations of high stress the symptom abates with removal from the home (Fine & Louie, 1979; Kuhnley, Hendren, & Quinlin, 1982; Shaw, 1966).

Once the setting for the intervention is agreed upon with family and in some cases court approval, a variety of treatment modalities can be considered, all of which have been touted as successful, but their "success" is evaluated over relatively short follow-up periods. At present there have not been any large-scale studies that have compared the efficacy of the following, most frequently cited, treatments aimed at juvenile firesetters: (a) counseling and psychotherapy, (b) family treatment, (c) behavioral management techniques, and (d) educative strategies. Behavioral management techniques are of particular interest to the school psychologist because they are most readily available for use.

Counseling and Psychotherapy

Although insight-oriented psychotherapy per se is not well adapted to most firesetters, who by the very nature of their symptom use action instead of words to express problems, a modified form of psychotherapy may be effective in some cases in which a particular capacity for insight and cognitive ability make the firesetter a good candidate for this form of intervention. The therapist would work in alliance with the child's ego strengths to develop more assertiveness on the part of the client and to foster social skills in general and verbal mediation abilities in particular. In effect the therapist tries to help the child to handle aggression directly (verbalizing anger at siblings instead of setting the barn on fire), to learn to mediate actions with words, and to be able to preview an act to comprehend the consequences. Supplementary family lessons in fire safety, or the design of a fire safety exit plan for the family by the client, could help the child develop a stronger and more positive role in the family. Also a prearranged visit to a fire station after the firesetting has stopped might be used as an incentive.

Family Treatment

When the locus of pathology of the firesetting symptom lies in the family or when the family is a stable, viable resource, a family intervention should be considered. The family can act as auxiliary therapists, can help to supervise the child, and can educate the child in fire safety measures. If family members value each other enough to give support and want to reach some homeostasis in the family system, and if the events precipitating the firesetting episode can be isolated and addressed, the family therapy treatment model is a most useful form of intervention (Eisler, 1972). Using a crisis intervention model of family treatment, Eisler worked successfully with the family of a 14-year-old boy firesetter. Through structured family tasks such as having family members write and discuss independent grievance lists about other family members, he successfully addressed issues of social relationships and confusing nonverbal communication among family members.

The strategic school of family treatment views the family as a system divided into other subsystems arranged in hierarchical order. The symptom of firesetting would be seen as an analogical expression of a dysfunction in one or more of these subsystems. The strategic school family therapist would try to reorganize or rearrange the subsystem organization around the symptom. The identified patient is thought to protect the family by containing the pathology of the family and also occupies a hierarchically low position in the family system. A cleverly designed strategic intervention with the family of a 10-year-old twin male firesetter involved reversing the boy's hierarchical family position of notoriety as a firesetter to help him become the resident fire safety expert. This was achieved by having the mother repeatedly reenact a scene designed by the therapist in which the mother pretended to be burned by a match and the boy pretended to put out the fire. The therapist also trained the boy in lighting matches and fire safety, then asked that he be given the special privilege of lighting the stove at home (Madanes, 1984).

Behavioral Management Techniques

Behavioral management runs the gamut from aversion therapy (having children close their eyes and hold lit matches until they feel the heat [Lowenstein, 1979]) to stimulus satiation (having children light twenty boxes of matches [Welsh, cited in Graziani, 1971]), to reward contingencies (paying a child to return unlit matches found around the house [Holland, cited in Schaefer & Millman, 1977]). In addition *The Juvenile Firesetter Handbook* (Federal Emergency and Management Agency, 1984) suggests (a) supervisory strategies or putting the child in charge of fire education for younger siblings or family, (b) contract strategies (the child cosigns a contract with an adult to gain special rewards for desired behavior), (c) behavior strategies in general, such as a reward/debit system for controlling behavior, (d) a restitution strategy in which the child earns money for repairs or actually does limited reparative work to compensate for damage inflicted by a fire, and (e) educational strategies stressing fire dangers and safety through films, readings, and practice.

Based on the school psychologist's assessment of the cognitive abilities of a client firesetter and the hypotheses of why the fire was set, an individual treatment package can be designed using humane combinations of the above techniques. Since firesetting behavior is usually infrequent, it is also useful to work on one or two coexisting behavioral problems that may be more immediately amenable to treatment and might make quick positive changes in the child's life. Patterson's book *Living With Children, New Methods for Parents and Teachers* is highly effective in quickly educating parents and teachers on behavior modification procedures.

Educative Strategies

Regardless of the specific mode of treatment, it is crucial that the school psychologist closely follow the family at agreed-upon intervals and reassess the situation with regularity. When working in a school, the psychologist can easily consult with teachers in designing age-appropriate educative strategies. One simple, effective way to respond quickly to the "curiosity" firesetter is to call in a respected figure from school or community to discuss the seriousness of the incident with the child and the family. The family should be instructed and helped by the school psychologist to support the child during this meeting. Schools can support the child's positive behavior by using a fire safety curriculum in the classroom (see National Firehawk Foundation Bibliography of Publications and Resources, 1986), encouraging puppet plays or skits with fire safety themes, and holding fire safety poster design contests. If the child is a "curiosity" firesetter, the school psychologist also has the option of referring the child to one of many nationwide Firehawk programs, in which specially trained fire fighters are paired with firesetters in a therapeutic surrogate parent or big brother type of relationship. Calling your state fire department or contacting the National Firehawk Foundation would allow you to locate these types of programs in your locality.

Whenever you do choose to work with a firesetter strictly within school bounds it is important to remember that the amount of time spent with the firesetter will be circumscribed, the time of initiating the intervention often delayed, and the risk of losing some of the facts in the family's attempt to protect the child's academic career will be restrictive.

SUMMARY

No matter what efforts are made to educate the public, or what treatment modalities are tried, the sobering fact remains that some children will continue to engage in firesetting that is neither benign, one-time only, or simple, nonpathological experimentation. This is true because most problem behavior produces secondary gain. Firesetting seems particularly noxious in this regard. It is immediately rewarding: "the sensory stimulation of the fire itself, the commotion of crowds, sirens and bells, and praise and recognition derived from the community if the firesetter turns in the alarm or helps put out the fire" (Vreeland & Levin, cited in Canter, 1980, p. 40). The way to assess whether firesetting is truly pathological is to consider (a) the frequency and duration of the symptom, (b) the deviance from age-appropriate norms, (c) the presence or absence of corollary behavioral problems, and (d) the circumstances preceding the behavior (Shekheim, 1978).

The key to helping a juvenile firesetter is to reduce stresses, teach alternative ways of solving problems and getting attention, encourage the child to monitor and verbalize aggression, and, most importantly, provide stronger rewards elsewhere. In addition, the child must learn to regain controls and reduce impulsivity. Fear and anxiety in relation to setting a fire must be raised to diffuse the firesetting impulse and halt the behavior.

We have come a long way from Prometheus to Smokey the Bear: from trying to imagine how man obtained fire to trying to help man contain fire. Now we have a new problem, the juvenile firesetter. It is not surprising that we have spawned a generation of firesetters. After all, we are a nation of fire watchers. We give news headlines to fires; dignitaries visit fires in progress. We equate fire with power and make sure it is easily accessible to all: Just a "flic of your bic." The fact that U.S. parents seem to be supervising children less, and the fact that children are less familiar with the positive uses of fire (warming the house and cooking the food) contribute to the problem. Perhaps today's children are more angry with fewer outlets for aggression. Perhaps we are just getting better at harvesting statistics. One point is certain; thousands of schoolchildren dramatically watched on television screens as the space shuttle Challenger burst into flames, burning up astronauts and a teacher. Will this mass media event lend firesetting a negative reputation? What effects will this and similar events have on incidence levels? Possibly a temporary decrease for the "curiosity" firesetter, but for the "pathological" firesetter the act is ignited by an intrapsychic spark of conflict and "the fire next time is only seconds away.

REFERENCES

American Psychiatric Association. (1980). *Diagnostic and statistical manual of mental disorders* (3rd ed.). Washington, DC: Author.

Arlow, A. (1955). Notes on oral symbolism. *Psychoanalytic Quarterly, 24,* 63–74.

Awad, G. A., & Harrison, S. J. (1955). A female firesetter: A case report. *Journal of Nervous and Mental Disease, 163*(6), 432–437.

Baizerman, M., & Emshoff, B. (1984, May–June). Juvenile firesetting: Building a community based prevention program. *Children Today,* pp. 8–12.

Bender, L. (1966). In C. R. Shaw. *Psychiatric disorders of childhood* (pp. 299–302). New York: Meredith.

Bumpass, E. R., Fagelman, F. D., & Brix, R. J. (1983). *American Journal of Psychotherapy, 37*(3), 328–345.

Chess, S., & Hassibi, M. (1978). *Principles and practice of child psychiatry.* New York: Plenum.

Chodorow, N. (1978). *The reproduction of mothering.* Berkeley: University of California Press.

Collins, G. (1984, October 1). Children who set fires. *New York Times,* P. C12.

Denholtz, M. S. (1972). At home: Aversion treatment for compulsive fire setting behavior: Case report. In R. B. Rubin, H. Fensterheim, & L. T. Ullman (Eds.), *Advances in behavior therapy* (pp. 235–246). New York: Academic.

Eisler, R. M. (1972). Crisis intervention in the family of a firesetter. *Psychotherapy: Theory and Practice, 9*(1), 76–79.

Fahy, R. (1986, January). *Fire Journal,* pp. 19–85.

Federal Emergency and Management Agency, United States Fire Administration. (1984). *Interviewing and counseling juvenile firesetters.* Washington, DC: Author.

Fine, S., & Louie, D. (1979). Juvenile firesetters: Do the agencies help? *American Journal of Psychiatry, 136*(4a), 433–435.

Fineman, K. (1980). Firesetters in childhood and adolescence. *Psychiatric Clinics of North America, 3*(3), 483–500.

Fisher, K. (1984). Volunteer program curbs juvenile arson. *APA Monitor, 15*(2), pp. 7, 12.

Freud, S. (1932). The acquisition of power over fire. *International Journal of Psychoanalysis, 13,* 405–410.

Gaynor, J., McLaughlin, P. M., & Hatcher, C. (1983). *The firehawk children's program: A working manual.* San Francisco: National Firehawk Foundation.

Gilligan, C. (1982). *In a different voice.* Cambridge: Harvard University Press.

Gruber, A. R., Heck, E. T., & Mintzer, E. (1981). Children who set fires: Some background and behavioral characteristics. *American Journal of Orthopsychiatry, 5*(3), 484–488.

Holland, C. J. (1977). In C. Schaefer & H. L. Millman (Eds.), *Therapies for children* (pp. 307–314). San Francisco: Jossey-Bass.

Jacobson, R. R. (1985). Child firesetters: A clinical investigation. *Journal of Child Psychology, 26*(5), 759–768.

Justice, B., Justice, R., & Kraft, G. (1974). Early-warning signs of violence: Is a triad enough? *American Journal of Psychiatry, 131*(4), 457–459.

Kafry, D. (1980). Playing with matches: Children and fire. In D. Cantor (Ed.), *Fires and human behavior* (pp. 47–61). New York: Wiley.

Kaufman, I., Heims, L. W., & Reiser, D. E. (1961). A re-evaluation of the psychodynamics of firesetting. *American Journal of Orthopsychiatry, 31,* 123–127.

Klein, M. (1975). *The psychoanalysis of children.* New York: Delacorte Press/Seymour Lawrence.

Kolko, D. J., Kazdin, A. E., & Meyer, E. C. (1985). Aggression and psychopathology in childhood firesetters: Parent and child reports. *Journal of Consulting and Clinical Psychology, 53*(3), 377–385.

Kuhnley, J. E., Hendren, R. L., & Quinlain, D. M. (1982). Firesetting by children. *Journal of the American Academy Of Child Psychiatry, 21*(6), 560–563.

Lewis, N., & Yarnell, H. (1951). Pathological firesetting. *Nervous and Mental Disease Monographs,* No. 82.

Lowenstein, L. F. (1979). *A study of child arsonists: Their diagnosis and treatment* (Report No. 120 128). Fair Oak, United Kingdom. (ERIC Document Reproduction Service No. ED175 199).

Macht, L. B., & Mack, J. E. (1968). The firesetter syndrome. *Psychiatry, 31,* 277–288.

Madanes, C. (1981). *Strategic family therapy* (pp. 84–85). San Francisco: Jossey-Bass.

Mavromatis, M., & Lion, J. R. (1977). A primer on pyromania. *Journal of Diseases of the Nervous System, 38*(11), 954–955.

McGrath, P., Marshall, P., & Prior, K. (1979). A comprehensive treatment program for a firesetting child. *Journal of Behavior Therapy and Experimental Psychiatry, 10,* 69–72.

McKinney, C. D., & Corral, E. A. (1985, October). *Fire Command,* pp. 32–33.

National Firehawk Foundation. (1986). *A bibliography of publications and resources.* Author.

National Firehawk Foundation. (1986, Spring). Up in smoke, school set fires. *Bulletin.*

Nurcombe, B. (1964). Children who set fires. *Medical Journal of Australia, 1,* 579–584.

Patterson, G. R. (1982). *Coercive family process.* Eugene, Oregon: Castalia.

Patterson, G. R., & Gullion, M. E. (1968). *Living with children, new methods for parents and teachers.* Champaign, IL: Research Press.

Rothstein, R. (1963). Explorations of ego structures of firesetting children. *Archives of General Psychiatry, 9,* 246–253.

Sakheim, G. A., Vigdor, M. G., Gordon, M., & Helprin, L. M. (1985). A psychological profile of juvenile firesetters in residential treatment. *Child Welfare, 64*(5), 453–476.

Sandrick, K. (1982, August 6). Psychiatrist's goal: Stop child arsonists. *American Medical News,* p. 35.

Sensor, C. (1985). Firesetting. In J. Grimes & A. Thomas (Eds.), *Psychological approaches to problems of children and adolescents* (pp. 3–19). Des Moines: Iowa Department of Public Institutions.

Shaw, C. R. (1966). *The psychiatric disorders of childhood.* New York: Meredith.

Shekheim, W. O. (1978). Letter to the editor on firesetting in children. *Journal of Clinical Psychiatry, 39*(30), 270.

Stekel, W. (1924). *Peculiarities of behavior* (Vol. 2). New York: Boni and Liveright.

Vandersall, T. A., & Weiner, J. M. (1970). Children who set fires. *Archives of General Psychiatry, 22,* 63–71.

Vreeland, R. G., & Levin, B. M. (1980). Psychological aspects of firesetting. In D. Canter (Ed.), *Fires and human behavior* (pp. 31–36). Chichester, United Kingdom: Wiley.

Welsh, R. S. (1971). The use of stimulus satiation in the elimination of juvenile firesetting behavior. In A. Graziani (Ed.), *Behavior therapy with children.* Chicago: Atherton Press, Altiri (Aldine).

Winget, G. N., & Whitman, R. M. (1973). Coping with problems: Attitudes toward children who set fires. *American Journal of Psychiatry, 130*(4), 442–445.

Wooden, W. S. (1985, January). The flames of youth. *Psychology Today,* pp. 22–30.

Wooden, W. S., & Berkey, M. L. (1984). *Children and arson: America's middle class nightmare.* New York: Plenum.

Yarnell, H. (1940). Firesetting in children. *American Journal of Orthopsychiatry, 10,* 272–286.

BIBLIOGRAPHY: PROFESSIONALS

Fineman, K. (1980). Firesetting in children and adolescence. *Psychiatric Clinics of North America, 3*(3), 483–500.
For a quick, comprehensive, and easily readable understanding of the state of the art in the field of firesetting research, turn to Fineman. His paper covers the scope of the current problem, a historical overview, research problems, current psychodynamic formulations, distinctions between normal and pathological firesetters, and suggested treatment modalities.

Gruber, A. R., Heck, E. T., & Mintzer, E. (1981). Children who set fires: Some background and behavioral characteristics. *American Journal of Orthopsychiatry, 5*(3), 484–488.
Ninety children identified as firesetters in residential treatment were studied ex post facto. Demographic variables, presenting behavior, history of placement contacts, and professional reports were analyzed. A profile of child firesetters was developed that emphasizes problems in the family constellation and academic history. Lack of adequate evaluation was noted.

Kafry, D. (1980). Playing with matches: Children and fire. In D. Cantor (Ed.), *Fires and human behavior* (pp. 47–61). New York: Wiley.
This researcher investigated firesetting behavior in a sample of public school boys (99) with a focus on the *normal* developmental phenomenon of fire-play in children. Parents and children were interviewed at home, parents were asked to complete a questionnaire, and mothers were observed teaching their children to boil water on a camp stove.

McGrath, P., Marshall, P., & Prior, K. (1979). A comprehensive treatment program for a firesetting child. *Journal of Behavior Therapy and Experimental Psychiatry, 10,* 69–72.
Demonstrates the application of a well-designed behavior modification program for an 11-year-old firesetter. On the basis of hypotheses generated to explain why the child set fires, a cleverly designed treatment package included a social skills training component, overcorrection exercises, a covert sensitization segment, and an educative project.

Wooden, W. S. (1985, January). The flames of youth. *Psychology Today,* pp. 22–30.
This lively, fascinating article is a condensed and updated version of *Children and arson: America's middle class nightmare,* which Wooden, a sociologist, coauthored with psychologist M. L. Berkey (Wooden & Berkey, 1984). Distinctions are made among four different types of firesetters: the curiosity firesetter,the plea-for-help firesetter, the delinquent firesetter, and the firesetter with severe psychopathology.

BIBLIOGRAPHY: PARENTS

National Firehawk Foundation Bulletin. P.O. Box 27488, San Francisco, CA 94127. (415) 922-3242.
This nonprofit organization serves as a national clearinghouse for current research and legislation related to juvenile arson. In addition to the *Bulletin,* which covers relevant programs and statistics of import, they publish educational materials such as *A working manual,* and a comprehensive bibliography on the subject. In addition they offer guidance in starting Firehawk Programs, in which firemen are trained in working with child firesetters.

Children and Foster Homes

Nancy A. McKellar
Wichita State University

BACKGROUND

Foster homes are one of several situations, including group homes, shelters, and other institutions, in which children live apart from their biological parents. Foster family care is defined by the Child Welfare League of America (1975) as "substitute *family* [italics added] care for a planned period for a child when his [sic] own family cannot care for him for a temporary or extended period, and when adoption is either not yet possible or not desirable" (p. 8). Except for the alternative of adoption, foster care seems to be selected more often than other forms of substitute care for younger children and for those with less serious behavior problems (Horejsi, 1979). In 1980, there were 281,053 children in foster homes in the United States, out of a total population of 63,536,058 persons under age 18 years (Bureau of the Census, 1984). Thus, about one of every 226 children in this country is in a foster home.

The common reasons given for why children are placed in foster homes touch on problems presented by one or both parents, typically the biological mother. These include unwillingness or inability either to continue or to assume care of the child; neglect or abuse; and mental or physical illness (Shapiro, 1976). The child's behavior or personality problems are stated as the reason for placement in only about a tenth of the cases. In many families, however, there are multiple problems that result in the need for foster care (Horejsi, 1979).

There are those who argue that children are removed from their biological homes and placed in foster homes more frequently than is necessary and for reasons other than the needs and best interests of the child (Cox & Cox, 1985). Such practices are attributed (a) to bureaucratic and governmental policies that include overworked, often inexperienced caseworkers who, therefore, are unable to give sustained attention to any one family; (b) to state and federal funding of out-of-home care as the only option for welfare departments dealing with troubled families; and (c) to the absence of clear judicial standards specifying acceptable reasons for removing children from the home. Norman (1985) discussed the characteristics of model family preservation programs that provide interventions aimed at preventing unnecessary placement of children in foster care.

Local variations in welfare policies and practices result in geographic differences in the characteristics of children in foster care (Cox & Cox, 1985). In general, however, the average age of these children is approximately 10.5 years, 4.5 years being the average age of entrance into foster care. Although males and females are fairly equally represented in foster care, a child of an ethnic minority, such as a Native American or a black, from a single-parent home, and/or from an extremely poor family is more likely to be placed in foster care than other children (Cox & Cox, 1985; Horejsi, 1979).

About half of all foster children are placed in more than one setting while they are in the foster care system (Norman, 1985). Once in foster care, children are more likely to stay in the system if they were placed because of the mental or emotional illness of their biological parent(s) or severe family disorganization, rather than the physical illness of the parent(s). The length of time that children spend in foster care is directly correlated with the probability of staying there. "Once a child has been in foster care for three years, it is highly unlikely that he or she will leave the foster care system prior to reaching maturity" (Horejsi, 1979, p. 17). Some children who cannot be reunited with their biological families are kept in foster care for long periods of time before finally being released for adoption. By that time, they are often too old and/or traumatized to be readily adopted (Bolles, 1984).

The author gratefully acknowledges the information on foster children in schools from Patricia Ryan and the recommendations regarding children's literature from Ann Wardell.

DEVELOPMENT

Foster children are first of all children with all the problems typical of others their age. Additionally, they have specific problems associated with their status as foster children. These problems concern their adjustment to separation from their biological families, the effects of the events that prompted foster care placement, and the difficulties associated with being in the foster care system.

Regardless of the age of the child or the circumstances of placement, a child reacts to the trauma of being separated from the biological family in much the same manner as persons who have lost loved ones in other ways (Horejsi, 1979; Jewett, 1982). These common reactions have been described as the stages of shock, protest, despair, and detachment (Norton, 1981). Foster children experiencing shock may appear to be adjusting adequately to the separation from their biological family, but their emotional involvement with their new situation is minimal. Sleep difficulties, teeth grinding, and upper respiratory infections may be observed. During the protest stage, foster children may experience anger, anxiety, and helplessness. These reactions are viewed as attempts to retain their former selves and prevent the emerging changes in themselves that result from their being in a new environment. Working with children in this stage can be very frustrating, because they may appeal for help in negative, inappropriate ways, yet reject such help when it is given. Foster children in the stage of despair react apathetically to the demands of their world, appearing to be disorganized and helpless and to lack motivation.

The detachment stage is a period of adjustment for foster children. They feel accomplishment in having adjusted and seek out new relationships in which they invest themselves emotionally. They may still hope to return to their biological family, but these ideas are more reality-based than previously. They may even adopt the traits, values, interests, or other attributes of their biological families (Jewett, 1982).

Traumatic events frequently precipitate foster home placement (Norton, 1981). The child may suffer long-term effects from previous abuse and/or neglect. Such children sometimes reason that if they were removed from their biological families, with whom they identify, because the family was unworthy, then they must also be unworthy (Norman, 1985). Using the Coopersmith Self-Esteem Test, Gil and Bogart (1982) found that the foster children in their study scored lower in self-esteem than would be expected for children their age. Foster parents, teachers, and caseworkers may expect the child to perform and behave in age-appropriate ways, forgetting the damage done by their earlier experiences (Norton, 1981).

Separation from the biological family in any case generally causes short-term emotional trauma and pain for the child, leading to confusion, uncertainty, problems of identity, conflicts of loyalty, and anxiety about the future (Horejsi, 1979). These immediate effects are not necessarily lasting, however. In their well-known longitudinal study of New York foster children, Fanshel and Shinn (1978) found that long-term placement in foster care, per se, did not lead to deterioration in IQ, school performance, or emotional adjustment. One explanation for this finding is that many persons and situations, not just the family, help to shape a child's development (Horejsi, 1979). Lahti et al., (1978) found that the foster children in their study showed greater adjustment when in a placement that they perceived to be permanent, whether it was actually permanent or not. However, any negative effects of long-term placement in terms of social and psychological development increase when the child is placed in many foster homes. Each new placement subjects the child to the harmful effects of separation (Horejsi, 1979).

As a result of being in the foster care system, children are identified to their peers as being different (Emlen, Lahti, Downs, McKay, & Downs, 1977). They always have a different name from the family with whom they live. Foster children may not have the information about their past that would be necessary to participate in class activities that involve family trees, baby pictures, and the like. Furthermore, payment of any extra school fees for items such as field trips and yearbooks will set the children apart from peers. In most states, foster parents are responsible for routine school expenses, but "extras" must be provided by state funds, which may be delayed, or through the generosity of the foster family. Payments to foster families vary widely among states (Select Committee on Children, Youth, and Families, 1983), are low, and typically do not cover the essential items for the child's care, let alone "extras" for school (Carbino, 1980).

By definition, placement in foster care will mean that a child must move into a new home and usually into a new school and community. Moving can be disruptive for any child in respect to education and social relationships, but the moves required of foster children entail the additional trauma of separation from their biological families. Some foster children must also deal with being moved from one foster home to another. Often these moves are sudden, at least from the child's viewpoint, making them particularly difficult to handle emotionally (Jewett, 1982; Kaplan & Seitz, 1980). The persistent uncertainty faced by foster children has been described as "growing up on standby, never knowing if you are to live with a family for only a short time more or until you have come of age" (Bolles, 1984, p. 179).

Moving results in several practical problems for foster children (Emlen et al., 1977). Handicapping conditions, such as a specific learning disability or a mild hearing loss, may not be identified and treated. Health records may not be accurate, so that the foster child either does not have up-to-date immunizations or has been given the same ones more than once. It may be difficult for these children to participate in some sports and other extracurricular activities if they are not in the same school all year. The prospect of a sudden move to a new foster home leaves the foster child not knowing until the last minute where important holidays will be spent.

Foster children may exhibit certain problematic behaviors in school. Those children who do not yet feel secure in their foster home may regress to immature behaviors, such as temper tantrums, whining, or clinging (Horejsi, 1979). A foster child may behave inappropriately in an attempt to disrupt the foster home placement and/or to cope with the grief of separation from the biological family. Foster children sometimes tell stories that teachers find unusual enough to doubt their truth. Their stories may be accurate accounts of bizarre things that really happened to them; or alternatively these children may be confused, fantasizing, or attempting to gain attention. Foster children's defenses against additional rejection may take the forms of chronic criticism of the teacher; withholding whatever they think the teacher wants, such as completed homework or compliance with classroom rules; and running away, truancy, or unexplained absences (Silin, 1978). Unfortunately, some foster children may show signs of current abuse or neglect; any suspicions of such must, of course, be reported.

PUTTING FOSTER CARE IN PERSPECTIVE

There are numerous reasons why foster children might have problems in school and thus come to the attention of the school psychologist through consultation and/or referral for evaluation. These include a change in educational placement after having moved; an unidentified handicapping condition; worries about their biological families and about their own futures; feelings of anger, of being lost, or of being overwhelmed; developmental lags resulting from the trauma of separation; and various consequences of having previously attended a school that was very different from the present one (Piers, 1984).

Gil and Bogart (1982) interviewed 50 children, aged 8–18 years, about their perceptions of foster care. "Many of the children interviewed could not read the questionnaire with comprehension or write responses" (p. 9). No child wrote a grammatically correct sentence. Many of the foster parents expressed frustration in their attempts to obtain specialized educational treatment for their children. Some reported that their child had been on waiting lists to receive services for what seemed to them to be quite a long time. The school psychologist needs to counteract any assumption on the part of the school that a child is "just passing through" and should, therefore, not be given the attention to which he or she is entitled.

In addition to understanding the needs of foster children, it is important to understand the roles of the foster parents, the biological parents, and the social service agency worker. Foster parents tend to be middle-aged, lower middle class, married, and with children of their own (Carbino, 1980). The foster parent attrition rate is high, particularly within the first year of fostering, and contributes to the problem that some children are placed in a number of different foster homes. Not all foster parents receive training for their new role and responsibilities (Carbino, 1980), even though trained foster parents are more likely to keep children in their care for longer periods of time (Boyd & Remy, 1978).

Much diversity and ambiguity exist concerning the role of foster parents (Carbino, 1980). Agencies typically expect foster parents to handle a wide range of emotional and behavioral problems and be flexible enough to accept a new child into the family on short notice and to work with a variety of caseworkers (Pasztor & Burgess, 1982). Yet foster parents often do not receive complete information about the children they take care of; then are not allowed input in case decisions affecting the children; and are required to have their foster children interviewed by caseworkers without being told of the reason for the talk. Pasztor and Burgess (1982) advocate redefining the role of foster parents to that of a valuable member of the social service agency team. They suggest that job descriptions be used to clarify such a role for foster parents in the agency.

The goal is usually to return foster children to the biological family. Therefore, biological parents are actively encouraged by the agency to visit their children (Bolles, 1984). The more frequent the contract between biological parents and their children, particularly early in the placement, the greater the likelihood that the children will eventually be reunited with their biological families (Horejsi, 1979). Strife can occur between the foster parents and the biological parents, particularly when the children appear upset after visiting with the biological parents. If foster children seem to have periodic difficulties in their behavior or work at school, teachers should ask the foster parents if these disturbances coincide with visits by the biological parents. In these cases, it may be helpful to have the foster parents inform the teachers when such visits occur so that the teachers can more easily recognize the cause of the children's periodic difficulties (Piers, 1984). It is important to remember that emotionally upsetting visits are less harmful to foster children than the devastating feelings of abandonment that result from no visits at all (Horejsi, Bertsche, & Clark, 1981).

The caseworker's duties include working with the foster parents and the biological family, maintaining all official records concerning the child's status, and developing a permanency plan for the child (Bolles, 1984). They are typically overworked, carrying 40 to 80 cases at a time, and are therefore unable to give individual attention to each foster child (Norman, 1985).

School personnel should ask caseworkers to explain the permanency plans that exist for foster children. It is helpful to know whether the agency has established a goal and accompanying plan for these children to be returned to their biological families or to be freed for adoption. Such plans should be established as early as possible to prevent these children from being left adrift in the system without a clear goal being set (Horejsi, 1979). If the plans are to return these children to their biological families, as it is for most foster children, the biological parents should be involved in the children's education to the greatest extent possible at that time. The foster parents should also be encouraged to take an active part as parents in the educational process, since they are caring for the children on a daily basis. Having a foster child in the classroom means that the teacher usually will need to work with more adults than is typical, but the potential long-term benefits to the child are great. The teacher can indicate to the caseworker the desire to have both sets of parents participate in the child's education and ask for specific guidelines for working with each of them at that stage of foster care.

Foster children have a right to their own family privacy, just as other children do. Foster parents are typically advised by the agency not to share information not pertinent to the children's education with the school and to refer such questions to the children's caseworkers (Kaplan & Seitz, 1980; Piers, 1984). However, the teacher should ask the foster parents whether they know of any special needs or problems that their children have. Teachers and other school personnel should also include new foster children in hobbies, sports, and social activities at school as soon as possible in order to help them feel included in the new school and experience success.

ALTERNATIVE ACTIONS

Foster children can be frustrating for school personnel to work with because they move in and out of the school, sometimes unexpectedly. They may move into the school district after the annual funding levels have been determined. Also, school multidisciplinary teams may find that just as they have completed the evaluation process and placed a foster child in the appropriate educational setting, the child is moved to another school. When this happens, a member of the team should check to see that the evaluation information and recommendations are received by the child's new school. It is important to remember that the child is the victim, not the cause, of the moving that inconveniences school personnel and should not become the scapegoat for these frustrations.

A mistake that teachers and other school personnel sometimes make is to blame a foster child's school problems on the biological family's situation (Piers, 1984). Care needs to be given to focusing on appropriate interventions for the child and avoiding any tendency to place blame.

Special consideration should be given to the disciplining of foster children. Any punishment techniques used with foster children should not be humiliating or degrading (Kaplan & Seitz, 1980). Such measures would be especially counterproductive to improving these children's self-respect. Corporal punishment is never an appropriate technique to use with foster children, regardless of the school's discipline policy (Kaplan & Seitz, 1980; Piers, 1984). Many foster children have been severely abused; thus, corporal punishment will be ineffective at best and potentially very traumatic for the child. In general, techniques to manage foster children's behavior should not include punishment of any type. Instead, natural consequences and positive reinforcement of appropriate behaviors should be emphasized.

Compared to biological parents and social service agencies, foster parents have, in general, few legal rights and responsibilities regarding their foster children (Carbino, 1980). "State laws vary as to what types of legal permission foster parents can give for special testing, school trips, or health examinations" (P. Ryan, personal communication, March 4, 1986). Typically, it is the agency that is authorized to give consent for psychological evaluation and special education services (Kaplan & Seitz, 1980). Thus, when situations arise in which parental consent is required by law, school officials will need to determine who can give such consent. Foster families should be requested to participate in the treatment plans for their children whenever appropriate, however (Kaplan & Seitz, 1980).

There are several difficult issues that need to be discussed with foster children (Gil & Bogart, 1982). First, they need to understand the reason for their placement in foster care (Horejsi, 1979; Jewett, 1982), which is typically not because of their own behavior (Shapiro, 1976). Unfortunately, many children believe that they are responsible for their placement in foster care (Gil & Bogart, 1982) and so blame themselves for what has happened. Second, foster children deserve to know what decisions are being made regarding their future. Often such information is withheld in an effort to protect them from further emotional pain. Unfortunately, children fill the void left by this lack of information with fantasies of their own and fail to begin the necessary grieving for the loss of their biological families. The person who discusses these issues with a foster child should be someone who is caring, empathic, and knowledgeable, whether this be the caseworker, school counselor, foster parent, or another adult.

In discussing guidelines for counseling foster children, Norton (1981) stressed that counselors need to be aware of the stages through which foster children pass in reacting to separation from their biological family. The child may desperately seek acceptance, yet reject it when offered. Because children are often convinced that they have caused their own losses, they can be quite reluctant to discuss their perceived failures (Jewett, 1982). Conflicts may arise when foster children generalize feelings they have toward their biological parents to all other adults. Norton (1981) emphasized the need for counselors to convey warmth and acceptance while taking a genuine interest in helping children deal with separation issues. Nonverbal techniques using life story books (Beste & Richardson, 1981), puppets, drawings, and toys are sometimes useful in helping foster children express their thoughts and feelings (Horejsi, 1979). Jewett (1982) provides a very helpful, specific discussion of how to help a child make sense out of past losses, both of the biological family and of previous foster homes.

Foster children need to develop self-esteem and a sense of identity as all children do, but they may do so at a slower pace because of the circumstances and impact of separation from their biological families (Piers, 1984). "Every effort should be made to help the child develop a relationship with at least one other person who really cares about him/her and can affirm the child's worth" (Horejsi, 1979, p. 131). This person may be someone at school, such as a teacher, school counselor, or teacher aide, or may be another adult, such as a foster parent or a relative. Such a relationship provides an opportunity for the child to talk about personal concerns and conflicts and helps to counter the child's feelings of being different, unworthy, and/or rejected.

SUMMARY

Most school psychologists have several foster children in each school that they serve, but they may not be aware of the special circumstances and needs of these children. Two things are certain. First, foster children have been removed from their families because of some severe, disruptive events, which usually were not their fault. Second, these children have suffered the trauma of one or more separations from loved ones. The grieving and self-blame related to separation may affect their ability to function up to their potential in school. At a time when these children could benefit greatly from involvement in a consistent educational program, they are likely to be moved. Thus, they cannot plan for future events or experience a sense of stability in other areas of life. Furthermore, foster children are set apart as different from peers by virtue of being in the foster care system. Finally, the school may ignore these children in the erroneous assumption that they are "just passing through" or because it is so frustrating to work with a child who may move suddenly.

Just as with all children, the parents of foster children should be involved as much as possible in the education of their children. In the case of foster children, however, there are two sets of parents, the biological and the foster parents, who need to be involved. In addition, when parental consent is required by law, it is usually the agency caseworker who must give it.

Foster children are likely to need emotional support, sometimes in the form of counseling. They need to understand the reasons for their placement in foster care and what decisions have been made regarding their future. Punishment, particularly corporal punishment, is not an appropriate disciplinary approach to use with foster children. Helping them to form a deep relationship with one other person is an excellent way to help foster children overcome feelings of being different, unworthy, or rejected.

Foster children have very little status or power in our society. Nonetheless, they will someday become adult members of our communities. It is, therefore, imperative that they be given the best help and support possible by the schools in their difficult path through childhood.

REFERENCES

Beste, H. M., & Richardson, R. G. (1981). Developing a life story book program for foster children. *Child Welfare, 60,* 529–534.

Bolles, E. B. (1984). *The Penguin adoption handbook: A guide to creating your new family.* New York: Viking.

Boyd, L. H., Jr., & Remy, L. L. (1978). Is foster parent training worthwhile? *Social Service Review, 52,* 275–296.

Bureau of the Census. (1984). *Living arrangements of children and adults* (Publication No. PC80–2–4B). Washington, DC: U.S. Government Printing Office.

Carbino, R. (1980). *Foster parenting: An updated review of the literature.* New York: Child Welfare League of America.

Child Welfare League of America. (1975). *Standards for foster family service* (rev. ed.). New York: Author.

Cox, M. J., & Cox, R. D. (1985). The foster care system: An introduction. In M. J. Cox & R. D. Cox (Eds.), *Foster care: Current issues, policies, and practices.* Norwood, NJ: Ablex.

Emlen, A., Lahti, J., Downs, G., McKay, A., & Downs, S. (1977). *Overcoming barriers to planning for children in foster care.* Portland, OR: Portland State University, Regional Research Institute for Human Services.

Fanshel, D., & Shinn, E. B. (1978). *Children in foster care: A longitudinal investigation.* New York: Columbia University Press.

Gil, E., & Bogart, K. (1982). Foster children speak out: A study of children's perceptions of foster care. *Children Today, 11,* 7–9.

Horejsi, C. R. (1979). *Foster family care: A handbook for social workers, allied professionals, and concerned citizens.* Springfield, IL: Thomas.

Horejsi, C. R., Bertsche, A. V., & Clark, F. W. (1981). *Social work practice with parents of children in foster care: A handbook.* Springfield, IL: Thomas.

Jewett, C. L. (1982). *Helping children cope with separation and loss.* Harvard, MA: Harvard Common Press.

Kaplan, B. L., & Seitz, M. (1980). *The practical guide to foster family care.* Springfield, IL: Thomas.

Lahti, J., Green, K., Emlen, A., Zadney, J., Clarkson, Q. D., Kuehnel, M., & Casciato, J. (1978). *A follow-up study of the Oregon Project.* Portland, OR: Regional Research Institute for Human Services.

Norman, A. (1985). *Keeping families together: The case for family preservation.* New York: Edna McConnell Clark Foundation.

Norton, F. H. (1981). Foster care and the helping professions. *Personnel and Guidance Journal, 60,* 156–159.

Pasztor, E. M., & Burgess, E. M. (1982). Finding and keeping more foster parents. *Children Today, 11,* 2–5, 36.

Piers, J. C. (1984). *Fostering the school age child: Instructor's manual.* Ypsilanti, MI: Eastern Michigan University, Institute for the Study of Children and Families, Foster Parent Education Program.

Select Committee on Children, Youth, and Families. (1983). *Supporting a family: Providing the basics* (Publication No. 26-101 0). Washington, DC: U.S. Government Printing Office.

Shapiro, D. (1976). *Agencies and foster children.* New York: Columbia University Press.

Silin, M. W. (1978). Why many placed children have learning difficulties. *Child Welfare, 57,* 243–248.

BIBLIOGRAPHY: PROFESSIONALS

Horejsi, C. R. (1979). *Foster family care: A handbook for social workers, allied professionals, and concerned citizens.* Springfield, IL: Thomas.
This comprehensive handbook contains clear, concise information on the foster care system, foster children, biological and foster parents, and legal and bureaucratic issues. The format is question-and-answer, making information easy to locate.

Jewett, C. L. (1982). *Helping children cope with separation and loss.* Harvard, MA: Harvard Common Press.
See the description of this book in the annotated bibliography for parents.

Piers, J. C. (1984). *Fostering the school age child: Instructor's manual.* Ypsilanti, MI: Eastern Michigan University, Institute for the Study of Children and Families, Foster Parent Education Program.
This is an instructor's manual for an 8-week foster parent training program. The Institute for the Study of Children and Families at Eastern Michigan University (Ypsilanti, MI 48197) is a valuable source of practical information related to foster children.

BIBLIOGRAPHY: PARENTS

Fleischmann, D. (Ed.). (1977). *The parents' handbook: A guide for parents of children in foster care.* New York: City of New York, Department of Social Services.
This booklet explains to the biological parents, in understandable language, their role, rights, and responsibilities while their child is in foster care.

Jewett, C. L. (1982). *Helping children cope with separation and loss.* Harvard, MA: Harvard Common Press.
Jewett's specific techniques and guidelines for helping children cope with grief over loss (of the biological family and/or previous foster families) will be very helpful to anyone, parent or educator, who is working with foster children on this issue.

Kaplan, B. L., & Seitz, M. (1980). *The practical guide to foster family care.* Springfield, IL: Thomas.
An excellent sourcebook for foster parents. Impacts of fostering on the child and the foster family are discussed, along with practical information on such topics as relating to the biological family, disciplining the foster child, dealing with the school and community, financing, and separating when the child leaves.

BIBLIOGRAPHY: CHILDREN

Byars, B. C. (1977). *The pinballs.* New York: Harper & Row.
The title of this book for 10 to 13-year-olds is taken from the emotions of Carlie, who has felt like a "pinball," an object having no control over itself. Carlie is one of three unrelated foster children with very unfortunate prior home lives who come to live with a loving family.

Little, J. (1965). *Home from far.* Boston, MA: Little, Brown.
This is an unsentimental account of the relationships among members of a family affected by death and the placement of foster children. The hurt, confusion, and resentment that different children experience are pictured clearly for 10-to 13-year-old readers. The parents show respect for each child's individuality.

MacLachlan, P. (1982). *Mama one, mama two.* New York: Harper & Row.
A little girl in a foster home is reassured about the eventual return of her mentally ill biological mother. The foster mother is depicted as loving and understanding. This book would be helpful in preparing a child aged 4–7 years for a foster home.

Paterson, K. W. (1978). *The great Gilly Hopkins.* New York: Crowell.
Gilly Hopkins has been abandoned by her mother and placed in two foster homes before her present one. She fantasizes about her mother and acts out against her latest foster parent. The main theme of this book for children aged 10–13 years is dealing with separation and rejection.

Stanek, M. N. (1981). *My little foster sister.* Niles, IL: Albert Whitman.
This first-person narrative encourages understanding among 4 to 9-year-old children of what it means to be a foster child or have a foster sibling. A little girl first resents and rejects a younger foster sister, then learns to love and enjoy her.

Children and Giftedness

Betty E. Gridley
Ball State University

BACKGROUND

> "A great gift is futile when its owner is not appropriately connected to the world" (Gruber, 1985, p. 301).

The most frequently cited definition of giftedness (Martinson, 1977; Tuttle & Becker, 1980) is that adopted by the United States Office of Education from The Gifted and Talented Children's Act of 1978 (PL 95-561, Section 902):

> Gifted and talented children are those identified by professionally qualified persons who by virtue of outstanding abilities are capable of high performance. These are children who require differentiated programs and/or services beyond those provided by the regular school programs in order to realize their contribution to self and society.
>
> Children capable of high performance include those with demonstrated achievement and/or potential ability in any of the following areas, singly or in combinations: (1) general intellectual ability, (2) specific academic aptitude, (3) creative thinking, (4) leadership ability, (5) visual and performing arts, (6) psychomotor ability. (Marland, 1972, p. 2)

Based on the above definition, the estimate of the incidence as gifted at any particular time is 3–5%. However, there are many different definitions leading to estimates ranging from 2% to 3%, based on performance on an IQ test alone, to 20%, based on other criteria (Freeman, 1985).

While practitioners must deal with legal definitions, there exists no universally accepted conceptual one. According to Hallahan and Kauffman (1982), beyond the statement that "gifted children are in some way superior to a comparison group of other children the same age," there is little agreement about how *gifted children* should be defined.

The focus of this chapter will be on giftedness as a multidimensional trait such as that proposed in the federal definition but, in addition, as one that is dynamic rather than static. Giftedness is not something that one "has" but rather a characteristic to be developed and used. This idea of a "promise of productivity" is shared with other observers such as Hagen (1980), who stated "the ultimate criterion for giftedness is not performance in school but the quality of the contribution that an individual makes as an adult" (p. 3). In addition, Tannenbaum (1983) emphasized that developed talent is found only in adults and that gifted children are those who have the "potential for becoming critically acclaimed performers or exemplary producers of ideas in spheres of activity that enhance the moral, physical, emotional, social, intellectual, or aesthetic life of humanity" (p. 86). This definition encompasses such aspects as intellectual and creative production and implies that this capacity can come to fruition only through appropriate interaction with the environment.

There is no federal mandate of gifted programs, and states have been free to develop their own legal definitions, which usually include, but are not limited to, children with exceptionally high intelligence. The cutoff score for this category varies, with a lower limit of about 120–132. Prior to 1971, only four states had laws or regulations in which giftedness was defined (Fox, 1981). By 1978, 42 states had developed their own definitions or had guidelines for the federal definitions (Karnes & Collins, 1978). General intellectual ability was specified in all of the 42 states. In 36 states, the definition included separate categories for specific academic aptitude and creative thinking (Fox, 1981).

Early definitions were narrowly focused on exceptional intellectual ability, for example, Terman's (1925) top 2–3% on an IQ test. While this narrow definition of giftedness remained fairly well entrenched for a number of years, even as early as the 1940s writers were concerned about the limitations of intelligence tests in defining and identifying the gifted. Guilford (1967) suggested that some types of thinking were not tapped by traditional IQ tests. Getzels and Jackson (1958) and Torrance (1962) urged that divergent thinking or creativity be included as part of the definition. The current trend is toward a multidimensional view such as that proposed by Renzulli (1979), who analyzed studies of giftedness and characteristics of gifted individuals and proposed a definition of giftedness that consists of three elements: (a) above-average (but not necessarily superior) ability, (b) high levels of creativity, and (c) high levels of task commitment.

While resources are often limited, this chapter will emphasize a policy of inclusion rather than exclusion. Perhaps children who are not "truly" gifted will be identified. However, the penalty in paying for programming for those who may not eventually contribute something of significance to society will be less than overlooking potentially gifted producers.

A primary need for these children is the acceptance of the importance of providing programming. While a majority of people seem to feel it is a moral responsibility to provide help for those at the other end of the spectrum, they question the need to help those who already have an advantage to become even better. However, as Gowan (1979) aptly stated:

> The continued understimulation of the potential talents of gifted students is stupidity of the same order as running a car on the freeway in low gear or using a racehorse to pull a dump cart. It destroys the capability of the agent, and it wastes the resources of the environment. The memorable achievements of mankind consist in actualization of these potential talents, not in their denial. (p. 71)

DEVELOPMENT

Neither legal nor conceptual definitions are very helpful in recognizing gifted children. Fairly consistent agreement about the need for early identification of gifted children exists (e.g., Johnson, 1983; Sellin & Birch, 1980). This is predicated on the rationale that these years represent a critical period for development. Without appropriate intervention at this stage, environmental influences cannot be maximized. Giftedness is neither a characteristic of the individual nor a function of the environment alone, but the interaction of the two.

Formal identification procedures are usually initiated prior to entrance into school only for those children who are unusually precocious or whose parents are especially attuned to their needs. Even after a child has entered the formal educational system, the costs of the multifaceted identification procedures recommended usually necessitate some assurance that a child is really gifted before an individual evaluation is initiated. Identification as a step-by-step process has been suggested (e.g., Alexander & Muia, 1982; Martinson, 1977). These steps are the following:

1. Initial screening through use of multiple methods such as group achievement and ability measures; teacher, parent, peer, and self-nominations; behavioral checklists, etc.

2. Compilation of data from various sources for a comprehensive picture of the student. A number of plans have been suggested for weighting both objective and subjective data. However at the present time none of these plans seems well enough validated to replace the final step of individual assessment.

3. Identification through use of individual assessment and case study.

A comprehensive treatment of screening procedures, individual assessment, and psychometric issues can be found in "Best Practices in the Evaluation of Gifted Children" (Fischman, 1985) for those wishing more detailed information.

However, there are certain behavioral characteristics that have been found to be displayed more often by those children who later become gifted producers. Unfortunately there is a paucity of substantive empirical research of a developmental nature. This is especially true of longitudinal studies comparing gifted youngsters with others not so identified. Even Terman's (1925) landmark studies, while of a longitudinal nature (e.g., Terman & Oden, 1959), included no control group. It is generally accepted that long-term predictions based on commonly used psychometric measures have not been very accurate. The closer one is to adulthood when evaluation takes place, the better the prediction about adult functioning.

Traditionally psychologists have agreed that gifted children can not be identified before the age of 3 years. Recent research (Flavell, 1985; Freeman, 1985) indicates, however, that even tiny infants remember and learn much more than had been previously assumed. Therefore, it is useful for professionals and parents alike to be aware of characteristics manifested even early in life that, when observed together, may be associated with outstanding future accomplishments. What are these behavioral characteristics that differentiate gifted children from their peers? It has long been recognized that gifted children start to do almost everything earlier than other children (Ginsberg & Harrison, 1977). Characteristics typical of gifted 3-year-olds identified by the Harvard Project 1965–1978 (White, 1985) included more role play, make-believe, and pretend than the average child. By age 6, these children evidenced a desire to compete, were more comfortable with adults than their nongifted peers, and had unusually well developed capacities to sense discrepancies or difficulties.

Many lists of characteristics of gifted children are available in a number of sources (e.g., Clark, 1979; Martinson, 1977; Tuttle & Becker, 1980; Hagan, 1980; Renzulli, Hartman, & Callahan, 1971; Whitmore, 1985). Table 1 gives a summary of observable characteristics often ascribed to gifted children.

The population of gifted children is an extremely heterogeneous group and not all children who are gifted will display all of these characteristics. That the gifted are individuals with unique personalities, interests, etc., cannot be discounted. Recognition of these behavioral characteristics by parents and teachers can add a dimension to identification of gifted students not evaluated by use of traditional psychometric procedures alone (Gridley & Treloar, 1984).

PUTTING CHILDHOOD GIFTEDNESS IN PERSPECTIVE

Gifted children tend to be superior in every way (Terman & Oden, 1959). While Terman's studies tended to dispel the stereotype of emotional and physical weakness as an accompaniment of intellectual superiority, there are some problems inherent in the foregoing generalization. The danger is that the opposite stereotype will develop. In the United States, this has been especially true in our expectations of the *Wunderkinder* or "superkids," who are expected to do everything well. What special deficiencies do false expectations produce? What children do we overlook because of these stereotypes?

Several obstacles to identification of and programming for gifted students are given below (this list is an expanded version of one that appeared in Whitmore, 1985):

1. Too much reliance on testing alone. Ability and achievement testing often identify only high achievers and good test takers.
2. Stereotypical expectations. Teachers and parents expect gifted children to excel in all areas.
3. Immaturity. Many teachers are reluctant to refer students whom they deem socially and/or emotionally immature for gifted programs. In addition, if some of these students have been identified to receive programming, their teachers and parents often do not see these children as being "truly" gifted.
4. Lack of apparent motivation. Students who seem unmotivated to succeed are often overlooked or dropped from gifted programs. Unfortunately, it may be the very lack of appropriate motivators found in an unchallenging curriculum that feeds this type of behavior. These are the students who often get into trouble because of boredom with regular programming.
5. Prior identification of a handicapping condition. In many school districts, students who have been identified as vision- or hearing-impaired, physically handicapped, or learning-disabled are often not considered for gifted programs.
6. Personality and learning characteristics. For example, girls often take fewer risks than their male counterparts and develop different value systems.
7. Language and other problems associated with certain culturally different groups.

ALTERNATIVE ACTIONS

Educational

Perhaps the most common questions school psychologists and other professionals are asked about gifted children deal with educational placement and decision making. There are many available programming options for gifted school children. The major options include (a) acceleration, (b) enrichment, (c) special class placement, and (d) independent study. An excellent review of types of programs that addresses the areas of curriculum, instructional strategies, and special grouping is given in Fox and Washington (1985).

One generally suggested procedure for educational decision making that applies equally well to gifted students as to others is a procedure often taught in beginning assessment classes and described in terms of the simple mnemonic scheme P-I-E-E-S (Weaver, 1984). This scheme provides for integration of (P)hysical, (I)ntellectual, (E)motional, (E)ducational, and (S)ocial aspects. Whether formal evaluation and referral proce-

TABLE 1

Characteristics of Potentially Gifted Children for Aid in Identification*

1. Curiosity
   Persistent curiosity: "bug" you with a lot of questions — more logical and searching questions; keen observational skills; desire to learn rapidly.

2. Memory
   Good memory; retention of an extraordinary quantity and variety of information; broad, changing spectrum of interests.

3. Higher-order thinking skills
   Ability to find and solve problems; understanding of complex concepts; ability to perceive relationships; ability to work with abstractions and to generalize; generate original ideas and solutions; strong critical thinking skills and self-criticism.

4. Language
   High level of language development; early, accurate use of advanced vocabulary; ability to reproduce stories and events with great detail at an early age.

5. Precociousness
   Precocity in physical and intellectual development such as early walking, talking, or reading; advanced expression of interest or talent in a specific area such as music.

6. Attention and concentration
   Longer attention span and ability to concentrate, for longer periods than normal for child's age; persistent goal-directed behavior; periods of intense concentrationl

7. Social maturity
   Tendency to prefer companionship of older children and adults; ability to converse intelligently with older children and adults; social maturity above that expected for age.

8. Sense of humor
   Keen sense of humor; often more insightful than peers; able to see subtle humor in a situation.

Note: Not all gifted children will exhibit all listed characteristics.

*Compiled from the following sources: Clark (1979); Ginsberg & Harrison (1977); Hallahan & Kauffman (1982); Hall & Skinner (1980); Renzulli (1979); Tannenbaum (1983).

dures are instituted or not, gathering information concerning these aspects of a child's functioning can help to make informed decisions. This holistic approach to evaluation reminds one that educational decisions must address cognitive functioning but be couched in terms of emotional, physical, and psychosocial maturity as well. An educational decision based on intellectual and achievement (educational) data alone may be inadequate in as much as the child's functioning in each area impacts on virtually all of the others. For example, the presence of sensory impairments such as hearing deficits may lead not only to language and cognitive delays but also to lack of maturity in social interactions as the child is unable to decode verbal cues. In addition, increased dependency because of the impairment may lead to lags in cognitive as well as social functioning.

Often the first contacts school psychologists have with gifted children and their parents are made in regard to early entrance into kindergarten, that is, before the legal entrance age has been reached. Research has shown that superior achievement but no real differences in adjustment are shown by children admitted early into kindergarten provided that special attention has been paid to socioemotional concerns (Obrzut, Nelson, & Obrzut, 1984). However, these same researchers pointed out that "early school entrance for intellectually superior children puts them 'at risk' in the social–emotional area of development" (p. 76).

Double promotion (grade skipping) was a common practice early in this century, but is rarely found today except in extreme cases. Critics cite social and emotional harm, as well as the missing of essential skills and/or blocks of curriculum. It is more likely that a student will be accelerated in a single subject area. Complete information should be gathered and counseling given the child and the parents about both positive and negative aspects prior to the decision.

Social/Emotional/Family

Educational programming for the gifted does not often address affective concerns included for other areas of exceptionality. While, as a group, these youngsters do not have more emotional problems and indeed seem to be more well adjusted than their peers, there are individual deviations from the mean. The most effective attitude to adopt is that no stereotypes apply. These are simply children like all others. No child should be denied programming to develop intellectual potential on the basis of emotional or social grounds. Instead, these areas of weakness should be dealt with in much the same way as strengths and weaknesses and addressed for other exceptional populations under PL 94-142. Each gifted child is an individual to whom individual decisions apply. However, there are some unique problems that seem to arise more often among gifted students than others.

Contrary to what many professionals may believe, not all middle-class parents look for giftedness in all of their own children. Often, parents will not be overjoyed at being told that their child is gifted. These parents sometimes feel inadequate and unsure of their own abilities and their abilities to deal effectively with this special child. Recent evidence (Cornell, 1983) suggests that the family structure is altered significantly when one child has been identified as being gifted. Problems arise from such individuals themselves. Emotional problems seem to be directly related to how they feel. The more different they feel, the more apt they are to develop emotional difficulties. This means that for highly intelligent children, emotional problems are likely to be more prevalent.

In addition, problems often develop because of inconsistent development in different areas. For example, intellectually mature children whose motor coordination has not developed to a comparably high level often feel frustrated when they can't perform up to their own expectations. Problems develop when parents expect that a child's emotional development will keep pace with the intellectual development. Contradictions occur when the child is curious about and able to deal with topics more advanced than others of his or her age one minute and the next reacts to a new sibling by returning to "babyish" patterns. Parents need to be counseled that this is probably perfectly normal behavior. This brings to mind the experience of the mother of a gifted first grader who thought she was emotionally disturbed because she was asking grown-up questions about death that her older siblings had never asked at this age. Parents as well as anyone may be frightened by what they don't understand.

Gifted children and adolescents have problems in accepting their own shortcomings as well as those of others. While they are hypersensitive to feelings about themselves and others, they seem to have trouble dealing with this awareness. This may lead to inadequate social interactions with a concomitant dearth of appropriate reward systems, resulting in isolation and loneliness.

Parental expectations range from putting rather extreme pressures on these children to succeed to a laissez faire attitude in which the feeling is that "they'll get it on their own." Parents must be encouraged to provide appropriate opportunities without accompanying pressures for success. Parents often forget that children do not always have the same interests and attitudes that they had at the same age; such children need latitude and encouragement to develop their own interests. Gifted children also often place unrealistic pressures on themselves. In adolescents this can lead to more serious emotional problems such as depression and thoughts of suicide. A student who is doing well academically is not exempted from having serious social or emotional problems. Too often parents and professionals alike discount the seriousness of problems that are found to arise. Professional counseling is recommended for these students and their parents.

Children's play is an important component in intellectual as well as emotional development for all children. Too often parents place undue emphasis on intellectual achievement without encouragement toward more imaginative exploits. Gifted children often have difficulty integrating high-level cognitive processes with lower levels of emotional maturity. Parents should allow them ample opportunity to daydream, fantasize, and engage in seemingly nondirected activities. Parents can extend play with suggestions for generalization of concepts and principles. For example, a young child may be encouraged to go beyond merely labeling to classifying according to different attributes. A parent may say "Yes, those are all farm animals," when the child names cow, pig, horse from pictures. Kaplan (1980) gives further examples of how a young child's play can be enhanced by adults without intrusion into the important world of the child. It is important that gifted children be allowed to help in guiding and planning their own endeavors. Flavell (1985) recently urged that "whatever other functions play might serve in the child's life (and there are probably quite a few), no one has ever doubted that it is a major vehicle for learning and mental development" (p. 23). Keeping this in mind, parents should be encouraged to allow their children to be "children." Time should be allowed for unstructured activities as well as the usual music lessons, clubs, organized sports, etc.

Another problem area for the gifted is sibling and peer relations (Grenier, 1985). Often rivalries develop when siblings or peers sense that the gifted child is being singled out for extra programs and attention. Parents should be encouraged to provide plenty of individual attention to all their children, no matter the individual child's capabilities. Each child has needs and individual strengths as well. Parents can encourage all of their children to pursue those areas in which their interests and abilities lie.

The consummate curiosity that gifted children display can be a handicap. Gifted children are sometimes a "pain in the neck" for both parents and teachers. They often ask insightful and probing questions; they seem reluctant to take rules and requests at face value and question the veracity of information presented to them. Parents and teachers sometimes resent this incessant questioning and what they see to be a questioning of their authority. The role of the professional here is to help parents find support groups composed of other parents and/or other sources of information (see annotated bibliography at the end of this chapter). The professional can reassure parents that their concerns are real, and that it takes gifted adults to recognize questions that are designed not so much to put them on the spot as to secure accurate information. Patience and understanding are needed to deal with the special foibles of these children.

Special Subpopulations

A handicapped gifted child represents a challenging overlap of categories. These children include those with visual and hearing impairments, physical handicaps, or learning disabilities. Some of our most gifted producers with such handicaps have included Itzhak Perlman, Helen Keller, Ray Charles, Thomas Edison, and Nelson Rockefeller. What a loss to society if their gifts had been overlooked because of their handicaps. A handicapping condition must not preclude students categorically from receiving gifted programming. However, in many school districts this is the practice. The intent of PL 94-142 was to provide for individual programming for students based on their strengths as well as their weaknesses. Identification of handicapped youngsters as gifted is impeded by the masking of their extraordinary abilities by other problems. For example, academic excellence may be limited by speed of production. In addition, greater dependence and generally lower levels of maturity may be misleading. In the process of teaching basic skills; higher-level thinking skills are often ignored. Those with communication difficulties are especially at a disadvantage. Whitmore (1985) suggested that handicapped youngsters be judged with regard to peers having similar handicaps and that a determination be made of those who are superior in various ways. More collaboration and sharing among various special educators is also called for in helping to identify these extra special youngsters.

Culturally different students including blacks, Mexican-Americans, Orientals, low-SES whites, etc., are also frequently overlooked in regard to gifted programs. Teachers are misled by language problems, lack of general types of knowledge, and different norms for social behavior. Different personality styles such as variation in activity or passivity, etc., are other barriers. Teachers need to become more aware of various cultural norms as a means of making more-informed decisions.

While there are slightly more males than females at either end of the normal distribution of intelligence (Maccoby & Jacklin, 1974), these differences do not account for the superiority of males in adult attainment. There is not sufficient evidence to support a thesis of biological and/or hormonal reasons for these differences. Instead, the research points to socialization experiences (Fox & Zimmerman, 1985). In addition, male and female choices for careers may depend more on value differences than on abilities or aptitudes. Girls must be encouraged to pursue careers regardless of societal pressures that tend to consign them to more traditional roles. The conflict between what a woman wants to do and what society tells her to do may result in anxiety and guilt. In addition, males are more often risk takers and are more often counseled to take advantage of special programming. Enrichment activities for females should focus on independence and risk-taking behavior as well as more cognitive pursuits. Support from teachers, counselors, and parents is vital for girls to facilitate development of their giftedness, competence, and self-confidence. Professionals must be aware and concerned about transmission of subtle messages about male–female differences. Differential expectations based on gender need to be guarded against.

SUMMARY

If our educational system were centered around and attuned to the individual differences of all children, it would not be necessary to attach labels, and the needs of all children would be addressed on an individual basis. Unfortunately, at the present time, individual educational programming is a reality only for those children to whom labels can be attached. There is ample evidence that unless gifted children receive appropriate educational experiences the promise of their gifts will never be fulfilled. This means that there is a need for informed, concerned professionals who can help identify gifted potential at an early age. This identification becomes especially important for those gifted individuals within certain subgroups who are often overlooked in traditional identification procedures. In addition, these professionals can help provide parents with appropriate information about programming, leadership, and support. These professionals are available to help match children's needs with appropriate programming and suggest challenges such as outside resources and mentors.

In addition, gifted children seem to have special needs in the area of emotional and social interactions and face as well particular dynamics within the family unit. As Janos & Robinson (1985) have asserted, the "most critical resource" for gifted children and their families may be school psychologists and counselors.

REFERENCES

Alexander, P. A., & Muia, J. A. (1982). *Gifted education.* Rockville, MD: Aspen Systems.

Clark, B. (1979). *Growing up gifted.* Columbus, OH: Merrill.

Cornell, D. G. (1983). Gifted children: The impact of positive labeling on the family system. *American Journal of Orthopsychiatry, 53,* 323–335.

Fischman, R. (1985). Best practices in the evaluation of gifted children, In A. Thomas & J. Grimes (Eds.), *Best practices in school psychology* (pp. 143–155). Kent, OH: National Association of School Psychologists.

Flavell, J. H. (1985). *Cognitive development* (2nd ed.). Englewood Cliffs, NJ: Prentice-Hall.

Fox, L. H. (1981). Identification of the academically gifted. *American Psychologist, 36,* 1103–1111.

Fox, L. H., & Washington, J. (1985). Programs for the gifted and talented: Past, present, and future. In F. D. Horowitz & M. O'Brien (Eds.), *The gifted and talented: Developmental perspectives* (pp. 197–221). Washington, DC: American Psychological Association.

Fox, L. H., & Zimmerman, W. Z. (1985). Gifted women. In J. Freeman (Ed.), *The psychology of gifted children* (pp. 219–243). New York: Wiley.

Freeman, J. (1985). A pedagogy for the gifted. In J. Freeman (Ed.), *The psychology of gifted children* (pp. 219–243). New York: Wiley.

Getzels, J. W., & Jackson, P. W. (1958). The meaning of "giftedness" — An examination of an expanding concept. *Phi Delta Kappan, 40,* 275–277.

Ginsberg, G., & Harrison, C. H. (1977). *How to help your gifted child: A handbook for parents and teachers.* New York: Monarch.

Gowan, J. C. (1979). The use of developmental stage theory in helping gifted children become creative. In *Issues in gifted education.* Ventura, CA: Ventura County Superintendent of Schools Office.

Grenier, M. E. (1985). Gifted children and other siblings. *Gifted Child Quarterly, 29,* 164–167.

Gridley, B. E., & Treloar, J. H. (1984). The validity of the Scales for Rating the Behavioral Characteristics of Superior Students for the identification of gifted students. *Journal of Psychoeducational Assessment, 2,* 65–71.

Gruber, H. E. (1985). Giftedness and moral responsibility: Creative thinking and human survival. In F. D. Horowitz & M. O'Brien (Eds.), *The gifted and talented: Developmental Perspectives* (pp. 301–330). Washington, DC: American Psychological Association.

Guilford, J. P. (1967). *The nature of human intelligence.* New York: McGraw-Hill.

Hagen, E. (1980). *Identification of the gifted.* New York: Teachers College Press.

Hall, E. G., & Skinner, N. (1980). *Somewhere to turn.* New York: Columbia University Teachers College.

Hallahan, D. P., & Kauffman, J. M. (1982). *Exceptional Children, Introduction to special education.* Englewood Cliffs, NJ: Prentice-Hall.

Horowitz, F. D., & O'Brien, M. (1985). *The gifted and talented developmental perspectives.* Washington, DC: American Psychological Association.

Janos, P. M., & Robinson, N. M. (1985). Psychosocial development in intellectually gifted children. In F. D. Horowitz and M. O'Brien (Eds.), *The gifted and talented, Developmental perspectives* (pp. 149–195). Washington, DC: American Psychological Association.

Johnson, L. G. (1983). Giftedness in preschool: A better time for development than identification. *Roeper Review, 5*(4), 13–15.

Kaplan, S. N. (1980). The role of play in a differentiated curriculum for the young gifted child. *Roeper Review, 3,* 12–13.

Karnes, F. A., & Collins, E. C. (1981). *Assessment in gifted education.* Springfield, IL: Thomas.

Maccoby, E. E., & Jacklin, C. N. (1974). *The Psychology of Sex Differences.* Stanford, CA: Stanford University Press.

Marland, S. P., Jr. (1971). *Education of the gifted and talented,* Vol. 1 (Report to the Congress of the United States by the US Commissioner of Education). Washington, DC: U.S. Government Printing Office.

Martinson, R. (1977). *The identification of the gifted and talented.* Ventura, CA: Ventura County Schools.

Obrzut, A., Nelson, B., & Obrzut, J. F. (1984). Early school entrance for intellectually superior children: An analysis. *Psychology in the Schools, 21,* 71–77.

Renzulli, J. S. (1979). *What makes giftedness: A reexamination of the definition of the gifted and talented.* Ventura, CA: Ventura County Superintendent of Schools.

Renzulli, J. S., Hartman, R. K., & Callahan, C. M. (1971). Teacher identification of superior students. *Exceptional Children, 38,* 211–214, 243–248.

Sellin, D. F.,& Birch, J. W. (1980). *Educating gifted and talented learners.* Rockville, MD: Aspen Systems.

Tannenbaum, A. J. (1983). *Gifted Children, Psychological and educational perspectives.* New York: Macmillan.

Terman, L. M. (1925). *Genetic studies of genius: Vol. 1: Mental and physical traits of a thousand gifted children.* Stanford, CA: Stanford University Press.

Terman, L. M., & Oden, M. (1959). *Genetic studies of genius, Vol. V: The gifted group at mid-life.* Stanford, CA: Stanford University Press.

Torrance, E. P. (1962). *Guiding creative talent.* Englewood Cliffs, NJ: Prentice-Hall.

Tuttle, F. B., Jr., & Becker, L. A. (1980). *Characteristics and identification of gifted and talented students.* Washington, DC: National Education Association of the United States.

Weaver, S. J. (1984). Introduction to the psychological assessment process. In S. J. Weaver (Ed.), *Testing children* (pp. 1–14). Kansas City, KS: Test Corporation of America.

White, B. (1985). Competence and giftedness. In J. Freeman (Ed.), *The psychology of gifted children* (pp. 59–73). New York: Wiley.

Whitmore, J. (1985). New challenges to common identification practices. In Freeman, J. (Ed.), *The psychology of gifted children* (pp. 93–113). New York: Wiley.

BIBLIOGRAPHY: PROFESSIONALS

Fischman, R. (1985). Best practices in the evaluation of gifted children. In A. Thomas & J. Grimes (Eds.), *Best Practices in school psychology* (pp. 143–155). Kent, OH: National Association of School Psychologists.
A very complete coverage of screening, assessment, and psychometric issues in identification of gifted students.

Hallahan, D. P., & Kauffman, J. M. (1978). Giftedness. In *Exceptional children. Introduction to special education* (Chapter 9, pp. 372–411). Englewood Cliffs, NJ: Prentice-Hall.
An excellent summary chapter looking at giftedness from the perspective of a category of exceptionality. Surprisingly complete coverage. If you only have time to read one source, read this.

Horowitz, F. D., & O'Brien, M. (1985). *The gifted and talented. Developmental perspectives.* Washington, DC: American Psychological Association.
An edited book that deals with many current issues in the entire field of gifted education.

Karnes, F. A., & Collins, E. C. (1981). *Assessment in gifted education.* Springfield, IL: Thomas.
A comprehensive compilation and analysis of instruments used in the assessment of gifted and talented students. Excellent sourcebook.

Tannenbaum, A. J. (1983). *Gifted children. Psychological and educational perspectives.* New York: Macmillan.
A scholarly work including a good literature review of the entire area. Includes appendix on methods, techniques, and educational programs for stimulating creativity.

BIBLIOGRAPHY: PARENTS

American Association for Gifted Children. (1978). *On being gifted.* New York: Walker and Company.
Written by a group of gifted and talented students. This provides an insightful look into the major problems and concerns as well as positive aspects of "being gifted."

Ginsberg, G., & Harrison, C. H. (1977). *How to help your gifted child: A handbook for parents and teachers.* New York: Monarch.
A practical, how-to book. Provides suggestions for coping, as well as specific activities and suggestions for parenting groups.

Hall, E. G., & Skinner, N. (1980). *Somewhere to turn.* New York: Teachers College, Columbia University.
One of a series of books published by The Gifted and Talented Project headed by Abraham J. Tannenbaum. Practically oriented to answer parents' questions and concerns. Includes activities and strategies.

Lewis, D. (1979). *How to be a gifted parent.* New York: Norton.
Must reading for *every* parent. Common sense approach to parenting, in general.

Children and Grades

William Strein
University of Maryland

BACKGROUND

Grading, especially the traditional A, B, C, D, F system, is one of the most pervasive practices of U.S. school systems (Evans, 1976). There is ample evidence that grading practices have significant effects on children's work habits, attitudes, and self-esteem. To the anguish of many educators, students are most often heard to ask "WAD-JA-GET?" (Kirschenbaum, Simon, & Napier, 1971) in response to returned papers, rather than focusing on the specific aspects of their own performance. Despite many efforts to the contrary, parents still attach more importance to the grades that their children receive than to written comments of the teacher or behavior-oriented checklists of strengths and weaknesses. Clearly, grading has a significant impact on the lives of children and adolescents.

Although grading seems natural and inevitable to virtually everyone in the United States, the practice of assigning a "mark" to a student's work is scarcely 100 years old. What is now considered traditional grading began at about the turn of this century as an attempt to make education more efficient, and in line with the then current belief that everything can be measured (Cohen, 1983). The practice of giving grades or marks is extremely widespread. Even the Soviet Union uses a 5-point system for evaluating students' work (Stewin, 1980).

A thoughtful analysis of grades must begin with a working definition of what is meant by the term *grade.* The following definition (adopted with revisions from Terwilliger, 1977, p. 22) will be used: A grade is a symbol (letter, number, word) that represents a value judgment concerning the relative quality of a student's achievement or performance.

Distinguishing between *measurement* and *evaluation* is also critical to understanding the issue of grading. Measurement is "the process that attempts to obtain a quantified representation of the degree to which a student reflects a trait" (Ahmann & Glock, 1981, p. 11), whereas grading and all other forms of evaluation always represent an *evaluative judgment* of the student's performance rather than an absolute measurement of the performance itself. For example, the same score of

---

The author wishes to express his sincere appreciation to Ms. Beverly L. Cohen, who provided invaluable research assistance in the preparation of this chapter.

80/100 on a difficult spelling test might be viewed as outstanding, receiving an A, in a school where few students excel academically but be viewed as merely average, receiving a B or C, in a highly competitive or select school. Typically, grades are assigned to convey one or more of four broad meanings: (a) certification of competency or mastery of a specific set of skills or knowledge, (b) improvement during some period of time, (c) perceived effort, or (d) ranking of a student's performance relative to others (Carpenter, Grantham, & Hardister, 1983). The meaning of any given grade, then, can only be correctly interpreted by knowing which of the four basic messages the teacher was trying to convey. Interpreting grades without additional information is particularly difficult, since different teachers put relatively more emphasis on each of the four basic meanings of grades, and even the same teacher may accent different aspects of grading from one time to another or from one student to another.

In addition to the differing meanings that grades convey, grades are intended to serve a wide variety of functions including providing corrective feedback to the student, motivating the student to learn, informing parents about their children's progress, and informing employers and postsecondary institutions about a student's mastery of the curriculum or abut the student's relative mastery compared to other students. Even strong proponents of traditional grading agree that no single system of evaluation can serve these diverse functions equally well (Terwilliger, 1977).

Before continuing to discuss grades, several technical terms need to be defined. *Norm-referenced* grading, more popularly known as "grading on the curve," is the practice of grading students relative to one another. In this system, only a limited number of students can receive top grades and a certain, small proportion of students will usually receive failing grades. The group to which a student is compared might be the student's own class, grade, all students in a particular course, or all students who have recently taken a given course. In *criterion-referenced* grading, sometimes called mastery of fixed-standard grading, students are assigned grades based on reaching some preset criterion. In principle, all students in a class in which criterion-referenced grading is used could receive A's if each student met the criteria set for an A. A newer wrinkle on the criterion-referenced model is *contract grading*. Here, each student receives a grade based on a preset criterion, but the criteria are individually set for each student by mutual agreement between the instructor and the student, occasionally including the student's parents. The *pass/fail* grading system can be used with either the norm-referenced or criterion-referenced models, but is usually used with the latter. As the name implies, the student in this system receives one of only two possible grades, P or F, depending on satisfactory or unsatisfactory performance.

Effects of Grades on Students and Teachers

Grading is a controversial topic that produces volumes of strongly stated opinion and relatively little research. The author's review of the professional literature for the past 10 years produced 42 articles, but only 10 of these reported any original research. Similarly, Yarborough and Johnson (1980) found only 23 research studies in a 30-year period that related grading practices to reading achievement. In the absence of a large body of research, it is fruitful to consider the philosophical and other arguments made for and against grading.

Most of the critiques of grading have focused on presumed positive or negative effects on students or teachers of using traditional letter grades. Although in theory one could assign grades based on either a purely norm- or criterion-referenced system, in practice most teachers use some combination of both systems, even when they think they are using only one or the other (Terwilliger, 1977). One of the most common objections to the traditional system is that it breeds competition among the students, inevitably creating "winners" and "losers" and fostering a climate in which "classroom success is a finite quantity to be distributed to a limited number of students on the basis of who crosses the finish line first" (Dilendik, 1978, p. 90). Many critics (Bresee, 1976) fear that traditional grading directs the student's attention from the learning task to a competition task, thereby reducing any intrinsic motivation that the learning task might have. In parallel fashion, traditional grading may lead teachers to believe that if most or all of their students are receiving good grades, then they are either weak teachers or soft graders (Bresee, 1976). Other critics have been concerned that grades cause students to be overly dependent on teachers, resulting in decreased self-initiation and creativity (Longstreet, 1975). The majority of critics of traditional grading have supported some more pure form of criterion-referenced grading as an alternative.

Defenders of traditional grading generally point to the motivational value of grades and to their efficiency in providing a succinct evaluation of students' progress (Rhine, 1975). In addition, Rhine (1975) observes that all evaluations effectively use comparative categories, such as "good" or "excellent," which are really no different than a letter grade. Terwilliger (1977) defends comparative grading on the grounds that the identification of the person's relative strengths and weaknesses is beneficial both to society and to the student, in that such information helps the student to identify areas of relative weakness and helps in making career or other choices.

Actual research on the effects of grades has been sparse, but what research does exist is generally not very supportive of traditional grading. Yarborough and Johnson (1980) identified 23 research studies between the 1950s and the 1980s that studied the effects of graded versus nongraded settings on reading achievement. Of these, 11 studies found advantages for nongraded settings, 9 found no differences, and 3 were inconclusive. None of the 23 studies found clear advantages for the graded settings. These researchers then conducted their own study of seventh-grade students who had completed six previous years in a nongraded, nonmarked school compared to a matched group of controls from traditional, graded schools. In results that were similar to those of previous studies, Yarborough and Johnson (1980) found no differences between the two groups on achievement in reading or language arts. A clear picture of the effects of giving grades is confounded in all of these studies because the experimental groups varied from the control groups in that they did not receive traditional letter grades and were enrolled in schools in which students were not assigned to traditional grade levels.

Although the research does not support, in general, the idea that grades have positive effects on pupils, some interesting differential effects likely exist. Perseley (1975) found that grades *do* function as motivators for motivated, upper elementary students but that they do not function similarly for low-achieving students. Similarly, Evans (1976) reviewed existing research and concluded that anxiety about grades increases grades of students already receiving good grades but lowers grades of students whose previous performance has been average. Interestingly, Yarborough and Johnson (1980) did not find differential effects on achievement but did find differential effects on affective variables such as attitudes toward school or self-concept. High-ability students benefited affectively from being in graded schools, whereas low-ability students benefited affectively from being in schools in which marks weren't given.

All of the research cited above can be criticized on the grounds that students in the different grading systems were also in different schools, may have been from different neighborhoods, and so on. One study did directly compare norm-referenced and criterion-referenced grading. Miller (1983) studied fifth- and sixth-grade students who were assigned to study French under one of the two grading conditions. Compared to students in the criterion-referenced condition, students who received norm-referenced grades scored lower on tests, studied and reviewed less at home, felt less confident about their abilities, were more anxious about taking tests, reported more negative attitudes toward French, and were less interested in taking more French.

Issues Relating to Traditional Grading

The most commonly addressed issue related to traditional grading has been the question of the subjectivity of grading. Numerous studies have shown that the same student performance will receive widely varying grades when rated by different teachers. This is particularly true for the grading of activities such as essays, which require a double judgment from the grader — first, a judgment about how the student performed, and second, what level of quality the performance represents. On "objective" tests in which there are clear right and wrong answers, such as a spelling test, the grader only has to judge the quality level of the performance. Clearly, in both cases there is some form of value judgment about the student's performance. In fact, all grading involves a value judgment, usually the classroom teacher's (Terwilliger, 1977), and all grading therefore includes a subjective element. The relevant question then becomes not whether grading is subjective but whether the subjective standards applied by the teacher and/or school are appropriate (Rhine, 1975).

Teacher's grades have been found to be influenced by such nonrelevant factors as penmanship, the student's voice characteristics (Crowl, 1984), the student's reputation, discipline problems, the student's membership in a class group, and sex and race (Leiter & Brown, 1985). One study (Crowl, 1984) even found that elementary teachers' need for social approval influenced their grading of essays, even though they did not know the students being graded. A recent comprehensive study of the determinants of reading and math grades in early elementary years (Leiter & Brown, 1985) suggested that grading is a complex process in which the students' and teachers' expectations of one another interact in subtle ways to produce a self-fulfilling prophecy. The same study also found that classroom grades are more related to specific classroom achievement than to broader measures of achievement in the subject area, such as scores on a standardized achievement test.

The latter finding from the Leiter and Brown (1985) study illustrates an important aspect of classroom grades. To the extent that a teacher's grades represent valid measurements of something, they are largely a measure of *classroom performance* rather than of skills or knowledge. A highly skilled student who is not motivated to perform in class or who has poor workhabits may get low grades, whereas a student who has somewhat lesser skills but who performs well in class may receive higher grades. In fact, in a massive study of high school grades Keith (1982) found that the average low-ability student who did as little as 1–3 hours of homework per week received grades that were comparable to the grades of average-ability students who did no homework.

A second commonly raised issue is whether grades in elementary or high school relate to anything important later on. The answer to this question largely depends on what later criteria one chooses. Elementary school grades do correlate with high school grades, and grades from year to year in high school are moderately related (r equals about .6) to one another. High school grades are about equally related to college grades (Evans, 1976) and are the best single predictor of college performance for most students. By contrast, research has generally found little or no relationship between college grades and "real-life" outcomes. However, research on the relationship between grades and adult accomplishments is plagued with numerous technical problems, and employers and colleges nevertheless do place a high value on grades (Evans, 1976). The common-sense belief that students who receive better grades in school generally have more opportunities available to them and are more likely to advance professionaly should not be quickly dismissed.

DEVELOPMENT

A common question in parents' minds is, "Are my child's grades likely to get much better or worse in the coming years?" This question is relatively easily answered in the abstract, but for any individual student the answer may be quite complex. In general, grades are moderately stable over time (Evans, 1976) and from one subject area to another (Leiter & Brown, 1985). In other words, using broad categories, students' grades don't change much. Most children, for example, who begin school as average students more or less remain so throughout their school years. The same is generally true for students considerably above or below average. Similarly, although most students do a bit better or worse in some subjects, they generally receive similar grades across the board. A student who receives A's in math usually doesn't receive D's in language arts. Since grades reflect some mixture of skills and performance and since both skills and work habits tend to change incrementally rather than suddenly, grades are likely to become more stable as the student progresses through school.

A significant change in grades not caused by any real change in the student, but caused by changing teachers must be considered. Grades always involve subjective judgments, and judgments clearly vary from teacher to teacher. Furthermore, since grading is probably a complex interaction between student and teacher (Leiter & Brown, 1985), there is ample room for so-called "personality conflicts" or other nonrelevant influences on the grading process. Students expect some teachers to grade harder than others and perceive that teachers give higher grades to students they like, but students generally perceive that teachers are fair in their grading (Hull, 1980). On an individual case basis, however, the possibility that one teacher gives lower grades than other teachers or is somehow biased against a given student needs to be investigated when trying to explain a decline in the student's grades.

Notwithstanding the general stability of grades over time and subject matter, there are some sharp and somewhat predictable deviations from the pattern of stable grades. Mastery of the curriculum objectives plays an important role in grading, and the demands of the curriculum change in predictable ways through the elementary and middle school years. In early elementary school the curriculum largely requires rote memory skills, such as learning phonics rules or number facts. Around third or fourth grade the curriculum begins to require some modest conceptual skills, such as the ability to comprehend reading material or to apply math facts to solve problems. A further increased demand for conceptual and analytic abilities occurs at about the seventh grade. Students who have an uneven development of abilities may experience rather abrupt changes in grades as a result of the shifting curriculum demands. Children who have a relatively good memory compared to their conceptual skills often receive satisfactory grades in the early years but show fairly rapid declines in grades around the third or fourth grade. This pattern is common for "slow learners," certain learning-disabled children, or even for mildly retarded children, if these children are motivated and have good memory skills.

At about the same points at which the curriculum shifts emphasis toward more conceptual objectives, demands also change in regard to students' self-sufficiency. Starting around the third grade, students are increasingly expected to work independently during "seatwork" periods or on homework assignments. As the students move into departmentalized structures in which each student has several teachers, demands for self-sufficiency and organizational skills take another leap. Most students are able to adjust to these shifting demands, but for those students who have difficulty working independently, who have strong needs for frequent approval from adults, or who are disorganized, these shifts can be disastrous, resulting in dramatically lower grades. Students with certain types of learning disabilities, especially attention deficit disorders or hyperactivity, and students with emotional problems frequently follow this pattern.

The foregoing discussion of the stability of grades has assumed that the student has either remained in the same school system or has moved within similar systems. Moving between dissimilar schools can have a significant impact on grades but does so in predictable ways. Schools vary tremendously in the average skill level of, and hence the expectations for, their students. Since classroom grades almost always contain some norm-referenced element, one can easily predict that a student who moves to a school with higher expectations will experience some decline in grades; transfer to a school with lower standards will likely result in higher grades. Such changes have little to do with changes in the student's mastery level but reflect a change in relative standing. Changes in grades caused by a change in expectations are most likely to occur for the broad range of average or above-average students. Outstanding students are likely to continue to excel. Conversely, students who receive low or failing grades usually do so because of very poorly developed skills and/or other factors that inhibit classroom performance. These difficulties are likely to result in low grades in any system, since although there are wide differences between schools in terms of expectations for students, the general demands for basic academic and self-sufficiency skills are quite similar. This is an important consideration because many parents whose child is failing attempt to cure the problem by moving the child to a less competitive school, for example by moving the child from a parochial to a public school. Such a move, in itself, seldom solves the problem. It is much more helpful to attempt to identify the causes of the student's low grades and to obtain the services and learning environment necessary to improve performance.

PUTTING GRADES IN PERSPECTIVE

Philosophical and well-reasoned academic arguments notwithstanding, grades are important because, as a society, we believe they are so. The use of grades, especially the traditional five-letter system, is extremely widespread and ingrained from kindergarten to graduate school. Grades clearly may have positive or negative effects on a student's achievement, motivation, and emotional well-being; they are surely not neutral. But, despite their obvious importance, grades should not be given more status than they deserve. For example, although grades are often thought of as motivators for student achievement, this appears to only be the case for high achievers (Yarborough & Johnson, 1980). Therefore, teachers and parents need not be overly fearful that alternate grading systems used with low-achieving students are detrimental to the students' motivation. Similarly, although grades are important factors in gaining admission to highly selective colleges, grades are only moderate predictors of college performance, and are questionable predictors of adult accomplishments (Evans, 1976).

An important perspective on grades is that they are relatively poor vehicles for communication, even though this is one of their primary purposes. Grades are meant to communicate to four different audiences, each of which interprets grades differently. Students expect that grades reflect their performance in class, parents often see grades as their sole source of information about their children's progress, school personnel see grades as providing an academic picture of the student, and post-secondary employers and schools see grades as indicators of future performance. If teachers intend to convey one of four basic meanings with their grades (mastery, effort, improvement, relative standing) and these grades are then interpreted in one of these four ways, it is clear that there are 16 possible sender/receiver combinations of which only 4 are correct matches. In other words, in about 75% of the cases there is some miscommunication (Carpenter, Grantham & Hardister, 1983). Grades should be interpreted cautiously. If one wishes to ask a specific question about a student's progress, information in addition to grades is needed.

Grades, or changes therein, do have diagnostic value but more as a general indication that something is going on rather than as an indication of what specifically is happening. As discussed above, a variety of factors influence the stability of grades. When grades are used as a diagnostic indicator, all of these factors must be considered. Do the changes in the grades primarily reflect changes in the student or changes in the evaluative standards occasioned by changing schools or teachers? Are lower grades primarily the result of a shift in the cognitive demands of the curriculum? If so, the change may suggest some problem with underlying learning aptitudes. Are the lower grades primarily the result of a shift in the self-sufficiency demands of the curriculum? If so, the change may suggest problems with ability to attend or with social/emotional development. Lower grades resulting from reduced classroom performance, rather than inadequate skills, may also result from more recent emotional concerns or trauma, such as parents' divorce, death of a loved one, child abuse, and so on. In the case of emotional trauma, grades may change precipitously, although gradual changes are also possible. Changes in grades caused by shifts in the curriculum are usually more gradual. On rare occasions, changes in grades may reflect neurological problems resulting from a degenerative condition, tumor, trauma to the nervous system. In the case of precipitous changes in grades that cannot be explained by transitions or emotional factors, the possibility of neurological problems should be investigated. Contrary to popular belief, however, damage to the nervous system may not have immediate effects on school performance but may adversely affect performance even several years later (Rourke, 1986).

ALTERNATIVE ACTIONS

Consulting With Teachers About Grading

Psychologists and counselors are often viewed as the measurement experts in the school (Fairchild, 1982) as well as being a sympathetic listener to teachers' problems. Given these two roles, grading could hardly be a more suitable consultation topic. Teachers are usually not free to choose the types of grades given, but they do decide on what basis to assign grades and make the evaluative judgments of the students' performance that all grading entails. Since grading issues are not primarily technical and since several viewpoints are legitimate, a collaborative consultation approach (Conoley & Conoley, 1982), in which consultant and consultee work as equal partners in the exploration and problem-solving process, would seem most appropriate when consulting about grading practices.

As unusual as it may seem, the place to start when consulting about grading is a discussion of the teacher's philosophy of education and an exploration of what grading system is most consistent with the teacher's beliefs. This is so because grades, as opposed to achievement tests, are a subjective evaluation of the students' performance (Rhine, 1975) and because grades are intended to serve several functions in addition to measuring performance. Tinkering with different labels for evaluative categories, such as using "excellent" instead of "A," or making minor changes in the width of the categories has little to do with the basic issues, which are the personal philosophy and practices of the teacher doing the grading (Terwilliger, 1977). Although it is necessary to help teachers sort through the nuances of their philosophies, Terwilliger (1977) offers a handy gross guide to matching philosophies and grading systems. Behaviorists, with their emphasis on mastering predefined goals and their general lack of interest in individual differences, are usually most comfortable with some form of criterion-referenced system. Humanists, who emphasize students' affective growth, generally shun grading if possible. If forced to grade, humanists usually prefer some form of self-referenced grading, assigning grades either on the basis of growth over time or in relation to the students' perceived abilities. Traditional grading is preferred by pragmatists, who emphasize the practical values and consequences of education.

Use of Alternative Grading Methods

Teachers and schools will probably continue to primarily use traditional letter grading, since it is a familiar system, it is arguably beneficial to high-achieving students, and it is well-suited to the school's administrative needs such as reporting pupil progress. Nevertheless, the use of alternate grading systems with low-achieving or handicapped students is highly recommended. Research (Perseley, 1974; Yarborough & Johnson, 1980) clearly suggest that traditional grading is not beneficial and may be harmful to such students.

Grading on effort, on achievement relative to ability, or on progress have been recommended as preferred ways to grade low-achieving students (Cohen, 1983), but all of these methods are plagued with technical problems and confuse the meaning of the grades assigned (Terwilliger, 1977). A much better system is to use a mastery approach in which criteria are set for each student and grades are assigned according to the degree to which criteria are met. This system may include a formal contract discussed with parents and included in a handicapped student's individualized educational plan (Borders, 1981). Mastery grading effectively includes evaluating progress, since new goals are set upon completion of earlier ones. One criticism of this system is that the grades would not accurately reflect students' relative standing compared to their peers, but since such information is primarily of interest to colleges this criticism is reduced at least for handicapped students (Vasa, 1981). An admitted disadvantage of this system is that it is relatively time-consuming and could cause problems in a heterogeneous class in which some students are being graded according to individualized goals while some are being graded in traditional fashion. An alternative system that addresses the latter concern is use of multiple marks for different aspects of performance within each subject area (Malehorn, 1984). For example, separate grades might be given for mastery, effort, and progress.

SUMMARY

Psychologists need to understand the grading process and view grades in the correct perspectives. Despite their many flaws, grades cannot be written off as irrelevant or meaningless. Grades are relevant because they impact on the lives of children and their parents, and affect the life of the school. Collectively, grades do have meaning but interpreting their multiple meanings requires careful thought and good detective work.

Although sure to persist, the traditional grading system works well for a relatively small proportion of students because the four basic meanings attached to grades — effort, mastery, improvement, relative standing — are highly correlated only for well-motivated, high achieving students. For students typically seen by psychologists, grades paint a murky picture of the students' performance and often work as a disincentive for improvement. Psychologists need to help children and parents understand and deal with the grading system, and help teachers develop creative, flexible grading procedures that validly depict student performance without destroying the conditions that promote academic and affective growth. Psychologists who successfully perform these two tasks surely deserve an A.

REFERENCES

Alhmann, J. S., & Glock, M. D. (1981). *Evaluating student progress: Principles of tests and measurement.* Boston: Allyn and Bacon.

Arcy, T. H. (1979). Philosophies of grading systems. *College Student Journal, 13,* 310–314.

Borders, J. (1981). Contract for success. *Vocational Education, 56,* 49–50.

Bresee, C. W. (1976). On "grading and the curve." *Clearing House, 50,* 108–110.

Carpenter, D., Grantham, L. B., & Hardister, M. P. (1983). Grading mainstreamed handicapped pupils: What are the issues? *Journal of Special Education, 17,* 183–188.

Cohen, S. B. (1983). Assigning report and grades to the mainstreamed child. *Teaching Exceptional Children, 15,* 86–89.

Conoley, J. C., & Conoley, C. W. (1982). *School consultation: A guide to practice and training.* New York: Pergamon.

Crowl, T. K. (1984). Grading behavior and teachers' need for social approval. *Education, 104,* 291–295.

Dilendik, J. R. (1978). Assumptions underlying criterion-referenced assessment are educationally sound. *Education, 99,* 89–96.

Evans, F. B. (1976). What research says about grading. In S. B. Simon & J. A. Bellanca (Eds.), *Degrading the grading myths: A primer of alternatives to grades and marks.* Washington, DC: Association for Supervision and Curriculum Development.

Fairchild, T. N. (1982). The school psychologist's role as an assessment consultant. *Psychology in the Schools, 19,* 200–208.

Hull, R. (1980). Fairness in grading: Perceptions of junior high school students. *Clearing House, 53,* 340–343.

Keith, T. Z. (1982). Time spent on homework and high school grades: A large-sample path analysis. *Journal of Educational Psychology, 74,* 248–253.

Kirschenbaum, H., Simon, S. B., & Napier, R. W. (1971). *Wad-Ja-Get?: The grading game in American education.* New York: Hart.

Leiter, J., & Brown, J. S. (1985). Determinants of elementary school grading. *Sociology of Education, 58,* 166–180.

Longstreet, W. S. (1975). The grading syndrome. *Educational Leadership, 32,* 243–246.

Malehorn, H. (1984). Ten better measures than giving grades. *Clearing House, 57,* 256–267.

Miller, D. L. (1983). Relationships of norm-referenced and content-referenced grading strategies to helplessness deficits in success- and failure-oriented students. *Dissertation Abstracts International, 43,* 2608A. (University Microfilms No. 83-00, 590)

Perseley, G. W. (1975). The effects of grading and previous academic achievement on subsequent academic achievement and student attitudes. *Dissertation Abstracts International, 35,* 7131A. (University Microfilms No. 75-10, 783)

Rhine, C. H. (1975). Grading and growth: Answer to an editorial. *Educational Leadership, 32,* 247–249.

Rourke, B. P. (1986, April). *Neuro-psychological assessment.* Workshop conducted in Washington, DC.

Stewin, L. L. (1980). A note on pupil evaluation in the Soviet Union. *Alberta Journal of Educational Research, 26,* 276–280.

Terwilliger, J. S. (1977). Assigning grades — Philosophical issues and practical recommendations. *Journal of Research and Development in Education, 10,* 21–39.

Vasa, S. F. (1981). Alternative procedures for grading handicapped students in the secondary schools. *Education Unlimited, 3,* 16–23.

Yarborough, B. H., & Johnson, R. A. (1980). How meaningful are marks in promoting growth in reading? *Reading Teacher, 33,* 644–651.

BIBLIOGRAPHY: PROFESSIONALS

Simon, S. B., & Bellanca, J. A. (Eds.). (1976). *Degrading the grading myths: A primer of alternatives to grades and marks.* Washington, DC: Association for Supervision and Curriculum Development.

This short book includes 19 essays written in an easy-to-read style on various topics related to grading. The authors have a clear orientation against traditional grading but present information useful even to teachers who favor such grades.

Terwilliger, J. S. (1977). Assigning grades — Philosophical issues and practical recommendations. *Journal of Research and Development in Education, 10,* 21–39.

In an exceptionally clear analysis of the issues surrounding grading, Terwilliger identifies the philosophical assumptions underlying various approaches to grading and analyzes on technical grounds several common grading procedures. Recommendations are made within an admitted pragmatic belief system.

Children and Grandparents

Timothy S. Hartshorne
Wichita State University

BACKGROUND

While "grandparent" may conjure up a romantic image of sleigh rides and summer vacations, of long walks and talks, of being spoiled, and perhaps of blueberry muffins, to the rational scientific mind this fanciful stereotype may have little relevance to children's needs. In fact, it was almost 45 years ago that the sociologist Talcott Parsons (1943) proclaimed that the nuclear family is isolated from its relations, thereby isolating the aged, and leaving older people with no role of any significance to play within the family. Early gerontologists supported this notion with the theory of disengagement (Cumming & Henry, 1961), suggesting that the aged promote their life satisfaction in old age precisely by intentionally and systematically reducing the frequency and number of their social contacts.

Early case studies did little to support the positive stereotype of grandparenthood. Vollmer (1937), for example, discussed the "extraordinarily pernicious influence on grandchildren" of grandmothers. Grandparents have been accused of having a role in neurosis (Abraham, 1955) and in behavior problems and delinquency (Bordon, 1946; Straus, 1943), of having a negative influence on child rearing (LaBarre, Hensner, & Ussery, 1960), and in fact of constituting a "syndrome" (Rappaport, 1958). These studies supported the notion of the "meddlesome" grandparent and would tend to endorse disengagement as a boon to child mental health.

The study of the grandparent–grandchild relationship is a recent development. The reasons for this increased interest likely stem from the gradual aging of the population and the breakdown of the stable nuclear family owing to divorce. Scientific interest in gerontology stems from the first, and grandparents' increased concern for their grandchildren and children from the second phenomenon (Bengtson & Robertson, 1985).

The importance of grandchildren to grandparents stems in part from the fact that the relationship is one of the few formal social roles actually available to older persons (Kahana & Kahana, 1971). However, not all grandparents are elderly; in fact, the median age of entry into grandmotherhood is in the range of 42–45 years (Sprey & Matthews, 1982). For this reason alone the grandparent–grandchild relationship would likely be "particularistic" as opposed to "global" (Matthews & Sprey, 1985). That is, the relationship has only a "latent potential" (Hagestad, 1981), depending less on formal social role factors and more on current family dynamics. Troll (1983) views grandparents as "family watchdogs" for whom grandparenting is typically a secondary activity, but who become active when they believe their values are not being handed down, or they discover there is trouble in their children's lives.

It is not unusual for grandparents to find trouble in their adult children's lives, and the readiness of the "kin-network" to provide mutual aid in times of personal difficulties is well established (Sussman, 1965). At such times the school psychologist may be most likely to encounter grandparents. A survey of Kansas school psychologists found that almost 25% of the 112 respondents had considerable contact with grandparents, and only 6% had no contact (Kansas Association of School Psychologists [KASP], 1984).

This chapter considers the relationship between grandparents and grandchildren, its significance to children, and the potential for intervention.

DEVELOPMENT

Development in the Absence of Family Crisis

There are two contexts in which the development of the grandparent–grandchild relationship can be considered: the presence and the absence of crisis. The latter provides a backdrop for the former. There are two aspects to the development of the relationship in the absence of crisis: its nature and its outcome.

The Nature of the Relationship in the Absence of Crisis. If a general conclusion can be drawn, it is that while the grandparent–grandchild relationship is extremely important to both parties (Hartshorne, 1979; Hartshorne & Manaster, 1982), there is considerable variation in the way the roles are played. Such variation is related to individual differences,but may also be due to the age of the participants, their sex, their ethnic or racial background, and the amount of contact between them.

Regarding age differences, Kahana and Kahana (1970) interviewed children of different ages about their favorite grandparent. The older children (11 and 12 years) reported no favorite. Children aged 4–5 years identified the grandparent who gave them the most presents, food, and demonstrations of love as the favorite. Children aged 8–9 years associated shared activities and special qualities of the grandparent with their decision of favorite.

Hartshorne (1977) found a similar developmental sequence with a small sample of college students. As a child, their relationship with grandparents was based on shared activities, for example, "She always let me do fun things and she would play cards with me and give me candy." During adolescence this changed to one of some annoyance: "She was my grandmother and she was sometimes irritating because she would tell me to 'be good' and 'act nice,' etc." As a young adult, a much closer relationship was described that was based on mutual affection and enjoyment of each other's company: "Now my communication with her is very important and I've learned a lot from her. I can appreciate her more now as a thinking human being."

Regarding age of grandparent, Neugarten and Weinstein (1964) found older grandparents to be more formal and younger grandparents more "fun-seeking" in their relationship. Cherlin and Furstenberg (1985) found the nature of grandparents' activities to change with length of time in the role. Their appreciation of the relationship followed the same trend as that reported by grandchildren, moving from baby-sitting, presenting gifts, and sharing fun, leisure-time activities to mutual assistance, advice giving, and discussion of problems, prior to letting go as the grandchildren entered adulthood.

Few differences have been found by sex of grandchild (Baranowski, 1984). Hartshorne (1979) found no difference by sex for adult grandchildren in the amount of contact they had with grandparents and their assessment of the importance of the relationship, but females did have a more personalized as opposed to formal role with their maternal grandmother than did males.

Considerable data support the importance of the maternal grandmother and the relative distance of the paternal grandfather (Hoffman, 1979-1980). Explanations generally point to age differences (the maternal grandmother is likely to be the youngest and the paternal grandfather the oldest) and to the closeness of mother–daughter linkages in families.

There are some ethnic and racial differences in the relationship, although even within each ethnic group there is considerable variability (McCready, 1985). Few differences have been found for blacks and whites; however, Mexican-American grandparents tend to be more involved with their grandchildren, provide more assistance, and report more satisfaction than grandparents from other groups (Bengtson, 1985).

Geographic mobility today makes contact between grandparents and grandchildren less frequent than it was in the past. Hartshorne and Manaster (1982) found that adult grandchildren (college students) had more contact with their grandparents in person than by telephone or letter, and saw them several times a year. However, they overwhelmingly reported a desire for more contact. Cherlin and Furstenberg (1985) found that increased contact was related to a more involved role, and less contact with a detached role.

Outcomes of the Relationship in the Absence of Crisis. The variables identified above appear to influence the kind of grandparent–grandchild relationship that exists, but what are the benefits of this relationship?

The benefits for grandparents are more apparent. As has been noted, grandparenthood is one of the few formal social roles still available to older persons, and so the relationship may be significant to their mental health (Kivnick, 1982). Hartshorne (1979) found a significant correlation between life satisfaction among grandmothers and being "involved" with their grandchildren.

The benefits for grandchildren can be more subtle. Baranowski (1982) has suggested that the potential exists for assistance with identity development, an improved relationship with parents, and a more positive attitude toward aging and the aged. Data to support the first two advantages are scanty, and primarily anecdotal, and data on the third are conflicting.

Kivnick (1982), in a major study of grandparenting and mental health, found that meaningful and positive experiences as a grandchild were related to the kind of grandparental role adopted later in life, and that "generationally appropriate grandparenthood related experience contributes to the success with which an individual is able to resolve developmentally successive psychosocial conflicts" (p. 123).

Other, basically clinical, data from Kornhaber (1985) indicated that close relationships with grandparents produced in grandchildren a sense of belonging, the absence of agist and sexist attitudes, and a lack of fear regarding old age.

Hartshorne (1979) found three general benefits to grandchildren that derived from their social interaction with grandparents. A personal relationship with their maternal grandmother was related to increased life satisfaction. In addition, the more contact these adult grandchildren had with their grandparents, the lower their death anxiety, and the more active they perceived the future to be.

One of the strongest proponents of the benefits of this relationship was Margaret Mead (1974). Because change in today's society is so rapid, she feared children might fail to understand the nature of change, and might take it for granted, whereas older persons might fail to grasp the results of change and fail to understand the world and the direction in which it is moving. These two generations, she suggested, have much to offer each other.

The present grandparental generation has observed more dramatic change than any other in history. In fact, Mead insisted, the aged have become living repositories of change. Having seen so much change, this generation has a deep faith in change, and a belief that real change for a better future is possible. This is not true of the present parental generation, which tends to view the world as "somehow finished,although possibly finished wrong" (1974, p. 245). Such a world, Mead suggested, becomes devoid of any belief in the future. It is through interaction between grandparents and grandchildren that a new belief in change and the future might be accomplished, "to restore a sense of community, a knowledge of the past, and a sense of the future to today's children" (p. 245).

Development in Crisis

Within normal family development, children may benefit from a relationship with grandparents. But as noted above, grandparents may become more involved in times of crisis. Two such crises will be discussed: divorce and death.

Divorce. Divorce poses a major challenge to families, producing with increasing frequency families that take on a number of forms from single-parent to a variety of stepparent families and blended families. This constitutes a challenge to intergenerational family continuity, and the job of maintaining generational integrity may be left to grandparents (Aldous, 1985).

Most grandparents are not terribly well informed about the quality of their children's marriages (Matthews & Sprey 1984), and thus may not be well prepared for divorce. However, in the best "family watchdog" style, they may suddenly find themselves involved. This is in spite of the widespread acceptance of the "norm of noninterference" (Cherlin & Furstenberg, 1985), the view that grandparents should not interfere with their children's families.

Johnson (1985) identified three issues for grandparents following their children's divorce. First, they have to decide how active they are going to be in the provision of supportive services. Second, they must decide on the nature of their future relationship with their past sons and daughters-in-law. Third, they must cope with value differences they experience between and among the three generations.

Aldous (1985) found that aging parents were more likely to stay involved with their single than with their married children, in giving financial aid, helping out with transportation, and providing emotional support. But if their married children subsequently divorced, they became involved, particularly when there were grandchildren. The major services provided by the grandparents were housework, childcare, and emotional support. These findings were particularly true when the grandmother was under age 62, and the adult divorced child was a female. Given the prevalence with which mothers are awarded custody of children, the latter finding is not surprising. Johnson (1985) obtained similar findings, concluding: "Because the divorce of parents created disruptions in family life, the grandmothers saw themselves as a 'back-up' person whose home was a 'safe harbor' or an 'island of security' for grandchildren of all ages" (p. 88).

According to Beal (1979), adult children may deny grandparents access to grandchildren when the divorce is not amicable or has created friction with their parents. Who received custody was found by Matthews and Sprey (1984) to influence the extent of contact with former daughter- and son-in-laws. It may be necessary for grandparents who wish to maintain contact with their grandchildren to consider the expediency of a working relationship with the former in-law. In certain cases, grandparents might form an alliance with the former in-law against their own child, for example, if their own child has been abusive, or if the grandparents view it as in the "best interests of the child" (Johnson, 1985). Because the grandparents may have had less invested in the marriage, it may be easier for them emotionally to maintain ties with the former in-law, but it can also be expedient, in the case of certain custody arrangements. A further complication is the presence of another set of grandparents. In cases of joint custody, and therefore the need for both parents to receive assistance from their parents, children may end up living in four different homes, rotating among mother, father, maternal grandparents, and paternal grandparents. Johnson (1985) found the two sets of grandparents sometimes forming a coalition to make arrangements for visitations and holiday gatherings.

Depending on their age and cohort group, there may be a number of value differences between the generations, particularly in their view of divorce and changing family lifestyles. A number of studies have found that such value differences tend to be issue- and cohort-specific (Armstrong & Scotzin, 1974). Interestingly, a review of the generation gap literature shows that differences between the first and the third generations are often not as extreme as between the second and first.

In fact, Kalish (1969) suggested that the first and third generations might be considered generation gap allies. He pointed out that both young and old belong to somewhat age-segregated groups, are constantly reminded of their nonproductive roles, have little influence on decision making, and live in a relatively unstructured time situation. The elderly, he insisted, can be particularly relevant to the young by providing a link with the past, by challenging attitudes and platitudes regarding the dignity of life, and, as grandparents, by offering a sense of family continuity and time perspective. This kind of a link may be particularly significant to children whose lives have been disrupted by divorce.

Death. Death is both an event and a concept. Grandparents often provide the first human experience children have with death, but they may also be able to assist children with the development of their attitude toward death. Most studies have found that children's concept of death follows Piaget's developmental stages, and that it is also strongly influenced by their parents' attitude (Zeligs, 1967). Hartshorne (1979) examined death anxiety as one variable influenced by the relationship with grandparents. While most studies have reported higher levels of death anxiety for females, he found the sample of grandmothers to have a lower level than his sample of adult grandchildren. He also found that present-time, in-person contact with grandparents was related to lower death anxiety in the grandchildren. Interestingly, there was also a significant and positive correlation of death anxiety scores for maternal grandmothers with those of their grandchildren. Thus, with contact, grandmothers may influence their grandchildren's death anxiety.

Wilcox and Sutton (1985) have noted that the subject of death is emerging in children's literature, although often in the form of an animal who dies; however, one exception is *My grandpa died today,* by Joan Fassler. Since they are often elderly, the loss of a grandparent may be the child's first experience with death. Kastenbaum and Aisenberg (1972) quoted a 4-year-old girl talking to her 84-year-old grandmother: "You are old. That means you will die. I am young, so I won't die, you know" (p. 18). Despite the age-appropriateness of their death, the loss of a grandparent can be traumatic for a child, particularly when a close relationship between the two has developed. Unfortunately, no literature has emerged addressing the death specifically of a grandparent.

Grollman (1977) identified a variety of children's reactions to death including denial, isolation, and withdrawal, physiological distress, guilt, hostility, replacement, and fear and panic. Grollman highlights the need for assisting children to express their feelings, to be listened to, and to be told about the death as honestly as possible.

Grandparents may be in an ideal position to do this. First, they bring a perspective based on greater experience with death and, as noted above, may have less death anxiety and so be able to talk with a child more honestly and directly than others. Second, as Bengston (1985) says, "Their presence serves to maintain the identity of the family and to provide a buffer against its mortality" (p. 21). In other words, in spite of death, the family, and life, goes on. Third, grandparents may also have a need to talk about the death, and as Mead (1974) and Kalish (1969) have noted, the first and third generations may have a lot they can learn from one another. In their role of "family watchdogs," one would expect that in the case of a death, as in the case of divorce, grandparents would, as Bengston (1985) put it, "be there."

Other Crises. While literature is lacking, the grandparental role in other family crisis such as child abuse, poverty, mental illness, handicapping condition, etc., can be essentially the same. In every case of family disruption, grandparents may be in a position to provide the kind of perspective and support that children need to cope successfully.

PUTTING CHILDREN AND GRANDPARENTS IN PERSPECTIVE

The preceding is essentially a presentation in support of a close relationship between grandparents and their grandchildren. There are, however, three conditions that may influence this judgment.

The first is the attitude of the grandparents. Not all grandparents want a close relationship with their grandchildren. Every study of grandparental roles has identified one group of grandparents who may be described as remote. These grandparents do tend to be older, but it is essential to recognize that grandparents are individuals and some may be uninterested in an active involvement with their grandchildren.

The second condition is the attitude of the middle generation. Kivnick (1982) suggested that this attitude is shaped by that generation's experience with their own grandparents, but it can also be affected by the relationship between them and their own parents. Regardless of the source, Robertson (1975) and others have noted the power of parents to control access to grandchildren and to shape attitudes toward grandparents.

The third condition is legal. Traditionally, grandparents have no legal rights (Wilson & DeShane, 1982). The landmark case of *Succession of Reiss* (cited in Wilson & DeShane, 1984) established the supremacy of parental rights over grandparents', and that a legal relationship between grandparents and grandchildren exists only when both parents are dead or incapacitated. Grandparents may, however, have some legal responsibilities. In a 1974 case a mother successfully sued the paternal grandparents for child support, since the ex-husband's disabilities prevented him from paying (Wilson & DeShane, 1982). Most states do now have laws allowing grandparents some visitation rights in the case of divorce, but entitlement may be based on the grandparents having petitioned for visitation rights prior to the divorce, and may not include stepchildren and adoptive grandchildren.

ALTERNATIVE ACTIONS

School psychologists frequently encounter children in crisis situations and recognize that family systems are invariably involved. Information on the nature of grandparental involvement with the family may help to assess strengths and weaknesses within the family system and may suggest intervention strategies. Data can be collected in an initial interview with the child and/or parents or other family members.

Assessment

1. The degree of grandparental involvement in a crisis situation may be related to the depth of the family crisis, the mediating role of the parents, or the remoteness of the grandparent from the family. Secondary factors would be the age and sex of the grandparents. An involved grandparent may be an adjunct to intervention; an uninvolved grandparent could represent family instability.

2. Data from statistics over the past 20 years is strongly supported by the view that the grandparent–grandchild relationship can be a positive influence in family affairs, but this depends on the extent to which grandparental actions serve to maintain family integrity. Is the grandparents' behavior appropriate to the age of the grandchildren? Does the contact detract from the relationship of children and parents? Does the relationship monopolize the child's time? Positive influences can be encouraged; negative ones could be a focus for intervention.

3. An interesting way to assess family strength during a crisis is to analyze the extent to which grandparents play the family watchdog role. Do grandparents who are not generally present appear on the scene during a crisis? What kind of services do they bring to the family, and what kind of support do they afford the grandchild?

Intervention

1. Involving a grandparent. If a child is in crisis, is there a grandparent available who is not involved but could be mobilized? Some grandparents may simply wait to be asked while the parents may hesitate to impose. Suggesting involvement might get things going. Being aware of state law regarding grandparental visitation is helpful. If there is not a grandparent, the involvement of another older adult may still be beneficial (Arch, 1978). There are many ways to be involved from visits to leisure time activities to the grandparent's attending school.

2. Using grandparents. Grandparents could be used to award reinforcements, to function as tutors, to volunteer in the classroom, to collect data, to provide family history, to read to the child, to monitor behavior, to provide encouragement and a cheering section. What is important to remember is that they may have the motivation and the time.

SUMMARY

Grandparents, when available, may be of considerable importance to children. Their relationship with the grandchildren may influence the children's development throughout their lives, their ability to cope with crises, and their perspective on family and family values. There are many ways of being a grandparent, and the role is mediated by parental attitudes. But grandparents themselves may hesitate between the norm of noninterference and the role of family watchdog. The school psychologist may break the stalemate by inquiring about a grandparent, providing information on the benefits of the relationship, and creatively utilizing the grandparent with interventions.

REFERENCES

Abraham, K. (1955). Some remarks on the role of grandparents in the psychology of neurosis. In H. C. Abraham (Ed.), *Selected papers and essays in psychoanalysis* (Vol. 1). New York: Basic Books.

Aldous, J. (1985). Parent–adult child relations affected by the grandparent status. In V. L. Bengtson & J. F. Robertson (Eds.), *Grandparenthood* (pp. 117–132). Beverly Hills, CA: Sage.

Arch, S. D. (1978). Older adults as home visitors modeling parenting for troubled families. *Child Welfare, 57,* 601–605.

Armstrong, B. N., & Scotzin, M. M. (1974). Intergenerational comparisons of attitudes toward basic life concepts. *Journal of Psychology, 87,* 193–304.

Baranowski, M. D. (1982). Grandparent–adolescent relations: Beyond the nuclear family. *Adolescence, 15,* 575–584.

Baranowski, M. D. (1984). *Sex differences in adolescents' relations with grandparents.* Paper presented at the meeting of the Gerontological Society of America, San Antonio, TX.

Beal, C. W. (1979). Children of divorce: A family systems perspective. *Journal of Social Issues, 35,* 140–154.

Bengtson, V. L. (1985). Diversity and symbolism in grandparental roles. In V. L. Bengtson & J. F. Robertson (Eds.), *Grandparenthood* (pp. 11–25). Beverly Hills, CA: Sage.

Bengtson, V. L., & Robertson, J. F. (Eds.). (1985). *Grandparenthood.* Beverly Hills, CA: Sage.

Bordon, B. (1946). The role of grandparents in children's behavior problems. *Smith College Studies in Social Work, 17,* 115–116.

Cherlin, A., & Furstenberg, F. F. (1985). In V. L. Bengtson & J. F. Robertson (Eds.), *Grandparenthood* (pp. 97–116). Beverly Hills, CA: Sage.

Cumming, E., & Henry, W. E. (1961). *Growing old: The process of disengagement.* New York: Basic Books.

Grollman, E. (1977). Explaining death to children. *Journal of School Health, 48,* 336–339.

Hagestad, G. O. (1981). Problems and promises in the social psychology of intergenerational relations. In R. Vogel, E. Hatfield, S. Kiesler, & R. Shanas (Eds.), *Aging: Stability and change in the family* (pp. 11–47). New York: Academic.

Hartshorne, T. S. (1977). [The relationship with grandparents at different ages]. Unpublished raw data.

Hartshorne, T. S. (1979). The grandparent and grandchild relationship and life satisfaction, death anxiety, and attitude toward the future (Doctoral dissertation, University of Texas at Austin, 1979).

Hartshorne, T. S., & Manaster, G. J. (1982). The relationship with grandparents: Contact, importance, and role conception. *International Journal of Aging and Human Development, 15,* 233–245.

Hoffman, E. (1979-1980). Young adults relations with their grandparents. An exploratory study. *International Journal of Aging and Human Development, 10,* 299–310.

Johnson, C. L. (1985). Grandparenting options in divorcing families: An anthropological perspective. In V. L. Bengtson & J. F. Robertson (Eds.), *Grandparenthood* (pp. 81–96). Beverly Hills, CA: Sage.

Kahana, B., & Kahana, E. (1970). Grandparenthood from the perspective of the developing child. *Developmental Psychology, 3,* 98–105.

Kahana, E., & Kahana, B. (1971). Theoretical and research perspectives on grandparenthood. *Aging and Human Development, 2,* 261–268.

Kalish, R. A. (1969). The old and the new as generation gap allies. *Gerontologist, 9,* 83–89.

Kansas Association of School Psychologists (KASP). (1984). [Survey of Kansas School Psychologists]. Unpublished raw data.

Kivnick, H. Q. (1982). *The meaning of grandparenthood.* Ann Arbor, MI: UMI Research Press.

Kornhaber, A. (1985). Grandparenthood and the "new social contract." In V. L. Bengtson & J. F. Robertson (Eds.), *Grandparenthood* (pp. 159–172). Beverly Hills, CA: Sage.

LaBarre, M. B., Hessner, L., & Ussery, L. (1960). The significance of grandmothers in the psychopathology of children. *American Journal of Orthopsychiatry, 30,* 175–185.

Matthews, S. H., & Sprey, J. (1984). The impact of divorce on grandparenthood: An exploratory study. *Gerontologist, 24,* 41–47.

Matthews, S. H., & Sprey, J. (1985). Adolescents' relationships with grandparents: Am empirical contribution to conceptual clarification. *Journal of Gerontology, 40,* 621–626.

McCready, W. C. (1985). Styles of grandparenting among white ethnics. In V. L. Bengtson & J. F. Robertson (Eds.), *Grandparenthood* (pp. 49–60). Beverly Hills, CA: Sage.

Mead, M. (1974). Grandparents as educators. *Teachers College Record, 76,* 240–249.

Neugarten, B. L., & Weinstein, K. K. (1964). The changing American grandparent. *Journal of Marriage and the Family, 26,* 199–204.

Parsons, T. (1943). The kinship system of the contemporary United States. *American Anthropologist, 45,* 22–38.

Rappaport, E. A. (1958). The grandparent syndrome. *Psychoanalytic Quarterly, 27,* 518–538.

Robertson, J. F. (1975). Interaction in three-generation families; parents as mediators: Toward a theoretical perspective. *International Journal of Aging and Human Development, 6,* 103–110.

Sprey, J., & Matthews, S. H. (1982). Contemporary grandparenthood: A systematic transition. *Annals of the American Academy of Political Science, 464,* 91–103.

Straus, C. A. (1943). Grandma made Johnny delinquent. *American Journal of Orthopsychiatry, 13,* 343–346.

Sussman, M. B. (1965). Relationships of adult children with their parents in the United States. In E. Shanas & G. F. Streib (Eds.), *Social structure and the family: Generational relations.* Englewood Cliffs, NJ: Prentice-Hall.

Troll, L. E. (1983). Grandparents: The family watchdog. In T. Brubaker (Ed.), *Family relations in later life* (pp. 63–74). Beverly Hills, CA: Sage.

Vollmer, H. (1937). The grandmother: A problem in child rearing. *American Journal of Orthopsychiatry, 7,* 378–382.

Wilcox, S. G., & Sutton, M. (Eds.). (1985). *Understanding death and dying.* Palo Alto, CA: Mayfield.

Wilson, K. B., & DeShane, M. R. (1982). The legal rights of grandparents: A preliminary discussion. *Gerontologist, 22,* 67–71.

Zeligs, R. (1967). Children's attitudes toward death. *Mental Hygiene, 51,* 393–396.

BIBLIOGRAPHY: PROFESSIONALS

Bengtson, V. L., & Robertson, J. F. (Eds.). (1985). *Grandparenthood.* Beverly Hills, CA: Sage.
This collection of articles by some of the leading researchers in the field should be an essential reference for anyone interested in the nature of grandparenthood. The first chapter, a review by Bengtson, is an outstanding summary of current thinking.

Kivnick, H. Q. (1982). *The meaning of grandparenthood.* ANN ARBOR, MI: UMI Research Press.
Reports on a major research study, including both clinical and survey data, on grandparental roles and mental health. It is not light reading but the case histories are particularly helpful in their illustration of the conclusions.

Mead, M. (1974). Grandparents as educators. *Teachers College Record, 76,* 240–249.
This theoretical and conceptual article represents one person's thinking about the role of grandparents and what they and grandchildren can learn from each other. Based both on her career as an anthropologist and on her experience as a grandmother.

BIBLIOGRAPHY: PARENTS

Goode, R. (1976). *A book for grandmothers.* New York: McGraw-Hill.
An extremely easy-to-read, practical guide for grandmothers. Excellent treatment of many of the same issues covered in this chapter, including the norm of noninvolvement, what grandparents offer, and dealing with divorce.

Kornhaber, A., & Woodward, K. L. (1985). *Grandparents/grandchildren: The vital connection.* New Brunswick, NJ: Transaction Books.
This is not light reading, but it is not difficult reading. The authors point to a "new social contract" that serves to keep grandparents and grandchildren apart. They discuss the necessity for, and the vitality of, the relationship in its potential for emotional well-being.

ADDITIONAL RESOURCE

Foundation for Grandparenting, 10 West Hyatt Ave., Mt. Kisco, NY 10549.
This relatively new organization publishes a newsletter, *Vital Connections.* The newsletter includes topics such as When your child divorces, Grandparents and child care, Resources for grandparents, Parent–grandparent problems.

Children and Head Injury

Robert Diamond
Albemarle County Schools, Virginia

BACKGROUND

Introduction

The school psychologist is the professional in the schools best prepared to recognize the learning and behavioral implications of head injury. In order to facilitate communication between the medical professionals who treat head injury and the educational professionals who deal with the head-injured child in the school, the school psychologist must know the epidemiology, terminology, and effects of head injury.

There is great diversity in the behavioral sequelae of head injury, and no single symptom is present in all head-injured children. Typical features include personality changes, impulse control deficits, attentional difficulties, and disruption of cognitive abilities. A head-injured child may become verbally or physically aggressive at minor frustrations, may have difficulty ignoring distractions, and may be unable to learn new academic tasks or to perform previously learned ones. The uniqueness of head injury is that the situation is not stable, and recovery is expected.

Incidence

Head injuries among adults and children are a surprisingly common event. Incidence figures range from 6.1 to 8.9 million individuals annually in the United States (Bakay & Glasauer, 1980; Caveness, 1979; Rimel et al., 1981). The frequency of head injuries serious enough to prompt an individual to seek medical attention is reported as 1.2–1.6 million annually (Kraus, 1980).

There is an inverse relationship of severity to frequency. Minor injuries are more common than severe ones. Bakay and Glasauer (1980) reported that for motor vehicle-related head injuries, 66% were classified as mild, 24% as moderate, and 10% as severe.

Caveness (1979) provided an analysis of head injury demographics from data of the National Center for Health Statistics. In 1976, more than 57% of head injury victims were under 17 years of age, a third being less than 6 years old. The epidemiological data also indicate that head injury is a more common event for younger children and for boys (Klonoff, 1971).

In children there are causes of injury that are not common in adults. These include injuries during free play, organized athletics, and child abuse (Jennett, 1972). The preinjury personality characteristics of children sustaining head injury have also been studied. Robarts (1971) noted that head-injured children are described as having been more adventuresome and daring than noninjured children. Mannheimer and Mellinger (1967) reported significant relationships between accident proneness and personality characteristics. Children at greater risk were more extroverted, daring, attention-seeking, and impulsive.

Skultety (1981) reported that sports with a higher incidence of head injury include football, soccer, gymnastics, diving, and horse riding. Roy and Irvin (1983) suggested that any sign of confusion or memory loss following head injury in an athletic event should be cause for immediate removal from the activity. They suggested the use of a serial sevens task as an appropriate screening device for adolescents. In this task, the individual is asked to begin at 100 and successively subtract seven from the result. Any difficulty in completing this task would be cause for removal and further medical attention.

DEVELOPMENT

Classificatory systems for head injury are based on severity or physiology of injury. The severity terminology (minor, mild, moderate, severe) is not objectively defined and may vary in application. The duration of loss of consciousness is commonly used to classify head injury according to severity. Researchers' criteria for a mild injury, however, may range from a moment up to a 20-min period of unconsciousness.

Head injury is also differentiated into closed and open injuries. In a closed head injury, the skull remains intact. An open head injury is one in which the protective surfaces of the brain (the meninges, the skull, and the scalp) are torn and fractured so that the surface of the brain is exposed. A penetrating head injury is a subtype of open head injury in which bone fragments and scalp tissue enter the surface of the brain. While serious and potentially life-threatening from the standpoint of infection, open injuries are paradoxically often less serious in terms of neurobehavioral outcome than closed injuries. The fracturing of the skull absorbs much of the force of impact. Open head injuries tend to produce a circumscribed loss of brain tissue, resulting in focal impairment or specific brain functions.

The brain has numerous protective mechanisms. The cerebrospinal fluid supports the weight of the brain and gives a hydraulic protection. The meninges provide a physical protection ranging from the soft and pliant pia mater adjacent to the brain to the rigid dura mater. The interior of the skull consists of ridged compartments that support and stabilize the brain.

Contusions, or bruising injuries of the brain surface, are produced by the sudden contact of the brain with these interior ridges and with folds in the dura mater. A coup contusion (Levin, Benton, & Grossman, 1982) is produced by direct physical trauma, such as being struck with a blunt object. The traumatic force causes the skull to impact on the brain. A contrecoup contusion occurs when, as a result of acceleration or deceleration forces such as in a fall, the brain moves in the cerebrospinal fluid and impacts upon the skull (Gurdjian & Webster, 1958). Thus, coup contusions are located at the site of trauma, while contrecoup contusions are located at some distance, often opposite to the point of impact (Jamieson, 1971).

Diffuse brain injury results from sudden movement of the brain within the skull. There is no impact between the brain and the skull; however, the rapid changes in momentum initiate shearing strains which can tear axons, cell bodies, and small vessels (Levin, Benton, & Grossman, 1982). Concussion is a form of diffuse injury. Diffuse injury may, however, be caused by rapid shaking of the head and does not require direct physical impact. For instance, whiplash, whether from a motor vehicle accident or child abuse, may cause diffuse brain injury.

PUTTING HEAD INJURY IN PERSPECTIVE

The most common functional consequence of head injury is a disruption of mental abilities (Jennett & Teasdale, 1981). Jennett and Teasdale reported that for diffuse injuries, verbal language abilities as assessed by the Wechsler Intelligence Scales, are less severely affected than are abilities measured by the Performance scale. They also state that verbal abilities are recovered more rapidly, often within 3–6 months, whereas nonverbal skills may take more than a year to reach maximum improvement.

The natural history of head injury follows a negatively accelerating recovery curve. Bond (1975) has reported a rapid early recovery of verbal skills within the first 6 months following severe head injury. In contrast, performance abilities did not reach a maximal recovery level until 24 months after injury.

There is less consistency in studies of memory functions, but the evidence suggests that memory deficits may be persistent and characterized by poorer incidental learning, increased caution, and decreased ability to use organizational cues. There is also evidence of persistent deficits of language, sensory abilities, and learning skills.

Because language abilities recover fairly quickly, head-injured persons may be in the difficult position of appearing more capable and recovered than they actually are. Fuld and Fisher (1977), in assessing head-injured children aged 1–8 years, found persistent intellectual deficits at 1 year following injury that were not evident to the children's parents. Most of these children also exhibited unspecified personality changes that the authors felt were secondary to stress.

Chadwick, Rutter, Thompson, and Shaffer (1981) studied 97 children 3–5 years after they had sustained open head injury. they found that intellectual levels were consistently lower for children who had had more severe injuries. There was a tendency for tests of reading achievement to show greater impairment both for children who had experienced left-hemisphere trauma and for children who were under 5 years of age at the time of injury.

The authors offered two hypotheses for the latter finding. They suggested that brain injury may interfere with the acquisition of unfamiliar skills rather than with the retention and refinement of well-learned skills. Older children, having already acquired basic reading skills, would be less vulnerable to reading difficulties following head injury.

The alternative hypothesis is that the younger head-injured children may have had an impaired development following injury. The plasticity concept proposes that head injury in infants and young children has less severe cognitive sequelae, since the areas of the brain have the potential to assume different functions. Boll and Barth (1983) have noted, however, that the plasticity concept suggests qualitative rather than quantitative differences in head injury sequelae for young children. They stated that it is outmoded as a basis for optimism regarding recovery from head injury in young children.

Klonoff and his associates reported on an initial assessment (Klonoff, Robinson, & Thompson, 1969) and a 5-year follow-up assessment (Klonoff, Low, & Clark, 1977) of 231 head-injured children. They found that a third of the children exhibited residual neuropsychological deficits at 5 years after injury. Over the 5-year study, a quarter of the children had either failed a grade or were placed in remedial or slow-learner classes. The children had been making normal to above-average educational progress before the injury.

Dillon and Leopold (1961) reported on the study of 50 head-injured children aged 3–13. The children were seen at varying intervals ranging from within a week to more than a year following injury. Almost two thirds of the children had sustained a minor head injury. Personality changes were the most prominent finding. Over 90% of the children had marked behavioral changes including increased aggressiveness, withdrawal, regression, deterioration of school performance, anxiety, and sleep disturbance. Enuresis was found in 26% of the cases.

Black and his associates (Black, Blumer, Wellner, & Walker, 1971; Black, Jeffries, Blumer, Wellner, & Walker, 1969) have reported a long-term follow-up of 105 children with head injuries of various severities. The dominant symptoms were behavioral. The most common problems were difficulty with anger control, hyperkinesis, and impaired attention. Approximately 20% of the children were described as having persistent adjustment difficulties.

The epidemiological data indicate that having a head injury is an excellent predictor of future head injury. Gronwall and Wrightson (1975) compared young adults with a second minor head injury to matched controls with a single concussion. They found that individuals with previous minor head injuries performed significantly more poorly on initial information-processing abilities and required more days to recover. Symonds (1962) suggested that the result of head injury might be a permanent and diffuse loss of neuronal function. He proposed that in normal individuals the number of available neurons is greater than that required for functional efficiency. In the head-injured, some fraction of that reserve has been lost so that successive injuries could result in more severe and persistent symptoms.

Todorow (1975) noted that in respect to the late behavioral sequelae of head injury, the interaction of physical, psychological, and environmental factors must be considered. He proposed that the relative importance of these factors may change depending on the amount of time following trauma. Immediately after injury, physical factors may be most important; as time passes, however, the psychological response and the environmental conditions become predominant in their effect on outcome.

Jennett and Teasdale (1981) proposed that early psychological response to head injury may be a complicating factor in the recovery of children and adults, particularly those with minor injuries. They noted that the extended loss of consciousness and posttraumatic amnesia of the more severely injured individual may preclude recall of the injury-producing event. In contrast, the individual with a minor injury may have both a clear recall of the traumatic event and be faced with what Jennett and Teasdale call the "facile reassurance that nothing serious has happened" (p. 262). Thus, for minor head injuries there is the potential for greater psychological distress.

ALTERNATIVE ACTIONS

The most important function of the school, the family, and others in the head-injured child's environment is to allow the natural process of recovery to occur to its maximal extent without interference. While rehabilitation programs are intuitively logical, there is no demonstrable evidence of their effectiveness. There is, however, evidence that adverse conditions such as a premature return to preinjury activities may have the negative effect of locking the child into a disabled self-concept. Goldstein (1952) proposed the term *catastrophic reaction* for that situation in which the injured person's perception of diminished intellectual proficiency contributes to emotional and behavioral disturbance. Gronwall and Wrightson (1974) believe that, in the worst case, this frustration and alarm may lead to a fixed reaction that persists long after the original organic disturbance has resolved.

The sequelae of head injury are often subtle and not evident without specialized testing. Oddey, Humphrey, and Uttley (1978) speculated that the disparity between an apparent complete recovery and the subjective recognition of impairment may be problematic for head-injured individuals.

Romano (1974) reported on 6-month to 4-year follow-up observations of 13 severe closed head injury subjects and their families. She stated that the families demonstrated persistent denial of the severity of the injury, and a refusal to acknowledge residual deficits or personality change. This was so even in those cases in which the patients were able to acknowledge their own limitations. She proposed that this inconsistency of the family message and the individual's subjective experience may contribute to depression.

Collier (1979) discussed the role of self-concept following head injury. He believes that traumatically injured individuals may excessively focus on their impairments. This focus generates an "impaired self" with a resultant loss of adaptability and flexibility. Collier also proposed that the interaction of the sense of impairment and the cognitive sequelae of head injury may generate a cycling phenomenon that intensifies and prolongs the disability caused by either.

The more severely injured child is likely to be gradually returned to school with careful medical consultation and support. In contrast, the child who has had a minor head injury is often rapidly returned to school with no special attention. Boll and Barth (1983) noted that even in cases of an obvious period of unconsciousness, a minor head injury has traditionally been assumed to produce no lasting impairment. The medical standard has been that patients with minor head injury should be immediately capable of resuming their preinjury activities.

There is an important difference in interpretive outlook between the psychologist and educator and the medical professional. Following a minor head injury, a child is clearly not at medical risk and therefore the medical professional may consider this a complete recovery. However, there is research evidence that subtle cognitive difficulties may persist for sometime following even a very minor injury. If this information is not shared with parents, teachers, and others who work with a head-injured child, their expectations may not be consistent with the child's capabilities. This discrepancy may engender the stress and negative conditions that are frequently mentioned as factors in prolonged difficulties.

The ideal situation would be to obtain regular comprehensive neuropsychological assessments in order to monitor the child's recovery and match expectations with abilities. If this is not possible, the school psychologist should monitor the child's abilities in the areas of information processing, memory, and attentional and concentration skills.This may require the use of instruments different from those used for a standard assessment of cognitive skills. Depending upon the specifics of the situation and the psychologist's competencies, any of a number of tests such as the Paced Auditory Serial Addition Test (Gronwall & Wrightson, 1974), the Visual Aural Digit Span Test (Koppitz, 1977), the Trail Making Test of the Halstead–Reitan Battery (Reitan, undated), and the Wisconsin Card Sorting Test (Heaton, 1981) may be appropriate. It will be important for school psychologists to take advantage of training opportunities in the field of neuropsychology. The focus on brain–behavior relationships and the multifactorial view of cognitive abilities are two particularly relevant aspects of neuropsychology as applied to school psychology.

Consultation with school personnel, parents, and the injured child is necessary. The important facts that all parties must understand are that there may indeed be some legitimate decline in intellectual efficiency, and that improvement is expected. This may range from a total recovery of preinjury abilities to a persistent and pervasive intellectual deficit. Head-injured children and their families find themselves in a difficult situation in which they will need compassionate,honest, and knowledgeable support. The task of all professionals must be to facilitate an attitude of realistic optimism.

Short-term counseling with these children, and possibly their parents, may be useful in dealing with emotional responses to the injury and its sequelae.

The dissemination of information to the public through opportunities such as PTO meetings would also be an appropriate activity. While preventive procedure such as using child safety restraints in automobiles and wearing helmets when riding off-the-road vehicles should be stressed, the goal would not be solely to prevent head injury but also to promote understanding of the importance of seeking proper treatment and of notifying the schools when a head injury has occurred. It is unlikely that we would be able, or even that it would be appropriate, to try to protect children from all possible causes of head injury. However, the potential long-term negative outcomes, especially of a minor head injury, can and should be prevented.

Another important activity would be to open lines of communication with other professionals. Within the schools we tend to see learning abilities as fairly stable. The sequelae of head injury, with the expectation of improving abilities and the need for regular alteration of expectations, do not fit neatly into that view. Outside the schools, medical professionals, with their different criteria, may precipitate difficulties by leading parents, children, and others to expect that everything will be just as it was before the injury. This expectation may then lead to the assumption that something more serious is occurring if the child encounters difficulty when returning to school.

SUMMARY

Head injuries, particularly "minor" injuries, happen to a substantial percentage of children. The school psychologist can promote recovery by helping to avoid complications that might interfere with the maximal gains following injury.

The major issues in relation to the schools are essentially psychological. We need to help children and their parents and teachers to avoid inaccurate expectations, and to avoid seeing the natural sequelae of head injury as an unusual occurrence. There is also a need to recognize that, following head injury, a child's abilities may be fluctuating and unstable for a period ranging from several months to 2 years. It is necessary that the children involved, their parents, and their teachers be aware that performance expectations will need to be adjusted to fit this pattern of changing abilities.

REFERENCES

Bakay, L., & Glasauer, F. E. (1980). *Head injury.* Boston: Little, Brown.

Barth, J. T., Macciocchi, S. M., Giordani, B., Rimel, R., Jane, J. A., & Boll, T. J. (1983). Neuropsychological sequelae of minor head injury. *Neurosurgery, 13,* 529–533.

Black, P., Blumer, D., Wellner, A. M., & Walker, A. C. (1971). The head injured child: Time course of recovery and implications for rehabilitation. In F. J. Gillingham, J. F. Shaw, J. Fraser, E. R. Hitchcock, & P. Harris (Eds.), *Head injuries: Proceedings of an international symposium held in Edinburgh and Madrid* (pp. 131–137). Baltimore: Williams & Wilkins.

Black, P., Jeffries, J. J., Blumer, D., Wellner, A. M., & Walker, A. C. (1969). The posttraumatic syndrome in children: Characteristics and incidence. In A. E. Walker, W. Caveness, & M. Critchey (Eds.), *The late effects of head injury* (pp. 142–149). Springfield, IL: Thomas.

Boll, T. J., & Barth, J. T. (1983). Mild head injury. *Psychiatric Developments, 3,* 263–275.

Bond, M. R. (1975). Assessment of the psychosocial outcome after severe head injury. CBA Foundation Symposium, *34,* 141–157.

Caveness, W. (1979). Incidence of craniocerebral trauma in the United States with trends from 1970 to 1975. *Advances in Neurology, 22,* 1–3.

Chadwick, O., Rutter, M., Thompson, J., & Shaffer, D. (1981). Intellectual performance and reading skills after localized head injury in childhood. *Journal of Child Psychology, Psychiatry, and Related Disciplines, 22,* 117–139.

Collier, H. (1979). The role of psychological follow-up in nervous system trauma. *Advances in Neurology, 22,* 149–166.

Dillon, H., & Leopold, R. L. (1961). Children and the postconcussion syndrome. *Journal of the American Medical Association, 175,* 110–116.

Fuld, P. A., & Fisher, P. (1977). Recovery of intellectual ability after closed head injury. *Developmental Medicine and Child Neurology, 19,* 495–502.

Gennarelli, T. A. (1982a). Cerebral concussion and diffuse brain injury. In J. S. Torg (Ed.), *Athletic injuries to the head, neck, and face* (pp. 93–105). Philadelphia: Lea & Febiger.

Gennarelli, T. A. (1982b). Head injury mechanisms. In J. S. Torg (Ed.), *Athletic injuries to the head, neck, and face* (pp. 65–73). Philadelphia: Lea & Febiger.

Goldstein, K. (1952). The effect of brain damage on the personality. *Psychiatry, 15,* 245–260.

Gronwall, D., & Wrightson, P. (1974). Delayed recovery of intellectual function after minor head injury. *Lancet, 2,* 605–609.

Gronwall, D., & Wrightson, P. (1975). Cumulative effects of concussion. *Lancet, 2,* 995–997.

Gronwall, D., & Wrightson, P. (1981). Memory and intellectual processing capacity after closed head injury. *Journal of Neurology, Neurosurgery, and Psychiatry, 44,* 889–895.

Gurdjian, C., & Webster, M. (1958). *Head injuries: Mechanisms, diagnosis, and management.* Boston: Little, Brown.

Heaton, R. K. (1981). *Manual for the Wisconsin Card Sorting Test.* Odessa, FL: Psychological Assessment Resources.

Jamieson, K. (1971). *A first notebook of head injury* (2nd ed.). London: Butterworths.

Jennett, B. (1972). Head injuries in children. *Developmental Medicine and Child Neurology, 14,* 137–147.

Jennett, B., & Teasdale, G. (1981). *Management of head injuries.* Philadelphia: Davis.

Klonoff, H. (1971). Head injuries in children: Predisposing factors, accident conditions, accident proneness, and sequelae. *American Journal of Public Health, 61,* 2405–2417.

Klonoff, H., Low, M. D., & Clark, C. (1977). Head injuries in children: A prospective five year follow-up. *Journal of Neurology, Neurosurgery, and Psychiatry, 40,* 1211–1219.

Klonoff, H., Robinson, G. C., & Thompson, G. (1969). Acute and chronic brain syndromes in children. *Developmental Medicine and Child Neurology, 11,* 199–213.

Koppitz, E. M. (1977). *The Visual Aural Digit Span Test.* New York: Grune & Stratton.

Kraus, J. F. (1980). A comparison of recent studies on the extent of the head injury and spinal cord injury problem in the United States. *Journal of Neurosurgery, 53,* 35–43.

Levin, H. S., Benton, A. L., & Grossman, R. G. (1982). *Neurobehavioral consequences of closed head injury.* New York: Oxford University Press.

Lezak, M. D. (1976). *Neuropsychological assessment.* New York: Oxford University Press.

Manheimer, D. I., & Mellinger, G. D. (1967). Personality characteristics of the child accident repeater. *Child Development, 38,* 491–513.

Oddey, M., Humphrey, M., & Uttley, D. (1978). Subjective impairment and social recovery after closed head injury. *Journal of Neurology, Neurosurgery, and Psychiatry, 41,* 611--616.

Reitan, R.M. (undated). *Instructions and procedures for administering the Neuropsychological Test Battery used at the Neuropsychology Laboratory, Indiana University Medical Center.* Unpublished manuscript.

Rimel, R. W., Giordani, B., Barth, J. T., Boll, T. J., & Jane, J. A. (1981). Disability caused by minor head injury. *Neurosurgery, 9,* 221–228.

Robarts, F. H. (1971). A summarized exposition of the causes of head injury in infancy and childhood: Precipitating factors and indications as to their prevention. In F. J. Gillingham, J. F. Shaw, J. Fraser, E. R. Hitchcock, & P. Harris (Eds.), *Head injuries: Proceedings of an international symposium held in Edinburgh and Madrid* (pp. 16–17). Baltimore: Williams & Wilkins.

Romano, M. D. (1974). Family response to traumatic head injury. *Scandinavian Journal of Rehabilitative Medicine, 6,* 1–4.

Roy, S., & Irvin, R. (1983). *Sports medicine: Prevention, evaluation, and rehabilitation.* Englewood Cliffs, NJ: Prentice-Hall.

Shaeffer, D., Chadwick, O., & Rutter, M. (1975). Psychiatric outcome of localized head injury in children. CBA Foundation Symposium, *34,* 191–213.

Skultety, M. F. (1981). Sports injuries of the head and neck. *Seminars in Neurology, 1,* 275–283.

Strich, S. (1961). Shearing of nerve fibres as a cause of brain damage due to head injury. *Lancet, 2,* 443–448.

Symonds, C. (1962). Concussion and its sequelae. *Lancet, 2,* 1–5.

Todorow, S. (1975). Recovery of children after severe closed head injury: Psychoreactive superimpositions. *Scandinavian Journal of Rehabilitative Medicine, 7,* 93–96.

BIBLIOGRAPHY: PROFESSIONALS

Note: At present there is very little material specifically designed for distribution to the general public. It is suggested that material be selected from the professional literature as appropriate for individual situations.

Collier, H. (1979). The role of psychological follow-up in nervous system trauma. *Advances in Neurology, 22,* 149–166.
Provides both a theoretical discussion of psychosocial factors in head injury recovery and practical suggestions for psychological follow-up in medical and mental health settings.

Fuld, P. A., & Fisher, P. (1977). Recovery of intellectual ability after closed head injury. *Developmental Medicine and Child Neurology, 19,* 495–502.
Specifically discusses intellectual deficits and recovery rates in both mild and severe head injury. There is also a limited discussion of the role of parental expectations.

Jamieson, K. (1971). *A first notebook of head injury* (2nd ed.). London: Butterworths.
Jamieson's work is designed as an introductory text for medical students, and is purposely basic in the presentation of material. It is thus a good source of information about the mechanisms of head injury for the professional without a background in physiology.

Levin, H. S., Benton, A. L., & Grossman, R. S. (1982). *Neurobehavioral consequences of closed head injury.* New York: Oxford University Press.
An excellent summary text that provides extensive discussion of all aspects of psychosocial sequelae of head injury.

Torg, J. S. (Ed.). (1982). *Athletic injuries to the head, neck, and face.* Philadelphia: Lea & Febiger.
The chapters by Gennarelli provide detailed information about head injury mechanisms and immediate effects. This book is a good source of information about incidence, etiology, and preventive measures.

Children and Health Promotion

Joseph E. Zins and Donald I. Wagner
University of Cincinnati

BACKGROUND

In recent years, there has been increasing recognition of the role that behavioral factors play in determining physical and emotional well-being, and the link between lifestyle, and health consequences has become well-established (e.g., Hankin & Oktey, 1979). Many of these health-related behavioral patterns which are developed in childhood and adolescence have been found to affect long-term physical and emotional health in adulthood (e.g., Roberts & Peterson, 1984a). Moreover, a number of the leading causes of physical and emotional disorders are associated with preventable risk factors.

In response to these issues, many people in the United States have become more health conscious in their quest for a higher quality of life (Manusco, 1985), and interest has increased regarding means to prevent the onset of health problems through the development of healthy lifestyles, and the elimination of specific unhealthy practices. Particular emphasis has focused on the development of health-enhancing behavior *early* in life. As Harris (1981a) has noted:

> It is almost self-evident that behavior is one of the principle determinants of health status. This is especially true with children, both because so many behavioral patterns established in childhood affect long-term health outcomes in adulthood, and because so many of the immediate dangers to children are those related to risk behaviors or situations that admit to behavioral . . . solutions. (p. 46)

Preventive and health promotion activities have significant potential for bringing about a decline in the prevalence of many disorders and concomitant improvement in general health (Perry, 1984; Rosen & Solomon, 1985). Consequently, *health promotion* has become an area of great promise for school psychology practitioners.

Health Promotion

What is health promotion? While no universal definition of the term exists, in this chapter health promotion is taken to mean measures intended to facilitate the emotional and physical well-being of individuals and groups of children and adolescents. From a broad perspective, the term is defined as "a combination of behavioral, educational, social, economic, and/or environmental efforts which support the establishment and maintenance of behaviors and lifestyles conducive to overall *emotional and physical well-being*" in healthy individuals [italics added] (Wagner & Zins, 1985, p. 5). Thus, there is an emphasis on eliminating or reducing unhealthy behaviors as well as on increasing and strengthening students' repertoires of skills and competencies. In other words, health promotion is a proactive approach that includes both reducing health-compromising behaviors and increasing wellness efforts. The potential focus of health promotion or preventive efforts is extremely broad and includes "practically every effort aimed at improved child rearing, increased communication, building inner control and self-esteem, reducing stress and pollution, etc. — in short, everything aimed at

---

The authors would like to thank Charlene R. Ponti and Sally Graumlich for their helpful comments on an earlier draft of this chapter.

improving the human condition, at making life more fulfilling and meaningful" (Kessler & Albee, 1975, p. 557). While technically there are differences between health promotion and prevention activities, and health promotion does not automatically have preventive effects (Price, Bader, & Ketterer, 1980), in this chapter the terms will be used more or less interchangeably.

An interest in health promotion is consistent with recent discussions within school psychology that emphasize the need for a paradigm shift from traditional diagnostic and remedial services to a preventive orientation. For example, the National Association of School Psychologists (NASP) recently adopted a resolution calling for greater emphasis on preventive efforts in education in order to serve more students effectively in mainstream settings before they are designated as handicapped ("Advocacy for Appropriate Educational Services," 1985). In addition, the NASP *Standards for the Provision of School Psychological Services* (1984) suggest that "school psychologists design and develop procedures for preventing disorders [and] promoting mental health" (p. 19).

Despite the increased interest in prevention and health promotion efforts in school psychology, minimal activity currently exists in day-to-day practice, and there appears to be a discrepancy between values and actions (Alpert, 1985). Therefore, the intent of this chapter is to help narrow this gap by sensitizing school psychologists and other mental health professionals to this emerging area of practice and by providing a description of health promotion with a specific focus on the contribution of psychological and behavioral factors. Issues regarding the development of healthy lifestyles, influences on their development, and examples of interventions that can be instituted to enhance students' emotional and physical well-being are discussed.

DEVELOPMENT

Consideration of the more salient influences on the development of health-enhancing and health-damaging practices is helpful not only in understanding the origins and development of these health-related behaviors, but also in formulating and implementing interventions. These influences are discussed next.

Learning Health-Related Behaviors

Most health-risk behaviors are learned, particularly early in a person's life, and are a result of a complex mixture of social, cognitive, personality, and developmental factors (e.g., Bandura, 1977). From a social learning perspective, it is the interaction of both intrapsychic and environmental influences that motivates one to engage in behavior that promotes or compromises health. As Bandura (1977) stated,

> behavior, other personal factors, and environmental factors all operate as interlocking determinants of each other . . . . The relative influences exerted by these interdependent factors differ in various settings and for different behaviors. There are times when environmental factors exercise powerful constraints on behavior, and other times when personal factors are the overriding regulators of the course of environmental events. (pp. 9–10)

An example of the application of this perspective follows. A 10-year-old girl may develop a sedentary lifestyle and become overweight as a result of the interaction of a number of factors. She may not have the physical coordination or skill necessary for many sports, or she may be reluctant to participate as a result of limited social competence. Her parents may model behaviors that do not include regular exercise regimens, or they may not reinforce the girl's athletic endeavors as a result of what they perceive to be her limited talents in this area or the minimal value they place on such activities. The child may not view exercise as important because it has not been emphasized as such to her, or because of attributions she makes about her own athletic skills. Thus, the relative power of personal, environmental, and/or behavioral aspects of the situation may vary in their influence, and it is the interaction among these factors that determines the girl's behavior.While all of these factors are important, the focus of our interest here is limited to the social and cognitive influences of this complex interaction.

An additional source of detrimental social influences is the modeling of unsafe driving practices, physical violence, or poor problem solving by "high-status" role models including peers, older siblings, influential adults, parents, or media figures. Cognitive factors include the intense concern for public image and the need for peer group acceptance that are frequently evident during the preadolescent and adolescent periods (Botvin & Dusenbury, in press) that may be associated with risk-taking behaviors such as use of tobacco and alcohol, excessive exposure to the sun, or consumption of fast foods on a frequent basis. These various influences, both individually and collectively, help to foster the image and legitimize the idea that engaging in such risk-taking behavior is socially acceptable and appropriate, or that it is highly effective in increasing one's social status. Thus, by observing the behavior of role models or through their influence, children learn to engage in similar behavior.

Alternatively, students also can imitate health-enhancing lifestyle behaviors modeled by others, and in this respect, school personnel can be especially influential. Consequently, many schools have developed programs directed toward helping students resist negative social influences and toward developing assertiveness skills (e.g., Botvin & Dusenbury, in press). Others have encouraged development of wellness behavior in teachers through school-sponsored employee health promotion programs (e.g., Blair, Collingwood, Smith, Upton, & Sterling, 1985). Although both approaches are important, the major "advances in child health in the past century have been accomplished primarily through efforts aimed at changing the behaviors of adults rather than children" (Maddux, Roberts, Sledden, & Wright, 1986, p. 31). Indeed, research on modeling (e.g., Bandura, 1977) suggests that changes are not as likely to occur in children's health without prior alteration of the behavior of adult models.

Controllable Health Risk Factors

Engaging in many of the health risk behaviors described in the chapter eventually can result in or contribute to premature death or serious illness. In fact, it has been estimated that lifestyle is a 50% contributing factor to disease (U. S. DHEW, 1979). Not only can serious negative long-term physical and/or psychological effects result from health-compromising behavior, but significant emotional as well as financial hardships may be experienced by families who must cope with chemical dependence, juvenile delinquency, adolescent suicide, or a myriad of stress-related disorders. Health promotion programs offer hope for decreasing the incidence of these lifestyle-related problems.

Health promotion programs can be directed both toward reducing the frequency of unhealthy behavior, and toward promoting daily behavior and habits that are associated with a healthier, better-adjusted life. The primary controllable, lifestyle health risk factors that are linked to childhood disorders and accidents can be classified into two categories. First are those risk factors that pose a threat of causing significant problems, injury, or even death during childhood. Second are those risk factors that contribute, over a longer period of time beginning in childhood and adolescence, to the development of chronic diseases and disorders that ultimately end in premature death or disability. Table 1 contains examples of various diseases and disorders and the related primary risk factors in both of these categories.

In addition to learned lifestyle behaviors, genetic predisposition, environmental hazards, and availability of health services also are important factors in health and may be the focus of intervention efforts. However, lifestyle usually exerts even greater influence on health than do these other factors.

In summary, many lifestyle behaviors that are not conducive to overall health and well-being are *learned* by children and adolescents, often early in life. Thus, many of these behaviors are appropriate targets of various change programs.

PUTTING HEALTH PROMOTION IN PERSPECTIVE

In the process of implementing health promotion interventions, two additional perspectives or influences on the development of health risk behavior are worthy of consideration. These are a developmental perspective and the influence of societal changes on health-related behavior.

Developmental Perspective

A developmental perspective is important in understanding all human behavior. In regard to children's health, there are two main elements in the developmental approach. First is the focus on specific periods in a child's life during which particular problems may arise. Second is an orientation that recognizes that early intervention is important because of the potential long-term effects of behaviors related to lifestyle (Maddux et al., 1986).

A developmental perspective recognizes that children undergo many significant changes as they grow and mature, and that interventions directed toward various developmental periods in a child's life have the potential for influencing behaviors that occur at "predictable" times (Roberts & Peterson, 1984a). For example, school entrance or transfer and the experience of divorce by parents typically are highly stressful times for children, and excessive stress has been recognized as potentially a major contributing factor to physiological, cognitive, emotional, and behavioral problems in children and adolescents (Forman & O'Malley, 1984). As a result, many schools have established orientation programs directed toward new students, and/or support groups for those whose parents are in the process of divorce, with the goal of minimizing the stress associated with these events and enhancing participants' competence to deal with the situation.

It also has been suggested that there are certain times during children's developmental years when they may be more susceptible to developing unhealthy lifestyles (Roberts, Elkins, & Royal, 1984). Specifically, for example, children in the age group 6–11 years often develop unsafe playground behavior and thus experience many injuries involving bicycles, skateboards, and playground equipment (Sweeney, 1979). Learning safe playground behavior may help them to avoid some of these accidents. Likewise, special approaches may be necessary for problems that have their origin during different developmental periods. These include interventions during the perinatal period (e.g., altering maternal nutritional practices), the elementary years (e.g., teaching social problem solving), junior high (e.g., providing information on contraception), and adolescence (e.g., teaching self-instructional techniques to increase assertiveness).

With regard to the second element of a developmental approach, early or forward-looking intervention, of special interest is the fact that the onset of many health risk and lifestyle behaviors such as insufficient exercise, poor sleep habits, neglect of dental care, inadequate nutrition, lack of social competence, failure to use contraceptives, and excessive television viewing begins during childhood and adolescence. For example, the greatest susceptibility to becoming a habitual smoker occurs around the age of 12, when children are entering a critical decision-making stage and are more inclined to develop smoking habits. Therefore, preventive interventions related to this serious health risk should be initiated prior to this age (Matarazzo, 1982).

A developmental approach, however, is not necessarily appropriate and effective in preventing all problems which occur at more than one developmental level. In such cases, a problem-oriented or setting-focused intervention may be preferable (Roberts & Peterson, 1984a). For more comprehensive discussion of other approaches, interested readers may wish to refer to Roberts and Peterson (1984b) and Felner, Jason, Morit-

TABLE 1

Primary Risk Factors

Selected Disease/Disorder	Known or suspected risk factor
Onset during childhood	
1. Heart disease	1. Hypertension; obesity; family history; elevated serum cholesterol; stress; juvenile diabetes
2. Cancers (leukemia, etc.)	2. Environmental carcinogens; overexposure to sun; exposure to sidestream smoke
3. Accidents: non-motor-vehicle	3. Alcohol; drug abuse; poor safety skills at home; smoking; stress
4. Accidents: motor vehicle	4. Alcohol; drug abuse; no seat belt use; speeding
5. Diabetes	5. Family history; obesity
6. Infectious disease (pneumonia, etc.)	6. Immunization status
7. Suicide	7. Stress; alcohol abuse; drug abuse; environmental factors (residence)
Onset during adulthood	
1. Heart disease	1. Diet; elevated blood lipids; smoking; hypertension; diabetes; lack of exercise; stress; family history
2. Malignant neoplasms (cancer)	2. Tobacco use; worksite exposure; environmental exposure; alcohol abuse; diet; overexposure to sun
3. Cirrhosis of the liver	3. Alcohol abuse
4. Stroke	4. Hypertension; smoking; elevated blood lipids; stress

Note: Based on *Health United States 1980* (Harris, 1981B).

sugu, and Farber (1983). However, in most interventions directed toward children and adolescents, a developmental perspective is helpful.

Influence of Societal Change

In recent years, a number of societal changes have led to increased maternal employment (Galambos & Garbarino, 1983), single-parent households (Harris, 1981b), and high childcare costs (U. S. DHEW, 1975), resulting in new demands for special efforts by schools (Howe, 1986). While most of the children affected by these changes receive adequate care and supervision, an increasing number of children and adolescents are being left on their own, either without or with minimal parental supervision. Consequently, these children may incur increased risk for inadvertent domestic and neighborhood mishaps and injuries from causes such as fires, drowning, playground accidents, poisoning, and kidnapping (Mori & Peterson, 1986). In other words, these children, by default, must assume greater responsibility for their own nutrition, safety, personal hygiene, social problem solving, and leisure activities (e.g., exercise, television viewing)(Peterson, 1984). Consequently, there are clear advantages to making these children, and particularly their caregivers, targets of change efforts in order to prevent the occurrence of potential health-related problems.

There also have been increases in health risk and lifestyle behaviors associated with other changes in U. S. society. These include teenage pregnancy, controlled substance abuse, suicide, motor vehicle accidents, sexually transmitted diseases, increased smoking by females (smoking among males is declining), and so forth. Furthermore, despite the large numbers of children living in poverty, which frequently is associated with poor nutrition, less health care, increased homelessness, and less education, the federal budget recently has been decreased in areas related to the poor (Howe, 1986). While the causes of these changes are exceedingly complex, these developments have had the result of placing greater responsibility on schools for the emotional, social, and physical, as well as the cognitive development of students. Consequently, there is increased support for incorporation of health promotion programs and activities into the educational system to meet these challenges by discouraging the development of unhealthy lifestyle behaviors.

ALTERNATIVE ACTIONS

There are a wide range of interventions that can be used to promote the emotional and physical well-being of students. Here we will review examples of various interventions that have demonstrated effectiveness and show promise for implementation by school psychologists and other mental health specialists. The interventions are categorized according to the organization level at which they can be delivered. While both organizational systems and practitioner-level interventions will be addressed, the emphasis is on actions that can be taken by school psychologists in their individual schools. Furthermore, in this discussion it is assumed that the need for health promotion programs has been adequately determined, and that administrative and caregiver sanction has been obtained prior to the initiation of these activities. It is acknowledged that the distinction between organizational and practitioner-level practices is somewhat arbitrary; they are separated herein for discussion purposes. For the interested reader, detailed discussion of relevant program planning and implementation issues is contained in several sources (e.g., Maher & Bennett, 1984; Maher, Illback, & Zins, 1984b). Moreover, it is acknowledged that health promotion programs are most effectively and efficiently provided when developed and implemented through the *collaborative* efforts of school personnel, students, parents, and community participants. Responsibility for these programs does not rest solely with any one group and a multidisciplinary approach is advantageous (Peterson & Lane, 1985).

Organizational Level

Schools, as organizations, can encourage the development and implementation of health promotion programs. Specifically, they can be structured so that their philosophies, policies, and services support a health promotion/problem prevention orientation. Consideration of these three aspects of the school organization is important since all health promotion efforts take place within a given organizational context.

Philosophy suggests the ideals that are valued by the school and that become intentions toward which the organization directs its efforts (Maher, Illback, & Zins, 1984a). For example, the school's philosophy may emphasize the importance of the social and affective development of its students; it may dictate that corporal punishment not be permitted owing to its potentially adverse effects on students and staff (Bongiovanni, 1979).

Policies are written statements, derived from the school's philosophy, that inform staff, pupils, and teachers about how health promotion efforts will be carried out (Maher et al., 1984a). A policy may stipulate that problem-solving and decision making skills are to be included in the curriculum for all students from kindergarten through high school. At a more concrete level, there may be policies that no junk food be sold or no smoking be permitted on school premises.

Services that are provided are the core feature of a school organization (Maher et al., 1984a). These services can be placed along a continuum ranging from preventive to remedial, and oftentimes they are a mixture of both emphases. For example, a program for pregnant students dealing with physical and psychological issues in pregnancy and parenthood may be provided through the collaborative efforts of the school nurse and the school psychologist; aerobics instruction could be included as part of the physical education program.

Another example would be for the school psychologist to promote faculty development and personal adjustment through presentation of various behavioral and cognitive–behavioral training programs. The relationship between productivity and the personal adjustment of staff has been recognized in the organizational literature (Katz & Kahn, 1978). Likewise, it is apparent that improvements in staff performance can lead to positive outcomes for students, and that staff can become better role models for students. Forman (1981, 1982), for example, has demonstrated that self-control programs combining relaxation and cognitive training can have positive effects on staff stress and anxiety. More detailed discussion of staff development is beyond the scope of this chapter (see Forman, 1984, for additional information), but these approaches are important components in comprehensive health promotion programs.

This brief discussion is intended to emphasize the fact that services are provided by individual practitioners within an organizational context. As such, the school organization exerts tremendous influence on health promotion efforts. School psychologists clearly can become involved in intervening at this level through organizational consultation to insure that school philosophies, policies, and services include a health promotion component. Not only can they consult with school boards, administrators, and other decision makers regarding these issues, but they can serve as members of various districtwide committees, such as for curriculum and policy development, act as resource persons for administrators and department heads, conduct in-service training and organization development programs, and become involved with community groups, such as social service agencies and juvenile courts, that interact with the school regarding health-related issues. Further, it recently has been demonstrated that health promotion programs for school staffs initiated in schools can result in considerable savings in personnel costs (Blair et al., 1985). Consequently, all of the above examples indicate that school psychologists operating at an organizational level can effectively and efficiently exert a major influence on the development of healthy lifestyles.

Practitioner Level

In this section, activities appropriate for the individual school psychologist who wishes to engage in health promotion efforts at the school building level will be described. Since the chapter has a preventive and not remedial focus, the primary emphasis is on the school psychologist in a consultative rather than a direct service role. Indeed, the primary function of the school psychologist in health promotion programs is to provide consultation services. In this capacity, the school psychologist engages in a mutual problem-solving process with other professionals to develop intervention strategies to benefit pupils.

Interdisciplinary Collaboration. There often are opportunities for school psychologists to consult with teachers and parents, as well as medical and allied health professionals, regarding problems that children experience. Thus, interdisciplinary collaboration frequently is the preferred mode of operation. Medical treatments that have behavioral components such as exercising, taking medication, or dieting, may be enhanced if developed and implemented collaboratively with parents and school personnel (Williams, Foreyt, & Goodrick, 1981). Furthermore, in the diagnosis and treatment of ailments such as attention deficit disorders, a cooperative relationship between medical and school personnel may be necessary for diagnostic purposes and to enhance treatment effectiveness and generalization. A thorough diagnostic assessment would establish whether a behavior such as hyperactivity or inattention occurs across settings and determine the antecedents and consequences of the behavior. Once treatment is initiated, whether it be behavioral, medical, or some combination of the two, it is necessary to ascertain compliance with intervention procedures and to determine outcomes. Collaboration between medical personnel and school psychologists can improve treatment effectiveness in such instances (Barkley, 1981) and extend generalization of the prescribed behavior.

Referral Out. Given the complex nature of health, school psychologists frequently collaborate with and make referrals to a variety of health-related agencies and professionals that provide health promotion services to children and families. In many instances, these services include educational programs, interventions designed to change health-related behavior (e.g., programs to reduce stress, stop smoking, reduce weight), and health screening services. It is important for school psychologists to become personally familiar with these resources, as such knowledge is crucial in influencing children and families to accept and follow through on referral recommendations (Zins & Hopkins, 1981).

Most communities, even in sparsely populated rural areas, have access to a variety of local or state health promotion community resources. There are five broad classifications of these community resource agencies.

1. Health agencies: These include primarily voluntary health agencies that are devoted to the elimination of selected diseases, such as the American Heart Association, American Cancer Society, Mental Health Association, and American Lung Association. These agencies have many written materials, curricula, films, and other teacher aids available at low or no cost. Also, voluntary agencies often sponsor peer-led, self-help activities such as smoking cessation or alcohol support groups.

2. Public health personnel: Often the local, county, or state health departments will have a variety of health promotion resources that are similar to those of the voluntary health agencies. Also, they have special expertise in respect to immunizations, infectious diseases (especially sexually transmitted ones), and environmental health hazards.

3. Health care programs: Many hospitals have developed health promotion services in an effort to diversify their services and to appeal to new health care markets. Programs for eating disorders, sports medicine, cardiovascular fitness, parenting, chemical dependence, stress management, weight control, and childbirth are some of the more common offerings by hospitals.

4. Youth services agencies: The YMCA and YWCA network continues to actively participate in promoting the health and well-being of children, adolescents, and adults (see Kuntzleman, 1985). Also, many 4-H Clubs, Scouts, churches, and other youth organizations are involved in helping youngsters develop healthy lifestyles.

5. Mental health centers: Expertise in chemical dependence, stress management, suicide prevention, and other mental health concerns is readily available from community mental health centers, alcohol treatment programs, and chemical dependency centers. Many of these agencies also offer employee assistance programs for local industry and businesses to deal with health-related concerns; therefore, they may be important resources for families.

Program Development Consultation. While there are a variety of health promotion interventions, this section describes several exemplary programs that have a social learning orientation as examples of the range of possible approaches, and it also includes a brief summary of three instructional media programs. As suggested in the previous section, the school psychologist can serve in a consultative capacity to school personnel as they implement these programs in the classroom.

A psychoeducational intervention approach developed by Botvin (Botvin, 1983, 1985; Botvin & Dusenbury, in press), *Life Skills Training* (LST), has been implemented successfully in several junior and senior high schools. This approach is based conceptually on social learning (Bandura, 1977) and problem behavior theories (Jessor & Jessor, 1977), and is intended to develop essential competencies in the areas of social skills, self-control, problem-solving, and study skills. LST primarily uses cognitive–behavioral strategies to facilitate skill development along with lectures and small group discussions. It is divided into three major components: (a) personal skills training, which deals with decision making and self-improvement, coping with anxiety, and resisting persuasive advertising; (b) a problem-specific component, which addresses the consequences of a health behavior and methods of resisting peer pressure; and (c) social skills training which considers communication skills, overcoming shyness, developing social contacts, and assertiveness. More specific information on Life Skills Training is included in Table 2, and a summary of empirical research supporting the efficacy of the program is found in Botvin and Dusenbury (in press).

Another program, *Health Is Basic* (Educational Development Corporation, 1983), is targeted to grades 7–12 and includes a curriculum guide to 16 health-teaching modules. Topics included in the program are (a) being fit; (b) eating well; (c) promoting health in families; (d) communicating in families; (e) having friends; (f) living with feelings; (g) handling stress; (h) protecting oneself and others — smoking, drinking, and drugs; (i) preventing injuries; (j) locating health resources; and (k) creating a healthful environment. The overall intent of the program is to improve students' ability to direct their own development in health-enhancing ways by expanding their knowledge, sensitivity, and understanding of relevant health-related behaviors and influences. Specific teaching strategies are provided for each module and include techniques such as the use of minilectures, group discussion, self-assessment, brainstorming, role playing, and self-directed activities.

Several relevant instructional media programs have been developed that are also based upon a social learning orientation. In several respects, the instructional media programs have goals and formats that are similar to those of *Life Skills Training* and *Health is Basic.* Consequently, they can serve as useful media resource supplements to both of these previously discussed programs. The modules included in the media programs —*Inside/Out* (National Instructional Television Center, 1973), *Self-Incorporated* (Agency for Instructional Television, 1975), and *On The Level* (Agency for Instructional Television, 1980) —also can be used as self-contained health promotion programs, or they can be integrated with individualized approaches. Major elements of each program are summarized in Table 3.

In summary, each of these programs, as well as other similar programs, usually include a focus on a combination of the following topics: (a) consideration of the underlying determinants of specific health behaviors; (b) importance of modeling healthy behaviors; (c) media and peer influences; (d) overcoming other negative social influences; and (e) promoting positive influence. School psychologists can encourage the use of these training activities as members of planning committees or in consultative capacities.

SUMMARY

This chapter presented an overview of health promotion interventions and the potential role of the school psychologist in this emerging and very promising area. Health promotion was broadly viewed as encompassing both emotional and physical well-being, and as emphasizing early intervention to eliminate unhealthy behavior and to reinforce healthy behavior. A primary focus was on lifestyle behaviors that are learned, often early in life, and that potentially have long-term consequences for the individual. Since many health risk factors associated with various disorders are learned, they often are controllable through behavioral intervention. It also was noted that a developmental perspective is useful and that numerous societal changes have contributed to the development of unhealthy lifestyles.

School psychologists have numerous opportunities to become involved in health promotion programs at both the organizational and the practitioner levels, primarily in a consultative capacity. They can encourage and influence school organizations to develop philosophies, policies, and services that support a health promotion orientation. In addition, they can collaborate and consult with teachers, related professionals, and parents

TABLE 2
Life Skills Training Program Overview

Component	Number of sessions	Content
Cognitive	4	Three sessions on short- and long-term consequences of tobacco, alcohol, and marijuana use; one session on physical effects of smoking
Decision making	4	Two sessions on decision-making processes and skills; two sessions on advertising techniques and consumer behavior
Coping with anxiety	2	Both sessions on relaxation techniques to use in anxiety-inducing situations
Social skills training (communication, relationships, assertiveness)	6	Two sessions on communication skills (verbal and nonverbal
		Two sessions on initiating social contacts (boy-girl, etc.) and overcoming shyness
		Two sessions on assertiveness skills
Self-improvement	2	Both sessions on self-image and self-improvement and methods to enhance them

Note: Based on Botvin (1985) and Botvin and Dusenbury (in press).

TABLE 3
Instructional Media Programs

Name of program	Target audience (age)	Number of programs	Length of each program (minutes)	Selected topics
Inside/out	8–10	30	15	Understanding feelings; dealing with group pressure; learning to be yourself; calculating safety risks
Self-incorporated	11–13	15	15	Making decisions; boy–girl relationships; everyday pressures; communication skills
On the level	14–17	12	15	Dealing with conflict; developing self-concept; coping with stress; peer group membership; love; friendship

regarding the implementation of health promotion programs. Finally, several programs were reviewed as examples of the range of possible approaches that can be incorporated into classroom health-related interventions. While it was beyond the scope of the chapter to provide an in-depth discussion of health promotion, the intent was to present an overview of the topic and to stimulate interest and practice. Readers desiring additional information are encouraged to consult the sources listed in the annotated bibliography and in the References section.

The potential of health promotion programs appears vast, but it is an area of practice that has been virtually untapped by most school psychologists. However, there are numerous opportunities for role expansion that would include involvement in this emerging area as an additional means of facilitating the learning and adjustment of *all* children.

REFERENCES

Advocacy for appropriate educational services for all children. (1985). *Communique, 13,* 9.

Agency for Instructional Television. (1975). *Guide to "Self-Incorporated"* [Film]. Bloomington, IN: Author.

Agency for Instructional Television. (1980). *Guide to "On the Level"* [Film]. Bloomington, IN: Author.

Alpert, J. L. (1985). Change within a profession: Change, prevention, and school psychology. *American Psychologist, 40,* 1112–1121.

Bandura, A. (1977). *Social learning theory.* Englewood Cliffs, NJ: Prentice-Hall.

Barkley, R. A. (1981). *Hyperactive children.* New York: Guilford.

Blair, S. N., Collingwood, T. R., Smith, M., Upton, J., & Sterling, C. L. (1985). Review of a health promotion program for school employees. In J. E. Zins, D. I. Wagner, & C. A. Maher (Eds.), *Health promotion in the schools* (pp. 89–98). New York: Haworth.

Bongiovanni, A. F. (1979). A review of the effects of punishment: Implications for corporal punishment in the schools. In I. Hyman & J. Wise (Eds.), *Corporal punishment in American education* (pp. 351–372). Philadelphia: Temple University Press.

Botvin, G. J. (1983). *Life Skills Training* (teacher's manual). New York: Smithfield.

Botvin, G. J. (1985). The Life Skills Training program as a health promotion strategy: Theoretical issues and empirical findings. In J. E. Zins, D. I. Wagner, & C. A. Maher (Eds.), *Health promotion in the schools* (pp. 9–24). New York: Haworth.

Botvin, G., & Dusenbury, L. (in press). Life Skills Training: A psychoeducational approach to substance abuse prevention. In C. A. Maher & J. E. Zins (Eds.), *Psychoeducational interventions in schools.* Elmsford, NY: Pergamon.

Educational Development Corporation. (1983). *Health is basic: An introduction to the teenage health teaching modules for teachers and students.* Newton, MA: Author.

Felner, R. D., Jason, L. A., Moritsugu, J. N., & Farber, S. S. (Eds.). (1983). *Preventive psychology.* Elmsford, NY: Pergamon.

Forman, S. G. (1981). Stress management training: Evaluation of effects on school psychological services. *Journal of School Psychology, 19,* 233–241.

Forman, S. G. (1982). Stress management for teachers: A cognitive–behavioral program. *Journal of School Psychology, 20,* 180–187.

Forman, S. G. (1984). Behavioral and cognitive–behavioral approaches to staff development. In C. A. Maher, R. J. Illback, & J. E. Zins (Eds.), *Organizational psychology in the schools* (pp. 302–322). Springfield, IL: Thomas.

Forman, S. G., & O'Malley, P. (1984). School stress and anxiety reactions. *School Psychology Review, 13,* 162–170.

Galambos, N. L., & Garbarino, J. (1983). Identifying the missing links in the study of latchkey children. *Children Today, 12,* 2–4, 40–41.

Hankin, J., & Oktey, J. (1979). *Mental disorder in primary medical care* (DHEW Publication No. [ADM] 78-661). Washington, DC: U. S. Government Printing Office.

Harris, P. (1981a). *Better health for our children: A national strategy. The report of the Select Panel for the Promotion of Child Health.* Washington, DC: U. S. Government Printing Office.

Harris, P. (1981b). *Health United States 1980* (Publication No. [PHS] 81-1234). Washington, DC: U. S. Government Printing Office.

Howe, H., II. (1986, April). *The prospect for children in the United States.* Keynote address presented at the annual meeting of the National Association of School Psychologists, Hollywood, FL.

Jessor, R., & Jessor, S. L. (1977). *Problem behavior and psychosocial development: A longitudinal study of youth.* New York: Academic.

Katz, D., & Kahn, R. L. (1978). *The social psychology of organizations* (2nd ed.). New York: Wiley.

Kessler, M., & Albee, G. W. (1975). Primary prevention. *Annual Review of Psychology, 26,* 557–591.

Kuntzleman, C. T. (1985). Enhancing cardiovascular fitness of children and youth: The Feelin' Good program. In J. E. Zins, D. I. Wagner, & C. A. Maher (Eds.), *Health promotion in the schools* (pp. 39–48). New York: Haworth.

Maddux, J. E., Roberts, M. C., Sledden, E. A., & Wright, L. (1986). Developmental issues in child health psychology. *American Psychologist, 41,* 25–34.

Maher, C. A., & Bennett, R. E. (1984). *Planning and evaluating special education services.* Englewood Cliffs, NJ: Prentice-Hall.

Maher, C. A., Illback, R. J., & Zins, J. E. (1984a). Applying organizational psychology in the schools: Perspectives and framework. In C. A. Maher, R. J. Illback, & J. E. Zins (Eds.), *Organizational psychology in the schools: A handbook for professionals* (pp. 5–20). Springfield, IL: Thomas.

Maher, C. A., Illback, R. J., & Zins, J. E. (Eds.). (1984b). *Organizational psychology in the schools: A handbook for professionals.* Springfield, IL: Thomas.

Manusco, J. (1981). Psychological services and health enhancement. In A. Broskowski, E. Marks, & S. H. Budman (Eds.), *Linking health and mental health* (pp.137–158). Beverly Hills, CA: Sage.

Matarazzo, J. D. (1982). Behavioral health's challenge to academic, scientific, and professional psychology. *American Psychologist, 37,* 1–14.

Mori, L., & Peterson, L. (1986). Training preschoolers in home safety skills to prevent inadvertent injury. *Journal of Clinical Child Psychology, 15,* 106–114.

National Association of School Psychologists. (1984). *Standards for the provision of school psychological services.* Washington, DC: Author.

National Instructional Television Center. (1973). *Inside/out: A guide for teachers* [Film]. Bloomington, IN: Author.

Perry, C. L. (1984). Health promotion at school: Expanding the potential for prevention. *School Psychology Review, 13,* 141–149.

Peterson, D. W., & Lane, B. (1985). The role of interdisciplinary teams in the promotion of physical and mental health. In J. E. Zins, D. I. Wagner, & C. A. Maher (Eds.), *Health promotion in the schools* (pp. 113–124). New York: Haworth.

Price, R. H., Bader, B. C., & Ketterer, R. F. (1980). Prevention in community mental health. In R. H. Price, R. F. Ketterer, B. C. Bader, & J. Monahan (Eds.), *Prevention in mental health* (pp. 9–20). Beverly Hills, CA: Sage.

Roberts, M. C., Elkins, P. D., & Royal, G. P. (1984). Psychological applications in the prevention of accidents and illnesses. In M. C. Roberts & L. Peterson (Eds.), *Prevention of problems in childhood* (pp. 173–199). New York: Wiley.

Roberts, M. C., & Peterson, L. (1984a). Prevention models: Theoretical and practical implications. In M. C. Roberts & L. Peterson (Eds.), *Prevention of problems in childhood* (pp. 1–42). New York: Wiley.

Roberts, M. C., & Peterson, L. (1984b). (Eds.). *Prevention of problems in childhood.* New York: Wiley.

Rosen, J. C., & Solomon, L. J. (1985). (Eds.). *Prevention in health psychology.* Hanover, NH: University Press of New England.

Sweeney, T. B. (1979). X-rated playgrounds? *Pediatrics, 64,* 961.

U. S. Department of Health, Education, and Welfare. (1979). *Healthy people: The Surgeon General's report on health promotion and disease prevention* (DHEW [PHS] Publication No. 79-55071). Washington, DC: U. S. Government Printing Office.

U. S. Department of Health, Education, and Welfare. (1975). *National childcare consumer study* (No. 105-1107). Washington, DC: Office of Child Development.

Wagner, D. I., & Zins, J. E. (1985). Health promotion in schools: Opportunities and challenges for special services providers. In J. E. Zins, D. I. Wagner, & C. A. Maher (Eds.), *Health promotion in the schools* (pp. 5–8). New York: Haworth.

Williams, B. J., Foreyt, J. P., & Goodrick, G. K. (Eds.). (1981). *Pediatric behavioral medicine.* New York: Praeger.

Zins, J. E., & Hopkins, R. A. (1981). Referral out: Increasing the number of kept appointments. *School Psychology Review, 10,* 107–111.

BIBLIOGRAPHY: PROFESSIONALS

Felner, R. D., Jason, L. A., Moritsugu, J. N., & Farber, S. S. (Eds.). (1983). *Preventive psychology: Theory, research, and practice.* New York: Pergamon.
Many leading researchers in prevention provide an extensive survey of preventive approaches within psychology. Although the focus of the book is not on children, the information on the theoretical bases of prevention, including competency-based and ecological/environmental perspectives, is essential to all practitioners. Other sections address issues such as stress, prevention in the community, training, and future directions.

Matarazzo, J. D., Weiss, S. M., Herd, J. A., Miller, N. E., & Weiss, S. M. (Eds.). (1984). *Behavioral health: A handbook for health enhancement and disease prevention.* New York: Wiley.
The editors have compiled a very comprehensive handbook on health enhancement and disease prevention. The content includes reviews of general strategies for health enhancement, training of health promoters, and future directions for health promotion programs. There also are sections of the book devoted to specific health enhancement program areas including exercise, smoking, nutrition, blood pressure, safety, alcohol, and dental health.

Roberts, M. C., & Peterson, L. (Eds.). (1984). *Prevention of problems in childhood: Psychological research and applications.* New York: Wiley-Interscience.
In this volume, a number of leading experts in prevention present theories, research, and interventions for physical and psychological problems. Three major intervention approaches are discussed by contributors: milestone, high-risk group, and population-wide prevention. The material is organized developmentally and shows how to prevent problems with various age groups in a variety of settings.

Severson, H. H., & Shellenberger, S. (Eds.). (1984). Behavioral health [Special issue]. *School Psychology Review, 13*(2).
This special issue is intended to provide information and direction for school psychologists regarding ways in which they can become involved in prevention and treatment programs that will have a major influence on the physical well-being of children. The contributors examine the various sources of decreased health and present numerous useful ideas for preventing these problems.

Zins, J. E., Wagner, D. I., & Maher, C. A. (Eds.). (1985). *Health promotion in the schools: Innovative approaches to facilitating physical and emotional well-being.* New York: Haworth.
This book provides information regarding the many opportunities that school psychologists and other special services providers have to be innovators and leaders in preventing physical and emotional disorders and in promoting health. Leading experts in a number of disciplines present up-to-date ideas and specific suggestions regarding a variety of activities that can be implemented by practitioners within educational settings.

BIBLIOGRAPHY: PARENTS

Elias, J., & Clabby, M. J. (1986). *Teach your child decision making.* New York: Doubleday.
This very readable book is based upon extensive research conducted by the authors in schools since 1979. It contains information designed to enable parents and educators to teach children the necessary skills for solving everyday problems on their own. The purpose is to enable children to respond to their problems with confidence in an active and positive manner.

Pantell, R. H., Fries, J. F., & Vickery, D. M. (1977). *Taking care of your child: A parent's guide to medical care.* Reading, MA: Addison-Wesley.
This book is perhaps the most comprehensive guide to understanding common childhood illnesses; as such, it should be helpful to parents in reducing anxieties associated with illness. The authors guide the reader through the process of deciding when homecare is advisable and when medical intervention is required. Also, immunization charts and other health-promoting information is provided.

Schaefer, C. E., & Millman, H. C. (1981). *How to help children with common problems.* New York: Van Nostrand Reinhold.
This practical manual provides specific advice to parents in a nontechnical manner on how to handle everyday problems of normal children from early childhood through adolescence. More than one way is presented for dealing with each of the common problems included. In addition to the problem-focused sections, the book describes preventive parenting techniques that are designed to avert or minimize behavior problems.

U. S. Department of Health and Human Services. (1985). *Medicine for the layman: Behavior patterns and health* (NIH Publication No. 85-2682). Bethesda, MD: Office of Clinical Reports and Inquiries.
A basic exploration of how individual behavior can contribute to the causation or prevention of various diseases. Specific risk factors are explored as they relate to the leading causes of death and disease. Overall, the book is a good primer on the behavioral aspects of health and should be a useful resource for the layperson.

Wynder, E. L. (1981). *The book of health: A complete guide to making health last a lifetime.* New York: Franklin Watts.
An excellent guide for exploring the preventive aspects of the leading causes of disease and death. Chapters on nutrition, exercise, stress, accidents, and environmental hazards provide important information for all parents to enable them to make more informed decisions regarding their children.

Children and Hearing

Susan M. Vess
University of Northern Colorado

Laura S. Gregory
Ouachita Parish Schools, Louisiana

Susan L. Moore
Northeast Louisiana University

BACKGROUND AND DEVELOPMENT

This chapter focuses on children with mild and/or fluctuating hearing losses (M/FHL). Until relatively recently, M/FHL children were ignored by educators and other professionals because they were not seen as having problems as a result of their hearing impairment. Their behavior was so like their peers that their learning and behavioral difficulties were attributed to mild mental impairment and/or emotional problems. Since they experienced problems irregularly, it was often concluded that these children performed "if they wanted to" of "if they paid attention" (Boothroyd, 1982; Berg & Fletcher, 1970; Proctor, 1963). Although the numbers involved are difficult to determine, about 60% of children have otitis media, the major cause of M/FHL, before 5 years of age, and approximately 20% of school-aged children have a fluctuating loss sometime during their school years (Webster, Saunders, & Bamford, 1984; Northern & Downs, 1984; Dobie & Berlin, 1979; Berg & Fletcher, 1970).

Hearing, the invisible sense, operates in the following manner. The external ear gathers sound waves from the environment and funnels them into the internal ear. These waves travel down the external auditory canal to the middle ear and cause the eardrum to vibrate. The vibrations in the middle ear amplify the sound waves and send them into the inner ear, where they are transformed into neural impulses. The Eustachian tube, the passage between the middle ear and the throat, permits ventilation and pressure equalization between the middle ear and the throat.

A conductive hearing loss occurs when the sound waves are unable to travel down the ear canal to the middle ear because of middle ear problems or abnormalities and/or the eardrum does not vibrate sufficiently to amplify the sounds. For example, when earplugs are used to block sounds, a temporary conductive hearing loss results. These losses arise when a foreign object such as beans or paper are stuck into the ear for "fun" by children. Parents may inadvertently cause conductive hearing losses by forcing objects, or earwax, deeper into the auditory canal when using tweezers or cotton swabs to clean the ear. The major cause of conductive losses in children is otitis media (OM) (Boothroyd, 1982). This inflammation of the middle ear, caused by failure of the Eustachian tube and/or by infection in the middle ear cavity, is generally associated with short-term or fluctuating hearing loss (Boothroyd, 1982). If it is left untreated or becomes chronic, OM can lead to permanent conductive hearing impairment. Conductive losses are usually remediable through medication and/or surgery. Persons with conductive losses hear as long as sound is loud enough to penetrate the blockage, but they experience difficulty hearing sounds whose volume is below the hearing threshold. Speech, language, and academic problems are consistent with the degree and timing of hearing loss. Individuals with a conductive loss can hear, but at less intense volume, and can learn to speak naturally. Conductive losses never cause total deafness because the blockage is bypassed when the volume is loud enough to cause the skull bones to vibrate.

The inner ear consists of the vestibular system, which is responsible for balance, and the snail-shaped cochlea, which generates neural impulses to the auditory processing areas of the brain. A sensorineural hearing loss occurs when the cochlea and/or the auditory nerve is damaged. Causes of congenital sensorineural losses include maternal bacterial and viral infections, drugs, radiation, metabolic disorders, RH incompatibility, and a variety of genetic conditions. Postnatal causes include common childhood illnesses such as measles, chicken pox, and mumps, as well as influenza, meningitis, viral pneumonia, otitis media that has spread into the inner ear, and exposure to loud noises from hunting, firecrackers, or music.

Mumps is a major cause of unilateral sensorineural hearing loss in children. Since both ears work together to judge sound localization and distance, a mild unilateral hearing loss is problematic. Both ears hear, but because the ears are not perceiving equally, the sound relationship between the ears is imbalanced (Northern & Downs, 1984). The consequences of a mild unilateral hearing loss in children include difficulties with sound localization and distance determination, following conversations in a noisy environment, and listening to sounds on the "bad" side. Although the differences are not statistically significant, children with mild unilateral hearing losses perform below grademates across academic areas, and approximately half fail a grade or require academic assistance (Bess & Tharpe, 1984; Keller & Bundy, 1980).

Sensorineural losses are usually permanent, because regeneration or repair of the cochlea or auditory nerve is beyond the scope of current medical technology.

Cochlear implants, which are sought by parents as a cure for their children's deafness, are not relevant to all kinds of hearing loss, do not enable children to derive meaning from sounds, and are not recommended by hearing specialists for most children (National Association of the Deaf, 1986). In sensorineural losses, not only is volume insufficient, but also sounds are distorted. Therefore, children with a sensorineural loss exhibit "deaf" speech. The consequences of a mild sensorineural hearing loss that occurs in the developmental years include poor academic performance and problems with speech and language, all of which intensify as the children grow older (Blair, Peterson, & Viehweg, 1985).

Sounds vary along the dimensions of intensity and frequency. On the audiogram, frequency is represented by vertical lines and intensity is plotted horizontally. Intensity, the audiologist's term for volume, is measured by determining the loudness level (dB) of a sound when it is first heard. The threshold designates the faintest volume at which a sound is perceived. For example, for a child with a 70dB hearing loss, the threshold is so high that normal conversation is not loud enough to be heard. Frequency, similar to pitch, is arranged like the keys on a piano with the low pitches on the left and the high pitches on the right. Continuing the comparison, the pitches associated with human speech are the octaves surrounding middle C. The threshold at each frequency is plotted for both ears on the same audiogram. Consequently, the pattern across frequencies and the difference between the two ears is readily apparent. Normal hearing sensitivity is indicated by thresholds that lie between 0 and 25dB. 0dB is the value that indicates the faintest volume perceived by most people with normal hearing. It does not mean an absence of sound. Beyond 25dB, severity of hearing loss is classified by the volume level indicated on the audiogram. For example, persons whose hearing loss ranges between 35 and 69dB are considered hard of hearing while those whose loss exceeds 69dB are identified as deaf (Moores, 1982). When a hearing loss exists, both corrected and uncorrected thresholds are measured, because it is important for communication and learning to know how well a person hears when using amplification, just as it is important for driving to know how well an individual sees with glasses. Since difficulty hearing and understanding speech is a common complaint, tonal tests measuring which sounds are heard and which are not heard are supplemented by tests that assess how well an individual understands speech in day-to-day situations. When only 50–60% of words are discriminated, the person has difficulty following conversation (Goetzinger, 1978).

It is common to hear that an individual has a particular percentage of hearing loss, but whether the deficiency is in volume or in comprehension is not specified. This percentage is the average of thresholds across three pitches, less 25 (the value for normal hearing), multiplied by 1.5. These percentages are analogous to mental ages, in that they are sufficiently unsophisticated to communicate, but they do not explain what skills are available to the person under discussion.

The audiogram, with pictures at the juncture of their intensity and frequency, illustrates the interplay between volume and pitch. Objects like the air conditioner located near the top of the audiogram have a softer volume than objects such as the chainsaw that are closer to the bottom. Objects like the vacuum cleaner on the left are lower-pitched than those, such as the telephone, on the right. Let's take a hypothetical case. If a horizontal line is drawn across the audiogram at 40dB, everything above the line is too quiet to hear. As indicated by the audiogram, the person with a 40dB hearing loss does not hear ocean waves, ticking clocks, the letters *f, g, h, p, k,* or *s,* or the *ch, sh,* and *th* sounds. If the line is drawn at 70dB, then the person has difficulty discriminating sounds, and only hears loud voices when they are within a foot of the ear; but perceives some environmental sounds. If a hearing loss occurs before a child is a year old, speech and language do not develop spontaneously, are defective, and may even deteriorate. When the line is drawn near the bottom of the audiogram, the individual hears tractor trailers, bands and jetplanes; but as anyone who has attended a rock concert can attest, it is very difficult to separate sound perception from vibrations. The dB ranges for conversational speech and dangerous noise levels are indicated on the audiogram. Time limits established by OSHA are also indicated because exposure to loud noises for a sustained period results in a permanent sensorineural hearing loss. Although adults are protected from din in the workplace, children suffer hearing losses from loud noises in their environment. Two common sources of noise leading to impaired hearing in adolescents are high school shop classes and using earphones to listen to loud music. The audiogram measures hearing only in the best listening environment. Therefore, depending on the amount of background noise, the hearing-impaired individual, like the hearing person, may have more difficulty distinguishing speech and environmental sounds than the audiogram suggests.

PUTTING HEARING IN PERSPECTIVE

A relatively small percentage of the hearing-impaired population experiences severe auditory loss or deafness. However, most children who are presumably without risk of a hearing impairment are susceptible to a fluctuating and/or permanent loss from a variety of childhood illnesses. A fluctuating hearing loss is one that varies in severity. Conductive losses that are due to OM fluctuate as the fluid in the middle ear increases or thickens or if the patient fails to take prescribed medication (Paradise, 1981). Allergies are another source of fluctuating hearing losses (McLaughlin, et al., 1983). In addition, when hearing aids are not worn consistently or if they are working poorly, hearing-impaired children experience an artificial fluctuating loss (Boothroyd, 1982). Chronic ear conditions such as OM can lead to a permanent mild to moderate loss if, for example, medication is discontinued too early because a child no longer has overt symptoms of illness, or the prescribed dosage was too low to eliminate infection (Meyerhoff, Liston, & Anderson, 1984).

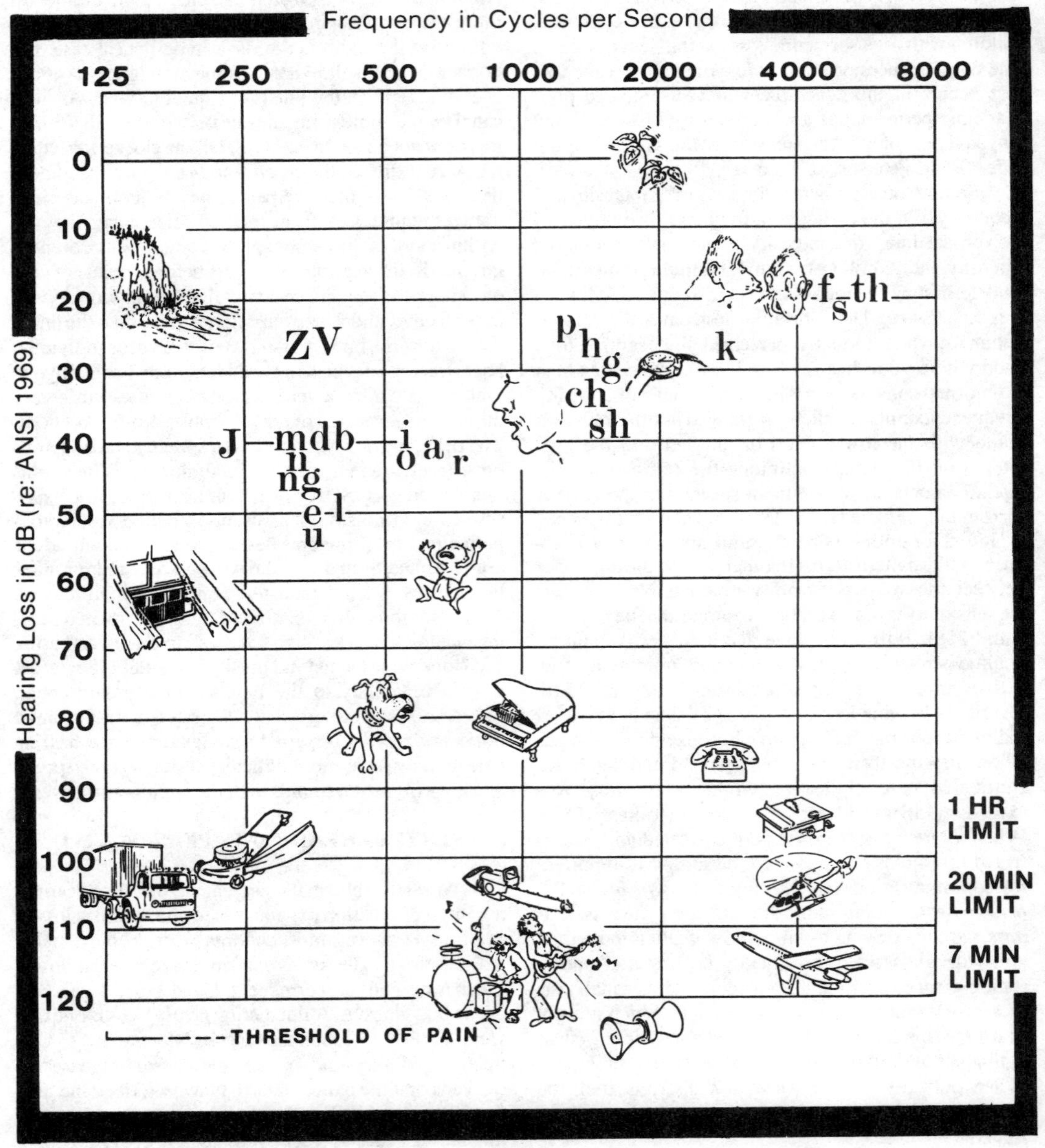

From: Northern and Downs: *Hearing in Children,* 3rd Edition, Baltimore: Williams and Wilkins, 1984. Reprinted by permission.

OM is second only to upper respiratory infections (URI) in frequency of occurrence in children, and it often results from spread of the URI to the ears (Meyerhoff, Liston, & Anderson, 1984). Contagion from a cold, for example, moves from the nose and throat to the ears when the nose is pinched shut during blowing. Additional causes of OM include allergies, sinusitis, and childhood illnesses such as measles and mumps. Children with impaired hearing, Down's syndrome, and cleft palate are very vulnerable to OM (Webster, Saunders, & Bamford, 1984). When hearing-impaired children undergo an episode of OM, fluid in the middle ear reduces the level of functioning obtained by amplification and the children's academic work and socialization are hurt. After an episode of OM, if hearing does not return to its former level, stronger amplification and additional problems in language, schooling, and socialization may result.

OM occurs most frequently during the preschool years, two-thirds of children having at least one episode before the age of 5 (Friel-Patti et al., 1982; Berg & Fletcher, 1970). Since most children have several episodes and 20% have OM chronically, recurrence is a major feature of this inflammation (Kudrjavcev & Schoenberg, 1979). In a study by Berg and Fletcher (1970), 30% of children with no symptoms of illness or allergy were found to have fluid in their ears during a follow-up or routine pediatric evaluation. Most children are expected to have a mild to moderate hearing loss for weeks or even months after the acute phase of OM. Following an episode of OM, children may regain normal acuity levels and health, but some experience chronic infection of their ears, tonsils, and adenoids. Table 1 presents common symptoms of OM.

Until recently, chronic OM and/or mild hearing losses were considered medical problems that necessitated little educational intervention. Consequently, children with either condition attended regular education classes. Although they had poor study habits, negative attitudes toward school, and conflicts with their teachers and classmates, most were perceived as unmotivated, inattentive, and perhaps even mentally or behaviorally impaired. Although hearing was continuously used in learning, these children often found their hearing sensitivity too faint or too variable for success at school. According to Glass (1981), there is a systematic relationship between middle ear infections and auditory learning disabilities, with 70% of children suspected of having OM at the time of evaluation. Moreover, other students with a history of ear effusions scored below age-mates on three measures of auditory learning (Glass, 1981). Even if they make a complete physical recovery, children with M/FHL may experience educational complications and have additional problems related to the noise level of activities and equipment in their classrooms, the lack of individual attention in large classes, the mannerisms and speech patterns of the teacher, and personal characteristics (Stevens, 1986; Bess, 1985; Downs, 1985; Northern & Downs, 1984; Webster, Saunders, & Bamford, 1984; Kirkwood & Kirkwood, 1983; Reichman & Healey, 1983; Boothroyd, 1982; Burgener & Mouw, 1982; Brandes & Ehinger, 1981). Table 2 lists symptoms of mild or fluctuating hearing loss (M/FHL).

Children need consistent auditory input to associate a sound with its source and to derive meaning from auditory stimuli. When M/FHL causes irregular or variable auditory perception, its victims miss the important contribution of hearing to learning and communication and rely more heavily on the other senses and on gestures. Consequently, they may develop secondary problems such as deficient auditory recognition and memory even after their hearing acuity has returned to normal. Furthermore, during periods of M/FHL, these children are also unable to monitor or gain control over their speech mechanisms. Therefore, although their speech is intelligible, they may not articulate all sounds clearly. M/FHL children communicate orally but learn language less well than their age-mates; thus they have difficulties with expressive vocabulary and cognition, including abstract, small, or distant concepts. Because they were unaware of the connotative properties of sound such as stress and intonation, these children may respond inappropriately when interacting with others. In summary, although the long-term impact of M/FHL is minimized by parents and teachers, children whose auditory input is incomplete may have problems with speech and language, cognitive development, socialization, and academic attainment despite relatively normal hearing acuity.

ALTERNATIVE ACTIONS

Parents who are unfamiliar with the impact of M/FHL yet recognize it has important and potentially dramatic consequences, need practical information about how to assist their children's development at home and at school. They are often dissatisfied and confused, however, by the diversity of recommendations made by medical and educational professionals and by the lack of communication between physicians and school personnel, which results in a time lapse between referral and placement in an intervention program. Finally, parents confront a significant lack of interest, understanding, and training about the educational needs of children with M/FHL that extends from the teacher education program to the policies and personnel of the local school district.

Academic modifications suggested by medical professionals focus primarily on preferential seating. However, it is important to broaden this recommendation to flexible seating. In general, children with M/FHL should sit near the teacher during instruction or close to the focal point of classroom activity. Additionally, M/FHL children often find group discussions particularly difficult to follow because they are slow to localize the speaker, especially when the flow of discussion moves rapidly or several children talk at one time, and they lose visual cues because of their classmates' movement and raised hands. Although hearing-impaired children are not reluctant to move closer to the focus of classroom activities, M/FHL children are less assertive about their right to hear and so often move away from

TABLE 1

Symptoms of Otitis Media

Symptoms of Otitis Media
Earaches and tugging at the ear
Drainage from the external ear
Low-grade fever
Cough and other symptoms of upper respiratory infection
General debility, irritability, and lassitude
Apparent hearing impairment including lack of responsiveness to auditory stimuli and puzzled facial expression
Complaints of physical discomfort

TABLE 2

Symptoms of Mild or Fluctuating Hearing Loss

Symptoms of Mild or Fluctuating Hearing Loss
History of recurrent ear disease, allergies, or upper respiratory infections
Academic difficulties especially in reading and language arts
Motivation problems
Behavior problems including unexpected changes in behavior
Inattentiveness and preoccupation
Poor articulation
Language problems including poor vocabulary and lack of idiomatic expressions
Frequent request for repetition of directions
Irrelevant or tangential responses to questions
Reluctance to participate in class discussions and general conversation
Use of gesture and facial expression to support speech and language

conversation and instruction. Therefore, the two most important adaptations made for children with M/FHL are awareness of the locations of these children relative to classroom activities and permission to move closer to an instructional activity without request.

Modified seating includes attention to the classroom environment. Extraneous noises from air conditioners, fans, and other equipment including the whirring of an overhead projector, overshadow speaking voices or the narration from a filmstrip. Moreover, these sounds, which are equivalent to white noise, are amplified and serve as a constant irritant to children wearing hearing aids. Favorable lighting helps children with M/FHL use vision to supplement auditory information. Glare from windows near their desks and the corona that surrounds the teacher standing in front of a window also impede reception of visual cues. Finally, both audition and vision are facilitated when the teacher attends to the children with M/FHL during instruction rather than talking to the blackboard or roving around the classroom.

Media aids such as overhead projectors provide a valuable visual supplement to instruction because they make concepts tangible. It is important for the teacher to stand toward the class while illustrating information on AV equipment. Additionally, concrete materials and experiential activities greatly enhance M/FHL children's understanding of class content and lessen their frustration with fill-in-the-blank formats. In the primary grades, a sight word approach enables children with M/FHL to learn to read more quickly and supports acquisition of phonetic word attack skills.

Children with M/FHL need special modifications of oral directives and assignments to facilitate communication and understanding. Although they are positioned so that M/FHL children derive meaning from facial expression and movement of the lips, speakers need only enunciate words normally, without exaggerated mouth movements, and talk at a normal rate. To verify learning, ask open-ended questions as M/FHL children, just like their hearing classmates, indicate more understanding of material than exists. Repetition of material often does not facilitate its acquisition. Therefore, when information is not learned, simplify instructions by modifying vocabulary and/or syntax. For example, the initial question "In what ways are a rabbit and a deer similar?" might be rephrased "How are a rabbit and deer alike?" In addition to oral directions, provide written instructions for classroom activities and homework. At the beginning of each week, supply an overview of the week's assignments such as new vocabulary and concepts to allow preparation and review at home. Since intercoms crackle and vary in volume and clarity, relay messages to M/FHL children. Finally, for children with M/FHL at the secondary level, arrange for provision of clear, complete carbon copies of class notes. It is impossible for these children to attend visually to lectures and simultaneously take notes.

A variety of health and school professionals can help children overcome the negative consequences of M/FHL. Physicians can monitor health and hearing status every few months. Audiologists and school nurses can regularly evaluate amplification needs to facilitate rapid implementation of educational suggestions, including the repair of hearing aids. While it is important to monitor the hearing of children with M/FHL or OM every 3 months, all children in the primary grades should be regularly evaluated because of the frequency of and potential dangers from OM and URI. Speech therapy in the school ensures continued development of language, corrects misarticulated speech sounds, and provides instruction in speech reading and attention to visual cues. Finally, the school psychologist helps parents and teachers adjust to the special needs of M/FHL children, evaluates their cognitive development, and makes suggestions about filling gaps in thinking and learning and assists these children with their frustrations over academics, communication, and social concerns.

Speech clinicians and audiologists are also a resource to the school psychologist. They are trained to evaluate children's hearing as well as its importance relative to academic performance, speech and language, and behavior. Therefore, they are important in the evaluation of children with a history of M/FHL. Like school psychologists, they select test instruments on the basis of presenting behaviors and diagnostic questions and thus have no specific tests designed to identify an auditory processing disorder. It is useful to include these professionals in conferences with parents and teachers to explain the impact of M/FHL on a particular child's learning and behavior.

Parents who overprotect their handicapped children may find it easier to reduce expectations rather than fight the communication problems associated with M/FHL. Nevertheless, they should set responsibilities at home that impress upon their M/FHL children that they are competent, productive, and valued members of their family. Participation in family interactions and chores supports these children's feelings of self-worth and importance, sets appropriate and realistic goals, and models interactions for those who are uncertain about the implications of M/FHL.

Unfortunately, parents of M/FHL children often are forced to fight not only for recognition that academic and behavioral problems are due to M/FHL, but also for provision of support service. Although they accept the possible consequences of their children's handicap, parents experience episodes of disappointment and frustration throughout the school years. They find transition periods especially difficult. First grade, with its introduction of language arts and reading skills; fourth grade, with its movement to textbooks and class content that includes science and social studies; and junior high, with its rotating class schedule that forces adaptation to a variety of teachers, students, and expectations are examples of these transition periods.

Gallagher, Beckman, and Cross (1983) reported that families with handicapped children have more financial problems, higher divorce rates, and a greater incidence of child abuse than those without disabled members. Some families feel unable to interact socially because of handicapped family members, so staying home becomes a ready option. Others are totally unrealistic in their demands; for example, they may expect M/FHL children to sit quietly in church. Families can use organizations and resource personnel in their area to provide service and information that facilitates integration of children with M/FHL into their families, schools, and communities. Schools as well as regional and national organizations can assist families to understand and respond to the needs of their handicapped members. Additionally, they can provide advocacy and support services.

Many siblings feel that their M/FHL brothers and sisters take up a disproportionate amount of their parents' time and attention, receive special privileges, and get out of household responsibilities. Some are sufficiently envious of their siblings that they wish they were also handicapped (Vadasy, Fewell, Meyer, & Schell, 1984). Siblings of the handicapped, including those with M/FHL, may express the following emotions: jealousy about attention, guilt over resenting handicapped siblings, embarrassment about their brothers' and sisters' difference, fear that they will be shunned by their peers, and concern that they will pass the disability on to their children. Additionally, many older siblings are delegated responsibility for their M/FHL brothers and sisters. Although they may contribute to the care of their handicapped siblings, they are rarely given an explanation of their M/FHL siblings' problems or needs that would facilitate their understanding and help them teach their peers about the handicap.

SUMMARY

The needs of children with M/FHL are often overlooked or discounted by parents, physicians, and educators. Consequently, it is necessary for all the significant adults in these children's lives to guard vigilantly against episodes of OM and other causes of M/FHL and to work aggressively for provision of remedial services so that these children can attain their linguistic, cognitive, social, and academic potential.

REFERENCES

Berg, F. S., & Fletcher, S. G. (Eds.). (1970). *The hard of hearing child.* New York: Grune & Stratton.

Bess, F. H. (1985). The minimally hearing impaired child. *Ear and Hearing, 6,* 43–47.

Bess, F. H., & Tharpe, A. M. (1984). Unilateral hearing impairment in children. *Pediatrics, 74,* 206–216.

Blair, J. C., Peterson, M. E., & Viehweg, S. H. (1985). The effects of mild sensorineural hearing loss on academic performance of young school-age children. *Volta Review, 87,* 87–93.

Boothroyd, A. (1982). *Hearing impairments in young children.* Englewood Cliffs: Prentice-Hall.

Brandes, P. J., & Ehinger, D. M. (1981). The effects of early middle ear pathology on auditory perception and achievement. *Journal of Speech and Hearing Disorders, 46,* 301–307.

Burgener, G. W., & Mouw, J. T. (1982). Minimal hearing loss' effect on academic/intellectual performance of children. Part I: Study 1. *Hearing Instruments, 33,* 7–8.

Dobie, R. A., & Berlin, C. I. (1979). Influence of otitis media on hearing and development. *Annals of Otology, Rhinology, and Laryngology, 88,* 48–53.

Downs, M. P. (1985). Effects of mild hearing loss on auditory processing. *Otolaryngological Clinic of North America, 18,* 337–344.

Friel-Patti, S., Finitzo-Hieber, T., Conti, G., & Brown, K. C. (1982). Language delay in infants associated with middle ear disease and mild, fluctuating hearing impairment. *Pediatric Infectious Diseases, 1,* 104–109.

Gallagher, J. J., Beckman, P., & Cross, A. H. (1983). Families of handicapped children: Sources of stress and its amelioration. *Exceptional Children, 50,* 10–18.

Glass, R. (1981). The association of middle ear effusion and auditory learning disabilities of children. *Rehabilitation Literature, 42,* 81–85.

Goetzinger, C. P. (1978). Word discrimination testing. In J. Katz (Ed.), *Handbook of clinical audiology* (2nd ed.). Baltimore: Williams & Wilkins.

Keller, W. D., & Bundy, R. S. (1980). Effects of unilateral hearing loss upon educational achievement. *Child: Care, Health, and Development, 6,* 93–100.

Kirkwood, C. R., & Kirkwood, M. E. (1983). Otitis media and learning disabilities: The case for causal relationship. *Journal of Family Practice, 7,* 219–227.

Kudrjavcev, T., & Schoenberg, B. S. (1979). Otitis media and developmental disability: Epidemiologic considerations. *Annals of Otology, Rhinology and Laryngology, 88,* 88–98.

McLaughlin, J., Nall, M., Isaacs, B., Petrosko, J., Karibo, J., & Lindsey, B. (1983). The relationship of allergies and allergy treatment to school performance and student behavior. *Annals of Allergy, 51,* 506–510.

Meyerhoff, W. L., Liston, S., & Anderson, R. G. (Eds.). (1984). *Diagnosis and management of hearing loss.* Philadelphia: Saunders.

Moores, D. F. (1982). *Educating the deaf.* (2nd ed.) Boston: Houghton-Mifflin.

National Association of the Deaf (NAD). (1986). Position paper: Cochlear implants. *N.A.D. Broadcaster, 8.*

Northern, J. L., & Downs, M. P. (1984). *Hearing in children* (3rd ed.). Baltimore: Williams & Wilkins.

Paradise, J. L. (1981). Otitis media during early life: How hazardous to development? A critical review of the evidence. *Pediatrics, 68,* 869–878.

Proctor, D. F. (1963). *The nose, paranasal sinuses and ears in childhood.* Springfield, IL: Thomas.

Reichman, J., & Healey, W. C. (1983). Learning disabilities and conductive hearing loss in children. *Journal of Learning Disabilities, 16,* 272–278.

Stevens, M. Q. (1986). *The effects of otitis media on children's achievement and behavior.* Paper presented at the National Association of School Psychologists, Ft. Lauderdale, FL.

Vadasy, P. F., Fewell, R. R., Meyer, D. J., & Schell, G. (1984). Siblings of handicapped children: A developmental perspective on family interactions. *Family Relations, 33,* 155–167.

Webster, A., Saunders, E., & Bamford, J. M. (1984). Fluctuating conductive hearing impairment. In: Hearing impaired children: their assessment and education [Special issue]. *Association of Educational Psychologists Journal, 6,* 6–19.

BIBLIOGRAPHY: PROFESSIONALS

Reichman, J., & Healey, W. C. (1983). Learning disabilities and conductive hearing loss involving otitis media. *Journal of Learning Disabilities, 16,* 272–278.
Reviews and critiques research studies on the prevalence of OM in LD children and the effects of both resolved and recurrent OM on children. It makes suggestions for future research as well as recommendations for current practice in serving children with OM.

Friel-Patti, S., Finitzo-Hieber, T., Conti, G., & Brown, K. C. (1982). Language delay in infants with middle ear disease and mild, fluctuating hearing impairment. *Pediatric Infectious Disease, 1,* 104–109.
Describes the efforts of the authors to identify the impact of OM on language development of children under 2 years. It proposes a method of language evaluation in these children.

Northern, J. L., & Downs, M. P. (1984). *Hearing in children.* (3rd ed.). Baltimore: Williams & Wilkins.
Discusses hearing, its measurement, and the kinds and causes of hearing loss. It is a basic text in understanding the role of hearing in children's growth and development.

BIBLIOGRAPHY: PARENTS

All the books listed are available from Gallaudet University in Washington, DC 20002.

Katz, Mathis, & Merrill. (nd). *The deaf child in the public schools: A handbook for parents.* PA002.
This paperback uses a question-and-answer format to answer parents' concerns about their hearing-impaired children.

Mendelsohn, J. Z., & Fairchild, B. (nd). *Years of challenge, a guide for parents of hearing impaired adolescents.* PA006. This book, which was written by parents of deaf children, describes adolescent concerns and family legislation.

Featherstone, H. (nd). *A difference in the family.* PA007. This book discusses parental reactions to a child's handicap.

Freeman, R., Carbin, C., & Boese, R. (nd). *Can't your child hear?* PA008. This excellent paperback describes the causes, treatment and education of the hearing impaired child. It helps the reader understand the needs and the promise of hearing impaired children.

Frederickson, F. (nd). *Life after deaf.* PA012. This is an excellent resource for anyone concerned about the impact of deafness on a family.

Children and Homework

Timothy Z. Keith
University of Iowa

BACKGROUND

The effect of homework was a controversial topic long before the latest round of educational reform, and long before homework was highlighted by the report of the National Commission on Excellence in Education (1983). The efficacy of homework has been debated since the early 1900s (Foyle & Bailey, 1985), and continues to be debated in both the professional (Strother, 1984) and popular (Wood, 1984) press. For example, a 1985 publication from Phi Delta Kappa, designed to review homework research and draw practical implications for teachers, concluded that little was known about the effects of homework (England & Flatley, 1985). On the other hand, the U.S. Department of Education's recent compilation of research concerning teaching and learning argues that both the quality and the quantity of homework affect student learning (1986). Given such inconsistency, this chapter will begin with a review of homework research, with the assumption that before they can develop coherent recommendations concerning homework, psychologists need to understand its effects. Homework is here defined as work assigned for completion outside the normal class period; it may be completed at home or at school, but it is assumed that most is completed at home. Further, it is assumed that the primary purpose of homework is to supplement and improve academic learning.

Effects of Homework on Achievement

Quantity. Does homework substantially improve achievement? If not, the reasons for assigning homework seem weak, at best. Thus, we need to turn to the research evidence. As we do, it may seem surprising that most homework research focuses on issues of quantity rather than quality. However, since quality of assignments is difficult to categorize, whereas time commitments are universal across all types of homework assignments, much of the homework research has understandably focused on time spent on homework, or homework versus no homework, and the effects of such conditions on learning.

Much of the available homework research has been conducted at the high school level, and many researchers have used large, representative data sets and nonexperimental research techniques for such analyses. For example, two recent analyses of the effects of homework in public and private schools both suggest that the amount of time the students spent working on homework had an important effect on their achievement (Coleman, Hoffer, & Kilgore, 1981; Page & Keith, 1981). Similarly, several recent, large-sample path analyses of the effects of homework have found similar results, suggesting that the amount of time high school students spent on homework influenced their achievement, whether it was measured by grades or by test scores, and even after important background characteristics were controlled (Keith, 1982; Keith & Page, 1985; Keith, Reimers, Fehrmann, Pottebaum, & Aubey, 1986; Natriello & McDill, 1986). Perhaps of most interest is the observation that many of the background variables used in such analyses (e.g., socioeconomic status and intellectual ability) are not easily manipulable by schools, whereas homework is manipulable by parents, by schools, and by students themselves. Nevertheless, not all research consistently supports the positive influence of homework on achievement. Several recent reports have shown smaller apparent effects for homework when more complex analyses were used (Walberg & Shanahan, 1983; Walberg, Pascarella, Haertel, Junker, & Boulanger, 1982). Still, the importance of homework for high school students has been further suggested in a recent well-designed quasi experiment using tenth graders and social studies assignments (Foyle, 1984). In this study, students who had been assigned homework achieved at a higher level than those assigned none.

There seems to be less research on the effects of homework for younger children, and the available research seems to be less consistent in its methodology and findings. Mathematics homework has been a popular topic of study, and a number of researchers have found significant positive effects for homework, even for elementary level students (e.g., Doane, 1973; Koch, 1965; Levine & Worley, 1985; Maertens & Johnston,

1972). Such results suggest that homework may improve arithmetic computation (Maertens & Johnston), problem-solving skills (Hudson, 1966; Maertens & Johnston), and concept understanding (Koch). But the findings of social science research are not always consistent. Other researchers have found no such differences between elementary-level groups assigned homework and those assigned none (Gray & Allison, 1971; Maertens, 1969; Whelan, 1966), although several such studies have used very narrow definitions of homework (e.g., Gray & Allison; Whelan). Thus, in a 1979 review of homework research in mathematics, Austin concluded that the results of homework studies in mathematics suggest the superiority of homework over no homework, at least down to the fourth-grade level.

Homework seems to have positive effects for elementary school students in other subject areas as well. Amount of time devoted to homework was found to be an important influence on the achievement of elementary (ten-year-olds) through high school level students, for a variety of subject areas (science, reading, literature) in an analysis of survey data of the International Association for the Evaluation of Educational Achievement (Wolf, 1979). Similar results have been demonstrated in analyses of the effects of homework on reading, mathematics concepts, writing, and other subject matter with students as young as fourth graders (Harnischfeger, 1980; Levine & Worley, 1985). Furthermore, it appears that the positive relation between homework and achievement exists even for gifted adolescents (Stanley, 1980).

Quality. It seems logical that the quality of homework assignments should also be important. And while quality is more difficult to define than quantity, there is evidence to support this assumption as well. There is considerable evidence, for example, that homework that is graded or commented on has a stronger impact on achievement than does homework that is not (Austin, 1976; Paschal, Weinstein, & Walberg, 1984). Evidence from in-class assignments suggests that *positive* comments are particularly beneficial (Page, 1958). Furthermore, well-planned, systematic homework that is closely tied to the instruction in the classroom appears to be more effective than vague, less well-planned assignments (Leonard, 1965). Finally, consequences for homework completion or noncompletion (Harris, 1973) and parental checking of homework (Maertens & Johnston, 1972) may add to its effectiveness. On the other hand, in one of the few studies designed to compare the effectiveness of various types of homework, Foyle (1984) found no difference in the effects of *practice* homework, that designed to review and reinforce skills and materials covered in class, and *preparation* homework, that designed to prepare students for an upcoming class topic. However, as noted by Keith (1986), such results do not necessarily mean that the two types of homework result in no meaningful differences; the lack of differences in the two experimental conditions may simply point to the need for the type of homework to be tied closely to the *purpose* of the assignment.

Other Time Variables, Effects, and Purposes

The contribution of homework to achievement is further suggested by research with other time variables (e.g., in-school learning time, time needed for learning, time spent learning) which generally supports their importance for learning (Fredrick & Walberg, 1980; Gettinger, 1984), and it appears that homework is an important influence on college achievement as well (Polachek, Kniesner, & Harwood, 1978). In addition, homework may have compensatory effects; less able students may be able to compensate for their lower ability through increased study (Polachek et al.). Homework seems to influence achievement for both gifted (Stanley, 1980) and low-ability youth (Keith, 1982), and the effects of homework may be greater for minority students than for youth in general (Keith & Page, 1985). Finally, some researchers speculate that homework may further improve achievement by reducing leisure TV viewing (Paschal et al., 1984), although a recent analysis of the effects of both variables found little support for this hypothesis (Keith et al., 1986).

Although the primary purpose of homework may be the improvement of learning, it may have other purposes and effects as well, although research support for such effects is generally limited. Parents see homework as developing responsibility, providing experience in independent study and preparation for future study, and strengthening the home–school bond (Friesen, 1978). Other possible advantages of homework include the development of good work habits, the opportunity for practice and review, and the assessment of students' understanding of classroom lessons (for a more detailed discussion of these purposes, see Keith, 1986). Homework may also aid in attempts to individualize instruction when individual students or small groups of students are given different assignments based on their instructional levels. There is, in fact, preliminary evidence that individualized homework assignments produce higher achievement than "blanket" assignments (Bradley, 1967).

DEVELOPMENT

It seems obvious that homework should be closely tied to the curriculum and to a child's instructional level. Homework assignments should have a clear purpose, with explicit, even foolproof directions. Similarly, the product of the assignment should be clear. Finally, homework should generally be evaluated in some way either by grading assignments, quizzing the students on the assignment topic, or commenting on their assignments (cf. Paschal et al., 1984). Whatever system is chosen, work completed outside of school should be followed up in school, both to correct problems that occur and to reinforce the learning that has resulted.

Education and school curricula are of a developmental nature, and thus it follows that homework should change at different ages and grade levels. At the simplest level, the time students spend working on homework should vary depending on their age and grade level. Guidelines for the "right" amount of homework are difficult because this depends a great deal on the individual community, school, and teacher. Even more important, there will be wide variability within a classroom for the same assignment; the assignment that takes one student 10 minutes may take another an hour. Despite such complications, the following time ranges have been suggested as guidelines for assignments for average students: 10–45 minutes per day in grades 1–3, 45–90 minutes per day in grades 4–6, 1–2 hours per day for grades 7–9, and 1½ to 2½ hours for grades 10–12 (Keith, 1986, p. 17).

Types of homework assignments should also vary by grade level and subject matter. Lee and Pruitt (1979) classified homework as falling into one of four categories. *Practice* homework, the most frequent type, is designed to review materials and reinforce skills developed in the classroom; *preparation* assignments are designed to prepare students for an upcoming class topic and often involve activities such as reading in a text or library research; *extension* homework is designed to extend or generalize concepts or skills learned from familiar to new situations (e.g., writing an essay on the similarities and differences in the causes of the U.S. and the French revolutions [Lee & Pruitt, 1979, p. 34]); and *creative* homework assignments require the integration, extension, and creative application of a variety of skills (e.g., a TV production on some topic). It is not the case that one type of assignment is always better than another (cf. Foyle, 1984); each serves its own purpose and has its own strengths and weaknesses. Practice, for example, while a necessary component of learning, tends to be the most frequently used type of homework assignment, and it can degenerate into busy work if overused. Preparation assignments, on the other hand, require considerable initiative and thought, but they may not be helpful if they are vague (e.g., read the next chapter in your social studies text).

While one type of assignment is not always better than another, it seems likely that both the purposes and types of assignments should vary by grade level. If one of the purposes of homework is to increase students' initiative and responsibility as they grow older, we should expect the mix of types of assignments to change as students enter higher grades. Thus, if we place the types of homework on a continuum from practice to creative assignments, we would expect to see the proportion of higher-order (extension and creative) assignments to increase as children enter higher grades. Similarly, some of the other purposes of homework would seem to become more important or less important as children grow. For example, the purpose of strengthening the home–school relation would seem more important at younger than at older grade levels, whereas the purpose of independent study would seem more important at higher grade levels. Individualization of homework is important for any student having learning difficulties.

PUTTING HOMEWORK IN PERSPECTIVE

Homework can be viewed from a variety of perspectives, depending on the nature of the question asked. On the one hand, homework can be viewed as the means to the end of raising achievement or improving learning. From this perspective, homework can be seen as the possible answer to a question concerning low achievement, or as a potential educational intervention (Keith & Page, 1985). Homework questions may also focus on homework itself, such as compliance with homework requests or the extent to which assigned homework is being correctly completed (Fish & Mendola, 1986). Parents' and teachers' questions commonly come from this perspective: Homework is being assigned; why isn't the student completing it?

Homework questions can arise in a group or an individual context. A child may be referred to a school psychologist for problems in homework or with a problem (such as low achievement) for which assignment of homework might be a suitable intervention. However, homework is a "hot topic" these days, and many school districts and schools are in the process of developing homework policies; school psychologists should be involved in designing such policies. Similarly, school psychologists' input would seem valuable when developing less formal policies at a school or classroom level.

Thus, the underlying perspective may be among the first considerations in dealing with homework problems brought to the school psychologist. In addition, the school psychologist will want to know if homework is being assigned, and if so, how much is being assigned. How long does it take the student to do the homework? What types of homework are being assigned? Are the types of assignments and the amount of homework appropriate for the child's grade and ability level? Is the purpose of the assigned homework clear? Do the children understand what they are to do and the expected product of the assignments? Is the homework being reviewed in some meaningful fashion in the classroom? Does the homework supplement classroom instruction?

Assigned homework will not fulfill any purpose if it is not completed; when homework problems arise, it may be valuable to assess patterns of homework completion. Is assigned homework generally being completed? Are there clear contingencies for the completion or noncompletion of homework? How much homework is being completed? Are there differences in the types of homework that students are completing compared to homework that is not completed? Is completed homework done accurately? If the concern is with an individual student, are other students in the class completing homework correctly? If homework is being completed, but inaccurately, adjustments may be needed in the directions or in types or difficulty level of homework assignments. Homework that is clearly defined, regularly assigned, of appropriate difficulty level, positively evaluated, and properly integrated into the curriculum will probably produce more learning, and be more likely to be correctly completed, than homework that is not. Furthermore, students will likely complain less about homework that is expected, relevant, and appropriate.

Student's attitudes toward homework are obviously important. What are students' reactions to the homework they are assigned? Do they have valid reasons for not completing assignments? What changes would they suggest?

Homework is a shared school–home responsibility, and thus assessment of what happens in the home is needed when homework problems arise. What are parents' and other family members' attitudes towards homework? Do the parents convey a belief that completion of homework, and learning in general, is important? There is evidence that such an orientation toward learning, called "the curriculum of the home," may be an important influence on learning (Walberg, 1984). Is there a quiet place — even if only the kitchen table — for the child to study? Is homework time planned, or is homework done hurriedly and only when there is extra time available? For some students specifying regular times for homework may be necessary; for other students it may be better simply to specify a time by which homework must be completed (Rosemond, 1984). Is a parent too involved with the child's homework, so that homework is viewed as a shared responsibility rather than the child's responsibility? Is it easy for parents to become overinvolved in children's homework, especially for children who are having academic difficulties. Listening to children read and discussing what has been read can be very beneficial for elementary school children (Epstein, 1984), and extensive involvement in older children's homework may be helpful on occasion, but in other cases direct parental participation in homework should probably be minimal.

ALTERNATIVE ACTIONS

The action taken towards a homework question will depend on the nature of the problem. It has been noted that homework questions may focus on homework as an intervention (homework as a means to an end) or on issues of homework completion (homework itself as the focus). In addition, homework questions may arise as group or individual problems. Possible actions can be grouped into four categories, although the overlap among the possible actions should be kept in mind.

Group Intervention

School districts are increasingly expressing an interest in the development of formal homework policies, and it seems appropriate that school psychologists be involved in the development of such policies. Informal policies at the district, school, or class level are also possible, and there are advantages and disadvantages to both approaches. For example, a districtwide policy creates consistent standards that let parents, children, teachers, and administrators know what is expected. On the other hand, informal policies or class level policies may provide greater flexibility for individual classes and individual students.

Whatever the approach taken, the policy developed should be flexible. It should communicate different expectations for different grade levels, and allow flexibility within grade levels, subject matter areas, and individual classes. An inflexible, unworkable homework policy is probably worse than none at all. The policy should be shared with students and parents to insure that they are aware of expectations as well; it may also provide guidelines for parental involvement in homework. The policy should emphasize the need for variety in homework assignments, and should encourage homework on a consistent basis. Such regularly assigned homework will likely produce more learning than less consistently assigned homework (Paschal et al., 1984), and students who expect homework on a regular basis will also likely complain less about assignments than those who do not expect homework. Homework policies should be developed with input from administrators, teachers, parents, and even students (Bond & Smith, 1965). Finally, when districtwide homework policies are developed, the establishment of a "homework hotline" to help answer student questions concerning homework should also be considered (Blackwell, 1979), although students can also be encouraged to call classmates with homework questions.

Any district or school that institutes a homework policy should be prepared to hear objections to that policy. Homework takes time for students to complete, and takes time for teachers to check over and grade. Some critics contend that students have too many other important out-of-school activities to spend time on homework, although the finding that many high school students spend more time watching TV per *day* than they spend per *week* on homework (Keith, 1986) would seem to suggest the fallacy of this concern. Students' objections to homework can be minimized if homework is expected, its purpose is clear, time requirements are not excessive, and the scope and product of the assignment are explicit. High school teachers may be advised to let students know in advance what their assignments will be for the week, to avoid having several classes "bunch up" their assignments.

Homework also requires a time commitment from teachers. Good homework assignments are well planned and an integral part of the curriculum. Most assignments should be graded, although practice homework may profitably be followed by a quiz or students may occasionally correct each other's assignments. Still, most objections to homework revolve around the issue of time commitment; but if it is decided that homework is important, then time will need to be budgeted for its assignment, completion, and correction.

Individual Intervention

Homework intervention for an individual child may best be illustrated by a hypothetical case. The school psychologist receives a referral from a teacher concerning a sixth-grade boy achieving below the level of his peers; the teacher questions whether special class placement is needed. Assessment reveals low average abilities and achievement, and a consistent history of marginal classroom performance. Special class placement is ruled out, yet some sort of classroom intervention is obviously needed. Further checking reveals the presence of low homework demands (or possibly, the regular assignment of homework that is too difficult and not completed). A homework intervention may be appropriate in such a case, and the efficacy of the intervention could be demonstrated using single-subject design techniques. For example, weekly quizzes could be instituted in math and reading with the scores for the first several weeks serving as a baseline for the intervention. The school psychologist would then work with the teacher to develop appropriate level, nightly mathematics homework and would work with the student and his parents to explain the mathematics intervention, to enlist their support, and to set up some guidelines at home for homework completion. Weekly quizzes would be continued in both mathematics and reading, the expectation being that the mathematics quizzes would improve while the reading quizzes would remain stable. After such a pattern emerged, reading homework assignments could similarly be started, with the expectation of subsequent improvement in the reading quiz scores. Such an intervention would keep the child in the regular classroom, would enlist the aid of the teacher, parents, and the child in improving his achievement, would clearly demonstrate whether the intervention was effective, and would require relatively little in-class individualization. Of course, several assumptions are made in this hypothetical case. The first is that the homework assigned is appropriate for the child's achievement level and that it is closely tied to the in-class curriculum; homework that does not meet these criteria will likely be ineffective. The second major assumption is that the child complies with the homework intervention; if not, adjustments would be needed in the intervention. The appropriateness of the level and time commitment of the assignments would need to be checked, as would the commitment of the parents and the student. It would also be relatively easy to build in some type of reinforcement for successful homework completion.

Insuring Homework Completion — Groups

Many questions about homework center around methods of insuring its completion. A teacher may explicitly ask the school psychologist about methods to insure completion of homework; more likely it will be apparent from other questions that the teacher asks that he or she is experiencing problems with homework completion. The school psychologist working with such teachers will want to encourage them to assign homework on a regular basis and to make every effort to insure that the assignments are consistent with in-class goals and activities.

Teachers should strive to convey the purpose of the assignment and to make sure that the directions and expected products of assignments are so clear that they are virtually foolproof. It may be worthwhile to start assignments in class to clear up any questions or problems that arise. Teachers should provide a mix of assignments; practice is necessary, but should not be overused. Other types of assignments will often fulfill the didadic purpose better than practice assignments. Teachers should be encouraged to individualize assignments for students who are unlikely to benefit from the normal assignment (Bradley, 1967). For example, the majority of the class might be given extension homework in science, whereas several low-achieving children might be better served by an assignment using some of the new, important science vocabulary in writing sentences. Excessively long assignments will also reduce compliance; teachers should be encouraged to think about how long a similar assignment would take in the classroom, and it may be worthwhile occasionally to ask a reliable student how long an assignment took to complete. Finally, grades and positive comments on homework assignments will likely produce more learning, and will convey that the teacher also thinks the assignments are important.

Insuring Homework Completion —Individuals

Teachers and parents are often concerned about a child who does not complete or poorly completes assigned homework. The first step in such a referral should be the assessment of the homework that is being assigned, using some of the guidelines presented for groups in the preceding section. The homework assigned should be appropriate for the individual child's ability, achievement, and in-class performance. Individualization of homework assignments may be needed for a child performing below the average classroom level. The purpose of the assignment and the directions should be clear and the products well defined; completed assignments should be graded or otherwise evaluated. Given the adequacy of the assigned homework, individual cases of noncompletion of homework will often require working with the child and the child's parents to increase percentage completion. The child may be questioned about reasons for noncompletion, and realistic objections and concerns should be addressed. Behavior management techniques can be used to increase homework compliance; self-instruction training has been shown to improve completion levels (Fish & Mendola, 1986), and a daily report card focusing on homework completion would likely be another worthwhile technique (Givner & Graubard, 1974, pp. 71–72).

Parental cooperation and support will also be important in such cases. If nothing else, parents should be informed of their child's noncompletion of homework, and the extent to which they should expect the child to bring assignments home. If parents do not know how often homework is assigned, it is easy for their children to pretend they have no homework. Thus, regularly assigned homework will help insure clear parental expectations as well. Parents should be encouraged to provide a relatively quiet, nondistracting place for their child to study, as well as a regularly scheduled time for study; they should be encouraged to convey a belief in the importance of homework and the expectation that homework will be completed well. The extent of parental involvement in a child's homework, while negotiable, should also be discussed. Extensive involvement should probably be rare; even when parents have the academic and teaching skills to help their children with homework, it is difficult to serve as teacher and parent at the same time. Parents should generally provide the structure and encouragement for homework completion and should be available to answer an occasional question and to review completed assignments, if they feel comfortable in this role.

Completion of homework is a first step; *successful* completion is obviously a more important goal. A child experiencing difficulty with homework may need adjustments in the nature and type of assignment and may also need help in developing good study skills. The school psychologist may need to work with the child to teach him or her basic organization and study strategies. For example, the SQ3R (survey, question, read, recite, review) approach is a valuable tool for insuring understanding of texts, and is easy to apply to a variety of situations (see also the chapter "Study Skills" in this volume).

SUMMARY

It is easy to view the currently heightened interest in homework as a fad; although always a part of school life, homework has recently received increased research and popular attention. Indeed, homework has been featured as an important influence on school learning in two U.S. Department of Education publications, *A Nation at Risk* (National Commission on Excellence in Education, 1983) and *What Works* (U.S. Department of Education, 1986). Fad or not, research evidence strongly suggests that homework has an important influence on academic learning, and it may fulfill other worthwhile purposes as well. Yet homework needs to be a well-planned part of the curriculum and needs to be appropriate for the students who are to complete it.

Questions concerning homework that are brought to school psychologists may focus on groups or individuals, and may focus on general achievement, with homework being a potential means of improving achievement, or may focus on homework itself (is homework being completed?). As with other types of referrals, school psychologists faced with homework questions will need to understand the perspective and needs of the person referring the problem, and will need to gather additional information about the child, the child's classroom, and the nature of the homework. Yet unlike many other types of school concerns, homework provides an excellent opportunity for working with the school, the child, and the home in an effort to improve a child's functioning.

Homework can be viewed as a cost-effective intervention for improving achievement or as a method of accomplishing other purposes. Yet homework requires a considerable time commitment, both from teachers and from the students. For this reason, care is needed to insure that homework assignments fulfill their purposes, and that they are clear, well-mated to the curriculum, and appropriate for the students who are to complete them. Such a focus on quality of homework assignments should help insure that assignments are treated as important rather than as busy work. Further, with such a focus on quality, and with appropriate feedback, it is likely that the effect of homework on learning will be even greater than that shown in research, where quality of assignments is rarely controlled.

REFERENCES

Austin, J. D. (1976). Do comments on mathematics homework affect student achievement? *School Science and Mathematics, 76,* 159–164.

Austin, J. D. (1979). Homework research in mathematics. *School Science and Mathematics, 79,* 115–121.

Blackwell, W. R. (1979, November). *An analysis of Dial-A-Teacher assistance program (Dataline).* Paper presented at the National Urban League Conference, Detroit. (ERIC Document Reproduction Service No. ED 183 647)

Bond, G. W., & Smith, G. J. (1965). Establishing a homework program. *Elementary School Journal, 66,* 139–142.

Bradley, R. M. (1967). An experimental study of individualized versus blanket-type homework assignments in elementary school mathematics. *Dissertation Abstracts International, 28,* 3874a.

Coleman, J. S., Hoffer, T., & Kilgore, S. (1981). *Public and private schools.* Washington, DC: U.S. Department of Education.

Doane, B. S. (1973). The effects of homework and locus-of-control on arithmetic skills achievement in fourth-grade students. *Dissertation Abstracts International, 33,* 5548A.

England, D. A., & Flatley, J. K. (1985). *Homework — And why.* Bloomington, IN: Phi Delta Kappa Educational Foundation.

Epstein, J. L. (1984, April). *Effects of teacher practices of parent involvement for change in student achievement in reading and math.* Paper presented at the annual meeting of the American Educational Research Association, New Orleans.

Fish, M. C., & Mendola, L. R. (1986). The effect of self-instruction training on homework completion in an elementary special education classroom. *School Psychology Review, 15,* 268–276.

Foyle, H. C. (1984). The effects of preparation and practice homework on student achievement in tenth-grade American history (Doctoral dissertation, Kansas State University, 1984). *Dissertation Abstracts International, 45,* 2474A.

Foyle, H. C., & Bailey, G. D. (1985, March). *Homework in the classroom: Can it make a difference in student achievement?* Paper presented at the annual meeting of the Association for Supervision and Curriculum Development, Chicago. (ERIC Document Reproduction Service No. ED 257 796).

Fredrick, W. C., & Walberg, H. J. (1980). Learning as a function of time. *Journal of Educational Research, 73,* 183–204.

Friesen, C. D. (1978). *The results of surveys, questionnaires, and polls regarding homework.* Iowa City, IA: University of Iowa. (ERIC Document Reproduction Service No. ED 159 174)

Gettinger, M. (1984). Achievement as a function of time sent in learning and time needed for learning. *American Educational Research Journal, 21,* 617–628.

Givner, A., & Graubard, P. S. (1974). *A handbook of behavior modification for the classroom.* New York: Holt, Rinehart and Winston.

Gray, R. F., & Allison, D. E. (1971). An experimental study of the relationship of homework to pupil success in computation with fractions. *School Science and Mathematics, 71,* 339–346.

Harnischfeger, A. (1980). Curricular control and learning time: District policy, teacher strategy, and pupil choice. *Educational Evaluation and Policy Analysis, 2*(6), 19–30.

Harris, V. W. (1973). Effects of peer tutoring, homework, and consequences upon the academic performance of elementary school children. *Dissertation Abstracts International, 33,* 6175A.

Hudson, J. A. (1966). A pilot study of the influence of homework in seventh grade mathematics and attitudes toward homework in the Fayetteville public schools. *Dissertation Abstracts International, 26,* 906.

Keith, T. Z. (1982). Time spent on homework and high school grades: A large-sample path analysis. *Journal of Educational Psychology, 74,* 248–253.

Keith, T. Z. (1986). *Homework.* West Lafayette, IN: Kappa Delta Pi.

Keith, T. Z., & Page, E. B. (1985). Homework works at school: National evidence for policy changes. *School Psychology Review, 14,* 351–359.

Keith, T. Z., Reimers, T. M., Fehrmann, P. G., Pottebaum, S. M., & Aubey, L. W. (1986). Parental involvement, homework, and TV time: Direct and indirect effects on high school achievement. *Journal of Educational Psychology, 78,* 373–380.

Koch, E. A. (1965). Homework in arithmetic. *The Arithmetic Teacher, 12,* 9–13.

Lee, J. F., & Pruitt, K. W. (1979). Homework assignments: Classroom games or teaching tools? *Clearing House, 53*(1), 31–35.

Leonard, M. H. (1965). An experimental study of homework at the intermediate-grade level. *Dissertation Abstracts International, 26,* 3782.

Levine, V., & Worley, W. R. (1985, April). *The impact of television and homework time on cognitive and noncognitive outcomes.* Paper presented at the annual meeting of the American Educational Research Association, Chicago.

Maertens, N. (1969). An analysis of the effects of arithmetic homework upon the arithmetic achievement of third-grade pupils. *The Arithmetic Teacher, 16,* 383–384.

Maertens, N., & Johnston, J. (1972). Effects of arithmetic homework upon the attitude and achievement of fourth, fifth, and sixth grade pupils. *School Science and Mathematics, 72,* 117–126.

National Commission on Excellence in Education. (1983). *A nation at risk: The imperative for educational reform.* Washington, DC: U.S. Department of Education.

Natriello, G., & McDill, E. L. (1986). Performance standards, student effort on homework, and academic achievement. *Sociology of Education, 59,* 18–31.

Page, E. B. (1958). Teacher comments and student performance: A seventy-four classroom experiment in school motivation. *Journal of Educational Psychology, 49,* 173–181.

Page, E. B., & Keith, T. Z. (1981). Effects of U.S. private schools: A technical analysis of two recent claims. *Educational Researcher, 10*(7), 7–17.

Paschal, R. A., Weinstein, T., & Walberg, H. J. (1984). The effects of homework on learning: A quantitative synthesis. *Journal of Educational Research, 78,* 97–104.

Polachek, S. W., Kniesner, T. J., & Harwood, H. J. (1978). Educational production functions. *Journal of Educational Statistics, 3,* 209–231.

Rosemond, J. (1984). *How to help with homework.* (Newspaper column available from John Rosemond, PO Box 4124, Gastonia, NC 28053)

Stanley, J. C. (1980). Manipulate important educational variables. *Educational Psychologist, 15,* 164–171.

Strother, D. B. (1984). Homework: Too much, just right, or not enough? *Phi Delta Kappan, 65,* 423–426.

U.S. Department of Education. (1986). *What works: Research about teaching and learning.* Washington, DC: Author.

Walberg, H. J. (1984). Improving the productivity of America's schools. *Educational Leadership, 41*(8), 19–30.

Walberg, H. J., Pascarella, E., Haertel, G. D., Junker, L. K., & Boulanger, F. D. (1982). Probing a model of educational productivity in high school science with National Assessment samples. *Journal of Educational Psychology, 74,* 295–307.

Walberg, H. J., & Shanahan, T. (1983). High school effects on individual students. *Educational Researcher, 12*(7), 4–9.

Whelan, J. A. (1966). An analysis of the effects of systematic homework in two fourth-grade subjects. *Dissertation Abstracts International, 26,* 5143.

Wolf, R. M. (1979). Achievement in the United States. In H. J. Walberg (Ed.), *Educational environments and effects: Evaluation, policy, and productivity.* Berkeley, CA: McCutchan.

Wood, T. (1984, August 24). School homework making a comeback. *Kansas City Star,* pp. 1, 2.

BIBLIOGRAPHY: PROFESSIONALS

Keith, T. Z. (1986). *Homework.* West Lafayette, IN: Kappa Delta Pi.
This short booklet summarizes current homework research and provides practical advice, primarily aimed toward teachers, on how to devise a homework policy and meaningful homework assignments. A section on parental involvement and homework is also included.

Walberg, H. J. (1984). Improving the productivity of America's schools. *Educational Leadership, 41*(8), 19–30.
An excellent synthesis of thousands of research studies on a number of variables, including homework, that affect academic learning. Must reading for any psychologist concerned with improving school learning.

Walberg, H. J., Paschal, R. A., & Weinstein, T. (1985). Homework's powerful effects on learning. *Educational Leadership, 42*(7), 76–79.
This article provides a discussion of a homework meta-analysis (see Paschal et al., 1984, in the reference list), discusses issues related to homework (students' time budgets, policy constraints), and practical suggestions for schools and parents concerning homework.

BIBLIOGRAPHY: PARENTS

Bond, G. W., & Smith, G. J. (1965). Establishing a homework program. *Elementary School Journal, 66,* 139–142.
Although more than 20 years old, this article provides an overview of some of the purposes of homework, advice on establishing a district homework policy, and suggestions to parents concerning children's homework.

England, D. A., & Flatley, J. K. (1985). *Homework — And why.* Bloomington, IN: Phi Delta Kappa Educational Foundation.
This short booklet provides some good suggestions for parents and students concerning homework expectations and homework assignments. Unfortunately, the research review is incomplete and dated, which affects some of the conclusions and recommendations.

Keith, T. Z. (1986). *Homework.* West Lafayette, IN: Kappa Delta Pi.
See discussion in Bibliography: Professionals.

Rosemond, J. (1984). *How to help with homework.* (Newspaper column available from John Rosemond, P.O. Box 4124, Gastonia, NC 28053).
This column presents six practical suggestions for parents on how to help with children's homework. This "six point plan" may also soon be available as a part of a cassette series for parents.

Children and Homosexuality

David C. Canaday
Unified School District #489, Hays, Kansas

BACKGROUND

Introduction

In recent years, the subject of homosexuality has generated increased attention from researchers and lay persons alike. Once a topic shunned and ignored, homosexuality has become a public issue. Signs point to a more positive change in societal attitudes toward homosexual self-expression, although gay men and women remain targets of fear and hostility.

Although much attention has been focused on homosexuality in adulthood, homosexuality in children and adolescence has been relatively ignored. Professional literature addressing the gay adolescent or homosexual behavior in youth is sparse (Ross-Reynolds & Hardy, 1985), and the existence of adolescent homosexuality is usually denied or avoided by adults (Woodman & Lenna, 1980). Yet groups of gay teenagers in school settings appear to be increasing, and more and more students are identifying themselves as gay and are seeking help in understanding their homosexuality (Woodman & Lenna, 1980). Given this phenomenon, understanding the issue of children and homosexuality is an important task for the professional who works with young people.

This chapter will discuss aspects of youthful homosexuality, including incidence, gay identity formation, characteristics of and issues confronting gay youth, and counseling gay youth. Since homosexual behavior in preadolescence has been virtually ignored in the professional literature, this discussion will be confined primarily to homosexuality in adolescence. Also, since little research on female adolescent homosexuality exists, much of this chapter will center on gay males, although many of the points raised apply to females as well. Although recognizing that many types of *homosexualities* and expressions thereof exist, in this chapter, homosexual refers to sexual acts between persons of the same gender, an erotic and affectational attraction toward someone of the same gender, or a self-identification with a gay lifestyle.

Incidence

Many researchers have examined the frequency of sexual activities between adolescent males. Kinsey, Pomeroy, and Martin (1948) found that 38–60% of males in their survey had engaged in some form of homosexual behavior, and that for 25% this behavior occurred on more than a few occasions. Sorensen's (1972) study reported that 5% of all boys 13–15 years old and 17% of all boys 16–19 years old have had one or more homosexual experiences. Karlen (1971) reviewed data suggesting that adolescent homosexual behavior is at least as great as that reported by Kinsey et al. Others (Saghir & Robins, 1973; Pillard, 1974) have recorded incidences similar to the Kinsey data. Kremer, Zimpfer, and Wiggers (1975), noting that these figures may in actuality be higher owing to the reluctance of teens to report stigmatized behavior, demonstrated that when one applies the Kinsey and Sorensen data, given a high school population of 500 males, "anywhere from 25 (in the 13 to 15 age group) or 85 (in the 16 to 19 age group) to 250 adolescent males have engaged in actual homosexual activities." (p. 96). These figures exclude those with gay feelings who do not act on their preferences.

These surveys indicate that homosexual behavior in adolescence is relatively common. Many teenage males experience sex with other males, and many of these do not label or consider themselves "homosexual" (Berger, 1983). Also, adolescent sexual behavior does not necessarily predict adult sexual behavior or preferences. Since Kinsey et al. (1948) estimate that approximately 10% of males are homosexual, it is apparent that a large number of adolescents who engage in homosexual behavior do not become adult gays. In addition, a large number of gay adults do not experience homosexual activity until after adolescence (Schofield, 1965). The available research indicates that there is no way of predicting from adolescent sexual behavior whether a male will engage in predominately homosexual or heterosexual activities (Kremer et al., 1975). On the other hand, large numbers of gay individuals self-identify as gay during their teenage years (Dank, 1971). In fact, adult homosexuality stems from gay feelings during adoescence (Bell, Weinberg, & Hammersmith, 1981a).

Homosexual and heterosexual feelings and behavior are not dichotomous but rather occur in varying degrees. For example, the Kinsey et al. (1948) data found that only 50% of males remained exclusively heterosexual throughout their lives of, and that only 4% were exclusively homosexual. Almost one half of the U. S. male population experiences both homosexual and heterosexual feelings and actions to varying degrees. From this perspective, homosexual behavior among male adolescents is far from atypical.

DEVELOPMENT

Gay Identity Formation

In understanding the gay young person, it is important to understand the processes involved in the formation of a homosexual identity. As Ross-Reynolds and Hardy (1985) point out, "although there is considerable societal support for the development of a heterosexual identity, the gay adolescent faces major obstacles on the path to developing a positive self-identity, particularly in the absence of role models, the existence of homophobic attitudes, and the fact that to be homosexual in American society constitutes a profound stigma" (pp. 307–308).

Consideration of various models and stages of gay identity formation involves several assumptions. First, gay identity formation follows a prescribed developmental process with relatively distinct yet often overlapping stages. Second, these stages do not necessarily occur in a rigid, step-by-step order; individuals may skip stages, advance or fail to advance to later stages, and regress to earlier stages, depending upon a myriad of events and self-interpretations of these events. Third, identity formation results from the interaction of the individual with his or her environment. Adjustment and socialization of the individual is greatly influenced by social forces (Erikson, 1956), and identity develops according to the nature of interpersonal relationships (Sullivan, 1953). Finally, the nature of the stages of gay identity formation is highly varied. The individual plays an active role in his or her identity formation. The nature of this process depends on factors such as age, gender, perception of societal and interpersonal pressures, and emotional adjustment.

Several models of gay identity formation have been proposed. Two models, proposed by Cass (1979) and E. Coleman (1982), serve to illustrate the process of acquiring a gay identity. Coleman describes five developmental stages, and Cass's six stage model emphasizes achieving a degree of congruence between one's self-perception, behavior, and perceptions of others' views.

Coleman terms the initial stage of gay identity acquisition the pre–coming out stage. A person in this stage may not be consciously aware of homosexual feelings but usually does recognize a sense of being somehow "different." The resulting alienation may lead to behavior problems, psychosomatic illnesses, or other symptoms. The person may not be aware of the reason for feeling alienated, or may employ ego defenses to avoid dealing with same-sex feelings. Cass's first stage is called identity confusion. In this stage a person encounters incidental information about homosexuality and assigns it personal significance, realizing that his or her feelings and behaviors may be called homosexual. The individual experiences a sexual identity crisis that he or she may seek to resolve by (a) seeking out more information about homosexuality to acquire a positive gay identity, (b) denying the possibility of homosexuality, or (c) rationalizing homosexual feelings and behavior, thereby disowning responsibility for them.

In the next stage, termed coming out by Coleman and identity comparison by Cass, the individual makes the first commitment to a homosexual self. Coleman emphasizes disclosure of gay feelings to trusted others as the first step toward self-acceptance. The reactions of those who are told can have a profound impact upon the individual's self-esteem. If confidants react negatively, the person may internalize much guilt and self-hatred; if reactions are favorable or at least nonnegative, self-worth and a positive identity will be enhanced. In Cass's second stage, the individual's self-statement of "I may be gay" results in alienation and may lead to an attempt to resolve the isolation by devaluing others' opinions, seeking a public image of heterosexuality or asexuality, or moving to a different location to gain anonymity.

The third stage of gay identity acquisition is characterized by the individual's seeking out other gay people, in order to experiment socially and sexually with the new identity. The tasks of Coleman's exploration stage are developing skills to socialize with other gays, acquiring a sense of sexual attractiveness, and exploring a gay way of life. In Cass's view, during the third, or identity tolerance, stage the individual seeks out other gays to reduce isolation. The quality of the homosexual social contacts at this stage is important: positive gay relations can facilitate subsequent development, whereas a negative experience may lead to devaluation of the gay lifestyle.

Increasing interaction with other gays comes during the next stage. Coleman notes that individuals establish their first intimate relationships during this period. These initial relationships are often characterized by intensity, possessiveness, and a lack of trust, and they may end on a turbulent note. In Cass's fourth stage, identity acceptance, gay persons may view their homosexuality as "ok" as long as it is kept private and undisclosed except to carefully selected associates. Many gays end the process of self-definition at this stage, choosing to live their lives in this manner rather than advancing to later stages.

Persons who have accepted their homosexuality and who interact with the gay community to some extent may move to the later stages of homosexual identity formation. In Coleman's final stage, identity integration, gays incorporate their public and private identities into one. They feel less of a need to hide their homosexuality, although most will exercise some degree of discretion because of society's negative views toward homosexual behavior. Relationships at this stage are more successful, and other developmental challenges, such as aging,can be more readily handled. In Cass's model, the individual may experience the identity pride stage, in which pride in being gay and anger toward society's homophobia may lead to vocal participation in gay rights activism. During Cass's final identity synthesis stage, incongruence between behavior, self-image and perceptions of others' views is reduced considerably, and the person acknowledges that his or her homosexuality is but one aspect of a total identity.

Models of gay identity formation delineate a process one undergoes in achieving a gay self-image. Homosexual feelings or experiences lead one to feel some sense of apartness, and eventually these feelings or behavior are labeled "homosexual." The individual begins an often agonizing process to deal with these feelings. An initial sense of shame or guilt is common, and as one attempts to deal with a potentially new identity in the context of a homophobic environment (particularly so in adolescence), the conflict between this guilt and one's sexual drive can be overwhelming. If this conflict is handled successfully, a positive self-image will result. Unresolved feelings of guilt may hinder emotional adjustment.

Research indicates that the early stages of gay identity formation are often experienced during adolescence. Dank (1971) found that 15% of his gay male sample had identified themselves as gay between ages 10 and 14, and that 79% had done so between the years 15 and 19, although in his under-30 sample, the percentages were 22% and 50%, respectively. Jay and Young (1979) noted that only 16% of their sample had self-identified during late adolescence, but that 29% had self-identified in early adolescence and 31% had self-identified in preadolescence. This study also found that lesbians identified themselves as homosexual at a later age. In Dank's sample, the mean age of a first homosexual contact was 13 and, on the average, a 6-year interval existed between first being aware of homosexual feelings and deciding that one was gay. Although research indicates that gay men usually do not come to a full realization of their homosexuality until age 19 or 20 (Dank, 1971; Harry & DeVall, 1978), homosexual interests seem to have an onset during late childhood and early adolescence (Saghir & Robins, 1973). Clearly, many individuals deal with the issue of their own homosexuality during their teen years.

PUTTING CHILDHOOD HOMOSEXUALITY IN PERSPECTIVE

Characteristics of Gay Youth

Gay preadolescents and adolescents are a heterogenous group. Seldom will a person be able to identify a homosexual or prehomosexual child or adolescent on the basis of observable behaviors, personality traits, interests, or other characteristics, despite the existence of popular stereotypes. However, many researchers have concerned themselves with distinguishing between the characteristics of gay and nongay youth. A brief overview of their findings is presented not so as to make it possible to "identify" potentially gay young people, but rather to highlight the unique issues involved in the lives of children who experience same-sex feelings.

Much of the professional research addressing homosexual youth has focused on "cross-gendered" behavior —gender-specific behavior that is deemed by a society to be inappropriate if displayed by the "wrong" gender (e.g., boys dressing in female clothes). Several studies surveying gay men about their childhood have reported cross-gender behavior in preadolescence. Saghir and Robins (1973) reported that 67% of the gay men in their sample reported having been "girllike" in childhood, compared to a 3% of their heterosexual sample. Harry (1982) found significant differences in reported childhood effeminancy between his homosexual and heterosexual groups, concluding that gender-role preference is strongly associated with later homosexual orientation. Whitam (1977) noted that 94% of his gay male respondents reported exhibiting at least one of six cross-gender characteristics. One of these characteristics dealt with sexual interest in other boys; not surprisingly, 80% of Whitam's exclusively homosexual respondents exhibited this characteristic. Other retrospective recall studies (Green & Money, 1969; Stroller, 1968) and longitudinal studies (Green, 1974; Zuger, 1970) have linked childhood cross-gender behavior with later homosexuality. However, because of serious methodological deficiencies such as bias, inconsistent terminology, and stereotyping, Jones (1981) concluded that no reliable model for predicting adult homosexuality in childhood exists. Also, significant numbers of gay respondents in the above surveys indicated childhood behaviors no different from that of heterosexual controls. One should therefore be extremely cautious in assuming subsequent homosexuality from gender-deviant childhood behavior.

Other studies (Harry, 1982; Stephan, 1973) have found that gay youths tend to be loners. Harry linked this alienation with cross-gendering, hypothesizing that (a) cross-gendered youngsters are rejected by their peers and hence become loners, or (b) cross-gendered youth prefer to be loners rather than interact with conventional adolescent culture. Harry's (1982) survey indicated other characteristics in youth recalled; by his gay respondents. Gays as adolescents were significantly less interested in girls than nongays and, to a lesser extent, were less interested in dating, although nearly half of the gays did report interest in these areas. Homosexuals as adolescents reported less interest in sports (22–33% reported interest), tended to be better students academically, and were less likely to engage in delinquent acts.

Finally, Tripp (1975), reporting unpublished Kinsey data, found that gay males tend to arrive at puberty earlier and become sexually active earlier than heterosexuals. Harry hypothesized that undergoing puberty at an early age "may be conducive to homosexual behaviors since social groups during early adolescence are still largely sex-segregated" (p. 15).

Issues Confronting Gay Youth

Young homosexuals face issues, dilemmas, and problems different from those encountered by their heterosexual peers. Although growing up gay is somewhat easier now than in previous years (Growing Up Gay, 1986), adolescents with homosexual feelings and identities usually encounter grave difficulties in achieving a positive self-identity (Ross-Reynolds & Hardy, 1985). An awareness of the unique issues confronting gay youth will enable the professional to help adolescent gays more effectively.

Lack of Information. Young people who begin the process of acquiring a gay identity have few sources to turn to regarding homosexuality and gay life. Sex education classes usually give little or no attention to homosexuality (Newton, 1982). Textbooks, when they do mention the topic, are often filled with biases and misinformation (Newton, 1979). Persons, institutions and support systems helping adolescents to socialize heterosexually are unavailable to the gay teenager (Malyon, 1981). Homosexual role models important for the development of personal identity are nonexistent. Parents, teachers, and peers, who are important sources of information about other topics, are seldom approached by the gay teenager because of their potentially negative reaction. Even adult gays are often reluctant to disseminate information to minors because of the "recruitment" stigma. Normally gay adolescents are left to their own resources to find information about their affectional orientations.

Guilt. Because of the stigma society places on homosexuality and the resulting homophobia, many adolescents experience conflicts and guilt regarding their same-sex feelings and actions. The intensity of this conflict may range from denial or rationalization to mild concern about homosexual interests to outright self-loathing. The especially intense homophobia within the adolescent subculture often exacerbates guilt among gay teenagers. This may prevent them from experiencing the social and developmental experiences necessary for the development of maturity and self-respect (Malyon, 1981).

Harry and Duvall (1978) found that 51% of their gay male sample were troubled as adolescents by the idea that they might be gay. Harry (1982) reported that those who exhibited cross-gendered behavior as children but were "defeminized" as teens were significantly more guilty than those who were not cross-gendered or were cross-gendered as adults. An important role of the psychologist will be to help gay teens deal with guilt feelings and to help them build a positive self-concept.

Socialization. Bell, Weinberg, and Hammersmith (1981a) demonstrated that gay men are much more likely than nongay men to have felt different from other boys during childhood and adolescence. Because heterosexual relations and sports activities are the two primary interests of adolescent life (J. Coleman, 1961), and because young gays' view of these activities are usually indifferent or negative (Harry, 1982), adolescent peer culture offers relatively few socialization options for homosexual teens. Gay adolescents therefore are more likely to be loners and to feel isolated and different from their peers (Harry, 1982; Saghir & Robins, 1973; Stephan, 1973). As Harry (1982) noted, adolescents may deal with this alienation in several ways. They may remain isolates uninterested in adolescent culture or peers. Conformity to peer expectations, at least on the surface, is another option. Many gays, for example, dated heterosexually as teens because "it was the thing to do" (Bell et al., 1981a), although they received little or no satisfaction from doing so (Saghir & Robins, 1973). A third, more desirable, option would be to develop involvement in alternative adolescent activities such as academics, dramatics, art and music, student government, and other interests. Harry's study (1982) discovered that large numbers of gay teens do become intensely interested in academics. As Gagnon (1979) states, the rejected homosexual adolescent "may find opportunities to be upwardly mobile, go to college, and become successful, while his classmates are still hanging around the corner tavern" (p. 237).

For the individual coming to grips with a gay identity, socialization with other gays is crucial in achieving self-acceptance (Berger, 1986). Berger states that homosexual "individuals who do not interact with other homosexuals are likely to suffer from poor self-esteem, since they are exposed to negative opinions about homosexuality without benefit of a homosexual reference group to counter with positive feelings" (p. 169). Yet for adolescents this interaction seldom occurs. Information about where to meet other gays is often unavailable to teens, and as noted above, many adult gays are hesitant to interact with gay minors. Psychologists and counselors may be helpful in referring the client to sources of information about homosexuality.

AIDS. No topic has generated the amount of concern within the gay community as has the disease AIDS (acquired immune deficiency syndrome). Although other population groups are at risk, gay men account for the majority of AIDS cases. Over half of all individuals afflicted with the disease have died. Fortunately, a wealth of information is available about AIDS, its symptoms, and its prevention. Although researchers know increasingly more about the disease, a cure for AIDS remains to be discovered. Meanwhile the epidemic has resulted in an upsurge of antigay sentiment.

The AIDS issue impacts on gay teens just as it does on adults. Gay adolescent males may adopt a cavalier, fatalistic, concerned, or fearful attitude about AIDS (Ross-Reynolds, 1987). But because it is a significant concern for these youngsters, helping professionals must address the subject in an objective manner. The nature of the disease, its symptoms, and especially its prevention is vital information that the gay adolescent must know.

Discussing AIDS prevention will involve candid explanation of explicit sexual practices, which will invariable elicit some degree of embarrassment from both counselor and client. Yet the ability to discuss sexual acts is important for two reasons. First, nonjudgmental discussion communicates to the teenager a feeling of acceptance. Second, practice in discussing sexual practices openly will help the teenager communicate with sexual partners regarding safe sex practices and previous sexual contacts. Although AIDS is an emotional topic, those who work with young gays have an obligation to provide information about AIDS and safe sexual practices to their clients.

ALTERNATIVE ACTIONS

Professionals may encounter the issue of youthful homosexuality in a wide variety of both crisis and noncrisis situations. Parents may discover their child engaged in a homosexual act and may react impulsively, precipitating a crisis within the family. School personnel, at a loss in dealing with the harassment of a student perceived by peers as gay, may consult counselors and psychologists. Students themselves may seek out professionals for advice or information. Introspection on the part of the helping professional is important, for as Ross-Reynolds (1982) explains, professionals faced with this issue are also confronted with their own attitudes and biases about homosexuality. Also, counselors must consider the reactions of others; few issues generate as much emotion and controversy even today as homosexuality.

Guidelines in Counseling

Therapists must confront their own attitudes and values about a number of issues. Homosexuality is no exception. Counselors who are asked to help young gays must recognize their potential biases and to judge whether these biases are likely to be imposed upon their clients (Daher, 1977). Assigning the client to another therapist may be in order; failing that, lack of therapy may be less harmful than that stemming from antihomosexual bias (Ross-Reynolds, 1982).

In discussing homosexuality with the client, Kremer et al. (1975) recommend the following:

1. Therapists should show openness in discussing homosexuality. Avoiding the topic sends a negative message to the client.
2. Counselors should take actions that will allow the client to feel comfortable in discussing homosexuality. This may include discussion of sexual fantasies and acts.
3. Counselors should be aware of the issues and feelings inherent in homosexuality.
4. Therapists should be aware that clients may ask them to give information about gay life, or ways of obtaining this information.
5. The counselor's position relative to superiors, parents, and school personnel should be considered, as should their possible reactions to the counseling of a gay youngster.

Counseling With the Client

The first step in counseling students who have stated that they are gay may be to clarify what the clients mean by the statement (Ross-Reynolds, 1982). Money and Ehrhardt (1972) differentiate between homosexuality as sexual acts and homosexuality as a long-term affectational preference. Is the client considering this possibility because of isolated incidents, labeling by others, or actual gay feelings, fantasies, and preferences? How does the person define "gay"? At some point the therapist may give information that same-sex behavior in adolescence is common and that many who experience such behavior are not necessarily gay. However, the therapist should not imply that the client's homosexual feelings and behavior are "just a passing phase" to be "grown out of." At the initial stage, expressing to the client that a homosexual, bisexual, or heterosexual identity is possible is important. A discussion of what it would mean to the person if he or she were gay is also useful.

An important role that the counselor may play is exploring with the student the possibility of a particular sexual orientation, which can fall anywhere along the Kinsey continuum (see Kinsey et al., 1948, pp. 638–641). Woodman and Lenna (1980) give several factors that are useful in exploring the likelihood of a homosexual orientation:

1. Greater sexual arousal by same-sex individuals than by the opposite sex. Examination of masturbation fantasies is especially important.
2. Preference for initiating and enjoying same-sex experiences, in which the person actively chooses these experiences.
3. The sex of the persons with whom the client *primarily* experiences or fantasizes about sexual acts and affectional relationships, recognizing that the client may have experiences and fantasies about both sexes.
4. The consistency in number, duration, and intensity of same-sex relationships, and their duration over time.
5. The sex of the partner who it is anticipated will help the individual obtain his or her life goals in the future — a significant indicator of gayness if this partner is to be of the same gender.
6. Preference for same-sex social interaction while engaging in pleasurable activities, such as movies, trips, etc.
7. Self-description with terms indicative of a gay identity. The difference between self-perception and labeling by others is important.
8. Reactions to and opinions about homophobic jokes and statements and pressure to conform heterosexually (dating, marriage, etc.)

Occasionally therapists may work with a person who may deny a homosexual identity even though he or she may frequently seek out homoerotic sexual acts. The counselor should be aware that this attitude is common in the early stages of gay identity formation and that, assuming identity foreclosure does not occur, the client will progress toward later stages. Berger (1986) cautions professionals thus:

> Efforts of the worker to label a client as homosexual when he does not label himself as such are misguided and are likely to result in a broken client-practictioner relationship. On the other hand, if the client is uncomfortable about the inconsistency between his self-perception and his behavior . . . the worker can facilitate resolution of this task by openly discussing the inconsistency and helping the client through the tasks of homosexual identity formation, if appropriate. In the case of the client who is convinced he is gay in the absence of any overt sexual experience with males, if the therapist urges dismissal of these feelings as "incidental" or "unimportant," the process of self-acceptance will be impeded. (p. 165)

Counseling With Parents

Many times parents will refer their child to a professional because they have discovered that he or she is gay. Parental reactions to this discovery can range from aplomb to violence (Silverstein, 1977). Woodman and Lenna (1980) advise that parents be brought to understand that homosexual behavior in childhood and adolescence is not confirmation that they will be gay adults, and that a continued negative focus on their homosexual behavior may harm their self-concept and adjustment. Should their homosexual experience, through therapeutic exploration, be found to be a consistent part of their identity rather than incidental, further work with parents may be to help them understand that their children still need their love and acceptance, and that gay men and women can lead happy, fulfilling lives. An important goal in family therapy is to return the family interactions to normal (Woodman & Lenna, 1980).

SUMMARY

In comprehending the plight of the gay adolescent in contemporary society, it may be useful to imagine a world where blue cars are the norm, and a preference for red automobiles is forbidden. Children grow up understanding that they are expected to play only with blue toy cars, and that when they mature they are to drive a blue automobile. But in late childhood and early adolescence, some discover that for some inexplicable reason they have strong preferences for red cars. They dream of red cars, and perhaps they and some of their friends secretly play with red cars. Later, they learn that those red car preferences are considered bad, and they acquire guilt and conflict over their red car urges. They feel different and isolated from their peers, and they may be ostracized by others. They have nowhere to turn to deal with their feelings; their friends, teachers, and parents shy away when they bring up the topic. Finally, they choose either to suppress their red car feelings and drive or to deal with them by "coming out." Neither choice will be easy.

As with the children in this fictitious world, young persons with same-sex feelings and sexual behavior are in need. Despite the fact that such adolescents constitute a significant segment of the teen population, they have generally been ignored or shunned by both professionals and lay persons. As they mature, gay young people undergo a developmental process in dealing with their homosexual identity. At some point in this process, intense feelings of guilt and self-hatred may occur, and some individuals continue to experience this throughout their lives. Gay teens usually feel different, apart from or isolated from their peer group because of their sexual feelings and their lack of interest in many particularities of adolescent culture. Some, especially those with cross-gendered behavior, may be targets of hatred, ridicule, and avoidance by peers and adults. Unlike heterosexual young people, gay youth must deal with unique issues such as acquiring information about homosexuality, coping with guilt and alienation, seeking out other gays, and AIDS. Professionals who wish to help gay teens must deal with their own feelings as well as the reactions of others toward this emotional topic. Yet the counselor can be of great benefit by helping the young person to explore same-sex feelings, move toward the acceptance of a homosexual identity, build self-confidence and self-esteem, and acquire information about homosexuality and gay life.

As society comes to understand homosexuality and to fear it less, growing up gay will be easier. Currently, however, adolescents with same-sex interests are faced with difficult tasks in a hostile environment. Those who have the interest and the courage can help gay young people face these tasks and mature into well-adjusted, competent adults.

REFERENCES

Bell, W., & Weinberg, M. (1978). *Homosexualities: A study of diversity among men and women.* New York: Simon and Schuster.

Bell, W., Weinberg, M., & Hammersmith, S. (1981a). *Sexual preference.* Bloomington, IN: Indiana University Press.

Bell, W., Weinberg, M., & Hammersmith, S. (1981b). *Sexual preference: Statistical appendix.* Bloomington, IN: Indiana University Press.

Berger, R. (1983). What is a homosexual: A definitional model. *Social Work, 28,* 132–135.

Berger, R. (1986). Gay men. In H. Gochros, J. Gochros, and J. Fischer (Eds.), *Helping the sexually oppressed* (pp.162–180). Englewood Cliffs, NJ: Prentice-Hall.

Cass, V. (1979). Homosexual identity formation: A theoretical model. *Journal of Homosexuality,4,* 219–235.

Coleman, E. (1982). Developmental stages of the coming out process. *Journal of Homosexuality, 7,* 31–43.

Coleman, J. (1961). *The adolescent society.* New York: Free Press.

Daher, D. (1977). Sexual identity confusion in late adolescence: Therapy and values. *Psychotherapy: Theory, Research and Practice, 4,* 12–17.

Dank, B. (1971). Coming out in the gay world. *Psychiatry, 34,* 180–197.

Erikson, E. (1956). The problem of ego identity. *Journal of the American Psychoanalytic Association, 4,* 56–121.

Gagnon, J. (1979). The interaction of gender roles and sexual conduct. In H. Katchadourian (Eds.), *Human sexuality* (pp. 225–245). Berkeley, CA: University of California Press.

Green, R. (1974). *Sexual identity and conflict in children and adults.* New York: Basic Books.

Green R., & Money, J. (Eds.) (1969). *Transsexualism and sex reassignment.* Baltimore: Johns Hopkins Press.

Growing up gay (1986, Jan. 13). *Newsweek,* pp. 50–58.

Harry, J. (1982). *Gay children grown up.* New York: Praeger.

Harry, J., & DeVall, W. (1978). *The social organization of gay males.* New York: Praeger.

Jay, K., & Young, A. (1979). *The gay report.* New York: Summit.

Jones, G. P. (1981). Using early assessment of prehomosexual boys as a counseling tool: An exploratory study. *Journal of Adolescence, 4,* 231–238.

Karlen, A. (1971). *Sexuality and homosexuality: A new view.* New York: Norton.

Kremer, E., Zimpfer, D., & Wiggers, T. (1975). Homosexuality, counseling and the adolescent male. *Personnel and Guidance Journal, 54,* 94–101.

Kinsey, A., Pomeroy, W., & Martin, C. (1948). *Sexual behavior in the human male.* Philadelphia: Saunders.

Malyon, A. (1981). The homosexual adolescent: Developmental issues and social bias. *Child Welfare, 60,* 321–330.

Money, J., & Ehrhardt, A. (1972). *Man and woman, boy and girl: Differentiation and dimorphism of gender identity from conception to maturity.* Baltimore: Johns Hopkins Press.

Newton, D. (1979). Representation of homosexuality in health science textbooks. *Journal of Homosexuality, 4,* 247–254.

Newton, D. (1982). A note on the treatment of homosexuality in sex education classes in the secondary school. *Journal of Homosexuality, 8,* 97–99.

Pillard, R. (1974). Incidence of teenage homosexual behavior. *Medical Aspects of Human Sexuality, 8,* 192.

Ross-Reynolds, G. (1982). Issues in counseling the "homosexual" adolescent. In J. Grimes (Ed.), *Psychological approaches to problems of children and adolescents* (pp. 55–88). Des Moines: Iowa Department of Public Instruction (ERIC Document Reproduction Service No. ED 232 082)

Ross-Reynolds, G. (1987). Intervention with the homosexual adolescent. In J. Sandoval (Ed.), *Crisis counseling, interventions, and prevention in the schools.* Hillsdale, NJ: Erlbaum.

Ross-Reynolds, G., & Hardy, B. (1985). Crisis counseling for disparate adolescent sexual dilemmas: Pregnancy and homosexuality. *School Psychology Review, 14,* 300–312.

Saghir, M., & Robins, E. (1973). *Male and female homosexuality.* Baltimore: Williams & Wilkins.

Schofield, M. (1965). *Sociological aspects of homosexuality.* London: Longmans, Green.

Silverstein, C. (1977). *A family matter.* New York: McGraw-Hill.

Sorenson, R. (1972). *Adolescent sexuality in contemporary America: Personal values and sexual behavior — ages 13–19.* New York: World.

Stephan, W. (1973). Parental relationships and early social experiences of activist male homosexuals and male heterosexuals. *Journal of Abnormal Psychology, 82,* 506–513.

Stoller, R. (1968). *Sex and gender.* New York: Science House.

Sullivan, H. (1953). *The interpersonal theory of psychiatry.* New York: Norton.

Tripp, C. (1976). *The homosexual matrix.* New York: Signet.

Whitam, F. (1977). Childhood indicators of male homosexuality. *Archives of Sexual Behavior, 6,* 89–96.

Woodman, N., &Lenna, H. (1980). *Counseling with gay men and women: A guide for facilitating positive lifestyles.* San Francisco: Jossey-Bass.

Zuger, B. (1970). The role of familial factors in persistent effeminate behavior in boys. *American Journal of Psychiatry, 126,* 1167–1170.

BIBLIOGRAPHY: PROFESSIONALS

Gonsiorek, J. (1982). *Homosexuality and psychotherapy: A practitioner's handbook of affirmative models.* New York: Haworth.
This book gives a general overview of the research, trends, and issues involving therapy with gay and lesbian clients. In particular, the chapters on stages of gay identity acquisition and counseling parents of young gay males are important.

Ross-Reynolds, G. (1982). Issues in counseling the "homosexual" adolescent. In J. Grimes (Ed.), *Psychological approaches to problems of children and adolescents* (pp. 55–88). Des Moines: Iowa Department of Public Instruction. (ERIC Document Reproduction Service No. ED 232 082)
A valuable document giving an overview of professional opinion and research about homosexuality in general and teenage homosexuality in particular. Provides important considerations in counseling gay adolescents. An excellent overview of the subject of homosexuality and adolescence.

Ross-Reynolds, G., & Hardy, B. (1985). Crisis counseling for disparate adolescent sexual dilemmas: Pregnancy and homosexuality. *School Psychology Review, 14,* 300–312.
In the portion of this article addressing homosexuality, the authors raise important points about teenage homosexual behavior and counseling gay young people. This is a good companion article to that by Ross-Reynolds (1982).

Spada, J. (1979). *The Spada report.* New York: Signet.
This book reports the results of a nationwide survey of gay men conducted between 1976 and 1978. It gives the professional an overview of the gay life experience, including sexuality, coming out, relationships, and views of ones-self. Particularly germane is the discussion of early childhood awareness of gay feelings and early sexual experiences.

BIBLIOGRAPHY: PARENTS

Borhek, M. (1983). *Coming out to parents: A two-way survival guide for lesbians and gay men and their parents.* New York: Pilgrim.
For parents and gay youth to use together, this book explores the feelings parents and children have about "coming out." The author provides suggestions to minimize the trauma of disclosure and offers support to both parents and child as they confront the issue of homosexuality.

Clark, D. (1977). *Loving someone gay.* Millbrae, CA: Celestial Arts.
This book is written for those whose child, sibling, relative, or friend is gay. It describes being gay, the issues and feelings confronted by gays, and how the reader may give help and support to their gay loved one.

Fairchild, B., & Hayward, N. (1979). *Now that you know: What every parent should know about homosexuality.* New York: Harcourt, Brace, & Jovanovich.
Written by two founders of Parents of Gays, this is an excellent book for parents who are dealing with their son's or daughter's disclosure of homosexuality. The authors relate accounts of parents and gay children that most parents will relate to. In addition, the writers discuss what homosexuality is, gay couples, religion, and the Parents of Gays organizations.

Katz, J. (1976). *Gay American history.* New York: Crawell.
This book will demonstrate to parents that many famous and influential personalities in history have been gay, and that their child can have a happy and productive life as well.

Silverstein, C. (1977). *A family matter: A parent's guide to homosexuality.* New York: McGraw-Hill.
An introductory book providing experiences of parents of gay children. This book encourages parents and children to discuss homosexuality together.

BIBLIOGRAPHY: CHILDREN

Alyson, S. (Ed.). (1980). *Young, gay and proud.* Boston: Alyson. A book for gay teens discussing coming out, sexuality, health, and finding support. Also included are vignettes by gay teenagers.

Fricke, A. (1981). *Reflections of a rock lobster.* Boston: Alyson.
An autobiography by the teenager who sought to bring a male date to his high school prom, this book tells of what it is like to grow up gay, to experience teenage love, and to deal with homophobia in and outside of high school. Gives a very positive outlook by a "survivor" of gay adolescence.

Hanckel, F., & Cunningham, J. (1979). *A way of love, a way of life: A young person's introduction to what it means to be gay.* New York: Lothrop, Lee & Shepard.
Discusses how to meet other gays (although the information is more useful for teens in large cities), family and friendships, relationships, sexual health, understanding homosexuality, legal issues, and historical perspectives on homosexuality. It also encourages the reader to seek out help in crises and in answering questions. A very good introduction for teenagers who are self-identifying as gay and who wish to find out more information about homosexuality.

Heron, A. (Ed.) (1983). *One teenager in ten: Writings by gay and lesbian youth.* Boston: Alyson.
In this book teenagers tell about their feelings and concerns about homosexuality, including telling parents and coping with alienation.

Institute for the Advanced Study of Human Sexuality. (1986). *Safe sex in the age of AIDS.* Secaucus, NJ: Citadel Press.
A candid, simply written short book outlining safe and unsafe sexual practices. It contains a section especially for adolescents.

Children and Hospitalization

Donald Brunnquell
Minneapolis Children's Medical Center

BACKGROUND

Approximately 3,650,000 children were discharged from hospitals in 1983 after an average stay of 4.6 days (McCarthy & Kozak, 1985). About one-third of all young people will have been hospitalized at least once before they reach adulthood (Prugh, 1983).

Many of these children had been hospitalized in "pediatric units" of community hospitals, and others in the 124 "children's hospitals" across the nation which offer an environment and psychosocial support network designed for children's needs. These hospitalizations can result from "short stay" or "same-day" procedures, one-time acute treatment, repeated or episodic care, or long-term, chronic service. Each type of hospitalization carries a different risk to the child's development. It should be noted that children with long hospitalizations fall under the protection of PL 94-142 and it's successor bills as orthopedically or other health-impaired (Office of Education, 1977). While state and local requirements differ (Walker & Jacobs, 1986), guidelines for educational and other psychosocial interventions do exist (ACCH, 1980, 1986).

The emphasis on the psychosocial aspects of preventive work with hospitalized children in part grows out of studies demonstrating long-term effects of hospitalization on psychological adjustment. The classic work of Spitz (1946) identifying minimal stimulation during long-term hospitalization in infants has led to considerable study of this issue. Douglas (1975) found an increase in psychiatric disturbance among adolescents with prolonged or repeated hospitalizations in early childhood.

Replication by Quinton and Rutter (1976) of these findings in 10-year-olds provides strong evidence that repeated hospitalization or hospitalization for more than 4 weeks is associated with an increased incidence of later psychiatric disturbance. Especially for children experiencing other risk factors such as poverty, family discord or significant loss, the well-documented immediate stress of hospitalization (Thompson, 1985) can have long-term psychological effects.

The short-term effects of hospitalization can be divided into immediate, in-hospital effects on behavior and posthospitalization changes. Thompson (1985) provides a comprehensive review of this literature. During a hospitalization, changes in behavior related to fear, pain, coping with pain, self-esteem, dependency, and cognitive organization have been found. In addition many studies have demonstrated a reduction in both psychological and physiological indicators of stress through hospital interventions. Shaw and Routh (1982) point out that such behavioral changes must be evaluated in the context of their adaptive value. For example, an increase in crying during an injection when parents are present may indicate an increased security and freedom of expression in the presence of parents.

The psychological effects of hospitalization in the weeks and months following the experience have also been clearly demonstrated. Thompson's (1985) review of this literature finds that upset in areas such as fears, eating, sleep, aggression, and apathy have been found immediately after discharge from the hospital, but these disturbances almost always subside within 2 months. There are clearly some individuals for whom the symptoms are of longer duration, and risk factors such as preexisting psychopathology, developmental crises, family crises, and prolonged or repeated hospitalization bear special attention (Prugh, 1983). Numerous studies have demonstrated that preparation for hospitalization and procedures and general supportive care are effective in reducing posthospitalization symptoms (Wolfer & Visintainer, 1975; Ferguson, 1979).

DEVELOPMENT

Hospitalization and Developmental Level

Both in assessing the needs of a hospitalized child and in antistress intervention the child's developmental level is recognized as the most important guide. This information has generally been presented in broad age categories, although clearly the actual mental age and developmental level outweigh chronological age in importance. Table 1 provides a summary of the major stressors and of suggested interventions by developmental level for parents and school personnel. The vast literature regarding hospital staff interventions is not included here but they have ancillary relevance and follow the same general principles.

For infants the major stressors of hospitalization are difficulty in attachment, separation from caregivers, disruption of routine, and impaired development of basic trust. Especially in the neonatal period, the first 2 months of life, a real threat to the strength and substance of parental attachment to the infant exists. The work of Klaus and Kennell (1976) demonstrates that early and prolonged separation from an infant and the emotional trauma that often accompanies an emotional crisis can affect the parent's long-term relationship with the child. Especially in families at risk due to age, poverty, family discord or violence, and lack of a support system, the relationship of the parent and the critically ill child placed in a neonatal intensive care unit should be closely monitored. Throughout infancy hospitalization may separate the child from the parent. Aside from the threat to attachment, this is most clearly stressful in the second 6 months of life when a child both recognizes primary caregivers and is wary of other contact. This stranger anxiety is variable in expression, but this has often been seen as a time of special vulnerability (e.g., Nesbitt, 1985; Prugh, 1986). One of the reasons separation is an issue is that it implies disruption of caregiving routine. Inconsistency of caregiver and routine combine with the intrusive aspects of many medical procedures to shake the basic trust in a stable and nurturant world that is the major psychosocial acquisition of infancy (Erickson, 1959).

The stresses on infants in the hospital can be lessened, if not eliminated, by active involvement of the parents in the caregiving. Many hospitals now permit "rooming-in," allowing a parent to stay overnight with a child, as well as providing 24-hour-a-day visitation policies for parents. In addition parents should be encouraged to communicate their child's routines, needs, and idiosyncrasies to the nursing staff. The parent should be an advocate both for adaptation of these routines into the hospital routine and for consistency of care by nurses, who over time come to know the child better.

For toddlers, roughly aged 12–30 months, the issues of separation and trust are compounded by disruption of the additional developmental tasks of this age. Individuation and autonomy are important themes at this age, which are met in the toddlers' life by predictability of routine and allowing the toddler control over moving to and from caregivers. Hospitalization, with its many strangers making nonroutine demands on the child, can throw this delicate equilibrium out of balance. As this happens the child may show regression in areas of emerging skills, especially in bowel and bladder control. Restriction of movement, an activity of great importance at this age, also contributes to regressive reactions, which are almost always temporary, although preventive work with the parents and with the child, through age-appropriate activities, is important. Also disturbing to parents is the child's tendency to focus anger at them. Not recognizing this as a sign that children feel "safe" with the parents, they often become anxious or angry on seeing this response in their child, further complicating the child's adjustment reaction. Separations and reunions are especially difficult and require time and understanding on the part of the parent (Prugh, 1983). The relative lack of coping mechanisms at this age, such as language, fantasy, and elaborated play, makes this an especially vulnerable age.

For toddlers, as for infants, parental involvement

TABLE 1

Developmental Issues and Hospitalization

Developmental phase	Stressors	Intervention strategy
Infancy (0–12 mo.)	Difficulty in attachment	Encourage early contact Crisis support Ongoing involvement in care
	Separation from parent	Regular contact Rooming-in
	Disruption of routine	Maintain home schedule Consistency of caregivers
	Impaired basic trust	Minimize intrusive procedures
Toddler (12–30 mo.)	Separation from parent	Involvement in noninvasive cares Rooming-in
	Loss of autonomy	Age-appropriate activities Maintain home routines Consistency of caregivers
	Restriction of movement	Age-appropriate activities
Preschool (30 mo.–5 yrs.)	Separation from parent	Parental involvement Rooming-in
	Fear of mutilation	Accurate information
	Magical thinking	Preparation for procedures Honest communication
	Loss of competence and initiative	Age-appropriate activities Play
School-age (6–12 yrs.)	Loss of bodily control	Preparation for procedures Honest communication
	Enforced dependence	Involvement in care
	Loss of competence	Age-appropriate activities
Adolescence	Lack of trust	Honest communication
	Enforced dependence	Parent involvement in care Parent involvement in decisions
	Threat to bodily competence	Realistic discussions of changes
	Threat to future competence	Age-appropriate activities
	Social isolation	Peer visits

throughout the hospitalization, sensitization of staff to routines, and a limited number of caregivers are all helpful. Additionally one can begin to use preparation and explanation with toddlers. While they may not entirely understand, the exposure at a nonthreatening time and the experience of seeing adults providing a calm approach to the situation are extremely valuable. Age-appropriate play materials and transitional objects brought from home are also essential to minimizing untoward reactions.

In the preschool years, roughly ages 30 months through 5 years, a child develops considerable linguistic skill, the ability to maintain some mental images and to use them in fantasy play, and remarkable social abilities. All of these provide a basis for coping with the separation and autonomy issues, which are often reduced in intensity although still clearly present. In addition to these issues one must attend to the fear of bodily mutilation, the concern with causation of illness (Bibace & Walsh, 1980; Perrin & Gerrity, 1981), magical thinking, and the threat to initiative that hospitalization can bring. The developing sense of body and awareness of sexuality that is seen in these years is easily affected by a hospital experience in which one must expose the body to numerous strangers and often allow the body to be changed. While these concerns should not be seen only in the sense of psychosexual development, certainly that element is present. When combined with the preschooler's concern with causation — the eternal question "why" of these years — and their egocentric assumptions about why things happen, a child may interpret hospitalization as punishment for some known or unknown thought or deed. This may be especially related to harm to the genitals or sensitive areas such as eyes or head (Prugh, 1983). The so-called magical thinking of these years may lead preschoolers to invent many explanations that would not even occur to an adult. An emphasis on honesty in information given to children helps the child feel permitted to worry about appropriate concerns, while ruling out worry about those things not involved in the hospitalization, and promotes trust and communication between child and caregivers.

The need to develop competence and initiative in these years is also clearly threatened by the restriction of activities and social interaction which are basic to this age-group. Opportunities for age-appropriate play and activities are essential to a positive adaptation to hospitalization for preschoolers. When possible this should involve social experiences. Accurate information and preparation before both major procedures such as surgery and minor procedures such as blood drawing are important. The child should also have permission to express fears and pain, but the adaptive value of talking about those problems should be emphasized. Parental involvement and maintenance of routine remain important, although the child's broader experiences in the world often allow more flexibility in these areas for the preschooler than for younger children.

School-age children, roughly aged 6–12 years, clearly have additional coping skills as their general understanding of causation, emotion, and relationships develops. Separation is much less of an issue for most of these children, but loss of control over their body or thoughts, especially during anesthesia, and fear of disfigurement are very prominent. These children generally handle brief hospitalizations well, and only in extended stays or painful and disfiguring procedures do they encounter difficulty with regression and a threat to their sense of self and their own competence and industry. Extended dependence on others, inability to carry out age-appropriate activities or social relations, or parental overindulgence and overprotection are factors that put the school-age child at greater risk.

Children in this age group are especially amenable to preparatory efforts, the beneficial effects of which have generally been demonstrated (Thompson, 1985). These children are also better able to develop and use relationships with caregivers within the hospital, lessening their dependence on parents during this time. They can accept information in a generally realistic and anxiety-reducing fashion if it is provided in a manner that fits their current phase of concrete operational development. Since these children are in a phase of developing mastery over their environment, continued educational and recreational activities are also effective preventive measures.

Adolescence is frequently considered to be a time in which the previously "resolved" developmental tasks all reemerge and are resolved, hopefully so as to produce a well-integrated, competent individual. While their expression is different, the major issues from each previous developmental phase reappear under the stress of hospitalization on the adolescent. The trust issues emerge in relation to the adults on the hospital staff and to parents, and the struggle for autonomy is beset by enforced dependency due to physical limitations and to the unfamiliar, difficult-to-control hospital system. While ideas of causation are well developed, magical thinking in the form of fantasies about both prowess and failure clearly affect the teenager's response to hospitalization. The threat to competence and effectiveness felt by the school-age child is compounded in adolescents by the development of a sense of the future and their place in the world. At the moment of greatest bodily change and need for control and a fantasy of invulnerability, the adolescent must face the fact of vulnerability. Social pressures also raise questions of how friends will understand or evaluate the hospitalization; it may be seen as a sign of weakness, or an unacceptable level of weakness, at least in the fantasy of the hospitalized adolescent. In addition, embarrassment with the opposite sex is a problem for many teens as they work with the hospital staff, and cooperation with authority figures may be interpreted as a sign of weakness. All of these factors lead to a threat to the task of late adolescence of developing a capacity for intimacy with others.

Because of the many issues that face adolescents and the dilemma posed by the necessity of giving help to someone insistent on independence, there are great challenges in helping teens meet the stress of hospitalization. Most important is openness and honesty in communication even of difficult news. Parents should be encouraged to use the occasion as an opportunity to reinforce the trusting aspects of their relationships. Involvement in their own care and as much independent activity as possible are also essential to teenagers. Since hospitals are filled with caregivers and since ambivalence may mark the teenager's responses to them, parents should be gentle advocates with both the staff and the teenager to encourage this autonomy. Providing age-appropriate activities, including ongoing educational efforts, is essential to a positive adaptation especially to longer hospital stays. Recognizing the meaning of resistant or noncompliant behavior is also important, along with efforts to help adolescent patients reframe their understanding so that cooperation becomes a sign of strength in face of illness instead of noncooperation being seen as a sign of strength in face of authority figures. Facilitating social contact during hospitalization and subsequently encouraging social reintegration both at home and at school are important tasks. Finally, helping the teenager successfully work through the threat to invulnerability implied in illness is a difficult but necessary task.

Assessing the Impact of Hospitalization

Since responses to stressors are idiosyncratic, a format for evaluation of disruption and adaptation is more useful than any list of symptoms. The impact of hospitalization can be broadly evaluated during the stay, and then in the short and the long term after the experience. Guidelines for assessing adaptation during the hospital stay are presented in Table 2. After discharge, short-term effects should be evaluated on behavioral disruption, especially sleep, appetite, activity level, limit-testing, and relationships with parents. Since these effects seem to return to normal spontaneously in most cases, continued supportive intervention and parent guidance is a useful level of intervention.

TABLE 2

Assessment of Adaptation During Hospitalization

1. Has the child maintained age-appropriate social relations?
2. Has the child maintained age-appropriate activities?
3. Has the child used defenses appropriate to age?
4. Has the child shown significant behavioral regression?
5. Has the child shown inappropriate dependency?
6. Are symptoms of psychopathology consistently present, especially depression or hyperactivity?
7. Is the child's response to pain commensurate with the physical stimulus in time of onset, magnitude, and duration?
8. Is the child able to use family, peer, hospital staff and cognitive resources in an age-appropriate manner?

Assessment of the long-term effects of hospitalization should include evaluation of specific concerns about hospitalization and medical settings, but it should be based on a broader view of the child's adaptation. Table 3 presents a set of questions for such an evaluation that look at cognitive, social, and behavioral changes as reflections of emotional upset or maladaptation. Major changes of more than 2 months duration should be seen as unusual and further intervention should be considered.

TABLE 3

Assessment of Adaptation After Hospitalization

1. Has the child shown ongoing fears of bodily harm?
2. Has the child shown ongoing fears of medical contact?
3. Has disruption of sleep or appetite continued?
4. Has there been marked change in activity level?
5. Have relationships with parents changed since the hospitalization?
6. Have relationships with siblings changed since the hospitalization?
7. Have peer relationships changed since the hospitalization?
8. Has school performance changed since the hospitalization?
9. Has the child's ability to attend to or complete tasks changed since the hospitalization?
10. Have symptoms of overt psychopathology been noted since the hospitalization?

PUTTING HOSPITALIZATION OF CHILDREN IN PERSPECTIVE

Parents clearly find hospitalization to be a time of high anxiety and face considerable uncertainty about their role in care and support (Thompson, 1985; Algren, 1985). Assistance in obtaining information, providing advocacy, maintaining caregiving, and avoiding overprotection is helpful, as is exploring the possibilities of rooming-in options and involvement in noninvasive procedures. While relatively few siblings show continued negative responses (Knafl, 1982; Knafl and Dixon, 1983) encouraging their inclusion in the process, receiving adequate information from parents, and visitation are helpful in reducing stress. Siblings are most at risk during long hospitalization with parent absence and inconsistency of caregivers. Changes in overall family role and structure can be seen during extended stays. When the hospitalization and illness dominate family life after an initial diagnostic period, family adaptation should be more closely examined.

ALTERNATIVE ACTIONS

Preparation and Preventive Measures

Research on the effects of hospitalization and widespread advocacy for the concerns of children have led to the development of preadmission preparation programs in many hospitals. A survey of such hospitals (ACCH, 1982) found that 76% of children's hospitals and 56% of general hospitals with pediatrics units offered preadmission preparation programs. Unfortunately the use of such programs by eligible families remains low, 23% in children's and 15% in general hospitals. One major effective intervention by the psychologist would be to assist families in exploring and using such programs.

There has been considerable research into the effectiveness of preparation programs and the relative efficiency of different types of preparation. The 65 studies reviewed by Thompson (1985) point to the general effectiveness of many types of preparation, compared to no preparation, in reducing anxiety before, during, and after hospitalization, in facilitating positive adjustment and cooperation during hospitalization, and in minimizing posthospital upset and behavior disturbance.

While many different types of preparation exist, perhaps most promising are multimethod forms of preparation, for example, the "stress point preparation" of Wolfer and Visintainer (1979). Their approach involves giving verbal and sensory information, behavioral rehearsal, and emotional support before and during stressful points of hospitalization. Many pediatric institutions have adapted a variety of these techniques to their own settings. For example, Minneapolis Children's Medical Center has devised a program that includes verbal and sensory information given on a tour of various stress-inducing service areas (e.g., anesthesia induction and recovery room), play opportunity combined with modeling by adult volunteer staff, and parental preparation. They provide a coloring book to encourage continued consideration of the hospital experience.

In another review of hospital preparation, Eiser (1985) has pointed out that the research is limited in that most preparation is aimed at the less vulnerable groups of school-age children undergoing brief or one-time hospitalization. She cited a study by Peterson and Shigetomi (1983) that found that 1 year after surgery, 67% of mothers reported that their children, who had undergone preparation, still spoke of their hospitalization. Of these children 62% recalled the positive aspects and only 22% recalled the negative. Eiser's own work found that healthy children between 5 and 10 years of age were generally ill-informed about the hospital and were extremely concerned about the social aspects of hospitalization such as missing school and separation from friends and family.

Especially when preparation programs are unavailable, one can assist children by working with parents to prepare the child adequately. Table 4 presents some essential points that parents can use in working with their child. This emphasizes the whole child, the process of hospitalization, establishing communication, giving information honestly, using developmentally appropriate methods of presentation, and viewing hospitalization as a possible mastery experience for the child. Many parents ask at what age preparation should be done. Generally even toddlers can use the sensory information and nonthreatening visit to the hospital; the parents' willingness to communicate also comes through even to young children. Specific preparation should take place shortly before a hospital stay. One clinically useful rule of thumb is that preparation should begin 1 day in advance of hospitalization for every year over 2 years of age in order to provide adequate time to process information without creating undue anxiety (Erbaugh, 1986). Work with parents on understanding the reasons and methods of preparation and any special difficulties they might have in helping their child is among the most valuable interventions that can be made on behalf of the child.

The Place of Education and School Personnel

Learning and education are basic to the general development of all children. For children in hospitals developmentally appropriate educational activity has not only its own intrinsic value but is helpful in promoting adaptation in a stressful situation. This is clearly recognized in the policy statements of advocacy organizations such as the Association for Care of Children's Health (ACCH, 1980). While the availability and type of service vary, the legal as well as the ethical obligation to provide such service is clear. While approximately 66% of pediatric hospitals have certified teachers working with patients and about 51% have specific classrooms, many other arrangements for individual tutoring, electronic assistance, or supervised independent work are possible. All contribute to both the in-hospital and posthospital adjustment of children.

A brochure published by ACCH (1983) provides suggestions for teachers on general education in the classroom about hospitals, and basic concepts of health and wellness, including explanation and activities when a child is ill and helping the ill child. It stresses teachers' maintenance of contact with the ill child, communication from classmates with notes and cards, and coordination of educational efforts during extended hospital stays and convalescence. The teacher can also invite hospital personnel to work with staff or classmates to provide information to facilitate reintegration.

By sensitizing the class through discussion and activities and anticipating special needs, teachers can facilitate social as well as cognitive adaptation. Teachers also have a role in monitoring a child's behavior on return to the classroom to assess any long-term effects of hospitalization. The role of the school nurse in interpreting medical data to the staff and students can be a real aid in reducing anxiety and uncertainty, which are major impediments to successful reintegration. Clearly other school professionals will be involved, depending on the system's structure.

It is essential to define the educational team for an individual child, to assure proper information for its members, and to choose one individual as a liaison with hospital personnel.

Contact With Hospital Personnel

As in a school system, there are many people within the hospital system who will have some role with a child. In larger pediatric settings one often finds child life specialists. Trained in child development, these staff members often have responsibility for developmentally appropriate activities during hospitalization; therefore they can be extremely helpful in coordinating with the school.Their nonintrusive contact with the child offers the haven of a nonthreatening relationship that can be of great assistance to a teacher coming into the hospital. In-house education programs are often part of the child life department of larger institutions. If such a program exists, the educational liaison can be a valuable inside resource who can coordinate contacts around educational and other psychosocial issues.

Contact with nurses is especially valuable in obtaining information about a child's current condition. It is helpful in most cases for a teacher to check regularly with the nursing staff to assess any changes in the child's condition, since the medical situation can change very rapidly. Nurses also may provide outreach services to the classroom, and thereby assist in reintegration efforts. Often a "primary nurse" is assigned to a patient. This nurse cares for the patient whenever possible and has the job of coordinating all nursing care to the child. In this role the nurse may be a primary contact person.

All hospitals are required by the Joint Commission on Accreditation of Hospitals to provide some social service to their patients, and in some institutions coordinating with outside agencies including schools falls to the social workers.

As in the school system, it is important to identify a single liaison person from the hospital who can coordinate the education interventions with other psychosocial and medical work. Requesting such a contact person explicitly both aids the school personnel and creates an advocate for the ongoing educational work within the hospital system.

TABLE 4

Preparation Guidelines for Parents

1. *Preparation is important:* The child can avoid being overwhelmed, and hospitalization can be a growth and mastery experience.
2. *The whole child:* Hospitalization affects the psychological and social well-being of the child as well as the body.
3. *The process:* Concern about hospitalization begins before the experience and extends afterwards, and parents should include those times in their work.
4. *Establish communication:* Most important, the parent should convey an attitude of openness and a desire to talk about the experience.
5. *Give information honestly:* Help the child limit fears to what is a real concern; let them know if something will hurt, why it must be done, and when it will be over.
6. *Give developmentally appropriate information:* All children need information, but they can absorb it in different ways, starting with sensory–motor for the toddler and adding basic verbal for the preschooler, specifics for the school-age child, and more abstract concerns for the adolescent.
7. *Find out what your child thinks:* Through play, drawings, observation, and casual conversation ascertain the child's thoughts: they are different from yours.
8. *Attend to feelings and thoughts:* Help the child be aware not just of medical procedures but also of feelings and thoughts about them.
9. *Get adequate support and information for yourself:* Adequate information allows you to help your child and reduces your own anxiety; support from family, friends, and professionals does the same.

TABLE 5

Information on the Hospitalized Child

I. Team composition
   A. Primary hospital liaison with the school during hospitalization.
   B. Other professionals involved in the case.
   C. Professionals who will provide outpatient follow-up.
   D. Contact person in case of emergency.

II. Medical condition
   A. Nature of the illness.
   B. Expected course of the illness and anticipated stress points.
   C. Specific, especially ongoing, procedures that the child may discuss.
   D. Limitations the illness will place on cognitive, social, and physical activities.
   E. Possible emergency situations that may arise and how to respond.
   F. Risks to others, both staff and student, especially possibilities of contagion.
   G. Expected length of hospital stay and home convalescence.

III. Psychosocial considerations
   A. Are changes in cognitive, emotional, or social skills anticipated?
   B. How has the child adapted to the illness and hospitalizaton?
   C. How will educational efforts aid adaptation?
   D. What does the child know and understand about the illness?
   E. How will parental and sibling responses affect school contact?
   F. What long-term adaptational issues are anticipated?

While confidentiality must be observed on both sides of the hospital–school system relationship, obtaining releases for free exchange of information is essential to coordinating those systems. While each case is different, some basic categories of information should always be addressed. Table 5 provides an outline of these categories. Obtaining this information serves not only the affected child, but helps to address anxieties of staff and students who will have contact with the child.

SUMMARY

Hospitalization is an experience that will affect up to one third of our children sometime before they reach adulthood. While the overall length of hospital stays is declining, children in hospitals are generally sicker and need more psychosocial services. Repeated or extended early hospitalization has been found to have long-term psychiatric effects. This has spurred a new attention to the psychosocial milieu in hospitals. Short-term post-hospitalization behavioral disruption is seen in areas such as sleep and eating disturbances, changes in activity, and increased anxiety, but these problems tend to spontaneously remit within a few weeks. If they do not, they should receive further attention. Children with developmental problems, recent losses or trauma, recent family discord, or repeated hospitalizations appear to be at special risk.

Analysis of the risks at each developmental phase is most helpful intervention in behalf of hospitalized children. The new environment, many unfamiliar people and demands, enforced dependence, and invasive procedures pose a threat to the attachment and trust infants must develop, to the autonomy and initiative of toddlers and preschoolers, to the growing sense of competence of the school-age child, and to the sense of self and of future achievement of the adolescent. The hospitalization may also affect parental competence, sibling adjustment, and overall family equilibrium. The centrality of the illness and hospitalization in the family life during times of relative stability in illness is an indicator of family adaptation.

It is clear that preventive measures such as preparation of children and parents before hospitalization and the beginning of medical procedures reduces anxiety and short-term behavioral disruption. Questions still exist about the optimal type of preparation and its effects on especially vulnerable populations. Provision of ongoing educational activities by school personnel is important to minimize disruption during extended hospitalization. It is also legally mandated under PL 94–142 and its successor bills. The issues that arise in the coordination of two large formal systems are numerous and best handled by designating a liaison from each system for on-going contact. By exchanging information, these systems can complement each other in providing continuity in a child's life that will minimize the stress of hospitalization and of reentry into the school. This helps the child achieve the sense of mastery over a stressful situation, which is the goal of hospital psychosocial intervention.

REFERENCES

ACCH. (1980). *Psychosocial policy guidelines for administration of pediatric health care facilities.* Washington, DC: Association for the Care of Children's Health.

ACCH. (1981). *Hospital school programs: Guidelines and directory.* Washington, DC: Association for the Care of Children's Health.

ACCH. (1983). *A guide for teachers: Children and hospitals.* Washington, DC: Association for the Care of Children's Health.

ACCH. (1986). *Children and hospitals week.* Washington, DC: Association for the Care of Children's Health.

Algren, C. L. (1985). Role perception of mothers who have hospitalized children. *Children's Health Care, 14,* 1–9.

Bibace, R., & Walsh, M. E. (1980). Development of children's conceptions of illness. *Pediatrics, 66,* 912–917.

Douglas, J. W. (1975). Early hospital admissions and later disturbances of behavior and learning. *Developmental Medicine and Child Neurology, 17,* 456–480.

Duval, E. M. (1977). *Marriage and family development.* Philadelphia: Lippincot.

Eiser, C. (1985). *The psychology of children's illness.* New York: Springer-Verlag.

Erbaugh, S. (1986). Personal communication, May 13.

Erickson, E. H. (1959). *Identity and the life cycle.* New York: International Universities Press.

Ferguson, B. F. (1979). Preparing young children for hospitalization: A comparison of two methods. *Pediatrics, 64,* 656–664.

Klaus, M. H., & Kennell, J. H. (1976). *Maternal-infant bonding.* St. Louis: Mosby.

Knafl, K. A. (1982). Parents' views of the response of siblings to a pediatric hospitalization. *Research in Nursing and Health, 5,* 13–20.

Knafl, K. A., & Dixon, D. M. (1983). The role of siblings during pediatric hospitalization. *Issues in Comprehensive Pediatric Nursing, 6,* 13–22.

McCarthy, E., & Kozak, L. (1985). *Hospital use by children: United States, 1983.* Washington, DC: National Center for Health Statistics.

Nesbitt, T. (1985). Psychosocial needs of infants and toddlers: Implications for care. In C. Fore & E. Poster (Eds.), *Meeting psychosocial needs of children and families in health care* (pp. 38–42). Washington, DC: Association for the Care of Children's Health.

Office of Education, DHEW. (1977). PL 94-142. *Federal Register, 42,* No. 163 (Tuesday, August 23).

Perrin, E. C., & Gerrity, P. S. (1981). There's a demon in your belly: Children's understanding of illness. *Pediatrics, 67,* 841–849.

Prugh, D. (1983). *The psychosocial aspects of pediatrics.* Philadelphia: Lea & Febiger.

Prugh, D. G., Staub, E. M., Souds, H. H., Kirschbaum, R. M., & Lenihan, E. A. (1953). A Study of the emotional reactions of children and families to hospitalization and illness. *American Journal of Orthopsychiatry, 23,* 70–106.

Shaw, E. G., & Routh, D. K. (1982). Effect of mother presence on children's reactions to aversive procedures. *Journal of Pediatric Psychology, 7,* 33–42.

Shore, M. F. (Ed.). (1965). *Red is the color of hurting: Planning for children in the hospital.* Washington, DC: National Institute of Mental Health.

Spitz, R. A. (1946). Hospitalism: An inquiry into the genesis of psychiatric conditions in early childhood. In *The Psychoanalytic Study of the Child,* (Vol. 1, pp. 53–74). New York: International Universities Press.

State of Minnesota (1982). *Patients and residents of health care facilities, Bill of rights; Statute 144.651.* St. Paul: State Government Printing Office.

Thompson, R. H. (1985). *Psychosocial research on pediatric hospitalization and health care: A review of the literature.* Springfield, IL: Thomas.

Walker, D. K., & Jacobs, F. H. (1985). Public school programs for chronically ill children. In N. Hobbs & J. Perrin (Eds.), *Issues in the care of children with chronic illness* (pp. 615–655). San Francisco: Jossey-Bass.

Wolfer, J. A., & Visintainer, M. A. (1975). Pediatric surgical patients' and parents' stress responses and adjustment. *Nursing Research, 24,* 244–255.

BIBLIOGRAPHY: PROFESSIONALS

Thompson, R. H. (1985). *Psychosocial research on pediatric hospitalization and health care.* Springfield, IL: Thomas.
A comprehensive review of 306 studies over the past two decades, looking at concepts of and responses to hospitalization, procedures and illness, the effectiveness of preparation, use of play, and effects on family of hospitalization in infancy through adolescence.

Eiser, C. (1985). *The psychology of childhood illness.* New York: Springer-Verlag.
A wide-ranging attempt to conceptualize and organize current knowledge regarding children's experiences in the hospital, knowledge of body and illness, and family impact of chronic illness. Chapters also address phenylketonuria, diabetes, asthma, and leukemia as models of chronic illness.

Association for the Care of Children's Health. (1984). *Preparing children and families for health care encounters.* Washington, DC: ACCH.
A collection of articles stressing practical approaches to psychological preparation of children for the hospital stay as well as a few research reports.

Association for the Care of Children's Health. (1981). *Hospital school programs: Guidelines and directory.* Washington, DC: ACCH.
After a brief rationale this book describes practical aspects of developing a hospital school program and lists all hospitals responding to a survey of educational programs and delineates available services.

Prugh, D. G. (1985). *The psychosocial aspects of pediatrics.* Philadelphia: Lea & Febiger.
A comprehensive review from the viewpoint of a nationally known physician specializing in the psychosocial aspects of pediatric medical care. It includes a chapter on hospitalization as well as information on development, psychopathology, and illness from a medical standpoint.

BIBLIOGRAPHY: CHILDREN

ACCH. (1982). *For teenagers: Your stay in the hospital.* Washington, DC: Association for the Care of Children's Health.
A brief pamphlet that helps teenagers understand and prepare for hospitalization; it is also a useful tool for discussion of these issues.

ACCH. (1984). *Selected books for children and teenagers about hospitalization, illness,and handicapping conditions.* Washington, DC: Association for the Care of Children's Health.
An annotated bibliography covering 98 books useful in working with children around psychosocial issues in illness and hospitalization.

Ciliotta, C., & Livingston, C. (1981). *Why am I going to the hospital?* Seacaucus, NJ: Lyle Stuart.
A book for preschool and school-age children dealing with the causes and experiences of hospitalization, including the emotional aspects.

Greenwald, A., & Heed, B. (1977). *Going to the hospital.* New York: Family Communications.
A Mr. Rogers' book for preschoolers and young school-age children. Informs readers generally about hospitalization and encourages further exploration and discussion.

Rey, H., & Rey, M. (1966). *Curious George goes to the hospital.* Boston: Houghton-Mifflin.
In this book for preschool and early school-age children the familiar monkey character Curious George models adaptive reactions to various aspects of hospitalization.

Richter, E. (1982). *The teenage hospital experience: You can handle it!* New York: Cowad, McCenn, and Geoghan.
A book for adolescents, based on interviews with teenagers and caregivers, that addresses the issues of independence and social support vital to teenagers.

Stein, S. (1974). *The hospital story.* New York: Walker.
This book for preschool and young school-age children follows the experience of a girl having a tonsillectomy and also contains a text for parents. It deals with the emotional as well as medical aspects of the experience.

Children and Household Chores

John R. Hester
Francis Marion College

BACKGROUND

The scene is familiar; parents have just complained about their children's noncompliant behavior. The psychologist begins to question the parents to identify the problem, expecting the disclosure of some unusual behavior. Instead the parents respond that their children will not take out the trash, clean their room, or complete similar tasks. While parents rarely initiate a referral because of household chores, it is remarkable how the failure to complete such everyday tasks as chores or homework takes on family importance. From the psychologist's perspective there may be a litany of more pressing concerns, but the parent's interest in chores offers an inviting consultation opportunity.

Thrall (1978) and White and Brinkerhoff (1981) reported that, not surprisingly, approximately 90% of the families surveyed required school-age children to regularly perform some chore. When asked, in a study by Griffths (as cited in Harris, Clark, Rose, & Valasek, 1954), how they could improve their behavior for parents, children cited chores as one of the most frequently mentioned behaviors. Parents continue to require chores despite growing concerns about the division of children's after-school time among homework, leisure activities, organized sports, and community activities. While parents' motivation for requiring chores may vary somewhat with the age of the child and the work needs of the family, the foremost reason for requiring chores is to build character through development of a sense of responsibility. This is true regardless of the child's sex or the parents' education, religion, or marital division of labor (White & Brinkerhoff, 1981).

Early research by Harris et al. (1954) found no relationship between chore requirements and responsibility. More recently, evidence has been derived (Whiting & Whiting, 1975) from cross-cultural investigations that cultures in which children exhibit higher levels of prosocial behavior have economics requiring children to assume more work responsibility. The economic involvement of mothers outside the home requires children to assume more home responsibilities. Such a relationship between chores and instrumental competence is reassuring to a country such as the United States, where a long-held tradition of chores for children may become more of an economic necessity now that 50% of mothers in two-parent families are employed (Hoffman, 1979). The percentage of mothers employed is even higher for the ever increasing single-parent family. Chore requirements, long a cultural norm, will surely increase in practical importance for families under increasing economic pressure.

Additionally, chores are important in sex-role socialization. Despite strong indication that household chores are assigned by sex, chores are often overlooked as a contributing factor in the socialization process. There is evidence that marital division of household labor has its roots in childhood (Thrall, 1978). Sex-role behaviors are being modeled and imitated everyday within the home.

For the psychologist, chores offer an opportunity to teach parenting skills. The psychologist can use chores to illustrate skills such as setting rules, conducting a task analysis, choosing and applying appropriate consequences, communicating task requirements, and involving children in family decisions. Chores are specific, important, and relatively amenable to intervention, so that success can be obtained without maximum investment of professional time. Successful assistance with chores can serve as a foot in the door for subsequent consultation with parents. The family benefits from completion of chores in that children learn important self-help skills, while developing a sense of responsibility and feelings of self-efficacy. Parents begin to witness compliant behavior, which contributes to more positive parent–child relationships.

Household chores will be defined as repetitive tasks assigned within the context of a child's or adolescent's family. No consideration will be given to either special work activities, such as working on an addition to the house, or to work for pay outside the home. Yard work, gardening, and car maintenance, when assigned as routine family work, will be discussed as household chores.

DEVELOPMENT

Prior to intervention, children's responsibility for doing household chores must be viewed from the perspective of the individual within the context of the family. Consideration must be given to individual factors such as a child's age and sex, as well as the ecological factors associated with maternal employment, the single-parent family, and rural residence. The sensitivity of the mental health professional to individual and ecological variables provides a clearer understanding of the significance of chores in context and enhances the likelihood of successful intervention.

Generally data collected on children's accomplishment of chores are based on the mothers' reporting of their children's chore activity for the day prior to an interview and the day after the interview (Sanik & Stafford, 1985). Only occasionally will children provide self-reports (Goldstein & Oldham, 1979) or will the data be collected through participant observation (Berheide, 1984).

Age

The percentage of children assigned household chores increases, across different household tasks, with increasing age. For school-age children Cogle and

Tasker (1982) found the percentage of children assigned chores to be as follows: ages 6–8, 78%; 9–11, 93%; 12–14, 95%; and 15–17, 96%. Even 40% of male and 36% of female preschoolers between the ages of 0–4 years were reported to be assigned chores (White & Brinkerhoff, 1981). Some research has indicated a slightly decreasing trend in the percentage participating during middle to late adolescence (Sanik & Stafford, 1985). While significant numbers of children are required to perform chores, the number of hours per week is typically modest. A median of 4 hr per week was found across all ages by White and Brinkerhoff. Cogle, Tasker, and Morton (1982) reported the average for adolescents was somewhat higher, at 64 min per day, whereas mothers spent 401 min per day and fathers 121 min per day. Concern that chores might interfere with homework or leisure appears to be unfounded, especially considering that less chore time is required on school days (Sanik & Stafford, 1985) and that children spend a substantial amount of time watching television.

A developmental trend has been noted in the type of task required (White & Brinkerhoff, 1981). Children until the age of 10 assume child-centered responsibilities such as making their bed, picking up their toys, or cleaning their bedroom. Around the age of 10 chores become more family-centered, in that children engage in work like food preparation, which serves the family as a whole. Parents' reasons for assigning chores change with age. Teaching responsibility remains the primary goal of chore assignment across ages, but it declines in importance for older children relative to other reasons, such as parents' need for help.

Sex

The sex of a child is the most important factor in determining which and how many household tasks will be assigned. White and Brinkerhoff (1981) found a higher participation rate across ages for males, but other research has yielded higher rates for females (Cogle & Tasker, 1982; Lynch, 1975). During the early years the amount of time spent is roughly equivalent, but by adolescence females are required to commit significantly more of their day to household chores than are males. Even including time spent by males on yard activities, females work approximately 60% (Cogle et al., 1982; Sanik & Stafford, 1985) to 100% (Lynch, 1975) more time at chores than do males. Apparently females bear a disproportionate amount of the increased workload parents place on older children.

The types of tasks children are assigned reflect traditional sex roles. Females are more likely to be assigned tasks such as housecleaning, dishwashing, grocery shopping, washing clothes and preparing meals. The only chores that males perform more often than females is a loosely grouped series of tasks that include household maintenance activities (such as housepainting), yard work, car maintenance, and pet care (Cogle & Tasker, 1982; Lynch, 1975). The males' tasks are not required as regularly, which helps to explain why males spend less time on chores. Females spend triple the amount of time males do on dishwashing and six times more time on grocery shopping (Cogle et al., 1982).

Such sex stereotyping of tasks for children and adolescents should not be surprising, given many of the adult models in the home. While Pleck (1985) has found significant involvement of fathers in household tasks, a recent survey of 164 couples by Nyquist, Slivken, Spence and Helmreich (1985) found that only 1.4% of the couples reported sharing equally or having husbands assume primary responsibility for traditionally assigned female tasks. Similarly, traditional male assignments were shared equally or assumed by women only 11.4% of the time. While the data are contradictory, the issue is important considering that Thrall (1978) concluded that adults' expectations concerning division of labor are shaped during childhood by their own parents.

Given the perception of current adolescents of marital division of labor, the trend may continue. While there is growing willingness to more equally share childcare, traditional views toward household labor are still very prevalent (Hansen & Darling, 1985). Keith and Brubaker (1980) reported that adolescent females have more egalitarian views than do males. Both sexes are more likely to accept the sharing of responsibility in others' marriages than in their own.

Children and adolescents also encounter extrafamilial sex-stereotyped models of household roles. In reviewing television programs of the day, Barcus (1983) found that women characters were approximately twice as likely as men to perform household tasks as their primary activity. Approximately three-quarters of children in catalogue pictures and on packages of housekeeping toys were found to be girls. Typically if a boy was shown, he was being served by a girl. All catalogues and packages for workbenches and tools showed boys using the toy (Schwartz & Markham, 1985). Division of labor between the sexes begins early and is modeled by many sources.

Maternal Employment and Single-Parent Families

Economic demands and social changes are altering the structure of the U. S. family. Women are seeking and finding employment in ever increasing numbers. Cogle et al. (1982) found adolescents spending the following time (minutes) per day on chores across maternal work status: fully employed mothers, 84; part-time employed mothers, 35; homemaker, 56. The authors suggested that part-time employed mothers, in attempts to be "supermom," require less household work of adolescents than mothers who are homemakers. Even when working mothers received increased assistance from adolescents and fathers, working mothers many times continue to shoulder a disproportionate amount of housework (Cogle et al., 1982).

Montemayor (1984), in investigating the influence of maternal employment, found that mothers are most likely to enter the work force when their children have reached adolescence. The results indicate that males had more conflict with their mothers if she was employed, the majority of the conflicts centering on everyday issues such as chores. No relationship was found between female children and either parent or between males and their fathers. Interestingly, fathers were found to have spent less free time with children when the mothers worked. Apparently employed mothers have less time to organize opportunities for father–child interactions.

Recent census data (U. S. Bureau of the Census, 1985) indicate that approximately 26% of all families are headed by single parents. In Weinraub and Wolf's (1983) study single-parent mothers, despite being more likely to be employed, received no more assistance with household work than mothers in a two-parent family. While single-parent and two-parent mothers reported similar abilities to cope with finances and childcare, single-parent mothers reported significantly less ability to cope with the stress of household responsibilities. Employment of the single-parent mothers increased both maternal demands on children and attempts at controlling children.

A pattern emerges of employed mothers demanding more household responsibility of their adolescent children, which results in conflict, especially between single-parent mothers and sons. Time constraints require mothers to demand that adolescent males perform tasks viewed by them as "women's work" at a time when they are sensitive about their masculinity. The ensuing conflict results in what has so aptly been described as the "coercive cycle" (Hetherington & Parke, 1986). The cycle involves a repetitious pattern of maternal demands and adolescent refusal.

Rural Residence

Rural children are required to perform both household and farm chores. Whiting and Whiting (1975) found that agricultural cultures are more likely to require work responsibility at a younger age. Assistance with household tasks peaks at 7–12 years of age and declines somewhat during adolescence (Light, Hertsgaard, & Martin, 1985). Apparently the increasing demands of farm chores decreases available time for household work.

PUTTING CHILDREN AND HOUSEHOLD CHORES IN PERSPECTIVE

Before implementing any intervention techniques, the psychologist must assess, in addition to individual and ecological factors, the meaning or importance of chores to the family, parenting style, and the likelihood of continued contact with the parent.

In researching 790 families White and Brinkerhoff (1981) assigned the rationales for assigning children household chores to five categories: (a) developmental (chores help develop character and responsibility); (b) reciprocal obligation (it is the child's duty to the family to help); (c) extrinsic (parents need help in completing household tasks); (d) task learning (children need to know how to perform certain tasks); (e) residual (all other reasons). Overall, approximately three-quarters of the families surveyed cited character development as a reason for assigning chores. Given that parents could cite more than one category, reciprocal obligation was mentioned by 25%, the extrinsic factor by 23%, task learning by 12%, and other reasons (residual) by 9%. Across sex and all age groups responsibility was the primary purpose attached to chores. Employed mothers and single-parent mothers were more likely than others to cite the extrinsic category. Apparently the work ethic and its value to children is still a prevalent theme in today's family.

Unfortunately many parents who have difficulty with their children and seek the assistance of a mental health consultant have a parenting style that Baumrind (1983) has characterized as either authoritarian or permissive. Neither of these two parenting styles are conducive to the development of social responsibility. The authoritarian family will not discuss standards; rather, parents hope to inculcate a respect for work. The permissive parent will be uncomfortable making demands for household responsibility. Hoffman (1984) has emphasized that parents who use a democratic or inductive style are more successful in encouraging internalization of moral standards, i.e., in building character. Parents establish standards, but the children are induced to understand and anticipate the effects of their behavior on others. The standard underlying the parental requirement is emphasized. In order to best assist a family with the time available, a psychologist must be armed with an understanding of both the meaning of chores in the family and parenting style.

ALTERNATIVE ACTIONS

Strategies for inducing and maintaining the performance of household chores require a multicomponent treatment plan that includes suggestions for selecting chores, communicating task requirements, providing consequences for fulfillment or nonfulfillment of assignments, and monitoring and adjusting the program. As with all good intervention strategies the various components are interdependent.

Selecting Chores

The best chores are those that can be completed with minimum supervision, can be regularly required, and do not interfere with important activities. In matching a child with specific chores, the cognitive, motoric, and social–emotional skills required by the task must be considered. Without outside intervention, parents of younger children usually chose tasks that require them to care for themselves. In choosing child-centered tasks parents sense the need for simplicity, realize the value of learning self-help skills, and know that parental freedom from such repetitive tasks is very beneficial. Studies have found that significant numbers of preschoolers are required to complete chores, and if there is adequate supervision, there is no reason to delay the assigning of chores (White & Brinkerhoff, 1981). The Vineland Adaptive Behavior Scales (Sparrow, Balla, & Cicchetti, 1984) at the 3-year level has an item concerning helping with chores, the assumption being that there are regularly assigned responsibilities at that age. As a child matures, more complicated chores directly contributing to the family's common good can be assigned. For all children, but especially handicapped children, skill level rather than chronological age is the important factor.

Parents should be sensitive to behaviors that indicate stress caused by too much responsibility. Complaining, dawdling, irritability, and unusual noncompliant behavior may indicate a child's discomfort with a task. Asking if there is anything else to be done or becoming angry with parental assistance may indicate not enough responsibility.

Reasons for having children engage in household chores influence the choice of tasks. Families using chores as a necessary labor source will be guided by family needs. Families that have the luxury of using chores solely to teach responsibility will have a wider range of possibilities, but should not assign contrived work.

In assisting families to select an appropriate chore, avoidance of sex stereotyping will present the most difficulty. Assigning males and females equally to tasks offers some significant advantages to both the children and the family. Children will develop a flexible, nonsexist perception of household work that will later assist them in assuming ever changing marital and parenting roles. From a practical standpoint males who can wash their clothes and prepare their meals, and females who can repair a car are being provided with survival skills that will contribute to their behavioral autonomy. The family benefits by having available flexible workers, which for an employed mother or single parent can be critical. Also, if chore assignment is more equitable, there develops a sense of collaboration and belonging. Fathers who commit minimal time to only certain yard and house activities act as a salient model that from a nonsexist viewpoint is destructive and must somehow be addressed. Certainly schools, other families in the community, and some television families can act as alternative models in respect to flexible work assignments.

Children and adolescents can be actively involved in the assignment process. Children who have participated in the assignment of chores are likely to make fewer complaints and see how their role fits into the context of the family. Parents and children together can compile a list of job possibilities and ask for volunteers. Unpopular jobs can be rotated among family members or assigned to more than one person. There is evidence that children view an unpleasant chore more favorably when two people are assigned the job together (Nichols & Berger, 1969). Parents can act as models by accepting undesirable jobs; alternatively, if no one will accept the job, assignment can be drawn with other jobs from a jar by family members (Dinkmeyer & McKay, 1973). If there are children of various ages or with handicapping limitations, a family meeting offers an opportunity for parents to discuss the fairness issue. The parents' utilization of a family meeting for chore assignment can provide an opportunity for a psychologist to discuss the advantage of regularly held family meetings and how to conduct them (Dinkmeyer & McKay, 1982). The success of such an intervention will depend on the family's ability to adopt more of a democratic/inductive parenting style.

Communicating Requirements of the Task

Primary to a successful household chore program is communication of the requirements to the children. Both children and parents must clearly understand the work contract. An important question for an involved psychologist to consider is why previous attempts to have children complete chores failed. Failure may have resulted because the children did not know how to perform a task (skill deficit), or did not wish to do the task (performance deficit). Especially for handicapped children a task analysis of the chore must be performed and the skill level of the child assessed. In training a blind client Brueske and Cuvo (1985) found that a relatively simple task such as cleaning the bathtub included five general and 42 specific component tasks. A psychologist's evaluation data and a special educator's individual education plan can be of assistance to parents in assessing a child's ability and in performing a task analysis.

Parents should always observe a child's initial performance of a new chore to determine if behavior must be prompted. If necessary, parents should move from modeling to more intrusive aids such as physical guidance. In modeling a task, adults should teach short subparts of the task and have the child perform each part before moving to the next component (Gillet, 1979). For inexperienced children chores should be short and simple.

Parents frequently report that chores are often completed only after frequent reminders. Verbal reminders to complete chores are often ineffective (Hall et al., 1972) and often are seen by children as nagging that occasionally results in unauthorized escape behavior by the child such as avoiding a parent or watching television. To avoid this, parents should list chores to be completed in some prominent place such as the refrigerator or the children's door. The wording of chores should be short, stated positively, and easy to remember (Becker, 1971).

Providing Consequences

As previously noted, parents overwhelmingly cite teaching of responsibility as the primary reason for assigning chores. It is important to parents that children not merely comply with parental demands but internalize the concept of responsibility. Parents want children to adopt a standard and generalize the principle to other life requirements. Compliance in respect to a particular consequence is not the parents' goal. Yet, some consistently applied consequence is often necessary to initiate the desired behavior. A psychologist assisting the parent with this dilemma should consider Lepper's minimal sufficiency principle: To change long-term behavior and assist in the internalization of the responsibility standard, external consequences should be powerful enough to secure the desired behavior without overwhelming the standard and its importance (Lepper, 1983). Excessive external coercion can cause a child to associate the chore behavior with the reinforcer or punisher rather than adopting it as an internalized norm.

One of the least intrusive consequences for the completion of chores is to simply record whether the task has been completed. On a chart that lists the child's name and obligations, adults indicate with a mark, star, or other indicator whether a chore has been completed. Such a simple system has been reported to have varying success with children. In one study the system improved completion of chores (Hall et al., 1972), but it had minimal success in another (Christophersen, Arnold, Hill, & Quilitch, 1972). Parents can review the chart at a specified time each day, providing praise for completed chores. Two more visual systems suggested by Eyre and Eyre (1984) are to utilize for each child a pegboard with a peg placed in a hole for each chore completed, or use a tagboard similar to those in classrooms, whereby a tag is turned around for each task completed. Even though additional consequences may prove necessary, some recording system is recommended as an initial step.

The Premack principle is a natural technique to use to gain fulfillment of chore obligations from a child. A simple contingency is that before engaging in a high-frequency behavior such as watching television or playing with a preferred friend or toy, the child must first engage in the low-frequency chore behavior. For this technique to be effective parents must be able and willing to control access to the reinforcing activity. Too often parents are inconsistent, or they choose an activity that is not valued by the child. Parents can occasion the timely completion of chores by applying a "limited hold" condition whereby the activity reinforcer is available only if the chore is completed within a specified time.

When necessary, material reinforcers can be added to increase program effectiveness. Money in the form of an allowance offers several advantages and disadvantages. Goldstein and Oldham (1979) reported that by the first grade most children are receiving an allowance that is usually earned by completing chores. The requirement of chores for an allowance is a concept that many families find comfortably fits their work ethic. Out of the allowance parents can both require children to pay for small expenses, and also encourage savings. The danger is that children may attribute chore completion to the very salient reinforcer of money. Family discussions on the value of each child's work contribution can keep the focus on the standard of responsibility.

For families who are moving toward providing material and activity reinforcers for younger children Jenson, Neville, Sloane, and Morgan (1982) have offered a simple and clever contingency management system called "spinners and chart" that can easily be adapted to use with chores. A chart containing a pattern of dots in the outline of a favorite picture such as an animal is made with randomly placed larger dots indicating reinforcement and smaller dots indicating no reinforcement. To add to the novelty of the system and discourage a postreinforcement pause, each dot is covered with scratch-off ink to be removed only when a chore has been completed and a line has been drawn to a new dot in the connect-a-dot pattern. The occurrence of the large dots is variable throughout, their scheduling being thinned as the program progresses. When a larger dot is uncovered, children use the spinner to discover their reinforcer. The spinner is divided into sections, each indicating a different reinforcer such as getting to stay up late.

Token economies such as those used at Achievement Place, a home-style rehabilitation setting for "predelinquent" boys have been demonstrated to be successful with household tasks (Phillips, Phillips, Fixsen, & Wolf, 1971). A similar program requiring 10 hours of parent training with a psychologist has been adapted for home use by Christophersen et al. (1972). Alvord (1973) has developed a home token economy that has extensive recordkeeping charts and offers the innovation of making the parents subject to being fined for not administering the program properly. Implementing token economies can be time-consuming and present generalization problems. To address generalization Phillips et al. (1971) offered an "adjusting consequence" procedure in which consequences accumulate between intermittent checkpoints. Such a procedure prevents reduction of both frequency and magnitude of the consequence and assists in gradually fading the contingency. The efficacy of a token economy will depend upon the parent's commitment and the psychologist's ability to follow up.

Monitoring and Adjusting

To maximize success, parents must be able to monitor completion of chores and adjust the program of change. Parents constantly complain about having to check to see if a child has completed a chore. Having children evaluate and accurately report their own behavior is desirable. Wood and Flynn (1978) offered a self-evaluation system by which children are reinforced for accurately reporting completion of chores. In the context of a token economy the authors offered children points for completion of a task and additional points for accurately evaluating and reporting their performance. Once children were consistently responding at an established accuracy criterion, that response level was found to be maintained even after accuracy points were no longer awarded. In fact, the self-evaluation group was more resistant to extinction even after reinforcement for both accuracy and chores was terminated. Self-evaluation procedures seem to assist in the shift from external attribution to self-attribution.

Another alternative is to assign monitoring of chore completion to a child assigned to be a manager (Phillips, 1968). The manager is reinforced on the basis of how well the chore has been completed by others under the manager's supervision. Group contingencies such as those used in the Good Behavior Game (Barrish, Saunders, & Wolf, 1969) can be adapted for home use. Separate chore teams can be established or all family members can serve on one team, with a group consequence provided only if everyone on a team has completed chores at an established criterion level. Children control each other through peer monitoring. While such programs have the danger of creating conflict, they can be effective.

A related issue is what to do when children are not completing, are partially completing, and/or are complaining excessively about their assignments. Parents should not provide any reinforcer for a task not completed at the specified criterion level. A general rule is that parents should not complete tasks for their children, although there are situations such as care of a pet where this is not advisable. Parents who constantly encounter the problem of unfinished chores should re-evaluate the requirements of the chores and the consequences being provided. Parents may need to adjust the amount, frequency, or type of work required; or remembering the minimal sufficiency principle, they may proceed to more powerful external consequences. Using chores as punishment is not recommended. Minor verbal complaints and whining should be ignored or fined, and more serious complaints can be discussed at a family meeting. Rotating chores and allowing children to have input into the decision-making process should help.

SUMMARY

The importance of the matter of household chores is that a family's orientation toward household chores reveals much about the dynamics of the family. In addition, chores offer a window of opportunity for intervention. Suggestions offered in this chapter can be used in short-term intervention or in ongoing parent training. Children benefit from the improved parenting skills, the development of prosocial behavior, and the enhancement of feelings of competency. Research indicates that a sense of competency fosters prosocial behavior (Midlarsky, 1984). As a result, the successful completion of chores tends to generate continuing completion of chores. Programs to modify chore behavior should stress assigning mutually agreed-upon assignments that are carefully defined and communicated to the child. Parents must assess the skill level of their children and when necessary provide training. Consequences should be simple, natural, and not excessive.

Household chores should be viewed within the context of overall family functioning. Parents must constantly be reminded that they act as the most salient models of work behavior. A family's values concerning the work ethic, sex roles, and cooperation will be mirrored in the division of labor within the home. Household chores are integral to the socialization of work and establishment of marital roles.

REFERENCES

Alvord, J. R. (1973). *Home token economy: An incentive program for children and their parents.* Champaign, IL: Research Press.

Barcus, F. E. (1983). *Images of life on children's television.* New York: Praeger.

Barrish, H. H., Saunders, M., & Wolf, M. M. (1969). Good behavior game: Effects of individual contingencies for group consequences on disruptive behavior in a classroom. *Journal of Applied Behavior Analysis, 2,* 119–124.

Baumrind, D. (1983). Socialization and instrumental competence in young children. In W. Damon (Ed.), *Social and personality development: Essays on the growth of the child* (pp. 121–138). New York: Norton.

Becker, W. C. (1971). *Parents are teachers: A child management program.* Champaign, IL: Research Press.

Berheide, C. W. (1984). Women's work in the home: Seems like old times. *Marriage and Family Review, 7,* 37–55.

Brueske, S. L., & Cuvo, A. J. (1985). Teaching home cleaning skills to a blind client. *Journal of Visual Impairment and Blindness, 79,* 18–23.

Christophersen, E. R., Arnold, C. M., Hill, D. W., & Quilitch, H. R. (1972). The home point system: Token reinforcement procedures for application by parents of children with behavior problems. *Journal of Applied Behavior Analysis, 5,* 485–497.

Cogle, F. L., & Tasker, G. E. (1982). Children and housework. *Family Relations, 31,* 395–399.

Cogle, F. L., Tasker, G. E., & Morton, D. G. (1982). Adolescent time use in household work. *Adolescence, 17,* 451–455.

Dinkmeyer, D., & McKay, G. D. (1973). *Raising a responsible child: Practical steps to successful family relationships.* New York: Simon and Schuster.

Dinkmeyer, D., & McKay, G. D. (1982). *The parent's handbook: Systematic training for effective parenting.* Circle Pines, MN: American Guidance Service.

Eyre, L., & Eyre, R. (1984). *Teaching children responsibility.* New York: Ballantine Books.

Gillet, P. (1979). Pointers for parents of the LD child. *Academic Therapy, 15,* 157–164.

Goldstein, B., & Oldham, J. (1979). *Children and work: A study of socialization.* New Brunswick, NJ: Transaction Books.

Hall, R. V., Axelrod, S., Tyler, L., Grief, E., Jones, F. C., & Robertson, R. (1972). Modification of behavior problems in the home with a parent as observer and experimenter. *Journal of Applied Behavior Analysis, 5,* 53–64.

Hansen, S. L., & Darling, C. A. (1985). Attitudes of adolescents toward division of labor in the home. *Adolescence, 20,* 61–72.

Harris, D. B., Clark, K. E., Rose, A. M., & Valasek, F. (1954). The relationship of children's home duties to an attitude of responsibility. *Child Development 25,* 29–33.

Hetherington, E. M., & Parke, R. D. (1986). *Child psychology: A contemporary viewpoint* (3 ed.). New York: McGraw-Hill.

Hoffman, L. W. (1979). Maternal employment: 1979. *American Psychologist, 34,* 859–865.

Hoffman, M. L. (1984). Parent discipline, moral internalization, and development of prosocial motivation. In E. Staub, D. Bar-Tal, J. Karylowski, & J. Reykowski (Eds.), *Development and maintenance of prosocial behavior: International perspectives on positive morality* (pp. 117–137). New York: Plenum.

Jenson, W. R., Neville, M., Sloane, H. N., & Morgan, D. (1982). Spinners and chartmoves: A contingency management system for school and home. *Child and Family Behavior Therapy, 4,* 81–85.

Keith, P. M., & Brubaker, T. H. (1980). Adolescent perceptions of household work: Expectations by sex, age and employment situation. *Adolescence, 15,* 171–182.

Lepper, M. R. (1983). Social-control processes and the internalization of social values: An attributional perspective. In E. T. Higgins, D. N. Ruble, & W. W. Hartup (Eds.), *Social cognition and social development: A sociocultural perspective* (pp. 294–330). New York: Cambridge University Press.

Light, H. K., Hertsgaard, D., & Martin, R. E. (1985). Farm children's work in the family. *Adolescence, 20,* 425–432.

Lynch, M. (1975). Sex-role stereotypes: Household work of children. *Human Ecology Forum, 5,* 22–26.

Midlarsky, E. (1984). Competence and helping: Notes toward a model. In E. Staub, D. Bar-Tal, J. Karylowski, & J. Reykowski (Eds.), *Development and maintenance of prosocial behavior: International perspectives on positive morality* (pp. 291–308). New York: Plenum.

Montemayor, R. (1984). Maternal employment and adolescents' relations with parents, siblings, and peers. *Journal of Youth and Adolescence, 13,* 543–557.

Nichols, A., & Berger, P. (1969). Guiding work of teenage girls. *Journal of Home Economics, 61,* 625–628.

Nyquist, L., Slivken, K., Spence, J. T., & Helmreich, R. L. (1985). Household responsibilities in middle-class couples: The contribution of demographic and personality variables. *Sex Roles, 12,* 15–34.

Phillips, E. L. (1968). Achievement Place: Token reinforcement procedures in a home-style rehabilitation setting for "pre-delinquent" boys. *Journal of Applied Behavior Analysis, 1,* 213–223.

Phillips, E. L., Phillips, E. A., Fixsen, D. L., & Wolf, M. M. (1971). Achievement Place: Modification of the behaviors of pre-delinquent boys within a token economy. *Journal of Applied Behavior Analysis, 4,* 45–59.

Pleck, J. H. (1985). *Working wives/Working husbands.* Beverly Hills: Sage.

Sanik, M. M., & Stafford, K. (1985).Adolescents' contribution to household production: Male and female differences. *Adolescence, 20,* 207–215.

Schwartz, L. A., & Markham, W. T. (1985). Sex stereotyping in children's toy advertisements. *Sex Roles, 12,* 157–170.

Sparrow, S. S., Balla, D. A., & Cicchetti, D. V. (1984). *Vineland adaptive behavior scales: Interview edition, survey form.* Circle Pines, MN: American Guidance Service.

Thrall, C. A. (1978). Who does what: Role stereotypy, children's work, and continuity between generations in the household division of labor. *Human Relations, 31,* 249–265.

U. S. Bureau of the Census. (1985).Household and Family Characteristics: March 1984 (Current Population Reports, Series P-20, No. 398). Washington, DC: U. S. Government Printing Office.

Weinraub, M., & Wolf, B. M. (1983). Effects of stress and social supports on mother–child interactions in single- and two-parent families. *Child Development, 54,* 1297–1311.

White, L. K., & Brinkerhoff, D. B. (1981). Children's work in the family: Its significance and meaning. *Journal of Marriage and the Family, 43,* 789–798.

Whiting, B. B., & Whiting, J. W. M. (1975). *Children of six cultures: A psycho-cultural analysis.* Cambridge, MA: Harvard University Press.

Wood, R., & Flynn, J. M. (1978). A self-evaluation token system *versus* an external evaluation token system alone in a residential setting with predelinquent youth. *Journal of Applied Behavioral Analysis, 11,* 503–512.

BIBLIOGRAPHY: PROFESSIONALS

Alvord, J. R. (1973). *Home token economy: An incentive program for children and their parents.* Champaign, IL: Research Press.

Parents are typically going to need the assistance of a professional to utilize this home-based token economy.Included in this program are a brief manual and contract sheets or charts that are quite complete. A unique feature of this program is the "child manages parent" section.

Blechman, E. A. (1985). *Solving child behavior problems at home and at school.* Champaign, IL: Research Press.

While written at a level that some parents may use alone, this book offers a wealth of practical ideas for the professional who is assisting parents with applied problems such as homework, temper tantrums, bedtime behavior, misbehavior away from home, and chores. Assigning and communicating chore requirements are discussed.

Sulzer-Azaroff, B., & Mayer, G. R. (1977). *Applying behavior-analysis procedures with children and youth.* New York: Holt, Rinehart and Winston.

This is one of the best professional resources on how to establish behavior programs for children. Behavior techniques are sometimes illustrated with household examples, and a family contracting program to modify chore behavior is presented (pp. 379–381).

BIBLIOGRAPHY: PARENTS

Becker, W. C. (1971). *Parents are teachers: A child management program.* Champaign, IL: Research Press.

Still one of the best books for introducing parents to behavioral techniques. It presents the concepts and language of behavioral techniques while using very vivid case illustrations. The book is not specific to chores, but the techniques can easily be adapted.

Eyre, L., & Eyre, R. (1984). *Teaching children responsibility.* New York: Ballantine Books.

An inexpensive book designed for parents that addresses a variety of responsibility issues including work. Several clever suggestions are offered for illustrating the importance of chores and encouraging successful completion of assigned work.

BIBLIOGRAPHY: CHILDREN

Berry, J. W. (1982). *Let's talk about being lazy.* Newark, NJ: Peter Pan Industries.
Offers suggestions to children on how to complete chores and attempts to help children understand the effect of their helpful or lazy behavior on others. If parents read to the child, it could be used at ages 3 or 4.

Wilt, J. (1979). *A kid's guide to managing money: A children's book about money management.* Waco, TX: Word.
Since allowance is a related issue, this book could be helpful even though it doesn't directly address chores. A very complete book that discusses why money is needed, how to obtain money, and the spending, donating, and saving of money. The book would be most appropriate for children of elementary school age.

Children and Humor

Frank J. Prerost
Western Illinois University

BACKGROUND

Every day, in any school yard during a recess break, children can be seen and heard sharing laughter. Humor is one of the most common experiences children observe or enter into each day. Laughing, smiling, joking, and grinning, most children confront humor before, during, or after the school day. Considering the prevalence of humor responses among children, laughter and its relatives are poorly understood by parents, teachers, and school psychologists. Everyone enjoys seeing children have fun as they laugh and play, but humor can be perceived as a problem. What teacher enjoys the class clown who consistently disrupts the educational climate with jokes and laughter? What parent has not been upset by a "dirty" joke overheard being told by a young child? Is the child who laughs at the misfortunes of others sharing a healthy attitude toward life? Should a child be laughing at aggressive cartoons and jokes? How many times have adults been frustrated in attempts at serious conversation with children or adolescents by constant joking or flippant remarks?

Humor, being such a common response, becomes a component in many problem behaviors and disorders. When gathering information about a child or adolescent, questions concerning humor and its responses often appear. Inappropriate laughter, hostile joking, lack of a sense of humor, and forced laughter frequently appear as part of the symptomology among students referred to the school psychologist. Yet the professional typically lacks formal education in the psychology of humor. What the normal course of development of humor responses is and how its development is influenced by various factors remain unanswered in most courses on child and adolescent development. Issues surrounding the relationship between humor and personal adjustment in childhood and adolescence are omitted in the major texts currently used for undergraduate and graduate instruction. These shortcomings can deprive the school psychologist of an additional useful tool in the diagnostic and remedial process. Understanding an individual's sense of humor allows the school psychologist to garner information relevant to a number of developmental and adjustment issues.

It is the purpose of this chapter to present the basic information required to make purposeful decisions about humor responses among children and adolescents. The significant patterns of development of the sense of humor are discussed and the normal changes to be expected are illustrated. Such normative data can be used to assess the humor exhibited by a child and allay the fears parents often have about scatological (i.e., focusing on excrement or urination) or sexual humor. It is also true that deficits in the sense of humor do appear in some children, who then do not benefit from the social exchange inherent in humor and may develop inhibited and/or restrictive lifestyles. This chapter shows the mechanisms of the humor response and how to identify problem areas that cause excessive or inhibited humor responsiveness. The process of laughter entails numerous factors that can be observed and assessed. A model for reviewing the possible problem areas is included. Finally, humor can be used by the school psychologist during interaction with students in individual sessions —a number of methods can be used to promote humor for therapeutic or diagnostic purposes. The individual session with a school psychologist can be a stressful event for a child; the child or adolescent may come to the session feeling forced to attend and resenting the adults involved. Hence, tension, resistance, and anger can cloud the session and lead to limited initial success with the child. This author has found humor to be an effective method to alleviate anxiety and resentment during the crucial initial sessions with a client. Skill in recognizing the opportunities for humor during individual or group sessions can be facilitated through use of specific laughter-inducing factors that are described below.

DEVELOPMENT

Stages of Humor

Researchers have demonstrated that a sense of humor is related to numerous normative developmental changes during childhood and adolescence, including cognition (McGhee, 1980), language (Shultz & Robillard, 1980), sex roles (Prerost, 1983), sexuality in adolescence (Prerost, 1984), and social interaction (Foot, Chapman, & Smith, 1977).

The underlying mechanism in the development of a sense of humor appears to be the ability to recognize incongruity in the world. Children normally progress through four stages of humor, beginning around 2 years of age, that are tied to their level of cognitive development. Once a child can represent objects with internal images, the first stage of humor is attained. Incongruous *actions* in relation to physical objects provoke laughter in a child. Pleasure is derived from creating in fantasy play a set of conditions known to be incongruous with reality, e.g., using a banana to write on a piece of paper (Piaget, 1962). Stage 2 humor manifests itself when the child uses *words* to create incongruities. Any inconsistency between verbal label, the real object, and the image combine to supply the source of humor. The most common type of Stage 2 humor involves giving names to objects or events that are known to be incorrect. Some children will laugh continually while using every word but the correct one to name a known object. Teachers have often been frustrated by this playful frame of mind in young children. Typically, children lose interest in this form of humor when they leave the preschool years. Parents and preschool teachers typically object to this name-changing game and view it as childish. But if children are punished for this tendency toward fantasy play, they may avoid such games and suffer later deficits in humor and/or fantasy life. Freedom to develop a playful frame of mind appears to encourage cognitive development during childhood (Fein, 1975).

The next stage in the development of a sense of humor involves *conceptual* incongruity. Stage 3 is more complex than the preceding stage of humor and involves understanding the classes of objects or events that have key defining characteristics. Stage 3 jokes center around the violation of the characteristics defining an object of a particular class. A picture of a pink elephant dressed in sneakers elicits a laugh. The Stage 2 child finds humor from calling the elephant in such a picture a horse. In the Stage 3 level of development, the child is still usually visually oriented. Cartoons produce the greatest humor when they violate a child's schema for an object. When working with a child in the late preschool or early elementary stage, attempts at humor benefit from the use of visual props. Many companies manufacture useful articles, such as a "rubber" ball that does not bounce, that can be used when working with this age group.

Shultz and Robillard (1980) have shown how a new form of language develops during stage three. Repetitious rhyming of words and the creation of nonsense words are common sources of humor. When a child begins with a common word and continues to slightly alter its sound with each repetition, it is the sound change that is humorous for the child. The generation of nonsense words is funny, simply because they do not sound like any word the child has ever heard before. Parents and teachers may interpret such behavior as regressive, worrying that their child is demonstrating poorer linguistic skills than they have already achieved. When such behavior is age-appropriate (ages 3–7), assurances need to be given to concerned persons that it is a positive sign of growth, not regression.

Logic begins to enter the humor equation as the child moves to Stage 4. This stage of humor is achieved by the acquisition of cognitive abilities referred to by Piaget as concrete operational thinking. Children at the beginning of elementary school can be cruel in their humor by laughing directly at another person's problem or unusual condition simply because it does not occur to them that they may be hurting someone's feelings. Having obtained cognitive capacity for operational thinking, older children are able to take another person's point of view; in consequence they have the capacity not to laugh directly at another person's shortcomings or oddities.

Stage 4 humor involves the understanding of *multiple meanings* in words, that two or more meanings are applicable to a key word in a joke. By the age of 7, the average child is more able to detect linguistic ambiguity (Shultz & Hoube, 1974) and able to enjoy riddles or puns. The more abstract or complex the ambiguities in the riddle, the older the child must be to comprehend and enjoy the joke. The general characteristics of Stage 4 humor remain into adulthood. Adolescents appear to favor anecdotes and spontaneous wit rather than memorized jokes. Puns are viewed with disdain among adolescents because of the simplistic nature of the play on words. It is during the late childhood and early adolescent periods that humor preferences begin to be firmly established and reveal the degree to which traditional sex roles are adopted (Prerost, 1984). Following Stage 4 humor, individual patterns of preference and the factors associated with them are more dominant than age or cognitive development effects.

Preschool Humor

During the preschool period, laughter is closely tied to play activities. Many times the enjoyment and excitement of play elicit laughter in the absence of any other humor-producing stimulus. Laughter is a highly contagious behavior at this age, and children in groups may break into laughter as a spontaneous manifestation of pleasure. Dangerous or frightening actions also produce laughter as a mechanism to reduce tension and achieve a sense of mastery.

Sherman (1975) has coined the term "group glee" to describe the humor spontaneously generated by children during play or challenging activities. Parents or teachers need not be concerned by the exaggerated laughter shown at this age when children play in groups.

The verbal humor of the preschool child centers on the misnaming of objects, simple riddles, and guessing games. Children experiencing normal development use outrageous names, juxtapose improbable elements, and invent unlikely events on a regular basis. Children particularly enjoy it when adults enter into the fun by giving silly answers to riddles and inventing unusual situations. The school psychologist can consider such behavior as good rapport-building devices.

Of particular concern to many parents during this period is the appearance of scatological humor. The content of the jokes depends on the child's natural concerns at the time and on the particular prohibitions or concerns expressed by parents. Jokes concerned with elimination are popular at this age because of the usual taboos related to defecation. When sexual curiosities emerge, words associated with this area become sources of enjoyment. This joking allows the child to express curiosity and derive pleasure from expressing the forbidden idea. Parents need to exhibit tolerance during this period and respond to the child with understanding. Once the novelty has waned, the humor diminishes.

Elementary School Humor

First or second grade is the usual point of transition away from the humor that has dominated the preschool years. Simple violation of logic in behavior and decision making begin to be funny. One of the important outcomes of the newly developed cognitive capacities at this transitional period concerns moral thinking. Moral judgments are closely related to a child's reaction to certain cartoons or jokes, because many have themes about bad people or evil forces. According to Piaget, after age 8 years children consider the intention of the perpetrator of an act before moral judgments are made. *Unintentional* actions causing highly damaging outcomes are humorous to older children, whereas the preschool individual does not discriminate in respect to intention. For example, in the preschool years a person purposely smashing a tray of dishes at a cafeteria is funny, but the 8-year-old sees humor only if the dishes are broken as a result of accidental tripping.

In the elementary years, the *joke facade* makes its appearance. In order to avoid social disapproval of the expression of sexual and aggressive impulses, children learn to disguise these impulses in jokes. Witty remarks directed toward someone can be a socially accepted way to release hostility toward the person without fearing retaliation. Using the joke facade, aggressive and/or sexual messages can be expressed publicly without major social disapproval or rejection. "I was only kidding." Skill in using the joke facade continues to evolve through adolescence and into adulthood. Theorists agree that its use is not a sign for alarm and only becomes a problem when used in excess or if the underlying intent is repeatedly poorly disguised.

Adolescent Humor

The adolescent with advancing cognitive development enjoys humor derived from multiple meanings and innuendo. The mental activity associated with the comprehension of the subtle meaning of words and situations produces enjoyment and laughter. Often a joke facade is constructed to conceal the true purpose of the joke teller. Story telling is often elaborate and involved as it leads to the unexpected punchline. Trying to figure out the story's conclusion is enjoyment in itself. Thus, the adolescent's newly developing skills in abstraction show in the construction and appreciation of humor.

Yet, adolescent humor has a distinct divergent quality. Many jokes centering on sex, physical appearance, aggression, and relationships are crude and blunt. When content reflects closely the worries and impulses of the developing adolescent, humor can become direct and lack an adequately constructed joke facade. In the social exchange of humor between peers, the adolescent attempts to use humor as a means to signal mastery over troubling concerns and impulses. A sense of superiority is achieved by the joke teller over the audience and the content expressed in the joke. Sexuality is flaunted in humor among adolescents without a joke facade in order to demonstrate mastery and superiority. Put-downs in the area of sex, appearance, and capabilities are commonly exchanged between adolescents. Once the teen is able to achieve a sense of competence and satisfaction with his or her own sexuality, the direct sexual humor with hostile thrust disappears (Prerost, 1983).

The observer who is sensitive to the reasons for humor in adolescence can gain insights into the needs and concerns of individuals by listening closely to humor content.

PUTTING CHILDREN'S HUMOR IN PERSPECTIVE

Gender Differences

When considering the appropriateness of a child's humor for his or her age, some gender differences need to be considered. Preschool boys and girls do not significantly differ in their verbal humor. At around the age of 6, gender differences begin to emerge toward a solidification of traditional patterns found in adulthood. At the start of elementary school, boys demonstrate more silly rhyming and use of "dirty" words than girls. The boys become preoccupied with a lot of joke-telling sessions and attempts at humor. Clowning, acting foolish, and various physical actions to elicit humor are traditionally attempted by boys to a greater extent than by girls. Boys initiate humor in the presence of either sex, which possibly reflects society's traditional acceptance of aggressive male behavior. The boys' enhanced experience with humor appears to increase their skill at creating humor (McGhee, 1974).

A traditional pattern has been identified, beginning in childhood in the preferences of males and females as to humor content. Sexual and aggressive jokes or cartoons have been the domain of males. They have been socially expected to be the joke tellers and initiate humorous situations. Also starting in childhood, females have learned to be the reactors to jokes, laughing at the stories of others. Self-disparagement was the common theme for female humor, a perfect example being Joan Rivers' comments about herself. This traditional divergence in humor content preferences among males and females has been documented for decades. Yet, Prerost (1984) has demonstrated that these patterns have disappeared among adolescents as traditional sex role restraints diminished. Sex role pressures in childhood can be recognized through the differential preferences of boys and girls.

The school psychologist can gain information on sex role learning among individual school-age boys and girls and the pressures on the children by reviewing their humor content preferences.

Adjustment Concerns

Theorists have long associated a good sense of

humor with sound emotional development. As was mentioned above, jokes can serve as safe releases for the impulses of sex and aggression. Children's and adolescents' most intense responses are often reserved for sexual and aggressive humor. The child or adolescent who demonstrates a general disdain for such humor is losing an opportunity of expression of natural tendencies. The inhibited client may benefit from the encouragement of developing humor as an outlet.

Children use jokes to express areas of concern in their lives. The school psychologist needs a sensitive ear to the joking comments of children and adolescents. The professional must search for repetitions of content and theme. The underlying sources of stress and anxieties confronting the client can emerge through review of jokes or cartoon preferences. Yorukoglu (1974) specifically questioned children abut their favorite jokes. In the jokes, conflicts emerge as the child attempts to minimize distress. Children without the capacity to find humor in distress are considered to be less well adjusted. Joking about one's shortcomings demonstrates a certain level of acceptance and willingness to compensate or cope with them.

Children's "gallows" humor usually has the function of diminishing worry and anxiety. Following large-scale disasters, such as floods, earthquakes, famines, nuclear reactor accidents and the shuttle explosion, children are quick to produce a wide variety of "sick" jokes about them. The jokes can upset adults and worry parents. Yet, the humor serves a useful function for the child. Anxiety produced by the disaster can be reduced in a safe manner through laughter. Disasters stimulate thoughts of personal mortality and/or concerns about the loss of loved ones. The anxiety can be relieved by "sick" jokes and the laughter they promote. Enjoyment of disaster jokes instills some sense of mastery and control over the unknown and the powerful forces of nature.

Adolescents also use "sick" jokes to express their independence. Anxiety associated with achieving separateness from parents is expressed in humor found unacceptable by society. When adolescents enjoy a joke evaluated by adults as "sick" or "disgusting," they demonstrate freedom while removing, to some degree, worries and anxiety.

The joking behavior described above may not be pleasant for adult listeners, but the humor serves a useful function in the overall development of the child and adolescent. Adults need to deal with the underlying anxieties producing the humor, rather than be overly concerned about the content.

Humor Production

Although a number of theories exist that attempt to explain humor development, certain common elements can be conflated to produce a model explaining responses to humor. The model presented in Table 1 can be used to assess the source of psychological problems in the sense of humor of a client and suggest strategies for using humor productively in remedial sessions.

Review of the factors outlined in Table 1 can assist the professional in analysis of the humor responses exhibited by both children and adolescents. The factors presented interact in producing specific responses to humor. Thus, a child's immediate level of anxiety, together with some personal conflict, can produce a peculiar form of excessive laughter in one setting and not another. The professional, when working with a child, needs to identify the regularities and irregularities in the individual's pattern of humor. The occurrence of unusual responses to humor can then be traced to processing factors in the response equation. For example, improvements in the behavior of the class clown may be accomplished by changing the student's work setting, or varying the cognitive challenge of activities, or finding less disruptive outlets for certain of the child's physiological states. Changes in the humor responses can then be used as a measure of the intervention's success.

Although personality is listed as component of the humor response model, consistent information from research is not readily available. Frequently cited is the work of Janus (1975), who examined the lives of famous comics. Humor development in the elementary years was fostered by exposure to tough and demanding situations in the home. Apparently, these children's expression of so much humor in their school years was a coping mechanism. The most striking aspects of their high levels of joking and clowning were physical and verbal aggressiveness. Expression of humor was also found to be associated with attempts to seek attention, affection, and emotional support. These children may have been uncertain about their parents' emotional commitment. It is safe to conclude that the home environment and how it has affected a child's personality growth should be addressed by the professional.

ALTERNATIVE ACTIONS

As discussed above, a healthy sense of humor can assist in facilitating social exchange, relieving tensions, and instilling a sense of mastery. Encouraging a good sense of humor in clients can involve extinguishing some maladaptive expressions of humor, removing underlying personal conflicts, or modifying environmental or familial conditions. Using the model for humor responses as a guideline, the school psychologist can make an assessment and strategy for intervention and then can consider employing a variety of responses that encourage humor during interaction with the child. When dealing directly with a child, certain statements and events can generate a humor response. The school psychologist can assist the inhibited or shy child in using humor as a coping mechanism; the attention-seeking aggressive child can be shown appropriate forms for expression of humor. Listed in Table 2 are a number of techniques that can promote beneficial humor during individual or group sessions with children or adolescents. Besides the rapport-building value of these techniques, they help in the process of therapeutic change.

In using humor during sessions with children or adolescents, it is important not to use sarcasm. Comments heard as criticism are detrimental to the professional relationship and care must be taken when exag-

TABLE 1
Model Summarizing Factors in the Humor Response

Factors to Consider: Potentially Humorous Stimulus Situations	Intervening Factors: Processing of Stimuli	Responses: Humor Outcomes
1. Content aggressive sexual neutral	1. Mental activity cognitive capabilities resolution of incongruity	1. Laughter appropriate excessive
2. Form or structure incongruity complexity presentation cognitive	2. Psychodynamic factors personal conflicts impulse expression inhibitions	2. Smiling/enjoyment
3. Novelty surprise	3. Physiological state anxiety/fear hostility	3. Mood changes pleasure/euphoria hostility
	4. Social context setting social exchange	4. Physiological changes arousal relief of tension
	5. Personality/gender/age	5. Verbal reactions joking criticism

TABLE 2
Techniques for Producing Humor

Technique	Procedure
Exaggeration	Overstate the obvious in regard to size, proportions, numbers, feelings, or facts. Understating the apparent is also useful. Preschool and early elementary students respond favorably.
Novelty	Rather than ignoring outside intrusions or events during an individual session, comment on it in an unusual fashion. Do not be afraid to think differently about an event.
Incongruity	Try to link two or more incompatible ideas, emotions, or objects. Remember to consider the child's cognitive level of development. Words with double meanings and puns are a good beginning in learning this technique. Word play through songs, quotes, or rhymes can be practiced.
Story-telling	Construct stories that may be true to life, fairy tales or allegories to illustrate important topics to the client. Include humorous passages in them. Adolescents often respond well to metaphorical constructions as they do not feel lectured-to. Or generate stories on the "human condition" and its problem.
Bodily actions	Illustrate points with excessive body animation. Show feeling and emotion in this way while joking about it, openly to the child. Remember, for young children most humor coincides with physical activity.

gerations or incongruities are employed. Humor with children should have the following characteristics. They must be based on acceptance and centered around the child's needs and must strengthen, reveal, alleviate, and lubricate; they must also be corrective and educational. If the humor encourages a questioning of self-worth, implies stupidity, stigmatizes, has a detrimental quality, or retaliates, then its use by the professional must be seriously questioned.

Trying to use humor during sessions with clients does not involve mere joke telling. The professional must be flexible and sensitive to situations appropriate for humor. Professionals are often uneasy during initial attempts at generating humor. Experience and self-confidence in one's professional capabilities smoothes the way for the beneficial introduction of humor-inducing remarks and procedures.

SUMMARY

Understanding the developmental aspects of the sense of humor provides the school psychologist with added insight into the psychological functioning of children and adolescents. The laughter and humor preferences appropriate for individuals at a particular age follow predictable developmental lines. Knowing the role of such variables as cognitive growth, impulse control, and moral reasoning in the developing humor response, the school psychologist can assist parents and teachers in dealing with frustrating and demanding childhood problems. Used as a gauge of psychological adjustment and a path into the source of problems, jokes reveal much to the trained professional. It is crucial to listen carefully to children's humor. Too often attention is focused on removing the behavior because it may be disruptive in the educational setting. Listen for the message conveyed and look at the timing and for the target of the humorous remark. Close attention to the content, time, and place of the laughter may reveal a child's emotional and cognitive life. Listening and recording the humor responses found among the children you serve may assist in enhancing service to them.

Seek connections among the various humor responses exhibited by an individual child. Compare how the child's responses vary from age-specific norms, and look for explanations for such differences, based upon the patterns of growth typical for humor responses. Some differences may be benign, for example, the accelerated cognitive growth in one child may produce humor that seems advanced compared to that exhibited by same-age peers. Once the professional can make educated judgments concerning the appropriateness of a particular child's humor, meaningful intervention strategies can be developed to reinstate a satisfying, healthy sense of humor.

Finally, the professional must be ready to accept that some of the humor shown by children and adolescents will be objectionable and cruel-sounding to adults. This is part of the normative developmental process. The shock the humor may elicit among adults is part of the reason for its use. Parents and those working with these age groups can benefit from reassurances of normality from professionals. The school psychologist can help parents deal with objectionable humor by making them aware of the underlying developmental issues present. As parents show sensitivity to the normal stresses of development, the degree of offensive humor can be modified.

REFERENCES

Fein, G. A. (1975). A transformational analysis of pretending. *Developmental Psychology, 11,* 291–296.

Foot, H. C., Chapman, A. J., & Smith, J. R. (1977). Friendship and social responsiveness in boys and girls. *Journal of Personality and Social Psychology, 35,* 401–411.

Janus, S. S. (1975). The great comedians: Personality and other factors. *American Journal of Psychoanalysis, 35,* 169–174.

McGhee, P. E. (1974). Cognitive mastery and children's humor. *Psychological Bulletin, 81,* 721–730.

McGhee, P. E. (1980). Development of the sense of humor in childhood: A longitudinal study. In P. E. McGhee & A. J. Chapman (Eds.), *Children's humour.* Chichester, England: Wiley.

Piaget, J. (1962). *Play, dreams, and imitation in childhood.* New York: Norton.

Prerost, F. J. (1983). Changing patterns in the response to humorous sexual stimuli: Sex roles and expression of sexuality. *Social Behavior and Personality: An International Journal, 11,* 23–28.

Prerost, F. J. (1984). A decade of change in humor appreciation among males and females: A relaxation of social and sex role restraints. In L. Mintz (Ed.), *Third International Conference on Humor Conference Book.* Washington, DC: American Humor Studies Association.

Sherman, L. W. (1975). An ecological study of glee in small groups of preschool children. *Child Development, 46,* 53–61.

Shultz, T. R., & Horibe, F. (1974). Development of the appreciation of verbal jokes. *Developmental Psychology, 10,* 13–20.

Shultz, T. R., & Robillard, J. (1984). The development of linguistic humor in children: Incongruity through rule violation. In P. E. McGhee and A. Chapman (Eds.), *Children's humour.* Chichester, England: Wiley.

Yorukoglu, A. (1974). Children's favorite jokes and their relation to emotional conflicts. *Journal of Child Psychiatry, 13,* 677–690.

BIBLIOGRAPHY: PROFESSIONALS

Chapman, A. J., & Foot, H. C. (1977). *It's a funny thing, humour.* Oxford: Pergamon.
This book is a series of brief articles on a wide range of topics associated with the psychology of humor. It is a good resource volume that provides significant information on a subject in a brief and readable format. Contributors to the volume address many topics relevant to school psychology.

Fisher, S., & Fisher, R. L. (1981). *Pretend the world is funny and forever: A psychological analysis of comedians, clowns, and actors.* Hillsdale: Erlbaum.
Provides details on the history and development of individuals professionally involved with humor. Insights into early childhood factors influencing development are vividly portrayed. Some of the examples may remind professionals of students they have worked with professionally.

McGhee, P. E., & Duffey, N. W. (1983). Racial–ethnic differences in the onset of children's appreciation of humor victimizing different racial–ethnic groups. *Journal of Cross Cultural Psychology, 14,* 29–40.
The ethnic joke used to make fun of a particular group is one of the most common humor forms found among children and adolescents. This article discusses the appearance of this joke form and the precursors to it. A valuable article to assist in understanding this continuing phenomena.

Prerost, F. J. (1984). Evaluating the systematic use of humor in psychotherapy with adolescents. *Journal of Adolescence, 7,* 267–276.
This is one of the few articles available that demonstrates the effectiveness of employing humor procedures therapeutically. The article describes a method of systematically inducing humor during psychotherapy. A good article demonstrating the positive benefits of humor production.

Zillmann, D., & Bryant, J. (1983). Uses and effects of humor in educational ventures. In P. E. McGhee & J. H. Goldstein (Eds.), *Handbook of Humor Research* (Vol. II) New York: Springer-Verlag.
This is a review of the previous attempts at enhancing the learning environment with humor. Numerous investigators have varied the presentation of material with humor searching for positive effects. Although written in a dry scientific fashion, the article provides useful information that can serve as a resource when consulting with teachers.

BIBLIOGRAPHY: PARENTS

Goodman, J. (1983). How to get more "smileage" out of your life: Making sense of humor, then serving it. In P. C. McGhee & J. H. Goldstein (Eds.), *Handbook of Humor Research* (Vol. 2). New York: Springer-Verlag.
This article discusses in lay terms the purposes of encouraging a healthy sense of humor in one's life. It includes many amusing anecdotes to illustrate its points of view. The chapter is an excellent resource for parents who may need some humor in their lives and is written in an interesting style.

Meryman, R. (1978, February). Carol Burnett's own story. *McCall's.*
Parents should enjoy this report on the early development of Ms. Burnett's sense of humor. Numerous aspects of her experience reflect on the major components of the development of a healthy sense of humor. Since many parents are familiar with this celebrity, they should find the article particularly intriguing.

Mindess, H. (1971). *Laughter and liberation.* Los Angeles: Nash.
This is an excellent book discussing the need for children and adolescents to develop a healthy sense of humor. The author describes those familial and environmental conditions that are detrimental to humor's development. Parents can gain insights into the value of humorous expression in childhood and adolescence through reading of this book.

Schwartz, T. (1978, April 3). Comedy's new face. *Newsweek,* pp. 60–71.
Appropriate for the general public as it discusses the development of humor among different current comedians. Facets of their upbringing and how they influenced their humor are discussed. A good article when trying to explain to parents some of the causes for "clowning" in class and other disruptive behaviors.

Singer, J. L. (1973). *The child's world of make believe.* New York: Academic.
Many parents are concerned about their child's fantasy life and potential for creativity. This is an excellent book for parents to learn about the significance of make-believe in a child's early development. The author shows how humor can promote creativity among children and enhance cognitive development.

Children and Hyperactivity

Betty P. Robertson
Hot Springs County School District, Thermopolis, Wyoming

BACKGROUND

Hyperactivity is defined as excessive motor activity accompanied by impulsivity, distractibility, and short attention span. The disorder has also been labeled hyperkinesis and minimal brain dysfunction, but more recently it has been subsumed under the classification attention deficit disorder which may or may not include physical hyperactivity. Regardless of the label used, the hyperactive student is one whom all school psychologists and teachers encounter at some point during their careers. Hyperactive students seriously disrupt the educational process for themselves and at the same time significantly disrupt the ongoing instruction of the other students in the classroom. Academic achievement usually falls below ability level (Lambert & Sandoval, 1980) and learning disabilities frequently occur (Safer & Allen, 1976).

Although the incidence of hyperactivity is accepted to be 4–5% (Kerasotes & Walker, 1981), it accounts for 30–40% of the referrals to child guidance clinics (Safer & Allen, 1976). Perhaps no behavioral disorder is more frustrating to school psychologists as to both assessment and management. Referred students cannot be regarded as a homogenous group since individual evaluation reveals a diverse group of disorders (Kenny et al., 1971).

Some students may be anxious, attention-seeking, or distressed whereas others may be inadequately socialized and have poor impulse control. Still others may evidence neurological pathology or serious emotional disturbance. Finally, some students are incorrectly viewed as hyperactive by adults with unrealistic notions of age-appropriate activity levels. Research has suggested the possibility of several different types of hyperactivity but as of the present, a clear, definitive description and delineation of such categories in the literature has not evolved (Kerasotes & Walker, 1981). The assessment of hyperactive students, therefore,varies significantly from one school psychologist to another, depending upon individual degree of knowledge and specific philosophical orientation.

In the interest of uniformity and consistency, it would appear feasible for the practical purposes of the school psychologist to roughly sort hyperactive students into three discrete groups on the basis of distinguishable behavioral characteristics and differential etiological factors: neurological hyperactivity, hyperactivity related to anxiety, and unsocialized hyperactivity. The distinct characteristics and etiology of each category indicates different recommendations in regard to medical, classroom, and home management.

DEVELOPMENT

Normal Development

Most children enter school with the ability to sit quietly, listen attentively, and comply adequately with teachers' requests. But students who are out of their seats, wriggly, inattentive, and distractible are unable to participate in or benefit from the educational process. For them learning is haphazard, sketchy, and sporadic and they may be unable to comply appropriately with situational demands (Cantwell, 1975). In addition, hyperactive students are frequently at risk for emotional, academic, and social problems in adolescence (Whalen & Henker, 1980). Pathological hyperactivity, however, needs to be differentiated from age-appropriate activity levels. It is possible, after all, for students to have higher than average activity levels and nonetheless fall within the average or normal range. Perhaps the single most decisive discriminating factor is the degree to which the activity level inhibits or interferes with the student's learning. Students who jiggle their legs while adequately concentrating on reading exercises or math problems are different in degree from students who are so active that they cannot sufficiently attend to academic work.

Types of Hyperactivity

Neurological Hyperactivity. Neurological hyperactivity results from dysfunctions of the central nervous system (CNS) although such dysfunctions may be too minimal to be detected by electroencephalograms. CNS dysfunctions may be of genetic origin or may be due to prenatal, perinatal, and postnatal complications. Common prenatal causes of neurological hyperactivity are bleeding during pregnancy, toxemia, trauma, or illness of the mother that causes delayed maturation. Birth and neonatal complications may involve anoxia (lack of oxygen after delivery), cerebral trauma from the use of forceps, prematurity, jaundice, or cerebral hemorrhage. Among the more common postnatal causes are encephalitis, meningitis, dehydration, cerebral tumors, degenerative disorders, and trauma. Since the range of neurological indicators is diverse, it is necessary to obtain a comprehensive developmental history from the parents as part of the assessment process.

As to behavior, the neurologically hyperactive child is usually described as having a high activity level from birth. Sleeping problems in the early years are frequent; many of these children establish a pattern of going to bed late, getting up early, and having difficulty with napping in the daytime. The constancy of the high activity level is characteristic not only throughout the student's day but also over the years. There may be a slightly lower activity level in one-to-one situations, however, in contrast with group situations, because of the decrease in environmental stimuli. In the classroom, the neurologically hyperactive student typically is almost constantly fidgety, inattentive, and distractible regardless of the type of activity in progress and regardless of the time of day.

Anxious Hyperactivity. The anxious hyperactive student, by contrast, usually has a developmental and social history that is devoid of neurological indicators and characteristic of normal development prior to an identifiable stressful event or situation. Developmental milestones are achieved at normal ages and there are no parental concerns with hyperactivity prior to the life stress. The state of anxiety can be sparked by such specific life events as divorce, parents' marital stress, a death in the family, illness, sexual abuse, physical abuse, and real or imagined fears. Perhaps the most distinguishing characteristic, however, is the parents' report of a normal activity level prior to the specific event precipitating the anxiety.

In the classroom, the anxiously hyperactive student behaves qualitatively differently from the neurologically hyperactive child. There is a variability in the activity level, which ranges from stillness to hyperactivity. There is greater activity and impulsivity in emotional-laden or unstructured situations, during which the student becomes preoccupied with the life stress situation. In more structured or emotionally neutral activities, the student often is temporarily weaned from the anxious preoccupation by immersion in an absorbing classroom function.

Unsocialized Hyperactivity. The unsocialized hyperactive student has an equally characteristic profile. As in the case of the anxiously hyperactive student, the developmental history reveals an absence of neurological indicators, and no hyperactivity is reported during the years prior to the beginning of school. However, unlike the anxiously hyperactive child who demonstrates an increased activity level with the onset of a specific life stress, the unsocialized student evidences hyperactivity at the beginning of formal schooling. The unsocialized hyperactivity is frequently given the label of *immaturity* by the teacher, who is repeatedly frustrated in attempts to have the student conform to classroom rules and limits, the most basic of which are to sit quietly, pay attention, and comply with the teacher's requests.

Interviews with the parents of unsocialized hyperactives indicate a similar disregard on the part of these children for rules and limits at home. They frequently report difficulties with getting their children to mind from a very early age (2 or 3 years) and the most typical comment made is "We've tried everything and nothing works." An assessment of the parenting styles often indicates a lack of or faulty social training within the family and significant inconsistency in parenting. In a two-parent family, a rigid, authoritarian parent may share a disciplinary role with a permissive parent. In a single-parent family, the parent may vacillate between firmness and permissiveness. Such inconsistency subsequently leads to serious problems for the child in adequately internalizing a stable set of rules and limits by which to govern behavior. The child usually develops a chameleon-like pattern of following the mother's rules when with the mother, the father's rules when with the father, and perhaps a third set of rules when with the teacher. None of the sets of rules of any one adult, however, are complied with sufficiently to accomplish adequate socialization.

In the classroom, the unsocialized hyperactive student has a fluctuating, variable activity level and attention span. If the activity is interesting to the student, it may be sustained for as long as 45–60 min with minimal fidgeting or distractibility. When the task is disliked or difficult, however, the student may wiggle and squirm, "forget" to stay in his seat, interrupt with irrelevant questions, and passively or openly fail to comply with the teacher's instructions to complete assignments satisfactorily.

PUTTING CHILDREN'S HYPERACTIVITY IN PERSPECTIVE

The school psychologist's assessment of hyperactivity is, of necessity, multifaceted. A variety of procedures are utilized and the student's parents as well as the teachers must be closely involved in the evaluation.

Development and Social History

A complete developmental and social history should be obtained from the parents. Special attention should be allocated to prenatal and postnatal factors, developmental milestones, early behavioral concerns, sleeping problems, and the student's overall compliance with rules and limits. A detailed history of activity level from the early years is needed as well as information about the student's current emotional and social functioning. An informal assessment of the parents' child-rearing skills and practices will also help the school psychologist begin to differentiate between the neurologically hyperactive and the unsocialized student. To assist in the identification of the anxiously hyperactive student, information should also be obtained about past and present life stresses that may be generating anxiety.

Interviews With Teachers

A vital component of the evaluation process consists of interviews with present and past teachers. Information should be obtained about the constancy or variability of the hyperactivity, length of attention span, and degree of distractibility. It is also frequently helpful to identify the teachers' emotional responses to the student. Neurologically hyperactive student typically engender feelings of frustration and impotence on the part of their teachers. Anxiously hyperactive students, by contrast, generate a sympathetic response, whereas unsocialized students invariably elicit feelings of anger.

It should be emphasized that experienced teachers are often able to differentiate students with the various types of hyperactivity on their own as a result of their extensive experience with such students. Since there is the probability of having one hyperactive student in the classroom per year, it is easy to see how a seasoned teacher who has encountered 10 such students in 10 years can become adept at identification of types of hyperactive disorders.

Teacher/Parent Rating Scales

In addition to information from the parent and teacher interviews, behavior rating scales are able to provide additional data about the student. Among the most widely used scales are the Teacher Rating Scale (Conners, 1969), the Parent Symptom Questionnaire (Goyette, Conners, & Ulrich, 1978), the Child Behavior Check List (Achenbach, 1982), the Walker Problem Identification Checklist (Walker, 1976), the Personality Inventory for Children (Wirt, Lacher, Klinedinst, & Seat, 1984), the School Behavior Checklist (Miller, 1977), and the Werry–Weiss–Peters Activity Rating Scale (Werry, 1968). The Conner scales, in particular, provide some discrimination among conduct problems, learning problems, psychosomatic disorders, impulsive–hyperactive problems, and anxiety disorders.

Classroom Observations

Several short observation periods (15–20 min) extended over several days will yield more differential information for assessment than one longer (40–60 min) observation. Of particular importance is the constancy versus the variability of the hyperactivity, in addition to an assessment of the length of the attention span and the degree of distractibility. Structured as well as unstructured observations allow the school psychologist or teacher to evaluate on–task versus off-task behavior and thus assess the extent of the effect on learning activities in the classroom.

Psychological Testing

Safer and Allen (1976) reported that 70–80% of hyperactive students have learning disabilities. In view of this fact, academic and intellectual evaluations are necessary to identify possible learning problems. The neurologically hyperactive student, in particular, may have areas of cognitive deficit that are contributing to poor academic performance in the classroom. The anxiously hyperactive student, by contrast, might be expected to have intact intellectual and academic functioning but a general lowering of academic performance after the onset of the life stress episode.

The unsocialized hyperactive student, by contrast, has relatively intact intellectual abilities, but academic performances is below ability level because of problems with motivation.

Dietary Factors

Dietary factors as causative agents in hyperactivity have been the focus of much discussion but much less substantive research. Although the theory that sugar and food additives stimulate hyperactivity and that their removal would thus eliminate such overactivity is intriguing, experimental studies thus far have reported minimal efficacy of specific dietary regimes (Barling & Bullen, 1985; Harley & Matthews, 1980). At best only a small number of hyperactive students respond positively to regimens such as the Feingold diet (Feingold, 1975).

ALTERNATIVE ACTIONS

Medication

Although medication has been used with all three types of hyperactivity, it would appear to be medically indicated primarily for neurological hyperactivity. Stimulant medication such as methylphenidate (Ritalin) or dextroamphetamine (Dexedrine) may be necessary to effect a normal activity level. Such medication is said to have a paradoxical effect: it activates the brain stem, cortical inhibitory systems, and cortex to produce a calming effect. Such medication for anxiously hyperactive and unsocialized hyperactive students is contraindicated, since it would function as a stimulant and thus exacerbate the hyperactivity. It should be emphasized, however, that even when medication is indicated, it should not be the only management strategy. Instead, the medication should be utilized in conjunction with classroom and home management programs and other procedures such as counseling.

Classroom–Home Behavior Programs

Structure and routine in the environment are beneficial for all types of hyperactive students although such order satisfies different needs in different students. For the neurologically hyperactive student, a structured routine imposes external order and consistency on a world that is difficult to organize sufficiently on one's own. For the anxious student, such routine provides a sense of security, sameness, and predictability that may be lacking in areas touched by the life stresses. For the unsocialized student, routine and consistency provide external limits by which behavior can be regulated since internal controls are weak.

In addition to structure and consistency at both school and home, classroom behavior programs for the neurologically hyperactive and unsocialized students are indicated. Although the programs may be similar in design, implementation, types of reinforcement, and data collection, the target behaviors will be different. For the neurologically hyperactive student, the behavioral focus is on remaining seated, staying at task, and completing assignments. For the unsocialized student, the focus is on compliance with classroom rules and limits, including such behaviors as requesting permission to leave one's seat, talking only with permission, and completing assigned work. The overall goal is to socialize the student by providing some incentive through a behavioral program supporting conformity and compliance. The parents will require extensive help in implementing similar social training procedures at home, although this is usually most effectively accomplished through parent counseling with the school psychologist rather than by teacher consultation.

Classroom management programs are not indicated for the anxious student. Instead counseling is the treatment of choice.

Counseling

Educative counseling is indicated for the parents and the student when hyperactivity is of neurological origin. Concerns with medication, the need for structure and routine in the environment, possible learning problems, self-esteem difficulties, and prognosis need to be discussed openly and clearly. Collaboration with the family physician is also indicated if the hyperactivity is pronounced enough to warrant medication.

For the unsocialized student, the counseling focus is on providing socialization training both at home and at school. The parents require basic skills in the areas of setting appropriate limits, maintaining consistency, and effectively using appropriate reinforcement contingencies. Progress will be slow for many families especially if the student is an adolescent, since the maladaptive behavior patterns will have persisted for a longer period of time.

The anxiously hyperactive student has perhaps the strongest need for counseling services. Help will be needed in learning to cope with the life stresses in appropriate, healthy ways as a means of decreasing the overall anxiety level and thus reducing hyperactivity. Adjunctive family counseling can be beneficial in helping parents understand the sources of the anxiety and in assisting them in providing emotional support to the student.

Cognitive–Behavioral Approaches

One specific approach advocated for use with hyperactive students that has been widely discussed and variously acclaimed or disclaimed is cognitive–behavioral therapy. Such procedures are designed to teach self-guidance and problem-solving strategies, which in turn are supposed to result in increased self-regulated behavior — that is, in the present context, decreased hyperactivity and distractibility and increased attention span. In a review of cognitive–behavioral therapies used with hyperactive children, Whalen, Henker, and Hinshaw (1985) reported limited efficacy as the therapies are presently used. The most consistent gains have been seen in the area of attention-cognition rather than in behavioral areas. Generalization of the strategies from the training situation to other environments appears to be a particular weakness. It would appear that the unsocialized hyperactive student would benefit the most from cognitive–behavioral strategies.

Parent Involvement

The complexity of hyperactivity as a behavior syndrome necessitates the active involvement of the parents in both the assessment and management phases. Unless parents clearly understand the student's disorder, they are limited in their effectiveness in helping their child adequately cope with the problematic behavior. In addition, research suggests that hyperactive students as a group present significant parenting problems in the family since there is more noncompliant and negative behavior than in most families (Befera & Barkley, 1985).

SUMMARY

The hyperactive student presents a challenge to the parent, teacher, and school psychologist in terms of assessment and management. Although all hyperactive students initially look the same, there appear to be discriminating characteristics in etiology and behavior that in turn indicate differential management. Assessment procedures include securing a complete developmental and social history from the parents, and using parent and teacher rating scales, classroom observations, and formal psychological testing. Factors such as neurological indicators, normal physical development, constancy or variability of the hyperactivity, cognitive deficits, and parenting styles need to be considered as carefully as the behavioral reports by the adults working with the students.

After a comprehensive assessment, it is usually possible to classify the hyperactivity pattern as one of three types. Neurological hyperactivity is characterized by a history with neurological indicators, a pattern of a constantly high activity level form the early preschool years, and possible areas of cognitive deficit on formal psychological tests. Management procedures may include stimulant medication, educative counseling for the student and parents, increased structure and routine at home and in the classroom, special help for learning disabilities if present, and behavior programs at home and school.

The anxiously hyperactive student, by contrast, is identified by an absence of neurological indicators in the developmental history and reports of a normal activity level prior to the onset of a life stress such as divorce, death, or a move. The parents' childrearing skills may be average to above average. Classroom observations indicate a variable activity level with increased hyperactivity in unstructured or emotional-laden situations. On psychological testing, the student shows intact intellectual functioning but a general lowering of academic achievement that commenced with the precipitating event. Management recommendations center primarily on counseling for the student with the goals of improving coping skills and decreasing the anxiety level. Adjunctive counseling for the parents enables them to better understand the stresses in the student's life and to provide additional emotional support. Classroom and home behavior programs are not necessary and medication for the hyperactivity is contraindicated.

The unsocialized hyperactive student demonstrates a different pattern of characteristics. There is an absence of neurological indicators, and the onset of the hyperactivity problems typically occurs with the entry into school. Interviews with the parents indicate a significant degree of interparent or intraparent inconsistency in discipline, with vacillations between authoritarianism and permissiveness. There is also a history of noncompliance with rules and limits that reaches problematic proportions at school age. In the classroom, the student's activity level and attention span are variable; sustained attention, concentration, and stillness are evident on preferred or high-interest tasks. Psychological testing evidences intact intellectual abilities, but academic achievement is significantly below ability level because of chronic motivational problems. Management recommendations include social training behavioral programs at home and school. Extensive family counseling is also a crucial component in effecting behavioral change in the student. As with the anxiously hyperactive student, medication is contraindicated.

In summary, the assessment and management of hyperactive students by school psychologists necessitates a collaborative effort with parents and teachers. Without such collaboration and cooperation, the management of hyperactivity in the school setting will be impaired by confusion and mystique, which frustrate successful intervention.

REFERENCES

Achenbach, T. M. (1982). *Developmental psychopathology* (2nd ed.). New York: Wiley.

Barling, J., & Bullen, G. (1985). Dietary factors and hyperactivity: A failure to replicate. *Journal of Genetic Psychology, 146,* 117–123.

Befera, M. S., & Barkley, R. A. (1985). Hyperactive and normal girls and boys: Mother–child interaction, parent psychiatric status and child psychopathology. *Journal of Child Psychology, Psychiatry and Allied Disciplines, 26,* 439–452.

Cantwell, D. P. (1975). *The hyperactive child.* New York: Spectrum.

Conners, C. K. (1969). A teacher rating scale for use in drug studies with children. *American Journal of Psychiatry, 126,* 884–888.

Feingold, B. F. (1975). *Why your child is hyperactive.* New York: Random House.

Goyette, C. H., Connors, C. K., & Ulrich, R. F. (1978). Normative data on revised Parent and Teacher Rating Scales. *Journal of Abnormal Child Psychology, 6,* 221–236.

Harley, J., & Matthews, C. G. (1980). Food additives and hyperactivity in children. In R. Knights & D. Bakker (Eds.), *Treatment of hyperactive and learning disabled children.* Baltimore: University Park.

Kenny, T. J., Clemmons, R. L., Hudson, B. W., Lentz, G. A., Cicci, R., & Nair, P. (1971). Characteristics of children referred because of hyperactivity. *Journal of Pediatrics, 79,* 618–622.

Kerasotes, D., & Walker, C. E. (1981). Hyperactive behavior in children. In C. E. Walker & M. C. Roberts (Eds.), *Handbook of clinical child psychology* (pp. 498–523). New York: Wiley.

Lambert, N., & Sandoval, J. (1980). The prevalence of learning disabilities in a sample of children considered hyperactive. *Journal of Abnormal Child Psychology, 8,* 33–50.

Miller, L. C. (1977). *School Behavior Checklist.* Los Angeles: Western Psychological Services.

Safer, D. J., & Allen, R. P. (1976). *Hyperactive children: Diagnosis and management.* Baltimore: University Park.

Walker, H. M. (1976). *Walker Problem Behavior Checklist.* Los Angeles: Western Psychological Services.

Werry, J. S. (1968). Studies of the hyperactive child: IV. An empirical analysis of the minimal brain dysfunction syndrome. *Archives of General Psychiatry, 19,* 9–16.

Whalen, C. K., & Henker, B. (Eds.). (1980). *Hyperactive children: The social ecology of identification and treatment.* New York: Academic.

Whalen, C. K., Henker, B., & Hinshaw, S. P. (1985). Cognitive–behavioral therapies for hyperactive children: Premises, problems, and prospects. *Journal of Abnormal Child Psychology, 3,* 391–410.

Wirt, R. D., Lachar, D., Klinedinst, J. K., & Seat, P. D. (1984). *Multidimensional description of child personality: A manual for the Personality Inventory for Children.* Los Angeles: Western Psychological Services.

BIBLIOGRAPHY: PROFESSIONALS

Kerasotes, D., & Walker, C. E. (1981). Hyperactive behavior in children. In C. F. Walker & M. C. Roberts (Eds.), *Handbook of clinical child psychology* (pp. 498–523). New York: Wiley.
Comprehensive overview of the current definitions of hyperactivity and the central issues involved in diagnosis and treatment.

Zins, J. E., & Ponti, C. R. (1982). Hyperactivity in children: Issues in definition, diagnosis, and intervention. In J. Grimes (Ed.), *Psychological approaches to problems of children and adolescents.* Des Moines: Iowa State Department of Public Instruction Division of Special Education, pp. 425–468.
Excellent review of assessment and management of hyperactivity intended as a manual for the school psychologist. Advocating a multifaceted approach to both evaluation and educational management, Zins and Ponti offer practical recommendations for school personnel.

Children and Language Development

Lynne Blennerhassett
Gallaudet University

BACKGROUND

> Greetings to the inhabitants of the universe from the third planet Earth of the star the Sun.
> Hello from the children of the planet earth.
> Messages on the *Voyager* Spacecraft

In 1977, two Voyager spacecraft were launched on an exploration of our solar system and beyond. On board were greetings in 55 different languages, selected to represent the majority of people whose cultures constitute the 193 principal languages of the world (Sagan, Drake, Druyan, Ferris, Lomberg & Sagan, 1978). It is *not* likely that the primary intent of the Voyager messages was interstellar communication; rather, the motivation was to secure public attention and support for NASA space programs. What better way to gain people's support than to lure them with the promise of interpersonal communication, that powerful force that gives rise to the development of languages. This chapter will examine the dimensions of language and the process of language development.

Defining Language

The intent to communicate is fundamental to the definition and development of language. Kretschmer and Kretschmer (1978, p. 1) define language as "an organized set of symbolic relationships, mutually agreed upon by a speech community to represent experience and facilitate communication." The symbolic relationships that must be mastered by a growing child include the pragmatic, semantic, and syntactic rule systems. Simply stated, pragmatic relationships deal with the rules that direct social discourse; semantic relationships deal with the meanings we ascribe to the symbols used in social discourse; and syntactic relationships deal with the rules used to order the symbols.

Pragmatic, semantic, and syntactic systems are not discrete, mutually exclusive domains. The pragmatic, or social discourse base, determines which semantic and syntactic forms are appropriate. One theoretical approach that gives precedence to the pragmatic basis of language is Speech Act Theory (Austin, 1962; Searle, 1970). This theory acknowledges the importance of social discourse by identifying "speaker's intentions" and "effects upon the listeners" as key theoretical concepts. More specifically, speech act theory identifies three types of speech acts that are fundamental to all communication situations: *illocutionary acts,* which convey speaker's intentions; *perlocutionary acts,* which express the effects upon the listener; and *locutionary acts,* which involve selecting and uttering the selected words and sentences. Figure 1 illustrates the pragmatic basis of language within which speakers select semantic and syntactic forms appropriate to the communication intention.

The pragmatic dimension of language includes the variety of ways in which we can use language, as well as the rules of social editing that apply to our language use. For example, language can be used to gain attention, greet, warn, question, demand, seek permission, protest, joke, describe, explain, assert, evaluate, identify, refuse, or answer (Dore, 1978).

The pragmatic dimension of language also includes "rules of social editing" such as: *accessing* (how to enter conversations); *topicalization* (how to establish, maintain and change topics); *turn-taking* (how to take-a-turn and pass-a-turn); and *closing* (how to terminate the conversation) (Kretschmer, 1986; Sacks, Schegloff, & Jefferson 1974). Indeed, pragmatic rules of social editing guide when, and with whom, it may even be an option to open a conversation, establish or shift topics, take or pass a turn, or engage in various social functions of the language. The developing child must learn the variety of social functions to which language may be applied, as well as the rules of social editing used to carry out those various functions. As will be discussed later, development of the pragmatic aspects of language is evidenced early in the first year of life, long before the first word is spoken.

The semantic dimension of language refers to the cognitive process of relating symbols, or words, to their referents. For example, children must come to understand that the word *mommy* means the one specific adult woman who bathes, feeds, and cares for them; likewise that *cookie* refers to those small, sweet, flat cakelike goodies, and that many different kinds of these goodies can be referred to by the same symbol, *cookie.*

But semantic mastery involves more than just the development of specific symbol reference. It also involves understanding the roles that symbols play in combination with other symbols. Among the semantic roles identified in language research are agent, patient, experiencer, entity, complement, possessor, action verbs, process verbs, stative verbs, and modifiers of time, manner, location, and attribute (Bloom & Lahey, 1978; Brown, 1973; Hasenstab & Laughton, 1982; Kretschmer & Kretschmer, 1978). Definitions and examples of each of these semantic roles are presented in Table 1.

To the developing child, semantic mastery involves learning specific symbol reference as well as learning the rules governing when, and if, words may act as agents, patients, experiencers, and so on. For example, children must learn the contexts within which *mommy* assumes the role of agent, patient, experiencer, possessor, or entity; likewise, they must learn the contexts within which *cookie* assumes the role of patient, complement, or entity. It has been argued that it is the verb cases (action, process, or stative) that determine the semantic roles of the noun cases (Chafe, 1970; Kretschmer & Kretschmer, 1978). Similarly, it has been argued that it is the action-based (verb-like) nature of parent–infant interactions that sets in motion semantic development (Bruner, 1974/1975, 1983). As with pragmatic development, semantic development originates long before the emergence of the child's first word.

The syntactic dimension of language is the ordering of the symbols (or words) according to the grammatical rules of the particular language. The length and grammatical complexity of the sentence is determined by the number of propositions, or ideas, that the speaker wishes to encode, and the social context within which the utterance occurs. For example, single-proposition expressions can be encoded in basic sentence patterns such as those described by Streng (1972). Table 2 presents definitions and examples of the five single-proposition sentence patterns identified by Streng.

The syntactic dimension of language also includes the rules that govern the ordering of morphological markers for verb tense (-ed, -ing, inclusion of auxiliary verbs, etc.), plurality (-s, -es), possessives ('s), and prepositions (in, on, etc.). Syntactic rules also govern the ordering of symbols in multipropositional, or complex, sentences. Examples of these grammatical constructions include coordination (or conjunction), embedding, and relativization. These grammatical forms will be defined and illustrated below.

Noticeably absent in the above definition is the inclusion of speech, or phonological development, as a component of language. In the discussion that follows, a distinction is made between speech and language: language is the knowledge and use of symbolic, rule-governed relationships (pragmatic, semantic, and syntactic), whereas speech is the verbal expression of the linguistic code (Carrow-Woolfolk & Lynch, 1982; McCormick, 1986). Although there is a close relationship between speech and language, language may or may not be expressed through speech. The most obvious example of this can be found with the American Sign Language which is used by a large number of deaf people. Even in spoken languages, Birdwhistle (1970) estimates that no more than 30–35% of the social meaning of conversations is conveyed by spoken expression; rather it is the nonverbal expressive channels such as facial expression, posture, proximity, and other visual–gestural forms of communication that convey illocutionary and perlocutionary acts. In summary, the discussion of language development that follows is guided by the definition of language as the knowledge and use of pragmatic, semantic, and syntactic relationships toward communicative ends. Readers interested in the area of phonological development are referred to Menn (1985).

Prevalence of Communication Disorders

Satisfactory estimates on the prevalence of problems related to language development are difficult to

FIGURE 1
Illustration of the pragmatic, or social discourse basis of language, including semantic and syntactic relationships

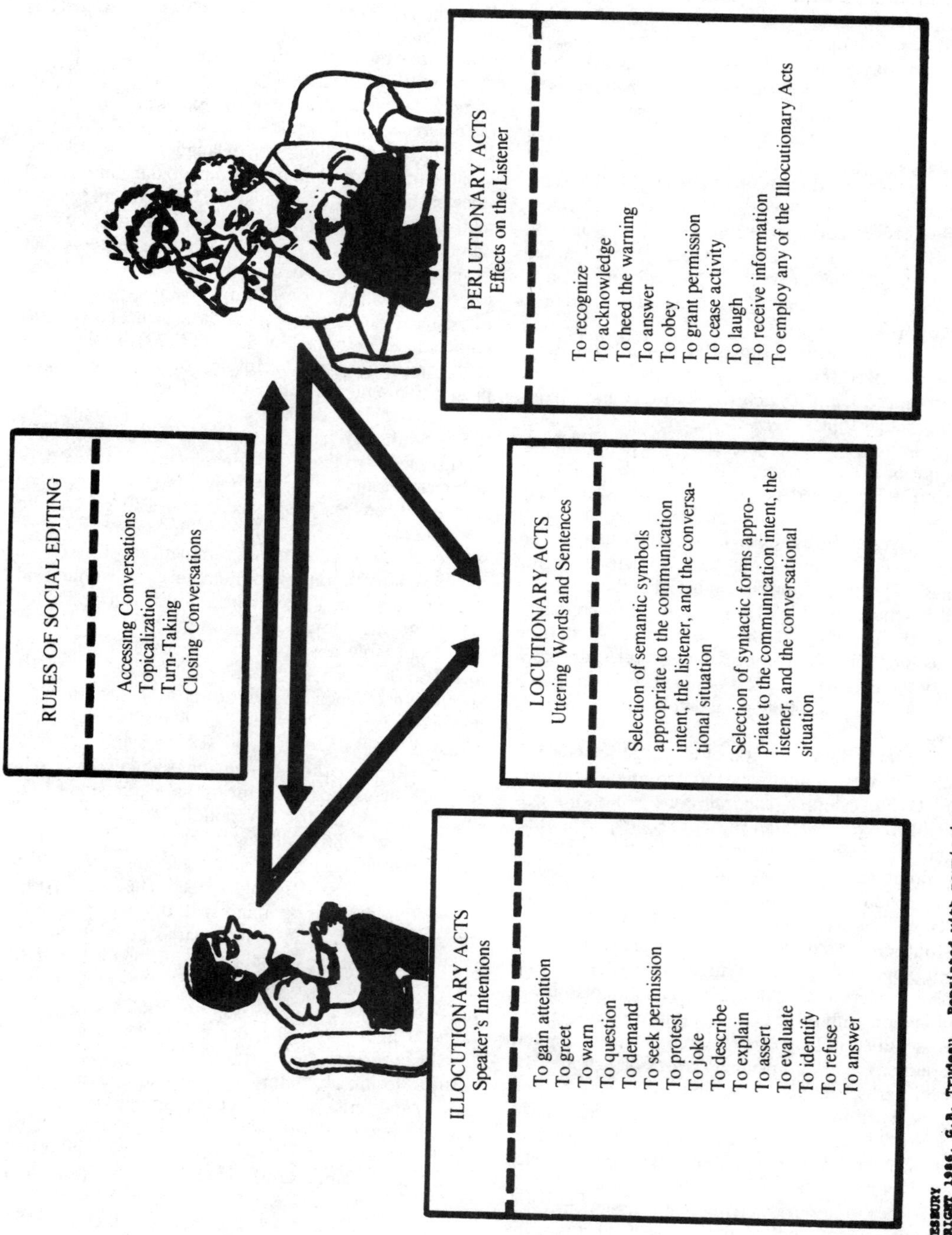

Adapted from Carrow-Woolfolk & Lynch, 1982; Dore, 1978; and Kretschmer, 1986. *Artwork:* Doonesbury, Copyright 1986, G. B. Trudeau. Reprinted with permission of Universal Press Syndicate. All rights reserved.

TABLE 1

Semantic Roles

Cases	Definition and examples
Noun	
Agent	Someone or something that initiates or causes an action. *Patty* hit Tom.
Patient	Someone or something that receives the effects of action or process verbs. Patty hit *Tom.*
Experiencer	Someone or something that performs process verbs. *Jack* thought about Mary.
Entity	Someone or something that is in a state of being. The *apple* is red. That's my *sister.*
Complement	That which comes into being as a result of the action or process berbs. Mom baked a *cake.* Mary thought up the *idea.*
Possessor	Someone or something that owns or has possession of other objects. *Patty's* bunny. *Mike* has a car.
Verb	
Action verbs	A specific movement, change in position or location, or act performed. Patty *hit* Tom.
Process verbs	Verbs of internal activity, change of state, or condition. Jack *thought* about Mary.
Stative verbs	Verbs that specify that someone or something is in a state or condition. The apple *is* red. Patty *is* cute.
Modifier	
Time	Indicates the time when action of verbs takes place. Mary got her letter *yesterday.*
Manner	Indicates how an action occurred. Patty hits *hard.*
Location	Indicates the place where verbs occur. Daddy is *at work.*
Attribute	Describes properties of an object, person, or event. The apple is *red.*

Adapted from Hasenstab and Laughton (1982), Kretschmer and Kretschmer (1978, and Laughton and Hasenstab (1986).

TABLE 2

Streng's Five Single-Proposition Sentence Patterns and Examples

1. Intransitive verb sentence: noun + intransitive verb
   Example: Mary laughed.
2. Transitive verb sentence: noun + transitive verb + noun
   Example: Bob cooked dinner.
3. Predicate nominal sentence: noun + verb *to be* + noun
   Example: Susan is president.
4. Predicate adjective sentence: noun + verb *to be* + adjective
   Example: Jack is sad.
5. Predicate adverbial sentence: noun + verb *to be* + adverb
   Example: Chris is in the park.

Adapted from Kretschmer and Kretschmer (1978), and Streng (1972).

obtain for at least three reasons: variations in definitions of delayed or disordered language; the overlapping or fusing of diagnostic categories within the general realm of communication disorders (phonological, morphological, syntactic, semantic, and/or pragmatic linguistic problems); and the practice of compiling prevalence statistics according to primary handicapping condition, when language disorders may frequently be present as secondary or tertiary problems (Carrow-Woolfolk & Lynch, 1982; Laughton & Hasenstab, 1986). Estimates of the prevalence of communication disorders in general range from a low 2–4% to a high of 15–20% of the school age population, with higher estimates at the younger age levels, and with language disorders secondary to speech disorders (Lilly, 1979). Other estimates specify that 2–4% of the school age population is speech-impaired, and up to 7–8% of the preschool population is language-disordered (Lilly, 1979; McCormick, 1986).

Regardless of whether the linguistic problem is primary or is secondary to other handicapping conditions, its impact must not be underestimated. A child with pragmatic, semantic, and/or syntactic language problems is at risk for interaction problems of a most significant nature, the loss or disruption of interpersonal communication.

DEVELOPMENT

Development Prior to the First Word

One of the most common misperceptions about language development is the belief that language begins with the emergence of a child's first word, or first approximation of words. Children not yet communicating with words are often said to "have no language." School psychologists and others who attempt to evaluate language development often mistakenly target the single-word stage as the entry level for identifying the onset for language development. In doing so, critical aspects of early language development are ignored, and valuable opportunities for evaluation and intervention are lost. Observational research of parent–infant interactions has provided insight into the early language-learning process and has offered alternative approaches for evaluation and intervention with language-delayed children.

Parent–infant interactions, especially mother-infant communication, have been the focus of much research regarding the early language-learning environment (Bates, Camaioni, & Volterra, 1975; Bruner, 1975, 1983; Snow, 1977a, 1977b). Early parent–infant interactions provide the social context within which children acquire five critical cognitive/linguistic abilities. During the first year of life, children learn to (a) perform perlocutionary acts; (b) engage in illocutionary acts; (c) practice rules of social editing; (d) actively experience semantic roles; and (e) focus attention within the linguistic boundaries that contain the semantic and syntactic codes.

During the first year of life, children are able to affect perlocutionary acts by the adults with whom they interact. Bates et al. (1975) have identified the period from birth to 10 months as the perlocutionary stage, in which infants have a systematic effect on their interactional partner without necessarily having intentional control over that effect. Infants come to the communication situation with a number of basic receptive, expressive and motor abilities such as smiles, burps, cries, coughs, head movements, gazes, and arm/leg movements. During interactions, attentive parents interpret these behaviors as the child's attempts to communicate, and respond to the child as if the child had taken a "conversational turn" (Snow, 1977b). Snow notes that mother–infant interactions during this period resemble "conversations," mothers actively working to interpret infant behaviors as questions, statements, demands, or expressions of feeling. And when infants are less active, mothers will "take the babys' turns" for them by supplying language rich in questions, answers, acknowledgments, commands, compliances, and so on. Thus, within these early interactions babies can effect perlocutionary acts by adults, while gaining exposure to the pragmatic process of turn-taking.

Bates et al. (1975) find children, at about 10 months of age but still before the first word, to be capable of engaging in intentional, illocutionary acts. More controlled behaviors such as pointing, gesturing, directing gaze, babbling, showing, and nodding enable children to communicate illocutionary intent. They can use these more controlled, intentional, communicative behaviors to engage in what Bruner (1975, 1983) refers to as "reciprocal modes" of interaction with their parents, marked by give-and-take games and more sophisticated turn-taking experience. Jargoning and vocal play during this period act to reinforce the "conversational" aspect of these early parent–child turn-taking exchanges.

Early parent–child interactions typically center around highly routinized activities such as bathing, eating, changing diapers, and playing with toys. These ritualized, shared activities involve both partners in focusing on the same object or activity, at the same time, for the same purpose (Bruner 1974/1975, 1975, 1983). By focusing attention and activities around a shared topic, the stage is set for the child to practice topicalization as well as gain experience with various semantic roles. For example, children can use their illocutionary, communicative behaviors to establish topics, comment on topics established by their partner, or change topics. There is some evidence (Bates, 1975; Blennerhassett, 1984) that children benefit from being exposed to a variety of communication partners at very young ages, especially with partners who are not equally skilled in interpreting the child's desired topic or intended illocutionary act. The benefit lies in motivating children to develop a variety of adaptive pragmatic language strategies that allow them to establish, change, and maintain topics with different discourse partners.

Once topics are established, the reciprocal, give-and-take interactions around those topics provide children with action-based experience at varying semantic roles (Bruner 1974/1975, 1975, 1983). Even before the emergence of their first word, children experience a sense of their own agency in establishing, maintaining, and changing topics. Further, within the context of give-and-take play and communicative interactions, children experience themselves as receivers of objects and actions (patients and possessors), givers of objects (agents), and experiencers of various states of being and internal feeling (entities, experiencers, process verbs and stative verbs). Such experiences lay the foundation for acquisition of semantic linguistic skills.

Not only do interactions during this stage provide active experience with semantic roles, but also parents' speech provides children with the linguistic symbols, semantic and syntactic, that are used to encode these experiences. Mothers' speech to babies, referred to as baby talk or "motherese," is different from speech to adults or older children (Snow, 1977a), in ways that are important for encouraging language development. Mothers' speech to language-learning children is slower, highly intonational, and more varied in pitch, and it contains more clearly segmented phrases. Also, mothers tend to speak in shorter sentences, use simplified vocabulary, and talk about things in the here and now. The prosodic, simplified features of "motherese" provide children with clearly organized linguistic boundaries within which to focus their attention. This then makes it easier for children to perceive the patterns, or rule systems, that govern expressive locutionary acts. That is, the features of the early language-learning environment assist the child in organizing, perceiving, and extracting the semantic and syntactic rules necessary for later expression of locutionary acts.

Because the period preceding the first word is so critical to later language development, it may be valuable to specify the preverbal behaviors that children bring to the communication situation, and use to participate as conversational partners. Hasenstab and Laughton (1982) developed an evaluation system that identifies nine early cognitive/motor behaviors and eleven communicative behaviors that are believed to represent significant early pragmatic and semantic linguistic acquisitions during the first year of life.

Table 3 presents a summary of these early pragmatic and semantic behaviors. The nine cognitive/motor behaviors include some very basic, but very fundamental abilities that are necessary for children to participate in successful interactions. For example, *eye contact* and *motor imitation* have been identified as powerful early means of turn-taking by which children can respond to mothers' calls for attention, establish topics themselves, and/or comment on topics already under discussion. Developing notions such as *causality, body image, object permanence,* and *relational concepts* help children understand their own agency and semantic role variability within the interaction.

The eleven communicative behaviors listed by Hasenstab and Laughton further develop the range of abilities children typically bring to the communication situation. Here, the more illocutionary behaviors are identified, including *pointing, gazing, tugging, facial expression,* and *posturing.* Although still not capable of single words, the children's contributions at this level may be vocal, such as *babbling, jargoning,* and *crying.* The cognitive/motor and communicative behaviors summarized by Hasenstab and Laughton function as the core abilities that children bring to the early communication situation, and it is with this repertoire of capabilities that they play an active, "conversational" role, establishing the pragmatic, semantic, and syntactic foundation for later language development.

In a somewhat different investigation of the early language-learning environment, Nelson (1973) reported on the role of maternal acceptance of children's conversational attempts in respect to rate of language development. More specifically, the rate of language development was found to be determined by three things: the child's style, the mother's talking style, and the mother's level of acceptance of the child's contributions. Children's styles were categorized as either expressive (socially oriented) or referential (interested in learning about objects in the environment). Likewise, mothers' talking styles were categorized as either expressive (predominantly socially oriented, game-like verbalization) or referential (giving the child information about objects, events, and activities in their environment). Finally, mothers' styles were characterized as either accepting (positive and uncritical) or rejecting (negative and critical) of the child's contribution to the interaction.

The rate of language development was positively correlated with referential talking styles and maternal acceptance of the child's linguistic contribution. The children most at risk for delays in language development were those for whom expressive talking styles dominated, coupled with maternal rejection of communication efforts. In summary, development toward the locutionary stage can be said to be influenced by the active nature of the parent–child interactions, the linguistic input of the parents, and parental acceptance of the child's communication efforts.

Development of Locutionary Acts

There is a wide age range which has been identified as the single-word stage of language development. For normal language-learning children, first words may emerge as early as 11–18 months (Bloom, 1973; Bloom & Lahey, 1978; Dore, 1974); for "language-disordered children" emergence of the first word may not appear until 27 months (Leonard, 1985). But more important than the age of onset is the nature of the development that occurs during this period. It would be a mistake to consider the accumulation of vocabulary or lexical items as the primary work of this period, because word counts alone fail to capture the significant semantic and pragmatic acquisition taking place. For example, Bloom (1973) and Bloom & Lahey (1978) have posited that early in the single-word stage, when children may have as many as 25 words, they tend to use only a limited number (fewer than 10) of these words when they are involved in the difficult cognitive work of developing understanding of the various semantic roles that words can play (agent, patient, experiencer, etc.). Once these semantic concepts are established, a rapid increase in the child's acquisition of words is enabled. Bloom referred to this as the "vocabulary spurt," but noted that even with this larger vocabulary a child may frequently use only a limited number (18–20) of words when communicating and working on new linguistic structures.

Another qualitative analysis of children's linguistic development at the single-word stage is that which examines pragmatic function achieved when children use their single words. Dore (1974) identified nine different social functions that the single-word user can achieve. They are labeling, repeating, answering, requesting action, requesting answers, greeting, calling, practicing, and protesting. In a later longitudinal study of single-word users, McShane (1980) identified additional social uses of single-word utterances, including describing, offering information beyond the here and now, accompaniments to social acts of giving and receiving, and adding a follow-on word to others' utterances. The last of these play an important role in permitting a child to have a conversational turn even when they have no new information to offer.

Rather than evaluate development of the single-word stage by counting the number of words acquired, Hasenstab and Laughton (1982) suggested that practitioners look qualitatively at the range of pragmatic and semantic roles that children express with the words they use in conversational situations. They have developed an evaluation system that analyzes infant and preschool language samples for the variety of pragmatic and semantic roles expressed in naturally occurring communication situations.

Development Beyond the Single Word

For normal language-learners, two-word combinations may appear as early as about 18 months of age; for "language-disordered" children, onset of two-word combinations may not occur until as late as 40 months of age (Leonard, 1986). But as at the single-word level, it is more informative to look at the nature and function of a

TABLE 3

Hasentab and Laughton's (1982) Semantic/ Pragmatic Descriptive Categories Prior to the Single Word

Cognitive/motor behaviors	
Motor imitation	Making a reasonable attempt to copy the gross motor movements of another person
Body image	Perceiving one's body as separate from others and capable of performing tasks
Eye contact	Visually focusing on another person with whom the child is interacting
Object permanence	Knowing objects exist in space and time even when the child no longer sees or acts on them
Ordering	Putting things into a specific, intentional order
Embedding	Inserting something into a previously established arrangement
Categorizing	Grouping things according to characteristics they have in common
Relational concepts	Making some association between or among things based on function or ownership
Causality	Noting that one event or action will regularly cause another event or action to take place
Communicative behaviors (preverbal but may be vocal)	
Pointing/gesturing	Conveying information or making known wants or needs by gesturing/pointing at persons or objects in the environment; may be used to refer to objects of actions or to show relationships between objects or actions
Crying	Differentiated to indicate need for attention, food, or removal of discomfort
Gazing	An early form of eye contact used for communication in which child and adult maintain eye contact; may be accompanied by smiling, touching, and vocalizing
Facial expression	Emotions can be easily observed in facial expression: fear, surprise, contentment, pleasure
Posturing	Turning body or head toward or away from adult in a social/ communicative fashion
Babbling/jargon/ vocal play	Series of vocalizations with or without intonation; short sentence-like utterances with no meaning; gurgles and chuckles
Turn-taking	Interaction in which an adult or child speaks or acts, waits to allow the correspondent a response (turn); the adult is permitted to take the child's turn if the child declines a turn
Touching/holding/ tugging	Social behavior that establishes a bond between child and adult, for example, pulling the adult to or away from a task to indicate wishes or needs
Showing	Taking objects to an adult or the adult to an object to indicate requests, wishes, or action
Requesting/ questioning	Bringing an object to an adult and questioning or requesting by facial expression and/or vocalizing
Negating/nodding	Shaking head to indicate nonexistence, denial, or rejection, or covering or throwing an object to remove it from the immediate environment

(continued next column)

(Table 3 continued)

From Hasenstab and Laughton (1982) pp. 234-235. "Bare Essentials in Assessing Really Little Kids (BEAR): An Approach." In M. S. Hasenstab & J. S. Hurner (Eds.), *Comprehensive Intervention With Hearing Impaired Infants and Preschool Children* (pp. 234–235), Rockville, MD: Aspen. Copyright 1982 by Aspen Publishers. Reprinted by permission.

child's multiple-word combinations rather than simply to characterize development along a chronological age time line.

Brown (1973) identified a number of developmental trends that characterize children's emerging mastery of semantic–syntactic, morphological, and syntactic forms. For example, Brown identified a set of minimal semantic–syntactic relations that children express with their early two-word combinations. Table 4 presents a listing of these relations along with examples.

As children expand their utterances beyond the two-word level, they begin to acquire mastery of simple morphological rules. For normal language-learning children, these developmental trends may be observed approximately between the ages of 27 and 34 months. Among the morphological forms that children acquire during this period are the present progressive verb form (-ing); prepositions (in, on); plurals; past tense of regular and irregular verbs; possessive form ('s); articles; third-person form of regular and irregular verbs (mommy eat*s*; daddy *has*); and contraction rules for the verb *to be* when functioning as either the main verb or the auxiliary verb.

Mastery of the syntactic rules that govern more complex sentence structures is generally the work of age 30–35 months and beyond. Coordination (or conjoining), embedding, and relativization are examples of multipropositional sentence constructions developed during this period. Developmentally, conjoining represents the earliest attempt at multipropositional expression, followed by embedding, and relativization (Brown, 1973; Tager-Flushberg, 1985).

TABLE 4

Summary of Brown's (1973) Semantic–Syntactic Relations at the Two-Word Level

Relations	Examples and context
Major semantic–syntactic relations	
Action and agent	mommy fix (mommy fix toy)
Action and object	hit ball (mommy hit ball)
Agent and object	mommy toy (mommy fix toy)
Action and location	put floor (put toy on floor)
Entity and location	lady home (the lady is home)
Possessor and possession	mommy chair (mommy's chair)
Entity and attribute	mommy big (mommy is big)
Additional two-word relations	
Nomination and (X)	that (kitty)
Recurrance and (X)	more (cookie)
Nonexistence and (X)	all-gone (mommy)

The subject of this relationship can assume many values, which are represented by (X).

Note:A First Language: The Early Stages, by R. Brown, 1973, Cambridge, MA: Harvard University Press. Copyright 1973 by Harvard University Press. Adapted by permission.

The complex grammatical construction of coordination (or conjunction) enables the child to express, in a single sentence, two or more propositions that are of equal importance or occur in sequence (Kretschmer & Kretschmer, 1978). Conjunctions typically involve the word *and,* as in "He bought a shirt *and* tie" or "She dressed herself *and* went to school." Other coordinating words such as *but* and *or* are used in complex sentence constructions that express the contradictory or competitive nature of the underlying propositions (Kretschmer & Kretschmer, 1978). Examples of such multipropositional constructions are "She'll eat the fruit *but* not the vegetables" and "You can buy the book *or* the toy." Other words used to conjoin propositions are *because, so, since,* and the like. Developmentally, the word *and* appears to be the most common term used in early coordination; words such as *but, so, or,* and *if* appear next, followed by *because* and *when,* which are used later for causal conjoining (Owens, 1986).

Embedding has been defined as the syntactic process of "placing a word, phrase, or clause in an existing sentence" (Shames & Wiig, 1986, p. 617). The syntactic process of complementation involves embedding, or inserting, a proposition into another, more central proposition. This developmentally is evidenced when children embed one proposition as the object of another proposition, as in "I hope I don't hurt it" (Brown, 1973, p. 21). This type of embedding often occurs in main sentences that use process verbs such as *think, know, mean,* and *hope.*

Multipropositional expression is also encoded in the syntactic form of relativization. Kretschmer and Kretschmer define relativization as "embedding one proposition into another in order to restrict or clarify specific arguments contained within the core proposition" (1978, p. 34). Terms such as *that, who,* and *which* are examples of relative pronouns used in this type of grammatical construction. In developing mastery of relativization, Limber (1973) and Menyuk (1971) report that children initially express the relative clauses that are connected to the object of a sentence, as in "He wrote the novel that I read on the train." Later, relative clause constructions are connected to the subject of a sentence, as in "The woman who wrote the novel visited the class." Tager-Flushberg (1985) reported that although children as young as 36 months may receptively understand relativization, it is not until they reach school age that production of this form is fully mastered. Further expansion of complex syntactic forms is evidenced throughout the late preschool and early school-age years, with multiple embedding, expanded relativization, and mixed conjoining and embedding occurring within same sentences (Owens, 1986).

ALTERNATIVE ACTIONS

Accepting a social discourse perspective of language requires that traditional assessment and intervention techniques be modified. Hasenstab (1982) has reminded us that "in language evaluation we are concerned with the child as a language user within the communicative world" (pp. 137–138). Yet, traditional, formal testing techniques place children in artificial contexts rather than natural conversational situations, and as such fail to provide evaluators with a picture of the children's functional communicative abilities (Kretschmer & Kretschmer, 1978). Gathering and analyzing language samples as they occur in natural communication situations offer an alternative approach to assessment of language development (Hasenstab & Laughton, 1982; Kretschmer & Kretschmer, 1978). Readers interested in a review of more traditional, testing approaches to language assessment are referred to Hasenstab (1982).

Working from the foundation that development of language is based within a social discourse context, Kretschmer (1986) cited the following as important features of assessment and intervention:

1. Engaging children in conversations as part of the assessment process.
2. Listening to children's responses and understanding that they are attempts at communication.
3. Recognizing that testing alone is not enough and that viewing the classroom is important.

4. Contextualizing language in recognition of the importance of functional, not taught language.
5. Allowing for developmental stages, that is, recognizing that children do not go from no language to perfect performance.

Rather than "teaching" language, the methods to be used during intervention activities must adhere to discourse rules and assumptions that are valid means for achieving communication (Conant, Budoff, & Hecht, 1983). For example, roles played by speakers and listeners should be reciprocal and discourse-based, both child and adult taking turns as both speakers and listeners, givers and receivers of information. And because speakers do not normally tell listeners information that they assume is already known, Conant, Budoff, and Hecht (1983) have stressed the importance of engaging in intervention activities in which "the speaker has information unavailable to the listener that the listener needs" (p. 9). These authors have developed a number of intervention activities that adhere to these discourse-based considerations (Conant, Budoff, and Hecht, 1983).

SUMMARY

Language development involves more than just *locutionary acts* (uttering words and sentences). It involves acquiring skill in expressing a variety of *illocutionary acts* (communicating intentions), and effecting desired *perlocutionary responses* (effects upon the listener). The development of these skills is fundamentally embedded within social discourse contexts, where reciprocal, conversational exchanges incorporate the pragmatic, semantic, and syntactic rule systems that must be mastered. In order for assessment and intervention of language development to be valid, the integrity of the communicative, social discourse base must be maintained.

REFERENCES

Austin, J. L. (1962). *How to do things with words.* Cambridge, MA: Harvard University Press.

Bates, E. (1975). Peer relations and the acquisition of language. In M. Lewis & L. A. Rosenblum (Eds.), *Friendship and peer relations* (pp. 259–292). New York: Wiley.

Bates, E., Camaioni, L., & Volterra, V. (1975). The acquisition of performatives prior to speech. *Merrill-Palmer Quarterly, 21*(3), 205–226.

Birdwhistle, R. L. (1970). *Kinesics and context.* Philadelphia: University of Pennsylvania Press.

Bloom, L. (1973). *One word at a time.* The Hague: Mouton.

Bloom, L., & Lahey, M. (1978). *Language development and language disorders.* New York: Wiley.

Blennerhassett, L. (1984). Communicative styles of a 13-month old hearing impaired child and her parents. *Volta Review, 86,* 217–228.

Brown, R. (1973). *A first language: The early stages.* Cambridge, MA: Harvard University Press.

Bruner, J. (1974/1975). From communication to language —A psychological perspective. *Cognition, 3*(3), 255–287.

Bruner, J. (1975). The ontogenesis of speech acts. *Journal of Child Language,* 2, 1, 1–19.

Bruner, J. (1983). *Child's talk.* New York: Norton.

Carrow-Woolfolk, E., & Lynch, J. I. (1982). *An integrative approach to language disorders in children.* New York: Grune & Stratton.

Chafe, W. (1970). *Meaning and the structure of language.* Chicago: University of Chicago Press.

Conant, S., Budoff, M., & Hecht, B. (1983). *Teaching language-disabled children: A communication games intervention.* Cambridge, MA: Brookline.

Dore, J. (1974). A pragmatic description of early language development. *Journal of Psycholinguistic Research, 3*(4), 343–349.

Dore, J. (1978). Variation in preschool children's conversational performance. In K. Nelson (Ed.), *Children's language* (Vol. 1 (pp. 397–444). New York: Gardner.

Hasenstab, M. S. (1982). Language evaluation. In M. S. Hasenstab & J. S. Horner (Eds.), *Comprehensive intervention with hearing-impaired infants and preschool children* (pp. 137–202). Rockville, MD: Aspen.

Hasenstab, M. S., & Laughton, J. (1982). Bare essentials in assessing really little kids (BEAR): An approach. In M. S. Hasenstab and J. S. Horner (Eds.), *Comprehensive intervention with hearing-impaired infants and preschool children* (pp. 203–320). Rockville, MD: Aspen.

Kretschmer, R. (1986, April). *Language as a communication process: Implications for assessment and programming.* Paper presented at the National Association of School Psychologists Convention, Hollywood, Florida.

Kretschmer, R., & Kretschmer, L. (1978). *Language development and intervention with the hearing impaired.* Baltimore: University Park.

Laughton, J., & Hasenstab, M. S. (1986). *The language learning process: Implications for management of disorders.* Rockville, MD: Aspen.

Leonard, L. (1986). Early language development and language disorders. In G. H. Shames & E. H. Wiig (Eds.), *Human communication disorders: An introduction* (pp. 291–330). Columbus, OH: Merrill.

Lilly, M. S. (1979). *Children with exceptional needs: A survey of special education.* New York: Holt, Rinehart & Winston.

Limber, J. (1973). The genesis of complex sentences. In T. Moore (Ed.), *Cognitive development and the acquisition of language* (pp. 169–185). New York: Academic.

McCormick, L. (1986). Communication disorders. In N. Haring & L. McCormick (Eds.), *Exceptional children and youth* (4th ed.) (pp. 201–232). Columbus, OH: Merrill.

McShane, J. (1980). *Learning to talk.* Cambridge: Cambridge University Press.

Menn, L. (1985). Phonological development: Learning sounds and sound patterns. In J. Berko Gleason (Ed.), *The development of language* (pp. 61–102). Columbus, OH: Merrill.

Menyuk, P. (1971). *The acquisition and development of language.* Englewood Cliffs, NJ: Prentice-Hall.

Nelson, K. (1973). Structure and strategy in learning to talk. *Monographs of the Society for Research in Child Development, 38*(1), 2.

Owens, R. E. (1986). Communication, language, and speech. In G. H. Shames & E. H. Wiig (Eds.), *Human communication disorders* (pp. 27–79). Columbus, OH: Merrill.

Sacks, H., Schegloff, E. A., & Jefferson, G. (1974). A simplest systematics for the organization of turn-taking for conversation. *Language, 50*(4), 696–735.

Sagan, C., Drake, F. D., Druyan, A., Ferris, T., Lomberg, J., & Sagan, L. (1978). *Murmurs of the earth: The voyager interstellar record.* New York: Ballantine Books.

Searle, J. R. (1970). *Speech arts.* Cambridge: Cambridge University Press.

Shames, G. H., & Wiig, E. H. (Eds.). (1986). *Human communication disorders.* (Columbus, OH: Merrill.

Snow, C. (1977a). Mothers' speech research: From input to interaction. In C. Snow & C. Ferguson (Eds.), *Talking to children* (pp. 31–49). Cambridge University Press.

Snow, C. (1977b). The development of conversation between mothers and babies. *Journal of Child Language, 4,* 22.

Streng, A. H. (1972). *Syntax, speech and hearing.* New York: Grune & Stratton.

Tager-Flusberg, H. (1985). Putting words together: Morphology and syntax in the preschool years. In J. Berko Gleason (Ed.), *The development of language* (pp. 139–172). Columbus, OH: Merrill.

BIBLIOGRAPHY: PROFESSIONALS

Berko Gleason, J. (Ed.). (1985). *The development of language.* Columbus, OH: Merrill.
Brings together a number of prominent researchers in the field of language development and would make an excellent reference for professionals interested in further reading. There are separate chapters on prelinguistic development, phonological development, development of morphological and syntactic rules, individual differences in language acquisition, and reading and written language.

Conant, S., Budoff, M., & Hecht, B. (1983). *Teaching language-disabled children: A communication games intervention.* Cambridge, MA: Brookline Books.
This reference provides readers with examples of language intervention activities that depart from "teaching" language to more communicative, turn-taking activities. The interventions are designed to be compatible with a pragmatic, social discourse base for language interventions.

Fey, M. (1986). *Language intervention with young children.* San Diego: College Hill.
Offers comprehensive treatment of the issue of language intervention. The bridge between theory and intervention is discussed, along with the role of the family in the intervention process. Child-oriented and trainer-oriented approaches to intervention are discussed, and the importance of a social–conversational basis for intervention is illustrated.

Hasenstab, M. S., & Horner, J. S. (1982). *Comprehensive intervention with hearing-impaired infants and preschool children.* Rockville, MD: Aspen.
Professionals interested in alternative assessment techniques are referred to the BEAR system of analyzing natural language samples, which is described in this text. Although the system was developed for use with hearing-impaired children, it can be used with other children who exhibit delays in pragmatic, semantic, syntactic, and morphological language skills.

Kretschmer, R., & Kretschmer, L. (1978). *Language development and intervention with the hearing impaired.* Baltimore: University Park.
This is a classic reference in the field of language development and hearing impairment, but its use is not limited to those who work with the hearing-impaired. The descriptions of children's language development, of assessment and educational procedures, and of reading and written language would be valuable reading for professionals who work with any language-delayed child.

Children and Learning Styles

Mary Elise Polce
Frederick County Public Schools, Virginia

BACKGROUND

The National Association of School Psychologists (1985) advocacy statement recognizes a prevalent "lack of regular education options designed to meet the needs of children with diverse learning styles." Unfortunately, educational interventions often focus on deficit labels rather than learning style needs. Matching instruction to each learner is obviously an unrealistic objective. However, parents and professionals can identify style patterns and external conditions that influence learning. Although a concise formula for identifying learning styles does not exist, it is possible to observe and describe qualitative style differences involving perception, conceptualization, and problem-solving abilities.

The impact of learning styles extends beyond the

classroom to various settings. This chapter provides an overview of learning styles and how they relate to the academic, social, and emotional development of children and adolescents. It includes informal ways to identify elements of style and suggests intervention guidelines for the classroom, counseling setting, and home.

DEVELOPMENT

Keefe (1979, p. 4) described learning styles as "characteristic cognitive, affective and physiological behaviors that serve as relatively stable indicators of how learners perceive, interact with and respond to their environment." Dunn, Dunn, and Price (1979) recognized 18 elements of learning style affecting the way individuals concentrate, absorb, and retain new information and skills. Learning styles are preferences that reflect mediation abilities. They range from flexible to rigid depending on developmental maturation, neuropsychological factors, genetic codes, and socioenvironmental experiences (Gregorc, 1979; Restak, 1979).

Perceptual modality is one element of learning style. This refers to tactile, kinesthetic, visual, and auditory modes of receiving information, for which learners have a preference that normally follows a developmental progression. Yet some individuals demonstrate consistent modality preferences despite maturation. For example, a tactile or kinesthetic learner internalizes best when involved in actual experiences, projects, or physical activity. Schools typically meet the needs of students with visual and auditory preferences, yet continued attempts to classify individuals as simply visual learners or auditory learners overlooks conceptualization and mediation processes. Learners exhibit unique cognitive, affective, and physiological behaviors mediated by the environment. Therefore, a more accurate description of learning style involves additional qualitative elements. Figure 1 presents a comprehensive table of considerations affecting child and adolescent learning styles. Psychologists, counselors, and teachers can use this as a summary or reference list.

Learning styles are essentially neutral, yet potential positive and potential negative effects of various style patterns exist (Guild & Garger, 1985). For example, a child who struggles with the phonetic approach to spelling and reading may have stronger simultaneous or global processing skills. Therefore, a visual whole-word approach might facilitate word recognition and spelling revisualization. The adolescent with strong abstract reasoning and weak verbal concept formation might better demonstrate mastery of course objectives through nontraditional activities such as creative individual projects, videotaping, and demonstrations. A distractible child in an open school setting needs external structure to function successfully. These examples suggest that alternative classroom experiences are essential. Some children and adolescents serendipitously compensate for learning style needs; others must be taught "to use their strengths to strengthen weaknesses" (Lawrence, 1982).

Cognitive Elements

An application of neuropsychological principals provides a systematic framework for understanding learning style strengths and weaknesses. Neuropsychological theory contributes a model of cognitive information processing that becomes valuable because it examines the way learners attempt to solve problems by focusing on process rather than product.

Most cognitive information processing models include three basic operations: reception, central processing, and output (Snart, 1985). *Reception* involves perceptual modality and is also affected by attention, concentration, and motivation. *Central processing* includes the analysis and synthesis of information. Many factors affect processing. Some of these are memory, conceptualization, and language development. *Output* communicates verbal and nonverbal responses, the main purpose being to execute tasks and report information. Unfortunately, output and "perceived intelligence" often rely on language. Yet it appears that language itself confers little in the way of sophisticated thinking. Other systems coexist to compute and make decisions; language merely reports on these (Gazzaniga, 1985). Response is also affected by conceptual tempo, which is the amount of time required to process a task and is frequently described as reflective or impulsive (Kagan, 1966).

Coding and planning strategies govern these three operations and are characterized by simultaneous and successive processes. Literature often interchanges the terms *simultaneous* and *successive* with *global* and *analytical,* respectively. Studies indicate that reflective children utilize analytic processing, whereas impulsive children use a more global cognitive style (Sinatra, 1982). Analytic and global cognitive styles are not mutually exclusive. Many learners are equally facile with both processing styles, but some children and adolescents have extreme preferences that require matched teaching or counseling styles. Carbo (1981) suggested that extremely analytic readers can often recall details easily but have difficulty understanding global ideas. They may learn more efficiently when information is presented in small, logical, sequential steps. Global readers often respond to emotional rather than logical appeals, benefiting from high-interest experiences to focus attention, maintain interest, and facilitate understanding.

Additional elements of style may affect problem solving, goal setting, and organization. Research on field independence/dependence suggests that field-dependent learners prefer external structure, goals, and reinforcement, whereas field-independent learners supply structure themselves and often prefer to work alone (Griggs, 1985; Whitkin, Moore, Goodenough, & Cox, 1977). Children and adolescents with superior cognitive abilities may receive failing grades in school because they are disorganized and often forget or lose assignments. These students could be field-dependent learners who require external structure, cues, and reinforcement in academic and social settings.

FIGURE 1

Interactive Parameters: How do the following considerations affect learning styles?

Cognitive Elements	References
• modality perceptions: tactile, kinesthetic, visual, auditory	• Barbe & Swassing, 1979
• coding: successive, simultaneous; global, analytical	• Das & Malloy, 1981; Carbo, 1981
• planning: flexible, rigid; field dependent/independent	• Kane, 1984; Whitkin, et al., 1977
• responding: reflective, impulsive, conceptual-tempo	• Kagan, 1966; Keefe, 1979
• conceptualization: concrete, abstract, verbal, nonverbal	• Gregorc, 1979; Snart, 1985
• language: receptive, processing, expressive	• Wiig & Semel, 1984
• achievement: academic, vocational	• Kaufman & Kaufman, 1983; Knaack, 1983
• creativity, intelligence	• Presbury, Benson & Torrence, this issue; Sternberg, 1985

Affective Correlates	References
• personality: style, temperament, type	• Kiersey & Bates, 1978; Myers, 1966, 1980
• motivation: self, peer, adult, academic, other	• Dunn, Dunn & Price 1979; Maslow, 1970
• self-concept: self-image, self-esteem	• Canfield & Wells, 1976; Dunn, 1983
• social: perception, judgment, interpersonal relations	• Schumaker, et al., 1982
• coping skills: adaptive, maladaptive; locus of control	• Lawrence, 1982; Rotter, 1966

Physiological Factors	References
• neuropsychological: related learning patterns	• Hynd, 1981; Rourke, Baker, Fisk & Strang, 1983
• biological health: diet, sleep, exercise	• Greenfield & Steinback, 1972
• attending ability: directing, focusing, sustaining	• Barkely, 1977; Thies, 1983
• physical: fine/gross motor skills, strength, coordination	
• mobility needs: active, passive	• Dunn, Dunn & Price, 1979

Environmental Effects	References
• physical setting: noise, lighting; time of day, structure	• Dunn, Dunn & Price, 1979; Lawrence, 1982
• psychological atmosphere: affect, interpersonal dynamics	• Chase, 1975
• socio-cultural: norms, attitudes, values	• Guild & Garger, 1985

Qualitative descriptions of creativity and intelligence are consistent with the concept of style. Sternberg (1985) used a multidimensional model to describe intellectual strengths and weaknesses. He suggested three metacomponents or executive processes govern thinking skills and performances, namely, componential, experiential, and contextual aspects of intelligence that reach beyond traditional quantitative measures. This triarchic model focuses on analysis, insight, and adaptation abilities. It is a practical application with diagnostic implications. By capitalizing on intellectual strengths and experiences, individuals can adapt, select, and shape their environment.

Affective Correlates

Differences in cognitive styles can manifest diverse personality dimensions. Planning strategies encompass the ability to monitor the actions of oneself and others (Das & Malloy, 1981). How an individual plans, monitors, and evaluates can affect interpersonal relationships and social behavior, as well as academic achievement. Additional factors such as interest level, motivation, and locus of control appear to be important affective dimensions that interact with learning styles (Keefe, 1979).

Personality theory and research suggest that children's temperament characteristics reflect unique personality styles that also interact with learning. Myers (1962, 1980) described specific personality dimensions and types. These include a matrix of polarities: extroversion-introversion, sensing–intuition, thinking-feeling, judgment–perception. Various experiences also help younger children develop different kinds of perception and judgment. For example, exact observation exercises sensing, whereas figuring out possible solutions to a problem exercises intuition. Anticipating unintended consequences of actions exercises thinking, and identifying people's emotions exercises feeling. By observing the relative ease and interest a child has in performing these activities, parents and teachers can detect early clues indicating type or style.

Self-concept and self-esteem have a special relationship to learning style. To establish a successful identity, children and adolescents need to develop an accurate self-perception of strengths and weaknesses. Individuals who experience academic difficulty often underestimate their potential or overgeneralize failure. Knowledge regarding personal learning style communicates a realistic reflection of abilities and limitations. Parents, teachers, and counselors are in a position to facilitate this process and nurture learning style differences.

Physiological Factors

A wide range of elements influence children's and adolescents' behavior. For example, specific biological and health-related factors may affect the ability to focus and sustain attention (Barkely, 1977; Thies, 1982). Physical strength, coordination abilities, and athletic prowess can become especially important for enhancing self-esteem. Lifestyle habits such as nutrition, exercise, and rest are additional considerations that may affect academic performances.

Environmental Effects

The environment has a dual role: It mediates learning and it reflects learning styles. Consequently, the environment has the potential to accommodate or frustrate a particular style. Social learning theory, enrichment experiences and reinforcement may also play a role in the development of style differences (Guild & Garger, 1985). Therefore, intervention strategies become significant environmental mediators.

PUTTING CHILDREN'S LEARNING STYLES IN PERSPECTIVE

An environment consistent with individual learning styles enhances achievement, performance, and self-esteem (Dunn, 1983). Similarly, academic underachievement, failure, and social or emotional problems often signal learning style discrepancies. Research reveals that learning styles differ among underachievers, the gifted, the learning-disabled, and the socially maladjusted (Griggs, 1985).

Learning style differences affect children and adolescents in family, education, and social systems. Yet instead of celebrating the diversity of style, current norms and practices often ignore unique perceptions, conceptual processes, and style characteristics. When learning styles interfere with academic success, an unresolved question emerges: "Who must change, the learner or the environment?" Unfortunately, the education system often decides this by expecting all children to learn with the same approach, at the same pace. McGuiness (1986) has suggested that labels such as dyslexia and hyperactivity result from the educational system's failure to accommodate learning style differences rather than the students' ability to learn.

The present state of research and assessment makes it difficult and impractical to identify each element of style. However, stylistic differences can be detected in students by utilizing observation and self-report techniques. Programs exist that use formal and informal assessment to implement learning style interventions in education and counseling settings (Learning Styles Network Annotated Bibliography, 1986).

Communicating learning style information and designing effective interventions can be a creative challenge in school or at home. However, organizational factors and interpersonal dynamics may inhibit action. Constraints in the educational system include lack of knowledge regarding learning styles, limited alternative teaching approaches, rigid curriculum policy, and general resistance to change. At the interpersonal level, conflicting styles, attitudes, or values may promote learning discrepancies.

Until higher education training programs and school curricula adopt learning style theory and practices, consultation services will be necessary. Parents, educators, and young people benefit from knowledge regarding personal style. An emphasis on learning styles, versus learning deficits, meets the needs of all individuals while developing positive and realistic expectations for students with learning difficulties.

ALTERNATIVE ACTIONS

Acting as consultants, school psychologists and other professionals can develop academic and social or emotional interventions utilizing learning styles. Psychologists are frequently asked to provide direct services such as counseling and academic therapy, or indirect services that involve individual consultations, in-service workshops, child study meetings, or teacher assistance teams. A consultation model utilizing a systems approach is the most effective way to design group or individual interventions. A consultant needs to gather information regarding interpersonal norms, values, and attitudes towards learning differences. Organizational structures should also be examined, since developing a new program or improving an old one may be necessary. Interviews, observations, discussion, and providing learning style information often result in minor accommodations or further evaluation and referral. The remaining section contains suggestions for the school psychologist or professional who considers that attention to learning styles is a valuable intervention tool.

Identifying Learning Styles

Cornett (1983) and Freeley (1983) reviewed standardized instruments used to identify elements of style in the general population. Among them are the Learning Style Inventory (Dunn, Dunn, & Price, 1979) and the Human Information Processing Survey (Torrence, 1984). Qualitative and quantitative data from individual neuropsychological and educational assessments provide school psychologists with valuable information for interpreting learning styles in referral populations (Hynd, 1981; Kaufman & Kaufman, 1983). *An Adult's Guide to Style* (Gregorc, 1982) and the Myers-Briggs Type Indicator (Myers, 1962) help adults gain insight into their own personal styles.

Informal methods also exist to help parents and educators describe learning styles in children and adolescents. The first step begins with awareness of style and interactive parameters. The next steps involve gathering readily available information. The following sources are valuable: (a) reviewing cumulative scholastic records and achievement performances, (b) examining various samples of classwork, (c) identifying learning patterns through content and error analysis, (d) observing behavior in academic and nonacademic settings, and (e) interviewing the child and significant others. Developing a checklist of various learning style characteristics helps parents and educators utilize their data to identify patterns that reflect internal perceptions and processes. A variety of resources provide information to develop such checklists and inventories (Butler, 1984; Lawrence, 1982; Vitale, 1982).

A profile of academic and nonacademic strengths and weaknesses yields practical learning style information (Figure 2). An intervention began for Mike, an eighth-grade boy, when the classroom teacher and student used a graph to rate diverse skills and abilities as weak, average, or strong. Work samples, report card grades, observations, and self-report techniques provided necessary information. The completed profile was a valuable communication tool because it summarized Mike's preferences for acquiring and expressing information. Content analysis of reading, math, and language skills revealed specific areas of strength and weakness rather than a global level of performance. This assisted the classroom teacher in developing classroom alternatives that tapped learning strengths. Overall, the profile helped develop realistic academic expectations while emphasizing frequently overlooked areas of success.

General Classroom Strategies

When current methods are not successful, alternative approaches do not require extensive teacher training or investment of time. For example, curriculum emphasis is traditionally verbal, analytic, and abstract. Complementary strategies that benefit all learners include concrete, nonverbal, global experiences. Sinatra (1982, p. 50) suggested the following techniques:

1. Present illustrations or objects prior to, during, and after activities to tie nonverbal experiences with language. Stick figures or student drawings can be effective.
2. Use drama, music, art, role-playing, and group projects to develop reading and writing activities.
3. Present figurational materials such as graphs, flow charts, time lines, and context clues to aid holistic comprehension.
4. Supplement visual/auditory presentations with tactile cues and kinesthetic "hands on" experience whenever possible. This includes lab activities, learning centers, and peer projects.
5. Involve the use of imagery and visual mnemonics to aid coding and recall.

Classroom structure and affective atmosphere can also accommodate learning style differences:

1. Use interest as a motivational aid.
2. Involve students in decision making and activity planning.
3. Provide a variety of assignments to facilitate and evaluate mastery of objectives.
4. When possible, remove time limits from in-class assignments or allow completion outside of class.
5. Introduce activities that enhance self-esteem and encourage positive attitudes towards learning differences (see So What's the Difference?, 1985).

The amount of structure needed for an activity or situation interacts with learning styles. Children and adolescents require varying degrees of structure. Hunt (1979) outlined characteristics and interventions for styles that require varied amounts of structure. (a) Those needing very much structure are active individuals with short attention spans who do not function successfully in group situations or discussions and who need a highly structured environment that is accepting and firm, with clear and consistent rules. Short-term goals and a variety of kinesthetic activities help direct energy constructively. Positive comments and immediate feedback provide external reinforcement. (b) Those needing moderate structure are children and adolescents oriented to the role of "good students," who usually prefer to work alone, seeking teacher approval and predictable schedules. These learners need a nonthreatening environment with opportunities for choice and risk-taking to encourage spontaneity, self-awareness, and cooperation. (c) Those needing less structure are imaginative, independent thinkers who often don't require a teacher's rewards and appear to be averse to details or step-by-step activities. They may be self-centered, needing reminders to be sensitive to others. These learners can approach material from an abstract discussion level, moving later to facts and details.

A classroom intervention begins by examining the interaction between teachers' personal teaching styles and students' learning styles. The key to a successful teaching/learning style match is an eclectic instructional program. Figure 3 presents an illustrative guide for accommodating diverse styles in the classroom. This chart is a heuristic model rather than a comprehensive guide to alternative approaches. Three general questions reveal possible content demands, and a list of activities, tests, and basic skills emphasize differences in learning styles. A psychologist or teacher can use this as a reference guide for classroom interventions. One example involves the exclusive use of written objective tests to determine mastery. This may actually prevent some learners from demonstrating their acquisition of knowledge because it taps a limited scope of skills. The most practical and efficient way to use this chart is to identify content demands for a given task and observe the students' performance. When a particular approach is repeatedly unsuccessful, another method with emphasis on a different learning style should be explored. A variety of presentation and evaluation methods accommodate learning style needs in both general and special education programs.

Basic Skills: Specific Strategies

Children and adolescents who experience academic difficulties may require an individualized teach-

FIGURE 2

An informal analysis of an individual's strengths and weaknesses communicates valuable learning style information to parents, educators, and students.

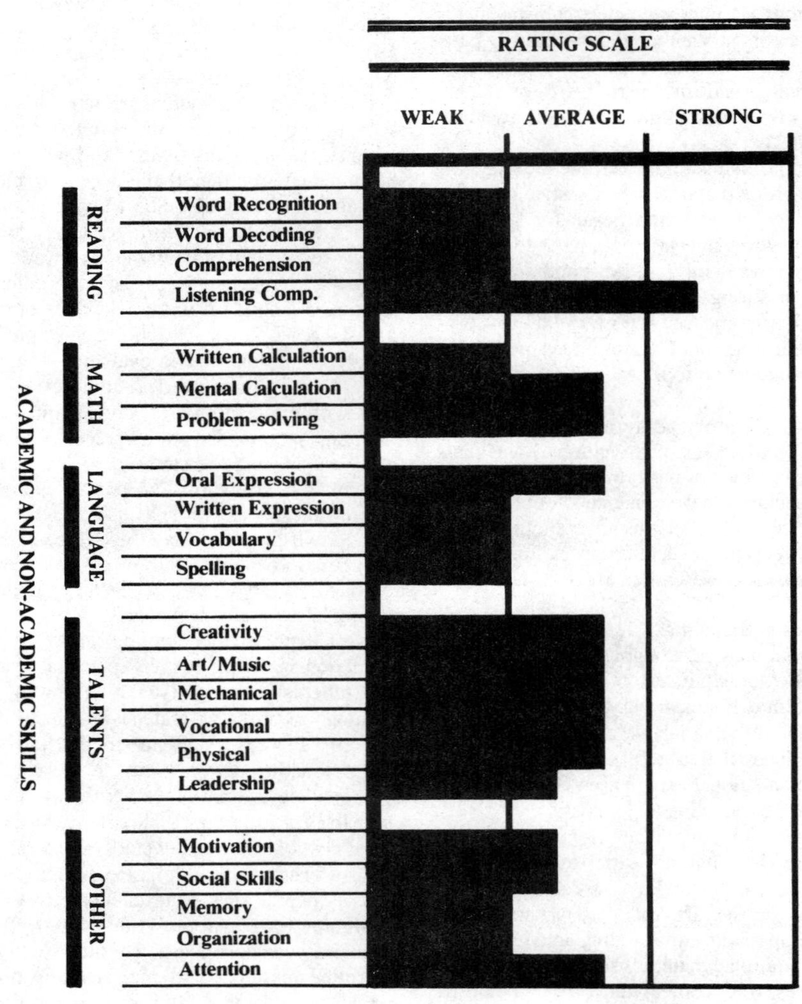

FIGURE 3

An illustrative guide for matching teaching and learning styles in the classroom, K–12

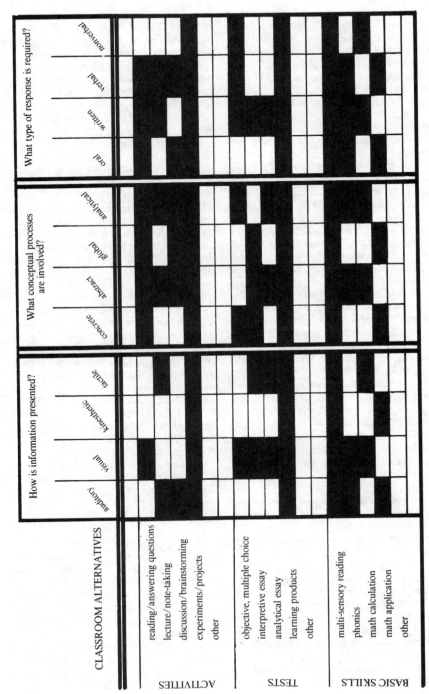

LEARNING STYLE EMPHASIS

CLASSROOM ALTERNATIVES		How is information presented?				What conceptual processes are involved?				What type of response is required?			
		auditory	visual	kinesthetic	tactile	concrete	abstract	global	analytical	oral	written	verbal	nonverbal
ACTIVITIES	reading/answering questions		■			■	■	■	■	■	■	■	
	lecture/note-taking	■			■		■		■		■	■	
	discussion/brainstorming	■					■	■	■	■		■	
	experiments/projects	■	■	■	■	■	■	■	■	■	■	■	■
	other												
TESTS	objective, multiple choice		■			■			■		■	■	■
	interpretive essay		■		■	■	■	■			■		
	analytical essay		■		■		■		■		■		
	learning products	■	■	■	■	■	■	■	■	■	■	■	■
	other												
BASIC SKILLS	multi-sensory reading	■	■	■	■	■	■	■	■	■	■	■	■
	phonics	■	■				■		■	■	■	■	
	math calculation		■		■		■		■		■		■
	math application	■		■		■		■		■		■	
	other												

ing/learning style match. Helping these learners acquire basic skills and concepts might involve work in the following areas.

1. Reading style: A review of previous instruction and an informal inventory can reveal strengths and weaknesses in word recognition, phonetic decoding, comprehension, and listening skills. This information helps select the "right method(s)" for elementary children, which might include language experience stories, multisensory techniques, phonics, or sight vocabulary; teaching reading through the content areas may be effective at middle and high school levels (Carbo, Dunn, & Dunn, 1986; Gunnison & Kaufman, 1982).

2. Mathematics: Work samples and math surveys can be combined to identify learning style patterns that affect computational skills, number concepts, and mastery of basic facts. A highly systematic and concrete approach to math concepts may be necessary for some children and adolescents, and providing verbal rules may facilitate acquisition of the visual–spatial skills required for computation (Kaufman, Kaufman, & Goldsmith, 1984; Rourke, 1985). Calculators and computers help compensate for weak basic facts while providing high-interest reinforcement and practice.

3. Written language: Observation of spontaneous writing samples identifies handwriting, word usage, theme maturity, and spelling skills. A general comparison of oral and written expression may reveal a more efficient mode of expression, and analysis of subskills can target specific learning style needs. Individuals with weak phonetic spelling ability may require a structured approach emphasizing visual word patterns such as "night, bright, delight." In contrast, learners with adequate phonetic skills need different exercises such as reading or "20 times each" to increase visual recall and letter sequence. Individuals with strong theme expression and weak punctuation/capitalization or handwriting might benefit from the Write-Right method. This allows the individual to free-write content of an assignment on a rough draft and edit corrections on the second draft. Word-processing programs are excellent compensatory or supplementary tools.

Learning Styles and Social–Emotional Development

Perhaps the people who most need to understand the concept of individual style are parents. As a child matures, parents who understand style patterns are better able to accept unique differences and set realistic expectations. This also helps parents manage school-related tasks and assist with future career goals.

Parents can identify differences in perception and judgment by observing unique adaptation modes during early developmental stages (Myers, 1980). Observation of children and adolescents in academic, social, and family settings provides a holistic perspective of style. As in the classroom, stylistic differences often require accommodation in the home or family. The impulsive, disorganized child needs a structured environment with consistent discipline. The adolescent who lacks academic success benefits from parents who provide nonacademic opportunities for success. And the talented or creative youngster grows from experiences at home that explore and encourage unique gifts.

Counseling. Therapeutic interventions that consider individual learning styles facilitate the counseling process. Awareness of cognitive information processes and personality style clearly assists with selection of treatment and intervention strategies. Griggs (1985) focused on four considerations when counseling through individual learning styles: (a) type of client (learning style, personality, sociocultural background); (b) setting (individual, group, peer, adult); (c) counseling approach (behavioral, cognitive, rational emotive therapy, reality therapy, etc.); (d) technique (verbal, visual, kinesthetic, structured, etc.).

A variety of presenting problems illustrate unique learning style approaches in counseling. For example, an aggressive child with weak verbal reasoning skills may not gain adequate insight into her or his behavior through traditional "talk through" approaches. This child requires concrete, experiential techniques such as creative arts therapy, multisensory imagery, or gestalt exercises. Adolescents with weak attending and organizing abilities might benefit from relaxation training, biofeedback, or cognitive behavior modification. Individuals who lack accurate social perceptions or judgment may respond to structured social skill training that emphasizes clearly defined behaviors and consequences. Academically gifted students with anxious, perfectionistic tendencies may dispel irrational thoughts through insight-oriented approaches and learn to manage physiological responses with relaxation exercises. Enhancing self-esteem in the kinesthetic learner could involve nonverbal approaches and unconventional techniques such as dance, running, team sports, or adventure experiences (Bass, 1985; Glasser, 1976).

This brief overview presents a sampling of isolated cases and hopefully emphasizes the value of examining learning styles in the counseling process. A variety of cognitive and behavioral approaches exist to accommodate different styles (Griggs, 1985). Counseling is also an effective way to help children and adolescents understand their learning style and develop realistic self-perceptions.

SUMMARY

This chapter invites parents and professionals to tap learning potential by developing style strengths and accommodating needs. Academic performance and interpersonal relations frequently reflect stylistic differences. Cognitive, affective, physiological, and environmental parameters are important considerations that affect learning styles.

A practical application of learning styles asks persons directly involved with children and adolescents (a) to become familiar with their own personal learning styles, (b) to develop a basic understanding of cognitive information processes and interactive parameters, (c) to identify unique perceptions and conceptual approaches, (d) to analyze content or situation demands, (e) to help students understand their styles and develop compatible learning strategies, and (f) to manipulate the environment when necessary to accommodate learning style needs. Indirect services include consultation at the organizational level to develop curricula based on learning styles and alternative teaching approaches. Pilot programs and in-service workshops can begin the planned change process in schools.

Attention to learning styles asks everyone to examine current practices and attitudes toward learning. People need to accept the concept of individual style and begin to recognize a range of learning styles that are all variations of "normal." The diversity of style yields various scholastic, artistic, and mechanical skills. Learning styles promote equity in young people by discovering how they learn, and how they fail to learn. Ultimately, this helps children and adolescents find ways to help themselves.

REFERENCES

Barbe, W. B., & Swassing, R. H. (1979). *Teaching through modality strengths: Concepts and practices.* Columbus, OH: Zaner-Bloser.

Barkely, R. A. (1977). A review of stimulant drug research with hyperactive children. *Journal of Child Psychology and Psychiatry, 18,* 1–31.

Bass, C. (1985). Running can modify classroom behavior. *Journal of Learning Disabilities, 18,* 160–162.

Bland, J. (Ed.) (1985). So what's the difference? Developing positive attitudes towards persons who learn differently. *Virginia Journal of Education, 78,* 24.

Butler, K. (1984). *Learning and teaching style: In theory and practice.* Maynard, MA: Gabriel Systems.

Canfield, J., & Wells, H. (1976). *100 ways to enhance self-concept in the classroom: A handbook for teachers and parents:* Englewood Cliffs, NJ: Prentice-Hall.

Carbo, M. (1981). Reading style inventory manual. Roslyn Heights, NY: Learning Research Associates.

Carbo, M., Dunn, R., & Dunn, K. (1986). *Teaching students to read through their individual learning styles.* Englewood Cliffs, NJ: Prentice-Hall.

Chase, L. (1975). *The other side of the report card: A how-to-do-it program for affective education.* Santa Monica, CA: Goodyear.

Cornett, C. (1983). *What you should know about teaching and learning styles.* Bloomington, IN: Phi Delta Kappa Educational Foundation.

Das, J. P., & Malloy, G. (1981). Of brain divisions and functions. *Academic Therapy, 16,* 349–358.

Dunn, R. (1983). Learning styles and its relation to exceptionality at both ends of the spectrum. *Exceptional Children, 49,* 496–507..

Dunn, R., Dunn, K., & Price, G. (1979). Identifying individual learning styles. In National Association of Secondary School Principals (Eds.), *Student learning styles: Diagnosing and prescribing programs* (pp. 39–54). Reston, VA: NASSP.

Freeley, M. (1983). Instrumentation Assessment Analysis: Interim Report. *Learning Styles Network.* Jamaica, NY: St. John's University and National Association of Secondary School Principals.

Gazzaniga, M. (1985). *The social brain: Discovering networks of the mind.* New York: Basic Books.

Glasser, W. (1976). *Positive addiction.* New York: Harper and Row.

Greenfield, N., & Steinback, R. (1972). *Handbook of psychophysiology.* New York: Holt, Rinehart & Winston.

Gregorc, A. (1979). Learning/teaching styles: Potent forces behind them. *Educational Leadership, 36,* 234–236.

Gregorc, A. (1982). *An adult's guide to style.* Maynard, MA: Gabriel Systems.

Griggs, S. (1985). *Counseling students through their individual learning styles.* Ann Arbor, MI: University of Michigan, ERIC Counseling and Personnel Services Clearinghouse.

Guild, P. B., & Garger, S. (1985). *Marching to different drummers.* Alexandria, VA: Association for Supervision and Curriculum Development.

Gunnison, J., & Kaufman, N. K. (1982). Reading remediation based on sequential and simultaneous processing. *Academic Therapy, 17,* 297–311.

Hunt, D. (1979). Learning style and student needs: An introduction to conceptual level. In National Association of Secondary School Principals (Eds.), *Student learning styles: Diagnosing and prescribing programs* (pp. 27–38). Reston, VA: NASSP.

Hynd, G. (Ed.). (1981). Neuropsychology in the schools. [Special Issue]. *School Psychology Review, 10*(3).

Kagan, J. (1965). Impulsive and reflective children: Significance of conceptual tempo. In J. D. Krumboltz (Ed.). *Learning and the educational process.* Chicago: Rand McNally.

Kagan, J. (1966). Reflection–impulsivity. The generality and dynamics of conceptual-tempo. *Journal of Abnormal Psychology, 71,* 17–24.

Kane, M. (1984). Cognitive styles of learning and thinking: Parts I, II. *Academic Therapy, 19,* 83–92; *20,* 527–536.

Kaufman, A., & Kaufman, N. (1983). *Kaufman Assessment Battery for Children (K-ABC) Manual.* Circle Pines, MN: American Guidance Service.

Kaufman, A., Kaufman, N., & Goldsmith, B. (1984). *Kaufman Sequential or Simultaneous: K-SOS. Participant's Packet.* Circle Pines, MN: American Guidance Service.

Keefe, J. W. (1979). School applications of the learning style concept. In National Association of Secondary School Principals (Eds.), *Student learning styles: Diagnosing and prescribing programs* (pp. 123–132). Reston, VA: NASSP.

Keirsey, D., & Bates, M. (1978). *Please understand me, character and temperament types.* Del Mar, CA: Prometheus, Nemesis.

Knaak, W. C. (1983). *Learning styles: Applications to vocational education.* Columbus, OH: National Center for Research in Vocational Education.

Lawrence, G. (1982). *People types and tiger stripes: A practical guide to learning styles* (2nd ed.). Gainesville, FL: Center for Application of Psychological Type.

Learning styles network: Annotated bibliography. (1986). Jamaica, NY: St. John's University and the National Association of Secondary School Principals.

Maslow, A. (1970). *Motivation and personality* (2nd ed.). New York: Harper and Row.

McGuinness, D. (1986). *When children don't learn: Understanding the biology and psychology of learning disabilities.* New York: Basic Books.

Myers, I. B. (1962). *The Myers-Briggs type indicator manual.* Princeton, NJ: Educational Testing Service.

Myers, I. B. (1980). *Gifts differing.* Palo Alto, CA: Consulting Psychologists.

National Association of School Psychologists. (1985). Advocacy for appropriate educational services for all children. *Communique, 13*(8), 9.

Restak, R. (1979). *The brain: The last frontier.* New York: Warner Books.

Rotter, J. B. (1966). Generalized expectancies for internal versus external control of reinforcements. *Psychological Monographs, 80*(10), 1–28.

Rourke, B. (1985). *The neuropsychology of learning disabilities.* New York: Guilford.

Rourke, B., Baker, D., Fisk, J., & Strang, J. (1983). *Child neuropsychology: An introduction to theory, research and clinical practice.* New York: Guilford.

Shumaker, J., Hazel, J., Sherman, J., & Sheldon, J. (1982). Social skill performances of learning disabled, non-learning disabled and delinquent adolescents. *Learning Disability Quarterly, 5,* 388–393.

Sinatra, R. (1982). Brain processing: Where learning styles begin. *Early Years, 12*(6), 49–51.

Snart, F. (1985). Cognitive processing approaches for the assessment and remediation of learning problems: An interview with J. P. Das and Reuven Feuerstein. *Journal of Psychoeducational Assessment, 3,* 1–14.

Sternberg, R. J. (1985). *Beyond IQ.* New York: Cambridge University Press.

Thies, A. P. (1983). The biology of attention. *Early Years, 13*(7), 18–19.

Torrance, E. P. (1984). *Human information processing survey.* Bensenville, IL: Scholastic Testing Service.

Vitale, B. (1982). *Unicorns are real: A right brained approach to learning.* Rolling Hills Estates, CA: Jalmar Press.

Wiig, E. H., & Semel, E. M. (1984). *Language disabilities in children and adolescents.* Columbus, OH: Merrill.

Witkin, H., Moore, C. A., Goodenough, D. R., & Cox, P. W. (1977). Field-dependent and field-independent cognitive styles and their educational implications. *Review of Educational Research, 47,* 1–64.

BIBLIOGRAPHY: PROFESSIONALS

Butler, K. (1984). *Learning and teaching style: In theory and practice.* Maynard, MA: Gabriel Systems.
Presents the concept of style with extensive applications for the classroom. Based on Gregorc's model of learning style, it is particularly useful for curriculum development and inservice training, K–12. Charts, checklists, and specific recommendations are included.

Griggs, S. (1985). *Counseling students through their individual learning styles.* Ann Arbor, MI: University of Michigan. ERIC Counseling and Personnel Services Clearinghouse.
Contains valuable information for counselors and psychologists. Chapters cover such subjects as identifying learning styles, prescribing counseling interventions, and consulting with parents and teachers. It also describes research and current programs utilizing learning style interventions.

Guild, P., & Garber, S. (1985). *Marching to different drummers.* Alexandria, VA: Association for Supervision and Curriculum Development.
Answers the question "How can knowledge about style help open educational opportunities to students who need it most?" It presents major research contributions, a summary of concepts, and a wide range of suggested applications. Recommended for parents, counselors, psychologists, and school personnel.

Lawrence, G. (1982). *People types and tiger stripes: A practical guide to learning styles.* (2nd ed.). Gainesville, FL: Center for Applications of Psychological Type.
This practical book presents ways to identify learning styles and motivation patterns. It includes readings, exercises, and applications of learning style theory. There is an expanded introduction to Jung's types, a question-and-answer section, and a chapter on introducing type theory into a school system.

Learning Styles Network Newsletter. St. John's University and the National Association of Secondary School Principals, School of Education and Human Services, Grand Central and Utopia Parkways, Jamaica, NY 11439.
The Network is a clearinghouse for learning style information. It publishes a newsletter providing current research, experimental programs, conference schedules, and a list of media explaining learning style to students and adults. The Network compiles an annotated bibliography annually.

BIBLIOGRAPHY: PARENTS

Barbe, W. (1985). *Growing up learning: The key to your child's potential.* Washington, DC: Acropolis Books.
A practical guide for parents and teachers, this book explains how to increase success based on individual strengths. It utilizes learning styles to teach discipline, reading, handwriting, math, spelling, and living skills.

Duncan, L. (1984, January). What's going on here? When bright kids don't learn. *Working Mother,* pp. 69–73.
Lois Duncan is a popular author who writes empathically about child and adolescent learning disabilities. She has a learning style weakness affecting visual memory, and chose the writing profession because of her strong verbal skills. This article helps parents identify and understand various academic and social problems related to learning style "disabilities."

Guild, P., & Hand, K. (1985). *Where did we get this one? A parents' guide to appreciating the individual personalities of their children.* Seattle, WA: The Teaching Advisory.
This booklet helps parents understand differences in children's style. It encourages parents to use this knowledge to improve parent–child relationships, to help children be successful in school, and generally to enhance self-esteem.

Schumann, W. (1983, October). Educators are finding some children need special help to develop basic skills for learning. *Parents,* pp. 42–50.
Helpful to parents with young children who experience learning difficulties. The author discusses educational alternatives, social adjustments, and opportunities for success. She includes a checklist for parents regarding language development, visual–spatial skills, motor skills, and general behavior.

Vitale, B. (1982). *Unicorns are real: A right-brained approach to learning.* Rolling Hills Estates, CA: Jalmar Press.
An illustrated activity book showing parents and teachers how to tap children's strengths. It includes creative strategies that complement traditional approaches. The author's use of "left-brain/right-brain" terminology serves to develop awareness and emphasize learning style differences rather than verify brain–behavior localizations.

BIBLIOGRAPHY: CHILDREN

Duncan, L. (1983). Learning disabilities: Why some smart people can't learn. *Current Health, 10*(1), 3–8.
Appropriate for grades 8–12. The author successfully presents LD boys and girls as intelligent individuals who "learn differently." Descriptions of famous and ordinary people who utilized their learning strengths to compensate for weaknesses are valuable for general and special education students.

Hedges, W. (1980, February). The labeling game. *Instructor,* 176.
This one-page article describes 10 persons who experienced social and academic problems during their early years. Although labeled in one way or another, they went on to become successful presidents, authors, and psychologists. This activity can be a springboard for discussion on the diversity of learning styles and is appropriate for parents and teachers, as well as adolescents.

Ulrich, C., & Guild, P. (1985). *No sweat! How to use your learning style to be a better student.* Seattle, WA: The Teaching Advisory.
Written for elementary and middle school students, this booklet helps children identify their own learning styles. It includes strategies for effective studying, ways to approach assignments, and how to ask for help from teachers and parents.

Children and Lying

Jan Hughes
Texas A & M University

BACKGROUND

Definitional and Conceptual Issues

A lie is a special type of untrue statement, and it is important to define *lie* in a manner that distinguishes it from other false statements. It is important because the psychologist must ascertain the type of falsehood before prescribing a treatment strategy. Children as young as 8 years of age and adults do not call an unintentional falsehood a lie (Wimmer, Gruber, & Perner, 1984). That is, children and adults are unwilling to define an assertion as a lie on the basis strictly of its accuracy. An untruthful statement made with no intention to deceive is not a lie. In a study of children's definitions of lying, Peterson, Peterson, and Seeto (1983) found that 80% of 9-year-olds and 95% of adults do not classify an erroneous guess as a lie.

For purposes of this chapter, *lie* is defined as an intentional falsehood that lacks prosocial motivation. The intentional/unintentional distinction refers to the congruence between the speaker's subjective experience of the truth and his or her assertion. If a person thinks A and says B, statement B is an intentional falsehood. Instrumental, or antisocial, lies are deliberate attempts to deceive another person in order to avoid blame, obtain a reward, or inflict harm. Examples of each of these instrumental lies follow: (a) A girl accidentally breaks a vase; her mother asks how the vase broke; the girl replies, "I don't know." (b) A boy falsely tells his mother that he has finished his homework; (c) A school child tells a girl classmate that another classmate is spreading unkind rumors about her, in hopes of starting a fight between the two classmates; the accusation, however, is false.

Compulsive lying and wishful thinking are examples of noninstrumental lies. In wishful thinking, the lie is motivated by a desire that things be different. A rejected girl tells her classmates that she has a close friend who lives in a nearby town and that they engage in many fun activities together. This child knows that no such friend exists, but she would very much like to have a friend. The lie harms no one; the imaginary friend is a substitute for the real friend she wants. Wishful thinking is different from falsehoods that are motivated by unconscious needs, as occurs in denial, which is described below.

In compulsive lying, a person lies excessively, without immediate or long-term gain. The individual recognizes the falseness of the assertion but experiences a subjective sense of compulsion, or lessened control over lying. Compulsive lying, like compulsive stealing, or kleptomania, is considered an impulse control problem (Fenichel, 1945). However, there is virtually no literature on the causes or treatment of compulsive lying.

Prosocial falsehoods are motivated by positive social motives, such as avoiding hurting another's feelings, entertaining another, and helping another. These intentional falsehoods are not classified as lies. Examples of each type of prosocial falsehood follow: (a) to avoid hurting feelings, a boy tells a friend that he likes his new hair style, when the friend asks him for his opinion. (b) To embellish a story, a girl says that the dog that chased her on her way to school was as "big as an elephant." (c) To prevent another person from getting hurt, a child claims, upon inquiry by the neighborhood bully, not to know where a smaller child is.

There are three types of unintentional falsehoods. First, a child may not distinguish reality from fantasy. For example, a boy says that two girls followed him all day at school, staring at him constantly and whispering about him. The boy believes this assertion, even though no one followed him all day.

Second, a child's false assertion may be the result of the unconscious defense mechanism of denial. For example, a 6-year-old denies ever trying to hurt baby brother, even after pinching him hard. Because the pain and discomfort that acknowledging the behavior would produce cannot be tolerated, there is a resort to denial. Although there are no data on the frequency of denial in children, it probably is common among children below the age of about 7 years. Young children's perceptions of others are often global (Flavell, 1985), that is, they evaluate people in global terms of good and bad. They may deny they have done something bad, because to admit to bad behavior is to believe oneself all bad. Children 6 years old do not believe that they can both be a good person and behave badly or have "bad feelings" (Harter, 1977). Because such psychological defenses occur at an unconscious level, there is no conscious attempt to deceive another.

The third type of unintentional falsehood is the accidental falsehood. Children often make a false statement accidentally because they are misinformed, or make an erroneous guess.

This classification scheme has important implications for intervention. When a teacher or parent reports that a child lies, the school psychologist must ascertain the type of falsehood that is being termed a lie. Prosocial falsehoods and accidental falsehoods require no intervention. The child whose perception of reality is distorted needs a comprehensive psychological or psychiatric evaluation to determine the presence of psychotic thinking. The child who relies on denial as a coping response may require no intervention, as this type of defense is common in children below the age of 7. Beyond about age 7, children who rely on denial may require counseling to help them develop a more realistic and integrated self-concept.

This chapter focuses on interventions for children who tell antisocial lies. In addition, wishful thinking and compulsive lying are briefly examined.

Incidence

Lying is a very common behavior. In fact, the item "I do not always tell the truth" is included on the Lie scale of the Minnesota Multiphasic Personality Inventory (Hathaway & McKinley, 1967). The purpose of the Lie scale is to detect persons who are not straightforward and honest in answering items on the test. In a study on developmental changes in conceptions of lying, Peterson et al. (1983) found that all children more than 11-years-old and adults admit to lying at least some of the time. Because everyone lies at least sometimes, the frequency and the severity of the consequence of the lying are important considerations in defining lying as a problem behavior. Because there are no data on the frequency of lying in normal populations, frequency cannot be defined as a statistical deviation from a norm. As to its consequences, lying is regarded as a problem behavior when it interferes with the development and maintenance of satisfying interpersonal relationships. This criterion for determining when lying is a problem behavior recognizes that lying is an interpersonal behavior that tends to destroy the trust that is essential to satisfying relationships with others.

There are no reliable data on sex differences in lying. Because lying and cheating are both dishonest behaviors, but studies on sex differences and cheating may be relevant to lying. The frequency of cheating is reported to be the same in school-aged boys and girls (Burton, 1976), and in a study on sex differences in self-reported shoplifting, Wright and Kirmani (1977) found that fewer girls than boys reported shoplifting.

Although moral reasoning and moral behavior are not the same, researchers investigating sex differences in moral reasoning relative to lying and stealing found no sex differences (Peisach & Hardeman, 1983).

Although there are no reliable data on age differences in lying, researchers have investigated developmental changes in children's definitions of lying and moral evaluations of lying. Young children's lexical definitions of lying are stricter than those of older children and adults (Peterson et al., 1983; Wimmer, Gruber, & Perner, 1984). Children under age 8 tend to define a lie strictly in terms of its adherence to the truth, whereas older children and adults define lies in terms of both factual accuracy and the speaker's intentions. All children, even 4-year-olds, tend to evaluate the morality, or badness, of statements in terms of the speaker's intentions rather than in terms of the truthfulness of the statement. Selfishly motivated falsehoods are evaluated as worse than unintended falsehoods and prosocial falsehoods (Peterson et al., 1983; Wimmer et al., 1984). Thus, even very young children know the difference between lying and telling the truth, know that it is wrong to lie, and evaluate selfish falsehoods as worse than other falsehoods.

Role of Lying in Other Childhood Problems

Lying is associated with several childhood problems, including poor peer relationships, conduct disorders, and disturbed parent child relationships. Thus, viewing lying as part of a constellation of behaviors is more useful than viewing lying as an isolated behavior problem.

Lying and Interpersonal Relationships. Trust is an essential characteristic of friendship, especially in later childhood and adolescence (Selman, 1980). Thus, the child who lies will have difficulty being accepted by peers and developing close friendships. In turn, satisfactory peer relationships are very important to a child's behavioral adjustment and learning. Children who are rejected by their peers achieve less well in school (Bonney, 1971; Laughlin, 1954) and are more likely to experience a wide range of adjustment difficulties in later adolescence and adulthood (e.g., Cowen, Pederson, Barbigian, Izzo, & Trost, 1973; Robbins, 1966; Roff, Sells, & Golden, 1972). The importance of satisfactory peer relationships increases in adolescence, as adolescents depend more on peers and less on parents for emotional support and approval. Because rejected or withdrawn children experience fewer opportunities to interact with peers, they lose opportunities to learn essential social skills for interpersonal relationships.

Lying and Conduct Disorders. According to the *Diagnostic and Statistical Manual,* Third Edition (DSM III) (American Psychiatric Association, 1980), lying is one of the criteria for a diagnosis of Conduct Disorder. The conduct-disordered child or adolescent violates societal norms of conduct by persistently engaging in behavior in which the basic rights of others or societal norms or rules are violated. In the conduct-disordered youth, lying is part of a pattern of antisocial behavior. The youth violates consensually defined standards of moral behavior by engaging in such behaviors as lying, stealing, truancy, and consumption of illegal drugs.

Lying and Oppositional Disorders. Also according to *DSM III,* lying is common in children found to have an Oppositional Disorder. However, the lying is not as persistent as in the case of the conduct-disordered child. In the child with a diagnosis of oppositional disorder, lying is a pattern of negativistic, rebellious, and hostile behavior toward the parents.

DEVELOPMENT

Because honesty is a moral behavior, theories of moral development are relevant to the development of honesty. The Swiss scientist Jean Piaget wrote extensively about the development of children's moral reasoning and moral behavior. Piaget's research emphasized the cognitive aspect of moral development. Piaget investigated the development of children's knowledge of ethical rules and their judgments of the goodness and badness of various acts. He claimed that children up to about age 9 judge the morality of informative statements only on the basis of their accuracy, a view referred to as *moral realism.* He believed that older children and adults use the speaker's intention to deceive as the main criterion in evaluating the morality of informative statements, a view he termed *subjective responsibility.* Recently, researchers have questioned Piaget's claim that young children are not capable of considering the speaker's intention in evaluating the goodness or badness of untrue assertions. These researchers believe that Piaget's findings were a result of certain methodological flaws (Peterson, et al., 1983; Wimmer et al., 1984). They have found that children's definitions of lying are based on moral realism, as Piaget found; that is, children below about 9 years of age define an assertion as a lie on the basis only of its accuracy. This finding is not surprising, considering that parents and teachers tell children a lie is "something that is not true." Contrary to Piaget's findings, in evaluating the goodness and badness of false assertions, even children as young as 4 years of age evaluate selfish lies as worse than accidental lies. Furthermore, a selfish lie that results in only a small negative consequence is evaluated more harshly than an accidental lie that results in a larger negative consequence. Thus, young children adopt a subjective realism view of the morality of lying.

Kohlberg (1969) offered a theory of moral development that extended and refined Piaget's theory. Kohlberg formulated a series of three broad levels of moral development, subdivided into six stages. At the first level, that of preconventional morality, there is no internalization of moral standards. Moral acts are judged on the basis of their consequences. "You should not lie because you would be punished" is an example of Level 1 moral reasoning. At Level 2, the conventional level, ethical standards are internalized and judgments of right and wrong are based on the approval or disapproval of others rather than on the physical consequences of the behavior. "You should not lie because other people will not trust you" is an example of Level 2 reasoning. At Level 3, moral judgments are based on a rational and internalized ethical code and are relatively independent of approval or negative sanctions of others.

Although the ages at which individuals attain each stage vary, Kohlberg believed that individuals progress through the stages in an invariant order and that a child's cognitive abilities determine the stage of moral development.

Kohlberg provided evidence that Level 1 prevailed in children below the age of about 9. However, recent investigators have questioned Kohlberg's conclusions. Peisach and Hardeman (1983) interviewed first graders regarding reasons for not lying. They found that 75% of first graders' responses reflected Level 2 moral reasoning.

The implications of research on the development of moral reasoning is that even young children know better than to lie. Of course, knowledge of the morally correct behavior does not guarantee morally correct behavior. Most evidence indicates that there is little relationship between moral judgments and moral behavior, such as cheating, among young children (Nelsen, Grinder, & Biaggio, 1969). Thus, knowledge of a child's moral judgments does not predict moral behavior. Children lie for reasons other than low levels of moral reasoning.

Although there are no data on the stability of lying, there are data on the stability of antisocial behaviors in general (Graham, 1979) that suggest that antisocial behaviors are relatively stable throughout childhood and adolescence. This stability increases the need to intervene instead of waiting for children to "outgrow" their antisocial behaviors. Another reason for intervening early in cases of problem lying is the likelihood that the lying will have negative consequences on children's development of interpersonal relationships.

PUTTING CHILDHOOD LYING IN PERSPECTIVE

When a teacher or parent asks for help regarding a child's lying, the psychologist must conduct an assessment of the lying behavior in order to know how to intervene. A problem-solving approach to the assessment of lying is recommended, in which the psychologist collects information that will answer a series of questions. Based on the answers to these questions, an individual model of the child's lying is constructed that helps the psychologist formulate hypotheses about the reasons the child lies and suggests intervention approaches. In turn, the success of the intervention provides evidence as to the clinical utility of the individual model. The following text presents the recommended series of questions as well as methods of obtaining the data needed to answer each question.

A Question-Answering Approach to Assessment

What behaviors does the referring adult classify as lying? In an interview with the adult, the psychologist asks for specific examples of the referred child's lying behavior. The classification scheme discussed above can be used to help the referring adult identify the behavior of concern.

How frequently does the child lie? There are very real problems in obtaining an accurate count of lying. Lying is difficult to observe; a child may be a skilled liar and only get caught on occasion. Nevertheless, an estimate of the frequency of lying helps the psychologist determine the seriousness of the problem and serves as an important baseline against which to evaluate improvement following the intervention. The psychologist asks the referring adult to maintain a written record of the child's lying for a period of 7–12 days. The definition of lying arrived at in the interview serves as the operational definition of lying. If possible, both the child's parents and the teachers record instances of lying in order to determine the specifics of the behavior. Because the adults will not be able to judge, with complete confidence, whether an assertion made by the child is true or false, they record all assertions they have just cause to believe are false. As a check on the accuracy of this count, the parents or teachers are instructed to select a small number of the recorded suspected lies to inconspicuously investigate.

With respect to detection of lying, there are several commonly held beliefs about cues associated with lying. For example, people believe broken eye contact is a behavioral cue associated with lying (Zuckerman et al., 1981). Research with adults, however, has demonstrated little correspondence between these cues and actual deception (e.g., Zuckerman, et al., 1981; DePaulo, Lanier, & Davis, 1983). There are no comparable studies on detection of lying in children.

What is the content and context of the child's lying? The answer to this question is critical to understanding the child's lying and selecting an intervention strategy. By analyzing the content of the child's lies and environmental antecedents and consequences, the psychologist formulates hypotheses about the child's motivations. To obtain information on the content of the child's lies, the psychologist asks the referring adult, as well as other adults who are in a position to observe the child, to write down each instance of lying. This recording yields a frequency count as well as a content analysis. For each recording, the observer writes down the following information: the actual content of the lie, antecedent events, and consequent events. Antecedent events here mean all the characteristics of the situation that obtained just before the lie occurred and the person to whom the lie was directed. Consequent events are simply whatever happened just after the lie occurred. Examples of antecedent situations: bragging by another child; criticism of the target child; an unstructured play situation. Examples of consequent events: someone calls the child a liar; the child avoids punishment; or another child is unjustly blamed. A notepad with three columns marked off facilitates the record keeping. In the center column, the observer writes the child's suspected false assertion, in the left column the antecedents, in the third column consequent events.

Do other children view the child as having a problem with lying? Given the importance of lying to interpersonal relationships, it is important to determine the extent to which the child's peers view the child as untrustworthy. The Guess Who technique is a sociometric procedure that yields information on children's perceptions of classmates (Asher & Hymel, 1981). All children in a classroom are asked to write the name of a classmate next to statements that begin with the words "Guess who." Example items are "Guess who is real smart on tests" and "Guess who is always being the class clown." One of the items could ask students "Guess who says things that are not true."

What other problems does the child have? In order to place the child's lying in perspective, problems in other areas must be identified. The lying may be related to poor academic achievement, truancy, stealing, cheating, aggression, peer rejection, or social withdrawal. There are several behavioral rating scales and checklists that are useful in assessing a child's behavior problems in different areas. For example, the Peterson-Quay Behavior Problem Checklist (Quay & Peterson, 1979) and the School Behavior Checklist (Miller, 1972) have good reliability and evidence of concurrent validity. The Achenbach Child Behavior Checklist (Achenbach & Edelbrock, 1983) is completed by a child's parents and has good reliability and evidence of validity. By taking a broad view of the child's behavior problems as well as areas of strength, the lying can be put into perspective. When lying is part of a pattern of delinquent behavior, the intervention should address the class of delinquent behaviors rather than only the lying. When the child who lies has poor social skills, intervention should attempt to improve the deficient skills.

What prosocial behaviors does the child lack or perform at a substandard level? The social skills deficit hypothesis of lying states that lying occurs because of a deficiency in important friendship-making skills. Social skills can be evaluated through behavioral observation, teacher ratings, and peer ratings, or sociometrics. Evaluations of these approaches can be found in Asher and Hymel (1981) and Gresham (1981).

What socialization influences has the child experienced? It is important to determine if the child's peer group and parents provide the child with models of honesty in interpersonal relationships. In delinquency subcultures, the values of the dominant culture are rejected, often because low-socioeconomic-status individuals often believe they are blocked from access to U.S. middle-class advantages (Cohen, 1955). A social history provides important information on the child's socialization history.

Integrating Assessment Data into an Individual Model: Two Case Examples.

Case 1. Phillip, age 10, was referred to the school psychologist by his classroom teacher for excessive lying. In the initial interview, the teacher recounted several of Phillip's recent lies, including the claims of having given a crippled child a ticket to Disneyland that he had won, having had a pet tiger when he was younger, having raised $1,000 for the American Red Cross in a marathon jumprope contest, and having lived in a mansion in Virginia before a flood washed it away. The teacher agreed to record Phillip's lying behavior, using the three-column technique, for seven school days. The teacher recorded an average of two lies a day. The lies were told to the entire class, usually during social studies, when class discussions were common. The lies often involved material possessions or outstanding accomplishments. Other children argued with Phillip, trying to prove that he was lying, but Phillip stuck to his assertions. His measured intelligence was average, and he earned grades of B and C. On the Guess Who item "Guess who says things that are not true" 13 of the 20 children in Phillip's class named him. He received no best friend nominations on a sociometric question administered to all children in his class, but he chose two of the most popular boys in class as his best friends. Phillip is aggressive in his play, bossing others and monopolizing the play equipment. He rarely gives compliments, shares, or offers help to classmates. On a self-report questionnaire, he described himself as lonely and unpopular with his classmates.

Phillip lives with his parents in a lower-middle-income neighborhood. His parents are concerned about his lying, but they blame the lying on other children who pick on Phillip and do not accept him.

On the basis of this assessment, the psychologist believed that Phillip's lying was a problem because it occurred frequently and interfered with his friendships. His lying appeared to be motivated by his desire to be accepted by his classmates. He lacked social skills for relating positively with peers, and he had a poor self-concept.

Case 2. Heather, a 12-year-old girl, was referred to the psychologist by her parents for lying. Example lies included saying she did not phone the emergency 911 number after calling it three times, spilling honey and then blaming it on her sister, and telling her parents she made 100 on a spelling test. The psychologist called a meeting with the parents and the teacher for the purpose of determining whether Heather also lied at school. The teacher said that Heather had made up some highly unlikely excuses for not turning in her homework. It was also discovered during the meeting that Heather had told lies that the teacher had not detected. Although her parents did not allow her to wear makeup to school, Heather wore a great deal of it at school, especially eye makeup. When the teacher asked her what her mother thought about her wearing so much makeup, Heather had responded that her mother did not mind. She was putting the makeup on when she got to school and washing it off before going home. Heather also had signed her mother's name to a note excusing her from dressing out for P.E. Her teacher and her parents agreed to record instances of Heather's lying for 2 weeks, and they agreed to communicate with each other two or three times a week to verify information that Heather had given one of them. The teacher detected five lies, four involving untrue reasons for not doing homework and one involving reasons for being tardy to class. The parents recorded ten lies at home, all of which were instrumental, or antisocial. These lies usually involved avoiding blame or obtaining a reward.

Heather was named by only two classmates as a person who says things that are not true. She received two best friends nominations. On the teacher version of the Child Behavior Checklist (Achenbach & Edelbrock, 1983) her teacher endorsed a large number of items reflecting the Externalizing syndrome, particularly within the Aggression scale (argues, disobeys at school, lies and cheats, stubborn). Although Heather's measured intelligence was average, she earned grades of C and D.

Heather's parents were controlling and rigid in their parenting approach. She had a long list of daily chores for which she was responsible. Her parents did not allow her to watch television programs that contained violence or that reflected values different from those of her parents. She was grounded for rather minor infractions of rules. Her parents did not want her to associate with "the wrong kind of kids" and only allowed her to invite children over to play whose parents were friends.

Based on this assessment, the psychologist hypothesized that Heather's lying was part of a pattern of child defiance against parental authority. Heather was rebelling against overly strict and rigid parental control. Family relationships were characterized by hostility and conflict.

ALTERNATIVE ACTIONS

In applied behavior analysis, specific target behaviors are identified, and principles of learning are applied to their modification. Recently, the concept of target behaviors in behavior therapy has been criticized on the grounds that it encourages a simplistic, static, and monosymptomatic view of client difficulties (Evans, 1985; Mash, 1985, Kanfer, 1985). The target behavior metaphor has particular problems when applied to a complaint of lying. Lying is the "decelaration" target behavior (the behavior to be eliminated or at least decreased in frequency), and telling the truth is the incompatible "acceleration" behavior that between them constitute the basis of this approach. According to applied behavior analysis, the problem behavior is either ignored or punished, and the incompatible behavior is rewarded. Yet, rewarding telling the truth is problematic. A child could easily obtain rewards by making truthful assertions while continuing unabated lying. But punishing lying behavior poses problems, too. If we punish for each lie a child tells, we may succeed only in making the child a more skillful liar. Also, "getting at the truth" places parents and teachers in the role of grand inquisitor and provides the child with attention that may inadvertently reinforce the lying behavior.

While a strict contingency management approach to lying may be unproductive, it is important to alter contingencies of reinforcement for lying and telling the truth so that the rewards for lying are lessened, and the rewards for telling the truth are increased. For example, when the child lies to avoid punishment and is detected in the lie, the punishment that would have been administered for the original behavior should stand, and a punishment for lying should be added. When a child admits to a wrongdoing on his or her own, the punishment for the wrongdoing should be less than it would be if the child had not admitted guilt.

Lying as Part of a Behavioral Constellation

Lying is not a unidimensional problem. Rather, it forms part of a behavioral constellation. Any intervention selected to decrease a child's lying must address the constellation of which it is a part. Summarized briefly below are interventions that attempt to effect a beneficial change in constellations of which lying typically may be a part.

Lying as Part of a Pattern of Antisocial Behaviors. Most published studies of the effectiveness of intervention programs for conduct-disordered children and juvenile delinquents have involved token economies in institutionalized settings (Ross, 1981). One of the best-known programs, Achievement Place (Phillip, 1968), is a comprehensive intervention carried out in community treatment facilities and based on operant principles. Studies of the program's effectiveness have shown outcomes to be impressive (Fixsen, Phillips, & Wolf, 1972).

School psychologists are more likely to be involved with the families of conduct-disordered children than with institutional programs such as Achievement Place. For families that have a conduct-disordered child a useful intervention is behavioral contracting, which involves a bilateral agreement between the child and his or her parents. In this intervention strategy a contract specifies the children's responsibilities and contingent privileges within the family. For example, adolescents who want the privilege of time to themselves may have to agree to take upon themselves the responsibility of going to school regularly. Children who want the privilege of visiting friends have to agree to keep parents informed of their whereabouts and return at a specified time. Response-cost procedures for specific prohibitions and bonuses for compliance with the contract are recommended parts of the behavioral contract (Stuart, 1971).

Studies of the effectiveness of behavioral contracts for conduct-disordered children generally reveal positive results (e.g., Alexander & Parson, 1973; Alexander, Barton, Schiavo, & Parson, 1976). In a review of behavioral contracting with families of delinquents, Ross (1981) concluded, "Contingency contracts drawn between the various members of these families with the aid of a skilled therapist appear capable of improving family interaction and to reduce the frequency of norm-violating offenses" (p. 179).

Lying as Part of a Pattern of Deficient Social Skills. Social skills training programs are based on the assumption that rejected and neglected children are deficient in the skills necessary for the development and maintenance of satisfactory peer relationships. Most current social skills training programs fall within one of the two categories. In behavioral social skills programs, modeling, coaching, behavioral rehearsal, performance feedback, and reinforcement are used to teach such skills as participation, cooperating, supporting others, leading, and assertion (Oden & Asher, 1977; Ladd, 1981). In interpersonal cognitive problem-solving training (ICPS) children are taught such problem-solving skills as alternative thinking, means–end thinking, and consequential thinking (e.g., Spivack, Platt, & Shire, 1976; Weissberg et al., 1981). Recent reviews of social skills training programs have revealed mixed but generally positive results, although long-term effectiveness and outcome generalization have not been conclusively demonstrated (Conger & Keane, 1981; Gresham & Lemanek, 1983; Urbain & Kendall, 1980).

Lying as a Part of Disturbed Parent–child Relationships. Several large-scale parent training programs have been implemented with parents of antisocial children (Conger, 1981). Behavioral parent training programs usually involve three steps. First, parents read materials on child management. Second, they are assisted in identifying, observing, and recording their child's behavior. Third, they are aided in applying operant techniques to the problems for which they have sought help (Patterson & Fleischman, 1979). Behavioral training programs have proven successful in modifying a range of child behaviors, including noncompliance, oppositionalism and general aggressive behavior (Bernstein, 1982).

In addition to behavioral parent training programs, programs based on improving communication and problem-solving skills have demonstrated effectiveness in improving child behavior and parent–child relationships (Robin & Foster, 1984).

Lying as a Result of Impulse and Control Problems. Compulsive lying, which involves no gain to the individual, may be the result of difficult self-control. Although there are no published studies of applying self-control training to compulsive lying, self-control training has been found to be effective with a range of impulse problems, including aggression (Kendall & Braswell, 1985).

Lying as Wishful Thinking. Children who state as fact what is really a wish, need help in learning how to express desires. Parents and teachers can rephrase an untrue assertion as a wish, accepting the child's feelings while gently confronting the factual accuracy of the statement. This rephrasing, or reframing technique, shows respect for the child and conveys empathy. For example, should a 9-year-old child say "My dad bought a red Trans Am car," the teacher might respond, "You're thinking about how much fun it would be to ride in a fancy sports car, and you wish you had one." If the child insists on the factual accuracy of the assertion, the teacher just moves on to another topic or activity.

SUMMARY

Lying in children is common. The frequency of the lying and the magnitude of its consequences for the child and others determine whether it is to be considered a problem. Problem lying is viewed as an interpersonal behavior that places the child at risk for poor interpersonal relationships with peers as well as adults.

Antisocial lying is not condoned at any age level. Even children as young as first graders know what a lie is and evaluate the morality of a lie in terms of its selfish intent.

When requested by a parent or teacher to help with a child's lying, the school psychologist needs to ask and answer a series of questions to determine if lying is the behavior of concern and to put the lying in perspective. Lying is rarely best treated as an isolated behavior; usually treatment should view lying as part of a pattern, or constellation, of behaviors that should be treated conjointly.

REFERENCES

Achenbach, T. M., & Edelbrock, C. (1983). *Manual for the Child Behavior Checklist and Revised Child Behavior Profile.* Burlington, VT: University of Vermont, Department of Psychiatry.

Alexander, J. F., Barton, C., Schiavo, R. S., & Parsons, B. V. (1976). Systems-behavioral intervention with families of delinquents: Therapist characteristics, family behavior, and outcome. *Journal of Consulting and Clinical Psychology, 44,* 656–664.

Alexander, J. F., & Parsons, B. V. (1973). Short-term behavioral intervention with delinquent families: Impact on family process and recidivism. *Journal of Abnormal Psychology, 81,* 219–225.

American Psychiatric Association. (1980). *Diagnostic and statistical manual of mental disorders* (3rd ed.). Washington, DC: Author.

Asher, S. R., & Hymel, S. (1981). Children's social competence in peer relations: Sociometric and behavioral assessment. In J. D. Wine & M. D. Smye (Eds.), *Social competence* (pp. 125–157). New York: Guilford.

Bernstein, G. S. (1982). Training behavior change agents: A conceptual review. *Behavior Therapy, 13,* 1–23.

Bonney, M. R. (1971). Assessments of efforts to aid socially isolated elementary school pupils. *Journal of Educational Research, 64,* 345–364.

Burton, R. V. (1976). Honesty and dishonesty. In T. Lickona (Ed.), *Moral development and behavior.* New York: Holt.

Cohen, A. K. (1955). *Delinquent boys.* Glencoe, IL: Free Press.

Conger, J. C., & Keane, S. P. (1981). Social skills intervention in the treatment of isolated or withdrawn children. *Psychological Bulletin, 90,* 478–495.

Conger, R. D. (1981). The assessment of dysfunctional family systems. In B. J. Lahey & A. E. Kazden (Eds.), *Advances in clinical child psychology* (Vol. 4). New York: Plenum.

Cowen, E. L., Pederson, A., Barbigian, H., Izzo, L. D., & Trost, M. A. (1973). Long-term follow-up of early detected vulnerable children. *Journal of Consulting and Clinical Psychology, 41,* 438–446.

DePaulo, G., Lanier, K., & Davis, T. (1983). Detecting the deceit of the motivated liar. *Journal of Personality and Social Psychology, 45,* 1096–1103.

Evans, I. M. (1985). Building systems models as a strategy for target behavior selection in clinical assessment. *Behavioral Assessment, 7,* 21–32.

Fenichel, O. (1945). *The psychoanalytic theory of neurosis.* New York: Norton.

Fixen, D. L., Phillips, E. L., & Wolf, M. N. (1973). Achievement Place experiments in self-government with predelinquents. *Journal of Applied Behavior Analysis, 6,* 31–47.

Flavell, J. H. (1985). *Cognitive development* (2nd ed.). Englewood Cliffs, NJ: Prentice-Hall.

Graham, P. J. (1979). Epidemiological studies. In H. C. Quay & J. S. Werry (Eds.), *Psychopathological disorders of childhood* (2nd ed.). New York: Wiley.

Gresham, F. M. (1981). Assessment of children's social skills. *Journal of School Psychology, 19,* 120–133.

Gresham, F. M., & Lemanek, K. L. (1983). Social skills: A review of cognitive–behavioral training procedures with children. *Journal of Applied Developmental Psychology, 4,* 239–261.

Harter, S. (1977). A cognitive–developmental approach to children's expression of conflicting feelings and a technique to facilitate such expression in play therapy. *Journal of Consulting and Clinical Psychology, 45,* 417–432.

Hathaway, S. R., & McKinley, J. C. (1967). *Multiphasic Personality Inventory.* New York: The Psychological Corporation.

Kanfer, F. H. (1985). Target selection for clinical change programs. *Behavioral Assessment, 7,* 7–20.

Kendall, P. C., & Braswell, L. (1985). *Cognitive–behavioral therapy for impulsive children.* New York: Guilford.

Kohlberg, L. (1969). *Stages in the development of moral thought and action.* New York: Holt.

Ladd, G. W. (1981). Effectiveness of a social learning model for enhancing children's social interaction and peer acceptance. *Child Development, 52,* 171–178.

Laughlin, F. (1954). *The peer status of sixth- and seventh-grade children.* New York: Teachers College Columbia, Bureau of Publications.

Mash, E. J. (1985). Some comments on target selection in behavior therapy. *Behavioral Assessment, 7,* 63–78.

Miller, L. C. (1972). School behavior checklist: An inventory of deviant behavior for elementary school children. *Journal of Consulting and Clinical Psychology, 38,* 134–144.

Nelsen, E. A., Grinder, R. E., & Biaggio, A. M. (1969). Relationships among behavioral cognitive–developmental and self-report measures of morality and personality. *Multivariate Behavioral Research, 4,* 483–500.

Oden, S., & Asher, S. (1977). Coaching children in skills for friendship making. *Child Development, 48,* 495–506.

Patterson, G. R., & Fleischman, M. J. (1979). Maintenance of treatment effects: Some considerations concerning family systems and follow-up data. *Behavior Therapy, 10,* 168–185.

Peisach, E., & Hardeman, M. (1983). Moral reasoning in early childhood: Lying and stealing. *The Journal of Genetic Psychology, 142,* 107–120.

Peterson, C. C., Peterson, J. L., & Seeto, D. (1983). Developmental changes in ideas about lying. *Child Development, 54,* 1529–1535.

Phillips, E. L. (1968). Achievement Place: Token reinforcement procedures in a home-style rehabilitation settinng for "pre-delinquent" boys. *Journal of Applied Behavior Analysis, 1,* 213–223.

Piaget, J. (1965). The moral judgment of the child (M. Gabain, Trans.). New York: Free Press. (Originally published 1932).

Quay, H. C., & Peterson, D. R. *Manual for the Behavior Problem Checklist.* Published by the authors, 59 Fifth St., Highland Park, NJ, 08904.

Robbins, L. N. (1966). *Deviant children grown up.* Baltimore, MD: Williams & Wilkins.

Robin, A. L., & Foster, S. L. 91984). Problem-solving communication training: A behavioral–family systems approach to parent–adolescent conflict. In P. Karoly & J. J. Steffen (Eds.), *Adolescent behavior disorders: Foundations and contemporary concerns* (pp. 195–240). Lexington, MA: Lexington Books.

Roff, M., Sells, S. B., & Golden, M. M. (1972). *Social adjustment and personality development in children.* Minneapolis: University of Minnesota Press.

Ross, A. O. (1981). *Child behavior therapy,* New York: Wiley.

Selman, R. L. (1980). *The growth of interpersonal understanding.* New York: Academic.

Spivack, G., Platt, J., & Shure, M. (1976). *The problem-solving approach to adjustment.* San Francisco: Jossey-Bass.

Stuart, R. B. (1971). Behavioral contracting with the families of delinquents. *Journal of Behavior Therapy and Experimental Psychiatry, 2,* 1–11.

Urbain, E. S., & Kendall, P. C. (1980). Review of social-cognitive problem-solving interventions with children. *Psychological Bulletin, 88,* 109–143.

Weissberg, R., Gesten, E., Carnrike, C., Toro, P., Rapkin, B., Davidson, E., & Cowen, E. (1981). Social problem-solving training: A competence-building intervention with second to fourth grade children. *American Journal of Community Psychology, 9,* 411–423.

Wimmer, H., Gruber, S., & Perner, J. (1984). *Journal of Experimental Child Psychology, 37,* 1–30.

Wright, T. L., & Kirmani, A. (1977). Interpersonal trust, trustworthiness, and shoplifting in high school. *Psychological Reports, 41,* 1165–1166.

Wright, T. L., & Kirmani, A. (1977). Interpersonal trust, trustworthiness, and shoplifting in high school. *Psychological Reports, 41,* 1165–1166.

Zuckerman, M., Koester, R., & Driver, R. 91981). *Journal of Nonverbal Behavior, 6,*(1), 105–114.

BIBLIOGRAPHY: PROFESSIONALS

Phillips, E. L. (1968). Achievement Place: Token reinforcement procedures in a home-style rehabilitation setting for "pre-delinquent" boys. *Journal of Applied Behavior Analysis, 1,* 213–223.
Programs based on this well-publicized and researched community intervention model view lying, cheating, aggression, and other delinquent behaviors as the result of inadequate social learning experiences. Social, academic, and self-help skills are taught in a group home setting, by operant techniques. Elements of this structured systematic model are transportable to other settings, such as alternative schools.

Robin, A. L., & Foster, S. L. (1984). Problem-solving communication training: A behavioral–family systems approach to parent–adolescent conflicts. In P. Karoly & J. J. Steffen (Eds.), *Adolescent behavior disorders: Foundations and contemporary concerns* (pp. 195–240). Lexington, MA: Lexington Books.
This model "involves multidimensional assessment and treatment techniques, guided by an evolving social learning theory of parent–adolescent conflict that blends cognitive–behavioral and family systems orientation with developmental considerations concerning adolescence" (p. 196). Behavioral assessment techniques are used to assess family communication, problem solving, developmental status, belief systems, family structure, and functional interaction patterns. Training involves social learning, cognitive restructuring, and family systems approaches.

Stuart, R. B. (1971). Behavioral contracting with the families of delinquents. *Journal of Behavioral Therapy and Experimental Psychiatry, 2,* 1–11.
A behavioral contract is a bilateral agreement between the parents and their child that provides a structured basis for the scheduled exchange of positive reinforcements. Stuart describes and evaluates his experiences with family behavior contracting in the Family and School Consultation Project, a community-based family intervention project for school-referred, predelinquent children.

Children and Maladaptive Habits

Bruce Pray, Jr.
Kansas Unified School District #489

Jack J. Kramer
University of Nebraska–Lincoln

BACKGROUND

Common maladaptive habits among children include fingernail biting, thumbsucking or fingersucking, hair pulling, self-destructive oral habits, tics, and nonfunctional clenching and grinding of the teeth (bruxism). These habits constitute a problem when the particular behavior is prolonged or habitual. Typically, maladaptive habits worsen when a child is stressed. These habit disorders are problematic because they often cause physical disorders, embarrassment, and social difficulties. For example, both chronic thumbsucking and bruxism are associated with dental problems, and hair pulling can cause bald spots as well as hair follicle damage. Some habits distract and irritate others. At times, siblings and peers mimic and make fun of a child's habit.

This chapter will explore treatment options available in the psychological, medical, and dental literature for maladaptive habits with emphasis on behavioral and cognitive–behavioral interventions. The data reveal that habit reversal (HR) (Azrin & Nunn, 1973, 1977) is the most effective treatment available for a wide range of habit disorders. This discussion will focus on the principles and applications of habit reversal treatment with children and provide information on when referral to a physician or dentist is appropriate.

An understanding of habit disorders begins with a description of the physical problems and social consequences of long-term habit behavior (Table 1). In most cases, with the exception of tic disorders, the long-term result of the habit is some form of damage to the body. Of equal concern are the psychological and social ramifications of the habit behavior. Although habits do not invariably have a serious effect on psychological or social functioning, habit disorders can interfere with interpersonal/social functioning by causing shame and embarrassment. To date, treatment for maladaptive habits has had two primary purposes: (a) stopping the habit to prevent further damage to the affected body area, and (b) training the individual to cope with generalized or environmentally specific stress in more adaptive ways (see the chapter on stress in this volume). As a result of treatment, an individual may experience improved interpersonal/social functioning and be viewed more positively when not exhibiting the annoying habit behavior.

DEVELOPMENT

Of the habits outlined above, only thumbsucking and transient tic disorder are considered developmentally normal behaviors. Nunn (1978) refers to thumbsucking as "the first and most common habit among children, with the age of four being the typical stopping point" (p. 351). Before the age of 4 years, the chronicity and dental complications of thumbsucking should be considered in determining if intervention is appropriate (see the chapter on thumbsucking in this volume).

Tics are another common habit among children. Survey results indicate that from 12% to 24% of schoolchildren have a history of tics (American Psychiatric Association [APA], 1980). A mild transient tic disorder is common in childhood and systematic treatment is usually unnecessary. The duration of transient tics is from at least 1 month to not more than 1 year. Usually the tics disappear after several months. The most common transient tic is an eye blink or other facial tic. Specific treatment of transient tics is problematic

TABLE 1

Habit Disorders of Children

Habit	Behavioral description	Physical consequence
Diurnal/nocturnal finger sucking, thumbsucking	Placing finger(s) or thumb in the mouth and sucking on them	Open bite, overjet, and closed bite dental malocclusions
Nail biting/nail picking	Biting or picking at fingernails	Partial or complete absence of nails, roughened skin area around nails
Hair pulling	Removing body hair by pulling, breaking, or rubbing hair with hands or by tangling hair in a brush or comb to pull out; may also involve eating hair after pulling it	Hair follicle damage and bald spots
Diurnal/nocturnal bruxism	A nonfunctional gnashing, grinding, clenching, or clicking of the teeth	Abnormal wear to teeth, facial pain, bulging masseter muscles, tooth mobility, malocclusions, periodontal disease
Motor tics	Recurrent, repetitive, rapid movement of a functionally related group of skeletal muscles	No physical effect except that chronic conditions may strengthen muscle, producing movement while antagonistic muscle weakens
Self-destructive oral habits	Biting, chewing, sucking, licking, or pushing of the cheeks, tongue, lips, teeth, or palate	Damage to soft oral tissue, tooth movement, malocclusions, swelling, soreness, chapping, infection, pain, teeth deformation

because of the variability in duration and intensity of symptoms. When treatment is necessary, general stress identification and management techniques (Herzfield & Powell, 1986) may be appropriate. Chronic motor tic disorder and Tourette's disorder (APA, 1980) which have symptoms of more than a 1-year duration, are referred more often for treatment and are more amenable to systematic treatment (Pray, Kramer, & Lindskog, 1986).

Nail biting, bruxism, self-destructive oral habits, and other miscellaneous habits are viewed as normal or as abnormal behavior depending on the chronicity and the physical problems caused by the habit. Hair pulling, or trichotillomania, is abnormal at any age and should be considered for possible intervention efforts. As with any behavior, maladaptive habits may simply disappear without any special attention or intervention effort. School psychologists who understand the developmental and normative patterns of habit behavior will be best prepared for evaluating the appropriateness of intervention efforts.

PUTTING MALADAPTIVE HABITS IN PERSPECTIVE

Parents and individual children often are embarrassed by a habit and reluctance to seek treatment. Referral may come only after dental, medical, or other services have proven ineffective or the habit disorder has resulted in a significant physical or social problem. On the other hand, some parents find a medical or neurological cause more acceptable than a behavioral explanation and prefer medical intervention.

Teachers and parents may also be reluctant to intervene because of a fear that treatment would place too much pressure on the child and exacerbate the habit. Caretakers should be informed that identifying environmental stressors related to the habit and, more importantly, helping the child manage these stressors is a critical component of treatment. Also, parents and teachers occasionally express concern about the child's adverse reaction to teasing from peers. Caretakers should be encouraged to direct their efforts toward an intervention for the particular child, rather than engage in an often difficult task of stopping peer teasing. Eliminating the habit is the purpose of treatment and ultimately the most effective treatment for teasing.

A detailed history of the child's habit is necessary in formulating an appropriate intervention plan. It is also necessary to involve the parents, child, and, in some cases, teachers in implementing a treatment plan (Pray et al., 1986). Behavioral consultation (Gresham, 1982) has proven effective in involving caretakers in developing, implementing, and evaluating a treatment plan. This model assumes that the child, parents, and teachers are the individuals who will implement the treatment with the psychologist serving as a consultant. This involvement of caretakers is necessary if treatment procedures are to be carried out in the child's everyday environment. In addition, treatment procedures must be continued over several weeks or months to prevent recurrence of the habit. Caretakers and the referred child must be the primary behavior-change agents if change is to occur and be maintained.

Treatment of habits can be a complicated and time-consuming endeavor for all persons involved, including the psychologist formulating the treatment plan. Eliminating a well-established habit of long duration requires much effort. In this respect, it is important to determine the motivation of both the child and significant others for treating the disorder. One effective way to accomplish this is through a "minimal effort response probe" (Alessi & Kaye, 1983, p. 61). This "probe" involves asking the interested behavior-change agents to collect data on habit occurrences for several days. The baseline data will provide clues to the nature of the habit, as well as probe the change agent's compliance with treatment tasks. If the persons responsible for treatment either won't or can't complete minimal baseline charting, they probably will not implement a treatment plan. Always obtain general compliance with basic treatment requirements before investing a lot of time in developing a comprehensive treatment plan.

ALTERNATIVE ACTIONS

Treatment Procedures

To understand the rationale behind treatment procedures it is necessary to describe the etiology of habits (Azrin & Nunn, 1973, 1977). Briefly, habits begin as low-frequency normal behavior that gradually increases in frequency, intensity, and duration over months and years. Often, individuals are unaware of the high frequency of the habit behavior and become habituated to the resulting annoyances, such as pain and injury, caused by the habit. As the habit persists, it becomes associated with other behaviors and eventually becomes part of an individual's daily behavioral repertoire. Maladaptive habits per se are not considered symptomatic of emotional or mental disturbance (Azrin & Nunn, 1977), although they are considered stress-related disorders.

To date, the most effective treatment for habit disorders has been habit reversal (HR). Azrin (1977) proposed that multicomponent behavioral treatments, such as HR, are necessary since no single procedure is capable of being generally effective for all persons seeking treatment. However, HR is a self-management program that is effective only for children capable of managing their own treatment with supervision from caretakers. Pray et al. (1986) have provided a detailed description of the HR treatment as implemented by a practitioner. A brief description of HR procedures is provided below in the following paragraphs.

Inconvenience Review. List the difficulties caused by the habit. What are the reasons to eliminate the habit? What are the situations in which the habit has caused problems?

Awareness Training. Noticing when a habit occurs is the first step in controlling the habit. Procedures to increase awareness include self-monitoring and performing the habit slowly and deliberately in front of a mirror while describing the habit aloud.

Habit-Promoting Situations. Identify the situations in which the habit is likely to occur in order to be prepared to use a competing behavior when entering these situations.

Competing reaction. Learn a reaction that is incompatible with the habit in order to stop the habit behavior (see Figure 1). The competing behavior can be maintained for several minutes without appearing unusual to others, does not interfere with normal activities, and increases self-awareness of the habit. The competing response is a critical component of HR (see Azrin & Nunn, 1977, for detailed procedures on competing response exercises for various habit disorders).

Corrective and Preventive Reaction. After learning the competing reaction, use it to interrupt the habit or prevent its occurrence in the first place.

Associated Behavior. Identify the behavior that precedes the habit behavior and use the competing reaction to stop this associated behavior.

Relaxation Training. Learn a method of relaxation in stressful or habit-promoting situations.

Social Support. The child should be assisted in increasing self-awareness of the habit and be encouraged to eliminate it. Parents should maintain a high ratio of positive statements to reminder statements.

Practice. Practice the competing reaction daily until it becomes routine behavior. Also, rehearse the competing response while imagining habit-promoting situations.

Records. Keep a daily record of the frequency of the habit to determine the progress of the treatment.

The following is a brief review of habit disorders with emphasis on HR treatment of these disorders. Included are analyses of the following habits: hair pulling, bruxism, tic disorders, destructive oral habits, and miscellaneous habits. Thumbsucking is reviewed by Jensen (this volume) and nail biting by De Francesco (this volume).

Hair Pulling

Trichotillomania, chronic hair pulling, is a disorder primarily of children and young adults that occurs more frequently among females than males. No systematic survey data are available on incidence; however, Azrin and Nunn (1977) estimate that 4% of the U. S. population are chronic hair pullers. The scalp is the most common area affected, although beards, eyelashes, eyebrows, and/or other body hair can be the focus of hair pulling (Friman, Finney, & Christophersen, 1984). Severe cases of trichotillomania result in almost total baldness and individuals sometimes wear hairpieces to cover bald spots. An additional habit associated with trichotillomania is trichophagy, eating one's hair after pulling it out (Azrin, Nunn, Frantz, 1980).

In a review article, Friman et al. (1984) reported that self-management strategies, facial screening, and the differential application of rewards and punishments have been used to treat hair pulling in diverse populations including preschool and retarded children. Price (1978) has recommended a medical examination of hair loss to rule out organic scalp disease prior to any treatment. The literature of trichotillomania, in contrast to that of other habits, contains studies of children as young as 2 and 3 years old, in addition to investigations with developmentally delayed individuals. Treatment for developmentally delayed hair pullers or developmentally normal preschool children typically has involved the differential use of rewards and punishments (Friman et al., 1984).

Barmann and Vitali (1982) used facial screening to treat hair pulling in three severely to moderately retarded children. This procedure involved placing a terrycloth bib over the children's faces for a short time contingent upon hair pulling. Facial screening was effective in eliminating hair pulling within 11 days with the subject's parents and caretakers serving as the primary behavior-change agents.

Sanchez (1979) treated a 27-month-old male with a 6-month history of hair pulling. Prior to formal treatment, the parents had attempted a variety of procedures to stop hair pulling, including shaving the boy's head. This caused the boy to start to pull out the hairs on his eyebrows and forehead until his scalp hair began to grow and then he resumed pulling scalp hair. A time out procedure was also used during formal treatment but was discontinued because the subject pulled out his hair in the time out area, his bedroom. It was noted during the study that fingersucking occurred along with the hair pulling. In an attempt to break the behavior chain, the parents used reprimands and taping of the three fingers he sucked for 10 minutes immediately following each fingersucking incident. This stopped finger sucking and, subsequently, the hair pulling.

Gray (1979) also resorted to punishment to prevent hair pulling. In this case, four hard slaps on the hand were used immediately following hair pulling. This procedure was implemented to decrease the behavior rapidly; it was used only after a variety of other treatment methods were unsuccessful. Gray (1979) provides excellent guidelines for the use of punishment in treating trichotillomania.

In a study comparing HR and negative practice, Azrin, Nunn, and Frantz (1980) reported that the HR group not only eliminated the overt behavior of hair pulling but also the subjects' reported covert or private urge to pull. At 22-month follow-up, however, several subjects noted a reappearance of the covert "impulse" to renew pulling their eyelashes owing to local sensitivity when the lashes started growing back, after the initial cessation of eyelash pulling. Additional treatment sessions and careful follow-up may be necessary for this particular form of trichotillomania. It appears that in other studies subjects' reported covert urge to pull hair declined at a slower rate than the overt behavior (MacNeil & Thomas, 1976; Anthony, 1978). In this respect, Anthony recommended self-monitoring of both the cognitive component and overt behavior associated with the habit to help promote long-term maintenance of treatment. In a more recent HR study, Rosenbaum and Ayllon (1981a) treated four hair pullers, including a 10-year-old girl with a mild case of trichotillomania. They reported that HR treatment was cost-efficient in obtaining maximum benefits from minimal professional time with mild cases of trichotillomania.

Altman, Grahs, and Friman (1982) treated a young girl's hair pulling that occurred in her bed at night and not in the presence of her parents. The subject also sucked her thumb while pulling her hair. Placing a bad-tasting substance on the thumb eliminated the thumbsucking and also presumed covarying behavior of hair pulling (see Baer, 1982, for an explanation of the process of stopping covarying behaviors in a behavioral chain). In another study involving private hair pulling, Anthony (1978) used a simple self-control procedure to treat a 9-year-old boy who pulled his hair when he was alone in his room. Dahlquist and Kalfus (1984) treated an 11-year-old girl with a reinforcement program for increase in hair growth, and a response prevention method for night time hair pulling that involved taping her index and middle finger together. Wulfsohn and Barling (1978) treated a preadolescent girl with a 7-year history of eyelash pulling. Initially, they used external control procedures in the form of a token economy and response cost; then they introduced self-instruction and self-monitoring to maintain treatment effects. This procedure was based on Bellack, Schwartz, and Rozensky's (1974) model demonstrating external control to be essential in developing and maintaining self-control.

In summary, trichotillomania has been treated successfully with a variety of behavioral interventions including self-management strategies for older children, facial screening for retarded populations, and a differential application of rewards and punishments for developmentally immature children (Friman et al., 1984). Future research should investigate the differential effectiveness of these techniques across different populations.

Bruxism

Bruxism, a nonfunctional clenching and grinding of the teeth, can occur while an individual is awake and/or asleep. Estimates of incidence of bruxism vary from 5% to 21% for the general population with no significant age or sex differences in incidence (Glaros & Rao, 1977). Blount, Drabman, Wilson, and Stewart (1982) estimated that 22% of institutionalized retarded persons engage in diurnal teeth grinding. Both diurnal and nocturnal teeth grinding produce loud clicking or grating

FIGURE 1

A pictorial representation of the various types of maladaptive habits or tics. The left-hand column illustrates the different tics or habits. The adjacent illustration shows the competing exercises. The arrows in each of the competing exercise illustrations show the direction of isometric muscle contraction being exerted by the client. From "Habit-reversal: A method of eliminating nervous habits and tics," by N. H. Azrin and R. G. Nunn, 1973, *Behavior Research and Therapy, 11,* p. 621. Reprinted by permission.

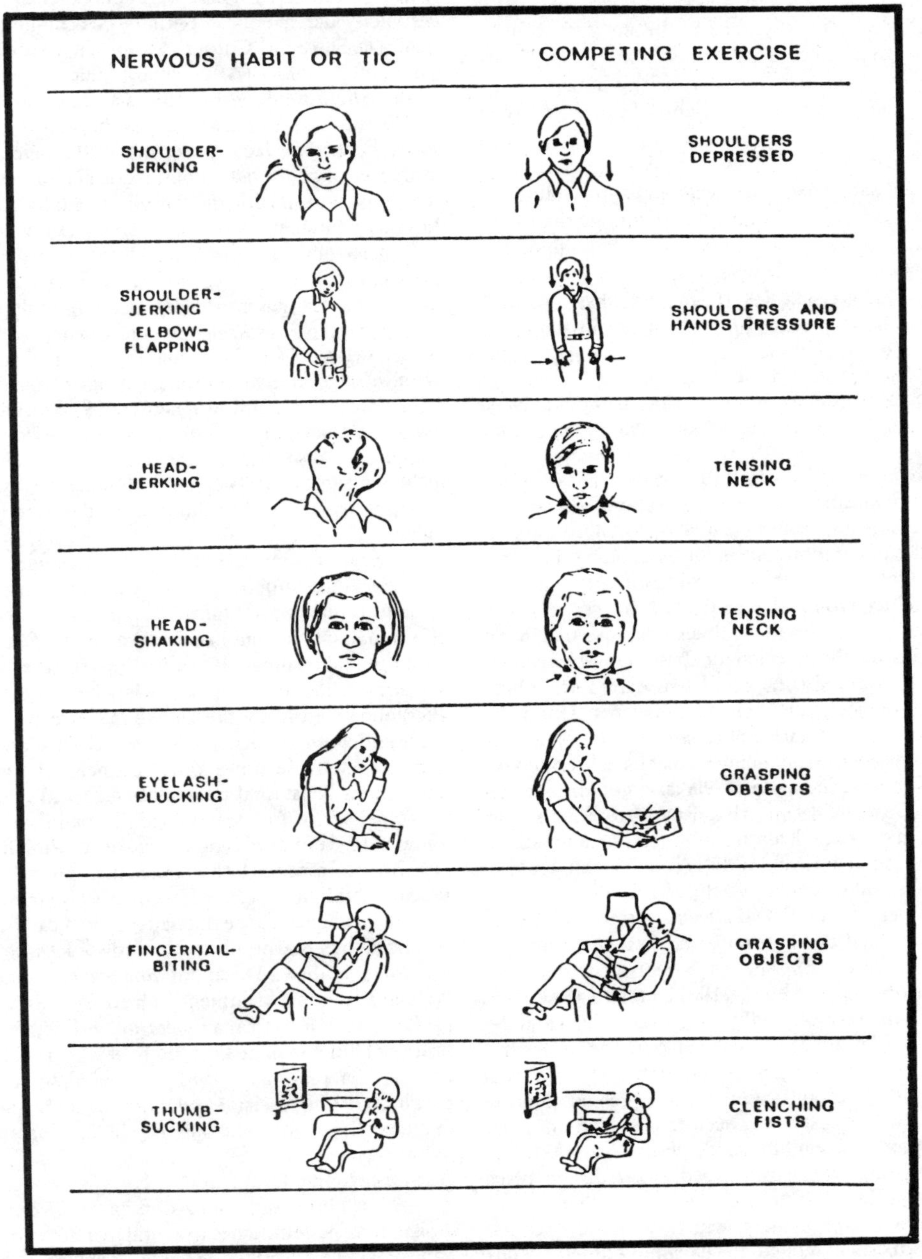

NERVOUS HABIT OR TIC	COMPETING EXERCISE
SHOULDER-JERKING	SHOULDERS DEPRESSED
SHOULDER-JERKING ELBOW-FLAPPING	SHOULDERS AND HANDS PRESSURE
HEAD-JERKING	TENSING NECK
HEAD-SHAKING	TENSING NECK
EYELASH-PLUCKING	GRASPING OBJECTS
FINGERNAIL-BITING	GRASPING OBJECTS
THUMB-SUCKING	CLENCHING FISTS

sounds. These sounds often irritate others during the day and even disturb the sleep of roommates at night. The grinding sounds, like those of snoring, do not awaken the bruxist. With the exception of retarded populations, daytime bruxing typically involves a silent, teeth-clenching action.

In a review article, Glaros and Rao (1977) report that bruxism has been viewed as primarily a dental problem by psychologists and often conceptualized in psychological terms by dentists. In any case, bruxists react to stress either from intrapersonal psychological sources or from situational sources by grinding, clenching, or clicking their teeth. A relationship exists between both diurnal and nocturnal bruxism and recognizable stressful events (McGlynn, Cassisi, & Diamond, 1985). Bruxing is damaging to the teeth and surrounding oral structures because bit forces exerted during bruxing episodes may be four to five times more than the normal forces exerted when chewing food.

McGlynn et al. (1985) proposed that bruxing is directly related to stress or to the interaction between stress and occlusal dysharmony. In this respect, psychological interventions must sometimes be coordinated with dental treatment and psychologists should always diagnose and treat individuals in collaboration with a dentist.

Dental treatments for bruxism include (a) muscle relaxant medication, particularly Valium; (b) occlusal appliances/adjustments to correct malocclusion; and (c) occlusal equilibration that involves grinding down the teeth surfaces in order to maximize remaining tooth surfaces (McGlynn et al., 1985). Medications are used as temporary or last-resort treatment because of adverse side effects and the potential for abuse of muscle relaxant drugs. It should also be noted that dental procedures primarily prevent, not eliminate, bruxism and individuals may persist in their habit (Glaros & Rao, 1977).

Psychological interventions that have been applied to bruxism include muscular relaxation training (Goldfried & Davison, 1976), HR (Rosenbaum & Ayllon, 1981b), and feedback alarms for nocturnal and diurnal bruxism (McGlynn et al., 1985). Aversive contingencies have been used with retarded children for diurnal grinding. Kramer (1981) trained a teacher to use contingent reprimands and tactile stimulation to the jaw for 2–3 seconds as punishers with an 8-year-old moderately retarded boy. Blount et al. (1982) utilized contingent "icing" with two profoundly retarded girls. In this study, "icing" entailed applying a cube of ice to the cheeks and chin following instances of grinding. The ice was removed 6–8 seconds after grinding ceased. During periods when bruxism was occurring at high rates, the ice was moved around the face to ease discomfort.

In summary, bruxism is a disorder that involves psychological stress factors in interaction with physical/dental problems. Treatment will vary according to the type of bruxism exhibited, the capability of individuals to manage stress themselves, and the severity of dental symptoms. A multidisciplinary approach to assessment and treatment is necessary.

Tic Disorders

The term *Tics* refers to both motor and phonic tic behavior. A motor tic is a recurrent, repetitive, rapid movement of a functionally related group of skeletal muscle; a vocal tic is the production of various abnormal vocalizations (APA, 1980). Golden (1982) noted that tic disorders "represent the same condition and differ only in degree of severity and probability of complete remission" (p. 215). These disorders range in terms of chronicity and severity across three tic conditions: Transient Tic Disorder, Chronic Motor Tic Disorder, and Tourette's Disorder (APA, 1980). Males are subject to all three tic conditions three times as much as females.

Tics are attributed to both organic and psychological or behavioral factors. Subsequently, there are two distinct treatment orientations, medical and behavioral (see Pray et al., 1986, and Turpin, 1983, for reviews). Medical treatment involves a complete examination by a physician or neurologist to rule out alternative medical conditions that might be the cause of the abnormal movement. Tic-like movements occur in multiple sclerosis, general paresis, schizophrenia, organic mental disorders (APA, 1980) and in a variety of static and progressive degenerative neurological disorders (Golden, 1982). However, medical treatment of tic disorder can involve medications that suppress tic behavior but do not cure the disorder. A variety of adverse side effects including lethargy and cognitive blunting are associated with pharmocological treatment of tic disorders (Hagin, 1984).

Behavioral treatment has been successfully utilized to combat tic disorders, HR having provided most effective in producing "clinically significant" treatment effects in single and multiple tics (Pray et al., 1986). Prior to behavioral treatment two steps must be taken: (a) An appropriate physical examination is necessary to rule out alternative reasons for the tic-like movements, and (b) the disorder must be accurately assessed and classified in order to determine appropriate treatment strategies.

Direct behavioral treatment of a child's transient tic(s), given the frequent variability in intensity and duration of symptoms, is probably unnecessary. Richard (1982) recommended that extinction procedures be used for children with tics of less than a 1-year duration, especially when tics are exhibited only in the presence of significant others. Chronic motor tic disorder with symptoms of more than a 1-year duration are more amenable to comprehensive treatment approaches. Pray et al. (1986) used HR to treat a 9-year-old girl with a 7-year history of head-shaking tic; a study in which behavioral consultation (Gresham, 1982) was used by a school psychologist to assist caretakers with developing, implementing, and evaluating the HR treatment.

Self-Destructive Oral Habits

Azrin, Nunn, and Frantz-Renshaw (1982) used the designation of self-destructive oral habits to describe habits that involve biting, chewing, or licking of the lips, cheeks, tongue, or palate. The small number of treatment studies have consisted of case studies lacking quantitative data, follow-up, and controlled comparison of alternative treatments. Azrin et al. (1982) utilized a group experimental design to compare HR with negative practice. Only one child was used in the HR treatment group. HR proved effective in eliminating a 9-year-old boy's chronic habit of pushing and flicking his tongue on the upper teeth and roof of the mouth. HR treatment was provided in a single 2-hour session. HR offers an alternative to more drastic treatments used, such as oral surgery and intraoral appliances (Azrin et al., 1982).

Miscellaneous Habits

A variety of annoying habits such as trembling hands, foot tapping, hand tapping, throat clearing, nonfunctional coughing, squinting, and eye blinking are experienced to a distressing degree by approximately 1% of the population. Arzin and Nunn (1977) have utilized HR treatment and have described competing reactions for these behaviors.

SUMMARY

Maladaptive habits may cause significant physical and social problems for a child or only minor discomfort and irritation among significant others. Psychologists will most likely be involved in cases in which the habit is a major problem. In many cases the "problem" will involve a habit disorder that has endured for many months and perhaps years before being brought to a psychologist's attention. Habit disorders often involve damage to a particular area of the body, necessitating treatment by dentists, physicians, and orthodontists. In contrast to behavioral treatments, medical or dental treatments prevent but seldom eliminate maladaptive habits. Communication with various professionals involved in treating habit disorders is essential. In some cases there is an interface between medical and/or dental and psychological treatments.

Practitioners face a variety of issues when developing treatments for maladaptive habits in children. A critical factor in determining an appropriate intervention is the children's motivation for treatment and capability to self-treatment procedures themselves. Some form of external control may be required to develop and maintain the self-control necessary to eliminate long-standing habits in children. External control by means of punishment is justified when the habit behavior is physically destructive or socially harmful to the child and when alternative methods of reducing or eliminating the behavior have proven unsuccessful. Punishment procedures may necessitate medical consultation as well as staff training and frequent monitoring of treatment (Blount et al., 1982).

Another important concern in implementing treatment programs is to always request that children or caretakers chart habit behavior. By asking for the collection of minimal baseline data, an assessment of motivation for participating in treatment can be made. Failure to chart behavior usually means that the responsible individuals are unwilling to devote the necessary time or effort to attain the desired change. Behavior charting is an essential element of HR. In some cases, simply self-monitoring a habit is the only treatment procedure necessary (Esveldt-Dawson & Kazdin, 1982).

In summary, maladaptive habits are conceptualized as learned, habitual physical reactions. Habits are often exacerbated by stress and sometimes interact with medical and dental factors. A relationship exists between maladaptive habits and environmental or intrapersonal stressors. The critical factor is not the amount of stress, but individual reactions to stressful events. Herzfeld and Powell (1986) noted that "virtually anything can cause a stressful reaction in someone" (p. 1). Thus, future research should investigate both procedures for eliminating specific habits and cognitive restructuring of children's responses to stressful life events (Goldfried, Decenteceo, & Weinberg, 1974). Clearly, the behavioral technology exists for psychologists to assist children in eliminating embarrassing and self-destructive habits.

REFERENCES

Alessi, G. J., & Kaye, J. H. (1983). *Behavior assessment for school psychologists.* Kent, OH: National Association of School Psychologists.

Altman, K., Grahs, C., & Friman, P. (1982). Treatment of unobserved trichotillamania by attention reflection and punishment of an apparent covariant. *Journal of Behavior Therapy and Experimental Psychiatry, 13,* 337–340.

American Psychiatric Association. (1980). *Diagnosis and statistical manual of mental disorders (3rd ed.).* Washington, DC: Author.

Anthony, W. Z. (1978). Brief intervention in a case of childhood trichotillomania by self-monitoring. *Journal of Behavior Therapy and Experimental Psychiatry, 9,* 173–175.

Azrin, N. H. (1977). A strategy for applied research: Learning based but outcome oriented. *American Psychologist, 32,* 140–149.

Azrin, N. H., & Nunn, R. G. (1973). Habit reversal: A method of eliminating nervous habits and tics. *Behavior Research and Therapy,11,* 619–628.

Azrin, N. H., & Nunn, R. G. (1977). *Habit control in a day.* New York: Simon and Schuster.

Azrin, N. H., Nunn, R. G., & Frantz, S. E. (1980). Treatment of hair pulling (trichotillomania): A comparative study of habit reversal and negative practice training. *Journal of Behavior Therapy and Experimental Psychiatry, 11,* 13–20.

Azrin, N. H., Nunn, R. G., & Frantz-Renshaw, S. E. (1982). Habit reversal vs. negative practice treatment of self-destructive oral habits (biting, chewing or licking of the lips, cheeks, tongue, or palate). *Journal of Behavior Therapy and Experimental Psychiatry, 13,* 49–54.

Baer, D. M. (1982). The imposition of structure on behavior and the demolition of behavioral structures. In D. J. Bernstein (Ed.), *Nebraska Symposium on Motivation, 1981* (Vol. 9, pp. 217–254). Lincoln, NE: University of Nebraska Press.

Barmann, B. C., & Vitali, D. L. (1982). Facial screening to eliminate trichotillomania in developmental disabled persons. *Behavior Therapy, 13,* 735–742.

Bellack, A. S., Schwartz, J., & Rozensky, R. H. (1974). The contribution of external control to self-control in a weight reduction program. *Journal of Behavior Therapy and Experimental Psychiatry, 5,* 245–249.

Blount, R. L., Drabman, R. S., Wilson, N., & Stewart, D. (1982). Reducing severe diurnal bruxism in two profoundly retarded females. *Journal of Applied Behavior Analysis, 15,* 565–571.

Dahlquist, L. M., & Kalfus, G. R. (1984). A novel approach to assessment in the treatment of childhood trichotillomania. *Journal of Behavior Therapy and Experimental Psychiatry, 15,* 47–50.

Esveldt-Dawson, K., & Kazdin, A. E. (1982). *How to use self-control.* Lawrence, KS: H & H Enterprises.

Friman, P. C., Finney, J. W., & Christophersen, E. R. (1984). Behavioral therapy of trichotillomania: An evaluative review. *Behavior Therapy, 15,* 249–265.

Glaros, A. G., & Rao, S. M. (1977). Bruxism: A critical review. *Psychological Bulletin, 84,* 767–781.

Golden, G. S. (1982). Movement disorders in children: Tourette syndrome. *Journal of Developmental and Behavioral Pediatrics, 3,* 209–216.

Goldfried, M. R., & Davison, G. C. (1976). *Clinical behavior therapy.* New York: Holt, Rinehart, & Winston.

Goldfried, M. R., Decenteceo, E. T., & Weinberg, L. (1974). Systematic rational restructuring as a self-control technique. *Behavior Therapy, 5,* 247–254.

Gray, J. J. (1979). Positive reinforcement and punishment in the treatment of childhood trichotillomania. *Journal of Behavior Therapy and Experimental Psychiatry, 10,* 125–129.

Gresham, F. M. (1982). *Handbook for behavioral consultation.* Des Moines, IA: Department of Public Instruction.

Hagin, R. (1984) *Tourette Syndrome and the school psychologist.* Bayside, NY: Tourette Syndrome Association.

Herzfeld, G., & Powell, R. (1986). *Coping for kids: A complete stress-control program for students ages 8–18.* West Nyack, NY: Center for Applied Research in Education.

Kramer, J. J. (1981). Aversive control of bruxism in a mentally retarded child: A case study. *Psychological Reports, 49,* 815–818.

MacNeil, J., & Thomas, M. R. (1976). The treatment of obsessive compulsive hair pulling (trichotillomania) by behavioral and cognitive contingency manipulation. *Journal of Behavior Therapy and Experimental Psychiatry, 7,* 391–392.

McGlynn, F. D., Cassisi, J. E., & Diamond, E. L. (1985). Bruxism: A behavioral dentistry perspective. In R. J. Daitzman (Ed.), *Diagnosis and intervention in behavior therapy and behavioral medicine* (pp.28–81). New York: Springer.

Nunn, R. G. (1978). Maladaptive habits and tics. *Psychiatric Clinics of North America, 1,* 349–361.

Pray, B., Jr., Kramer, J. J., & Lindskog, R. (1986). Assessment and treatment of tic behavior: A review and case study. *School Psychology Review, 15,* 418–429.

Price, V. H. (1978). Disorders of the hair in children. *Pediatric Clinics of North America, 25,* 305–320.

Richard, J. (1982). Tic disorders. In J. Grimes (Ed.), *Psychological approaches to problems of children and adolescents* (pp. 277–292). Des Moines, IA: Department of Public Instruction.

Rosenbaum, M. S., & Ayllon, T. (1981a). The habit reversal technique in treating trichotillomania. *Behavior Therapy, 12,* 473–481.

Rosenbaum, M. S., & Ayllon, T. (1981b). Treating bruxism with the habit-reversal technique. *Behavior Research and Therapy, 19,* 87–96.

Sanchez, V. (1979). Behavioral treatment of chronic hair pulling in a two-year-old. *Journal of Behavior Therapy and Experimental Psychiatry, 10,* 241–245.

Turpin, G. (1983). The behavioral management of tic disorders: A critical review. *Advances in Behavior Research and Therapy, 5,* 203–245.

Wulfsohn, D., & Barling, J. (1978). From external to self-control: Behavioral treatment of trichotillomania in an eleven-year-old girl. *Psychological Reports, 42,* 1171–1174.

BIBLIOGRAPHY: PROFESSIONALS

Azrin, N. H., & Nunn, R. G. (1977). *Habit control in a day.* New York: Simon & Schuster.
A treatment handbook for maladaptive habits that provides detailed procedures for implementing HR. The etiology of habit disorders is explained. Methods for treating behavioral precursors to habits are included. Guidelines for parents to assist young children in eliminating habits are provided. This book is essential reading for psychologists who are developing treatment plans.

Friman, P. C., Finney, J. W., & Christophersen, E. R. (1984). Behavioral treatment of trichotillomania: An evaluative review. *Behavior Therapy, 15,* 249–265.
Presents a brief review of prevalence, assessment methods, and etiological factors along with a comprehensive review of behavioral treatments of hair pulling. Specific procedures to treat trichotillomania in preschool and developmentally delayed children along with self-management treatments for older children are enumerated.

Goldfried, M. R. & Davison, G. C. (1976). *Clinical behavior therapy.* New York: Holt, Rinehart, & Winston.
Chapter 5 provides a description of muscle relaxation training, which is important in treating habit disorders. Details on the mechanics of relaxation training including a transcript of a tension-relaxation induction and methods to extend relaxation skills to clients' stressful life situations are provided.

McGlynn, F. D., Cassisi, J. E., & Diamond, E. L. (1985). Bruxism: A behavioral dentistry perspective. In R. J. Daitzman (Ed.), *Diagnosis and intervention in behavior therapy and behavioral medicine* (pp. 28–81). New York: Springer.
Presents an extensive review of the theories, dental and psychological factors, assessment methods, and treatments, both dental and psychological, of bruxism. The dental signs of bruxism are explained along with methods for psychologists to assess the relationship between stress and bruxist behavior.

Pray, B., Jr., Kramer, J. J., & Lindskog, R. (1986). Assessment and treatment of tic behavior: A review and case study. *School Psychology Review, 15,* 418–429.
Reviews the medical and psychological treatments for children's tic disorders. A case study is presented that details the procedures for implementing HR treatment of tics within a behavioral consultation framework. Methods for involving parents and teachers in a home/school treatment plan are provided.

BIBLIOGRAPHY: PARENTS

Azrin, N. H., & Nunn, R. G. (1977). *Habit control in a day.* New York: Simon & Schuster.
This treatment handbook is written in nontechnical terms for the general public. It is intended to be used for self-treatment. It can be used by parents or older adolescents for self-treatment. Consultation with a psychologist in developing a specific treatment plan should be encouraged.

Esveldt-Dawson, K., & Kazdin, A. E. (1982). *How to use self-control.* Lawrence, KS: H & H Enterprises.
This brief manual for parents and teachers explains procedures to help people manage their own behavior. This information will be helpful in assisting caretakers and individual children in maintaining and generalizing treatment gains, especially when external control is faded.

Herzfeld, G., & Powell, R. (1986). *Coping for kids: A complete stress-control program for students ages 8–18.* West Nyack, NY: Center for Applied Research in Education.
Provides a step-by-step program of techniques, exercises, and activities for teaching children to control stress. Lessons and over 45 reproducible activity worksheets can be used by teachers and parents to help children control stress.

Tourette Syndrome Association (TSA), Inc. 41-02 Bell Boulevard, Bayside, NY, 11361.
This organization provides a variety of educational material on Tourette syndrome and related tic disorders. Resources include brochure and flyers, research and scientific materials, educational kits, video tapes and films, and the TSA *Newsletter.* TSA is an important resource for both parents and professionals.

Children and Masturbation

Marcia B. Shaffer
Steuben - Allegany Board of Cooperative Educational Services, Bath, New York

BACKGROUND

"Masturbate: to manipulate the genitals for sexual gratification" (Webster's New World Dictionary, 1982).

For hundreds of years, the word *masturbation* has had an unclean and sinful connotation in the Judeo-Christian world; the act itself has been condemned as dirty and ugly. Parents slap little hands that wander toward genitals. School-age children are told that masturbation will lead to blindness, insanity, the falling-off of one's penis, and/or the depletion of one's sperm supply. Adolescents who masturbate in surreptitious solitude are ever aware that they may elicit dire consequences. While it is said that there are small groups of people in the United States who teach their toddlers to masturbate as a means of keeping them quiet, those rumors are not mentioned by recognized authorities. For most people in the United States, indeed for most of the Western world, the taboo against masturbation is well established, usually through religious prohibitions.

The tenet operant in the United States has been that sexual functions are intended for procreation only. Onan, an Old Testament character, was said to have "spilled his seed," a statement that for centuries was interpreted to mean that he had masturbated. Thus the term *onanism* has been used as a synonym for masturbation and as a reference to the prodigal use of sexual substance.Recent translations by theologians allege that Onan was more likely indulging in coitus interruptus. This sustains the onus of wrongdoing on Onan and does nothing to improve the reputation of masturbation. Some religious leaders have attempted to reconcile church dogma with scientific information, urging more acceptance of, and pleasure in, "normal" sexual activity. Despite their efforts, the stigma on "self-abuse" remains.

Leading authorities on sexual matters say little about differences in beliefs among socioeconomic classes or various cultures. One reference states that the lower class may view masturbation as unmanly (Stone & Church, 1973), and another (McCandless, 1961) notes that persons with less education tend more to mutual than to solitary sexual behavior, but few others comments on class differences were noted. An ERIC search produced no references involving class or cultural differences.

It is presumably middle-class convictions that are most often encountered in public schools. There, the idea that masturbation is wicked is deeply entrenched, with an intensity that is cause for wonderment. The Old Testament, after all, exhorts Jews and Christians to honor their parents, refrain from coveting their neighbors' spouses, and desist from annihilating their fellows. Not one of these sins seems to evoke such panic as does the very thought of masturbation. In this author's experience, teachers of both sexes exhibit near-hysteria when children appear to be touching their genitals or rubbing against a piece of furniture. "Liberal" parents may react with righteous indignation and undue severity to masturbatory activity. As recently as December 1985, a mother in a southern city led a successful crusade to remove one of Judy Blume's books from a school library because the book contained the word *masturbate.* Even some social scientists take on a moral tone when discussing masturbation. Freud believed that it was acceptable in youngsters, but childish, immature, and undesirable for adults except in extraordinary circumstances. Haim Ginott (1969) described it as a self-centered and lonely act, indicating that it is an expression of immaturity. Although sex expert Sol Gordon may announce, from the depths of his loving soul, that "masturbation is ALL RIGHT" (seminar at The Rehabilitation Center of Cattaraugus County, Allegany County, NY), the situation does not appear to have changed since Boyd McCandless wrote, a quarter of a century ago, regarding the goals of childhood sex training in the United States: "The first . . . is to inculcate the taboo against incest; the second . . . is training against masturbation" (McCandless, 1961, p. 92).

Research on the subject of masturbation is not plentiful. Since it is a subsection of the vast topic of sex in general, its investigation is hampered by the same uncontrollable variables: the scarcity of possibilities of observation; the idiosyncracies that lead a person to become a subject in such surveys; the suspicion that reports of behavior or reactions may not be accurate. The research is also quickly outdated. Work that seemed daring, results that were shocking, even 30 years ago seem risible in the light of recent changes in sexual mores. Available bibliographies list sociological and criminological treatises, plus case histories, discussions of masturbatory fantasies, and answers to questions that adults think adolescents would like to ask. About the only scientifically reputable knowledge available is medical evidence that masturbation does not bring on the results suggested by traditional superstitions. None of this is very helpful to the school psychologist who is seeking solid data on which to base advice to clients.

The most professionally respectable pragmatic approach, in this writer's opinion, is to adapt to one's own purposes the advice of the recognized and accepted "experts" in the field of sex education. Those relied upon here are Mary Calderone, Sol Gordon, and Eric Johnson. These three are probably the nation's most prominent purveyors of information to the general public. These are the people to whom the ensuing text refers as "experts."

DEVELOPMENT

Experts agree that masturbation is a natural act, a normal sexual expression for humans as well as for other primates. A very young baby may find his or her genitals while being bathed or diapered, as early as 6 months of age. Bedtime masturbation is quite common, beginning late in the first year of life. A child no more than 18 months old may become sexually excited through self-stimulation. Masturbatory activity usually reaches its initial peak at age 4 years. The 4-year-old, who has been described as "plunging" and "intrusive" by authorities on child development, is likely to have her or his hands in every conceivable orifice. After that, masturbation usually diminishes until puberty.

Many sexologists and sex therapists are of the opinion that early masturbation has a specific part to play in the sexual evolution of the human being; that it is a healthy rehearsal for later sexual roles. They are also of one mind in declaring that the myths associated with masturbation are untrue. Boys and girls who masturbate do not, as a result, become blind or insane, or do any damage to their sexual anatomy.

"Spontaneous lust," sexual excitement without discernible external stimulus, probably rarely occurs before the end of the latency period, roughly age 10–13 years. After puberty, both boys and girls derive pleasure from handling their genitals. During adolescence, almost 100% of males are believed to masturbate more or less regularly. The percentage for girls has been estimated at 10–75%, the latter figure being the most recent. Clearly masturbation is not an unusual act. Conversely, there are many people who never masturbate. Boys and girls who do not do so should not consider themselves peculiar or undersexed.

For the older boy or girl, as well as for little ones, masturbation is "rehearsal play," getting ready to be adult. Through masturbation, girls may learn how their bodies react, how to achieve orgasm; boys may learn how to delay orgasm. Those are advantages beyond the exploration, the pleasure, and the tension reduction that are masturbation's anticipated accompaniments.

Can Masturbation Be Harmful?

Ginott (1969) was of the opinion that persistent masturbation might become a "too ready consolation for mishaps." Current writers concur. They say that masturbation may occur because of conflicts in young people's lives that are not sexual (boredom, frustration, loneliness); that masturbation should not be used only as a reaction to depression; and that compulsive masturbation (that which a child or adolescent seems unable to resist) may be a sign of serious emotional conflict. A further word regarding compulsive masturbation may be useful. If a person feels driven to masturbate, if it is done more than he or she really likes, it is not pleasant —in the same way that too many ice cream cones may make one ill, even though eating is natural.

Masturbation is also harmful, in the social sense, when it is done publicly by someone old enough to know better. Most children of school age are aware of the social disapproval accorded public masturbation, so any demonstration beyond the age of 6 or 7 years must be viewed as a sign of emotional distress.

PUTTING CHILDREN'S MASTURBATION IN PERSPECTIVE

Those readers who wish to consider masturbation on a more theoretical level will find many sources of information in the bibliographies of the books listed at the end of this chapter. Some may want to investigate the writings of Freud and his followers, including the current journals of psychoanalytic persuasion. Even those who do not espouse Freudian theory are likely to be indebted to the concept of the unconscious for enabling them to understand the intense reactions of adults to the idea of masturbation. Unconscious yearnings and/or guilt seem to be the most feasible explanation for the agitation shown by teachers and parents in response to almost any sexual move by children, masturbation in particular.

Experts on child development and human sexuality are in accord in their attitudes about masturbation. To a person, they emphasize that it is a normal form of sexual release, not only in childhood but throughout life. At least one authority (Gordon, 1975) advises that even married people should not worry if they masturbate from time to time. Experts also state that the myths that have grown up around masturbation should be discounted precisely as myths. The real problem, they contend, is the guilt that masturbation engenders; the problem lies not in masturbation, but in attitudes about it. Mothers usually begin reprimanding, in varying degrees and ways, when their babies first touch themselves. Mothers' and fathers' attitudes are thought to have lasting effects. "One of the main sources of failure to achieve sexual satisfaction in adult life is interference by parents early in life with the child's discovery of its own body as a source of pleasure" (Calderone and Johnson, 1981, p. 27). Gordon (1975) is persuaded that most of a child's future attitudes toward sex are formed by the age of 6.

Unfortunately, parents have been the victims of the biases and guilt of their own parents. Memories of punishment for masturbating, whether the memories are conscious or not, may influence a person's reaction toward his own child's behavior. So, in spite of extravagant assurances that masturbation is harmless, that the myths are untrue, and that the act is no longer to be seen as a sin, parents may not be comfortable in regard to occurrences of it in their offspring. Although sex experts acknowledge the deleterious effect of early negative experiences on adult sentience and conduct, there is a blithe quality to their observations and opinions that gives the impression that they do not recognize that there are still many people who have great concern over masturbation.

Masturbation, in the writings of authorities, is usually attributed to a desire for bodily pleasure or a need to suppress or repress extreme anxiety. Rarely are simple reasons for masturbating mentioned. This omission leaves a gap in the knowledge of the practicing school psychologist, who may be asked to solve the "problem" of a given child's suggestive fidgeting. Lawrence Balter, who is the resident child psychologist at the CBS Television Network, submits that masturbation may follow the witnessing of an excessive amount of adult sexual activity, as on television or, in some cases, between one's parents; and that it may be a way of alleviating specific fears, as in the situation of a little boy who saw his baby sister unclothed, realized that she had no penis, and felt constrained to assure himself frequently that his own penis remained intact (Balter, 1985). The thoughtful school psychologist will consider such idiosyncratic factors when a teacher reports that a child is masturbating. Furthermore, having ruminated over possible causes such as individual worries, sexual release, and anxiety, the professional will inquire into other conceivable causes: inadequate personal hygiene; genital infection; genital irritation, which *may* be the result of sexual abuse; and too-tight undergarments.

Masturbation and the Disabled

Persons with disabilities, physical or mental, have the same basic drives as other people, including sexual sensations. We expect retarded adults, for example, to be hungry and thirsty and sleepy, but may thoughtlessly assume that they are nonsexual. School psychologists are among those who have the opportunity to make the needs of the handicapped clear to those about them.

Perhaps because they are more aware of the details of their children's lives than the parents of the nonhandicapped, parents of disabled children are reputed to spend more time trying to discourage masturbation. The handicapped who do not live at home are equally restrained. Staff members in institutions are inordinately vigilant, expending much effort to be certain that patients do not have enough privacy to masturbate. Sol Gordon, who is full of ardor and sympathy for every aspect of human sexuality, believes that prohibition of masturbation is "a devastating restriction" on handicapped young people who lack the usual outlets of dating, kissing, hand-holding. He warns that those who are not permitted to explore their sexuality by means of masturbation may suffer serious emotional consequences. He adds, with characteristic practicality, that "for persons who do not have sufficient motor control to masturbate themselves, vibrators can be used with satisfying results" (Gordon & Gordon, 1983, p. 186).

Masturbation is as acceptable for the retarded as for anyone, but they may not be perceptive about good manners. The austitic child likewise may be wanting in social comprehension, and in understanding the language in which sexual information is conveyed. Such young persons may need more than words to learn that masturbation in public is not to be tolerated. Behavior modification is recommended. Any infraction, any public display, should result in immediate loss of privileges, or whatever negative reinforcement is most useful for a given individual. Gordon and Gordon (1983) remind their readers that anyone who is toilet-trained can be taught that masturbation must be carried out in private.

Not only the retarded, but other disabled youths

may be overly enthusiastic about masturbating and may find it an easy refuge. Their parents and teachers must make sure that masturbating is not an emotional retreat, a solution to any and every problem, the surcease for every stress. How to achieve a "happy medium" will need to be settled case by case.

ALTERNATIVE ACTIONS

Although many people do it, masturbation is a "rare incidence" problem in schools, one to which most school psychologists, and their books and journals, give minimal attention. The first step for the school psychologist, therefore, is understanding. Some of the authors listed in the bibliography at the end of this chapter have devoted their professional lives to promulgating facts about sex and urging people to enjoy rather than deplore it, masturbation included. Only one or two of their books need be read to absorb their viewpoint. Their writings may also be recommended to parents and teachers; in fact, many of them have written specifically for the general public. When appropriate, it would be useful for the school psychologist to discuss healthy attitudes toward masturbation at meetings of parents' groups or school staff. Brief articles might be placed in the local newspaper or the school bulletin.

Professional associations could aid in publicizing information, too. An organization might develop a brochure dealing with data on sexuality, with a section delineating major opinions on masturbation. To provide such a brochure for general distribution would be a service to school psychologists as well as to the public.

Disseminating information about masturbation is no different from telling people about child-rearing practices or learning problems. However, masturbation is a subject that even professional people may not be able to discuss easily. The teacher who is upset over a child's masturbation may be embarrassed, perplexed, angry, disgusted. Many people find it impossible to abandon their notions that this is an evil and filthy act, and that the child who does it is tainted. For those persons, school psychologists must adopt a semitherapeutic role, exercising sensitivity with regard to each individual's personal attitudes. School psychologists must also be especially alert to the influence of their own feelings about masturbation on their responses to clients.

If the adult asking how to handle observable or suspected masturbation is reasonable, a calm, factual presentation will be helpful. A teacher or parent should be told that, while severe scoldings or punishment are emotionally damaging to a child, a request to stop masturbating is unlikely to leave permanent scars on small psyches. The best treatment, if one has determined that the masturbation does not have an extraneous cause such as an emotional conflict or a physical ailment, may be to ignore it.

Parents should be requested not to discourage explorations of the body, to permit freedom of exploration without giving masturbation more importance than it deserves. Balter (1985) has suggested that, should a pre-school child embarrass parents socially by masturbating, the parents simply say "It's a stage he's going through." That response may not come naturally, but is worth practicing.

The one restriction posited by all authors is that masturbation should be a private act, belonging only to oneself. Actually, in view of our societal mores, it seems ill-mannered, dull-witted, or psychotic to masturbate in the presence of others. Public masturbation will make a child an object of scorn or ridicule, or at the very least, curiosity. Schoolmates will stare or jeer or giggle or all three. For parents to permit a child to be exposed to such hurtful experiences would be cruel.

Parents should be reminded to avoid being derisive and causing humiliation to their children. Gordon (1975) has suggested also that parents be admonished that, even if they were raised to believe that masturbating is wrong, they should try not to show disapproval and to refrain from severe punishment, since either of those actions will give the child a negative message. Acceptance of masturbation as natural is one of the benefits parents may not have had but can give to their own children.

Given the opportunity to talk with a child directly, school psychologists will want to use a correct vocabulary, defining words in slang terms if necessary. In addition, they will want to confirm the privacy of the act, and investigate the possibility of anxiety as a causative factor. Above all, in every contact with teachers or parents or children, school psychologists will want to make one point very clear: It is natural and normal to masturbate; it is also natural and normal *not* to masturbate.

SUMMARY

Masturbation is a normal form of sexual release for human beings of all ages. It is to be expected, developmentally, in tiny babies, reaching a peak at age 4 years and again in adolescence. It is still widely regarded as wicked, although sexologists and theologians have tried to remove the sense of disgrace that often accompanies it.

To deal with situations that may arise in practice, the school psychologist will want to keep in mind that masturbation is not harmful; that if it is done excessively or compulsively, physical ailments or emotional disturbance should be considered as possible causal factors; that the disabled have entirely normal sexual needs and should be provided or permitted ways to satisfy them; and that considerable sensitivity is required in discussing masturbation with individual parents or teachers as well as with children.

REFERENCES

Balter, L. (1985). *Dr. Balter's child sense.* New York: Simon and Schuster.

Calderone, M. S., & Johnson, E. W. (1981). The family book about sexuality. New York: Harper and Row.

Ginott, H. G. (1965). *Between parent and child.* New York: Avon Books.

Ginott, H. G. (1969). *Between parent and teenager.* New York: Avon Books.

Gordon, S. (1975). *Let's make sex a household word.* New York: John Day.

Gordon, S., & Gordon, J. (1983). *Raising a child conservatively in a sexually permissive world.* New York: Simon and Schuster.

McCandless, B. R. (1961). *Children and adolescents.* New York: Holt, Rinehart and Winston.

Stone, L. J., & Church, J. (1973). *Childhood and adolescence* (3rd ed.). New York: Random House.

BIBLIOGRAPHY: PROFESSIONALS AND PARENTS

Calderone, M. S., & Johnson, E. W. (1981). *The family book about sexuality.* New York: Harper and Row.
Covers almost every conceivable aspect of sexual functioning in a dignified style. It includes sex information for the handicapped and covers sexual conditions which have legal implications. It deals thoughtfully with the emotional side of sexuality.

Fischer, H. L., Krojicek, M. J., & Borthick, W. A. (1973). *Sex education for the developmentally disabled.* Baltimore: Park Press.
Consists of a series of pen and ink drawings illustrating sexual activities, including masturbation by both sexes. The drawings are shown to the subject; words of explanation are provided. There is a lengthy bibliography and suggestions for a one-day workshop on sexuality and the mentally retarded. It is suitable for use with the mentally retarded, the organically dysfunctional, the physically handicapped, and the emotionally disturbed.

Gordon, S. (1975). *Let's make sex a household word.* New York: John Day.
Like all of Dr. Gordon's publications, this one is forthright. It is addressed to parents, and covers topics of concern for children of preschool age through adolescence. It contains chapters regarding handicapped children, including the retarded, and discusses the roles of schools and organized religion on sex education. It provides an excellent bibliography, including books for the parents of disabled children.

Gordon, S., & Gordon, J. (1983). *Raising a child conservatively in a sexually permissive world.* New York: Simon and Schuster.
Written with Dr. Gordon's customary courage, compassion, and comprehensibility, and supported by his wife's social work philosophy, this book places more than the usual emphasis on social relationships and "sexual integrity." It provides a fine bibliography, listed by topics.

Johnson, C. B., & Johnson, E. W. (1970). *Love and sex and growing up.* Philadelphia: Lippincott.
Written in the expert Johnson style, this volume presents sexual information in a gentle, direct way. It makes clear the Johnson philosophy, which is that sexual information should be available to young people, but that they should feel free to embrace old-fashioned morality if they so choose.

A resource guide in sex education for the mentally retarded. (undated). A joint project of the Sex Information and Education Council of the United States and the American Association for Health, Physical Education, and Recreation.
The writer received this material, xeroxed, from the California State Department of Education, and has no further information about its publication. It appears to have been compiled circa 1979–80. In addition to lesson plans, the "Guide" contains lists of printed materials, films, transparencies, teaching aids, tapes, and organizations which will give additional assistance.

Children and Medication

Teresa A. Hutchens
University of Georgia

BACKGROUND

There are over 10,000 prescription drugs and 100,000 nonprescription or over-the-counter (OTC) products available to the U. S. market (Silverman & Lee, 1974). Many of these medications are commonly used with school-aged children in treatment for desired physical and/or behavioral changes. The behaviors that may be altered by these drugs are often those reflected in school performance, attention, emotionality, etc. It is important for the school psychologist and professional educators to be familiar with the medications most commonly administered to school-aged children and their potential effects on behavior. The relevance of these considerations is even greater for the psychologist who works in close association with special education students, among whom there is a relatively greater incidence of medication therapy (Gadow, 1986). Owing to the vast number of precipitating conditions and medications for treatment, it appears necessary to focus on general concepts, broad classes of medicines that are commonly used, and resources for specific information and individual case questions.

Medications are identified in three ways: by chemical name, by generic or nonproprietary name, and by trade name. The latter two are commonly used, the trade name being generated by the manufacturer holding the patent for production. Once this patent has expired, other companies may produce the same drug under its generic label, often at a lower cost (Gadow, 1986; McKim, 1986). References are usually made to both, relying on the generic name for greater consistency for consumers.

The effects of medications are categorized in three ways: direct or indirect effects (physical or psychological changes for improvement of the presenting condition), side effects (secondary changes that may or may not be observed), and emanative effects (cognitive or social changes often subsumed under side effects) (Ross & Ross, 1982). This terminology is an integral part of reference listings and comes up in communication with medical professionals. It can be particularly relevant to parents and teachers as medication for a physical disorder may produce side effects that influence school or social behavior. Likewise, some psychotropic drugs, those designed to produce psychological changes, may promote physical changes, such as headache or nausea. An awareness of potential side effects may contribute to more precise and relevant observations both at school and at home. Treatment decisions are often contingent on feedback obtained from teachers and parents, especially when the presenting problem is more behavioral than physiological.

DEVELOPMENT

The effects of a given medication can be influenced by a number of factors, such as sex, genetic background, presence of other medications, etc. (McKim, 1986; Sarason & Sarason, 1984). A primary influence is age. In adults, medication effects are fairly predictable; however, children demonstrate much greater variability in their reactions. Generally pediatric patients are reported to be less sensitive and may require larger dosages per unit body weight to achieve a given effect (Minde, 1977). This is due to developmental factors such as metabolic rate and ratio of body fat to muscle mass, which affect the dose and frequency of administration (Tatro, 1985).

The same physiological and developmental variables may influence the extent to which adverse or negative reactions are observed. Some adverse reactions may appear with greater frequency in the younger age groups (Tatro, 1985). Among the most common concerns are the effects of drugs for long-term use on growth patterns and developing tissue, such as tooth and bone and long-term effects of continuous medication into later adolescence.

The effects of psychopharmacological medications, which influence behavior and cognitive, academic, and social functioning, also appear to be influenced by developmental factors. Children under 10 years tend to react qualitatively differently than do adults (Minde, 1977). For example, stimulants may produce a paradoxical effect in some children, causing a decrease in motor activity as opposed to the increase more often seen in adults. The variability of reactions to psychoactive medications is greater in children; empirical evaluation is required for each individual child (Gualtieri, Golden, & Fahs, 1983). Prescribed use of drugs for more psychological or behavioral effects should be only one component of treatment, to be complemented with nondrug interventions such as behavior therapy or environmental manipulation (Gaddes, 1985; Gualtieri et al., 1983; Ross & Ross, 1983; Sarason & Sarason, 1984).

PUTTING CHILDREN'S MEDICATION IN PERSPECTIVE

The study of the influence of medications on behavior is broadly defined as psychopharmacology (Sarason & Sarason, 1984). Controversy continues to surround the prescribing of drugs for behavior control in children. Critics discuss the practice as a "band-aid approach," whereby drugs treat only behavioral symptoms for ease in management rather than addressing the underlying source of behavior disturbances (Minde, 1977). Despite such criticism, the value of psychotropic medication is increasingly recognized and is evidenced by widespread use in the school-age population. Rather than a "cure" for disturbances in behavior, these drugs are now viewed as valuable assets within a comprehensive educational or treatment program.

Medication for behavior control also raises the question of the lack of consistency in defining problem behaviors for which drug treatment is appropriate. Evaluation procedures, criteria for diagnoses, and decisions regarding medication are usually made by physicians whose knowledge, experience, and theoretical orientation vary; therefore, procedures and treatment decisions may differ (Gaddes, 1985). Most valid evaluation procedures require comprehensive information about a child's behavior in his or her natural environment. Information is usually obtained from parents and/or teachers to identify a child's typical behavior rather than that observed only in a clinical setting (Minde, 1977). Different methods of acquiring such information can be used, such as behavior rating checklists, structured interviews, and ongoing consultation with primary caretakers, including classroom teachers (Gadow, 1986). School psychologists may also be asked to provide referral or evaluation information.

Prescription medications for behavior control include the major tranquilizers, also called antipsychotics or neuroleptics; the antidepressants; and the other minor tranquilizers or antianxiety drugs. Within the pediatric age group, stimulants or analeptics are also included.

Major Tranquilizers (Neuroleptics)

The major tranquilizers (listed in Table 1) are frequently referred to as antipsychotics, especially when used in adult populations. The incidence of psychosis in children is low, increasing to approximately adult proportions in late adolescence. Therefore, a relatively small number of the major tranquilizers are used in the pediatric age group and may be targeted for specific behavioral effects (White, 1977). For example, use with the mentally retarded, usually adolescents and adults, has been shown to suppress maladaptive behaviors, such as self-injury (Gadow, 1982; Minde, 1977). Other treatment effects include mood regulation, decrease in aggression, and reduced motor agitation (Gadow, 1986; Gilman et al., 1985; White, 1977). Primarily, the control of behavior contributes to greater effectiveness of concurrent intervention strategies (Alderton, 1977; White, 1977).

Although a characteristic of neuroleptic medication is reduced agitation and motor activity, this is not usually the treatment of choice for hyperactivity (Ross & Ross, 1982; White, 1977). Mellaril (thioridazine) is considered, particularly with children who do not react favorably to stimulants. When used, close monitoring of medication administration and effects is recommended.

In the pediatric population, Navane (thiothixene) is used for treatment of psychoses (White, 1977; Barnhart, 1985). The effects include less sedation with a decrease in motor agitation. Haldol (haloperidol) has also been found to be effective for pediatric use in cases of chronic aggression (Maxwell, 1984) and more frequently for the control of tic behavior, as in Gilles de la Tourette's syndrome (White, 1977). For more general effects, as in decrease of motor agitation, Thorazine (chlorpromazine) can be used because of its wider margin of safety in administration.

All major tranquilizers have the potential for side effects, such as unusual motor behaviors, including muscle spasms, resting tremors, and poor muscle tone (Gilman et al., 1985; Tatro, 1985). Sedation is commonly observed early in the course of these medications, but tolerance frequently develops against this effect within several days (Gadow, 1986). Other side effects include dry mouth, blurred vision, and infrequently, adverse reactions (Gadow, 1986). To review potential effects, consultation with a physician with reference to the specific medication is recommended.

Antidepressants

Although antidepressants include two main categories, tricyclic antidepressants (Table 2) and monoamine oxide (MAO) inhibitors, only the former are commonly used with children (Sarason & Sarason, 1984). Tricyclics are prescribed for a variety of pediatric disorders, including depression, which is increasingly recognized as an affective disorder in childhood (Gualtieri et al., 1983).

Of the antidepressants, Tofranil (imipramine) is the most frequently prescribed in children, often for enuresis (Gadow, 1986; Wright, Schaefer, & Solomons, 1979). Successful use in treatment of nocturnal enuresis is documented, which approximately 50–60% of children achieving nocturnal dryness; however, it should be noted that 50% of those successful may relapse with discontinuance of the drug (Ack, Norman, & Schmitt, 1983). Even less effectiveness is reported with daytime wetting and with use in adolescents (Ack et al., 1983; Minde, 1977).

Antidepressants, particularly Tofranil and to a lesser extent Elavil (amitriptyline), have been used effectively for other conditions in childhood. Treatment programs for hyperactivity, depression, and school phobia may effectively include this type of medication (Gilman et al., 1985; Gualtieri et al., 1983). Effective use has also been reported for anorexia nervosa in adolescents (Gualtieri et al., 1983).

Side effects may be observed with the use of antidepressants, particularly with prolonged use. Initial effects may be relatively minor,such as blurred vision or constipation; however, the potential for more significant effects increases with length of administration, which may include mood swings, sleep disturbances, and even electrocardiographic and electroencephalographic changes (Ack et al., 1983; Gilman et al., 1985). Ongoing monitoring of medication effects is therefore warranted. Supervision in administration is also strongly recommended, for consuming an excessive amount may prove lethal (Ack et al., 1983; Minde, 1977). Because drug effects may be influenced by the presence of other medications, parents should be cautioned to consult with their physician before providing other medications to a child already taking antidepressants.

TABLE 1
Neuroleptics (Major Tranquilizers)

Generic name	Trade name
Phenothiazines	
Acetophenazine	Tindal
Chloropromazine[1]	Thorazine
Fluphenazine	Prolixin, Permitil
Mesoridazine	Serentil
Perphenazine	Trilafon
Piperacetazine	Quide
Promethazine[1]	Phenergan
Thioridazine[1]	Mellaril
Trifluoperazine[1]	Stelazine
Triflupromazine	Vesprin
Thioxanthenes	
Chlorprothixene	Taractan
Thiothixene	Navane
Butyrophenones	
Droperidol	Inapsine, Innovar
Haloperidol[1]	Haldol

[1]Most commonly used.

TABLE 2
Tricyclic Antidepressants

Generic name	Trade name
Imipramine	Janimine, SK-Pramine, Tofranil
Amitriptyline	Elavil, Endep
Nortriptyline	Aventyl, Pamelor

Minor Tranquilizers (Antianxiety Agents)

Antianxiety medications include sedatives or minor tranquilizers (Table 3). They are frequently drugs of choice in the treatment of adult anxiety or other psychiatric symptoms; however, they are not routinely prescribed for this purpose in children (Minde, 1977). Pediatric applications include use to relax muscles as in cerebral palsy (Gadow, 1986), to reduce anxiety, which may aggravate conditions of ulcers or epilepsy (McKim, 1986; Vess & Goldberg, 1985), to control seizure activity (Gadow, 1986), etc.

Of all these medications, Benadryl (diphenhydramine) is the most commonly used with children. Cold symptoms as well as symptoms of upper respiratory illnesses, hay fever, and allergies are usually alleviated by the antihistamine properties of the medication (Vess & Goldberg, 1985; White, 1977). A sedative effect often accompanies its use. This is important to note, as a child's classroom behavior may reflect lethargy and drowsiness. The drug is frequently in use; previously available by prescription, Benadryl is now approved for over-the-counter purchase. Teachers and psychologists may be advised to consult parents if a student displays lethargy that is inconsistent with previously observed behavior.

All minor tranquilizers produce similar sedation, muscle relaxation, and anticonvulsant effects; however, they differ in the intensity to which these relative effects are produced. It would therefore be ill-advised for the education process to alter activities or expectations of performance upon knowledge that a student receives such medication. Classroom observation and consultation with parents should produce more valuable information as to the individual child's reactions.

Stimulant Medication (Analeptics)

The use of stimulants (Table 4) is one of the most controversial issues in the field of medication for behavior control. In the early 1970s, reports suggested that as many as 10% of all elementary school children were being prescribed stimulants, used most frequently and effectively in the control of hyperactivity (Ross & Ross, 1982). Inconsistencies were noted in diagnosis and prescription, involving a range of labels that included min-

TABLE 3

Minor Tranquilizers (Anti-anxiety Medications)

Generic name	Trade name
Benzodiazipines	
Diazepam[1]	Valium
Chlordiazepoxide	Librium
Clonazepam	Clonopin
Clorazepate	Tranxene
Flurazepam	Dalmane
Oxyazepam	Serax
Diphenylmethane Derivatives	
Hydroxyzine hydrochloride	Atarax
Hydroxyzine pamoate	Vistaril
Diphenhydramine	Benadryl
Propanediols	
Meprobamate	Equanil

[1]Most commonly used.

TABLE 4

Analeptics–Stimulants

Generic name	Trade name
Amphetamine sulfate	Benzedrine
Deanol	Deaner
Dextroamphetamine[1]	Dexedrine
Magnesium Pemoline	Cylert
Methylphenidate[1]	Ritalin

[1]Most commonly used.

imal brain dysfunction, hyperactivity, hyperkinesis, and psychogenic impulse control (Kanter, 1982). Children who were identified as conduct-disordered were often given trials of stimulant medication, and found to show little or no improvement (Minde, 1977).

These issues have been greatly clarified and the limitations of stimulant medication have been recognized. The term "hyperactivity" is basically a descriptive label for excessive and aimless motor activity, impulsiveness, and problems with directed attention for which medical referral may be appropriate (Minde, 1977; Ross, 1976). It is included among the clinical diagnoses of DSM-III and may be contrasted with conduct disorders and/or adjustment problems (American Psychiatric Association, 1980). Stimulant medication is not appropriate or effective with all children; however, when used appropriately, stimulants are an effective component of a more comprehensive treatment approach (Gadow, 1986; McKim, 1986; Ross & Ross, 1982).

Recent surveys estimate that 1–2% of the elementary school population receive stimulant medication (Ross & Ross, 1982). Not all children respond in the same way. Approximately 70% respond positively during the initial trial period; improvement in behavior may not be observed with the first dose or the first medication tried (Ross & Ross, 1982). A child's response to medication does not reflect the cause of his or her behavior problem. Even if improvement is achieved with stimulant medication, it does not mean that the child has a neurological dysfunction (Ross, 1976).

The trial period of stimulant medication is usually about 2 weeks for a determination of effectiveness, regulation of dosage, and evaluation of side effects. Parent and teacher reports of a child's behavior are recommended (Berkow & Talbott, 1977; Gadow, 1986). A positive response is regarded to be an increase in directed attention and a decrease in motor activity when the child is placed in a structured environment, such as a classroom (Barkley, 1977; Smith, 1983). Observations by classroom teachers are noted to be particularly valuable during this time. The physician may determine how such observations are to be reported. Behavior rating scales can be used, but they are frequently applied inconsistently and with uncertain reliability for this specific need (Smith, 1983).

Most commonly prescribed is Ritalin (methylphenidate). Effects are much like those of Dexedrine (dextroamphetamine), which is the next most commonly prescribed (Minde, 1977; Ross & Ross, 1982). With appropriate dosage, a child's activity level may appear unchanged in an unstructured setting (Gadow, 1986); however, when task demands require greater concentration and reduced motor activity in a structured environment, a positive response to the medication can be inferred (Barkley, 1977; Ross, 1976). A positive response also includes improvement in performance on short-term memory tasks and in psychological testing. It is thought that the improvement results from the child's heightened ability to use problem-solving strategies and past knowledge. These medications do not produce learning but facilitate conditions necessary for learning to occur (Barkley, 1977; Gadow, 1986). Social benefits may accrue that include an increase in positive social interactions, in peer relationships, and in positive self-image (Ross, 1976).

Improvements in behavior are observed only as long as the medication is taken; when it wears off, activity returns to premedication levels (Sarason & Sarason, 1984). Classroom teachers are in primary positions to observe increases in activity levels, which suggest the length of time a particular dose is effective. This is valuable information for the attending physician for an optimum schedule of administration.

Observations of side effects are also important to report to parents and physician; approximately 30% of children taking stimulants report varying degrees of these effects (Minde, 1977). The most frequently reported are loss of appetite, sleep disturbances, sadness, and stomach upset; headaches have also been reported (Ross & Ross, 1984). Severe side effects are rare but have been more often reported with Dexedrine than with Ritalin (Ross & Ross, 1984; Tatro, 1985).

Concern has been expressed regarding suppression of growth as a side effect; relatively small gains in height and weight are sometimes observed (Minde, 1977; Ross & Ross, 1982). This effect is reported to be temporary. Children are reported to display a rebound effect upon discontinuation of the medication. Greater than normal gains in height and weight have been reported during drug-free periods and upon termination of the medication (Gadow, 1986; Minde, 1977; Sarason & Sarason, 1984). To alleviate this concern, many physicians recommend drug "holidays," drug-free periods during weekends or school vacations.

Anticonvulsants

Children of all ages and levels of intellectual ability may have seizure disorders. Incidence is estimated at approximately 2% of children in regular education classes, increasing to 20% in TMR students (Frank, 1982). There are many types of convulsive disorders; medication is usually prescribed on the basis of the type of seizure and tendency to recur (Connor, Williamson, & Siepps, 1978). The effects of such medication (Table 3) are individually determined, close monitoring of patients' behavior being necessary (Frank, 1985). Approximately 50% of children taking anticonvulsants are free of seizures and another 25% have fewer seizures, which are less severe; in 15% medication has no effect (Gadow, 1986).

Medication therapy usually begins with a single drug; other drugs may be added or substituted systematically to achieve optimal functioning (Connor, 1978). Anticonvulsants may have secondary effects on cognition and memory, influencing school behavior (Matthews & Barabos, 1985). Side effects such as drowsiness, lethargy, confusion, and mood changes may be observed; physical sequelae such as nausea, vomiting, and dizziness may also be seen (Frank, 1985; Gadow, 1986; Matthews & Barabos, 1985). Such effects vary with individual patients, and are dependent on the type, dosages, and combinations of drugs prescribed. More information is available in the chapter on Children and Seizures elsewhere in this volume.

Antibiotics

More viral and bacterial infections are found in the pediatric population than in adults. Prescriptions are based on a specific diagnosis of the presenting condition (Berkow, 1977). Too wide a range of antibiotic medications are available for pediatric use to come within the scope of this discussion. The most frequently used medications will be addressed briefly.

Two classes of antibiotics used in the school-age group are penicillin, including ampicillin, penicillin G, and amoxycillin, and the tetracyclines. The penicillin group is frequently prescribed for infectious diseases in childhood, including otitis media, the most common (Cupit, 1984; Gilman et al., 1985). In contrast, tetracyclines are prescribed frequently for adolescents, at higher doses for infections and low doses for acne control (Gilman et al., 1985). Tetracyclines are now used in younger children with caution, owing to possible harm and discoloration of tooth and bone tissue during the formative years (Ball, Gray,& Murdock, 1978; Maxwell, 1984). Erythromycin is also a commonly used medication, frequently prescribed for strep (streptococcal) and staph (staphylococcal) infections, as well as otitis media (Cupit, 1983; Gilman et al., 1985; Maxwell, 1984).

Each of these antibiotic groups can cause adverse reactions, presenting as skin rashes, nausea, vomiting, or muscle spasms (Gilman et al., 1985). Reactions are varied and are usually observed by parents because of the infectious nature of the presenting condition. Each type of antibiotic medication can produce specific reactions. Because of this and the multitude of drugs available, consultation between parents and the attending physician is advised. Further consultation with parents and teachers may be warranted if long-term medication or school-day administration is required. References are available to provide information about specific medications.

TABLE 5
Antiepileptic Drugs

Generic name	Trade name	Common use	Possible side effects	Unacceptable side effects
Clonazepam	Clonopin	Absence (petit mal, akinetic, myoclonic	Lethargy, dizziness, nausea/vomiting	Hypersensitivity, allergic reaction
Valproic Acid	Depakene	Absence (petit mal), generalized tonic-clonic	Nausea/vomiting, indigestion, sedation/dizziness, hair loss, tremor	Hypersensitivity, allergic reaction
Phenytoin	Dilantin	Any seizures except absence (petit mal)	Body hair increase, gum overgrowth, tremor, anemia, loss of coordination, double vision, nausea/vomiting, confusion, slurred speech	Hypersensitivity, allergic reaction
Phenobarbital	No trade name commonly used	Most types	Drowsiness, lethargy, hyperactivity	Hypersensitivity, allergic reaction
Primidone	Mysoline	Complex partial (psychomotor, temporal lobe), generalized tonic-clonic (grand mal), elementary partial	Drowsiness, appetite loss, irritability, nausea/vomiting, dizziness, loss of coordination	Hypersensitivity, allergic reaction
Carbamazepine	Tegretol	Complex partial (psychomotor, temporal lobe, generalized tonic-clonic (grand mal), elementary partial	Drowsiness, dizziness, blurred vision, double vision	Hypersensitivity, allergic reaction

Note: Data from *Epilepsy: Medical Axpects* (p. 5) by the Comprehensive Epilepsy Program of the University of Minnesota, Minneapolis: The University of Minnesota. Copyright 1979 by the Comprehensive Epilepsy Program of the University of Minnesota. Reprinted by permission of Florence Gray, Program Coordinator.

OTC Medications

Nonprescription drugs are generally available over-the-counter and have widespread availability. Because there are no legal restrictions on purchase and use, the dangers associated with these medications can be overlooked. Deviation from recommended dosage, the presence of other drugs, and accidental poisoning are of concern, particularly to parents. This is of greatest importance in respect to young children, because of their curiosity and possible access to such medications stored in the home.

The most common accidental poisoning in children is from aspirin, toxic reactions to which depend on the child's size and the amount consumed (Berkow & Talbott, 1977). Soon after a child ingests a large amount, symptoms of nervous agitation may appear, accompanied by vomiting, rapid breathing, and elevated temperature. Convulsions may follow. It is critical to empty the child's stomach, which may be facilitated by administering ipecac syrup (Berkow & Talbott, 1977). Because symptoms may worsen and can be fatal, medication attention should be sought immediately.

Aspirin is recommended for children because of its anti-inflammatory and analgesic properties. It is often used over extended periods of time, as in cases of juvenile arthritis or for brief periods for fever reduction (Baum, 1983; Gilman et al., 1985). Caution is recommended in use with children if fever results from viral infections, such as varicella or chicken pox. Though the incidence of development of Reye's syndrome is low, from 0.37 to 6 cases per 100,000, this syndrome has been linked to the use of aspirin in the presence of viral infection (Hall, 1984). Reye's syndrome is a serious condition that affects the nervous system and liver; the potential risk warrants serious consideration in the use of aspirin. Parents should be advised to be cautious, especially when educators are aware of a known virus, such as chicken pox, in the student population.

All nonprescription drugs should be treated with the same care as any prescription medication. The possibility of adverse reactions and danger in combining drugs exists with OTC medications also. Symptoms associated with sensitivity reactions may be observed during the school day. Medicine given before a child leaves home may not become fully effective until he or she reaches school. Teachers and other education professionals can assist parents by informing them of potential problems when medication is a factor.

ALTERNATIVE ACTIONS

Medication can influence many aspects of a student's school performance. Changes can be observed in behavior, physical skills, social interaction, and even academic performance. Many schoolchildren require medication therapy for extended periods; many more require short-term medication for a wide range of physical complaints. The potential influence on school performance and frequency of their use suggest a need for educators to be aware of their students' medication and its possible effects. Communication between parents and teachers is vital to meet this need. The school psychologist presents a valuable resource to both, as well as to the medical professional in optimizing this communications network.

The school psychologist is also involved in referral and evaluation procedures, which include assessment in all areas possibly related to a presenting problem. This includes the area of health and involves several means of collecting information. Information about a child's medication status may be extremely relevant to the evaluation process. To the degree that medication influences a student's participation in the academic program, either facilitating or hindering academic progress, the acquisition of such information is relevant to procedures of evaluation and assessment.

The expertise of the psychologist can be utilized by conducting parent–teacher workshops about student medications. Parent education programs might include recommendations for informing teachers of children's current medication. It might also be suggested that initial administration of the medication take place in the home, under parental supervision, prior to its being administered during the school day. Many schools have strict policies prohibiting self-medication by students, even for OTC drugs. Policy restrictions and guidelines should be clearly communicated to parents, who should also be cautioned against permitting self-medication by their children without supervision in all other settings. Further information might be provided to parents regarding the importance of informing teachers that a student is taking a specific medication. The possible effects of drugs, such as decongestants, which frequently produce stimulation, or antihistamines, which may produce drowsiness (Harkness, 1977), should be explained, as they influence a child's behavior in school. Parents should be encouraged to report any side effects that are likely to be observed as a result of current medications in order that school personnel might modify student activities or expectations accordingly.

With the use of any drugs, guidelines are recommended. Conveying the guidelines in Table 6 to parents may be helpful in increasing their awareness.

TABLE 6

Guidelines for Parental Supervision of Children's Medication

1. Know your child's medication. Learn the generic and trade name as well as the specific reason for its use.

2. Administer medication exactly as directed. "More" does not mean "better." The dosage is determined for your individual child's age and weight. Altering the amount or schedule can be dangerous.

3. Observe your child after administering medication. Ask the doctor what side effects to expect and consult her or him in the event of unexpected results.

4. Avoid mixing medications, either prescription or nonprescription, unless specifically advised by your doctor.

5. Store medicines wisely, out of the reach of children. A medicine cabinet that locks is a good safety precaution. Never store more than one drug in a single container.

6. Discard unused medications. They can lose their beneficial effects and may become dangerous if too old.

7. Supervise your child's regular medication, even in the case of long-term regimen. Children may not be responsible or attentive and may not be able to remember the details of their dosage.

8. Inform your child's teacher or other school personnel when medication has been given. Include the type and amount in case such information is needed.

9. Know school policy regarding medication or drugs at school. Discuss the policy with your child and assist in its being enforced.

School administration usually assumes responsibility for developing and executing policy on medication and drug use in the schools. School psychologists, as a liaison between educational and medical professionals, may be called upon to help develop or modify such guidelines. Committees composed of teachers, school nurses, administrative personnel, and psychologists may present considerations particular to the needs of the student population. Questions to be considered also include where the medication is to be stored during the school day, who is authorized to have access, who is to administer the medications, etc. Administrative guidelines might also require written parental and/or medical permission for medication. In all cases, it is imperative that the school psychologist and school personnel be familiar with such policy and its enforcement. Strict adherence is required to insure responsible practice in the school setting.

REFERENCES

Ack, M., Norman, M. E., & Schmitt, B. D. (1985, January). Enuresis: The role of alarms and drugs. *Patient Care, 19*(1), 75–90.

Alderton, H. R. (1977). Psychoses in childhood and adolescence. In P. O. Steinhauer & Q. Rae-Grant (Eds.), *Psychological problems of the child and his family* (pp. 165–190). Toronto: Gage.

American Psychiatric Association. (1980). *Diagnostic and statistical manual of mental disorders* (3rd ed.). Washington, DC: Author.

Ball, A. P., Gray, J. A., & Murdoch, J. M. (1978). *Antibacterial drugs today.* Baltimore: University Park Press.

Barkley, R. A. (1977). A review of stimulant drug research with hyperkinetic children. *Journal of Child Psychology and Psychiatry, 18,* 137–165.

Barnhart, E. R. (Ed.). (1986). *Physicians' desk reference.* Oradell, NJ: Medical Economics Company.

Baum, J. (1983, March). Treatment of juvenile arthritis. *American Family Physician, 27*(3), 133–139.

Berkow, R., & Talbott, J. H. (1977). *The Merck manual for diagnosis and therapy* (13th ed.). Rahway, NJ: Merck, Sharp, & Dohme Research Laboratories.

Connor, F. P., Williamson, G. G., & Siepps, J. M. (1978). *Program guide for infants and toddlers with neuromotor and other developmental disabilities.* New York: Teachers College Press.

Cupit, G. C. (1984, November). Pediatric drug therapy. Parts I and II. *American Druggist, 190*(5), 81–96.

Frank, B. B. (1985). Psycho-social aspects of educating epileptic children: Roles for school psychologists. *School Psychology Review, 14,* 196–203.

Gaddes, W. H. (1985). *Learning disabilities and brain function: A neuropsychological approach* (2nd ed.). New York: Springer-Verlag.

Gadow, K. D. (1986). *Children on medication* (Vols. 1, 2). San Diego: College-Hill.

Gilman, A. G., Goodman, L. S., Rall, T. W., & Murad, F. (1985). *Goodman and Gilman's the pharmacological basis of therapeutics* (7th ed.). New York: Macmillan.

Gualtieri, C. T., Golden, R. N., & Fahs, J. J. (1983). New developments in pediatric psychopharmacology. *Developmental and Behavioral Pediatrics, 4,* 202–209.

Hall, S. (1984). A review of Reye's Syndrome. In J. Hallman, L. Goldman & G. R. Fryers (Eds.), *Aspirin Symposium 1983* (pp. 37–41). London: The Royal Society of Medicine and Oxford University Press.

Kanter, D. R. (1982). Etiological considerations in childhood hyperactivity. In P. Karoly, J. J. Steffer, & D. J. O'Grady (Eds.), *Child health psychology: Concepts and issues* (pp. 211–228). New York: Pergamon.

Matthews, W. S., & Barabos, G. (1985). Recent advances in developmental pediatrics related to achievement and social behavior. *School Psychology Review, 14,* 182–187.

Maxwell, G. M. (1984). *Principles of pediatric pharmacology.* New York: Oxford University Press.

McKim, W. A. (1986). *Drugs and behavior.* Englewood Cliffs, NJ: Prentice-Hall.

Minde, K. (1977). The role of drugs in the treatment of disturbed children. In P. O. Steinhauer & Q. Rae-Grant (Eds.), *Psychological problems of the child and his family* (pp. 413–426). Toronto: Gage.

Ross, A. O. (1976). *Psychological aspects of learning disabilities and reading disorders.* New York: McGraw-Hill.

Ross, D. M., & Ross. S. A. (1982). *Hyperactivity: Current issues, research, and theory.* New York: Wiley.

Sarason, I. G., & Sarason, B. R. (1984). *Abnormal psychology: The problem of maladaptive behavior* (4th ed.). Englewood Cliffs, NJ: Prentice-Hall.

Silverman, M., & Lee, P. R. (1974). *Pills, profits, and politics.* Berkeley: University of California Press.

Smith, C. R.(1983). *Learning disabilities: The interaction of learner, task and setting.* Boston: Little, Brown.

Tatro, D. S. (1985) Adverse drug reactions in children. In L. A. Pagliaro & R. H. Levin (Eds.), *Problems in pediatric drug therapy* (pp. 119–142). Hamilton, IL: Drug Intelligence Publications.

Vess, S. M., & Goldberg, I. B. (1985). Medications commonly used with children. In A. Thomas & J. Grimes (Eds.), *Best practices in school psychology* (Appendix V, pp. 554–566). Kent, OH: National Association of School Psychologists.

White, J. H. (1977). *pediatric psychopharmacology: A practical guide to clinical application.* Baltimore: Williams & Wilkins.

Wright, L., Schaefer, A. B., & Solomons, G. (1979). *Encyclopedia of pediatric psychology.* Baltimore: University Park Press.

BIBLIOGRAPHY: PROFESSIONALS

Barnhart, E. R. (Ed.). (1986). *Physicians' desk reference.* Oradell, NJ: Medical Economics, Co.

Information is provided by manufacturers for comprehensive descriptions of medications, including product name, generic name, and drug category, and pictorial presentations in a cross-referenced format. Indicated use, contraindications, precautions, and possible side effects are included for each drug. One of the greatest values in the use of this reference is its annual publication. Supplements are provided throughout the year after publication to provide additional and most current information. This reference is one of the most useful available.

Berkow, R., & Talbott, J. H. (1977). *The Merck manual of diagnosis and therapy* (13th ed.). Rahway, NJ: Merck, Sharp, & Dohme Research Laboratories.

This classic reference is used primarily by referencing the medical condition precipitating drug use. Entries include a discussion of effects in the pediatric and adolescent population as well as in adults. Some psychological as well as physical conditions are included with symptomatology, diagnoses, and treatment approaches commonly recommended in medical intervention. Recommended medications, both prescription and nonprescription, are included, usually by generic or class reference though occasionally by product name. The *Merck Manual* can be used effectively with the *Physician's Desk Reference* for comprehensive information about both conditions and medications influencing behavior.

Gilman, A. G., Goodman, L. S., Ross, T. W., & Murad, F. (1985). *Goodman and Gilman's The Pharmacological Basis of Therapeutics* (7th Edition). New York: Macmillan.

This text provides comprehensive discussion of the full range of pharmacological therapies. Current research and advancements are included in this most recent edition. An extensive discussion of medications, their mechanism of action, and therapeutic applications is provided. As a reference, this text serves to present information surrounding a medication's physiological and psychological effects. It is especially advisable for use by those who serve as a liaison between medical professionals and mental health or educational agencies.

Graef, J. W., & Cone, T. E. (Eds.) (1980). *Manual of pediatric therapeutics* (2nd ed.). Boston: Little, Brown.
This collection stems from work at the Children's Hospital Medical Center (Boston) and reviews therapeutic approaches applicable to the neonate to the adolescent. The format is most useful as a reference for classes of disorders and a range of specific conditions therein. Particular value for the school psychologist lies in the range of diagnostic information as well as treatment approaches, including maintenance recommendations and possible complications of treatment. Because of its medical orientation and reference format, a general background in medical terminology is recommended for most beneficial use.

McKim, W. A. (1986). *Drugs and behavior.* Englewood Cliffs, NJ: Prentice-Hall.
This brief but comprehensive volume includes general information on research and analysis of drug effects. Of greatest importance is the emphasis given to psychopharmacology, the effects of drugs on behavior, in both human and animal models. Treatment of general principles of drug action and research serves as a foundation for more specific discussion of the most commonly used drugs, alcohol, caffeine, and tobacco, as well as those requiring medical supervision, such as barbiturates, stimulants, and antianxiety medications. Drugs highly subject to abuse are also included. The format is readable and informative, especially for those requiring a broad understanding of drug action and research.

Wright, L., Schaefer, A. B., & Solomons, G. (1979). *Encyclopedia of pediatric psychology.* Baltimore: University Park Press.
A range of pediatric disorders is presented in a concise, easily referenced format presenting both medical and psychological/behavioral information. Historical aspects, status of research, and treatment approaches are presented for each condition. Medication therapy as well as other approaches are discussed. A glossary of terminology is included. Those involved in psychometrics may be interested in the inclusion of a "test glossary," reflecting the broad information base of psychological functioning as well as medical.Not only medication information but a discussion of childhood disorder and treatment plans are presented. This volume is included here because of its broad utility, ease of use as a reference, and applicability.

BIBLIOGRAPHY: TEACHERS AND PARENTS

Benovicz, R. J. (1983). *Non-prescription drugs and their side effects.* New York: Putnam.
Over 700 over-the-counter medications are reviewed, as are common classes of disorders. General information about each condition is followed by recommendations for accurate diagnoses, guidelines for self-treatment, and contraindications. The format is readable and concise. The volume presents excellent recommendations for consultation with a physician, cautions against use of certain medications in the presence of other conditions, and supplies charts for reference use. This is an excellent reference for consumers.

Gadow, K. D. (1986). *Children on medication* (Vols. 1, 2). San Diego, CA: College-Hill Press.
This two-volume set is specifically directed toward an understanding of the use of medication in the field of education. Information is provided especially for those likely to receive special education services, children with disorders requiring long-term treatment. In Volume 1, attention is given to hyperactivity, learning disabilities, and mental retardation; Volume 2 addresses epilepsy, emotional disturbance, and adolescent disorders. These volumes are highly recommended for the parent, teacher, and school psychologist because of their emphasis on behavioral effects specifically relevant to academic and social performance.

Harkness, R. (1977). *OTC handbook: What to recommend & why.* Oradell, NJ: Medical Economics Co.
This volume serves as a reference in self-medication, the selection and use of nonprescription drugs. Medications are discussed by their active ingredients, as well as common brand names, in order to be useful in evaluating regional-distribution drugs and new brands using the same chemical basis of action. This is strictly a reference book that presents information to consumers about easily accessible medications, their use, and common contraindications. The *OTC Handbook* presents general, concise information about conditions familiar to all, especially those in contact with young children. In-depth discussion is not provided but the volume is broadly informative.

Shirkey, H. C. (1977). *Pediatric drug handbook.* Philadelphia: Saunders.
This is an excellent reference volume for prescription medications most frequently used in the pediatric population. Drugs are listed by class and by generic names, amid their commonly recommended dosages. Conditions for which they are usually prescribed, contraindications, and precautions in their reactions are also given. The text makes use of medical terminology and may be most helpful for those familiar with medical terms or in consultation with physicians.

FOR FURTHER INFORMATION

A. H. Robbins Company
1407 Cummings Drive
Richmond, VA 23320

Allergy Foundation of America
801 Second Avenue
New York, NY 10017

Department of Public Health
Division of Maternal & Child Health Services
Washington, DC 20402

Health Education Council
78 New Oxford Street
London WC1, England

J. B. Lippincott Company
East Washington Square
Philadelphia, PA 19100

Ross Laboratories
Department of Nursing Services
Columbus, OH 43216

Abbot Laboratories
14th Street & Sheridan Road
North Chicago, IL 60644

Department of Medicine
Children's Hospital New Medical Center
Boston, MA

Epilepsy Foundation of America
1729 F Street, NW
Washington, DC 20005

Information Specialists
Division of Chronic Diseases
U.S. Public Health Department
Washington, DC 20540

Riker Laboratories
19901 Nordhoff Street
Northridge, CA 91324

U.S. Department of Health, Education & Welfare
Public Health Service
4040 North Fairfax Drive
Arlington, VA 22203

Children and Moral Responsibility

G. G. Bear
University of Delaware

BACKGROUND

> "To be a real boy . . . It's entirely up to you. Prove yourself brave, truthful, and unselfish . . . You must learn to choose between right and wrong" (the Good Fairy, 1940).

According to the Good Fairy in Walt Disney's classic movie *Pinocchio* (Disney, 1940), moral responsibility is the essence of being human, and although influenced by one's environment, it evolves from within the individual. This view is shared by Plato, Aristotle, Piaget, Durkheim, Dewey, Kohlberg, and many other philosophers, psychologists, and educators. These writers agree that truthfulness, unselfishness, and more importantly the ability to choose between right and wrong are among the characteristics of the morally responsible person. They also agree that moral development is a complex process, and that the understanding of how a child develops into a morally responsible citizen should be a primary concern of education.

As also noted in *Pinocchio* by another well-known counselor and philosopher, Jiminy Cricket, there are many, many obstacles in the straight and narrow path to moral behavior. Temptation is one of them. Speaking to Pinocchio, Cricket succinctly states the nebulous nature of temptation:

> You see, the world is full of temptations. They're the wrong things that seem right at the time. But even though the right things may seem wrong sometimes, sometimes the wrong things may be right at the wrong time or vice versa. Understand? [To which Pinocchio responds: "No, but I'm going to do right."]

Cricket recognized not only the importance of temptations in determining moral behavior, but also a serious problem with the psychoanalytic approach to moral development. Cricket understood that although the superego, or one's conscience, should guide moral behavior, it rarely does so. As noted by Cricket: "A conscience is that still small voice that people don't listen to. That's just the trouble with the world today."

The Gallup Poll has consistently shown that the majority of the U.S. public support moral education. However, few educators readily admit that they teach "moral" responsibility or "moral" behavior. And perhaps this is for good reasons. In recent years the term "moral" has become too emotionally laden for educators. Unfortunately, it is perceived by a vocal minority of the public as being associated with either religious education or "secular Humanism." Nevertheless, aspects of moral responsibility are taught in the schools via the hidden curriculum, moral education programs, or programs designed to teach social skills, social problem solving, social competence, or discipline. An ach of these aim of eprograms is to teach at least one of the different criteria that have been used by psychologists to define personal morality. These criteria are (a) behavior that helps another human being, (b) behavior in conformity with societal norms, (c) the internalization of social norms, (d) the arousal of empathy or guilt or both, (e) reasoning about justice, and (f) putting another's interests ahead of one's own (Rest, 1983).

Behavior in conformity with societal norms is perhaps the most common criterion used to evaluate the effectiveness of popular educational approaches that teach responsible behavior. For example, assertive discipline and social skills training programs are designed to train children to conform to specific classroom rules. Conformity to group norms is certainly an important part of morality and an important goal of the classroom. And assertive discipline and social skills training provide valuable methods of teaching compliance with authority and social norms. However, like the other five criteria used to evaluate morality, the criterion of social conformity, and the training strategies used to achieve this criterion, are limited. Socrates, Jesus Christ, Ghandi, and Martin Luther King were not conformists. The Nazis were. Although most parents do not expect, or desire, that their children reason and act like Socrates, they also do not want them to be blind conformists when faced with such issues as the Vietnam War, apartheid, drug use, and abortion. Instead, they hope that their children will not only recognize social norms, but also choose right from wrong and act in just ways whenever social norms are unclear or whenever norms conflict with moral values.

DEVELOPMENT

An important determinant of moral behavior, particularly in situations involving conflicting values, is moral reasoning. To act in a morally responsible manner implies behavior choice that is influenced by reasoning. Indeed, research links moral reasoning to classroom conduct problems (Bear & Richards, 1981; Richards, Stewart, & Bear, 1984), sociopathic behavior (Haines & Miller, 1980), cheating (Harris, Mussen, & Rutherford, 1976), prosocial behaviors (Bar-Tal, 1982; Eisenberg, 1982), and a variety of other moral and social behaviors (see Blasi, 1980, for a review of 75 studies, 57 of which reported a significant relationship between moral reasoning and behavior).

Different theoretical models and research paradigms have been used to describe the developmental, or age-related, nature of moral reasoning. Although there is a considerable disagreement among researchers regarding the question whether reasoning develops in "stages," there is a general consensus that the quality of moral reasoning changes with age. It changes from an orientation based on self-interest and the consequences of behavior to an orientation toward internalized norms and moral principles. Such changes are explained in Kohlberg's cognitive–developmental theory of moral development, which has dominated the research on moral development for the past 20 years.

According to Kohlberg (1981, 1984, 1986), all individuals develop through natural stages of moral reasoning. The progression of stages occurs in an invariant order, which means that children do not skip stages or reverse the order of growth. In his earlier writings Kohlberg claimed six natural stages, but as a result of his own longitudinal research he recently recognized that Stage 6 does not appear to be part of the normative developmental continuum (Colby, Kohlberg, Gibbs, & Lieberman, 1983). Kohlberg and his associates found no Stage 6 reasoners and very few Stage 5 reasoners. The longitudinal findings provided strong support for the invariant assumption of stage growth, but only in respect to the first four stages. The characteristics of these four stages, which describe the development of reasoning from childhood to adulthood, follow.

Stage 1. Punishment and Obedience Orientation. The behavior of children who reason at Stage 1 is based on physical consequences and not respect for the interests of others. Good behavior is rewarded and bad behavior is punished. Avoiding physical punishment and obeying those in positions of power and authority are the two primary motives for moral behavior. The intentions of others are not considered in the judgment of behavior.

Stage 2. Instrumental Relativist Orientations. The reasoning of children at Stage 2 is hedonistic and instrumental in perspective. Behavior is determined by self-interests and personal benefits, although children at this stage may occasionally act to satisfy the desires of others. Pragmatic reciprocity appears: "You scratch my back and I'll scratch yours."

Stage 3. Interpersonal Concordance, or "Good Boy–Nice Girl," Orientation. Children and adolescents who reason at Stage 3 are concerned about helping and pleasing others. The approval of others is more important than concrete rewards or punishment. They realize that in order to gain this approval they must be perceived by others as being "good boys and girls," which means they must conform to societal standards and expectations. Stage 3 reasoners understand that self-interest is not as important as group interests, rules, and laws, and that people's intentions should be a primary consideration in the judgment of their actions.

Stage 4. Law and Order Orientation. Adolescents who reason at Stage 4 consider themselves full members of society. Right behavior is behavior that follows society's standards and maintains the given social order for its own sake. Social order requires doing one's duty and respect for authority. In certain circumstances, however, laws should be violated if they conflict with other more important social duties.

Growth through the stages does not occur simply as a result of learning new content such as social skills, rules, and consequences of behavior. It develops as a child gradually restructures his or her present stage of moral reasoning. Cognitive restructuring results from interactions with the environment, especially those interactions that provide role-taking opportunities. In findings that are consistent with this view, research shows that moral reasoning is positively correlated with those factors that influence the quantity and/or quality of role-taking opportunities, including socioeconomic status, level of formal education, intelligence, and perspective-taking ability (Rest, 1983).

Although all children advance through stages of moral reasoning in the same order, they do not advance at the same rate. Neither do all children attain the same moral stage at the end of childhood, adolescence, or adulthood. Whereas "average" children exhibit dominant Stage 1 and Stage 2 reasoning during the lower elementary grades, Stage 2 and Stage 3 during the upper elementary and intermediate grades, and Stage 3 and Stage 4 during high school, other children in the normal population develop more slowly or more quickly. More deviant rates of growth in moral reasoning occur among handicapped children. Mentally retarded (Perry & Krebs, 1980), emotionally disturbed (Selman & Jacquette, 1977), and learning-disabled children (Derr, 1986) exhibit less developed moral reasoning strategies than their peers. On the other hand, a more rapid rate of moral development is found among intellectually gifted children (Bear, 1983).

PUTTING MORAL RESPONSIBILITY IN PERSPECTIVE

As discovered by Pinocchio, it is not easy to be moral. Moral thoughts do not always translate into moral deeds, and vice versa. Moral responsibility is influenced by a variety of factors that are not accounted for in single-process theories of moral development, such as Kohlberg's theory or behavioral theories. Moral responsibility involves learning social norms, reasoning about justice, and experiencing empathy and guilt. It also involves the integration of each of these processes and much more.

The various intrapersonal, interpersonal, and situational complexities that influence moral responsibility and behavior are represented in the following three-step interactional model. The model incorporates the research of various social psychologists, cognitive-developmentalists, and social learning theorists. Although similar to other multicomponent frameworks that have emerged in recent years, especially those of Rest (1983), Widaman and Little (1985), and Schwartz and Howard (1982), it differs from these models in its greater emphasis on those variables that help explain why some children fail to act in a morally responsible manner. The model also differs in its emphasis on research findings that have direct and practical implications for the teaching of moral responsibility.

Step I. Situational Awareness and Arousal. Various personal and situational factors interact to determine whether a child perceives that a given situation involves matters of right or wrong, and that the situation requires a decision to act responsibly. Personal and situational variables also determine the degree of emotional arousal or anxiety that is experienced in response to awareness of the situation. Personal variables include previous experiences; alertness to situational cues; sensitivity to the feelings, thoughts, and needs of others (Selman, 1980); empathy (Hoffman, 1984); and attributions of responsibility. Situational variables include the perceived severity and clarity of the situation, the physical distance between the child and others involved, the child's similarity to and emotional involvement with others in the situation, and the length of exposure to the situation (Piliavin, Dovidio, Gaertner, & Clark, 1982).

Awareness and the degree of arousal determine whether the child will act immediately, after the activation of complex cognitive processes, or not at all. In most situations that involve sociomoral issues, awareness and emotional arousal trigger the activation of complex moral reasoning and problem-solving processes. These processes determine the course of behavior that follows. However, in some situations a child might act prior to the engagement of complex thinking processes. In such cases sociomoral reasoning might actually follow the behavior, relieving or producing cognitive conflict, or it might not occur at all.

Step II. Moral Reasoning and Interpersonal Problem Solving. Although arousal may lead directly to right or wrong behavior, such as helping someone in an emergency or hitting someone, it is usually mediated by complex cognitive processes. Most, but not all, cognitive developmentalists argue that in order for a behavior to be "moral," it *must* follow moral reasoning. Moral reasoning determines what ought to be done —the moral ideal. Interpersonal problem-solving skills determine the various alternatives and one's choice of alternatives — what one intends to do. Moral judgments (Blasi, 1980), the generation of various alternatives and evaluation of their consequences (Spivack & Shure, 1983), goals (Staub, 1984) and intentions (Ajzen & Fishbein, 1980) are related to sociomoral behavior.

Moral reasoning and social problem solving are often interrelated and occur simultaneously. Alternatives are generated and their implications are evaluated in reference to both nonmoral criteria, such as social convention and costs and benefits, and moral criteria. The stage of moral reasoning applied influences the alternatives generated and the intended course of action. Alternatives that are not consistent with one's present stage of moral reasoning are likely to be rejected. However, this does not always happen — what one intends to do does not always conform with one's moral ideal. The response of a 10-year-old girl from the Bronx aptly exemplifies how moral reasoning does not necessarily translate into moral intentions. When asked the WISC-R Comprehension question, "What should you do if you find a wallet lost in a store?" she replied: "I know what you're supposed to do — take it to the police station. But you don't do this in New York. Just take the money and throw the rest away. You know what they say 'Findehs-keepehs, losers-weepehs.' You're supposed to find out whose it is, but you have to be out of your mind to do this in New York."

Children may mean well, but in a situation of moral conflict, lower-stage values or other nonmoral values and interests can preempt values based on their present stage of moral reasoning. This happens whenever anticipated costs and benefits or situational determinants override decisions based on their dominant stage of moral reasoning. Nevertheless, their current stage of moral reasoning is one of the strongest determinants of what children intend to do in a situation of moral conflict.

Step III. Morally Responsible Behavior. After a moral decision has been made, morally responsible behavior is likely to follow. But just as intentions do not always conform with moral reasoning, neither does behavior always conform with intentions. All too often, school psychologists encounter children and adolescents who verbalize moral reasoning, social-problem-solving skills, and intentions that are inconsistent with their actions. Although children might fail to exhibit morally and socially appropriate behavior because of deficits of social skills, inappropriate behavior is more likely to result from the lack of ego strength or self-regulation.

In order for moral reasoning and social-problem-solving skills to be consistent with moral behavior, children must successfully develop and execute action plans that are based on moral goals derived from Step 2 cognitive processes. Such plans would include sequential steps leading to the behavioral goals and the anticipation of and possible solutions to whatever pitfalls and obstacles that might lie ahead. These obstacles may be personal, such as the lack of performance skills, lack of perseverance, frustration, or impulsiveness, or they may be situational, such as physical and social distractions.

One obstacle to reasoning–behavior consistency, as well as to reasoning–intention consistency, that has been the focus of considerable interest among attributional theorists in recent years is the use of denial defenses (Schwartz & Howard, 1982). Children rationally defend inconsistencies in thinking or behavior by denying moral responsibility. They might deny any responsibility in order to conform to moral judgments and social conventions ("I know it's not right but everyone else is doing it"), deny the ability to act ("I couldn't help if I tried"), or deny the need to act in a morally responsible way ("Someone else will help the person"). The role of judgments of responsibility in reasoning–behavior consistency has received increased emphasis in recent revisions of Kohlberg's theory (Colby, Kohlberg, Gibbs, & Lieberman, 1983). A Substage B is now used at each stage in Kohlberg's theory to characterize persons who orient toward issues of fairness and responsibility, as opposed to rules or pragmatics.

ALTERNATIVE ACTIONS

The complex interactional nature of moral responsibility necessitates a multicomponent approach to moral education. Whether working at the preventive level with children in the regular classroom, or at a direct or indirect level of intervention with children and adolescents who exhibit serious deficits in one or more of the areas related to the three steps to moral behavior, it behooves the school psychologist to implement strategies and activities that address each of the three steps. The degree of emphasis school psychologists should place on training procedures related to each step depends on the strengths and weaknesses of the specific child or group. Whereas some children are ready to discuss sociomoral problems and brainstorm and evaluate alternative solutions to such problems, others require immediate and intensive changes in their present behavior before intervention can focus on the self-regulation of behavior.

School psychologists are accustomed to using a variety of behavioral techniques that focus on the environmental control of behavior. They are less familiar with techniques used to teach children why rules exist and why certain behaviors might not always be appropriate. For this reason, the following action plans are presented that focus on the development of moral reasoning.

Moral discourse, or the interactive discussion of moral issues and problems of justice, is the most effective means of fostering the growth of moral reasoning (Berkowitz, 1985). Although most commonly practiced in regular classrooms and at home, moral discussion strategies have also been used in special education classrooms (Gardner, 1983), social skills training groups (Goldstein & Pentz, 1984), and "Just Community" projects designed to improve the overall moral atmosphere of the school (Kohlberg, 1985). If a goal of school psychologists is to develop cognitive processes that are related to moral behavior, then moral discussion should be an important component of their prevention or intervention plans.

Moral discussions develop children's ability to recognize and appreciate the rights and responsibilities of others. Effective discussions create cognitive conflict and stimulate students to take social perspectives — promoting stage growth in moral reasoning. To successfully conduct moral discussions requires an adequate understanding of developmental theory, including some knowledge of the stages of moral reasoning and the nature of moral conflict. The role of the school psychologist during moral discussions is to facilitate the kind of discussion that generates moral conflict. This is done by challenging children's reasoning based on their present social and moral perspective. Because this role can also be performed by parents and peers, school psychologists should seek their support and provide them with necessary training and consultation.

Socratic dialogue characterizes discussions that successfully promote moral conflict. This entails the use of effective questioning strategies — questioning that probes and challenges the child's moral reasoning and problem-solving processes. The discussion facilitator acts as a devil's advocate, voicing the perspectives of others and why a discussant's reasoning and intentions might not lead to desired behavior. Whenever appropriate, the facilitator also uses role-playing activities to further encourage perspective taking. For example, the issue of shoplifting would be addressed by asking students in the intermediate grades to consider the perspectives of all characters in a shoplifting situation, including that of the store owner, customers, the shoplifter, and the shoplifter's parents and friends. Students who express Stage 1 and Stage 2 reasoning, characterized by an egotistic viewpoint, would be challenged by other students, or the teacher. They would be asked to examine the impact of shoplifting on all characters as well as on society as a whole. The situation would be role-played with variables added, as needed, to foster cognitive conflict. Many reasons, both for and against shoplifting, would be discussed with an emphasis on the perspectives of everyone involved and the need for laws that protect individuals and society.

Hypothetical and real-life dilemmas are typically used to generate moral discussions. Real-life dilemmas are preferred because they tend to be more meaningful and stimulating to children and adolescents. Materials and guidelines for conducting moral discussions are available in a variety of subject and topical areas, including social studies (Frankel, 1980), guidance and personal growth in high school (Sullivan, 1980), creative problem solving in elementary school (Bear & Callahan, 1984), computer ethics (Bear, 1986), and general classroom use (Reimer, Paolitto, & Hersh, 1983).

When developing and implementing moral discussions, school psychologists should consider the following research findings:

1. Discussions in which Socratic dialogue is frequently used yield greater gains in moral reasoning than discussions in which active listening predominates (Berkowitz, 1985).

2. A mixture of discussants at different stages of moral reasoning within groups is necessary for effective moral discussions (Berkowitz, 1985).

3. Moral growth occurs slowly. The amount of growth in moral reasoning that is typically produced in most moral discussion programs is about $\frac{1}{3}$ to $\frac{1}{2}$ of a stage (Enright, Lapsley, & Levy, 1983).

4. Teachers, peers, and parents can be effective discussion leaders. Although teacher-led moral discussions are necessary at the elementary level, there is no convincing evidence that teacher-led discussions are any more effective than peer-led discussions at the high school level (Kavanagh, 1977).

5. The use of real-life and hypothetical dilemmas is more effective than the use of content-specific dilemmas, such as issues in history or literature (Higgins, 1983).

6. The frequency of moral discussions appears to be related to program success. Colby, Kohlberg, Fenton, Speicher-Dubin,and Lieberman (1977) found that 20 discussions produced greater results than 10 discussions. However, a comprehensive review of moral education programs by Schlaefli, Rest, and Thoma (1985) reported that programs lasting more than 12 weeks are no more effective than those lasting 3–12 weeks.

7. Extensive training in Kohlberg's theory is not necessary in order for teachers to conduct moral discussions successfully. Teachers who complete workshop training are no more effective than those who simply read a training manual (Colby, Kohlberg, Fenton, Speicher-Dubin, & Lieberman, 1977).

8. Transition from Stage 2 to Stage 3 appears to be easier to achieve than at any other stages (Lockwood, 1978).

9. The younger the students, the more difficult it is to produce stage change (Enright, Lapsley, & Levy, 1983). However, this may be more a reflection of the limitations of the measures used in moral education research than a reflection of the effectiveness of moral education with young children.

10. Teaching students Kohlberg's theory often results in immediate pretest to posttest gains in moral reasoning. However, few researchers believe that such gains are truly developmental (Schlaefli, Rest, & Thoma, 1985).

11. Moral discussions are more effective in producing stage growth than other popular strategies used in humanistic approaches to moral education. Kohlberg's approach has been shown to be more effective than the values clarification approach (Leming, 1981) or Gordon's youth effectiveness (Bear, Shever, & Fulton, 1983).

Although Kohlberg's moral discussion model is the most researched and widely recognized approach to moral education in the regular classroom, it is not the only worthwhile approach. Two other useful models of moral education that emphasize the development of cognitive processes are value analysis and rationale building (Hersh, Miller, & Fielding, 1980). As with Kohlberg's model, neither of these models is sufficient for the task of teaching moral responsibility. However, each one offers the school psychologist different strategies that promote moral reasoning and problem solving. When these strategies are combined with other strategies that focus specifically on actual behavior, such as the social action model for normal and gifted students (Hersh, Miller, & Fielding, 1980) and social skills training for children with serious behavior problems, the school psychologist is able to provide a comprehensive program that teaches moral responsibility.

SUMMARY

Moral responsibility is influenced by both developmental and nondevelopmental factors. These factors can be grouped according to three basic steps to moral behavior: situational awareness and arousal, moral reasoning and interpersonal problem solving, and morally responsible behavior. This chapter focused on moral reasoning, an important component of the second step. If children and adolescents are expected to act in morally responsible ways of their own accord, it is important that strategies designed to foster moral reasoning and interpersonal problem solving be incorporated into educational programs. Moral discussion is one such strategy. But just as moral reasoning is not sufficient for explaining or predicting moral behavior, neither is the use of moral discussions sufficient for teaching children and adolescents to be morally responsible citizens.

Lickona (1983) gives nine major concepts that succinctly summarize both research and theory that are related to the three steps to moral behavior. Although developed mainly for parents, they can be used by school psychologists and other educators in the teaching of moral responsibility.

1. The core of morality is respect for self and others. Children should be taught to respect the rights, dignity, and worth of all persons.

2. A morality of respect develops slowly and through stages. While moral discussions should be consistent with the children's current developmental level, they should also challenge the discussants to begin to reason at the next higher stage of moral reasoning.

3. Teach mutual respect. Children should not only be respected, but should also be required to show respect toward others.

4. Set a good example. This means providing a positive moral example and monitoring other models that children are exposed to in their environment.

5. Teach by telling. Parents and educators should not only practice what they preach, but also preach what they practice. Lickona cites research that shows that parents who frequently "moralize" by stressing moral issues in given situations have children who are beyond their peers in their stage of moral reasoning.

6. Help children learn to think for themselves. Research shows that children who are raised by parents

who use "induction" — other-oriented reasoning — as their primary method of discipline tend to be more flexible in their moral reasoning. Their decisions are based more on the intentions of others and the spirit of the law rather than the letter of the law. On the other hand, children raised by parents who frequently use power assertion or love withdrawal tend to have children with rigid moral reasoning.

7. Help children take on real responsibilities. (See "Children and Responsibility" in this volume.)

8. Balance the need to exercise control and the child's desire to be independent. Parents and educators need to be both firm and democratic in their disciplinary practices.

9. Love children. Warmth and nurturance foster moral development.

REFERENCES

Ajzen, I., & Fishbein, M. (1980). *Understanding attitudes and predicting social behavior.* Englewood Cliffs, NJ: Prentice-Hall.

Bar-Tal, D. (1982). Sequential development of helping behavior: A cognitive-learning approach. *Developmental Review, 2,* 101–124.

Bear, G. G. (1983). Moral reasoning, classroom behavior,and the intellectually gifted. *Journal for the Education of the Gifted, 6*(2), 64–71.

Bear, G. G. (1986). *Computers in your life: Face the social issues.* Portland, ME: J. Weston Walch.

Bear, G. G., & Callahan, C. M. (1984). *On the nose: Fostering creativity, problem solving,and social reasoning.* Hartford, CT: Creative Learning Press.

Bear, G. G., & Richards, H. C. (1981). Moral reasoning and conduct problems in the classroom. *Journal of Educational Psychology, 73,* 644–670.

Bear, G. G., Shever, K. L., & Fulton, D. (1983). Usefulness of Y.E.T. and Kohlberg's approach to guidance. *Elementary School Guidance and Counseling, 17,* 221–225.

Berkowitz, M. W. (1985). The role for discussion in moral education. In M. W. Berkowitz & F. Oser (Eds.), *Moral education: Theory and applications* (pp. 197–218). Hillsdale, NJ: Erlbaum.

Blasi, A. (1980). Bridging moral cognition and moral action: A critical review of the literature. *Psychological Bulletin, 88,* 1–45.

Colby, A., Kohlberg, L., Fenton, J., Speicher-Dubin, B., & Lieberman, M. (1977). Secondary school moral discussion programs led by social studies teachers. *Journal of Moral Education, 6,* 90–111.

Colby, A., Kohlberg, L., Gibbs, J. C., & Lieberman, M. (1983). A longitudinal study of moral judgment. *Monographs of the Society for Research in Child Development, 48* (1-2, Serial No. 200).

Derr, A. M. (1986). How learning disabled adolescent boys make moral judgments. *Journal of Learning Disabilities, 19,* 160–164.

Disney, W. (Producer). (1940). *Pinocchio* [Film]. Buena Vista, FL: Walt Disney Productions.

Eisenberg, N. (1982). The development of reasoning regarding prosocial behavior. In N. Eisenberg (Ed.), *The development of prosocial reasoning* (pp. 219–249). New York: Academic.

Enright, R. D., Lapsley, D. K., & Levy, V. M. (1983). Moral education strategies. In M. Pressley & J. R. Levin (Eds.), *Cognitive strategy research: Educational applications.* New York: Springer-Verlag.

Frankel, J. R. (1980). *Helping students think and value: Strategies for teaching social studies* (2nd ed.). Englewood Cliffs, NJ: Prentice-Hall.

Gardner, E. M. (1983). *Moral education for the emotionally disturbed early adolescent: An application of Kohlbergian techniques and spiritual principles.* Lexington, MA: Lexington.

Goldstein, A. P., & Pentz, M. A. (1984). Psychological skill training and the aggressive adolescent. *School Psychology Review, 13,* 311–323.

Haines, A. A., & Miller, D. J. (1980). Moral and cognitive development in delinquent and nondelinquent children and adolescents. *Journal of Genetic Psychology, 137*(1), 21–35.

Harris, S., Mussen, P. H., & Rutherford, E. (1976). Some cognitive, behavioral, and personality correlates of maturity of moral judgment. *Journal of Genetic Psychology, 128,* 123–135.

Hersh, R. H., Miller, J. P., & Fielding, G. D. (1980). *Models of moral education: An appraisal.* New York: Longman.

Higgins, A. (1980). Research and measurement issues in moral education interventions. In R. L. Mosher (Ed.), *Moral education: A first generation of research and development* (pp. 92–107). New York: Praeger.

Hoffman, M. L. (1984). Empathy, its limitations, and its role in a comprehensive moral theory. In W. Kurtines & J. Gewirtz (Eds.), *Morality, moral behavior, and moral development* (pp. 283–302). New York: Wiley.

Kavanagh, H. (1977). Moral education: Relevance, goals and strategies. *Journal of Moral Education, 6,* 121–1330.

Kohlberg, L. (1981, 1984, 1986). *Essays on moral development.* New York: Harper & Row.

Kohlberg, L. (1985). The just community approach to moral education in theory and practice. In M. W. Berkowitz & F. Oser (Eds.), *Moral education: Theory and applications* (pp. 27–87). Hillsdale, NJ: Erlbaum.

Leming, J. S. (1981). Curricular effectiveness in moral/values education. *Journal of Moral Education, 10*(3), 147–164.

Lickona, T. (1983). *Raising good children.* New York: Bantam.

Lockwood, A. L. (1978). The effects of value clarification and moral development curricula on school-age subjects: A critical review of recent research. *Review of Educational Research, 48*(3), 325–364.

Perry. J. E., & Krebs, D. (1980). Role-taking, moral development and mental retardation. *Journal of Genetic Psychology, 136,* 95–108.

Piliavin, J. A., Dovidio, J. F., Gaertner, S. L., & Clark, R. (1982). Responsive bystanders: The process of intervention. In V. J. Derlega & J. Grzelak (Eds.), *Cooperation and helping behavior: Theories and research* (pp. 281–305). New York: Academic.

Reimer, J., Paolitto, D. P., & Hersh, R. H. (1983). *Promoting moral growth: From Piaget to Kohlberg.* New York: Longman.

Rest, J. R. (1983). Morality. In J. H. Flavell & E. M. Markman (Eds.), P. H. Mussen (Series Ed.), *Handbook of child psychology* (4th ed.): Vol. 3. *Cognitive development* (pp. 556–629). New York: Wiley.

Richards, H. C., Stewart, A., & Bear, G. G. (1984, August). *Moral reasoning and classroom conduct: A replication.* Paper presented at the meeting of the American Psychological Association, Toronto.

Schlaefli, A., Rest, J., & Thoma, S. J. (1985). Does moral education improve moral judgment? A meta-analysis of intervention studies using the defining issues test. *Review of Educational Research, 55,* 319–352.

Schwartz, S. H., & Howard, J. (1982). Helping and cooperation: A self-based motivational model. In V. J. Derlega & J. Grzelak (Eds.), *Cooperation and helping behavior: Theories and research* (pp. 328–356). New York: Academic.

Selman, R. (1980). *The growth of interpersonal understanding: Developmental and clinical analyses.* New York: Academic.

Selman, R., & Jacquette, D. (1977). Stability and oscillation in interpersonal awareness: A clinical developmental analysis. In C. B. Keasy (Ed.), *Twenty-fifth Nebraska symposium on motivation,* pp 261–304. Lincoln: University of Nebraska.

Spivack, G., & Shure, M. (1983). The cognition of social adjustment: Interpersonal cognitive problem-solving thinking. In B. Lahey & A. Kazinn (Eds.), *Advances in clinical child psychology* (Vol. 5, pp. 323–372). New York: Plenum.

Staub, E. (1984). Steps toward a comprehensive theory of moral conduct: Goal orientation, social behavior, kindness, and cruelty. In W. Kurtines & J. Gewirtz (Eds.), *Morality, moral behavior, and moral development* (pp. 241–260). New York: Wiley.

Sullivan, P. (1980). Moral education for adolescents. In R. L. Mosher (Ed.), *Moral education: A first generation of research and development* (pp. 165–187). New York: Praeger.

Widaman, K. F., & Little, T. D. (1985). Contextual influences on sociomoral judgment and action. In J. B. Pryor & J. D. Day (Eds.), *The development of social cognition* (pp. 115–152). New York: Springer-Verlag.

BIBLIOGRAPHY: PROFESSIONALS

Kurtines, W. M., & Gewirtz, J. L. (1984). *Morality, moral behavior,and moral development.* New York: Wiley.
A comprehensive collection of recent writings on important topics in the study of moral development. Articles are written by prominent scholars and researchers representing various theoretical perspectives.

Kohlberg, L. (1981, 1984, 1986). *Essays on moral development.* New York: Harper & Row.
Three volumes make up the essay series: *The philosophy of moral development: Moral stages and the idea of justice* (Vol. 1), *The psychology of moral development: The nature and validity of moral stages* (Vol. 2), and *Education and moral development: Moral stages and practice* (Vol. 3). The most authoritative source for those who desire an in-depth study of Kohlberg's theory and research.

Mussen, P., & Eisenberg-Berg, N. (1977). *Roots of caring, sharing, and helping: The development of prosocial behavior in children.* San Francisco: Freeman.
An excellent introduction to prosocial development. Biological, cultural, cognitive and situational points of view are presented. Emphasizes research and theory on the development of altruism, generosity, personal consideration, and sharing.

Reimer, J., Paolitto, D. P., & Hersh, R. H. (1983). *Promoting moral growth: From Piaget to Kohlberg.* New York: Longman.
Perhaps the best introduction to Kohlberg's theory and the cognitive-developmental approach to moral education. The theory and its practical implications are presented clearly. Provides excellent teaching suggestions, guidelines for curriculum development, and a good review of Kohlberg's just community approach.

Carroll, J. L., & Elliott, S. N. (1984). *School Psychology Review, 13,*(3).
This special issue is devoted to the topic of the development, assessment, and intervention of social competence and social skills. Two excellent articles provide a developmental perspective on social competence, another article reviews techniques for assessing social skills from a behavioral perspective, and four articles review or present research on social skills intervention.

BIBLIOGRAPHY: PARENTS

Lickona, T. (1983). *Raising good children.* New York: Bantam.
Presents parents with practical advice derived mainly from cognitive-devlopmental theory and research. Emphasizes the development of moral reasoning and prosocial behavior from birth through adolescence. Methods of discipline, communication, and teaching basic values are included. An excellent guide and reference for parents. Includes an annotated bibliography of recommended books for children and adolescents.

Schulman, M., & Mekler, E. (1985). *Bringing up a moral child.* Reading, MA: Addison-Wesley.
Written for parents by a clinical psychologist and a school psychologist, this book stresses three key concepts related to the moral growth of young children and adolescents: internalizing the rules of parents, learning to empathize with others' feelings, and developing personal standards.

Children and Moving

Douglas F. Goldsmith and Elaine Clark
University of Utah

BACKGROUND

For many children in the United States moving has virtually become a way of life. Although families with no children or preschoolers move twice as often as families with children between the ages of 5 and 18 years (Long, 1972), there are still approximately 8 million school-age children who move to new schools in new communities each year (U. S. Bureau of the Census, 1983). Consequently, it is incumbent upon school psychologists to be aware of, and to anticipate, potential adjustment problems when the lives of children are disrupted by moving. At the same time that these children are coping with their feelings of loss, they are simultaneously faced with unfamiliar school environments, in which the expectations of both teachers and peers are unknown. Unfortunately, as parents attempt to cope with their own feelings about moving, they are often not as available to their children for emotional support. Of course some children experience only minimal distress in response to this challenge and respond by becoming more self-reliant (Blair, Marchant, & Medway, 1984). Others, however, experience anxiety and situational depression (McAnarney, 1979). Even though there is little agreement about which children will be negatively affected by moving itself, and in what ways, those who lack the necessary coping skills may require the school psychologist's services.

Although no single factor has been associated with a child's response to moving, the best predictor seems to be the child's status at the time of the move. Because moving tends to exaggerate a child's existing strengths and weaknesses (Shaw & Pangman, 1975; Whalen & Fried, 1973), it is generally most advantageous to well-adjusted, adaptable children who have made consistent progress in school (Turner & McClatchey, 1978) and detrimental to those who have had difficulties before moving (Schaller, 1974). But difficulties prior to moving do not always predict problems following the transition. For example, some children following a move enroll in a more suitable school or begin to associate with healthier peer groups, both of which may facilitate a positive adjustment.

Parents and professionals alike are primarily concerned about the negative impact of moving on children, as considerable press has been given to the few studies that have suggested that moving has adverse effects. Although the concern is understandable, it is curious that the professional's beliefs in the deleterious effects of moving persist without empirical support. In fact, it has been largely ignored that some children actually benefit from moving in terms of their academic, social, and emotional development (Shaw & Pangman, 1975), and many emerge from the disruption of a move with greater adaptive skills (Shaw & Pangman, 1975), strengthened family bonds (Douvan & Adelson, 1966), and increased independence (Mann, 1972). Perhaps attempts to deal with the complex phenomenon of moving have resulted in the adherence to preconceived notions rather than empirical evidence precisely because there is so little evidence.

There seems to be a consensus that mobility, generally defined in the literature as one or more moves, is context-mediated (Stokols & Shumaker, 1982). However, researchers have often failed to take into account that moving is a multivariate phenomenon and thus recognize the need to study it as such. Few investigators have even attempted to control the factors thought to be related to moving that would enable them to isolate the more direct effects of relocating and specify the conditions under which moving might interfere with a child's school progress and emotional and social development (Turner & McClatchey, 1978). Methodological flaws and the reliance on small, nonrepresentative samples (e.g., military families), have left unanswered a number of questions. While it is certainly possible that moving has serious consequences for some children, assigning responsibility for a child's difficulties to moving may actually mask the contribution of factors that are more directly responsible and thus provide an excuse for poor academic performance and psychological maladjustment. Additionally there is little evidence to conclude that difficulties resulting from a move are long-lasting; on the contrary, whatever the effects, they appear short-lived (Mackay & Spicer, 1975).

Unfortunately, there have been very few studies reported recently in the literature. Professionals are therefore forced to rely primarily on data collected several years ago. It is unclear, however, how much has actually changed over the past decade in terms of the factors thought to be related to moving itself. School psychologists are in a unique position to attempt to unravel this puzzle by providing pertinent information about the individual needs of mobile children. Since professionals working in the schools are often uninformed about the ways moving might affect children's psychological adjustment and academic achievement, this chapter addresses issues pertaining to the geographic relocation of children and provides an overview of intervention strategies.

DEVELOPMENT

In assessing the emotional impact of mobility on children, school psychologists need to be aware that moving can potentially exacerbate any preexisting stage-appropriate conflict. While there might be certain developmental stages during which children are more vulnerable to disruptions in their life, there is little agreement as to when this might be. Some observers contend that moving is more stressful for very young children, 5 or 6 years of age, who are preoccupied with the developmental task of separating from parents and transferring their allegiance from home to school (Tooley, 1970). Others assert that it is during the period of middle childhood (Inbar, 1976) or adolescence (Rubin, 1980) that children are more vulnerable to the effects of moving. For instance, Schaller (1975) found that children who were older than 11 years at the time of a family move experienced greater adjustment problems than those who moved at younger ages. Older children and adolescents are particularly at risk because they are faced with overwhelming personal and social demands, and moving means forming new friendships in peer groups that often appear impenetrable. In fact, teenagers report that the most difficult aspect of mobility is leaving friends and making new ones (Brett, 1982). In a study of 229 school-age children, Barrett and Noble (1973) found that 31% of children 11 years and older reported having difficulty forming friendships. In contrast, only 10% of children between the ages of 6 and 10 had such difficulty. As adolescents rely on a peer group in their attempt to increase their independence and formulate their own identity, the loss of a peer group may hamper the developmental process.

In an attempt to better understand the factors that effect the outcome of moving, researchers have studied the attitudes toward moving of both children and parents. Schaller (1975) asked 335 mobile children and 514 of their nonmobile peers to respond to questions regarding a hypothetical move. The findings indicated that while both mobile and nonmobile children anticipated adjustment problems, the mobile children generally had more positive attitudes about moving than their nonmobile peers. It was also noteworthy that the worries of the children who had moved frequently pertained more to hypothetical concerns than those actually recalled from past moves. Some researchers have found that when asked about their children's adjustment to moving, parents responded that moving had had a positive effect (Barrett & Noble, 1973); other researchers have found that parents viewed moving as detrimental to their children's social and academic adjustment (Brett, 1982). In the study by Brett, parents indicated that compared to their nonmobile counterparts, mobile boys aged 6–14 years were less persistent on school tasks and that mobile girls in the same age group had a slightly higher number of behavior problems.

Since a child's adjustment is often related to parental attitudes, it is reasonable to expect that the beliefs of mothers and fathers about moving will influence their children's attitudes and subsequent adjustment (Whalen & Fried, 1973; Lehr & Hendrickson, 1968). Parental attitudes, as one might expect, are influenced by the reason for moving, whether the move is for economic advancement or a result of economic failure (Turner & McClatchey, 1978). Obviously not all parents have negative attitudes about the impact of moving and even when negative parental attitudes do exist, the relationship between their attitudes and a child's actual adjustment to moving is not consistent (Barrett & Noble, 1973; Shaw & Pangman, 1975). For a number of children the reason for moving has been shown at least indirectly to affect their adjustment, whether it be academic, social, or emotional (Kirschenbaum, 1970). This is especially true when a family moves following a separation or divorce. Wallerstein and Kelly (1980) found that two thirds of the children in their study had moved three or more times during the first two or three years following a divorce. Most of the moves were due to economic factors and many of the children reported a great deal of anxiety with each move. If the move was due to remarriage of the custodial parent, however, some of the children were more likely to be enthusiastic about the prospect of moving.

Some experts maintain that high socioeconomic status places a mobile child at an advantage academically compared to nonmobile peers (Lacey & Blane, 1979), but others feel it has a negligible effect (Blane & Spicer, 1978). The mobile child from a low socioeconomic background, on the other hand, is thought to be educationally disadvantaged by a move (Blane & Spicer, 1978). In terms of social relationships, when socioeconomic status has been controlled for, it has been found that mobile children are less well adjusted socially than their nonmobile peers (Wooster & Harris, 1972). Actually, when the educational status of the parents and the intellectual functioning of the child is controlled for, the relationship between moving and socioeconomic status becomes less certain (Long, 1975; Turner & McClatchey, 1978).

Of additional concern for the school psychologist is the academic adjustment of mobile children. Generally it appears that moving may enhance the academic performance of the more capable student and hurt those who are less capable (Whalen & Fried, 1973). Although mobile and nonmobile children perform similarly on intelligence tests, mobile children with higher scores tend to achieve above the level of their nonmobile high-IQ peers, whereas those with lower scores achieve at a level below that of their nonmobile, low-IQ peers (Schaller, 1974, 1975). Perhaps the brighter children have greater confidence in their ability to succeed in a new environment, and thus are stimulated by a move; the less able children, on the other hand, might be immobilized by the overwhelming demands of moving (Turner & McClatchey, 1978). Unfortunately, even the academically successful child may not be able to fully enjoy the benefits of success, given the difficulties presented by a move (Brett, 1982).

While some might suppose that a higher incidence of school-related problems is to be found among those children who move more frequently or move a greater distance, the effects of both the frequency and distance of a move seem to be mediated by the individual ability levels of the children. Children of lower ability who move more frequently (Schaller, 1975) or move the furthest (Long, 1975) have the greatest adjustment problems. Again, the school psychologist needs to be cognizant that for some children even the most modest changes, such as a move from elementary to middle school, can cause adverse reactions (Miller et al., 1972).

The process of adjusting to a new school is strongly influenced by the attitudes of the administrators, the teachers, and the students. Administrators have a tendency to regard mobile students as a source of problems and may attribute any academic, social, and emotional difficulties of mobile children to their moving (Medders, 1972). The effects of school personnels' attitudes about moving, however, have yet to be documented, as have the attitudes of the children who make up the classroom into which a child moves. Although student attitudes are not necessarily predictive of their behavior toward newcomers, their attitudes have been found to vary by grade level. Schaller (1975) reported that fifth graders were found to be much more positive toward newcomers of the opposite sex than were fourth graders, and on the whole girls tended to be more accepting of mobile children than boys, regardless of the newcomer's gender.

PUTTING CHILDREN AND MOVING IN PERSPECTIVE

Given the limited nature of the available research, it seems inadvisable to build a core curriculum based on the unproven and possibly false assumption that moving interferes with school progress. However, for some children, namely those of low IQ who come from disadvantaged homes and have experienced prior school-related difficulties, interventions may be beneficial. Additionally, even children who are unlikely to suffer negative consequences from moving may benefit from immediate and brief preventive measures.

Interventions for mobile children range from elaborately planned, schoolwide programs to consultation with students, teachers, and parents. Schools in areas of highly mobile populations require structured interventions tailored to the ongoing needs of students moving into or out of the school. In more stable communities, interventions can be planned that are based on the individual needs of the mobile students. This might involve direct services with a small group of mobile children or consultation with the classroom teacher. Consultation with parents is another important, yet often overlooked intervention. Prior to a planned family move, the parents can be given information to help them adequately prepare their children for the transition. Because the stress of a family move may entail a need for therapy (Tooley, 1970), the school psychologist can also be instrumental in helping the family locate appropriate resources in the community.

ALTERNATIVE ACTIONS

School-Based Interventions

Several school-based programs for mobile children have been designed and implemented with a high degree of effectiveness. An annual Summer Visitation Program was developed to meet the needs of one highly mobile community (Crabbs & Crabbs, 1980). The goals of the program focused on reducing the social and emotional problems associated with moving to a new school. This was achieved by introducing families to the counseling staff and acquainting the new students with the school, classroom, community, and their peers before the first day of school. The program was introduced to the community by using the resources of the local Welcome Wagon, public service announcements, and advertisements in the local newspaper. Each family that responded was contacted by a counselor who made arrangements for a home visit. The home visit gave the counselor an opportunity to introduce the family to the school's policies and procedures. Additionally, the counselor led discussions regarding fears and concerns about entering a new school. The families were then invited to the school where they toured the building, became acquainted with administrators and faculty, and met other new families. In order for the students to develop friendships prior to the first day of school, the final activity involved a new-families picnic and swimming party. During the picnic the counselors conducted a series of games and activities that encouraged communication between the adults and children. A follow-up evaluation of the program compared new students from the previous year who had not participated in the orientation program with students who were involved in the Summer Visitation Program. The results indicated that participating students experienced a lower rate of absenteeism than their nonparticipating peers. Participating students also rated themselves as significantly happier, reported fewer physical illnesses, knew a significantly larger number of peers, and were more likely to know their teacher's name on the first day of school. Questionnaires were given to parents of mobile children from the previous year who had not been involved in the program and to parents who had participated in the Summer Visitation Program. Parents of participating students were very enthusiastic. Their children were perceived as less reluctant to attend school on the first day and less likely to make excuses to avoid going to school. In addition, the parents felt that their children were greatly helped by the establishment of relationships prior to attending school and as a result were less likely to dwell on the loss of their former home and friendships. The efficacy of the program supports its utilization as a schoolwide intervention for schools that have a large number of mobile students.

Another schoolwide program that effectively assisted mobile students was entitled Operation SAIL, for Students Assimilated Into Learning, (Panagos, Holmes, Thurman, Yard, & Spaner, 1981). This program was implemented in a district in which over 70% of incoming students manifested academic and behavioral deficits. The primary emphasis of Operation SAIL was on remediation of academic deficits, which was achieved by tailoring interventions to the individual needs of the mobile children. Teachers received special training in the areas of assessment strategies, remediation, and classroom management techniques. Parental involvement was considered an integral component to the success of the program. Following orientation to the goals of Operation SAIL, the parents conferred with their children's teachers regarding past educational experiences and current needs. Students who qualified for the program were placed in a SAIL learning center for one period a day. The learning center focused on the individual needs of each child that had been identified during the assessment phase. Once academic deficiencies were remediated, students were released from the program. Evaluation of the students' progress revealed gains in reading, spelling, and arithmetic.

Support Groups

One of the greatest worries for mobile children is the prospect of difficulty in developing new friendships. While social skills training groups are typically utilized for students manifesting behavioral problems, they can also be used to effectively meet the needs of mobile children who lack social skills. Thus, children who are anticipating a move, or those who have recently moved, may benefit from a time-limited social skills group. The group can focus on those skills that are deemed necessary for the development of friendships and thus decrease some of the anxiety associated with making friends. In order to determine the direction of intervention it is important to evaluate at the onset whether the children lack familiarity with the skills that are prerequisite to initiating contact with peers, or simply lack experience in practicing the skills (Gresham, 1985). Several useful programs are available that contain lessons for teaching children how to initiate contact with peers (McGinnis & Goldstein, 1985; Walker, McConnell, Holmes, Todis, Walker, & Golden, 1983).

Support groups for mobile children have also been used to help reduce the stress associated with moving, while being sensitive to the developmental issues that might affect elementary and secondary students differently (Singer, 1982). To early elementary school children who are in the process of resolving separation conflicts and coping with new authority figures, support groups can offer help in adjusting to the move and facilitate the transfer of their allegiance from the home to the school. Storybooks about children who have moved to a new home can be used to elicit the children's feelings about their own experiences. Since children in the lower grades are particularly upset by change in routine and adjusting to new surroundings, support groups can serve as a predictable, supportive component of their environment during their initial adjustment.

Young adolescents are also occupied with working to decrease dependence on their parents, but the transfer of their allegiance is to a peer group (Tooley, 1970). Since the loss of a peer group can seriously disrupt the developmental process, the use of a peer support group can reduce an adolescent's possible tendency to become overly dependent on the parents and encourages them to gain support from their peers. Moreover, for some adolescents, the family move can place them in a different socioeconomic milieu in which there are new expectations. Those having trouble adapting to a new social situation could utilize peer input to learn about new norms and possible lifestyle changes. It is helpful to integrate students who are already familiar with the school and the community into the support group, as they can provide useful information regarding the local culture.

Classroom Interventions

Interventions in the classroom must focus on the needs of both exiting and entering children. Children who are leaving need help saying goodbye to their classmates and require assurances and support in coping with the anticipated move to a new home and school. Children who are moving into the classroom have different needs, especially if they enter after the school year is under way. At the beginning of the school year, the teacher and students in a classroom simultaneously become acquainted with one another as the rules and procedures are laid out. Even though new students who enter at the beginning of the year have the disadvantage of not having close friends from the previous year, they share with their peers the process of getting to know the teacher, and learning how their new classroom functions. The children who enter the classroom following the first quarter of school are understandably at a much greater disadvantage. Since classroom rules and procedures are already established, the students are likely to feel quite uncomfortable. The new students must experience the entire process on their own and are often expected to adapt to their new environment within a few days. The needs of the child in this situation are easily overlooked as the teacher and students have forgotten how difficult the initial adjustment process might have been for them. The school psychologist, being in a more objective position, might be able to sensitize teachers to the predicament of the mobile child.

Teacher Consultation

At the preschool level the school psychologist can be most helpful by assisting teachers with interventions geared to help children cope with an impending move. At this age it is unlikely that children will be able to create a visual representation of exactly what a move to a new home and school entails. Play sessions can be used to effectively assist the children in understanding the moving process by actually acting out a move by using two doll houses. It is also difficult for the preschooler to conceptualize what it means to move to a new city or state. Helping the children draw a map of the classroom, followed by drawing a map of the building, allows them to begin to comprehend even larger areas such as the new state (Beem & Prah, 1984). Writing stories about the events that will lead up to and follow the move may also be helpful for the young child (Beem & Prah, 1984). The school psychologist can assist teachers in devising methods to help children express their feelings about moving by using various toys. Dolls and puppets are an especially effective tool with preschoolers. By having a puppet talk about its fears of making new friends, the preschoolers can be encouraged to help the puppet solve the problem. This may also serve to stimulate a teacher-led discussion.

Elementary school children tend to worry about their ability to handle the schoolwork in their new classroom (Lehr & Hendrickson, 1968). The school psychologist can play an important role in assisting classroom teachers who have newly arrived students in assessing these children's current ability levels. Even more importantly, the teachers can be encouraged to have the children explain what type of arithmetic or reading assignments they were working on in their former classroom. This enables the teacher to pinpoint potential areas of concern for the children. Programming continuity between the old and the new schoolwork is comforting to mobile children and relieves fears about succeeding in the new classroom.

Several procedures can be instrumental in helping mobile children integrate themselves into a regular classroom. For instance, the teacher can assign a peer to be a mobile child's guide during the first week of school. In addition, the mobile children can write a brief story about their last school and their former community and can share some information regarding hobbies, pets, and their favorite sports. Similarly, all members of the class can write a brief sketch about themselves that can then be shared with the new child. Schools with a large number of mobile children can have students prepare a brief videotape presentation about the school and its various rules and regulations. For students who are moving away and leaving a classroom, a scrapbook can be made, each child in the class contributing a separate page. The book can become a comforting support during the transition between the old and the new school.

The transition between elementary and middle school is often a frightening one for students. Even though it may not involve a change in residence, these children have many of the same needs as their mobile peers. The school psychologist can actively assist these children by helping teachers find ways to elicit students' worries and concerns about the move. Story writing can be used to encourage children to express their thoughts about the new school. As one of their greatest concerns is getting lost in the new, and usually considerably larger building, activities using maps of the new school are also possible. A variety of games can be designed to help children feel more confident about finding their way around the new school.

Parent Consultation

The school psychologist may also be able to intervene with parents to assist mobile families in their adjustment prior to and following a move, but not without an understanding of the reasons behind the move. Although the majority of family moves are for a job promotion or job transfer (U. S. Department of Labor, 1977), a move may also result from the separation or divorce of parents. In either situation, the family may experience a socioeconomic change and consequent change in lifestyle. Prior to planning the most appropriate intervention, the school psychologist must be sensitive to the needs of each family's situation.

Certainly one of the most significant stressors for a family is a move by a family previously affected by divorce. For very young children, moving might evoke memories of the earlier separation from a parent that is remembered as a painful transition associated primarily with loss. Since discussions about moving might cause these children to worry that during an upcoming move the remaining parent might also leave, parents may need suggestions on ways to elicit their children's feelings about the move and reassure the child that the family will stay together. To alleviate concern about when the move will take place, the date of the move can be clearly marked on a calendar. This allows a child to anticipate the move and possibly worry less about being left behind.

Parents can also be advised to allow their children to pack their own belongings in order to maintain some control over the impending move. Parents also need to be cautioned not to throw away too many of their children's old toys and belongings. These items assure continuity for children and provide a sense of security during transition. Finally, parents should be advised to help their children say goodbye to their friends. Collecting addresses and exchanging photos helps children maintain positive feelings about their old friends and enables them to be more open to meeting new ones.

SUMMARY

Despite inconclusive results in the literature on the effects of mobility, it is safe to assume that moving can exacerbate any already existing educational or psychological problems. Children who might be considered at risk for negative effects of moving are typically from disadvantaged areas, have low IQs and manifest academic or behavioral problems prior to the move. The school psychologist can assess the needs of the mobile child and utilize interventions designed to remediate potential problems. Children who are not experiencing difficulties prior to moving might also benefit from early interventions as a preventive measure. It is important for school psychologists to anticipate the concerns of children and focus on these worries both prior to and following the move. Interventions geared to providing mobile children with adaptive skills can be utilized to ease the stress during their transition into a new school. Even more importantly, it is incumbent on the school psychologist to sensitize parents and teachers to the needs of mobile children in order to make moving to a new home and school an exciting and positive experience.

REFERENCES

Barrett, C., & Noble, H. (1973). Mothers' anxieties versus the effects of long distance moves on children. *Journal of Marriage and the Family, 35*(2), 181–188.

Beem, L. M., & Prah, D. W. (1984). "When I move away, will I still be me?" *Childhood Education, 61,* 310–314.

Blair, J. P., Marchant, K. H., & Medway, F. J. (1984). Aiding the relocated family and mobile child. *Elementary School Guidance and Counseling, 18*(4), 251–258.

Blane, D., & Spicer, B. (1978). Geographic mobility, educational attainment and adjustment: Which children are at risk? *Education Australia, 3,* 51–64.

Brett, J. M. 91982). Job transfer and well-being. *Journal of Applied Psychology, 67,* 450–463.

Crabbs, M. A., & Crabbs, S. K. (1980). New kid on the block: How one district extends a helping hand. *National Elementary Principal, 69,* 42–44.

Douvan, E., & Adelson, J. (1966). *The adolescent experience.* New York: Wiley.

Ferri, E. (1976). *Growing up in a one-parent family.* Windsor: NFER Publishing Company, Ltd.

Gresham, F. (1985). Best practices in social skills training. In A. Thomas & J. Grimes (Eds.), *Best practices in school psychology.* Kent, OH: National Association of School Psychology.

Inbar, M. (1976). *Social science frontiers: The vulnerable age phenomenon.* New York: Russell Sage Foundation.

Kantor, M. B. (1965). *Mobility and mental health.* Springfield, IL: Thomas.

Kirschenbaum, A. B. (1970). Family mobility: An examination of factors affecting migration. (Doctoral dissertation, Syracuse University, 1970.) *Dissertation Abstracts International, 32,* 1087A.

Lacey, C., & Blane, D. (1979). Geographic mobility and school attainment: The confounding variables. *Education Research, 21*(3), 200–206.

Lehr, C. J., & Hendrickson, N. (1968). Children's attitudes toward a family move. *Mental Hygiene, 52,* 381–385.

Long, l. H. (1972). The influence of number and ages of children on residential mobility. *Demography, 9*(3), 371–382.

Long, L. H. (1975). Does migration interfere with children's progress in school? *Sociology of Education, 48,* 369–381.

Mackay, L. D., & Spicer, B. J. (1975). *Educational turbulence among Australian servicemen's children.* Canberra: Australian Government Publication Service.

Mann, P. A. (1972). Residential mobility as an adaptive experience. *Journal of Consulting and Clinical Psychology, 39,* 37–42.

McAnarney, E. R. (1979). Adolescent and young adult suicide in the Untied States: A reflection of societal unrest? *Adolescence, 14*(56), 765–774.

McGinnis, E., Goldstein, A. P., Sprafkin, R. P., & Gershaw, N. J. (1985). *Skillstreaming the elementary school child. A guide for teaching prosocial skills.* Champaign, IL: Research Press.

Medders, J. L. (1972). Problems related to student mobility in elementary and secondary schools: United States Dependent Schools, European Area. (Doctoral dissertation, University of Southern California, 1972). *Dissertation Abstracts International, 33,* 4017A.

Miller, l. C., Barrett, C. L., Hampe, E., & Noble, H. (1972). Comparison of reciprocal inhibition, psychotherapy and waiting list control for phobic children. *Journal of Abnormal Psychology, 79,* 269–279.

Panagos, J. L., Holmes, R. L., Thurman, R. L., Yard, G. L., & Spaner, S. D. (1981). Operation SAIL: One effective model for the assimilation of new students into a school district. *Urban Education, 15,* 451–468.

Schaller, J. (1974). Experienced and expected problems reported by children after a family move. *Goteborg Psychological Reports, 4,*(16).

Schaller, J. (1975). The relation between geographic mobility and school behavior. *Man–Environment Systems, 5,* 185–187.

Shaw, J. A. (1975). Geographic mobility and the military child. *Military Medicine, 140*(6), 413–416.

Singer, M. (1982). Moving groups. *School Counselor, 29,* 416–417.

Stokols, D., & Shumaker, S. A. (1982). The psychological context of residential mobility and well-being. *Journal of Social Issues, 38*(3), 149–417.

Tooley, K. (1970). The role of geographic mobility in some adjustment problems of children and families. *Journal of the American Academy of Child Psychiatry, 9,* 366–378.

Turner, I., & McClatchey, L. (1978). Mobility, school attainment and adjustment: A review of recent research. *Association of Educational Psychologists Journal, 4*(9), 45–50.

U. S. Bureau of the Census. (1983). *Geographical mobility: March 1980–March 1981* (Current Population Report No. 377, Series P-20). Washington, DC: U. S. Government Printing Office.

U. S. Department of Labor. (1977). *Handbook of women workers.* Washington, DC: U. S. Government Printing Office.

Walker, H. M., McConnel, S., Holmes, D., Todis, B., Walker, J., & Golden, N. (1983). *The Walker social skills curriculum: The Accepts program.* Austin, TX: Pro-Ed.

Wallerstein, J. S., & Kelly, J. B. (1980). *Surviving the breakup.* New York: Basic Books.

Whalen, T. E., & Fried, M. A. (1973). Geographic mobility and its effect on student achievement. *Journal of Experimental Education, 67*(4), 163–165.

Wooster, A. D., & Harris, G. (1972). Concepts of self and others in highly mobile service boys. *Educational Research, 14,* 195–199.

BIBLIOGRAPHY: PARENTS

United Van Lines (1978). *Moving with children.* United Van Lines, 1 United Drive, Fenton, MO, 63026.
This is an excellent brochure for parents that provides helpful suggestions regarding how to talk to children and prepare them for moving. It is available by writing to United Van Lines.

BIBLIOGRAPHY: CHILDREN

Brown, M. B. (1967). *Pip moves away.* California: Golden Gate Junior Books.
Portrays a young boy on moving day who is watching the moving van pack up his belongings while he plays with his best friend the last time. After moving to the new home, he finds that although he still misses his old friend, he meets a new child right across the street.

Green, P. (1980). *Gloomy Louie.* Chicago: Whitman.
Louie is very distressed when he is told that his family is moving to Arizona. However, a series of events occur that help Louie develop the needed optimism and self-confidence to view the move in a more positive light.

Hurwitz, J. (1979). *Aldo Applesauce.* New York: Morrow.
Aldo is a fourth grader who finds that making friends at a new school is a frightening process. The experience, however, becomes exciting when he meets DeDe, a unique girl who always wears a fake moustache. A humorous and sensitive book about the process of integrating into a new school.

Nida, P. C., & Heller, W. M. (1985). *The teenager's survival guide to moving.* New York: Atheneum.
Explains how to survive and adapt to the stressful life changes related to moving. Issues such as how to keep old friends and make new ones, how to adapt to a new school and community, and how to cope with an overseas move are discussed.

Zolotow, C. (1973). *Janey.* New York: Harper and Row.
Janey's friend misses her deeply since she moved away. The story recalls fond memories of their friendship, but shows how two children who no longer live near each other can still be friends.

Children and Nailbiting

John J. DeFrancesco
Connecticut Department of Children and Youth Services

BACKGROUND

Nailbiting is a behavior that has perplexed researchers and practitioners for years. There is confusion about the meaning and severity of the behavior, whether the behavior can or should be treated, and what treatment or intervention, if necessary, is most effective. Unlike similar types of behavior such as thumbsucking (Jensen, this volume) and hairtwisting (Pray, this volume), nailbiting, particularly childhood nailbiting, has not received much exposure in the research literature. Nevertheless, it is one of the most frequent and persistent behaviors among children and adolescents. Although nailbiting can begin as early as 1 year of age (Malone & Masler, 1952), the behavior typically does not manifest itself before the age of 4 (Malone & Masler, 1952). Between the ages of 4 and 6 approximately 38% of all children bite their nails. By 10 years of age this increases to 60% (Malone & Masler, 1952; Bawkin & Bawkin, 1972). Nailbiting behavior peaks at age 13 for males, when 62% of males bite their nails, and for females at age 11, when 51% engage in this behavior (Clark, 1970; Birch, 1955). The incidence of nailbiting behavior then decreases to 20% in college-age men and 19% in college-age women (Coleman & McCalley, 1948). As the nailbiter enters adulthood the incidence stabilizes at about 10–20% (Pennington, 1945; Klatte & Deardorff, 1981).

There have been studies investigating the incidence of nailbiting (Pennington, 1945), exploring strategies employed to treat the behavior (DeLuca & Holborn, 1984), and attempting to identify personality characteristics of nailbiters (Walker & Ziskind, 1977). Many of these studies lack a comprehensive and cohesive definition of what nailbiting is, and others do not attempt to define the physical act of nailbiting at all. However, before a behavior can be researched and treated it must be accurately identified. Some studies that do address the act of nailbiting define it as simply inserting a finger into the mouth (Perkins & Perkins, 1976) or touching the lips with a finger and making contact with one or more teeth (Vargas & Adesso, 1976). Nunn and Azrin (1976) define the behavior as any hand movement that results in damage to the nails or surrounding cuticles and skin, and Malone & Master (1952) define it as the actual biting of the fingernails with the teeth.

Nailbiting is a behavior that will sometimes go unnoticed; however, it can cause social embarrassment (Azrin & Nunn, 1977), parental concern and anxiety (Grant, Carr, & Berman, 1983), dental problems (Odenrick & Brattstrom, 1985), and infections (Levine, Carey, Crocker, & Gross, 1983), and it can indicate underlying emotional problems (Dreikurs, 1972). Generally, it is a behavior that should not be ignored once it becomes persistent and/or severe.

DEVELOPMENT

During the course of what is considered age-appropriate development most children will engage in some form of nailbiting. In fact, the frequency of nailbiting behavior in children who exhibit developmental delay or distortions in development is quite similar to the frequency in those who do not exhibit distortion or delay (Clark, 1970). Nailbiting is a fairly pervasive behavior that is evident in males and females of all ages, social strata, and levels of functioning. It has been termed an "everyday problem of the everyday child" (Kanner, 1972, p. 528). Indeed, episodic mild nailbiting behavior is innocuous and should not be considered to indicate developmental problems or underlying psychopathology (Kanner, 1972; Anthony, 1970). Not until nailbiting becomes persistent and severe does it pose an issue of concern for the child, parent, psychologist, or other professionals.

Malone and Masler (1952), in a comprehensive study of nailbiting, developed a typology of nailbiters. They categorized children as nonnailbiters, definite nailbiters, and indefinite nailbiters. Nonnailbiters were defined as persons who do not bite any of their nails. Definite nailbiters were characterized as those who bite all 10 nails, and indefinite nailbiters those who bite one to nine nails. They also rated the severity of the nailbiting as not bitten, mildly bitten, moderately bitten, and severely bitten. Their rating of not bitten indicates that the nails are intact, and mildly bitten indicates that the nails are mainly intact although the free edge of the nail may be irregular. Moderately bitten designates that the free edge has been bitten off to the skin line. Severely bitten nails are those that have been bitten off below the free edge beyond the soft tissue border (Hadley, 1984).

While mild cases of nailbiting, as just defined, may cause some concern among parents, most children outgrow the behavior (Bawkin & Bawkin, 1972). Moderate and severe nailbiting, however, can be considered developmentally inappropriate and require investigation and treatment (Grant, et al., 1983). The probability of underlying emotional problems in children with severe and moderate cases of nailbiting is great (Spock & Rothenberg, 1985). Social (Azrin & Nunn, 1977) and medical/dental issues (Odenrick & Brattstrom, 1985; Levine et al., 1983) should also be addressed in these cases. In short, moderate and severe nailbiting must be scrutinized, not only as a means of treating the behavior, but because it may be indicative of other difficulties that can significantly affect the psychological, physical, and social development of the child.

PUTTING NAILBITING IN PERSPECTIVE

Nailbiting is a behavior that, in most instances, is first noticed by parents. It is so prevalent, however, that most parents will dismiss it as a behavior that every child engages in and will soon outgrow. In many situations, particularly in cases of mild, infrequent nailbiting, this is considered the best and most effective way to deal with the behavior. However, when parents or teachers begin to notice that the nailbiting is persistent and/or severe, there is reason for concern, particularly if the nails are severely bitten (Malone & Masler, 1952), the fingers are sore and bleeding, and/or infections develop (Levine et al., 1983). In this situation a physician is often consulted because of the bleeding and/or infections. After the medical condition is treated, parents will usually not immediately seek further assistance. Only after many days and weeks of frustration and perhaps the recurrence of soreness and/or bleeding will the parents seek the help of a psychologist or other mental health professional. An astute teacher can often assist the parents in this regard.

In order to determine appropriate treatment, the psychologist must assess the child's background, including family history and functioning, peer and other social relationships, academic functioning, and medical history. This assessment is done to diagnose any stress, conflict, or problems the child may be experiencing that could contribute to or cause the nailbiting behavior.

Parents must be involved in the assessment because the behavior may be a reaction to familial conflict. Furthermore some research indicates that nailbiting may have a genetic base (Bawkin & Bawkin, 1972), or develop through imitation (Langford, 1972). Teachers and other pertinent school personnel should be contacted to determine if the academic environment is particularly stressful for the child. Finally, the child must be assessed to determine if the nailbiting behavior is a reaction to an interpersonal conflict. This evaluation can be made by a variety of techniques including, but not limited to, clinical interviews, testing, and observational methods. After the assessment has been completed a plan of action can be developed. If the source or sources of internal or external tension, conflict, or stress can be diagnosed, treatment will be more expedient and successful. Once this has been accomplished, the psychologist can provide for a course of systematic treatment strategies to ameliorate the nailbiting. Typically, the psychologist will act as a consultant to parents and teachers, although psychotherapy or counseling may be indicated in some instances.

ALTERNATIVE ACTIONS

There are a variety of methods available to parents and professionals for treating the moderate and severe nailbiter. In order to comprehend the rationale behind the treatment methods, however, an understanding is needed of the etiology of nailbiting, on which research is scarce and varied. One view holds that the causes of nailbiting are linked to psychodynamics, particularly the unresolved Oedipal conflict (Pierce, 1975). The behavior occurs because of hostile feelings and impulses toward the opposite-sex parent. If those feelings and impulses were actualized, however, nailbiters would destroy a requisite source of psychological support. They engage in nailbiting as a way of discharging this inner tension, specifically as a means of denying their hostility, punishing themselves, expressing anger and aggression, but sparing the object of their aggression (Pierce, 1975).

Nailbiting is also thought to be a form of regression to infantile sources of gratification when there is environmental conflict (Henderson & Gillespie, 1977). Menninger (1938) indicated that the behavior was the equivalent of masturbation with displacement from the genitals to the fingers. He also believed that the behavior could be considered a form of "focal suicide," since it involved destruction of only a part of the body.

Other studies appear to indicate a genetic basis for nailbiting. Research with twins reveals that monozygotic twins are concordant for the behavior four times as often as dizygotic twins. Further investigations indicate that there is a strong probability that any given nailbiter has a relative who also is a nailbiter. The closer the genetic relationship the greater the probability (Bawkin & Bawkin, 1972).

Imitation, modeling, and observational learning (Bawkin, 1971; Hadley, 1984) are also thought to contribute to nailbiting. The imitation of nailbiting behavior, particularly in families, is frequent.

Bevans (1945) identified nailbiting as resulting from the discomfort associated with poorly manicured fingers. She maintained that the child with dirty hands, broken nails, or long nails attempts to relieve the discomfort by biting off the rough edges and ends.

According to Azrin and Nunn (1977) nailbiting is a nervous habit that has its beginnings in normal behavior. The behavior may originally have been a reaction to a trauma or may have started as an infrequent behavior that increased in frequency over time. The behavior is then classified as a habit when it continues consistently after the original trauma or stressful event. The individual becomes accustomed to the annoyances of the behavior because the acquisition of the habit takes place gradually (Hadley, 1984).

Another commonly accepted causal theory is that nailbiting is a response to stress and is indicative of internal tension (Malone & Masler, 1952). Severe nailbiting results from especially stressful and anxiety-inducing situations (Spock & Rothenberg, 1985; Viets, 1931; Grant et al., 1983). Children exhibit the behavior at particularly stressful moments, for example, when leaving for school, waiting to be called on in class, listening to their parents argue, being teased on the playground, or going home to a punitive family situation. The behavior has also been linked to unrealistic parental expectations and demands that the child cannot fulfill (Cava et al., 1979). A study by Viets (1931) found that nailbiters, in contrast to nonnailbiters, come from stressful, conflict-ridden home situations. Billig (1942) indicated that children in his study reported nervousness as the reason they bite their nails. Bowley (1943) in consultation at a school because of the prevalence of nailbiting in one particular classroom, found that all the pupils were biting their nails because the teacher was so strict that the entire class was under extreme stress. Authorities (Spock & Rothenberg, 1985; Hadley, 1984; Malone & Masler, 1952) indicate that nailbiting is a response to stress and a sign of anxiety.

Treatment methods, like the explanations, are varied. Insight-oriented psychotherapy (Mahler & Luke, 1946), hypnotherapy (Bornstein et al., 1980; K. L. DeFrancesco, personal communication, April 17, 1986), and play interventions (Mulick, Hoyt, Rojahn, & Schroeder, 1978) might be the choice of those who adhere to the psychodynamic school of thought. Pharmacological treatment (Connell, Corbett, Horne & Matthews, 1967) has also been attempted, although with little success. Other pragmatic interventions include wearing gloves to prevent biting, chewing gum as a substitute for the nailbiting (Bawkin & Bawkin, 1971), and using a manicure set to become involved in improving one's appearance (Bevans, 1945). Applying bitter substances to the nails is a popular technique with parents but is rarely effective (Spock & Rothenberg, 1945).

Most of the aforementioned treatment methods are not successful in cases of severe nailbiting, for which the most successful method of treatment is a combination of stress reduction and behavioral techniques. When nailbiting is seen as a response to stress and tension it becomes imperative to assess and then try to relieve the causes of the stress in the child's life. Chandler's (1982) stress response system, which identifies internal and external stress arising from a variety of sources, is a valuable technique that is able to pinpoint sources of stress by obtaining information from parent and child interviews, testing, rating scales, and behavioral checklists. Developmental, medical, academic, family, and social information is obtained. The child, teacher, and parent can be asked to note when the child actually bites in order to determine in which situations the nailbiting occurs. Once the source of stress is identified, the parent and psychologist must develop strategies to relieve the stress in the child's life. For example, if parents' expectations are too high, they should be encouraged to decrease their expectations; if the child feels rejected because of the arrival of a new sibling, rigorous attempts should be made to include the child in more family activities (see Chandler, 1982, for a comprehensive step-by-step listing of stress-reducing strategies for parents, schools, and psychologists).

Relieving significant sources of stress in a child's life, however, may be a time-consuming process. Considerable efforts by parents, school, and psychologist may be necessary to promote change. When the source of a child's stress is identified, psychological consultation will be necessary to develop strategies that parents and school will use to help the child decrease the nailbiting behavior. When these strategies are developed and implemented, it may take time before the behavior is eliminated because the nailbiting and its causes are probably of long duration. However, parents of severe nailbiters may be extremely impatient and want immediate results. For the benefit of the child and the parents it becomes necessary in the interim to implement behavioral interventions as a way of immediately decreasing/stopping the overt behavior. This will also indicate to the parent, child, and teacher that the problem is soluble. It must be emphasized, however, that the use of behavioral methods alone to treat the overt behavior will only produce short-term benefits and will not relieve the causal stress and inner tension.

Many behavioral techniques have been used, with varying degrees of success, to treat nailbiting. Treatments have included overcorrection (Barmann, 1979), negative practice (Azrin, Nunn & Frantz, 1980), contingency contracting (Ross, 1974), and covert sensitization (Paquin, 1977). Self-monitoring techniques (McNamara, 1972) as well as aversive methods (Vargas & Adesso, 1976) have also been used.

The habit reversal technique developed by Azrin and Nunn (1973) has been the most successful behavioral intervention for nailbiting. Indeed, follow-up studies (Nunn & Azrin, 1976; Glasgow, Swaney, & Schafer, 1981) have indicated that the technique is quite successful. A 90% reduction in nailbiting was reported the first day following treatment with the HR method (Nunn and Azrin, 1976). All subjects ceased the activity completely at the one month follow-up.

In the habit reversal procedure, individuals practice physical movements that are incompatible with nailbiting such as the grasping or clenching reaction. They are also taught to be aware of each time they engage in the behavior and to be aware of the situations in which it is likely to occur. The individual is reinforced for not engaging in the nailbiting behavior. The four major criteria of the habit reversal technique are that the competing action(s) should not interfere with typical everyday activities, should be suited to being performed without attracting attention, should be incompatible with the nailbiting behavior, and should increase the individual's awareness of the problem (Hadley, 1984).

While behavioral techniques, particularly habit reversal, are effective in treating nailbiting behavior, they do have the reputation of not producing long-term effects (Fischer & Gochros, 1975). In contrast, the combination of behavioral and stress reduction techniques produces both short- and long-term results. The source of stress, not just the overt behavior, is eliminated. Often, extinguishing the overt behavior without knowing and dealing with the stress that is causing the behavior will result in symptom substitution. Once the nailbiting is extinguished by the habit reversal method alone, another similar type of behavior such as thumbsucking or toenail biting may develop. The two techniques used concomitantly can produce long-term results and a happier child, family, and school situation.

Of course, for the severe nailbiter medical treatment may also be necessary for any infections, soreness, or bleeding that may develop. Parents should also inform their dentist if their child is a nailbiter. This can be done at the child's regularly scheduled checkups.

SUMMARY

Nailbiting is one of the most frequent behaviors in children and adolescents. Mild cases of nailbiting can be considered developmentally appropriate and treatment is typically not necessary. Only when the nailbiting becomes severe is there reason for concern and treatment.

While the behavior has been linked to the unresolved Oedipal conflict, genetics, imitation, and regression, most authorities would concur that the behavior is most often caused by underlying tension and anxiety resulting from internal or external source(s) of stress.

The most effective method of treating nailbiting behavior combines behavioral techniques (habit reversal) in conjunction with stress-reducing intervention. Noting environmental stimuli and/or inner feelings each time nailbiting takes place will assist in determining which events trigger the nailbiting. It may also be beneficial to reinforce the individual when a situation that would have previously caused nailbiting is avoided. Although other interventions such as psychotherapy and pharmacological treatment have been used, they are not as effective. Medical or dental treatment may be necessary at times.

If primary care givers are willing to help the child, the behavior will stop. Concerted efforts must be made to identify and relieve the source(s) of stress that are causing the behavior and to simultaneously treat the nailbiting by means of habit reversal. This will provide satisfactory, long-term results.

REFERENCES

Anthony, E. J. (1970). The behavior disorders of childhood. In P. H. Mussen (Ed.), *Carmichael's manual of child psychology*, (Vol. 2, pp. 667–764). New York: Wiley.

Azrin, N. H., & Nunn, R. G. (1973). Habit reversal: A method of eliminating nervous habits and tics. *Behavior Research and Therapy, 11,* 617–628.

Azrin, N. H., & Nunn, R. G. (1977). *Habit control in a day.* New York: Simon & Schuster.

Azrin, N. H., Nunn, R. G., & Frantz, S. E. (1980). Habit reversal vs. negative practice treatment of nailbiting. *Behavior Research and Therapy, 18,* 281–285.

Barmann, B. (1979). The use of overcorrection with artificial nails in the treatment of chronic fingernail biting. *Mental Retardation, 17,* 309–311.

Bawkin, M. (1971). Nailbiting in twins. *Developmental Medicine and Child Neurology, 13,* 304–307.

Bawkin, H., & Bawkin, R. (1972). *Behavior disorders in children* (4th ed.). Philadelphia: Saunders.

Bevans, G. (1945). Biting the fingernails. *Women's Day,* pp. 58–59.

Billig, A. (1942). Finger nailbiting: It's incipiency, incidence, and amelioration. *Journal of Abnormal and Social Psychology, 37,* 406–408.

Birch, L. (1955). The incidence of nailbiting among school children. *British Journal of Educational Psychology, 25,* 123–128.

Bornstein, P. H., Rychtarik, R. G., McFall, M. E., Winegardner, J., Winnett, R. L., & Paris, D. (1980). Hypnobehavioral treatment of chronic nailbiting: A multiple baseline analysis. *The International Journal of Clinical and Experimental Hypnosis, 28,* 208–217.

Bowley, A. (1966). *The natural development of the child.* London: Livingstone.

Cava, E., Girone, J., Hipp, T., Rothstein, E., Schiller, R., Schlackman, N., & Souder, R. (1979). *A pediatrician's guide to child behavior problems.* New York: Masson.

Chandler, L. (1982). *Children under stress.* Springfield, IL: Thomas.

Clark, D. F. (1970). Nailbiting in subnormals. *British Journal of Medical Psychology, 43,* 69–81.

Coleman, J., & McCalley, J. (1948). Nailbiting among college students. *Journal of Abnormal and Social Psychology, 43,* 517–525.

Connell, P., Corbett, J., Horne, D. J., & Matthews, A. (1967). Drug treatment of adolescent tiqueurs: A double blind trial of diazepam and haloperidol. *British Journal of Psychiatry, 113,* 375–381.

DeLuca, R. V., & Holborn, S. W. (1984). A comparison of relaxation training and competing response training to eliminate hair pulling and nail biting. *Journal of Behavior Therapy and Experimental Psychiatry, 15,* 67–70.

Dreikurs, R. (1972). *Coping with children's misbehavior: A parent's guide.* New York: Hawthorne.

Fischer, J., & Gochros, M. (1975). *Planned behavior change: Behavior modification in social work.* New York: Free Press.

Glasgow, R., Swaney, K., & Schafer, L. (1981). Self-help manuals for the control of nervous habits: A comparative investigation. *Behavior Therapy, 12,* 177–184.

Grant, Q. R., Carr, R. P., & Berman, G. (1983). Common syndromes in child psychiatry. In P. D. Steinhawer & Q. R. Grant (Eds.), *Psychological problems of the child in the family* (pp. 168–196). New York: Basic Books.

Hadley, N. H. (1984). *Fingernail biting.* New York: Spectrum.

Henderson, D., & Gillespie, R. D. (1950). *A textbook of psychiatry.* London: Oxford University Press.

Kanner, L. (1972). *Child psychiatry* (4th ed.). Springfield, IL: Thomas.

Klatte, K. M., & Deardorff, P. A. (1981). Nailbiting and manifest anxiety of adults. *Psychological Reports, 48,* 82.

Langford, W. (1972). Abnormalities of psychologic growth and development. In H. L. Barnett & A. H. Einhorn (Eds.), *Pediatrics* (pp. 3–66). New York: Appleton-Century-Crofts.

Levine, M., Carey, W., Crocker, A., & Gross, R. (1983). *Developmental-behavioral pediatrics.* Philadelphia: Saunders.

Mahler, M., & Luck, J. (1946). Outcome of the tic syndrome. *Journal of Nervous and Mental Disorders, 103,* 433–445.

Malone, A. J., & Masler, M. (1952). Index of nailbiting in children. *Journal of Abnormal and Social Psychology, 47,* 193–202.

McNamara, J. R. (1972). The use of self-monitoring techniques to treat nailbiting. *Behavior Research and Therapy, 10,* 193–194.

Menninger, K. (1938). *Man against himself.* New York: Harcourt, Brace.

Mulick, J., Hoyt, P., Rojahn, J., & Schroeder, S. R. (1978). Reduction of a nervous habit in a profoundly retarded youth by increasing toy play. *Behavior Therapy and Experimental Psychiatry, 9,* 381–385.

Nunn, R. G., & Azrin, N. H. (1976). Eliminating nailbiting by the habit reversal method. *Behavior Research and Therapy, 14,* 65–67.

Odenrick, L., & Brattstrom, V. (1985). Nailbiting: Frequency and association with root resorption during orthodontic treatment. *British Journal of Orthodontics, 12,* 78–81.

Paquin, M. J. (1977). The treatment of a nailbiting compulsion by covert sensitization in a poorly motivated client. *Journal of Behavior Therapy and Experimental Psychiatry, 8,* 181–183.

Pennington, L. A. (1945). The incidence of nailbiting among adults. *American Journal of Psychiatry, 102,* 241–244.

Perkins, D. G., & Perkins, F. M. (1976). *Nailbiting and cuticle biting: Kicking the habit.* Richardson, TX: Self Control Press.

Pierce, C. M. (1972). Nailbiting and thumbsucking. In A. M. Freedman & H. I. Kaplan (Eds.), *The child: His psychological and cultural development* (pp. 210–212). New York: Atheneum.

Ross, J. (1974). The use of contingency contracting in controlling adult nailbiting. *Journal of Behavior Therapy and Experimental Psychiatry, 5,* 105–106.

Spock, B., & Rothenberg, M. B. (1985). *Dr. Spock's baby and child care* (rev. ed.). New York: Pocket Books.

Vargas, J. M., & Adesso, V. J. (1976). A comparison of aversion therapies for nailbiting behavior. *Behavior Therapy, 7,* 322–329.

Viets, L. E. (1931). An inquiry into the significance of nailbiting. *Smith College Studies in Social Work, 2,* 128–145.

Walker, B. A., & Ziskind, E. (1977). Relationship of nailbiting to sociopathy. *Journal of Nervous and Mental Disorders, 164,* 64–65.

BIBLIOGRAPHY: PROFESSIONALS

Azrin, N. H., & Nunn, R. G. (1973). Habit reversal: A method of eliminating nervous habits and tics. *Behavior Research and Therapy, 11,* 617–628.
The initial study that presents the theory and rationale behind the development of the habit reversal method of treating nailbiting behavior.

Chandler, L. (1982). *Children under stress.* Springfield, IL: Thomas.
Discusses the development of the stress assessment system and indicates how childhood emotional adjustment/behavioral reactions result from internal and external sources of stress. Identifies methods of assessing source(s) of stress and provides specific strategies for parents, teachers, and psychologists to reduce/relieve childhood stress.

Hadley, N. H. (1984). *Fingernail biting.* New York: Spectrum.
A comprehensive and objective text on fingernail biting providing an extensive treatise of research, definition, theories, and methods of treatment. A reference list that includes many of the major studies on nailbiting is included.

Malone, A. J., & Masler, M. (1952). Index of nailbiting in children. *Journal of Abnormal and Social Psychology, 47,* 143–202.
An older study but one of the most comprehensive investigations of nailbiting to date. Incidence, definitions, types of nailbiters, and severity of the behavior are examined.

BIBLIOGRAPHY: PARENTS

Azrin, N. H., & Nunn, R. G. (1977). *Habit control in a day.* New York: Simon & Schuster.
A self-help book based on the habit-reversal method developed by the authors in 1973. Specific instructions on how to implement the method are provided. The book is a generalized approach to treating nailbiting behavior and similar types of behaviors such as stuttering, hairpulling, and tics.

Chandler, L. (1982). *Children under stress.* Springfield, IL: Thomas.
Discusses the development of the stress assessment system and indicates how childhood emotional adjustment/behavioral reactions result from internal and external sources of stress. Identifies methods of assessing source(s) of stress and provides specific strategies for parents, teachers, and psychologists to reduce/relieve childhood stress.

Kanner, L. (1972). *Child psychiatry* (4th ed.). Springfield, IL: Thomas.
A general psychiatry textbook that includes a concise, pragmatic, and straightforward account of the meaning, causes, and treatment of nailbiting behavior from various points of view.

Perkins, D. G., & Perkins, F. M. (1976). *Nailbiting and cuticle biting. Kicking the habit.* Richardson, TX: Self Control Press.
A manual designed to help individuals control nailbiting behavior. The manual presents a basic behavioral approach to treating the behavior by methods such as contingency contracting, self-awareness, self-monitoring, and visualization.

Children and Nutrition

Charles W. Paskewicz
West Virginia College of Graduate Studies

BACKGROUND

The phrase "you are what you eat" represents the concern that parents and school professionals sometimes share regarding the nutritional status of children they help nurture. Many parents recognize the preference their children have for sugared and processed foods even to the extent of causing conflicts both during and in between meals about what the child will and will not eat.

Children view over 11,000 low-nutrition "junk" food ads a year on television, and they tend to recall the ads and request foods that are highly advertised. Ads for products of low nutritional value are more effective than ads for nutritional products which had little measurable impact on children's total calorie consumption (Jeffrey, McLellaren, & Fox, 1982).

There appears, however, to be a recent rise in health food advertising that parallels the rise in health consciousness and fitness. These commercials stress the reduction of sugar content, the elimination of additives, the use of lead-free canned packaging, and an emphasis on hypoallergenic products. These areas — sugar, food additives, metal toxins, and food allergies — are becoming areas of focus as researchers seek to establish relationships between food and behavior as a means to explain and alleviate behavior and learning problems in children.

Children who are exhibiting behavioral and learning problems in school are often referred by teachers and parents to school psychologists for assessment and intervention recommendations. These school problems may be related not only to psychological, but also to medical, physical, nutritional, or environmental problems. Thus, it is helpful to entertain multiple hypotheses about the factors that may influence a child's problems until they are systematically ruled out. In dealing with children who exhibit problems, medical management, nutritional readjustment, psychological counseling, and environmental management may all have to be tried (Smith, 1976).

School psychologists have not generally been exposed in their training to the medical and nutrition literature on the relationship between diet and behavior and learning. There has been in the 1980s a growing professional and popular interest in the effects of diet and nutrition. Summarized here are four areas of current interest.

DEVELOPMENT

Sugar and Processed Foods

Most nutritionists are alarmed at the amount of nonnutritive, high-calorie foods being consumed by children. Children now consume more cake, cookies, and donuts than meat, more candy than eggs, and more soda than milk (Mindell, 1981). The consumption of sugar in children aged 5–12 averages over 100 pounds each year (Morgan, Zabik, Cola, & Luveille, 1980). Given the increased rate of consumption of processed foods and sugars, many children may have marginal nutrition imbalance, which can have a considerable impact upon intellectual abilities (Latham & Cobos, 1971).

The following adjectives have been applied in various articles to children affected by excessive sugar consumption: hyperactive, aggressive, headachy, nervous, irritable, anxious, highly variable as to mood swings, obese, hungry all the time for sweets, depressed, inattentive, and sleepy (Green, 1969; Powers, 1973–1974; Von Hilsheimer, 1974). Buchannon (1984) called for sugar to be considered as and to be studied as a toxin.

Several studies have found a positive relationship between behavior problems and ingestion of sugar. Prinz, Roberts, and Hartman (1980) investigated the effects of sugar in hyperactive children. Seven-day dietary records and independent observations of hyperactive behavior were kept on children 4–7 years old. Both the amount of sugar and the ratio of sugar to nutritional foods were significantly correlated with destructive–aggressive and restless behavior observed during free play. Conners and Blovin (1982) found that in normal and disturbed children 9–11 years old, the omission of breakfast and an increase in sugar was related to attentional problems and increased motor behavior. The ratio of refined carbohydrates (white flour and sugar products) to total food calories was negatively correlated with IQ and school achievement (Latham & Cobos, 1971; Lester, Thatcher, & Monroe-Lord, 1982). Harper (1982) reported an unspecified study by Thatcher, Lester, Monroe-Lord and McAlaster that found significant negative correlations of the amount of refined, low-nutrient foods in the diet of children with their IQs and their reading and mathematics achievement scores.

Oliver (1983) conducted a 3-year double-blind study to determine the validity of the premise that refined carbohydrates (simple sugars) impair children's learning at school and at home. When sugars were removed from the diet, classwork improved, IQ and achievement test scores rose, and various physical symptoms including sinus problems, indigestion, and skin problems decreased.

Schoenthaler and Doraz (1983) conducted a crossover double-blind experiment to reduce aggressive behavior in incarcerated juveniles by reducing sugar intake. Soft drinks and junk food snacks were replaced with fruit juice and nutritive snacks, and high sugar-content desserts and cereals were eliminated. In this 2-year study, the incidence of antisocial behavior decreased 50%.

Other studies, however, have found no relationship between sugar intake and behavior. Barling and Bullen (1985), in a replication of the Prinz et al. (1980) study with a group of 9-year-old children, found no significant relationship between sucrose consumption and hyperactivity or aggression. They suggested that age may be a medicating variable, younger children being more susceptible to behavioral effects of sugar.

Behar (1984) evaluated 21 boys (aged 6.5–14 years) who were considered by their parents to have adverse behavioral reactions to dietary sugar. Sugar challenges produced no significant or consistent change in observers' behavior ratings or measures of attention and memory. They doubted the clinical significance of sugar intake in the etiology of behavior disturbance.

Rapoport (1982–1983) generalized on the basis of her research that in pediatric populations a variety of cognitive and behavioral tasks failed to show excitatory effects of sugar in a supposedly vulnerable population. Similarly, Brody and Wolitzky (1983), using a group of 16- to 24-year-olds, found no indication of an effect of sugar ingestion on measures of anxiety, cognitive loss, depression, fatigue, quiet or hostility.

None of the above studies showed that the ingestion of refined sugar products enhanced behavior or learning. Arnold (1984), in a review of the sugar studies, concluded that the impact of diet on behavior and learning problems — such as attention deficit disorders, conduct disorders, and learning disabilities — has not yet been adequately studied. However, it is reasonable that sugar might be involved in behavior abnormalities in some children (Wurtman, 1984).

Additives

Feingold (1975) asserted that a diet that excluded artificial colors, flavors, or preservatives may benefit hyperactive children. Teachers, who sometimes refer parents to physicians for medication, tend to rate hyperactive children as hostile–aggressive and vice-versa (Smith, 1985). Thus, food additives may affect both children seen as hyperactive as well as conduct disordered. Holborow, Elkins, and Berry (1981) found that 8.5% of normal school children on the diet improved significantly in areas of distractibility, attention span, and demands for attention. Harper (1982) reported an unreferenced study by Williams that found that 25% of hyperactive children were diet-responsive to some extent.

There are several conclusions that can be drawn from existing reviews of the literature (Harper, 1982; Weiss, 1982; Connors, Gazette, & Newman, 1980) concerning the effect that the Feingold additive-elimination diet has on behavior. First, there is an effect for some children, regardless of whether research shows significant group differences. Second, younger children seem more sensitive to additives and the diet than older children. Third, some children respond to the diet only after a period of several months. Fourth, the diet may work because a food allergen has been removed. Fifth, stimulating drug therapy is more effective in controlling hyperactive behavior. Sixth, no study reported a positive effect for the increase of food additives.

Weiss (1982) suggested that in applying nutritional therapy in cases of childhood behavior disorders the best way to proceed is to encourage parental experimentation. Since some children are helped, whether because of the diet itself, the removal of a food allergen, or increased attention with a reduction of blaming, such experimentation appears warranted.

Toxic Materials

The presence of minerals and metals in the brain affect behavior and learning. Many populations functioning at lower than optional levels (delinquents, learning-disabled [LD], mentally retarded [MR]) have been reported to exhibit abnormal levels of minerals, particularly heavy metals (Rimland & Lawson, 1983). It has long been known that lead poisoning is related to brain damage and mental retardation. Levels of lead previously considered to be nontoxic, however, may effect learning ability (Marlow, Cossairt, Welch, & Ephera, 1984).

Rimland and Lawson (1983) found that LD and MR groups showed increased levels of lead, and that higher-IQ children had low levels of lead. Pihl, Parkes, and Stevens (1979) separated an LD and a normal group in terms of a significant higher concentration of lead. There is also evidence of lead-related deficits in psychological and classroom performance (Needleman et al., 1979), in impairment in cognitive and sensorimotor functioning (Perine & Ernhart, 1974), and in lowered school achievement (Thatcher & Lester, 1985; Moor, Marlow, Stellern, & Errern, 1985).

Ernhard, Lands, and Wolf (1985), however, has maintained that previously reported positive findings of the relationship between lead and academic deficits were not substantiated.

A dietary deficiency of zinc has been found to increase toxicity of lead (Detering, 1978; Mahaffey, 1981). When LD and normal groups are compared, the LD group has a significantly lower concentration of zinc (Phil, Parkes, & Stevens, 1979). Rimland & Lawson (1983) found that children with a high IQ had an increased zinc level. Thatcher, McAlaster, Lester, and Centor (1984) found that higher concentrations of zinc are related to increased reading achievement. Zinc deficiency is also associated with moodiness, depression, irritability, antagonism, temper tantrums, and learning problems (Kronick, 1975).

Refined foods are low in zinc (Schooeder, 1971). Caffeine (in the form of coffee, tea, cola-flavored soft drinks, and chocolate) can cause zinc to be depleted. A dietary deficiency of calcium also has been shown to enhance toxicity of lead (Petering, 1978). Teenagers are known to have low calcium intake (Trusuell & Darnton-Hill, 1981). Caffeine also prevents the proper assimilation of calcium.

Food Allergies

An allergy is defined as an abnormal response to a substance well tolerated by most people. Levin and Zellerback (1983) have categorized two types of allergies: Type 1 includes the familiar hayfever, asthma, and skin disorders, as well as food-related gastrointestinal problems. Type 2 symptoms, however, include changes of mood or behavior such as depression, suspiciousness, fatigue, hyperactivity, delusions, hallucinations, panic, phobic and aggressive responses, irritability, and distractibility. These psychological symptoms may mask a hidden food allergy.

Harper (1982) investigated the literature on the relationship between food allergies and behavioral symptoms. The studies reviewed the effect of diet on the functioning of outpatient and inpatient psychotics and learning-disabled and hyperactive children. He concluded that there exists a strong cognitive–emotional effect of allergens. The allergens that were studied were milk (the most common food allergen) and wheat, but other common allergens include eggs, corn, and chocolate products.

Food allergies are common disorders among children, especially those younger than 3 years of age (Baker & Herry, 1986). It is cautioned, however, that allergies do not account for all cerebral symptoms.

PUTTING CHILDREN'S NUTRITION IN PERSPECTIVE

Although each of the researched areas produced conflicting results or cautious conclusions, all recommended that nutrition be investigated as a cause of disturbed behavior. Of course, even though medication and behavioral techniques in some degree have been found effective in controlling some problem behaviors, elimination of the cause of the problem may be the more effective intervention at least for some children. Thus, it remains important to acquire information relating behavior problems and nutrition.

Since individual tolerances for foods are highly variable, individual assessment and experimentation is recommended. Hence, a measure of a given child's problem behavior is necessary. Parents can rate the referred behavior of the child at home, using a simple 1–10 scale (a rating of 1 meaning the behavior has been acceptable, and a rating of 10 meaning the child's behavior was a disaster). Preparing a set of dated index cards makes it convenient for the parents to keep the data. The child's teacher should also be asked to rate how the child behaved in school on a similar scale. If the reason for any referral was hyperactivity, use of any hyperactivity rating scale may be useful. If assessment is used in connection with a dietary project, whether the teacher knows about the project conducted at home or an attempt is made to keep the teacher "blind" to the experiment, depends on the intent of the school psychologist in using the information (Paskewicz, Clark, & O'Keefe, 1982).

Sugar

To investigate the relationship between sugar and its behavioral and learning effects for any individual child, it is necessary for the parents to keep a daily sugar diary (a daily record of the amount of *all* sugar eaten). To do this it may be necessary to list all foods eaten because sugar appears in many foods in various forms. It is useful to read the list of ingredients of prepared foods to check for the presence of the various sugars. Ingredients are listed in decreasing order of the amount present, but the amount of sugar is not necessarily given. Carbohydrate information combines contributions from both starches and sugars, so that the contribution from sugar alone may be hidden. It may be necessary to write the food companies or use their 800 telephone number to obtain the amount of sugar contained in a serving of any particular food.

The sugar content of some foods can be surprisingly high. Breakfast cereals may contain as much as 4.2 teaspoons of sugar per 1-oz serving (¾–1 cup of cereal). In this case the sugar constitutes 56% of the content of the cereal product. Sugar is found in some granolas (up to 31% sugar), fruit-flavored drinks (12%), flavored gelatin (83%), canned vegetables (up to 11%), and ketchup (29%). Twelve ounces of cola beverage may contain up to 10 teaspoons of sugar. One-fourth of a teaspoon of sugar equals 1 gram. Pennington and Church (1985) provide a reference for the sugar content of various foods.

Help parents convert all food information that has been collected to teaspoons of sugar. After baseline data are collected on the amount of sugar in foods typically eaten by the child, have parents eliminate sources of

FIGURE 1

Relationship Between Sugar Intake and Behavior Ratings

TEASPOONS SUGAR	BEHAVIOR RATING				
100	10				
90	9				
80	8				
70	7				
60	6				
50	5				
40	4				
30	3				
20	2				
10	1				
0	0				
		M T W T F S S	M T W T F S S	M T W T F S S	M T W T F S S

FIGURE 2

Log of Foods and Food Additives Consumed

	Artificial Color	Artificial Flavor	Preservative
Food #1			
Food #2			

sugar. Start by eliminating a few and eventually try to get rid of most sugar sources over a period of a few weeks.

Prepare a graph of the compiled data (see Figure 1). For each day, put teaspoons of sugar in red, home behavior rating in blue, and school behavior rating in pencil.

There is a significant relationship if problem ratings decrease with a decrease in sugar consumption. Check if there are withdrawal problems when sugar is first eliminated. Statistical analysis of the data may also be useful, noting the problems of sugar withdrawal which may confound the data. Review these results with parents, as they can make judgments about what they will do with the information.

One parent, with whom the author counseled, found a decline in hyperactive behavior and an increase in classroom achievement following the elimination of sugar from the diet. Other parents interviewed had already learned about the effects of sugar in some children and had already eliminated it but without noticeable effect. Sugar reduction can be expected to help some, but not all, children.

Food Additives

To investigate the relationship between behavior and food additives, collect information from food packaging on the presence of artificial colors, flavors, and preservatives on a daily basis. List the foods eaten and which type of additive is included, using the form shown in Figure 2. This can be used as a guide to alert parents to the presence of these additives in the diet, and for recording the amounts of additives consumed after the attempted elimination of additives is begun. The data then are used to relate recorded behavior changes to changes in levels of additives. A graph can be prepared to demonstrate this relationship, additives being substituted for sugar. Sometimes behavior changes don't immediately follow reduction of additives, but take 2–5 months of intervention.

Metal Toxicity

Short of the measurement of blood mineral levels or hair mineral analysis, the reviewed research points to (a) the elimination of canned food products sealed with the use of lead, (b) the addition of zinc and calcium (either in food or supplements), and (c) the elimination of processed foods (white flour and sugared products) from the diet.

Food Allergy

The symptoms of Type 2 allergy referred to in the previous section may be associated with the addictive reaction pattern. A test for food addiction is a "yes" answer to two or more of the following five questions: (a) Do you ever feel a strong craving for a particular food? (b) Do you ever feel desperate for that food? (c) Do you feel weak, irritable and frustrated until you satisfy that craving? (d) Do your symptoms disappear when you eat that food? (e) Do you wonder why you eat and eat and not feel full?

If a child displays Type 2 symptoms, have the parents use this test. If positive, help them make a list of the child's favorite foods that are repeatedly eaten. It is possible that one or more of these foods are the allergen responsible for the undesirable behaviors, since allergy-related illnesses are usually based on repeated exposure (Mitchell, 1984).

In an elimination challenge, help the parents eliminate all the foods that might be causing symptoms. Then, if the symptoms disappear, add foods back one by one to note which causes the symptoms to reappear. Do this by keeping a food diary – a daily record of everything eaten, how much was eaten, and what symptoms resulted. List *all* ingredients in mixed dishes and combination foods. Reading labels that list ingredients is especially recommended, as commonly allergenic foods are found in many food products, especially milk (milk solids, nonfat dry milk, dairy whey), corn (corn sweeteners), and wheat (as a filler). Use the diary to note patterns (immediate as well as possibly delayed reactions) and relationships among foods and behavioral symptoms (Maleskey, 1986). Eliminate foods that have been shown to be related to the identified problems.

ALTERNATIVE ACTIONS

Although in the previous section diagnosis was intimately related to treatment, there are a number of general interventions that appear to be helpful.

Importance of Breakfast

Breakfast is the prime nutritional charge for the energy that children and teenagers need for a school day (Mindrell, 1981). Children who miss breakfast or have too much sugar in their morning meal won't do as well in school. Missing breakfast shortens attention span and decreases task performance (Morrell & Atkinson, 1977), increases decision-making time, and decreases sociability (Mindrell, 1981). A simple nutritional intervention is the monitoring of breakfast eating.

Reduction or Elimination of Sugar Products From the Diet

Given the current state of knowledge about nutrition and its effects on behavior, decreasing the use of refined sugar and processed foods, while increasing proteins to which children are not allergic, is unlikely to harm and may help behavior (Arnold, 1984). Sugar here means sweeteners of all forms: white, brown, powdered, raw, and turbinado sugar, as well as corn and maple-flavored syrups, and sucrose, dextrose, fructose, maltose, and all other "—oses." All forms of sweetness have the same effect. The body does not distinguish among the sugars for energy. It merely converts them to glucose, or blood sugar.

Food and Vitamins

Variety in a child's diet is the best defense against overconsumption or deficiency of any nutrient. Increase in the consumption of unprocessed foods is recommended. Thus, fresh or frozen foods are preferred to canned. Whole wheat products are preferred to products with white flour. Although a varied diet, high in unprocessed foods, should offer enough nutrients, the average diet of children at present would benefit from minimal vitamin supplementation.

Nutrition Education

Charlton-Seibert, Stratton, and Williams (1980) concluded that better nutrition is dependent, in part, on the encouragement of nutritional education programs as part of the school curriculum. Johnson and Johnson (1985) reviewed studies of the effect of programs of nutrition education, investigating the relationships among knowledge of nutrition, attitude toward nutrition, and consumption of nutritious foods. They concluded that nutrition education promotes greater knowledge of and positive attitudes toward nutrition and increased consumption of nutritious foods.

Children's eating behavior may best be changed, not by lecture, but by modeling. Immediate behavior change influences long-term eating changes more than increased knowledge alone (Edwards, Acock, & Johnston, 1985). What parents prepare greatly influences what children will eventually try and will eat. The elimination of foods that have been found to be harmful is best accomplished simply by not buying them or allowing them to be purchased. Parents' explanations concerning the food variation that will be tried in the family, the results obtained from the experimentation, and the permanent dietary changes to be made on the basis of these results should be repeated as often as necessary to their children. Patience during the changeover will be rewarded only over time, as children's food preferences are unrelated to their "good-for-you" nutrient content ratings (Eiser, Eiser, Patterson, & Harding, 1984).

Charlton et al. (1980) also recommend banning junk foods (soda pop and sugared, processed snacks) from schools. Dertz and Putnam (1982) call for the substitution of those snacks with nutritional foods. Vending machines that offer fruit juice (as well as school-sponsored popcorn snacks) are becoming increasingly available and popular.

SUMMARY

Nutritional variables are important enough to be

included in the assessment of referred children, and nutritional intervention also may be important for some clients. Despite controversial approaches, conflicting data, and contradictory conclusions, nutrition assessments and interventions are cautiously recommended. The caution stems from the lack of consistently positive group results. A number of children, however, respond well to nutritional intervention, and there is some evidence that supports the effectiveness of nutrition intervention with the more disturbed and disabled groups of children. Parents can sometimes be counseled to substitute natural foods for processed ones, and to monitor the effects of nutritional changes on their children's behavior, so as to check on the effectiveness of the intervention in reducing maladaptive behavior and learning problems, which are sometimes associated with the consumption of excessive amounts of sugar, lead, additives, and foods frequently found to cause allergic reactions.

School psychologists should consider suggesting nutritional interventions either when behavioral assessments fail to turn up an understandable pattern explaining problem behavior or when behavioral interventions have failed to alleviate the problem behavior. Nutritional interventions require of the school psychologist not only increased consultation time to be devoted to parents, but a mental set that allows for the inclusion of another set of variables in the assessment of problem behavior.

REFERENCES

Arnold, L. E. (1984). Diet and hyperkinesis. *Integrative Psychiatry, 2*(5), 188–194.

Baker, S., & Henry, R. (1986). *Parent's guide to nutrition.* Reading, MA: Addison-Wesley.

Barling, S., & Buller, G. (1985). Dietary factors and hyperactivity: A failure to replicate. *Journal of Genetic Psychology, 146*(1), 117–123.

Behar, D. (1984). Sugar challenge testing with children considered "sugar reactive." *Nutrition and Behavior, 1*(4), 277–288.

Brody, S., & Wolitzky, L. (1984). Lack of mood changes following sucrose loadings. *Psychosomatics, 24*(2), 155-162.

Buchannon, S. (1984). The most ubiquitous toxin. *American Psychologist, 39*(1), 1327–1328.

Charlton-Seibert, J., Stratton, B., & Williams, M. (1980). Sweet and slow: Diet can affect learning. *Academic Therapy, 16*(2), 211–217.

Conners, C. K., & Blouin, A. (1982–1983). Nutritional effects on behavior of children. *Journal of Psychiatric Research, 17*(2), 193–201.

Conners, C. K., Goyette, C., & Newman, K. (1980). Dose–time effect of artificial colors in hyperactive children. *Journal of Learning Disabilities, 13*(9), 512–516.

Edwards, D. K., Acock, A. C., & Johnston, R. L. (1985). Nutrition behavior change: Outcomes of an educational approach. *Evaluation Review, 9*(4), 441–459.

Eiser, J. R., Eiser, C., Patterson, D. J., & Harding, C. M. (1984). Effects of information about specific nutrient content on ratings of "goodness" and "pleasantness" of common foods. *Appetite, 5*(4), 349–359.

Ernhard, C., Lands, B., & Wolf, A. (1985). Subclinical lead levels and developmental deficit: Re-analysis of data. *Journal of Learning Disabilities, 18*(8), 475–479.

Feingold, B. F. (1975). *Why your child is hyperactive.* New York: Random House.

Fuchs, N. K. (1985). *The nutrition detective.* Los Angeles: Jeremy D. Tarcher.

Green, R. (1969). Reading disability. *Canadian Medical Association Journal, 100,* 586.

Harper, G. M. (1982). Diet and behavior: Is there a relationship? In J. Grimes (Ed.), *Psychological approaches to problems of children and adolescents* (pp. 123–156). Des Moines, IA: Iowa Department of Education.

Holborow, P., Elkins, J., & Berry, D. (1981). The effect of the Feingold diet on "normal" school children. *Journal of Learning Disabilities, 14*(3), 143–147.

Jeffrey, D. B., McLellarn, R., & Fox, D. (1982). The development of children's eating habits: The role of television commercials. *Health Education Quarterly, 9*(2–3), 174–189.

Johnson, D. W., & Johnson, R. T. (1985). Nutrition education: A model for effectiveness. A synthesis of research. *Journal of Nutrition Education, 17*(2), 51–144.

Kronick, D. (1975). Case history: Sugar, fried oysters and zinc. *Academic Therapy, 11,* 119.

Latham, M. C., & Cobos, F. (1971). The effects of malnutrition on intellectual development and learning. *American Journal of Public Health, 61,* 1307–1324.

Levin, A., & Zellerback, M. (1983). *The Type 1/Type 2 allergy relief program.* New York: Berkley Books.

Mahaffey, K. (1981). Nutritional factors in lead poisoning. *Nutritional Reviews, 39,* 353–362.

Maleskey, G. (1986). Find your food pals and discover relief. *Prevention, 38*(4), 97–112.

Marlow, M., Cossaint, A., Welch, K., & Errera, J. (1984). Hair mineral content as a predictor of learning disabilities. *Journal of Learning Disabilities, 17*(7), 418–421.

Mindell, E. (1981). *Vitamin bible for your kids.* New York: Ransor, Wade.

Mitchell, D., & Aldous, K. (1974). Lead content of food stuffs. *Environmental Health Perspectives, 1,* 59–64.

Mitchell, J. (1984). *Help for the hyperactive child through diet and love.* White Hall, VA: Betterway.

Moor, C., Marlow, M., Stellern, J., & Errern, J. (1985). Main and interaction effects of metallic pollutants on cognitive functioning. *Journal of Learning Disabilities, 18*(4), 217–221.

Morgan, K. J., Zabik, M. E., Cola, R., & Leveille, G. A. (1980). *Nutrient intake patterns for children ages five to twelve years based on seven-day diaries* (Research report No. 406). East Lansing, MI: Michigan State University Agriculture Experiment Station.

Mornell, G., & Atkinson, D. R. (1977). Effect of breakfast programs on school performance and attendance of elementary school children. *Education, 98,* 111–116.

Natlow, A., & Heslin, J. (1985). *No-nonsense nutrition for kids.* New York: Pocket Books.

Needleman, H. L., Gunnoe, C., Leviton, A., Reed, R., Perseie, H., & Barrett, C. (1979). Deficits in psychologic and classroom performance of children with elevated routine lead levels. *New England Journal of Medicine, 300,* 689–695.

Oliver, B. (1983). The children who should have been passing but didn't. *Journal of Orthomolecular Psychiatry, 12*(3), 235–241.

Paskewicz, C. W., Clark, R. D., & O'Keefe, S. L. (1982). *School experimentation and the school psychologist.* Des Moines, IA: Iowa Department of Public Instruction.

Pennington, J. A. T., & Church, H. N. (1985). *Bowes and Church's food values of portions commonly used* (14th ed.). Philadelphia: Lippincott.

Perino, J., & Ernhart, C. (1974). The relation of subclinical lead levels to cognitive and sensorimotor impairment in black preschoolers. *Journal of Learning Disabilities, 1,* 616–620.

Pertz, D., & Putnam, L. (1982). An examination of the relationship between nutrition and learning. *Reading Teacher, 35*(6), 702–706.

Petering, H. G. (1978). Some observations on the interaction of zinc, copper, and iron metabolism in lead and cadmium toxicity. *Environmental Health Perspectives, 25,* 141–145.

Pihl, R. O., Parkes, M., & Stevens, R. (1979). Nonspecific interventions with learning disabled individuals. In R. Knights & D. Bakker (Eds.), *Rehabilitation, treatment and management of learning disorders.* Baltimore: University Park Press.

Powers, H. (1973–1974). Dietary measures to improve behavior and academics. *Academic Therapy, 9,* 203–214.

Prinz, R., Roberts, W., & Hartman, E. (1980). Dietary correlates of hyperactive behavior in children. *Journal of Consulting and Clinical Psychology, 48*(6), 760–769.

Rapoport, J. (1982–1983). Effects of dietary substances in children. *Journal of Psychiatric Research, 17*(2), 187–191.

Rimland, B., & Lawson, G. E. (1983). Hair mineral analysis and behavior: An analysis of the literature. *Journal of Learning Disabilities, 16,* 279–285.

Schoenthaler, S., & Doraz, W. (1983). Types of offenses which can be reduced in an institutional setting using nutritional intervention: A preliminary empirical evaluation. *International Journal for Biosocial Research, 4*(2), 74–78.

Schroeder, H. A. (1971). Losses of vitamins and trace minerals resulting from processing and preservation of foods. *American Journal of Clinical Nutrition, 24,* 562–573.

Smith, L. (1976). *Improving your child's behavior chemistry.* New York: Pocket Books.

Thatcher, R., & Lester, M. (1985). Nutrition, environmental toxins and computerized EEG: A mini-max approach to learning disabilities. *Journal of Learning Disabilities, 18*(5), 287–297.

Thatcher, R. W., McAlaster, R., Lester, M. L., & Contor, D. S. (1984). Comparisons among EEG, hair minerals and diet predictions of reading performance in children. *Annals of the New York Academy of Sciences, 433,* 87–96.

Truswell, A. S., & Darnton-Hill, I. (1981). Food habits of adolescents. *Nutrition Reviews, 39*(2), 73–88.

Von Hilsheimer, G. (1974). *Allergy, toxins and the learning disabled child.* San Rafael, CA: Academic Therapy Publications.

Weiss, B. (1982). Food additives and environmental chemicals as sources of childhood behavior disorders. *Journal of the American Academy of Child Psychiatry, 21*(2), 144–152.

Wurtman, R. (1984). Diet and hyperkinesis: Commentary. *Integrative Psychiatry, 2*(5), 195–196.

BIBLIOGRAPHY: PROFESSIONALS

Harper, G. M. (1982). Diet and behavior: Is there a relationship? In Jeff Grimes (Ed.), *Psychological approaches to problems of children and adolescents.* Des Moines, IA: Iowa State Department of Public Instruction. (ERIC Document Reproduction Service No. ED 232082).
Reviews research on dietary deficiencies and excesses. It also looks at research problems in evaluating the relationship between various nutritional problems and behavior learning. It provides resources for a more in-depth investigation and understanding of the biological side of nutritional functioning.

Johnson, D. W., & Johnson, R. T. (1985). Nutrition education: A model for effectiveness, a synthesis of research. *Journal of Nutrition Education, 17*(2), 51–144.
This issue of the journal is devoted to looking at the effectiveness of nutrition education programs, which would be helpful for school psychologists looking for not only individual interventions but organizational change regarding nutrition and education.

Eighth Annual Marabou Symposium. (1981). Nutrition in adolescence. *Nutrition Reviews, 39* (2).
This edition of *Nutrition Reviews* is dedicated solely to the topic of nutrition in adolescence. It covers topics such as medical problems, growth and maturation, nutritional requirements, and food habits. Problems in nutrition are also discussed in articles on obesity, anemia, anorexia nervosa, and acne. This issue is useful for school psychologists dealing with middle (junior high) and high school students.

BIBLIOGRAPHY: PARENTS

Mindrell, E. (1981). *Vitamin bible for your kids.* New York: Rawsor, Wade.
This easy-to-read book begins by describing the basics of nutrition, reviewing all the vitamins and minerals, including general information, what they can do for your child, what foods they are contained in, and dosages. There is a section entitled "Special Foods for Special Kids," which describes various categories of children and helpful hints on what to eliminate and to add to their diets. There is a section on physical and medical problems in relation to nutrition. It is the best available primer on nutritional information regarding children.

Natow, A., & Heslin, J. (1985). *No-nonsense nutrition for kids.* New York: Pocket Books.
A nutritionally conservative work that is not overwhelmed by fads or fanaticism. It has a question-and-answer format that deals with nutrition and toddlers, preschoolers, school-age children, and preteens. It has a section on nutritional needs in special situations, which include feeding during illness, dental health, weight control, feeding the junior athlete, and allergies. Although the prevalence of sugar in the diet is emphasized in a chart in the appendix presenting nutritional analyses of fast foods, no column about sugar content is presented.

Smith, L. (1976). *Improving your child's behavior chemistry.* New York: Pocket Books.
A first-person look at diet and nutrition in this physician's attempts to solve body and behavior problems. An often-quoted work, it recounts Dr. Smith's experiences with and theories about problems of children referred to him. His emphasis is on prevention, and he takes a strong position against sugar and white flour.

Boston Children's Hospital, with Baker, S., & Henry, R. (1960). *Parents' Guide to Nutrition.* Reading, MA: Addison-Wesley.
This recent book reviews basic nutritional needs of children, as well as eating problems, foods and diets, and special diets for children with special problems, including allergies and reactions to additives. It provides practical help to parents to aid their children attain proper nutrition.

Children and Obesity

David N. Bolocofsky
University of Northern Colorado

BACKGROUND

Overview

Children's poor eating habits have long been of special interest to psychologists, educators, and parents, not only because of their high frequency but also because of their potentially harmful effects. There is scarcely a parent who has not expressed concern over the quantity or the quality of the food his or her child eats. Maladaptive eating can be viewed in the contexts of obesity, poor nutrition, and in the extreme case eating disorders. This chapter reviews the incidence, effects, causes, and treatments of child overeating and obesity. The areas of nutrition and eating disorders are examined in other chapters of this book.

Definition and Incidence

Being overweight is the result of storing excessive fat in the body (Fox, Switzky, Rotatori, & Vitkus, 1982). Being significantly overweight, called obesity, is defined as body weight in excess of desirable weight by 20% or more. It has been estimated that up to 80 million persons in the United States, including 30% of the children, are overweight (Southam, Kirkley, Murchison, & Berkowitz, 1984; Wolf, Cohen, & Rosenfeld, 1985), and that approximately 80% of overweight children become overweight adults (Kingsley & Shapiro, 1977). In spite of myths to the contrary, it seems clear that children do *not* typically "grow out of it" solely through increases in height (Lansky & Brownell, 1982). If obese children do not achieve a more normal weight by the end of adolescence, the odds of their remaining obese as adults are 28 to 1 (Coates & Thoresen, 1978).

Effects

Obesity exacts a severe toll both in physical health and psychosocial adjustment. Overweight children are more likely than children of normal weight to show carbohydrate intolerance (Coates & Thoresen, 1978; Wolf et al., 1985), lowered growth hormone release, elevated blood pressure, and risk of cardiovascular disease (DeWolfe & Jack, 1984; Southam et al., 1984), and a higher probability of developing diabetes, gout, and angina (Southam et al., 1984). Mortality among adults is also positively correlated with obesity and has been reported to be as much as 700% higher for grossly overweight men (Stults, 1977).

In addition to the physical effects of being overweight, obese children receive less acceptance from their peers and more discrimination from significant adults in their lives (Coates & Thoresen, 1978), and exhibit a greater sense of failure and rejection, poorer interpersonal relationships with others, limited group and social interest (Werkman & Greenberg, 1967), more passivity, a higher level of anxiety and depression, and a greater incidence of personality disturbances (DeWolfe & Jack, 1984). Overweight children may also be viewed as "weak-willed gluttons" and suffer from intense social pressure from their family and friends (Stults, 1977; Wolf et al., 1985).

Being overweight may also be related to underachievement. One study found that obese individuals equal in intelligence, grades, and socioeconomic status to their thinner counterparts were significantly less likely to attend college, even though they had similar acceptance rates (Canning & Mayer, 1966).

DEVELOPMENT

It is not clear whether obese children have heavier birth weights than nonobese children. However, there is general agreement that obese individuals have a greater rate of weight gain during childhood (Stults, 1977). Three peaks have been identified as related to the onset of juvenile obesity: one between birth and 4 years of age, the second between 7 and 11 years, and the third in adolescence (Stults, 1977). However, because children may show vastly different rates of physical development, it is virtually impossible to identify age-appropriate weights. A height and weight table (e.g., Metropolitan Height and Weight Tables, 1983) can be used to identify desired weights.

PUTTING CHILDHOOD OBESITY IN PERSPECTIVE

Types of Obesity

Obesity is an increase in fat tissue that may result from an increase in the *number* of fat cells (endogenous obesity) or the *size* of the cells (exogenous obesity). Although fat cells grow in number during childhood and adolescence, there is no additional increase in adulthood. Adults with a history of childhood obesity often have a greater number of fat cells than individuals who became overweight during adulthood. In fact, in some children the number of fat cells exceeds the normal adult cell numbers by midchildhood and early adolescence (Stults, 1977). Decreasing the number of fat cells, which is necessary for achieving a normal weight, forces these people to remain in a biologically abnormal state. And because these cells pressure the organism to be filled, they are driven to remain obese. Further, since the number of fat cells in a person's body can never be decreased other than through radical surgery (Coates & Thoresen, 1978), adults with juvenile-onset obesity have a much poorer prognosis for attaining a normal weight than persons who became overweight as adults.

Food Intake and Obesity

Although it is commonly believed that people are obese because they eat more than their nonobese counterparts, several studies suggest that many overweight individuals actually eat *less* (Stults, 1977). Nor is there any truth to the belief that overweight children eat more high-calorie foods (Cohen, Gelfand, Dodd, Jensen, & Turner, 1980). Rather than overeating, a significant source of obesity appears to be underactivity. Further, as they grow older, obese children show greater declines in activity than their thinner peers.

Psychosocial Factors

A variety of psychosocial variables has been found to be related to obesity. In general, overweight individuals show lower motivation and emotional maturity (Werkman & Greenberg, 1967), poorer self-control, lower self-concepts (Southam et al., 1984), and a more external locus of control (Cohen et al., 1980). Several factors have also been identified that may influence weight change. Individuals most likely to lose weight show lower anxiety, an internal locus of control (Cohen & Alpert, 1978), a later age of onset of obesity, and greater self-reliance (Bolocofsky, Coulthard-Morris, & Spinler, 1984).

Parental Involvement

Parents are important influences of their children's weight and the likelihood of successful weight loss. On the one hand, parents may inadvertently interfere with their child's progress by a lack of recognition of the seriousness of the problem, a failure to lend support to adaptive weight change (Kingsley & Shapiro, 1977), or by modeling inappropriate eating habits (Cohen et al., 1980). On the other hand, parental involvement in the child's weight program can facilitate adaptive changes such as controlling the amount and type of food available in the home (Kingsley & Shapiro, 1977) and modeling desirable eating habits (Cohen et al., 1980).

The child's age is a crucial variable in determining the nature and extent of parental involvement. Older children and adolescents may be trying to establish independence from their parents. Thus, parental regulation of eating behavior could become a significant source of family conflict, and the children may rebel against parental control by deliberate overeating (Cohen et al., 1980).

ALTERNATIVE ACTIONS

Since fewer than 5% of obese persons are overweight because of biological factors or metabolic disorders (Stults, 1977), most weight treatments have focused on self and environmental change. These include diets, appetite suppressants, exercise programs, therapy, and behavior modification. Unfortunately, the majority of these programs have been relatively unsuccessful (Bolocofsky, Spinler, & Coulthard-Morris, 1985). Even when clients have shown significant weight loss during treatment, they have often regained most or all of it within a year after treatment was terminated (Graham, Taylor, Hovell, & Siegel, 1983). However, some of the more recent approaches, which integrate several treatment strategies, have shown greater promise.

Diets

Although perhaps the most common approach to weight loss, diets are among the least effective over the long run. While many dietary programs can result in significant weight change during the treatment phase, the likelihood of regaining the lost weight has been as high as 80% (Lloyd, Wolff, & Whelen, 1961).

The assumption underlying most diet programs is that if calorie intake is reduced below energy expenditure, the body will draw its needed calories from fat deposits, resulting in a reduction in weight (Coates & Thoresen, 1978). However, there is increasing evidence that when food intake is severely reduced, the metabolic rate and, therefore, energy expenditure substantially decrease. As a result, dieters have to significantly reduce their food intake just to *maintain* their present weight. In order to lose any weight by dieting, individuals may have to eat as little as 50% of their usual caloric intake.

A second difficulty with diet programs is that they are rarely successful unless contact with a diet therapist is frequent and the treatment is intensive. Even then, the weight loss only persists as long as the contact continues (Leon, 1976). Thus, successful dieters often must follow their diet or some variation of it for the rest of their lives.

In addition to the lack of effectiveness of most dietary programs for both children and adults, health hazards such as anemia, lowered adrenal functioning, and retarded growth have been associated with certain popular diets. Some authors of diet books have been the target of lawsuits from readers who followed the diet program presented and suffered personal injury or death (e.g., Dr. Robert Linn's "Last Chance Diet," *Pacific Indemnity Co. v. Linn,* 1985). The extent of permanent impairment can be significantly aggravated for children, who are still experiencing important physical changes. Coates and Thoresen (1978), thus, concluded that "dietary counseling, as practiced, is ineffective in the long run . . . [and] by itself, is an inefficient use of patient and professional time" (pp. 144–145).

Hospitalization and Weight Loss Camps

Another popular, but expensive, weight treatment is attendance at a special residential camp. By spending all of their time in the camp, individuals can focus on eating healthy, low-calorie, nutritious meals; engage in structured exercise programs; and receive counseling on appropriate eating behaviors. Residential camps have excellent short-term results. Most individuals show a significant weight loss and decrease in percentage of body fat (Coates & Thoresen, 1978). However, within a year these clients are often as heavy as or heavier than when they entered the camp (Nathan & Pisula, 1970). A further deficiency is that the failure to maintain weight loss even after being hospitalized or entering a residential setting may convince the participants that they are unable to lose weight and maintain the reduction under normal circumstances and that they are doomed to remain obese.

Of greater promise for children are day camps that focus on exercise, behavior modification, and self-control of maladaptive eating habits, rather than dietary change. These programs allow treatment within the child's natural psychosocial environment and can enlist the assistance of significant persons in the child's life such as family and friends (Southam et al., 1984). Although limited data exist on the effectiveness of these camps, they appear to have the potential for greater and more lasting weight loss and fewer drop-outs.

Appetite Suppressants

A third approach to weight loss is the use of diet pills. These medications, whether prescribed or over-the-counter, are designed to act as appetite suppressants by stimulating the central nervous system or affecting the appetite centers of the brain. However, little effect on juvenile obesity has been found (Coates & Thoresen, 1978). The short-term effect of these drugs is comparable to that of a placebo (Raynor & Court, 1974), and even when they successfully promote weight loss, the recidivism rate is still extremely high (Lloyd, Wolff, & Whelan, 1961). Furthermore, long-term use of such medication has been implicated in several significant physical problems, including the increased risk of strokes, as well as the danger of abuse and dependence (Coates & Thoresen, 1978).

Exercise

Although obese children may not eat more than their nonobese peers, they often show a significantly lower activity level (Coates & Thoresen, 1978). And since it is generally believed that regular physical activity can expend enough calories to burn off excess fat, an increasingly common treatment has been a formalized exercise program. When used properly, such programs appear to be an effective way to lose weight. On the positive side, a formalized exercise regimen can result in better health and a significant decrease in body fat. On the negative side, although frequent exercise causes an increase in metabolic rate, food intake may also increase. Since the effectiveness of the exercise program lasts only as long as the individual continues exercising, if he or she ceases regular exercise but does not correspondingly decrease food intake, weight *gain* is likely to occur. This has been particularly true for ex-athletes, including joggers.

Unfortunately, few individuals continue exercising once the structured programs are terminated; thus, exercise alone is rarely a viable treatment for long-term weight change (Coates & Thoresen, 1978). However, when exercise is combined with behavioral self-control procedures, long-term efficacy can substantially increase. For example, as little as a 10-minute prelunch series of activities coupled with verbal praise and tokens for appropriate eating has been shown to decrease food intake at lunch for 5- to 6-year-old children (Epstein, Masek, & Marshall, 1978). And a program of 18 50-minute meetings, conducted once every six school days, which incorporated behavior modification, or exercise and nutrition, resulted in significant weight loss for obese junior high school students (Lansky & Brownell, 1982).

Group Treatment

A variety of support models and self-help groups have been developed to facilitate weight loss. Support groups such as Overeaters Anonymous are often premised on the assumption that overeaters are incapable of losing weight on their own. The support of other individuals who share the same problem is therefore necessary before overeaters can learn better ways of eating and lose weight. When overeaters have the urge to return to former inappropriate eating habits, they call on other members for support and guidance. However, although many individuals are quite successful as long as they diligently maintain contact with the group, they usually regain most or all of the lost weight after leaving the group (Leon, 1976). Few support groups are available for children.

Self-help groups such as TOPS (Take Off Pounds Sensibly) provide strong group pressure to lose weight. Individuals who remain in the group usually show significant weight reduction (Leon, 1976). However, the 75% of the group who typically drop out generally do not maintain their weight loss. These groups have been relatively ineffective for children (Mees & Keutzer, 1967).

Individual Therapy and Hypnosis

Therapeutic treatment of obesity often focuses on uncovering conflicts assumed to underlie overeating (Leon, 1976). Thus, obesity is viewed as a symptom of a deeper psychological problem and best treated by some form of insight-oriented therapy. Unfortunately, there is little evidence, other than case studies, of the effectiveness of this often expensive and time-consuming approach.

Hypnosis, viewed by many people as having special properties, has long been a popular treatment for weight loss. However, despite the proliferation of weight programs primarily relying on hypnosis, there is little evidence that hypnotic suggestion alone can successfully effect long-term weight change (Leon, 1976). In the absence of a formalized weight treatment, hypnosis appears to have little permanent effect on appetite, diet, or eating habits (Leon, 1976). A more promising use of hypnosis has been as an adjunct to a behavioral weight program (Bolocofsky et al., 1985).

Behavior Therapy

To date the most effective nonmedical treatment for weight change has been behavioral intervention (Lansky & Brownell, 1982; Leon, 1976; Wolf et al., 1985). These procedures are designed to reduce food intake and increase energy expenditure by training clients to modify variables in their environment that influence eating behaviors and activity level. It is assumed that if the individual learns more appropriate food intake and energy expenditure behaviors, *long-term* weight change will result (Weiss, 1977). Clients may receive training in effectively controlling stimuli that trigger maladaptive eating such as watching television, responding to internal cues such as hunger and taste rather than external cues such as food on the plate, slowing down the rate of eating and increasing internal control, and using rewarding consequences for following the weight program (Wolf et al., 1985).

Behavioral weight treatments have been as successful as other approaches over the short run and generally more effective over the long run (Coates & Thoresen, 1981). Weight maintenance for as long as 2 years has not been uncommon (Bolocofsky et al., 1985; Leon, 1976). These programs have often been even more successful for children than adults (Coates & Thoresen, 1978; Zakus, 1982). Because children's eating habits are more easily modified than adults', early intervention is likely to result in greater and more enduring change.

The effectiveness of behavioral weight loss programs has been substantially enhanced when parents were involved as coparticipants but not when the parents were used solely as support systems for their children (Kingsley & Shapiro, 1977; Lansky & Vance, 1983). Obese children are highly likely to have overweight parents (Cohen et al., 1980). When parents do not participate in the weight program, their own behaviors may contradict those they are encouraging the child to follow. The discordance between what the parents say and what they do may significantly reduce the credibility of their instructions (Mischel & Liebert, 1966). Furthermore, parents cannot continuously monitor their children's eating behavior (Cohen et al., 1980). On the other hand, actively involving the parents in the weight programs not only increases the sources of reinforcement for practicing adaptive eating patterns, but it also provides a better model of appropriate behavior.

Long-term success in a behavioral weight treatment has also increased when imagery techniques or hypnosis has been included (Bolocofsky et al., 1985), self-control procedures have been incorporated (Jeffrey, 1974), client self-attributions of success have been increased (deCharms, 1968), and locus of control training has been added (Bolocofsky, Lindsey, & Mean, 1986). Finally, better results have been reported when exercise has been included in behavioral weight treatments (Stalonas, Johnson, & Christ, 1978) and nutritional education has been provided (Ikeda, Fujii, Fong, & Hanson, 1982).

School-Based Intervention

The school has increasingly been recognized as an ideal environment for the prevention and treatment of obesity. Schools have daily contact with children over long periods of time, are more cost-effective, facilitate early identification and treatment, have the potential for reaching large numbers of persons, and include important social aspects of children's environment (Lansky & Brownell, 1982; Wolf et al., 1985). Not surprisingly, school-based programs, particularly those incorporating behavior change and exercise, have been notably successful in promoting weight loss (Lansky & Brownell, 1982; Wolf et al., 1985). For example, successful weight reduction has resulted from school programs that involved monitoring weight and rate of food consumption and modeling appropriate eating behaviors for seventh and eighth graders (Botvin, Cantlon, Carter, & Williams, 1979), and emphasizing self-monitoring and techniques for changing dysfunctional eating habits (Zakus, Chin, Cooper, Makovsky, & Merrill, 1981). Including school personnel, the family, and children's peers in weight programs offers even more promise (Southam et al., 1984).

Surgical Intervention

Surgical intervention has been employed as a last resort for grossly obese patients not responding to other treatments. Suction, in which excess fat cells are surgically removed, can result in significantly lowered weight; but unless the client's eating habits change, rapid weight gain is common. Intestinal bypass surgery reduces caloric production by limiting the amount of food entering the body through the small intestine. However, these techniques have rarely been used with children because of their potentially dangerous side effects (Stults, 1977).

Exceptional Populations

Special education populations show a greater incidence of obesity but little difference in responsiveness to weight treatment compared with nonhandicapped individuals (Fox et al., 1982). Neither diets, exercise programs, therapy, nor weight groups show much success in effecting long-term weight change, particularly for retarded individuals. On the other hand, behavioral approaches have shown significant potential. "At present, the development of [behavioral] self-control skills throughout the program with the support of those in the client's natural environment appears to be a crucial element to success" (Fox et al., 1982, p. 243).

SUMMARY

The alarming incidence of childhood obesity and the physical, academic, and psychosocial toll of being overweight strongly point to the need for its prevention and early treatment. If individuals remain obese into adulthood, there is little likelihood of their ever permanently attaining a normal weight. Furthermore, there is a high probability that their own children will suffer from obesity as well. "The vicious cycle of obesity may then be not only perpetuated, especially in the obese adolescent girl, but also transmitted to her children . . . since she is more likely to live in a lower socioeconomic class and to marry a male who is obese or who has obese relatives" (Stults, 1977, p. 123).

Unfortunately, most weight programs have had a limited long-term effectiveness. Treatments that have emphasized dietary change, appetite suppressants, residential camps, support or self-help groups, or exercise alone have sometimes resulted in clinically significant weight change, but only as long as the clients continued with the treatment or group. When the clients returned to their normal, everyday environment, they typically regained most or all of the lost weight.

In contrast, behavioral weight approaches, whether provided in day camps, individual treatment, or in the schools, have shown considerable success in effecting long-term weight change with children. This has been equally true for handicapped and nonhandicapped individuals. The best programs have incorporated an exercise component, nutritional training, and frequent therapist contact both during and after treatment. Parental involvement has also been a crucial factor in promoting weight change, at least for children and preadolescents. However, parents must be active participants in the program. Where parents are only used for support, they often inadvertently inhibit successful weight loss.

School psychologists, along with other school health personnel, are in an excellent position to promote effective weight change. They have frequent, systematic, and continual contact with children over an extended period of time, all of which are necessary components of successful programs of long-term weight loss. Further, they can enlist the assistance of important social support systems such as the children's teachers, family, and friends. A behavioral weight program incorporating a peer support group appears especially promising and would require as little as an hour per week of the psychologist's time.

Aside from resorting to a formalized weight program, parents can assume an important role in preventing childhood obesity. First, they can ensure that their family eats healthy, nutritious meals. Regular and frequent exercise is another way to promote better weight as well as health. Food should never be used as a means of combating depression or as a substitute for love. Similarly, children should not be forced to "clean their plates" when they are truly no longer hungry. Finally, parents can serve as models for proper eating habits. It is important to remember that food primarily serves four purposes: (a) satisfying hunger, (b) stimulating taste buds, (c) providing the body with energy, and (d) creating or filling fat cells. Before encouraging a child to eat, the parent should ensure that one of the first three purposes are being met. A multidisciplinary approach to weight management, perhaps including the school psychologist, counselor, and nurse, is likely to assist parents in developing an effective weight prevention program.

REFERENCES

Bolocofsky, D. N., Coulthard-Morris, L., & Spinler, D. (1984). Prediction of successful weight management from personality and demographic data. *Psychological Reports, 55,* 795–802.

Bolocofsky, D. N., Lindsey, D., & Mean, N. (1986). *Improving behavioral weight management by modifying locus of control.* Manuscript submitted for publication.

Bolocofsky, D. N., Spinler, D., & Coulthard-Morris, L. (1985). Effectiveness of hypnosis as an adjunct to behavioral weight management. *Journal of Clinical Psychology, 41,* 35–41.

Botvin, G. J., Cantlon, A., Carter, B. J., & Williams, C. L. (1979). Reducing adolescent obesity through a school health program. *Journal of Pediatrics, 95,* 1060–1062.

Canning, J., & Mayer, J. (1966). Obesity: Its possible effect on college acceptance. *New England Journal of Medicine, 275,* 1172–1174.

Coates, T. J., & Thoresen, C. E. (1978). Treating obesity in children and adolescents: A review. *American Journal of Public Health, 68,* 143–151.

Coates, T. J., & Thoresen, C. E. (1981). Behavior and weight changes in three obese adolescents. *Behavior Therapy, 12,* 383–399.

Cohen, E. A., Gelfand, D. M., Dodd, D. K., Jensen, J., & Turner, C. (1980). Self-control practices associated with weight loss maintenance in children and adolescents. *Behavior Therapy, 11,* 26–37.

Cohen, N. L., & Alpert, M. (1978). Locus of control as a predictor of outcome in treatment of obesity. *Psychological Reports, 42,* 805–806.

deCharms, R. (1968). *Personal causation.* New York: Academic.

DeWolfe, J. A., & Jack, E. (1984). Weight control in adolescent girls: A comparison of the effectiveness of three approaches to follow-up. *Journal of School Health, 54,* 347–349.

Epstein, L. H., Masek, B. J., & Marshall, W. R. (1978). A nutritionally based school program for control of eating in obese children. *Behavior Therapy, 9,* 766–788.

Fox, R., Switzky, H. Rotatori, A. F., & Vitkus, P. (1982). Successful weight loss techniques with mentally retarded children and youth. *Exceptional Children, 49,* 238–243.

Graham, L. E., Taylor, C. B. Hovell, M. F., & Siegel, W. (1983). Five-year follow-up to a behavioral weight-loss program. *Journal of Consulting and Clinical Psychology, 51,* 322–323.

Ikeda, J. P., Fujii, M., Fong, K. A., & Hanson, M. (1982). Two approaches to adolescent weight reduction. *Journal of Nutrition Education, 14,* 90–92.

Jeffrey, D. B. (1974). A comparison of the effects of external control and self-control on the modification and maintenance of weight. *Journal of Abnormal Psychology, 83,* 404–410.

Kingsley, R. G., & Shapiro, J. (1977). A comparison of three behavioral programs for the control of obesity in children. *Behavior Therapy, 8,* 30–36.

Lansky, D., & Brownell, K. D. (1982). Comparison of school-based treatments for adolescent obesity. *Journal of School Health, 52,* 384–387.

Lansky, D., & Vance, M. A. (1983). School-based intervention for adolescent obesity: Analysis of treatment, randomly selected control, and self-selected control subjects. *Journal of Consulting and Clinical Psychology, 51,* 147–148.

Leon, G. R. (1976). Current directions in the treatment of obesity. *Psychological Bulletin, 83,* 557–578.

Lloyd, J. K., Wolff, O. H., & Whelen, W. S. (1961). Childhood obesity: A long-term study of height and weight. *British Medical Journal, 2,* 145–148.

Mees, H. L., & Keutzer, C. S. (1967). Short term group psychotherapy with obese women. *Northwest Medicine, 66,* 548–550.

Metropolitan Height and Weight Tables. (1983). New York: Metropolitan Life Insurance.

Mischel, W., & Liebert, R. M. (1966). Effects of discrepancies between observed and imposed reward criteria on their acquisition and transmission. *Journal of Personality and Social Psychology, 3,* 45–53.

Nathan, S., & Pisula, D. (1970). Psychological observations of obese adolescents during starvation treatment. *Journal of the American Academy of Child Psychiatry, 9,* 722–724.

Pacific Indemnity Co. v. Linn, 766 F.2d 654 (3rd Cir. 1985).

Raynor, P. H. W., & Court, J. M. (1974). Effect of dietary restriction and anorectic drugs on linear growth in childhood obesity. *Archives of the Disabled Child, 49,* 822.

Southam, M. A., Kirkley, B. G., Murchison, A., & Berkowitz, R. I. (1984). A summer day camp approach to adolescent weight loss. *Adolescence, 19,* 855–868.

Stalonas, P. M., Johnson, W. G., & Christ, M. (1978). Behavior modification for obesity: The evaluation of exercise, contingency management, and program adherence. *Journal of Consulting and Clinical Psychology, 46,* 463–469.

Stults, H. (1977). Obesity in adolescents: Prognosis, etiology, and management. *Journal of Pediatric Psychology, 2,* 122–126.

Weiss, A. R. (1977). A behavioral approach to the treatment of adolescent obesity. *Behavior Therapy, 8,* 720–726.

Werkman, S. L., & Greenberg, E. S. (1967). Personality and interest patterns in obese adolescent girls. *Psychosomatic Medicine, 29,* 72–80.

Wolf, M. C., Cohen, K. R., & Rosenfeld, J. G. (1985). School-based interventions for obesity: Current approaches and future prospects. *Psychology in the Schools, 22,* 187–200.

Zakus, G. (1982). Obesity in children and adolescents: Understanding and treating the problem. *Social Work in Health Care, 8,* 11–29.

Zakus, G., Chin, M. L., Cooper, H., Makovsky, E., & Merrill, C. (1981). Treating adolescent obesity: A pilot project in a school. *Journal of School Health, 51,* 663–666.

BIBLIOGRAPHY: PROFESSIONALS

Coates, T. J., & Thoresen, C. E. (1978). Treating obesity in children and adolescents: A review. *Journal of Public Health, 68,* 143–151.

This article is a thorough overview of the incidence, effects, and prognosis for childhood obesity. Treatment approaches are reviewed and strategies are presented for developing effective weight programs for children.

Fox, R., Switzky, H., Rotatori, A. F., & Vitkus, P. (1982). Successful weight loss techniques with mentally retarded children and youth. *Exceptional Children, 49,* 238–243.

This article reviews the incidence and treatment of obesity in retarded children. The major causes of obesity are reviewed and the implications for providing effective weight reduction interventions are discussed. Behavioral approaches are emphasized.

Stults, H. (1977). Obesity in adolescents: Prognosis, etiology, and management. *Journal of Pediatric Psychology, 2,* 122–126.

This article is a medical approach to understanding the etiology and treatment of adolescent obesity. The prognosis and etiology of childhood obesity are thoroughly reviewed from a physiological perspective, and the health and psychosocial effects are discussed. Treatment strategies are briefly reviewed.

Wolf, M. C., Cohen, K. R., & Rosenfeld, J. G. (1985). School-based interventions for obesity: Current approaches and future prospects. *Psychology in the Schools, 22,* 187–200.
This article is a review of school-based approaches to childhood obesity. The comparative effectiveness of behavior modification, dietary control/nutrition education, and formalized exercise programs is discussed. Implications for the successful provision of a school-based weight program are presented.

BIBLIOGRAPHY: PARENTS AND ADOLESCENTS

Eden, A. N. (1975). *Growing up thin.* New York: McKay.
This integrated approach to weight loss emphasizes exercise and behavior change and was written for parents and older children. A unique feature is a discussion of the relationship of weight and weight loss techniques to different stages of the children's development.

Ellis, L. E., & Ellis, C. A. (1976). *Lose weight without dieting.* Jacksonville, FL: Heritage Press.
This book is an overview of the benefits and risks of surgical approaches to weight loss, particularly intestinal bypass surgery. The discussion is written in language readily understandable by mature adolescents and adults.

Ferguson, J. M. (1976). *Habits, not diets: The real way to weight control.* Palo Alto, CA: Bull.
This book focuses on basic behavioral approaches to weight loss and includes techniques that are appropriate for children and adults.

Stuart, R. B., & Davis, B. (1972). *Slim chance in a fat world.* Champaign, IL: Research Press.
This is one of the classic nondiet weight loss books. The authors' extensive experience in behavioral weight management techniques is clearly evident in their thorough discussion of the factors underlying effective and permanent weight change and the presentation in a simple, step-by-step approach. The book is somewhat dated but still highly recommended.

Children and Organization

Gail Epstein Mengel
Longmeadow Public Schools, Massachusetts

BACKGROUND

Disorganized children are no strangers to the school psychologist. Perhaps referred initially for their lack of motivation, irresponsibility, or even "spacey" behavior, these children are frequently discovered to have some basic difficulties in organization and planning that contribute to, exacerbate, or even foster their unmotivated learning postures. All too often, however, the organizational deficit is overlooked, especially when academic, diagnostic, and intelligence test scores indicate that these children could in fact succeed. Not a function of intelligence, organizational deficits permeate all levels of abilities and may be permanently disabling to those unprepared to acknowledge and cope with them. Unlike basic skills, which are tapped at specific times and places, organizing deficiencies are pervasively influential in children's personal styles of behaving (deHirsch & Jansky, 1980).

Considering the far-reaching impact of such a disability, attention to organizational deficits is surprisingly meager in the educational and psychological literature as well as in curricular materials that might be expected to address them (Slade, 1986). The education system seems to acknowledge organization needs only as they pertain to specific study habits and test-taking. While this presents a necessary beginning to assist the disorganized child in the school setting, it is not sufficient in scope for dealing with the myriad of organizational challenges faced in all settings by the child who must cope with this learning disability.

Perhaps the lack of research attention to organization results from its amorphous nature, as "organization" traverses many planes. Perceptual, conceptual, and possibly psychic organization seem to be compromised in the child with organizational deficits (deHirsch & Jansky, 1980). Central to understanding and addressing organization problems is a definition that incorporates its many aspects and that can thus provide direction for the school psychologist.

On a behavioral level, the activity of organizing implies an ability to structure and order objects, procedures, information, and communication in a meaningful way. Idiomatically, a "place for everything and everything in its place" and a "time for everything, everything in its time" are maxims that address this aspect of organization. From a Gestalt perspective, this structuring ability is dependent on figure–ground separation, one of the essential mechanisms by which individuals organize their environment. It requires perceiving order from chaos, configuration from confusion, pattern from randomness, and the relationship of the parts to the whole (Hall & Lindzey, 1957). Organization is only as effectual as the underlying ability to interpret and catalogue stimuli (Combs & Snygg, 1959).

To disorganized children, information they take in from their senses seems impervious to sorting, classification, and categorization in meaningful ways to make its retrieval and use more efficient and effective (Smith, 1979). These children often are personally disheveled, manage their time poorly, exhibit clumsiness, get lost in space, lose possessions, submit "messy" work, have difficulty in prioritizing, and fail to see the patterns and routines of daily life (Smith, 1979). This constellation of behaviors can make successful adaptation very difficult both in school and out.

It is the intent of this chapter to offer some insights into what may influence the development of organization ability, how deficiency of organizational ability can be diagnosed, and what alternatives for action are available to address this deficit. It is hoped that this chapter will broaden the recognition of organizational deficits as a significant factor in the lives of the children with whom school psychologists deal.

DEVELOPMENT

The etiology and development of organizational ability in children has not yet been clearly established by developmental and cognitive psychologists. Although there is no evidence of significant neurological impairment per se, it has been hypothesized that patterning and organizational deficits may be a consequence of neurointegrative makeup, potentially present from birth (deHirsch & Jansky, 1980). This hypothesis has led to some recent investigation of ways to measure infant functioning that may ultimately predict the potential for future organizational problems (Als, 1985). Considered an important aspect to this development is the child's interaction with the environment, both through affective involvement (deHirsch & Jansky, 1980) and sensory–motor experience (Ginsburg & Opper, 1969).

From a social-developmental perspective, Elkind (1986) suggested that lack of organization may be related to prematurely curtailing children's direct (sensory motor) learning and experience in the interest of teaching them to read and write at an earlier age. Imposed on them by adults who believe — on the basis of faulty data — that earlier academic teaching accelerates learning, this academic pressure thwarts fulfillment of the children's natural curiosity. Initiative to self-organize for learning loses momentum, resulting in reliance on the adult world for structure. An inactive learner is the consequence.

Elkind's (1986) postulate dovetails with that of cognitive psychologists who view learning-disabled children as nonactive problem-solvers. In spite of their possession of the appropriate cognitive strategies for organizing information, these children tend not to deploy them spontaneously. It is not until their use is prompted that their organizational performance becomes indistinguishable from their nondisabled peers. Inconsistency in routinely generalizing these strategies to similar learning situations compounds this deficiency (Hall, 1980). This viewpoint assumes that underutilized cognitive processing is basic to the lack of organizational problem-solving ability.

DeHirsch and Jansky (1980) maintained that an inadequate infant–mother bond and a chaotic environment are significant factors in the development of organizational deficits in children. Their Gestalt interpretation proffers that "mother" does not stand out as figural against a chaotic background. This, in turn, has consequences for how well these children discern what is important to attend to, and it contributes to their pervasively obfuscated sense of boundaries and relationships.

Factors That Influence Organizational Ability

Although organizational skills have yet to be comprehensively understood, factors that are considered influential to their development have been proposed. That language skills may affect planning and organizing has been suggested by Kops and Belmont (1985). Other observers have found that it is the developmental level of conceptual language that discriminates between the organized and nonorganized problem-solvers (Tomlinson-Keasey, Crawford & Eisert, 1979). Specifically, higher-order classification skills are critical elements in organizational thinking, as they assist categorization of the information to be processed. Inadequacy in sorting and categorizing information is the very weakness that a child with organizational deficits experiences.

Anxiety can potentially have a cyclical impact on organizational skills. Acredolo (1982) has found that emotional insecurity debilitates spatial reasoning, a basic weakness in the disorganized child. Conversely, deHirsch and Jansky (1980) view organizational deficits as contributors to emotional insecurity. As a result of their inability to sort out their experiences coherently and get a "fix" in space and time, organizationally deficient children often experience overwhelming anxiety. Thus, anxiety may not only compound disorganization, but be a result of it as well. Concordant with this, a stable, nurturing, and emotionally secure environment that fosters independence and decision making positively influences organizational thinking and an organized sense of self (Stern, 1985; Torgesen, 1977). However, life situations that lack these qualities occasion disorganized functioning.

Behaviorally, an environment that models, cues, and reinforces good organization provides better conditions for learning how to organize than one in which disorganization prevails. Indeed, children rarely invent their methods of organizing; they have incorporated strategies and techniques imparted by organized teachers and parents. An organized and structured household is an influential factor in creating a sense of order, predictability, and routine, allowing the disorganized child to function more optimally (Smith, 1979).

PUTTING CHILDREN AND ORGANIZATION IN PERSPECTIVE

Basic Considerations

Disorganization can be a common trait among students (and their parents and teachers) at any given time. Indeed, adolescents especially can be quite puzzling to the school psychologist for this reason. With the onset of hormonal changes that upset equilibrium and the stress so common to the age, some degree of disorganization is typical during this stage of development. It thus becomes necessary to discriminate at what point intervention is indicated. But, while a genuine disability is more pronounced, extensive, and enduring (Smith, 1979), what constitutes a sufficient duration or number of disorganized behaviors to justify special services? To determine this, school psychologists must each calibrate their own yardsticks. One basic principle should probably underlie all decisions, however: To the extent that disorganization threatens effective progress, organizational deficits become important to address. Thus, these questions need to be asked: Does the disorganization cause failure in one area only? Is promotion to the next grade in jeopardy? Is the youngster likely to "drop out of life?" The comprehensiveness of action taken depends on the answers to these questions.

Organizatinal deficiency is often mistaken for lack of motivation, especially when basic skills and achievement test results provide evidence that academic progress is obtainable with moderate effort. Indeed, disorganization can create an attitude of hopelessness that culminates in low motivation. Motivation energy can be difficult to recoup and sustain in these cases unless specific organizational strategies are instituted as part of remedial therapy. Consequently, referrals for motivational problems should automatically signal a need to assess for underlying organizational deficits.

Too, disorganization can be a byproduct of depression (Beck, 1967). Here, energy efficiency is reduced and diluted, and impetus and momentum to structure, order, and plan activities of daily living are diminished. Assessment of clinical indicators of depression often becomes necessary for discriminating appropriate treatment.

Differential diagnosis may be required to separate out those with organizational deficits from those whose symptoms resemble borderline schizophrenia (Bender, 1966, cited in deHirsch & Jansky, 1980). While there may be considerable overlap in the diagnostic impressions of each category, children with organizational deficits have, in particular, affective depth. They can form relationships and respond well — often dramatically — to remedial therapy. In addition, their human figure drawings, though diffuse and often spatially disorganized, lack the bizarre features seen in samples from the schizophrenic group (deHirsch & Jansky, 1980).

Areas of Specific Observation and Assessment

While younger children with organizational problems often manifest many behavioral symptoms, older children and adolescents frequently manage to disguise or compensate for these difficulties (deHirsch & Jansky, 1980). Some accomplish this by assuming an insouciant attitude or by learning splinter skills that obscure the basic deficiency. For this reason it becomes important for the school psychologist to evaluate the extent of organizational deficit from several diagnostic perspectives. Among these are the physical-behavioral dimensions, language and academic functioning, and the observations, parent reporting, and test indicators of space and time disorganization.

Behavior. Disorganized behavior is difficult to overlook, since it tends to result in intrusion on the space, time, and patience of others. The noteworthy behaviors include messy workspace, loss of possessions, personal untidiness, difficulty in sustaining focused attention, poor time management, difficulty in recalling the daily schedule or weekly routine, dependency on others for structure and cues, poor motor organization and clumsiness, general confusion, inflexibility, spatially disorganized paperwork, confusion of left and right, and difficulty following the sequence of events (Ferrald & Schamber, 1973; Smith, 1979; Haman & Isaacson, 1985).

Language and Academics. Disorganization in language processes tends to accompany an organizational deficit, which is considered a sub-category of learning disability (deHirsch & Jansky, 1980). The following observations, consistent with a finding of language learning disability, are frequently reported by teachers: word-finding difficulties, loose and disjointed discourse, poor sequencing of stories or jokes, syntax errors, inability to make a point, difficulty in following directions in sequence, and disorganized written language (deHirsch & Jansky, 1980; Smith, 1979). Disorganized children also evidence the same reading, writing, and spelling problems as learning disabled children show, for example, reversal, inversion, or missequencing of letters, loss of place on the page, disregard of punctuation, and poor visual recall and recognition of spelling and reading words. Handwriting suffers from poor spatial organization, characterized by words often running into each other, poor alignment of columns, inaccurate formation of letters, mixture of capital and lower case letters, difficulty staying on the line, slow letter formation, and overall illegibility. Lack of proficiency in use of the dictionary, indexes, or telephone book, and weak apprehension of the chronology of historical events may be present. Difficulty with geometry, fractions, decimals, computional borrowing and carryng may surface in addition (Smith, 1979).

Formal Assessment

Short of direct observation, little has been reported in the literature regarding more formal diagnostic assessment of organizational deficits. Formal assessment, however, becomes particularly important in the case of the child or adolescent who has masked or compensated for the deficit, especially when lack of motivation accompanies the disorganization. It is helpful in the accurate determination of appropriate remediation and fosters a greater understanding of the more pervasive needs of the child.

Psychological Evaluation. In diagnostic testing the school psychologist has many means of assessing a child's apprehension of spatial and temporal elements in addition to evaluating the child's purposeful and incidental oral language. Weak scores in the WISC-R spatial subtests of Block Design and Object Assembly have been associated with organizational deficits (deHirsch & Jansky, 1980). A weak score in Information can sometimes be traced to errors on questions related to spatial or temporal knowledge or to word-finding difficulties. For diagnostic purposes the following guidelines are appropriate: seek all information related to sequencing (numbers; days of the week; months and seasons of the year), time-telling, spatial planning and organization (Bender designs); to spatial problem solving (Block Design and Object Assembly) and problem-solving efficiency (trial-and-error, methodical, systematic); to flexibility (Object Assembly), directional sense (geographical, right/left), height estimation; and to self-organization.

Because emotional insecurity can affect spatial reasoning (Acredolo, 1982) and "crises" of withdrawn love and approval can lead to greater disorganization and inflexibility (Viney & Clarke, 1974), their potential impact on a child with organizational deficits is great. For the school psychologist, assessment of the level of stress experienced by children may reveal how much of the disorganization is stress-induced. Thus, the impact of family dynamics, structure, and management on the disorganization of children must not be underestimated.

Developmental History. A developmental history makes it possible to investigate characteristics of the child that are associated with organizational deficits, such as deficiencies in space and time appreciation, language use, and motor development. Is the child's room chaotic? Can the (young) child get dressed with clothes put on the right way? Is handedness well-established or ambiguous? Were feeding and sleeping routines readily established in infancy? When was language acquired and what was its quality? Can the child relate a story in good sequence? A joke in good sequence? Can the child recall a series of directions given? Does the child have difficulty finding the right word to express the thought intended? Was motor coordination smooth? Were/are there signs of clumsiness? Was learning to ride a bicycle without training wheels an arduous task? Is a sense of the order of the day's or week's events internalized? Is there a sense of time and its duration? Does the child know intuitively when to come home for lunch or dinner? Does the child confuse right and left? Is getting "lost" a concern for the child? (Smith, 1979; deHirsch & Jansky, 1980). Parents can often offer good insights into this practical assessment.

Information from Other Specialists. Although they are called upon to share their observations and assessments perhaps too infrequently, other specialists also often have valuable input. The physical education teacher can provide a normative assessment about general coordination, balance, sense of self in space, and body boundaries in relation to the child's peers. Any special need on the part of the child for well-defined rules or extra spatial structure in large-group activities in gym may be a significant indicator.

The art teacher can give insights into how well organized the child's art production is. Are parts of the whole spatially integrated and related? Is figure–ground perception well developed? In fathoming the characteristics and needs of a child with organizational deficits, the school psychologist can pose knowledgeable diagnostic questions to virtually any person who has continuous contact with the child.

Knowing the configuration of relevant diagnostic clues affords the school psychologist the insights to propose that organizational difficulties — not motivation, laziness, stubborness, or irresponsibility — are a significant factor in school failure. This end justifies the expenditure of time and energy in observation and diagnostic assessment, particularly because these children respond so positively to appropriate remediation.

ALTERNATIVE ACTIONS

Overview

Helping a child with organizational deficits can be a full-time job. In need of structure in all aspects of their lives, these children require that boundaries be constantly projected, limits judiciously determined, and priorities and alternatives reduced and clarified for them. Pragmatic, specific strategies offer the most immediate solution to the difficulties that interfere with everyday functioning. Some clinicians (deHirsch & Jansky, 1980; Smith, 1979) advocate a more holistic approach that facilitates the internal organization of the child by reframing life experiences into more organized, comprehensible patterns. Achieved within the context of an emotional bond, this approach strives to foster more organized behavior through restructuring perceptual interpretation. More recently, interest in metacognition, which is the awareness of cognitive strategies and their use, has generated some methods for increasing organizational problem solving (Loper & Murphy, 1985; Messerer, Hunt, Meyers, & Lerner, 1984). Although the emphasis here is on the more pragmatic, direct approach to remediation, it in no way is meant to diminish the importance and promise of metacognitive contributions, which are subsequently addressed in brief.

Principles of Organizing

Pragmatic approaches to getting organized are guided by some basic principles. Among them are the following, many of which are consistent with Winston (1977):

1. The first step to becoming better organized is to recognize, acknowledge, and specifically identify disorganization where it occurs. Winston (1977) has suggested that all notes taken during this process be recorded in a single notebook.

2. Determine priorities in addressing problems according to need. What is most upsetting to the child, to the teacher, to the parent? What interferes most and least with successful daily living? With long-term objectives?

3. If initiating the reorganization process is aversive, begin with the task or procedure that stands out as most readily organizable. This builds a sense of gratification more immediately with less sense of effort.

4. Break down the task or process into its component steps. Start first by discriminating gross steps (for example, prepare an outline for a term paper) or categories (for example, select out "discard" from "keep" items, or science from history notes). Then move to finer discriminations (identify reference materials; science lab notes from science lecture notes).

5. Approach the job systematically. Work on one place, step, or category at a time until the organization within it is completed. Move to the next step only at that time.

6. Always take a step, no matter how small, to progress toward overcoming the disorganization. This "swiss cheese method" starts small and requires only small bits of time, but gains cumulative results.

7. Do not leave a task without first identifying and writing down what the next step to take will be. This makes the task more approachable the next time.

8. If it becomes unclear what the next step to be taken is, decide what further information is needed to determine the next step and write that down.

9. Make certain that there is in fact a place for everything that is being physically reorganized and that each is readily accessible and identified, perhaps with a label. Specific identities for things can be obtained by the use of file folders, baskets, cups, jars, boxes, cubbies, bookends, etc. Fasteners —staples, all sizes of paper clips, spring clips, etc. — are indispensable aides.

10. Make a "plan of attack" before becoming immersed in trying to sort through excessive disorganization. This avoids frustration and confusion, which can undermine the organizing effort. Putting this plan into writing is beneficial, and affords a more visible sense of how detailed the job is. Checking off each step as it is done also provides reinforcement, and marks progress in a systematized fashion.

Some Basic Strategies for Organizing. Common to children with organizational deficits are physical disorderliness and difficulty in starting and completing tasks. The guidelines in Chart 1, some of which are obvious, provide some structure for approaching these difficulties. Adult supervision and modeling are needed to teach these to the disorganized child.

Some Specific Approaches and Recommendations. As can be deduced from the preceding principles, the major tasks confronting the organizer are breaking down the task into its component parts, perceiving the important elements, and categorizing, sequencing, and making decisions. Slade (1986) added to these organizational skills the important components of following routines and managing time.

Developing the skills that underlie organizational ability is best accomplished by eliciting the active participation and ego involvement of the students. Slade (1986) suggested evoking interest in organizational efforts by timing the retrieval, in game-like fashion of items specified by the teacher from the students' own workspaces. Maintaining possessions in an orderly condition is the key to efficient retrieval and requires that a place be available for every (category of) item. This serves to motivate students to develop an organizational scheme or "blueprint" for their desks, a miniproject that can be undertaken by the class and facilitated by the teacher. Use and labeling of "containers" for each type of item should be encouraged to separate categories of objects more clearly for children. Bins, crates, cubbies, cans, shelves, etc., can be helpful. Three-ring notebooks should have tabbed dividers, a pencil case, a pocket file, a homework pad, a space for adhering a schedule card, etc.

If teachers model and discuss how tasks are broken into segments, their students can begin to discern how the steps relate to the whole process. Conversely, prac-

TABLE 1

Strategies for Organizing

Organizing Objects or Information
(cleaning up a desk, sorting papers)

1. Choose the pile or mass of information that feels most approachable.
2. Use one of the following guidelines to sort through the material: (a) Preview to discern the categories or groupings represented and assign preliminary labels for each; (b) or, if categories are not readily apparent, determine and label one category only and sift through all the objects or information for items included in that category; (c) or, as in dealing cards, take each item one at a time and create or add to a pile in accordance with the item's relatedness, assigning labels as soon as they become apparent.
3. Assign final category labels that reflect the general contents of each, for example, Tests, Projects, Special Interests, Personal, Recreation, Supplies, References.
4. While sorting the objects and information into the various categories defined, put whatever finds no "fit" into a Miscellaneous category.
5. After all sorting is completed, try to discern any objects or data that seem to cluster together logically within the Miscellaneous category.
6. Label these groups and research this pile for additional members.

Organizing Steps of a Task
(term paper, preparation to get a license)

1. Brainstorm all steps that can be anticipated for the task and write them down.
2. Sequence them, or, if the sequence is not readily apparent...
3. Select the step that appears to be first, Label it "1."
4. Compare each step with every other step in rotation — using a forced-choice comparison — and derive which come first. Label each of these "first" steps consecutively, as they are determined, resuming with "2.".

Organizing to Accomplish a Project
(science lab, cooking project)

1. Identify and gather all supplies and materials needed as indicated in the directions.
2. Determine and gather all utensils and tools needed to handle those supplies and materials.
3. Preplan procedures as in Organizing Steps of a Task.

tice in brainstorming all the possible steps to a task and then sequencing them provides a format to follow that can be generalized to other tasks and procedures. Identifying when these procedures are appropriate to utilize and practicing their use in these situations fosters more active problem solving and an organized approach to performance.

Categorizing skills can and needs to be taught through continuous practice in sorting. Objects, pictures, symbols, words, and ideas all offer possibilities for this purpose. The finding that organizing ability is related to development and use of higher-order classification skills (Tomlinson-Keasey et al., 1979) appears to make activating these particular skills a prerequisite to organization.

Routines are essential to developing organized behavior and should be discussed, each activity or stage being related to the next as meaningfully as possible. Previewing the activities of the day, posted on the blackboard or a personal schedule card, and of the week, posted on a "special" calendar, can provide an overall sense of how the parts (activities) relate to the whole (day or week). On a smaller scale, labeling procedural stages *within* activities ("direction time," "work/play time," "clean-up time") and generalizing these labels to other activities as well helps develop a sense of sequence and routine. To do this, Slade (1986) has suggested initially providing a step-by-step explanation of a procedure, moving on to using shortened verbal or visual cues to evoke procedural recall, and ultimately fading out the cuing. Perceiving routines *between* activities on a larger scale is occasioned by chaining, by which one activity's culmination is arranged to signal the beginning of the next (Slade, 1986). Through raising consciousness of routines, a sense of structure and predictability is engendered.

Providing opportunities for decision making encourages self-exploration and self-reliance. For the less secure or younger child, the choices should be limited to two. Gradually, and at older ages, the number of options can be increased. This simplifies evaluation of options while still fostering independent thinking. In addition, it reduces dependency on adult structure,and provides a sense of autonomy and control in contrast to helplessness and inability to "take charge." The youngster who feels in control is more likely to actively attempt organizing and to invest in securing an outcome.

Time management, a consistent weakness in children with organizational deficits, can be addressed by first making the child aware of the passage of time. Estimating the amount of time a task will take, timing various activities or chores, and having a "race against time" all provide feedback that relates time to a child's more personal experience. Slade (1986) has also suggested that keeping a log of these time periods spurs motivation to become better organized by inviting record setting.

For adolescents, not only is involvement in the organizational planning important, but checklists, too, are integral to a successful effort to organize. Each step of each task or chore needs to be recorded to highlight the overall process and to check off each step as completed. Smith (1979) applied this technique with adolescents who had experienced difficulty in mastering the skills of daily living that most others accomplish with facility. As a means of building confidence and self-sufficiency, it reinstates a sense of mastery and control over one's life. This can in turn encourage more active coping, and reduce the anxieties that can inhibit organization and organized thinking (Viney & Clarke, 1974). Because this strategy makes no assumptions about what the adolescent *should* know to do, it can prevent frustration and conflict between the disorganized child and parents and teachers. Although frustration with these children can be great, it is important to remember that acceptance, positive regard, and empathy are essential elements in a successful approach to children with organizational deficits (Ferrald & Schamber, 1973); withdrawal of approval can fuel disorganization (Caplan, 1969).

While building organizational skills is considered important to the disorganized child, deHirsch and Jansky (1980) view it as insufficient to address the more basic deficiencies present. These clinicians advocate using the services of an educational therapist who can develop an emotional bond with the child. Mediated by the educational therapist, experiences are distilled, regrouped, and magnified to reflect the patterns, routines, and consistencies which belie their basic organization. Through this relationship deHirsch and Jansky believe learning becomes more ego-involving and memorably internalized. Helping these children to subsequently organize themselves and their environment can thus be achieved more readily.

Adults need to structure all aspects of the disorganized child's life by projecting clear boundaries, setting well-considered limits, and presenting priorities and alternatives in a clarified and abridged way(Ferrald & Schamber, 1973). School psychologists can suggest practical recommendations to parents which might include, for example, assistance in the physical organization of their child's bedroom. By insuring that everything has a designated place, organization becomes easier to maintain. Also important are such practices as upholding routines and pointing out their order by labeling what comes first, next, and last, explaining the steps in a procedure, providing limited choices instead of a vast array of alternatives, clarifying what is and is not acceptable behavior, and being specific and terse in directions and explanations. The parents of disorganized children can be easily strained by the excessive demands for order and organization. Praise, helpful direction, and brainstorming assistance from the school psychologist may be necessary to maintain parents' optimism and sense of humor, which are essential for confronting the frustrations of parenting a child with organizational deficits (Smith, 1979).

Metacognitive Contributions

Difficulty in organizing incoming and outgoing information is a hallmark of organizational deficits. For this reason, it is pertinent to consider information-processing models, in which organization plays a central role. Indeed, metacognitive research, which has studied the exceptional child's use of cognitive strategies and their deficiencies, has generally found that these strategies — including self-questioning, self-charting, self-instruction, self-reinforcement, and self-monitoring — are not deployed spontaneously in exceptional children, but can be prompted with positive results (Cort, 1980). Important means of generating strategic success in these children include facilitating their assessment of tasks' demands, increasing their recognition of what they do or not know about the strategies, and sensitizing their awareness of which learning strategy to use to match the demands of the task (Wong, 1985).

Feuerstein's instrumental enrichment approach has also offered some metacognitive direction for working with disorganized children. Believing that human cognitive development is modifiable at all ages and stages, Feuerstein's model first identifies and then remediates cognitive deficiencies through a formal instructional program (Feuerstein, 1979, 1980). Specific to the needs of the organizationally deficient child, training in aspects of the instrumental enrichment approach has been found, in preliminary studies, to increase organizational thinking and problem-solving ability (Messerer et al., 1984).

Although the study of organizational deficiencies in children is still young, some viable approaches to curtailing their effects are on the horizon. Perhaps with the passage of time and the recognition of their importance to success both in school and in life, a comprehensive body of knowledge will be generated that can address these difficulties with proven effectiveness on all planes.

SUMMARY

The child with an organizational deficit is indeed a disadvantaged learner. Frequently viewed as unmotivated or "lazy," these children have a learning disability that is both pervasive and yet elusive to those who seek reasons for performance failure. Ability and achievement test scores may even reveal adequate capacity for successful learning. It is the disorganized approach to that learning and to daily performance, however, that is too often overlooked, particularly in the older child or adolescent who has learned to mask or compensate for organizational problems.

The school psychologist is in a pivotal position to assist these children. Recognition of the telltale clues of organizational deficits revealed in academic and language assessment, psychological testing, and developmental and social history avails the school psychologist of rich confirmation data even if the physical-behavioral manifestations are obscured. Knowledge of the variables that can influence organizational ability provides direction for intervention, perhaps involving both teacher and family in consultation and support.

Assisting children with organizational deficits requires a comprehensive effort. In need of structure in all aspects of their lives, they demand conscious and deliberate management: boundaries need to be clearly projected, limits judiciously set, and priorities and alternatives simplified and reduced for them. Consciousness of routines, task analysis, time management, and classification skills needs to be facilitated. For disorganized children to distinguish the important from the unimportant, to identify the steps in relation to an entire task, and to sort and categorize information, they must depend on others to show them how to structure and interpret their world, until they are able to internalize this themselves.

The school psychologist who is aware of the needs of this group of children can help others to appreciate the difficulty these children have in coping with the myriad of organizational challenges that most persons take in stride. The problem is not one of lacking motivation necessarily, but rather of not knowing where to begin, what to do next, and what to put where. The world may seem unpredictable and confusing. Stress may unravel attempts to cope efficiently. Success may appear hopelessly remote or unattainable. The school psychologist who can gain empathy and understanding of the disorganized child has achieved an important step toward remediating the problem: that of reinstating the child's self-worth.

If in fact education's goal is to prepare its students for the real world, organization — so pervasively important to all aspects of life — needs to become a more central focus for educational study. School psychologists need to be aware of its impact, be able to identify a deficiency, and lend direct and indirect support to the children who suffer from its disabling effects. Teacher training programs need to incorporate methods which teach how to teach organization skills, as well as when and how to model them. Guides to getting organized and using organizational strategies for learning and daily "survival" need to be created and introduced into curriculum materials. More integrally, the judgment that early inducement toward academic learning may contribute to disorganization occasions a point of departure for justifying more development-conscious instruction.

REFERENCES

Acredolo, L. P. (1982). The familiarity factor in spatial research. In R. Cohen (Ed.), *Children's conceptions of spatial relationships.* San Francisco: Jossey-Bass.

Als, H. (1985). Patterns of infant behavior: Analogues of later organizational difficulties? In F. H. Duffy & N. Geschwind (Eds.), *A neuroscientific approach to clinical evaluation.* Boston: Little, Brown.

Beck, A. T. (1967). *Depression.* New York: Harper and Row.

Bender, L. (1966). The concept of plasticity in childhood schizophrenia. In L. Bender (Ed.), *Psychopathology of schizophrenia.* New York: Grune and Stratton. Cited by K. deHirsch and J. Jansky (1980), Patterning and organizational deficits, *Bulletin of the Orton Society, 30,* 227–239.

Caplan, G. (1969). Opportunities for school psychologists in the primary prevention of mental disorders in children. In A. J. Bindman & N. D. Spiegel (Eds.), *Perspectives in community mental health* (pp. 420–436). Chicago: Aldine.

Combs, A. W., & Snygg, D. (1959). *Individual behavior.* New York: Harper and Row.

Cort, R.H. (1980). *Effects of training on recall and use of organizational strategies by learning disabled and non-disabled youngsters.* Unpublished doctoral dissertation, Columbia University Teachers College, New York.

DeHirsch, K., & Jansky, J. (1980). Patterning and organizational deficits in children with language and learning disabilities. *Bulletin of the Orton Society, 30,* 227–239.

Elkind, D. (1986). Formal education and early childhood education: An essential difference. *Phi Delta Kappan, 67,* 631–636.

Ferrald, R. H., & Schamber, R. G. (1973). *ADAPT: A diagnostic and prescriptive technique, Handbook I.* Sioux Falls, SD: ADAPT Press.

Feuerstein, R. (1979). *The dynamic assessment of retarded performers.* Baltimore: University Park Press.

Feuerstein, R. (1980). *Instrumental enrichment: An intervention program for cognitive modifiability.* Baltimore: University Park Press.

Ginsburg, H. & Opper, S. (1969). *Piaget's theory of intellectual development.* Englewood Cliffs, NJ: Prentice-Hall.

Hall, C. S., & Lindzey, G. (1957). *Theories of personality.* New York: Wiley.

Hall, R. J. (1980). Information-processing skills of exceptional children. *Exceptional Education Quarterly, 1,* 9–15.

Haman, T. A., & Isaacson, D. K. (1985). Sharpening organization skills. *Academic Therapy, 21,* 45–50.

Kops, C., & Belmont, I. (1985). Planning and organizing skills of poor school achievers. *Journal of Learning Disabilities, 18,* 8–14.

Loper, A. B., & Murphy, D. M. (1985). Cognitive self-regulatory training for underachieving children. In D.L. Forrest-Pressley, G. E. Mackinnon, & T.G. Waller (Eds.), *Metacognition, cognition, and human performance,* (Vol. 2). Orlando, FL: Academic.

Messerer, J., Hunt, E., Meyers, G., & Lerner, J. (1984). Feuerstein's instrumental enrichment: A new approach for activating intellectual potential in learning disabled youth. *Journal of Learning Disabilities, 17,* 322–325.

Slade, D. L. (1986). Developing foundations for organizational skills. *Academic Therapy, 21,* 261–266.

Smith, S. L. (1979). *No easy answers: Teaching the learning disabled child.* Cambridge, MA: Winthrop.

Stern, D. N. (1985). *The interpersonal world of the infant.* New York: Basic Books.

Tomlinson-Keasey, C., Crawford, D. G., & Eisert, D.C. (1979). Organization facilities memory — if you have the appropriate classification skills. *Journal of Genetic Psychology, 134,* 3–13.

Torgesen, J. K. (1977). The role of nonspecific factors in the task performance of learning disabled children: A theoretical assessment. *Journal of Learning Disabilities, 10,* 33–40.

Viney, L. L., & Clarke, A. M. (1974). Children coping with crisis: An analogue study. *British Journal of Social and Clinical Psychology, 13,* 305–313.

Winston, S. (1978). *Getting organized.* New York: Warner Books.

Wong, B. Y. L. (1985). *Metacognition and learning disabilities.* In D. L. Forrest-Pressley, G. E. MacKinnon, & T. G. Waller, (Eds.), *Metacognition, cognition, and human performance* (Vol. 2). Orlando, FL: Academic.

BIBLIOGRAPHY: PROFESSIONALS

Ferrald, R. H., & Schamber, R. G. (1973). *ADAPT: A diagnostic and prescriptive technique, Handbook I.* Sioux Falls, SD: ADAPT Press.
This compendium of diagnostic and remedial suggestions represents a multidisciplinary approach to teaching exceptional children, focusing on psychosocial characteristics (of which disorganization is one) and skills of auditory, visual, and verbal expression. Its annotated bibliography of instructional materials is quite thorough, though undoubtedly outdated for 1986.

Smith, S. L. (1979). *No easy answers: Teaching the learning disabled child.* Cambridge, MA: Winthrop.
Provides a comprehensive everyday portrait of the disorganized learning-disabled child, describing many situations with which the reader can identify. Addressing learning disabilities problems in a realistic and practical way, it is perhaps the only in-depth descriptive resource on disorganized learners available. The appendices include extensive listings of reference books, journals, and films.

Wadsworth, F. J. (1978). *Piaget for the classroom teacher.* New York: Longman.
For the professional concerned with maintaining academic expectations at an appropriate developmental level for children, this book offers a clear and practical translation of Piagetian theory. It articulates theoretical foundations, assessment procedures, and teaching principles and practices that make it an excellent resource for both the psychologist and teacher.

Winston, S. (1978). *Getting organized.* New York: Warner Books.
Provides practical, action-oriented, step-by-step methods for physically organizing all aspects of personal living, including time management, setting up and reorganizing a desk, establishing a filing system, organizing storage, and facilitating children's personal organization. Although not educationally oriented, many of its principles and ideas can be generalized to the classroom setting.

BIBLIOGRAPHY: PARENTS

Smith, S. L. (1979). *No easy answers: Teaching the learning disabled child.* Cambridge, MA: Winthrop.
This detailed description of the disorganized child is so complete and untechnical that it is an excellent resource for parents who need and want to understand their learning-disabled child thoroughly. It addresses parents' feelings and concerns, and suggests practical methods of dealing with these children at home.

Winston, S. (1978). *Getting organized.* New York: Warner Books.
Provides practical, action-oriented, step-by-step methods for physically organizing all aspects of personal living, including time management, setting up and reorganizing a desk, establishing a filing system, organizing storage, and facilitating children's personal organization. Its value to parents lies in the organizational model that it can create and the structure within a household that it can help foster.

Children and Peer Relations

Kathryn Gerken
University of Texas at Dallas

BACKGROUND

> Friends do matter. Friends serve central functions for children that parents do not, and they play a crucial role in shaping children's social skills and their sense of identify. (Rubin, 1980, p. 12)

Psychologists such as Piaget and Sullivan proposed that peer relations were the source of critical characteristics such as sense of equality, interpersonal sensitivity, need for intimacy, and mutual understanding (Youniss, 1980). Duck, Miell, and Gaebler (1980) believe that for theoretical work and social policy all aspects of childhood friendships need to be seen as functionally related to personality development and individual growth.

Hartup (1983) reported that scientific interest in children's peer relations began with the investigations of the effects of social groups on human behavior. Between 1830 and 1930 systematic observation and sociometric methods were developed and became major tools for assessing peer relations. Yet, following World War II observational studies of children focused on family-oriented theories of aggression and dependency, and work on peer relations during the 1950s and 1960s languished. A surge of interest in peer relations appeared in the 1970s, and the literature of the 1970s and 1980s contains an abundance of descriptive studies, new techniques in observational recording and data reduction, examinations of special friendships, analysis of group structures, and new strategies for enhancing social skills (Hartup 1983).

Duck (1983) has suggested that children face two problems when developing friendships: (a) learning to relate in a way acceptable to peers or contemporaries in current circumstances, and (b) learning the skills of friendship that will be necessary for relationships in later life.

The definitions and expectations of friendships change with age and under different environmental and organizational emphases. Rubin (1980) stated that friendship, in the sense that it matters to us, is what a child makes it out to be. For the purposes of this chapter, *friends* will be viewed as voluntarily selected associates who form a primary group and whose roles change depending on age and situational variables: whereas *peers* will be viewed as a larger population, or secondary group, of voluntary or involuntary associates from which friends are usually chosen. *Collectives* are bands of children that range from two or three individuals to a dozen or more. Hartup (1983) held that a collective becomes a *group* when social interaction occurs regularly, there are shared values beyond those maintained by society at large, individual members have a sense of belonging, and a structure exists to support the attitudes members should have toward one another. *Cliques* are often viewed as one form of friendship groups. Table 1 provides an overview of processes that govern clique (or group) formation. Propinquity and similarity are major factors in group formation.

This chapter will review normal development in peer relations and friendships, problem areas, assessment of peer relations and friendships, and appropriate intervention.

DEVELOPMENT

The constructivist view of interpersonal relations, which is also called the interactionist view (Corsaro, 1985; Gottman, 1983; Youniss, 1980) is that children interpret, organize, and use information from the environment and in the process construct adult skills and knowledge. The child's perspectives are thought to be continually changing and are related to the child's level of cognitive development and the stable features in the child's life world. Children work out for themselves what social reactions are all about on the basis of their actual encounters with others. As children attempt to cooperate with one another they learn to appreciate the capabilities, desires, and values of others.

The behaviorist view is that adult caretakers are of primary importance in children's development of friendship, as children learn how to relate to others because of their reinforcement history. Both the behaviorist and the constructivist views recognize functional changes and age-related differences in the conceptions and develop-

TABLE 1

Processes Governing Clique Formations

Source	Description
Dyad	Clique evolves around close friendship between two individuals — friends of dyad are included
Single individual	Central figure has certain skills, talents, or resources valued by others. This figure often becomes the leader
Formal structure	Students in the group are homogeneous with respect to a particular characteristic
Informal group	Students who share a common interest form a group to engage in their preferred activity

Adopted from Hallinon (1980).

TABLE 2

Onset Grades for Increasing Friendship Expectations With Age

Onset Grade	Dimension
2	Friend as help-giver
2	Share common activities
3	Propinquity
3	Stimulation value
3	Organized play
3	Demographic similarity
3	Evaluation
4	Acceptance
4	Admiration
4	Increasing prior interaction
5	Loyalty and commitment
6	Genuineness
6	Friend as receiver of help
7	Intimacy potential
7	Common interests
7	Similarity in attitudes and values

Adapted from Bigelow and La Gaipa (1975) and Bigelow (1977).

ment of friendship and peer groups (Bigelow & La Gaipa 1975, 1980; Corsaro, 1985; Hartup, 1983; Selman, 1980; Youniss, 1980).

Table 2 illustrates the developmental differences in friendship expectations that Bigelow and La Gaipa (1975, 1980) and Bigelow (1977) found and confirmed through interviews with children and adolescents. Bigelow and La Gaipa (1980) do not believe that the social skills needed to maintain a friendship can be explained solely in terms of cognitive development.

This general developmental pattern of child–child interactions goes from simple "interacts" to more complex and coordinated interactions and from the primitive awareness of the needs of others to reciprocities based on complex attributions and utilization of multiple sources of information (Hartup, 1983). By adolescence the amount of time spent with peers exceeds the time with other socialization agents.

Cooperation and intimacy emerge in childhood and adolescence, but personal support is especially strong in adolescence. Similarities in demographic characteristics are strong determinants of friendship selection, yet behavioral similarities determine selection and socialization outcomes among adolescents.

Table 3 provides a brief overview of major changes in peer relations from infancy to adolescence. If these changes normally occur, what happens to prevent children from having positive peer relations?

Factors Affecting Development

Cross-Age Peer Relations and Friendships. Observations have confirmed that the age differences existing between children may affect the quality and quantity of their interactions even when they are well acquainted (Hartup, 1983). Young children appear to enjoy and accommodate successfully to the demands of cross-age interaction, and older children in such situations console, entertain, and help care for younger classmates. Children with younger siblings tend to be more helpful and nurturant than children without.

Cross-age friendships can have a negative side too. Bullying of younger peers can appear as well as rejection by own peers. It is important to have the opportunities to make friends across age lines, but an exclusive preference for older or younger friends could be a "danger" signal. Hartup (1983) believes that both same- and mixed-age socializations contain constructive challenges for individual children.

Cross-Sex Peer Relations and Friendships. From the age of 3 years, children interact more frequently with members of their own sex and express verbal preference for them. Rejection of the opposite sex occurs and avoidance of the opposite-sex peer is salient feature of the social organization in middle childhood. Friendships between males and females may have beneficial and satisfying consequences, but there are serious barriers to opposite-sex friendships (Newman, 1982).

Cross-Race Peer Relations and Friendships. Hartup's (1983) review of race and social interaction reveals that in mixed-race situations, same-race contacts are more frequent than cross-race contacts. This occurs from preschool years through early adolescence. Same-race sociometric choices are also more common than other-race nominations. The race cleavage becomes even more pervasive as children grow older, and it is more evident in friendship choices than in acquaintance or work choices. Negative attitudes toward other-race children is

TABLE 3

Patterns of Normal Development in Peer Relations

Time Period	Observed Behaviors	Comments
First year	Look at each other Touch and reach Coordinated social acts Social contacts are relatively infrequent Reciprocation of actons are rare	The appearance of these social elements parallel an infant's reactions to the mother and to inanimate objects
Second year	Amount and complexity of interaction increases Positive and negative affect becomes more evident in the interactions	Observation of infants and toddlers occurred in home or "lab" setting
Preschool years (age 3–5 years)	Frequency of positive and negative social interaction increases Dyadic situations occur more often among 5-year-olds than 3-year-olds Studies of the 1930s suggested that play progresses from parallel play to associative play to cooperative play Recent studies reveal that preschool children still spend considerable amounts of time by themselves or in noninteractive contact with other children Utilization of more sophisticated social skills occurs Some cliques are formed There is a discrepancy in social cognition studies (interviews) vs. observational studies on who is a friend Preschoolers frequently ignore, exclude, and desert each other Level of aggression (beyond exclusionary behavior) in preschool setting is low Increase in verbal behaviors and in fantasy play Overall increase in contacts with peers	Observation occurred most frequently in daycare and preschool setting
Middle childhood (age 6–12 years)	Recognition of differences in peers Increase in effectiveness of communication skills Decrease in overall aggression	
Early adolescence	Highest level of conformity appears in the 11- to 13-year age range — gradual decrease in susceptibility to group pressure from then on Unisexual cliques	
Adolescence	Conformity affected by status in peer group and by self-blame Adolescents seek friends who share their values and understand their questions	

Sources: Adcock and Sergal (1983); Coleman (1980); Hartup (1983); Hodapp and Miller (1982); Howes (1983); Newman 1982).

also present in early childhood, especially among the majority children.

An extensive review of the literature on interracial acceptance in the classroom (Carter, Detine-Carter, & Benson, 1980) revealed that white children preferred white children and that in earlier studies black children also preferred white children. Variables such as the number of years in integrated schools, the black–white ratios in the classroom, the grade, the age of children, the school, and the teachers' attitudes all influence interracial peer acceptance. Athletic ability also influences interracial acceptance, especially among boys. Regardless of race, reciprocity governs children's friendships. Hallinan and Smith (1984) have reported that both black and white students choose friends who are similar to themselves in gender and age and who choose them as a friend.

Setting Conditions and Peer Relations and Friendships. Certain setting conditions affect child–child interactions differently than others, yet all aspects of the setting (space, toys, materials, group size, familiarity of setting, presence of adults) need to be considered in order to understand differences in interactions. For example, it has been found that the presence of toys change the nature of interactions, considerable literature suggests ideal sizes for child care facilities and elementary classrooms. Although the literature on setting conditions present conflicting results, attention to these conditions is mandatory (Hartup, 1983). Conditions within single classroom as well as within the entire school influence students' social relationships. Therefore, concern with the impact of the school setting is justified (Busch-Rossnagal and Vance, 1982; Epstein & Karweit, 1983).

PUTTING PEER RELATIONS IN PERSPECTIVE

Peer Acceptance and Rejection

Terms such as likable, popular, unpopular, friendly, rejected, and neglected are used to describe children's sociometric status. Status is conceived as the extent to which a child is sought by others for association. Children are judged to be popular by the number of choices they receive; friendliness is measured by the choices the children make; friendships are measured by the mutual choices; rejection is measured by negative choices; neglected children are not noticed and receive few positive or negative choices.

Berndt's (1983) conclusions regarding individual differences in sociometric status indicate that (a) children are liked and become popular when they are cooperative and friendly in their interactions, and are disliked and rejected when they are aggressive or disruptive in their peer interactions; (b) children are neither liked nor disliked when they rarely interact with peers; (c) rejected and neglected children are often unsuccessful when they try to join a group of peers already engaged in an interaction; (d) the social environment influences the distribution of sociometric status; and (5) children's sociometric status may be increased following social skills training.

Correlates of Peer Acceptance and Rejection. Few experimental and/or longitudinal studies have been conducted to determine the causes of acceptance or rejection. Most of the research has focused on what makes a person initially attractive to another such as physical attractiveness, nonverbal behaviors, and personality characteristics (Duck, Miell, & Gaebler, 1980; Zakin, 1983). There is limited information about the connection between popularity and social–cognitive skills or about friendship formation after initial attraction.

What is clear from Hartup's (1983) literature review is that friendly, prosocial, and competent social behaviors predict social acceptance, and devious, aversive reactions to others increases one's chances of social rejection. Intelligence and academic and athletic achievement contribute significantly to the variance in social status. Children are also at a social advantage if they possess an attractive face and body, are a later-born child in a middle-class or upper-class family, have an ordinary in contrast to an "offbeat" name and do not have any physical, emotional, or learning disabilities.

Peer Relations and the Socialization of the Individual Child

There is little doubt that children exert powerful influences over one another. There has been massive evidence to indicate the importance of friendship in delinquency, but disagreement as to the nature of the influence that having friends, or lacking friends, has on individuals' delinquent activities. It appears that social clusters in adolescence may result partly from self-selection. Friendship networks may dispose an individual adolescent toward more adult forms of crime and may maintain criminal behavior through the adolescent period; however, such associations may not be prognostic indicators of delinquency in early and middle childhood. Hartup (1983) maintained that delinquency among adolescents and young adults can be predicted mainly from one dimension of early peer relations — "not getting along with others" (p. 165). Yet there are delinquents who are highly social individuals with strong positive bonds to their friends and other delinquents who are "loners," incapable of forming lasting affectional bonds with others.

Hartup (1983) suggests that criminal behavior emerges developmentally from disturbed family relations, followed by troubled peer relations, and finally by exposure to delinquent norms. If failure to form effective social relationships within the family disposes the individual child to trouble in peer relations, it follows that these difficulties would contribute to further lowering of self-esteem, more alienation, and less social effectiveness, which may increase the motivation to seek self-enhancement outside the core culture.

Correlational data clearly show that peer difficulties and antisocial behavior are associated with conduct and affective disorders. Evidence of poor peer relations is embedded in the life histories of individuals who are "at risk" for emotional and behavioral disturbance. Yet childhood indicators of adult maladjustment include many other variables, and the poor peer relationships may simply reflect general difficulties in life course development. Findings on the relationship between the family and peer culture can be summarized succinctly:

> (a) Secure family relations are the basis for entry into the peer system and success within it. (b) Family breakdown interferes with adaptation to the peer culture. (c) Parent and peer values are mainly concordant, especially on issues "that matter." (d) Normative opposition is more acute in early adolescence; the most intense oppositional experience surrounds antisocial behavior. (e) Most adolescents remain attuned to parental norms. (f) Dissonance may be considerable when adolescents are alienated from their parents and associate with agemates who endorse misconduct. (g) The majority of

adolescents are able to synthesize their understandings and expectations of their families and their peers. (Hartup, 1983, p. 172)

ALTERNATIVE ACTIONS

There is no doubt that poor peer relations are involved in the etiology of a variety of emotional and social maladjustments (Hartup, 1983, Michelson, Sugai, Wood, & Kazden, 1983). Thus, it is of major import to identify those children who have poor peer relations and attempt to provide appropriate intervention.

Assessment

Dodge (1985) has suggested that there are major aspects of social competence that must be assessed if relevant intervention is to be conducted. One must consider the unconscious influences (goals, set, format), the problematic tasks (entry into groups, etc.), the processing of social information (encoding, interpretation, response search, response evaluation, enactment, and self-monitoring), the behaviors displayed (list of behaviors), and the evaluations of others (parent and teacher ratings, peer status). He believes that an aggregated assessment of all five areas will lead to strong prediction of actual social success and ratings of competence by peers. Figure 1 is a concrete example of this assessment scheme.

Hops and Finch (1985) believe that assessment of social competence must include consideration of the factors that may contribute to a child's difficulties in peer relations. They suggest that one assess the specific social skills needed to establish and maintain social contact, the language skills that form the essential prerequisites of effective social communication, the physical or motor skills that allow children to more effectively explore the world of objects with their peers, and the parents' child-rearing skills that provide the child with the socially adaptive behaviors needed for entering and adapting to social situations.

Both the assessment of children's peer relations and intervention to change those relations need to be individualized and contextually relevant in order to be most effective.

Sociometric evaluations, which are defined as measures of personal attraction among members of a specified group, (Hymel, 1983) have been used extensively to identify "popular," "rejected," and "neglected" children. Hymel (1983) reviewed the use of nomination measures, paired-comparison measures, and rating scale measures when assessing preschoolers' peer relations. The review revealed that any type of sociometric data obtained for children younger than 4 years of age may be questionable as to reliability, concurrent and predictive validity, and utility of the measures. For children older than 4, there was clear support for the use of rating scales over the use of the other techniques.

A major disadvantage of rating scale measures is that they do not distinguish isolated and rejected chilren and cannot assess a child's visibility among peers. Hymel (1983) offered a note of caution about the overall usefulness of sociometric measures, as they do not provide data as to the cause of peer judgments. In fact, Asher (1983) points out that neither sociometric data nor behavioral observation have provided us with the reasons for the acceptance of "social errors" committed by some children and not others. He suggests that peers' perception of the intentions of other children may influence the way the behavior is viewed. No assessment instrument is available to accurately assess those perceptions. Hymel and Franke (1985) stress the importance of also obtaining children's self-perceptions. Children who exhibit similar patterns of social behavior may perceive and interpret their social situations differently. The data available currently support ratings by others and naturalistic observation as the most appropriate techniques for assessing social skills (Gresham & Elliott, 1984; Hymel, 1983). There is a need for multimethod assessment of social skills whether one is assessing for identification or intervention.

Intervention

Parents influence their children's peer relations (Lewis, 1984; Rubin & Sloman, 1984) and often need to be involved in the intervention process. Parents set the stage for peer relations by choosing a neighborhood, school, and adult associates, and by arranging social contacts, coaching, and providing models of social relationships and a home base. There are times when parents must step in to remove a child from a negative friendship or group, but usually they are needed to help children understand friendship and peer breakups and separations. Rubin (1980) suggests that parents may take these experiences too lightly and not provide security and support.

Gurian and Formanek (1983) have provided many suggestions for parents to help their children develop satisfactory peer relationships from early childhood through adolescence, with specific suggestions for "troubled" times (moving, divorce, friendship decay). Stocking, Arezzo, and Leavitt (1980) provided specific guidelines for parents to teach social skills deemed important for entry into a group, and to teach children to act positivly toward others, resolve conflicts, and be sensitive and empathetic. Cartledge and Milburn (1980) emphasized the need to individualize the selection of skills to be taught and to task-analyze the desired social behavior into subcomponents. Discussions based on a variety of materials, grouping, using humor and fun, and setting expectations are all techniques they use to effect change. They also made suggestions for a cognitive approach to either altering self-statements or developing problem-solving skills. Both Cartledge and Milburn (1980) and Sobol and Earn (1985) have stressed the importance of using age-appropriate techniques.

The preponderance of intervention literature has dealt not with friendships, but with training in insufficiently developed skills and changing general social behavior with peers. The assumptions have been that children with poor peer relations lack social skills, that children can learn social skills from social skills training, and the skills thus learned lead to improved peer rela-

FIGURE 1

Illustration of the Assessment Scheme of Dodge (1985)

Unconscious Influences

"Shy Sarah" views herself as clumsy. She has never been "welcomed" into a group, but wants to belong. (goals, set, format)

Problematic Task

"Shy Sarah" wants to play with others. (entry into dyad)

Processing of Social Information

"Shy Sarah" approaches 2 children and sees them whispering. (encoding)

She decides the children are whispering about her. (interpretation)

She thinks about what she should do. (response search)

She thinks about the very best thing for her to do. (response evaluation)

She turns to run away from the children and falls down. (enactment)

Sarah believes that she is unattractive and clumsy. (self-monitoring)

Behaviors Displayed

"Shy Sarah" ran away.

The two children watch Sarah run away.

Evaluation by Others

The children say Sarah is not any fun.

Sarah's teacher says she is shy.

Sarah's parents say Sarah will never have friends unless she talks to other children.

---

tions (Ladd, 1985). The deficit model contains these steps: define the behaviors to be taught, assess the level of competency, teach the behaviors that are found to be lacking, evaluate, reassess, practice, and generalize to new situations. Furman (1984) has discussed subject-oriented interventions such as reinforcement, modeling, and social–cognitive approaches as well as peer and environmental-oriented interventions such as reinforcement of peers, cooperative interactions, mixed-age socialization, and play material. An integrative approach to intervention may be more effective than either subject-oriented or peer-oriented approaches alone.

Several authors have described their approaches to social skills training (SST) (Argyle, 1985; Asher, 1985; Michelson, Sugai, Wood, & Kazden, 1983) and some of the problems they encountered. Argyle (1985) suggests that SST be augmented by training students to send nonverbal signals, to perceive nonverbal signals, to be able to use conversational sequences, to assume the role of others, to present self (positive appearance and voice), to focus on situations, and to focus on relationships.

Michelson et al. (1983) have provided detailed training modules that have been supported by research. They suggest that the following procedures be used in order to promote generalization: Teach behaviors that will be rewareded or reinforced in the natural environment; teach a variety of responses; train loosely under varied conditions; train across many persons and settings; fade the training consequences; reinforce accurate self-reports of performance; train the ability to generalize by reinforcing new appropriate applications; use peers; and focus on approach or cognitive style of child. Training appears to be most effective when the trainees are younger children, when there has been a multifaceted approach and practice outside the training sessions, and when persons who can support the new skills are incorporated into the training (Asher, 1985; Michelson et al. (1983); Schneider & Byrne, 1985; Strain, 1985).

Evaluations of the effectiveness of social problem-solving programs are mixed (Weissberg, 1985), but at a minimum the professional needs to structure the program to fit the realities of the school or other setting in respect to time, space, materials, and methods for training trainers.

Intervention in the School. The organization of schools and classrooms limits or extends students' contacts and the potential selection of friends, through the assignments made, the procedures for classwork, and the opportunities for interaction that occur before, during, and after the academic program. Miller (1983) has maintained that the procedures in some schools promote racial intolerance, disrespect, and rejection, rather than promoting positive across-race relations. He emphasized the need to incorporate cooperative goal structures into class and school activities and to directly involve the children in the process. School personnel need to recognize their power to determine patterns of peer interaction and friendship choice. Rewards can be built into classroom organizations for inclusiveness rather than exclusiveness, and for cooperative and tolerant behavior rather than competition and intolerance. The decision to use or not use peer groups in the classroom should be based on the teacher's knowledge of organizational structure and group processes and on the desired outcomes of educational activity. School policies regarding new students, new populations, and new programs will influence the successful entrance of students.

There are two major types of peer relationship interventions that occur in the schools: friendship therapy or coaching and organizational reform. Coaching strategies fit the skills deficit model. It is necessary to accurately identify the students and provide training that will not decrease their self-esteem. Most coaching studies have shown only short-term results. The social organization reform model requires that the classroom be managed as a social system. The leader/teacher needs to be aware of the goals for the group and individuals and find ways to use the classroom structure to obtain the goals. The students must be given important common tasks to complete that will require that the students work together and recognize the contributions, talents, and powers of others. The teacher needs to insure the likelihood of success and rewards for all participants. Peer tutoring has been viewed as both a coaching and social reform technique. The social reform model is based on differential assets rather than deficits. There are also student-oriented interventions, such as organized clubs, in which social skills are developed. The best intervention would utilize an integrated approach.

SUMMARY

There is a need to look at peer interactions across time and across settings and to use more than one method to measure relationships. The environments in which peer interactions occur, and the ages and developmental stages of students, affect peer relations and patterns of selection and influence. Nonbehavioral and behavioral correlates of peer acceptance and rejection have been identified, but the majority of intervention programs have dealt with behavioral correlates. It has been assumed that if these behaviors change, peer relations wil also change. However, the psychologist must not forget the power of the nonbehavioral correlates: Even minor changes in appearance, name, and setting have had positive results in affecting initial interactions.

The positive and negative influences of friendship must be recognized and dealt with. Too much emphasis on friendship can result in rejection, sterotyping, cruelty, jealousy, and resentment if the desired friends are not obtained, and some students may learn negative behaviors in order to keep friends. Schools and other environments need to provide opportunities for both unique personal development and for conforming, cooperative effort.

In the area of peer relations there has been an overabundance of peer status data gathered but not enough information about causes of the phenomona these data reflect. There have not been systematic investigations of the impact of specific assessment techniques and intervention techniques across ages. Tactics for intervention have been written about extensively, but the content of instruction remains a major unresolved issue. The search continues for the critical link between children's cognitive development, family relations, school organization, instructional techniques, and social behavior. School psychologists needs to make sure that they have investigated each of these areas before attempting to help a student improve peer relations and friendships.

REFERENCES

Adcock, D., & Segal, M. (1983). *Making friends.* Englewood Cliffs, NJ: Prentice-Hall.

Argyle, M. (1985). Social behavior problems and social skills training in adolescence. In B. H. Schneider, K. H. Rubin, & J. E. Ledingham (Eds.), *Children's peer relations: Issues in assessment and intervention.* New York: Springer-Verlag.

Asher, S. R. (1983). Social competence and peer status: Recent advances and future directions. *Child Development, 54,* 1427–1434.

Asher, S. R. (1985). An evolving paradigm in social skill training research with children. In B. H. Schneider, K. H. Rubin, & J. E. Ledingham (Eds.), *Children's peer relations: Issues in assessment and intervention.* New York: Springer-Verlag.

Berndt, T. J. (1983). Correlates and causes of sociometric status in childhood: A commentary on six current studies of popular, rejected, and neglected children. *Merrill-Palmer Quarterly, 29*(4), 439–448.

Bigelow, B. J. (1977). Children's friendship expectations: A cognitive–developmental study. *Child Development, 48*(1), 246–253.

Bigelow, B. J., and La Gaipa, J. J. (1975). Children's written descriptions of friendship; A multidimensional analysis. *Developmental Psychology, 11*(6), 857–858.

Bigelow, B. J., & La Gaipa, J. J. (1980). The development of friendship values and choice. In H. C. Foot, A. J. Chapman, & J. R. Smith (Eds.), *Friendship and social relations in children.* Chichester, England: Wiley.

Busch-Rossnagel, N. A., & Vance, A. K. (1982). The impact of the schools on social and emotional development. In B. B. Wolman (Ed.), *Handbook of developmental psychology* Chapter 25,pp. 452–467. Englewood Cliffs, NJ: Prentice-Hall.

Carter, D. E., Detine-Carter, S. L. & Benson, F. W. (1980). Interracial acceptance in the classroom. In H. C. Foot, A. J. Chapman, & J. R. Smith (Eds.), *Friendship and social relations in children.* Chichester, England: Wiley.

Cartledge, G., & Milburn, J. F. (Eds.). (1980). *Teaching social skills to children.* New York: Pergamon.

Coleman, J. C. (1980). Friendship and peer groupin adolescence. In J. Adelson (Ed.), *Handbook of adolescent psychology* (Chapter 12, p. 431). New York: Wiley.

Corsaro, W. A. (1985). *Friendship and peer culture in the early years.* Norwood, NJ: Ablex.

Dodge, K. A., & Richard, B. A. (1985). Peer perceptions, aggresion and the development of peer relations. In J. B. Pryor and J. D. Day (Eds.), *The development of social cognition.* New York: Springer-Verlag.

Duck, S., Miell, D. K., & Gaebler, H. C. (1980). Attraction and communication in children's interactions. In H. C. Foot, A. J. Chapman, & J. R. Smith (Eds.), *Friendship and social relations in children.* Chichester, England: Wiley.

Epstein, J. L., & Karweit, N. (Eds.). (1983). *Friends in school. Patterns of selection and influence in secondary schools.* New York: Academic.¢

Furman, W. (1984). Enhancing children's peer relations and friendships. In S. Duck (Ed.), *Personal relationships: Repairing personal relationships.* New York: Academic.

Gottman, J. M. (1983). How children become friends. *Monographs of the Society for Research in Child Development, 48*(3, Serial No. 201).

Gresham, F. M., & Elliott, S. N. (1984). Assessment and classification of children's social skills: A review of methods and issues. *School Psychology Review, 13*(3), 292–301.

Gurian, A., & Formanek, R. (1983). *The socially competent child.* Boston: Houghton Mifflin.

Hallinan, M. T. (1980). Patterns of cliquing among youth. In H. C. Foot, A. J. Chapman, & J. R. Smith (Eds.), *Friendship and social relations in children.* Chichester, England: Wiley.

Hallinan, M. T., & Smith, S. S. (1984). Students' same-race and cross-race friendships. *Advances in Group Processes* Vol. 1, 229–255.

Hartup, W. W. (1983). Peer relations. In P. H. Mussen (Series Ed.), E. M. Heatherington (Vol. Ed.), *Handbook of child psychology: Vol. 4, Socialization, personality, and social development* (chap. 2, pp. 102–196). New York: Wiley.

Hodapp, R. M., & Mueller, E. (1982). Early social development. In B. B. Wolman (Ed.), *Handbook of developmental psychology* (chap. 16, pp. 284–300. Englewood Cliffs, NJ: Prentice-Hall.

Hops, H., & Finch, M. (1985). Social competence and skill: A reassessmenht. In B. H. Schneider, K. H. Rubin, J. E. Ledingham (Eds.), *Children's peer relations: Issues to assessment and intervention.* New York: Springer-Verlag.

Howes, C. (1983). Patterns of friendship. Child Development, 54, 1041–1053.

Hymel, S. (1983). Preschool children's peer relations: Issues in sociometric assessment. *Merrill-Palmer Quarterly, 29*(3), 237–260.

Hymel, S., & Franke, S. (1985). Children's peer relations: Assessing self-perceptions. In B. H. Schneider, K. H. Rubin & J. E. Ledingham (Eds.), *Children's peer relations: Issues in assessment and intervention.* New York: Springer-Verlag.

Ladd, G. W. (1985). Documenting the effects of social skill training with children's process and outcome assessment. In B. H. Schneider, K. H. Rubin, & J. E. Ledingham (Eds.), *Children's peer relations: Issues in assessment and intervention.* New York: Springer-Verlag.

Lewis, M. (Ed). (1984). *Beyond the dyad.* New York: Plenum.

Michelson, L., Sugai, D. P., Wood, R. P., & Kazdin, A. E. (1983). *Social skills assessment and training with children.* New York: Plenum.

Miller, N. (1983). Peer relations in desegregated schools. In J. L. Epstein & N. Karweit (Eds.), *Friends in school* (chap. 12, pp. 201–217). New York: Academic.

Newman, P. R. (1982). The peer group. In B. B. Wolman (Ed.), *Handbook of developmental psychology* (chap. 29, pp. 526–536). Englewood Cliffs, NJ: Prentice-Hall.

Rubin, Z. (1980). *Children's friendships.* Cambridge, MA: Harvard University Press.

Rubin, Z., & Sloman, J. (1984). How parents influence their children's friendships. In M. Lewis (Ed.), *Beyond the dyad* (chap. 10, pp. 223–250). New York: Plenum.

Schneider, B. H., & Byrne, B. M. (1985). Children's social skills training: A meta-analysis. In B. H. Schneider, K. H. Rubin, & J. E. Ledingham (Eds.), *Children's peer relations: Issues in assessment and intervention.* New York: Springer-Verlag.

Selman, R. L. (1980). *the growth of interpersonal understanding: Developmental and clinical analyses.* New York: Academic.

Sobol, M. P., & Earn, B. M. (1985). Assessment of children's attributions for social experience. Implications for social skills training. In B. H. Schneider, K. H. Rubin, & J. E. Ledingham (Eds.), *Children's peer relations: Issues in assessment and intervention.* New York: Springer-Verlag.

Stocking, S. H., Arezzo,D., & Leavitt, S. (1980). *Helping kids make friends.* Allen, TX: Argus Communications.

Strain, P. S. (1985). Programmatic research on peers as intervention agents for socially isolated classmates. In B. H. Schneider, K. H. Rubin, & J. E. Ledingham (Eds.), *Children's peer relations: Issues in assessment and intervention.* New York: Springer-Verlag.

Weissberg, R. P. (1985). Designing effective social problem-solving programs for the classroom. In B. H. Schneider, K. H. Rubin, & J. E. Ledingham (Eds.), *Children's peer relations: Issues in assessment and intervention.* New York: Springer-Verlag.

Youniss, J. (1980). *Parents and peers in social development.* Chicago: University of Chicago Press.

Zakin, D. F. (1983). Physical attractiveness, sociability, athletic ability, and children's preference for their peers. *Journal of Psychology, 115,* 117–122.

BIBLIOGRAPHY: PROFESSIONALS

Epstein, J. L., & Karweit, N. (Eds.). (1983). *Friends in school. Patterns of selections and influence in secondary schools.* New York: Academic.
Deals specifically with the school as a social organization in which peer relations occur. It offers practical guidelines for intevention.

Foot, H. C., Chapman, A. J., & Smith, J. R. (Eds.). (1980). *Friendship and social relations in children.* Chichester, England: Wiley.
Each chapter provides an excellent reveiw of a particular aspect of friendships and/or peer relations.

Hartup, W. W. (1983). Peer relations. In D. H. Mussen (Series Ed.), E. M. Heatherington (Vol. Ed.), *Handbook of child psychology: Vol. 4. Socialization, personality, and social development* (chap. 2, pp. 103–196). New York: Wiley.
An extensive review of the peer relations literature is provided. This chapter should serve as a valuable resource until the next *Handbook of Child Psychology* is published.

Michelson, L., Sugai, D. P., Wood, R. P., & Kazdin, A. E. (1983). *Social skills assessment and training with children.* New York: Plenum.
The purpose of this book is to provide readers with knowledge regarding social skills assessment and training so that the reader can implement and evaluate social skills training. It contains 16 detailed training modules and appendices with assessment instruments and films (parts appropriate for parents).

Schneider, B. H., Rubin, K. H., & Ledingham, J. E. (Eds.). (1985). *Children's peer relations: Issues in assessment and intervention.* New York: Springer-Verlag.
Excellent and current compilation of research findings on assessment and intervention in peer relations. Basic assumptions are challenged, and new issues are raised.

Children and the Perception of Time

Robert J. Cattoche
Bethel School District, Eugene, Oregon

BACKGROUND

Time pervades all aspects of children's lives. Children must adapt to the cycles of day and night, respond to the rhythms of physiological needs, and follow the clock-driven schedules and demands of parents and teachers. But young children's perception of time is subjective, rooted in concrete actions and in the specific events of the day. At age 8 most children learn clock time, but they have difficulty grasping the adult concept of objective time. An abstract notion of time as continuous, linear, and measured by equal intervals does not develop until adolescence (Fraisse, 1963).

The abstract nature of time makes it difficult to define. Impalpable and invisible, time can neither be directly perceived nor directly measured. Time is experienced as a perception of changes, consisting of duration and succession (Fraisse, 1963). Succession is the ordering of events, whereas duration is the period between events or changes.

Piaget (1969) initiated the most systematic and empirical studies of the acquisition and development of children's concepts of duration and succession. Piaget's research postulated that children's concepts of time emerge as cognitive constructions, transformed through experience and action.

Although normal development of time perception in children has been well researched, fewer studies are available concerning disorders in time perception. Anecdotal accounts and observations of learning-disabled (LD) children and adolescents include descriptions of their difficulty in meeting time limits and schedules and their delay in acquiring time concepts (Smith, 1979). Hyperactivity is associated with an impairment in time estimation and time orientation (Walker, 1982; Goldman & Everett, 1985). Delinquent and culturally different adolescents develop a significantly different future time perspective, a different expectation of achievement and success in the future. Future time perspective is also affected by social class, age, and sex (Cottle, Howard, & Pleck, 1969).

Through the development of language, children incorporate temporal vocabulary and concepts into their cognitive systems and begin to relate these concepts to their daily activities and lives. A language-disordered child who lacks the subtleties and complexities of the language of time may experience disorientation in time and confusion with daily routines and schedules.

DEVELOPMENT

Developmental Psychology of Jean Piaget

According to Piaget (1969), the development of a child's concept of time begins as an infant's awareness of the before and after sequence of the events of feeding. During the sensorimotor period extending from birth to the age of 2, a child develops an understanding of the sequence of events and the duration of time intervals. Memory makes possible internal representations of external events and the anticipation of future events, thus establishing the rudimentary concepts of temporal relations.

In the preoperational period, lasting until the age of 7 or 8, children's ideas of time are not separated from the concepts of distance and velocity. Children use distances and speed to measure the passage of time. For example, a preoperational child's observation of two toy trains having the same starting point and traveling on unequal lengths of track would result in a unique conclusion when the trains arrive simultaneously at the ending point. Although the train moving along the longer track would have to travel faster to reach the ending point, the child would comment that neither train traveled faster, because both trains took the same amount of time.

Children in the preoperational stage perceive the objective passage of time as dependent on the activities in which they are involved. Preoperational children actually perceive the hands of a clock moving more quickly or slowly depending on whether they are engaged in slow or rapid activities. Because of their egocentric view of external events, objective time is not understood as a constant flow. During this period of development, children also have difficulty coordinating age and date of birth. They can know which of two persons is the younger or the older but remain unable to determine who was born first. A preoperational child confuses age with height: Once a person has stopped growing, they have stopped aging. This can be attributed to the child's focusing on the single characteristic of height.

It is only through the coordination of duration and sequence that the child at the concrete-operational level, at the age of 7 or 8 years, understands the notion of clock and calendar time. Throughout this stage of development, the child's conception of time is practical and workable, but it lacks the sense of personal and historical time. This abstract notion of time does not occur until adolescence, when formal-operational thought appears. At the formal-operational level of cognitive development, the adolescent is able to use logic and reason to consider various possibilities and solutions to hypothetical problems. The adolescent attempts to integrate past, present, and future into a personally meaningful time perspective (Gorman & Wessman, 1977).

The development of these stages is related to intelligence. Children classified as mentally retarded acquire these concepts at a much later age than children with average intelligence, but these stages occur generally in the same sequence (Wallace & Rabin, 1960; Lovell & Slater, 1960).

Development of Language

Through language, children communicate their thoughts, information, and feelings to influence the actions of others. Children use language in their internal thinking and respond and react to inner speech and ideas (Gorman & Wessman, 1977). As language develops, a child begins to amass a large vocabulary of temporal words, and acquires temporal concepts needed to order and coordinate activities in reference to past, present, and future.

Ames (1946) systematically studied and charted children's verbalizations of time concepts. Children tell the time of the occurrence of an event in relation to a specific activity before they can give the actual clock time. Use of specific-time words, which refer to specific contexts, precedes use of generalized time words. For example, the term, "this day" appears long before the term, "every day." Expressions of duration appear after age 3, when children begin to use phrases such as "for two weeks" or "all day."

Ames observed that complete mastery of a time concept is acquired gradually in three stages. In the first stage, children are able to respond suitably to a temporal expression, in the second stage they can use the term in spontaneous conversation, and finally they can correctly answer questions related to a time concept.

In a review of children's development of language, Harner (1982) noted that very young children talk first about specific needs and experiences. They live very much in the present and have little awareness of the past or of the future. During the acquisition of time words, verbs usually come before adverbs. Use of the present tense in conversation precedes use of either past or future verbs, and the initial use of the past and future verbs varies with individual children. After children learn temporal adverbs such as *now, later,* and *yesterday,* they may experience difficulty in combining the correct time reference for both adverb and verb, as revealed in the statement "I will go yesterday."

The terms *before* and *after* can have either a spatial or temporal reference that shifts depending on the context of their expression. These terms are found early in children's speech, *after* preceding *before* (Ames, 1946), but their full meanings are not comprehended until later. By the age of 5 children have acquired a large time vocabulary, and at this age they are usually able to produce time words on appropriate occasions (Harner, 1982).

In his comprehensive book, *The Psychology of Time,* Paul Fraisse (1963) summarized the ages at which children are thought to acquire the more important time concepts:

TABLE 1
Ages at Which Children Acquire Certain Time Concepts

Time concept	*Age (years)*
Recognize special day of week	4
State whether it is morning or afternoon	5
Correctly use the words *yesterday* and *tomorrow*	5
Indicate day of week	6
Indicate month	7
Indicate season	7–8
Indicate year	8
Indicate day of month	8–9
Estimate duration of conversation, duration since the holidays, and duration until the holidays	12
Give the time within 20 min.	12

Note: From *The Psychology of Time* (p. 188) by P. Fraisse, 1963, New York: Harper and Row. Copyright 1963 by Harper and Row. Reprinted by permission.

Disorders in the Concepts of Time

The mechanism that regulates temporal perception is not well understood, and the search for an internal clock in the brain has produced few results (Gorman & Wessman, 1977). Ornstein (1969) presented the argument that time perception, rather than having a specific biological location, is the result of cognitive processes. According to Ornstein, individual differences in time perception can be best understood in terms of information processing and of memory.

Research with brain-injured adults would seem to support the position that no specifically localized time organ exists in the brain. Benton (1968) found that patients who had sustained damage to the bilateral frontal lobes of the brain experienced a greater degree of temporal disorientation than those with unilateral damage. Benton also observed that the bilaterally injured patients showed more concrete and less abstract thinking compared to the unilaterally injured patients, suggesting that time perception is related to cognition.

In a study of affective disorders and time perception, Tysk (1984) found that depressed and manic adult patients misjudged the estimation of time intervals. Schizophrenic adult patients demonstrate significant impairment in their ability to estimate time (Densen, 1984), and exhibit a high degree of disorientation in their concepts of time compared to normal individuals. The temporal disorientation experienced by schizophrenic patients may be related to broader cognitive problems and not limited to the experience of time (Gorman & Wessman, 1977).

Very few studies with children have investigated the effects of brain damage or severe emotional disturbance on their concepts of time. Two such studies (Farnham-Diggory, 1966; Drisko, 1977) reported that emotionally disturbed and brain-damaged children displayed an impaired sense of future time. Most studies have focused on students having learning disabilities, hyperactive children, mentally retarded children, and delinquent youths.

Time Orientation, Learning Disabilities, and Hyperactivity

In her study of the development of the time sense in children, Ames (1946) noted that some children "are so poorly oriented as to both time and space that we believe this lack of orientation may constitute a genuine handicap which has not hitherto been given sufficient consideration." Temporal disabilities are associated with educational difficulties in reading, writing, spelling, and language (Bateman, 1968). Knights and Bakker (1980) observed that deficits in temporal concepts are a common disability in learning-disabled children. These deficits affect their judgment about the length of discussion of a subject, their determination of how much time to allocate to complete a task, their capability of prediction, and their knowledge of past, present, and future, and their place in time.

Whether temporal understanding reflects specific perceptual disabilities (Kephart, 1971) or is part of a generalized learning problem is an issue still under investigation. Forer and Keogh (1971), in their study of students with learning disorders, concluded that LD children have less mastery of time concepts than normally achieving children. An analysis of the results of the performance of the LD children suggested a generalized disability.

The Time Appreciation Test (Buck, 1946), when administered to students as a measure of learning disabilities, has aided in the accurate identification of LD students (Kass et al., 1982). And Dodd, Griswold, Smith, and Burd (1985) have developed an updated measure, the Functional Time Estimation Scale. They found on the basis of a comparison of the scores of LD and nonhandicapped children, that LD children experienced more difficulty with time orientation than regular education children, and that this pattern was consistent across grade level and age.

Hyperactive children are characterized as highly distractible, having a short attention span and being impulsive in their cognitive tempo. Behavior modification techniques are common methods for shaping longer periods of attention, but these techniques depend on the ability to estimate time (Cappella, Gentile, & Juliano,

1977). If hyperactive children are impaired in this ability, they may have difficulty knowing if they have been attending long enough for a reinforcement. Walker (1982) reported significant differences between impulsive and reflective cognitive tempo children in time estimation tasks.

Reflective children tend to have a more highly developed understanding of time than impulsive children; impulsive children subjectively overestimate time intervals of 3 minutes and longer. Knowledge of time concepts and accuracy of time estimation have been shown to increase with age for both the reflective and impulsive groups (Goldman & Everett, 1985).

The Language-Disordered Child

The time schema is difficult for children to learn because the point of reference in temporal events is constantly changing. The present flows into the future and becomes the past, as today will become yesterday tomorrow (Carrow-Woolfolk & Lynch, 1982). Children who have not developed an understanding of terms such as *later, now, before, after, in a little while,* and *in a few minutes* will have difficulty responding to parent and teacher requests and keeping track of time schedules and demands.

Researchers have given little attention to the specific effects of temporal language deficits on children's communications and interactions with others. An impairment in the ability to sequence temporal events may affect social interactions and peer relationships. A child unable to recount events in a logical, sequential order will have difficulty communicating memories and past actions to peers and adults. This inability to integrate and express memories coherently in the present may result in miscommunication and in being perceived by others as confused and disorganized.

Mentally Retarded Children and Adolescents

Using tests devised by Piaget, Lovell and Slater (1960) assessed normal and mentally retarded students' understanding of various aspects of the concept of time. Lovell and Slater concluded that the mentally retarded students of 16–17 years of age had an understanding of time equal to that of the average 9-year-olds tested. These time concepts developed in approximately the same sequence in both groups of children. A follow-up study, which measured individual IQs of normal and mildly retarded children and used similar tests of time concepts, reported that the development of the understanding of time occurred at generally the same mental age in both groups (Montroy, McManis, & Bell 1971). It should be noted, however, that both of these studies measured mentally retarded children's acquisition of time concepts within a developmental framework, and without the benefit of systematic instruction. When mentally retarded students have received systematic teaching, they have made substantial gains in their understanding and use of clock time, but have not reached the level of average-ability students receiving the same instruction (Thurlow & Turnure, 1977).

In a study of future and past extension in mildly retarded and normal adolescents, Roos and Albers (1965) found that the mildly retarded subjects differed from the normals by having a shorter orientation to the future and a longer orientation to the past. The mildly retarded adolescents viewed the past more negatively, but associated pleasant experiences with the present. The foreshortened future orientation may explain why long-range incentives are often unsuccessful in motivating mentally retarded adolescents and adults.

Age, Gender, and Other Influences in Time Perception

Future time perspective is the mental space in which motivational needs and anticipations are processed cognitively into long-term goals (Nuttin, 1985). As a cognitive process affected by an individual's interaction with family, school, and culture, future time perspective is influenced by developmental experiences. In a study of normal children and children with behavior problems, Klineberg (1967) reported that orientation to the future increased from childhood to adolescence in normal subjects, but orientation to the future decreased among the behavior-problem subjects in the study. No difference in time perspective appears to exist between adolescent boys and girls considered to be delinquents (Davids, Kidder, & Reich, 1962), and both groups were significantly more oriented to the present than normal adolescents.

Delinquent and behavior-problem adolescents' orientation towards the present can be understood as a response to what is perceived as a hopeless future and as a need to gain immediate satisfaction in the present. Students with poor grades share this pessimism and lack of confidence in the future, and, compared to high-achieving students, low-achieving students are less oriented toward the future. High motivation and assumption of responsibility for future achievement are closely related to an extended future time perspective (Wolf & Savickas, 1985).

Male and female preadolescents and adolescents perceive the future differently. Because of socialization factors, female preadolescents appear to be more oriented towards the present. Their perception of time is highly associated with levels of self-esteem and self-concept (Panides, 1984). Male preadolescents are more oriented towards the future and future achievement than are female preadolescents, and these social role demands and time orientations continue throughout adolescence and adulthood (Cottle, 1976).

Members of minority group cultures may experience an orientation to time at odds with the majority culture's. Native American and Latino students are less likely to relate the passage of time to achievement, and these cultural differences in time concepts may be the cause of some of the school-related difficulties of these minority groups (Shannon, 1976). Compared to students from the majority culture, Native American students lack time estimation skills that are expected in the school system. A deficit in these skills would inhibit the successful completion of the many tasks demanded of students throughout the school day.

PUTTING CHILDREN'S PERCEPTION OF TIME INTO PERSPECTIVE

In order to determine whether a student is affected by a disorder in time concepts, time estimation, or time orientation, a school psychologist needs to consider a number of influencing factors: (a) whether a lack of instruction has caused the skill deficit; (b) whether the intelligence and developmental level of the child or adolescent is involved; (c) whether remediation is indicated, or the teaching of compensation techniques; (d) how cultural factors affect the child's or adolescent's motivation and attitude toward time.

Rather than accepting maturation and incidental learning as the most important component in the acquisition of time skills, Bateman (1968) proposed that teachers systematically evaluate and teach time concepts. In addition to an evaluation of time skills, an assessment of intelligence and developmental level can give valuable information about difficulties a student might experience in learning the more abstract concepts of time, such as historical time or the relationships within eras.

Whether to remediate or teach compensation techniques is a difficult decision for a school psychologist or teacher. If a child or adolescent appears to be unable to develop an adequate sense of time despite intensive instruction, teaching techniques that compensate for this disability become paramount.

Cultural differences in student attitudes and motivation require sensitivity and understanding from school personnel. Modification of timetables for achieving goals may be beneficial for some minority group children who do not view future time in fundamentally the same way as do students from the majority culture (Shannon, 1976).

ALTERNATIVE ACTIONS

It is highly unlikely that a teacher would refer a student specifically because of difficulties in time orientation or lack of time concepts. Disorders in time concepts may be associated with learning problems, behavior disorders, emotional disturbance, mental retardation, hyperactivity, or language disorders. Behavioral manifestations are characterized by an inability to complete tasks within an assigned time period, a sense of being "lost in time," or a lack of awareness of the time of day, month, or year. A language-disordered child may become confused when hearing phrases such as "in a little while" and "much later," or be unable to sequence events from the past. A school psychologist should view these indicators in the context of the student's developmental level, intelligence, and cultural background.

If a school psychologist suspects a language delay or language disorder in a child or adolescent, a referral to a speech and language specialist is the appropriate action. In addition to school-based speech and language intervention, parents and teachers can also teach children the language of time. Harner (1982) has described many useful activities for classroom and home.

Because no currently normed standardized test of time concepts exists, school psychologists will need to develop their own evaluation instruments. In *Temporal Learning,* Bateman (1968) presented various categories of questions on time facts and concepts from which a school psychologist can develop a criterion-referenced survey of time concept skills and prerequisite quantitative skills and develop suggested remediation strategies for both parents and teachers. Parents can structure the home environment so that daily routines occur predictably. By continually referring to specific events in the past and future and to clock and calendar time, parents can encourage in their children an interest in and orientation to time.

Regular and special education teachers can help a child gain an understanding of time by flexibly structuring classroom routines, carefully developing the vocabulary and language of time, and including systematic instruction in time telling and time use (Moyer, 1983; Burton & Edge, 1985). Teachers can improve time estimation skills in hyperactive children and minority group children through instruction and practice (Friedman, 1977). Screening of low-achieving children for time estimation skills would identify students needing assistance to master these important concepts. If these skills are lacking, the curriculum should include the teaching of time estimation and time use. Alternatively, school personnel should change the educational demands on children who lack these skills (Shannon, 1976).

A mentally retarded child will acquire an understanding of time at a slower rate than a child of average ability, but this should not preclude the teaching of time facts and clock and calendar time (Partington, Sundberg, Iwata, & Mountjoy, 1979), and embedding a sense of past and future time in the context of specific activities and personally significant events. Reward systems for mentally retarded adolescents should take into account their limited sense of future time, and any rewards should be based on short-term payoffs.

Compensation strategies for students who prove to be unresponsive to remediation might include wearing a digital watch constantly, using an electronic timer to measure elapsed time, relying on a "talking clock" to tell time, or asking others for help in time. These compensatory techniques may assist an individual to cope in a clock-driven society.

Attempts to increase future time orientation and achievement motivation may encounter resistance from adolescents because of attitudes derived from culturally determined experiences. It is important to attempt to connect present activities to future achievement, but it is equally important to acknowledge that the aspirations of adolescents, from the majority or minority cultures, are closely adapted to the opportunities provided by society (Moerk, 1972).

SUMMARY

In Western society, time is valued as a commodity. The successful individual saves time and deplores the idle wasting of time. As the pace of modern life increases, so too does the pressure to organize time and schedule more activities into the confines of the 24-hour day. Students must learn the prescribed curriculum within the time limits defined by schools, or be considered academic failures.

Children and adolescents rarely experience disorders in time without concomitant problems in learning or behavior. Although little attention has been given to the role of time perception in school-related difficulties, a school psychologist can include assessment of time concepts, time facts, and time estimation when a student exhibits an inability to sense the passage of time, or to plan and use time effectively. Using this evaluative information, the school psychologist can develop intervention strategies for the home and the classroom and can help a child or adolescent cope with the expectations of a time-oriented society.

REFERENCES

Ames, L. B. (1946). The development of the sense of time in the young child. *Journal of Genetic Psychology, 71,* 97–125.

Bateman, B. (1968). *Temporal learning.* San Rafael, CA: Dimensions.

Benton, A. L. (1968). Differential behavioral effects in frontal lobe disease. *Neuropsychologia, 6,* 53–60.

Buck, J. N. (1946). *Time appreciation test.* Los Angeles, CA: Western Psychological.

Burton, G., & Edge, B. (1985). Helping children develop a concept of time. *School Science and Mathematics, 85*(2), 109–120.

Cappella, B., Gentile, J. R., & Juliano, D. B. (1977). Time estimation by hyperactive and normal children. *Perceptual and Motor Skills, 44,* 787–790.

Carrow-Woolfolk, E., & Lynch, J. I. (1982). *An integrative approach to language disorders in children.* New York: Grune and Stratton.

Cottle, T. J. (1976). *Perceiving time. A psychological investigation with men and women.* New York: Wiley.

Cottle, T. J., Howard, P., & Pleck, J. (1969). Adolescent perceptions of time: The effect of age, sex, and social class. *Journal of Personality, 37,* 636–650.

Davids, A., Kidder, C., & Reich, M. (1962). Time orientation in male and female juvenile delinquents. *Journal of Abnormal and Social Psychology, 64*(3), 239–240.

Densen, M. E. (1977). Time perception and schizophrenia. *Perceptual Motor Skills, 44,* 436–438.

Dodd, J. M., Griswold, P. E., Smith, G. H., & Burd, L. (1985). A comparison of learning disabled and other children on the ability to make functional time estimates. *Child Study Journal, 15*(3), 189–197.

Drisko, J. W. (1977). Time-limited therapy with children: The impact of emotional disturbance on time understanding. *Smith College Studies in Social Work, 48,* 107–131.

Farnham-Diggory, S. (1966). Self, future, and time: A developmental study of the concepts of psychotic, brain-damaged, and normal children. *Monographs of the Society for Research in Child Development, 31* (1, Serial No. 103).

Forer, R. K., & Keogh, B. K. (1971). Time understanding of learning disabled boys. *Exceptional Children, 37,* 741–743.

Fraisse, P. (1963). *Psychology of time.* New York: Harper and Row.

Friedman, E. R. (1977). Judgments of time intervals by young children. *Perceptual and Motor Skills, 45,* 715–720.

Goldman, A. P., & Everett, F. (1985). Delay of gratification and time concept in reflective and impulsive children. *Child Study Journal, 15*(3), 167–179.

Gorman, B. S., & Wessman, A. E. (1977). *The personal experience of time.* New York: Plenum.

Harner, L. (1981). Children's understanding of time. *Topics in Language Disorders, 2*(1), 51–65.

Kass, C. E., Lewis, R. B., Havertape, J. F., Maddux, C. D., Horvath, M. J., & Swift, C. A. (1982). A field test of a procedure for identifying learning disability. *Journal of Learning Disabilities, 15,* 173–177.

Kephart, N. C. (1971). *The slow learner in the classroom* (2nd ed.). Columbus, OH: Merrill.

Klineberg, S. (1967). Changes in outlook on the future between childhood and adolescence. *Journal of Personality and Social Psychology, 7*(2), 185–193.

Knights, R. M., & Bakker, D. J. (1980). *Treatment of hyperactive and learning disordered children.* Baltimore: University Park Press.

Lovell, K., & Slater, A. (1960). The growth of the concept of time: A comparative study. *Child Psychology and Psychiatry, 1,* 179–190.

Moerk, E. L. (1974). Age and epogenic influences on aspirations of minority and majority group children. *Journal of Counseling Psychology, 21*(4), 294–298.

Montroy, P., McManis, D., & Bell, D. (1971). Development of time concepts in normal and retarded children. *Psychological Reports, 28,* 895–902.

Moyer, M. B. (1983). Let's teach "time-using" as well as "time-telling." *Academic Therapy, 18*(4), 453–456.

Nuttin, J. (1985). *Future time perspective and motivation: Theory and research method.* Hillsdale, NJ: Leuven University Press.

Ornstein, R. (1969). *On the experience of time.* Baltimore: Penguin.

Panides, W. (1984). The perception of the past, present, and future in preadolescent asthmatic children: An exploratory study. *Sex Roles, 11*(11/12), 1141–1152.

Partington, J. W., Sundberg, M. L., Iwata, B. A., & Mountjoy, P. T. (1979). A task-analysis approach to time telling instruction for normal and educably mentally impaired children. *Education and Treatment of Children, 2*(1), 17–29.

Piaget, J. (1969). *The child's conception of time.* New York: Basic Books.

Roos, P., & Albers, R. (1965). Performance of retardates and normals on a measure of temporal orientation. *American Journal of Mental Deficiency, 69,* 835–838.

Shannon, L. (1976). Age change in time perception in Native Americans, Mexican-Americans, and Anglo-Americans. *Journal of Cross-Cultural Psychology, 7*(1), 117–122.

Smith, S. L. (1979). *No easy answers: The learning disabled child at home and at school.* New York: Bantam.

Thurlow, M. L., & Turnure, J. E. (1977). Children's knowledge of time and money: Effective instruction for the mentally retarded. *Education and Training of the Mentally Retarded, 12*(3), 203–212.

Tysk, L. (1984). Time perception and affective disorders. *Perceptual and Motor Skills, 58,* 455–464.

Walker, N. W. (1982). Comparison of cognitive tempo and time estimation by young boys. *Perceptual and Motor Skills, 54,* 715–722.

Wallace, M., & Rabin, A. S. (1960). Temporal experience. *Psychological Bulletin, 57,* 213–236.

Wolf, F. M., & Savickas, M. L. (1985). Time perception and causal attributions for achievement. *Journal of Educational Psychology, 77*(4), 471–480.

BIBLIOGRAPHY: PROFESSIONALS

Bateman, B. (1968). *Temporal learning.* San Rafael, CA: Dimensions.
Provides a thorough review of children's development of time concepts and perceptual causes of time disorders. The author also discusses the evaluation and teaching of time concepts in the context of a unique time schema.

Burton, G., & Edge, B. (1985). Helping children develop a concept of time. *School Science and Mathematics, 85*(2), 109–120.
Contains suggestions and hints for teaching the language of time, developing time sense, helping children understand duration and sequence, and telling time. This article emphasizes teaching time understanding and application of time concepts.

Harner, L. (1981). Children's understanding of time. *Topics in Language Disorders, 2*(1), 51–65.
Reviews language development of time concepts and vocabulary within the framework of the developmental psychology of Piaget. The article lists intervention strategies for parents and teachers to help children understand time.

BIBLIOGRAPHY: PARENTS

Engelmann, S., & Engelmann, T. (1981). *Give your child a superior mind.* New York: Simon and Schuster.
Parts of this book present detailed instructions for teaching certain time concepts and teaching time-telling skills.

Schaefer, C. E., & Millman, H. L. (1981). *How to help children with common problems.* New York: Van Nostrand Reinhold.
Contains a section about how parents can help children use time more effectively. The emphasis of this book is on emotional and behavioral causes of children's problems. In the section on time, the authors discuss the reasons why these problems occur, how to prevent such problems, and what to do about them.

Stevens, S. H. (1983). *The learning-disabled child: Ways that parents can help.* Winston-Salem, NC: Blair.
Suggests ways parents can help a learning-disabled child or adolescent compensate for a lack of time sense and time concepts.

Children and Physical Abuse

M. Patricia Brockman
Louisiana State University Medical Center

BACKGROUND

Physical abuse is the most noticeable and life-threatening form of child abuse. It is a problem of international proportions that dates to ancient times. Although physical abuse is not a new issue and no longer takes people by surprise, the number of cases continues to rise and more children are murdered or seriously injured each year. There is perhaps no social challenge that poses a greater need for close cooperation among professionals in education, medicine, social service, psychology, and the law than the multi-faceted problem of physical child abuse.

Although there is no standard definition of physical abuse, it is commonly interpreted as the nonaccidental use of physical force or an act of omission on the part of a parent or caretaker that results in injury to a child. The most common injuries that abused children sustain are bruises, abrasions, lacerations, and, to a lesser extent, burns and fractures (Gil, 1970). The decision about whether a parent or caretaker is abusive is generally based on subjective professional judgment rather than objectively defined criteria (Goldstein, Keller & Erne', 1985).

Incidence

Because of differing interpretations of abuse and variations in states' reporting procedures, it is difficult to accurately report the actual incidence of physical abuse in the United States. According to the 1984 statistics

TABLE 1

Types of Physical Injuries by Degree of Severity

Major	Minor	Unspecified
Brain damage, skull fracture Subdural hemorrhage or hematoma Poisoning Internal injuries Burns, scalds Bone fracture Dislocation, sprains Severe cuts, lacerations, bruises Freezing, exposure Other major physical injury	Minor cuts, bruises, welts, twisting, shaking Other minor injury Unspecified/mixed minor physical injuries	Unspecified, mixed injury Unspecified/mixed major physical injuries

Types of abuse defined by the American Association for Protecting Children (1986).

collected by the American Association for Protecting Children (1986), 1,726,649 children were reported nationwide because of various suspected forms of abuse or neglect, including (a) major, minor, and unspecified types of physical injury (see Table 1 for examples), (b) sexual maltreatment, (c) deprivation of necessities, (d) emotional maltreatment, and other types of abuse. This represented an increase of 158% since 1976. One of the above three types of physical injury was cited in approximately one-fourth of all investigated abuse cases, major injuries constituting 3.3% of all cases investigated.

The situation may be even more serious than statistics indicate. According to survey research, incidence reports significantly underestimate the actual number of children who are physically injured (Gelles & Strauss, 1985). Also, approximately half of these children are likely to have been previously abused or will be abused again (Herrenkohl & Herrenkohl, 1979), indicating that the use of physical force within reported families is likely to be a part of their general pattern of child rearing, rather than just a single isolated episode.

Fatalities

Physical child abuse in its most severe form results in greater than 1,000 deaths per year in the United States (Burgdorf, 1981). The percentage of fatal cases involving major physical injuries has increased from 40% in 1983 to 47% in 1984 (American Association for Protecting Children, 1986).

Infancy is a period of especially high risk of fatal abuse. Bruises, abrasions, and internal and multiple injuries that are common in all age groups more often result in death at younger ages. Children fatally abused in 1984 were 2½ years old on the average, and were more often boys than girls. Parents who fatally abused their children tended to be young and inexperienced and from a low socioeconomic group (Jason & Andereck, 1983).

Predictors Related to Abuse

Despite the confusion in the literature produced by varying definitions and differences in incidence reporting, there is some agreement about demographic characteristics related to child abuse (Friedrich & Einbender, 1983). Many of the reported risk factors fall into these categories: characteristics of the child; skill, knowledge, and attitudinal deficits of the parent(s); and environmental situations that may combine to create high levels of stress within families and negatively affect parent–child interactions. These predictors of abuse are presented in Table 2.

No single event or circumstance can be said to cause abuse, but the presence of several of these risk factors makes it increasingly likely that abusive treatment will result. In about five of every six cases of physical abuse, children are injured by their own parents; however, other abusers include stepparents, mothers' boyfriends, baby-sitters, and foster parents. Having a child with special needs is likely to increase stress in families, especially for parents or caretakers who lack child management skills or have difficulty controlling their anger. Marital instability and other environmental situations, such as unemployment, may also contribute to the creation of a potentially violent and abusive situation.

Whether these stressors actually lead to child abuse often depends on the parents' coping skills and the support available from extended family members, friends, and/or community social service professionals. Child abuse occurs at all socioeconomic and educational levels, although it is more often reported in families of low educational and occupational status.

The most consistent and insidious finding in the child abuse literature is that abusing parents have frequently been physically or emotionally abused as children (Goldstein et al., 1985). In fact, merely observing violence in the home as a child was noted to be an

TABLE 2

Personal and Demographic Factors That Pose a Risk of Physical Child Abuse

Children's characteristics

Prematurity and low birthweight

Handicapping condition or chronic illness

Being difficult — for example, hyperactive or noncompliant

Age (major injuries most frequently occurring from birth to 3 years and from 12 to 16 years)

Parents' characteristics

Personal history of abuse during childhood

Lack of knowledge of child development, resulting in unrealistic expectations of children

Poor parenting skills, including inadequate child management techniques and an overreliance on commands, threats, and physical punishment

Poor personal coping skills and lack of impulse control

Emotional and social isolation

Poor interpersonal and marital skills

Inability to distinguish feelings of self and others, particularly in relation to the child

Inaccurate attributions about intent or personal responsibility

Frustrated dependency needs

Immaturity and a tendency to choose mates who have similar background and emotional difficulties

Environmental factors

Unemployment

Large family size

Inadequate spacing of children (having too many children too quickly)

Marital instability

important factor in later abuse behavior. For example, those individuals who reported that they had witnessed their parents hit one another or another sibling showed a much higher rate of violence toward their own children than people whose parents were not observed to be violent (Gelles, 1980). The fact that many abusive parents report having been abused as children does not mean that children who are maltreated will necessarily grow up to be abusive parents (Goldstein et al., 1985). The presence of other risk factors, coupled with skill deficits and lack of emotional support for parents, are more likely to affect whether an abusive situation develops.

DEVELOPMENT

It is important to understand the developmental consequences of child abuse for at least two practical reasons. First, knowledge of the particular developmental difficulties that abused children face should lead to more effective treatment methods. Second, understanding the nature and extent of these deficits and their long-term costs to society should help professionals and the public make more intelligent decisions about allocating the needed resources to address this complex social problem (Toro, 1982).

Unfortunately, much of the research on the developmental effects of abuse has been poorly controlled and is fraught with the same definitional problems that plague incidence reporting. It is often not clear, except in prospective research, whether problems observed in abused children are the result of physical maltreatment or whether they existed prior to the abuse. Despite such methodological problems, it is apparent that the harmful effects of physical abuse range from superficial wounds to permanent neurological, cognitive, and behavioral–emotional damage, and to death.

Neurological Impairments and Intellectual and Cognitive Deficits

Chronic subdural hematoma, possible retardation, microcephaly, and diffuse and nonfocal neurological signs result from the abusive shaking and rough handling of infants (Caffey, 1974).

Clinically, it has generally been assumed that physical abuse results in lowered intelligence (Lynch, 1978) and delays in language development (Blager & Martin, 1976). Children subjected to continual maltreatment have been punished for investigating or challenging their environment, a condition that has an inhibiting effect on intelligence (Morgan, 1976). In a review of hospital records, Buchanan and Oliver (1977) reported that 3–10% of mental retardation in children may have been caused by abuse. While retardation may not always be the result, physically abused children have consistently been found to have significantly lower scores on measures of intellectual and cognitive functioning.

In studies comparing nonabused accident victims with physically abused children, Elmer (1977, 1978) suggested that the pervasive and stressful consequences of abused children's impoverished environment may be more detrimental to their development than the injuries they suffered. However, in a controlled study, Barahal, Waterman, and Martin (1981) found significant impairments in intellectual functioning of abused school-aged children who were not from economically disadvantaged families. It is therefore apparent that children who are physically maltreated are at risk for cognitive difficulties as a direct or indirect result of the injuries they receive.

Behavioral, Emotional, and Personality Consequences

While there is no single behavioral style that is characteristic of abused children, the presence of social–

TABLE 3

Social-Emotional Problems of Abused Children

Low self-esteem
Oppositional behavior
Compulsivity
Unresponsiveness to praise
Lack of motivation
Social withdrawal
Hypervigilance to adult cues
School learning problems
Fearfulness, clinging
Haphazard dress, messy work
Difficulty in making decisions
An impaired ability to enjoy life, apparently due to ineffective and anxious efforts to please others
Psychiatric symptoms such as enuresis, tantrums, hyperactivity, depression, and bizarre behavior
Inability to depend on or trust others
Little confidence in their ability to influence their own experiences, particularly in avoiding negative outcomes
Excessive avoidance and denial in anxiety-provoking situations (such as presenting in front of the class)
Inability to understand subtle and complex interpersonal relationships — rigid and literal in orientation
Pseudo-adult or precocious behavior
In older students a tendency to be troublesome, selfish, boisterous, and chronically dissatisfied

emotional problems is well documented. Some of these are included in Table 3.

Behaviorally, abused children have been described as either very withdrawn and passive or very active and aggressive (Martin & Beezley, 1976). George and Main (1979) found that young abused children showed significantly more aggression toward peers and daycare staff, fewer approaches toward staff, and more avoidance of peers and staff. Physically abused children have also been found to be significantly more self-destructive, evidencing more suicide attempts and self-mutilation (Green, 1978). The amount of aggression measured on psychological tests was found to be directly related to the severity of abuse experienced by the child (Kinard, 1982).

The consequences of abuse will vary with the children's developmental levels, the duration and intensity of the abuse they have experienced, and the quality of their subsequent home environment, treatment efforts, and community support. Negative effects are also experienced by the siblings of abused children even those who are not the direct victims of physical injury. Nonabused siblings as well as the physically abused children have significantly more negative perceptions of their parents and family members than children from nonabusive families (Halperin, 1981).

PUTTING PHYSICAL CHILD ABUSE IN PERSPECTIVE

Detection and Reporting

It is essential that school professionals be sensitive to the possibility of abuse, since parents and children rarely report themselves. A general awareness of abuse, together with the understanding that it is usually possible to protect the child and treat the family, will set an attitude of cooperative detection (Brummitt, 1985). This is especially true if children are identified when they show the earliest signs of abuse, so that help can be made available at a stage when problems can be more readily resolved. Too often, referrals to child protective services are not made until the conditions of abuse become so acute and intolerable that it is extremely difficult to successfully treat the family.

School professionals are in key positions to detect and report suspected abuse because of their prolonged contact with children and because of their firsthand knowledge of specific children's development. They may be the only ones with whom an abused child has a trusting relationship, and an empathic response may encourage disclosure. Most children, however, are usually hesitant to discuss the problem for fear that they might bring shame to their family or betray their parents (Rose, 1980). In this case, the use of observation, free play, and games, along with a structured interview, might be useful to elicit the child's feelings and perceptions about the home situation.

When physical abuse is detected, it is often the nature of the injury itself that raises initial suspicion. When inquiring about how an injury has occurred, school staff should become wary if differing explanations are offered, if the reports are discrepant with direct observation of the injury, and/or if the injuries are multiple and in varying stages of healing. The child's manner and behavior as well as the parents' may also provide useful clues when gathering information. Some examples of "red flags" or indicators of a child's potential need for protection are presented in Table 4. The evidence of one or more indicators in a child or parent should arouse concern for the child's welfare. Whether there is truly a need for protection, however, is a determination that child protective services will make after it has explored the situation.

Notes detailing the injuries, verbal statements from the child and parents, observations of parent–child interactions, observation of the student with his or her peers, changes in the child's behavior, and any other information that raises the question of abuse should be written as the events occur so that they can provide an ongoing record to the child protective team in their investigation. These notes should be objective descriptions and observations rather than subjective judgments based on conjecture about the parents. Since actions

TABLE 4

Indicators of a Child's Possible Need for Protection

Child's physical condition
- History of previous injuries
- Reports of injuries discrepant with physical appearance
- Unexplained bruises (in various stages of healing), welts, human bite marks, bald spots
- Unexplained burns, especially cigarette burns or immersion burns (glove-like)
- Unexplained fractures, lacerations, or abrasions

Child's behavior
- Self-destructive
- Withdrawn and aggressive — behavioral extremes
- Uncomfortable with physical contact
- Arrives at school early and stays late as if afraid to be at home
- Repeated absences from school
- Chronic runaway (particularly adolescents)
- Complains of soreness or moves uncomfortably
- Wears clothing inappropriate to weather to cover body
- Refuses to dress for physical education classes or sports

Parental attitudes
- Parents aggressive or defensive when approached about problems concerning their child
- Parents delay seeking medical attention or refuse to accept medical attention
- Parents apathetic or unresponsive
- Observation of parent-child interaction by school personnel seems bizarre or strange
- Parents show little concern for child
- Parents fail to show an interest in what child is doing
- Lack of participation in school activities or refusal to permit child to participate

Note: Adapted in part from *Early childhood programs and the prevention and treatment of child abuse and neglect,* The User Series, by D. D. Broadhurst, M. Edmunds, & C. A. MacDicken, 1979, Washington, DC: U.S. Department of Health, Education, and Welfare. Copyright, 1979 by U.S. DHEW. Adapted by permission.

taken by these agencies and by the courts often take long periods of time, written documentation made at the time of the events will ensure accuracy and objectivity.

Once suspected, abuse must be reported. Since the mid 1960s, state laws have made it mandatory for all professionals, including educators, to report suspected child abuse. There is civil and criminal liability protection for those who report suspected incidents. With the passage of the Child Abuse Prevention and Treatment Act (PL 93-247), many states operate toll-free child abuse prevention and information lines. Reports of suspected abuse and neglect originate with physicians, hospitals, schools, police, social workers, and others. School personnel currently make up the largest group of professionals reporting suspected abuse to child protective service agencies (American Association for Protecting Children, 1986).

An essential point to remember is that without early detection and reporting, the child will not be protected either through treatment by most of the family or by removal from the abusive environment. Furthermore, the abuse will likely be repeated, often frequently and with increasing severity. Severe penalties such as jail sentences and large fines have been imposed on professionals for failure to report. In some states, individuals can be held liable for damages from subsequent injuries to a child after failure to report suspected abuse.

Reports are usually made to the state or county child protective agencies and occasionally to the police. Each school should have a written set of policies and procedures that guide the reporting process. These policies should include (a) a general overview of abuse, including causative factors and intervention strategies, (b) indicators for identifying potentially abusive situations, (c) relevant legislation, (d) procedures to follow when abuse is suspected, and (e) guidelines for documentation. A *Guidelines for Schools* pamphlet is available from the American Humane Association detailing some of this information. Because the legal procedures vary in each state, the Council for Exceptional Children (1979) has recommended that an attorney or the state's attorney general be consulted when developing the school's policy. A model plan for handling cases at both state and local levels is available from the Education Commission of the States (1976).

The report may be made by the person who initially suspected the abuse or in conjunction with another school professional, such as the principal, community counselor, or school nurse delegated to assist in reporting. If the delegated school representative chooses not to file a report, it is still the responsibility of the individual who initially suspected the abuse to do so.

Once a report has been filed, the school professional(s) will often be asked to assist the child protective workers and others who are involved in the assessment and management of the child and family. The multidisciplinary team may include physicians, mental health professionals, and lawyers, as well as representatives from the child's school School professionals can make a valuable contribution to this team because of their unique ability to meet the child's academic and developmental needs (Brummitt, 1985).

ALTERNATIVE ACTIONS

Teachers, unlike many other professionals who are required to report suspected cases of child abuse, are in the unique position of having continuous contact with abused children and their families before, during, and after the report has been filed. Therefore, the aftereffects of the reporting process, the investigation and treatment phases, are also of particular interest to them.

Talking With the Parents

Although they may well be skillful in conducting parent conferences about academic issues, most teachers have not been trained how to handle the stressful situation of confronting parents who have possibly mistreated their children. Physicians who deal with this situation more frequently suggest that school professionals be frank, but sympathetic, first stating that the child has been injured nonaccidentally, that both the teacher and the parents obviously want the child to be cared for properly, and that the teacher and school staff want very much to help the parents achieve these goals (Rose, 1980). This three-pronged statement works well, since abusive parents tend to see themselves as trying to provide for their children but at the same time being up against insurmountable obstacles in their effort.

The parents should be reminded that the school staff will not be called upon to make decisions regarding parental fitness or child custody, and that the school is not an enemy of the family but needs to ensure the safety of the child. Anger and hostility toward the professional, however uncomfortable at the receiving end, should be expected from a parent who faces the consequences of a report of child abuse. By acknowledging these feelings, school professionals can more readily help the parents work through their possible feelings of being persecuted by the reporting agent and begin to address the central issue of abuse.

Investigation

During the investigation, a juvenile probation office may be called upon to determine whether the case must go to court. Court proceedings involve an adjudicating hearing during which the judge determines whether abuse has occurred. If abuse has been found to occur, a dispositional hearing will be conducted to determine the family's ability or inability to care for the child. A court order for treatment may also be made at the dispositional hearing based on the recommendations offered by the social service worker.

Treatment of Abuse

Experts in the area of child maltreatment agree on a general approach to the dysfunctional family. This should include a multidisciplinary, multiservice team for each family. What has been learned from 20 years of working with abused children and their families is that treatment of abusive parents can be long and it is sometimes ineffective. Treatment efforts should not just be geared to the parents, but also be aimed specifically at the child through a collaborative effort by social workers, therapists, and teachers.

Foster Care. It is clear that abused children and their siblings will require some kind of therapeutic intervention and may need to be removed from the parents (Kempe, 1982). Removal of children from the home is advocated when they appear to be in danger of further injury, if there is evidence of repeated abuse, if the children are unable to protect themselves, or if parents are unable or unwilling to cooperate with the involved agencies. The compulsion felt by some therapists and judges to "keep the family together" may well be fatal (Helfer, 1982). Helfer (1982) has suggested that when it is apparent that a safe family will never exist for the children with their own parents, parental rights should be terminated as quickly as possible by the courts to improve the chances that the children can be adopted by caring individuals.

In cases in which the children must remain in foster care, the number of foster home placements the child experiences should be minimized, since lack of stability has a detrimental effect on psychosocial development (Pardeck, 1983). Foster care alone should not be considered as "treatment." Although it can be therapeutic,it regrettably often is not. Some abused children are not easy to care for, however, and appropriate training and professional support/supervision is not always given to foster parents to ensure a therapeutic and positive placement.

Intervention Efforts in the School. School is the setting, second only to home, in which children spend a great amount of time. For this reason, it will be important and necessary for school professionals to become involved beyond the recognition and reporting process and participate directly in treatment efforts. Teachers should have an understanding of how, and to what degree, the consequences of abuse interfere with learning. They also need strategies for working with the social–behavioral problems of abused children in the classroom.

The sometimes violent and abrupt separation from their parents can be another trauma for abused children, who invariably feel abandoned and often responsible. The school can provide a supportive and stabilizing situation for children at this time, especially when other aspects of their lives have changed so dramatically. In addition to providing stability, it has been suggested that the classroom is the natural place to help these children learn needed social skills and group relationships. Teachers and other school personnel can also be appropriate models of caregiving for children who may not have experienced a trusting relationship and positive interactions at home.

Teachers should be aware that abused children often come from homes where performance, progress, and "being good" were the only ways they could get approval or keep from being abused by their parents. Children may well react to their teachers' demands for performance and progress as they did to their parents' demands for performance and progress. This may take several forms (a) total acquiescence out of fear (fear of rejection, fear of pain), (b) overt opposition to the teacher's requests, and/or (c) subtle passive–aggressive behavior (Martin & Miller, 1976).

It is important for school professionals to communicate the following attitudes when working with abused children. First, that they like the children whether or not they can do all the things asked of them. Second, that the teachers are most concerned with helping them learn and overcome problems that are bothering them. Third, that their teachers "hang in there" with them despite inappropriate or uncooperative behavior. Finally, that their teachers will not be upset, but will listen and participate, if they want to discuss feelings about past injuries, their parents, or the consequences of the abuse (Martin & Miller, 1976).

The social–behavioral problems of physically

abused children may make it extremely difficult to work with them in a regular classroom especially when they are chronically unmotivated and uncooperative students. Morgan (1976) has suggested utilizing the existing system of special education and resource classrooms to address these problems by providing remedial learning and psychological support services for abused children. This individualized assistance (for example, social skills training, academic skill enhancement, teaching appropriate ways of expressing emotions, focusing on the children's strengths to improve self-image) should be aimed toward increasing the chances that these students will learn to interact in the regular classroom as successfully as possible.

Intervention for Abusive Parents. Treatment strategies for abusive parents need to be focused on long-term and highly supportive interventions. Short-term interventions, basic information, and referral services focused solely on parenting skills will, in all likelihood, have little impact on these clients. The services that are likely to have the greatest impact are interventions that include "resocialization" tasks designated to break patterns of isolation and facilitate the development of interpersonal relationships and support. Such services could include self-help groups such as Parents Anonymous, parent aides to augment parental care, "shared parenting" (Gabinet, 1983), and intervention strategies that focus on reparenting. The most common areas addressed in parent treatment groups include isolation, deficiency of marital skills (such as communication with spouse), impatience and/or temper, inadequate child management, and unemployment.

Service personnel currently working with abusive families need to emphasize the development of the broadest possible range of services for their clients in the community. Given current funding realities, this emphasis will necessitate community resource development that builds a public and private partnership in working with parents who abuse their children (Anderson & Lauderdale, 1982).

Prevention Efforts in the Schools. School personnel have important roles in the prevention of abuse. As professionals specifically trained in the developmental needs of children, they can effectively advocate for children's rights, for treatment programs for families, and for community resources to reduce the environmental stresses associated with abuse.

Helfer and Kempe (1976) have suggested several ways in which schools can become involved in abuse prevention. First, provide an adult education program designed to develop parenting skills and knowledge of early childhood development. Second, implement a continuing interpersonal skills training program for students, beginning with simple skills in grade school and advancing to courses in sexuality and parenting in high school. Third, include information on family planning in health education classes. Fourth, sponsor a parent support group and make available accessible information from community groups such as Parents Anonymous and services such as Parent Hotlines. Fifth, encourage the development of early childhood programs to provide preschoolers with age-related activities. And, sixth, teach students problem solving and crisis prevention and resolution.

SUMMARY

The physical abuse of children is a shocking problem of staggering proportions that results in continued suffering and even death for some victims. Professionals working in the schools have a unique opportunity and a mandated obligation to become sensitive and responsive to the needs of these children and their families. Inservice and preservice training programs are needed to educate school professionals about physical abuse. Written school policies and procedures should be developed and implemented to ease the difficult task of reporting, investigating, and treating the victims of physical abuse and their families. A good deal of work lies ahead, and schools can take a leading role by actively supporting community agencies and public policies that serve these families.

REFERENCES

American Association for Protecting Children. (1986). *Highlights of official child neglect and abuse reporting, 1984.* Denver, CO: American Humane Association.

Anderson, S. C., & Lauderdale, M. L. (1982). Characteristics of abusive parents: A look at self-esteem. *Child Abuse and Neglect, 6,* 285–293.

Barahal, R. M., Waterman, J., & Martin, H. P. (1981).The social cognitive development of abused children. *Journal of Consulting and Clinical Psychology, 49,* 508–516.

Blager, F., & Martin, H. P. (1976). Speech and language of abused children. In H. P. Martin (Ed.), *The abused child: A multidisciplinary approach to developmental issues and treatment* (pp. 83–92). Cambridge, MA: Ballinger.

Broadhurst, D. D., Edmunds, M., & MacDicken, R. A. (1979). *Early childhood programs and the prevention and treatment of child abuse and neglect.* The User Series. Washington, DC. U. S. Department of Health, Education and Welfare.

Buchanan, A., & Oliver, J. E. (1977). Abuse and neglect as a cause of mental retardation: A study of 140 children admitted to subnormality hospitals in Wiltshire. *British Journal of Psychiatry, 131,* 458–467.

Brummitt, J. R. (1985). Child abuse. In R. A. Haslam & P. J. Valletutti (Eds.), *Medical problems in the classroom: The teacher's role in diagnosis and management* (pp. 299–307). Austin, TX: Pro-Ed.

Burgdorf, K. (1981). *Recognition and reporting child maltreatment: Study findings. Natural study of the incidence and severity of child abuse and neglect.* (DHHS Publication No. 81-30325). Washington, DC: National Center on Child Abuse and Neglect.

Caffey, J. (1974). The whiplash shaken infant syndrome: Manual shaking of the extremities with whiplash induced intracranial and intraocular bleedings, linked with permanent brain damage and mental retardation. *Pediatrics, 54,* 396–403.

Council for Exceptional Children (1979). *We can help: Specialized curriculum for educators on the prevention and treatment of child abuse and neglect.* Reston, VA: Author.

Education Commission of the States. (1976). Child abuse and neglect: Model legislation for the states. Denver, CO: Author.

Elmer, E. (1977). A follow-up study of traumatized children. *Pediatrics, 59,* 273–279.

Elmer, E. (1978). Effects of early neglect and abuse on latency age children. *Journal of Pediatric Psychology, 3,* 14–19.

Friedrich, W. N., & Einbender, A. J. (1983). The abused child: A psychological review. *Journal of Clinical Child Psychology, 12,* 244–256.

Gabinet, L. (1983). Shared parenting: A new paradigm for the treatment of child abuse. *Child Abuse and Neglect, 7,* 403–411.

Gelles, R. J. (1980). A profile of violence toward children in the United States. In G. Gerbner, C. J. Ross, & E. Zigler (Eds.), *Child abuse; An agenda for action.* New York: Oxford University Press.

Gelles, R. J., & Strauss, M. A. (1985). *Is violence toward children increasing? A comparison of 1975 and 1985 National Survey Rates.* Durham, NH: Family Violence Research Program.

George, C., & Main, M. (1979). Social interactions of young abused children: Approach,avoidance, and aggression. *Child Development, 50,* 306–318.

Gil, D. G. (1970). *Violence against children.* Cambridge, MA: Harvard University Press.

Goldstein, A. P., Keller, H., & Erne', D. (1985). *Changing the abusive parent.* Champaign, IL: Research Press.

Green, A. H. (1978). Self-destructive behavior in battered children. *American Journal of Psychiatry, 135,* 579–582.

Halperin, S. L. (1981). Abused and non-abused children's perceptions of their mothers, fathers, and siblings: Implications for a comprehensive family treatment plan. *Family Relations, 30,* 89–96.

Helfer, R. E. (1982). A review of the literature on the prevention of child abuse and neglect. *Child Abuse and Neglect, 6,* 251–261.

Helfer, R., & Kempe, C. H. (Eds.). (1976). *The family and the community.* Cambridge, MA: Ballinger.

Herrenkohl, E. C., & Herrenkohl, R. C. (1979). A comparison of abused children and their nonabused siblings. *Journal of the American Academy of Child Psychiatry, 18,* 260–269.

Jason, J., & Andereck, N. D. (1983). Fatal child abuse in Georgia: the epidemiology of severe physical abuse. *Child Abuse and Neglect, 7,* 1–9.

Kempe, C. H. (1982). Changing approaches to treatment of child abuse and neglect. *Child Abuse and Neglect, 6,* 491–493.

Kinard, E. M. (1982). Experiencing child abuse: Effects of emotional adjustment. *American Journal of Orthopsychiatry, 52,* 82–91.

Lynch, M. A. (1978). The prognosis of child abuse. *Journal of Child Psychology and Psychiatry, 19,* 175–190.

Martin, H. P., & Beezley, P. (1976). Personality of abused children. In H. P. Martin (Ed.), *The abused child: A multidisciplinary approach to developmental issues and treatment* (pp. 105–110). Cambridge, MA: Ballinger.

Martin, H. P., & Miller, T. (1976). Treatment of specific delays and deficits. In H. P. Martin (Ed.), *The abused child: A multidisciplinary approach to developmental issues and treatment* (pp. 179–188). Cambridge, MA: Ballinger.

Morgan, S. R. (1976). The battered child in the classroom. *Journal of Pediatric Psychology, 1,* 47–49.

Pardeck, J. T. (1983). An empirical analysis of behavioral and emotional problems of foster children related to replacement care. *Child Abuse and Neglect, 7,* 75–78.

Rose, B. C. (1980). Child abuse and the educator. *Focus on Exceptional Children, 12,* 1–13.

Toro, P. A. (1982). Developmental effects of child abuse: A review. *Child Abuse and Neglect, 6,* 423–431.

BIBLIOGRAPHY: PROFESSIONALS

Council for Exceptional Children. (1979). *We can help: Specialized curriculum for educators on the prevention and treatment of child abuse and neglect.* Reston, VA: Author.
Presents information that will be helpful to school professionals in a variety of ways including in-service on the general topic of abuse, specific guidelines for developing and implementing policies and procedures for reporting potentially abusive situations, descriptions of abuse investigation procedures, and the role of school professionals in the prevention and treatment of abuse.

Fairorth, J. W. (1982). *Child abuse and the school.* Palo Alto, CA: R & E Research Associates.
Includes an excellent overview of the dynamics of child abuse and specifics on school professionals' roles in treatment and prevention.

Goldstein, A. P., Keller, H., & Erne', D. (1985). *Changing the abusive parent.* Champaign, IL: Research Press.
Provides an excellent comprehensive and updated overview of the area of child abuse in the first chapter and a description of various intervention programs that have been implemented in the area of abuse in the second chapter. The remainder of the book focuses on the use of the Structured Learning Approach for working with abusive parents. Very complete instructions are provided for training paraprofessional and professional therapists to conduct Structured Learning Treatment groups. The treatment program is skills-oriented and designed to address deficits in the following areas: self-control skills, parenting skills, marital skills, and interpersonal skills.

Martin, H. P. (Ed.). (1976). *The abused child: A multidisciplinary approach to developmental issues and treatment.* Cambridge, MA: Ballinger.
An excellent resource that contains 22 well-written chapters that provide an overview of the needs and treatment of abused children from a number of discipline perspectives. Some of the primary areas covered include neurodevelopmental and psychological problems experienced by abused children, the entire abusive environment as a dysfunctional system, risk factors associated with abuse, the usefulness of developmental assessment and consultation, and advocacy and treatment for abused children and their families.

Toro, P. A. (1982). Developmental effects of child abuse:A review. *Child Abuse and Neglect, 6,* 423–431.
Provides a critical overview on the effects of physical child abuse on children's development by examining studies in the area and pointing out methodological and logical flaws. Some general suggestions are made to improve the quality and clarity of future research in terms of definition, generalization, causality, and statistical analysis.

Audiovisual Aids

The following audiovisual aids are available from:

Child Abuse and Neglect Resource Center
Department of Special Education
California State University, Los Angeles
5151 State University Drive
Los Angeles, CA 90032
Telephone: (213) 224-3283

Film: *The Interview* (35 min)
Presents an actual interview between a parent suspected of child abuse and a physician. The film demonstrates interviewing principles for the medical interview and outlines one approach to gather important medical, social, and psychological information with which to conduct an assessment and treatment plan. In the discussion session after the film, viewing groups are encouraged to review the film's content, reactions to and feelings about the film, and the interview process demonstrated.

Film: *Abusive Parents* (30 min)
Includes excerpts from a panel discussion by four women incarcerated at the California Institute for Women for crimes involving child abuse, followed by an interview with the former director of a therapeutic daycare center for abused children and their families. The interview covers the social context of abuse, personal and family dynamics that may contribute to abuse, and a generic profile of abusers.

Filmstrip: *Medical Indicators of Abuse and Neglect*
Five short filmstrips. One is focused on the medical indicators to be aware of in diagnosing physical abuse.

Filmstrip: *Child Abuse and Neglect:What the Educator Sees* (15 min)
Depicts the physical and behavioral indicators of abuse and neglect that children are likely to display in a school setting. Also discusses the unique vantage point that teachers and other educators have in identifying and responding to abused and neglected children.

Filmstrip: *Physical Indicators of Abuse, Signs of Alert: Part A; Physical Abuse, What Behavior Can Tell Us: Part B.*
An overview of physical and behavior indicators of physical abuse. Part A looks at major external and internal physical manifestations. Part B looks at child behavior and interactions between children and parents that may indicate abuse. (Each run about 14 minutes).

BIBLIOGRAPHY: GENERAL

Publications

The following publications and pamphlets are available from

National Committee for Prevention of Child Abuse
332 South Michigan Ave. Suite 950
Chicago, IL 60604-4357

Physical Child Abuse by Anne H. Cohn
Maltreatment of Adolescents by James Garbarino & Anne Garbarino
It Shouldn't Hurt to Be a Child
The Disabled Child and Child Abuse by Donald F. Kline
Selected Child Abuse Information and Resources Directory

Audiovisual Aids

The following audiovisual aids are available from:

Child Abuse and Neglect Resource Center
Department of Special Education
California State University, Los Angeles
5151 State University Drive
Los Angeles, CA 90032
Telephone: (213) 224-3283

Film: *Fragile: Handle with Care* (narrated by Bill Cosby) (26 min)
Depicts the battering parent, the results of child abuse, and the help society can offer, by focusing on three families. The situations portrayed are all reenactments of authentic case histories.

Film: *War of the Eggs* (27 min)
A sensitive exploration of the child-battering syndrome. A young lawyer and his wife have taken their son to the hospital because he was critically injured in "an accidental" fall. With gentle probing by the hospital psychiatrist, the truth emerges and the parents take responsibility for what they have done and face the fact that they need help.

Film: *Cipher in the Snow* (24 min)
The true story of a little boy no one thought was important until his sudden death one morning. A film to motivate concern for the needs of every child.

Film: *Cradle of Violence* (20 min)
A film about the problem of child abuse and the solutions to the frustrations of parenthood that bring about violence against children. The film gets actual child abusers to explore their problems. The tone of the film is very positive and provides motivation to continue to help with the problems whether they are professional personal or concerned citizens. It is a documentary film designed for school, library, church, and community group programs.

Film: *Don't Give Up on Me* (28 min, 16mm, color)
Produced for use in caseworker awareness training, the program uses real people in real situations to probe the reasons behind the child abuse pattern. Included are recreated scenes from a case history and scenes from actual counseling workshops. In addition to its primary audience, the program is designed for mental health agencies, social work-oriented college curricula, health care centers, law enforcement agencies, libraries, civic groups, and the concerned public.

Slide Presentation: *The Administrator's Role in Combating Child Abuse and Neglect* (10 min)
Used by administrators to develop both board and administrative policies to initiate a program against child abuse and neglect. Information concerning reporting laws, immunity laws, and the misdemeanor penalty for failure to report is presented, along with a suggested procedure for referring suspected cases of abuse or neglect.

Organizations to Contact for Further Information

The American Humane Association — Children's Division
9725 East Hampden Avenue
Denver, CO 80231

Parents Anonymous, Inc.
2810 Artesia Boulevard
Redondo Beach, CA 90278

Children and Play

Peter R. Burzynski
Vincennes University

BACKGROUND

The expression is so casual, *just playing*. There is a tendency to trivialize, to minimize, to ignore the activities described under the general rubric of *play*. But evidence from research conducted by scientists from a variety of backgrounds is mounting that play serves many functions, that it is characterized by many types of activities, and that in all its complexities, it is far more important in the lives and development of children than was ever previously acknowledged.

Definitions

While play appears to be universal, it is not easy to explain, define, or describe in an exact way. However, play can be examined in several dimensions that can be helpful to those who might wish to interact or affect the play of children. It will be the intent of this chapter to examine these dimensions of play.

Scientific investigations of play began in a serious vein only in the last hundred years. These studies have resulted in at least five theoretical positions on the nature of play.

The first of these is the *surplus energy theory*, stating primarily that play is the aimless expenditure of exuberant energy. The second, the *recapitulation theory*, was formulated by G. Stanley Hall (1906), and takes a Darwinian view that a child's play is a reflection of the behavioral evolution of the species, whereby it mirrors the activities of the race during past eons. The third theory of play, the *instinct–practice theory*, holds that play is a necessary preparation for adult life and that through modeling and imitation children acquire the skills of adulthood (Groos, 1901). Fourth, play was theorized by Patrick (1916) to be pure activity, spontaneous and free, that is pursued for its own sake; this was known as the *relaxation theory*. Fifth, the *psychoanalytic theory* suggested that play is cathartic and allows for the release of unpleasant emotions. This perspective includes not only the original Freudian explanation that play is a projection of an *inner life* over which the child desires to gain mastery (Freud, 1922), but also the more contemporary views of Erikson (1950) that a child uses play experiences to form better understanding of the world. Piaget (1962) has combined Freudian and Eriksonian ideas by suggesting that play is both motivated by pleasure and capable of adding to an accumulating knowledge in the intellectual development of the child.

Together, these theories of play provide a comprehensive, though nonunified understanding of play. As Frost suggested, "the need for an integrated theory of play is perhaps greatest in education and child development, for these disciplines are deeply concerned with the practical consequences of development" (Frost, 1984, p. 14). This unification of understanding of play is, unfortunately, still not readily available.

Characteristics of Play. A useful definition of play can be based on the following listing of its characteristics (adapted from Frost, 1984):

1. Play is pleasureable, as evidenced by expressions of joy and excitement.
2. Play is intrinsically rewarding and motivating.
3. Play is free from externally imposed rules.
4. Play is spontaneous and voluntary.
5. Play requires active involvement.
6. Play is simulative, symbolic behavior, bridging fantasy and reality.
7. Play that is social and gamelike is bounded by rules.

Consequences of Play. Additionally, play can also be defined by its consequences, including the following:

1. Play is a means of overcoming fears, anxieties, and tensions.
2. Play is a means of developing readiness for mastery of elements of the environment — for example, by (a) providing opportunities for novel situations; (b) leading to formation of schemas, the precursors of concepts;

(c) leading to discovery, verbal judgment, and reasoning; (d) promoting language development; (e) serving as a vehicle of culture transmission; (f) leading to divergent thinking, improving problem solving; (g) leading to creative ideation; and (h) supporting prosocial behavior and cooperation.

Play is also cited by several researchers (Garvey, 1977; Huizinga, 1950; Ellis, 1973; Frost & Klein, 1984) for its relationship to nonplay and/or work. Garvey (1977, p. 5) indicated that "the very idea of play depends on contrasts; we can only speak of play when we can contrast it with other orientations or states." Frost (1984, p. 16) added, "Work comes closest to representing the antithesis of play[, and] although pure play and pure work may be theoretically possible, in practice play may contain elements of work and vice versa."

Functions of Play

Jerome Bruner (1983) named five fundamental functions of play in the activity of children:

1. Play is an activity that is for itself and not others; it is a reduction in the seriousness of the consequences of errors.
2. Play activity permits a looseness between means and ends. Children often change their goals en route to suit new means or change the means to suit new goals.
3. Play is very rarely random or by chance. Bruner quoted Joyce in saying that play "is often . . . an epiphany of the ordinary, and idealization, a pure dilemma" (Bruner, 1983, p. 61).
4. Play projects the interior life onto the world, as opposed to learning, in which we interiorize the external world and make it part of ourselves.
5. Play gives pleasure, perhaps even to the point of the erections of obstacles within play; the obstacles even seem necessary to avoid boredom.

The real import of any theory or definition of play lies in the degree to which it can be used to aid parents and educators to guide and control the play of children. It will be a further purpose of this chapter to report research evidence offering relationships between the effects of play and children's social, emotional, and cognitive development. Finally, there will be a review of training and therapeutic programs that have been designed to change children's play in order to promote growth, alleviate emotional problems, or enhance specific skills.

DEVELOPMENT

The Kinds and Nature of Play

Play is not a subject, learned by children as they learn how to reduce a fraction, diagram a sentence, or pronounce a new word. Play proceeds from a child simultaneously as a consequence of and nurturant to growing. "Play is an experimental dialogue with the environment" (Eibl-Eibesfeldt, 1967). And Garvey (1977, p. 27) suggested that play "increases the chances of survival for the individual as well as for the group." As Piaget (cited by Frost, 1984) indicated,

> On the one hand play is active repetition and consolidation, and in this sense it is . . . growth through functioning. On the other hand, it is mental digestion, i. e., perception or conception of the object in so far as it is incorporated into the real or possible . . . . it is by repeating his behaviors through reproductive assimilation that the child assimilates objects to actions and that these becomes schemas. These schemas constitute the functional equivalent of concepts and of the logical relationships of later development. (p. 27)

A baby smiling may be the first reflection of play behavior. The entertainment of the motion and sensation provided by adults, animals, or objects is easily seen to be pleasing to infants.

The developmental sequence of play behaviors may be an important yardstick by which to measure a child's growth. One summary of the developmental sequence of play is given by Papalia and Olds (1986). This formation, adapted from earlier researchers' work, has two major classification systems or models: *social play* and *cognitive play.*

Social Play. In the classification system or model described as social play, early researchers like Parten (1932) used samples of behavior of 2- to 5-year-olds in free play periods to obtain observations of play. The general result of her observations was the finding that children mature in their play from less to more social play. *Unoccupied play,* reflecting the lowest level of maturity, is characterized by watching the activity of others or playing with one's own body, getting on and off chairs, or just standing around. *Onlooker behavior* involves passive noninteractive observation by one child of the play of another child or group of children. The onlooking child may make comments or suggestions to another, but will not receive responses. In *solitary play,* a child will pursue some activity in which she or he will be engrossed, often in the midst of other children who are playing independently or in groups. *Parallel play* is much like solitary play, but the emphasis is on a child's choosing to play with toys similar to those of children nearby; there is no attempt to change the play behavior of others. *Associative play* is the first truly interactive play of the maturing child, and the emphasis is on the associational or relational aspects of play. Children in associative play perform similar play activities, often giving and exchanging materials, and sometimes trying to influence each other, but not sharing or planning their play goals or end products. The highest level of maturity of social play is *cooperative play,* in which children play together to make something, play in dramatic roles, play in competition, or play a game with formal rules.

Analysis of Social Play. The developmental sequence of social play can be used as a general gauge for assessing children's social–emotional development. For example, children who are approaching the age of 5 who spend a majority of their play time in unoccupied play may be socially immature or have an emotional problem that prevents them from playing in more complex ways. A 3-year-old who consistently demonstrates associative or cooperative play is reflecting early maturation of social behavior and is more likely to have good social–emotional development.

Cognitive Play. Cognitive play is a model of play that, unlike the social play system, reflects intellectual growth as the predominant theme. It is a model that is independent of the social play model. *Functional play* (or as Piaget (1962) described it at times, exercise play) is the first play of children and can consist of any simple repetitive muscular movement with or without objects. Garvey (1977) goes so far as to suggest that smiling, laughter, and glee may be the first precursors or precedents of functional play. This level of play corresponds with Piaget's sensorimotor stage (the period from birth to 2 years) of the cognitive development of a child. *Constructive play* is the manipulation of objects to create or construct something. Much research, as will be reported, has centered on the use of objects in play as a reflection and determiner of mental growth. Constructive play might be thought to coincide with Piaget's preoperational stage of cognitive development. The acquisition of Piaget's concept of *object permanence* is a fundamental prerequisite of progression through constructive play and into dramatic play. *Dramatic play,* often called *symbolic play, imaginative play, make-believe play, or pretend play,* will usually appear soon after the initiation of constructive play. This is play that allows for the representation of missing or absent objects or people, or, as Frost (1984, p. 24) puts it, "playgrounds of the mind." (*Rough-and-tumble* play can be found within dramatic play, in which children enjoy nonaggressive simulations of battle and competition or revel in the sensations of physical closeness.) Closely associated with this kind of play is the development of children's imaginary playmates, humor (jokes and riddles), story telling, and childhood lore. Finally, playing *games with rules* brings about a period in which children cooperate to form a game with rules and which has a goal or goals. This requires the ability to act in socially acceptable ways and to get along with others. It becomes highly elaborated and predominant in the adolescent years.

Analysis of Cognitive Play. A reflection of cognitive development or intellectual skill is apparent in this ordered progression of play activities. Children simply smiling or laughing in a passive sense at activities going on around them are showing less mature thinking skills than children involved within play or creating play activities. Symbolic thinking, as evidenced through symbolic play, requires memory and imagination. When children can "play" at fighting (as in rough-and-tumble play), they are demonstrating an ability to represent ideas from memory and use them in a present context.

A child who, among playmates who are acting out ideas and employing imaginative "dramas," consistently reacts with true anger or fear to the feigned attacks or simulated competition may not be intellectually mature compared with agemates. This may be difficult for an observer to differentiate from a child who is reflecting poor emotional adjustment, or who may be emotionally disturbed and intellectually slow.

Children who spend large amounts of time in interactive games, and who use and respect rules for the completion of their games, are exhibiting a high degree of intellectual development. The recognition of the importance of "another" in an intellectual sense corresponds to a lessening of the egocentricism of earlier thinking.

A Social–Emotional–Cognitive Analysis of Play. It is not always easy to determine whether a child's play behavior, if not similar to that of agemates, is a reflection of differences in social–emotional development, intellectual development, or both. As an example, an older child's frequent onlooking behavior may be the result of difficulties in making friendships and a weak sense of self or of personal worth. Or, the child may not have the mental capacity for more mature constructive play.

Analysis of play behaviors alone may not be sufficient for an accurate description of a child's overall developmental state.

Evidence From Play Research

Can we see research evidence supporting the above-mentioned relationships between play and developmental characteristics? What does it mean to a child's development to have more or fewer opportunities for play? What effect does television watching, and/or video game playing have on a child? Can a child be encouraged to play in more healthful, beneficial ways? Some answers to these questions and others can come from an examination of play research. Papalia and Olds (1986), Garvey (1977), Frost (1983), and Fein (1981) have reviewed research of play. Their findings can be summarized in the following rubrics:

1. Play and Physical Development
2. Play and Social Development
3. Play and Language
4. Play and Objects
5. Play and Adults
6. Play and Sex Differences
7. Play and Its Context
8. Play and Television
9. Play and Siblings

Research into these areas of play can be briefly summarized as follows

Play and Physical Development. While it may seem mundane and self-evident, research evidence supports the contention that physical play appears to have a positive influence on motor development, both for large and small muscles (Wolfgang & Stekenas, 1985).

Social or Nonsocial Play. Children who play by themselves may be, in general, at risk for a number of social, mental health, and educational problems. At the same time, however, recent evidence indicates that much nonsocial play may consist of constructive or educational activities and contribute to a child's cognitive, physical, and/or social development. It is probably more important to ascertain the kind of play (whether it is solitary and yet goal-directed, fine-muscle, or education-related, as opposed to solitary and random and transient) than whether the play is simply solitary or social.

Play and Language. Play has been found to stimulate innovation in language, introduce and clarify new words and concepts, motivate language use and practice, develop language awareness, and encourage verbal thinking (Levy, 1984).

Piaget and Vygotsky, as reviewed in Isenberg and Jacob (1983), suggested a relationship between symbolic play and the later use of symbols involved in literacy activities. Several different empirical studies point to the conclusion that engaging in symbolic play and incorporating literacy into symbolic play can have a positive influence on early literacy development.

Play and Objects. Sylva (1976) has determined that children who engage in play with objects are better able to find creative problem-solving solutions involving the objects than children who are either shown modeled uses of the objects by adults or children who were given specific training with the use of the objects. It appeared that the *free handling* of the objects in play gave the children an opportunity to explore alternative steps in the problem-solving process and that they had a more relaxed attitude towards the task.

Play and Adults. Several studies have determined that play involving adults — not necessarily as trainers or teachers, but simply as interactive participants — is most profitable for children, for example, play that produces prolonged concentration and rich elaboration (Bruner, 1983), sustained and rich play, with complexity of action and language (Sylva, 1984), and enhanced sociodramatic play (Fein, 1981; Tower et al. 1979). In these studies the children were playing without an intrusive, watching-over-the-shoulder adult, but, rather, with sensitive, question-answering adults who were in the background, yet available.

Play and Sex Differences. Sex differences have been noted in many research investigations of play. Boys chose to play outdoors more often, girls indoors. Boys more frequently chose competitive physical activities than do girls (Stoneman, Brody, & MacKinnon, 1984). Boys were more likely to choose toys representing constructions and transportation (trucks, planes, boats) than girls, who were more likely to choose dolls (Fein, 1981). Boys tended to show more solitary behavior than girls; girls interacted with each other as playmates more often than boys (Stoneman et al., 1984). When play was observed in *activity centers,* boys showed significantly greater preferences for woodworking, manipulatives, and language (books, audiotapes), whereas girls preferred housekeeping, painting, and games.

An important summative finding was that sex-role training appeared to occur early in life and was reflected in play. Even preschoolers' toy choices tended to be related to sex-typed behaviors, that is, children chose toys that are in keeping with their pattern of sex role adoption or training (Cameron, Eisenberg, & Tyron, 1985).

Play And Its Context. Play in *adventure playgrounds* —those play areas with child-created and -constructed materials or nontraditional play materials in them — has been found to result in more, and more active, participation by children than adult-made, traditional, and static play structures or areas (Naylor, 1985; Burzynski, 1971).

Play and Television. U. S. children, 98% of whose homes have television, show an increasingly common tendency, beginning in the preschool years, to reflect television content in their play. Children's inclusion of television content seemed most often to reflect (a) a need to add diversity and fun to their play, (b) a vehicle by which to self-explore roles or behaviors, and (c) social uses, for example, gaining attention and friendships, and maintaining friendships. While some aspects of children's television-related play reflected sex-role stereotypes, an overall finding was that the use of television-related play had positive consequences on children's understanding of their feelings and abilities (James & McCain, 1982).

Sibling Play. Play with siblings tends to follow clear role definitions as pertains to age; that is, older children tend to direct or manage the play of younger siblings. In nonsibling play, however, younger children do not show a tendency to be managed by older children; the preference for the younger nonsiblings is to escape to solitary play or other activities (Stoneman et al., 1984).

PUTTING CHILDREN'S PLAY IN PERSPECTIVE

Of what use to the school psychologist, educator, or parent are the definitions, theories, and empirical findings just presented? In fact, several different uses can be considered.

General Suggestions

Perhaps the most significant suggestion is that adults *can* be involved in the play of children. It can be as simple as being active listeners, attuning themselves to observe many of the developmental characteristics that children reflect through their play. In this way, adults can recognize the extent to which they might be either underestimating or overestimating the children's ability. Or, in its fuller, more meaningful way, adult involvement in child play can be to provide a background assurance that the environment is stable and continuous (Bruner, 1983). Adults can offer a nonintervening, noninterfering source of reassurance and information.

The play activities that are thought best to support overall cognitive development are constructional play, that is, use of either fluid or structured materials that can be used to produce representational products. This can include paints, clay, blocks, Lego blocks, and puzzles (Wolfgang & Stakenas, 1985).The specific cognitive skill of memory appears to be best enhanced by symbolic play, that is, play that uses toys or objects to represent reality. Perceptual–motor skill development is highly associated with play using clay, paints, or water. Block play or other structured forms as playthings have been associated with better quantitative thinking skills. Problem-solving skills have been found to relate to play that puts an emphasis on curiosity, exploration, freedom of choice, and creativity (Cecil, Gray, Thornburg, & Ispa, 1985).

Children's selection of toys has been found to be associated with the sex role stereotyping of their adult caretakers; this often occurs during the years form infancy through age 2–3 years. The development of non-sex-typed toy selection behavior could thus be expected to occur in children of caretakers who showed androgynous behaviors and attitudes to their children (Peretti & Sydney, 1984).

To contemporary Americans, video game play has become an emerging area of concern. A consensus on this topic by several researchers reveals two major conclusions: (a) Children who play video games do *not* show reduced participation in active sports, poor school performance, or increased measures of aggressive behavior; but (b) the potential for abuse in video game play (compulsiveness, deviancy, low self-esteem) is not fully explored (Ellis, 1984; Dominick, 1984; Egli & Meyers, 1984).

Specific Areas and Ideas for Training

Anyone concerned with the development of children can be advised that an imperfect understanding of the relationship between play and work in the United States and other industrialized societies may be the biggest hurdle to placing greater emphasis on play behavior among our children. The views held by society about play — that it is seen as frivolous and unessential — have precluded its investigation and inclusion as a major topic in curricular designs of preschool or school programs (Sutton-Smith, 1967). In countries where the work ethnic prevails, play is usually thought of as something occurring primarily under conditions of surplus time and energy, and that anything as pleasureable as play could not possibly be directly useful (Green, 1984).

Preschool and regular school educators should be aware that the most effective promotion of play for children involves *play intervention;* this requires a specialized effort by the educator, ranging from being a facilitator of play to that of passive and active participant in play. The facilitator role requires the provision and careful arrangement of selected objects, materials, props, and preparatory experiences (reading of stories, explanations, etc.) related to selected themes. Intervention comes in when teachers become involved with and participate in the children's play and help children to recognize crucial elements that may be missing. Teachers can be revitalizing, by clarifying and expanding the play (Green, 1984). Passive participatory roles for teachers can involve making intervening suggestions and asking questions from outside of the play; active participatory behavior consists of assuming a role in play by modeling appropriate behaviors.

Parents and others relating to children can be aided by the following suggestions:

1. Parental involvement in play in a nonintrusive, nondirective way is a key to enhanced child development. Adults can encourage, demonstrate, and assist. They can preview play, monitor it, and help to review it. Reluctance by an adult to participate in play cannot be justified by claiming that play is better left to children or that an adult playing with a child would render the child unable to differentiate fantasy and reality.
2. Assessing the value of any one piece of play equipment is extremely difficult, but generally the better equipment is that which has multiple physical, social, or imaginative uses. Expense has little or nothing to do with qualitatively superior characteristics of the play equipment. Play areas need to ideally combine both indoor and outdoor settings, with some provision for isolation.
3. Early active communication with an infant in a playful dialogue can enhance development. This includes labeling and identifying objects or describing aloud the activities the adult is performing. Encouraging verbal response can be helpful to children throughout their lives. As children grow into adolescence, the roles of elaborator and appreciative audience can be added to the parent.
4. Children playing singly or in groups of three or more do not benefit as much from play as do those in a dyadic playgroup. Two children can exchange ideas, negotiate their intentions, elaborate as need be, and go on for as long as necessary; one child becomes lonely or bored and three or more offer too many distractions and unresolved dilemmas (Bruner, 1983).
5. Specific play training programs have been shown to help children cognitively through enhancing imaginative play, exploratory play, and self-esteem (Kuzovich & Yawky, 1982).

ALTERNATIVE ACTIONS

The Psychologist and Play

While much of the above information is most appropriately directed to teachers and parents, school psychologists might also benefit from this brief summary of play theories and research data. In a comprehensive perspective, the school psychologist might use play in both diagnosis and therapy for development. The outline in Table 1 might be helpful in a diagnostic evaluation of play.

Play was described above as a medium of cathartic self-expression. Play can thus be seen as therapeutic facilitator; this is often found in the psychoanalytic conception of play by Freud and others. Axline (1969, p. 9) suggested that "play is an opportunity which is given to the child to 'play out' his feelings and problems, just as, in certain types of adult therapy, an individual 'talks out' his difficulties." She further feels that nondirective play therapy allows a child to bring out negative feelings, face them, deal with them, and learn to control them or abandon them.

TABLE 1
A Psychodiagnostic Evaluation of Play

I. Cognitive dimensions
   1. Language use
   2. Literacy
   3. Choice of objects
   4. Quantification
   5. Symbolism
   6. Perceptual–motor/use & integration
   7. Creativity

II. Social dimensions
   1. Nonsocial
      a. Unoccupied
      b. Solitary
      c. Parallel
      d. Associative
   2. Social
      a. Functional
      b. Constructive
      c. Dramatic
      d. Games with rules

III. Emotional dimensions
   1. Psychoanalytic or other interpretations of content
   2. Sociodramatic play analysis
   3. Choice of partners (Sex, age, role)
   4. Fantasy content

V. Other factors
   1. Time on task
   2. Contributing variables
      a. SES
      b. Birth order
      c. Space
      d. Race or culture
      e. Geography, weather, etc.

IV. Physical dimensions
   1. Large- or small-muscle
   2. Active or inactive
   3. Perceptual–motor development

Play to the emotionally disturbed child is a seemingly ideal medium for expression of conflicts and the potential reduction of tensions, anxieties, and fears. What play therapy does, then, is to simply provide an optimum environment for a child's play to do the *work* of emotional maturation. Without play therapy, a child's emotions may not find resolution or healthy expression and release.

A caution to the school psychologist contemplating play therapy is that the therapist's role in most of the play therapies is not easy to establish or maintain. Play therapy requires large commitments of time and extensive training, and it usually requires a large inventory of play materials and a facility in which they can be used by children.

SUMMARY

Play is acknowledged to be a difficult aspect of human behavior to define and describe, but it can be characterized through several dimensions. It is a universal behavior of children, beginning in infancy and extending throughout life in various forms. Various theories describe play as a release of surplus energy, instinctive practice for adult life, a reflection of evolution, or as having a relaxing and self-serving function or a psychoanalytically cathartic and healing role.

Play is primarily pleasureable and rewarding; it is spontaneous, active, and symbolic; and it contributes to numerous components of cognitive maturation, among them concept formation, language development, literacy, problem-solving skills, creativity, socialization skills, quantitative skills, symbolic logic, perceptual–motor skills, and physical development.

Play can be either social or nonsocial and represent various degrees of social interaction and maturity. It is varied in its reflection of social backgrounds and sibling and peer relationships.

Play can involve a variety of objects or physical apparatus. It can be realistic, modeled, or dramatic, involving symbols, pretense, or fantasy. It can take place in many external environments, outdoors or indoors.

The evidence from play research has revealed many relationships between play and human behavior. It was found to promote physical development, perceptual–motor integration, memory, concentration, and language. Sex differences appeared often in children's play, and sex typing of toy selection by children was found to relate to parental sex role stereotypes. A child's sex determined which play centers would be used more, and boys displayed more physically active play behaviors than girls.

Television and video arcade game playing have not been shown to present any significant negative consequences on children's development as it relates to aggression, deviancy, or school success. Play based on TV themes has been related to enhanced self-understanding of feelings.

Older children seem likely to direct the play of younger siblings, but not that of younger unrelated playmates.

Adults can enhance the quality of children's play by including themselves in their play, by providing multipurpose playthings, and by talking about play activities during children's play. Two-children playgroups are better for children than solitary or three-person or larger playgroups. Play training programs for adults can improve the quality of play in children under their supervision.

Finally, school psychologists can use a diagnostic

various degrees oapproach to assessing childrens' play, and can choose play therapies as a method of providing treatment for social–emotional problems.

REFERENCES

Axline, V. (1969). *Play therapy.* New York: Houghton Mifflin.

Bruner, J. (1983). Play, thought and language. *Peabody Journal of Education, 3,* 60–69.

Burzynski, P. (1971) *Observations on various European preschool child-care facilities.* Unpublished master's thesis. Indiana State University, Terre Haute.

Cameron, E., Eisenberg, N. & Tyron, K. (1985). The relations between sex-typed play and preschoolers' social behavior. *Sex Roles, 12,* 601–615.

Cecil, L., Gray, M., Thornburg, K., & Ispa, J. (1985). Curiosity–exploration–play–creativity; The early childhood mosaic. *Early Child Development and Care, 19,* 199--217.

Egli, E., & Meyers, L. (1984). The role of video game playing in adolescent life: Is there reason to be concerned? *Bulletin of the Psychonomic Society, 22,* 309–312.

Eibl-Eibesfeldt, I. (1967). Concepts of ethology and their significance in the study of human behavior. Cited in H. Stevenson, E. Hess, & H. Rheingold (Eds.), *Early Behavior.* New York: Wiley.

Ellis, D. (1984). Video arcades, youth, and trouble. *Youth in Society, 16,* 47–65.

Ellis, M. J. (1973). *Why people play.* Englewood Cliffs, NJ: Prentice-Hall.

Fein, G. (1981). Pretend play in childhood: An integrative review. *Child Development, 52,* 4.

Freud, S. (1959). Beyond the pleasure principle. In J. Strachey (Ed.), *The standard edition of the complete psychological works of Sigmund Freud,* London: The Institute of Psychoanalysis (original work published 1922).

Frost, J. L. (1984, June). *Toward an integrated theory of play.* Paper presented at the meeting of the Music in Early Childhood Conference, Provo, UT.

Frost, J. L., & Klein, B (1984). *Children's play and playgrounds.* Austin, TX: Playgrounds International.

Garvey, C. (1977). *Play.* Cambridge, MA: Harvard University Press.

Green, P. (1984). Teachers and the play curriculum: Issues and trends. *Early Child Development and Care, 17,* 13–22.

Groos, K. (1901). *The play of man.* New York: Appleton.

Hall, G. S. (1906). *Youth.* New York: Appleton.

Huizinga, J. (1950). *Homo ludens: A study of the play element in culture.* London: Routledge and Kegan Paul.

James, N., & McCain, T. (1982). Television games preschool children play: Patterns, themes and uses. *Journal of Broadcasting, 26,* 783–800.

Kuzovich, C., & Yawky,T. (1982, April). *Play programs at home to stimulate growth.* Paper presented at the Study Conference of the Association for Childhood Education International, Atlanta, GA.

McCloyd, V. (1980). Verbally-expressed modes of transformation in the fantasy play of black preschool children. *Child Development, 51,* 1133–1139.

Naylor, H. (1985). Outdoor play and play equipment. *Early Child Development and Care, 19,* 109–130.

Papalia, D., & Olds, S. (1986). *Human development.* New York: McGraw-Hill.

Parten, M. (1932). Social play among preschool children. *Journal of Abnormal and Social Psychology, 27,* 243–269.

Patrick, G. T. W. (1916). *Psychology of relaxation.* New York: Houghton Mifflin.

Peretti, P., and Sydney, T. (1984). Parental toy choice stereotyping and its effects on child toy preference and sex-role typing. *Social Behavior and Personality, 12,* 213–216.

Piaget, J. (1962) *Play, dreams and imitation in childhood.* New York: Norton.

Soper, W., & Miller, M. (1983, September). Junk-time junkies: An emerging addiction among students. *School Counselor.*

Stoneman, Z., Brody, G., & MacKinnon, C. (1984).Naturalistic observation of children's activities and roles while playing with their siblings and friends. *Child Development, 55,* 617–627.

Sutton-Smith, B. (1967). The role of play in cognitive development. *Young Children, 22,* 361–370.

Sylva, K. (1976). Play and Learning. In B. Tizard & D. Harvey, (Eds.), *The biology of play.* London: Heinemann.

Sylva, K. (1984). A hard-headed look at the fruits of play. *Early Child Development and Care, 15,* 171–184.

Tolman, E. C. (1932). *Purposive behavior in animals and men.* New York: Century.

Tower, R., Singer, D., Singer, J., & Biggs, A. (1979). Differential effects of television programming on preschoolers' cognition, imagination, and social play. *American Journal of Orthopsychiatry, 49,* 265–281.

Wolfgang, C., & Stakenas, R. (1985). An exploration of toy content in preschool children's home environments as a predictor of cognitive development. *Early Child Development and Care, 19,* 291–307.

BIBLIOGRAPHY: PROFESSIONALS

Axline, V. (1969). *Play therapy.* New York: Houghton Mifflin. Axline's book is the classic on play therapy and gives a careful, clearly written description of the emotional content of children's play. It could provide the impetus for a practitioner to enter into therapeutic play for the first time.

Bruner, J. (1983). Play, thought and language. *Peabody Journal of Education, 3,* 60–69.
In a short, interesting article, the reader is given a reflection of the seminal thinking from the famous educator at the New School for Social Research, Jerome Bruner. The words of this man seem to carry more poignancy and impact than other writers'.

Fein, G. (1981). Pretend play in childhood: An integrative review. *Child Development, 52,* 4.
A comprehensive review of the literature concerning the topic of pretense or pretend play in childhood. It offers a narrower but more accurate description of an arena of play behavior and provides significant new thought.

Frost, L. (1984, June) *Toward an integrated theory of play.* Paper presented at the meeting of the Music in Early Childhood Conference, Provo, UT.
Attempts to develop a more comprehensive theory of play after reviewing five major theoretical orientations in the literature. It also looks at play through five perspectives: characteristics, motives, processes, functions, and content. Thorough and summative.

Garvey, C. (1977). *Play.* Cambridge, MA: Harvard University Press.
The approach in this book is fresh and absorbing. The author tells of numerous experiments with children in microscopic detail, providing a believable assessment that adds new dimensions to our understanding of play.

BIBLIOGRAPHY: PARENTS

Allen, M. (1968). *Planning for play.* London: Thames and Hudson.
Illustrates a number of different adventure playground designs, from which a parent can model the construction of a backyard play area or equipment. What is so appealing is that these play designs can be constructed inexpensively and attractively, and most importantly they are well liked and used by children.

Axline, V. (1972). *Dibs: In search of self.* Cambridge, MA: Houghton Mifflin.
Presenting her play therapy concepts in the form of an intriguing mininovel and case history, Axline makes for very informative, heart-warming reading.

Papalia, D., & Olds, S. (1986). *Human development.* New York: McGraw-Hill.
This up-to-date text covers not only the topics of play extremely well, but is an excellent overall resource of child development in a "student text" format. This text is used in college classrooms throughout the country.

Children and Prejudice

Joan R. Walton
Framingham Public Schools, Massachusetts

BACKGROUND

In schools, prejudice may be expressed in the books that distort the multicultural reality of the United States, in student racial epithets and fights, in staff remarks about "those -- !", in differential treatment of the sexes in class, or in differential treatment of children and parents who are poor or minority or bilingual.

What is prejudice? Allport (1958, p. 10) said, "prejudice is antipathy based upon faulty and inflexible generalization. It may be felt or expressed." Pelligrew (1982) flippantly and succinctly said, "Prejudice is being down on something you're not up on" (p. 1). Prejudice involves attitudes, as well as cognitions, as in statements: "I hate ——s!" and " ——s are stupid." Prejudice may be acted out in a continuum of actions from verbal insults, to avoidance, to segregation, to attack, to extermination.

This chapter looks at prejudice generically. Racial, religious, ethnic, and sex prejudice are the most frequently studied, but school professionals find prejudice against handicapped, fat, ugly, and poor children and old people as well. It is not certain that research findings about one target of prejudice generalize to all prejudice.

Extent of Prejudice

How widespread is prejudice? In Sydney, Australia, where middle school children represent 57 ethnic groups, Phillips (1982) concluded that children from all ethnic groups were prejudiced against some others on a survey of attitudes. Research on the extent of prejudice gives different answers depending on what measures are used, where it is done, when it is done, and what targets are studied. Allport (1958) estimated from research that 80% of the U.S. population harbored prejudice against Jews, blacks, and Roman Catholics of a degree "that would influence their daily conduct" (p. 77). Epps (1974) summarized more recent studies that suggest that "a sizable minority of white Americans, perhaps as large as a fifth of the adult population, persists in harboring racist attitudes in their most vulgar and naive forms" (p. 11). Porter's (1971) study in Boston showed an increase in children aged 3 years (50%) to 5 years (70%) who chose a black doll as "lazy" or "stupid" over a white doll (cited in Ehrlich, 1973).

Glock, Wuthrow and Piliavin (1975) reported that by high school age, school children's acceptance of negative Jewish stereotypes ranged from 34% to 45% of adolescents in three cities. Acceptance of negative black stereotypes was greater, ranging from 49% to 64%. Historically, Bettelheim and Janowitz (1964) reported a decrease in both anti-Jewish and anti-black prejudice in the United States, according to polls and surveys, but they felt a "hard core" of prejudiced persons remained.

Denial of Prejudice

It is usual for school personnel to deny a problem of prejudice. Glock et al. (1975) reported a teacher survey in three high schools showing a range of 1–11% who felt there was a religious prejudice problem in their school and 11–27% who felt racial prejudice was a problem. These numbers were much lower than the percentages of students who expressed prejudice that were cited earlier. Few teachers, without evidence or consciousness raising, would believe that they treat boys and girls differently in class. Most administrators feel a pressure to contain problems and tend to deal with them, as they are forced to, with the least amount of publicity. But denial makes systemwide prevention and/or treatment less likely. School staff rarely come to the school psychologist or counseling personnel asking for help with prejudice.

DEVELOPMENT

Theories of the Development of Prejudice

Historians, psychologists, and sociologists who have studied the origins of prejudice have advanced various theories of which Katz (1982) and Moran (1974) have provided compact summaries. Theoretical models include (a) the psychodynamic, (b) the personality type, (c) the cognitive factors, (d) the learning factors, and (e) the social factors theories. Most writers attempted systheses of several models, but there is a clear need for integrated theory and research to test out integrated theories.

Bird (1957) clearly stated the psychodynamic model, which today is less credited and appears less useful for work in schools. The scapegoating model, which proposed that prejudice comes out of misplaced anger, is an extension of this view. Cognitive factors and intelligence also have been related to measures of prejudice (Glock et al., 1975; Sussman & Thompson, 1971).

All other views give much more weight to learning and environment as causes of prejudice in people. Authoritarian parents have been posited to exhibit and teach prejudice (Adorno, 1950; cited by Katz, 1982). Correlations between mothers' authoritarian attitudes and children's prejudices have been found (Harris, Gough & Martin, 1950). Parents' prejudice correlates with children's prejudice (Ehrlich, 1973) and siblings' levels of prejudice correlate even more highly (Murphy, 1973; cited in Ehrlich, 1973). Overt verbal learning of prejudice was described by Orost (1971) in kindergartners. One white child, referring to black children, said, "No I don't even play with them, 'cause I don't like. My family hates them too, 'cause they all tell me . . . 'cause they're black. And that isn't their favorite color" (p. 12).

More subtle learning factors like modeling and observation are also at work (Katz, 1980). Bishop (1976) demonstrated that textbooks can covertly teach prejudice. The schools' role in teaching sex prejudice was documented by Serbin, O'Leary, Kent, and Tonick (1973), in whose studies differential treatment of boys and girls was found in 15 preschool classes.

A social–psychological explanation of prejudice includes many factors. Prejudice must be seen in the light of historical factors, such as slavery; sociocultural factors, such as urbanization, war, and colonization; and economic factors, such as whose job is threatened by a new immigration or a new working population (women) (Allport, 1958). Clark (1963) suggested that the U.S. history of immigration, in which nearly everyone came to escape poverty and/or persecution with great drive for success, made a good seedbed for prejudice based on competition. Sherif and Sherif (1953) expressed the "group norm" theory as an explanation of prejudice; attitudes of prejudice are "functionally related to becoming a group member — to adopting the group and its values (norms) as the main anchorage in regulating experience and behavior" (p. 161).

Wilner (1985) summarizes a social-psychological view of prejudice: "Prejudice is seen as . . . the almost inevitable result of the socialization of the child within an environment in which prejudiced attitudes are commonly held rather than solely a consequence of individual personality dispositions" (p. 31). Ehrlich's (1973) summary conclusion was even broader:

> The primary cause of the transmission of ethnic attitudes from parent to child and the primary mechanism for the maintenance of ethnic prejudice in society are not to be found in the psychology of people or in the social psychology of their interpersonal relationships. It is to be found in the particular historical conditions and present political economic structures out of which intergroup relations develop and are sustained (p. 161).

Prejudice in children, parents, and school personnel grows, and is nurtured in the climate of differential power relationships between groups in the community. Some people avoid adopting prejudiced feelings, attitudes and behaviors because they (a) do not experience the psychological needs answered by prejudice; (b) have the cognitive structures to distinguish individuals from groups, see through untrue stereotypes, and understand reasons behind true stereotypes; (c) have been overtly and covertly taught values of nonprejudice and how to respond to prejudiced cultural norms, (d) have self-identity and group identity that is not dependent on prejudice, and (e) have positive multicultural experiences that are valued by important people in their lives.

Stages of Development and Prejudice

When does prejudice develop? Katz (1982) reported no studies about the development of prejudice before the age of 3 years. By ages 3 and 4, racial differences are distinguishable by black and white children. Sex differentiation is also well established by that age. Other differentiations, such as religious, come to children's awareness much later. Differential racial valuing was reported by Katz in a group of 4-year olds. One black

4-year-old said, "the people that are white they can go up. The people that are black they have to go down."

By the age of middle school, differences are well noted and many children show negative affect about the differences. In Sydney, Australia, Phillips (1982) showed a distinction between developmental egocentric responses to other races such as "They are not like us" and prejudiced responses such as "They are wogs — I hate 'em." Piaget and Weil (1951) identified stages in children's development of distinction between in-groups and out-groups. Children may not logically be able to conceive, in the face of manifest differences (black/white), of a more general sameness (human, American) without sufficient cognitive development.

In adolescence the developmental drive for identity fosters same-group preferences and rejection of outsiders (Bettelheim & Janowitz, 1964). Prejudice here seems a defense against identity diffusion. *West Side Story* is a play in which heroes and cliques dominate to give gang members identity and selfhood. Glock et al. (1975) found adolescents in three communities to be more prejudiced than adults surveyed nationally at the same time. The economic status of these adolescents, and their cognitive sophistication, were highly correlated with prejudice. The more secure adolescents, academically and financially, did not need this defense.

Prejudice appears to develop in children naturally according to their stage and their psychological needs. It begins as differences are distinguished. It becomes translated into specific prejudiced beliefs, feelings, and behaviors, or not, as the child and the culture interact.

Assessment of Prejudice

There are at least five different methods of assessing prejudice in children. Many are group-administered and others require individual assessment. Many have been adapted for different age levels.

Ehrlich (1973) described three classic measurement areas and methods. Part of prejudice is conceptual, and it involves stereotypic thinking. Measurements of acceptance of stereotypic thinking probe for this dimension of prejudice. Part of prejudice is conative, or behavioral, and this aspect has been measured by self-reports on social distance scales or friendship patterns. Part of prejudice is affect, and some studies have used measures of galvanic skin reaction (GSR) to statements or stories or pictures designed to measure affect.

Measures for direct observation of differential teacher behavior come from sex discrimination literature (Serlin et al., 1973; Sadker, 1984). Wilkins and Velicer (1980) tried another measurement model by using four scales of the semantic differential to measure children's attitudes toward three groups of handicapped persons.

Discussion and examples of preschool and kindergarten measures can be found in Katz (1978), Serbin et al., (1973), Orost (1971), Westphal (1974), and Paulsen and Balch (1984). Nonverbal measures involving doll choices have frequently been used. Katz (1978) warned that in measuring for stereotypic attitudes or social distance with dolls of different skin colors, the color of hair and eyes should remain constant or they will be confounding. Paulsen and Balch (1984) found that in a preschool group (31–72 months) only two of four prejudice measures correlated. They warned against trying to assess or understand prejudice "unidimensionally." Ehrlich (1973) reported that studies show low but positive correlations for an older group of children between stereotypic thinking, social distance, and GSR measures.

Discussion and examples of measures for elementary-age children can be found in Sadker (1984), Wurzel (1980), Salvo (1980), Houser (1978), Frech (1975), Schaefer and Brown (1976), Wilkins and Velicer (1980), and Phillips (1982). Phillips's questionnaire included reliability data and some validity data.

Discussion and examples of measures for secondary school use can be found in Glock et al. (1975), Phillips (1982), and Martinez (1972).

A school mental health person may assess the need for individual intervention more simply, by interview and observation. Does a child show prejudice in all three areas of thinking? feeling? behaviors? Does the perspective go beyond noticing differences between people? Are significant others in the child's life concerned about the adoption of prejudiced attitudes? With positive answers to these questions an individual intervention may be helpful and effective. An analysis of the source of prejudice for this particular child leads to the most effective action.

The assessment of a need for intervention in a school or class may come also from experience and observation. Teachers' room conversations, student verbal and physical interactions, and patterns of ethnic or racial differentiation in discipline centers may all show a crying need for increased intergroup acceptance. Wherever there are groups that have differential power relations there is a need for programatic, instructional, and curriculum intervention. Because of the problem of denial of prejudice, school mental health workers need to be proactive in this advocacy rather than reactive.

PUTTING PREJUDICE IN PERSPECTIVE

The Victim

What happens to a child who is a victim or target of prejudice? Saenger (1953), in an early review of the literature, found that victims of race prejudice tended to (a) adopt majority views of their own inferiority, (b) playact the stereotype, (c) identify with the oppressors, and (d) assimilate if possible.

In contrast, according to Allport (1958) prejudice victims tended to become either intrapunative or extrapunitive. Intrapunitive victims, he found, tended variously to (a) deny membership with the target group, (b) behave passively and withdraw, (c) hate themselves and identify with the dominant group, (d) hate, or make class distinctions within, the target group, (e) have sympathy with other victims, (f) strive for symbolic status, and (g) become neurotic or mentally ill. Extrapunitive victims, in his view, tended to (a) have strong in-group ties and support, (b) be sly and cunning in survival and revenge tactics, (c) hold prejudice against other victims, (d) fight back militantly, and (e) strive to overcome the "handicap" and to prove themselves. In either case, Allport noted some healthy as well as some less healthy responses, in contrast to Saenger's view.

Black children, as they grow older, move to more favorable ratings of their own race and less favorable ratings of whites. Black kindergartners are still more likely than whites not to identify with their own race (Morland, 1973).

Cottle (1974), who had established long-term relationships with several black families in Roxbury, Massachusetts, learned about the fear of victims of prejudice. He quoted the ghetto mother of one of his young friends:

> Nobody . . . really wants us to have our children. They don't want these children around here . . . They go making all sorts of rules and laws about welfare. Then they come back to us with ideas of contraception . . . Because we're a burden to this country and to all those men who make the rules . . . What they'd really like is to get rid of us. Yesser, everyone of us. (p. 123)

The ultimate fear of the victim is annihilation. The feeling is often that of worthlessness.

Young victims can make healthy responses even in the midst of the overt dangers, for example, of school desegregation (Coles, 1967). Ruby, age 10, black, reflected on her past experience while helping to integrate a white school:

> When you get older you see yourself and the white kids; and you find out the difference. You try to forget it and say there is none; and if there is you won't say what it be. Then you say it's my own people and so I can be proud of them instead of ashamed. (p. 51)

And John, age 15, described some of his family's feelings about integration of facilities and stores:

> They (my parents) wanted me to be glad I could walk on the sidewalk . . . But I told them that once you walk on the sidewalk, you look in the windows of the stores and restaurants, and you want to go there too (p. 82).

The Victimizer

What happens within the prejudiced child? Saenger (1953) described a dynamic understanding of the defensive coping of the victimizer: Prejudice helps (a) increase self-esteem, (b) alleviate guilt, (c) give an outlet for aggression and frustration, (d) build up a sense of security, and (e) project the "bad" part of oneself.

Clark (1963) built his arguments for desegregated schools on his conclusion that prejudice is harmful to the victimizer as well as the victim. He argued that if white parents realized that prejudice "distorts and damages the core of personality" (p. 4) they would not demand segregation. He wanted *all* children to be "saved from the corrosive effects of racial prejudice" (p. 130).

Coles (1967) quoted the words and feelings of an archsegregationist: "It's like anything you've grown used to and depend on and believe in: if it's going to be changed right from under you, against your will, you'll be angry and you'll try to do something about it" (p. 362). However, there is a lack of hard data about the psychodynamics of the victimized and causal relationships remain unclear.

Prejudice and Learning

Does prejudice affect learning? The only evidence concerns the victims of prejudice. Wilner (1975) summarized research on black achievement in integrated schools. He concluded that black students generally did better in integrated schools than in compensatory segregated education alone. He warned that some studies had failed to control for differences in socioeconomic status. Segregated compensatory programs may also have been too little and too late. However, the increased black achievement was gained despite greater academic and social stress experienced by black students in desegregated schools.

ALTERNATIVE ACTIONS

Actions for Individuals

Research generally has shown that victimizers' prejudice is so much a social phenomenon that individual therapeutic work is not effective unless the client is "sick" in some other way. Prejudice is not a disease of this individual but a social disorder. Group work in classrooms, schools, and communities are the best options for treatment.

Sometimes a victim of prejudice will benefit from individual attention if there is pain or breakdown in coping skills. If such a condition is suspected, the school psychologist should be equipped to do an assessment that will help raise staff awareness of the experience of prejudice. Castaneda (cited in Epps, 1974) advocated that assessment should distinguish culturally preferred modes of learning, relating, reinforcement, and problem solving, and help teachers to respond to them. The assessment should be culturally sensitive and cautious in identifying intellectual deficits and learning handicaps. The assessment should identify any need for counseling, and counseling should be culturally relevant.

Katz (1982) reported studies of the period from 1974 to 1981 during which young children's doll choices (with eye and hair color constant) showed improved self-concepts in black children, perhaps as a result of the civil rights movement as well as from the improved testing. Community and group work aimed at raising pride may be more effective than individual work for victims, but evidence is confounded.

For a potential victimizer there are suggestions for individual interventions (Goodman, 1963). Parents and teachers can (a) actively teach their own pluralistic values, (b) discuss prejudice by age-appropriate means, (c) introduce multicultural experiences in books, television, and trips, and provide exposure to different cultural groups, (d) encourage family and child–child or child-adult multicultural friendships, and (e) build up prejudice-vulnerable students' self-esteem and sense of personal identity.

Actions in Schools

School psychologists and counseling staff in

schools can advocate what Allport (1958) described as a democratic school climate as a step to combat prejudice. It is hypothesized that prejudice-vulnerable students will have less need to use their defenses in this environment. It would model fairness and respect for individuality.

Contact between different groups has generally led to lessened prejudice (Epps, 1974; Smith, 1969; Bullock, 1976) although Bettelheim and Janowitz (1964) suggested that numerically unbalanced mixes of majority- and minority-group students may not help. Smith (1969) found that ninth-grade majority students who chose more minority friends came from a racially balanced eighth grade. In the same study there was found to be more stereotyping of Jews where a Jewish population dominated. Orost (1971), however, found white preschoolers' attitudes toward blacks to be unaffected by contact. Mussen (1950) found an interracial camp experience actually increased prejudice in the campers. School psychologists can consult with school personnel about the quantity and quality of intergroup contacts.

Programs of instruction for appreciating a pluralistic world and combating prejudice have been advocated by nearly all researchers. There is powerful evidence that programs of instruction are effective (at least in the short run) in changing attitudes (Katz, 1978; Wurzel, 1980; Westphal, 1974; Guttentag, 1976; Houser, 1978). Sussman and Thompson's (1971) work suggested that both victims' and victimizers' attitudes were changed by instruction. In a large study comparing 3,000 high schools Corder (1954) found less prejudice in those that had programmed education about race and minority issues. School psychologists can advocate and help implement programs of instruction that promote multicultural values and combat prejudice.

Not all programs, however, have been effective. Orzech (1979) suggested that high school students who sign up for a course on the nature of prejudice and ethnic studies may already be low on prejudice scales and experience no real change. A values clarification program with eighth graders did not improve scores on one student multicultural survey (Dunbar, 1980). A program for cognitive flexibility reported by Bronzo (1970) did not change prejudiced attitudes of high school students but a prejudice reduction curriculum did. Research suggests that programs need to be specific in advocating values of multiculturalism and in combating prejudice and need to be built into existing curriculums so that all students are exposed. Several curriculums are listed in the annotated bibliography for professionals.

Actions in the Community

School mental health personnel can effectively join community forces that are working for multicultural goals. In the past segregation and discrimination laws have been successfully targeted (Coles, 1967; Epps, 1974; Clark, 1963). Mass media instruction to counter prejudice as well as the monitoring of textbooks for covert teaching of prejudice also have been considered important projects (Allport, 1958).

In 1986, in Boston, a coalition of the Anti-Defamation league of B'nai B'rith (ADL), the Greater Boston Civil Rights Coalition, the Shawmut Banks, and WCVB TV 5 initiated a campaign to reduce prejudice with the theme of *A World of Difference. The Boston Globe* of January 27, 1986, put out a complete section of the paper to announce and publicize the campaign. The Shawmut bank gave money. WCVB donated massive air coverage and expertise for spots and documentaries. The ADL provided expertise for producing a teacher–student guide for use in schools. Children participated in artwork projects and in writing of experiences of prejudice. Massive campaigns like this have great potential to affect whole communities.

SUMMARY

Prejudice of some form is probably familiar to all humans. It is not a disease, but it can be lethal and limit the full development of both victims and victimizers. Education and cognitive sophistication hinder its growth, but the presence of prejudice in schools probably increases the chances of failure and dropout for its victims. Victims include ethnic groups, girls, bilingual students, religious minorities, the handicapped, and the fat, old, ugly, and poor.

Prejudice seems multidetermined, perhaps under a broad umbrella of differential power relationships transmitted through learning and socialization. Psychodynamic, personality, cognitive, learning, and social–psychological factors may all help explain particular expressions or feelings of prejudice. Race and color prejudice appears to grow early in life, and develops along with perceptual and cognitive structures when the necessary variables are present. Victims have an uphill life battle and many fail in the schools. Given support for self-esteem and identity, victims may become strong survivors. Victimizers show signs of limited or constricted personality development. They also can change.

In order to combat prejudice and help both the victim and the victimizer, group work seems to be most effective and efficient. Schools, organized around democratic principles of respect for differences, model the ideal. Curricula specifically designed to develop multicultural interests and discourage prejudice seem to change attitudes at all ages.

REFERENCES

Allport, G. (1958). *The nature of prejudice* (abridged). Garden City, NY: Doubleday/Anchor Books.

Baratz, S., & Baratz, J. (1970). Early childhood intervention, the social science basis of institutional racism. *Harvard Educational Review, 40,* 29–50.

Bettelheim, B., & Janowitz, M. (1964). *Social change and prejudice including dynamics of prejudice.* Glencove, NY: Free Press.

Bird, B. (1957) A consideration of the etiology of prejudice. *Journal of the American Psychoanalytic Association, 5,* 493.

Bishop, B. (1976). Learning prejudice in schools. *Topics in Cultural Learnings, 4,* 6–9.

Bronzo, A. (1970). Changes in prejudice and cognitive behavior in high school students as a function of instruction. *Dissertation Abstracts International, 31,* 2697A.

Bullock, C. (1976). *School desegregation, inter-racial contact and prejudice, final report.* (Report No. BBB 0621). Washington, DC: NIE (DHEW). (ERIC Document Reproduction Service No. ED 128524)

Clark, K. (1963). *Prejudice and your child.* (2nd ed.) Boston: Beacon.

Coles, R. (1967). *Children of crisis.* Boston: Little, Brown.

Corder, R. (1954). A factoral approach to antidemocratic attitudes. *Purdue University Studies in Higher Education, 82.*

Cottle, T. (1974). *Black children, white dreams.* Boston: Houghton Mifflin.

Dunbar, L. (1980). Utilization of values clarification in multicultural education. *Dissertation Abstracts International, 41,* 920A.

Ehrlich, H. (1973). *Social psychology of prejudice.* New York: Wiley.

Epps, E. (Ed.). (1974). *Cultural pluralism.* Berkeley, CA: McCutcham.

Frech, W. (1975). The effects of cognitive training in anthropology on ethnocentric attitudes. *Psychology in the schools, 12,* 364–370.

Glock, C., Wuthrow, R., & Piliavin, M. (1975). *Adolescent prejudice.* New York: Harper and Row.

Goodman, M. (1963) *A primer for parents educating our children for good human relations.* New York: ADL of B'nai B'rith. (Eric Document Reproduction Service No. ED001988)

Guttentag, M., & Bray, H. (1976). *Undoing sex stereotypes.* New York: McGraw-Hill.

Harris, D., Gough, H., & Martin, W. (1950). Children's ethnic attitudes: Relationship to parental beliefs concerning child training. *Child Development, 21,* 169–181.

Houser, B. (1978). An examination of the use of audio visual media as an instructional technique for altering ethnic attitudes among young children. *Psychology in the Schools, 15,* 116–122.

Katz, P. (1978). Modification of children's racial attitudes. *Developmental Psychology, 14,* 447–461.

Katz, P. (1982). Development of children's awareness and intergroup attitudes (Report No. BBB18183). Washington, DC: NIE. (ERIC Document Reproduction Service No. ED 207675)

Lipsit, S. (1969). Prejudice and politics in the American past and present. In C. Glock, & E. Siegelman (Eds.), *Prejudice USA.* New York: Prager.

Martinez, M. (1972). Reaction of high school students to desegregation in a southern metropolitan area. *Psychological Reports, 30,* 543–550.

Moran, R. (1974). *The roots of prejudice: Also reflections on the book "Racial awareness in schools."* Rio Piedras, Puerto Rico: Puerto Rico University. (ERIC Document Reproduction Service No. ED 090324)

Morland, J. (1973). *Racial attitudes in school children: from kindergarden through high school. Final report* (Report No. BBB07237). Washington, DC: National Center for Education Research. (ERIC Document Reproduction Service No. ED 072173)

Morse, C., & Allport, F. (1952). The causation of antisemitism: An investigation of seven hypotheses. *Journal of Psychology, B4,* 197–233.

Mulenz, C. (1979). Non-prejudiced caucasian parents and attitudes of their children toward Negroes. *Journal of Negro Education, 48,* 84–91.

Mussen, P. (1950). Some personality and social factors related to change in children's attitudes towards Negroes. *Journal of Abnormal and Social Psychology, 45,* 433–444.

Orost, J. (1971). Racial attitudes among white kindergarten children from three different environments (Report No. ETS-ICM-71-1). Princeton, NJ: Educational Testing Service (ERIC Document Reproduction Service No. ED 4650)

Orzech, M. (1979). Attitudes of high school students towards three selected ethnic groups as affected by participation in an ethnic studies program. *Dissertation Abstracts International, 35,* 1979A.

Paulson, K. & Balch, P. (1984). A note on the assessment of ethnic attitudes in pre-school children. *Journal of Community Psychology, 12,* 288–290.

Pelligrew, T., Frederickson, G., Knoble, D., Glazer, N., & Veda, R. (1982). *Prejudice.* Cambridge, MA: Belknap Press/Harvard University Press.

Phillips, S. (1982). Prejudice in middle school. *Journal of Psychology, 110,* 91–99.

Piaget, J., & Weil, A. (1951). The development in children of the idea of the homeland and of relations with other countries. *International Social Science Bulletin, 3,* 570.

Sadker, D. (1984). Teacher reactions to classroom responses of male and female students (Report No. EDN00001). Washington, DC: NIE. (ERIC Document Reproduction Service No. ED 245839)

Saenger, G. (1953). *The social psychology of prejudice.* New York: Harper and Row.

Salvo, D. (1980). Logic for children: An exploratory tool to affect stereotypic levels. *Dissertation Abstracts International, 40,* 499A.

Schaeffer, C. & Brown, S. (1976). Investigating ethnic prejudice among boys in residential treatment. *Journal of Social Psychology, 100,* 317–318.

Serbin, L., O'Leary, K., Kent, R., & Tonick, I. (1973). A comparison of teacher responses to the preacademic and problem behaviors of boys and girls. *Child Development, 44,* 796–804.

Sherif, M., & Sherif, C. (1953). *Groups in harmony and tension.* New York: Harper and Row.

Silberman, C. (1969). The schools and the fight against prejudice. In C. Glock, & E. Siegelman (Eds.), *Prejudice USA* New York: Prager.

Smith, M. (1969). The schools and prejudice, findings. In C. Glock & E. Siegelman (Eds.), *Prejudice USA.* New York: Prager.

Sussman, E., & Thompson, G. (1971). *Prejudice as a function of intellectual level and cultural information.* Address prepared for Educational Research Association Convention. New York: ERA. (ERIC Document Reproduction Service no. ED 048421)

Westphal, R. (1974). The effects of primary grade level interethnic curriculum on racial prejudice. *Dissertation Abstracts International, 35,* 3534–3535A.

Wilkins, J., & Velicer, W. (1980). A semantic differential investigation of children's attitudes towards three stigmatized groups. *Psychology in the Schools, 17,* 364–371.

Wilner, D. (1975). *Children and race:* Middlesex, England: Penguin Books.

Wurzel, S. (1980). Reduction of prejudice and stereotyping. *Dissertation Abstracts International, 40,* 5877B.

BIBLIOGRAPHY: PROFESSIONALS

Gabelko, N., & Michaels, J. (1981). *Reducing adolescent prejudice.* New York: Teachers College Press, Columbia University.
A study guide made up of eight units to fit into high school curricula in U.S. history, sociology, or psychology. Makes much use of discussion and fostering adolescent thinking.

Ehrlich, H. (1973). *Social psychology of prejudice.* New York: Wiley.
This author examined over 600 pieces of literature about prejudice and the bibliography is worth copying. He makes clear judgments about what research can tell us about prejudice.

Epps, E. (Ed.), (1974). *Cultural pluralism.* Berkeley, CA: McCutchan.
Gives professionals an opportunity to read eight views of cultural pluralism in schools and how each might look from different minority viewpoints.

Martinez, J., & Walters, A. (1977). *U. S. cultural mosaic. A multicultural program for primary grades.* ADL of B'nai B'rith, 823 UN Plaza, New York, NY, 10017
Two hundred forty activities for children aimed at teaching self-acceptance through presentation of celebrations, heroes, and stories of the multicultural world. Organized about goals with clear objectives. Written by educators from California.

Shiman, D. (1979). *The prejudice book; activities for the classroom.* ADL of B'nai B'rith, 823 UN Plaza, New York, NY, 10017.
A series of activities for children aged 9–13, focusing on thinking of and perceiving differences, human relations training, and multicultural learning.

BIBLIOGRAPHY: PARENTS

Goodman, M. (1963). *A primer for parents educating our children for good human relations.* ADL of B'Nai B'Rith, 823 UN Plaza, New York, NY, 10017. (ERIC Document Reproduction Service No. ED001988)
Advocates active parental teaching and modeling for cultural pluralism. A 30-page pamphlet.

Clark, K. (1963). *Prejudice and your child* (2nd ed.) Boston: Beacon.
Written to advocate desegregation to all parents. It gives historical, social, and psychological reasons for prejudice and suggests ways to combat it.

Coles, R. (1967). *Children of crisis.* Boston: Little, Brown.
A well-written and moving account of Coles's experience with children and families who were leading the school integration movement in the South. Also gives voice to their opponents.

BIBLIOGRAPHY: CHILDREN

Kindergarten to Second Grade

Adoff, A. (1973). *Black is brown is tan.* New York: Harper and Row.
A picture book with simple illustrations about a biracial family.

Goble, P. (1984). *Buffalo woman.* New York: Bradbury.
A native American legend about the intimate relationship between buffalo and people.

Nye, L. *What color am I?* (1977). Nashville, TN: Abingdon.
From a religious point of view this picture book celebrates God's gift of diversity of colors among humans.

Spier, P. (1980). *People.* New York: Doubleday.
A joyful, colorful presentation of differences and essential humanness of all people.

Third to Fifth Grade

Estes, E. (1984). *The hundred dresses.* New York: Harcourt Brace Jovanovich.
Deals with class prejudice. Girls tease a poor girl about her fantasy of having 100 dresses. There is some growth and change in the victimizing girls.

Godden, R. (1972). *The diddakoi.* New York: Viking.
A gypsy girl tries to fit into a new life in a village after losing her grandmother caretaker. Feelings of being different are well explored.

Konigsburg, E. (1971). *Altogether one at a time.* New York: Atheneum.
Four short stories involving prejudices against the learning-disabled, fat people, old people, and different races.

Lord, B. (1984). *In the year of the boar, and Jackie Robinson.* New York: Harper and Row.
A new immigrant Chinese girl enters a multiracial class in NYC. A funny and comfortable way to explore differences in customs and feelings of newness.

Sixth to Eighth Grade

Blume, J. (1970). *Iggie's house.* New York: Bradbury.
A white sixth-grade girl and her family and friends meet new black neighbors. Issues of change and prejudice are portrayed.

Cohen, R. (1968). *The color of man.* New York: Random House.
Wonderful photos by Ken Heyman. Offers a scientific approach, as well, to understanding differences. Nonfiction.

Frank, A. (1952). *Anne Frank: The diary of a young girl.* New York: Pocket Books.
Memories of an adolescent Jewish girl hiding out with her family to escape Nazi extermination. Adolescent issues and the ultimate fear of victims of prejudice evoked.

High School

Griffin, J. (1961). *Black like me.* Boston: Houghton Mifflin.
A white man travels the south as a black to experience prejudice firsthand.

Lee, H. (1960). *To kill a mockingbird.* New York: Lippincott.
White Alabama children go through crises and danger when their lawyer father defends a black man accused of rape.

Rivera, G. (1978). *A special kind of courage: Profiles of young Americans.* New York: Bantam Books.
Eleven young people with different backgrounds show common and heroic courage.

Other Sources for Children's Literature

Dreyer, S. (1977–1985). *Bookfinders* (Vols. 1–3). Circle Pines Minneapolis, MN: American Guidance Service.

Multi-Ethnic Books for Young Children: An annotated bibliography. National Association for the Education of Young Children, 1834 Connecticut Avenue, NW, Washington, DC 20009.

Children and Prematurity

E. Jeanne Pound
Griffin Regional Educational Service Agency, Georgia

BACKGROUND

During the past two decades, the emergence of neonatology as a specialized branch of pediatrics and the concomitant development of neonatal intensive care units have been associated with dramatic increases in the survival rate of preterm infants. Estimates of the incidence of premature births in the United States range from 6% to 8% of all births; roughly 250,000–300,000 infants whose gestational ages are less than 37 complete weeks and birthweights are below 2,500 g are born annually (Harrison, 1983; Nance, 1982). While the vast majority of premature infants exhibit normal development by the age of 2–3 years (Henig, 1983), as many as 20% may continue to display difficulties ranging from mild forms of learning disabilities, muscular incoordination, and poor socialization to severe forms of cerebral palsy, mental retardation, and sensory deficits (Koops & Battaglia, 1984).

Researchers have identified various risk factors that may be associated with premature labor and delivery. Among these risks are maternal complications such as toxemia, high blood pressure, cervical and uterine abnormalities, placental problems, urinary tract and vaginal infections, polyhydramnios (excessive accumulation of amniotic fluid), premature rupture of the membranes, and exposure to diethylstibestrol (DES) (Harrison, 1983; Henig, 1983). Other contributing factors include low socioeconomic status, poor nutrition, drug and alcohol abuse, single parenthood, maternal age less than 18 years or greater than 40 years, previous history of miscarriages or abortions, multiple pregnancy, and prior preterm delivery. However, in approximately 50% of all premature births, the specific causes remain unknown (Harrison, 1983). Consequently, the parents of a premature infant may be ill prepared to confront the anxiety and stress surrounding the various challenges of their infant's struggle for survival. Feelings of fear, helplessness, guilt, anger, denial, failure, frustration, disappointment, and depression are not uncommon among the reactions of the parents of preterm infants (Nance, 1982; Harrison, 1983; Klaus & Kennell, 1982).

Due to the immaturity of their organ systems, premature infants are particularly vulnerable to traumas during the perinatal and postnatal periods. Respiratory difficulties are common and pose a serious threat to the premature baby, since a diminished supply of oxygen to the brain tissue is a prime cause of brain injury and neurological impairment (Perlman & Volpe, 1985). Babies born prior to the 35th week of gestation are especially susceptible to respiratory distress syndrome (RDS), because their immature lung tissue is unable to produce sufficient amounts of surfactant to inhibit their lungs from collapsing during the breathing process. Boys with a gestational age between 28 and 38 weeks, infants who are the product of complicated deliveries, the latter born of twins, and the offspring of diabetic mothers are also at high risk for developing RDS. Approximately 35% of all preterm infants born in the United States each year suffer from RDS (Harrison, 1983). Premature infants afflicted with RDS may also experience episodes of apnea (Fitzhardinge, 1973), during which they cease to breathe for periods in excess of 20 seconds. Apnea may be a result of the immature development of the respiratory centers of the brain, which monitor the concentration of blood gases and regulate the rate and depth of respiration. Episodes of bradycardia or slowed heart rate often occur concurrently with apneic episodes. Prior to the advent of neonatal intensive care units and the technological advances in respiratory therapy, approximately 75% of the infants afflicted with RDS succumbed before attaining one month of age (Koops & Battaglia, 1984). Today, with oxygen hoods, continuous positive airway pressure (CPAP) that prevents the lungs from collapsing, and mechanical ventilation, the recovery rate approaches 80% (Henig, 1983). Respiratory therapy is not without its complications, though. The extended use of a respirator can cause damage to the lungs and result in a chronic lung condition referred to as bronchopulmonary dysplasia or BPD (Harrison, 1983). In this condition, the formation of scar tissue obstructs the airway and interferes with the aeration of the blood. Premature infants with BPD often require lengthy confinement in a neonatal intensive care unit (Landry et al., 1984); such an extended separation may have a negative impact upon bonding and attachment. Retrolental fibroplasia (RLF), which causes damage to the retina of the eye, is another complication of respiratory therapy. It is thought that the administration of oxygen may be associated with mild, moderate, and severe forms of visual impairment, which include myopia, partial loss of the field of vision, and blindness. The incidence of visual impairment due to RLF is greatest among very low birthweight infants: 22–42% of infants with birthweights below 1,000 g are afflicted with some degree of visual impairment, whereas 2% of infants with birthweights ranging from 1,000 to 1,500 g experience visual impairment. It is also estimated that 5–11% of the very low birthweight group suffers from blindness (Harrison, 1983; Henig, 1983; Moore, 1981).

Brain bleeding or intraventricular hemorrhage (IVH) occurs in approximately 30% of neonates under 1,500 g (Koops & Battaglia, 1984). Premature infants between 24 and 34 weeks of gestation are particularly susceptible to IVH owing to the immaturity and lack of protection of the blood vessels surrounding the ventricular system (Henig, 1983). Birth asphyxiation, extreme alterations in the infant's blood pressure during a difficult delivery, and pressure against the head in the birth canal can cause the fragile capillaries to rupture. Brain bleeds are classified from Grade I to Grade IV, depending upon their severity and extent; Grade IV bleeds are the most severe and are usually associated with serious neurological problems (Landry, Fletcher, Zarling, Chapieski, & Francis, 1984; Harrison, 1983). Many premature infants with less severe bleeds recover without major neurological impairment; however, a fair proportion of these babies may experience problems such as hydrocephalus, cerebral palsy, mental retardation, and hearing or visual impairment (Koops & Battaglia, 1984).

Hyperbilirubinemia or physiologic jaundice afflicts nearly 70% of preterm infants (Henig, 1983). During the breakdown of fetal red blood cells following birth, bilirubin is released along with iron and protein. Prior to its excretion from the body, bilirubin is transported to the liver, where it is conjugated from a potentially toxic substance into a harmless waste product. As a result of the immaturity of the liver, the premature infant is unable to convert bilirubin adequately and, thus, it accumulates in the bloodstream (Moore, 1981). Careful monitoring of the bilirubin concentrations and the timely treatment of hyperbilirubinemia with phototherapy and, in severe cases, exchange transfusions, have been successful in limiting the incidence of kernicterus, a syndrome characterized by mental retardation and severe forms of cerebral palsy. Inner ear damage resulting in a sensorineural hearing loss is a more common consequence of elevated bilirubin levels (Koops & Battaglia, 1984; de Vries, Lary, & Dubowitz, 1985).

Due to the immaturity of the immune system and the shortened length of gestation, which reduces the amount of maternal antibodies transferred through the placenta, the preterm infant is also highly susceptible to bacterial, viral, and fungal infections (Moore, 1981). Male infants appear to be more vulnerable to infections than female infants. It has been hypothesized that this phenomenon may be attributed to the association between the X chromosome and factors responsible for the regulation of the immune system (Moore, 1981; Harrison, 1983). Infections may be conveyed to the infant while in the uterus, during passage through the birth canal, and through exposure to infections in the neonatal intensive care unit. Punctures of the skin during the birth process and during hospital procedures, such as the insertion of an intravenous feeding tube or an arterial catheter, provide potential sites for the invasion of infections. Among the various intrauterine infections, toxoplasmosis, rubella, cytomegalovirus, and herpes appear to be the most serious (Harrison, 1983). Infants afflicted with such infections may be small for their gestational ages and display signs of neurological impairment, which include mental retardation, seizure disorders, and neuromuscular disease. In addition, they may sustain sensory handicaps that affect their hearing and vision (Koops & Battaglia, 1984). Exposure to infections may also cause illnesses such as pneumonia, sepsis, and meningitis in the neonatal period. When severe, pneumonia can result in respiratory failure and hypoxia, which require treatment similar to that for RDS (Harrison, 1983). Sepsis, a bacterial infection of the bloodstream, may be accompanied by symptoms that include irritability,lethargy, apnea, problems with thermoregulation, feeding difficulties, and abdominal distention. Treatment may consist of administering antibiotics and exchange transfusions (Moore, 1981). Among those treated for sepsis, 20–30% may experience such difficulties as developmental delays, mental retardation, and hearing impairment (Koops & Battaglia, 1984). Meningitis, which has a high mortality rate among neonates, may develop in 25–40% of the infants afflicted with sepsis (McIntosh & Lauer, 1984). The morbidity rate for survivors approaches 50% and includes abnormal electroencephalograms (EEGs), seizure disorders, cognitive deficits, speech problems, and perceptual–motor difficulties (Koops & Battaglia, 1984).

DEVELOPMENT

Significant deviations in the attainment of developmental milestones by premature and full-term infants with identical chronological ages may persist until the premature infant has attained a chronological age of 2–3 years. In order to better evaluate the development of preterm infants, a correction for gestational age is usually made until the infant's second birthday (Henig, 1983; Harrison, 1983). To accomplish this, the number of weeks that the baby was premature is subtracted from the chronological age. Thus, a 6-month-old infant born at 32 weeks of gestation would more closely resemble a full-term baby at 4 months of age than one of a similar chronological age. It is suggested that parents be adequately informed about the adjustment for gestational age, and that a statement regarding such an action be included in the body of the psychological report.

The general sequence in which premature infants attain the various developmental milestones is similar to that of full-term infants. Therefore, standard developmental charts can be employed as guidelines to evaluate the progress of a preterm infant, provided that the infant's age has been corrected for the degree of prematurity. A summary of the major developmental milestones attained during the first year and their corresponding corrected ages is outlined by skill area in Table 1. For many premature infants, the pattern of development during the first year may be uneven; while they may exhibit adequate cognitive and social functioning for their corrected ages, their acquisition of various motor skills may be somewhat delayed (Harrison, 1983). Henig (1983) offers a framework within which to evaluate the developmental progress of a preterm infant during the first 12 months following the expected due date; an infant who has not mastered the skills of visual tracking, responding to the voice of the caregiver, rolling over, crawling, and sitting within 3–4 months beyond the corrected age for attaining such skills may warrant concern about such delays in development. A preterm infant who exhibits a preference for one side of the body over the other during the first year may also be at greater risk for developmental difficulties (Harrison, 1983).

Researchers investigating the development of preterm infants have focused on the medical complications surrounding birth, neurological and developmental assessments of the infant, and the interactions between the infant and the environment (Sigman & Parmelee, 1979). In general, the medical complications surrounding the birth of premature infants appear more likely than birthweight or gestational age to influence their development at 24 months of age. Beyond 24 months, environmental variables, such as socioeconomic status, parent education levels, and the quality of the caregiver–infant interaction, have a significant impact upon the preterm infant's development. While normalization of preterm infants without severe sequelae has been observed on global indices of development at 24–36 months, subtle learning problems may emerge in the preschool or school-aged child (Harrison, 1983).

Much of the research on preterm infants has focused on the sensorimotor period of development. Siegel et al. (1982) compared the development of 80 preterm infants weighing less than 1,501 g at birth with that of 68 full-term infants at 4, 8, 12, 18, and 24 months of age. Approximately 12.5% of the preterm group exhibited serious problems, which included blindness, cerebral palsy, and severe developmental delay; these were excluded from the developmental testing at 24 months. When scores were corrected for the degree of prematurity, the preterm group, whose birthweight was appropriate for gestational age (AGA), resembled their full-term counterparts at 24 months of age on the Mental Scale of the Bayley Scales of Infant Development and the Reynell Developmental Language Scale. The performance of the full-term group significantly exceeded that of the preterm group on the Motor Scale of the Bayley Scales, however, which is consistent with the findings of other researchers (Field, Dempsey, & Shuman, 1979). Specific factors that were associated with the prediction of cognitive, language, and motor delays in the preterm group included lower socioeconomic status, lower educational level of the parents, maternal smoking, number of previous miscarriages, later birth order, degree of prematurity, asphyxia, hyperbilirubinemia, and apnea. In addition, episodes of severe apnea appeared to be related to delays in expressive language development. Landry et al. (1984) studied the effects of various major medical complications upon the development of preterm infants with gestational ages less than 37 weeks and birthweights below 1,501 g. Such medical complications included respiratory distress syndrome, intraventricular hemorrhage, bronchopulmonary dysplasia (BPD), and hydrocephalus (HYD). At 24 months of age, infants afflicted with RDS, with or without IVH, exhibited functioning within the average range on both the Mental and Motor scales of the Bayley Scales of Infant Development. Significant delays in cognitive and motor development were evident in both the BPD and HYD groups. Length of hospitalization in excess of 16 weeks was also associated with a poorer developmental outcome in the BPD group. A more recent study by Meisels, Plunkett, Roloff, Pasick, and Stiefel (1986) also revealed differential developmental outcomes during the second year of life for groups of premature infants afflicted with respiratory distress syndrome or bronchopulmonary dysplasia. While infants who were small for their gestational ages, or below the 10th percentile in birthweight, were excluded from the study, those with BPD exhibited significant growth retardation in their second year. To assess cognitive, sensorimotor, and language development, the researchers employed the Mental and Psychomotor Scales of the Bayley Scales of Infant Development, several scales from the Uzgiris–Hunt Ordinal Scales of Psychological Development, and the Receptive–Expressive Emergent Language Scale. The developmental outcome of the infants in the RDS group significantly exceeded that of the infants in the BPD group in all of the areas assessed; the mean scores of the RDS group were within the Average range of ability, while those of the BPD group fell within the Low Average range of ability. It was also determined that the nature of the respiratory illness accounted for more of the variance in developmental

TABLE 1

Major Developmental Milestones With Ages Corrected for Degree of Prematurity

Skill Area	Corrected Age
Gross-motor	
Rolls from stomach to back	5 months
Rolls from back to stomach	6 months
Sits without support when placed	7 months
Crawls	8 months
Pulls up to a standing position using furniture	9 months
Stands alone	11 months
Walks alone	12.5 months
Fine-motor	
Reaches for object beyond his immediate grasp	6 months
Uses pincerlike grasp to secure small objects; transfers objects between hands	8 months
Uses prehensile grip to secure small objects	12 months
Language	
Coos, squeals, and gurgles	3 months
Babbles	6 months
Imitates sounds in response to caretaker	7 months
Recognizes name	8 months
Appears to understand the meaning of "no"	11 months
May have a 2–5-word vocabulary	12 months
Mental	
Tracks slowly moving objects within his field of vision	3 months
Recognizes caretakers	5 months
Recognizes self and smiles at reflection in mirror	8 months
Attempts to uncover hidden objects	10 months
Develops a beginning concept of object permanence	11 months
May construct tower of 2–3 blocks	12 months
Social skills	
Smiles purposively in response to others	3 months
Smiles upon recognition of familiar person	5 months
Engages in playing peek-a-boo	7 months
Repeats behaviors that have been positively reinforced	9 months
Plays pat-a-cake	10 months
Recognizes distinction between self and others	12 months

Note: Adapted from Bayley (1969), Caplan (1982), and Henig (1983).

outcomes than did gestational age or birthweight. Sigman, Cohen, Beckwith, and Parmelee (1981) attempted to identify the social and familial variables that were associated with the development of preterm infants whose gestational ages were equal to or less than 37 weeks and birthweights were below 2,500 g. An infant's birth order and the quality of the caregiver–infant interaction were the factors most closely associated with performance on the Gesell Developmental Scale and the Mental Scale of the Bayley Scales between 4 and 24 months of age. The provision of responsive caregiving and much social, verbal, and object stimulation may have accounted for the superior performance of firstborn infants. Higher socioeconomic status and English language background were also significantly related to higher levels of competence at 24 months of age.

Investigating the relationship between prematurity and the cognitive, perceptual, and personal–social development of preschoolers from predominantly middle-class backgrounds, Jacob, Benedict, Roach, and

Blackledge (1984) discovered that children who had been born at term scored significantly higher on the Perceptual–Performance Scale of the McCarthy Scales of Children's Abilities than those who had been born prematurely. When the scores of the 3-year-olds in the premature group were adjusted to reflect their postconceptual ages, however, such discrepancies were not apparent. An analysis of the individual subtests that comprise the McCarthy Scales indicated some impairment on the Draw-A-Design subtest for the preterm group. Given the association that others have found between drawing tasks involving visual–motor coordination and integration, and measures of arithmetic achievement, the researchers speculated upon the possibility that the preterm group may be at higher risk for the emergence of arithmetic disabilities at school age. No significant differences were detected between the preterm and full-term groups in the areas of verbal ability, memory, articulation, self-direction, ability to plan, impulsivity, task persistence, and personal–social development.

In a longitudinal study that addressed the intellectual and emotional development of premature children from 1 to 7 years of age, Grigoroiu-Serbanescu (1984) found that deficits were associated with the degree of prematurity until the age of 3. Boys with birthweights below 1,500 g and gestational ages between 27 and 29 weeks exhibited the most pronounced cognitive deficits. Between the ages of 3 and 5 years, the various preterm groups exhibited normal developmental progress, which was consistent with that of the full-term group (Grigoroiu-Serbanescu, 1981). Although the preterm and full-term groups of children displayed normal intelligence at ages 6 and 7, boys with birthweights between 1,500 and 1,999 g and gestational ages between 30 and 33 weeks, as well as boys and girls with birthweights below 1,500 g and gestational ages between 27 and 29 weeks, displayed significantly lower mean IQs than did the full-term children. Boys and girls in both of these lower birthweight groups also exhibited more signs of emotional immaturity, whereas the emotional maturity of preterm children with birthweights between 2,000 and 2,500 g and gestational ages between 34 and 36 weeks resembled that of full-term children. School adjustment difficulties, as documented by measures of language, reading, writing, and mathematics achievement, attention, fatigability, emotional maturity at school, and social behavior, were also more prevalent among the lower birthweight preterm children. The interaction among the variables of degree of prematurity, IQ, perinatal and postnatal medical complications, emotional maturity, and cultural and income levels of a child's family appeared to contribute to school adjustment (Grigoroiu-Serbanescu, 1984).

Vohr and Garcia Coll (1985) conducted a longitudinal study of very low birthweight (≤ 1,500 g) preterm infants, whose gestational age averaged approximately 30 weeks. Based upon a neurological examination during the first 12 months following birth, the infants were categorized as normal, suspect, or abnormal. The suspect group included infants who displayed aberrations of muscle tone, posture, movement, reflexes, cranial nerves, or head circumference. Infants in the abnormal group were afflicted with cerebral palsy or severe sensory deficits. During the course of the study, referrals to infant stimulation or preschool special education programs were initiated. At the age of 7 years, assessment consisted of a neurological examination and a psychoeducational evaluation, which utilized the Stanford–Binet Intelligence Scale, the Developmental Test of Visual–Motor Integration, the Reading subtest from the Wide Range Achievement Test, and the Picture Completion and Block Design subtests from the Wechsler Intelligence Scale for Children–Revised. The criteria for placement in the normal group at 7 years of age were the absence of neurological or developmental handicaps and an IQ score ≥ 80. Those in the suspect group exhibited delayed language development, fine- or gross-motor problems, or seizure disorders, and those in the abnormal group had obvious neurological impairment that included cerebral palsy, blindness, deafness, and hydrocephalus. Roughly 23% of the children who had originally been viewed as normal manifested subtle neurological deficits in the areas of fine- and gross-motor development. Problems with balance were particularly notable, and, as the authors suggest, may be indicative of minor cerebellar insults. While 58% of those in the suspect group at 1 year of age continued to exhibit soft neurological signs, 41% were classified as normal at 7 years of age. All of the children designated as abnormal at 1 year of age continued to be categorized as such at school age. With respect to cognitive abilities, both the normal and suspect groups had mean IQ scores within the Average range on the Stanford-Binet. Although the mean IQ score of the abnormal group was significantly lower, the children in this category experienced the most dramatic cognitive gains over time. Learning difficulties were discovered in all three groups; 54% of all of the very low birthweight infants required special education or remedial services at school age. A high incidence of visual–motor integration difficulties was noted in all three groups, and significant decoding problems were apparent among the members of the suspect and abnormal groups. While socioeconomic status did not appear to be associated with neurological sequelae, a higher proportion of children from lower-socioeconomic-status families received special education placement.

PUTTING PREMATURITY IN PERSPECTIVE

Early identification of preterm infants considered at risk for developmental problems is imperative, in order to provide early intervention that may limit the severity and chronicity of such problems. Screening at birth consists of an Apgar evaluation of the neonate's heart rate, breathing effort, muscle tone, reflex irritability, and color at 1 minute and 5 minutes following birth. Healthy, full-term babies typically receive Apgar scores between 8 and 10, whereas preterm infants who are moderately depressed may be assigned Apgar scores ranging from 5 to 7. Apgar scores of 4 and below are indicative of severe distress and may be associated with poorer developmental outcomes (Koops & Battaglia, 1984). Preterm infants thought to be at risk may also be evaluated by the Brazelton Neonatal Assessment Scale, a behavioral instrument that focuses on an infant's muscle tone, reflexes, motor responses, organization, habituation, irritability, startle responses, and self-quieting skills (Koops & Battaglia, 1984; Harrison, 1983). A neonatal neurological exam may also be warranted for infants displaying overt signs of possible impairment.

Preterm infants who do not exhibit any of the severe sequelae or obvious indications of neurological impairment may come to the psychologist's attention through physician- or parent-initiated referrals. Massive screenings of preschool and kindergarten populations are another source of potential referrals. In order to determine an appropriate course of action for a particular preterm child, it is fundamental to obtain data relative to the child's medical, developmental, psychosocial, familial, and, if appropriate, educational histories; to screen for possible sensory deficits; and to conduct a comprehensive interdisciplinary assessment of the child's developmental progress. While some of the historical information can be ascertained through interviews with the child's parents or primary caregivers, such data should be supplemented by the medical records of the hospital, neonatologist, and pediatrician. Formal assessment should be conducted by an interdisciplinary team that, ideally, would consist of a pediatrician, neurologist, psychologist, social worker, speech and language therapist, physical therapist, occupational therapist, early childhood or special educator, and the child's parents. Specific areas to be addressed during formal assessment include medical and neurological status, receptive and expressive language development, cognitive development, fine- and gross-motor functioning, social–emotional functioning, and adaptive behavior. It is important that an evaluation of the physical and social–emotional aspects of the child's home environment also be included in the comprehensive assessment, since environment has a significant impact upon developmental outcome beyond the age of 2 years. A selected list of instruments suitable for the early identification of children considered to be at risk is included in Table 2. An interdisciplinary assessment should enable the evaluation team to obtain an estimate of global functioning, to determine specific strengths and weaknesses, to develop general and specific developmental and educational goals, and to devise an appropriate program of intervention for a given child and his family.

ALTERNATIVE ACTIONS

Early intervention for at-risk premature infants and children is of paramount importance in eliminating or curtailing the effects of prematurity upon development. Among the courses of action that might be pursued are referrals to infant stimulation programs, the development of preschool and school-age special education programs, the organization of parent support groups, and the education and training of parents.

Various researchers have examined the relationship between tactile–kinesthetic, auditory, visual, or multimodal stimulation of preterm infants in the neonatal intensive care unit and subsequent development. Tactile–kinesthetic stimulation, consisting of cuddling, rocking, stroking, and flexing of the limbs, has been shown to yield better habituation, improved muscle tone, better head control, and significant weight gain in the preterm infant. A reduction in the frequency of apneic episodes has also been associated with the utilization of oscillating water beds. Studies employing auditory stimulation, such as the tape recording of the mother's voice; visual stimulation, such as pictures and mobiles; and multimodal stimulation have also documented benefits that include weight gain, neurological maturation, increased levels of attention, and the facilitation of motor development. Long-term stimulation programs, which continued for a year or more beyond the period of hospitalization and emphasized the quality of the caregiver–infant relationship, produced the most significant results. Although there are some methodological problems in this body of research, it appears clear that early sensory stimulation is an integral factor in the development of the premature infant (Masi, 1979).

Other infant stimulation programs are individualized and reflect the specific needs of high-risk infants and their families. Programs may be home-based, center-based, in which case the child is transported to an appropriate agency or educational facility; or a combination of the two. The goal of such programs is to effect changes in the parent or caregiver's behavior that will engender optimal development in the infant. Through the use of modeling techniques, an infant specialist can assist parents in improving the quality of interaction with their child, as well as discovering specific activities and materials that might enhance the child's development at a given stage (Bromwich & Parmelee, 1979).

Depending upon particular state mandates, high-risk preterm infants may become eligible for special education placement during their preschool years or upon entering kindergarten. Following a comprehensive assessment, an individualized educational plan (IEP) designating general and specific goals to be attained within a prescribed time frame would be devised by members of the evaluation team. Preschool programs may be home- and/or center-based; programs for school-aged children are more likely to be school-based. Parental participation can be encouraged through the development of activity packets to be employed at home and through a flexible policy regarding classroom visitation. Children with severe handicaps, whose needs may extend beyond the scope of the school's special education program, can be referred to appropriate community agencies.

Support groups for the parents of premature infants have propagated across the United States, but are primarily concentrated in urban areas. Such groups offer peer counseling and support to parents and are designed to help allay feelings of anxiety and guilt, as well as to assist parents in coping with the demands of a premature infant. In addition, these groups may sponsor discussions with professionals on topics relevant to prematurity,

TABLE 2

Instruments Suitable for the Developmental Evaluation of High-Risk Preterm Infants and Children

Tests	Age range	Description
COGNITIVE		
Bayley Scales of Infant Development — Mental Scale	2 months–30 months	Evaluates sensorimotor skills, visual and auditory discrimination, object permanence, memory, problem-solving skills, and early speech and language development
Kaufman Assessment Battery for Children	2½ years–12½ years	Assesses ability to perform tasks that involve sequential and simultaneous cognitive processing
McCarthy Scales of Children's Abilities	2½ years–8½ years	Measures cognitive functioning through Verbal, Perceptual–Performance, Quantitative, and Memory Scales
Stanford-Binet Intelligence Scale: Fourth Edition	2 years–23 years, 11 months	Evaluates crystallized abilities, fluid-analytic skills, and short-term memory
Uzgiris Hunt Ordinal Scales of Psychological Development	2 weeks–2 years	Assesses visual tracking, object permanence, imitation, causality, means for obtaining goals, object relations in space, and schemata for relating to objects
Wechsler Intelligence Scale for Children — Revised	6 years–16 years	Scales assess verbal and nonverbal abilities, and provide an estimate of global intelligence
LANGUAGE		
Assessment of Children's Language Comprehension	3 years–6 years 5 months	Assesses the understanding of words and phrases through a pictorial format
Clinical Evaluation of Language Functioning	6 years–18 years	Evaluates the ability to process and produce oral language; provides diagnoses in the areas of phonology, syntax, morphology, semantics, memory, word finding, and retrieval
Receptive Expressive Emergent Language Scale	Birth–36 months	Utilizes a parent interview to assess receptive and expressive language
Reynell Developmental Language Scales - Revised Edition	1½ years–6 years	Employs toys and pictures to analyze receptive and expressive language development
Test for Auditory Comprehension of Language	3 years–6 years, 11 months	Uses a pictorial format to measure understanding of oral vocabulary, morphology, and syntax
Test of Early Language Development	3 years–7 years, 11 months	Evaluates semantic and syntactic areas of receptive and expressive language
Test of Language Development — Primary Edition	4 years–8 years 11 months	Assesses semantic, syntactic, morphological, and phonological aspects of receptive and expressive language
MOTOR		
Bayley Scales of Infant Development — Motor Scale	2 months–30 months	Measures control of the body, locomotion, gross-motor, and fine-motor skills
Bruininks–Oseretsky Test of Motor Proficiency	4½ years–14½ years	Assesses gross- and fine-motor development in areas that include agility, speed, balance, strength, bilateral coordination, dexterity, and visual–motor control

(Table 2 continues on following page)

(Table 2 continued)

Tests	Age range	Description
MOTOR (continued)		
McCarthy Scales of Children's Abilities — Motor Scale	2½ years–8½ years	Evaluates fine- and gross-motor coordination, balance, visual–motor integration, and visual tracking
Developmental Test of Visual–Motor Integration	2 years–15 years	Utilizes a paper-and-pencil design-copying task to assess visual–motor integration
SOCIAL-EMOTIONAL		
Burks' Behavior Rating Scales–Preschool and Kindergarten Edition	3 years–6 years	Ratings by the child's parent or teacher elucidate significant behavior patterns; the subscales of dependency, coordination, intellectuality, attention, and impulse control may be particularly relevant
Conners Parent and Teacher Rating Scales	3 years–17 years	Assesses magnitude of conduct problems, hyperactivity, and inattention–passivity through parent or teacher ratings; useful, along with behavioral observations, in the evaluation of a child suspected of having an attention deficit disorder
Early School Personality Questionnaire	6 years–9 years	Administered directly to the child, this instrument yields data regarding 13 dimensions of personality; in addition, scores may be calculated for the second-order factors of extraversion, anxiety, tough poise, and independence
Home Observation for Measurement of the Environment	Infancy–preschool age	Using direct observation and parent report, data are obtained relative to parent involvement with the child, amount of language and cognitive stimulation, variety of experience, availability of learning materials, and warmth, affection, and acceptance of the caregiver
Personality Inventory for Children	3 years–5 years; 6 years–16 years	Utilizes information provided by the parent or primary caregiver to analyze the personality and behavior of the child; the scales of adjustment, development, family relations, social skills, achievement, somatic concern, and hyperactivity may be of particular interest in the evaluation of the preterm child
Vineland Adaptive Behavior Scales	Birth–Adulthood (for Interview editions)	Through an interview with a parent or primary caregiver, adaptive behavior is evaluated across the domains of Communication, Daily Living Skills, Socialization, and Motor Skills

provide information about community resources and specific programs for children at risk, assist parents in developing advocacy skills, and maintain a file of child-care workers trained in cardiopulmonary resuscitation and apnea monitoring.

While nurses, neonatologists, and pediatricians may serve as parent educators during an infant's confinement in the neonatal intensive care unit, the need for parent education extends far beyond the period of hospitalization. Parent education is particularly vital for those with limited formal schooling and those from lower socioeconomic classes, who may not avail themselves of relevant literature and resources. Recognizing the needs of the parents of premature infants, a psychologist or other health care professional may attempt to initiate parent education and training groups that focus on the normal development of a preterm infant, deviations in development requiring immediate attention and intervention, health-related problems of preterm infants, materials and experiences designed to enhance development, and effective parenting skills.

SUMMARY

Current medical and technological advancements in the field of neonatology are largely responsible for the increased survival rate of premature infants with low birthweights and assorted medical complications. Research regarding the association between prematurity and developmental outcome suggests that approximately 20% of all preterm infants experience difficulties that span the continuum from subtle learning disabilities to overt forms of serious neurological impairment. The early identification and subsequent provision of appropriate intervention programs are critical in limiting the severity and chronicity of developmental difficulties. Psychologists can be instrumental in helping to identify children at risk and in developing effective and appropriate programs of intervention. Through a preventive model, which emphasizes parent involvement, support, and training, psychologists and other education or health-related professionals may assist in curbing the incidence of gross developmental delays and severe behavioral difficulties.

REFERENCES

Bayley, N. (1969). *Bayley Scales of Infant Development.* New York: Psychological Corporation.

Beery, K. E., & Buktenica, N. A. (1982). *Revised administration, scoring, and teaching manual of the developmental test of visual-motor integration.* Cleveland: Modern Curriculum Press.

Bromwich, R. M., & Parmelee, A. H. (1979). An intervention program for pre-term infants. In T. M. Field (Ed.), *Infants born at risk* (pp. 389–411). Jamaica, NY: Spectrum.

Bruininks, R. H. (1978). *Bruininks–Oseretsky Test of Motor Proficiency.* Circle Pines, MN: American Guidance Service.

Burks, H. F. (1983). *Burks' Behavior Rating Scales.* Los Angeles: Western Psychological Services.

Bzoch, K. R., & League, R. (1974). *The Bzoch–League Receptive–Expressive Emergent Language Scale.* Gainesville, FL: Tree of Life Press.

Caldwell, B. M., & Bradley, R. H. *Home Observation for Measurement of the Environment.* Little Rock, AR: University of Arkansas at Little Rock, Center for Child Development and Education.

Caplan, F. (1982). *The first twelve months of life.* New York: Perigree Books.

Carrow-Woolfolk, E. (1973). *Test for Auditory Comprehension of Language.* Austin, TX: Learning Concepts.

Coan, R. W., & Cattell, R. B. (1976). *Early School Personality Questionnaire.* Champaign, IL: Institute for Personality and Ability Testing.

de Vries, L. S., Lary, S., & Dubowitz, L. M. S. (1985). Relationship of serum bilirubin levels to ototoxicity and deafness in high-risk low-birth-weight infants. *Pediatrics, 76*(3), 351–354.

Drorbaugh, J. E., Moore, D. M., & Warren, J. H. (1975). Association between gestational and environmental events and central nervous system function in 7-year-old children. *Pediatrics, 56*(4), 529–537.

Field, T. M. (Ed.) (1979). *Infants born at risk.* Jamaica, NY: Spectrum.

Fitzhardinge, P. M. & Ramsay, M. (1973). The improving outlook for the small prematurely born infant. *Developmental Medicine and Child Neurology, 15,* 447–459.

Forslund, M., & Bjerre, I. (1985). Growth and development in preterm infants during the first 18 months. *Early Human Development, 10,* 201–216.

Foster, R., Giddan, J., & Stark, J. (1983). *Assessment of Children's Language Comprehension.* Palo Alto, CA: Consulting Psychologists Press.

Gerken, K. C. (1983). Assessment of preschool children with severe handicaps. In K. D. Paget & B. A. Bracken (Eds.), *The psychoeducational assessment of preschool children* (pp. 387-416). New York: Grune & Stratton.

Goyette, C. H., Conners, C. K., & Ulrich, R. F. (1978). Normative data on revised Conners parent and teacher rating scales. *Journal of Abnormal Child Psychology, 6,* 221–236.

Grigoroiu-Serbanescu, M. (1981). Intellectual and emotional development in premature children from 1 to 5 years. *International Journal of Behavioral Development, 4,* 183–199.

Grigoroiu-Serbanescu, M. (1984). Intellectual and emotional development and school adjustment in preterm children at 6 and 7 years of age: Continuation of a follow-up study. *International Journal of Behavioral Development, 7,* 307–320.

Harrison, H. (1983). *The premature baby book.* New York: St. Martin's.

Henig, R. M. (1983). *Your premature baby.* New York: Rawson.

Hresko, W. P., Reid, D. K., & Hammill, D. D. (1981). *Test of Early Language Development.* Austin, TX: Pro-Ed.

Jacob, S., Benedict, H. E., Roach, J., & Blackledge, G. L. (1984). Cognitive, perceptual, and personal–social development of prematurely born preschoolers. *Perceptual and Motor Skills, 58,* 551–562.

Kaufman, A. S., & Kaufman, N. L. (1983). *Kaufman Assessment Battery for Children.* Circle Pines, MN: American Guidance Service.

Klaus, M. H., & Kennell, J. H. (1982). *Parent–infant bonding.* St. Louis: Mosby.

Koops, B. L., & Battaglia, F. C. (1984). The newborn infant. In C. H. Kempe, H. K. Silver, & D. O'Brien (Eds.), *Current pediatric diagnosis and treatment* (pp. 40–95). Los Altos, CA: Lange Medical.

Landry, S. H., Fletcher, J. M., Zarling, C. L., Chapieski, L., & Francis, D. J. (1984). Differential outcomes associated with early medical complications in premature infants. *Society of Pediatric Psychology, 9*(3), 385–401.

Largo, R. H., Molinari, L., Weber, M., Comenale Pinto, L., & Duc, G. (1985). Early development of locomotion: Significance of prematurity, cerebral palsy and sex. *Developmental Medicine and Child Neurology, 27,* 183–191.

Masi, W. (1979). Supplemental stimulation of the premature infant. In T. M. Field (Ed.), *Infants born at risk* (pp. 367–387). Jamaica, NY: Spectrum.

McCarthy, D. (1972). *McCarthy Scales of Children's Abilities.* New York: Psychological Corporation.

McIntosh, K., & Lauer, B. A. (1984). Infections: Bacterial and spirochetal. In C. H. Kempe, H. K. Silver, & D. O'Brien (Eds.), *Current pediatric diagnosis and treatment* (pp. 825–882). Los Altos, CA: Lange Medical Publications.

Meisels, S. J., Plunkett, J. W., Roloff, D. W., Pasick, P. L., & Stiefel, G. F. (1986). Growth and development of preterm infants with respiratory distress syndrome and bronchopulmonary dysplasia. *Pediatrics, 77*(3) 345–352.

Moore, M. L. (1981). *Newborn family and nurse.* Philadelphia: Saunders.

Nance, S. (1982). *Premature babies.* New York: Priam Books.

Newcomer, P. L., & Hammill, D. D. (1982). *Test of Language Development–Primary.* Austin, TX: Pro-Ed.

Perlman, J. M., & Volpe, J. J. (1985). Episodes of apnea and bradycardia in the preterm newborn: Impact on cerebral circulation. *Pediatrics, 76*(3), 333–338.

Reynell, J. K. (1977). *Reynell Developmental Language Scale–Revised Edition.* Windsor, England: N.F.E.R. - Nelson.

Ross, G. (1985).Use of the Bayley Scales to characterize abilities of premature infants. *Child Development, 56,* 835–842.

Semel, E. M., & Wiig, E. H. (1980). *Diagnostic battery examiner's manual for the Clinical Evaluation of Language Functions.* Columbus, OH: Merrill.

Siegel, L. S., Saigal, S., Rosenbaum, P., Morton, R.A., Young, A., Berenbaum, S., & Stoskopf, B. (1982). Predictors of development in preterm and full-term infants: A model for detecting the at risk child. *Journal of Pediatric Psychology, 7*(2), 135–148.

Sigman, M., Cohen, S. E., Beckwith, L., & Parmelee, A. H. (1981). Social and familial influences on the development of preterm infants. *Society of Pediatric Psychology, 6*(1), 1–13.

Sparrow, S. S., Balla, D. A., & Cicchetti, D. V. (1984). *Vineland Adaptive Behavior Scales.* Circle Pines, MN: American Guidance Service.

Taub, H. B., Goldstein, K. M., & Caputo, D. V. (1977). Indices of neonatal prematurity as discriminators of development in middle childhood. *Child Development, 48,* 797–805.

Thorndike, R. L., Hagen, E. P., & Sattler, J. M. (1986). *The Stanford-Binet Intelligence Scale: Fourth Edition.* Chicago: The Riverside Publishing Company.

Uzgiris, I. & Hunt, J. Mc V. (1975). *Assessment in infancy.* Urbana, IL: University of Illinois Press.

Vohr, B. R., & Garcia Coll, C. T. (1985). Neurodevelopmental and school performance of very low birth weight infants: A seven-year longitudinal study. *Pediatrics, 76*(3), 345–350.

Wechsler, D. (1974). *Wechsler Intelligence Scale for Children–Revised.* New York: Psychological Corporation.

Winton, P. J., Turnbull, A. P., & Blacher, J. (1984). *Selecting a preschool: A guide for parents of handicapped children.* Baltimore: University Park.

Wirt, R. D., Lachar, D., Klinedinst, J. E., Seat, P. D., & Broen, Jr., W. E. (1982). *Personality Inventory for Children, Revised Format.* Los Angeles: Western Psychological Services.

BIBLIOGRAPHY: PROFESSIONALS

Field, T. M. (Ed.). (1979). *Infants born at risk.* Jamaica, New York: Spectrum.
This volume is a compilation of research from the fields of obstetrics, neonatology, psychiatry, and developmental psychology. Sections on prematurity, prematurity plus other complications, interactions of high-risk infants, and intervention programs may be of particular value.

Harrison, H. (1983). *The premature baby book.* New York: St. Martin's.
Along with practical information for parents, this book contains much research concerning low and very low birthweight infants, specific medical complications, and developmental sequelae.

Kempe, C. H., Silver, H. K., & O'Brien, D. (Eds.). (1984). *Current pediatric diagnosis and treatment.* Los Altos, CA: Lange Medical.
Revised every 2 years to reflect current technology and research, this is an invaluable resource for psychologists and other professionals who work with children experiencing health-related problems. The specific chapters that concentrate on the newborn infant and developmental disorders may be of interest to those working with preterm infants and children.

Paget, K. D., & Bracken, B. A. (Eds.). (1983). *The psychoeducational assessment of preschool children.* New York: Grune & Stratton.
In addition to chapters that address specific instruments for evaluating language development, cognitive abilities, fine- and gross-motor functioning, and social–emotional development, the chapter focusing on the assessment of preschool children with severe handicaps is applicable for professionals serving a high-risk population.

BIBLIOGRAPHY: PARENTS

Caplan, F. (1982). *The first twelve months of life.* New York: Perigree Books.
Written primarily for parents, this book incorporates much research in discussing the sequence of development during the first year of life,as well as activities to stimulate development. In applying this developmental framework to the preterm infant, a correction should be made for gestational age.

Growing child/Growing parent. Lafayette, IN: Dunn & Hargitt.
Monthly newsletters provide information on developmental stages and activities from birth to 6 years, and on various aspects of caregiving.

Harrison, H. (1983). *The premature baby book.* New York: St. Martin's.
This book is a fundamental resource for parents as well as professionals. Interwoven with research about medical complications and developmental outcomes are personalized accounts from the parents of preterm infants. In addition, the book provides practical information about caregiving both in the neonatal intensive care unit and at home. An appendix of resources for parents contains lists of organizations and publications that focus on specific sequelae associated with prematurity, as well as the addresses of parent support groups in the United States and Canada.

Henig, R. M. (1983). *Your premature baby.* New York: Rawson.
Essentially a handbook for parents, this book includes both research and practical information. Of particular interest are the chapters focusing on neonatal medical complications, hospital procedures,and developmental concerns during the first year of life. Appendices include a metric chart for converting grams into pounds, a glossary of medical terminology, addresses of self-help groups and organizations that deal with special-needs infants, and a developmental chart for the first year.

Winton, P. J., Turnbull, A. P., & Blacher, J. (1984). *Selecting a preschool: A guide for parents of handicapped children.* Baltimore: University Park.
Reports from the parents of preschool handicapped children, research on preschool programs for children with special needs, and information about federal and state mandates are included to help parents make informed decisions about educational placements.

Children and Psychiatric Involvement

Tony D. Crespi
Altobello Psychiatric Hospital, Meriden, Connecticut

BACKGROUND

It is estimated that 63.4 million children are under the age of 18 in the United States. Silver (1982) speculated that 3.2 million will have major emotional problems, of whom he estimated, 90% will not receive any treatment. Lerman (1980) noted that "while the commitment of all other age groups to psychiatric facilities has decreased appreciably in public facilities, the number of young persons admitted since the early 1960s into these facilities has increased."

Since serious psychiatric illness often begins in childhood or adolescence and since it is generally accepted that early intervention increases the likelihood of successful treatment (Koret, 1980), it is important to expand our understanding and knowledge in this area.

The range of symptoms reported in the literature for children with psychiatric involvements includes suicide, homicide, assorted acts of violence, various psychotic features, substance abuse, and acts of crime (Silver, 1982). Some will merit psychiatric intervention; others will be treated by clinics and schools. The accompanying affective features may include depression, anger, fear, or a sense of isolation. It is important to realize that most youths referred because of psychiatric emergencies typically demonstrate urgent behavioral symptoms, often in response to some precipitating incident (Smith & Morrison, 1975).

School psychologists are in a position to address many of these conditions. Since the widespread existence of mental disorders remains an urgent problem, and since early identification efforts can be of considerable benefit, school psychologists can be extremely helpful with respect to early identification, preventive intervention, and appropriate referral. The remainder of this chapter will treat the information that is often considered in the identification of children manifesting psychiatric involvements, discuss the classification of childhood psychopathologies, and consider three major psychiatric interventions: psychiatric medication, day-treatment hospital services, and inpatient psychiatric services.

DEVELOPMENT

Typically, the onset of psychiatric problems occurs at adolescence (Wilson & Soth, 1985). Recently published data compiled through the National Institute of Mental Health indicate that of the 81,532 individuals under the age of 18 who were admitted to psychiatric facilities for inpatient care in 1980 approximately 67% were between the ages of 15 and 17, 28% were between the ages of 10 and 14, and 5% were under the age of 19 (Milazzo-Sayre et al., 1986).

Simply stated, primary prevention measures consist of attempts to reduce the incidence of mental disorders in the community. Caplan and Grunebaum (1967) have explained that this can be accomplished by "modifying the environment and strengthening individual capacities to cope with situations." Visotsky (1967) suggested that prompt intervention may be helpful by "counteracting the stressful or potentially harmful social conditions which produce mental disorders." But recognition of mental illness in children is difficult because of the extremes of normality and development.

Although any youngster may enter into a crisis if an emotionally traumatic incident is potent enough, certain individuals seem more susceptible than others. Caplan (1970) defined a crisis as an "imbalance between the difficulty and the importance of the problem and the resources immediately available to deal with it." Therefore, crisis behavior should not be confused with symptomatic behavior. In a school situation we might observe a loss of interest school, withdrawal, or an explosive outburst.

In fact, a crisis situation, alone, is an atypical cause of referral. Multiple behavioral difficulties and repeated occasions of difficulty are important clues for parents and professionals. The general symptoms reported in the literature that have been exhibited by children manifesting psychiatric conditions include overactivity, aggressiveness, impulsivity, unpredictability, anxiety, temper outbursts, depression, excessive passivity, and psychosis (Silver, 1982; Smith & Morrison, 1975). Lapouse and Monk (1958), reporting on characteristics often associated with psychopathology in a general population of school children, speculated about a tendency for transient symptomatic behavior. And most youngsters seen as psychiatric referrals have demonstrated long-standing behavioral problems. Hence, the school psychologist is in an important position to distinguish between normal variations in development and abnormality.

During primary school years more boys than girls are referred for psychiatric assistance (Connell, 1972). This is in contrast with adult psychiatric disturbances, which affect females predominantly. Earlier research by this writer (Crespi, 1985) suggested that societal factors may partially explain this phenomenon: Briefly, rates for incarceration for men far outnumber rates for women. Guttridge and Warren (1983) concluded that a shifting in populations from one arm of the social control system to another sometimes occurs and can result in inappropriate placements. Since males typically act out toward the environment they may be sent off to prison. Women, on the other hand, may express their emotions inwardly and be sent to a psychiatric facility. Early identification and prevention may be helpful with both types of behavior.

PUTTING CHILDREN'S PSYCHIATRIC INVOLVEMENT IN PERSPECTIVE

The specific circumstances of psychiatric involvement vary from one client to another. As a rule, psychiatrists complete a mental status examination with a client and gather a considerable array of diagnostic and interview material. This may include the results of a psychological examination, educational evaluation, psychosocial and family history, and speech and language evaluation. The psychiatrist will review this information and make a diagnosis based on the nomenclature of the American Psychiatric Association's *Diagnostic and Statistical Manual of Mental Disorders* (3rd ed.), the DSM III (1980).

Since so many youngsters are being referred to psychiatric clinics and admissions to psychiatric facilities are increasing steadily for youths, it is important to become familiar with the DSM and with the multiaxial model it utilizes for the classification of psychopathology. The five axes that make up a complete diagnosis follow:

DSM III's Five-Axis System

Axis I: Clinical psychiatric syndromes (conditions that are not attributed to a mental disorder but are a focus of treatment)

Axis II: Personality disorders and specific developmental disorders

Axis III: Physical disorders

Axis IV: Severity of psychosocial stressors

Axis V: Highest level of adaptive functioning during the past year

Table 1 presents an outline of the overall classification system emphasizing disorders first observed in infancy, childhood, and adolescence. Table 2 provides a more detailed guide and is intended as a reference for the school psychologist confronted with specific problems and/or psychiatrically troubled children. Table 2 outlines common developmental variations, contains data on prevalence, and provides specific information used both in making classifications and in designing intervention programs. Table 2 may also be helpful in interpreting reports received from various agencies.

ALTERNATIVE ACTIONS

After the necessary background information has been obtained and diagnostic decisions have been made, intervention strategies are developed. School psychologists, typically, are in the position either of being a part of the referral leading to such interventions or of being consulted when a psychiatrically involved child is being re-enrolled in the school system after receiving some sort of psychiatric treatment. In either situation three major interventions often utilized in psychiatry are as follows: psychiatric medications, partial hospital services, and inpatient treatment.

Psychopharmacology: Psychiatric Medication

Psychopharmacology has brought hope to many people struggling with mental illness. Information on psychopharmacology is not, however, a typical component of a school psychologist's graduate training. Such information, though, is vital to understand one major treatment intervention utilized for children with psychiatric illnesses. The following is not an encyclopedic review of the pharmacology literature. Excellent reviews are available by both Biederman and Jellinek (1984) and Werry (1982). It is the intention of this section to provide the reader with an overview of the treatments that are commonly used with children and adolescents. Milazzo-Sayre et al. (1986) have noted that medication is a major treatment intervention for children receiving inpatient psychiatric treatment. It is also commonly used on an outpatient basis. In consequence it is important to provide practicing professionals with information about this important treatment modality.

Many mental health professionals are in disagreement about psychotropic medications. Their effectiveness in severe psychotic conditions and in cases of

TABLE 1

Psychiatric Disorders First Observed in Infancy, Childhood, or Adolescence

Category	Subcategory
Intellectual disorders	Retardation (mild, moderate, severe, profound)
Developmental disorders	Pervasive developmental disorders Specific developmental disorders
Behavior disorders	Attention deficit disorders (short concentration span) Conduct disorders (persistent patterns of antisocial behavior) Oppositional disorder (a 6-month pattern of disobedience/tantrums, etc.) Separation anxiety disorder Avoidant disorder (shrinking from contact with strangers)
Emotional disorders	Overanxious disorder (persistent worry about future/past/competence) Reactive attachment disorder of infancy (lacks signs of responsiveness) Schizoid disorder (no friends or interest in friends) Identity disorder (severe distress over identity issues) Affective disorders (disturbances of mood including depression)
Physical disorders	Eating disorders (anorexia nervosa, bulimia, pica) Stereotyped movement disorders (disregulation of motor movements) Stuttering Functional enuresis or encopresis Sleepwalking disorder Sleep terror disorder

severely disorganized thinking and behavior has been profound. Their utility with disruptive behavior, though, remains controversial.

Generally, five groups of drugs are used in connection with psychiatric disorders. These are stimulants, antipsychotics, antidepressants, lithium, and the sedative hypnotics. The first four groups are generally used with children.

Stimulants. These drugs have been discussed in the literature as to their effectiveness with hyperactive or disruptive behaviors felt to be related to attention deficit disorders, for which they are used extensively. Two recent reviews were completed by Rapoport (1983) and by Cantwell and Carlson (1978). Common drugs include methylphenidate (Ritalin), dextroamphetamine (Dexedrine), and pemoline (Cylert).

The short-term effects are well documented but the long-term effects are not. Direct observation has revealed reduced movements by hyperactive children and an improvement in forethought and planning. Werry and Sprague (1974) emphasized the importance of dosage in improving concentration and attention. Barclay (1977) reported an impact on mood. Werry et al. (1980) reported an improvement in self-image.

However, Gettelman-Klein and Klein (1974) found a lack of academic improvement, and Taylor and Sandburg (1984) reported that activity levels may be reduced but defiance may not be. In a famous experiment by Schachter and Singer (1962), students were provided with amphetamines and consequently exposed to different emotional situations. The authors reported that emotional intensity was affected by the drug but that knowledge of the emotion was determined by the situation and the students' knowledge about what was prescribed. The question, then, is whether children will attribute school and/or behavioral success to the drug or to themselves.

The important effects of stimulants raised hopes that scientists could learn more about the physical bases of symptoms. However, cogent arguments have been articulated regarding activation of generalized inhibitory systems, activation of midbrain arousal systems, action on frontal centers controlling stimulus sampling, and stimulation of motor centers. Individual differences in drug metabolism and side-effects will greatly enhance our understanding of such biological actions.

The side-effects of stimulants include abdominal pain, headaches, and sleeplessness. Increased heart rate, depression, and growth retardation have all been reported as well. The growth retardation has not been permanent when administration is alternated with periods of drug removal. Typically children have growth spurts and simply catch up.

Overall, stimulants have been helpful for children with attention deficit disorders with or without hyperactivity, but it is important to keep in mind that aggression, defiance, and academic difficulty by themselves are not symptoms that warrant use of such medication.

Antipsychotics. Sometimes referred to as major tranquilizers or neuroleptics, antipsychotics help control hallucinations and delusions and restore order to disorganized thinking. The classes of drugs used include the phenothiazines (e.g., Thorazine, Mellaril), butyrophenones (e.g., Haldol), and the thioxanthenes, (e.g., Navane).

Another action of these drugs, particularly halo-

TABLE 2

Common Psychiatric Disturbances in Children and Adolescents

1. Common Developmental Variations
   A. Temperamentally difficult (Thomas & Chess, 1984)
   B. Bladder and bowel weaknesses
      1. By age 3 most children have daytime bladder control
      2. By the age of 4–5 years 75–80% of children have nocturnal control
   C. Childhood fears
      1. Types: animals, strangers, water, getting lost, death
      2. Fears of some type displayed by a large proportion of normal children
   D. Social withdrawal
   E. Temper tantrums
      1. Interventions: time-outs and contingencies
   F. Aggressive behavior
      1. A common source of control but an important aspect of socialization (Clarizio & McCoy, 1983)
      2. Interventions: role-modeling (Bandura, 1973); time-outs
   G. Noncompliance
      1. The most frequent complaint at clinics (Forehand & McMahon, 1981)
      2 A normal aspect of development in a mild form (Campbell, 1983)
   H. Thumbsucking
      1. Found in 90% of all normal infants
      2. Declines with age
      3. Remedies: bitter-tasting applications, self-monitoring
   I. Nightmares
      1. Experienced by 28% of all normal 6- to 12-year-olds
      2. Distinct from night terrors
         a. Night terror (pavor nocturnus): Characterized by disorientation, feelings of terror, heavy breathing, perspiration, and other symptoms of severe distress; occurs rarely beyond puberty

2. Pervasive Developmental Disorders
   A. Infantile autism: A pervasive lack of responsiveness to other people, gross deficits in language, bizarre responses, absence of delusions or hallucinations; onset before 30 months of age
      1. Treatments: behavior modification (Steffan & Karoly, 1982) and pharmacology (Geller, Titvo, Freeman, & Yuwiler, 1983)
   B. Childhood onset pervasive developmental disorder: Characterized by failure to develop social relationships, a number of bizarre behaviors that can include excessive anxiety, constricted affect, resistance to change, oddities of motor movement, abnormalities of speech, hyper- or hyposensitivity, self-mutilation, absence of delusions, and onset before the age of 12
      1. Treatment: behavior modification
   C. Developmental reading disorder
   D. Developmental arithmetic disorder
   E. Developmental language disorder

3. Schizophrenic Disorders
   Criteria: At least one of the following: (a) bizarre delusions such as thought insertion or delusions of being controlled; (b) delusions with or without persecutory or jealous content; (c) autiroty hallucinations; (d) incoherence or loosening of associations. The diagnostic criteria also include continuous signs for 6 months
   Prevalence: About 3–4 children in 10,000 (Neale & Oltmanns, 1980)
   Treatment: Behavior modification, drug treatment, psychotherapy
   Note: The DSM III criteria also include criteria for diagnosing various subtypes. These include a disorganized type (disorganization in speech, blunted or silly affect), a catatonic type (motor disturbances such as rigid postures), a paranoid type (delusions or hallucinations dominate), and an undifferentiated type

4. Psychotic Disorders/Disorders with Psychotic Features That Do Not Fit the Criteria for Organic Mental, Schizophrenic, Paranoid, or Affective Disorders
   A. Schizophreniform disorder: Meets all the criteria for schizophrenia aside from duration, which is more than 2 weeks but less than 6 months
   B. Brief reactive psychosis: Characterized by emotional turmoil and psychotic symptoms following a stressful event
      1. Symptoms: At least one of the follwoing: (a) loosening of associations, (b) delusions, (c) hallucinations, (d) grossly disorganized behavior
      2. Duration: More than a few hours but less than 2 weeks
   C. Schizoaffective disorder: Retained in the DSM III for instances in which the clinician cannot distinguish between an affective disorder and schizophrenia
   D. Atypical psychosis: psychotic symptoms are present (delusions, hallucinations, loosening of association, illogical thinking, disorganized behavior) but does not meet the criteria for a specific mental disorder. Two examples follow:
      1. Psychosis with confusing clinical features
      2. Psychosis with unusual features
         a. Psychosis accompanying the menstrual cycle

      Note: This is a residual category. Psychotic symptoms must be present but functioning may not be impaired.

5. Affective disorders
   Criteria: Disturbance of mood accompanied by related symptoms and persisting for at least 1 week. Can involve extremes of depression or elation and can range from mild to severe conditions
   A. Manic disorders: one or more distinct periods with elevated, expansive, or irritable mood accompanied by three of the following: (a) increase in activity, (b) more talkative, (c) flight of ideas, (d) inflated self-esteem (e) decreased need for sleep, (f) distractibility, (g) excessive involvement in activities with possibly painful consequences
   B. Major depressive episode: Loss of interest or pleasure in almost all usual activities and characterized by depression, sadness, blueness, hopelessness, or irritability. Mood disturbances must be pronounced and persistent and include at least four of the following: (a) poor appetite or significant weight loss, (b) insomnia, (c) psychomotor agitation, (d) loss of pleasure in activities, (e) loss of energy, (f) feelings of worthlessness, (g) difficulty concentrating, (h) recurrent thoughts of death or suicide

1. Prevalence: 15–20% of children referred for psychiatric assistance can be expected to display a depressive disorder (Pearce, 1977)
2. General data: 1.9% of a sample of normal children evidenced depression although 18% evidenced depressed affect (Kashani & Simonds, 1979)
3. References: Cantwell (1982) and Petti (1983) for information on conceptual issues in childhood depression
4. Treatment: Psychotherapy, drug treatment, institutionalization

C. Other specific affective disorders
   1. Cyclothymic disorder: Periods displaying both depressive and manic syndromes
   2. Dysthymic disorder: Symptoms of depression but not of sufficient severity and duration to meet the criteria for a major depressive episode

6. Conduct Disorders (five types)
   A. General criteria: A repetitive pattern of aggressive or nonaggressive behavior in which either the basic rights of others are violated or major age-appropriate societal rules are violated, as evidenced by one of the following: (a) physical violence against a person or object such as breaking and entering, rape, vandalism, or assault; (b) stealing; (c) violations of rules at home or school; (d) repeated running away; (e) persistent lying. Differentation of the subcategories involves a review of behavior associated with signs of social attachment. Two categories require the exclusion of at least four of the following and two categories require at least two of the following: (a) friendships lasting more than 6 months, (b) extending self to others when no advantage is evident, (c) feeling guilt or remorse, (d) avoiding blaming others, (e) sharing concern for others
      1. Duration: At least 6 months
      2. Age: Under 18 years
      3. References: Quay (1979) and Ellis (1982)
      4. Treatment: Institutionalization, behavioral approaches such as contingencies, psychotherapy (particularly group therapy), and miscellaneous approaches such as depicted in the television program "Scared Straight," which was reported to be effective with 80–90% of the several thousand youths who participated. Another novel approach includes the various outward-bound type of programs
   B. Types
      1. Conduct disorder: undersocialized, aggressive
      2. Conduct disorder: Undersocialized, nonaggressive
      3. Conduct disorder: Socialized, aggressive
      4. Conduct disorder: Socialized, nonaggressive
      5. Atypical conduct disorder: A residual category of which the predominant disturbance involves a pattern of behavior that involves violation of either the basic rights of others or major age-appropriate societal rules but that cannot be classified into one of the aforementioned categories

---

peridol (Haldol), has been the suppression of certain repetitive movements, sometimes found in Tourette syndrome.

Engelhardt et al. (1972) found that a number of drugs are successful in reducing activity levels and in increasing tolerance of frustration. General mood and sleeping also improved with psychotic patients. These drugs included the phenothiazines (e.g., chlorpromazine, thioridazine, prochlorperazine, and fluphenazine).

Generally, the research has demonstrated a reduction in certain behaviors and improvements in the symptoms noted above. Common short-term side-effects are hypotension, hypersensitivity to the sun, and Parkinsonian symptoms. Other side-effects include jaundice, overeating, impaired learning, and some hormonal side-effects, particularly with girls. Edwards (1981) provided a very useful review of side-effects for those seeking more detailed information. Certainly the risks of such medications need to be assessed. During the first week, acute dystonic reactions have commonly been reported (Werry et al., 1976). Treatment with anticholinergic agents such as Cogentin or Benadryl are effective in treating or reducing dystonias and estrapyramidal side-effects.

The most serious long-term side-effect is tardive dyskinesia, which is characterized by involuntary movements of the face, tongue, neck, shoulders, and arms. Common facial features include tongue protrusions and grimaces. Unfortunately, it may be irreversible and can occur in children treated for long periods with antipsychotic medications (Paulson et al., 1975; Gualtieri et al., 1980). Withdrawal dyskinesias, which look similar to tardive dyskinesia, have also been reported in children. McAndrew et al., (1972) has discussed these features, noting that arm and body movements are more common than oral or facial movements.

Overall, it can be stated that antipsychotic medication can be beneficial in the control of psychotic conditions such as schizophrenia and there is evidence that it can help in other disorders such as Tourette syndrome. Note must be taken of the side-effects such as tardive dyskinesia. Careful monitoring and periodic withdrawal of medication is useful to assess its efficacy. Rebound effect may partially explain certain withdrawal emergent symptoms, but a sufficiently controlled period that allows the body to adjust to the withdrawal can provide an important gauge of behavior.

Antidepressants. In the past few years interest in childhood depression has increased remarkably. Petti (1978) and Petti and Connors (1983) have reported some promising information, including data on the benefits of imipramine, a tricyclic antidepressant. The value of tricyclic medication, it should be noted, remains controversial; studies have yielded conflictual data. The tricyclics have been most effective for adults with depression.

Depression, as a symptom seen in children, is typically manifested by somatic complaints, insomnia, and hyperkinesis. The use of antidepressants in hyperactive children, although less successful than stimulants, has been effective (Werry et al., 1980).

Antidepressant medications are of two main kinds: the tricyclics and the monoamine oxidase inhibitors (MAO inhibitors). Commonly used tricyclics include Elavil and Tofranil. Nardil and Parnate are common MAO inhibitors.

With respect to side-effects, tricyclics are chemically similar to the phenothiazines and share many side-effects with them. Those most pronounced with tricyclics are dry mouth and constipation. These may be treated with medication that enhances the action of acetycholine. The tricyclics may also produce low blood pressure, arrhythmias of the heart, decreased sweating, retention of urine, and dilation of pupils. The MAO inhibitors have some anticholinergic-type side-effects. A patient may experience difficulty in urinating, impotence, and constipation. Agitation is common. MAO inhibitors are rarely used with children.

Lithium. Lithium is unique. It is commonly used with a diagnosis of manic-depression (Steinberg, 1980), and is the first drug that can prevent an emotional illness. It generally has no effect on mood but stabilizes it within normal limits. It has been used most successfully to prevent episodes of mania and less consistently in the prevention of depression.

There are drawbacks to the use of lithium. First, it does not work with all manic–depressives. Second, it must be taken indefinitely. Finally, it is not commonly used with children, but more commonly with older adolescents and adults. The long-term effects include thyroid disorders. Nausea often occurs within a few days and vomiting, diarrhea, and tremors must be watched for. Schwartz and Johnson (1985) noted that there is less research on these drugs with respect to their side-effects on children than on adults.

Day-Treatment or Outpatient Psychiatric Services

Child guidance clinics, primary prevention programs, and various day-treatment programs provide an assortment of potentially valuable services for youngsters not necessarily in need of inpatient treatment. Drug therapy, of course, requires the active involvement of a psychiatrist. In situations requiring the use of medication, then, referral to a program with a psychiatrist on staff will be a necessity.

The primary advantage of day-treatment or partial hospital services lies in the possibility of keeping children united with their families. Bentovim and Landown (1973) noted that such treatment is valuable in keeping families united and by creating less disruption of family and peer group relationships. Gritzka (1970) noted some overlap between partial-hospital programs and special education day-treatment programs. The key differences, according to these investigators, lies in the realm of treatment strategy. Typically, a partial hospital program is established by psychiatric personnel and is oriented toward psychiatric treatment, adjunctive services being construed to include education. In school-based programs, though, special education and education in general is the focus of treatment and psychiatric and other mental health services are considered to be support services.

Separation from the family and the availability of more stringent behavioral interventions are two advantages of a partial-hospital program or day-treatment program. Bentovim and Boston (1973) and Cooklin (1984) noted the success of such programs. Lansing and Schopler (1978) observed that day-treatment programs with specialized techniques have been helpful for children with psychotic disorders.

Perlmutter (1983) noted that since more than half of all cases seen in a psychiatric emergency service present with family members, the use of family therapy is critical. Family therapy, group therapy, individual therapy, drug therapy, and social skills training all can be incorporated into day-treatment.

Cooklin (1984) observed that where families may experience boundary difficulties, the day-treatment program affords endless opportunities for change through task sharing and modeling. Asen et al. (1982) noted that intensive attendance may be required of families in some programs but be less necessary in others. This underscores the variability that cuts across the wide spectrum of programs for youth. Day-treatment, partial-hospitalization, and school-based treatment services vary widely among both services and philosophy. Typically, what is shared is the use of behavior management systems (e.g., token economies, point systems), the use of individual and group therapy, and some type of family contact. Psychopharmacologic interventions, as noted, are the province of the psychiatrist and are more common in hospital-affiliated programs. Some schools, though, have contracted for such services.

Inpatient Hospitalization

Recently published surveys by the National Institute of Mental Health report that an estimated 81,532 persons under the age of 18 years were admitted to inpatient psychiatric care during 1980 (Milazzo-Sayre et al., 1986). Nonpsychotic disorders and preadult disorders accounted for almost one-half of all diagnoses. Family and friends were the most likely referral source for children (approximately one-third). Courts and correction agencies accounted for another quarter of the referrals.

The leading types of treatment that the above-mentioned children received were individual therapy (89%), activity therapy (73%), group therapy (62%), drug therapy (42%), family therapy (38%), social skills training (36%), and educational training (35%).

In this survey group 23% of all admissions under the age of 18 were hospitalized for a week or less, 60% for 28 days or less, 78% for 56 days or less, and 87% for 90 days or less. Length of stay did not vary significantly by sex, although certain racial differences were observed (whites tended to be released more readily).

In sum, inpatient treatment for children and adolescents is still expanding. The primary goal of such an intervention is to return the child to a normal life in his or her school and community (Palmer et al., 1983). Inpatient treatment is, increasingly, being discussed by researchers as one facet of a continuum of care that may include outpatient psychotherapy after discharge, psychiatric medication, and possibly special education services.

Variability in size and physical plant, increasingly all-adolescent units, and an interdisciplinary treatment team model are the ingredients that typify inpatient psychiatric units for youth. Although parents are the cornerstone of the referral process, most admissions are facilitated through a physician at an emergency room. Courts constitute another process or avenue for admission.

Payment is a complicated issue. In some instances insurance carriers will pay all or the majority of the cost of treatment. Different carriers, including health maintenance organizations, offer varying rates of coverage. Some will cover 60 days, others 90 days. Providers often require certain institutional accreditations such as that acquired through the Joint Commission on Hospital Accreditation (JCAH). Title 19 or various state departments of children and youth services can be valuable resources for parents. The options are complicated and require careful attention. One valuable resource may lie in the admissions officer at a local mental health facility.

Typically, each psychiatric program has a person responsible for admissions. Often a trained psychiatric nurse or clinical social worker, this individual will probably work in concert with a resident psychiatrist.

The basic rationale behind inpatient treatment is to restore order to disorganized thinking or to address serious or potentially life-threatening situations. Whether a child needs outpatient or partial-day services or inpatient treatment, most psychiatric care institutions utilize a highly structured environment and a multidisciplinary treatment team model, consider the appropriateness of medications, and utilize an assortment of psychotherapeutic interventions. The drawbacks include the cost, the disruption to the family, and possible scapegoating by peers.

SUMMARY

Understanding the dynamics of childhood and adolescent psychiatric involvement is one of the more imposing challenges facing school psychologists. Medications for psychosis, depression, and assorted disorders are but one facet of child psychiatry. Often, day-treatment or inpatient psychiatric hospitalization is necessary to assist a child troubled by psychiatric problems.

The increase in the numbers of youngsters manifesting psychiatric difficulties requires an expansion of knowledge on the part of practicing school psychologists. Often the school psychologist can be helpful either during the referral process leading toward such interventions by psychiatric professionals or during the home–school transition following some psychiatric intervention. Choices as to use of drug therapy, day-treatment, level and intensity of psychotherapy, and possibly inpatient hospitalization will depend upon the specific needs of each child.

In contrast to many issues faced by educators, psychiatric involvement typically requires intervention on the part of the medical community. In order to make the referral process or the transitional phase back to the home most effective the school psychologist requires a working knowledge about four important areas of child and adolescent psychiatry: diagnosis and psychopathology (including behavioral symptoms), psychotropic medications (including the long-term and short-term side-effects), day-treatment, and inpatient hospital services.

It does seem evident that an increasingly complex world and expanding numbers of youth with psychiatric difficulties will make knowledge about child and adolescent psychiatry increasingly important to the school-based mental health professional.

REFERENCES

American Psychiatric Association (1980). *Diagnostic and statistical manual of mental disorders* (3rd ed.). Washington, DC: Author.

Asen, K., Stein, R., Stevens, A., McHugh, B., Greenwood, J., & Cooklin, A. (1982). A day unit for families. *Journal of Family Therapy, 4,* 345–358.

Bandura, A. (1973). *Aggression: A social learning approach.* Englewood Cliffs, NJ: Prentice-Hall.

Barkley, R. (1977). A review of stimulant drug research with hyperactive children. *Journal of Child Psychology and Psychiatry, 18,* 137–166.

Bentovim, A., Boston, M. (1973). A day centre for disturbed young children and their parents. *Journal of Child Psychotherapy, 3,* 46–60.

Bentovim, A., & Lansdown, R. (1973). Day-hospitals and centres for disturbed children in the London area. *British Medical Journal, 4,* 536–538.

Biederman, J., & Jellinek, M. S. (1984). Medical intelligence: Current concepts — Psychopharmacology of children. *New England Journal of Medicine, 310* (15), 968–972.

Blotcky, M. J., Dimperio, T. L., & Gossett, J. T. (1984). Follow-up of children treated in psychiatric hospitals: A review of studies. *American Journal of Psychiatry, 141*(12), 1499–1507.

Campbell, S. B. (1983). Developmental perspectives in child psychopathology. In T. Ollendick & M. Hersen (Eds.), *Handbook of child psychopathology.* New York: Plenum.

Cantwell, D. P. (1982). Childhood depression: A review of current research. *Advances in Clinical Child Psychology.* New York: Plenum.

Cantwell, D., & Carlson, G. A. (1978). Stimulants. In J. S. Werry (Ed.), *Pediatric psychopharmacology: The use of behavior-modifying drugs in children* (pp. 171–207). New York: Brunner/Mazel.

Caplan, G. (1970). *The theory and practice of mental health consultation.* New York: Basic Books.

Caplan, G., & Grunebaum, H. (1967). Perspectives on primary prevention. *Archives of General Psychiatry, 17,* 331–346.

Clarizio, H. F., & McCoy, G. F. (1983). *Behavior disorders in children* (3rd ed.). New York: Crowell.

Clark, W. G., & del Giudice, J. (1970). *Principles of psychopharmacology.* New York: Academic.

Connell, H. M. (1972). Depression in childhood. *Child Psychiatry and Human Development, 4,* 71–85.

Conners, C. K. (1977). Methodological considerations in drug research with children. In J. M. Wiener (Ed.), *Psychopharmacology in childhood and adolescence.* New York: Basic Books.

Cooklin, A. (1984). The family day unit. In C. Fishman & B. Rosman (Eds.), *Festschrift for Salvador Minuchin.* Boston: Harvard University Press.

Crespi, T. D. (1985). *The development of the Inventory of Adolescent Well-Being: A follow-up study of the effects of psychiatric hospitalization on adolescents.* Unpublished doctoral dissertation, University of Massachusetts, Amherst.

Edwards, J. G. (1981). Unwanted effects of psychotropic drugs and their mechanisms. In J. M. Van Praag, M. H. Lader, O. J. Rafaelsen, & E. J. Sachar (Eds.), *Handbook of biological psychiatry* (Part 6). New York: Marcel Dekker.

Ellis, N. R. (1970). Mental processes in retardates and normals. In N. R. Ellis (Ed.), *International review of research in mental retardation* (Volume 4). New York: Academic.

Ellus,, P. L. (1982). Empathy: A factor in antisocial behavior. *Journal of Abnormal Child Psychology, 10,* 123–124.

Engelhardt, D. M., Polizos, P., & Argolis, R. A. (1972). The drug treatment of childhood psychosis. In W. Smith (Ed.), *Drugs, development, and cerebral function* (pp. 224–234). Springifled, IL: Thomas.

Forehand, R., & McMahon, R. J. (1981). *Helping the noncompliant child.* New York: Guilford.

Geller, E., Ritvo, E. R., Freeman, B. J., & Yuwiler, A. (1982). Preliminary observations on the effect of fenfluramine on blood serotonin and symptoms in three autistic boys. *New England Journal of Medicine, 307,* 165–169.

Gittelman-Klein, R., & Klein, D. (1976). Methylphenidate effects in learning disabilities: Psychometric changes. *Archives of General Psychiatry, 33,* 655–664.

Granato, J. E., Stern, B. J., Ringel, A., Karim, A. H., Krumholz, A., Coyle, J., & Adler, S. (1983). Neuroleptic malignant syndrome: Successful treatment with dantrolene and bromocriptine. *Annals of Neurology, 14,* 89–90.

Gritzka, K. (1970). An interdisciplinary approach in day treatment of emotionally disturbed children. *Child Welfare, 49,* 468–472.

Gualtieri, C. T., Barnhill, J., McGimsey, J., & Schell, D. (1980). Tardive dyskinesia and other movement disorders in children treated with psychotropic drugs. *Journal of the American Academy of Child Psychiatry, 19,* 491–510.

Gualtieri, C. T., Breuning, S. E., Schroeder, S. R., & Quade, P. (1982). Tardive dyskinesia in mentally retarded children, adolescents, and young adults: North Carolina and Michigan studies. *Psychopharmacology Bulletin, 18,* 62–65.

Gualtieri, C. T., Wargin, W., Kanoy, R., Patrick, K. Shen, C. P., Youngblood, W., Mueller, R. A., & Breese, G. R. (1982). Clinical studies of methylphenidate serum levels in children and adults. *Journal of the American Academy of Child Psychiatry, 21,* 19–26.

Guttridge, P., & Warren, C. (1983). Adolescent psychiatric hospitalization and social control. *Crime and Delinquency.*

Hartmann, H. (1958). *Ego psychology and the problem of adaptation.* New York: International Universities Press.

Howlin, P. (1982). The education and management of autistic children. In J. Wing, & L. Wing (Eds.), *Handbook of psychiatry: Vol. 3. Psychoses of uncertain aetiology* (pp. 246–250). Cambridge, MA: Cambridge University Press.

Klein, D. F., & Davis, J. M. (1969). *Diagnosis and drug treatment of psychiatric disorders.* Baltimore: Williams & Wilkins.

Knitzer, J. (1984). Mental health services to children and adolescents: A national view of public policies. *American Psychologist, 39,* 905–911.

Koret, S. (1980). Follow-up study on residential treatment of children ages six through twelve. *Journal of the National Association of Private Psychiatric Hospitals, 11*(3), 43–47.

Lansing, M. D., & Schopler, E. (1978). Individualized education: A public school model. In M. Rutter & E. Schopler (Eds.), *Autism: A reappraisal of concepts and treatment* (pp. 439–453). New York: Plenum.

Lapouse, R., & Monk, M. M. (1958). An epidemiologic study of behavior characteristics in children. *American Journal of Public Health, 48,* 1134–1144.

Lerman, P. (1980, July). Trends and issues in the deinstitutionalization of youth in trouble. *Crime and Delinquency,* pp. 281–298.

Lerman, P. (1982). *Deinstitutionalization and the welfare state.* New Brunswick, NJ: Rutgers University Press.

McAndrew, J., Case, Q., & Treffert, D. (1972). Effects of prolonged phenothiazine intake on psychotic and other hospitalized children. *Journal of Autism and Childhood Schizophrenia, 2,* 75–91.

Milazzo-Sayre, L. J., Benson, P. R., Rosenstein, M. J., & Manderscheid, R. W. (1986). Use of inpatient psychiatric services by children and youth under age 18, United States, 1980 (Statistical Note No. 175, DHHS Publication No. [ADM] 86–1451). Washington, DC: National Institute of Mental Health.

Morris, J. B., & Beck, A. J. (1974). The efficacy of antidepressant drugs. *Archives of General Psychiatry, 30,* 667–674.

Neal, J. M., & Oltmanns, T. (1980). *Schizophrenia.* New York: Wiley.

Palmer, J. O. (1983). *The psychological assessment of children* (2nd ed.). New York: Wiley.

Paulson, G., Rizvia, A., & Crane, G. (1975). Tardive dyskinesia as a possible sequel of long-term therapy with phenothiazines. *Clinical Pediatrics, 14,* 953–955.

Perlmutter, R. A. (1986). Emergency psychiatry and the family: The decision to admit. *Journal of Marital and Family Therapy, 12*(2), 153–162.

Petti, T. A. (1978). Depression in hospitalized child psychiatry patients: Approaches to measuring depression. *Journal of the American Academy of Child Psychiatry, 17,* 49–59.

Petti, T. A. (1983). *Childhood depression.* New York: Haworth.

Petti, T. A., & Conners, C. K. (1983). Changes in behavioral ratings of depressed children treated with imipramine. *Journal of the American Academy of Child Psychiatry, 22,* 355–360.

President's Commission on Mental Health. (1978). *Report to the President From the President's Commission on Mental Health.* Washington, DC: U.S. Government Printing Office.

Quay, H. C. (1979). Classification. In H. C. Quay & J. C. Werry (Eds.), *Psychopathological disorders of childhood* (2nd ed.). New York: Wiley.

Quay, H. C. (1979). Residential treatment. In H. C. Quay & J. S. Werry (Eds.), *Psychopathological disorders of childhood* (2nd ed.). New York: Wiley.

Rapoport, J. L. (1983). Stimulant drug treatment of hyperactivity: An update. In I. B. Guze, F. J. Earls, & J. E. Barrett (Eds.), *Childhood psychopathology and development.* New York: Raven.

Schachter, S., & Singer, J. E. (1962). Cognitive, social, and physiological determinants of emotional states. *Psychological Review, 69,* 379–399.

Schwartz, S., & Johnson, J. H. (1985). *Psychopathology of childhood: A clinical-experimental approach* (2nd ed.). New York: Pergamon.

Silver, L. B. (1982). *Mental health care for children and youth: A national perspective.* Unpublished manuscript (available from Larry B. Silver, National Institute of Mental Health, Department of Health and Human Services, Rockville, MD 20857).

Smith, U. R., & Morrison, G. C. (1975). Family tolerance for chronic, severe, neurotic, or deviant behavior in children referred for child psychiatry consultation. In G. C. Morrison (Ed.), *Emergencies in child psychiatry.* Springfield, IL: Thomas.

Steffen, J. J., & Karoly, P. (1982). *Autism and severe psychopathology: Advances in child behavioral analysis therapy* (Vol. 2). New York: Lexington Books.

Steinberg, D. (1980). Annotation: The use of lithium carbonate in adolescence. *Journal of Child Psychology and Psychiatry, 21,* 263–271.

Stores, G. (1978). Antiepileptics (Anticonvulsants). In J. S. Werry (Ed.), *Pediatric psychopharmacology* (pp. 274–315). New York: Brunner/Mazel.

Taylor, E., & Sandburg, S. (1984). Hyperactive behavior in English schoolchildren: A questionnaire survey. *Journal of Abnormal Child Psychology, 12,* 143–156.

Thomas, A., & Chess, S. (1984). Genesis and evolution of behavioral disorders: From infancy to early adult life. *American Journal of Psychiatry, 141,* 1–9.

Tramontana, M. G. (1980). Critical review of research on psychotherapy outcome with adolescents: 1967–1977. *Psychological Bulletin, 88,* 429–450.

Visotsky, H. M. (1967). Primary prevention. In A. D. Freedman & H. I. Kaplan (Eds.), *Comprehensive textbook of psychiatry.* Baltimore: Williams & Wilkins.

Werry, J. S. (1982). An overview of pediatric psychopharmacology. *Journal of the American Academy of Child Psychiatry, 21,* 3–9.

Werry, J. A., & Lampen, E. (1976). Haloperidol and methylphenidate in hyperactive children. *Acta Paedopsychiatrica, 42,* 26–40.

Werry, J. S., Aman, M., & Diamond, E. (1980). Imipramine and methylphenidate in hyperactive children. *Journal of Child Psychology and Psychiatry, 21,* 27–35.

Werry, J., & Sprague, R. (1974). Methylphenidate in children: Effect of dosage. *Australian and New Zealand Journal of Psychiatry, 8,* 9–19.

Wilson, M. R., & Soth, N. (1985). Approaching the crisis in adolescent long-term psychiatric hospitalization: Current problems and treatment innovations. *Psychiatric Annals, 15*(1), 556–595.

BIBLIOGRAPHY: PROFESSIONALS

Gossett, J. T., Lewis, J. M., & Barnhart, F. D. (1983). *The outcome of hospital treatment of disturbed adolescents.* New York: Brunner/Mazel.
Describes the long-term results of a follow-up study of adolescents treated at a psychiatric hospital. A thorough review of the literature on follow-up studies is also presented. The authors conclude that of 100 discharged adolescents approximately 50% were functioning well 5 years later.

Guze, S., Earls, F., & Barrett, J. (1983). *Childhood psychopathology and development.* New York: Raven.
Presents 16 papers on the following areas: epidemiology, diagnosis, treatment, neurbiology, and genetics as related to child psychiatry. Each paper includes comments by professionals useful in clarifying particular points. Information on early indicators of vulnerability to schizophrenia or routes to teenage psychiatric symptoms is included.

Smith, R. J., & Steindler, E. M. (1983). The impact of difficult patients upon treaters: Consequences and remedies. *Bulletin of the Menninger Clinic, 47*(2), 107–116.
Difficult patients and successful treatment models have been the focus of many discussions. The authors identify types of patients and suggest specific techniques for professionals. Specific strategies, such as anticipation of consequences, is of a type that school psychologists might present to parents either during meetings or during supportive counseling sessions.

BIBLIOGRAPHY: PARENTS

Bloom, B., & Asher, S. (1982). *Psychiatric patient rights and patient advocacy.* New York: Human Sciences.
This volume is part of the American Psychological Associations Community Psychology Series and is potentially helpful to parents or professionals concerned about patient rights as related to institutionalization. Issues such as involuntary committment, right to refuse treatment, restraint and seclusionary measures, and admission status are all discussed. An outstanding and helpful resource.

Lamb, R. (1982). *Treating the long-term mentally-ill.* San Francisco: Jossey-Bass.
The needs of long-term, mentally ill patients, reasons for their plight, appropriate living arrangements, and treatment services are all issues confronted by this very readable book. The discussion on living arrangements could be quite helpful in discussions of long-range plans for disturbed youngsters. The final section contains information on supplemental security income. A gentle and moving reminder of why mental illness is such an unfortunate and disconcerting part of our lives.

Children and Psychological Abuse

Pamela B. Rogers
Norwood Public Schools, Massachusetts

BACKGROUND

Psychological abuse has been described as the case issue in the broader picture of abuse and neglect (Garbarino & Vondra, in press). A variety of terms are used to indicate psychological abuse, including psychological maltreatment, emotional abuse, emotional maltreatment, and emotional neglect. In this chapter the term *psychological abuse* will be used to include emotional abuse or maltreatment and neglect. Historically, psychological abuse has not been easy to define. For this reason, Garbarino (1978) referred to it as the "elusive crime."

In 1983 at the International Conference on the Psychological Abuse of Children and Youth, a working definition was agreed upon (Proceedings, 1983):

> Psychological maltreatment of children and youth consists of acts of omission and commission which are judged on the basis of a combination of community standards and professional expertise to be psychologically damaging. Such acts are committed by individuals singly or collectively, who by their characteristics (e.g., age, status, knowledge, organizational form) are in a position of differential power that renders a child vulnerable. Examples of maltreatment include acts of rejecting, terrorizing, isolating, exploiting, and missocializing. Such acts damage immediately or ultimately the behavioral, cognitive, affective, or physical functioning of the child. (p. 2)

Children and youths who are most vulnerable to psychological abuse include those who are handicapped, hyperactive, or unwanted and unplanned, as well as those who are much brighter or much duller than their en parents (Brenner, 1984). Older childrof single parents, and children of teenage parents are at risk (Landau, 1984). Children who have been physically and/or sexually abused are also included in the psychologically abused population. The effects of maltreatment in the form of emotional scarring last well beyond the actual abusive incidents (Germain & Hart, 1985). Conditions which have been found to be associated with psychological maltreatment include poor appetite, guilt, lying, stealing, reduced emotional responsiveness, low self-esteem, incompetence and/or underachievement , misuse of drugs, withdrawal behaviors sometimes leading to suicide, violent aggression sometimes leading to homicide, and tendencies to psychologically maltreat others.

DEVELOPMENT

Psychological maltreatment of young people occurs in homes, neighborhood, and in a variety of community settings. Increasing attention is being given to the psychological maltreatment which children experience in school settings. Hyman (1985) proposed an educator-induced psychological abuse category which he conceptualized as an identifiable clinical entity. Characterized as a stress-related series of physical and psychological manifestations, symptoms can include vomiting, nausea, headaches, stomach aches, nightmares, difficulty concentrating, hyperactivity/anxious behaviors, and avoidance of school and school-related activities.

Hart and associates (Hart, 1985; Hart, Brassard, & Germain, in press) have identified five categories into which psychological maltreatment in an educational setting may fall. These include: (a) discipline and control through fear and intimidation, (b) low quantity and quality of human interaction, (c) limited opportunities to develop competency and self-worth, (d) encouragement to be dependent, and (e) denial of opportunities for healthy risk taking. This chapter will illustrate some examples of the kinds of abuse that occur in the school, and then focus on approaches to identification, evaluation, and prevention.

Verbal abuse may take the form of sarcasm, constant harrassment, or humiliation of a child in front of peers, as well as subjection of the victim to undue criticism.

Nonverbal abuse is more subtle but may be just as damaging. A child who does not meet a teacher's socioeconomic standards, or a child who in the eyes of the teacher looks or acts different from a perhaps unconscious norm, may be overlooked, for example, when a messenger is needed to go to the office. Another child, musically talented, may be passed over for the lead in the school play because he or she is deemed not attractive enough. Over time, these children receive a clear message that they are somehow not "good enough."

Another form of psychological abuse is the sabotaging of a youngster's educational plan, whether for counseling, remedial reading, speech, or other special service. When the youngster leaves the room, the teacher may remark that the morning's work is not finished. The child is then caught between leaving the room and probably worrying about the uncompleted papers, or staying in the classroom and missing the special class.

An indifferent attitude on the part of school staff members towards scapegoated children is another form of psychological abuse. Peers as well as adults may reject a child for any number of reasons. An adult in the school who takes no action to support the scapegoat tacitly encourages rejection by the other children, a clear case of blaming the victim.

Psychological Abuse and Competence

Psychological abuse significantly impairs a child's sense of competence, four major areas of which have been cited by Garbarino (1980): (a) communications skills — the ability to accurately transmit and receive verbal and nonverbal messages; (b) patience — the ability to delay gratification; (c) moderate goal setting —the ability to commit oneself to realistic challenges; and (d) ego development — the confidence to handle day-to-day challenges. Furthermore, children subjected to negative affective experiences over a period of time are discouraged from investigating their environment, a condition that has an inhibiting effect on intelligence (Fairorth, 1982).

Psychological abuse in the classroom not only impedes academic progress, by turning enthusiastic learners into resentful underachievers; it also adversely affects social interaction among peers. Children who are socially immature, impulsive, and lacking in judgment may be scapegoated by the other youngsters. The adult who punishes scapegoated children for their inability to get along with their peers is neglecting their real need for lessons in social skills. Children who have not learned socialization skills need to be carefully and explicitly taught (Osman, 1979).

Not all children who are exposed to psychological abuse in the classroom will show signs of stress. Research on self-esteem (Coopersmith, 1967) has provided clues to prevention of psychological abuse, as well as a way to distinguish between the child or youth who is more vulnerable than others to psychological maltreatment, whether at home or at school.

The child who exhibits a high degree of self-confidence is less likely to be affected by verbal and nonverbal abuse. Coopersmith cited four antecedents of self-esteem: acceptance by parents, appropriate limit setting, respect for the individual, and parental self-esteem. Not every antecedent is necessary to the development of self-esteem, as long as there is a minimum experience of devaluating situations such as rejection, ambiguity of limits, and disrespect.

In the school setting, it would seem obvious that youngsters who are confident of their abilities and worth are less likely to be affected by psychologically abusive situations. Conversely, children and adults who lack self-esteem become helpless, vulnerable, and inadequate in stressful situations.

Elkind (1981) delineated the characteristics of the invulnerable child. Such a child seems to be impervious to even the most stressful family situation, is socially competent, manages to impress adults so that they are supportive, and remains confident, independent, and achievement-oriented. Elkind warned, however, that even children and youths who do not fit into the categories of those commonly thought to be the most vulnerable to psychological abuse — those who have been physically and/or sexually abused, the handicapped, children of divorce, and those who have not had the benefits of parenting conducive to self-esteem — are nevertheless vulnerable to emotional stress. In particular this is true of those who suffer from the effects of the "abuse of hurrying," in which children and youths are pushed beyond the limits that can ordinarily be expected at any given developmental stage, and are depleted of their adaptive energy by adults who manipulate the youngsters to meet their own needs (Elkind, 1981).

PUTTING PSYCHOLOGICAL ABUSE OF CHILDREN IN PERSPECTIVE

Consider the following case study:

> Jimmy, age 6, came to the attention of the school psychologist in the fall of his first grade year. Both the teacher on duty at recess and the school nurse were concerned about his increasingly negative behavior. He was always in trouble on the playground, and he was becoming a regular visitor to the nurse's office for no apparent reason.

In this example, frequent trips to the school nurse and increased squabbling at recess, might suggest a chaotic classroom. However, since behavioral problems are usually a result of a number of factors, it is important to first evaluate thoroughly the youngster's developmental and educational history, as well as to investigate relationships both in school and at home.

Next, it is important to learn more about the teacher's teaching style, and to observe how disciplinary issues are handled. Does the teacher repeatedly blame one particular youngster when something goes wrong, without taking the time to find out if others were involved? Is this particular child always assumed to be the guilty one? Other factors in the classroom environment, such as the amount of structure vs. that required by the child, would be important to ascertain.

Complete evaluation of a troubled child's emotional state requires answers to many more questions regarding the psychological environment. Parents should be interviewed to determine whether they have noted any changes in the child's behaviors at home or attitudes towards school. For example, the youngster may be having trouble getting to sleep at night, as well as complaining more about school, which the parents see as a change. The existence of any chronic or acute medical/ health concerns should also be investigated.

Once other factors have been ruled out, a hypothesis might be made that the child's stress level is beyond what would be expected from occasional angry outbursts by the teacher.

In the present case, in talks with the kindergarten teacher, it was learned that Jimmy was often into mischief, but that his behavior had not impeded classroom activities. However, the first grade teacher had frequently chastised him when he was in kindergarten for running in the halls. This same teacher had heard the kindergarten teacher tell stories of Jimmy's wild antics. By the time Jimmy entered the first-grade classroom, the teacher had already decided he was a troublemaker and treated him accordingly. By October, although a competent child, Jimmy could do nothing right in the teacher's eyes. Raising his hand to be excused or to sharpen his pencil became a control issue.

On the other hand, what may appear to be an abusive situation may be so only in the perception of the student. Consider the case of Jennifer, who cried no matter how tenderly the teacher corrected her. After an exploration of the family situation, it was learned that the teacher was not being abusive; Jennifer was overly sensitive to adult criticism no matter how it was presented, owing in part to an abusive foster home placement several years previously.

Psychological Abuse and Motivation

Before one can conclude that psychological abuse has occurred in the classroom, a careful assessment of the expectations of the classroom relative to the developmental and cognitive levels of the youngsters must be made. Requiring a capable third grader to copy over a messy math paper, or periodically keeping careless youngsters in from recess to finish the homework they have forgotten to bring in, are not considered to be abusive acts.

It is important to differentiate between psychological abuse and techniques of motivation. Ginott (1972) suggested that the difference between psychological abuse and motivation is in the child's response to further learning. Fear is the greatest inhibitor of learning —"fear of failure, fear of criticism, fear of appearing stupid" (Ginott, 1972, p. 248). On the other hand, techniques that allow a child to risk making mistakes are psychologically motivating.

Ginott cited an example of how a typical classroom situation can easily disintegrate into an abusive incident: A teacher is frustrated because his repeated lengthy explanation of an algebra problem is not understood by a pupil. The exasperated teacher remarks, "You have to be bright to understand algebra!" The student ends up angry and hurt. A positive way to motivate the student might have been for the teacher to state that he, himself, may be having trouble making his point, and to suggest that they try another approach (Ginott, 1972).

While common sense would lead one to believe that students are best encouraged to learn by giving positive reinforcement of their efforts, and ignoring inappropriate behavior, Brophy (1976) has pointed out that criticism is an integral motivational tool, provided it is offered in a supportive manner. For example, a paper that is full of mistakes should not be ignored; good teachers bring mistakes to the students' attention. Criticism that is judgmental — "you're so sloppy" — is counterproductive and leaves students hurt and resentful. In contrast, good teachers remind students to slow down and work more carefully. This accomplishes two goals: It tells students what to do to improve, and at the same time helps them understand that it was their *approach* that was inappropriate.

Attacking a youngster's personality — "you're lazy, sloppy, a nuisance" — is not simply counterproductive; it leads to negative consequences over time in respect to the child's self-image. Posit the classical case of spilled milk, for example. Criticism can be negative or positive. Too many adults might comment, "You're clumsy and always have been." If enough incidents are handled by ridiculing a child's efforts, her or his self-confidence is affected. The positive way to handle mishaps is to assess the situation and to offer a solution; the obviously appropriate comment is, "The milk is spilled. Let's find a sponge and clean it up" (Ginott, 1965). Youngsters learn to view themselves positively and realistically when criticism is offered constructively.

Psychological Abuse and the Home

A critical component in the assessment of a case of psychological abuse is the developmental and family history. The most common trait among psychologically abusive parents is that they were psychologically abused in their youth. Surprisingly, most report that they "never had a hand laid on them as children" (Landau, 1984, p. 10). It is a chilling fact that the parent or teacher who is psychologically abusive need never have been either sexually or physically abused.

In evaluating the home situation, the school psychologist should ascertain the extent to which a referred child is being burdened with excessive responsibility and whether the student is being forced to conform to unrealistic expectations (Landau, 1984). Role reversal, in which the youngster is used to meet adults' emotional or physical needs, is common among the older children in single-family homes, and among children of teenage parents. These factors are associated with psychological abuse.

Mayhall and Norgand (1983) have identified four central themes in the psychologically abusive family: (a) positive normal growth is not affirmed (smiling, manipulation of toys, exploring, are either ignored or negatively reinforced); (b) in some way babies are discouraged from bonding (attachment); (c) positive self-esteem is penalized; (d) interpersonal skills are not encouraged.

In the families of psychologically abused adolescents, two family patterns are evident: (a) children are subjected to excessive generalized criticism that usually has begun in early childhood; the parents predict the child will be a failure; (b) adolescents are in a "double bind": they are encouraged to succeed but in reality they can do nothing right. They may be allowed to participate, for example, in after-school activities but are punished if they are 15 min. late for dinner. The parenting style is rigid; parents overreact to losing control of teenagers as they become more and more independent, at a time, perhaps, when the parents themselves are developmentally less able to exercise control in their adult lives.

When overcontrolling parents find themselves faced with a resistant teenager, the result may be rejection or even assault. Overcontrol at best tends to rob adolescents of opportunities for making decisions and learning from normal mistakes (Garbarino & Gilliam, 1980). Overcontrolling parents may withhold recommended treatment of emotional problems; they may even encourage antisocial behavior on the part of the adolescent, by denying that a problem exists (Mayhall & Norgand, 1983).

ALTERNATIVE ACTIONS

What can be done to prevent psychological abuse, as well as to ease its damaging effects, at school and in the home?

1. Improve the school climate: Better student achievement, attendance, behavior, discipline, motivation, and self-esteem can result from efforts to improve the climate of the school (Wilson, 1985).
2. Promote development of psychological processes as proper educational goals. "The facilitation of interchange with adults and peers [should] become *as* central a concern as the learning of basic facts" (Holt, 1982, p. 132).
3. Provide stress reduction workshops for staff and students. Relaxation techniques should be included. Brenner, among others, offers specific strategies for helping schools cope with stress — by removing one stressor at a time (the child who comes to school hungry can be given a snack) and by teaching children specific coping strategies usually reserved for adults (Brenner, 1984).
4. Provide support for staff around issues concerning special education. The stress level and subsequent psychological abuse of these youngsters naturally escalates when teachers are expected to individualize curriculum, as well as rearrange classroom activities and schedules around children who are scheduled to leave the class to work with specialists.
5. Provide a workshop on disciplinary techniques for all staff, including administrators, to sensitize staff to verbal and nonverbal situations in which psychological abuse is taking place. Discuss the appropriateness of various disciplinary strategies to the developmental level of the youngsters. Agree to guidelines to be used in crises, as well as on a day-to-day basis. Teachers who feel supported in their efforts to deal with behavior problems will be less likely to use psychologically abusive methods to control youngsters.
6. Teach socialization skills to youngsters, thereby decreasing scapegoating of those who have difficulty interacting with peers. "Reverse mainstreaming," in which regular education students join their special education peers in structured activity groups, lessens the socially deficient youngsters' fears of rejection and increases appropriate interaction skills.
7. Educate parents and the larger community about the consequences of psychological abuse.

SUMMARY

Psychological abuse has been considered an elemental factor, if not the key issue, in all situations of abuse and neglect. Researchers and educators have recently begun focusing on the emotional and physical consequences of psychological maltreatment that occurs in the school. This chapter has described some of the types of abuse that may occur and the correlative factors that are affected by such maltreatment. In addition, some of the elements that must be considered when evaluating a child who may be experiencing an abusive situation in the school setting are explored.

A positive school climate can make a real difference in preventing negative interactions among students and adults, as well as among peers and even among siblings. When there is respect for individual differences (emotional, cognitive, physical, cultural and socioeconomic), staff can concentrate on creative ways to cope with the inevitable stress of living with growing human beings. In such schools, students feel that teachers are "on their side" (Wilson, 1985).

Research has shown that the cycle of abuse can be broken: It is up to personnel in the schools, working together with parents and the larger community, to point the way.

REFERENCES

Brenner, A. (1984). *Helping children cope with stress.* Lexington, MA: Heath.

Brophy, J., & Everston, C. (1976). *Learning from teaching: A developmental perspective.* Boston: Allyn & Bacon.

Coopersmith, S. (1967). *The antecedents of self-esteem.* San Francisco: Freeman.

Elkind, D. (1981). *The hurried child: Growing up too fast too soon.* Reading, MA: Addison.

Fairorth, (1982). *Child abuse and the school.* Palo Alto, CA: R & E Research Associates.

Frude, N. (Ed.). (1981). *Psychological approaches to child abuse.* Lotowa, NJ: Rowman & Littlefield.

Garbarino, J. (1978). The elusive "crime" of emotional abuse. *Child Abuse and Neglect, 2,* 89–99.

Garbarino, J., & Gilliam, G. (1980). *Understanding abusive families.* Lexington, MA: Lexington Books.

Garbarino, J., & Vondra, J. (in press). Psychological maltreatment: Issues and perspectives. In M. R. Brassard, R. Germain & S. N. Hart (Eds.), *Psychological maltreatment of children and youth.* Elmsford, NY: Pergamon.

Germain, R., Hart, S., & Brassard, M. (1985). Crisis intervention for maltreated children. *School Psychology Review, 14*(3), 291–299.

Ginott, H. (1965). *Between parent and child.* New York: Macmillan.

Ginott, H. (1972). *Teacher and child.* New York: Macmillan.

Hart, S. (1985). *Psychological maltreatment and schooling.* A paper presented to the Annual Convention of the American Educational Research Association in Chicago.

Hart, S., Brassard, M., & Germain, R. (in press). Psychological maltreatment and education/schooling. In M. R. Brassard, R. Germain, & S. N. Hart (Eds.), *Psychological Maltreatment of children and youth.* Elmsford, NY: Pergamon.

Holt, J. (1982). *How children fail.* New York: Delacorte.

Landau, E. (1984). *Child abuse: An American epidemic.* New York: Julian Messner.

Mayhall, P. D., & Norgand, K. E. (1983). *Child abuse and neglect: Sharing responsibility.* New York: Wiley.

Osman, B. (1979). *Learning disabilities: A family affair.* New York: Random House.

Proceedings of the International Conference on Psychological Abuse of Children and Youth. (1983). Indianapolis: Indiana University, Office for the Study of the Psychological Rights of the Child.

Steele, B. (1980). The psychodynamics of child abuse. In Kempe (Ed.), *The battered child.* Chicago: University of Chicago Press.

U.S. Department of Health and Human Services. (1981). *National study of the incidence and severity of child abuse and neglect. Study findings* (DHHS Publication No. OHDS-81-30325). Washington, DC: U.S. Department of Health and Human Services.

Wilson, M. (1985). Best practices in improving school climate. In J. Grimes & A. Thomas (Eds.), *Best practices in school psychology* (pp. 485–492). Kent, OH: National Association of School Psychologists.

BIBLIOGRAPHY: PROFESSIONALS

Brenner, A. (1984). *Helping children cope with stress.* Lexington, MA: Heath.
A highly readable book on all aspects of child abuse. Included are specific treatment strategies for school personnel to use in working with children (and adolescents).

Frude, N. (Ed.). (1981). *Psychological approaches to child abuse.* Lotowa, NJ: Rowman & Littlefield.
An excellent summary of the latest research on child abuse.

Hyman, I. A. (1985). *Psychological abuse in the schools: A school psychologist's perspective.* Paper presented to the annual convention of the American Psychological Association, Los Angeles.
A school psychologist cites specific examples of the proliferation of psychological abuse in the schools.

Mayhall, P. B., & Norgand, K. E. (1983). *Child abuse and neglect: Sharing responsibility.* New York: Wiley.
A good overview of the subject. Provides helpful hints on interviewing abusive parents.

Office of the Study of the Psychological Rights of the Child (OSPRC), Indiana University, 902 West New York Street, P.O. Box 647, Indianapolis, IN 46223.
OSPRC is a good source of further information on all aspects of the needs of children and youth.

BIBLIOGRAPHY: PARENTS AND TEACHERS

Brenner, A. (1984). *Helping children cope with stress.* Lexington, MA: Heath.
Highly readable overview of the subject; includes specific strategies to use with children (and adolescents).

Elkind, D. (1981). *The hurried child: Growing up too fast too soon.* Reading, MA: Addison.
A good discussion of stress in children's (and adolescents') lives.

Ginott, H. (1965). *Between parent and child.* New York: Macmillan.
Concrete examples of how to communicate positively with children and adolescents so that self-esteem is enhanced.

Ginott, H. (1972). *Teacher and child.* New York: Macmillan.
Specific examples of psychologically abusive situations in the classrooms are discussed, together with ways to avoid such abuse.

Osman, B. (1979). *Learning disabilities: A family affair.* New York: Random House.
The author suggests ways in which youngsters who lack socialization skills can be helped to interact more positively with peers.

Children and Reactions to Death

Charles P. Heath
Deer Valley Unified School District, Phoenix, Arizona

BACKGROUND

Children must deal with the separation and loss of significant others more often than most adults realize. Divorce, family mobility, hospitalization, and death are all instances in which a child must cope with and try to understand the loss of a loved one. Each situation has the same results; all are accompanied by grief. Jewett (1982) has reported that no matter how trivial a loss, individuals must go through the same process of grief resolution, though the length and intensity will differ. Loss is viewed as a cumulative process in which, without complete resolution of a minor loss, subsequent less significant losses are likely to provoke similar stress.

While exact figures are not known, it is estimated that 5% of the children in the United States (1.5 million) lose one or both parents by age 15 (Kliman, 1979). This chapter will discuss children's reactions to the death of a parent; however, it should be remembered that similar reactions are seen when a close relative or other loved one dies.

DEVELOPMENT

The child's level of cognitive development plays a primary role in the extent to which a child will understand the loss of a parent. Krupnick (1984) reports that the tendency to impose adult models of death resolution on children has led to misunderstandings about children's grieving. Specific manifestations or reactions as well as their duration are different for adults and children. These differences necessitate an understanding of childhood grieving on the part of the school psychologist and others and one should not expect that children will express their emotions as adults do. Children's overt behaviors during the grieving process are often misinterpreted because they often do not reveal their internal distress.

A child's need to ask the same questions about the death over and over is more of a need for reassurance that the story has not changed rather than a need for factual accuracy. Reactions that appear to be unemotional such as telling strangers, "My daddy died" is the child's way of seeking reactions so that they can gauge their own reactions. Emotions may be expressed as angry outbursts or misbehaviors that are often not recognized as grief-related. Children are likely to manifest such grief-related behavior and affect on an intermittent basis for many years after a loss occurs. Such behavior reflects the cognitive and emotional capacity of the child.

Kastenbaum (1967) reported that an understanding of the developmental concept of death in a child is only one factor that must be addressed in understanding the grieving process in children. The second major factor is "ourselves" or the adult's view of death. The adult's own problems in coming to terms with death can have a significant effect upon the child and may complicate rather than facilitate the child's quest for understanding.

Developmental Phases in Understanding Death

While it is generally agreed that prior to the age of 3 or 4 years children are not able to achieve complete mourning, controversy remains over the years between early childhood and adolescence. The controversy centers around the question of whether a healthy resolution can be reached and the similarity between adults' and children's bereavement reactions. Before discussing children's reactions to death based upon chronological age, two points need to be made. First, the specific age references are not rigid but are to be used as rough guides. Second, children may regress to an earlier stage when emotionally threatened.

Given that infants and toddlers seem to lack conceptions of death, they nevertheless seem to explore the state of nonbeing. Maurer (1966) held that the infant experiments with the idea of death in games such as peek-a-boo, in which the baby risks and experiments with being and nonbeing. Another example is the familiar phenomenon of a child sitting in a high chair and throwing objects on the floor for others to retrieve. Gradually the child comes to realize that not all things come back and some may be "all gone." These early experiments with being and nonbeing may be a child's first steps in understanding death. The preschooler believes that self-identity has no limit in time. Periodically, one's condition changes somewhat in the same manner as one might sleep and later be awake. So also, one is "made dead" and later returns to ordinary life.

Children between the ages of 3 and 5 years deny death as a final event; death is seen as reversible. The dead are simply considered "less alive." But children functioning in Piaget's preoperational level of development tend not to recognize the irreversibility of death (Piaget, 1951). During this early stage of development of thought, the child seems to regard death mainly as a separation, a departure. As such, they make statements such as "Daddy will be back soon."

Between the ages of 5 and 9 years a child begins to comprehend the finality of death (Nagy, 1948). A seemingly detached inquiry into death is accompanied by two important assumptions. First, that death is accidental rather than inevitable. A child may report that "If you get run over, then you would be dead" or "He is so old, that is why he is dead." Individuals die under certain circumstances and if those circumstances do not occur then one cannot die. Children at this age do not believe that one must necessarily encounter a death-dealing situation at all. Their second assumption is that they themselves will not die. Death is seen as something that will happen to others.

Children around the age of 4 to 6 years are prone to misinterpret superficial events as being intrinsically involved in death. For example, children who have known someone who died in a hospital feel a need to stay away from hospitals to avoid death. Such children seek to isolate any events that "mean" or "cause" death (Kaustenbaum, 1967).

Jewett (1984) pointed out that children process information differently from adults. Young children, prior to age 7, use "magical thinking" during the egocentric stage of life. Personal thought, wishes, and actions are believed to be the causes for what happens. Children walking down the street carefully avoiding the cracks out of fear that "step on a crack, you break your mother's back" is an example of magical thinking. Young children who experience a loss will almost always display magical thinking ("If only I would have stayed home, it would not have happened"), and often adults display magical thinking in times of crisis.

Between the ages of 5 and 9 years, children can neither deny or accept death as an authentic aspect of their life. A compromise becomes necessary involving an acknowledgment that death is "real" but only in an external and distant sense (Kaustenbaum,1967). For this age group there is a tendency to interpret death in anthropomorphic terms; death is a person. Only those die whom the death-man carries off. The death-man is usually regarded as a creature of the night.

After the age of 10 years children have generally made the transition in both mental development and emotional security to express an understanding of death as a final and inevitable event that is associated with the cessation of bodily functions. The death-man is no longer feared.

Children need to develop some understanding of what is alive before they can fully understand the concept of death. Researchers disagree somewhat concerning the process by which children learn to distinguish the living from the nonliving, as well as the exact age when this understanding may occur. However, there is evidence to suggest that most children are capable of approximating an adult's view of the living and nonliving by age 10 (Huang & Lee, 1945; Klingberg, 1957; Russell, 1940; Strauss, 1951). As a child reaches adolescence there is a capability of understanding life and death in a logical manner (Anthony, 1940; Piaget, 1930).

Adolescence presents a new set of problems in the children's understanding of death. As the adolescent begins to gain more independence and starts looking forward to the future, there is the realization that all future plans require time, and death may come at any time to prevent these plans from reaching fruition. The adolescent soon realizes that each person grows up only to die.

Developmental Phases of Grief Resolution

Age not only affects children's understanding of death, but also determines how they might react to the loss of a parent. Comprehension of this fact is vital for the school psychologist or other helping professionals working with children. Natural reactions to death need to be understood so that those working with grieving children will be better able to support them during this time. Jewett (1982) identified three phases that children, as well as adults, go through in order to reach some resolution. It must be understood that these three phases are not discrete stages and some overlap may be seen. Anniversaries such as birthdays or special holidays may bring on a temporary regression to a previous phase. Also, the length and intensity of each phase is dictated by the seriousness of the loss and the children's coping capabilities.

During the initial phase of early grief, children's reactions are shock and numbing. The realization that a parent has died results in a mechanical process of completing daily activities; one seems to be simply "going through the motions." A flat affect is observed that may be combined with sudden outbursts of panic. Children will ignore friends and not get involved in activities that were pleasurable prior to the parent's death.

After the shock has subsided, there is typically a reaction of alarm. The alarm results because a child who loses a parent has questions of who is going to care and provide a safe environment. Physiological changes occur, such as an increased heart rate and muscle tension. Insomnia, as well as susceptibility to illness, are also common reactions. Such symptoms are likely to occur on an intermittent basis as the child processes the reality of the situation.

Denial and disbelief are also behaviors that may be exhibited during the initial phase of grief. Children may not accept the loss and may report that the deceased was seen or that his or her voice was heard. This denial allows children to shut out the hurt if it is overwhelming and to deal with the loss when they are feeling less threatened. The denial can be exhibited in many ways. Deprecation, contempt, or other efforts to devalue the lost person are all forms of the denial process. Adults may also see such children as hyperactive and unable to sit and attend for any length of time. Keeping busy is the child's way of avoiding the possibility of having to think about the loss.

Phase two, acute grief, has several characteristic behaviors such as yearning, searching, disorganization, despair, and ultimately reorganization. The death of a parent leaves a child wishing for a different ending. A child's world is filled with make-believe and fairy tales of which the endings are always happy. Children identify with those they read about or see on television and naturally wish for a reunion after a loss. This yearning is a stage of grief that will recur for some time. Resolution is reached gradually as the repeated yearnings are not met and the child understands the reality of the loss and separation. It is the mastering of these feelings about the loss that ultimately leads to resolution.

This phase is often characterized by strong feelings of sadness, anger, guilt, and shame. Adults who allow a child to experience these feelings as natural will be greatly facilitating the grieving process. The supportive adult during this phase must realize that it will take a long time before the child feels better. Once the stage of intense feeling starts, it can take 6–12 weeks for the worst pain to subside, and as much as 2 years before the grief process is completed (Jewett, 1982).

The last phase involves the integration of loss and grief in which the child begins to reorganize daily activities. Acceptance of the loss results in less frequent and less intense crying. Often the child is able to verbalize an awareness of their experience of grief, and a feeling of growth is evident.

PUTTING CHILDREN'S REACTIONS TO DEATH IN PERSPECTIVE

While an understanding of developmental trends and behavioral reactions of a child to the loss of a parent are important to know, there are also several other factors that need to be considered. How to explain the death of a parent to children, the circumstances when children should attend funeral services, and the effect of religious beliefs affect our interventions. Also, the child's age, sex, and prior relationship with the deceased as well as the circumstances of the death need to be considered.

When a child has lost a parent or loved one, there is always the question of how to explain the death. The death of a parent is best imparted by the adult to whom the child feels closest. If one parent dies and the remaining parent is unable to tell the child, then the child should be informed by another adult who is close to the child.

A clear message needs to be given to children that it is not their fault that the parent has died. They need to know that there is nothing that could have been done or can be done to make things different. Adults also need to realize that past experiences help them deal with the loss of a loved one but children often have no such experience. Two important things to tell children who have experienced the loss of a parent through death are first, that the dead person will never return and second, that the dead person's body will be buried in the ground or burned to ashes (Jewett, 1982).

If a parent has died, the emotional reaction of the remaining parent must be a prime consideration. A parent who is struggling with personal bereavement and shock must not deny a child an opportunity to share in the expression of pain. Talking to their children is often painful for bereaved adults and therefore many parents avoid it. Such an approach may be more to protect themselves from further upheaval than to protect their children. But by not talking to their children, these parents deny them the opportunity to confront their grief and reach resolution.

Adults' concern over interacting with their children is often greater than necessary. Adults need to be reassured that in times of great stress there is a shutting down of awareness on an emotional, intellectual, and even a physical level. A defense mechanism works that tends to prevent the individual from becoming overwhelmed in times of stress. A child's initial reaction may be apparently casual acceptance, followed by crying at a later time period. It may be necessary later to repeat the message that there has been a death of a parent.

During such emotionally trying times there is a tendency for adults to rely upon their children for comfort and understanding. Adults should avoid using their children as confidants; when this is not possible they should seek outside help such as a psychologist or counselor for youngsters involved. Parents should also remember that if they inadvertently say something that they later regret, they can always approach their children again and reexplain or clarify what was previously said.

The single most important message to relay to a child who has lost a parent is "You are not alone; I am with you." Touching or holding a child may do more than any words to relay a parent's message. The facts of the loss should be conveyed in as straightforward a manner as possible. Also, it should be remembered that children get their understanding of life primarily through their senses rather than through their intellects. It is helpful to tie the news to a sensory or bodily connection. Relating news back to what the child has heard or seen makes the information more real.

Once a child has been told of a parent's death, a decision must be made concerning the funeral. Having children attend funeral services is very important (Jewett, 1982; Rando, 1984) as they are thus allowed to share their grief with those whom they love. Not allowing children to attend the funerals may add feelings of insecurity and abandonment. However, the final decision on whether to attend should be the child's. Once a child makes the decision, it should be respected..

Prior to the funeral someone should explain to children who are to attend what will take place, who will be there, and how people are likely to react. (Rando, 1984). This information will help them put personal behavior into perspective. The choice of whether to view or to touch the deceased should also be left up to the child. Adults need to keep in mind that funeral rituals, in and of themselves, entail nothing for the child to fear. Children's fears are often the result of adults' reactions during the grieving process.

The beliefs, meanings, and values that individuals hold for life, death, and the life after death are greatly affected by prior religious training (Rando, 1984). Often adults' statements about "heaven" or "God" in relation to the death of a parent are viewed as efforts to protect the adult, not the child. Adults are often tempted to blame God when unsure of what else to say (Vogel, 1975). While it is understandable, it is also wrong and can have serious adverse effects for the child. Statements such as "God took your father to heaven" or "God wanted him" only serve to make God appear an enemy. Such statements may lead to resentment of God. Linking suffering and death with sin, punishment, or reward is likewise inappropriate (Grollman, 1976).

Besides funeral attendance and religious beliefs, the age and emotional stability of the child as well as the sex of the deceased and of the child need to be considered in order to understand a child's reactions to the death of a parent. Early adolescence also appears to be a particularly vulnerable time to lose a parent (Black, 1978). Children who have had parental relationships characterized by ambivalence or dependence tend to experience more difficult reactions to loss (Raphael, 1983). Preadolescent children, unlike adults or adolescents who have a number of close relationships outside the family, invest love almost exclusively in parental figures (Furman, 1974). Thus, preexisting relationships and the age of the child may be interacting factors in the grieving process.

Inconsistent results have been noted in studies in which the sex of the deceased parent and the child was investigated. Kliman (1979) reported that from about age 3 and older, a more overt yearning takes place when the opposite-sex parent dies. However, unique anxieties may develop when the same-sex parent dies, especially if the child views his or her role as one of replacing the deceased parent. Studies also suggest that girls are more vulnerable than boys to parental bereavement in general and especially during adolescence more affected than boys are by the loss of a father (Birtchell, 1972; Black, 1978). Kaffman and Elizur (1983), on the other hand, found few differences between boys and girls who had lost a father.

When there is a death in the family, chaos and disorganization usually preside rather than an atmosphere of stability and consistency. The major source of support for children is the parents, but during the period after a death they are often unable to provide an environment that is conducive to healing. When a father dies, the mother's capacity to remain assertive while coping with the loss, as well as the availability of a supportive father figure, influence a child's later responses to the loss (Elizur & Kaffman, 1983). How the surviving parent handles the grieving process and the extent of dependency placed on the child also affect future responses of the child (Hilgard, et al., 1960).

A final factor that affects the grieving process in children is the circumstances of the death. Whether one dies as a result of an extended illness or an accident, in the home or in a hospital, influences the bereavement process. Generally, it is easier for a child to deal with an expected death than a sudden death because of time allowed to prepare. Suicide is generally considered the most difficult type of death to accept (Schneidman, 1972). Specific information regarding children and suicide is reported in this volume, which should be consulted for a thorough review of the literature on death by suicide.

Before considering possible interventions, it is important to discuss whether children can even complete the grieving process. There is considerable controversy as to whether children are capable of mourning (Worden, 1982). Krupnick (1984) believes that complete mourning can only occur if a child has some understanding of death, is capable of forming a real attachment, and has a mental representation of the attachment figure. All of these can occur in children as early as 3 years. Bowlby (1980) held that children can resolve the death of a parent if, first, the parent–child relationship has been reasonably secure prior to the death; second, the child is given accurate information about the death as soon as possible and is allowed to ask questions and receives honest answers; third, the child participates in the family grieving process, including attending the funeral if the child desires; and fourth, a trusted adult can aid in comforting the child on a continuing basis.

On the other hand, Wolfenstein (1966) took an opposite position, saying that children cannot mourn until there is a complete identity formation, which occurs at the end of adolescence, when the individual is fully differentiated. A clear definition of mourning seems to be the basis for much of the controversy, which leads to the question of whether mourning is a detachment/identity process or is an interactional process as discussed by Bowlby.

ALTERNATIVE ACTIONS

It is important to establish continuity in the daily routines of children who have lost a parent. Likewise, families should avoid additional stresses immediately after a major loss. Changing to a new school or moving away to a new neighborhood should be postponed. Losing a parent is traumatic enough; compounding this loss with the loss of friends will only further hinder the grieving process.

Individuals may be unsure of exactly where to start in helping children deal with the death of a parent. There really is not a starting place; one should follow the lead of the child by responding to the questions that are asked and the behaviors that are exhibited.

Additional assistance may be necessary for children who do not appear, over time, to be progressing through the expected phases, as discussed earlier, after the loss of a loved one. However, it is crucial to distinguish normal from pathological grief. To overreact may tend to give children a message that there is something wrong with them, thus delaying resolution of grief. On the other hand, a lack of recognition may delay needed professional help. Intensity and duration are two important factors to consider but the limits can be difficult to establish (Krupnick, 1984). Bowlby (1980) established the following warning signals: the presence of persistent anxieties, hopes of reunion, or a desire to die and persistent blame and guilt, as well as patterns of overactivity with aggressive and destructive outbursts, compulsive caregiving and self-reliance, euphoria with depersonalization and identification symptoms, and accident proneness.

There is evidence that childhood bereavement can be a precurser of later emotional difficulties. The experience of prior emotional problems and the existence of a dysfunctional family system are factors that dictate whether more severe pathological developments might occur after the loss of a parent (Elizer & Kaffman, 1983).

Bowlby (1980) reported that the loss of a parent early in life may render a child vulnerable to future depression. Gay and Tonge (1967) suggested that depression associated with early bereavement tends to be reactive rather than endogenous. However, factors such as the quality of the relationship with the caretakers after the loss may be more influential in determining risk of later depression than the actual experience of bereavement (Birtchnell, 1980). In summary, data are inconclusive regarding the long-term consequences of bereavement during childhood and adolescence. Potential problems are indicated but there is a lack of understanding as to what puts a bereaved child at risk (Krupnick, 1984).

Interventions/Strategies

Once it is determined that a child is experiencing pathological grief, parents or other helping professionals need to decide upon appropriate interventions. Grief therapy, as defined by Worden (1982), involves the use of specialized techniques to resolve the conflicts of separation that preclude the completion of the mourning process.

One approach is bibliotherapy, in which books are used as an avenue to help explain death in an understandable way. Using bibliotherapy can be helpful; however, several cautions need to be noted. First, before giving them to the children, adult caregivers should read the books to be used for the therapy. This assures that the content is consistent with their own approach to death. It also makes it possible to better respond to the children's questions. Second, consideration should be given to the children's age and development so that they can be given books of an appropriate level. Third, the content of the books should coincide with the loss the children have experienced. Fourth, after reading the books, the children should have an opportunity to discuss them with adults. This allows for questions to be answered and misconceptions corrected (Heath, 1986).

Behavioral techniques such as relaxation, systematic desensitization, cognitive rehearsal, and contingency contracting may all be useful in resolving conflicts. Psychodrama techniques of role playing with pictures of the deceased to facilitate the goals of therapy as well as Gestalt techniques such as the "empty chair" can also be helpful.

Melges and DeMaso (1980) discussed using present-time guided imagery for reliving, revising, and revisiting scenes once shared with the deceased. This technique stresses the ability to address the deceased in the first person and in the present time context.

Rofes (1985) discussed approaches such as writing a paper about the earliest experiences with death, drawing pictures of how death is imagined to look, writing poems about the deceased, or writing down what it is like after death. All of these could be done on an individual or group basis.

Finally, it should be noted that while many techniques are not age-specific, others need to be geared directly to the children's age or cognitive capabilities. To implement techniques that are beyond the children's capabilities will only tend to further confuse them and hinder grief resolution.

SUMMARY

Children who experience the death of a parent or loved one often need a support system beyond the extended family. School psychologists and other helping professionals are in a unique position to assist children in grief resolution. Understanding age-related behaviors and children's cognitive understanding of death are both crucial in working with children who have lost a parent. Children will go through certain phases of grief that lead to resolution, and factors such as age, sex, and prior relationships with the deceased, as well as circumstances of the death will all affect bereavement. Additional factors such as how the death is explained to the bereaved children and who remains close to them as a source of emotional support also affect the grieving process.

While most children will proceed through the grieving process without major difficulties, some may need specific help to facilitate grief resolution. There does not appear to be any single intervention that is "most appropriate." Several techniques are useful and can be selected with an eye to the child's age, interests, and cognitive capabilities. The single most important message to relay to a child is that support is available and that as adults we are willing to follow the lead of the child during this critical time.

REFERENCES

Anthony, S. (1940). *The child's discovery of death.* New York: Harcourt.

Birtchnell, J. (1972). Early parent death and psychiatric diagnosis. *Social Psychiatry, 7,* 202–210.

Birtchnell, J. (1980). Women whose mother died in childhood: An outcome study. *Psychological Medicine, 10,* 699–713.

Black, D. (1978). The bereaved child. *Journal of Child Psychology and Psychiatry, 19,* 287–292.

Bowlby, J. (1980). *Loss.* New York: Basic Books.

Elizur, E., & Kaffman, M. (1983). Factors influencing the severity of childhood bereavement reactions. *American Journal of Orthopsychiatry, 53.* 668–676.

Furman, E. (1974). *A child's parent dies.* New Haven, CT: Yale University Press.

Gay, M.,& Tonge, W. (1967). The late effects of loss of parents in childhood. *British Journal of Psychiatry, 113,* 753–759.

Grollman, E. (1967). Prologue: Explaining death to children.In E. Grollman (Ed.), *Explaining death to children* (pp 3–27). Boston: Beacon.

Grollman, E. (1976). *Talking about death: A dialogue between parent and child.* Boston: Beacon.

Heath, C. (1986). Understanding death through bibliotherapy. *Techniques, 2,* 88–92.

Hilgard, J., Newman, M., & Fisk, J. (1960). Strength of adult ego following childhood bereavement. *American Journal of Orthopsychiatry, 30,* 788–799.

Huang, I., & Lee, H. (1945). Experimental analysis of child animism. *Journal of Genetics and Psychology, 66,* 69–74.

Jewett, C. (1982). *Helping children cope with separation and loss.* Harvard, MA: The Harvard Common Press.

Kaffman, M., & Elizur, E. (1983). Bereavement responses of kibbutz and non-kibbutz children following the death of a father. *Journal of Child Psychology and Psychiatry, 24,* 435–442.

Kastenbaum R. (1967). The child's understanding of death: How does it develop. In E. Grollman (Ed.), *Explaining death to children* (pp. 89–108). Boston: Beacon.

Kliman, G. (1979). Facilitation of mourning during childhood. In I. Gerber, et al., (Eds.), *Perspectives on bereavement.* New York: Arno.

Klingberg, G. (1957). The distinction between living and not living among 7–10-year-old children with some remarks concerning the so-called animism controversy. *Journal of Genetics and Psychology, 105,* 227–238.

Krupnick, J. (1984). Bereavement during childhood and adolescence. In M. Osterweis, et al. (Eds.), *Bereavement: Reactions, consequences, and care* (pp. 99–141). Washington, DC: National Academy Press.

Maurer, (1966). Maturation of concepts of death. *British Journal of Medicine and Psychology, 39,* 35–41.

Melges, F., & DeMaso, D. (1980). Grief-resolution therapy: Reliving, revising, and revisiting. *American Journal of Psychotherapy, 34,* 51–61.

Nagy, M. (1948). The child's theories concerning death. *Journal of Genetic Psychology, 73,* 3–12.

Piaget, J. (1930). *The child's conception of physical causality.* (M. Gabian, Trans.). New York: Harcourt.

Piaget, J. (1951). *The child's conception of the world.* London: Routledge and Kegan Paul.

Rando, T. (1984). *Grief, dying and death: Clinical interventions for caregivers.* Champaign, IL: Research Press.

Raphael, B. (1983). *The anatomy of bereavement.* New York: Basic Books.

Rofes, E. (Ed.) (1985). *The kid's book about death and dying: By and for kids.* Boston: Little, Brown.

Russell, R. (1940). Studies in animism: II. The development of animism. *Journal of Genetics and Psychology, 56,* 353–366.

Shneidman, E. (1972). Forward. In A. Cain (Ed.), *Survivors of suicide.* Springfield, IL: Thomas.

Strauss, A. (1951). The animism controversy: Re-examination of Huang-Lee data. *Journal of Genetics and Psychology, 78,* 105–113.

Vogel, L. (1975). *Helping a child understand death.* Philadelphia: Fortress.

Wolfenstein, M. (1966). How is mourning possible? *Psychoanalytic Study of the Child, 21,* 93–123.

Worden, J. (1982). *Grief counseling and grief therapy: A handbook for the mental health practitioner.* New York: Springer.

BIBLIOGRAPHY: PROFESSIONALS

Berlinsky, E., & Biller, H. (1982). *Parental death and psychological development.* Toronto: Heath.
A review of over 200 studies to determine immediate or long-term effects on an individual who experiences parental loss during childhood. Information is presented in a research fashion. Topics discussed include emotional disturbance, cognitive effects on the child, family and situational variables, and characteristics of the child such as age and sex at time of parent's death.

Jewett, C. (1982). *Helping children cope with separation and loss.* Harvard, MA: Harvard Common Press.
Discusses how to tell a child of a loss and likely reactions to separation and loss. Information not only on death but also divorce and the similarity of children's reactions to various losses. Practical intervention approaches are presented that facilitate the grieving process.

Osterweis, M., Solomon, F., & Green, M. (Eds.). (1984). *Bereavement: Reactions, consequences, and care.* Washington, DC: National Academy Press.
Presents information primarily on reactions to the death of a closely related family member. Areas discussed include health consequences of bereavement, adult and children's reactions to bereavement, and reactions to different types of losses, as well as interventions to assist in bereavement.

Rando T. (1984). *Grief, dying and death: Clinical interventions for caregivers.* Champaign, IL: Research Press.
Discusses the issue of bereavement, why it is necessary, and how to work with families and individuals. Issues of terminal illness care are presented. Contains a good chapter on funeral practices from a psychological and sociological perspective. Several chapters have exercises at the end that are helpful in exploring personal reactions to grief and death.

Worden, J. (1982). *Grief counseling and grief therapy: A handbook for the mental health practitioner.* New York: Springer.
Describes the mechanisms of grief and procedures to facilitate the process of normal grieving. Also explains how unresolved grief can lead to more serious problems. Distinction is made between grief counseling, which is used during normal grieving, and grief therapy, which is used to work through unresolved grief.

BIBLIOGRAPHY: PARENTS

Grollman, E. (Ed.) (1967). *Explaining death to children.* Boston: Beacon.
Information on both death and dying is presented by several professionals. Authors include a rabbi, minister, priest, sociologist, anthropologist, school psychologist, and others. Each discusses death on the basis of his or her background and perspective.

Grollman, E. (1976). *Talking about death: A dialogue between parent and child.* Boston: Beacon.
The narrator explains death to a child whose grandfather has died. This explanation is accompanied by a Parent's Guide, which suggests various ways to use the book. Also listed are agencies that may be of assistance plus further readings on the topic of death.

Kopp, R. (1983). *Where has grandpa gone?* Grand Rapids, MI: Zonderman.
Discusses different aspects of death and grief including the function of funerals. Ideas are presented on helping the child to grieve and reach appropriate grief resolution. Includes a special "read aloud" section for adults to read to children to help explain the meaning of death and ways to cope with grief and loss.

LaTour, K. (1983). *For those who live: Helping children cope with the death of a brother or sister.* Dallas, TX: Kathy LaTour.
Designed to help with the readjustment by the family after the death of a child or sibling. Examines how surviving children react to the death of a sibling. Discusses problems that both parents and children are likely to encounter during the grieving process.

Manning, D. (1984). *Don't take my grief away: What to do when you lose a loved one.* New York: Harper & Row.
Written more from the perspective of the bereavement of a spouse when losing a husband or wife. Stresses the natural process of grieving from the initial shock to recovery. Assists in understanding what happens when someone dies, dealing in a realistic yet healing way with the necessity of accepting the loss and facing the feelings of loss, separation, and even guilt that we experience.

BIBLIOGRAPHY: CHILDREN

Hazen, B. (1985). *Why did grandpa die? A book about death.* New York: Western.
A sensitive story that shows children the comfort of sharing feelings and how lasting memories can help wash away the sadness of a death. The introduction presents some "do's and don'ts" about talking with children about death.

Krementz, J. (1981). *How it feels when a parent dies.* New York: Knopf.
Eighteen children of various ages and ethnicity write about their thoughts and feelings when a parent has died. Helps children realize that many of their feelings are normal and shared by others in similar situations.

Mellonie, B., & Ingpen, R. (1983). *Lifetimes: The beautiful way to explain death to children.* New York: Bantam Books.
Beautifully written and illustrated. Explains life and death in a sensitive and caring way. It is a book about beginnings and endings, and about living in between. Uses plants, animals, and people to explain that dying is as much a part of living as being born.

Nystrom, C. (1981). *What happens when we die?* Chicago, IL: Moody.
Explains death from a Christian or religious perspective. Talks about God's role in life and death and heaven as an afterlife. Scripture citations are listed throughout the book for further reference on specific aspects of death.

Stiles, N. (1984). *I'll miss you, Mr. Hooper.* New York: Random House/Children's Television Workshop.
Discusses Big Bird's efforts to understand the death of Mr. Hooper. Shows how Big Bird's memories of Mr. Hooper help him to say good-by. Big Bird's confusion and questions are typical of what many children go through when they have lost a loved one.

Children and Reading

Gerald J. Spadafore
Idaho State University

BACKGROUND

It has been reported that 10–15% of school-aged children in the United States will encounter reading difficulties (Harring & Bateman, 1977). To illustrate this point in clearer terms, approximately four students in most elementary classes qualify for some type of reading assistance; 63% of all individualized educational programs (IEPs) feature reading goals, according to a national survey of individualized educational programs.

The critical issue, therefore, is what can be done to enhance reading development so as to lessen the negative consequences of inadequate reading skills? Before dealing with this concern, it is important to stress that the process of becoming a proficient reader requires one to travel through various developmental stages, each stage consisting of specific development tasks. Hence, the temptation to overreact to unexpected reading difficulties during the initial stages of reading development should be avoided. It is anticipated that many children will exhibit an assortment of beginning reading errors enroute to acquiring their adult-level reading skills.

When analyzing early reading difficulties, it is crucial to keep in mind that although beginning reading skills are substantially dependent on the home environment, the actual formal teaching of reading is usually reserved for public schools.

Reading curricula in the public schools generally reflect a specific philosophical orientation, different schools emphasizing their own particular preference. For this reason, a brief review of reading approaches associated with differing philosophical positions will be presented.

Stoner (1981) has identified four basic approaches to the teaching of reading. Although they are not mutually exclusive, they do emphasize different characteristics of the reading process.

Sight Words. The sight word approach teaches children to recall simple whole words through repeated exposure and practice. With this method children generally memorize key words that are repeated throughout a reading passage, such as:

See Dick.
See Dick run.
See Dick run fast.

Prior to reading a story, children are taught new words. Eventually they learn a variety of new words which will enable them to read more complicated materials on the basis of their expanded vocabulary.

Phonics. When the phonics approach is utilized, individual letter sounds are taught and later they learn how to blend these sounds to form new words. While the sight approach generally stresses visual skills, the phonics approach relies on auditory cues. This procedure not only emphasizes letter sounds, but also prepares children to employ a word-attack mode to decode new and unfamiliar words. Children who master phonic analysis skills are able to decode untaught words; this greatly enhances their reading ability.

Linguistics. The linguistics approach has many similarities to phonics; however, the linguistics approach employs a system that groups letters to form word families. For example:

CAT
NAT
SAT
MAT

Psycholinguistics. The primary emphasis of the psycholinguistics approach is on allowing children to use their own language to predict the sequence of events within a story. Children are initially taught how to read songs and stories they are familiar with, such as Humpty Dumpty. This approach permits a child to relate reading to past experiences and thereby increases the relevancy of that reading activity. In psycholinguistics, however, reading miscues are not always corrected unless they drastically alter the content of the story. The close relationship between reading and language makes this an appealing approach.

The majority of reading curricula will emphasize one approach while permitting the teaching of relevant components of all the other approaches. Because reading is so dynamic, rigidly adhering to one approach only may dilute the quality of the reading program.

DEVELOPMENT

For most children the acquisition of age-appropriate reading skills is a simple process; however, there are some children who experience some momentary setbacks. A good way to examine the procedure of learning how to read is to provide an overview of reading as a group of developmental skills by identifying general age and grade levels that correspond to the specific development of skills. Table 1 illustrates the stages of reading.

Typically, a student's reading patterns are influenced by a variety of variables such as ability, motivation, and encouragement at home. Whenever any of these variables becomes significant, the child's progress on the developmental scale may be altered in one direction or the other. Therefore, the information provided in Table 1 should be regarded as a general sequence for an average child.

PUTTING READING IN PERSPECTIVE

The ultimate goal of teaching children to read is to "turn them on" to reading so that they become so enthusiastic that they create self-imposed reading obligations. Reading activities flourish when the content is related to children's interests. These interests frequently supply the impetus to extramural reading. Children who are curious about something are more likely to pursue their interest through reading than are those who are indifferent.

Identifying and cultivating interests, therefore, is a natural procedure for encouraging children to engage in fact-gathering activities. Reading is by far the most productive means by which to quickly acquire vast amounts of knowledge from a variety of sources.

One way to evaluate children's interest is to have them complete a reading interest inventory. Three such inventories have been prepared (Table 2): one for primary (1st to 3rd), one for intermediate (4th to 6th), and one for secondary (7th to 12th) students.

Children are asked to read each of the questions and then provide a short response. Once the inventory is completed, a general pattern of interest areas will become evident. Reading activities should then be geared to these interest areas.

Structuring learning opportunities so as to galvanize children's interest in reading may be more complex than imagined. Often, well-meant intentions by both teachers and parents may actually extinguish children's enjoyment of reading.

Callaway (1984) examined both the positive and the negative factors that influence reading acquisition by asking 223 college students to respond to four basic questions. They were asked to identify events in and outside of school that sharpened as well as those that dulled their desire to read. The results are presented in Table 3.

ALTERNATIVE ACTIONS

Much has been written and said about reading and how it can be improved, yet teachers and parents still express a fair amount of dissatisfaction regarding development. As recently as 1985, the National Academy of Education submitted a report to the Commission on Reading in which they listed 17 recommendations. Five of their recommendations have been selected for discussion because they tie into the basic theme of this chapter.

Parents' Reading to Preschool Children and Informal Teaching About Reading and Writing

Parents should promote reading in the home as a natural habit. This is best achieved by communicating to their children that reading is not restricted to school assignments, but is also entertaining as well as enriching. Much satisfaction and fulfillment can be derived from reading.

Parents should let their children know that reading is important by modeling reading as a way to solve problems. For example, children who have questions

TABLE 1

Stages of Reading Development

Stage	Age	Grade
I. Prereading stage	2–5	Preschool
A. Language development		
1. Expressive language		
2. Receptive language		
B. Sensory skills	2–6	Preschool to 1st
1. Auditory processing		
2. Visual processing		
C. Social maturation	4–7	Preschool to 2nd
1. Attention span		
2. Curiosity stage		
II. Beginning reading stage	6–7	Preschool to 2nd
A. Decoding		
1. Letter naming		
2. Letter sounds		
3. Sound–symbol relationship		
4. Sight word reading		
5. Structural analysis blending		
B. Language comprehension–expression		
III. Basic reading stage		
A. Decoding	6–9	1st to 4th
1. Word attack skills		
2. Silent reading		
3. Oral reading		
4. Reading speed and accuracy		
5. Word list reading		
6. paragraph reading		
B. Comprehension	8–11	3rd to 6th
1. Silent reading comprehension		
a. Literal meaning		
b. Inferential meaning		
c. Evaluative		
2. Listening comprehension	6–11	1st to 6th
a. Literal meaning		
b. Inferential meaning		
c. Evaluative		
3. Vocabulary skills	8–13	3rd to 8th
a. Root words		
b. Prefixes and suffixes		
c. Word meaning		
IV. Applied reading stage		
A. Interest areas	6–17	1st to 12th
B. Attitude towards reading	6–9	1st to 4th
C. Reading for problem solving	9–17	4th to 12th
D. Reading for pleasure	6–17	1st to 12th
E. Reading for fact finding	11–17	6th to 12th
F. Reading assigned materials	8–17	3rd to 12th
G. Motivation to learn through reading	11–17	6th to 12th
H. Vocabulary development	11–17	5th to 12th

TABLE 2

Reading Interest Inventory

Primary

1. What is your favorite game?
2. If you could get someone to read out loud to you, what kind of story would you choose?
3. What kind of TV programs do you enjoy the most?
4. What kind of stories do you enjoy reading?
5. Do you have a library card?
6. What kind of comic books do you enjoy reading?
7. What do you enjoy doing the most outside of school?
8. What kind of activities do you do for recreation?
9. If you could choose to do anything you wanted to do, what would it be?
10. What are your interests?

Intermediate

1. How much time do you spend reading school-related materials?
2. How much time do you spend reading material of your choice?
3. Do you read the newspaper on a regular basis? If yes, what sections are you most interested in?
4. What kind of TV programs do you enjoy the most?
5. Do you have a library card?
6. What kind of books do you enjoy reading the most?
7. What do you enjoy doing the most outside of school?
8. What kind of activities do you do for recreation?
9. If you could choose to do anything you wanted to do, what would it be?
10. What are your interests?

Secondary

1. If you had to solve a problem, how much reading would you be likely to do?
2. Do you subscribe to or read a magazine on a regular basis? If yes, what kind of magazine?
3. Do you read the newspaper on a regular basis? If yes, which sections are of most interest to you?
4. How many library books do you read during an average month?
5. What kind of TV programs do you enjoy the most?
6. What kind of movies do you enjoy the most?
7. What do you enjoy doing the most outside of school?
8. What kind of activities do you do for recreation?
9. If you could choose to do anything you wanted to do, what would it be?
10. What things really interest you?

TABLE 3

Experiences Within and Outside the School That Fostered or Discouraged Students' Desire to Read

Positive experiences in school

The treatment of the material by the teacher; the nature of the material made less difference than the way it was presented.

Teachers' efforts to make reading enjoyable and meaningful. Teachers' encouragement, praise, and interest.

Use of library without forced choices.

Providing school time to allow children to read.

Paperback book clubs.

Oral reading to children on a regular basis was also helpful.

Negative experiences in school

Oral reading, "round robin reading."

Difficult material, boring material, isolated drill, and irrelevant or biased material.

Required reading, book reports, lack of time and lack of purpose for reading certain materials.

Treatment by teacher, fear that the teacher would send home poor workbook pages.

Sense of stigma when given easy books to read, placed in remedial reading classes, or placed in the low reading group.

Programmed materials, kits, and forced summer reading and library programs.

Positive outside of school experiences

Encouragement by parents and making books available.

Allowing students to select reading materials that appealed to them; no censorship, permitting reading of magazines, newspapers and comics.

Parents reading to them, especially when the subject was of interest.

Summer reading programs and clubs that were not forced.

Trips to libraries.

Movies, television, and advertising.

Negative outside of school experiences

Unrealistic expectations or being forced to read.

Difficulty in finding interesting books to read.

Lack of time for pleasure reading.

Church reading, *Reader's Digest*-type books, speed reading courses, forced reading programs.

Negative attitudes of parents, who did not seem to know their children were not the only ones with learning problems.

regarding a certain topic, should be guided to appropriate reading materials that can provide the answers. Parents should also convey a positive attitude towards reading by demonstrating an enthusiastic attitude towards reading themselves.

Parents should read to their younger children every day if possible. This is a valuable experience for both parent and child and it should be continued through elementary school. It is recommended that younger children be allowed to hold the book during such reading. After a story is read, questions should be asked to clarify understanding.

It is important for children to have a current library card, and frequent visits to the library are a must. Older children may choose to go to the library on their own.

Parental Support of School-Aged Children's Continued Growth as Readers

Parents should promote and try to cultivate in their children specific interest areas; later these areas can serve as an excellent incentive for reading.

Every home should have a quiet time for reading and studying. To really make this effective, all members of the household should be expected to read during "quiet time." A 15–20 minute daily reading time is manageable and will help to communicate the idea that reading is important.

Reading does not thrive in a vacuum; there must be an ample support of interesting reading material in the home if a child is to engage in reading on a frequent basis. Subscribing to various magazines, book clubs, or any other system that insures availability of current reading materials in the home is advisable.

If at all possible, each child should have a personal collection of books. This practice can be greatly enhanced if a child also has his own bookcase because it promotes the sense of ownership. It will also teach a child that books are to be treasured.

Parents should engage in activities that specifically stimulate reading. Reading games that involve story titles, names, characters, or plots can be fun and enriching. Reading ads or signs in the child's immediate environment emphasizes the value of reading.

Conferring rewards for reading can be an effective procedure for encouraging children to read without conflict. Parents could reward reading in terms of time spent reading or number of pages read. The important factor is to make sure there is a mutually acceptable criterion.

It is important for parents to devote time to listen to their children read aloud. This will achieve several desirable purposes. First, it will provide parents with an opportunity to monitor their child's reading behavior and to correct mispronounced words. Simply telling the child the correct pronunciation of a word is just as effective as using a more elaborate word attack system (Meyers, 1982). Second, it will communicate to the child that reading is important; Otherwise why would a parent spend so much of their time.

Comprehension Instruction in the School

Teachers can substantially improve the quality of reading comprehension by treating it as a specific reading skill. The old assumption that comprehension occurs automatically once decoding skills are mastered is no longer tenable. Balaythy (1984) suggested using student-constructed questions to improve reading comprehension. Self-questioning will arouse interest and direct the reader's attention, especially under adverse conditions such as requiring to read lengthy or uninteresting material. Self-questioning can trick the mind into maintaining attention and ultimately enhance the process of reading for meaning.

Reading comprehension can also be improved by teaching students to skim over difficult material prior to reading it. Pauk (1983) has developed a four-step procedure for students to follow whenever they are assigned textbook-type reading.

The first step is to read the title of the chapter out loud and think what the title promises. The second step is to go back and read the title of the previous chapter and think how it relates to the present chapter. Third, go to the beginning of the chapter that follows the assigned chapter and relate one to the other. In the last step, skim the assigned chapter by reading all the headings and subheadings and the first sentence under each heading. Also, read the summary of the chapter. This procedure should only take about 10 minutes.

Independent Reading

The value of independent reading cannot be overstressed. Whether in or out of school, it should always be encouraged. As previously mentioned, students who have specific interests are more inclined to explore new learning through reading materials that are related to their interest areas.

All kinds of independent reading activities are desirable. Those who enjoy reading comic books should be permitted to do so. If possible, however, a child's reading list should include classics as well as modern works of fiction and nonfiction.

Importance of Well-Stocked and Well-Managed Libraries

Easy access to interesting and informative books is a critical component of a successful reading program. Librarians should be regarded as an essential member of the faculty. They should be expected to assume direct responsibility in motivating students to read. This can be achieved by creating a physical environment that is stimulating and conducive to learning. Also of equal importance is the social climate of the library.

Children should not regard library time as boring or punitive. A friendly and supportive librarian will make a positive contribution to a child's reading habits. Using library time as a study hall is not recommended. Children should be encouraged to pursue new materials and engage in independent reading.

SUMMARY

Reading is judged to be a basic ingredient for learning in Western civilization. Its importance cannot be overstated. An appealing factor of reading is that while reading is of upmost importance, it is also a positive self-rewarding skill. No one has ever regretted learning how to read, nor can anyone accurately say that they have not gained from reading.

Reading is one of those skills that is an all-win proposition. Yet there are some children who have developed marginal reading skills, and even worse, there are children who possess functional reading skills but do not fully utilize these skills.

The advancement of reading will require the coordinated efforts of teachers, parents, and support staff, such as school psychologists. Parents, and the home setting, have the responsibility of providing a fundamentally sound language base; they must also actively promote reading in the home. Parents should monitor their children's progress in school by supporting homework, buying children books, encouraging reading as a full-time activity, and being enthusiastic readers themselves.

Teachers must regard reading as one of the primary goals of education. They should select a quality reading program, one that yields consistent results. They should devote sufficient time to teaching reading, with heavy emphasis on reading comprehension. They also must experiment with innovative teaching methods to help the hard-to-teach students.

School psychologists, like all support staff, must be prepared to contribute to the improvement of reading by focusing their services on related factors. They should design treatment programs to improve self-concept, motivational levels, attitudes toward school and learning, and a variety of other areas of concerns that go beyond instructional activities.

REFERENCES

Anderson, R., Hiebert, E. H., Scott, J. A., & Wilkinson, I.A.G. (1985). *Becoming a nation of readers.* Washington, DC: National Institute of Education.

Balaythy, E. (1984, February). Using student constructed questions to encourage active reading. *Journal of Reading,* pp. 408–411.

Callaway, B. (1984). What turns children "on" or "off" in reading. *Reading Improvement, 21,* 214–217.

Haring, N. G., & Bateman, B. (1977). *Teaching the learning disabled child.* Englewood Cliffs, NJ: Prentice-Hall.

Meyer, L. A. (1982). The relative effects of word analysis and word-supply correction procedures with poor readers during word-attack training. *Reading Research Quarterly, 4,* 544–555.

Pauk, W. (1983). A new way to skim. *Reading World,* pp. 252–254.

Stoner, M. (1981). *Reading at school and at home.* West Haven, CT: National Education Association of the United States.

BIBLIOGRAPHY: PROFESSIONALS

Culyer, R. (1985). Project read, *Early Years,* May, 24–32.
Provides teachers with a step-by-step sequence in formulating stimulating reading activities for children. This procedure will enable teachers to motivate their students to participate in a variety of reading activities.

DiSibio, R. (1984). Parents: A teacher's partner, *Education,* Spring, Vol. 104, N. 3, 296–299.
Stresses the role of the parents in developing their child's cognitive skills. It provides parents with a self rating scale so they can modify their home environment to enhance the quality of learning. Most parents will respond favorably to the helpful suggestions that are listed.

Greenwood, S. (1985). Use contracts to motivate and manage your secondary reading class. *Journal of Reading,* March, 187–491.
A complete overview of contracting and how it can be utilized to teach reading is presented. It will assist teachers in developing and implementing a fairly comprehensive reading program which can be augmented with contracts.

Kann, R. (1983). The method of repeated reading: Expanding the neurological impress method for use with disabled readers. *Journal of Reading Disabilities, 16,* 90–92.
Explains how two reading intervention activities, neurological impress method and method of repeated readings, can be employed to enhance children's reading skills. These procedures can be implemented by either teachers or parents.

Munns, K. (1983). Why can't Johnny's parents read? *Reading Improvement, 21,* Fall, 144–148.
A step-by-step procedure is presented to improve parents' reading skills. Often poor readers come from homes of non-reading parents. The training program consists of nine hours of lecture and practice periods covering three weeks. The results yield positive growth in reading skills for parents. The format is workable and does not require an unreasonable time commitment.

Children and Religion

Harriet Cobb
James Madison University

BACKGROUND

A surprising diversity of religious beliefs are currently practiced in the United States, from the informal, spare Quaker meeting to the ceremony of a Roman Catholic Church. Census data on religious beliefs have not been taken since the 1930s, and few religions other than Christianity attempt to maintain statistical records of membership. The most common religious groups in the United States are Protestants, Roman Catholics, Jews, Eastern Churches, Old Catholic, Polish National Catholic, Armenian Churches, and Buddhist Churches of America.

Within Protestantism, there is a significant variability in beliefs, customs, and practices. A brief review of "mainstream" religions, as well as some of the more common smaller sects would be useful. The reader is referred to Williams (1969), listed in the annotated bibliography, for elaboration.

It is not unusual for the school psychologist to encounter issues related to religion when working with children. Regardless of the personal attitudes and beliefs of the school psychologist, an understanding of the developmental perspective of this topic is important. It can have implications for developing rapport, understanding psychological dynamics, and generating interventions for children.

In completing a psychological assessment, knowledge of sociocultural factors is clearly important for a total understanding of a child's individual psychological development. This includes values, beliefs, and religious practices of the family. It is essential for school psychologists to become acquainted with beliefs and practices that are foreign to their own experience. This knowledge can assist in establishing rapport with a child or parent and help to avoid discomfort when certain issues are raised. For example, this author previously worked in a small Amish elementary school administering screening instruments for a research project. A comment to a young Amish girl that her hair was pretty would have been inappropriate because of the religious attitude toward vanity or personal pride. Asking a member of the Jehovah's Witnesses about a birthday celebration or a Jewish child about Christmas vacation would also be perhaps well-meaning but insensitive questions.

The Roman Catholic Church

Roman Catholicism, like all of Christianity, is monotheistic. Roman Catholics, as do most Protestants, also believe in the Holy Trinity of the Father, Son, and Holy Spirit. Jesus Christ is believed to be a man as well as God, having a human nature and a divine one. This doctrine is known as the dogma of the dual nature of Jesus Christ, and is considered a transcendent mystery. The belief in the existence of miracles and the supernatural is strong in the Catholic Church. Angels are purely spiritual beings, with important functions, such as arrangements of things in the universe and the execution of God's orders.

Regular attendance at the Roman Catholic Mass, which is considered the reenactment of the Last Supper, is obligatory. According to the Catholic Church, all children at birth are touched by original sin for which reason they must be baptized. Most people do commit sins during their lifetimes, and penance is handled through confession to a priest. Other beliefs about the spiritual universe include the possible repositories of the soul after death: Heaven, Hell, and Purgatory. As most people are sinners, these souls go to Purgatory after death for cleansing before entering Heaven.

The authority of the Church rests with the Pope, whose pronouncements are law, since Catholics believe he is the agent of Christ. The Pope is believed to be incapable of making a mistake when he speaks officially about faith or morals, although noncompliance with the official church position on birth control is widespread in the United States. Other positions that remain controversial include the forbidding of divorce and abortion.

Protestantism

There are well over 200 Protestant denominations in the United States, although most of them belong to the following groups: Lutheran, Presbyterian, Episcopal, Congregational, Baptist-Christian, and Methodist. Protestant beliefs range from the agnosticism of the Unitarians to the fundamentalism of the Southern Baptists.

Protestants generally believe that prayer and individual devotion are the best ways to approach God. Protestant churches tend to place considerable importance on the Bible, although with the exception of the Fundamentalists, they are not Bible literalists.

The more liberal Protestants accept the scientific method to the point that they do not believe in miracles. Instead they believe that Nature's laws are God's laws. There is less of an emphasis on man as sinner,more on the value of altruism.

A large group of Protestants, however, are Fundamentalists, who consider themselves "true" Christians. They believe in the infallibility of the Bible, the virgin birth of Jesus Christ, and the second coming of Jesus in bodily form. The concept of original sin is emphasized, and Fundamentalists share with Catholics a belief in a literal Heaven and Hell. Much of their missionary zeal is related to "saving" people from damnation. Additionally, they do not believe in the theory of evolution, as it contradicts the first chapter of Genesis. This insistence on the infallibility of their dogma, and the complete rejection of known scientific findings, have led to their activism in the public school regarding the science curriculum. Revival meetings as a way of boosting faith are common, and evangelical churches have taken advantage of television in reaching more people.

Seventh Day Adventists are extremely Fundamentalist, celebrating the Sabbath on the seventh day of the week as directed by the Old Testament. They also believe in the gift of prophecy, and the doctrine of conditional immortality, which states that if one is judged to be worthy, resurrection by Christ at his second advent will occur. They are vegetarian, abstain from tobacco and alcohol, and avoid card playing, dancing, and elaborate clothing or jewelry.

Jehovah's Witnesses believe that they will be saved by knowledge, and that the Truth is available in their literature, which they distribute as widely as possible. Satan, who actually exists, is the child of the demons, although Hell does not exist, since according to the Witnesses, it is not taught in the Bible. Witnesses oppose the celebration of birthdays, Mothers Day, the use of Christmas trees, the salute to the American Flag, and "religion" as practiced in all other churches. They also forbid blood transfusions even when a life may be saved, since the Bible does not allow "eating" blood. Women in this sect are almost completely subordinated. Members are usually from the lower socioeconomic groups.

The Amish, a very conservative denomination of the Mennonite Church, believe in the importance of living materially austere lives. They are primarily a rural agricultural society. The Old Order are known for their plain clothes and travel by horse and buggy, although farm equipment is permitted. Education beyond the eighth grade is not allowed, and early marriage is encouraged. Movies and photographs are forbidden and violation of the rules can result in "shunning" — a very harsh form of ostracism. Government aid is not accepted. Humility is stressed; any perceived pride or vanity is strongly disapproved of. Like the Quakers, the Amish are pacifists.

Quakers believe that the true church is spiritual and not of a formal nature. Religion is considered to be a personal experience, everyone having within themselves the source of inspiration. This philosophy has contributed to their advocacy for equal rights for women, humane treatment of the mentally ill, and pacifism.

Judaism

As within Protestantism, there are distinct differences among the major branches of Judaism: Orthodox, Reform, and Conservative. The highest concentration of this predominately urban population is in the North Atlantic area.

Orthodox Jews strive to maintain the traditional culture and follow the Torah (law) closely. The Bible (which Christians refer to as the Old Testament) is considered to be the word of God. There are numerous and complex commands of the Torah that must be followed. No work is allowed on the Sabbath, which begins at exactly sundown on Friday and ends at sundown on Saturday. No food can be prepared, no fires kindled; the lights must be turned on before Friday Sundown or a gentile must be hired to turn them on. Many laws involve food: certain foods may not be eaten at all, including pork and shellfish. Two sets of dishes are required to avoid mixing meat and dairy products. The processing of "kosher" food is supervised by specifically trained rabbis. The rituals of orthodox Judaism have been largely abandoned by the Reform Jews, who are more liberal yet than Conservative Jews.

Jews are monotheists and believe that the Christian trinity is a denial of monotheism. They believe that human nature is both good and bad, and that Jews are a "chosen people." This dogma of specialness to God is shared by many religious groups, however.

Naturalistic Humanism

In contrast to the religions are the beliefs of naturalistic humanism, which are shared by many atheists and agnostics. Some of the premises of this philosophy are that nothing exists but Nature and, until proven otherwise, human beings are its highest form. The source of knowledge is not faith, but reason in conjunction with experience. The existence of a soul or afterlife is doubted and the improvement of human welfare is what is considered to be of prime importance. Most humanists regard supernaturalism and traditional religious practices to be superstitious. They reject organized spirituality, which accounts for the lack of connectedness among those with these beliefs. However, even since the 1930s many scientists, writers, and students in colleges of superior reputation do not believe in a God to whom one may pray and expect an answer, nor in personal immortality (Williams, 1969).

DEVELOPMENT

Ratcliff (1985) comprehensively reviewed studies relating child development to religious beliefs. There have been numerous studies that have examined the concept of God and other religious issues by a variety of approaches, including clinical interviews, projective techniques, structured inventories, and standardized tests. Studies have been conducted across numerous cultures, both Eastern and Western; the vast majority of these studies included children whose parents are members of formal religions, as opposed to children of agnostic or atheistic parents. Regardless of specific religious background or training there are clear similarities among children's concepts, particularly prior to the third or fourth grade. This research demonstrates that religious concepts are highly correlated with cognitive development, following a pattern comparable with other classes of abstract concepts. Table 1 depicts religious stages in relation to Piaget's cognitive development stages and Kohlberg's stages of moral development.

A recent study specifically examined the development of the concept of God in children and found it to be compatible with Piaget's stages of cognitive development (Nye & Carlson, 1984). They asked Protestant, Jewish, and Catholic children between the ages of 5 and 16 years questions such as "Where does God come from?" "What does God look like?" "Can God see and hear you?" The children's responses were classified as

TABLE 1
A Comparison of Concepts by Developmental Stages

Piaget (cognitive development)	Kohlberg (moral development)	Harms (concept of religion)	Heller (concept of God)	Fowler (stages of faith)
I. Preoperational	Punishment–reward	Fairy tale (3–6 years)	Good vs. bad God — unquestioning acceptance	Intuitive, projective faith (imitation of adults; 3–7 years)
II. Concrete operational	Instrumental hedonism (reciprocal fairness)	Realistic (7–12 years)	Personalization of God (preadolescence)	Mythic, literal faith (literal interpretation; 7–12 years)
III. Early formal operations	Interpersonal expectations & concordance	Individualistic (13–18 years)		Synthetic, conventional (reliance on authority; 7–15 years)
IV. Formal operations	Societal perspective; reflective relativism or class-biased universalism			Individuating reflexive (personal reference pint; adolescence)
V. Formal operations	Prior to society, principled higher law (universal and critical)			Paradoxical, consolidative faith (acceptance of religions and objective paradox; adolescence)
VI. Formal operations	Loyalty to being			Universalizing faith; (acceptance of the oneness of being)

either "concrete" or "abstract." The criterion for a "concrete" level response was tangibility or measurability; the criterion for abstract responses was its generality, the absence of relation to specific descriptors. As was expected, the younger children were significantly more concrete in their responses than the older children. The more abstract concept of a deity is more dependent on developmental level rather than on religious training. Although the Jewish children in the 5- to 8-year-old group gave significantly more abstract responses than those in the other two groups, no other differences were found among the three groups.

Some differences related to gender were noted, however. Both girls and boys perceived a masculine deity, although girls tended to include more esthetic qualities, for example, drawing God surrounded by flowers. Boys tended to emphasize the physical prowess and strength of God. When asked, "What if God were the opposite sex?" Boys tended to completely reject the idea, whereas some girls took a decidely feminist perspective. One girl stated that there would be less violence if God were a woman.

The results of this study are consistent with Goldman's (1964) study, which assessed the readiness of children to learn certain religious concepts. Both of these studies support the notion that religious instruction has little impact on the child's concrete concept of God before the age of 10.

In a study of 4,800 children from different religious backgrounds, religious development progressed through three major stages: (a) fairy tale at age (3–6 years); (b) realistic stage (7–12 years); and (c) individualistic stage (13–18 years) (Harms, 1944, cited in Ratcliff, 1985).

Heller (1986) studied children's conceptions of God and how these constructs change with normal intellectual growth. He interviewed children brought up in homes affiliated with Judaism, Catholicism, Protestantism (Baptists), and Hinduism. The 4-6-year-old children tended to associate God with a happy state and, in an attempt to reconcile "bad" things, constructed a "bad" God. Children at the preoperational level gradually perceive God as being on about the same level of significance as their parents, whom they perceive as responsible for providing for their needs. Young children often imagine God as looking like their grandfather, or that he lives in the clouds. Children at this stage tend to unquestioningly accept statements about God.

As children approach adolescence, they tend to protect their own emotions and issues onto God. According to Heller (1985) this occurs when they observe that God does not always operate as they had originally concluded. At this point they will change the deity to meet their individual psychological needs.

These findings are similar to the observations of Deconchy (cited in Elkind, 1971, p. 673) whose 8-10-year-olds associated God with strength, beauty, and goodness. Older adolescents expressed worries related to doubt, fear, obedience, and love.

The Roman Catholic children in Heller's study interpreted God as an active participant in family events.

They were also more likely to stress the importance of informal dialogues with God. Jewish children were more likely to bring in rituals; Hindu children preferred chanting. Most of the preadolescent children expressed a dislike of rituals, especially silent prayer, which they perceived as "obsessive routine."

Other studies have found the belief that prayer actually produces results decreases with age (cited in Elkind, 1971, p. 673–674). Children's concept of prayer transforms from a magical to a sacramental orientation. As Elkind's research indicated, the children aged 5–7 did not understand prayer, although they recited certain phrases as expected of them and used the word "God" frequently. After the age of 7, these children usually focused on making specific requests. At approximately age 10–12, the children conceptualized prayer as a conversation with God, and became generally more satisfied with it.

Goldman (1964, cited by Ratcliff) also researched prayer in children and identified several stages. Younger children tended to believe that immediate answers from God were to be expected. Unanswered prayer was explained by misbehavior or an incorrect manner of responding. Superstitiously, events occurring soon after prayer were attributed to the prayer and not from other causes.

In the second stage, extending until the age of 12, Goldman's subjects believed failure of prayer to be a consequence of selfish or materialistic requests. In the third stage answers to prayer were attributed to the faith or effort of the individual praying. Later in adolescence, a lack of results was explained as "God knows best."

The concept of God as judge in children and adults has also been examined (Ratcliff, 1985). Children perceived God as using rewards and punishment, such as good weather or conversely flood or fire, in a concrete manner. At the highest level, about half of the adult respondents focused on the uniqueness of God's judgments, and resorted to more abstract descriptions of love and justice.

The specific activities of God as perceived by children was researched by Piaget (1929, cited by Ratcliff). During the preoperational stage, all origins are thought to be caused by a deity: Clouds are made by God's smoking a pipe. During the concrete stage, natural explanations are included with supernatural solutions.

Beginning at about age 10, God is perceived as a controller of nature. Understandably, the rational and scientific approach comes into direct conflict with the authoritative and miraculous aspects of religion, which remain contradictory.

At about the age of 12, children attempt to understand God as working within the known laws of nature, divine communication being an internal event.

Fowler (1981) (who might be described as a theistic developmentalist) has studied how faith changes with age, defining faith broadly as the individual's construction of "ultimate conditions of existence"; and he seems to assume that everyone possesses "faith." He has developed a six-stage progression of faith; using Kohlberg's theory of moral development as one of his themes, Fowler proposed that faith is necessary for the justification of a moral position.

Stage 1 (ages 3–7) is primarily the imitation of adults through story and example, with fantasy playing a major role. Stage 2 (7–12) is characterized by increasing distinction between fantasy and reality, with literal interpretation of symbols. The concrete thinking of this stage personalizes the beliefs and rituals. Adolescence brings more self-awareness, and according to Fowler, faith progresses through stages similar to Kohlberg's moral development sequence. Stage 3 continues to be authority-bound, whereas Stage 4 requires responsibility for one's actions. Stage 5 individuals act affirmatively upon their espoused values and beliefs. The final stage, which Fowler states is rare, is characterized by a sense of oneness of all persons.

According to Goldman (1964) children also progress through stages in perceiving the concept of "church." At first, children focus on the physical building, as the place God lives. Later, until they are approximately 14, church attendance is seen as a place to pray, learn about God, or receive help. In the third stage, church attendance is associated with fellowship, altruism, and spirituality.

With regard to identification with a particular church denomination, as would be expected, Elkind (1971) found that the onset of formal operations is associated with the abstract concept of holding specific beliefs. Prior to this stage children first perceive their denomination as a name, confusing it with nationality or race, and later associating it with the characteristic rituals.

The conclusion to be drawn from the research summarized above is that the child's perspective on religion is a reflection of developmental stage and should be recognized as such.

PUTTING CHILDREN AND RELIGION IN PERSPECTIVE

To what extent is the actual moral behavior of children related to religion? According to Kohlberg (1981), exhaustive studies indicate that no significant differences as a result of religious instruction have been found. All children progress through similar stages of moral development, which are detailed elsewhere in this book (see the chapter on children and moral responsibility).

Cross-cultural comparisons of honesty, for example, have found that religious education is neither necessary nor sufficient for the expression of honest behavior. Dishonesty and theft are low in some atheistic societies such as the Israeli atheistic kibbutzim, as well as some Christian and Buddhist groups, but high in some strongly religious countries such as Italy and Mexico.

Furthermore, college students who are conservative in their Christian faith are less likely to attain higher-stages ratings of moral reasoning than students who are liberal in their religious beliefs (Clouse, 1985).

Parents who frequently use the threat that "God will punish" to ensure compliance in their children tend to punish their children more frequently than parents who do not form an alliance with a punitive God. Catholic parents and those with Protestant fundamentalist beliefs tend to use this threat more than other Protestant denominations (Nelson & Kroliczak, 1984).

However, many religions communicate the values of self-actualization and of love and charity toward others. Affiliation with a religious institution can provide individuals with a sense of belonging and emotional support through life crises, although children's attitudes may differ from their parents' regarding beliefs in religious practices. While religious institutions do offer guidelines for human behavior, there is no evidence that any particular religious belief is necessary or sufficient for ethical behavior.

It must be recognized that some religions specifically promulgate values that are problematic from the perspective of psychological health. A dilemma that may be encountered by school psychologists whenever they counsel children is the difficulty of reconciling certain religious beliefs with accepted notions of what promotes psychological well-being. Much research has been conducted documenting the importance of developing a positive self-concept in children (see the chapter on children and self-concept in this volume). Yet some religions espouse a belief in the "evil nature" of humankind, which is logically incongruent with self-esteem and reinforces feelings of guilt. Additionally, the emphasis placed upon altruism at times comes at the expense of any self-interest, in some cases encouraging a denial of individuality or self-direction.

Most counseling theories place a value on the development of good problem-solving or coping skills (Ivey & Simek-Downing, 1980). Decision-making models emphasize the importance of considering several alternatives to solving a problem; there is often not just one "right" way. This is in direct conflict with Fundamentalists' teaching that there *is* only one right way to live, which is based on their literal interpretation of the Bible. In some of these religions there is an explicit assumption of the moral superiority of one religious sect over all others, discouraging acceptance of those with different belief systems. The emphasis on dogma and acceptance of authority in the more fundamentalist denominations can make the individuation tasks of adolescence even more difficult.

Inherent in the ethical guidelines for counseling is the avoidance of imposing one's own values on the client. However, mental health professionals accept certain premises, such as the promotion of self-esteem and acceptance of individual differences. Counseling is not totally value-free. In consequences, school psychologists may encounter some of the following specific situations.

1. A parent who refuses counseling services on religious grounds.
2. A divorced parent, with custody of a child, who does not want the school psychologist to talk with the noncustodial parent, who is "evil" (having left the church).
3. An adolescent who is depressed and suicidal because of the rejection of her or his family for committing a "sin."
4. A child who refuses to attend church and whose parents ask for some suggestions as to how to attain compliance.
5. An adolescent facing identity and autonomy problems, who asks "Is it wrong to question the beliefs of my church?"
6. Children or parents who ask the school psychologist about his or her religious affiliation.
7. Parents who approach the school psychologist for advice about how to prevent their daughter from associating with children of the "wrong" faith.
8. An adolescent who believes she is pregnant and wishes to obtain an abortion when her parents disapprove on religious grounds.
9. The parents of an adolescent who believe their children is "speaking in tongues" as a part of religious revelation rather than experiencing a psychotic episode.
10. A child of atheist parents who is confronted with peer pressure to attend the religious education classes provided during school time.

These are but a few of the ethical dilemmas related to religion that a psychologist who works with children may face.

ALTERNATIVE ACTIONS

As stated previously, it is important for school psychologists to learn as much as possible about the children's environment in the community in which they work. This means acquiring an understanding of the various cultural beliefs, including those related to religion. This is particularly relevant if a school psychologist is employed in an area with unfamiliar or less common religious practices. An overview of U. S. religions by Williams (1969) may be helpful in gathering information about specific religions. Although members of some religious sects are reluctant to talk with "outsiders," speaking with various community members or former believers is another way to learn about local customs and beliefs.

Without offering their own judgment of a belief or practice at issue, school psychologists can assist older children or adolescents in clear thinking about a particular problem. However, the school psychologist must appreciate that encouraging individuals to come to their own conclusions about a particular matter has certain risks. The adolescent, for example, may begin to experience considerable distress during the process of considering alternative choices that are in conflict with religious teachings. The school psychologist must be sensitive to the client's dilemma; the warmth and caring of a good counselor–client relationship is especially important. However, the parents themselves may not accept the services of a professional who is not affiliated with their religious institution. Many of these parents seek the counseling services of their church leaders, who may or may not be trained in professional counseling, and who may not make any attempt at being objective.

If a parent does choose to seek services elsewhere, it is important to appreciate how powerful a hold some authoritarian religions have on their members. It is understandable why a parent or child might be reluctant to disobey a church teaching when the consequences are believed to be so harsh.

SUMMARY

The topic of children and religion is a controversial one. Most people, school psychologists included, have strong beliefs in this realm, and there is a wide range of positions on the various issues that have been raised in this chapter.

A knowledge of the world view that children and their parents possess is essential for truly understanding the psychological dynamics involved in many emotional problems. Practicing psychologists should acquire extensive information on the children with whom they work, including their religious practices, beliefs, and customs. Additionally, it is suggested that school psychologists thoroughly explore their own values as part of the general self-awareness that is expected of a mental health professional. This can be important in reconciling any differences in the value system of the client and the professional in a way that emphasizes the child's best interest.

REFERENCES

Clouse, B. (1985). Moral reasoning and Christian faith. *Journal of Psychology and Theology, 13*(3), 190–198.

Elkind, D. (1971). The development of religious understanding in children and adolescents. In M. Strommen (Ed.), *Research on religious development: A comprehensive handbook.* New York: Hawthorn Books.

Fowler, J. (1981). *Stages of faith.* San Francisco: Harper & Row.

Goldman, R. (1964). *Religious thinking from childhood to adolescence.* New York: Seabury.

Heller, D. (1986). *The children's God.* Chicago: University of Chicago Press.

Ivey, A., & Simek-Downing, L. (1980). *Counseling and Psychotherapy: Skills, theories and practice.* Englewood Cliffs, NJ: Prentice-Hall.

Kohlberg, L. (1981). Moral and religious education and the public schools: A developmental view. In Kolberg, L. (Ed.), *Essays on moral development: Vol. 1: The philosophy of moral development* (pp. 294–306). San Francisco: Harper & Row.

Munsey, B. (Ed.). (1980). *Moral development, moral education, and Kohlberg: Basic issues in philosophy, psychology, religion and education.* Birmingham, AL: Religious Education Press.

Nelson, H. M. & Kroliczak, A. (1984). Parental uses of the threat "God will punish": Replication and extension. *Journal for the Scientific Study of Religion, 23*(3), 267–277.

Nye, W. C., & Carlson, J. S. (1984). The development of the concept of God in children. *Journal of Genetic Psychology, 145,* 137–142.

Ratcliff, D. (1985). The development of children's religious concepts: Research Review. *Journal of Psychology and Christianity, 4*(1), 35–43.

Williams, J. P. (1969). *What Americans believe and how they worship.* New York: Harper & Row.

BIBLIOGRAPHY: PROFESSIONALS

Munsey, B. (ed.). (1980). *Moral development, moral education, and Kohlberg: Basic issues in philosophy, psychology, religion and education.* Birmingham, AL: Religious Education Press.
A good collection of essays regarding moral development, several of them specifically focusing on the issue of religion.

Williams, J. P. (1969). *What Americans believe and how they worship.* New York: Harper & Row.
A comprehensive overview of most of the various religions practiced in the United States. The book is quite readable, providing history, structure, and custom related to each religion.

BIBLIOGRAPHY: PARENTS AND CHILDREN

Lickona, T. (1983) *Raising good children.* New York: Bantam Books (paperback).
Integrates moral development theory into a consistent approach to parenting. It focuses on assisting parents in helping children through the stages of moral reasoning, without relating to specific religious ideology.

Blume, J. (1970). *Are you there God? It's me, Margaret.* New York: Bradbury. (Ages 10–16)
The story of an 11-year-old girl who decides to investigate different religions for a school project. She looks into some of the differences, but gives up on her project when her grandparents come for a visit and start an argument with her about her religious views. Margaret is upset by this and gives up talking to God for a time.

Coutant, H. (1974). *First snow.* New York: Knopf. (Ages 7–9)
This story provides a reflection on the Buddhist faith, specifically with the belief that "life and death are but two parts of the same thing." A young girl has recently moved to New England from Vietnam and faces various types of adjustments.

Heiman, C. (1976). *The difference of Ari Stein.* New York: Harper & Row. (Ages 9–12)
The story of an 11-year-old Jewish boy learning to stand up for his own beliefs. Jewish customs are well described and the story is told in the boy's own voice. Tells the story of a boy adjusting to a new neighborhood and friends, and discovering some of the more significant differences between them.

Children and Responsibility

Cynthia M. Sheehan
West Islip,, New York

BACKGROUND

On a recent visit to a bookstore, this author noted a total of 32 offerings of the "How to" variety purporting to assist educators and parents in the development of responsible, morally upstanding, young people. Such a display reflects an increasing societal focus on the development of responsibility in children. The vast and somewhat confusing array of offerings underscores the complexity of this deceptively simple concept. It is clear that there is no single, easy, practical pathway to the development of responsible children but, rather, that in this endeavor parents and educators are left to grapple with values, educational priorities, theories of motivation, and developmental expectations.

Over the past several decades, there has been a natural pendulum swing of the cultural norms regarding the teaching of responsibility. The authoritarian approach and the permissive approach were dramatic oppositions that were thoroughly studied throughout the 1950s and 1960s. Sociological analyses that linked inflexibility and self-centered personalities to these polar "extremes" in child-rearing measures prompted a gradual and thought-provoking evolution in society's values and resources in the raising of children. In response to an increasing cultural awareness of personal rights, a large part of current child management theory is addressed to the instilling of morality and responsibility. In parallel with movements to secure women's liberation, gay rights, and minority group equality, a concern to improve the inferior status of children has given birth to a newfound interest in more democratic methods of interaction between adults and children. The recent recognition and publication of the appalling facts of child abuse have led to a societal reaction against the denial of children's equal status in dignity and human rights. With the recognition of these intrinsic rights comes the demand for responsible behavior. The child of 30 years ago who was excused from responsibility and "spoke only when spoken to" no longer exists. Likewise, children's recognition of their own rights and status poses a challenge to adults to teach and guide them while providing opportunities for problem solving, decision making, and exploration of their place in the family and in society.

It is of little wonder that parents and teachers, who for generations have been raised in an autocratic atmosphere, find themselves lacking in skills and techniques that encourage children to be independent and internally motivated towards responsible behavior. Fortunately, there has been a helpful response from the professional community regarding the myriad of factors to be considered in establishing a democratic and respectful climate for teaching, caring for, and interacting with children. Certain theorists with an intrapsychic orientation (Rogers, 1969; Gordon, 1974; Harris, 1969; Holt, 1983) emphasized development of optimal personal growth through an accepting, supportive environment. Others, with a more behavioral orientation (Kozloff, 1974; O'Leary & O'Leary, 1977; Meichenbaum, 1977; Goldstein, Sprafkin, & Gershaw, 1980), have stressed the need for external structure reinforcement, and contingencies in child management skills. However, the specific concept of "responsible" behavior and the techniques to encourage it have been most frequently defined and addressed within the humanistic theories of social interaction growing from an Adlerian orientation.

Personal responsibility can be viewed as encompassing many levels of social, moral, and legal obligations. Piaget (1965) and Heider (1958) have stressed intention and judgment as factors that define differing levels of subjective and objective responsibility. For the purpose of this chapter, responsibility will be viewed as that sphere of behavior that demonstrates personal accountability and respect for the rights of others as defined by social norms. Within the framework of the social interactionist model (Dreikurs & Soltz, 1964; Dinkmeyer & McKay, 1973), this chapter explores issues influencing the development and assessment of responsibility, including needs and values, developmental profiles, appropriate expectations, classroom priorities, natural consequences, problem-solving techniques, communication style, and group management skills.

DEVELOPMENT

From birth, individuals in our society are asked to delay gratification and begin to take responsibility for their interaction with their social environment: Newborns are to regulate their systems in response to feedings, sleep times, and care giving; toddlers are expected to pick up their toys, refrain from smearing food, and respond to adults in polite conversation; preschoolers are required to take responsibility for a "lie," and given consequences for striking out at a playmate; school-age children must balance work and play time, and are expected to respond to others' feelings in the socialization process. By the time of adolescence, responsibility becomes the main battleground between parents and child and often between school and child. Adolescents are drawn to the process of establishing their identity, which usually includes major conflicts with parents and teachers in regard to the priorities of responsibility to self, peers, family, school, and the common good.

Values versus Needs

Parents and teachers wishing to promote responsible behavior in children are often surprised and frustrated to find themselves in what feels like an endless power struggle with their charges despite benign intentions, sincere effort, and appropriate modeling. The risk of a potentially negative effect on the adult–child relationship is great in such a frustrating, defeating situation.

In addressing this problem, it is crucial to examine the underlying needs and values of teachers and parents. Foremost in this process is clarification of the adult's ultimate goal. It is to foster an independent, decision-making, responsible person, or is it first to maintain order, discipline, and power? Not always, but, at times these goals are mutually exclusive.

Children learn responsibility only if they are given responsibility. The task of raising and guiding responsible children requires an awareness of the separateness of the child from the adult's sphere of control. However, this distinction is often overlooked in a society that has for years held the adult ultimately responsible for the child's behavior, or more importantly, misbehavior! The stigma that results from seeing a child's responsibility as a reflection of an adult's inadequacy is a strong, often unrecognized factor in the counterproductive, high-control needs of parents and teachers. The culture sends a double message: Produce a self-sufficient, independent, responsible, moral individual, but remember all the while that you are responsible for every act of the child in your care. Such a philosophy tends to lead to two unfortunate circumstances: The child is left with very little real responsibility to "practice" with, and the adult tries to teach responsibility through external pressure.

Lasting responsibility, as opposed to conformity, is an internally motivated characteristic. The importance of encouraging a child's own resources and confidence is stressed by Dreikurs (1971):

> The greatest obstacle to growth and development, to learning and to an improved function . . . is discouragement, doubt in one's own ability. Our present methods of raising children confront them with a series of discouraging experiences. One either does for them what they could do for themselves, protecting and spoiling them, or one scolds and punishes. In either case the child is deprived of the experience of his own strength. He cannot use his inner resources if he is convinced he has none. (p. 8)

Recognizing the active role children must play in determining their own behavioral responses often helps a parent or teacher to take the perspective that adult and child spheres of responsibility are complementary, rather than competitive. Through extensive research on children natural temperament, theorists such as Chess, Thomas, and Birch (1965) have done much to support the concept of the important, but naturally limited, influence of the adult on the ultimate determination of the child's personality development. The identification of characteristics that show an early and lasting pattern of temperament in children has underscored the fact that adults are responsible *not* for a child's difficult behavior, but for providing an environment most conducive to that child's personal growth.

In providing a child with opportunities for developing responsibility, it is necessary to lay to rest the "good teacher" whose class is always on task and the "good mother" whose child's spotless room always has clothes laid out the night before school. This is sure to initially strike terror into the hearts and souls of those parents and educators who value safety, order, and respect. Visions of children learning to be responsible through classroom brawls, messy rooms, and blank homework papers will surely race through their heads. Such disorder likely would be the inevitable result of giving over all responsibility to children to fend for themselves. And, this anarchy would no more allow for the development of responsibility than the oppressive authoritarian methods of previous decades. Optimum opportunity for the development of independent, responsible persons lies in the carefully orchestrated sharing of responsibility based on democratic principles of appropriate leadership, mutual respect, and developmental readiness for responsibility.

Developmental Readiness/Appropriate Expectations

Giving preschoolers the task of scheduling the day's activities is likely to result in a chaotic, overactive mess in which teachers and children alike experience a discomforting sense of disorganization. However, asking a group of preschoolers to choose between two acceptable activities such as finger painting or play-dough sculptures fosters a sense of competence and accountability. The "developmental discipline" espoused by Ilg, Ames, and Baker (1981), the emphasis on increasing independence and awareness of the young child, proposed by Brazelton (1974), and Dreikurs and Soltz's (1964) proposals for stimulating self-sufficiency and making "reasonable requests," all stress the necessity of giving only responsibility that is in accordance with the children's developmental capabilities. Children faced with expectations that are cognitively, motorically, and emotionally beyond their maturational limits will surely experience a sense of failure and resentment that are highly counterproductive to the development of a responsible attitude.

In requesting responsible behavior in the context of a respect for the child and a recognition of order,the issue of normative expectation versus developmental expectation becomes crucial. Normative expectations are those applicable to the "average 4-year-old" or "average 10-year-old." As those with even a little experience working with children know, the "average" child is a mythical figure only to be found in dated textbooks and on "The Brady Bunch" reruns. Owing to each child's unique developmental progression and constantly changing capabilities, an individual evaluation of developmental readiness for responsibility is essential in establishing appropriate goals and expectations. Ames, Gillespie, Haines, and Ilg (1979) and Oppenheim, Boegehold, and Brenner (1984) are useful and practical resources in this regard.

It is important to note that in making developmental assessments, some skills and abilities are more important than others, specifically with regard to the acceptance of responsibility. A 10-year-old child with poor motor control, unable to button clothing or write legibly, may have the cognitive development and impulse control necessary to responsibly follow a time schedule, make choices about appropriate free-time activities, and participate in class problem-solving exercises. Encouragement of a responsible and confident attitude in children demands that one begin with the individual child's capabilities, rather than the needs of the adults. The following is a brief survey of the crucial stages of development highlighting the specific capabilities to be examined within those stages in order to formulate appropriate expectations.

Infancy. Many parents are unfamiliar with the abilities and needs of the typical infant. The extended family is no longer around with sage advice for the new parents. A confusing array of books, advice columns, and magazine articles offer contradictory advice that may well cause a parent to ignore their own child's readiness in favor of the "average" expectation. Trying to make a child adapt to a rigid schedule may cause parents to become frustrated and view their new baby's attempts to meet basic needs as stubborn refusal to accommodate to their routine. Many parents worry about "spoiling" an infant and,with good intentions, withhold comfort or care for brief periods only to end up feeling frustrated and defeated by their unhappy infant.

Specific attention to the following developmental abilities in infancy can be helpful in guiding parents and caregivers in making demands appropriate for encouraging the child's development while respecting an individual pace.

- Ability to delay gratification
- Ease of adaptability to routine
- Response to stimulation and comfort
- Interest in the environment
- Attachment to caregivers

Preschool. Preschool years are a time of using the newfound skills of toddlerhood to master the universe. Usually still within a small protected sphere of family or nursery school, these children explore the world's responses to their running, talking, doing, until exhaustion or overactivity set in. A child at this age often conforms to rules and exhibits some responsibility out of cooperation and attempts to please caregivers rather than from a real understanding of need for order. Preschoolers seem to change rapidly in ability, even within a 6-month period. A confident 3-year-old can turn into a fearful, testy 4-year-old almost overnight. It is essential to take a close look at the rapidly changing skills in the following areas in order to assure appropriate expectations.

- Attention span
- Ability to predict structure
- Development of sense of time
- Awareness of feelings of self
- Awareness of the feelings of others
- Ability to make choices between two alternatives
- Level of impulse control
- Reaction to new or exciting stimuli (Excessive shyness or overactivity)
- Ability to respond to transitions in activity or structure

Early School Years. The striving for social independence and the increased conceptual awareness of youngsters in the primary grade levels make them likely to understand a need for social rules and personal responsibility. The developmental issues of mastery in relation to the skills of others sharpen the importance of peer pressure at this age. Children who feel socially inadequate may tend to pursue a sense of importance or attract attention through disruptive means. Special attention to the following factors can guide the adult in presenting a child with opportunities for social self-assertion while encouraging respect for group rules.

- Social reciprocity: ability to see cause and effect in social situations
- Response to competition
- Self-image regarding academic and social mastery
- Maturing judgment of right and wrong in respect to effects on others
- Intensity of bodily awareness and sex-related exploration

Intermediate School Years. Preadolescents remain primarily concerned with the family as a source of their value systems. With developing self-control and cognitive growth, more expectations can be placed on a child to respond to situations with personal responsibility and morality. However, a growing self-consciousness may produce a strong temptation in the child to choose peer influence over personal responsibility. At this age a strong child–adult communication pattern is still possible and necessary in developing internally motivated values.

Preadolescents are ready and able not only to take responsibility for their actions, but weigh the consequences against their desire for increased independence. The following specific maturational factors should be considered in allowing a child to make decisions with social consequences, as a means of affording the child opportunities to learn the delicate balance of rights and responsibilities in preparation for the turbulent adolescent years ahead.

- Ability to predict how someone will feel as a consequence of an act
- Beginning of independence from family sphere: testing of limits
- Ability to conceptualize far-reaching moral implications of social acts
- Ability to sustain effort on task over a period of days
- Matured response to competition
- Self-consciousness about physical or social differences from "the norm"

Adolescence. Perhaps the most frustrating stage for parents and teachers to deal with in encouraging personal responsibility is adolescence. The developmental task of adolescence is to solidify independence. With this comes a certain amount of rejection of traditional orientations and values in order to explore the limits of personality and individuality. It is likely that parents who feel they had raised a responsible and caring preadolescent may experience a major disappointment and confusion as they encounter the differing priorities and values their adolescent child has developed. Understanding the following factors of adolescent development will often help to lessen the personalization of the adult–adolescent struggle and allow adults to encourage self-expression within an atmosphere of mutual respect.

- Exploration of a personal value system, often with rejection of "traditional values"
- Intense peer involvement, replacing the previous primary focus on family
- Increased awareness of long-term life planning; career exploration
- Sexual maturation, changing body image
- Increased awareness of role definition with regard to sexuality and relationships

PUTTING CHILDREN AND RESPONSIBILITY IN PERSPECTIVE

Priorities in the Classroom

Consider the following scenario, which is most likely being acted out somewhere at this very moment by unwilling participants:

> Mrs. Simon, a sixth-grade teacher has only 25 minutes allotted library time for her class on this particular day. Possibly because of the arrival of the first truly nice spring day, the mood of the class is somewhat "high." A large part of Ms. Simon's first hour has been devoted to reminding certain students of the rules, waiting for appropriate quit before speaking, and providing usually unneeded admonishing for the distracting behavior of a small group of boys. The class is already late on their way to the library, because Ms. Simon had to wait for orderliness before proceeding down the hall. Ms. Simon feels an extra pressure today, as she had planned on having the students finish the research on their "Peoples of Other Nations" paper so that she can focus on writing style during tomorrow's class, in conjunction with the rest of her English curriculum.
>
> As the class moves down the hallway, John and Jason begin poking each other playfully in the back. Ms. Simon shoots them a look, which goes unheeded. By the time the students have reached the library, John and Jason's playfulness has contaminated Andrew, who is always ready for a good time. The children are giggling and talking loud enough to be heard in adjacent classrooms. Ms. Simon feels herself growing angry and embarrassed, particularly as she notices a disapproving glance from the librarian. Her dismay increases as she realizes that Mr. Hessel, whose class is always a model of respect, responsibility, and politeness, has just closed his classroom door.

The disturbing components of this type of situation, in which children disrupt classroom routine and teachers feel angry, defeated, and drained of their resources, are perhaps the most commonly presented problems facing professionals providing support and guidance in schools today. Very often, these concerns do not come to a psychologist on the official "referral for service" form. It is much more likely that a casual comment will be thrown out in the faculty lounge: "This is the worst group I've had in all my teaching experience," or as a follow-up comment to an official referral regarding academic deficiency: "Oh, and another thing is that Jean is very stubborn. She will wait for me to remind her three times before clearing her desk, or giving in her homework. In a large class this kind of thing can get very frustrating."

The fact that oppositional, disrespectful, or irresponsible behavior of students is brought up in an emotional, informal forum reflects a misunderstanding that the primary, if not the sole, purpose of the teacher is to impart facts, teach students skills, and promote cognitive development. This dangerous assumption leaves teachers feeling frustrated and defeated when they must take time out of their academic lessons to address interpersonal or behavioral concerns. However, the fact that schools are by nature structured, social settings demands that response to authority, rules of group membership, personal responsibility and respect, or lack of it, for peers and adults be part of every school experience.

Unless teachers recognize that school is a much broader experience than the assimilation of academic facts, it is unlikely that the development of responsibility can be dealt with effectively. Owing to the interpersonal nature of this issue and the intrinsic involvement of attitudes, needs, and values of both adults and children, the consultation model, most fully described by Caplan (1970) and later modified to specifically address school issues (Meyers, Parsons, & Martin, 1979), may be seen as the most effective modality of intervention. It is only after issues of responsibility have been framed as a valid part of the classroom agenda, and the complex interactional phenomena are fully explored, that teachers will be able to respond effectively to ever present opportunities for the development of responsibility in students. In consultation the psychologist can assist in defining the issues, determining ownership of behavioral and attitudinal problems, and devising thoughtful methods of dealing with them. This type of mutual, objective exploration of issues can greatly reduce the paralyzing personalization of defeat experienced when students disrupt routine, and can free teachers to develop the skills and understanding necessary to successfully confront similar problems in the future.

Assessment of Responsibility

If Ms. Simon had viewed the children's disruptive hallway behavior as a reflection of their personal responsibility and as a matter worthy of as much time and attention as the "People's of Other Lands" library research, she may well have given herself permission to take the time to deal with the issues facing her. But if she had chosen to deal with the lack of responsible behavior, what should she have done? After a parent or teacher has been helped to recognize the validity of dealing with irresponsible behavior and has made a commitment to a planned response, the consultant begins to identify and formulate an understanding of the problem. To be useful, any assessment of such a complex issue must define specific behaviors and examine the environmental and interpersonal context in which they occur.

Problem Identification. The first stage of an assessment should involve an investigation of the nature of the disturbing behavior. Problem behaviors can be defined as "irresponsible" if their consequences violate the rights of others directly or indirectly, or demonstrate a lack of personal accountability to appropriate expectations. Parents and teachers have the right to personal respect, respect for belongings, and respect for group rules and structure. The disturbing behavior of the boys in Ms. Simon's class can legitimately be viewed as irresponsible because they are interfering with the rights of their classmates to proceed with the planned morning instruction, violating the rights of other classes to conduct lessons with little unnecessary distraction, and disregarding their personal accountability for adherence to group rules.

Examination of Expectations. The second stage of the assessment should involve an evaluation of the appropriateness of expectations. Are the situational demands within the child's emotional, cognitive, and motoric developmental capabilities? Have those expectations been communicated clearly and explicitly? The previous section on developmental readiness for responsibility delineates the specific factors to be examined in this regard. Oftentimes modifying adult expectations to conform to a child's abilities is all that is required to reduce "irresponsible" behavior. Most children wish to seek adult approval and will respond favorably to opportunities to demonstrate their independence and personal resourcefulness. If the determination is made that a child with apparent resources and maturity remains unresponsive in the face of appropriate expectations, an analysis of the motives for the disturbing behavior is indicated.

Goals of Behavior. It is a well-recognized fact that the behavior of human beings is goal-directed and purposeful (Adler, 1957). Even the seemingly random head banging or finger-flicking of the most delayed children can be seen as an attempt to stimulate senses that may be dulled to the normal perceptual excitations. Viewing disruptive or irresponsible behavior as purposeful can give teachers and parents an objective perspective and, more importantly, a way to proceed that is based on their understanding of the act, rather than their personal reaction to the act.

Dreikurs (1968), who bases his work on an Adlerian concept of human motivation, classified the goals of a child's disturbing behavior into four categories: attention getting, the struggle for power, the desire to retaliate, and the display of inadequacy in order to escape expectations. In diagnosing the purpose of a child's unacceptable behavior, an awareness of the adult's reaction and the response of the child to adult intervention is required. In the aforementioned scenario, Ms. Simon's anger and feeling of defeat may well signal that she is unwittingly and unendingly engaged in a power struggle for orderliness with a small group of the students in her class. Viewed in this manner, one can see the ineffectiveness of her reminders to follow the rules. In fact, such an intervention is likely to escalate the problem.

Children who are bent on gaining attention may respond temporarily to reminders and coaxing, but their eventual return to disturbing behavior is likely to leave the targeted adult feeling annoyed and frustrated. Parents or teachers feeling discouraged by the passivity or continuing inadequacy of a child in meeting appropriate expectations may be responding to the child's wish to avoid responsibility through a display of incompetence. Children who elicit anger and dislike from adults may present irresponsible behavior in the pursuit of revenge against authority.

Within a somewhat different theoretical base, Ross (1980) also stressed an examination of environmental consequences and "private events," such as the experience of anger and sadness, in the analysis of undesirable behavior.

Regardless of one's theoretical approach to the dynamics of behavioral interaction, it is imperative that in evaluating responsibility in children, one assess some understanding of the motives for behavior. It is only within this objective perspective that teachers and parents can extricate themselves from power struggles, avoid discouragement, and provide environments conducive to the development of personal responsibility.

Intensity and Persistence of Behavior. An important factor in assessing problem behavior is the level of interpersonal discord created by the specific behavior. To what degree is the irresponsible behavior upsetting the home routine or interfering with classroom structure? Behaviors that cause serious disruption reflect an intensity and persistence on the part of the child or group that indicate a significant need for intervention. If, on the other hand, a child appears occasionally irresponsible, and the particular offending behavior is judged not to be a grievous violation of personal rights, the parent or teacher may be counseled to view the situation as within the developmental norms of children's behavior. A particular focus of parent or teacher consultation should be to design the intensity of an intervention or response to be in direct proportion to the seriousness and frequency of the presenting problem.

Problematic children whose history has shown them to be responsible in the past are of particular interest in this regard. Regression in responsibility may well signal a problem in adjustment to a life event rather than an attitudinal or behavioral difficulty. The birth of a sibling, a move to a new school, or death of a close relative are some of the more common occurrences that may precipitate a regression of this sort.

In the illustrative case, Ms. Simon's admonishments are described as "usually unneeded," except on this particularly nice spring day. This may indicate an isolated instance of "spring fever" among the children. However, the intensity of Ms. Simon's emotional reaction suggests that she could use, at the least, some assistance in depersonalizing this type of behavior. Furthermore, the violation of the rights of students in other classes and the library demands that the seriousness of this kind of behavior be discussed with the offending parties.

Opportunities for Responsibility. An often overlooked factor in determining the level of responsibility in a child is the amount of opportunity the child has to demonstrate responsibility. Is the teacher or parent willing to allow a child the freedom to make responsible choices? Is there a conscious effort on the part of the adult to encourage responsibility for belongings, free-time activities, and personal preferences in clothing and food? How strong is the peer pressure for conformity rather than responsibility?

The psychologist as an objective observer can be invaluable in assessing the environmental opportunities for responsible choice and behavior offered in the home or school. A determination can then be made as to the proportion of occasions on which a child acts responsibly, considering the amount of opportunity offered for such a response. A child who meets with no openings for responsible choices will not demonstrate responsibility. In such a situation environmental or organizational interventions would be called for. Conversely, a youngster consistently choosing irresponsible alternatives in the face of adequate opportunities may well be in need of social consequences and individualized interventions.

ALTERNATIVE ACTIONS

By actively determining priorities, and understanding the motives of disturbing behavior in children, adults who are dedicated to encouraging responsibility in children and are aware of their own needs can choose to respond to behaviors and situations in ways that increase the probability of eliciting responsible behavior. Because of the complex and interactional nature of responsibility, there exists a broad range of areas of influence to be tapped to afford opportunities for responsible behavior. The following areas of practical application encompass the use of particular interpersonal skills, child management techniques and group process phenomena. To be most effective, a consultant must design an individualized intervention exploring the most judicious use of these techniques. Practical suggestions must be guided by an understanding of the adult's receptivity, personal style, and values; the child's or group's developmental level, interests,and abilities; and the nature, structure, and ambiance of the home or school.

Involvement

One of the necessary, but not sufficient, factors in encouraging responsibility in children is involvement by adults. This factor is labeled differently in different spheres of educational management or parental guidance literature as "love," "dedication to students," "identification," "investment," but there appears to be a consensus that a strong adult–child bond must exist if the adult is to have a lasting impact on the child's development of responsibility (Rogers, 1969; Adler, 1957). Glasser (1965, 1969), who bases a therapeutic approach for antisocial behavior on the development of responsibility by allowing choices to eventuate in their natural consequences, believes that careful analysis will show that every responsible individual has been exposed to a relationship with love and discipline. The teaching of responsibility is hard work and requires consistent and calculated, planned responses to children. It is unlikely that someone without investment in a child will be willing to provide the energy and consistency that the child requires. Furthermore, a child who senses a lack of involvement from an adult may be much less likely to withdraw from power struggles and retaliatory behavior that preclude responsible behavior.

The concept of involvement implies an interest in and awareness of the specific personal traits and experiences of another. Adults can demonstrate this to students through relatively simple acts such as calling them by name or remembering to acknowledge special events in their lives: birthdays, sports awards, or involvement in school plays or recitals. Offering appropriate support during such extraordinary circumstances as divorce, remarriage, death, or birth of a sibling demonstrates an active caring, as does an interest in a child's special skills, pets, hobbies, or talents. Reciprocating by sharing one's own interests further invites a close relationship and demonstrates a sense of trust necessary for the successful implementation of techniques designed to encourage responsibility.

Communication

Even highly motivated, capable children will fail to meet reasonable requests responsibly if they don't know what is expected. In order to set the stage for responsible behavior, adults must clearly and confidently communicate their expectations to children. With younger or handicapped children, this may necessitate visual reminders of rules, perhaps including pictures for non-readers. Expectations should be stated positively and with acknowledgment of personal rights, rather than as threats or lists of *don'ts.* A sign reading "Please handle our pets gently" or a quiet reminder "We must hold hands in the parking lot" are more likely to elicit a positive response than "Don't squeeze the hamster" or "John, I've told you a million times, don't run in the parking lot."

Communication is not only giving information, but receiving it as well. When students are assured that they are understood and accepted, it is more likely they will afford others respect and acknowledgment. At times, an active listening approach (Gordon, 1970, 1974) can be a valuable tool in demonstrating respect for students, acknowledging their feelings, and laying the foundation for responsible behavior.

Modeling

Modeling is recognized as an effective tool in changing behavior (Miller & Dollard, 1941; Bandura, 1962). Whether one views this phenomenon from a behavioral viewpoint or focuses on the process of identification, it seems there is a consensus that children do not learn responsible behavior from irresponsible adults. Children are good observers and there is much research to show that they increase or decrease behaviors in accordance with that of a valued adult (Bandura & Huston, 1961).

This may appear to be an elementary principle, especially for those adults committed to encouraging responsible behavior. However, modeling self-respect and respect for others may go against some of the double standard criteria adults often apply to themselves. A teacher may have to strictly avoid occasional late arrivals when attempting to instill a sense of promptness in students. Parents tempted not to return extra change at the cash register should be aware of the impact that the decision will have on their observant 8-year-old. Teachers who allow students to downgrade and curse at them under the guise of "free expression" will have little effect promoting a sense of pride and self-respect in their students. In large part, assisting teachers and parents in becoming effective examplars of responsible behavior lies in sensitizing them to inconsistencies between words and action so that congruent models are presented to children.

Natural and Logical Consequences

When providing opportunities for responsible behavior, a parent or educator must be willing to allow children to experience the natural consequences of their actions. Dinkmeyer and McKay (1973) stress the advantages of this technique:

> The parent does not threaten the child, argue or concede, but rather he permits the child to discover on his own the advantages of respect for order. He replaces stimulation from without with stimulation from within. By experiencing consequences the child develops a sense of self-discipline and internal motivation. He respects order not because he will be punished otherwise but because he has learned that order is necessary for effective functioning. (p. 108)

Allowing for natural and logical consequences disengages the adult from power struggles and takes advantage of naturally occurring opportunities for the development of responsibility. Children refusing to clean their rooms will experience the consequence of disorderly surroundings; a teenager unwilling to take responsibility for clothes washing may find no clean jeans to wear on a Friday night out with friends; a preschooler not putting toys away may find that some favorite items have been put in storage until they can be cared for more thoughtfully.

Allowing for natural consequences is a valuable, although limited tool for the adult. One would not wish to expose a preschooler to the health risks associated with eating art materials or the possibility of getting hit by a car when carelessly crossing a street. In these instances, logical consequences which relate to the irresponsible action may be imposed by adults who continue to assume responsibility for the well-being of the child or group in their care.

Shared Responsibility

The true test of commitment to the development of responsibility lies in the willingness to share responsibility. When dealing with children, most parents and teachers readily accept the necessity of involvement, clear communication, modeling respect, and sometimes allowing children the option of paying consequences. However, the suggestion of relinquishing some control over class or family responsibilities can result in anxious feelings that undermine apparently sincere attempts to provide children with opportunities for assuming responsibility.

Several approaches can be taken in successfully preparing an adult to share responsibility. First, the adult's feelings about changing their style of interaction with children must be fully explored. In asking their child or student "How can *we* make our living and learning experience more beneficial?" is the adult prepared to take suggestions seriously? The confidence and acceptance with which the adult engages the child in this venture will have a great impact on eventual outcome.

It is often helpful to share the probable positive outcomes of children's increased responsibility with a teacher or parent. Although the effects of democratic interactions with children have not yet been fully researched, the available information points to encouraging results. Tollefson, Tracy, Johnsen, Farner, and Buenning (1984) have reported that learning-disabled junior high students who were trained to set realistic goals and accept personal responsibility for their accomplishments tended to attribute achievement to the amount of personal effort expended more often than youngsters not so trained. In a study assessing the helping behaviors of school-age children, Peterson (1983) found increased altruism with increased feelings of competence and responsibility. Nash (1979, 1984) described strategies for teaching young children how to plan classroom learning activities that positively influenced their perception of being in control of their own learning.

The anxiety experienced by some parents and teachers at the mere contemplation of shared responsibility may be relieved with assurances that the adult appropriately maintains a leadership role with the children. Shared responsibility does not mean that rights to a safe, secure, productive environment must be relinquished. Quite the contrary, the concept of "sharing" responsibility with children assumes that the adult has that responsibility in the first place! A sense of safety and order must be established by the adult through the judicious use of physical structure, time scheduling, behavioral limits, and the demand for a sense of respect for oneself and for others. Within such a context, children can experience the security, predictability, and acceptance that readies them for the challenge of handling responsibilities at their level.

In changing any style of interaction with a child, a planned and gradual approach must be designed to provide new opportunities only when the child demonstrates a readiness for making responsible decisions. The following areas of practical application can be explored for use with youngsters able to conceptualize alternatives and make even elementary decisions.

Choices. Allowing children to choose between acceptable alternatives accomplishes three goals in a framework of democratic interaction. First, it allows the adult to maintain the leadership role by determining the of "acceptable" choices. Second, it offers an explicit opportunity for children to participate in shaping their own environment and experience the natural consequences of their choices. Third, giving children an active decision-making role is very likely to increase their level of compliance because of their personal investment in the course of action.

Simon and Olds (1977) presented a "clarifying grid" exercise that formalizes the decision-making process for children. In this model, child and adult together discuss and write down the options, consequences, values, and personal and social impact related to a given decision. A format such as this, which makes the relevant factors explicit, helps give young children an understanding of the ramifications and importance of their choices.

Adults may need some guidance in determining areas in which children can be productive and responsible decision makers. In the home, choices of clothing, preferred foods, television offerings, free-time activities, and room decoration can be considered. In the classroom, decisions as to use of class money, field trips, recreation time, and wall displays are relatively simple ways to allow children to exercise valuable input. More advanced decisions may be appropriate for more mature students. Appropriate choices can be made within a curriculum, such as selecting which novel to read or which community resource to explore in a social studies or civics lesson.

Goal Setting. Encouraging children to participate in setting the goals of an activity clarifies its purpose and encourages personal involvement. Interest, cooperation, and responsibility are likely to be encouraged by an adult's responsiveness to children's involvement in this area. In the classroom, a contract system can be used to decide on specific academic achievements the children set out to accomplish within a lesson. Slow learners or underachievers may choose fewer or less challenging goals from alternatives presented. Their resulting contracts may be shorter and more frequently drawn up than those of children willing and able to accept more academic responsibility.

At home, parents may involve children in setting goals regarding home management, such as maintenance tasks, or interpersonal issues such as the need to improve communication patterns. Displaying goals mutually agreed on by means of a chart or contract stresses the importance of the children's personal commitment. Further elaboration of steps towards achieving the desired goal can serve to direct and encourage young or immature children in the fulfillment of their responsibilities.

Problem Solving. If children are presented with choices and are involved in determining the goals of activities, it is logical that they should be involved in resolving conflicts arising from the activities they choose. Encouraging children to participate in the systematic analysis of a problem exposes them to a skill that allows them to handle conflicts in a responsible fashion. The following six steps of conflict resolution, originally proposed by John Dewey in relation to the scientific method, and more recently applied specifically to the classroom by Gordon (1974), can easily be taught to children so that they may participate more fully and responsibly in class and family decision making: Step 1, identifying and validating the issue; Step 2, gathering information, generating possible solutions; Step 3, considering alternatives and consequences; Step 4, deciding on a course of action; Step 5, specifying how to implement the decision; Step 6, evaluating the results.

It is quite likely that even those familiar with problem-solving methodology will need direction in recognizing when it is most applicable. Many opportunities for thoughtful, responsible resolution of conflicts between adults and children are lost because divisive issues are not designated as problems involving conflicting needs. Instead, either an adult or a child attempts to dominate the situation, often precipitating a covert power struggle or a passive-resistant response. The psychologist who sensitizes parents or teachers to these dynamics and assists in initial problem identification greatly increases the probability that problem-solving methodology will be used most productively in developing responsible behavior.

Group Format. Properly developed groups can be an experiential format for the constructive exchange of ideas, positive self-expression, development of problem-solving strategies, and recognition of each member's rights and responsibilities. Levels of cognitive development and social maturity will determine how directive an adult must be when organizing and participating in such groups. Young children may use an adult-directed "circle time" to exchange ideas and role-play problem solutions. More mature students may be able to organize a class council or may successfully process a problem arising during the day with little assistance from a teacher. At any developmental level, it is of utmost importance that the group process reflect a responsible use of power, respect for the individual members, and appropriate opportunities for open communication. Teachers may find it helpful to engage students in an initial session designed to embody these concepts in group determined rules using developmentally appropriate language and signs.

Group discussion or role-playing can provide children with valuable experience in the examination of responsibilities and consequences that serves to prepare them for decisions they will make outside the sphere of family or school life. There is evidence that group discussions of moral dilemmas popularized by Kohlberg can serve to increase the sociomoral reasoning of even delinquent youngsters (Gibbs, 1984). Mattox (1975) and Hall (1979) provide exercises based on values clarification and moral conflicts that can be easily adapted to group discussion to encourage problem-solving strategies, communication skills, and examination of responsible behaviors.

Class councils and family roundtable discussions can afford children practice in recognizing another person's rights and ideas, as well as providing a forum for them to express their opinions in an appropriate fashion. Teachers and parents employing the group format concretely demonstrate their respect for the children's ideas, the value in open communication, and a responsible approach to problem solving.

SUMMARY

Over the past several decades, there has been an increasing societal focus on personal responsibility. Despite the development of child-rearing techniques that emphasize mutual respect and personal accountability, the encouragement of responsible behavior in children remains a confusing and elusive goal for many of today's parents and teachers. Well-intentioned adults often undermine their own attempts at teaching responsibility because of unrecognized control needs or an authoritarian value system.

The school psychologist is in a unique position to assist interested parents and teachers in examining their attitudes, interactional style, and child development priorities as they relate to the explicit goal of fostering responsibility in youngsters. Through a consultative relationship the foundation can be laid for complementary, rather than competitive, spheres of responsibility among children and adults. Once an adult is prepared to offer the opportunity for responsibility, assessment of the developmental readiness of the child becomes crucial. Just as an adult must be prepared and have a plan about sharing responsibility, a child must be cognitively and emotionally ready to accept it. Individualized interventions encompass a variety of interpersonal skills, child management techniques, and group process phenomena that must be tailored to the adult's receptivity, the group's ability, and the general atmosphere of the home or school.

The encouragement of responsibility necessitates the difficult orchestration of a delicate interplay of needs, values, expectations, motivations, priorities, personal rights, capabilities, and opportunities. It is clear that the demands of the task are great, as are the rewards: independent, responsible, young persons.

REFERENCES

Adler, A. (1957). *Understanding human nature.* New York: Premier Books.

Ames, L. B., Gillespie, C., Haines, J., & Ilg, F. (1979). *The Gessell institute's child from one to six: Evaluating the behavior of the preschool child.* New York: Harper & Row.

Bandura, A. (1962). Social learning through imitation. In M. R. Jones (Ed.), *Nebraska symposium on motivation.* Lincoln: University of Nebraska Press.

Bandura, A., & Huston, A. C. (1961). Identification as a process of incidental learning. *Journal of Abnormal Social Psychology, 63,* 1–9.

Brazelton, T. B. (1974). *Toddlers and parents.* New York: Dell.

Caplan, G. (1970). *The theory and practice of mental health consultation.* New York: Basic Books.

Chess, S., Thomas, A., & Birch, H. (1965). *Your child is a person.* New York: Viking.

Dinkmeyer, D., & McKay, G. (1973). *Raising a responsible child.* New York: Simon and Schuster.

Dreikurs, R. (1968). *Psychology in the classroom* (2nd ed.). New York: Harper & Row.

Dreikurs, R., Grunwald, B., & Pepper, F. (1971). *Maintaining sanity in the classroom: Illustrated teaching techniques.* New York: Harper & Row.

Dreikurs, R., & Soltz, V. (1964). *Children: The challenge.* New York: Hawthorn/Dutton.

Gibbs, J., Arnold, K., Ahlborn, H., & Chessman, F. (1984). Facilitation of sociomoral reasoning in delinquents. *Journal of Consulting and Clinical Psychology, 52*(1), 37–54.

Glasser, W. (1965). *Reality therapy: A new approach to psychiatry.* New York: Harper & Row.

Glasser, W. (1969). *Schools without failure.* New York: Wyden.

Goldstein, A. P., Sprafkin, R. P., Gershaw, N. J., & Klein, P. (1980). *Skillstreaming the adolescent.* Champaign, IL: Research Press.

Gordon, T. (1970). *P.E.T.: Parent effectiveness training.* New York: Wyden.

Gordon, T. (1974). *T.E.T.: Teacher effectiveness training.* New York: Wyden.

Hall, R. T. (1979). *Moral education: A handbook for teachers.* Minneapolis: Winston.

Harris, T. A. (1969). *I'm O.K. — You're O.K.: A practical guide to transactional analysis.* New York: Harper & Row.

Heider, F. (1958). *The psychology of interpersonal relations.* New York: Wiley.

Holt, J. (1983). *How children learn* (rev. ed.). New York: Dell.

Ilg, F., Ames, L., & Baker, S. (1981). *Child behavior* (rev. ed.). New York: Harper & Row.

Kozloff, M. A. (1974). *Educating children with learning and behavior problems.* New York: Wiley.

Mattox, B. A. (1975). *Getting it together: Dilemmas for the classroom.* San Diego: Pennant.

Meichenbaum, D. H. (1977). *Cognitive–behavior modification: An integrative approach.* New York: Plenum.

Meyers, J., Parsons, R. D., & Martin, R. (1979). *Mental health consultation in schools.* San Francisco: Jossey-Bass.

Miller, N. E., & Dollard, J. (1941). *Social learning and imitation.* New Haven: Yale University Press.

Nash, B. C. (1979). Kindergarten programmes and the young child's task orientation and understanding about time scheduling. *British Journal of Educational Psychology, 49,* 27–38.

Nash, B. C. (1984). Kindergarten task management and grade two perceptions of teacher–learner roles. *British Journal of Educational Psychology, 54,* 221–222.

O'Leary, K. D., & O'Leary, S. G. (1977). *Classroom management: The successful use of behavior modification* (2nd ed.). New York: Pergamon.

Oppenheim, J., Boegehold, B., & Brenner, B. (1984). *Raising a confident child.* New York: Pantheon.

Peterson, L. (1983). Influence of age, task competence, and responsibility focus of children's altruism. *Developmental Psychology, 19*(1), 141–148.

Piaget, J. (1965). *The moral judgement of the child.* New York: Macmillan.

Rogers, C. R. (1969). *Freedom to learn.* Columbus, OH: Merrill.

Ross, A. (1980). *Psychological disorders of children.* New York: McGraw-Hill.

Simon, S. B., & Olds, S. W. (1976). *Helping your child learn right from wrong.* New York: McGraw-Hill.

Tollefson, N., Tracy, D. B., Johnsen, E. P., Farmer, A. W., & Buenning, M. (1984). Goal setting and personal responsibility training for LD adolescents. *Psychology in the Schools, 21*(2), 224–233.

BIBLIOGRAPHY: PROFESSIONALS

Dinkmeyer, D., & McKay, G. (1976/1983). *Systematic training for effective parenting STEP & STEP/Teen.* Circle Pines, MN: American Guidance Service.
This parent training kit is available in two levels: STEP, for preschool through middle school children, and STEP/Teen, for junior and senior high school students. A variety of materials including a manual, parent handbook, audiocassettes, discussion cards, charts, and posters allow the professional to lead a practically oriented parent training course. The focus is on decision making, natural consequences, motives of behavior, and communication skills.

Dreikurs, R. (1968). *Psychology in the classroom* (2nd ed.). New York: Harper & Row.
Principles such as social adequacy, motives of behavior, and the teacher's role in a democratic classroom are discussed. Practical application of natural consequences and group practices in the classroom are presented.

Dreikurs, R., Grunwald, B., & Pepper, F. (1971). *Maintaining sanity in the classroom: Illustrated teaching techniques.* New York: Harper & Row.
Presents a motivational theory of behavior, practical applications of democratic process in the classroom, and suggestions for dealing with learning deficits, behavior problems, and parent–teacher communication problems.

BIBLIOGRAPHY: PARENTS

Crary, E. (1979). *Without spanking or spoiling: A practical approach to toddler and preschool guidance.* Seattle: Parenting Press.
This brief handbook of child management skills is designed to guide the parent through practical application of behavioral techniques, conflict resolution and communication skills. There is a focus on children's temperament and developmental expectations that adds a useful framework for the techniques suggested.

Dinkmeyer, D., & McKay, G. (1973). *Raising a responsible child.* New York: Simon and Schuster.
The authors provide a useful blend of theoretical and practical information regarding motivations for misbehavior, communication patterns, natural and logical consequences, problem solving, and family relationships. There is a focus on avoiding self-defeating patterns of behavior and providing concrete opportunities for children to engage in responsible behavior.

Dinkmeyer, D., & McKay, G. (1982). *The parent's handbook: Systematic training for effective parenting.* Circle Pines, MN: American Guidance Service.
Provides some background and theoretical information on motivation, communication, and values orientation, but the majority of the handbook is devoted to a systemic presentation of child management skills. Readings, charts, and exercises allow parents to explore behavioral interventions and attitude changes designed to encourage responsible behavior in children.

Dreikurs, R., & Soltz, V. (1964). *Children the challenge.* New York: Hawthorn/Dutton.
A philosophy of child rearing that emphasizes mutual respect and social adequacy is discussed. A focus on the goals of children's behavior and parental responses that stimulate independence provides information that is useful for practical application in the family.

Oppenheim, J., Boegehold, B., & Brenner, B. (1984). *Raising a confident child.* New York: Pantheon.
Presents an explicit overview of sequential development in children that is useful in forming appropriate expectations.

Children and Running Away

James R. Deni
Appalachian State University

BACKGROUND

Children's running away from home is not a new phenomenon, but since the mid-1960s, there has been increased interest and concern for the growing numbers of children who leave home before they are of legal age. Runaway behavior throughout the literature is perceived as reaching epidemic proportions.

It is categorized in the juvenile legal codes as a "status offense," not conceptually applicable to adults. It is defined as leaving the home of one's parent(s) (or guardian(s)) for longer than one night without parental consent (American Psychiatric Association, 1981; Lambert, Rothschild, Atland, & Green, 1978; Opinion Research Center [OR], 1976). Most definitions of the term *runaway* include age, absence of parental permission to leave home, and the time away from home.

The focus of prior research and definitions of runaways involves the 10- to 17-year-old age group. According to the *National Statistical Survey* (ORC, 1976), in 47% of the reported cases of children's leaving home overnight, the parents did not conceptualize the event as runaway behavior. They explained that they knew where their children had gone and expected them home the next day. Parents apparently reserve the term *runaway* for youths who have voluntarily left home permanently and are therefore less likely to report incidences of one-day absence.

Each year in the United States approximately 1 million children run away from home (Ostensen, 1981). Many runaways are not included in official tabulations because of underreporting stemming from parental neglect, embarrassment, or indifference. According to the National Center for Health Statistics, the actual count may easily be three times as high, since so many runaways are not reported. The *National Statistical Survey* (ORC, 1976) found that the incidence was higher in more heavily populated cities and small towns, and lower in rural and suburban areas. Runaways were almost equally divided between males (53%) and females (47%). Based on the survey data, it is estimated that one child in eight will run away from home overnight before his or her 18th birthday.

Approximately half the youths who run away from home appear to stay within their general city or community area (Beyer, Reid, & Quinlan, 1973; Gold & Reimer, 1974). The most common destination is a relative's or friend's house (Beyer et al., 1973; Gold & Reimer, 1974). Shellow, Schamp, Liebow, and Unger (1967) reported that most runaway episodes are brief, and a study by Tobias (1970) indicated that 41% of runaways return home within a day, the average stay being 3 days. However, the length of time of a runaway episode tends to increase with age.

Brennan et al. (1978) reported a direct relationship between the age of the runaway youth and the distance traveled from home. There is a tendency for older runaways to travel longer distances which reflects their greater skills and survival ability. However, the majority of runaways travel between 100–200 miles away from home.

For many of the million youths who run away annually, an attempt to scratch out a life on the streets can lead to insurmountable obstacles. Hunger, drug addiction, alcohol abuse, and theft may become a way of life. The longer the youth stays away from home, the more difficult it becomes to survive. Sources of money include theft, violence, selling drugs, forgery, and even prostitution.

Typologies of Runaways

Various schemata for classifying runaways have been reported in the literature (Dunford & Brennan, 1976; English, 1973; Green & Esselstyn, 1972; Homer, 1973; and Brennan et al., 1978). They do not accurately describe the heterogeneous population of runaway youths and are therefore very inadequate and misleading. Brennan et al. (1978) has provided a detailed description of most of the criticisms leveled at taxonomic classification systems. Orten and Soll (1980) stated that to be useful to practitioners typologies must avoid the two pitfalls of oversimplification and excessively detailed categorization.

Three types of runaways are consistently described: those who run away from an "intolerable family situation," those seeking "adventure," and those with "school problems." The authors mentioned above all seem to be applying different labels to the same type of runaway behaviors. Adolescents who have run away because of family conflicts have been referred to as *running from* children by Homer (1973), sometimes as *runaways* by English (1973), and as *anxious runaways* by Green and Esselstyn (1972).

English (1973) presented a four-leveled system for classifying runaways consisting of *floaters, runaways, splitters,* and *hard road freaks.* He defines *floaters* as a large group of adolescents who frequently think of running away. The usual length of time away from home for a floater is 2–3 days. Sometimes they run to test their parents or relieve tension, but usually they return with a little urging. *Runaways* can be distinguished from floaters by their duration of time away from home and by the presence of more complex problems. Usually they will be away from home for weeks or even months. *Splitters* escape to the streets to avoid minor problems. Eventually, running away becomes the habitual strategy for dealing with problem situations. Usually the *splitters* are reinforced for their behavior by special attention from parents and peers, thus making it easier the next time. They usually learn how to survive and adapt to street life for a few days, then return home only to run away again when they can no longer cope with the problems associated with school and home. The *hard road freaks* are the most streetwise of the four categories. They are usually older teenagers, falling into the 17- to 20-year-old age range, who sever ties with family and exploit their younger counterparts. Most runaways avoid becoming splitters and hard road freaks, but the absolute numbers continue to increase.

Homer (1973) studied 20 runaway girls who were between the ages of 13 and 16. Two types of runaways were distinguished: girls who were running away from family problems and those who seemed to be pleasure seekers. Within the "running from" category, six of the seven girls indicated that they could not tolerate their home situation or one or both parents any longer. The "running to" group enjoyed running away and making new friends on the run. The girls in the "running from" category appeared to benefit from individual and family therapy and stopped running. In contrast, the girls in the "running to" group continued to run away frequently and "usually did not return until they were picked up by the police."

Orten and Soll (1980) offered a classification system with a focus on the degree of alienation between home and the child, as well as a gauge of how much the child has internalized running as a response to stressful situations. They claimed that alienation is determined by a clinical judgment, rather than a precise measurement, that is based on such factors as the quality of the relationship between parents and child, the duration of problems precipitating the runaway response, and the emotional exchange between parents and child. They offer a three-tiered system, each level being associated with higher levels of alienation between parents and child.

First-degree runaways, as the name implies, are first-time runners and are still usually psychologically dependent on their homes. Within this group there are two subtypes known as *walkaways* and *fugitives.* Walkaways are usually in their middle teens and are quite normal adolescents. They usually run once and learn from their experience. Walkaways usually do not feel powerless and are not fleeing intolerable situations. For many, fleeing simply becomes a learning experience. The second subtype within the first-degree group, known as *fugitives,* are generally younger than walkaways. They run because of their perceived powerlessness.

Second-degree runaways may have only run once but they perceive that they have strongly alienated the family (e.g., because of complications with drugs or pregnancy). Although they may run as a result of a single disapproved behavior, there is usually a history of family conflict. They are also in conflict as to whether they can or want to live at home.

Finally, the *third-degree* runaway is categorized by family rejection that is caused by strong alienation. They are usually 16 years of age or older and streetwise, and they usually are gone from home a year or more. There is usually no motivation on the part of the child, or encouragement by the parents, to return home.

In a recent study, Elliot (1984) interviewed over 250 runaways in Fort Lauderdale, and 250 additional runaways in other cities. Running away hasn't been illegal in Florida since 1975. His findings are as follows: (a) Most runaways will return home within 72 hr; (b) about 1 in 3 runaways are "throwaways" forced to leave home, and 2 of 3 runaways voluntarily leave home; (c) most juvenile prostitutes — both boys and girls — are runaways; (d) the age range for juvenile prostitution is from 14 to 21, and while girls hustle for shelter, young men frequently hustle for cash to support the girls they often life with; (e) for young children, street prostitution can be especially brutalizing, dehumanizing, and often violent; (f) there is a high incidence of violence and sexual abuse among runaways who turn to the streets for survival; (g) runaways and prostitutes are prey to a whole range of illnesses, from upper respiratory infections to venereal diseases, that go untreated; (h) runaways adopt street names and phony IDs that create problems of identification; (i) runaways rapidly lose a sense of identity, which frequently disrupts emotional development; (j) runaways adopt a nomadic and transient lifestyle; (k) runaways lie about the past and present, finding security in living the lie that their condition is temporary and that luxury awaits their return; (l) 62% of the runaways in the study came from broken homes and 85% claimed to have been victims of abuse; (m) both boy and girl runaways have a low sense of self-esteem in social interaction; (n) prior truancy is a significant indicator of runaway behavior; (o) Florida runaways are overwhelmingly white and most often middle-class; (p) Fort Lauderdale is the runaway "capital" for the State of Florida; (q) there is a high correlation between runaways and drug and/or alcohol use; (r) most runaways have negative reactions to the legal remedies that social services offer them, finally; (s) runaway youngsters live from day to day, and meal to meal, instantly gratifying their needs, with no realistic thought about adulthood or the future.

DEVELOPMENT

According to Bakan (1979), industrialization has brought societal changes that have made running away both more likely and more problematic for young people. The increased mobility and urbanization that has accompanied industrial growth has brought new problems that have fragmented and isolated families, resulting in increased alienation among family members. Orten and Soll (1980) have suggested that television may have created barriers to communication, thus adding to the level of alienation in families. If the television set is on for a high percentage of the time, family members may not have adequate time to talk to each other. Certainly, other sociological and industrial changes have contributed to the fragmentation of families, thus increasing the number of runaways.

Olson, Liebow, Mannino, and Shore (1971) provided data on a 12-year follow-up of 14 youths who had run away from home in the mid-1960s. The results indicated that these runaways had experienced serious behavior problems at school, exhibited chronic truancy, and felt boredom, frustration, and defeat. Evidence was also reported of strained relations between the former runaways and their parents early in life. All the runaways in the study reported being beaten by at least one parent several times prior to their running. Many of the runaways had poor work histories including unemployment and irregular attendance at work. One major finding was that youths who repeatedly ran away had continued problems into adult life, that required special attention from families and community agencies. In contrast, those who had run away only once seemed to have little or few problems as adults. However, future research needs to address differences between one-time runners and repeaters.

Beyer (1974), comparing runaways with their nonrunaway siblings, found that runaways had recurring patterns of low self-esteem, loneliness, friendlessness, rejection, and depression. Their low self-esteem and depression centered around the school and home. For such youths running may be the easiest coping strategy to escape their perceived or real problems.

A large majority of the studies reviewed by Walker (1975) between the 1930s and 1950s utilized a psychopathological model to explain runaway behavior. Running away was seen to be symptomatic of mental illness. More recently runaway behavior has been explained in the literature from three theoretical perspectives, each with its own explanation for runaway behavior (Brennan et al., 1978).

The psychological personal explanation of runaway behavior searches for some special trait or psychological characteristic to explain the runaway behavior. A large number of studies, mainly of clinical orientation and dealing with small samples of youths, provide a basis for this theory. A second theory is a social structural/environmental explanation of running. Unlike the psychological explanation, which clearly assigns responsibility to the child, the social structural/environmental theory locates causality not in any single personality characteristic of the runaway youngster, but in situations in the environment that cause or contribute to runaway behavior. The assumption is that anyone might reasonably try to escape from a dreadful environment.

A third explanation, and one that has gained considerable professional support (Brennan et al., 1978), is the social–psychological theory, which explains runaway behavior as a result of an interaction between personal and environmental effects. The basic assumption is that runaway behavior results from an interaction between certain kinds of social structural/environmental conditions (e.g., family, school, and the peer group) and the individual personality of the runaway child. This perspective recognizes the importance of both the individual and the environment, thus avoiding the narrow focus of the other two orientations. Although it appears that the social–psychological approach has gained favor, there are still only a few published studies using this orientation.

Home Environment and Family

The most consistently reported factor underlying runaway behavior is poor parent–child relationships (Adams & Munro, 1979; Van Hauten & Golembieski, 1978; Wolk & Brandon, 1977). Homes of runaways are typically scarred by high rates of internal conflict, divorce, and residential mobility. Their parents tend to discipline these children in physical and psychologically abusive ways, including beatings and social isolation. Runaways themselves most frequently cite problems at home as the major reason for their flight. The exact nature of home conditions leading to runaway behavior, however, is not completely understood.

Family conflict leading to runaway behavior usually results in an erosion of family bonds or prevents an adequate initial development of family bonds. In large-sample comparisons between homes of runaways and nonrunaways (Opinion Research Corporation, 1976) it was found that runaways (a) are provided with limited and/or poor supervision; (b) seldom obtain help with school work; (c) infrequently discuss problems with their parents; and (d) experience less emotional support from parents. Parents of nonrunaways generally appear to be more cooperative with their children and each other than parents of runaways (Roberts, 1981).

PUTTING THE PROBLEM OF RUNAWAYS IN PERSPECTIVE

In light of current research on runaway behavior, it seems unlikely that we can establish any single primary reason for running away. However, the single factor most cited in literature today as having a causal role in runaway behavior is parent–child relationships. Adolescents themselves cite communication problems as a major source of conflict in their home. In a study by Grieco (1984), it was found that although nonrunaway adolescents may not feel totally understood, strong feelings of love and high positive regard made a critical difference with respect to the adolescent's relationship with their parents. It seems that a strong sense of being loved and cared for can compensate for the feeling of not being totally understood. This also gives the family members a sense of self-worth and dignity.

In this connection, it is noteworthy that husband–wife relationships appear to have a considerable effect on running away (Opinion Research Corporation, 1976). Rates are much higher in single-parent families and in families in conflict. The reduction of such conflict and the enhancement of parent–child relationships can have a considerable effect on runaway youths.

Clearly, the majority of runaways are trying to escape circumstances that they perceive as problems they cannot or will not deal with. They run because they are unhappy with the existing environment, sometimes to avoid abusive and insensitive parents. Some merely escape; others run searching for a utopia. Current research leaves no doubt as to the importance of conflicts and alienation between adolescents and their parents and school. Although these young people are called runaways and have indeed left home, many of them feel they have been "pushed out" or "thrown away." Essentially, "throwaways" result from the inability of parents to cope with such adolescent behaviors as drugs, sexual activity, defiance of authority, and poor academic performance, as well as parental behaviors such as incest, child abuse, and inadequate response to economic pressures.

Given current research on runaway behavior, it appears that helping professionals should look for early warning signs, especially since many of the factors contributing to running away will not be found in a single source or given age. The events precipitating running away will, in most cases, be cumulative and there will be prior indications or warning signs. Some youths may have made earlier attempts to seek help or talk with their parents. Friends and relatives are the most frequent choices by runaways in seeking outside help. School personnel are also chosen by youngsters as potential sources of help prior to the actual runaway episodes. Many of these children will be seeking help with their family problems and will be in need of, and want, understanding, sympathy, and someone to talk to. Some children even talk about running away prior to acting, whereas others run without warning. School personnel and parents should be particularly aware and trained to look for (a) early warning signs of angry rejection by a child, (b) verbal threats of running away, (c) constant battles over autonomy, (d) alcoholism, (e) school failure, (f) parent–child conflict, (g) drug abuse, (h) truancy, (i) juvenile delinquency, (j) child abuse, (k) communication problems, (l) sharp changes in behavior or personality, (m) inadequate or poor peer relationships, (n) low self-esteem, and (o) poor social skills. Certainly, these warning signs are not unique to only runaway behavior, however, one or more could elicit a runaway response. A simple measure of conflict and alienation is the number of times a youth has run away.

Before deciding on courses of actions, helping professionals will want to consider the age of the youth, options available within the school and community, numbers of runaway episodes, and interaction effects between youth, parents, and school.

ALTERNATIVE ACTIONS

Since the literature (Benalcager, 1982; Gordon, 1979; Homer, 1983; Jorgensen, Thoenburg, & Williams, 1980) reports a lack of communication between youths and their families as correlates of runaway behavior, supportive counseling seems to work best. Such individual and/or group counseling needs to be consistent to be of any effect. In some cases, these youths just need a friend whom they can trust and who has the time to listen. In time, the counseling can develop into teaching problem-solving strategies, as well as conflict resolution, social skills, and communication skills. The treatment should also communicate an empathetic understanding of the child and his or her problems. This can best be achieved through reflective or active listening. It is just as critical not to be judgmental about their problems. Although to adults the problems of youth may seem minor and certainly not a reason to run, for adolescents they can be devastating. Remember also that many of these youths are saddled with low self-esteem. This suggests that individual and supportive counseling should focus on helping them understand and feel better about themselves. Getting them involved in extracurricular activities or varsity athletics might help reach this goal. Also, role playing and structured activities can help facilitate and focus discussions.

Many writers (Lappin & Covelman, 1985; Ostensen, 1981) feel that running away is symptomatic of general problems within the family, implying that treatment of runaways should include the entire family. These writers recommend various forms of family therapy directed toward changing the interrelationships between children and parents and teaching communication skills and methods of conflict resolution. Family therapy may help to clarify hidden expectations of the parents. It can also, in many cases, lessen the demands that parents place on their children, many of which center around school achievement, and that the children place on their parents. In fact, many youths who are returned home without any type of family intervention are considered a high risk for recidivism.

Crisis and help lines have also been used to provide referral information and some counseling to youngsters who are in trouble. One example is Phone-A-Home, a service for teenagers who wish to leave home for a night. Youth can obtain written permission to leave home for a night staying at a friend or neighbor's. A similar concept might be an emergency shelter for youth who might need to be away from the home for one or two days. However, at times a crisis line, hot line, or help line providing counseling might resolve the problem without the adolescent having to leave home.

The goal of counseling for first time runners (Orten & Soll, 1980) should be to bring stability back to the family that has been disrupted by the child's running away. The first meeting between the child, parents, and helping professional should follow the child's return as soon as possible. In the meeting the helping professional should show the child support and model effective communication and problem solving but individual sessions should also be held with the child. Orten and Soll (1980) also suggest that second-degree runners, if living at home is not practical, will require separate living arrangements, in which case therapeutic attention should focus on independent living and maintaining a friendly relationship with the family.

Thomas (1982) has suggested that helping professionals work with the juvenile courts system in an attempt to provide conditions for probation that will assure family involvement, including counseling. He further suggested that helping professionals develop a working relationship with juvenile court judges and probation officers, who frequently seek psychological and treatment recommendations for runaways. Finally, he suggested that helping professionals should pay particular attention to ethical and legal issues in working with youth. Psychologists and other helping professionals working as direct service providers to youths should be familiar with such issues as privileged communication and informed parental consent. Professionals should review the National Association of School Psychologists Principles for Professional Ethics or the American Psychological Association Code of Ethics.

Another key to treating runaway behavior is prevention. Helping professionals should develop prevention programs that center around the number of runaway episodes, methods of survival, illness, deaths, and reasons for running away. Since many youths who run away have an unrealistic expectation of a perfect carefree life away from the problems of school and home, school programs should be devised that are designed to bring students to realize that running is not as glamorous as it may first seem, and certainly not a solution to one's problems. School children should also be informed about available local, state, and national hotlines where information, counseling, and assistance will be provided. They should be made aware of the steps involved in getting back home if they or a friend do run away. Trailways Bus Lines, for example, sponsors a program called Operation: Home Free. A runaway child needs only to approach a police officer, who then checks to verify his or her status. The officer then goes to the nearest Trailways terminal, arranges for a free ticket home, and sees the child onto the bus. Parents and hometown police are notified of the arrival time. There are no arrests or fines, and the child is treated as a full-fare paying passenger. Trailways, whose fleet of 1,500 buses serves more than 12,000 cities, towns, and communities, has undertaken its own campaign to advertise the Home Free program.

Prevention should also include programs aimed at parents that point out how current research reports that family problems are seen as the most common cause of runaway behavior. Parents should be encouraged to listen to their children and be aware of some of the early warning signals of a runaway episode. Parents and professionals must remember children run away from home for a variety of reasons. In running away, a child may be attempting to exert his or her sense of independence or adventure, but usually whether they run because of parental marriage problems, child abuse, or just basic communication problems, the underlying cause is that the child feels the home situation is out of control. Tested parenting techniques (e.g., Parent Effectiveness Training, Tough Love) can train parents in communication skills to serve as a means of primary prevention. However, they should also be provided with information about the National Runaway Switchboard and the National Center for Missing and Exploited Children.

Helping professionals should provide children with coping strategies to deal with the day-to-day stress in life. These should include both physiological, psychological, and physical tactics. Examples could include biofeedback, relaxation, meditation, self-talk, thought stopping, problem solving, self-instruction training, running, swimming, biking, and other large muscle activities. All of these techniques, and more, could be used singly or in combination to reduce stress and serve as a means for youths to cope and keep their lives under control.

Finally, helping professionals should take leadership roles in their cities and communities to find out available resources for troubled and runaway youths. It is imperative that comprehensive planning for this eventually be initiated; this should include prevention problems, communication networks, runaway centers, shelters, crisis homes, and other meaningful efforts directed toward serving the runaway, as well as modifying such basic social institutions as the school and the family for the betterment of runaways and all other children.

SUMMARY

Weeks before her own murder, a young 18-year-old female wrote the following poem and called it "Runaway."

> Some runaways run to be free
> which is something they'll probably never be.
> Others run away from a bad life at home.
> They run, then walk in the streets all alone.
> A few don't run.
> They get kicked out.
> Then they're on their own and full of doubt.
> But I know one of those who ran to be free.
> Free, he is, his funeral is at three.

This poem expresses the feelings of many runaways — but how poignantly it is expressed by this young female. There are numerous examples today of the hurt and frustration felt by youths abandoned by parents and suffering the erosion of the family. Witness today the increase in the divorce rate and the decrease in marriages, adverse social changes that continue to be a detriment to the mental health of children. More and more, youths encounter the same struggles, problems, and frustrations as adults, trying desperately to find their own identity. The important point to remember is that children who stay away from home become delinquent, either by choice or necessity, but delinquent (at least status offenders) nevertheless. Rotating from street to street and city to city, the little world they form has no home, little future, and less opportunity.

The helping professional must recognize the problems of runaways and understand why they exist. Prevention information, crisis lines, shelters, group homes, and safety valves are needed. Amnesty for our runaway youth must be granted, as legislation to protect them is approved and enforced. To ignore a child as a runaway today is to deal with that child as a delinquent in the future. In essence, to ignore a delinquent child is to breed a criminal adult.

For parents and helping professionals, a need exists to recognize that children have feelings, too, although they may not have the language or vocabulary to express them. Experience and the scientific literature tell us that what most runaways are searching for is someone who cares and has the time to listen. Love, dreams, and hopes are also important to children. *We* must find the time to listen now, because the problem is *ours,* today and tomorrow.

REFERENCES

Adams, G. R., & Munro, G. (1979). Portrait of the North American runaway: A critical review. *Journal of Youth and Adolescence, 8,* 359–373.

American Psychiatric Association. (1981). *Diagnostic and statistical manual of disorders* (3rd ed.) Washington, DC: Author.

Bakan, D. (1975). Adolescence in America: From idea to social fact. *Daedalus, 100,* 979–995.

Beyer, M., Reid, T. A., & Quinlan, D. M. (1973, May). *Runaway youth: Families in conflict.* Paper presented at the meeting of the Eastern Psychological Association, Washington.

Brennan, T. M., Brewington, S., & Walker, L. (1974). A study of issues relating to runaway behavior. Washington, DC: Department of Health, Education, and Welfare, Office of Youth Development.

Brennan, T., Huizinga, D., & Elliot, D. (1978). *The social psychology of runaways.* Lexington, MA: Heath.

Dunford, F. W., & Brennan, T. (1976, September). A taxonomy of runaway youth. *Social Services Review,* pp. 457–470.

Elliot, N. (1984). *No place to run: A study of runaways in America.* Unpublished manuscript, U.S. Department of Justice, Office of Justice and Delinquency Prevention.

Elliott, N. (1984). *No Place to Turn: A Study of Runaways in America.* Paper presented for the U.S. Department of Justice, Office of Juvenile Justice and Delinquency Prevention.

English, C. J. (1973). Leaving home: A typology of runaways. *Transactions, 10,* 22–24.

Foster, R. M. (1962). Intrapsychic and environmental factors in running away from home. *American Journal of Orthopsychiatry, 32,* 486–491.

Gold, M., & Reimer, D. J. (1974, May 1). *Testimony on the Runaway Youth Act,* to the Subcommittee on Equal Opportunity of the United States House Committee on Education and Labor, May 2, 1974.

Gordon, J. S. (1979). Running away: Reaction or revolution? *Adolescent Psychiatry, 7,* 54–70.

Green, N. B., & Esselstyn, T. C. (1972). The beyond control girl. *Juvenile Justice, 23*(3), 13–19.

Grieco, E. (1984). Characteristics of a helpful relationship: A study of empathetic understanding and positive regard between runaways and their parents. *Adolescence, 73,* 74.

Hilderbrand, J. A. (1963). Why runaways leave home. *Journal of Criminal Law, Criminology, and Police Science, 54,* 211–216.

Homer, L. E. (1973). Community-based resources for runaway girls. *Social Casework, 54*(8), 473–475.

Johnson, R., & Carter, M. (1980). Flight of the young: Why children run away from their homes. *Adolescence, 58,* 486.

Jorgensen, S. R., Thornburg, H. D., & Williams, J. K. (1800). The experience of running away: Perceptions of adolescents seeking help in a shelter care facility. *High School Journal, 64*(3), 87–95.

Lambert, B. G., Rothschild, B. F., Atland, R., & Green, L. B. (1978). *Adolescence: Transition from childhood to maturity.* Monterey, CA: Brooks/Cole.

Lappin, J., & Covelman, K. W. (1985). Adolescent runaways: A structural family therapy perspective. In M. P. Mirkin & S. L. Koman (Eds.), *Handbook of adolescents and family therapy* (pp. 343–362). New York: Gardner.

Libertoff, K. (1976, September). *Runaway children and social network interaction.* Paper presented at the meeting of the American Psychological Association, Washington, DC.

Nye, F. S., & Short, F. (1957). Scaling delinquent behavior. *American Sociological Review, 22,* 326–331.

Nye, F. L. (1980). Theoretical perspective on runaways. *Journal of Family Issues, 2,* 274–299.

Olson, L., Liebow, E., Mannino, F. V., & Shore, M. F. (1980). Runaway children twelve years later: A follow-up. *Journal of Family Issues, 1*(2), 165–187.

Opinion Research Center. (1976, June). *National Statistical Survey on Runaway Youth,* Part I. Prepared for the Office of Youth Development and Office of Human Development, Department of Health, Education, and Welfare.

Orten, J. D., & Soll, S. K. (1980). Runaway children and their families: A treatment typology. *Journal of Family Issues, 1*(2), 249–261.

Ostensen, K. W. (1981). The runaway crisis: Is family therapy the answer? *American Journal of Family Therapy, 9*(3), 342.

Roberts, A. R. (1981). *Runaways and non-runaways in an American suburb: An exploratory study of adolescent and parental coping,* New York: John Jay.

Shellow, R., Schamp, J. R., Liebow, E., & Unger, E. (1967). Suburban runaways of the 1960s. *Monographs of the Society for Research in Child Development, 32*(3), University of Chicago.

Thomas, A. (1982). Runaways. In J. Grimes (Ed.), *Psychological approaches to problems of children and adolescents* (pp. 157–177). Des Moines: Iowa State Department of Public Instruction.

Tobias, J. L. (1970). The affluent suburban male delinquent. *Crime and Delinquency, 3,* 273–279.

Van Hauten, T., & Golembiewski, G. (1978). *Adolescent life stress as a predictor of alcohol abuse and/or runaway behavior.* Washington, DC: Youth Alternatives Project, 1346 Connecticut Avenue.

Walker, D. K. (1975). *Runaway youth: Annotated bibliography and literature overview.* Washington, DC: Office of Social Services and Human Development, Department of Health and Human Services.

Wolk, S., & Brandon, J. (1977). Runaway adolescents' perceptions of parents and self. *Adolescence, 12,* 175–188.

BIBLIOGRAPHY: PROFESSIONALS

Brennan, T., Huizinga, D., & Elliot, D. S. (1978). *The social psychology of runaways.* Lexington, MA: Heath.
This excellent text provides a review of social science literature, helping to explain the problems of runaway youth. The author demonstrates that runaway behavior does not occur in a psychological vacuum. The book is based on empirical data from large-scale studies conducted by these researchers for the Office of Youth Development.

Lappin, J., & Covelman, K. W. (1985). Adolescent runaways: A structural family therapy perspective. In M. P. Mirkin & S. L. Komeen (Eds.), *Handbook of adolescents and family therapy.* New York: Gardner.
An excellent text for helping professionals working in family therapy. It is current and well written, providing the reader with valuable information for use in bringing runaways and their families together.

Nye, F. I. (1980). A theoretical perspective on running away. *Journal of Family Issues, 1*(2), 274–299.
A very comprehensive overall review of current perspectives on runaways. The article offers a general explanation for running and/or expulsion from families. It will help the reader better understand the very diverse phenomenon of running away.

Ostensen, K. W. (1981). The runaway crisis: Is family therapy the answer? *American Journal of Family Therapy, 9*(3), 3–12.
Presents research on the relationship of two family counseling models, the first with temporary foster placement and the second without. The article provides data on the Brief Family Intervention counseling model. Additional descriptive data provide a profile of the teenage runaway.

Orten, J. D., & Sall, S. K. (1980). Runaway children and their families: *Journal of Family Issues, 1*(2), 249–261.
Provides the helping professional with detailed information couched in a three-tiered classification system. The authors stress two components in the assessment of runaway behavior: alienation and extent of previous running. Both components help determine the extent and direction of treatment.

Thomas, A. (1982). Runaways. In J. Grimes (Ed.), *Psychological approaches to problems of children and adolescents* (pp. 157–177). Des Moines: Iowa State Department of Public Instruction.
An excellent chapter particularly for school psychologists working with runaway youths. The author cites as examples two cases from personal experiences and one from a government publication. The entire text would be beneficial to any helping professional.

Resources

National Center for Missing and Exploited Children. 202-634-9821.
Provides assistance to parents and law-enforcement agencies in locating missing children and preventing child exploitation.

Operation: Home-Free. 214-655-7895.
Call for more information on the Trailways program.

Runaway or parents can telephone: National Runaway Switchboard, toll-free: 800-621-4000.
Provides counseling and referral services 24 hours; free and confidential.

Runaway Hotline Toll-free: 800-231-6946 (in Texas, 800-392-3352).
Provides confidential relay of messages from youths to parents without revealing locations.

Children and School Entry Decisions

Ronald E. Reeve and Ilene J. Holt
University of Virginia

BACKGROUND

> One of the first questions is at what age children should be sent to school, for they should neither be delayed too long, so that time is lost, nor hastened on too soon, at the risk of their bodies and the quickness of their wits jointly. What the age should be I cannot say, for ripeness in children does not always come at the same time.
> (Mulcaster, cited in Cole, 1950. p. 269.)

The issue of when children should begin formal schooling is neither new nor is it a uniquely American question. The writer quoted above was the 16th century English educator Richard Mulcaster. At different points in time and in different parts of the world mandatory school entry age has varied from 4 years to 8 years, providing an example in public policy of the uncertainty Mulcaster expressed. During spring and summer months parents are likely to ask psychologists who work with children for help with one decision more than any other: "Should my child start school in September?"

Readiness is a deceptively simple concept. In an educational context the term refers to the attainment of a developmental level at which one is capable of learning. Thus, "reading readiness" would be the point at which a child could learn to read. Readiness for entry into school, however, is not nearly that simple. The complexity occurs because of the multiple demands of the school. The child must be ready to learn to read, write, and count; to sit still and follow directions; to interact appropriately with peers; to dress, feed, and toilet; and so forth. The situation is further complicated by the considerable range among kindergartens/first grades in respect to expectancies. Some school personnel expect children to come in the door and begin academic work; others see the first year of school as a time primarily for social development, with little or none of the three R's.

Whether or not a child is ready for the multiple requirements imposed by school often is a moot point, in practice. While the notion that a child should enter the formal education system when and only when "ready" is appealing, the reality is that the criterion for entrance into school typically is chronological age, with admission only allowed once per year, in September. The simple criterion of chronological age is administratively convenient. Under this procedure, schools take all children whose birthdates fall within a specified 12-month period, ready or not. Supposedly, the school program then adapts to the developmental readiness of the children rather than requiring the children to be prepared to handle task demands of a rigidly circumscribed program.

What is the optimal age for school entry? A surprising lack of consensus is found on this point. This is illustrated by the range of five calendar months among entrance age requirements of various states. As shown in Table 1, the 42 states that set a specific cut-off date use 14 different dates.

Kindergarten teachers appear to believe that children should be at least 5 years old before entering school (e.g., Peterson & Ayabe, 1982), and that an even higher entry age would be better.

TABLE 1

Kindergarten Eligibility: Age Criterion/Cutoff Dates in the United States

Age	State
Local discretion	CO, IN, KS, MA, MT, NH, VT
5 by Aug. 1	CA, NJ
5 by Aug. 31	NC, WA
5 by Sept. 1	AZ, FL, GA, MN, NM, OK, SD, TX, UT, WV
5 by Sept. 15	IA, WY
5 by Sept. 30	MO, NH, OH, TN, VA
5 by Oct. 1	AL, AR, KY
5 by Oct. 15	ID, MD, NE
5 by Oct. 16	NC
5 by Nov. 1	SC
5 by Nov. 2	AK
5 by Nov. 15	PA
5 by Dec. 1	IL, MI, NY, WI
5 by Dec. 31	HI, ME, MD, RI
5 by Jan. 1	CT, DE, OR

From The Status of Kindergarten: A Survey of the States by M. Whaley, 1985, Springfield, IL: Illinois State Board of Educatoin: Copyright 1985 by the Illinois State Board of Education.

DEVELOPMENT

Normal human development occurs in fits and starts, spurts and plateaus, across skill areas. "Problems" may disappear over time, or they may arise. The correlation between children's developmental status in the first 2 years of life and later school performance is suprisingly low, except in the case of severely disabled children (Rubin & Balow, 1979). Knowing that a child began to talk or walk at a certain age is of virtually no use in predicting eventual school success. While predictions are better for the 3- to 5-year-olds, one must exercise caution in interpreting poor performance by a child on a developmental measure at any time during the preschool years. Part of the inadequacy of predictive validity of assessments at this age is due to limitations of the measurement methodology available for young children and to the fact that young children's behavior varies considerably depending on situational demands. However, the major problem in prediction from early to later childhood results from the considerable irregularities across skill areas inherent in normal child development.

PUTTING SCHOOL ENTRY DECISIONS INTO PERSPECTIVE

Does chronological age at the time of school entry make a difference in likelihood of success in school? What other factors are important? The following is a very brief summary provided by a review of the literature on key variables often considered to relate to success in school.

Chronological Age. Most states use chronological age of the child to establish when a child may and/or must enter school. A "magic" date thus is set by the state, and all children who achieve a certain age by that date are expected to enter school. Given the existence of this date, plus the fact that children are admitted only in the fall of the year, practically guarantees that students in a given grade will vary in age by at least 11 months and 30 days. At kindergarten entry, the relatively older students may have lived 20% longer; a year is a large increment at this age, both in terms of physiological maturity and opportunities for learning.

Not surprisingly, when comparing old and young ends of a kindergarten class, the older students generally do better on achievement tests at the conclusion of their first year in school. As Gredler (1980) has pointed out, one cannot say that the relatively older children learned more than the younger ones, and that they therefore were more "ready" for school, by looking at achievement scores at only one point in time. Probably the older children knew more at the beginning of school, too. Thus rate of gain is the relevant variable; how much was learned by the child since entering school should be the criterion for evaluating readiness.

The achievement gap between older and younger students in the same class typically attenuates throughout elementary school and disappears by teenage years (e.g., Davis, Trimble, & Vincent, 1980; Kalk, Langer, & Searles, 1981; Miller & Norris, 1967). Along the way, however, a disproportionate number of relatively younger students are retained at least 1 year and/or are referred for special education services (Donofrio, 1977), perhaps explaining why the differences in achievement tend not to be seen in later grades.

Chronological age per se, however, does not seem to be the critical element. Rather, it is age relative to peers in the same class that is important. Gray (1985) cites three studies conducted in states that use school entry cutoff dates varying from September 1 to December 1. The "problem" groups in each case were the youngest one-quarter of the population, though in some cases these were children with fall birthdates and in others children born in the late spring and summer were seen to be the ones "at risk." Apparently, teachers set standards for achievement and behavior normed to the group of children actually present in their classes. Regardless of the entry date set, the relatively youngest group will be more likely to include children who do not meet school personnel's expectations. Requiring children to be older by raising the minimum school entry age will not solve the problem — a relatively younger group will always be present.

Sex. Generally speaking, girls function better than boys of the same chronological age on school readiness tests and on later academic achievement, at least through the elementary school years (Beattie, 1970). In fact, the achievement differences found between younger and older children in the same grade often were present only for boys in the groups studied (Gredler, 1980).

Socioeconomic status. A strong relationship has been reported between socioeconomic status (SES) and academic success. For example, Gredler (1978) noted that SES was a much more powerful predictor of success in first grade than was relative chronological age.

Intelligence. Intelligence long has been considered the most powerful single predictor of academic success. Research results concur with this view. Beattie (1970), for example, in a study of 84 school districts, found significant relationships between intelligence and achievement in first grade in all districts studied.

Race. Blacks, as a group, tend to do less well than whites of the same age on readiness measures and on later school achievement tests. Blacks also are retained more frequently at each grade level (Langer, Kalk, & Searles, 1984). Within racial groups, comparing relatively younger and older youngsters in the same grade, a similar pattern emerges regardless of race. The oldest students do significantly better at least through age 13; then differences in achievement between younger and older students within the same grade become negligible (Langer et al., 1984)

Preschool Experience. Studies comparing children with and without experience in preschool yield mixed results. Generally, children who have attended preschool do better in subsequent years in both academic and social areas (Busch-Rossnagel & Vance, 1982). Some indications are present, however, that preschool does not have as great a benefit for middle and upper SES as for lower SES children (McKinnon, Flieger, & Patterson, 1982). Thus, the favorable results reported for those with preschool experience may be artifacts of the socioeconomic status of the subjects.

Conclusions From the Literature. Chronological age, not readiness, is the typical criterion for school entry because of its administrative convenience. Fourteen different cutoff dates for initial school entry presently are in effect in this country, spanning a range of 5 months. In addition, several states leave entry age decisions up to local education agencies, further increasing the variability in age of initial school entry. Children as young as 4 years and 8 months may enter kindergarten in four states, whereas they must be at least 5 years old in almost one-third of the other states. Despite many educators' beliefs that children should reach a certain age before beginning school, no compelling evidence supports the view that any particular age is the best age at which to start. Research studies repeatedly have indicated that the relatively younger children in a kindergarten or elementary school class do less well academically and socially than their relatively older classmates and are referred more frequently for special education services.

These differences typically are not found in later grades, though perhaps this is because of attrition of the lower-functioning younger students. However, it is important to note that, even among the youngest children in the youngest entering groups, the majority perform adequately in school from the start.

Two groups of students are at a relative disadvantage compared to their peers who enter at the same chronological age. Boys and blacks who are relatively young for their grade are at risk for retention, referral to special education services, and eventual dropout from school (Langer, Kalk, & Searles, 1984). Because relatively poor functioning compared to peers may lead to lowered self-esteem and hence, in a downwardly spiraling manner, to devaluing of school and to a subsequent lack of effort, special attention to young-for-grade males and blacks appears warranted.

ALTERNATIVE ACTIONS

1. Raising the minimum age for school entry is currently a popular "solution" to the problem of having a high proportion of children arriving in school unprepared for the demands of the academic program. While this approach may help ease the teachers' burden slightly, several problems will remain if that action is taken. One is that lower SES children will be less likely than their peers to spend their extra, "red-shirt" year of preschool time in good learning situations, and the result will be that the gap between themselves and more

advantaged children will widen. Also, handicapped children may not come to the attention of school personnel as quickly. Furthermore, there always will be at least a 12-month spread among children in an entering class, and the younger children as a group always will be substantially less "ready." Thus, changing the entry age is, at best, a partial answer.

2. Many school systems are admitting all age-eligible children to school, then retaining those who have difficulty in their first year. One popular model is a "transition" or "K-1" classroom. Children spend three years to complete the first two grades. This approach resolves many difficulties present in the first alternative. If retention is to occur, it is preferable for it to happen as early as possible in a child's school career (Germain & Merlo, 1985). However, if the retention is viewed as a "failure" by the child, there is danger of negative emotional reactions including damage to the child's self-concept. Also, the K-1 classes often consist primarily of low-functioning students who therefore are poor models for one another, and the curriculum sometimes involves simply a repeat of material covered the previous year. When this alternative is utilized, care should be taken to avoid these pitfalls.

A variant of this approach is the "junior kindergarten." Children who are relatively young compared to their kindergarten peers or are seen as being at risk for kindergarten failure are placed in a prekindergarten program with the intent of having them move to regular kindergarten the following year, then to first grade. Thus 3 years again are given to complete kindergarten and first grade; but the connotation of failure is removed, and the curriculum tends to be more developmentally appropriate.

3. More recently a number of schools have moved toward early screening programs, sometimes for children as young as 3 years old (Lichtenstein & Ireton, 1984). This has the obvious advantage, under the mandates of PL 94-142, of allowing for early identification of handicapped children. Furthermore, children with visual, auditory, or other physical problems can have these evaluated and corrected when possible. Such early contact with children also can be used to find candidates who could benefit from preschool education programs. Included would be children who are not able, for financial or other reasons, to participate in privately or other publicly funded programs, as well as those who are technically old enough to attend kindergarten but who are judged to be at risk for failure. In some localities public schools have cooperated with Head Start and other agencies to jointly sponsor these programs. Of course, intervening with children who are not yet legally old enough for school is expensive. However, compared to other alternatives, this approach appears to offer the best chance to head off later school failure with virtually none of the potentially aversive features of other approaches. If a child is likely to have to repeat a grade later unless this option is adopted, the net costs are similar. It can be argued, too, that such approaches will keep some children out of the even more expensive special education system, further increasing the cost effectiveness of the program.

4. The preceding "alternatives" are systems-level approaches. Often the situation is much more focused and individualized: Given the legal entry date and the nature of the school program in existence in a particular school system, should Billy/Susie begin school now or wait a year? In such specific cases the best approach is to obtain as clear a picture as possible of Susie'/Billy's level of functioning in several skill areas (intelligence, receptive and expressive language, perceptual processing, gross- and fine-motor functioning, and social–emotional skills). If the child is well below average, say by a standard deviation or more compared to the average child entering school in one or more areas, delaying entry should be considered. Other "risk factors" that should enter into the decision are (a) history of significant medical problems, such as serious recurrent ear infections; (b) a family history of major learning problems; (c) being male and/or black; and (d) being young relative to peers entering this particular school. Any decision to delay entry must be made on the basis of the knowledge that quality preschool programming or its equivalent will be available during the year prior to entering school. Just sitting around waiting to mature is unlikely to be productive for Billy/Susie; if that is the only option, it almost always is better to begin school.

Screening Programs

These are certain common features to programs that are committed to early identification. First, a preschool screening program needs to be integrated within an overall service network. Consequently, the most effective screening programs are the results of cooperation among various personnel within a school system, collaboration among agencies, and involvement of parents. Specific goals, careful planning, and commitment by professionals involved are also necessary for a successful screening program. Three sample screening programs described by Lichtenstein and Ireton (1984, pp.34–41) illustrate these themes.

Three Models. The children in Bloomington, MN (primarily white children from well-educated and financially secure families) are screened at two age levels: 3–4 years and 4½–5½ years old. The program is coordinated by a licensed school nurse, the actual screening being done at neighborhood schools. Three possible outcomes may result from the screening: (a) No physical problems or developmental delays are apparent and the child passes screening; (b) screening results are incomplete or questionable and rescreening is indicated; (c) screening results suggest possible problems/delays and further assessment is recommended. Therefore, valuable information is obtained that can be used to decide about early or delayed entrance to school.

The children in Madison, WI, (primarily white children from middle-income, white collar families) may participate in two screening programs: (a) for preschool children "who may be suspected of having a disability or handicapping condition"; and (b) a kindergarten screening program. The coordinator is a social worker. Preschool screening is done throughout the year; kindergarten screening is done annually. If the child's performance on screening instruments suggests problems, she or he is referred to a multidisciplinary team for further evaluation.

For the children in Holyoke, MA (primarily minority children from low-income families), screening takes place at the request of parents of 3- to 5-year-olds. A major part of this program involves cooperation among several agencies. Parental involvement is emphasized in kindergarten screening. Children identified may then be placed in one of several programs (special needs, non-special needs, or a Head Start program).

The programs just described illustrate how school systems and other agencies may vary in approach to screening and providing services. They differ with respect to age ranges, population, and the types of services they provide. However, the main goals and objectives are similar across programs.

How to Design a Screening Program. Designing and implementing a screening program can be a major undertaking. An effective preschool screening program requires careful thought and planning. However, there are steps to pursue (Lichtenstein & Ireton, 1984, pp.42–44) to assist in implementing a preschool screening program. Following such guidelines can reduce the amount of frustration and needless energy spent on this task.

Step 1: Select a coordinator. At a minimum, this person should possess considerable knowledge about young children and their parents as well as the ability to function effectively within a larger system.

Step 2: Establish a planning group, a multidisciplinary team composed of members with specialized areas of expertise. Ideally, this team as a unit should have knowledge of (a) the community, community resources, and the public communication network; (b) administrative operations within the school system or agency; (c) young children, child development, and developmental problems; (d) early childhood education and special education; (e) psychological and educational measurement and evaluation; and (f) communication with parents.

Step 3: Clarify general goals. Of particular importance at this stage is specifying the purposes of screening and the population to be served.

Step 4: Plan the specific elements of the screening process. The "nuts and bolts" of the program evolve at this level. Communication with parents and professionals, coordination with other agencies, logistics, content, and personnel training are among the matters to deal with.

Step 5: The screening itself takes place at this phase. This requires collecting data, making screening decisions, reporting results, and follow-up.

Step 6: Evaluate the program and procedure. This step is critical, though easy to overlook. Critiqueing the screening program yields valuable information regarding the rate of success of the procedure.

Readiness Tests

Many tests are available to help school personnel decide if a child is ready to begin school. No single test can be recommended without answers to at least the following questions: Are the results to be used to exclude some children from school entry at this time, or to help teachers know what to concentrate on in planning an instructional program? What are the expectations for children in this school's program? Is there a heavy academic emphasis for everyone, or is the program designed primarily to provide opportunities for social, physical, and preacademic skill development?

Readiness tests all suffer from problems inherent in assessing children this age. The marked fluctuations in attention and mood from hour to hour, the lack of experience with the assessment situation, and the spurts and plateaus of development typical of young children combine to compromise the reliability and validity of test results. No completely satisfactory solution to this problem exists. The best that can be done is to use multiple measures of important skills and to gather information from as many different sources, such as parents and preschool teachers, as possible. In ideal situations, gathering information at several different times also would help improve the accuracy of the results.

How to Select Readiness Tests. Selecting instruments to use with preschool children is a challenge. Because readiness tests are regularly used to make important educational decisions about individual children, it is important that these tests meet high technical standards, but there is a relatively narrow array of such test instruments on the market.

To begin identifying instruments that fit the service program, consulting sources that provide information on special tests and measures should be helpful; the following references are suggested as starting points in this process: Goodwin and Driscoll (1980), Lichtenstein and Ireton (1984), Mitchell (1985), Salvia and Ysseldyke (1985), and Southworth, Burr, and Cox (1981).

Readiness tests can be viewed from one of two orientations (Salvia & Ysseldyke, 1985). A *skills* orientation espouses that readiness involves basic skills development; that is, academic and social readiness is viewed as mastery of directly school-related skills. For example, assessing ability to hold a pencil or to count or to name letters would implement the skills orientation. The second perspective is a *process* orientation. From this point of view, readiness tests are viewed as to underlying processes (e.g., intelligence) that are believed to be necessary for acquisition of skills and knowledge.

Historically, readiness assessment has dealt with academic-process testing. These tests tend to be norm-referenced and the abilities generally tested are those thought to underlie all, or at least most, academic skills. Consequently, tests with a strong cognitive component are often included in readiness testing. Perceptual–motor ability and language development are also thought to underlie school achievement and thus often are included on tests of readiness.

SUMMARY

Deciding whether a child is ready to begin school is not as simple a process as it might appear to be.The decision must involve consideration of the legal, sociological,and educational context, the measurement issues, and then the characteristics of the specific child in question.

The chronological age at which a child is expected to enter school is determined by state or local mandate. With very few exceptions, entry is offered only in September, guaranteeing that children varying in age by at least 12 months will be present in each class. Generally, relatively older children perform better on end-of-year tests, as would be expected, since as a group they enter school knowing more. Among children of the same relative chronological age, girls, upper SES children, whites, more highly intelligent children, children with preschool experience, and children without significant medical histories do better academically, at least in the early years of school. However, most children do quite well in school, regardless of age at entry.

No convincing evidence supports raising the overall school entrance age for children. To the contrary, handicapped children, children with undetected sensory problems, and other children in need of cognitively stimulating experiences likely will go without service for an additional year when that approach is taken. Part of the difficulty can be ameliorated by instituting a quality preschool screening program, including evaluation of multiple skills by several raters over several periods of time, if possible.

When the question gets down to the level of the individual child, an individual assessment usually is called for. Skills levels in intellectual, language, motor, perceptual, and social-emotional functioning should be considered along with medical status and information about the expectations of the specific school program being considered. Such factors as age relative to peers in the class, sex, and so forth may become relevant issues if concerns arise from other parts of the evaluation. In every case, delaying school entry should be considered only if a quality preschool experience is available as the option to school entry.

REFERENCES

Beattie, C. (1970). *Entrance age to kindergarten and first grade: Its effect on cognitive and affective development of students.* Urbana, Illinois. (ERIC Document Reproduction Service No. ED 133 050)

Busch-Rossnagel, N. A., & Vance, A. K. (1982). The impact of the schools on social and emotional development. In B. Wolman (Ed.), *Handbook of developmental psychology* (pp. 452–470). Englewood Cliffs, NJ: Prentice-Hall.

Cole, L. (1950). *A history of education: Socrates to Montessori.* New York: Rinehart.

Davis, B. G., Trimble, C. S., & Vincent, D. R. (1980). Does age of entrance affect school achievement? *Elementary School Journal, 80*(3), 133–143.

Donofrio, A. F. (1977). Grade repetition: Therapy of choice. *Journal of Learning Disabilities, 10,* 349–351.

Germain, R., & Merlo, M. (1985). Best practices in promotion and retention decisions. In A. Thomas & J. Grimes (Eds.), *Best practices in school psychology* (pp.171–180). Kent, OH: National Association of School Psychologists.

Goodwin, W. L., & Driscoll, L. A. (1980).Handbook for measurement and evaluation in early childhood education. San Francisco: Jossey-Bass.

Gray, R. (1985). *Criteria to determine entry into school: A review of the research.* Springfield, IL: Illinois State Board of Education. (ERIC Document Reproduction Service No. ED 260 826)

Gredler, G. R. (1978). A look at some important factors in assessing readiness for school. *Journal of Learning Disabilities, 11*(5), 284–290.

Gredler, G. R. (1980). The birthdate effect: Fact or artifact? *Journal of Learning Disabilities, 13*(5), 239–242.

Johnson, O. G. (1976). *Tests and measurements in child development: Handbook II.* San Francisco: Jossey-Bass.

Kalk, J. M., Langer, P., & Searles, D. (1981, December). Trends in achievement as a function of age of admission (Report No. AY-AA-51). Denver: National Assessment of Educational Progress, Education Commission of the States.

Langer, P., Kalk, J. M., & Searles, D. T. (1984). Age of admission and trends in achievement: A comparison of blacks and caucasians. *American Educational Research Journal, 21,* 61–78.

Lazar, I., & Darlington, R. (1982). Lasting effects of early education: A report from the constorium for longitudinal studies. *Monograph of the Society for Research in Child Development, 47* (2-2, Serial No. 195).

Lichtenstein, R., & Ireton, H. (1984). *Preschool screening: Identifying young children with developmental and educational problems.* Orlando, FL: Grune & Stratton.

McKinnon, J., Flieger, S., & Patterson, M. (1982). *A comparative study of the effects of preschool education on middle class children.* Puce, Ontario: Lakeside Montessori School. (ERIC Document Reproduction Service No. ED 221 179)

Miller, W., & Norris, R. C. (1967). Entrance age and school success. *Journal of School Psychology, 6,* 47–60.

Mitchell, J. V. (Ed.). (1985). *The ninth mental measurements yearbook.* Lincoln, NE: University of Nebraska Press.

Peterson, S., & Ayabe, C. (1982). *Kindergarten age requirements.* Mesa, AZ: Mesa Public Schools (Mesa Public Schools Research and Evaluation Technical News).

Rubin, R. N., & Balow, B. (1979). Measures of infant development and socioeconomic status as predictors of later intelligence and school achievement. *Development Psychology, 15,* 225–227.

Salvia, J., & Ysseldyke, J. (1985). *Assessment in special and remedial education* (3rd ed.). Boston: Houghton Mifflin.

Southworth, L. E., Burr, R. L., & Cox, A. E. (1981). *Screening and evaluating the young child: A handbook of instruments to use from infancy to six years.* Springfield, IL: Thomas.

Whaley, M. (1985). *The status of kindergarten: A survey of the states.* Springfield, IL: Illinois State Board of Education. (ERIC Document Reproduction Service No. ED 260 835)

BIBLIOGRAPHY: PROFESSIONALS

Boehm, A. E., & Sandberg, B. R. (1982). Assessment of the preschool child. In C. R. Reynolds & T. B. Gutkin (Eds.), *The handbook of school psychology* (pp.82–120). New York: Wiley.
Presents a context for early assessment, and then deals with six types of instruments: cognitive, language and communication, motor, perceptual, preschool performance profiles, and social and emotional. For each, specific tests are described, along with lists of other references for more detailed information.

Gray, R. (1985). *Criteria to determine entry into school: A review of the research.* Springfield, IL: Illinois State Board of Education. (ERIC Document Reproduction Service No. 260 826)
An excellent, concise review is provided of the literature on school entry variables and their relationship to later school success. Included is a summary of kindergarten entry eligibility dates in the United States.

Lichtenstein, R., & Ireton, H. (1984). *Preschool screening: Identifying children with developmental and educational problems.* Orlando, FL: Grune & Stratton.
An extraordinarily valuable reference for anyone who wishes to implement or improve a screening program. Comprehensively covered are conceptual issues, selecting instruments, involving parents, and making and implementing decisions. Detailed descriptions are included of selected instruments and of "model" screening programs.

Nagle, R. J. & Paget, K. D. (Eds.). (1986). Mini-series on preschool assessment [Special section of issue]. *School Psychology Review, 15*(2).
Six articles make up this mini-series. Following a thoughtful overview and conceptual model presentation are solid articles on assessment of cognitive, social–emotional, and neuropsychological functioning, along with two pieces on topics not well dealt with elsewhere in the preschool literature —curriculum-based assessment and family assessment.

BIBLIOGRAPHY: PARENTS

Frith, T. (1985). *Secrets parents should know about public schools.* New York: Simon and Schuster.
An educator–parent gives direct, practical, inside information about how to make schools work for your individual child. Advice covers initial enrollment options, parent–teacher conferencing, conflict with teachers, and ways to gain and use influence in the social and political environment of the school.

Larrick, N. (1982). *A parent's guide to children's reading* (5th ed.). Philadelphia: Westminister.
A plea to parents to develop love of reading in their children, this book includes sections on the development of prereading skills, on getting access to good books, and on resources for choosing quality books and magazines to aid children's learning.

Patterson, G. R. (1975). *Families: Applications of social learning to family life* (rev.ed.), Champaign, IL: Research Press.
Presents the basics of social learning theory, utilizing a programmed instruction format. In clear language, in the context of common as well as more complicated behavior management problems, the author shows exactly how behavioral technology can be useful to teach children appropriate behavior in the family environment.

Rice, M. F., & Flatter, C. H. (1979). *Help me learn: A handbook for teaching children from birth to third grade.* Englewood Cliffs, NJ: Prentice-Hall.
Designed primarily for parents, this book also is an excellent resource for teachers and "all friends of children." Numerous short insightful sections on topics ranging from preparing for travel to divorce to creative writing are followed by well-selected reference lists, including books appropriate for children on most subjects.

Children and Seizures

Timothy B. Whelan and John F. Todd
University of Texas at Austin

BACKGROUND

Seizures are defined as intermittent disruptions of the nervous system due to the sudden, excessive, disorderly discharge of cerebral neurons (Adams & Victor, 1981). *Epilepsy* simply means subject to recurrent seizures. Given that seizures are the second most common neurological disorder in the United States, affecting 1–4% of the general population (Wright, 1975), and that three-quarters of those with epilepsy will manifest seizures by the end of adolescence (Epilepsy Foundation of America, 1978), the significance of these conditions for the school psychologist cannot be overstated.

Seizure Types and Etiology

The common causes of seizures in children of various ages reflect the differential incidence of various neurological diseases and disorders across the age span. The onset of seizures during infancy will probably be due to conditions such as maternal infection, congenital brain maldevelopment, birth injury, metabolic disorders, vitamin deficiency, or phenylketonuria. From ages 2 through 10, common causes include perinatal anoxia, injury, infections, blockage of blood supply to the brain, and indeterminate causes (idiopathic epilepsy). Onset of seizures in later childhood through midadolescence is most often due to congenital defects, trauma, or unknown causes. Frequent causes of seizures among young adults include trauma, tumor, and withdrawal from alcohol or sedative–hypnotic drugs. Meningitis may be a cause of seizures at any age (Adams & Victor, 1981).

Seizures are now classified according to the degree to which abnormal neuronal discharge is contained within a given brain region. Seizure activity that remains relatively localized is classified as partial; activity spreading throughout the cortex, subcortex, and/or brainstem is classified as generalized. It should be remembered that the same person can have more than one type of symptom or seizure.

Generalized tonic–clonic (or grand mal) seizures are common at all ages. They are often associated with alterations in consciousness before the obvious seizure manifestations: a "prodrome" with no detectable brain electrical abnormalities but alterations in mood, and/or an "aura" reflecting early electrical changes and resulting in slight movements or unnatural sensations. These are followed by an immediate loss of consciousness in the *tonic* phase of general muscular contraction, a *clonic* phase of synchronous muscle jerking, and a *terminal* phase involving fatigue, confusion, and disorientation.

Absence (petit mal) seizures may be the classic example of seizures not involving major motor convulsions. This form of generalized seizure is most common among 6- to 14-year-old children and results in behavioral changes, such as losing awareness, slight twitching, staring, and blinking, that last only a few seconds. These subtle alterations may be mistaken for daydreaming or inattentiveness.

Partial seizures may occur at any age. In some cases, consciousness is not lost, but "elementary" sensory (somatic sensory, visual, auditory, olfactory, vertiginous) or motor symptoms are present. "Complex" partial (temporal lobe) seizures may be accompanied by altered consciousness or confusion, repetitive motor action (e.t., buttoning and unbuttoning clothes, pacing, hand rubbing), or sensory and affective symptoms.

Diagnosis of Seizures

The accurate diagnosis and classification of seizures is the province of the neurologist. A family history is taken that is designed to inquire about epilepsy in the family, to accurately assess the nature of seizure manifestations, to gain a complete history of illnesses and injuries, and to determine if the behavioral signs and symptoms are indeed reflections of seizure activity. A physical examination including blood, urine, and other laboratory tests is intended to evaluate physiological abnormalities that are related to central nervous system malfunction.

It is important to gain diagnostic information by assessing the status of the central nervous system itself. The electroencephalogram (EEG), a measure of brain electrical activity, is employed in virtually all cases of suspected seizures. In this painless, noninvasive technique, brain electrical rhythms that are detected through electrodes placed on the scalp are amplified and displayed on paper or, more recently, condensed by statistical analyses or transformed to computer-enhanced images. While ordinary EEG recordings are made during a relaxed state with eyes closed, others are conducted under conditions designed to enhance the probability of detecting abnormal neuronal activity: hyperventilation, sleep, and strobe light stimulation. EEG tracings can be made during normal activity or over a prolonged period by having a patient wear portable headgear with electrodes in place that transmit to a recording device. On rare occasions, electrodes are surgically implanted deep into the brain tissue to detect abnormalities that don't register on surface recordings. Neuroradiological techniques such as CAT scans, magnetic resonance imaging, and cerebral angiograms may be employed to assess the brain anatomy and underlying structural integrity. A detailed appreciation of the neurological events related to less common seizure types, etiology, and diagnosis can be gained from neurology texts (Adams & Victor, 1981; Strub & Black, 1981) and attached references.

DEVELOPMENT

Biological Development

One of the major questions posed by those involved with epileptic children is how long can it be expected that the seizures will persist and require treatment; in other words, will they outgrow the seizures, or will they always need to contend with them in some way? In some cases, seizures may indeed cease if there is a known and treatable cause such as metabolic disorder or brain infection. Seizures that are coincident with high fever affect approximately 3% of infants and young children, and they typically do not progress to epilepsy in later years. Idiopathic seizures tend to diminish in frequency. Similarly, absence seizures may disappear in approximately 50% of affected children by age 20, though many times other forms of epilepsy take their place (Happe, 1985). Less common forms of generalized seizures that begin in infancy may evolve into tonic–clonic or absence varieties by middle childhood (Adams & Victor, 1981).

Psychological Development

Intellectual Functioning. Because seizures reflect brain dysfunction, there is a natural suspicion that they are accompanied by intellectual deficit. Only in the grossest sense is this true. For instance, Corbett and Harris (1974) reported that fully 32% of a sample of children with IQs less than 50 had a history of seizures. In a review of studies of epileptic children and adults, Hartlage and Telzrow (1984) reported a mean IQ of 87 across studies. However, as pointed out by Corbett and Trimble (1983), early studies of the correlation between seizures and intelligence typically evaluated selective samples and failed to distinguish between those with structural brain disorders and those with "uncomplicated" epilepsy. Mean IQs for those without other detectable signs of nervous system damage have often been reported in the average range (Rodin, 1968; Rutter, Tizard, & Whitmore, 1970). Lennox and Lennox (1960), Tarter (1972), and Corbett, Harris and Robinson (1975) review this literature.

In addition to the etiological concerns mentioned above, there is evidence that an earlier onset age, a longer duration (length of seizure episode and years of epilepsy), a more generalized classification (especially tonic–clonic), and more frequent seizures may all contribute to a greater probability of intellectual impairment, though the evidence is weak or inconsistent (Dodrill, 1981). Dodrill and Clemmons (1984) administered the WAIS, neuropsychological tests, and the Minnesota Multiphasic Personality Inventory (MMPI) to high school students with epilepsy and predicted employment and degree of independent living status 6 years later. Seizure-related and personality variables were not related to outcome measures, but a test of language ability and the Halstead Impairment Index (a summary measure indicative of level rather than pattern of performance) were positively correlated with overall adjustment in adulthood. In a study of medical variables related to early brain injury and their relation to intelligence in children affected by brain insults, Dennis (1985) reported that some seizure types were predictive of lower IQ, but others were predictive of higher IQ. Moreover, later-onset afebrile seizures were found to influence IQ, but early seizures were not. She concluded that a single–variable brain basis for any aspect of psychometric intelligence was unlikely, and that even the most powerful predictive set of neurological variables could account for only 25% of the variance in the intelligence test scores of children with early brain injury. Application to the single case is therefore inappropriate.

Nevertheless, it remains a goal to prevent the emergence and to limit the frequency and severity of seizures because of the potentially deleterious effects of seizures on cognition. In a follow-up study of 64 epileptic children and adolescents, Rodin, Schmaltz, and Twitty (1986) reported that gains of at least 10 IQ points were found only in those whose seizures had remitted, whereas losses were found mainly among those with unremitted seizures.

What is more important is that intellectual development and test performance are not totally contingent upon brain variables. Fearful and alienating reactions of other people to the condition of epilepsy, disruptions in developmental sequences, barriers to acquisition of self-control, and mediated learning difficulties may all impact negatively on cognitive development (Mearig, 1985).

Learning Disabilities. In comparison with global level of intelligence, the *pattern* of abilities of children with seizures may be of potentially greater significance regarding psychoeducational diagnosis and intervention. For instance, in Rutter, Graham, and Yule's (1970) Isle of Wight study, 18% of children with uncomplicated epilepsy were reading-disabled versus 6% of the general population. Sixteen percent of Holdsworth and Whitmore's (1974) sample of epileptic children in ordinary schools were experiencing educational difficulties, and half had consequently been referred to school psychologists. The incidence of learning problems among epileptic children was reported to be as high as 80% by Rangaswami (1980). Others have also noted a high incidence of reading and arithmetic disabilities (Bagley, 1971; Long & Moore, 1979).

Psychoeducational disabilities associated with academic achievement are generally more common among seizure-disordered groups of children, whether the area of concern is memory (Fedio & Mirsky, 1969), attention (Stores, Hart, & Peran, 1978; Fedio & Mirsky, 1969), language disorder (Cooper & Ferry, 1978), tactile perceptual abilities (Bolter, Berg, Ch'ien, Williams, Lancaster, & Cummins, 1982), or perceptual–motor skills (Morgan & Groh, 1980).

In a study noteworthy for its design, Hawkins, Hubler, and Geis (1986) studied 20 epileptic children and their seizure-free siblings by using neuropsychological and personality measures. The epileptic children were more impaired on 17 of the 20 measures relative to seizure-free siblings, whose mean scores were within normal limits on all measures. Relative to the normative population, those with seizures scored in the impaired range on measures of Verbal and Full Scale IQ, math, general information, and total achievement. Rather than displaying localized deficits on the Halstead-Reitan Battery, impairment was of a global, cognitive–integrative nature.

Affective Development. There has probably always been concern about the relationship between seizures and emotion, and it is even reflected in our linguistic tradition by the phrase "a fit of rage." Indeed, there is a very large literature on changes in emotion and personality in adults with epilepsy (Pritchard, 1983; Hermann & Whitman, 1984). The literature on the affective development of epileptic children is less substantial but still noteworthy. The best prevalence estimates are those from epidemiological studies, which indicate that 2–29% of school children with epilepsy have behavioral or emotional disorders (Rutter, Graham, & Yule, 1970; Mellor, Lowit, & Hall, 1971). In a recent study of children with tonic and/or clonic seizures using the Personality Inventory for Children (PIC), Berg, Bolter, Ch'ien, and Cummings (1984) noted that while there was no sample mean greater than 70 on any PIC scale, one-third of the subjects had two or more scale scores above that level.

Christ (1978) suggested that neurologically impaired children in psychotherapy view themselves as different, weird, or defective at least from the time peer comparisons are made in grade school or preschool. In addition, our discussions with adults in epilepsy support groups indicate that the potential exists for depression, anxiety, excessive shyness, exaggerated self-consciousness, and lifelong feelings of failure and inadequacy to develop early in childhood and to be maintained.

Parental ratings of their children with seizures have revealed deficits in self-concept and social competence. In addition, while a group of 12- to 16-year-old girls did report impaired self-esteem, they apparently did not display overt behavior problems to the same degree as boys or younger girls. Increases in "internalizing" and "externalizing" behavior problems were revealed on the Child Behavior Checklist (Hawkins et al., 1986).

While attempts have been made to ascribe specific thought and affect disorders to specific locations of epileptic activity in adults (Flor-Henry, 1976; Bear & Fedio, 1977; in opposition, see Dodrill, 1981), Rutter's (1977) review indicated that the forms of psychiatric disorder seen among epileptic children are similar to those seen in the general school-aged population. While the literature on the consequences of seizures in adults is of potential heuristic value, any simple extrapolation to brain dynamics in children is unwarranted. Thus, a clear understanding of the psychological functioning of epileptic children requires integration of data from biological and psychosocial domains.

PUTTING SEIZURES IN PERSPECTIVE

Biological Treatment

Actions to be Taken During a Seizure. Once a seizure begins, a few simple actions may be taken to minimize difficulties. First, the child should be eased to the ground and the surrounding area cleared of objects that may be injurious if struck. If not in a clearly dangerous area, the child does not need to be moved. Clothing should be loosened and glasses removed, and then the head should be gently turned to the side to allow fluid to drain safely. *Never* try to force the mouth open; victims of seizures will not swallow their tongue and normal breathing will return. Let the seizure run its course, and then provide calm reassurance during reorientation, allowing time for rest or sleep if it is desired. Ordinarily, it is not necessary to call a doctor, but if the child seems to have one attack after another without regaining consciousness, or if the seizure lasts longer than 10 minutes, emergency medical personnel and an ambulance should be called (Epilepsy Foundation of America, 1978).

Medication. Anticonvulsant drugs constitute the major form of treatment for seizures; approximately 50% of medicated children become seizure-free (not "cured"), and another 25–35% have significant decreases in seizure frequency or severity (Happe, 1985). Six anticonvulsant drugs account for the majority of the medical management of seizures: carbamazepine, phenytoin, phenobarbital, primidone, valproic acid, and ethosuximide. Many others are used occasionally, and drug combinations are common. Table 1 lists generic and trade names of major drugs, mechanisms of physiological action, the types of seizures effectively treated by each drug, and major side effects. Readers are referred to Browne and Feldman (1983) for more information.

Phenobarbital may result in subtle disturbances of cognitive functioning and may, in turn, cause a decline of school performance. A significant negative correlation between IQ and phenobarbital level has been reported, even though there were no clinical signs of toxicity in the subjects (Rodin et al., 1986). Consequently, serial psychological assessments indicating a decline in performance may provide valuable clues for drug management. Subtle affective changes marked by depression and a lack of interest or ambition are also occasionally present (Mattson, 1983). The other anticonvulsants also have side effects that may affect school performance. For example, valproic acid may result in hand tremor that can be severe enough to interfere with handwriting and drawing.

It should be noted that the severity of side effects typically decreases the longer an individual has received a drug. In addition, the breakthrough of seizures after a period of good medication control is probably not indicative of a worsening in seizures per se, but of changing body biochemistry; such occurrences are not uncommon during puberty.

Drug side effects that result in decreases in school performance and test achievement can invalidate unqualified interpretation of test results in psychoeducational assessments. School psychologists should be aware of the medications taken by children they are assessing as well as their effects on performance during classroom observation. Peer relations should also be closely monitored because of the affective changes associated with some of the drugs. Possible influences of medication should be clearly noted in test reports.

With regard to parental supervision of medication, substantial proportions of parents in the Hawkins et al. (1986) sample endorsed test items contrary to medical recommendation: (a) taking extra medication after a seizure (14%); (b) no harm to skip a day (9%); (c) can stop medication if patient feels good (11%) or if no seizures for several months (28%).

Biofeedback. Biofeedback based on EEG data has been utilized with persons whose seizures are poorly controlled by medication (Cleeland, 1981). In some studies epileptics have been trained to increase EEG activity in normal frequency ranges (Sterman, Macdonald, & Stone, 1974; Kaplan, 1975; Lubar & Bahler, 1976; Kuhlman, 1978). Other researchers provide feedback when epileptiform activity is present (Cott, Pavloski, & Black; 1979). All of the biofeedback programs require a lengthy training period and daily practice of about 30 minutes. It should be noted that this research has not been without criticism that the studies involved methodological faults, such as small *N*, placebo effect, confounding of relaxation techniques, and occasional lack of medication control, and that biofeedback is not effective with all types of epilepsy (Feldman, Ricks, & Orren, 1983).

Diet. A "ketogenic" diet very high in calories and fat may be useful to children with severe epilepsy that is refractory to anticonvulsants (Hopkins, 1981). In addition, the seizure threshold may be reduced by common

TABLE 1
Anticonvulsant Drugs

Generic name	Trade name	Mechanism	Type of seizures	Side effects
Carbamazepine	Tegretol	Unknown	Partial and secondarily generalized	Drowsiness, dizziness, ataxia, nystagmus, irritability, and hyperactivity*
Phenytoin	Dilantin	Inhibits excitory transmitter release by depressing sodium and calcium conductance	Focal-onset secondarily generalized tonic–clonic and generalized–onset tonic–clonic	Gum tissue growth, double vision, drowsiness, balance difficulties, nystagmus, ataxia, tremor, gastrointestinal discomfort
Phenobarbital		Unknown	Tonic–clonic	Aggravates hyperactivity, drowsiness, disturbance of cognitive functioning, affective changes
Primidone	Mysoline	Unknown	Tonic–clonic partial	Sedation, dizziness, incoordination, plus all of the side effects of phenobarbital†
Valproic Acid	Depakene Valontin	Increases GABA‡ in the brain	Petit-mal myoclonic atonic	Nausea, vomitting, sedation, hand tremor
Ethosuximide	Zarontin	Unknown	Absence	Nausea, vomitting, drowsiness

*Less than 5% of persons taking carbamazepine develop disabling symptoms.

†The side effects of primidone are usually more severe than those of phenobarbital.

‡GABA (gamma-aminobutyric acid) is an inhibitory neurotransmitter.

Note: Data from Browne (1983), Browne and Pincus (1983), Hopkins (1981), Mattson (1983), Mattson and Cramer (1983), Middleton, Attwell and Walsh (1981), and Rodin (1983).

stimulants such as coffee, tea, and cola drinks, and their intake may need to be reduced or eliminated (Freeman, 1979). Other major factors in seizure breakdown are loss of sleep and alcohol excess (Adams & Victor, 1981).

Surgery. In a small number of cases not responsive to the above treatments, seizures persist with sufficient frequency and severity to threaten cerebral integrity and to markedly interfere with daily activities. In a subset of these cases, there may be a clearly defined brain area, usually in the temporal lobes, that is the focus of the seizure activity. Surgical removal of the irritating brain tissue may then be considered and employed with success (Davidson & Falconer, 1975; Delgado-Escueta, Treiman, & Walsh, 1983a, 1983b).

Direct Psychological Intervention

While medication is the major form of treatment and is often effective in reducing seizures, it fails to address the emotional components of epilepsy. Individual, family, and group therapy are much needed but often neglected aspects of treatment because they focus on emotional support. Relevant issues follow below.

Individual. Quite apart from the changes in behavior, affect, or cognition that may be *generated by* abnormal brain functioning, there are common personal *reactions to the condition* of epilepsy. The core dynamic, in our view, involves a profound loss of control. The seriousness of this loss, and the depth of anxiety that it may generate, stand in direct opposition to the basic developmental tasks of attaining mastery and autonomy, and negatively impact upon the child's sense of self and self-esteem. This difficulty may be augmented by the fact that the loss of control (or episodic regression) occurring with some seizures is pervasive and primitive, involving both body and mind. In the words of one mildly retarded 8-year-old with poorly controlled seizures, "I turn into an animal"; she meant it quite literally. The continued stress of her unpredictable situation led to family dissolution, devastating anger in both mother and child, and periods of destructive acting out that the mother could not distinguish from actual seizure activity.

Lack of self-control may also alter attributions and

attitudes in the classroom. Compared with diabetic and normal controls, seizure-disordered children have been found to more often attribute success or failure in school to sources of control such as luck or fate, and to hold less positive feelings about school and self-worth in school (Matthews, Barabas, & Ferrari, 1983).

Being different from other children in the classroom is an additional source of anxiety and contributes to lowered self-esteem. Parental expectations of epileptic children are often lower than those held for nonepileptic siblings, and these lowered expectations may in turn be related to the child's lowered self-esteem (Ferrari, Matthews, & Barabas, 1983; Kerns & Curley, 1985). Since the epileptic child is "different" from classmates, self-esteem is threatened even more by peer rejection.

Forced dependence on external sources (medication, parents) for self-control, especially for older children and adolescents, may conflict with steps of self-assertion and independence. Stores and Piran (1978) note that epileptic boys are especially dependent on others. This dependence may be related to the compliant behavior noted by Richie (1981) and contribute even further to the helplessness of the child.

If one accepts a dynamic definition that depression is a response to a loss (in this case of normality, of autonomy, of internal control), or the cognitive–behavioral view of the relationship between helplessness and depression, it is not surprising that in one study 81% of epileptic children's parents believed that epileptic patients often become depressed and 56% believed that some epileptics become suicidal because of their condition (Hawkins et al., 1986). Individual therapy may be required to address these issues in the context of a relationship not easily available in the school.

Family. There is a reciprocal relationship between the functioning of the family and the epileptic child. Analyses of communication styles have indicated tendencies for epileptic children to withdraw and for mothers to be more prominent in the family hierarchy (Richie, 1981). This organizational form was viewed as minimizing disagreement and simultaneously providing the family with secure structure and a means of meeting the child's dependency needs. The need for security can be partly understood in relation to the unpredictability of the seizures, leading to a lack of individual and family control (Ferrari et al., 1983). It thus appears that the epileptic's family is similar to some with chronically ill or handicapped children, in which disagreement is minimized to protect the parents as well as the child.

The analysis of family interactions might also consider the characteristics of psychosomatic families described by Liebman, Minuchin, Baker, and Rosman (1976): (a) *enmeshment,* in which family members are overinvolved with and overresponsive to one another, fostering little autonomy and privacy for individuals; (b) *overprotectiveness;* (3) *rigidity* of interaction and behavior patterns; (d) *lack of conflict resolution* associated with stress and tension; and (e) *involvement of the child in parental conflict,* the child's symptoms functioning as a conflict-avoiding and detouring mechanism. Additionally, cognitive–affective skills are inhibited, and there is a lack of capacity for requesting support when needed (Minuchin, 1974). Thus the tasks of family therapy may include helping to establish clearer boundaries and foster more autonomous behavior.

Siblings. Long and Moore (1979) reported that while 58% of their parent sample rated their epileptic children as "disturbed," fully 26% of their nonepileptic children were so rated. Hoare (1984) reported that while children with newly diagnosed epilepsy were significantly more disturbed than seizure-free siblings (who were typical of the normal population), there were no differences between chronic epileptics and their siblings who were emotionally impaired with the same high frequency. Parents of epileptics were not found to be more disturbed than adults in the general population, though there was a trend for mothers of chronic epileptic children to have higher rates of psychopathology. Hawkins et al. (1986) have reported that an earlier age of onset of seizures in the epileptic child was associated with higher intellectual and academic achievement of seizure-free siblings, possibly supporting the notion that a lengthy period of family interaction with an epileptic child leads to negative perceptions of that child (thus affecting their cognitive and social competence), and a simultaneous "compensatory" or "deidentification" effect for the healthy sibling.

Educational Intervention

One of the most meaningful interventions with the seizure-disordered child is to convey an appropriate sense of what seizures *are* and *are not,* but even well-intentioned attempts at explanations may produce undesirable consequences. For instance, the explanation that epilepsy is excess "electricity" in the brain may conjure up parental admonitions regarding wall sockets, shocks, and terminal consequences (Whitt, Dykstra, & Taylor, 1979). We have also seen one adolescent boy in therapy who was terrified that during a seizure he would suffer such a loss of ego (but not bodily) control that he might kill the younger children at home. The above authors recommend metaphorical explanations aided by diagrams to assist children who are not likely to have a sense of the anatomy and physiology of the unseen nervous system. An alternative explanation provided by these authors is that the brain is like a telephone that sends messages to all parts of the body, and, just like a telephone, the brain during a seizure sometimes gets a "wrong number" by sending messages to ________ (substitute perceptual cues, perhaps those from the aura); just like a telephone after a wrong number, the brain later works fine again.

It is important not to assume that past explanations have been accurately or adequately internalized and integrated, regardless of a child's age or cognitive sophistication. While cultural differences limit generalization, more than one-half of a sample of British *parents* of epileptic children had never read about epilepsy, and their explanations for the cause of seizures included correlative medical events (injections, measles) as well as various cognitive states (worry, stress, nerves, excitement) (Long & Moore, 1979). In a report on parents of epileptics in the United States (Hawkins et al.,1986) mothers of epileptic children displayed more accurate knowledge of seizure first aid, less fear of seizures than adult epileptics,and less sense of social stigma than college students. Nevertheless, parental fears and anxieties were very high: 42% agreed that the risk of sudden death increases with seizures and 73% believed seizures caused brain damage. Reflecting persisting social stigma, 96% of nonepileptic college students believed that seizures cause stress and anxiety, 92% felt that children hide epilepsy from others (vs. 17% of parents), and 72% felt that other children were reluctant to play with epileptic children (vs. 8% of parents). Comprehension of the "meaning" of epilepsy is therefore a lengthy contextual process that shifts with developmental challenges.

ALTERNATIVE ACTIONS

The school psychologist's role has been expanded over the past decades to encompass a greater degree of indirect service to the student client (Whelan & Carlson, 1986). One aspect of this expansion is consultation, a problem-solving approach to remediation and prevention (Gutkin and Curtis, 1982). According to the Specialty Guidelines for the Delivery of Services by School Psychologists, the duties of the school psychologist include "interventions to facilitate the functioning of individuals or groups, with concern for how schooling influences and is influenced by their cognitive, conative, affective, and social development" (American Psychological Association, 1981, p. 672). These guidelines also note that "consultation with teachers and other school personnel to enhance their understanding of the need of particular pupils" is also part of the role (p. 672). Lombard (1979) notes that legal changes now place the school psychologist in a direct relationship with families when working with school-based problems. These guidelines have sweeping implications for the school psychologist in regard to the difficulties experienced by the epileptic child in school.

Workshops for training teachers and parents can present valuable and timely information designed to overcome misinformation and fear. These workshops can focus on what to do during a seizure (including demonstrations), the side effects of drugs and how to compensate for them, and stress management for both the teachers and parents as well as the children. Teacher workshops could also provide methods and materials to inform other students about epilepsy. The school psychologist should serve as a resource to provide further education or to refer to an appropriate source (See below). A small library that includes epilepsy information for children, parents, and teachers could be established as a ready resource.

The school psychologist's role should also include that of a liason between parents, teachers, physicians, agencies, and organizations to provide timely services according to the children's needs. In this context, the monitoring of drug therapy is an extremely important task, and the school psychologist can reduce detrimental effects by serving as a liason between the teachers and physicians. Careful observation of potential side effects of particular anticonvulsant drugs will then help the physician choose the minimum dose of the most effective drug with the least amount of learning disruption.

Liason with local agencies and organizations will serve to provide epileptic children and their families with necessary resources for support. If a local epilepsy organization does not exist, the school psychologist can serve as an advisor to parents wishing to form one. The psychologist may serve as a consultant or an officer of an existing organization in order to be familiar with local service delivery and to assist in expansion of services.

Thus the school psychologist's role as consultant leads far beyond the classroom in dealing with epilepsy, involving teachers, administrators, families, physicians, and other agencies, and forming a focal point for integration and action.

When to Refer to Whom

Ethical practice involves recognition of the limitations of one's competence, and school psychologists may wish to seek consultation regarding children with seizures. When seizures are suspected but not yet diagnosed, referral to a neurologist, preferably one with pediatric expertise, is necessary. This would also be the case when there are concerns regarding seizure control and medication effects. Dental intervention may be appropriate for those taking Dilantin. Referral to a neuropsychologist is also recommended in order to gain a better appreciation of brain–behavior relationships in individual cases or for general consultation regarding questions of assessment and intervention. Since there is no unique licensing for neuropsychologists, inquiry regarding depth and breadth of professional training is suggested. Family and child therapists experienced with clients with neurological disorders may also provide needed support.

Community Agencies

There are over 135 separate epilepsy organizations in the United States (Shaw, 1983). These organizations offer the epileptic's family a variety of resources and can usually make referrals to other agencies and professionals when necessary. They often have support groups based on the buddy system, and can be utilized to share common experiences and to provide families with much needed emotional support.

SUMMARY

After it has been determined that a child has experienced seizures, it can be assumed that his or her internal life and interactions with the environment will be changed. Cognitive and affective development, the quality of social and family relationships, and educational attainment may all be affected. But the precise nature of the effects remains *potential,* and the interactions among these functional domains are both variable and complex. The school psychologist can be uniquely well equipped and well placed to be aware of and active in avenues of prevention, assessment, consultation, and intervention, and thus to enhance the psychological health of these children and their families.

As a final caveat, seizures and epilepsy are generic terms indicating a broad class of biological conditions that result in diverse psychological changes and pressures; a systems perspective is a necessary starting point for an understanding of the child with seizures. In respect to evaluation of an individual child or appraisal of the literature, reliance on generalities without due consideration of complexity is likely to divert one from good practice.

REFERENCES

Adams, R. D., & Victor, M. (1981). *Principles of neurology.* New York: McGraw-Hill.

American Psychological Association. (1981). Specialty guidelines for the delivery of services by school psychologists. *American Psychologist, 36,* 670–681.

Bagley, C. (1971). *The social psychology of the epileptic child.* Coral Gables, FL: University of Miami Press.

Bear, D. M., & Fedio, P. (1977). Quantitative analysis of interictal behavior in temporal lobe epilepsy. *Archives of Neurology, 34,* 454–467.

Berg, R. A., Bolter, J. F., Ch'ien,L. T., & Cummins, J. (1984). A standardized assessment of emotionality in children suffering from epilepsy. *International Journal of Clinical Neuropsychology, 6,* 247–248.

Bolter, J. F., Berg, R. A., Ch'ien, L. T., Williams, S. J., Lancaster, W., & Cummins, J. (1982). *Tactile–perceptual functioning and academic performance in children with chronic seizures.* Paper presented at the meeting of the National Academy of Neuropsychologists, Atlanta.

Browne, T. R. (1983). Ethosuximide (Zarontin) and other succinimides. In T. R. Browne & R. G. Feldman (Eds.), *Epilepsy: Diagnosis and management* (pp. 215–224). Boston: Little, Brown.

Browne, T. R., & Feldman, R. G. (Eds.). (1983). *Epilepsy: Diagnosis and management.* Boston: Little, Brown.

Browne, T. R., & Pincus, J. H. (1983). Phenytoin (Dilantin) and other hydantoins. In T. R. Browne & R. G. Feldman (Eds.), *Epilepsy: Diagnosis and management* (pp. 175–190). Boston: Little, Brown.

Christ, A. E. (1978). Therapy of the child with true brain damage. *American Journal of Orthopsychiatry, 48,* 505–515.

Cleeland, C. S. (1981). Biofeedback as a clinical tool: Its use with the neurologically impaired patient. In S. B. Filskov & T. J. Boll (Eds.), *Handbook of clinical neuropsychology.* New York: Wiley.

Cooper, J. A., & Ferry, P. C. (1978). Acquired auditory verbal agnosia and seizures in childhood. *Journal of Speech and Hearing Disorders, 43,* 176–184.

Corbett, J. A., & Harris, R. (1974). Epilepsy in children with severe mental retardation. In P. Woodford (Ed.), *Epilepsy and mental handicap* (Report of Symposium No. 16). London: Institute for Research into Mental and Multiple Handicap.

Corbett, J. A., Harris, R., & Robinson, R. G. (1975). Epilepsy. In J. Wortis (Ed.), *Mental retardation and developmental disabilities* (Vol. 7). New York: Brunner/Mazel.

Corbett, J. A., & Trimble, M. R. (1983). Epilepsy and anticonvulsant medication. In M. Rutter (Ed.), *Developmental neuropsychiatry.* New York: Guilford.

Cott, A., Pavloski, R. P., & Black, A. H. (1979). Reducing epileptic seizures through operant conditioning of central nervous system activity: Procedural variables. *Science, 302,* 73.

Davidson, S., & Falconer, M. A. (1975). Outcome of surgery in 40 children with temporal lobe epilepsy. *Lancet, 1,* 260.

Delgado-Escueta, A. V., Treiman, D. M., & Walsh, G. O. (1983a). The treatable epilepsies. *New England Journal of Medicine, 308,* 1508–1514.

Delgado-Escueta, A. V., Treiman, D. M., & Walsh, G. O. (1983b). The treatable epilepsies. *New England Journal of Medicine, 308,* 1576–1584.

Dennis, M. (1985). Intelligence after early brain injury I: Predicting IQ scores from medical variables. *Journal of Clinical and Experimental Neuropsychology, 7,* 526–554.

Dodrill, C. B. (1981). Neuropsychology of epilepsy. In S. B. Filskov & T. Boll (Eds.), *Handbook of clinical neuropsychology.* New York: Wiley.

Dodrill, C. B., & Clemmons, D. (1984). Use of neuropsychological tests to identify high school students with epilepsy who later demonstrate inadequate performances in life. *Journal of Consulting and Clinical Psychology, 52,* 520–527.

Epilepsy Foundation of America. (1978). *What everyone should know about epilepsy.* South Deerfield, MA: Channing L. Bete.

Fedio, P., & Mirsky, A. F. (1969). Selective attention deficits in children with temporal lobe or centracephalic epilepsy. *Neuropsychologia, 7,* 287–300.

Feldman, R. G., Ricks, N. L., & Orren, M. M. (1983). Behavioral methods of seizure control. In T. R. Browne & R. G. Feldman (Eds.), *Epilepsy: Diagnosis and management* (pp. 225–234). Boston: Little, Brown.

Ferrari, M., Mathews, W. S., & Barabas, G. (1983). The family and the child with epilepsy. *Family Process, 22,* 53–59.

Flor-Henry, P. (1976). Lateralized temporal–limbic dysfunction and psychopathology. *Annals of the New York Academy of Sciences, 280,* 777-795.

Freeman, S. W. (1979). *The epileptic in home, school and society.* Springfield, IL: Thomas.

Gutkin, T. B., & Curtis, M. J. (1982). School-based consultation: Theory and techniques. In C. R. Reynolds & T. B. Gutkin (Eds.), *The handbook of school psychology* (pp. 796–828). New York: Wiley.

Happe, D. (1985). Seizure and convulsive disorders. In J. Grimes & A. Thomas (Eds.), *Psychological approaches to the problems of children and adolescents.* Des Moines, IA: Department of Public Instruction.

Hartlage, L. C., & Telzrow, C. F. (1984). Neuropsychological aspects of childhood epilepsy. In R. Tarter & G. Goldstein (Eds.), *Advances in clinical neuropsychology* (Vol. 2). New York: Plenum.

Hawkins, R. C., Hubler, D. W., & Geis, S. (1986). Comprehensive neuropsychological and psychological assessment in treatment planning for children with epilepsy: A technical report. San Antonio: Epilepsy Center South Texas.

Hermann, B. P., & Whitman, S. (1984). Behavioral and personality correlates of epilepsy: A review, methodological critique and conceptual model. *Psychological Bulletin, 95,* 451–497.

Hoare, P. (1984). The development of psychiatric disorder among school-children with epilepsy. *Developmental Medicine and Child Neurology, 26,* 3–13.

Holdsworth, L., & Whitmore, K. (1974). A study of children with epilepsy attending ordinary schools. *Developmental Medicine and Child Neurology, 16,* 746–758.

Hopkins, A. (1981). *Epilepsy: The facts.* New York: Oxford University Press.

Kaplan, B. J. (1975). Biofeedback in epileptics: Equivocal relationship of reinforced EEG frequency to seizure reduction. *Epilepsia, 16,* 447.

Kerns, R. D., & Curley, A. D. (1985). A biopsychosocial approach to illness and the family: Neurological diseases across the life span. In D. C. Turk and R. D. Kerns (Eds.), *Health, illness and families: A life-span approach* (pp. 146–182). New York: Wiley.

Kuhlman, W. N. (1978). EEG biofeedback training of epileptic patients: Clinical and electroencephalographic analysis. *Electroencephalographic Clinic Neurophysiology, 45,* 699.

Lennox, W. G., & Lennox, M. A. (1960). *Epilepsy and related disorders.* Boston: Little, Brown.

Liebman, R., Minuchin, S., Baker, L., & Rosman, B. (1976). The role of the family in the treatment of chronic asthma. In P. J. Guerin (Ed.), *Family therapy: Theory and practice.* New York: Gardner.

Lombard, T. J. (1979). Family-oriented emphasis for school psychologists: A needed orientation for training and professional practice. *Professional Psychology, 10,* 687–696.

Long, C. G., & Moore, J. R. (1979). Parental expectations for their epileptic children. *Journal of Child Psychology and Psychiatry, 20,* 299–312.

Lubar, J. F., & Bahler, W. W. (1976). Behavioral management of epileptic seizures following EEG biofeedback training of sensorimotor rhythm. *Biofeedback Self Regulation, 1,* 77.

Matthews, W. S., Barabas, G., & Ferrari, M. (1983). Achievement and school behavior among children with epilepsy. *Psychology in the Schools, 20,* 10–12.

Mattson, R. H. (1983). Phenobarbital, primidone (Mysoline), and mephobarbital (Mebaral). In T. R. Browne & R. G. Feldman (Eds.), *Epilepsy: Diagnosis and management* (pp. 191–202). Boston: Little, Brown

Mattson, R. H. & Cramer, J. A. (1983). Valproic acid (Depakane, Valontin). In T. R. Browne R. G. Feldman (Eds.), *Epilepsy: Diagnosis and management* (pp. 225–234). Boston: Little, Brown.

Mearig, J. (1985). Cognitive development of chronically ill children. In N. Hobbs and J. M. Perrin (Eds.), *Issues in the care of children with chronic illness.* San Francisco: Jossey-Bass.

Mellor, D. H., Lowit, I., & Hall, D. J. (1971). *Are epileptic children different from other children?* Paper presented at Annual Meeting of British Group of Pediatric Neurologists, Oxford.

Middleton, A. H., Attwell, A. A., & Walsh, G. O. (1981). *Epilepsy.* Boston: Little, Brown.

Minuchin, S. (1974). *Families and family therapy.* Cambridge: Harvard University Press.

Morgan, A. M., & Groh, C. (1980). Visual perceptual deficits in young children with epilepsy. In B. M. Kulig, H. Meinardi, & G. Stores (Eds.) *Epilepsy and behavior '79.* Lisse, the Netherlands: Swets & Zeitlinger.

Pritchard, P. B. (1983). Personality and emotional complications of epilepsy. In K. M. Heilman & P. Satz (Eds.), *Neuropsychology of human emotion.* New York: Guilford.

Rangaswami, K. (1980). Educational difficulties and adjustment problems of epileptic adolescents. *Child Psychiatric Quarterly, 16,* 19–25.

Richie, K. (1981). Research note: Interaction in the families of epileptic children. *Journal of Child Psychology and Psychiatry, 22,* 65–71.

Rodin, E. A. (1968). *The prognosis of patients with epilepsy.* Springfield, IL: Thomas.

Rodin, E. A. (1983). Carbamazepine (Tegretol). In T. R. Browne & R. G. Feldman (Eds.), *Epilepsy: Diagnosis and management* (pp. 203–214). Boston: Little, Brown.

Rutter, M. (1977). Brain damage syndromes in childhood: Concepts and findings. *Journal of Child Psychology and Psychiatry, 18,* 1–21.

Rutter, M., Graham, P., & Yule, W. (1970). A neuropsychiatric study in childhood (Clinics in Developmental Medicine Nos. 35–36). London: Spastics International Medical Publications/Heinemann Medical Books.

Rutter, M., Tizard, J., & Whitmore, K. (1970). *Health, education and behavior.* London: Longmans.

Shaw, E. B. (1983). Resources available to the patient with epilepsy. In T. R. Browne & R. G. Feldman (Eds.), *Epilepsy: Diagnosis and management* (pp. 139–143). Boston: Little, Brown.

Sterman, M. M., Macdonald, I. R., & Stone, R. K. (1974). Biofeedback training of the sensorimotor electroencephalogram rhythm in man: Effects on epilepsy. *Epilepsia, 15,* 395.

Stores, G., Hart, J. & Piran, H. (1978). Inattentiveness in school children with epilepsy. *Epilepsia, 19,* 169–175.

Stores, G., & Piran, N. (1978). Dependency of different types of school children with epilepsy. *Psychological Medicine, 8,* 441–445.

Strub, R. L., & Black, F. W. (1981). *Organic brain syndromes.* Philadelphia: Davis.

Tarter, R. E. (1972). Intellectual and adaptive functioning in epilepsy: A review of fifty years of research. *Diseases of the Nervous System, 33,* 763–770

Whelan, T. B., & Carlson, C. (1986). Books in school psychology: 1970 to the present. *Professional School Psychology, 1,* 283–293.

Whitt, J. K., Dykstra, W., & Taylor, C. (1979). Children's conceptions of illness and cognitive development. *Clinical Pediatrics, 18,* 327–339.

Wright, G. N. (1975). Rehabilitation and the problem of epilepsy. In G. H. Wright (Ed.), *Epilepsy rehabilitation.* Boston: Little, Brown.

BIBLIOGRAPHY: PROFESSIONALS

Browne, T. R., & Feldman, R. G. 1983). *Epilepsy: Diagnosis and management.* Boston: Little, Brown.
An excellent handbook that collates research findings and discusses seizure types, underlying causes, and precipitating factors in detail. Specific medications and alternative treatments are also covered in depth.

Corbett, J. A., & Trimble, M. R. (1983). Epilepsy and anticonvulsant medication. In M. Rutter (Ed.), *Developmental neuropsychiatry.* New York: Guilford (pp. 112–129).
This brief but well-referenced chapter by prominent figures in the field reviews emotional and behavioral disorders of children with epilepsy, effects on cognition, and anticonvulsant medications. Of particular benefit, the chapter is embedded in a comprehensive text that ought to be examined by anyone working with neurologically impaired children.

Dodrill, C. B. (1986). Psychosocial consequences of epilepsy. In S. B. Filskov & T. J. Boll (Eds.), *Handbook of clinical neuropsychology* (Vol. 2), New York: Wiley (pp. 338–363).
This chapter is included here for two reasons: (l) It is written by perhaps the most prominent neuropsychologist in this field; and (2) its focus is the interrelationship between neurological disorder and psychosocial functioning. The information will be most applicable with adolescents and young adults still in the school system.

Kerns, R. D., & Curley, A. D. (1985). A biopsychosocial approach to illness and the family: Neurological diseases across the life span. In D. C. Turk & R. D. Kerns (Eds.), *Health, illness, and families: A life span perspective.* New York: Wiley (pp. 146–182).
Only a portion of this chapter is directly concerned with children and seizures. However, its emphasis on a systems approach to understanding the dynamics of neurological disease within a family context is sufficiently important to warrant its inclusion on this list.

BIBLIOGRAPHY: PARENTS

Freeman, S. W. (1979). *The epileptic in home, school, and society: Coping with the invisible handicap.* Springfield, IL: Thomas.
An excellent source for parents, educators, administrators, and adolescents with epilepsy. Utilizing a question-and-answer format, it clearly provides a fairly comprehensive overview of epilepsy and its consequences.

Hopkins, A. (1981). *Epilepsy: The facts.* New York: Oxford University Press.
This book begins with an elementary description of the brain and then discusses the causes of epilepsy, treatment, long-term outlook, practical points regarding living with epilepsy, and the promise of the future. It is clearly written and appears to be an excellent source for parents.

Middleton, A. H., Attwell, A. A., & Walsh, G. O. (1981). *Epilepsy.* Boston: Little, Brown.
A slightly dated but comprehensive presentation of information regarding epilepsy. The material, presented in question-and-answer format, is aimed at parents but can also be useful to professionals. It contains directories of national organizations and a comprehensive reading list.

Sands, H., & Minters, F. C. (1977). *The epilepsy fact book.* New York: Scribner.
Written for the lay reader with a focus on learning to cope with the problems associated with epilepsy. A chapter on the child with epilepsy will be particularly helpful to parents.

BIBLIOGRAPHY: CHILDREN

There are a variety of pamphlet-sized publications providing appropriate and sound information for children, adolescents, and parents available from the Epilepsy Foundation of America (4351 Garden City Drive, Landover, MD 20785) and its local affiliates; they are available in Spanish. Geigy Pharmaceuticals (Ardsley, New York 10502) also provides information for parents and adolescents in brief format. Very basic information on seizure First Aid in comic book style ("Seizure Man") is published by the Comprehensive Epilepsy Program, Bowman Gray School of Medicine, Wake Forest University, Winston-Salem, NC 27103; this may be useful in elementary schools.

Children and Self-Control

Robin Boren, Lass Weir, Cynthia Benegar
Jefferson County Public Schools, Colorado

BACKGROUND

Most adults can readily identify children who seem to be lacking in self-control. These children are disruptive at home, at school, or in the community. They exhibit characteristics that include poor impulse control, low frustration threshold, off-task behavior, disorganization, and distractibility. However, when educators are asked to isolate the components inherent in good self-control, there is rarely agreement on the elements of this construct.

Self-control is defined as specific skills or "sets of behaviors needed in order to maintain goal-directed behavior" (Rosenbaum & Baker, 1984). Not only are these skills overt and identifiable, they can also be taught. Children's environments can be modified to facilitate the learning of self-regulating behavior, whether in a clinical setting, in the home, or in the classroom (Honig, 1985; Humphrey, 1982).

O'Leary and Dubey (1979) discussed the importance of teaching children self-controlling behavior: (a) our culture values independent behavior; (b) significant adults may be unable to provide external controls; (c) when children are able to regulate their behavior themselves, adults' time is freed for guidance and other teaching; (d) when direct adult supervision is not possible, children will be able to learn and behave appropriately; and (e) self-controlled children sustain desirable behavior more reliably than children solely dependent on external means of reinforcement. Additionally, children who have internalized the value of self-control in their lives can apply this skill in new and different situations (Drabman, Spitalnik, & O'Leary, 1982; Epstein & Goss, 1978). They also gain the ability to evaluate their own activities by giving themselves feedback as in self-talk (Ammer, 1982) or self-assessment (O'Leary & Dubey, 1979).

For children to successfully exhibit self-management, teachers and parents must be consistently available and intervene to reinforce successive approximations of self-control. When adults provide clear expectations and external prompts and when they strengthen children's positive attempts through social praise or tangible rewards, significant progress toward desired behavior will be noted (Honig, 1982; Katkovsky, Crandall, & Good, 1967). Children become more willing to test new skills in diverse situations, eventually without direct adult cues and reinforcers.

Mastery of self-control occurs when children identify a goal and confidently manage their behavior to accomplish their purpose. Additionally, they risk taking the initiative and making independent choices in new situations. Children with good self-control are self-reliant learners who accept daily challenges with increased confidence (McGhee & Crandall, 1968).

DEVELOPMENT

Too limited a research base exists to precisely identify the developmental stages of self-control (Mischel & Mischel, 1983; Wilson, 1984). The existing literature concentrates on behavioral management plans — often in a clinical setting (Kendall, 1984; Pressley, 1979). In actual practice, a lack of objective criteria for evaluating children's self-control strategies has prevented systematic assessment (Mischel & Mischel, 1983). Table 1 presents a developmental continuum that illustrates the stages of self-control and facilitates identification and evaluation of children's current levels of self-control functioning. This continuum is based on extensive daily observations of children's behavior.

In the top block of entries in Table 1, specific behavioral descriptors serve to enhance adults' ability to accurately identify children's developmental placement. The second block provides a perspective on children's internal reasoning at each stage. Adults' responsibilities and roles are clarified in the third block. In the last block, stage goals and behaviors prerequisite to the next level of growth delineate levels of mastery. By studying the continuum as a whole, parents, therapists, and teachers can gain an overview of children's growth that will be useful in planning appropriate and effective interventions.

Progress through the continuum occurs sequentially. No definite time spans are associated with the stages.As a result of differences in motivation, environmental influences, adult commitment, and other variables, children will display unique growth patterns. Given the fluid nature of self-control development, periodic regression can be anticipated (Honig, 1985). Adults must expect to reteach self-control strategies learned at earlier levels. This occurs because children continually face new situations with immature skills not yet fully internalized.

Self-control training appropriately begins when children separate from adults and decrease their dependence on direct adult supervision. As children explore and experiment with their environment, Stage 1 characteristics are manifested. Given normal maturation, this occurs during the preschool years. However, if guidance and support have not been provided consistently at home, the training necessary to Stage 1 success can be undertaken at school (O'Leary & Dubey, 1979; Rosenbaum & Drabman, 1979).

At each successive phase of development, the stage goals simultaneously reflect increasing demands on children and the gradual release of adults' responsibility. Increased independence is apparent as progress through the stages occurs. When children can reliably duplicate taught routines, transition from Stage 1 to Stage 2 begins. The goal for Stage 2 children is to attend to self-control requisites in familiar situations and apply them

TABLE 1

Self-Control Developmental Continuum

	Stage 1	Stage 2	Stage 3	Stage 4
Behavior descriptors	Needs Routines modeled	Knows routines when directed	Often initiates routines	Self-initiates routines
	Impulsive	Delays impulsivity when directed	Often regulates impulses voluntarily	Self-regulates
	Off-task	Remains on-task for short duration	Remains on-task for expected time limits	Remains productive beyond expected time limits
	Easily distracted; daydreams	Distracted by selected stimuli	With effort, sustains attention despite environmental distractions	Remains focused consistently despite distractions
	Poor problem-solving strategies; requires adult direction	Problem-solving approaches emerge; relies on adult reminders	Usually initiates reliable strategies; dependent on adult evaluation	Mentally prepared to anticipate, initiate, complete problem-solving strategies
	Disorganized; does not complete tasks; quality of work poor	Minimally organized; dependent on adult for task assistance; erratic accuracy	Organized; works independently; improved accuracy	Self-starts; completes tasks consistently; self-evaluates quality
Child's internal reasoning	Discomfort with adult expectations that conflict with familiar behavior patterns	Willing to comply with adult expectations when the reward is enticing	Trusts environment; meets adult behavioral expectations	Shares adult expectations; confidently risks adopting learned strategies
	"I don't want to do it. . . .do I have to?"	"I'll do what you want if . . ."	"I understand why you want me to do this."	"I trust myself to handle this well."
Adult role	Supplies motivation; models valued behaviors	Provides opportunities for rehearsal	Maintains high expectations	Serves as mentor
	Builds in opportunities for practice		Commends successful strategies	
	Gives tangible and intangible rewards for successive approximations	Regularly implements external rewards/prompts	Replaces regular, predictable reinforcement with intermittent reinforcement	Provides encouragement and guidance when needed
Stage goal	Begins to identify and build awareness of behaviors	Masters expected routines	Begins to value and internalize adult behavioral values	Self-control becomes a satisfying, internalized working system
	Duplicates taught behaviors and expected routines	Often predicts adult expectations and initiates appropriate behavior	Often generalizes previous learning	Behaviors reliably transfer across situations
	Develops one or two problem-solving approaches	Reaches transition between external predictable rewards and internal motivation	Sustains independent effort	Self-appraises realistically
				Risks making independent choices

independently. The expected outcome for Stage 3 children is to extend their ability to initiate and sustain self-regulating behavior in more situations. Growing appreciation of adult values and expectations encourages internalization of these standards. The ultimate goals of self-control training are expressed in Stage 4 outcomes. Children achieve a more complete internalization of expectations and are possessed of a personalized value system (Epstein & Goss, 1978; O'Leary & Dubey, 1979). Expanded confidence encourages children to design strategies to attain self-set goals. With success, and specific attention to generalization training they are increasingly willing to transfer learned tech niques from familiar to unfamiliar situations (Eastma & Rasbury, 1981; Kendall & Braswell, 1982).

PUTTING CHILDREN AND SELF-CONTROL IN PERSPECTIVE

Teachers, parents, and therapists bear the respons bility of ensuring that children acquire self-contr (Miller, 1984; Wilson, 1984). According to O'Lea and Dubey (1979), "children must be taught, not just told, to use self-controlling skills" (p. 461). Whether a child receives regular or special education, the need for self-control training is generally valued (Miller, 1984).

The Self-Control Developmental Continuum is effective in evaluating children's current levels of functioning and in planning appropriate interventions. For example, hyperactive children largely exhibit Stage 1 traits and usually struggle the most to overcome the physical interferences that impede progress. Exceptional adult perseverance and patience are needed to help these children compensate for their extreme lack of inner structure (Rosenbaum & Baker, 1984).

Likewise, withdrawn and passive children typically demonstrate Stage 2 behavior. They are often reluctant or unable to initiate task approaches and are dependent on continuous adult prompts for direction. Withdrawn children may appear to be detached or unmotivated. They expend minimal effort when presented with a learning goal. The adult's challenge is to engage these children by providing a consistent and secure interpersonal relationship so that trust can develop (Honig, 1982).

Significant adults in children's lives function as effective change agents (Katkovsky, Crandall, & Good, 1967). Sometimes, however, these adults are only minimally involved in their children's development. Circumstances such as transiency, economic pressure, family membership changes, substance abuse, or extended working hours often impact upon adults' ability to actively commit themselves to their children's development (Kanfer & Karoly, 1972). Other primary sources of interference not often cited include poor parenting skills and the generally decreased esteem in which schooling and school values are held.

Children affected by these environmental deficits can nevertheless benefit from appropriate self-control training. Often teachers or therapists can productively intervene by providing external structure. For example, children who are largely unsupervised at home can be taught at school to organize their approaches to tasks. Through the commitment of the adults at school, children experience a predictable, secure environment. With help, children can learn to internalize that stability to create their own routines and structures outside the academic milieu (Humphrey, 1984).

Children may be confused when school and home interpretations of self-control conflict. Adults' differing expectations impact on children's attempts to adapt to their environments. Overt conduct may reflect this confusion, as when children transpose a permissible home behavior to the school, where it may not be acceptable: for example, a child's parents may value physical retaliation while the school promotes nonviolent problem-solving. The school can minimize this confusion for children by clarifying the contexts for these differing expectations and helping children recognize that these differences are situation-specific.

When significant adults agree on values and expectations and collaborate to impart them to children, the conditions for success are optimal.However, if these conditions are not in place, mastery of self-control will likely take longer to achieve (Maphet & Miller, 1982).

To facilitate children's learning of self-control, adults must be sensitive observers, understand the developmental nature of self-control, and possess a working repertoire of strategies that emphasize behavioral training (Honig, 1982, 1985; Katkovsky, Crandall, & Good, 1967). Adults equipped with these tools can undertake self-control training despite the variety of behaviors and backgrounds children present.

ALTERNATIVE ACTIONS

Once children's placement on the developmental continuum has been determined, a practical application model for teaching self-control can be implemented. Four recurrent themes emerge in all stages. Adults must consider environment, language patterns, reward systems, and trust building when they undertake self-control training.

Initially, a dependable home or classroom environment needs to be established in which task routines and expectations are clearly stated. Adults in that setting need to communicate and enforce consistent and predictable standards (Humphrey, 1984). This structure promotes steady progress if children's tasks are realistic and age-appropriate. For example, a functional room arrangement, procedures for storage of materials, assigned chores, and appropriate strategies for requesting assistance promote a sense of continuity and security (Miller, 1984). Standards to evaluate performance must be specified and enforced.

A second consideration is the nature of the adult language to be used to interact with children (Honig, 1982). This must be characterized by careful word choice, firm intent, a nonjudgmental voice tone, and language patterns that encourage self-evaluation and self-monitoring. In this way attention stays focused on the desired behavior and responsibility remains with the child. To promote these objectives, effort should be made to rephrase statements into questions and to use one-word cues whenever possible.

A third principle is to encourage the progression of reward systems from tangible and external to intangible and internal reinforcers. Systematic use of immediate tangible rewards theoretically gives way to an intermittent reinforcement schedule of intangible reinforcers such as verbal praise. Although not a primary emphasis in the following model, these reinforcers support the goals of self-control training by encouraging transfer from an external to an internal locus of control (Hisama, 1976; Rothbaum, Wolfer, & Visintainer, 1979).

Finally, the role of trust between children and adults is of critical importance. When children can depend on the predictability of their environment and the sustained commitment and sensitivity of an adult, a supportive interpersonal child–adult relationship develops. Three aspects of this critical relationship are close interpersonal contact, empathetic understanding, and unconditional acceptance (Shapiro, 1983). When mutual caring and respect flourish, children grow in self-

TABLE 2

Model for Teaching Self-Control

	Possible strategies	Person responsible: Examples
1. Identify target behavior	Verbalize desired behavior	Adult: When the project is done, supplies must be put away.
	Provide rationale	Adult: If supplies are put away, we'll know where to find them next time.
	Validate feelings	Adult: It's frustrating when things are out of order.
	Develop common understanding	Adult/Child: What would happen if I needed a tool and it was missing?
2. Model desired behavior	Clarify expectation	Adult: Mouthing off is not acceptable behavior.
	Explore options	Adult: Better ways to tell me you're angry are to signal quietly or give an I-message.
	Verbal rehearsal/think aloud	Adult: When I feel mad, I want to swear. That causes trouble and hurts feelings.
	Compare/contrast	Adult: (models angry backtalk and contrasts with appropriate expressions of anger.)
	Elicit feedback	Adult: How does that make you feel?
		Child: (acknowledges hurt feelings.)
	Apply logical/natural consequences	Adult: I will ignore you until you talk politely.
3. Build opportunities for practice	Restate rules	Adult: I expect you to organize your time so the assignments are done by 10:30.
	Provide advance organizers	Adult: What will you do if you get stuck?
	Generate options	Child: When I get stuck, I can come to you for help or ask a friend.
	Role-play	Child: (models confusion and determines solution.)
	Self-talk	Child: I can't remember how to do this. I wonder if Susan knows.
	Give evaluative feedback	Child/Adult: Is the work getting done?
	Give reinforcement (tangible or intangible)	Adult: You came up with a good strategy. (Tangible reward may be offered.)
4. Monitor new behavior for consistent use	Self-monitor/record	Child: (charts completion of homework assignments.)
	Give evaluative feedback	Child: I turned my homework in on time.
		Adult: I like the way you have been remembering your homework this week
	Anticipate problem situations	Child: I have soccer practice tonight. When will I do my homework?
	Determine options, consequences	Child: If I wait until afterwards, I'll be tired and won't do it.
	Continue training	Adult/Child: Let's think together about your options.
	Continue reinforcement	Adult: I trust you to make a good decision this evening.
5. Encourage transfer	Affirm self	Child: I trust myself to work despite distractions.
	Generate options independently	Child: To get this report done, should I work at the library or use headphones?
	Select and implement option	Child: I'll work at the library where there are fewer distractions.
	Self-evaluate	Child: It feels good to have made that choice because my report is done.
	Give reinforcement (tangible)	Child: I've earned a night at the movies.
	(intangible)	Adult: Your work has noticeably improved. Your strategies must be working.

esteem; progress toward self-management is enhanced.

Current research and best practices in education describe an effective teaching/learning model (Hunter, 1967) that includes clear expectations and high standards of performance. These are first conceived by the significant adults so that children can eventually adopt standards of excellence for themselves. The teaching of self-control draws from the same model, which optimizes the interactive characteristics of a large group setting. The essential components are identified in Table 2. The five steps in Table 2 apply to skills being taught at all stages of development on the continuum. The adult progresses through these steps *each time* a new skill is introduced. The model reflects the importance of the gradual release of responsibility from the training adult to the maturing child.

The following discussion, with examples, illustrates the application of this model.

1. *Identify a specific target behavior.* The purpose of this step is to focus attention on one specific behavior, although many behaviors may need modifying. The adult role is to describe and clarify expected behaviors and explain their relevance and contribution to the school, home, or community. With adults' assistance, a common understanding of expectations is achieved. Children begin to make connections and realize that a relationship exists between actions and outcomes. The foundation for an appreciation of the value inherent in

these behaviors is established.

> Michael, age 8, throws a tantrum whenever he is not chosen first, complaining to a supervising adult that this is not fair. He punishes the "favored" child by punching, kicking, spitting, or name calling. The adult identifies the target behavior for Michael as learning acceptable strategies for dealing with anger. The adult directly says to Michael, "Your behavior is not acceptable here. People get hurt when you express your anger that way." The discussion continues until Michael can describe the consequences of his actions and their impact on the other child: "I hurt him when I kicked and punched him."

2. *Model desired behavior.* Once the behavior has been identified and a common understanding established, the adult is responsible for demonstrating what the prescribed behavior looks like. First the behavior is verbally described, with age-appropriate vocabulary. Then the behavior is modeled by the adult,often with peer assistance. A verbal account of the internal thinking process and of the external actions must accompany the demonstration. In this manner even language-deficient children attach labels to actions that then clarify their understanding. The adult checks for comprehension by modeling undesirable behavior and inviting children to offer constructive feedback. Frequent opportunities for reviewing standards can be easily integrated into subsequent situations.

> At the earliest opportunity, when Michael is calm, the adult explains appropriate alternatives for expressing anger: walk away, count to ten, express disappointment in words. Michael's outburst is twice reenacted by the adult, once as it originally occurred and then with a more acceptable course of action. The adult monologues, "I'm mad because I wasn't chosen first. I want to hit him but he will get hurt. I'll try counting to ten." The adult encourages Michael to identify what was wrong with his original action. Michael summarizes the two approaches modeled and highlights the differences. He must explain what he could do next time. "I guess I could count to ten or I could walk away." Then he is asked why that would be more appropriate: "Then no one would get hurt."

3. *Build opportunities for practice.* This step allows children to practice what has been demonstrated. They may role-play a situation drawn from actual experience. Other children and the adult provide verbal summaries of what was done well and what needed improvement. If even one child performs poorly, further rehearsals are immediately implemented. The purpose of this is to underscore the high value assigned to the expected behavior while simultaneously focusing children's attention and energy on applying the behavior successfully. As opportunities arise for practice, the adult prepares children in advance to apply what they have just learned. In selecting an appropriate strategy, children take a first step in internalizing the targeted behavior.

> The adult identifies a hypothetical situation and asks Michael to role-play, applying his newly learned skills. The adult asks, "What if you and another child both want the last empty swing?" Michael and the adult evaluate his role play, focusing on use of correct strategies. "When you chose to talk it over and not hit, you made a good choice." The adult anticipates potentially troublesome situations and reminds Michael to try out his strategies. "When you go out to play on the swing, what skill will you remember to use?" Successive approximations of the desired behavior are systematically reinforced with tangible or intangible rewards.

4. *Monitor the new behavior for consistent use.* In subsequent activities, the adult needs to carefully monitor behavior and provide positive feedback. More rehearsals may be required. Even as children give evidence of reliable understanding in selected situations, erratic performance can be expected. Care must be taken to keep the level of training intensive until the behavior is gradually internalized.

> On the baseball diamond, Michael is called "out" at first base. He sullenly trudges off the field. The alert adult takes advantage of this approximation of the targeted behavior by pointing out his progress. "In the last game, you argued with the umpire when you were called out. Today, you controlled your temper." Michael is asked to give additional examples of children who displayed self-restraint. The adult continues to prompt Michael to spot other incidents where good self-control was demonstrated until he can identify similar situations independently.

5. *Encourage transfer.* Now that the behavior has become somewhat routine, the adult must encourage spontaneous transfer. As children experience and are reinforced for their awareness of appropriate behavior, self-confidence builds. Children increasingly apply the new behavior without benefit of adult prompts. They learn to anticipate "red flag" situations and mentally rehearse a plan of action. Although this initially requires deliberate effort, the process eventually becomes automatic. Success is now its own reinforcer. Children trust themselves to generate positive alternatives and they become realistic evaluators of their own performance. Successful transfer of appropriate behavior is thus advanced.

> Michael has generally improved in controlling his anger although occasional regressions are observed. He is called a name and, without thinking, retaliates in kind. Later, when his anger subsides, Michael is able to take an objective view of what occurred. "I blew it by calling him a name back. Next time I should just walk away." When he tries this plan under similar circumstances and averts a negative outcome, Michael feels satisfied. The adult provides Michael with opportunities to debrief by asking about his performance and reinforcing good decisions. "I know it's hard to walk away when you're mad, but I trust you can handle it." This acknowledgment serves to sustain Michael's attention on the target behavior and boost his self-esteem. Gradually, as Michael is more consistently successful, external reinforcers are replaced by self-evaluating statements, such as "I'm getting better at this." Michael is increasingly likely to apply this new skill independently.

SUMMARY

Parents and school personnel experience extreme frustration when children underachieve in school; these children are not realizing their potential. Such children often have difficulty following rules and fail to internalize adult expectations. They appear less able to focus energy on problem solving and are often unable to complete tasks on a consistent basis.

Self-control is a highly valued measure of individual character, but self-management skills do not develop instinctively; they can and must be deliberately taught. The method presented is a systematic approach for successfully teaching self-control in nonclinical settings. The techniques described represent an ongoing process that can be used by adults with all children in various environmental circumstances.

A significant component of the process of self-control training is the fluctuating dynamic of children's progress in achieving self-control. Regression can be expected and is regarded as normal in the developmental process.

Another important consideration is that reponsibility for monitoring behavior should gradually shift from adults to children. In this way, children progress beyond externally imposed control toward the internalized and independent setting and attaining of goals.

The deliberate teaching of self-control skills gives children the essential tools for optimizing their interaction with their environment. As children grow in self-control, they develop the ability to identify realistic goals, to design strategies to accomplish goal-related tasks, and to follow through effectively. All children share the need for self-control training.

REFERENCES

Ammer, J. J. (1982). Managing learning disabled students' academic frustration through self-control. *Pointer, 27*(1), 17–20.

Anderson, L., Fodor, I., & Alpert, M. (1976). A comparison of methods for training self-control. *Behavior Therapy, 7,* 649–658.

Buffington, P. W., & Stilwell, W. E. (1980). Self-control and affective education: A case of omission, *Elementary School Guidance and Counseling, 15*(2), 152–156.

Drabman, R., Spitalnik, R., & O'Leary, K. D. (1973). Teaching self-control to disruptive children. *Journal of Abnormal Psychology, 82*(1), 10–16.

Eastman, B., & Rasbury, W. (1981). Cognitive self-instruction for the control of impulsive classroom behavior: Ensuring the treatment package. *Journal of Abnormal Child Psychology, 9*(3), 381–387.

Epstein, R., & Goss, C. (1978). A self-control procedure for the maintenance of nondisruptive behavior in an elementary school child. *Behavior Therapy, 9,* 109–117.

Hisama, T. (1976). Achievement motivation and the locus of control of children with learning disabilities and behavior disorders. *Journal of Learning Disabilities, 9*(6), 387–392.

Honig, A. S. (1982). Prosocial development in children. *Young Children, 37*(5), 51–62.

Honig, A. S. (1985). Compliance, control, and discipline. *Young Children, 40*(3), 47–52.

Humphrey, L. L. (1982). Children's and teachers' perspectives on children's self-control: The development of two rating scales. *Journal of Consulting Clinical Psychology, 50,* 624–633.

Humphrey, L. L. (1984). Children's self-control in relation to perceived social environment. *Journal of Personality and Social Psychology, 46*(1), 178–188.

Hunter, M. (1967). *Retention theory for teachers.* El Segundo, CA: Theory Into Practice Publications.

Kanfer, F. H., & Karoly, P. (1972). Self-control: A behavioristic excursion into the lion's den. In Mahoney, M. J. & Thoresen, C. E. (Eds.), *Self-control: Power to the person* (pp. 200–217). Monterey, CA: Brooks/Cole.

Katkovsky, W., Crandall, V., & Good, S. (1967). Parental antecedents of children's beliefs in internal–external control of reinforcements in intellectual achievement situations. *Child Development, 38,* 765–776.

Kendall, P. C. (1984). Cognitive–behavioral self-control therapy for children. *Journal of Child Psychology and Psychiatry, 25*(2), 173–179.

Kendall, P. C., & Braswell, L. (1982). Cognitive–behavioral self-control therapy for children: A component analysis. *Journal of Consulting and Clinical Psychology, 50*(5), 672–689.

Lickona, T. (1983). *Raising good children.* Toronto: Bantam Books.

Maggiore, R. P. (1983). Helping the impulsive pupil use self-control techniques in the classroom. *Pointer, 27*(4), 38–40.

Mahoney, M. J., & Thoresen, C. E. (1974). *Self-control: Power to the person.* Monterey, CA: Brooks/Cole.

Maphet, H. W., & Miller, A. L. (1982). Compliance, temptation, and conflicting instructions. *Journal of Personality and Social Psychology, 42*(1), 137–144.

McGhee, P., & Crandall, V. (1968). Beliefs in internal–external control of reinforcements and academic performance. *Child Development, 39*(1), 91–102.

Meichenbaum, D., & Goodman, J. (1971). Training impulsive children to talk to themselves: A means of developing self-control. *Journal of Abnormal Psychology, 77*(2), 115–126.

Miller, C. S. (1984). Building self-control: Discipline for young children. *Young Children, 40*(1), 15–19.

Mischel, H., & Mischel, W. (1983). The development of children's knowledge of self-control strategies. *Child Development, 54*(3), 603–619.

Morgan, S. R. (1986). Locus of control and achievement in emotionally disturbed children in segregated classes. *Journal of Child and Adolescent Psychotherapy, 3*(1), 17–21.

O'Leary, S. G., & Dubey, D. R. (1979). Applications of self-control procedures: A review.*Journal of Applied Behavior Analysis, 12*(3), 449–465.

Pressley, M. (1979). Increasing children's self-control through cognitive interventions. *Review of Educational Research, 49,* 319–370.

Rosenbaum, M., & Baker, E. (1984). Self-control in hyperactive and nonhyperactive children. *Journal of Abnormal Child Psychology, 12*(2), 303–318.

Rosenbaum, M. S., & Drabman, R. S. (1979). Self-control training in the classroom: A review and critique. *Journal of Applied Behavior Analysis, 12*(3), 467–485.

Rothbaum, F., Wolfer, J., & Visintainer, M. (1979). Coping behavior and locus of control in children. *Journal of Personality, 47*(1), 118–135.

Shapiro, D.H. (1983). Dimensions relevant to the health care and therapeutic use of self-control strategies: A system model for applied research. *Perspectives in Biology and Medicine, 26*(4), 568–586.

Wilson, R. (1984). A review of self-control treatments for aggressive behavior. *Behavioral Disorders, 9*(2), 131–140.

Workman, E. A. (1982). *Teaching behavioral self-control to students.* Austin, TX: Pro-Ed.

BIBLIOGRAPHY: PROFESSIONALS

Ammer, J. J. (1982). Managing learning disabled students' academic frustration through self-control. *Pointer, 27*(1), 17–20.
Presents a six-step series of interrelated skills taught to special education students to better ensure successful mainstreaming. Useful strategies for teachers and therapists include modeling, shaping, fading, and rehearsal to enhance students' problem-solving skills and reduce frustration.

Drabman, R., Spitalnik, R., & O'Leary, K. D. (1973). Teaching self-control to disruptive children. *Journal of Abnormal Psychology, 82*(1), 10–16.
Describes an extensive token reinforcement program undertaken in an after-school remedial class to reduce off-task behavior and increase academic output. Presents procedures in a step-by-step manner. Generalization of desired behavior was obtained during the control periods.

Epstein, R., & Goss, C. (1978). A self-control procedure for the maintenance of nondisruptive behavior in an elementary school child. *Behavior Therapy, 9,* 109–117.
Describes a single-subject case study designed to reduce the highly disruptive classroom behavior of a 10-year-old boy. This successful procedure was implemented with a minimal amount of direct teacher intervention. Self-evaluation and rewards for honest appraisal as well as contingent and noncontingent reinforcements were components of this systematic behavior modification program.

Mahoney, M., & Thoresen, C. (1974). *Self-control: Power to the person.* Monterey, CA: Brooks/Cole.
A practical handbook for the professional on a variety of self-control topics. Includes chapters on self-control principles, behaviors, assessments, and applications. Summarizes relevant research through selected readings.

Rothbaum, F., Wolfer, J., & Visintainer, M. (1979). Coping behavior and locus of control in children. *Journal of Personality, 47*(1), 118–135.
Distinguishes between inward and outward coping behaviors and relates them to locus of control. Clarifies that consequences are perceived by children either as resulting from random adult action over which children have no control or as directly related to their own antecedent behaviors.

BIBLIOGRAPHY: PARENTS

Honig, A. S. (1982). Prosocial development in children. *Young Children, 37*(5), 51–62.
Summarizes the training practices that are most effective in helping children develop prosocial behaviors: role-taking, maternal responsive care, parental modeling of warmth and nurturance, inductive discipline techniques. Also examines status variables of age, sex, culture, and socioeconomic placement.

Honig, A. S. (1985). Compliance, control, and discipline. *Young Children, 40*(3), 47–52.
Discusses the effects of preschool and daycare experiences on children's experiences in children's development of compliance. Calls for deliberate teaching of self-regulation in these settings. Provides adult strategies that address expectations, affect, environmental adaptations, and techniques for directing appropriate behavior.

Lickona, T. (1983). *Raising good children.* Toronto: Bantam Books.
Identifies in clear, readable style the stages of moral reasoning from early childhood foundations through adulthood. Offers practical suggestions for helping children master the developmental tasks of each stage. An extension of the work of Lawrence Kohlberg.

Miller, C. S. (1984). Building self-control: Discipline for young children. *Young Children, 40*(1), 15–19.
Distinguishes between discipline and punishment. Encourages parents and teachers to examine interaction style, environment, schedule, and expectations. Uses a how-to approach to natural consequences, problem-solving, redirection, and time out.

Children and Sexual Abuse

Linda C. Caterino
Mesa, Arizona

BACKGROUND

Definitions

Sexual abuse of children is a topic that receives much attention in the media. However, it is still considered the most underdiagnosed type of child abuse (Kempe, 1978). The National Center on Child Abuse defines sexual abuse as "contacts or interaction between a child and an adult when the child is being used for sexual stimulation of that adult or of another person" (U. S. Department of Health, Education, and Welfare, 1978).

Child sexual abuse is usually described as the sexual exploitation of a child by an adult or a significantly older peer (usually five or more years). It is a broad term and includes genital exposure, kissing, fondling, oral–genital contact, digital penetration, and vaginal or anal intercourse as well as child pornography and child prostitution. The abuse may be a single act committed by a stranger or incest with a family member carried on for many years. Key terms in sexual abuse include the following: sexual molestation, which is defined as sexual contact short of intercourse, such as exposure, touching, or masturbation; sexual neglect, the failure to prevent someone from engaging in sexual activities with a child; pedophilia, the adult preference for sexual relations with children; rape, sexual intercourse without the consent of the victim; statuatory rape, sexual intercourse with a child under the age of consent (usually age 16, depending on state law); and incest, sexual activity between a child and a related adult.

Incidence

A national incidence study of child abuse was conducted in 1978–1979 (as described in Finkelhor & Hotaling, 1984) and included all cases known to child protective services as well as schools, hospitals, and major agencies. It estimated 10.7 cases of child sexual abuse a year per 1,000 children as compared to 3.4 cases of physical abuse and 2.2 cases of emotional abuse. According to the National Center for Child Abuse and Neglect there were only 44,700 substantiated cases of sexual exploitation for 1979 (Russell, 1983). However, it is estimated that the actual incidence is much higher owing to problems in reporting and substantiation (Luther & Price, 1980). A report from the American Humane Society estimates that there are between 200,000 and 300,000 cases per year, 5,000 cases being incest (Summit & Kryso, 1978), and Sarafino (1979) estimates 336,200 cases per year.

Post hoc surveys indicate even higher percentages of sexual abuse (Russell, 1983; Finkelhor, 1979). Russell conducted a random sample of 930 adult women in San Francisco. She found that 16% of the women reported at least one intrafamilial sexual abuse before the age of 18 and of these, 12% were abused before the age of 14. In addition, 31% of the sample reported at least one extrafamilial incident of sexual abuse before 18 and 20% of these were before the age of 14. In Finkelhor's study of 796 college students, 19.2% of the women and 8.6% of the men indicated that they had been sexually victimized as children.

Child Victims

The typical sexually abused child is a female approximately 10–12 years of age. DeJong, Emmett, and Hervada (1982) found the mean age to be 10.2. Although there are reported cases of abuse at all ages, Finkelhor and Hotaling (1984) found that 33% of the children are less than 6 years old. Girls are reported to be abused four times more frequently than boys (Conte & Berliner, 1981; Kempe & Kempe, 1984). Yet, this may be due to underreporting. Carolyn Swift (1979, as cited in O'Brien, 1980) stated that only 10.5% of the male victims told their parents, compared with 43% of the females.

Nasjleti (1980) has hypothesized that boys may be less likely to report sexual abuse because they may not want to be seen as victims or because they may feel that by admitting to the abuse they may be admitting to homosexuality. Yet Groth and Birnbaum (1978) found no homosexual orientation in a group of 175 males convicted of sexual assault against children. Neilsen (1980) also noted that "a cultural double standard" may make some parents less concerned with a son's molestation than a daughter's and thus less prone to report the incident.

Offenders

Groth (1978) reported that 99% of the offenders are male. Russell (1983) reported that 11% of the assailants in her study were strangers, 60% were known but unrelated, and 29% were relatives of the victim. Of the relatives, Russell found 24% to be biological, step-, foster, or adoptive fathers and 26% to be uncles. Finkelhor (1979), however, found only 4% of the assailants to be fathers and 9% to be uncles. The difference, in part, may be due to the fact that Russell defined abuse as direct physical or attempted physical contact rather than less severe forms of abuse such as exhibitionism.

Contrary to popular mythology, pedophiles are usually not "drunken, dirty old men" who are strangers to the child. On the contrary, they are usually young. Groth (1978) reported that 11 of his clients committed their first offense before age 40 and 80% had committed the first offense by age 30. He also stated that the majority of the offenders knew their victims and noted that most did not use drugs or alcohol at the time of the offense.

Groth has classified offenders into two main

groups, the fixated pedophile and the regressed pedophile. Fixated pedophiles are persons who from adolescence have been sexually attracted primarily or exclusively to children. They usually avoid typical activities with peers, such as dating or sports. Generally, they do not initiate or actively pursue adult sexual relations, since they may fear rejection by adults. Almost half of the fixated offenders were victims of child sexual abuse, usually by nonfamily members in a violent manner. Fixated pedophiles become almost compulsively addicted to sexual experiences with children. Groth hypothesizes that the abuse behavior may be an attempt to resolve their own childhood victimization by repeatedly reliving the experience.

In contrast, the regressed offender usually does not demonstrate sexual interest in children until the time of the offense. He originally preferred peers for sexual gratification and is usually married. However, when under stress, he may turn to children to fulfill his sexual needs. The abuse is usually an impulsive act that is symptomatic of his own inability to cope. Groth indicates that the prognosis is better for the regressed offender, since in the past they have had satisfying peer relations.

The adolescent offender may not yet have had enough experiences to be classified as either a fixated or a regressed offender. The adolescent offender is usually nonviolent and is acquainted with his victims in 80% of the cases (Sanford, 1982). Usually, there are problems in peer relations that limit the offenders' normal sexual exploration. Typically, the teens' father is absent or aloof, which tends to limit the development of appropriate modeling. Approximately half of the adolescent offenders had been abused themselves. Since the adolescent is just beginning his pattern, he appears to be more amenable to treatment than the adult offender.

PUTTING CHILD SEXUAL ABUSE IN PERSPECTIVE

Dynamics of Child Sexual Abuse

Groth also described two basic motivations for sexual abuse of children. These are sex pressure offenses and sex force offenses, based on whether force, or the threat of force, was employed. This dichotomy was employed in a study by Burgess, Holstrom, and McCausland (1978). They reported that 39% of their sample could be classified as committing sex pressure crimes. This type of offender usually represents an authority figure who is known to the victim and may be related. The offender entices the child into going along with the sexual activity. He may bribe the child materially with candy or money, or with affection and attention, and then take advantage of the situation so that the child feels indebted or obligated. His goal is to gain control of the child by developing a willing sexual relationship. Here, sexuality is seen as satisfying the offender's need for physical contact and affection.

Sex force offenders use intimidation or physical aggression. No attempt is made to form an emotional relationship with the child and the child is seen strictly as an object for sexual gratification for the offender. When force is used, it is usually to gain control of the child in order for the sexual act to progress. However, a small group of sex force offenders may torture or physically subdue the child as the goal itself.

Incest

Many cases of intrafamilial sexual abuse, or incest, are committed by a father against his children. When the offender is not the natural father but occupies a parental rule such as stepfather or foster or adoptive father, or a mother's live-in lover, the act is called functional incest.

While there is a wide variety of incest patterns, Groth reports that in the majority of cases dependency needs are exaggerated. The husband may be overly dependent on his wife and later on his daughter. In other situations, the wife may be excessively dependent on her husband emotionally and/or financially. Raphling, Carpenter, and Davis (1967) described the incestuous father as an "ineffectual, nonaggressive, dependent man who assumes little responsibility for his family."

Usually, the incest relationship continues over time (3–5 years) (Sanford, 1982). While there are documented cases in infancy and preschoolers, the peak age for the beginning of such relationships is around 5–8 years for a girl. Sgroi, Blick, and Porter (1982) described a typical incest pattern of (a) engagement, (b) sexual interaction, (c) secrecy, (d) disclosure, and frequently (e) suppression.

During the engagement phase, the offender develops opportunities for private interaction with the child and selects appropriate inducements or establishes a threat of force to coerce the child into compliance. In the sexual interaction phase, the sexual relationship may progress from exposure to masturbation, fondling, kissing, and then oral, anal, or vaginal penetration. After the sexual activity, the children are cautioned not to tell anyone so that the offender (usually the father) may be able to continue the relationship for months or years. The secret is usually kept in compliance with the offender's direct order. But even if the secret is not explicit, a child may be afraid to tell because of the father's power or out of fear of destroying the family. The child may have been told, for example, that if the mother knew of the incest she could become ill or divorce the father or the father might be imprisoned. In addition, the child may have enjoyed the initial stages of the molestation since this attention may represent the only affection and feelings of "specialness" he or she had ever received. Thus, the child may feel, in some way, responsible for the abuse. The child may also fear that telling would be fruitless, since no one would believe the story anyway. It takes much to break the secret and allow for disclosure. At times, an adolescent may tell out of concern for a younger sibling or because of an unrelated issue such as an argument with the father concerning adolescent freedom and dating, since often incestuous fathers are very possessive and restrictive with their children. Accidental disclosure may also occur as a result of observation by others, physical injury to the child, pregnancy, or the contraction of a sexual disease. In the suppression phase, the child is pressured by the family to withdraw any complaint by making her or him feel guilty and isolated or even by the use of force or physical harm.

The parents in incest cases may be experiencing marital problems, although the couple may still be sexually active. In some cases, the mother is aloof and may actually be out of the home, at work, at school, or elsewhere, even hospitalized, allowing the relationship between father and daughter to grow. There may be a great deal of role confusion (Summit & Kryso,1978), the oldest daughter assuming many domestic tasks and childcare, and also the primary responsibility for socializing with the father. As the relationship between father and daughter grows, the sexual relationship may be seen as a method of lessening familial problems and as a method of keeping the family together. Indeed, the decision for disclosure usually causes the separation of the family (Burgess, Holmstrom, & McCausland, 1977). Frequently, the family is socially or even physically isolated (Finkelhor, 1979; Reimer, 1940; Nakashima & Zakus, 1977; Kempe, 1980) so that there may be fewer opportunities for sexual contact outside the home and less censure by society. There may be strong feelings of fundamental religiosity and strict moralism, extrafamilial affairs or divorce being seen as unacceptable so that the father does not look for sex outside of the home.

On occasion, the father is very dominant and sees his wife and children as property that may be used to satisfy his needs (Herman, 1971; Nakashima & Zakus, 1977). Implicitly, the incestuous father assumes that the family should serve him. If his wife is unavailable, he expects the daughter to substitute rather than assuming his own responsibility for family needs.

Stepfathers appear to be more likely to abuse their stepchildren than are natural fathers. Finkelhor (1979) found that the rate of father–daughter incest was almost five times greater in families with stepfathers than in natural father families. In the Russell (1983) survey, 17% of the women who had been abused had been abused by stepfathers compared to 2% by their biological fathers. In addition, the type of molestation was more severe with stepfathers. For example, 47% of stepfathers involved in incest perpetrated forced penile vaginal penetration compared to 26% of such biological fathers. However, a study using a very small sample (26 cases) found that the biological father was the most common abuser of children (Vander Mey & Neff, 1984).

Father–son abuse tends to be more disturbed than father–daughter abuse and sometimes violent. Typically, the homosexual aspect is not the primary motivation, but rather, as in father–daughter abuse, the behavior is characterized by an attempt to fulfill the father's feelings of inadequacy. Grandfather–granddaughter abuse is similar to father–daughter abuse, and indeed the granddaughter's mother may have been a previous victim of abuse (Goodwin, Cormier, & Owen, 1983). Sexual abuse by the mother (Goodwin and Divasto, 1979) is very rare, less than 1%. Abuse, if it does occur, usually takes the form of fondling or exposure. It usually occurs in those homes where the father is absent, owing to death or divorce. The boy victim typically has a more difficult time in these situations, since he cannot claim that he was overpowered by force and he usually feels intense guilt. In mother–daughter abuse, there appears to be a role reversal, the mother seeking emotional support, attention, and affection from the daughter. The mother may also not see a clear separation between herself and her daughter. Usually, these mothers are characterized as having severe emotional problems or as psychotic.

Much has been written about the role of the mother in father–child incest. Some writers have stated that the abuse may, in part, be the mother's fault or at least that she was aware of the abuse (Kempe, 1978, 1980) and may have actively or passively encouraged it. Russell (1984), however, indicated that mothers frequently may not know of the incest and they may indeed act to support the child upon disclosure.

Finkelhor (1979) and Herman (1981) reported that mothers in incest situations are usually absent, sick, or alienated from the child. Herman reported that occasionally, mothers do collude in incest. However, she noted that when this happens, it is a measure of maternal helplessness, for the mother herself may be victimized by the father. In any case, girls without strong mothers to protect them are more vulnerable to sexual abuse. In Finkelhor's study (1979), 58% of the girls who had lived without their mothers at some time had been sexually victimized three times more often than girls who had been with their mothers. He also found that 35 percent of girls whose mothers were often ill had been sexual victims almost two times the rate of the average girl.

James and Nasjleti (1983) described four types of mothers of incest victims. These are (a) the passive child–woman mother who is very dependent and immature; (b) the intelligent, competent, emotionally distant mother who may not provide her daughter with adequate nurturing; (c) the rejecting, vindictive mother who is openly hostile and threatening and who refuses to admit to herself that the incest has occurred; and finally, (d) the psychotic or retarded mother, who is unable to protect her children and is more likely to actively participate in the molestation of her children than other mothers.

Sibling abuse is thought to be the most common form of sexual abuse although it is not usually reported. The problems grow more severe with greater disparity in age. When the age difference between siblings is 5 years or more, there is greater imbalance in power; especially with an older brother and a younger sister, the dynamics are more similar to father–daughter incest.

Who are the victims of sexual molestation? Finkelhor (1986) suggested that the following factors make a child more vulnerable to sexual abuse: emotional deprivation, social isolation, prior knowledge of the adult, fondness for the adult, vulnerability to the incentives offered by the adult, feelings of helplessness and powerlessness, ignorance, sexual repression, curiosity, and coercion.

Typically in child sexual abuse the child is not the aggressor although interestingly, Bender and Blau (1937) stated that child victims may be very attractive and seductive. Nevertheless, it is the adult who is obligated to exercise judgment and restraint.

Severity Factors

Various factors appear to influence the long-term effects on child victims of sexual abuse. These include the relationship between the offender and the victim, the duration of the abuse, the type of abuse, the child's age and developmental level, and the reaction of parents and significant others.

While much of the research in this area is still in the initial stages, there does appear to be less trauma if the crime is committed by a stranger (Landis, 1956), since abuse by a family member seems to be symptomatic of family dysfunction in general, as well as raising significant trust issues. Finkelhor (1979) found no difference in the impact of intra- and extrafamilial abuse in general. However, he did find that abuse by a father or stepfather was significantly more traumatic than any other form of sexual abuse.

Studies that have looked into the duration of sexual abuse appear to be the most contradictory. Finkelhor (1979), using a self-report format, found no relationship with duration. However, Bagley and Ramsey (1985) found that the general mental health status of adult victims was worse in cases of abuse of longer duration. Yet Courtois (1979) found that adult victims with the longest-lasting experiences had the least trauma.

The effects of type of abuse are clearer. It appears that children who have endured penetration or experienced physical injury suffer greater trauma than those involved in mutual masturbation or exhibitionism. De Francis (1968) found that if there was an element of attack or if the child was disgraced or punished, there was more trauma. Russell (1983) found that 59% of her sample who reported completed or attempted vaginal or anal intercourse, fellatio, cunniligus, or analingus, said that they were extremely traumatized as compared with only 36% of those who experienced sexual touching or unclothed body parts and 22% of those who reported unwanted kissing or touching of clothed body parts. A study by Tufts University personnel (1984) found that physical injury was the single most important factor related to the degree of behavioral disturbance manifested by the child victims.

A child's age and developmental level also appear to have an inconsistent relationship to the amount of trauma the youngster experiences. Gomes-Schwartz, Horowitz, and Sauzier (1985), using the Louisville Behavior Checklist, indicated that their preschool and adolescent child samples showed fewer signs of serious disturbance than did the school-aged child (7–13 years). Common symptoms were angry, destructive behavior or internal anxiety and fear. However, the authors did suggest that the relatively fewer problems displayed by adolescents could be an artifact of their sample since severely disturbed adolescents might be institutionalized or runaways and not receiving outpatient services. Meiselman (1978) found that 57% of those who had experienced incest before puberty were severely disturbed, compared with only 17% of those abused after reaching puberty. The Tufts study found that age bore no systematic relationship to the degree of trauma but did agree that elementary-age school children appeared to be the most disturbed. Browne and Finkelhor (1986) suggested that there is no clear relationship between age of onset and degree of trauma, since while some youngsters may be "protected by naivete, others may be more traumatized due to their impressionability."

Parental reaction appears to be an important variable although only a few studies have looked at this area. The Tufts study (1984) found that when mothers' reactions to disclosure were anger and punishment, the children demonstrated more behavioral disturbance, but there was no systematic relationship between a positive parental reaction and the degree of adjustment.

Effects of Sexual Abuse

Browne and Finkelhor (1986) have reviewed the effects of sexual abuse on females. They found that some of the initial effects of child sexual abuse included fear, anxiety, depression, anger, and hostility, as well as inappropriate sexual behavior. Long-term effects as measured by retrospective responses of adults who were childhood victims of sexual abuse included depression, self-destructive or suicidal behavior, anxiety, feelings of isolation and stigma, poor self-esteem, and a tendency toward revictimization and substance abuse. They also found some indications of the following behaviors, although there was less agreement by researchers: difficulties in trust; sexual maladjustment; sexual dysfunction; impaired sexual self-esteem; and prostitution. Slager-Jorne (1979) reported that two-thirds of children who are sexually abused appear to suffer emotional difficulties. Mrazek and Mrazek (1981) reported short-term problems in learning and problems in sexual adjustment and interpersonal relations. They also reported loss of self-esteem, obesity, depression, character disorders, suicidal ideation, and psychosis and schizophrenia as effects of sexual abuse.

Symptoms of Sexual Abuse

The school psychologist needs to be aware of the symptoms of sexual abuse that are manifested by sexually abused children and be willing to impart this information to other members of the school staff and to parents. Parents and teachers may seek assistance without realizing that a child they have referred has been molested. They should be directed to note any serious changes in the child's behavior. Some typical symptoms that they may be advised to look for are changes in eating and sleeping habits, including nightmares and insomnia. Emotional reactions such as excessive fearfulness about particular people or places, clinging, withdrawal, and regressive behavior may also be observed. Other symptoms are various reactions toward school, including refusal to attend, excessive absenses, a drop in grades (although high achievers may also have been victims of abuse), an unwillingness to change for and participate in physical education, and arriving early and leaving late from school, perhaps out of fear of being at home. Physical symptoms include difficulty in sitting or walking; pain, swelling, or itching in the genital area; frequent urinary tract infections, painful urination, and vaginal or penile discharge; bleeding in the genital or anal area; torn, stained, or bloody underwear; and bruises. Venereal disease, particularly in a child younger than 13, and pregnancy should also be investigated. A child may also demonstrate a knowledge of sexual behavior far too advanced for his or her age and education, as well as masturbation and changes in fantasy play. Peer relations may also be poor. The child may engage in indiscriminate hugging, kissing, or seductive behaviors with other children and adults, as well as excessive aggression (Harrison, 1985; Watson, 1984; Rosenfeld, 1982; Pettis & Hughes, 1985; Brassard, Tyler & Kehle, 1983b).

Sexual Abuse Legislation and the Development of School Policies

The school psychologist should also be aware of the legal aspects of sexual abuse and work to develop appropriate school policies. Public Law 933-247 (as cited in Erickson, McEvoy & Colucci, 1984), passed in January, 1974, provided for a demonstration program for the prevention, identification, and treatment of child abuse and neglect, including child sexual abuse. This federal law serves as a model for individual state laws, since in order to qualify for federal financial assistance the states must develop appropriate legislation.

The school child abuse policy should not only document and describe the content of the specific state law but it should encourage school personnel to actively implement the law. The policy should state the legal obligations of reporting known and suspected cases of abuse and neglect and should specify the legal immunity from civil and criminal liability for those who report. Presently, 37 states name schools and school personnel specifically among those mandated to report child abuse. The remaining states require that any person suspecting abuse and neglect report those cases. Most states make provisions to protect those who report in good faith from both civil and criminal liability (O'Brien, 1980). However, if cases of child abuse and neglect are *not* reported to child protection agencies, or the police, the negligent party is guilty of a class B misdemeanor and may be fined or even be liable for damages in some states (Brassard, et al., 1983b). Suspected abuse should be reported immediately. Most states usually require only an oral report that can be done by telephone, but a few states require a follow-up written report. The national hot line is 1-800-A-CHILD and some states also provide a 24-hour toll-free telephone number for reporting.

ALTERNATIVE ACTIONS

Interviewing

The school psychologist may not be called upon to interview suspected child sexual abuse victims. This is usually conducted by child protection or police officials. However, the children may request that the school psychologist be present at the interview. They may also bring up such information during the course of a counseling session and the school psychologist should allow the abuse to be described. It is usually very difficult for children to disclose incidents of sexual abuse and if the adult they initially attempt to confide in is not empathetic or willing to listen, they may discontinue any attempt at disclosure and the abusive situation may continue.

Very often children will make hints or bring up issues concerning "a friend," and they should be allowed to speak freely. Once such students sense a positive response from the psychologist, they may be willing to discuss the abuse and the psychologist can then ask for further clarification.

At the start of the interview, the psychologist needs to reassure these children that they are safe and this may be accomplished initially by providing them with a private setting so that their conversations cannot be overheard. The children need to be given permission to say whatever they want to without fear of judgment. The psychologist must be careful not to respond with shock, horror, disgust, pity, or disbelief but to reflect back the child's statements and feelings. It may be necessary to employ the language of the interviewed children, since very often they do not know the appropriate anatomical terms. They may need to define them by pointing to specific areas on the psychologist's body, or their own, by drawing a picture, or by using anatomically correct dolls. Books such as *Red Flag, Green Flag People* (Williams, 1983) have appropriate pictures that can be used during the interview phase.

For younger children, a playhouse with small people or puppets may be quite effective (Faller, 1984). Clay and playdough can also be used to help children act out their stories. While psychologists can play with the children, they must be very careful not to lead them by indicating certain persons ("Was it Daddy?") or by supplying specific behaviors. Interviewers should ask general, open ended questions, such as "What happened next?" rather than "Where did he touch you?"

The psychologist should take good notes and if possible employ audio and/or video tapes. In some states, video tapes are permissible in court (Melton, 1985). Interviewers should attempt to get as much information as possible without upsetting the children. Specifics such as where the abuse happened, who was present, and when it happened, can be obtained by using birthdays or special occasions as time markers. The children's behavior, changes in mood, topics avoided, and so forth should be noted. Psychologists should tell the children in the interview that they will communicate the information to the school child abuse committee and to the authorities. Some children may feel relief at this point, but others will need more reassurance that they will be protected by the authorities.

Children who are suspected of having undergone sexual abuse are usually referred to medical personnel. However, there is gross physical evidence of sexual abuse in less than 15% of the cases (Jones & McQuiston, 1985). Cantwell (1983), however, indicated that there may be more subtle findings that medical personnel can look for, such as the size of the vaginal opening in females. Medical examination alone cannot refute a child's complaint of sexual abuse. The interview, if it is done correctly, is the most powerful technique in gathering evidence of sexual abuse.

Interviews, however, are subject to validation procedures that include examining the children's statements for specific detail, noting their sentence structure and vocabulary, and determining if they are consistent with the children's age or developmental level, as well as checking for the typical progression in cases of incest (e.g., from fondling to intercourse) and looking for motivations for possible false statements. Other validation procedures include speaking with other adults, such as teachers, concerning the children's behavior at the time of the suspected abuse and checking the consistency of the children's stories with known facts such as work schedules, opportunities, etc.

Intervention Procedures

After an initial report of suspected abuse is made and the victim is interviewed by a caseworker or police, the investigator will make the decision as to possible placements. For example, the investigator may determine that the child is in danger and may request that the child be immediately removed from the home and placed in foster care or that the father or stepfather (in cases of father–child incest) be removed.

After initial placement procedures are made, therapy should be implemented. School psychologists may, on occasion, work with the children and families directly, but in most cases their role will be more of a referral agent. They should be aware of treatment programs available in their community so that appropriate referrals can be made.

In the forefront of treatment programs for incestuous families is the Child Sexual Abuse Treatment Program of Santa Clara County California or CSATP (Giaretto, 1976, 1982). The first stage of the father–daughter incest rehabilitation program is individual therapy that progresses to marriage counseling and then family counseling. In conjunction with these programs, individual family members are involved with peer group counseling in Parents United and Daughters and Sons United programs. These peer group programs are now available in many communities. The goal of Giaretto's program is reunification of the family and his rate of success is quite high. He has stated that approximately 90% of the child victims have been returned to their families with a recidivism rate of less than 1% (Giaretto, 1982; Kroth, 1979).

James and Nasjleti (1983) also have described an in-depth program for victims of sexual abuse and their families. Their program includes individual crisis therapy, peer group therapy, and father–child and conjoint family therapy. Mayer (1983) details similar procedures for incest victims and lists specific methods for use with children and adolescents such as art and writing techniques, sociograms, desensitization programs, play therapy, and bibliotherapy. Art (Kelly, 1984), movement, mime, and music therapy (Naitove, 1982) are other methods used with child victims of sexual abuse. Relaxation techniques may also be useful in initial sessions with victims (Caterino, 1985), and Beck and Skinner (1982) reported the success of behavioral techniques with a 4-year-old incest victim in alleviating symptoms of anxiety and fearfulness.

Burgess, Holstrom, and McCausland (1978) stressed the importance of encouraging the victim of sexual abuse to talk about the experience to help the child "settle his or her feelings" about the sexual abuse, so that the encounter will be integrated into the child's life experience. They indicated that talking about the abuse will help all family members. Discussion of the abuse also helps the therapist to understand and deal with any misconceptions the child may have.

Play sessions can be particularly useful for preschool and elementary-aged children. Recommended toys for play include puppets, aggressive toys such as play guns, and art supplies such as crayons or paints, clay, and playdough. Older children may also enjoy board games.

Anatomically correct dolls are also useful in that they may allow children to repeat abusive incidents in play and to develop more appropriate resolutions. For example, a 3-year-old client of the author who was a victim of extrafamilial sexual abuse repeatedly acted out sexual experiences with dolls. Initially, she also displayed a great deal of aggressive play. After several sessions, the child stopped in the midst of acting out a sexual episode and loudly said "No! She's too little and she doesn't want to 'ride'!" She then tightly hugged the doll. It appeared that she had developed some control over the sexual abuse by developing an appropriate assertive response. Interestingly, the child's mother reported that after that session the child showed much less anxiety and aggressive behavior.

Commercially prepared books, such as *Something Happened to Me* (Sweet, 1981) and *No More Secrets for Me* (Wachter, 1983), can also be used to stimulate conversation with a shy or reticent young client. They are helpful in allowing the child to feel less isolated and/or different from other children. Issues such as guilt and responsibility need to be discussed during the course of therapy with abused children. They may wonder why the offender is being punished and they are not. They may also seek a great deal of reassurance from the therapist and their parents and may ask to be told repeatedly that the abuse was not their fault and that they are still loved and accepted. They may need to be reminded that their body is still intact and that no permanent physical damage was done. Children's perceptions of sexual activity may also be probed, as they may require help in distinguishing between sexual abuse and normal sexual and love relations. Sexually abused children may undergo typical psychological stages such as denial, guilt, and anger before they are able to reach a positive resolution. In addition, they and their parents should be made aware that supportive counseling may be necessary during critical periods such as when they reach puberty, when they begin dating and engaging in normal sexual relations, and when they marry and have children.

Prevention and Media Programs

The school psychologist can be a key person in organizing prevention programs in the schools. They can speak to classes and parent–teacher organizations or arrange for speakers from outside agencies such as rape crisis centers to come to the schools.

Various media programs have been developed that may help to facilitate these sessions. A comprehensive list of films is given by Erickson et al. (1984). These include, for both parents and teachers *Child Molesters: Fact and Fiction* (1976); *Incest: The Hidden Crime* (1979); *Incest: The Victim Nobody Believes* (1976); *The Last Taboo* (1977); and *Sexual Abuse of Children: America's Secret Shame* (1980). In addition, *Child Abuse: What Your Child Should Know* (reviewed by Hart, Kinder, & Mrazek,1985) is a comprehensive videotape program designed for parents and children from preschool to high school.

These films and tapes,many of which were television documentaries, should be reviewed first by district personnel and representatives of the school board and parent–teacher organizations. While they should not make up an entire session, they can be quite useful as springboards for the discussion of sexual abuse. Parents and teachers should also be taught to look for symptoms of abuse and urged to give their children appropriate techniques to help them in avoiding some forms of sexual abuse. Reactions of parents to children's disclosure should also be thoroughly reviewed for appropriateness. Parents need to be cautioned to believe and support their children if they report that they have been sexually abused.

Teachers, school counselors, and psychologists can also benefit from viewing the above-mentioned tapes. They may also find useful the slide and tape presentation *Lift a Finger: The Teacher's Role in Combating Child Abuse and Neglect* (no date) and the film *A Time for Caring: The School's Response to the Sexually Abused Child* (1978) in helping them to identify child abuse and to understand what legal steps to take. *The Sexually Abused Child: Identification/Interview* (1978) and *Child Abuse and the Law* (no date) may also be useful in teaching school personnel appropriate interviewing techniques.

School psychologists should also consult with teachers in developing appropriate sexual abuse curricula for children. Handicapped children may be particularly vulnerable and Ryerson and Sundem (1981) give a description of a specific curriculum that can be effective for this student group.

Media programs for youngsters include the *Bubbylonian Encounter* (Mackey, 1981), which is available as a play or videotape. It tells the story of Bub, an alien from the planet Bubbylonia who visits Earth and learns about the sense of touch. Other programs are *No More Secrets* (Wachter, no date), *Touch* (Kessler, no date), *What Tadoo* (no date), *Who Do You Tell?* (1978), *This Secret Should Be Told* (Waller, no date), *Now I Can Tell You My Secret* (Engel, no date), *Little Bear* (Bridgework Theater, no date), *No Easy Answers* (Kent, 1982), and *The Touching Problem* (Kleven, no date). Brassard, Tyler, and Kehle (1983a) describe another program "You're in Charge," which helps children learn that their bodies are their own and that they should report abuse immediately.

In addition to the previously mentioned books, the following books may be beneficial for children in the elementary age group: *It's My Body* (Freeman, 1982), *Private Zone* (Dayee, 1984), *Stranger Danger* (Quiri & Powell, 1985), *My Very Own Book About Me* (Stowell & Dietzel, 1979), *Never Say Yes to a Stranger* (Newman, 1985), *My Very Own Special Body Book* (Bassett, 1981), and *My Body Is Private* (Girard, 1984), which can be used by parents with their children.

Adolescent programs include: *Top Secret, Sexual Assault Information for Teenagers Only* (Fay & Flerchinger, 1982), and *Sexual Abuse Prevention* (Fortune, 1984). The *Child Abuse Help Book* (Haskins, 1982) and *Child Abuse* (Dolan, 1980) are good reference books on the subject for teenagers and older elementary school children.

All prevention programs should also provide information concerning reporting techniques and school and community resources. Aside from exposure to media and books, the best prevention is to help build children's self-esteem, their ability to trust their own judgment, and their confidence in using assertiveness skills. Nurturing parents and school personnel can probably be one of the best defenses children can have against the negative effects of sexual abuse.

SUMMARY

Sexual abuse has become one of the most serious problems facing children today. Usually the assailants are known or related to the victims. The long-term effects of childhood sexual abuse can be quite serious, including depression and self-destructive behavior. Being members of school staffs, school psychologists have the opportunity to be involved in the prevention and identification of sexual abuse of children. They need to be aware of symptomology and should conduct inservice training with teachers and other school personnel so that they, too, can objectively monitor children's behavior. School psychologists should be knowledgeable about state child abuse laws and help to develop school policies. They may be called upon to assist in interviewing and treating child victims and their families and should be cognizant of appropriate referral agencies in their community.

REFERENCES

American Humane Association, (1982). *Estimated number of sexual maltreatment victims in the United States reported to child protective services.* Denver, CO: American Humane Association.

Bagley, C., & Ramsey R. (1985). *Disrupted childhood and vulnerability to sexual assault: Long-term sequels with implications for counseling.* Paper presented at the Conference on Counseling the Sexually Abused, Winnepeg, Canada. Cited in Browne, A., & Finkelhor, D., (1986). Impact of child sexual abuse: A review of the research. *Psychological Bulletin, 99,* 66–77.

Bassett, K. (1981). *My very own special body book.* Redding, CA: Hawthorne.

Beck, J. V., & Skinner, L. S. (1982). Treatment of a four year old victim of incest. *American Journal of Family Therapy 10*(9), 41–46.

Bender, L., & Blau, A. (1937). The reaction of children to sexual relations with adults. *American Journal Of Orthopsychiatry, 7,* 500.

Brassard, M. R., Tyler, A. H., & Kehle, T. J. (1983a). School programs to prevent intrafamilial child sexual abuse. *Child Abuse and Neglect, 7,* 241–245.

Brassard, M., Tyler, A., & Kehle, J. (1983b). Sexually abused children: Identification and suggestions for interviewing. *School Psychology Review, 12,* l.

Browne, A. B., & Finkelhor, D. (1986). Impact of child sexual abuse. A review of the research. *Psychological Bulletin, 99,* 66–77.

Burgess, A., Holmstrom, L., & McCausland, M. (1977). Child sexual assault by a family member: Decisions following disclosure. *Victimology: An International Journal: 2*(2), 236–250.

Cantwell, H. (1983). Vaginal inspection as it relates to child sexual abuse in girls under 13. *Child Abuse and Neglect, 7,* 171–176.

Caterino, L. C. (1985). *Working with sexually abused children and their families.* Paper presented at the National Association of School Psychologists Meeting, Las Vegas, Nevada.

Child abuse and the law [film]. (no date). Evanston, IL: Perenial Education.

Child molesters: Fact and fiction [film]. (1976). Toronto: Summerhill Productions.

Conte, J. R., & Berliner, L. (1981). Sexual abuse of children: Implications for practice. *Social Casework, 62,* 601–606.

Courtois, C. (1979). The incest experience and its aftermath. *Victimology: An International Journal 4,* 337–347.

Dayee, F. S. (1982). *Private zone.* Edmonds, WA: Charles Franklin.

DeFrancis, V. (1969). *Protecting the child victim of sex crimes committed by adults.* Denver, CO: American Humane Association.

DeJong, A., Hervada, A., & Emmett, G. (1983). Epidemiological variations in childhood sexual abuse. *Child Abuse and Neglect, 7,* 155–162.

Dolan, E. (1980). *Child abuse.* New York: Franklin Watts.

Engel, E. (Producer). (no date). *Now I can tell you my secret* [film] No city given: Hallinan Plus Productions.

Erickson, E., McEvoy, A., & Colucci, N. (1984). *Child abuse and neglect: A guidebook for education and community leaders.* Holmes Beach, FL: Learning Publications.

Faller, K.C. (1984). Is the child victim of sexual abuse telling the truth? *Child Abuse and Neglect, 8,* 473–481.

Faye, J., & Flerchinger, B. J. (1982). *Top secret: Sexual assault information for teenagers only.* Renton, WA: King County Rape Relief (booklet and tape).

Finkelhor, D. (1979). *Sexually victimized children.* New York: Free Press.

Finkelhor, D. (1986). *A sourcebook on child sexual abuse.* Beverly Hills, CA: Sage.

Fortune, M. (1984). *Sexual abuse prevention: A study for teenagers.* New York: United Church Press.

Freeman, L. (1982). *It's my body.* Seattle, WA: Parenting Press.

Giaretto, M. (1976). Humanistic treatment of father–daughter incest. In R. Helfer & C. Kempe (Eds.), *Child abuse and neglect. The family and the community.* Cambridge, MA: Ballinger.

Giaretto, H. (1982). A comprehensive child sexual abuse treatment program. *Child Abuse and Neglect, 6,* 263–278.

Girard, L. W. (1984). *My body is private.* Nilen, IL: Albert Whitman.

Gomes-Schwartz, B., Horowitz, J., & Sauzier, M. (1985). Sexually abused preschool-age and adolescent children. *Hospital and Community Psychiatry, 36*(5), 503–508.

Goodwin, J., Cormier, L., & Owen, J. (1983). Grandfather–granddaughter incest: A trigenerational view. *Child Abuse and Neglect 7,* 163–170.

Goodwin, J., & DiVasto, P. (1979). Mother–daughter incest. *Child Abuse and Neglect 3,* 953–957.

Groth, A. N. (1978). Patterns of sexual assault against children and adolescents. In A. W. Burgess, A. N. Groth, L. Holmstein, & S. Sgroi (Eds.), *Sexual assault of children and adolescents.* Lexington, MA: Heath.

Groth, A. N. (1982). The incest offender. In S. Sgroi (Ed.), *Handbook of clinical intervention in child sexual abuse.* Lexington, MA: Heath.

Groth, A. N., & Birnbaum, H. J. (1978). Adult sexual orientation and attraction to underage persons. *Archives of Sexual Behavior; 7*(3), 175–181.

Harrison, R. (1985). How you can help the abused child. *Learning, 14*(1), 74–78.

Hart, S., Kinder, R., & Mrazek, P. (1985). Child sexual abuse; What your children should know (videotape reviews). *School Psychology Review 14*(3) 385–390.

Haskins, J. (1982). *The child abuse help book.* Reading, MA: Addison-Wesley.

Herman, J. (1981). *Father–daughter incest.* Cambridge, MA: Harvard University Press.

Incest: The hidden crime [film]. (1979). No city given: CBS News.

Incest: The victim nobody believes [film]. (1976). No city given: Mitchel-Gebhardt Film Co.

James, R., & Nasjleti, M. (1983). *Treating sexually abused children and their families.* Palo Alto, CA: Consulting Psychologists Press.

Jones, D., & McQuiston, P. H. (1985).Interviewing the sexually abused child (booklet) Denver, CO: Kempe Center.

Kelley, S. (1984). The use of art therapy with sexually abused children. *Journal of Psychological Nursing, 22,* 12–18.

Kempe, C. H. (1978). Sexual abuse, another hidden pediatric problem: The 1977 C. Anderson Aldrich lecture. *Pediatrics 62*(3), 381–389.

Kempe, C. H. (1980). Incest and other forms of sexual abuse. In C. H. Kempe & R. E. Heyfer (Eds.), *The battered child* Chicago: University of Chicago Press, 198–214.

Kempe, R. S., & Kempe, C. H. (1984). *The common secret: Sexual abuse of children and adolescents.* New York: Freeman.

Kent, C. A. (1982). *No easy answers — A sexual abuse program for junior and senior high students* [videotape]. Minneapolis: Illusion Theater.

Kessler, T. (no date). *Touch* [film]. Deerfield, IL: MTI Teleprograms.

Kleven, S. (no date). *The touching problem.* [videotape]. Bellingham, WA: Coalition for Child Advocacy.

Kroth, J. (1979). *Child sexual abuse: Analysis of a family therapy approach.* Springfield, IL: Thomas.

Landis, J. T. (1956). Experiences of 500 children with adult sexual relations. *Psychiatric Quarterly Supplement 30,* 91–109.

The last taboo [film]. (1977). Wheaton, IL: Calvacade Productions.

Lift a finger: The teacher's role in combatting child abuse and neglect [slide and tape presentation]. (no date). Houston, TX: Consortium C.

Little Bear [videotape]. (no date). Goshen, IN: Bridgework Theater.

Luther, S., & Price, J. (1980). Child sexual abuse: A review. *The Journal of School Health 50,*(3), 161–165.

Mackey, G. (1981). *Bubbylonian encounter.* [videotape]. Overland Park, KS: Bubbylonian Production.

Mayer, A. (1983).Incest: A treatment manual for therapy of victims, spouses, and offenders. Holmes Beach, FL: Learning Publications.

Meiselman, K.C. (1978). *Incest: A psychological study of causes and effects with treatment recommendations.* San Francisco: Jossey-Bass.

Melton, G. (1985). Sexually abused children and the legal system; some policy recommendations. *The American Journal of Family Therapy; 13*(1), 61–71.

Mrazek, P., & Mrazek, D. (1981). The effects of child sexual abuse: Methodological considerations. In P. Mrazek & C. H. Kempe (Eds.), *Sexually abused children and their families.* New York, NY: Pergamon.

Naitive, C. (1982). Arts therapy with sexually abused children. In S. Sgroi (Eds.), *Handbook of clinical intervention in child sexual abuse.* Lexington, MA: Lexington Books.

Nakashima, T. I., & Zakus, I. E. (1977). Incest: Review and clinical experiences. *Pediatrics, 60,* 696–701.

Nasjleti, M. (1980). Suffering in silence: The male incest victim. *Child Welfare, 59*(5), 269–275.

Newman, S. (1985). Never say yes to a stranger: What your child must know to stay safe. Toronto: General Publishing Co.

Nielsen, T. (1983). Sexual abuse of boys: Current perspectives. *Personnel and Guidance Journal, 62,* 139–142.

O'Brien, S. (1980). Child abuse: A crying shame. Provo, UT: Brigham Young University Press.

Pettis, K., & Hughes, R. (1985). Sexual victimization of children: Implications for educators. *Behavioral Disorders,* 175–182.

Quiri, P. R., & Powell, S. (1985). *Stranger danger: A safety guide for children.* New York: Julian Messner.

Raphling, D., Carpenter, B., & Davis, A. (1967). Incest: A genealogical study. *Archives of General Psychiatry, 16,* 505--511.

Reimer, S. (1940). A research note on incest. *American Journal of Sociology, 45,* 566.

Rosenfeld, A. (1982). Sexual abuse of children, perspectives and professional response. In E. Newberger (Ed.), Child abuse (pp. 57–87). Boston, MA: Little, Brown.

Russell, D. E. H. (1983). The incidence and prevalence of intrafamilial and extrafamilial sexual abuse of female children. *Child Abuse and Neglect, 7,* 133–146.

Russell, D. (1984). *Sexual exploitation, rape, child sexual abuse, and workplace harassment.* Beverly Hills, CA: Sage.

Ryerson, E., & Sundem, J. (1981). Development of a curriculum on sexual exploitation and self-protection for handicapped students. *Education Unlimited, 3*(4), 26–31.

Sanford, L. T. (1982). *The silent children. A parent's guide for the prevention of child abuse.* New York: McGraw-Hill.

Sarafino, E. P. (1979). An estimate of nationwide incidence of sexual offenses against children. *Child Welfare 57*(2), 127–134.

Sexual abuse of children: America's secret shame [film]. (1980). Van Nuys, CA: TGL Productions AIMS.

The sexually abused child: Identification/interview [film]. (1978). Wheaton, IL: Calvacade Productions.

Sgroi, S., Blick, L. & Porter, F. (1982). A conceptual framework for child sexual abuse. In Sgroi, (Eds.), *Handbook of clinical intervention in child sexual abuse.* Lexington, MA: Heath.

Slager-Jorne, P. (1979). Treating sexual abuse in children. *Child abuse and neglect 3,* 285–290.

Stowell, J., & Dietzel, M. (1979). *My very own book about me.* Spokane, WA: Lutheran Social Services Press.

Summitt, R., & Kryso, J. (1978). Sexual abuse of children: A clinical spectrum. *American Journal of Orthopsychiatry, 48,* 237–250.

Sweet, P. (1981). *Something happened to me.* Racine, WI: Mother Courage.

A time for caring: The school's response to the sexually abused child [film]. (1978). No city given; Profile Films.

Tufts New England Medical Center Division of Child Psychiatry. (1984). *Sexually Exploited Children Service and Research Project* (Final Report of the Office of Juvenile Justice and Prevention. Cited in A. Browne & D. Finkelhor (1986): Impact of child sexual abuse: A review of the research. *Psychological Bulletin, 99,* 66– 77.

U. S. Department of Health, Education, and Welfare. (1978). *Child Sexual Abuse: Incest assault and sexual exploitation.* Washington, DC: A National Center on Child Abuse and Neglect.

Vander Mey, B. J., & Neff, R. L. (1984). Adult–child incest: Sample of substantiated cases. *Family Relations 33,* 549–557.

Wachter, O. (no date). *No more secrets* [film]. New York: O. D. N. Productions.

Wachter, O. (1983). *No more secrets for me.* Boston: Little, Brown.

Waller, G. C. (Producer). (no date). *This secret should be told* [videotape]. Boston: WBZ-TV.

Watson, J. (1984). Talking about the best kept secret — Sexual abuse and children with disabilities. *Exceptional Parent 14,*(6), 15–16, 18–20.

What tadoo? [videotape]. (no date). Deerfield, IL: MTI Teleprograms.

Who do you tell? [videotape]. (1978). Deerfield, IL: MTI Teleprograms.

Williams, J. (1983). *Red flag, green flag people.* Fargo, ND: Rape and Abuse Crisis Center of Fargo-Moorehead.

BIBLIOGRAPHY: PROFESSIONALS

Burgess, A. W., Groth, A. N., Holmstrom, L. L., & Sgroi, S. (1978). *Sexual assault of children and adolescents.* Lexington, MA: Heath.
Edited chapters detail theoretical and practical information on offenders, victims, and available services. Also presents information concerning police investigations, interviewing techniques, and the court process.

Erickson, E. L., McEvoy, A., & Colucci, N. (1984). *Child abuse and neglect: A guidebook for educators and community leaders.* Holmes Beach, FL: Learning Publications.
Legal information on child abuse and a discussion of methods involving school personnel in policy development, identification, referral, and prevention are given. Appendices include federal laws, forms, reading, and audiovisual lists.

Finkelhor, D. (1986). *A Sourcebook on child sexual abuse.* Beverly Hills, CA: Sage.
Presents the latest research on child abuse. Reviews the effects of abuse and describes prevention programs.

James, B., & Nasjeleti, M. (1983). *Treating sexually abused children and their families.* Palo Alto, CA: Consulting Psychologists Press.
Presents a good description of sexually molested children, victims, and mothers of incest victims. Describes the cycle of sexual abuse and presents detailed treatment programs.

Sgroi, S. (1982). *Handbook of clinical intervention in child sexual abuse.* Lexington, MA: Heath.
A theoretical framework for child sexual abuse is described, as well as practical chapters on treatment issues, including discussions of individual, group, and family therapy.

BIBLIOGRAPHY: PARENTS

Adams, C., & Fay, J. (1981). *No more secrets: Protecting your child from sexual assault.* San Luis Obispo, CA: Impact Publications.
A practical guide for parents to help them discuss sexual assault with their children. The primary emphasis is on prevention, discussion topics, and games. It also attempts to aid parents whose children have already experienced sexual assault.

Calao, F., & Hosanky, T. (1983). *Your children should know.* New York: Berkley Books.
This book, using personal stories from victims and their families, describes sexual molestation of children and methods of prevention, including self-defense techniques. It also describes techniques for dealing with sexual abuse after it occurs.

Newman, S. (1985). *Never say yes to a stranger: What your child must know to stay safe.* New York: Putnam.
Meant to be read by parents and children, this book illustrates different situations in which children are approached by strangers and ways to deal with the encounters including specific practical techniques.

O'Brien, S. (1980). *Child abuse: A crying shame.* Provo, UT: Brigham Young University Press.
This book, written for parents and educators, presents the basic facts concerning child abuse and neglect. It provides suggestions for preventing and solving the problem.

Sanford, L. (1980). *The silent children: A parent's guide to the prevention of child sexual abuse.* Garden City, NY: Doubleday.
Written for parents, this book presents an overview of child molestation and incest. It presents specific techniques parents can use to prevent child sexual abuse as well as methods of discussing sexual abuse with children. A separate section is provided for parents with specific needs such as parents of developmentally disabled children.

BIBLIOGRAPHY: CHILDREN

Hyde, M. O. (1984). *Sexual abuse: Let's talk about it.* Philadelphia, PA: Westminster.
This book meant for adolescents defines sexual abuse and gives examples of what to do in case of an abuse situation. It also lists the addresses of child sexual abuse treatment centers in each state.

Kyte, K. (1983). *Play it safe: The kid's guide to personal safety and crime prevention.* New York: Knopf.
Written for upper elementary and older children, it tells children how to protect themselves in various situations. It also discusses prevention and reporting rape and child abuse.

Stowell, J., & Dietzel, M. (1982). *My very own book about me.* Spokane, WA: Lutheran Social Services of Washington.
This workbook, designed for elementary school-aged children, describes good and bad touches and presents hypothetical situations for children's responses.

Sweet, P. (1981). *Something happened to me.* Racine, WI: Mother Courage.
A sensitive, beautifully illustrated book meant for younger children. It is particularly helpful in eliciting responses from sexually abused children.

Terkel, S., & Rench, J. (1984). *Feeling safe, feeling strong: How to avoid sexual abuse and what to do if it happens to you.* Minneapolis, MN: Lerner.
Presents short vignettes concerning sexual abuse situations ranging from unwanted touches to incest, obscene phone calls, and rape along with a brief discussion of each topic.

Children and Sexual Interest

Deborah J. Tharinger
The University of Texas at Austin

BACKGROUND

Children are developing sexual beings; they are developing physically, biologically, cognitively, emotionally, socially, morally, and behaviorally in relation to their sexuality. Sexual development is a natural, necessary, and complex process that begins at conception and continues throughout the life cycle (Chilman, 1983; Masters, Johnson, & Kolodny, 1982). During the prenatal period, sexual development is controlled mainly by biological factors. But from the moment of birth, a child's sexual development is profoundly influenced by psychosocial factors, primarily parents and extended family, schooling, peers, and media, all interacting with the child's biological heritage. This process of being acculturated about sexuality is called sexual socialization (Calderone, 1983) and it cannot be prevented — it happens in one way or another. However, it can be weighted toward the positive or the negative. The goal is sexual adjustment, that is, individuals who, at every stage of their life cycles, are confident, competent, and responsible in their sexuality (Calderone, 1983).

Although Freud's rich insights into infant and child sexuality were first published in 1905, and there has been a marked liberalization in adult attitudes toward sexuality over the past 30 years (Yates, 1982), little change has occurred in cultural attitudes toward childhood sexuality. The child with an active curiosity about sexuality elicits concern, anxiety, and reprimands from parents and educators (Allgeier & Allgeier, 1984). Adults are concerned and fearful that allowing the natural expression of childhood sexuality and educating children about sexuality encourages permissive attitudes, resulting in active sexual involvement or sexual behaviors that deviate from a pattern normally accepted by society (Walters & Walters, 1983). Most adults defend against these concerns and fears by denying and prohibiting the existence of childhood sexuality. As a result, although there is nothing inherently evil, disgusting, dirty, or frightening about sexuality, many adults implant such negative emotions in children about sexuality from infancy onward. Even if they realize that some of their own unhappiness comes from negative parental attitudes in their histories, adults often are unable to control repeating such negative socialization practices, surrendering to what has been called "the inner child of their past" (Missildine, 1963) and an unconscious process (Gagnon, 1965). Consequently, the child's natural sexual feelings and curiosity may be transformed into feelings of shame, guilt, embarrassment, fear, and helplessness — an affective state that may persist, resulting in emotional pain and impaired intimate relationships (Missildine, 1963).

Furthermore, many children are left uneducated or inaccurately informed about sexuality. The implications of ignorance of the sexual process are well documented. Children who are more knowledgeable about sexual behavior are more responsible sexually than those whose sexual knowledge is limited (Hansson, Jones, & Chernovetz, 1979). Moreover, evidence suggests that parents who engender fear and guilt about sex in their children have children who are least prepared for sexual encounters and the development of healthy attitudes toward sexuality (Walters & Walters, 1983).

A permissive "do what feels good" attitude about sexual socialization is not advocated (Gordon & Gordon, 1983). The extremes of sexual expression can have results that are as undesirable as the extremes of sexual repression (Calderone, 1983). An approach to childhood sexuality is recommended that is open, acknowledges the complex nature of sexuality, and is respectful and conservative. The task for parents, educators, and school psychologists is to be knowledgeable, comfortable, approachable, communicative, allowing, and yet age-appropriately protective.

The Role of School Psychologists

School psychologists, by the nature of their psychological knowledge and professional role in the schools, are in a key position to reinforce parental and societal acceptance of children as sexual persons. They also can educate parents and teachers about what is normal, can serve to defuse parents' and teachers' fears that sexual expression in children leads to irresponsible or pathological sexual conduct in adult life, and can facilitate communication between adults and children about sexuality. However, school psychologists typically have little experience in this area, perhaps because of the long-held attitude that sexual matters are not part of the school curriculum (Brassard, Tyler, & Kehle, 1983). Although school psychologists interview and consult with parents and teachers about children's physical, intellectual, educational, social, and emotional development, they typically do not inquire about children's sexual development. In addition, school psychologists are rarely asked questions about children's sexuality, although almost all parents and teachers have questions or concerns in this area. To begin communication, children's sexuality should be considered a domain of human life that can be discussed with both adults and children; not a difficult and embarrassing topic to be avoided (Jensen, 1979).

To be responsive, school psychologists must be approachable. They must be open and comfortable with the topic, which requires obtaining knowledge and examining and clarifying personal attitudes about sexuality (Juhasz, 1983). In addition, they constantly must examine the effects of changing sexual mores with the broader social context. Once permission is given and comfortableness is modeled, many questions will be raised by parents and teachers. Most will pertain to behavior within the normal range, that is, questions about children who are manifesting basically normal behavior that adults regard as wrong, abnormal, deviant, or inappropriate for a given setting. For most of these situations, parents and teachers can be helped by education, reassurance, and brief counseling — interventions that help them respond to children in a manner that does not create a problem or exacerbate a minor problem. However, other questions asked can suggest a more serious problem because some children suffer genuine sexual problems, as exemplified by sexual preoccupations and compulsions, inappropriate exhibitionism, and behaviors related to having been sexually abused. These disturbances require thorough assessment and intervention for the child and family, and they may involve referral to outside mental health agencies.

To aid the school psychologist to be equipped to respond to the questions and needs of parents, teachers, and children, this chapter focuses on children's sexual interest. Sexual interest is defined broadly as curiosity and concern about the physical, biological, cognitive, emotional, social, moral, and behavioral aspects of sexuality. The natural course of children's sexual development is traced and discussed, from infancy through middle childhood, along with central aspects of the sexual socialization process. Guidelines for assessment, intervention, and prevention activities for school psychologists are addressed. The need for school psychologists to be capable and comfortable in supporting the healthy sexual development of children is emphasized.

DEVELOPMENT

Viewing sexual interest as developmental is useful in understanding the range of behavior included in the concept of normalcy rather than perceiving all childhood sexual behavior and variations as abnormal. In addition, knowing what is normal is essential to determining what is abnormal. The normal developmental progressions of children's sexual interest can be organized into the stages of infancy, early childhood, and middle-to-late childhood. Sexuality in adolescence is not reviewed owing to space limitations and to the belief that if parents and professionals are more knowledgeable about childhood sexuality, many of the sex-related problems that arise during adolescence can be prevented. Methods used by parents to socialize and to respond to children's sexual interest are discussed, aspects of children's sexual interest that are of concern to parents and teachers are reviewed, and practices designed to promote healthy sexual development are offered. An analysis of the types of concerns parents and teachers express completes the section.

Sexuality in Infancy

Sonograms show that the sexual response system begins functioning in utero, as shown by periodic erections of the penis and the findings that the vagina of the infant girl lubricates cyclically from birth on, by the same mechanism that operates later on in sexual responsiveness (Langfeldt, 1980). Also, orgasm-like behavior clearly is apparent in very young infants (Kensey, Pomeroy, & Martin, 1948; Kensey, Pomeroy, Martin, & Gebhard, 1953). Furthermore, the discovery of various parts of the body inevitably leads a baby of around 6 months to discover its sexual pleasure area, the penis in the boy and the clitoris and vulva in the girl. Baby boys and girls rub their genitals as soon as they develop the necessary motor coordination. There appears to be a genuine sense of pleasure leading to repetition of self-stimulation in infancy. The potential to respond to sexual stimuli in infancy suggests that the foremost "principle" in childhood sexuality is that "genital stimulation feels good" (Abramson, 1980).

The infant's interactions with primary caregivers, consisting of sensuous closeness through holding, clinging, and cuddling, are thought to greatly influence the development of sexuality (Higham, 1980). This parent–child bonding begins at birth and extends to include nursing, bathing, dressing, and other physical interactions between parents and their newborn child. These interactions correspond to Bowlby's (1969) concept of attachment and to Erikson's (1968) first psychosocial stage of development, trust versus mistrust, and they are viewed as the beginnings of sexual education (Bettelheim, 1981). Children who are deprived of warm, close bonding during infancy can experience later difficulties in forming intimate relationships and perhaps in being comfortable with their sexuality (Harlow & Harlow, 1962; Trause, Kennell, & Klaus, 1977).

As infants develop social attachment and seek to secure and maintain closeness and trust, they begin to regulate self-stimulation to conform to external reactions. Thus, early parental reactions to an infant's genital exploration set the stage for the regulatory character of his or her principles for acceptable sexual conduct (Abramson, 1980). As the infant grows, sensorimotor intelligence also unfolds and matures, and genital stimulation becomes a predetermined rather than a random response, making the connection between genital play and positive feelings more assured. However, as this sequence becomes more practiced, parental awareness of this behavior also is more likely. Again, the behavior conforms to external regulation, now being accompanied by a more conscious recognition of the relationship between genital play and a specific parental reaction.

Thus, although self-stimulation begins early in infancy, many parents even today continue to regard masturbation as wrong and unhealthy and are fearful of imagined consequences (Jensen, 1979). Conscious self-pleasuring of the genitals can upset a parent who has not been prepared for acceptance of its occurrence as normal; it can lead to constant interference by well-meaning but uninformed adults who, because of their fear, do not permit children to "own" their bodies and the pleasure that can be derived from them. As a result of parental interference many children stop the behavior, but the experience may leave a lasting negative outlook on their own sexuality and can restrict their sense of freedom to pleasure themselves later in life (Calderone, 1978; Masters & Johnson, 1970).

It is important for parents and educators to understand and accept that self-stimulation is a normal part of growing up and now is viewed as an important step in the development of the erotic response (Yates, 1982). The instances in which parents and teachers need to give children special guidance are those in which the child masturbates in situations that are felt to be inappropriate, e.g., in public, in the presence of persons outside the family, or even in the view of parents who are upset by it. The parent or teacher can be advised to tell the child simply to confine pleasuring to a private place — an appropriate place. This brings out a major principle in the sexual socialization of children, applicable from infancy on. Socialize for privacy; that is, the child's sexual interest, curiosity, or behavior should not be labeled "bad," but simply not appropriate for the time, place, or person (Calderone, 1983).

Instances occur in infancy and later stages of development when masturbation is not an aspect of healthy development and necessitates more than guidance for privacy. This is when masturbation is excessive and/or compulsive, that is, not under the rational control of the child. When this is the case, the behavior can be viewed as a means of warding off anxiety or other distressing feelings and can be interpreted as defensive behavior (Jensen, 1979) or as emotional disturbance, especially when coupled with withdrawn behavior (Chilman, 1983). In these instances, more extensive intervention is needed.

Sexuality in Early Childhood

The onset of language signals a critical new stage in the development of sexual interest (Gadpaille, 1978; Money & Ehrhardt, 1972). Children seek and are provided with labels for sexual feelings, functions, and organs that can serve to initiate a unified sense of sexuality (Abramson, 1980). It is important for adults to provide appropriate accurate labels (Calderone, 1983), and professionals can be helpful by enabling parents and early childhood educators to have a suitable vocabulary that is easily understood by the child. Furthermore, from this stage on, children are able to articulate what they understand has been presented to them as standards for acceptable sexual conduct.

During early childhood, most children begin asking questions about how babies are made and how birth occurs (Martinson, 1980). When parents are open, honest, and emotionally positive, the child senses that future question asking is welcomed. Parents also can anticipate questions and be prepared. The use of picture books to provide information and elicit questions is helpful. Some parents respond to their children's questions with matter-of-fact and developmentally appropriate answers, but others are obviously uncomfortable and reluctant to discuss sexual information at any length. Recent research has suggested that U.S. children are lagging in their knowledge of the facts and language of sexuality. In a cross-culture study, U.S. children were shown to be significantly delayed in the area of sexual thinking compared with Australian, British, and Swedish children but to be equal on tests of general cognitive reasoning (Goldman & Goldman, 1982).

At the same time that parents need to provide their children with accurate information, they need to be advised to be cautious about how much information they give a youngster when a question is asked and to remember the child's age and developmental level. It is helpful to determine what the child really wants to know, which may be very different from the answer the adult is inclined to give (Bettelheim, 1981). The young child is ready for only a little information at a time. A study on the thinking of children aged 3–12 about how people get babies is recommended as an excellent source for understanding what children know and can understand at various stages of development (Bernstein & Cowan, 1975).

By age 5, most children are fascinated with learning words about sexual body parts. Jokes about sex and genital function begin to make their rounds, often heard first from an older child or adult and then repeated. Obscene words, especially "fuck," are used. The fascination and use continue into the school years. These words are not used in an erotic way. Rather, they are used as part of growing up, of being like one's peers, or they are used to convey status, anger, or frustration. Unfortunately, since even young children quickly learn the difference between a "clean" and a "dirty" word or joke, the idea that sex is dirty is reinforced.

Children also form ideas about sexuality based on their observation of physical interactions between their parents. Parents are both conscious and unconscious role models to their impressionable youngsters. Seeing mommy and daddy hugging and kissing, and obviously enjoying it, is a good advertisement for the pleasure of physical and emotional intimacy. On the other hand, seeing parents constantly fighting and not being mutually responsive can have just the opposite effect.

Children continue to be curious about body parts, and unless harshly reprimanded for the behavior in infancy, they engage in genital stimulation, first as a solitary activity and later in social games like "show me yours and I'll show you mine" and "doctor." Children also continue to be aware of parental attitudes of disapproval of genital play and can be confused by parental encouragement to be aware of their bodies but to exclude the genitals from such awareness. A study of 3-and 4-year-olds found that the area between the belly button and the knees appeared to exist for the children as "not me" (Blackman, 1980). This attitude is compounded by many children's assumption that their genitals are "dirty" from messages received during toilet training.

Genital exhibitionism, a concern of some parents, is common and normal among 3- and 4-year-olds when it is occasional (Jensen, 1979). It generally indicates pride in one's body — a wholesome trait. Boys and girls up to 3 or 4 years enjoy being nude either at nursery school or in public. After that age, however, the public frowns on it, and they get the message and cover up. Normal genital exhibitionism is best accepted by parents for what it is —a healthy behavior. Parents simply need the education and reassurance to ignore the behavior or to act appropriately, and to avoid overreacting and creating a problem for the child.

It is normal for young children to want information about sexuality, to become fascinated by "dirty" words, to be influenced greatly by their parents' affectional behavior toward each other and toward them, to continue to self-stimulate and engage in social games involving sexual exploration, and to feel proud of their bodies and want to exhibit them. What is not normal is excessive or compulsive self-stimulation or exhibitionism; coercive and aggressive sexual behavior toward others; and detailed and age-inappropriate understanding of adult sexual behavior. It is likely that children manifesting these types of behavior have been overly sexually stimulated for their age. They may be victims of sexual abuse (see the chapter on sexual abuse in this volume); they may have sleeping arrangements that result in sexual overstimulation (Jensen, 1979); or they may have witnessed on television or in person sexual activity that they cannot comprehend or integrate and that preoccupies and disturbs them.

Sexuality in Middle to Late Childhood

A natural and continuing aspect of sexual development during this stage is sexual play between same-sex and opposite-sex peers. In most instances, sexual play is normal and healthy. It generally occurs between playmates of like age, is cooperative, and is limited to a few episodes (Kinsey et al., 1953). It may consist of mutual touching or imitating intercourse. However, if sexual exploration involves an older child, such as an adolescent with a school-age or younger child, or coercion or aggression, it is not a case of sexual play. It is sexual abuse, and needs to be handled accordingly.

Sexual play is usually secretive, conducted out of the sight of adults. Boys initiate sex play more often than girls (Kinsey et al., 1948; 1953). In a recent survey, parents noted that 76% of their daughters and 83% of their sons had participated in some sex play (Kolodny, 1980). By ages 8 or 9 children have awareness of the erotic element of self-stimulation and sexual play (Masters, Masters, & Kolodny, 1982). Engaging in these experiences can help children learn how to relate to others, with important consequences for their adult psychosexual adjustment (Broderick, 1968; Gadpaille, 1975; Martinson, 1976).

Thus, ordinary sex play is not psychologically harmful; it is simply a stage of development. The harm generally comes from any ensuing crisis that might arise — the punishment and guilt induced by the parents' and neighbors' reactions. The child who has been expressing normal sexual curiosity can come to feel bad and shameful. The episode can be traumatic; it can shape attitudes that interfere with healthy adult sexuality. Parental reactions to the discovery of sex play in children frequently operate on a double standard. Girls often are cautioned strongly against sexual play, especially with boys. Boys, on the other hand, tend to get mixed messages from their parents; they may be warned or even punished for such activity, but there is a hint of resignation or even pride in the attitude that "boys will be boys." The unspoken permission for boys to follow their sexual curiosity — except in homosexual situations, where parents consistently react in a negative way — is only rarely found directed to school-age girls in U.S. society (Allgeier & Allgeier, 1984).

Many parents are unaware that homosexual play among children is a normal part of growing up. Homosexual experiences have been reported by more than half the boys and more than a third of the girls in a study of children of ages 4–14 (Elias & Gebhard, 1969). These homosexual activities are a common part of sexual development in this culture, and such experiences are unrelated to preferences for sexual partners of the same or other gender in adulthood (Bell, Weinberg, & Hammersmith, 1981).

The above discussion calls into question Freud's concept of a period of sexual latency — a time when sexual interests and impulses are diverted into nonsexual behaviors and interests — during late childhood. The existence of a period of sexual latency is not widely accepted (Money, 1980). During late childhood, children play primarily with members of their own sex, but research indicates that they discuss sex-related topics frequently, show keen interest in the opposite sex, desire to be in the presence of the opposite sex, and under certain circumstances desire to engage in activities with members of the opposite sex. In a study of 10- 12-year-olds, it was found that 75% of the girls and 64% of the boys reported having a girlfriend or boyfriend of the opposite sex, 59% and 53% of the girls and boys, respectively, reported having been in love, and 31% and 25% of the girls and boys, respectively, reported having been on a date (Ruppel, 1980). In addition, cross-cultural studies clearly show that if a society is not repressive toward childhood sexual rehearsal, sexual play continues and may even be more frequent during the preadolescent than in earlier years (Ford & Beach, 1951; Marshall & Suggs, 1971). Kinsey's data also show that sexual experimentation does not stop or even slow down during this period (Kinsey et al., 1948; 1953).

Analysis of Parents' and Teachers' Concerns About Children's Sexual Interest

From an examination of the common anxieties of adults about childhood sexuality presented in the literature and briefly described here, four levels of concern are proposed by the author as an integrated and descriptive framework from which to conceptualize perceived sexual problems of children. Each progressive level represents a more serious problem and the need for more extensive intervention.

Level 1: Lack of Knowledge. The concern parents or teachers voice is due to their lack of knowledge about the normal development of child sexuality. Because of the lack of knowledge, the adult thinks of the child's interests and behaviors as abnormal.

Level 2: Lack of Effective Communication. The concern parents or teachers voice is due to poor communication with children about sexuality. They are confused about how to respond to children's behavior and questions. They are unsure about how to sexually socialize children — how to educate and yet protect. They are fearful of childhood sexuality and perhaps affected by their own sexual issues.

Level 3: Fear of Premature Sexual Activity and/or Social Rejection. The concern parents or teachers voice is due to the emotional and social consequences they fear for their children and, in the case of parents, themselves. Parents and teachers want to protect children from engaging in behavior that they cannot handle cognitively and emotionally, for example intercourse. They also want to protect children from engaging in thoughts, behaviors, and interests that would render them victims of social prejudice, for example, homosexuality and pervasive cross-gender behavior.

Level 4: Presence of Disturbed Sexual Behavior. The concern parents or teachers voice is due to emotional and behavior disturbance being expressed sexually by the child. The child's inappropriate sexual expression, self-directed or directed at others, is related to past or present sexual abuse or sexual overstimulation, to severe stress or neglect, or to inability to regulate sexual behavior as a result of being retarded, autistic, or psychotic.

PUTTING CHILDREN'S SEXUAL INTEREST IN PERSPECTIVE

A number of factors must be considered when evaluating a child's sexual interest as being possibly inappropriate and in need of intervention. The framework presented to guide assessment is ecological (Bronfenbrenner, 1979) and takes into account the various aspects of the child's sexual interest, the characteristics of the child, the features of the systems and culture that the child is part of, and the resulting interactions. In each of these areas, the factors that the school psychologist needs information about in order to evaluate the level of concern and the seriousness of the referred problem are proposed. The primary assessment method is an interview with parents, teachers, and the child. Suggestions for how to ask specific interview questions are provided by Walen and Vanderhorst (1983). Observation of the child, in classrooms and in play sessions, also can be valuable, especially with young children. In addition, the child's school files and other records can yield useful information. Furthermore, knowledge of the school climate, or peer group functioning, and of the attitudes of the local community, typically obtained through experience working in the community, is essential.

Following data gathering, the school psychologist integrates the ecological findings and determines the type of problem present, guided by the four levels of concern presented above. In addition, the degree of fit or lack of fit between the child, his or her sexual interest, and the expectations and values of the involved systems (family, school, and peers) is evaluated. The higher the level of concern and the poorer the fit, the more serious the problem is and the more difficult change will be. The goal of the evaluation is to recommend and provide appropriate intervention. The specific factors to be assessed include the following.

Aspects of the Sexual Interest

- Type, frequency, intensity, duration, and context of sexual interest the child is displaying.

Aspects of the Child

- Age, sex, and physical, cognitive, social, and emotional level of the child.
- Degree of distress experienced by the child as a result of his or her sexual interest.
- Child's level of understanding of his or her sexuality.
- Current stressors present in the child's life.
- Presence of current or previous sexual abuse.
- Motivation of the child to participate in an intervention.

Aspects of the Family

- Family composition.
- Degree of distress experienced by family members as a result of the child's sexual interest.
- Degree of accurate parental knowledge of childhood sexuality.

- Parents' ability to communicate effectively about sexuality with their child.
- Parental attitudes and values regarding sexuality, including cultural and religious attitudes.
- Presence of recent or current family stressors, including birth of a sibling, death of a loved one, parental separation or divorce, parental dating and sexual behavior, disclosure of adoption, parental alcoholism, and physical, emotional, or sexual abuse.
- Appropriateness of family sleeping arrangements.
- Motivation of the parents to participate in an intervention.

Aspects of the School Environment

- Teachers' and administrators' knowledge of sexuality, ability to communicate, and attitudes and values.
- Cultural and religious influences on the school environment.
- Degree of distress experienced by school personnel as a result of the child's sexual interest.
- Quality of the relationship between the family and the school.
- Motivation of the teacher(s) to participate in an intervention.

Aspects of the Peer Group

- Characteristics, behavior, and strength of influence of the child's peer group.

ALTERNATIVE ACTIONS

As part of the evaluation, the school psychologist determines the degree of need for intervention and recommends specific actions that fit with the level of concern and the degree of seriousness of the problem. The available interventions are not unique to the topic of children's sexual interest and are familiar to school psychologists. They include education; mental health or behavioral consultation; crisis intervention and related problem-solving techniques; school-based individual, group, and family counseling and therapy; and referral to mental health professions for similar and additional services. However, school psychologists need to be informed and comfortable about applying these interventions to sexual issues with children, parents, families, and educators. To be effective, school psychologists must examine their own personal attitudes about sexuality, must gain knowledge about child sexuality and sexual socialization, must consider the consequences of entering an area where cultural denial and prohibition continue to be strong, and must seek out school district and parental support. Interventions are described that are appropriate at each of the four levels of concern described above, followed by prevention activities.

Interventions for Level 1: Lack of Knowledge

If the evaluation reveals that the perceived sexual problem is a result of lack of knowledge on the part of the parents or teacher regarding what is developmentally appropriate, information needs to be provided, either directly by the school psychologist through a one-to-one format, or by referring the parents to a course and the teacher to an in-service training workshop focused on childhood sexuality. Providing reading materials also can be a helpful adjunct. Programs to help parents participate more effectively and comfortably in their children's sexual socialization have been reported since 1970 (Gripton, 1980). Suggested goals for a parent program (Walters & Walters, 1983) include the following: (a) Parents need to think carefully about their own attitudes and the attitudes about sexuality that they wish to transmit to their children; (b) the home should be acknowledged as the locus of the transferral of attitudes; (c) parents and children need to talk more about sexuality; (d) fathers, in particular, need to talk more with their children about sexuality; (e) of all the attitudes that parents need to communicate to children, one of the most important is their willingness to support their children; (f) in their conversations with their children, parents need to resist the inclination to be shocked or frightened by what they hear; and (g) although the family is only one of many sources of sexual education, the power of families to shape attitudes is great enough that it appears unnecessary for families to be overly concerned about the possibility that sexual education in schools will change their children's basic attitudes.

Another set of goals for a parent program (Gripton, 1980) that also seem applicable to programs for teachers include helping adults (a) to acquire a cognitive framework for their role in the sexual education of children that is based on relevant and accurate knowledge of the sexual development of children and that is integrated with their sexual values; (b) to overcome the anxiety that impedes effective communication with children about sexuality; and (c) to acquire specific communication-behavior competence in talking to children about sexuality. Other sources on sexual education programs for parents and teachers include D'Souza (1979) and Yates (1980).

Interventions for Level 2: Lack of Effective Communication

If the evaluation reveals that a child's perceived sexual problem is a result of poor or negative communication between parents and child, or teacher and child, it is appropriate for the school psychologist to intervene by directly working with the parents or teacher to aid them in feeling knowledgeable, confident, comfortable, and secure in talking to children about sexuality. A mental health consultation format can be effective. Many of the goals of the programs described above can be incorporated into individual and group programs. Referral to a parent group or communication group within the school or to a local mental health facility also can be effective. Suggestions on how to train parents to be educators on sexuality are offered by Drake, Nederlander, and Mercier (1980). If the parent or teacher appears to be seriously distressed by the idea of communicating about sexuality, a referral for individual or couple counseling may be timely.

It also can be beneficial for school psychologists to work directly with children, individually or in groups, to provide them with age-appropriate information about sexuality and the means to feel comfortable in communicating about their sexuality, especially if their parents are unwilling or unable to do so. Examples of treating sexual communication problems using a cognitive, rational–emotive approach with parents and children are provided by Walen and Vanderhorst (1983) and by Ellis (1980).

Interventions for Level 3: Fear of Premature Sexual Activity and/or Social Rejection

If the evaluation reveals that a child's perceived sexual problem is a result of the child's engaging in behavior that parents and/or teachers believe he or she cannot cognitively and emotionally handle, such as being sexually active, and the problem cannot be resolved by providing knowledge and communication skills to the adults and child involved, crisis intervention (Ross-Reynolds & Hardy, 1985) and family therapy, most likely outside of the school are recommended. Family therapy is the ongoing treatment of choice because the whole family's functioning, and how it may be supporting or even encouraging the child's behavior, can be reviewed and targeted for change.

In the case of children for whom evaluation reveals that the perceived sexual problem is a result of their engaging in thoughts, interests, and behaviors that can render them and perhaps their family victims of social prejudice, such as homosexual or excessive cross-gender behavior (see the chapters on homosexuality and gender identity in this volume), multiple interventions are in order. In the case of homosexuality, for example, the children need the psychological protection of a counseling or therapy relationship from which to explore these interests and determine their meaning (Ross-Reynolds & Hardy, 1985). Education about the normality of homosexual fantasies and behavior in childhood can relieve fears and distress and perhaps end the crisis. Children who determine that their sexual preference is exclusively or primarily toward members of the same gender need continued support to integrate this information into their identity and relationships in the world. In this case, parents also need support, through outside counseling and community support groups, to cope with what they will perceive as a loss and rejection and to reach the stage of acceptance. Family therapy also can be effective. In addition, school psychologists can aid teachers by providing consultation to allow them to work on their own emotional reactions to homosexuality and to assist them with other students' reactions.

Interventions for Level 4: Existence of Disturbed Sexual Behavior

If the evaluation reveals that a child's perceived sexual problem is due to emotional or behavioral disturbance, child and family therapy usually is warranted, and teacher consultation is recommended. If the child's inappropriate sexual interest is related to having been sexually abused, individual, family, and group therapy are needed. Sexual abuse has serious initial emotional and behavioral consequences for the child that continue if untreated and also endanger others (Vevier & Tharinger, 1986). If the child is continuing to be abused or is not sufficiently protected from the possibility, removal of the abuser from the home or foster placement for the child is required. In the case of sexual abuse, the designated protective service agencies must be contacted and they are responsible for securing protective and intervention services. Although school psychologists are not major figures in the in-depth treatment of child sexual abuse, they are in a key position in the schools to participate in the identification and prevention of child sexual abuse (Vevier and Tharinger, 1986).

If a child's inappropriate sexual interest is due to having been sexually overstimulated, a form of sexual abuse, environmental changes are in order, as well as family evaluation and possibly therapy. If the behavior is due to the child's being extremely stressed or neglected, and presents as excessive, compulsive, and nonregulated masturbation or exhibitionism, behavioral approaches can be effective in eliminating the behavior (Rekers, 1980), and family therapy can be useful to identify and eliminate the source of the distress. If the problem is due to the child's being unable to regulate sexual behavior because of retardation, autism, or psychosis, educational and behavioral management programs for the child at home and in the classroom need to be instituted by parents and teachers (Morgan, 1983).

Prevention Activities

In addition to providing intervention services, school psychologists can be involved actively in school-based prevention programs by conducting parent groups on childhood sexuality and communication skills, and by providing workshops for teachers and administrators on sexual development and on ways that school personnel can respond more positively and effectively to children's sexual interest. School psychologists also can meet a prevention need by supporting and being involved in sexual education programs for children in the schools. Although the first programs of sex education in U.S. schools began in the second decade of this century, the development of school-based sex education since that time has been characterized by slow and cautious expansion, periodically interrupted or reversed by well-organized attacks from right-wing religious and political groups (Gripton, 1980). It is estimated that substantially less than 10% of high school students in the United States receive a separate sex education course (Kirby, Alter, & Scales, 1979). The percentage of elementary school pupils receiving such instruction, the stage of development where it is thought to be essential, is minuscule (Chaltas, 1978). Suggestions for a sex education program for 10-to 12-year-olds are offered by Barrett, Bean, and Budden (1980).

In addition, school psychologists work extensively with children who have handicapping conditions. The handicapped child requires sex education and has the same needs, desires, rights, and responsibilities as the nondisabled child (Geist & Geist, 1980). To teach sex education to handicapped children, it is necessary to have a positive attitude toward disabled children and to know the particular medical and psychosocial implications of the disability. Suggestions for providing sex education for emotionally disturbed, behavior-disordered, mentally retarded, sensory-handicapped, and orthopedically impaired children are provided by Geist and Geist (1980) and Monat (1982).

SUMMARY

School psychologists have the opportunity to be involved in the identification and prevention of ignorance and silence about childhood sexuality. Although most people associate sexuality solely with adolescence and adulthood, infants and children are developing sexual beings and they express natural interest and curiosity about their sexuality. Most adults, however, find it difficult to accept and to allow expression of childhood sexuality, to communicate with children about sexuality, and to provide a positive sexual socialization experience for children. As a result, many children repress their positive feelings about sexuality, associate the negative feelings of shame, guilt, embarrassment, fear, and helplessness with sexuality, and later experience psychological pain and impaired intimate relationships. Ironically and unfortunately, as parents these children will pass on to their offspring similar attitudes and feelings.

Contrary to general belief, it is normal and healthy for infants to engage in and enjoy self-stimulation. It is normal for young children to seek information about sexuality, to become fascinated with "dirty words," to continue to self-stimulate and to engage in social games involving sexual exploration, and to feel proud of their bodies and want to show them off. It is normal for school-aged children to participate in sexual play between same-sex and opposite-sex peers, and to show keen interest in members of the opposite sex. It is not normal or healthy at any age for a child to engage in excessive or compulsive self-stimulation or exhibitionism, or in coercive or aggressive sexual behavior toward others, or to be sexually overstimulated or sexually abused.

School psychologists are in a key position to reinforce parental and societal acceptance of children as sexual persons, to educate adults and children about sexual development, and to promote honest, accurate, and open communication about sexuality between adults and children. In addition, school psychologists need to be able to evaluate adults' concerns about children's sexual interest and to recommend and provide appropriate interventions. The goal for school psychologists is to support and promote practices that allow children to feel confident, competent, accepting, and responsible about their sexuality. To be effective, school psychologists must be knowledgeable, comfortable, approachable, and willing to enter a controversial area.

To aid school psychologists in their work in the area of childhood sexuality, this chapter presented the normal developmental progressions of children's sexual interest from infancy through middle childhood, reviewed parental sexual socialization practices, and discussed concerns that parents and teachers express about children's sexual interest. Practices designed to promote healthy sexual development were described, and four progressive levels of concern about childhood sexuality were proposed. In addition, guidelines for conducting comprehensive assessments were provided, suggestions for appropriate interventions under each of the four levels of concern were offered, and a plea for school psychologists to be involved in prevention activities was made.

REFERENCES

Abramson, P. R. (1980). Cognitive development and sexual expression in childhood. In J. M. Samson (Ed.), *Childhood and sexuality: Proceedings of the international symposium on childhood and sexuality* (pp. 137–142). Montreal: Editions Etudes Vivantes.

Allgeier, E. R., & Allgeier, A. R. (1984). *Sexual interactions.* Lexington, MA: Heath.

Barrett, A., Bean, B., & Budden, S. (1980). Theoretical basis for a sex education program for pre-pubertal boys and girls. In J. M. Samson (Ed.), *Childhood and sexuality: Proceedings of the international symposium on childhood and sexuality* (pp. 418–425). Montreal: Editions Etudes Vivantes.

Bell, A. R., Weinberg, M. S., & Hammersmith, S. K. (1981). *Sexual preference: Its development in men and women.* Bloomington: Indiana University Press.

Bernstein, A. C., & Cowan, P. A. (1975). Children's concepts of how people get babies. *Child Development, 46,* 77–91.

Bettelheim, B. (1981, July). Our children are treated like idiots. *Psychology Today,* pp. 28–43.

Blackman, N. (1980). Pleasure and touching: Their significance in the development of the pre-school child. In J. M. Samson (Ed.), *Childhood and sexuality: Proceedings of the international symposium on childhood and sexuality.* Montreal: Editions Etudes Vivantes.

Bowlby, J. (1969). *Attachment.* New York: Basic Books.

Brassard, M. R., Tyler, A. H., & Kehle, T. J. (1983). School programs to prevent intrafamilial child sexual abuse. *Child Abuse and Neglect, 7,* 241–245.

Broderick, C. B. (1968). Preadolescent sexual behavior. *Medical Aspects of Human Sexuality, 2,* 20–29.

Bronfenbrenner, U. (1979). *The ecology of human development.* Cambridge, MA: Harvard University Press.

Calderone, M. S. (1978). Is sex education preventative? In C. B. Qualls, J. P. Wincze, & D. H. Barlow (Eds.), *The prevention of sexual disorders* (pp. 139–155). New York: Plenum.

Calderone, M. S. (1983). Childhood sexuality: Approaching the prevention of sexuality dis-ease. In G. W. Albee, S. Gordon, & H. Leitenberg (Eds.), *Promoting sexual responsibility and preventing sexual problems* (pp. 333–344). Hanover and London: University Press of New England.

Chaltas, V. (1978). New approaches to sex education: Kindergarten and elementary grades. In H. Oho (Ed.), *The new sex education* (pp. 51–67).

Chilman, C. S. (1983). The development of adolescent sexuality. *Journal of Research and Development in Education, 16,* 16–26.

Drake, L. W., Nederlander, C., & Mercier, R. G. (1980). Teaching sexual assertiveness training: Sex education between parent and child. In J. M. Samson (Ed.), *Childhood and sexuality: Proceedings of the international symposium on childhood and sexuality* (pp. 426–430). Montreal: Editions Etudes Vivantes.

D'Souza, A. A. (1979). *Sex education and personality development.* New Delhi: Usha.

Elias, J., & Gebhard, P. (1969). Sexuality and sexual learning in childhood. *Phi Delta Kappan, 3,* 401–405.

Ellis, A. (1980). The rational–emotive approach to children's and adolescents' sex problems. In J. M. Samson (Ed.), *Childhood and sexuality: Proceedings of the international symposium on childhood and sexuality* (pp. 513–524). Montreal: Editions Etudes Vivantes.

Erikson, E. H. (1968). *Childhood and society* (rev. ed.). New York: Norton.

Ford, C. S., & Beach, F. (1951). *Patterns of sexual behavior.* New York: Harper.

Gadpaille, W. J. (1975). *The cycles of sex.* New York: Scribner.

Gadpaille, W. J. (1978). Psychosexual developmental tasks imposed by pathologically delayed childhood: A cultural dilemma. In S. Feinstein & P. Giovacchini (Eds.), *Adolescent psychiatry* (Vol. 6). Chicago: University of Chicago Press.

Gagnon, J. H. (1965). Sexuality and sexual learning in the child. *Psychiatry, 28,* 212–228.

Geist, C. S., & Geist, G. O. (1980). Sex education for the handicapped child. In J. M. Samson (Ed.), *Childhood and sexuality: Proceedings of the international symposium on childhood and sexuality* (pp. 504–508). Montreal: Editions Etudes Vivantes.

Goldman, R., & Goldman, J. (1982). *Children's sexual thinking: A comparative study of children aged 5 to 15 years in Australia, North America, Britain and Sweden.* London: Routledge & Kegan Paul.

Gordon, S., & Gordon, J. (1983). *Raising a child conservatively in a sexually permissive world.* New York: Simon and Schuster.

Gripton, J. (1980). Preparing parents for participating in the sexual development of their children: An innovative program and a research design. In J. M. Samson (Ed.), *Childhood and sexuality: Proceedings of the international symposium on childhood and sexuality* (pp. 431–441). Montreal: Editions Etudes Vivantes.

Hansson, R. O., Jones, W. H., & Chernovetz, M. E. (1979). Contraceptive knowledge: Antecedents and implications. *Family Coordinator, 28,* 29–34.

Harlow, H. F., & Harlow, M. (1962). Social deprivation in monkeys. *Scientific American, 473,* 1–11.

Higham, E. (1980). Sexuality in the infant and the neonate: Birth to two years. In B. B. Wolman & J. Money (Eds.), *Handbook of human sexuality* (pp. 16–27). Englewood Cliffs, NJ: Prentice-Hall.

Jensen, G. D. (1979). Childhood sexuality. In R. G. Green (Ed.), *Human sexuality: A health practitioner's text* (2nd ed). Baltimore: Williams & Wilkins.

Juhasz, A. M. (1983). Variation in sexual behavior. *Journal of Research and Development in Education, 16,* 53–59.

Kinsey, A. C., Pomeroy, W. B., & Martin, C. E. (1948). *Sexual behavior in the human male.* Philadelphia: Saunders.

Kinsey, A. C., Pomeroy, W. B., Martin, C. E., & Gebhard, P. H. (1953). *Sexual behavior in the human female.* Philadelphia: Saunders.

Kirby, D., Alter, J., & Scales, P. (1979). *An analysis of U.S. sex education programs and evaluation methods.* Washington: U.S. Department of Health, Education, and Welfare (No. CDC-2021-79-DK-FR).

Kolodny, R. C. (1980). *Adolescent sexuality.* Paper presented at the Michigan Personnel and Guidance Association Annual Convention, Detroit.

Langfeldt, T. (1980). Aspects of sexual development, problems and therapy in children. In J. M. Samson (Ed.), *Childhood and sexuality: Proceedings of the international symposium on childhood and sexuality.* Montreal: Editions Etudes Vivantes.

Marshall, D., & Suggs, R. (1971). *Human sexual behavior.* New York: Basic Books.

Martinson, F. M. (1976). Eroticism in infancy and childhood. *Journal of Sex Research, 12,* 251–262.

Martinson, F. (1980). Child sexuality: Trends and consequences. In J. M. Samson (Ed.), *Childhood and sexuality: Proceedings of the international symposium on childhood and sexuality.* Montreal: Editions Etudes Vivantes.

Masters, W. H., & Johnson, V. E. (1970). *Human sexual inadequacy.* Boston: Little, Brown.

Master, W. H., Johnson, V. E., & Kolodny, R. C. (1982). *Human sexuality.* Boston: Little, Brown.

Missildine, W. H. (1963). *Your inner child of the past.* New York: Simon and Schuster.

Monat, R. K. (1982). *Sexuality and the mentally retarded: A clinical and therapeutic guidebook.* San Diego: College-Hill.

Money, J. (1980). *Love and love sickness.* Baltimore: Johns Hopkins University Press.

Money, J., & Ehrhardt, A. A. (1972). *Man and woman, boy and girl.* Baltimore: Johns Hopkins University Press.

Morgan, S. (1983). Counseling with teachers on the sexual acting-out of disturbed children. *Psychology in the Schools, 21,* 234–242.

Rekers, G. A. (1980). Therapies dealing with the child's sexual difficulties (behavioral approach). In J. M. Samson (Ed.), *Childhood and sexuality: Proceedings of the international symposium on childhood and sexuality* (pp. 525–538). Montreal: Editions Etudes Vivantes.

Ross-Reynolds, G., & Hardy, B. S. (1985). Crisis counseling for disparate adolescent sexual dilemma: Pregnancy and homosexuality. *School Psychology Review, 14,* 300–312.

Ruppel, H. J. (1980). Socio-sexual development among preadolescents. In J. M. Samson (Ed.), *Childhood and sexuality: Proceedings of the international symposium on childhood and sexuality* (pp. 128–135). Montreal: Editions Etudes Vivantes.

Trause, M. A., Kennell, J., & Klaus, M. (1977). Parental attachment behavior. In J. Money & H. Musaph (Eds.), *Handbook of sexology* (pp. 789–799). New York: Elsevier/North-Holland.

Vevier, E., & Tharinger, D. J. (1986). Child sexual abuse: A review and intervention framework for the school psychologist. *Journal of School Psychology, 24,* 293–311.

Walen, S. R., & Vanderhorst, G. K. (1983). A rational–emotive approach to childhood sexuality. In A. E. Ellis & M. E. Bernard (Eds.), *Rational–emotive approaches to the problems of childhood* (pp. 311–330). New York: Plenum.

Walters, J., & Walters, L. H. (1983). The role of the family in sex education. *Journal of Research and Development in Education, 16,* 8–15.

Yates, A. (1980). The effect of commonly accepted parenting practices on erotic development. In J. M. Samson (Ed.), *Childhood and sexuality: Proceedings of the international symposium on childhood and sexuality* (pp. 367–373). Montreal: Editions Etudes Vivantes.

Yates, A. (1982). Childhood sexuality in the psychiatric textbook. *The Journal of Psychiatric Education, 6,* 217–226.

BIBLIOGRAPHY: PROFESSIONALS

Bernstein, A. C., & Cowan, P. A. (1975). Children's concepts of how people get babies. *Child Development, 46,* 77–91.
This article reports the results of a study in which children aged 3–12 were interviewed on their concepts of how people get babies. The results indicated that children's concepts of how people get babies appears to follow a Piagetian developmental sequence. The important point for practitioners is that information about sexuality is not simply taken in by children; it is transformed to fit into the child's present level of thinking

Masters, W. H., Johnson, V. E., & Kolodny, R. C. (1986). *Masters and Johnson on sexual human loving.* Boston: Little, Brown.
This recent book is a well-written, integrated overview of current perspectives on the biological, psychological, and social aspects of sexuality. It covers childhood, adolescent, and adult sexuality and discusses the future of sexuality. Written for a general audience, it will be of interest to both professionals and parents.

Samson, J. M. (1980). *Childhood and sexuality: Proceedings of the international symposium on childhood and sexuality.* Montreal: Editions Etudes Vivantes.
This book is an excellent collection of conceptual, research, and applied articles on childhood sexuality, written by experts in the field. Topics include sexual development, sexual socialization, sex education, and treatment of perceived sexual problems. It may be the most comprehensive edited volume available. The majority of the articles are in English; the remainder are in French.

Walen, S. R., & Vanderhorst, O. K. (1983). A rational–emotive approach to childhood sexuality. In A. Ellis & M. E. Bernard (Eds.), *Rational–emotive approaches to the problems of childhood* (pp. 311–330). New York: Plenum.
This chapter provides excellent suggestions for interviewing parents and children about developing sexuality and sexual socialization practices. In addition, the application of the rational–emotive approach to therapy with problems involving sexuality is discussed.

BIBLIOGRAPHY: PARENTS

Bernstein, A. C. (1978). *The flight of the stork.* New York: Dell.
This book is written for parents and describes the levels of understanding that children have about how people get babies. Most importantly, the book gives suggestions for how to talk to children about reproduction at different stages of thinking and reviews the types of questions children are most likely to ask.

Gordon, S., & Gordon, J. (1983). *Raising a child conservatively in a sexually permissive world.* New York: Simon and Schuster.
This is an excellent book for parents who want to be the principal sexuality educators of their children, who want their children to grow up with healthy attitudes, and who want to get across their own values. It covers such topics as adults coming to terms with their own sexuality, becoming an askable parent, and determining what children need to know about sexuality in the preschool, preteen, and adolescent years.

Pogrebin, L. C. (1980). *Growing up free: Raising your child in the 80's.* New York: Bantam Books.
Written by a feminist, this book presents parents with information designed to promote nonsexist child rearing. A chapter on children's sexuality is included and the topic of how to raise children in a nonsexist manner and not be a homophobic parent is addressed.

BIBLIOGRAPHY: CHILDREN

Blank, J., & Quackenbush, M. (1983). *The playbook for kids about sex.* Burlingame, CA: Down There/Yes Press.
This is a light-hearted playbook that invites prepubescent children to explore aspects of sexuality such as nudity, touching, sexual anatomy, and masturbation. Children can respond to questions in the workbook by writing in answers and drawing pictures. Designed for the family that is already open to communicating about sexuality.

Blank, J., & Quackenbush, M. (1984). *A kid's first book about sex.* Burlingame, CA: Down There/Yes Press.
This is a book for children to read. It clearly separates reproduction from the parts of sexuality that are important to the young child. It should be welcome in homes where sexuality is treated openly.

Gardner-Loulan, J., Lopez, B., & Quackenbush, M. (1981). *Period.* San Francisco: Volcano.
This is an excellent, well-written book about menstruation, designed for girls in middle childhood. It is illustrated with humorous drawings, discusses how bodies and emotions change during puberty, and describes what to expect in general from adolescence.

Gitchel, S., & Foster, L. (1985). *Let's talk about . . . s-e-x.* Fresno, CA: Planned Parenthood.
This book is intended to help parents and their 9- to 12-year-old children develop better communication about sexuality. The first section prepares parents and the latter sections contain information for children. Topics covered include puberty, what's normal, making sense of love and sex, and self-esteem.

Sanchez, G. J., & Gerbino, M. (1984). *Let's talk about sex and loving.* Burlingame, CA: Down There/Yes Press.
This book is designed to be a young child's introduction to sexuality and love. The information is presented in a thorough and sensitive way. It is read to the child and the format encourages children to ask questions on reproduction, childbirth, privacy, and gender differences.

Children and Shyness

David W. Peterson
LaGrange Area Department of Special Education, Illinois

BACKGROUND

Shyness may well be the most common social problem encountered by U.S. school children. Surveys conducted by the Stanford Shyness Clinic indicate that 80% of the general population considers themselves to have been shy at some point in their lives, leading Zimbardo (1977) to characterize it as a "universal experience". An understanding of this trait is important, as excessive shyness reduces both the amount and the quality of a child's social interactions (Harris & Brown, 1982) and its behavioral and psychological correlates have been shown to affect children's overall social development and level of acceptance by peers (Hops et al., 1978), academic achievement (Kohn, 1977), and later adult adjustment (Wanless & Prinz, 1982). Despite a lack of attention to shy children in comparison with other groups (Wanless & Prinz, 1982) shyness, because of its prevalence and far-reaching effects, offers school psychologists and other special service providers a challenge to provide information, consultation, and effective interventions that will help to alleviate its deleterious impact on children.

Defining and Conceptualizing Shyness

No consensual definition of shyness exists and the lack of specific, agreed-upon, diagnostic criteria has hampered the development of effective interventions (Wanless & Prinz, 1982). Terms often used synonymously or in conjunction with the label of shyness include social isolation or withdrawal, communication apprehension (Harris & Brown, 1982), and reticence (Phillips, 1977). The existence of the overlapping categories of Shyness Disorder and Introverted Disorder of Childhood in DSM-III (American Psychiatric Association, 1979), both of which include avoidance of peers and other social interactions, exemplifies the lack of consensual agreement on a usable definition.

Leary (1986) has identified three general categories of shyness definitions: those that view shyness as an internal and subjective experience characterized by anxiety and selfdoubt; those that take a predominantly behavioral perspective as exemplified in Pilkonis's (1977) definition of shyness as a "tendency to avoid social interactions and to fail to participate appropriately in social situations" (p. 596); and definitions that combine elements of both of the above, incorporating concepts of social anxiety and constrained interactional behavior in social situations.

In reaching a useful conceptualization of shyness in children it is helpful to consider that children's fears generally consist of three elements (Morris & Kratochwill, 1983); a *motoric* or *behavioral* component, which in shy children reflects avoidance of others; a *cognitive* element, which in this case involves negative self-evaluations and attributions (Glass & Shea, 1986); and a *physiological/arousal* component, which is reflected in a shy child's reports of "butterflies" and accelerated pulse rates (Zimbardo, 1977). Additionally, within the behavioral component, it is useful to view the shy child's deficits in interactional skills as representing either skill deficits (the child has not learned or mastered necessary prosocial behaviors) or performance deficits (the child has acquired the necessary behaviors but does not demonstrate them consistently) (Gresham & Elliot, 1984).

Consequently, shyness in children can be defined, not as a discrete set of behaviors, but as a behavioral inhibition and avoidance of social situations accompanied by negative cognitions and, in most cases, unpleasant physiological arousal or anxiety. Specifically excluded from this definition are other forms of extreme social withdrawal resulting from intense phobic reactions, autism, or childhood schizophrenia.

Incidence

While estimates of its incidence vary, shyness is self-reported in approximately 42% of children between the ages of 9 and 13 years, 50% of the junior high population, and 40% of high school-aged youth (Zimbardo & Radl, 1981). Except at the junior high level, where greater numbers of shy females account for most of the reported increases, prevalence figures were the same for males and females. Generally, these findings are consistent with those of other studies. For example, Lazarus (1982) found that 38% of a group of fifth graders labeled themselves as shy, although he found greater proportions of females (49%) than males (26%). While incidence studies with younger children are rare, Zimbardo and Radl (1981) reported that parents, teachers, and observers similarly rate approximately 33% of preschoolers as shy. It should be noted that estimates of chronic and severe shyness (i.e., shyness in all situations with all people) are considerably lower, involving approximately 4% of the adult population (Zimbardo, 1977). Clearly, these figures indicate that a significant proportion of the school-aged population experience shyness and indicate the need for professionals working with children to have a thorough knowledge of the implications of shyness.

DEVELOPMENT

Normal Aspects of Shyness

Given the fact that approximately 80% of the population label themselves as having been shy at one time or another, it follows logically that some degree of shyness in children at some time in their growth and development is to be expected and is in fact normal. Zimbardo (1977) aptly pointed out that shyness "spans a wide psychological continuum" (p. 29), ranging from occasional reticence in a limited number of situations with a limited number of peers to chronic and severe shyness in all social situations.

While very few studies describing normal aspects of shyness exist (Asendorf, 1986), Zimbardo and Radl (1981) suggested that certain degrees of shyness serve as normal "protective" devices that enable children to adapt and acquire information about unfamiliar situations. Such normal wariness of strangers can be expected in children younger than 3 years of age (Greenberg & Marvin, 1982). Zimbardo (1977) further has asserted that shyness can be viewed as a positive trait, citing that between 10% and 20% of shy adults evaluate their shyness positively. Zimbardo suggested that this estimate may be a result of the increased privacy and protection afforded to those who are shy and of the fact that shy persons may be viewed by others as being introspective and as good listeners. Zimbardo also pointed out that certain degrees of shyness can be associated with positive descriptors including thoughtfulness and reserve and that shyness can serve an adaptive function by affording children an opportunity to interact selectively in social situations.

Given the dearth of research on normal aspects of shyness and the wide continuum of behavior encompassed within this construct, the practitioner must assess a child's shyness in relation to the expectations of normally occurring social situations and the degree to which the shy behavior inhibits the initiation and maintenance of appropriate and functional social relationships.

Correlates and Implications of Shyness

In contrast to the normal aspects of shyness, a number of its correlates can have significant negative implications for social and emotional development in children. For example, Zimbardo (1977) reported shyness in children to be strongly related to poor self-concept, feelings of failure, and negative self-statements.

Briggs, Cheek, and Jones (1986), in a review of the literature on shyness, enumerated a number of studies suggesting relationships between shyness and "depression, neurosis, fear, communication apprehension, shame, alienation, and self-conciousness" (p. 7). They also reported that shyness is reflected in less effective conversational skills. Similarly, Pilkonis (1977) found consistent negative differences in the ability of shys to initiate and structure conversations. Zimbardo (1977) also asserted that the anxiety accompanying shyness impairs memory and concentration and inhibits children from asking for needed help in school, consequently impairing academic progress. The current research clearly establishes the negative impact that shyness can have.

PUTTING SHYNESS IN PERSPECTIVE

This section provides an overview of a model and accompanying methodologies for the assessment of shyness in children. The purposes of such assessments are to first determine whether a child's shyness requires intervention and if treatment is warranted, to gather data that will be useful in designing and implementing effective interventions. Questions that should be addressed include what situations elicit the child's shyness and is the shyness reflected across a variety of situations, or only in a few? What social skills does the child need to demonstrate to reduce the impact of the shyness? To what extent is the child's shyness interfering in his or her social relationships?

As a result of limited research and the lack of agreement over the specific characteristics and definitions of shyness, clear guidelines for assessment are difficult to establish and the practitioner must select modes of assessment that sample the various dimensions of shyness, including (a) the cognitive and behavioral characteristics of the child, (b) components of the environments and elicitors within those environments in which the child's shyness is exhibited, and (c) the degree or severity of the shyness being exhibited. This model recognizes the situational nature of shyness (Asendorf, 1986) and the need to examine the interactions among behavioral and cognitive components of shyness and the social environments in which those characteristics are exhibited.

Zimbardo (1977) established the importance of identifying shyness elicitors, which are those specific social situations and/or individuals that precipitate shy behavior. Zimbardo and Radl (1981) obtained teacher and parent ratings of shyness elicitors and found agreement that "being the focus of attention" and "meeting strangers" are the most frequently identified elicitors of shyness in children. However, they also found that teachers rated peer interaction as the third most powerful elicitor, whereas parents ranked it last. This difference apparently reflects the situational specificity of shyness as well as the increased opportunities that teachers have to observe peer interactions (Asendorf, 1986).

Given this situational variance, the assessment of a child's shyness should include clear definitions of the specific environments and elicitors within those environments to aid in focusing intervention efforts. Certainly, children exhibiting shyness across many environments and to a variety of elicitors are more likely candidates for intervention than those who are shy in a limited number of situations. With younger children, this type of data can be obtained most efficiently through naturalistic observations and interviews with parents and teachers. When assessing older shy children, interviews and self-report inventories like the Stanford Shyness Scale (Zimbardo, 1977) can be used.

When assessing shyness, pertinent child characteristics include the absence or presence of relevant social skills, the cognitive attributes of the child's shyness, and the extent to which anxiety and its physiological correlates inhibit the child's performance. First, it is important to assess the contribution of any social skills deficits to the child's shyness. The shy child's lack of necessary prosocial behaviors may be the result of either skill *acquisition* deficiencies or *performance* deficits (Gresham & Elliot, 1984). The child having skills acquisition deficits has not learned or mastered the necessary social behavior (or subcomponents of that behavior); children with performance deficits are able to demonstrate the relevant behavior but do not do so consistently. In assessing a child's shyness, it is important to differentiate between these two categories of social skills, as performance deficits may be the result of interfering anxiety (Kratochwill & French, 1984) and thus require interventions geared to anxiety reduction rather than the direct social skills training used to treat acquisition deficits. Direct observation in naturalistic settings can be used to assess social skills and can include measures of verbal initiations and responses, proximity to peers, and rate and quality of interactions with peers and adults (Kratochwill & French, 1984). Interviews with parents and teachers and role playing can also provide data for identifying relevant social skills.

While they are considerably less amenable to direct assessment, effort should be made to determine the extent to which negative or unpleasant cognitions are contributing to a child's shyness. The tendency of shy children to utilize negative self-statements (Briggs, Cheek, & Jones, 1986) is a common characteristic, and if identified, it should be a target of intervention. With young children, interviews with parents and teachers can provide information regarding the content of a child's self-statements, and interviews or the use of "think-aloud" techniques with older children can elicit such data.

Self-report shyness measures (e.g., the Stanford Shyness Survey) have been used extensively with adult populations (Briggs & Smith, 1986; Zimbardo, 1977) but have not been adapted for children; thus they have limited utility for the school practitioner. However, normative data useful in determining the severity of shyness can be obtained through the use of behavior rating scales. The Behavior Problem Rating Scale (Quay, 1983) includes an "anxiety–withdrawal" scale that reliably measures a number of traits correlated with shyness.

The comprehensive evaluation of the shy child involves the assessment of ecological variables to determine specific shyness elicitors, social skills, and cognitive and affective correlates of shyness. Because shyness involves a number of interacting dimensions, careful specification of relevant variables within each is important and frequently necessary to design and implement intervention.

The following example illustrates this multidimensional approach and involves an 8-year-old male whose parents were concerned with what they felt to be his excessive shyness. Interviews with the parents and the student's teachers revealed that the child displayed extremely low rates of verbal interaction, specifically in group settings involving more than three or four peers or adults. When in familiar small-group settings the student generally displayed appropriate rates of interaction. The large-group settings identified included school, community, and family situations, and the child's shyness was elicited by both nonfamiliar adults and peers.

Observations confirmed the reported low rates of interaction in these settings. In an attempt to assess whether the child's shy behavior was a result of deficits of social skills acquisition, a series of role plays requiring a variety of verbal interactions were contrived. The student's successful performance in these role plays suggested that his lack of interaction in large-group situations was the result of performance deficits and that he had acquired the social skills needed to interact effectively. Cognitive correlates of the shyness were assessed through interviews with the child and they suggested a pattern of negative self-talk (e.g., "I don't know what to say"; "they'll make fun of me"), reflecting anxiety that was apparently contributing to the performance deficits. Given the pervasiveness of this child's shyness in a variety of large-group settings, interventions (to be described in the following section) were designed to reduce his anxiety, to change his negative cognitions, and to reinforce performance in large groups.

ALTERNATIVE ACTIONS

A variety of intervention strategies have been used to treat shyness in children (Wanless & Prinz, 1982; Kratochwill & French, 1984; Zimbardo & Radl, 1981). However, little data comparing the relative efficacy of these different procedures is available, and the selection of a specific technique or combination of techniques is dependent upon the variables and behaviors identified during assessment.

Operant Procedures

The use of operant and contingency management procedures assumes that the shy child does not receive sufficient naturally occurring reinforcement for appropriate social interaction. Treatment frequently requires teachers to contingently reinforce targeted interactive behaviors. While these types of intervention have produced increased rates of interaction during treatment, gains often decline significantly when the contingency procedures are withdrawn (Wanless & Prinz, 1982) and generalization of skills to other settings has not been consistently demonstrated (Kratochwill & French, 1984). Strict reinforcement strategies are also probably less likely to be effective with highly anxious shys whose anxiety inhibits social behavior, thereby reducing the opportunity for reinforcement. Such interventions may also not respond to the needs of shy students with deficits of social skills acquisition, unless instruction in appropriate skills is provided.

Cognitive Behavioral Interventions

Interventions utilizing cognitive behavior modification (CBM) are being increasingly used to treat shyness and have resulted in reduction of fear in social situations and public speaking (Harris & Brown, 1982). CBM techniques involve the modeling of appropriate self-statements and subsequent imitation by the child of those statements both overtly and privately (Craighead, 1982). Cognitive behavioral techniques offer considerable promise in the treatment of shyness as they can be applied to the treatment of the social anxiety (Forman & O'Malley, 1984) experienced by the shy child and also attempt to directly intervene in dysfunctional self-statements. Glass and Shea (1986) have pointed out that while CBM-oriented techniques can reduce anxiety and avoidance in social situations, they may not be as effective with children with social skills deficits.

Shy children who report high levels of anxiety or exhibit physiological symptoms of stress may also profit from progressive relaxation training and systematic desensitization (Forman & O'Malley, 1984). These techniques involve relaxation training accompanied by visualization of anxiety-producing social situations in a hierarchy of gradually ascending intensity.

Structured Activity Interventions

Wanless and Prinz (1982) reviewed a number of studies involving the structuring of play and activity situations and suggested that such interventions offer a potentially effective method for group treatment of social isolation requiring relatively little expenditure of effort. These interventions typically involve participation in plays, use of toys that enhance social play, and role taking in stories. While positive results are reported, maintenance and generalization of gains has not been demonstrated, and Wanless and Prinz (1982) do not recommend this type of intervention when it is not combined with other techniques.

Zimbardo (1977) recommended the use of similar, but more clearly structured cooperative learning strategies. Cooperative learning strategies (Miller & Peterson, in press) like "jigsaw" are specifically designed to promote interdependence and cooperation among children by using structured group formats to complete academic tasks. For example, "jigsawing" involves dividing a task into a number of components and making individual group members responsible for assuring that other members of the group learn the information that is assigned to each individual. While there is no research on cooperative learning's effects on shy children, it offers a variety of methods for structuring opportunities that will encourage interaction by shy or withdrawn children during instructional activities in the classroom.

Social Skills Interventions

Social skills training interventions employing instructional coaching have also been used to treat isolated children who were assumed to be deficient in necessary social skills (Kratochwill & French, 1984). Coaching entails instruction, rehearsal, reinforcement, and feedback on performance during training sessions (Wanless & Prinz, 1982). Target skills have included cooperation (Gresham & Nagle, 1980), assertive behavior (Bornstein, Bellack, & Hersen, 1977), and sharing and complimenting (LaGreca & Santogrossi, 1980). A more recent study (Christoff, Scott, Kelley, Schlundt, Baer, & Kelly, 1985) combined social skills training and social-problem-solving training to improve conversational skills and social-problem-solving abilities in shy adolescents. Coaching interventions are probably best suited to shy children with skills acquisition deficits. However, they may be useful for shy children with performance deficits if paired with some type of anxiety reduction technique.

Classroom Interventions

While the previously described interventions are suitable for individual children or small groups, the PEERS (procedures for establishing effective relationship skills) program (Hops, et al., 1978) was designed to be implemented on a classwide basis with primary grade children. PEERS incorporates elements of direct social skills training, contingency management procedures, joint task interactions with a variety of peers, and self-reporting of interactive play activities. The program is implemented through a consultant model and employs group rewards to increase the involvement of classmates in interaction with the target child. These procedures have demonstrated positive results and offer an integrated approach to intervention in the natural classroom environment.

Strategies for Parents

A number of strategies that parents can employ to minimize the effects of shyness are discussed by Zimbardo and Radl (1981) in a volume that is a source of detailed discussion of parental issues and shyness. Briefly, they stress the need for parents to communicate realistic expectations and to provide shy children opportunities for independence and the demonstration of responsibility. They also recommend that parents seek out and provide activities that will enable the shy child to experience success in social environments. They further recommend a number of specific teaching procedures, games, and structured social interactions that parents can employ to help alleviate shyness.

Budd (1985) has suggested that parents can serve as adjunct trainers to professionals when social skills training programs are being implemented. Parents can reinforce targeted social skills, provide opportunities for the rehearsal of skills, and provide professionals with evaluative data.

SUMMARY

The social, affective, and cognitive implications of shyness have an impact upon a large proportion of school-aged children. Mental health and educational professionals should be sensitive to the need to assess its influence on the children they serve and, when appropriate, develop interventions to minimize its negative effects.

Shyness and social withdrawal in children have only recently begun to receive research attention proportional to that devoted to children's aggression and acting out. As a result, definitional and conceptual ambiguities in the literature abound and research is hampered by the lack of agreement regarding the specific characteristics associated with this construct. In general shyness can be defined as behavioral inhibition in social situations that in most cases is accompanied by negative cognitions and anxiety.

The mental health practitioner should keep in mind that most children experience shyness during their growth and development and that occasional shyness in reaction to strangers or unfamiliar surroundings occurs with high frequency, especially among younger children. Nevertheless, research clearly establishes the negative implications of shyness among many children and a thorough knowledge of assessment and intervention techniques is warranted.

The assessment of shyness should include evaluation of the environments in which the shyness is exhibited, identification of shyness elicitors, examination of an affected child's social skills, and, if possible, evaluation of the cognitive attributes of the child's shyness. The selection of intervention strategies, when warranted, will be dependent upon the relative contributions of each of these dimensions to the composite picture of the child's shyness.

Interventions applied to the treatment of shyness include contingency management procedures, modeling, cognitive behavioral techniques, structured activity approaches, and social skills training models. While all of these intervention techniques have demonstrated success in certain situations, little research comparing their relative efficacy is available, and research on generalization and maintenance of gains is woefully lacking.

A great deal more must be known about shyness in children before the mental health practitioner can be provided clear guidance regarding its identification and treatment. Despite the lack of consensus regarding definitions and effective treatments, it is imperative that mental health professional in schools begin to more carefully consider its impact on the children they serve.

REFERENCES

American Psychiatric Association. (1979). *Diagnostic and statistical manual of mental disorders* (3rd ed.). Washington, DC: Author.

Asendorf, J. (1986). Shyness in middle and late childhood. In W. H. Jones, J. M. Cheek, & S. R. Briggs (Eds.), *Shyness: Perspectives on research and treatment* (pp. 91–104). New York: Plenum.

Bornstein, M. R., Bellack, A. S., & Hersen, M. (1977). Social skills training for unassertive children. *Journal of Applied Behavior Analysis, 10,* 183–195.

Briggs, S. R., Cheek, J. M., & Jones, W. H. (1986). Introduction. In W. H. Jones, J. M. Cheek, & S. R. Briggs (Eds.), *Shyness: Perspectives on research and treatment* (pp. 1–14). New York: Plenum.

Briggs, S. R., & Smith, T. B. (1986). The measurement of shyness. In W. H. Jones, J. M. Cheek, & S. R. Briggs (Eds.), *Shyness: Perspectives on research and treatment* (pp. 47–60). New York: Plenum.

Budd, K. S. (1985). Parents as mediators in the social skills training of children. In L. L'Abate & M. Milan (Eds.), *Handbook of social skills training and research* (pp. 254–262). New York: Wiley.

Christoff, K. A., Scott, W. O., Kelley, M. L., Schlundt, D., Baer, G., & Kelly, J. A. (1985). Social skills and social problem solving training for shy young adolescents. *Behavior Therapy, 16,* 468–477.

Craighead, W. E. (1982). A brief clinical history of cognitive–behavior therapy with children. *School Psychology Review, 11,* 5–13.

Forman, S. G., & O'Malley, P. L. (1984). School stress and anxiety interventions. *School Psychology Review, 13,* 162–170.

Glass, C. R., & Shea, C. A. (1986). Cognitive therapy for shyness and social anxiety. In W. H. Jones, J. M. Cheek, & S. R. Briggs (Eds.), *Shyness: Perspectives on research and treatment* (pp. 315–328). New York: Plenum.

Greenberg, M. T., & Marvin, R. S. (1982). Reactions of preschool children to an adult stranger: A behavioral systems approach. *Child Development, 53,* 481–490.

Gresham, F. M., & Elliot, S. N. (1984). Assessment and classification of children's social skills: A review of methods and issues. *School Psychology Review, 13,* 292–301.

Gresham, F. M., & Nagle, R. J. (1982). Social skills training with children: Responsiveness to modeling and coaching as a function of peer orientation. *Journal of Consulting and Clinical Psychology, 18,* 718–729.

Harris, K. R., & Brown, R. D. (1982). Cognitive behavior modification and informed teacher treatments for shy children. *Journal of Experimental Education, 50,* 137–143.

Hops, H., Guild, J. J., Fleischman, D. H., Paine, S. C., Street, A., Walker, H. M., & Greenwood, C. R. (1978). *PEERS: Procedures for establishing effective relationship skills, Consultant manual.* Eugene, OR: Center at Oregon for Research in the Behavioral Education of the Handicapped, Center on Human Development.

Jones, W. H., Cheek, J. M., & Briggs, S. R. (Eds.). (1986). *Shyness: Perspectives on research and treatment.* New York: Plenum.

Kohn, M. (1977). *Social competence, symptoms, and underachievement in childhood: A longitudinal perspective.* Washington, DC: Winston.

Kratochwill, T. R., & French, D. C. (1984). Social skills training for withdrawn children. *School Psychology Review, 13,* 331–338.

LaGreca, A. M., & Santogrossi, D. A. (1980). Social skills training with elementary school students: A behavioral group approach. *Journal of Consulting and Clinical Psychology, 48,* 220–228.

Lazarus, P. J. (1982). Incidence of shyness in elementary school-aged children, *Psychological Reports, 51,* 904–906.

Leary, M. R. (1986). Affective and behavioral components of shyness: Implications for theory, measurement, and research. In W. H. Jones, J. M. Cheek, & S. R. Briggs (Eds.), *Shyness: Perspectives on research and treatment* (pp. 27–38). New York: Plenum.

Miller, J., & Peterson, D. W. (in press). Peer mediated academic interventions. In C. A. Maher & J. E. Zins (Eds.), *Psychoeducational interventions in schools: Methods and procedures for enhancing student competence.* Elmsford, NY: Pergamon.

Morris, R. J., & Kratochwill, T. R. (1983). *Treating children's fears and phobias: A behavioral approach.* Elmsford, NY: Pergamon.

Philips, G. M. (1977). Rhetoritherapy versus the medical model: Dealing with reticence. *Communication Education, 26,* 34–43.

Pilkonis, P. A. (1977). The behavioral consequences of shyness. *Journal of Personality, 45,* 596–611.

Quay, H. C. (1983). A dimensional approach to behavior disorder. *School Psychology Review, 12,* 244–249.

Wanless, R. L., & Prinz, R. J. (1982). Methodological issues in conceptualizing and treating childhood social isolation. *Psychological Bulletin, 92,* 39–55.

Zimbardo, P. G. (1977). *Shyness: What it is, what to do about it.* Reading, MA: Addison Wesley.

Zimbardo, P. G., & Radl, S. L. (1981). *The shy child: A parent's guide to preventing and overcoming shyness from infancy to adulthood.* New York: McGraw-Hill.

BIBLIOGRAPHY: PROFESSIONALS

Hops, H., Guild, J. J., Fleischman, D. H., Paine, S. C., Street, A., Walker, H. M., & Greenwood, C. R. (1978). *PEERS: Procedures for establishing effective relationship skills. Consultant manual.* Eugene OR: Center at Oregon for Research in the Behavioral Education of the Handicapped, Center of Human Development.

The PEERS program provides the practitioner with a classroom-based intervention designed to be delivered primarily through a consultant model. Detailed procedures for social skills tutoring, joint task activities, a classroom contingency program, and student self-reporting are provided.

Jones, W. H., Cheek, J. M., & Briggs, S. R. (Eds.). (1986). *Shyness: Perspectives on research and treatment.* New York: Plenum.

This comprehensive text provides the professional with an excellent overview of the research on shyness. It includes well-written chapters by established shyness researchers on a wide variety of topics including etiology and development, treatment, and a number of other relevant conceptual variables important to a thorough understanding of the area.

Kratochwill, T. R., & French, D. C. (1984). Social skills training for withdrawn children. *School Psychology Review, 13,* 331–338.

While focusing on the somewhat broader category of withdrawn children, this article provides a concise overview of behavior theory-oriented assessment and intervention strategies that are applicable to shy children. Contingency management, modeling, coaching, and cognitive techniques are briefly reviewed.

Wanless, R. L., & Prinz, R. J. (1982). Methodological issues in conceptualizing and treating childhood social isolation. *Psychological Bulletin, 92,* 39–55.

While again focusing on a somewhat more inclusive concept (social isolation), this article provides a review of the literature on a variety of treatment techniques including operant techniques, modeling, and activity and socialization approaches that are relevant to shyness in children.

BIBLIOGRAPHY: PARENTS

Zimbardo, P. G. (1977). *Shyness: What it is, what to do about it.* Reading, MA: Addison-Wesley.

While not specifically focused on the needs of shy children, this text provides an excellent general reference for both parents and professionals. Although it is written in language suitable to the lay reader, its practical recommendations are based upon the pioneering research completed at the Stanford Shyness Clinic and it is an important text for the professional concerned about shyness.

Zimbardo, P. G., & Radl, S. L. (1981). *The shy child: A parent's guide to preventing and overcoming shyness from infancy to adulthood.* New York: McGraw-Hill.

This excellent text, coauthored by Philip Zimbardo, one of the foremost experts on shyness, offers parents a readable and practical resource in dealing with the shy child. Strategies for minimizing shyness at all age levels are offered and a chapter for older shy students is also provided.

Children and Siblings

Bruce C. Foster
Kern County Schools, Bakersfield, California

BACKGROUND

Despite recent demographic trends toward smaller families with one child or no children, sibling relationships must be considered significant to the development of children when one considers that 80% of all children grow up with at least one brother or sister (Dunn, 1983; Falbo, 1984; Hacker, 1983). In addition, during early childhood, children frequently spend more time interacting with their siblings than they do with their parents (Dunn, 1985). Thus, sibling interactions constitute one of the more common interpersonal relationships among humans. Clearly, this relationship plays an important role in the development of children's sociocognitive skills, providing them with a means for experimenting with various life roles such as competitor, teacher, protector, friend, and aggressor, as well as putting them into a relationship in which feelings such as love, affection, jealousy, and anger must be dealt with on a daily basis. However, only recently have researchers begun the task of directly examining the developmental processes that take place in sibling relationships (Dunn, 1983; Lamb & Sutton-Smith, 1982).

Until the 1970s, much of the literature characterized sibling interactions as rivalrous, being typified by intense feelings of jealousy and hostility (Levy, 1937; Adler, 1959). There was also much interest in the relationship between birth order and variables such as intelligence, personality, and achievement (Sutton-Smith & Rosenberg, 1970). While these two bodies of research certainly suggested that sibling interactions were developmentally important, they did not provide direct evidence of the extent of sibling influences on development (Dunn, 1983).

Since the 1970s, increasingly more descriptive and observational research has focused on the processes by which sibling relationships develop (Lamb, 1982). Several theories on the developmental influences of sibling relationships have evolved from this research. Behavioral geneticists have attributed differences in sibling personality and cognitive levels to a process in which siblings create different environments for one another within the family system (Daniels & Plomin, 1985; Scarr & Grajek, 1982). Clinicians have concluded that siblings relationships have a significant impact on identity development, particularly when there is high access between the siblings and insufficient parental influence (Bank & Kahn, 1982). Other psychologists have focused on the differential identification processes of siblings to explain their seemingly different personalities (Schachter, 1982). Finally, the pioneering researchers in naturalistic observations of siblings have proposed that interactions between siblings alternate between unilateral domination of the relationship by one sibling and interaction by both siblings on an equivocal, mutually satisfying basis (Dunn, 1983; Abramovitch, Corter, Pepler, & Stanhope, 1986).

DEVELOPMENT

Early Childhood

Much of the developmental research on sibling interactions has been conducted on sibling dyads during early childhood in the home, in which the older sibling ranged in age from 18 months to 6 years and the younger sibling ranged between newborn and 3 years of age (Dunn, 1983).

Upon the birth of the second child into the family unit, several noteworthy behavior patterns in the firstborn child have been observed. Specifically, the firstborn's reactions toward the newborn are typically characterized by ambivalence, with alternating reactions of great interest and great resentment being noted (Dunn, 1985; Nademan & Begun, 1982). Dunn (1985) found that firstborns rarely directed their hostility toward the newborn, being much more likely to exhibit a significant increase in noncompliant and aggressive behavior directed toward the mother. This oppositional behavior usually occurred when the mother was occupied by caregiving activities with the newborn. In addition, many firstborns were likely to exhibit clinging behavior, sleep disturbances, and a breakdown in toileting skills. Nademan and Begun found that younger firstborns less than 40 months old were more likely to engage in regressive behavior. However, older firstborns did exhibit a high degree of proximity maintenance such as not letting the mother out of sight. Dunn (1985) reported that the disturbances in the firstborn's behavior generally began disappearing by the time the secondborn was 2 months old. Firstborns who, before the birth of the second child, exhibited "difficult" temperament characteristics such as irritability, moodiness, and noncompliance, were likely to have the most behavioral disturbances after the arrival of the new sibling.

While firstborns may frequently exhibit behavioral disturbances during the infancy of the secondborn, many positive behavioral changes may also be demonstrated. According to Dunn (1985), firstborns frequently exhibit increased levels of mature and independent behavior during this period. She also reported that many firstborns express a willingness to engage in or assist in caregiving activities. Supporting this finding is the research of Stewart (1983) and Stewart and Martin (1984), who found that preschoolers capable of anticipating their younger siblings' behavior — perspective-taking — could adequately engage in caregiving and teaching behavior with those siblings.

Dunn (1985) also reported that the behavior of the mother toward the firstborn during this period could have lasting effects on the relationship of the siblings.

Specifically, it was discovered that in families in which mothers talked with the firstborn about the infant as a person — as someone having emotional and physical needs — the relationship between the siblings was likely to remain positive during early childhood.

As firstborns approach preschool age and secondborns enter into toddlerhood, several interesting interaction patterns have been observed to arise. Studies during this period suggest that interaction frequencies among siblings are very high, with a variety of prosocial, agonistic, and imitative behaviors being displayed (Dunn & Kendrick, 1982; Abramovitch, Pepler, & Corter, 1982). During observations of sibling interactions in the home, Pepler, Abramovitch, and Corter (1982) found that 44% of all behavior initiated between sibling dyads consisted of prosocial behaviors such as helping, cooperation, and affection. Agonistic behaviors, which included physical and verbal aggression as well as struggles over material possessions, constituted 29% of all behavior initiated. Imitative behavior made up the remaining 27%.

These rates of prosocial, agonistic, and imitative behaviors were consistent regardless of the sex of the siblings and regardless of the size of interval (1–2 years or 2.5–4 years) between the siblings. This finding is in contrast to the experiences of White (1985), who has asserted that siblings spaced less than 3 years apart exhibit a higher frequency of hostile interactions than those spaced more than 3 years apart. With respect to individual differences, Pepler et al. (1982) found that older siblings initiated a much higher frequency of prosocial behavior than their younger counterparts. In contrast, the younger siblings exhibited a higher frequency of imitative behavior. Older sisters were found to initiate more prosocial behavior than older brothers.

Pepler et al. (1982) also discovered that preschool-aged older siblings exhibited a much higher frequency of initiating agonistic behavior than their younger siblings. Physical aggression was initiated significantly more often by older brothers in same-sex dyads than older sisters in same-sex dyads during this period.

With the older siblings approaching school age and the younger siblings approaching preschool age in their longitudinal study, Pepler, et al. (1982) found that the developmental trends noted at earlier ages were still apparent. Social interaction between the siblings remained at high levels; prosocial behavior was observed 61% of the time, agonistic behavior 25% of the time, and imitative behavior 13% of the time. The older siblings continued to initiate more prosocial and more agonistic behavior, and the younger siblings still initiated more imitative behavior. However, with respect to prosocial and agonistic behavior, the younger siblings had become more competitive, initiating more prosocial behavior than when they were younger and initiating close to the same number of physically aggressive actions as their older counterparts. Older siblings initiated more verbally aggressive actions. The younger siblings' gains were attributed to their growing sophistication in social interaction skills as they became older.

In observations that were consistent with their findings at earlier ages, Pepler et al. (1982) found no effects for the size of age interval between the siblings. In addition, no differences were noted by sex. However, there were some interesting effects for the sex composition of the dyads. While the levels of imitative behavior within same-sex dyads virtually remained the same as was found at the earlier age levels, they fell dramatically in mixed-sex dyads, leading to speculation that sex typing was already taking place. Finally, it was noted that aggressive behavior was more prevalent in mixed-sex dyads than same-sex dyads.

Many of these findings have more recently been replicated by Berndt and Bulleit (1985). However, these researchers also found that children who tended to be aggressive or socially withdrawn in the sibling relationship exhibited similar behaviors in peer interactions. It was concluded that these behaviors may be due to social skills deficits. Another plausible explanation is that these behaviors were due to the temperamental characteristics of the individual children (Chess & Thomas, 1984).

Middle Childhood

Several observational studies have also been conducted with siblings during the middle childhood period, with the ages of the older sibling ranging between 6 and 12 years, and the age of the younger sibling ranging between 4.5 and 8 years (Abramovitch et al., 1986; Brody, Stoneman, MacKinnon, & MacKinnon, 1985; Minnet, Vandell, & Santrock, 1983). In addition, there have been some studies that have directly elicited the attitudes/perceptions of children about their sibling relationships (Furman & Buhrmester, 1985; Sutton-Smith & Rosenberg, 1968).

Abramovitch et al. (1986), in a longitudinal follow-up of previous studies (Abramovitch et al., 1982; Pepler et al., 1982), found the developmental trends established during early childhood to be continuing into middle childhood. The older siblings still initiated prosocial and agonistic behavior more frequently, and the younger siblings engaged in a higher frequency of imitative behavior. It was also found that older siblings initiated more play-related behavior than younger siblings. Consistent with previous findings were the observations that neither the sex of the child nor the size of age interval between the two siblings had a significant effect on their behavior. Same-sex dyads continued to exhibit more prosocial behavior than mixed-sex dyads, and mixed-sex dyads continued to exhibit more agonistic behavior than same-sex dyads.

In contrast to the findings of Abramovitch et al. (1986), Brody et al. (1985) found that school-age female siblings engaged in more prosocial and play behavior than school-age males. In observations that were consistent with the findings of earlier studies in a laboratory setting (Cicirelli, 1973, 1975), they also found that school-aged females assumed a teaching role more frequently than other experimental groups. In addition, it was found that the younger school-aged sisters were more willing to accept teaching attempts from the older sister than were their male counterparts. The researchers speculated that these differences might have been due to parental emphasis on teaching caregiving skills to females rather than males or to differences in temperamental characteristics.

Minnet et al. (1983), in an observational study done in a school setting without the mothers present, also obtained results that conflicted with those of Abramovitch et al. (1986). While it was clear that the older sibling engaged in more prosocial behavior, there was an age interval effect, with more prosocial behavior being exhibited when the siblings were spaced farther apart in age. Additionally, it was found that aggressive behavior between siblings increased in frequency as the age interval between the siblings became smaller, giving credence to the previously mentioned findings of White (1985). Finally, negative behaviors such as aggression and cheating were more likely to occur within same-sex dyads than mixed-sex dyads. The researchers suggested that these conflicting findings were due to the different observational environments in the two studies.

Self-report studies corroborate many of the findings of direct observational studies. Sutton-Smith and Rosenberg (1968) found that preadolescents consistently rated the firstborn as having more power than the secondborn, with the firstborn exhibiting more bossy behaviors and the secondborn exhibiting more submissive behaviors such as crying, pouting, and appealing to others to intervene. These results are consistent with the direct observational research findings of the older sibling's dominance of the sibling relationship.

Furman and Buhrmester (1985), in a factor analysis of self-report data from preadolescents, found four distinct dimensions within the sibling relationship: warmth/closeness, relative status/power, conflict, and rivalry. Again, older siblings were rated as having more relative status/power. It was also found that feelings of warmth and closeness were more prevalent in same-sex dyads than in mixed-sex dyads, a finding consistent with those of Dunn and Kendrick (1982) and Abramovitch et al. (1986). Conflict was found to be more prevalent in siblings who were closer in age, a finding more consistent with the research of Minnet et al. (1983).

Adolescence

Research on the developmental qualities of sibling relationships during adolescence is sparse. Adolescent siblings appear to play an important role in development, being likely to act as role models for younger siblings, serving in such altruistic and prosocial roles as caretaker and teacher, and providing friendship and companionship (Rice, 1978). Indeed, research suggests that the vast majority of adolescents feel close to their younger siblings, with relatively few viewing their relationship as being characterized by intense conflict or hostility (Bowerman & Dobash, 1974).

PUTTING CHILDREN AND SIBLINGS IN PERSPECTIVE

The previous section of this chapter primarily focused on the "normal" developmental aspects of sibling relationships during childhood. However, there are several situational factors that must be taken into account before determining what actions should be taken toward a presenting problem involving sibling interactions.

Other than the behavior and temperaments of the siblings themselves, perhaps the most important factor to consider before designing an intervention is the behavior of the parents toward the siblings. Specifically, interactions between siblings can be influenced significantly in either a positive or negative direction by the mother (Dunn, 1983). Thus, her behavior toward the siblings could potentially sabotage any intervention efforts or could be used as a major agent of change in improving the sibling relationship.

It must also be emphasized that most of the research on the developmental aspects of sibling relationships has focused on white middle-class intact families containing a nonworking mother with two children spaced less than 4 years apart. Thus, it is possible that the developmental trends noted in this research are not applicable to situations involving nonwhite families, families containing more than two children, families in which the age interval between siblings is very large, families in lower socioeconomic groups, single-parent families, or families in which both parents work. Indeed, some research suggests that the additional stresses present in the latter two situations can influence the sibling relationship (Kelly & Main, 1979; Long & Long, 1983). Other research suggests that the sibling interactions within step-families (Carlson, 1985), families with handicapped children (Burton, 1987), and families with twins (Lytton, 1980) may have their own unique qualities. In addition, the single-child family, in which no siblings are present, has been found to have significant implications for the development of the child (Falbo, 1984). Professionals who plan to intervene in any of these situations should be familiar with the family system dynamics involved.

Finally, it should be recognized that the developmental research reviewed in the previous section primarily focused on the general trends observed in sibling interactions. Sibling experiences vary widely and are influenced by a number of variables (Minnet et al., 1983). The research of Bank and Kahn (1982), although focusing on some extraordinary situations, vividly illustrates that sibling relationships can be incredibly complex as well as difficult to modify.

ALTERNATIVE ACTIONS

In the childhood behavior management literature, there are preciously few volumes that address sibling interactions. While much of the literature focuses on the rivalrous aspects of sibling relationships (Dobson, 1978; Millman & Schaefer, 1982; White, 1985), there are also some works that take a more holistic view (Calladine & Calladine, 1979; Dunn, 1985). Interventions drawn from this literature for some of the more common sibling management problems will be discussed briefly. Readers wishing more information should consult the publications listed in the annotated bibliographies.

During a firstborn's early childhood, the parent's

concerns frequently focus on her or his reactions toward and acceptance of a newborn. Dunn's research suggested several relatively simple interventions that can help to alleviate the stress that may occur during this period. Her studies indicated that the largest single source of stress at this time is the sharp reduction in maternal attention toward the firstborn. Actions by the mother that were found to alleviate this stressful situation include the provision of materials such as books and puzzles to the firstborn before infant caregiving activities are to take place; talking to the firstborn about the newborn's emotions, wants, and needs; and allowing the firstborn to assist in caregiving activities (Dunn, 1985).

While Dunn's research suggests that the behavioral disturbances of the firstborn on the arrival of a sibling may be a bid for the attention of the parent, research by Felson (1983) and Prochaska and Prochaska (1985) suggests that fighting among siblings is primarily due to conflicts over property, uneven division of chores, and/or simply a bad mood on the part of one of the siblings.

Felson's study implied that conflict could be reduced if parents set clear rules on access to common property and specifically define the division of labor in the household. In contrast, Prochaska and Prochaska solicited the opinions of fourth- and fifth-grade students on what interventions were effective in reducing sibling conflict and found that these students rated virtually all parental interventions as relatively ineffective. Such interventions as positive reinforcement for appropriate behavior, punishment, and keeping the siblings occupied with fun activities were judged to be only minimally effective.

As suggested by Felson's research, many childcare specialists stress that the key to relatively harmonious sibling relationships is the establishment of a system of justice and responsibilities within the family (Dobson, 1978; Millman & Schaefer, 1982). This system involves the clear delineation of household rules and responsibilities backed up with consistent consequences and a willingness on the part of the parents to mediate any quarrels involving rules and/or responsibilities.

Many childcare professionals would probably be adamantly opposed to the noninterventionist approach to sibling management suggested by the views of the students in the study of Prochaska and Prochaska. Calladine and Calladine (1979) suggested that parents take an active role when aggression is occurring or about to occur. When physical aggression is occurring, they recommend separating and then isolating the participants. When verbal aggression is escalating or physical aggression is about to occur, channeling the siblings into another activity or becoming involved in an activity with them are suggested interventions. Calladine (1983) has also reported positive results from taking away the object or privilege that is the source of the squabbling.

Millman and Schaefer (1982) have strongly advocated the use of group rewards and penalties to reduce aggressive and antagonistic behavior among siblings. They advise parents to encourage cooperative play by offering both siblings a reward if they are able to interact for specified periods of time without engaging in argumentative, aggressive, or teasing behavior. If the siblings engage in any of the undesirable behaviors, neither one gets the reward, no matter who initiated the inappropriate behavior. A similar procedure is used with penalties such as time out, with the parent emphasizing that both siblings will be penalized regardless of who initiates the inappropriate behavior. The advantage of this system is the elimination of the need to fix blame.

Another aspect of sibling management that has been emphasized in the literature is the treatment of siblings as individuals with unique characteristics and needs (Calladine & Calladine, 1979; Dobson, 1978; Millman & Schaefer, 1982). These authors recommend that parents recognize and appreciate the unique qualities of each child, but avoid making overt comparisons between siblings and showing any evidence of having a "favorite" child. This is particularly important when one sibling is not as physically attractive and/or talented as the other sibling. One of the more effective ways of emphasizing each sibling's individuality is for each parent to periodically spend time alone interacting with each child.

Since much of the observational research indicates that the relationship between brothers and sisters is primarily characterized by prosocial behaviors such as affection, sharing, cooperating, and helping, it may also be beneficial to refocus the parent's attention on this aspect of sibling interactions. All too often parents tend to focus on the negative or rivalrous aspects of their children's behavior because this type of behavior is very irritating. To counteract this situation, the parents' predominantly negative perspective on sibling interactions may be changed to a predominantly positive perspective if they are simply asked to quietly and unobtrusively observe the relative frequency of prosocial and agonistic behaviors that occur among the siblings.

While it would appear that the majority of sibling relationship difficulties can be managed through relatively brief consultations between mental health professionals and parents, the research of Bank and Kahn (1982) indicated that pathological sibling relationships requiring intensive intervention do exist. More intensive interventions such as long-term counseling or psychotherapy seem to be indicated when the relationship is dominated by intense feelings of attachment, competition, and/or jealousy on the part of one or both siblings. Traumatic experiences among siblings such as acts of extreme violence or incest are also likely to require more intensive interventions.

SUMMARY

The available research on sibling relationships suggests that interactions among siblings have a significant influence on the development of sociocognitive skills. During the formative early childhood years, the high frequency of interaction among brothers and sisters suggests that sibling influence may be comparable to parental influence. While much of the popular literature on siblings focuses on rivalry, current research clearly indicates that the relationship between siblings is primarily a positive one, and that high frequencies of altruistic, affectionate, and cooperative behavior take place throughout childhood.

Predictably, the older sibling has been found to dominate the relationship, consistently initiating more prosocial and more agonistic behaviors. In contrast, the younger sibling has been found to be more submissive and likely to take the role of the learner, engaging in a much higher frequency of imitative behaviors than the older sibling.

When attempting to improve sibling relations, the most effective interventions have involved modifying the parents —particularly the mother's — communication and behavioral interaction patterns with the siblings.

While the findings of observational research have enhanced the understanding of the dynamics of sibling relationships and validated the propriety of certain interventions, it is through the simultaneous consideration of situational factors, parental interaction factors, temperament factors, and sibling interaction factors that research will discover the actual impact of the sibling relationship on human development.

REFERENCES

Abramovitch, R., Corter, C., Pepler,C. J., & Stanhope, L. (1986). Sibling and peer interaction: A final follow-up and a comparison. *Child Development, 57,* 217–229.

Abramovitch, R., Pepler, C., & Corter, C. (1982). Patterns of sibling interaction among pre-school age children. In M. Lamb & B. Sutton-Smith (Eds.), *Sibling relationships: Their nature and significance across the lifespan* (pp. 61–86). Hillsdale, NJ: Erlbaum.

Adler, A. (1959). *Understanding human nature.* New York: Fawcett.

Bank, S. P., & Kahn, M. D. (1982). *The sibling bond.* New York: Basic Books.

Berndt, T. J., & Bulleit, T. N. (1985). Effects of sibling relationships on preschooler's behavior at home and at school. *Developmental Psychology, 21,* 761–767.

Bowerman, C. E., & Dobash, R. M. (1974). Structural variations in inter-sibling affect. *Journal of Marriage and the Family, 36,* 48–54.

Brody, G. H., Stoneman, Z., MacKinnon, C. E., & Mackinnon, R. (1985). Role relationships and behavior between preschool-aged and school-aged sibling pairs. *Developmental Psychology, 21,* 124–129.

Burton, S. L. (1987). Children and siblings of the handicapped. In J. Grimes & A. Thomas (Eds.), *Children's needs: Psychological perspectives.* Washington, DC: National Association of School Psychologists.

Calladine, C. (1983). Sibling rivalry: A parent education perspective. *Child Welfare, 57,* 421–427.

Calladine, C., & Calladine, A. (1979). *Raising siblings.* New York: Delacorte.

Carlson, C. (1985). Best practices in working with single-parent and stepfamilies. In A. Thomas & J. Grimes (Eds.), *Best practices in school psychology* (pp.43–60). Kent, OH: National Association of School Psychologists.

Chess, S., & Thomas, A. (1984). *Origins and evolution of behavior disorders.* New York: Brunner/Mazel.

Daniels, D., & Plomin, R. (1985). Differential experience of siblings in the same family. *Developmental Psychology,21,* 767–760.

Dobson, J. (1978). *The strong willed child.* Wheaton, IL: Tyndale House.

Dunn, J. (1983). Sibling relationships in early childhood. *Child Development,54,* 787–811.

Dunn, J. (1985). *Sisters and brothers.* Cambridge, MA: Harvard University Press.

Dunn, J., & Kendrick, C. (1982). *Siblings: Love, envy, and understanding.* Cambridge, MA: Harvard University Press.

Falbo, T. (Ed.). (1984). *The single-child family.* New York: Guilford.

Felson, R. B. (1983). Aggression and violence between siblings. *Social Psychology Quarterly, 46,* 271–285.

Furman, W., & Buhrmester, D. (1985). Children's perceptions of the qualities of sibling relationships. *Child Development, 54,* 448–461.

Hacker, A. (1983). *U/S: A statistical portrait of the American people.* New York: Viking/Penguin Books.

Kelly, F. D., & Main, F. O. (1979). Sibling conflict in a single-parent family: An empirical case study. *The American Journal of Family Therapy, 7,* 39–47.

Lamb, M. E. (1982). Sibling relationships across the lifespan: An overview and introduction. In M. E. Lamb & B. Sutton-Smith (Eds.), *Sibling relationships: Their nature and significance across the lifespan* (pp. 1–12). Hillsdale, NJ: Erlbaum.

Lamb, M. E., & Sutton-Smith, B. (Eds.). (1982). *Sibling relationships: Their nature and significance across the lifespan.* Hillsdale, NJ: Erlbaum.

Levy, D. M. (1937). Studies in sibling rivalry. *American Orthopsychiatric Association Research Monographs, 2.*

Long, L., & Long, T. (1983). *The handbook for latchkey children and their parents.* New York: Arbor House.

Lytton, H. (1980). *Parent–child interaction.* New York: Plenum.

Millman, H., & Schaefer, C. (1982). *How to help children with common problems.* New York: Plenum.

Minnet, A. M., Vandell, D. L., & Santrock, J. W. (1983). The effects of sibling status on sibling interaction: Influence of birth order, age spacing, sex of child, and sex of sibling. *Child Development, 54,* 1064–1072.

Nadelman, L., & Begun, A. (1982). The effect of the newborn on the older sibling: Mother's questionnaires. In M. E. Lamb & B. Sutton-Smith (Eds.), *Sibling relationships: Their nature and significance across the lifespan* (pp. 13–37). Hillsdale, NJ: Erlbaum.

Pepler, D., Corter, C., & Abramovitch, R. (1982). Social relations among children: Comparison of sibling and peer interaction. In K. H. Rubin & H. S. Ross (Eds.), *Peer relationships and social skills in childhood* (pp. 209–227). New York: Springer-Verlag.

Prochaska, J. M. & Prochaska, J. O. (1985). Children's views of the causes and "cures" of sibling rivalry. *Child Welfare, 54,* 427–433.

Rice, F. P. (1978). *The adolescent.* Boston: Allyn and Bacon.

Scarr, S., & Grajek, S. (1982). Similarities and differences among siblings. In M. E. Lamb & B. Sutton-Smith (Eds.), *Sibling relationships: Their nature and significance across the lifespan* (pp. 357–382). Hillsdale, NJ: Erlbaum.

Schachter, F. F. (1982). Sibling deidentification and split-parent identification: A family tetrad. In M. E. Lamb & B. Sutton-Smith (Eds.), *Sibling relationships: Their nature and significance across the lifespan* (pp. 123–151). Hillsdale, NJ: Erlbaum.

Stewart, R. B. (1983). Sibling interaction: The role of the older child as teacher for the younger. *Merrill-Palmer Quarterly, 29,* 47–68.

Stewart, R. B., & Martin, R. S. (1984). Sibling relations: The role of conceptual perspective-taking in the ontogeny of sibling caregiving. *Child Development, 55,* 1322–1332.

Sutton-Smith, B., & Rosenberg, B. G. (1968). Sibling consensus on power tactics. *Journal of Genetic Psychology, 112,* 63–72.

Sutton-Smith, B., & Rosenberg, B. G. (1970). *The sibling.* New York: Holt, Rinehart & Winston.

White, B. L. (1985). *The first three years of life.* Englewood Cliffs, NJ: Prentice-Hall.

BIBLIOGRAPHY: PROFESSIONALS

Abramovitch, R., Corter, C., Pepler, D. J., & Stanhope, L. (1986). Sibling and peer interaction: A final follow-up and a comparison. *Child Development, 57,* 217–229.
Provides a comparative summary of the findings of the authors' longitudinal and observational studies of sibling relationships during early and middle childhood.

Bank, S. P., & Kahn,M. D. (1982). *The sibling bond.* New York: Basic Books.
Presents a clinician's-eye view of sibling relationships, detailing the authors' in-depth study of 100 unusual sibling relationship situations. The authors also propose the theory that strong sibling bonds develop when siblings have high access to one another and parental influence is limited.

Dunn, J. (1983). Sibling relationships in early childhood. *Child Development, 54,* 787–811.
Provides an excellent review of the research on sibling relationships during the early childhood period and examines this research in the context of the author's conceptualization of reciprocal and complementary interactions.

Dunn, J., & Kendrick, C. (1982). *Siblings: Love, envy, and understanding.* Cambridge, MA: Harvard University Press.
A compilation of the findings of the authors' pioneering observational studies on sibling relationships during early childhood.

Lamb, M. E., & Sutton-Smith, B. (Eds.). (1982). *Sibling relationships: Their nature and significance across the lifespan.* Hillsdale, NJ: Erlbaum.
An edited volume that provides an excellent compendium of research on sibling relationships as they develop and evolve throughout the lifetime. Chapters are written by a variety of authorities in the areas of behavioral genetics, developmental psychology, clinical psychology, and comparative psychology.

BIBLIOGRAPHY: PARENTS

Calladine, C., & Calladine, A. (1979). *Raising siblings.* New York: Delacorte.
Drawing on the professional and practical experiences of two social workers, this book provides advice on the management of sibling interactions. Information is presented in a logical, thoughtful, and sometimes humorous way.

Dunn, J. (1985). *Sisters and brothers.* Cambridge, MA: Harvard University Press.
Written with the parent in mind, this book provides a thorough accounting of the ways in which siblings influence one another and how they frequently come to be so different from each other. Provides some practical behavior management suggestions based on empirical research.

Millman, H., & Schaefer, C. (1982). *How to help children with common problems* (pp. 248–257). New York: Plenum.
This chapter from the authors' excellent book on parental management of children's behavior problems provides an array of practical suggestions in dealing with sibling rivalry.

Children and Siblings of the Handicapped

Sally Linton Burton
University of Idaho

BACKGROUND

Introduction

The diagnosis of a handicapping condition brings about a variety of changes not only for the child but for all members of the family, both nuclear and extended. Most of the research to date has focused on the impact that the handicapping condition has on parents, but recent studies have shown that siblings are also significantly affected by the presence of a family member with a handicap (McKeever, 1983; Cleveland & Miller, 1977). Especially significant are the relationships between nonhandicapped siblings and their brother or sister with a handicap. The way non-handicapped siblings perceive the world, adapt to key developmental changes, and cope with stress is often directly related to their family experiences with siblings and parents. When a sibling is handicapped, the lifestyle of all family members changes, causing parents to depend more on their nonhandicapped siblings to provide special care and support services than on outside agencies and/or services. The purpose of this chapter is to identify the special needs of siblings of the handicapped and demonstrate how support groups can help this population to better understand and cope with this special relationship.

Currently, approximately 12% of all students in public school are receiving special education services, and another 3–17% of preschool children are also receiving some type of special education services (Haring, 1982). Most of these special education students have siblings who are significantly affected by their handicapping condition, although statistics on the extent of this indirect problem are currently unavailable.

Because of the large numbers of individuals believed to be affected by family members with handicapping conditions school psychologists should find useful an inquiry into this question designed to accomplish two purposes: (a) to provide information about the special needs and concerns of siblings of the handicapped and (b) to suggest specific techniques on how to develop a support system for siblings as well as how to implement these services.

Effects of a Family Member's Handicapping Condition on Siblings

In order to understand the impact the special requirements of a handicapped person on family dynamics and specific family members, it is first necessary to develop an understanding of normal family dynamics and then assess how a family member with a handicap may disrupt family dynamics, particularly in respect to siblings. Siblings play a significant role in the dynamics of family interactions. Duvall (1977) has described eight developmental tasks that families must perform to be productive: (a) physical maintenance, (b) allocation of resources, (c) division of labor, (d) socialization of family members, (e) maintenance of order and establishment of communication, (f) reproduction, release, and recruitment of members, (g) placement of members in a larger society, and (h) maintenance of motivation and morale.

Families with a handicapped child may find it difficult to perform many of these tasks. Although not every family functions less effectively because of a handicapped child, its group dynamics and processes may be dramatically different from those of other families. Thus, it is necessary to understand how accomplishment of the above-named tasks is altered by handicaps with notable impact on siblings, and how these effects may change the dynamics and functioning of the family unit.

Physical Maintenance. Physical maintenance includes providing the basic necessities of life, such as food, clothing, and shelter, to all family members. When families include a handicapped child, the task of physical maintenance is compounded greatly, usually including additional responsibility for providing special care, treatment, therapy, and/or medication to the affected family member. These extra responsibilities place a drain on family resources, often forcing siblings to fulfill "caregiver" roles in meeting the special needs of their handicapped brother or sister. Often financial or logistical concerns necessitates that siblings be trained to provide educational, behavioral, or physical therapy programs for the handicapped child, thus greatly increasing their role in family maintenance (Lobato & Tlaker, 1986; Schreibman, O'Neill, & Koegel, 1983).

Allocation of Resources. The added expenses incurred with a handicapped or chronically ill child can significantly strain family finances, particularly when the handicapping condition demands daily nursing care. Strained finances may force the mother to enter the work force, creating significant changes in the family system. The financial strain of a handicapped child may force nonhandicapped siblings to cut out many important extracurricular activities, such as music lessons or sports, in order to save money, thus creating envy and hostility toward their handicapped brother or sister owing to the unequal distribution of family funds.

Division of Labor. When there is a child in the family with special needs, the division of labor is often dramatically altered. Parents, particularly mothers, often become preoccupied with the needs of the child with a handicapping condition out of necessity, especially if special diets or treatments are required. The burden of other domestic responsibilities such as housework or childcare is often thrust on nonhandicapped siblings. Nevertheless, research has shown that families that share responsibilities and achieve a balanced division of labor by making cooperative family decisions through systematic family planning will normally foster more open communication and role acceptance from all family members (Turnbull, Summers, & Brotherson, 1983; Olson, Russell, & Sprenkle, 1979).

Socialization of Family Members. A handicapped child is a special challenge to other family members because of the extra love, attention, and energy that is required. Appropriate socialization of siblings is aided if parents convey a sense of encouragement to the family when they share the news that the child has some type of handicapping condition. Siblings are sensitive and will generally adopt the type of attitude, positive or negative, that they perceive in their parents (Fischer & Roberts, 1983). However, if parents have a tendency to overinvolve themselves with the special child, it may limit the energy available to also meet the needs of other family members, particularly siblings.

Siblings of the handicapped may miss out on normal family activities such as vacations if their parents fail to balance their time and energy expenditure to include time with their nonhandicapped siblings. Siblings find their lives significantly affected by a brother or sister with a handicap in positive as well as negative ways. In fact, Cleveland and Miller (1977) revealed that there are several positive benefits of being the sibling of a handicapped brother or sister. In their study, adult siblings reported greater flexibility and adaptability and achieved better relationships with their parents, siblings, and peers as a result of growing up with a handicapped family member.

Maintenance and Order. The presence of a handicapped child strains family maintenance of order, altering the dynamics between family members and the way the family functions (Turnbull, Summers, & Brotherson, 1983). Siblings of the disabled child may also have behavioral and self-concept problems that contribute to family stress and dysfunction. Breslau, Weitzman, and Messenger (1981) found, for example, that younger male siblings acted out by engaging in attention seeking, whereas the oldest female siblings exhibited coping problems linked to the inordinate amount of responsibility placed on them for the care of handicapped and nonhandicapped siblings. Trevino (1979) and McKeever (1983) both have labeled siblings of the handicapped and chronically ill as a "population at risk" because of the high incidence of psychological problems related to daily coping among this group. For example, Crain (Crain, Sussman, & Weil, 1966) found that siblings of diabetics were faced with stress levels significantly higher than normal because of the variety of extra demands placed on them by their sibling's illness as well as the reduction in parental attention they received because of the extra demands placed on their parents' time by the diabetic sibling. Siblings of diabetics may also be required to act as informants, reporting to their parents when siblings fail to comply with diet and/or medication instructions.

Inadequacy in social situations and eating and sleeping disorders have also been linked to the experience of being a sibling of a handicapped brother or sister. For example, Israelite (1986) demonstrated that siblings of the hearing-impaired felt unusually inadequate in social situations, whereas McKeever (1983) found psychosomatic complaints including eating and sleeping disorders to be typical of siblings of the handicapped and chronically ill.

Communication has been positively linked to the effectiveness with which a family copes with a crisis. Positive communication for siblings begins with accurate, age-appropriate information concerning the handicapping condition of their brother or sister (Powell & Ogle, 1985). Open communication also allows siblings to express their feelings, particularly feelings of sadness or guilt. Siblings may have some difficulty getting in touch with their feelings about having a handicapped brother or sister, and they need both the opportunity to express those feelings and the type of sensitive, supportive atmosphere that allows such a process to be productive. Some siblings are also sensitive to the difficulty their parents are having dealing with a handicapped child, and this awareness often inhibits them from discussing their own adjustment problems in order to avoid burdening their parents with questions that may provoke further guilt or sadness (McKeever, 1983).

Reproduction, Recruitment, and Release of Family Members. The birth of a child with a handicapping condition presents a dilemma to parents. If the possibility of another handicapped child is likely, they may question whether they should have another child. Advanced technology such as genetic counseling, amniocentesis, and ultrasound may provide parents with additional information that can help them render an appropriate and logical decision about having another child. Unfortunately, the fear of conceiving another handicapped child does not end with the parents. Both male and female siblings may worry, perhaps needlessly, that they "carry" a genetic defect that they may pass on to their own children.

Another future-related fear of all family members is whether the child with a handicap will ever be able to function independently in the community. Not only are the parents worried about this autonomy issue, but siblings are affected by the level of self-sufficiency attainable by the handicapped child and his or her ultimate placement. Siblings are particularly concerned with autonomy issues because responsibility for a brother or sister with a handicap may revert to them upon the death of their parents.

Special planning is necessary to prepare the entire family for the time when the individual with the handicapping condition is to move out of the home and into a new living situation. When the handicapped individual leaves home, a significant change will occur in family life. Parents and siblings may find that special routines they have religiously followed for years, providing for the special needs of the handicapped or disabled individual, are now no longer necessary. A time of transition is usually necessary for most families. Problems and family quarrels that had been ignored for years because the family's time and energy were spent dealing with the needs of the handicapped family member may now surface, particularly hostility and jealousy on the part of other siblings. On the other hand, the move of a handicapped family member to a new residential location can also provide the family with a new beginning; families may now use their new-found freedom to go on outings or take vacations that they have postponed since the handicapped child's condition was first diagnosed. Families who focus on the positive family growth that may occur because of increased time and resources should adjust to such a move more effectively than families who can only dwell on the negative aspects of such a move.

Family Members in the Larger Society. Many times families cut themselves off from friends and family when they have a child with a handicap. This self-imposed isolation considerably reduces the number of support systems that they can use in times of need. Even though the school system and specifically the special education teacher normally provide positive support for parents of handicapped children, isolation remains a significant problem faced by parents with a son or daughter with a handicap. Parents often feel that no one will understand what it is like to have a handicapped child and are reluctant to burden others with their problems. For this reason, there is a significant need for hospitals, community agencies, and school systems to organize support programs for parents of the handicapped.

Parents are not the only family members who experience a sense of isolation. Siblings, too, may feel very embarrassed and sad about their handicapped brother or sister. They want to talk about their sibling, but they are unsure whether their friends will understand. Siblings also need to establish firm support systems so they can express and work through their feelings.

Maintenance of Morale and Motivation. If the family has fostered strong bonds and positive relationships among all family members by developing an atmosphere characterized by openness, honesty, and a positive attitude towards the handicapping condition, then family members should be well prepared to enjoy full and happy lives.

As can be seen from the previous discussion, maintenance of the family unit is a complex task involving many developmental tasks. If the family spends too much time on any one of these developmental obligations, tasks in other areas will suffer. Thus, it is important that families with a child who has a handicap learn how to balance their time and energy so that all siblings feel loved and supported.

DEVELOPMENT

Needs and Concerns of Siblings

Parents, educators, and professionals are often uninformed of the special needs and unique concerns of their nonhandicapped members of the family, particularly siblings, of a handicapped child. Meyer, Vadasy, and Fewell (1985a) have suggested that awareness needs to be increased about the concerns of these nonhandicapped family members. Typical problems confronting siblings are overidentification, embarrassment, guilt, isolation, need for accurate information, concern about the future, resentment of caregiving, and pressure to achieve.

Overidentification. Some siblings worry that there may be something wrong with them because they have a brother or sister with a handicap. For instance, some such siblings might think that because they are not good at math they are handicapped, too.

Embarrassment. Siblings often accompany their brother or sister with a handicap to church, school, shopping, and throughout the community. The child with a handicap may embarrass the sibling by having a seizure, throwing a tantrum, or calling attention to himself or herself through some unusual behavior or simply by drawing the attention of peers, neighbors, or strangers, who might be so rude as to stare at their brother or sister with a handicap.

Guilt. Siblings on occasion get angry at their brother or sister with a handicap and may suffer feelings of guilt because they realize that their anger has been directed toward behavior that their sibling could not control. Most of all they may feel guilty that they can live a normal life that is impossible for the brother or sister.

Isolation. Siblings may feel a sense of isolation, wanting to tell their friends about their handicapped brother or sister but choosing, because they are afraid of the reaction they might get, not to talk about the problem. It may be difficult for siblings to explain to their friends about why their brother or sister has seizures or has to take special education classes. Siblings may often have to restrain their enthusiasm about an accomplishment that a sibling with a handicap has achieved with their friends because they might laugh at what, to them, seems a trivial achievement.

Need for Accurate Information. Siblings need to have age-appropriate information about their brother's or sister's handicapping condition. Siblings are usually not present when the diagnosis is made to the parents, so this information usually must be obtained secondhand. If siblings are not given accurate information, they will often invent their own explanations for the disability, sometimes even imagining that it is their fault. One excellent source of information about different handicapping conditions for young readers aged 10 years and above is a book written by Donald J. Meyer, Patricia Vadasy, and Rebecca R. Fewell entitled: *Living with a brother or sister with special needs: A book for sibs,* which is published by the University of Washington Press.

Concerns About the Future. Siblings have very real concerns about the future of their handicapped brother or sister. Siblings may want to know the answers to questions such as (a) Who will be responsible for the individual with the handicap? (b) Who will pay for the living accommodations of the handicapped brother or sister? (c) Should I live nearby in case of an emergency? (d) If an appropriate living situation is not found for the individual with a handicap, will she or he have to live with me? (e) What do individuals with handicaps do in group homes or institutions? Parents should begin as soon as possible to address these questions that siblings might have, although the parents themselves often have to find answers to these questions first.

Siblings are also often worried that they might have a handicapped child themselves when they have a family. This is a significant concern that needs to be addressed as siblings get older with accurate, expert information on the potential risks of a hereditary link to the handicapping condition.

Resentment. Siblings may sometimes resent the reduced amount of their parents' time they receive because of the special needs of the child with a handicap. Parents do not necessarily want to devote more time to the child with a handicap but often their special needs dictate a larger time commitment. Unfortunately, siblings may misinterpret their parents' priorities and engage in inappropriate behavior in an attempt to get their share of their parents' attention. As siblings get older, they may transfer this frustration and hostility into direct rebellion against teachers and other authority figures (Breslau, Weitzman, & Messenger, 1981). By being aware of siblings' needs, parents and teachers may be able to avoid some of these problems by making a special point to directly confront these issues and appropriately channel them.

Caregiving. Siblings are normally the best equipped and most convenient babysitters for their brother or sister with a handicapping condition, but such responsibilities may directly or indirectly conflict with the siblings' own needs. Parents need to plan interim respite care to avoid having their non handicapped children assume child care responsibilities inappropriate for their ages. Recent research demonstrates that siblings and specifically the oldest female in the family often carries the largest child care burden (Trevino, 1979; Gath, 1974; Grossman, 1972). If excessive child care responsibilities deprive siblings of the opportunity to have time to themselves (e.g., socializing with their friends), they may resent both their parents and their handicapped brother or sister.

Pressure to Achieve. Parents unconsciously or consciously develop expectations about what they hope their children can become. When a child is diagnosed as having a handicapping condition, parents often experience a sense of loss about the hopes and dreams for that child that will now go unfulfilled. Often these expectations are transferred to siblings, who experience increased parental pressure to achieve. Siblings quickly become aware of the increased parental expectations and emotional investment that compel them to excel in areas such as academics or sports to make up for their brother's or sister's handicapping condition. These increased expectations can create stress if parents and/or sibling expect more than is realistically possible. This pressure to achieve is no doubt one plausible explanation why Powell & Ogle, (1985) found that the larger the family the fewer the coping problems because of increased peer social support and a diffusion of the pressure to achieve among the siblings of the family.

PUTTING SIBLINGS OF THE HANDICAPPED IN PERSPECTIVE

Benefits and Burdens of Living With a Handicapped Child

Growing up in a family with a handicapped child is an experience that offers family members both benefits and burdens. While it is generally agreed that a child with a disability makes more work for everyone, these altered family roles and family dynamics do not have to result in a negative experience, and the family that develops strong support systems will have fewer problems and experience more positive family dynamics than those whose support systems are poorly developed (McCubbin et al., 1980). In fact, growing up with a brother or sister with a handicap may help develop many positive personality attributes. Some of the positive qualities reported in siblings who have grown up with an individual with a handicap are humor, tolerance, patience, maturity, dependability, teaching skills, and behavioral and emotional flexibility.

Humor. Out of necessity many siblings of the handicapped develop a sense of humor. They may be faced with situations in which they could respond by either laughing or crying. Over time many siblings have learned that it is easier and less stressful to see the humor in situations that they have no control over. Many siblings are put in difficult situations like this from an early age and they learn the value of a positive attitude in coping effectively with potential public embarrassment.

Tolerance. Siblings of the handicapped not only learn to accept differences in their brother or sister, but they also develop greater tolerance for differences in others. Meyer, Vadasy, and Fewell (1985a) have suggested that such acceptance of differences often generalizes to larger social situations and makes such siblings more tolerant of minorities or other diverse or oppressed groups. Consequently, they see people's capabilities rather than their deficiencies.

Patience. Developing the patience to allow a handicapped sibling to perform a task or household chore can be very difficult. The sibling could complete the same task in a fraction of the time and do it much more efficiently. Nevertheless, siblings know the value that performing tasks independently has for the handicapped, so they develop the patience to wait for their brother or sister to finish a task or, for example, color a picture unaided.

Maturity. Maturity is a personal quality that develops as a result of the realization that life is not perfect but it still deserves one's best efforts to make things as good as they can possibly be. Such maturity typifies many siblings and the relationship they develop within their families. Siblings learn that the needs of the family member who is handicapped will often have to come first, even though they themselves are important members of the family who have pressing needs, too. Often siblings learn how to recruit reinforcement from parents by acting in a dependable manner with their handicapped brother or sister. Bank and Kahn (1982) have noted that such siblings have an enhanced self-concept and a way of looking at life that is more positive and realistic than individuals without a handicapped sibling.

Teaching Skills. Siblings often successfully teach social and recreational skills to their handicapped sister or brother (Turnbull, Brotherson, & Summers, 1983). Several factors are responsible for this success: (a) They are more demanding of accomplishments; and (b) they can relate the skill better because they are closer to their sibling's age. Siblings also sometimes assist their brothers and sisters in academic and remedial tutoring. Many siblings later enter careers in teaching as a result of their lifetime exposure to a brother or sister with a special need.

Flexibility. Siblings of the handicapped learn to live their life one day at a time. Family plans often have to be changed because of problems or special considerations associated with the handicap. For instance, a change of medications for a special sibling might make a family outing or vacation impossible until the effects of the medication have stabilized. Because siblings are so often forced to change plans at a moment's notice, they develop flexibility and adaptability, not because they necessarily want to, but because they have to.

ALTERNATIVE ACTIONS

Designing a Community Support System for Siblings

Although siblings provide numerous skills and services to the handicapped family member, they also have their own special needs that must be considered. Consequently, support systems for siblings of the handicapped should be set up as natural outgrowths of these very real concerns.

The best people to start support systems are those who are most directly affected by a handicapped individual such as an adult sibling. It is also important to have a special education or counseling professional available to assist in the formation of the group. It is suggested that the facilitator of the group have some experience in counseling. Powell and Ogle (1985) have suggested that effective counselors must be mature, interested in people, honest, capable of establishing rapport with people, empathic, accepting, involved, ethical, and possess knowledge of handicapping conditions. Nevertheless, the most important prerequisite for organizing a group such as this is time, energy, and commitment.

Participants can be notified about meetings of the support group through the special education director or principal, who will mail out pertinent information about meeting time and place to parents and siblings of the special education students enrolled in the school district. A meeting location should be found that the participants will find comfortable but not tend to associate with any stigma, which might result from selection of a special education facility. After the group is well established, the location could rotate in order to equalize the distance traveled by participants.

The three major purposes of the sibling support group include: support, involvement and education (Meyer, Personal communication), but keeping meetings fun and interesting is equally important. Thus recreational activities such as cookouts, overnights, and roller skating parties often serve as the focal point of sibling support meetings. Good snacks or cooking projects are always popular and help to create an atmosphere for informal sharing.

The educational component is an important part of each sibling support meeting. Because interests and needs differ from one group to the next, a needs assessment can be done to identify the group interests and needs, although these concerns usually revolve around the implications of the family member's handicapping condition. The siblings should determine by consensus the primary group concerns to focus the planning of the educational component of each meeting.

Meyer, Vadasy, and Fewell (1985b) have identified four goals for working with sibling support groups that have provided the basis for many contemporary programs. These goals include creating a social support network, sharing experiences, developing behavior management skills, and learning about handicapping conditions.

Suggested Sibling Support Group Goals

Creating a Social Support Network. The first goal of a sibling support group is to create a social support network by providing members an opportunity to meet peers from their area who have similar experiences with a handicapped sibling. Meetings should stress a casual atmosphere that is conducive to the sharing of concerns.

Sharing Experiences. Another important goal of sibling support groups should be to provide members with an opportunity to share information about their family member who is handicapped. Participants should feel free to discuss both the positive and negative aspects of life with a family member who is handicapped. The support group should provide a setting in which members can seek information and discuss concerns openly with one another. The siblings' negative comments should be allowed and even encouraged because these feelings may need to be expressed and the participant may not have another opportunity to share their feelings with individuals they respect and trust. However, the positive aspects of life with a family member who is handicapped and the personal enrichment from such experiences can also be reinforced by the facilitator and the other participants.

Developing Behavior Management Skills. Another important goal of sibling support groups is the development of skills that will make it easier to deal with the handicapped family member. The support group can be a place where siblings learn how to deal with the behavior of their handicapped brother or sister by sharing with and learning from other participants what has worked in the past. New skills can be taught by special education professionals. Although many siblings will have had some experience with these skills, such educational sessions should improve these skills by encouraging participants to practice them with their siblings or fellow group members and receive feedback.

Learning About Handicapping Conditions. The final goal of support groups is to give all participants the opportunity to learn about the handicapping conditions of their siblings as well as the implications that the handicapping condition has on them and the rest of the family. Guest speakers can be invited to discuss various handicapping conditions that are of particular interest to the group members.

These goals should provide the general direction for organizing a support group, but specific goals should be revised on the basis of the group's makeup, needs, and personalities.

SUMMARY

The needs and concerns of siblings of the handicapped are very real yet are often ignored by both parents and professionals. School psychologists and counselors probably deal with this population indirectly through parent and staff meetings but could further benefit from learning about siblings and their unique needs and concerns. Because this population is considered to be "at risk," schools might consider some preventive measures with siblings of the handicapped, such as the organization of a sibling support program based on the goals outlined in this chapter.

The purpose of establishing a sibling support group is primarily to let these individuals know that they are not alone in their special concerns and joys. Moreover, these support groups can assist the participants in making friends with others who have common problems and concerns as well as learning more about handicapping conditions and developing skills that can assist them in working more effectively with the handicapped family member.

REFERENCES

Bank, S., & Kahn, M. D. (1982). Intense sibling loyalties. In M. E. Lamb & B. Sutton-Smith (Eds.), *Sibling relationships: Their nature and significance across the lifespan.* Hillsdale, NJ: Erlbaum.

Breslau, N., Weitzman, M., & Messenger, K. (1981). Psychological functioning of siblings of disabled children. *Pediatrics, 67,* 344–353.

Cleveland, D. W., & Miller, N. (1977). Attitudes and life commitments of older siblings of mentally retarded adults: An exploratory study. *Mental Retardation, 15,* 38–41.

Crain, A., Sussman, M., & Weil, W. (1966). Family interaction, diabetes and sibling relationships. *International Journal of Social Psychiatry, 12,* 35–43.

Duvall, E. M. (1977). *Marriage and family development.* Philadelphia: Lippincott.

Fischer, J., & Roberts, S. C. (1983). The effects of the mentally retarded child on his siblings. *Education, 103,* 399–401.

Gath, A. (1974). Sibling reactions to mental handicap: A comparison of the brothers and sisters of mongol children. *Journal of Child Psychology and Psychiatry, 15,* 187–198.

Grossman, F. K. (1972). *Brothers and sisters of retarded children: An exploratory study.* Syracuse, NY: Syracuse University Press.

Haring, N. G. (1982). *Exceptional children and youth (3rd ed.).* Columbus, OH: Merrill.

Israelite, N. K. (1986). Hearing impaired children and the psychological functioning of their normal-hearing siblings. *Volta Review, 88,* 47–53.

Lobato, D., & Tlaker, A. (1986). Sibling intervention with a retarded child. *Education and Treatment of Children, 8,* 221–228.

McCubbin, H. I., Joy, C. B., Cauble, A. E., Comeau, J. K., Patterson, J. M., & Needle, R. H. (1980). Family stress and coping: A decade review. *Journal of Marriage and Family, 42,* 855–871.

McKeever, P. (1983). Siblings of chronically ill children: A literature review with implications for research and practice. *American Journal of Orthopsychiatry, 53,* 209–218.

Meyer, D. J., Vadasy, P. F., & Fewell, R. R. (1985a). *Living with a brother or sister with special needs: A book for sibs.* Seattle: University of Washington Press.

Meyer, D. J., Vadasy, P. F., & Fewell, R. R. (1985b). *Sibships: A handbook for implementing workshops for siblings of children with special needs.* Seattle: University of Washington Press.

More New Games and Playful Ideas From the New Games Foundation. (1981). Garden City, NY: Headlands Press/Doubleday.

Olson, D. H., Sprenkle, D. H., & Russell, C. (1979). Circumplex model of marital and family systems. I: Cohesion and adaptability dimension, family types and clinical applications. *Family Process, 18,* 3–28.

Powell, T. H., & Ogle, P. A. (1985). *Brothers and sisters — A special part of exceptional families.* Baltimore: Brookes.

Sabbeth, B. F., & Leventhal, J. M. (1984). Marital adjustment to chronic childhood illness: A critique of the literature. *Pediatrics, 73,* 762–768.

Schreibman, L., O'Neill, R. E., & Koegel, R. L. (1983). Behavioral training for siblings of autistic children. *Journal of Applied Behavior Analysis, 16,* 129–138.

Trevino, F. (1979). Siblings of handicapped children: Identifying those at risk. *Social Casework, 60,* 488–493.

Turnbull, A. P., Summers, J. A., & Brotherson, M. J. (1983). *Working with families with disabled members: A family systems approach.* Lawrence, KS: University of Kansas, Research and Training Center of Independent Living.

BIBLIOGRAPHY: PROFESSIONALS

Meyer, D. J., Vadasy, P. F., & Fewell, R. R. (1985). *Living with a brother or sister with special needs.* Seattle, WA: University of Washington Press.
Living with a brother or sister with special needs is a book written for young readers. The book offers factual information and emotional support to brothers and sisters with handicaps. This book provides useful and clear explanations about specific handicapping conditions. The book constitutes an excellent resource book for siblings, parents, and professionals as well.

Powell, T. H., & Ogle, P. A. (1985). *Brothers and Sisters — A Special Part of Exceptional Families.* Baltimore, MD: Paul H. Brookes.
The authors are special educators who have combined a review of research on siblings of children with handicaps, together with their own experiences and recommendations, to produce a book which will be of considerable value to parents and professionals alike. The chapters include discussions on the unique needs of siblings with specific strategies to help them.

Seligman, M. (Ed.) (1983). *The family with a handicapped child.* New York: Grune and Stratton, Inc.
This volume focuses on a range of topics including legal issues, community service providers, working with families, counseling and therapeutic inverventions. There is a chapter entitled "Siblings of Handicapped Persons" by the author which includes an overview of research findings and discusses psychological prospects for siblings.

GROUPS FOR SIBLINGS

SEFAM Sibling Project
Experimental Education Unit WJ-10
Child Development and Mental Retardation Center
University of Washington
Seattle, WA 98195

Siblings Helping Persons with Autism Through Resources and Energy (SHARE)
National Society for Children and Adults with Autism
Suite 1017
1234 Massachusetts Avenue, NW
Washington, DC 20005

Sibling Information Network
Department of Educational Psychology
Box U-64
The University of Connecticut
Storrs, CT 06268

Siblings Understanding Needs (SUN)
Department of Pediatrics C-19
University of Texas Medical Branch
Galveston, TX 77550

Siblings for Significant Change
823 United Nations Plaza, Rm 808
New York, NY 10017

Special Siblings
Special Education Department
College of Education
University of Idaho
Moscow, ID 82843

Youth Advocates for Retarded Citizens
5522 University Avenue
Madison, WI

Children and Single-Parent Homes

Cindy Carlson
University of Texas at Austin

BACKGROUND

It is estimated that a majority of U. S. children will at some point in their lives live in a single-parent family (Glick, 1979). Currently, one of every five white children and one of every two black children under the age of 18 years live with a single parent. Over 90% of children in single-parent families live in households headed by their mothers. Alarmingly, more than 50% of these female-headed one-parent families fall below the poverty line in the United States, and as many as 50% of the children in single-parent homes reside with a parent who has not completed high school (Thompson & Gongla, 1983). Two-thirds of single-parent homes are created by divorce; one-fourth consist of never married mothers. Although the rate of divorce has slowed in recent years, the proportion of single-parent households is expected to remain constant owing to an upsurge of families maintained by never married mothers (Thompson & Gongla, 1983).

As the single-parent family represents a major child-rearing lifestyle within the United States, it becomes imperative that school psychologists be knowledgeable regarding the strengths and vulnerabilities of this variation of family structure for the functioning of children in school. A cautionary note, however, is appropriate. A focus on single-parent homes as a family "type" presents school psychologists with a deceptively simple view of complex parent–child relationships. The goals of this chapter are to increase knowledge of the "generic" properties of single-parent homes that impinge upon child development but also to heighten sensitivity to the complexity of mediating factors, which to a greater extent than family form, determine children's progress in the schools.

Single-Parent Homes: Variations and Commonalities

A single-parent family is one in which someone raises his or her children alone without the household presence of a second parent or a parent substitute (Weiss, 1979). Although no consistently accepted typology is available, several variables are assumed to characterize single-parent homes. These include: (a) the cause of parental absence (death, separation or divorce, never married status); (b) the degree of parental absence (total, partial, irreversible), duration of parental absence, and availability of a parental surrogate; (c) the age, sex, and education level of the custodial parent; (d) the age, sex, and birth order of children; (e) racial composition and socioeconomic status. A summary of the characteristics and variations in single-parent families, based on the antecedent to single parenthood, appears in Table 1. As can be seen from Table 1, single-parent homes vary in their vulnerability to stress, depending to a large extent upon social and economic resources, with the never-married single parents, a group largely resulting from illigitimate births to adolescents, presenting the greatest deficits.

Despite diversity, single-parent homes may be more likely to have certain problems and experiences than intact families. The commonality of experiences in single-parent homes can best be explained by viewing the structure of the single-parent family system. Certain roles must be accomplished by all families, regardless of membership. These include survival roles of economic support, childcare, child socialization, and housekeeping, as well as companionship roles of recreation and leisure, therapeutic support, and sexual satisfaction (Rollins & Galligan, 1978). The single-parent home represents an "understaffed" family system in that the same number of roles, with a comparable level of quality as an intact family, must be accomplished by one adult, typically on a single income. The common characteristic of single-parent homes is task or role overload that requires adaptations, very distinct from the experience of the sociocultural mainstream, in the utilization of available resources.

DEVELOPMENT

The single-parent, primarily mother-headed, family has typically been viewed as a "broken" and "deficient" family structure with expected adverse consequences for the development and socialization of children. The impact of the single-parent home on children's cognitive and personality development is reflected primarily in the clinical and empirical literature on father absence. This body of research is notable for its methodological shortcomings, including failure to differentiate the cause of the father's absence, failure to control for involvement of a male surrogate, and failure to determine the duration of the father's absence. Thus our information on the effects of father absence on children deserves cautious interpretation. Although mothers may also be absent in single-parent homes, the literature on maternal deprivation has not been considered here, as demographics indicate that (a) father-headed homes represent only a small percentage of the single-parent population, (b) mothers, to a greater extent than fathers, remain highly involved with their children following divorce, and (c) remarriage rates are higher among father heads (Grief, 1985). Thus the primary focus of the subsequent discussion is the effects of absence of the father on children's development over time in stabilized mother-headed single-parent homes; the reader is referred to the chapter "Children and Divorce" in this volume for discussion of acute postdivorce reactions.

School Learning and Achievement

In a comprehensive review of the research on the role of paternal absence and children's cognitive development, as measured by school grades, achievement tests, and IQ tests, Shinn (1978) concluded, "the evidence shows that rearing in father–absent families or in families in which fathers have little supportive interaction with their children is often associated with poor performance on cognitive tests" (p. 320). A summary of selected research findings reported by Shinn and others appears in Table 2.

As is evident in Table 2, the research findings regarding the effects of paternal absence are less than conclusive, with lowered cognitive performance frequently being more strongly associated with race or socioeconomic status than with absent-father or single-parent status. On the other hand, cognitive performance deficits emerge fairly consistently when children are under 5 years old at the time of parental separation (Radin, 1979) and in homes where a male surrogate remains unavailable over time (Fry & Scher, 1984). There is stronger support for the hypothesis that growing up in a fatherless home leads to a "feminine," although not necessarily deficient, cognitive pattern consisting of lowered quantitative and higher verbal scores on aptitude tests and more externalized and global thinking. Similarly, performance on a variety of nonintellective, but achievement-related, school behaviors appears to suffer in father-absent homes. Again mediating variables are significant, with low socioeconomic status and marital disruption being high-risk factors especially for male children. Absence of the father owing to death appears to have less impact on cognitive functioning or school success unless exacerbating circumstances exist.

Personality and Social Development

Research into the impact of single-parent homes on children's personality and social development has centered on three areas: sex-role orientation and heterosex-

TABLE 1

Single-Parent Family Variations and Characteristics

	Postdivorce mothers	Postdivorce fathers	Widows	Never married parents
Incidence	55%	11%	7%	25% and increasing
Economic well-being	Income falls 73%; income remains 50% below single fathers	Less than 20% report income drop	Income falls 31%	Lowest income expected due to low age, education, lack of child support, and high percentage of minorities
Social response	Reactions negative. Home viewed as broken, often blamed. Little support.	Reactions mixed; admired, engenders support but also viewed as counter-normative.	Reactions sympathetic; engenders support.	Reactions variable and changing with SES and race factors mediators.
Social support	Able to create diverse social support; success variable, cost high.	Use paid social support more frequently and with less guilt than mothers.	Family provides strong support; adequate unless financial devastation or high parent dependency.	Rely on family of origin with mixed results. High father desertion. Fewer than 25% use social programs.

Note: Primary sources are Weiss, K. (1979) and *Single Parent Fact Sheet* (1985).

TABLE 2

Children's Cognitive Performance and School Behavior

1. Cognitive performance deficits range up to 1.6 years lower on achievement tests, up to 0.9 standard deviations lower on IQ subtests, and up to 0.8 lower in GPA (Shinn, 1978).
   a. Cognitive deficits are larger for white than for black children.
   b. Cognitive performance deficits are seldom obtained when SES factors are controlled.
   c. More damaging cognitive decrements associated with loss of father through divorce than through death or desertion.
   d. Cognitive deficits with death of father occur only when followed by significant and chronic family stress.
2. A "feminine" cognitive style, characterized by lower quantative and higher verbal scores, as well as greater field dependence, is more typical of children raised in mother-headed homes.
   a. Effect is most observable in middle to upper SES families (Belz & Geary, 1984; Goldstein, 1982; Shinn, 1978).
3. Achievement motivation (e.g., competitiveness, desire for mastery, persistence) of boys declines significantly over a 5-year period, when SES is controlled (Fry & Scher, 1984).
4. Loss of father through divorce significantly lowers children's academic and social performance on nonintellective but school-related criteria (Guidabaldi, et al., 1984; Guidabaldi & Perry, 1984).
   a. Boys in mother custody homes appear to be most adversely affected (Guidabaldi & Perry, 1984; Warshak & Santrock, 1979).
5. Cognitive and school performance deficits may not appear in preschool or early school-aged children but may increase over time (Fry & Scher, 1984; Shinn, 1978).

ual relations; moral development and the development of self-control; and psychological adjustment. A summary of research findings appears in Table 3.

To summarize findings, paternal absence has been associated with a less secure masculine orientation, but not with homosexuality, in males. Boys from single-mother families are less masculine in sex-role preference but more masculine with regard to sex-role adoption as evidenced by behaviors such as independence or aggression (Stevenson & Black, 1983). Mother-headed single-parent homes (no studies have investigated female sex-role development in father-headed homes) have no measurable impact on the sex-role development of girls but are associated with difficulties in heterosexual relations. Absence of the father is strongly associated with a variety of externalizing behavior patterns, particularly for males. Again, the strength of effect, however, is mediated by socioeconomic status, by degree of parental supervision, and by cause of the father's absence; separation and divorce are most strongly associated with aggressive behavior. Finally, single-parent homes have differential effects regarding children's personal adjustment; gains in independence, maturity, and empathy are evidenced but personal costs may appear in self-esteem, sense of personal control and anxiety.

Discussion

Several conclusions appear to be warranted from the preceding discussion. First, observed differences in cognitive performance and social development in father-absent versus father-present homes attest to the importance of the father's (or male) role in children's development. This is further substantiated by research that finds cognitive and social competence to improve when a male surrogate, including stepfathers and older brothers, is available to children (Warshak & Santrock, 1979). Availability of a father or male surrogate can be expected to vary considerably across single-parent homes. Second, a variety of factors mediate the effects on child development of rearing in a single-parent home. A mediational model assumes that loss of a parent influences both the external stressors and the internal dynamics of the single parent family, and thus, indirectly impacts on children's behavior and learning in school (Brook et al., 1984). A discussion of critical mediating variables associated with children's psychological growth in single-parent homes follows.

PUTTING SINGLE-PARENT HOMES IN PERSPECTIVE

Socioeconomic Status

Socioeconomic status is frequently more strongly associated with adverse consequences for children's development in single-parent homes than parental absence. In 1979, the median income of two-parent families with two children was $23,000; that of single-mother families with two children was $8,314 and the income differential appears to be widening (Thompson & Gonglia, 1983). Single-mother families are more likely than two-parent families to experience the kinds of strains — income instability, residence change, and household composition change — commonly associated with being poor, black, and comparatively less educated (McLanahan, 1983). One longitudinal study found that only in single-mother families with an adequate standard of living did children's behavior improve over time (Ambert, 1985).

Socioeconomic status reflects a summary of the environmental resources affecting the child and the parent including social and educational opportunities, environmental stimulation and attention, parental attitudes, expectations, and child-rearing styles, as well as parents' intellectual capacity, education, and wage-earning potential (Goldsmith, 1982). Obviously these factors are interrelated and effects cannot be determined separately. Younger age, lower maternal education, and especially teen-age single-parenting, for example, are typically associated with the worst child development outcomes. Kinard and Reinharz (1984), however, found that maternal age, as well as marital status, impacted on children's developmental progress only indirectly, through maternal education, which had the far greater effect.The implications are clear — increasing the competence of single parents is paramount to their children's well-being.

Race

Race influences parenting style with differential effects on single-parent children. In one of the few available research studies comparing parental competence across ethnic groups, findings supported the greater efficacy of black and Mexican-American working (white-collar) single-parent mothers (Espinoza & Naran, 1983). Specifically, both minority groups reported significantly fewer discipline and control problems than Anglo mothers. Anglo mothers were overrepresented among the inadequate and no-control parenting styles, whereas black mothers typically fell within the authoritarian style and Mexican-American mothers within the authoritative style. Moreover, parenting style predicted school involvement, with authoritarian and authoritative single-parent mothers being highly involved in school, whereas no-control parents were found to have low school involvement.

A diverse sociocultural picture of single-parent–child relationships emerges in the above study. Black single-parent working mothers appeared to cope significantly better than either Anglos or Mexican-Americans. They reported fewer discipline problems, higher school involvement, higher career involvement, and higher expectations for independence and success for their children. The academic competence of black children reared in mastery-oriented single-parent homes has been supported in previous studies (Wilkinson & O'Connor, 1977). Anglo and Hispanic single-parent mothers, in contrast, appeared to be less psychologically prepared for the dual role of worker and mother. For the Mexican-American single parent, family ties and subsequent status within their culture and family declines following divorce, resulting in fewer social supports and greater intrafamilial conflict. Anglo women, although

TABLE 3

Children's Personality and Social Development: Selected Findings

Sex-Role Orientation and Heterosexual Relations

Boys

1. Boys in mother-headed homes appear less secure with their masculinity. Findings include behavior that alternates between exaggerated masculine and feminine behavior; a compensatory masculine style; higher verbal than physical aggression; less masculine self-concepts; less gender differentiation in drawings; play patterns and preferences more typical of girls than boys; less popularity with male peers (Biller, 1981; Santrock & Warshak, 1979).

2. Father absence before ages 4–5, but not later, appears to have a retarding effect on masculine behavior development (Biller, 1981). Father absence prior to age 2, presents the most handicapping conditions (Santrock & Warshak, 1979).

3. Sex role orientation is more likely to be affected than sex-role preference or heterosexual style except when combined with an intense maternal relationship and early female toy preference (Biller, 1981).

4. Father death is related to high maternal dependency, particularly if the mother does not remarry (Biller, 1981).

Girls

1. No effect on sex-role preference.

2. Associated with heterosexual insecurity in lower SES groups. Differential behavior evident in that father's absence due to divorce results in sexual aggressiveness, whereas father's death results in shyness and timidity (Hetherington, 1972). Effects strongest for father's absence before age 5, with no surrogate males present in home.

Development of Self-Control

Boys

1. Higher rates of impulsivity, inattention, inability to delay gratification, and antisocial behavior (Biller, 1981; Hetherington, Cox, & Cox, 1978).

2. Lower moral development and moral maturity (Biller, 1981).

3. Higher rates of school discipline problems, juvenile delinquency, and substance abuse (Biller, 1981; Brook, et al., 1985).
   a. Family supervision and socioeconomic status mediate rates of school discipline problems, delinquency, and substance abuse (Biller, 1981; Brook, et al., 1985; Goldstein, 1984). Low family supervision and lower social class status increase conduct-disordered behavior.

Girls

1. Differences in externalizing behavior between father-present and father-absent homes are less marked or seldom found (Hetherington et al., 1978).
   a. School discipline problems higher for girls in father-absent homes in the lower socioeconomic class (Goldstein, 1985).

Personal Adjustment

1. Associated in both sexes with early maturity, including greater independent functioning, acceptance of responsibility, awareness and sensitivity to adult concerns, sense of competence (Weiss, 1979b) and higher Vineland daily living scores (Guidabaldi & Perry, 1984).

Boys

1. Father's absence, especially early or postdivorce absence, associated with lower self-esteem (Biller, 1981; Parish & Young, 1985).
   a. Male self-esteem is higher in father-absent situations than in homes where the father is present but passive, ineffective, and unnurturing.

2. Ego strength, self-esteem, and internal locus of control were found to deteriorate over a 5-year period in father-absent homes (Fry & Scher, 1985).

Girls

1. Father's absence associated with lower feelings of personal control and higher anxiety (Hetherington, 1972).

2. Lower self-esteem found with absence of father due to divorce but not due to death (Hetherington, 1972).

less negatively affected by intrafamilial conflict or reduced family support, appeared to be stressed by trying to maintain a family life that would include all the advantages of their previous two-parent household. Anglo women, because of their desire to maintain an independent, separate family unit, frequently take on more roles than do black women with similar financial and time constraints and thus experience considerable childrearing difficulty. The black sociocultural milieu is viewed as providing greater support and positive role models for the single working parent.

Parental Psychological and Social Resources

It has been argued that when one parent is absent, the remaining parent will have a more intense effect upon the child (Hetherington, Cox, & Cox, 1978). Thus, the personal adjustment and emotional stability of the single parent is a critical factor in single-parent–child relations. A number of studies have shown that demographic characteristics such as low income, poor education, and the presence of young children are negatively related to mental health and well-being (McLanahan, 1983). Long-term single mothers report higher rates of depression, psychosomatic symptoms, and loneliness than married or remarried mothers (Wallerstein, 1986). Single-parent mothers report lower self-esteem, lower efficacy, a lower sense of personal control, and much less optimism about the future than intact-family mothers (McLanahan, 1983). Divorced mothers' self-concept has been found to predict the quality of mother–child interaction, the quality of father–child interaction, the quality of the ex-spouse relationship, and children's self-esteem (Kanoy, Cunningham, White, & Adams, 1985). Parental distress significantly relates to lowered maternal nurturance in both single and intact families (Weinraub & Wolf, 1983).

The availability and adequacy of social support systems can significantly mediate the psychological distress of the single parent (McLanahan, Wedemeyer, & Adelberg, 1981; McLanahan, 1983). Compared with married mothers, single-parent mothers work longer hours, face more frequent and stressful life changes, tend to be more isolated and less consistent in their social contacts and less involved in organizations and parenting groups, and tend to be less supported emotionally and in their parenting roles (Thompson & Gongla, 1983). Santrock & Warshak (1979) found that single fathers used organized social support systems, such as day care centers and paid housekeepers, more frequently than single mothers. Single mothers, on the other hand, are reportedly more capable of establishing buddy exchange systems than their male counterparts (Grief, 1985).

The role of social support must not be underestimated for the single-parent family; however, the benefits to be derived are dependent upon the match between single-parent needs, child needs, and social network demands (see Carlson, 1985). McLanahan et al. (1981) found that white middle-class single mothers created diverse social support structures. The supportiveness of these networks was moderated by the role orientation of the mother. Single parents who wanted to maintain their previous roles (of wife or mother) benefited most from close-knit, family or conjugal networks; single parents who were attempting to establish new careers and identities found loose-knit, extended friendship or multiple based networks optimal. Differential benefits from social support have also been observed in black, low-income, single-parent families, dysfunctional homes being characterized by more frequent contact with kin, greater reliance upon boyfriends and upon children no longer living at home, and network relationships characterized as lacking reciprocity (Lindblad-Goldenberg & Dukes, 1985).

Gender and Parental Competence

Eiduson (1984) found that stress in the single-parent family did not adversely affect children unless it was centered on the parent–child interaction. Investigators concur that measures of parent–child processes relate more strongly to child outcomes than single-parent status (Hetherington, Cox & Cox, 1978). High-quality mothering can compensate for loss of the father in the single-parent homes, whereas low-quality fathering can negatively influence children's development in intact homes (Biller, 1981).

Single-parent child-rearing techniques that have beneficial effects on both boys and girls include (a) adequate control and supervision and (b) adequate nurturance and warmth. A parenting strategy of warmth, clear setting of rules, and extensive verbal interaction significantly correlates with higher warmth, self-esteem, maturity, sociability, and social comformity in children in both mother- and father-headed homes, according to Santrock and Warshak (1979). On the other hand, these same investigators found that when single-parent fathers used an authoritarian style, children were low in independence, whereas no negative effects were found for mothers' use of authoritarian strategies; conversely, single-parent mothers' use of permissive child-rearing strategies was found to be negatively related to children's competence, whereas fathers' employment of these same strategies had no negative effects.

Fathers in contrast to mothers obtain greater compliance from children in both intact and single-parent homes (Hetherington, Cox, & Cox, 1978; Hanson, 1985); seldom do single-parent fathers report child-rearing difficulties (Grief, 1983; Ambert, 1985). Single-parent mothers, in contrast, frequently report child behavior problems, are observed to engage in permissive or laissez-faire parenting styles, and are significantly overrepresented among externalizing disordered children (Patterson, 1982; Santrock & Warshak, 1979). Clearly, the differential authority relations found in the roles of mothers and fathers in our society mediates the effects of single parenting.

Child Characteristics and Supports

The bidirectionality of influence in parent–child interactions is well documented. Several child characteristics have been found to ease or strain the single-parent–child relationship: age, gender, and genetic endowment. Younger children create more stress for parents than do older children (Hetherington, Cox, & Cox, 1979), and single mothers are more likely to have custody of younger children, both male and female (Hanson, 1985). Children with difficult temperaments or a history of maladjustment are less equipped to handle the greater number of life event stressors that afflict many single-parent families.Single mothers of retarded children report greater difficulty coping and more frequently opt for institutional placement than married mothers. Difficult children also contribute to the social isolation of single parents. The incidence of divorce and desertion by husbands is high among families with an exceptional child or complicated childbirth (Allen, Affleck, McGrade, & McQueeney, 1984), and remarriage is lower among single parents with difficult children (Ambert, 1985).

A child's gender also influences the single-parent–child relationship. In both intact and single-parent homes,boys are more likely to develop coercive behavior with parents, to approach parents with egotistic demands, and to get into a battle of wills (Maccoby & Martin, 1983). In postdivorce single-parent homes,boys consistently exhibit more aggression, antisocial and uncontrolled behavior than do girls (Hetherington, et al., 1978), although girls, in low-socioeconomic-status single-parent families, have been found to be equivalently aggressive verbally with their mothers (Ambert, 1985). Same-sex parent–child dyads may provide the best single-parent child-rearing situation for equivalent parent competence (Warshak & Santrock, 1979).

TABLE 4

Summary of Child Problems and Risk Factors Associated With Single-Parent Homes

Boys
1. Externalizing behavior disorders at home and at school.
2. Lowered achievement motivation, academic performance, and performance of nonintellective tasks.
3. Lowered quantitative performance.
4. Less secure masculine sex role identity.
5. Peer difficultues.
6. Lower self-esteem.

Girls
1. Lowered quantitative performance.
2. Adolescent heterosexual insecurity.
3. School discipline problems (low SES only).
4. Lower self-esteem, lower sense of personal control, and higher anxiety.

HIGH-RISK FACTORS
1. Mother-headed homes
2. Causation divorce
3. Male children
4. Younger children
5. Greater numbers of children
6. Inadequate financial and social support
7. Low maternal education
8. Lack of father or male surrogate involvement
9. Nonauthoritative parenting style
10. White or Hispanic

ALTERNATIVE ACTIONS

The Child

Children in single-parent homes are not automatically at risk for school adjustment, learning, or personality problems as their child-rearing environments vary dramatically. However,children often face problems that are associated with being reared in a single-parent home; these are summarized in Table 4. An interrelated constellation of externalizing behavior problems, peer difficulties, and uncertain self-esteem characterize males in single-parent homes, whereas girls, in the middle and upper socioeconomic classes, typically evidence fewer adjustment problems before adolescence. Both boys and girls exhibit lowered quantitative performance.

Regarding intervention, it would appear that children in single-parent homes might benefit from particular encouragement in mathematics and the sciences. Sensitizing teachers to the impact of the absent-father household on performance in these subject areas may be helpful in soliciting their assistance with single-parent children. The documented sex-role development difficulties of boys and girls suggest that opportunities for children to establish close relationships with an adult of the same sex as the absent parent would be helpful especially for boys. The importance of same-sex role models might be considered in classroom placement decisions, involvement in athletics, assignment of counselors, and linkages with community resources such as Big Brothers and Boy Scouts. Involvement in sports appears to be particularly important for males in female-headed households, as athletic competence is so centrally related to self-esteem and popularity in the male peer culture of school-aged children. Finally, children in single-parent homes appear to be at risk for low self-esteem and may benefit from programs that focus on building personal efficacy. Some schools have incorporated family-change classes into their elementary and secondary curriculums (Holdahl & Caspersen, 1977). These classes are designed to help children recognize the inevitability and normality of family changes, acknowledge the associated feelings, and develop skills for coping. Depending upon the severity and chronicity of children's problems, of course, individual child therapy may be warranted.

The expression of difficulties by single-parent children may reflect increased anxiety that is associated with their family circumstance. Fulmer (1983) noted that many of the behavior disorders exhibited by children in single-parent families can be viewed as "collusion mischief" triggered by the single parent's depression, apathy, or expressed helplessness, which engenders anxiety that propels the child to "impel" the parent to action in behalf of the child. It may be helpful, when school problems occur, to search for the possible hidden functions of maladaptive behavior within the single-parent family system.

The Single Parent

Certain problems are consistently reported by single parents who maintain independent households. A summary of single-parent concerns appears on Table 5.

Single-parent problems center on role overload and loneliness. Single mothers and fathers, regardless of financial status, report stress and a dearth of energy as a result of juggling the demands work, parenting, and socializing (Hanson, 1985; McLanahan, 1983). Single parents also report that their employment has been compromised by increased absence from work and by late arrival or early departure (Grief, 1985; Hanson, 1985). While school psychologists can do little to alleviate the role overload of single parents, the consistency with which this problem appears suggests that (a) child interventions that decrease rather than increase single-parent overload are likely to meet with greatest cooperation and (b) a single parent's failure to follow through on requested parent intervention may be a signal to refocus intervention to extrafamilial resources.

A second area of single-parent concern centers on meeting needs for intimacy, sexual gratification, and adult contact. Both single-parent mothers and fathers report that loneliness, regardless of the quality of their social networks, remains a primary dissatisfaction. The highest rates of anxiety and loneliness (approaching 100%) are reported by women over 40 years of age (Wallerstein, 1986). In coping with loneliness, many single parents date or socialize. Dating by single mothers and fathers can present child-rearing challenges. Problems are particularly acute with adolescent children, as both parent and child are thrust into the same life cycle transition, facing identical problems of intimacy, sexuality, and self-esteem. Younger children, in contrast, fearing the abandonment of their remaining parent, often act out their anxious feelings in front of dates or when parents are leaving for dates, thus increasing parental guilt and frustration. Assistance to professionals in helping single parents with dating issues is provided by Cantor and Drake (1983).

Finally, all single parents report difficulties in finding adequate childcare and experience uncertainty, at times, regarding the adequacy of their parenting. Fathers express most worry about parenting their teenage daughters, and mothers express greatest difficulty with child management, particularly of sons.

Based on reported single-parent concerns, intervention priorities include support and education, which can be accomplished by the school psychologist through a variety of modalities including individual parent consultation, bibliotherapy, structured groups, or linkage with community resources. A model for conducting single-parent support groups is provided by Garrison et al. (no date). These investigators have also developed a Single Parent Questionnaire (Stolberg & Ullman, no date), designed to measure skills at single parenting, and thus reveal need for parent intervention. A variety of community parent education, single-parent support, and single-parent organizations exist that may also benefit single parents. Parents Without Partners remains the largest existing organization. It provides local chapters with education and social programs and information dissemination, including a monthly newsletter with articles and resources that are helpful to the single parent as well as to the professional working with single parents. Since role overload and social isolation characterize single parents, their involvement in community groups may be facilitated by proactive organization by the school psychologist of networks or buddy systems consisting of single parents who have children in the same school or grade level.

TABLE 5

Single Parent Concerns

SINGLE MOTHERS AND FATHERS

1. Role strain/fatigue.
2. Loneliness and social isolation.
3. Dissatisfaction with social life.
4. Lack of role clarity.
5. Obtaining adequate, inexpensive child care.
6. Stereotyped social perceptions.
7. Keeping home organized.
8. Handling dating relationships.

PRIMARILY SINGLE MOTHERS

1. Child behavior problems (especially sons).
2. Financial stress.
3. Low self-esteem, depression, self-recrimination.

PRIMARILY SINGLE FATHERS

1. Lack of knowledge of child development.
2. Coping with adolescent daughter's sexual concerns.
3. Providing adequate nurturance.
4. Discomfort with identity as a single person.
5. Employment advancement constrained.

The Single-Parent–Child Relationship

Two main problems characterize the single-parent family system: (a) resolution of emotional loss and (b) reorganization of roles to cope with a vacuum in the family system. How these interrelated difficulties are resolved will be reflected in the single-parent–child relationship.

Resolution of Loss. Both the single parent and the child must resolve the emotional loss associated with parental absence. Children's resolution of loss in postdivorce single-parent homes is hampered (a) when the noncustodial parent remains minimally and intermittently involved and (b) when the coparenting relationship remains undifferentiated from the previous spousal relationship or remains conflictive. Resolution of loss following parental death is hampered when the absent parent is idealized by the remaining parent. Such idealization may undermine separation–individuation of the child and may fuel depression if idealized expectations cannot be met (Adams et al., 1985).

When unpredictable and irregular contact is maintained, the child is placed on a reinforcement schedule with regard to longing for and idealization of the absent parent that is most difficult to extinguish. This situation predicts single-parent–child conflict in which the child blames the custodial parent for the loss, externalizes anger in misbehavior, and may verbally undermine the remaining parent with invidious comparisons with the absent parent. Intervention is recommended with both the parent and child. Parent intervention should strengthen the single-parent's child-management skills and emotional resilience to their child's verbal manipulations. Interventions with the child should focus on resolution of the emotional loss and feelings of rejection (see also the divorce chapter in this volume).

When either an emotionally close or a highly conflictual spousal (versus cooperative coparental) relationship continues following marital dissolution, the likelihood is increased for the development of child-centered pathological triangle relationships, in which school problems serve a homeostatic family system function. Intervention in this situation is most appropriately targeted to the coparents or family system (see Carlson, in press, and Minuchin, 1974,for additional discussion of assessment and intervention with pathological parent–-child triangles).

Role Reorganization and Clarity. Failure to resolve emotional loss by the single parent may influence the degree to which single-parent children remain free to pursue their own developmental needs instead of being compelled to meet parental needs. Anxiety, loneliness, and dependency in custodial parents may encourage a blurring of the parent–child boundaries. In the cross-sex single-parent–child relationship, an oversexualized bond may occur that compromises the normal psychological heterosexual development of the child. Although most single parents can be expected to maintain appropriate sexual boundaries with children, the adult vacuum encourages greater exchange of self-disclosure and intimacy between parents and their children than is typical in intact families (Weiss, 1979a). Being the recipient of parental disclosure appears to increase the emotional sensitivity of single-parent children but may also increase their anxiety and inappropriately exaggerate feelings of responsibility regarding the well-being of their remaining parent.

Blurred generational boundaries may also emerge when functional requirements compromise emotional needs in single-parent homes. Children who are expected to play a considerable role in the rearing of siblings, for example, may become "parentified" children (Minuchin, 1974; Weiss, 1979a, 1979b). The parentified child, given adult responsibilities and power in specific childcare situations, may rebel when treated as a child. Thus, single parents with a parentified child are likely to report high levels of family conflict.

Children who are overtly or covertly expected to assume adult roles that are beyond their maturity can be expected to present symptoms of peer difficulties, low extracurricular involvement, excessive maturity and worry, and possibly concentration problems, depression, or behavior disorders, as well as frequent school absences. Parentified children may report that their peers are immature.

A lack of appropriate and well-defined parent and child roles in the single-parent home calls for utilization of intervention that (a) links the single parent with adult support systems and (b) educates them regarding the developmental needs of their children, permitting the establishment of clear and appropriate parent and child roles. With relatively well-functioning parents, education in child development and in normal single-parent family processes, as well as mutual exploration and problem solving regarding adequacy of family social support, is likely to be adequate. With more disturbed single parents, who are unable to differentiate their emotional needs from their children's, family and/or individual therapy is recommended (see, for example, Weltner, 1982). In all families, but especially in multiproblem single-parent homes, intervention that focuses on supplementing the parental role with extrafamilial resources should help free children from excessive involvement in inappropriate developmental roles.

In addition to the above parent–child relationship problems, several difficulties are common to particular single-parent–child constellations. Single-parent mothers and sons are most likely to present problems reflecting a lack of authoritative parenting that can result in uncontrolled behavior. The coercive family process cycle, which sometimes becomes established between aggressive boys and inadequately dominant single mothers, has also been carefully documented (Patterson, 1982; Phelps & Slater, 1985). The appropriate intervention is parent training in authoritative family management techniques (Patterson, 1982).

Single-parent fathers, while seldom reporting child-rearing problems associated with authority, do evidence potentially detrimental sex-role stereotyping in their relationships with daughters. Single-parent fathers have been found to rely significantly more heavily upon daughters than sons to fill the household and child-rearing vacuum created by an absent mother (Grief, 1985; Mendes, 1979). Most daughters relish their "special" role in the family; however, this role may restrict their social development with peers and may create considerable emotional distress if the single father becomes involved in a dating relationship or remarriage. In this situation, implications for intervention are similar to those described for blurred generational boundaries. Emotionally healthy single fathers are likely to be responsive to brief parent consultation or education regarding the developmental needs of their daughters, whereas dysfunctional single fathers are likely to require referral to an outside agency for individual therapy.

The Home–School Relationship

Single-parent home–school problems are most likely to emerge in situations when the capacity of each system is stressed. A mutual adversarial posture may be encouraged by the conflicting needs of the single-parent family and the school system. *Functional single-parent homes must rely upon social support outside the family.* Single parents, to a greater extent than intact families, are likely to look to the school to augment their role as child socializer. Additionally, single parents may be severely constrained by finances and employment in ways that adversely affect home–school communication. Single parents often cannot afford to be telephoned at work, to leave work early or arrive late, or to attend school conferences or functions during school hours. Paid before- and after-school childcare is often financially unmanageable, leaving few options except dropping children off early at school, relying on children to independently get ready for school, and leaving children unsupervised in the afternoon. Single-parent solutions to role overload and financial constraints are often viewed by school personnel as reflections of inadequate, unconcerned parenting. In short, a vicious home–school cycle can evolve in which single parents look to the school system for support but receive negative discrimination; the schools look to single parents to manage their children and find evasion or belligerance. The child in school becomes the victim of both systems.

School psychologists can play key mediational and advocacy roles in the single-parent home–school link with the goal of establishing a positive, supportive partnership and a problem-solving orientation between the systems. In addition, a critical view toward the impact upon single parents of traditional school system rules and regulations, with subsequent organizational consultation and intervention, may be beneficial in alleviating the social stigma that often falls on the children of single parents in school.

SUMMARY

Because of our cultural heritage, it is tempting to think of the intact, two-parent family as optimal and by logical extension, the single parent family as a deficient family system that predicts problems for the children. Rather, the structure of the single-parent home, in contrast with the intact family system, suggests that a different family model and measures of functioning are appropriate. Mendes (1979) has suggested that the single parent be viewed essentially as a "contributing coordinator" who does for the children what she can or he can manage without due stress and who coordinates the allocations of some of the other functions usually assigned to parents to competent persons within and outside the family. In this model, the keys to adaptive single-parent family functioning and child rearing are competent parent problem solving in obtaining adequate resources over time, and availability of adequate resources in the social environment. In the Mendes model, children are also regarded as contributing coordinators, not merely as recipients and reactors, which is typical of the intact family system. Adoption of a different family model for the single-parent home focuses school psychology assessment and intervention on maximizing the capacity of parents and children to identify, utilize, and maintain a level of resources optimal for development. Such a view dramatically balances the burden of child socialization between the sole parent and the social environment. In summary, schools and school psychologists are faced with a critical choice — retain the intact family model, which posits distinct, albeit coordinate, socializing roles for family and school, or join in partnership with single parents in the task of socializing children.

REFERENCES

Adams, P. L., Milner, J. R., & Schrepf, N. A. (1984). *Fatherless children.* New York: Wiley.

Allen, D. A., Affleck, G., McGrade, B. J., & McQueeney, M. (1984). Effects of single-parent status on mothers and their high-risk infants. *Infant Behavior and Development, 7,* 347–459.

Ambert, A. (1985). Custodial parents: Review and a longitudinal study. In B. Schlesinger (Ed.), *The one-parent family in the 1980's: Perspectives and annotated bibliography, 1978–1984* (pp. 13–34). Toronto, University of Toronto Press.

Belz, H. F., & Geary, D. C. (1984). Father's occupation and social background: Relation to SAT scores. *American Educational Research Journal, 21*(2), 473–478.

Biller, H. B. (1982). Father absence, divorce, and personality development. In M. E. Lamb (Ed.), *The role of the father in child development* (2nd ed.) (pp. 489–552). New York: Wiley.

Brook, J. S., Whiteman, M., & Gordon, A. S. (1985). Father absence, perceived family characteristics and stage of drug use in adolescence. *British Journal of Developmental Psychology, 2,* 87–94.

Burns, C. W., & Brassard, M. R. (1982). A look at the single parent family: Implications for the school psychologist. *Psychology in the Schools, 19,* 478–494.

Cantor, D. W., & Drake, E. A. (1983). *The divorced parent: A professional's approach to divorcing families.* New York: Springer.

Carlson, C. I. (1985). Best practices for working with single-parent and stepfamilies. A Thomas & J. Grimes (Eds.), *Best practices in school psychology* (pp. 43–60). Kent, OH: National Association of School Psychologists.

Carlson, C. I. (in press). Family assessment and intervention in the school setting. In T. R. Kratochwill (Ed.), *Advances in School Psychology* (Vol. 6). Hillsdale, NJ: Erlbaum.

Clay, P. L. (1981). *Single parents and the public schools: How does the partnership work?* National Committee for Citizens in Education.

Eiduson, B. T. (1983). Conflict and stress in nontraditional families: Impact on children. *American Journal of Orthopsychiatry, 53,*(3), 426–435.

Espinoza, R., & Naron, N. (1983). *Work and family life among Anglo, Black and Mexican-American single-parent families.* Austin, TX: Southwest Educational Development Laboratory.

Fry, P. S. & Scher, A. (1984). The effects of father absence on children's achievement motivation, ego-strength, and locus-of-control orientation: A five-year longitudinal assessment. *British Journal of Developmental Psychology, 2,* 167–178.

Garrison, K. M., Stolberg, G., Carpenter, J. G., Mallonee, D. J., & Antrim, Z. D. (no date). *Single parent support group: Leader's manual.* (DHEW No. 1 R01 MH34462-02). Washington, DC: National Institute of Mental Health.

Glick, P. C. (1979). Children of divorced parents in perspective. *Journal of Social Issues, 35*(4), 170–181.

Goldstein, H. S. (1982). Fathers' absence and cognitive development of 12- to 17-year-olds. *Psychological Reports, 51,* 843–848.

Goldstein, H. S. (1984). Parental composition, supervision, and conduct problems in youths 12 to 17 years old. *Journal of the American Academy of Child Psychiatry, 23*(6), 679–684.

Grief, G. L. (1985). *Single fathers.* Lexington, MA: Lexington Books.

Guidabaldi, J., & Perry, J. D. (1984). Divorce, socioeconomic status, and children's cognitive-social competence at school entry. *American Journal of Orthopsychiatry, 54*(3), 459–468.

Hanson, S. M. H. (1985). Single fathers with custody: A synthesis of the literature. In B.Schlesinger, *The one-parent family in the 1980's: Perspectives and annotated bibliography, 1978–1984* (pp. 57–96). Toronto. University of Toronto Press.

Hetherington, E. M. (1972). Effects of paternal absence on personality development in adolescent daughters. *Developmental Psychology, 7,* 313–326.

Hetherington, E. M., Cox, M. & Cox, R. (1978). The development of children in mother-headed families. In H. Hoffman & D. Reiss (Eds.), *The American family: Dying or developing* (pp. 117–145). New York: Plenum.

Holdahl, S., & Caspersen, P. (1977, October). Children of family change: Who's helping them now? *The Family Coordinator.* pp. 472–477.

Kanoy, K. W., Cunningham, J. L., White, P., & Adams,S. J. (1984). Is family structure that critical? Family relationships of children with divorced and married parents. *Journal of Divorce, 8*(2), 97–105.

Kinard, E. M., & Reinharz, H. (1984). Behavioral and emotional functioning in children of adolescent mothers. *American Journal of Orthopsychiatry,54*(4), 578–594.

Lindblad-Goldenberg, M., & Dukes, J. L. (1985). Social support in Black, low-income, single-parent families: Normative and dysfunctional patterns, *American Journal of Orthopsychiatry, 55*(1), 42–58.

Maccoby, E. E., & Martin, J. A. (1983). Socialization in the context of the family: Parent–child interaction. In P. H. Mussen (Ed.), E. M. Hetherington (Vol. Ed.), *Handbook of child psychology (4th ed.): Vol. 4. Socialization personality, and social development* (pp. 1–102). New York: Wiley.

McLanahan, S. S. (1983). Family structure and stress: A longitudinal comparison of two-parent and female-headed families. *Journal of Marriage and the Family, 45*(2), 347–357.

McLanahan, S. S., Wedemeyer, N. V., & Adelberg, T. (1981, August). Network structure, social support, and psychological well-being in the single-parent family. *Journal of Marriage and the Family,* 601–612.

Mendes, H. A. (1979, May). Single-parent families: A typology of life-styles. *Social Work* 193–200.

Minuchin, S. (1974). *Families and family therapy.* Cambridge, MA: Harvard University Press.

Parish, T. S., & Taylor, J. C. (1979). The impact of divorce and subsequent father absence on children's and adolescents' self-concepts. *Journal of Youth Adolescence, 8*(4), 427–433.

Patterson, G. R. (1982). *A social learning approach: Vol. 3. Coercive family process.* Eugene, OR: Castalia.

Phelps, R. E., & Slater, M. A. (1985). Sequential interactions that discriminate high- and low-problem single mother–son dyads. *Journal of Consulting and Clinical Psychology, 53*(5), 684–692.

Radin, N. (1979). The role of the father in cognitive, academic, and intellectual development. In D. J. Reiss (Ed.), *The American family in transition.* New York: Plenum.

Rollins, B. C., & Galligan, R. (1978). The developing child and marital satisfaction in parents. In R. M. Lerner & G. B. Spanier (Eds.), *Child influences on marital and family interaction.* New York: Academic.

Santrock, J. W., & Warshak, R. A. (1979). Father custody and social development in boys and girls. *Journal of Social Issues, 35*(4), 112–125.

Shinn, M. (1978). Father absence and children's cognitive development. *Psychological Bulletin, 85*(2), 295–324.

Single Parents Fact Sheet. (1985). Bethesda, MD: Parents Without Partners.

Stolberg, A. L., & Ulman, A. J. (no date). *Single Parenting Questionnaire: Development, validation, and application manual.* (DHHS R01 MH35562). Washington, DC: National Institute of Mental Health.

Svanum, S., Bringle, R. G., & McLaughlin, J. E. (1982). Father absence and cognitive performance in a large sample of six-to eleven-year-old children. *Child Development, 53,* 136–143.

Wallerstein, J. S. (1986). Women after divorce: Preliminary report from a ten-year follow-up. *American Journal of of Orthopsychiatry, 56*(1), 65–77.

Weiss, R. (1979a). *Going it alone.* New York: Basic Books.

Weiss, R. (1979b). Growing up a little faster: The experience of growing up in a single-parent household. *Journal of Social Issues, 35*(4), 97–111.

Weltner, J. S. (1982). A structural approach to the single-parent family. *Family Process, 21*(2), 203–210.

Wilkinson, C. B., & O'Connor, W. A. (1977). Growing up male in a Black single-parent family. *Psychiatric Annals, 7*(7), 356–362.

Young, E. R., & Parish, R. S. (1977). Impact of father absence during childhood on the psychological adjustment of college females. *Sex Roles, 3*(3), 217–227.

BIBLIOGRAPHY: PROFESSIONALS

Clay, P. L. (1981). *Single parents and the public schools: How does the partnership work?* National Committee for Citizens in Education.
This report of a national survey succinctly clarifies what school programs, school policies, and school attitudes adversely affect single-parent ;families. It also provides an invaluable listing of resources, including filmstrips and structured programs, for professionals, single parents,and their children.

Grief, G. L. (1985). *Single fathers.* Lexington, MA: Lexington Books.
This book both reviews the existing literature on single fathers and reports findings from the author's national survey. Coverage is comprehensive and includes chapters on the single father's relationship with his children, children's perceptions of their mother and father, the ex-wife's relationship with the children, and the emotional and social needs of this form of single-parent family.

Patterson, G. R. (1982). *A social learning approach: Vol. 3. Coercive family process.* Eugene, OR: Castalia.
This book is essential reading for the school psychologist who wants to understand the dynamics underlying the single-parent mother and unmanageable son. The first half of the book is a comprehensive documentation of research on anti-social children, which provides dramatic testimony to the benefits of practice derived from careful research; however, school psychologists may find the later chapters (10–13) most helpful for intervening in the coercive parent–child cycle.

Weiss, R. (1979). *Going it alone: The family life and social situation of the single parent.* New York: Basic Books.
Sensitive and comprehensive coverage of single-parent family issues is provided. The book is particularly useful for heightening awareness of the problems and concerns of the single parent. Available in paperback.

BIBLIOGRAPHY: PARENTS

Gardner, R. A. (1978).The boys and girls book about one-parent families. New York: Bantam Books.
A book written to help children cope with some of the common problems likely to arise in their single-parent family. Coverage of issues is comprehensive and attention is given to the different problems associated with variations in single-parent homes. The book is written at the third- or fourth-grade reading level. Discussion between parent and child while reading is recommended.

Parents Without Partners, Inc. 7910 Woodmont Avenue, Suite 1000, Bethesda, MD 20814. (800) 638-8078.
Largest national organization of single parents. Provides a monthly newsletter with articles informative to single parents and professionals. Provides up-to-date statistics on single parents and guides to informational materials for this population. Useful to professionals working with single parents as well.

Rodgers, J. E., & Cataldo, M. F. (1984). *Raising sons: Practical strategies for single mothers.* New York: Signet. Available in paperback.
In contrast to much of the research literature, this book presents single-mother–son childrearing positively in light of more androgenous social roles within society. The techniques of child management espoused borrow heavily from behavior theory. The limitation of the book is a high reading level, making it most suitable for college-educated single mothers.

Children and Stealing

R. Michael Weger
Mississippi Bend AEA, Iowa

BACKGROUND

Stealing is not widely studied because of practical and ethical considerations in its detection and treatment (Miller & Klungness, 1986; Rosen & Rosen, 1983). However, children with identified stealing problems are at greater risk for later adjustment and legal problems than youngsters identified by other means. In fact, they are far more likely to be involved with the police or court system, as are oppositional or aggressive children. Children who present problems of control or management are not nearly as likely to be involved with the law as those who engage in covert social actions such as lying and stealing. Parent-reported stealing is highly predictive of later delinquent status (Moore, Chamberlain, & Mukai, 1979).

The literature on stealing by school-aged children focuses on shoplifting and describes thievery that is usually indirect and without force. Such behavior is related to two childhood conduct disorders (i.e., Socialized/Nonaggressive and Undersocialized/Nonaggressive) defined in the Diagnostic and Statistical Manual of Mental Disorders, Third Edition (DSM III) (American Psychiatric Association, 1980). Aside from a diagnostic guideline of 6 months duration for these two conduct disorders, there is little in the literature to define normal stealing behavior in school-aged children. Most recently, Patterson (1982) has suggested that *stealer* be defined as a "child who is between the ages of 6 and 12 who has been caught stealing about once every three or four months" (p. 260) and whose stealing behavior has occurred for approximately 1 year.

Despite this lack of definitional specificity and normative data, childhood stealing (much of which is shoplifting) is a pervasive and most expensive problem in the United States today. Belson (1976) reports that during the school years approximately 9 of every 10 boys indulge in stealing. Klemke (1982), however, feels that most youths have only "limited involvements." Although the rate of stealing in general is internationally lower for females than males (Hampton, 1975), an informational pamphlet by the C. L. Bete Company (1983) indicates that shoplifting is a major form of stealing in the United States, that young people (under 18) make up one-half of all shoplifters and that girls greatly outnumber boys.

Not all observers agree that girls are more involved in shoplifting. However, the contradictions may simply relate to differences in the time of life sampled. Klemke (1982) suggested that males may shoplift more than females early in life, whereas females become more active in later adolescence and young adulthood. He also found that males got caught more frequently. Hindelang (1974) reported that only 26% of apprehended shoplifters are reported to the police; it is especially unlikely that a child under the age of 10 will be formally processed (Klemke, 1982). However, prosecution for theft is an accelerating phenomenon, with an average 25% reduction in time between convictions (Crockett, 1973). The likelihood of chronicity is increased with each offense. Moore, Chamberlain, and Mukai (1979) found that 92% of first offenders commit a second offense, 91% of these commit a third, and 80% of third offenders commit a fourth.

FBI crime reports (Department of Justice, 1979) indicate a 19% increase in shoplifting from 1974 to 1978. It is the fastest-growing form of larceny. Currently, $5 billion is reported lost every year, and two to three cents of every dollar spent is needed to cover these losses and pay for security and legal costs (C. L. Beta Company, 1983). The United States Bureau of the Census (1979) reported that juveniles are involved in 59.5% of all car thefts, 52.3% of all breaking and entering cases, 37.8% of the larceny, and 29.5% of all robberies committed in the United States.

The prevalence of stealing in school-aged children and its predictive value for later legal maladjustment underscores the need for early identification and intervention. School psychologists are in a key position to provide effective treatment to children and families.

DEVELOPMENT

It usually appears that an act of stealing has been committed to effect some material gain, but this is not always the case. Reinforcers supply needs, and needs are individual and not always apparent from the behavior or consequences involved in their satisfaction. A variety of factors are involved in the development of stealing behavior.

Behavioral Perspective

The majority of behavior, is, to some degree, acceptable and tends to be expected and overlooked. It is not nearly as often or as strongly reinforced as a successful theft. Stealing behavior is subject to inconsistent positive consequences and therefore develops the strength found in an intermittent schedule of reinforcement. Stealing is usually reinforced immediately by possession of the item stolen, by any internal conditions (feelings of triumph, control, power), and often by peers and/or teachers (Stumphauzer, 1976). Successful theft has an immediate payoff, and thus certain stimuli both internal and external will recur coincidentally with this behavior and acquire discriminative or secondary reinforcing properties. This yields a chaining effect that draws the subject to repeated acts of theft (Henderson, 1981).

The usually subtle but powerful reinforcing effects of either direct or unconscious parental approval must also be considered in respect to learning and maintenance of stealing behavior (Johnson, 1949; Renshaw, 1977; Stumphauzer, 1976). Additionally, the increasing isolation of families within neighborhoods makes it difficult for parents to get feedback about their child's behavior out of the home. Stealing is usually not confined to the home and thus punishment of out-of-the-home stealing is weak or nonexistent. This makes it possible for stealing behavior to become established before it can be treated (Reid, Rivero, & Lorber, 1980).

Sociological Perspectives

The *deviant vulnerability hypothesis* suggests increased susceptibility to delinquent involvement such as stealing by youths experiencing financial, home, and/or school problems. This relationship is supported by research findings for all three problem areas (Polk & Schafter, 1972; Rezvani, 1983; Zabezynska, 1977).

The *deviant labeling hypothesis* suggests that stigmatizing reactions by others may foster the formation of a deviant self-concept and involvement in delinquency and therefore in stealing. Klemke (1982) found a relationship, particularly for lower blue-collar class youth, between shoplifting and being labeled a "troublemaker" by oneself ($r = .40$) and by one's teachers ($r = .45$). Some authors believe the apprehension–labeling process has a deterrent effect (Cameron, 1964; Gold, 1970; Rezvani, 1983), but others do not (Applebaum & Klemmer, 1973; Klemke, 1982). In fact, Klemke (1982) found that youths recently apprehended by the police self-reported more instances of shoplifting and more recent instances than did nonapprehended youths. Hirschi (1975), however, asserts that there is more evidence to favor the possibility that deviant behavior increases the likelihood of labeling.

A final sociological perspective relates to deviant socialization. Klemke (1982) reports that youth are more likely to shoplift *with* someone and that there is a weak but positive relationship between number of friends and shoplifting ($r = .11$). Additionally, Linden and Hackler (cited in Klemke, 1982) report a relationship between recent shoplifting and "knowing" significant others who shoplift and between shoplifting and having friends labeled as troublemakers by teachers.

Internal Conflicts

In adults, unfulfilled emotional needs, especially those connected with early deprivation and feelings of unfulfillment, are thought to relate to shoplifting (Russell, 1973). A variety of reasons, many of which are similar, are advanced for stealing by children also.

Just as some observers feel that suicide behaviors are misguided attempts to draw attention to personal problems, there are those who believe the same about stealing. Millman, Schaefer, and Cohen (1982) feel that stealing is a plea for help with psychological problems, and Beck and McIntyre (1977) describe stealing as a "covert call for adjustment assistance."

Many authors speak of stealing as a way to get attention (Dreikurs, 1964; Millman et al., 1982; Stumphauzer, 1976). Salk (1972) feels that stealing is one way for a child to "penetrate his parents' attention barrier." Mack (1978) feels some children are "anal retentive" and become "pack rats." Once they feel rejected some children get into *things* instead of *others.* They steal all sorts of little items so they can *have* them as if these possessions might bring happiness. Peer pressure is an important factor, as it can motivate not only stealing but what is stolen as well (Belson, 1976; Levine & Kozak, 1979; Mack, 1978). Thus, a child may steal in order to buy friends with the act or the merchandise.

Stealing has been related to depression engendered in the first three stages of psychosexual development (Beck & McIntyre, 1977), to poor ego strength and consequent difficulty in resisting temptation (Revere, 1982), and to a desire for fun and excitement (Belson, 1976; Renshaw, 1977). Dreikurs (1964) agrees that some children delight in not getting caught. Renshaw (1977) believes that stealing may also be a consequence of poor impulse control, a substitute for sex (housebreaking in teens who report ejaculation upon entry of a house), a way for a child to assert some independence or the result of reality distortion as in psychosis. That is, some children may poorly perceive and navigate situations involving questions of ownership and belonging because of perceptions distorted by severe emotional problems.

Thus, both real and perceived needs motivate stealing. A child with a stealing problem who does not have obvious real needs is likely to be an emotionally needy person. Such children find independent thinking difficult. They are easily influenced by peers and often feel inadequate and unable to satisfy their emotional needs in more appropriate ways. They sometimes get caught up in their folly, not knowing how to stop (Mack, 1978). Stealing is the only way they have succeeded in obtaining the attention and recognition they seek.

Emotional neediness yields an egocentric orientation and feelings of a right to anything desired. Thieves often view the world from the viewpoint of how it can satisfy them (Dreikurs, 1964; Hudgins & Prentice, 1973). Such self-centeredness or self-love is viewed analytically under the label narcissism. Stealing, say some psychoanalysts, appears to have frank symbolic meaning even when superficially this is obscured by realistic gain. The act of stealing has a variety of discernible meanings, all of which are restitutive (Tedesco, 1974). That is, it serves to undo a loss that is subjectively perceived as a theft of which the thief has been the victim. It is also seen as an opportunity for revenge, for settling a score. Tedesco (1974) believes stealing and revenge are closely linked and that stealing is a way of taking initiative, of secretly converting a passive experience into an active one. Dreikurs (1964) feels that if a child denies his stealing behavior, his motive is power; and several authors have indicated that theft may possibly be related to anger at parents or authority in general (Mack, 1978; Millman et al.,1982; Revere, 1982). Stealing can also be a way of controlling a frightening and dangerous person or situation by reinstating a long-lost but cherished sense of omnipotence (Tedesco, 1974). The feelings of omnipotence come from the power, triumph, and possession that follow a successful theft. Stealing is often preceded by the fantasy of having been the victim of a prior theft. This prior theft is not necessarily of a material object but may be stolen love, attention, respect, etc.

Thieves who steal without apparent guilt must convince themselves that they need not feel bad about stealing because of the privation and damages they have experienced. Thus, they develop a sense of being exceptional, that the world owes them and that they have a right to what they want because of prior losses. These feelings of "being owed" are a "regressive maldevelopment" related to a lack of empathetic understanding by cool and distant, perhaps even cruel and hateful, parents according to Kligerman (1974). He suggests that a child may therefore fail to adequately internalize values of his parents necessary for a sense of completeness and self-esteem. Such children do not develop a set of ideals that will protect them from delinquency nor do they have the ego strength necessary to protect themselves against narcissistic hurt.

Emotional neediness in these situations can yield poor judgment, theft, and a consequent guilt which further reduces self-esteem and exacerbates the original neediness. It becomes a downward circle of inappropriate attempts toward fulfillment (Karson & O'Dell, 1976). Stealing temporarily makes a thief feel good, powerful, whole, etc., but in the long run it only further damages self-esteem.

Moral Development: The Impact of Family and Management Style

One's values come about largely through the process of identification with parents and significant others. The families of stealers appear to have certain distinguishing characteristics that impact on the development of stealing in their children. Stealers show more coercive behavior than nonstealers and family members seem less cohesive and more distant from one another (Loeber,

Weissman, & Reid, 1983; Patterson, 1982; Reid & Hendricks, 1973). Patterson (cited in Reid, Rivero, & Loeber, 1980) found mothers of stealers in particular to be less intensively engaged with their children, less anxious, and more sociopathic than the mothers of social aggressors. The importance of such sociopathic trends relative to the intrinsic value of parental antecedents in the development of moral behavior is underscored by Johnson's (1949) concept of superego lacunae. That is, some parents find gratification in the delinquent behavior of their children and unconsciously foster its continuance. This may be very subtle, a slight smile and a comment on how clever a theft was, or it may be more open and direct. It is parental pathology acted out by and through the child. The parents obtain vicarious pleasure from the child's stealing (Renshaw, 1977), although there may be a "show" of discipline. Parents of stealers also appear to have relatively poor control over their children (Reid, 1975). This makes it hard to teach them how to use immediate consequation in treating their child's stealing. Finally, the parents of stealers, just as they seem less involved with their children, have been shown to drop out of treatment more often than families of social aggressors (Holleran, 1981) and too often require therapy for marital problems and other conflicts in the home in addition to the child's stealing (Phillips, 1981).

Modeling by parents also plays an important role. Awareness that a parent steals has more impact than awareness of peer stealing according to Dituri (1977). He found that 10-year-olds view adult lying and stealing as worse than the same behavior by peers. Thus, the behavior is underscored and the lesson is heightened. The desensitization to stealing is greater if a child is aware that the parent does so.

Disciplinary style has also been linked to level of moral development. Hoffman (1977) describes three styles: assertion of power, withdrawal of love, and induction. The first threatens the child, who fears a punitive reaction by the parent. The child's focus is on the consequences to the self. Thus the child perceives moral standards to be external and learns behavior controls based on threat and fear. A threatened loss of love uses emotional elements such as fear and anxiety. A child's compliance to this style is again self-centered and a result of external forces. Induction, however, the explaining of the "why" part of the "shoulds" and "oughts" emphasizes the possible consequences of behavior. This makes the child aware of the relationship of his or her behavior to others. This knowing how behavior contributes to the distress of others aids the development of guilt feelings, which are an internal sense of moral guidance.

Miller and Swanson (cited in Eisikovits & Sagi, 1982) found a positive relationship between induction and ability to resist temptation in adolescent boys. Katovsky, Crandal, and Good (1967) found that internal control and induction were positively related, and Hoffman (1977) and Saltzstein, Diamond, and Belenky (1972) found that induction methods are related positively to higher moral development. Eisikovits and Sagi (1982) reported less induction with delinquents and a positive relationship between induction and most moral measures. Additionally, Peisach and Hardeman (1983) found that young children could show moral reasoning at a level higher than expected from a developmental perspective such as Lawrence Kohlberg's (1976). Thus, how parents behave and teach their children could increase their risk for stealing or, more appropriately, help them resist it despite external forces.

Other Factors: Biology, Intelligence, and Television

Biochemistry and neurology are discovering characteristics unique to a variety of personality types, syndromes, and behaviors. Stealers are no exception. A previous review of the literature (Weger, 1985) offers several suggestions that stealers may indeed be affected by specific biological substrates, some of which may even be predictive of stealing behavior.

The literature regarding the impact of intelligence on delinquent behavior ranges from findings supporting a positive relationship to ambiguous data to reports that constitute outright denial of any connection. Most recently, Austin (1978) studied adolescent theft in relation to school variables and found a weak and complex positive relationship between stealing and intelligence. Kohlberg (1976) has argued that moral reasoning is related to cognitive development. Comer (1980) and Renshaw (1977) more specifically indicated that children of normal intelligence are approximately 7 or 8 years of age before they understand concepts such as ownership, buying, selling, permission to use others' property, etc. They feel that a child must be able to comprehend such concepts before they can be regarded as stealers. Additionally, Jackson and Haines (1982) found that 12-to 14-year-old retardates responded like 6- and 7-year-old children to moral dilemmas and situations of impulse control. Thus, younger and/or intellectually limited children will need some special consideration.

Television has long been understood to influence the emotions and behavior of its viewers. Goldsen (1977) has described it as "the first mass effort at behavior-mod via electronic hookup" (p. 66). The average U.S. television set is on approximately 7 hours a day and has an enormous impact on our lives. Whatever children see and hear on television relative to crime, delinquency, or theft in particular will influence their perception of reality in regard to that behavior and the feelings they have about it and their own similar behavior (Goldsen, 1977; Hennigan, 1982).

PUTTING SCHOOL-AGE STEALING IN PERSPECTIVE

Answers to the following questions will clarify the extent of the problem, the level of intervention needed, and the direction it should take. Each child is unique, however, and the details of each treatment must be individualized.

I. Family
  A. General
    1. Is the family's financial status related to the child's stealing?
    2. Are there any siblings with similar problems?
  B. Parents
    1. To what level will the parents cooperate with treatment?
    2. How does the management style and capability of the parents relate to the child's behavior?
    3. How do the parents' histories and personalities relate to the child's stealing?
    4. How well are the child's emotional needs met by the parents?
    5. How have the parents dealt with the problem so far?
    6. Intellectually and practically, how complex a management program could the parents handle?
  C. Child
    1. Does the child have any intellectual limitations?
    2. How long and involved is the history of stealing? How extensive and how strong a behavior is it?
    3. What are the emotional needs of the child, how strong are they, and how do they relate to family dynamics?
    4. How does the child express anger?
    5. What level of legal involvement is there?
    6. What does the child do with stolen articles?
    7. Will the child cooperate with treatment?

II. School
    1. Is the child stealing at school, and what are the details?
    2. What has been tried and what resources in terms of personnel, cooperation, time, structure, and reinforcers are available?

III. Community
    1. Are there any peers whose influence must be considered?
    2. Are there any parents in the neighborhood who might help in terms of structure and feedback regarding out-of-home stealing?
    3. Do local social or legal agencies offer any organized programs or general support for stealers and their families?

ALTERNATIVE ACTIONS

In their critique of published treatment approaches for nonconfrontive stealing in school-age children, Miller and Klungness (1986) divided these efforts into five major categories: aversive contingency management, positive contingency management, parent training, self-control procedures, and a general school and communities category. They have additionally written about issues concerning the diagnosis and behavioral assessment of nonconfrontive stealing (Klungness & Miller, 1986; see also Bibliography: Professionals).

In general, intervention can involve any one or any combination of the following: individual counseling, parent training/counseling, a behavior management program for home and/or school, or referral to community agencies or programs.

Most interventions at school have been behavior-oriented, using tokens, discriminative stimuli, locker and desk searches, group rewards based on individual performance, reinforcers such as free time, money, personal time with an adult, and so on. Interveners are limited only by their expertise, available resources, and ethical/legal restraints.

Space considerations necessitate referring the reader to other articles for an overview and critique of a variety of treatment approaches (Miller & Klungness, 1986; Weger, 1985). Instead, some important considerations for parent involvement will be discussed. Parent participation is most important but often requires extensive knowledge and effort to maximize and maintain results. Although directed toward parents, the following guidelines are important for all managers of children referred for stealing.

Reid (1975) indicates some important necessities in preparing parents for cooperation in their child's treatment. They *must* define stealing *consistently* as "the child's taking or being in possession of anything that does not clearly belong to him/her" (p. 137) and *not* be swayed by doubts about proof or reduced concern because of the minimal value of the item. Parents are the sole judges who label the stealing. They may label an act as stealing by witnessing it themselves, by viewing the stolen property, or by report from a reliable informant. There is no arguing about whether the child is guilty. The child may be unjustly accused at times but it is their job to avoid being accused. Any time the child is "given" something or "borrows" an item, they *must* be able to prove it. Reid suggests that children refrain from bringing anything home until the stealing problem is under control.

The parental reaction is crucial (Comer, 1980; Dreikurs, 1964). They must respond and not deny or cover up the situation. Such a casual response suggests condoning. However, the reply needs to be in a calm and matter-of-fact style. It is important to use at least correction and punishment. Parents should be alert to the possibility that stealing may be a symptom of some underlying problem and the importance of an inductive style of management.

Additional details of this parent program can be found elsewhere (Reid, 1975; Reid & Patterson, 1976). An important point for any intervener, however, is Reid's recommendation that nonstealing *not* be reinforced, as covert and undetected stealing may be getting paid off. Additionally, Reid and Patterson (1976) have found the use of extrinsic reinforcers to help increase parent motivation and participation in the treatment program.

SUMMARY

Although most youngsters have only limited involvement with stealing and grow up to be responsible and law-abiding citizens, others will follow a social and legal agency path of chronic maladjustment.

Youths steal for a variety of reasons both real and perceived. There is considerable information available to guide intelligent evaluation of each case and to design an effective and individualized program of treatment. Most reported treatments have been largely behavioral. Parent cooperation in treatment efforts is a desirable but often difficult goal to achieve. Successful intervention requires structure and patience.

School psychologists are part of the second-largest continuing experience of children — education. Their training and this potential level of contact with each child combines to make the school psychologist a key figure in the treatment of any child referred for a problem of theft.

REFERENCES

American Psychiatric Association. (1980). *Diagnostic and statistical manual of mental disorders* (3rd ed.). Washington, DC: Author.

Applebaum, A. W., & Klemmer, H. (1973). Shoplifting-risk taking and anti-social behavior. *Meniger Perspective,* Fall, 1973.

Austin, R. L. (1978). Intelligence and adolescent theft. *Criminal Justice and Behavior, 5*(3), 211–225.

Beck, E. A., & McIntyre, S. C. (1977). MMPI patterns of shoplifting within a college population. *Psychological Reports, 2,* 103–104.

Belson, W. A. (1976). Juvenile stealing: Getting the record straight. *Bulletin of the British Psychological Society, 29,* 113–116. (From *Psychological Abstracts, 61,* Abstract No. 8624)

Cameron, M. D. (1964). *The booster and the snitch.* London: The Free Press of Glencoe, Colier-MacMillan.

Channing, L. Bete Company. (1983). *What everyone should know about shoplifting* (Research Rep. No. 1636B-2-78). South Deerfield, MA: Author.

Comer, J. P. (1980, June). If a child steals. *Parents Magazine,* p. 96.

Crockett, R. (1973). Habituation to criminal behavior. *British Journal of Criminology, 13,* 384–393.

Department of Justice. (1979). FBI uniform crime reports, pp. 27–31. Washington, DC: Author.

Dituri, J. (1977). Ten year olds moral judgment of similar peer and adult behavior. *Graduate Research in Education and Related Disciplines, 9*(1–2), 5–21. (From *Psychological Abstracts, 63,* Abstract No. 7330)

Dreikurs, R. (1964). *Children the challenge.* New York: Hawthorne Books.

Eisikovits, Z., & Sagi, A. (1982). Moral development and discipline encounter in delinquent and non-delinquent adolescents. *Journal of Youth and Adolescents, 11*(3), 217–230.

Gold, M. (1970). *Delinquency in an American city.* Belmont, CA: Brooks/Cole.

Goldsen, R. K. (1977, September). Changing channels: How TV shapes Americans minds. *Human Behavior,* pp. 63–67.

Hampton, R. E. (1975). *Sentencing in a Children's Court and Labeling Theory* (Research Series Number 5, Research section, Department of Justice, New Zealand).

Henderson, J. Q. (1981). A behavioral approach to stealing: A proposal for treatment based on ten cases. *Journal of Behavioral Therapy and Experimental Psychiatry, 12*(3), 231–236.

Hennigan, K. M. (1982). Impact of the introduction of television on crime in the United States: Empirical findings and theoretical implications. *Journal of Personality and Social Psychology, 42*(3), 461–477.

Hindelang, M. J. (1974). Decisions of shoplifting victims to invoke the criminal justice process. *Social Problems, 21*(April), 580–593.

Hirschi, T. (1975). Labeling theory and juvenile delinquency: An assessment of the evidence. In W. Grove (Ed.), *The labeling of deviance: Evaluating a perspective* (pp. 181–204). New York: Wiley.

Hoffman, M. L. (1977). Moral internalization: Current theory and research. In L. Berkowitz (Ed.), *Advances in experimental and social psychology,* Vol. 10. New York: Academic.

Holleran, P. A. (1981). *Prediction of treatment dropouts for families who steal.* Unpublished manuscript, Oregon Social Learning Center.

Hudgins, W., & Prentice, N. M. (1973). Moral judgment in delinquent and nondelinquent adolescents and their mothers. *Journal of Abnormal Psychology, 82*(1), 145–152.

Jackson, M. S., & Haines, A. T. (1982). A comparative study of the responses of young normal children and older retarded children in hypothetical temptation to steal situations. *Australia and New Zealand Journal of Developmental Disabilities, 8*(2), 85–91.

Johnson, A. M. (1949). Sanctions for super-ego lacunae of adolescents: In K. R. Eissler (Ed.), *Searchlights on delinquency.* New York: International Universities Press.

Karson, S., & O'Dell, J. W. (1976). *A guide to the clinical use of the 16 PF.* Champaign, IL: Institute for Personality and Ability Testing.

Katovsky, W., Crandal, V. C., & Good, S. (1967). Parental antecedents of children's beliefs in internal-external control of reinforcements in intellectual achievement situations. *Child Development, 38,* 765–776.

Klemke, L. W. (1982). Exploring juvenile shoplifting. *Sociology and Social Research, 67*(1), 59–75.

Kligerman, C. (1974). A discussion of the paper by Pietro Castelnuovo-Tedesco on stealing, revenge and the Monte Cristo complex. *International Journal of Psycho-Analysis, 55,* 179–181.

Kohlberg, L. (1976). Moral stages and moralization. In T. Lickona (Ed.), *Moral development and behavior theory, research and social issues.* New York: Holt, Rinehart & Winston.

Levine, E. M., & Kozak, C. (1979). Drug and alcohol use, delinquency and vandalism among upper middle-class pre- and post-adolescents. *Journal of Youth and Adolescence, 8*(1), 91–101. (From *Psychological Abstracts, 47,* Abstract No. 3501)

Loeber, R., Weissman, W., & Reid, J. B. (1983). Family interactions of assaultive adolescents, stealers and non-delinquents. *Journal of Abnormal Child Psychology, 11*(1), 1–14.

Mack, D. (1978, January). Stealing. *Teacher,* pp. 72–74.

Miller, G. E., & Klungness, L. (1986). Treatment of nonconfrontative stealing in school-age children. *School Psychology Review, 15*(1), 24–35.

Millman, H. L., Schaefer, C. E., & Cohen, J. J. (Eds.). (1982). *Therapies for school behavioral problems.* San Francisco: Jossey-Bass.

Moore, D. R., Chamberlain, P., & Mukai, L. H. (1979). Children at risk for delinquency: A follow-up comparison of aggressive children and children who steal. *Journal of Abnormal Child Psychology, 7*(3), 345–355.

Patterson, G. R. (1982). *Coercive family processes.* Eugene, OR: Castalia.

Peisach, E., & Hardeman, M. (1983). Moral reasoning in early childhood: Lying and stealing. *Journal of Genetic Psychology, 142,* 107–120.

Phillips, S. (1981). *Untitled.* Unpublished doctoral dissertation, University of Oregon.

Polk, K., & Schafter, W. (1972). *Schools and delinquency.* Englewood Cliffs, NJ: Prentice-Hall.

Reid, J. B. (1975). The child who steals. In G. R. Patterson, J. B. Reid, R. Jones, & R. E. Conger (Eds.), *A social learning approach to a family intervention: Vol. 1. The socially aggressive child* (pp. 135–138). Oregon: Castalia.

Reid, J. B., & Hendricks, A. F. C. J. (1973). A preliminary analysis of the effectiveness of direct home intervention for treatment of pre-delinquent boys who steal. In L. A. Hamerlynck, L. C. Hardy, & E. J. Mash (Eds.), *Behavior therapy: Methodology, concepts and practice.* Champaign, IL: Research.

Reid, J. B., & Patterson, G. R. (1976). The modification of aggression and stealing behavior of boys in the home setting. In E. Ribes-Inesta & A. Bandura (Eds.), *Analysis of delinquency and aggression* (pp. 123-–145). NJ: Erlbaum.

Reid, J. B., Rivero, G. H., & Lorber, R. (1980). *A social learning approach to the outpatient treatment of children who steal.* Unpublished manuscript, Oregon Social Learning Center.

Renshaw, D. C. (1977). Stealing and school. *Pointer, 21*(3), 9–13.

Revere, V. L. (1982). *Applied psychology for criminal justice professionals.* Chicago: Nelson-Hall.

Rezvani, F. (1983). Economic factors in juvenile crime. *Dissertation Abstracts International, 44*(5), Order No. DA8319793.

Rosen, H. S., & Rosen, L. A. (1983). Use of stimulus control with an elementary student. *Behavioral Modification, 7*(1), 56–63.

Russell, D. H. (1973). Emotional aspects of shoplifting. *Psychiatric Annals, 3*(5), 77–86.

Salk, L. (1972). *What every child would like his parents to know.* New York: David McKay.

Saltzstein, H. D., Diamond, R., & Belenky, M. (1972). Moral judgment level and conformity behavior. *Delinquency Psychology, 7*(3), 327–336.

Stumphauzer, J. S. (1976). Elimination of stealing by self-reinforcements of alternative behavior and family contracting. *Journal of Behavior Therapy and Experimental Psychiatry, 7,* 265–268.

Tedesco, C. P. (1974). Stealing, revenge and the Monte Cristo complex. *International Journal of Psycho-Analysis, 55,* 169–177.

U.S. Bureau of the Census. (1979). *Statistical abstract of the United States* (100th ed.). Washington, DC: U.S. Government Printing Office.

Weger, R. M. (1985). Stealing. In J. Grimes & A. Thomas (Eds.), *Psychological approaches: Vol. 2. Problems of children and adolescents* (pp. 83–134). Des Moines, IA: Iowa Department of Public Instruction.

Zabezynska, E. (1977). A longitudinal study of development of juvenile delinquency. *Polish Psychological Bulletin, 8*(4), 239–245. (From *Psychological Abstracts, 61,* Abstract No. 11149)

BIBLIOGRAPHY: PROFESSIONALS

Klemke, L. W. (1982). Exploring juvenile shoplifting. *Sociology and Social Research, 67*(1), 59–75.
Klemke reports shoplifting patterns of 1,189 nonmetropolitan high school youths in regard to sex, age, social class, frequency, and value of items taken. These self-report data are considered more accurate than store records and support the sociological hypotheses that deviant vulnerability labeling, and socialization are related to shoplifting.

Klungess, L., & Miller, G. E. (1986, April). *Non-confrontative stealing in school-aged children: Issues in assessment.* Paper presented at the National Association of School Psychologists convention, Hollywood, FL.
Klungess and Miller discuss important issues in this area, and suggest diagnostic interviews as the most appropriate assessment tool. A copy can be obtained from Gloria Miller, Department of Psychology, University of South Carolina, Columbua, SC 29208.

Miller, G. E., & Klungness, L. (1986). Treatment of nonconfrontative stealing in school-age children. *School Psychology Review, 15*(1), 24–35.
Miller and Klungness offer a critical review of published behavioral approaches for the reduction of nonconfrontive stealing behavior in school-aged children. Legal and ethical issues, approach efficacy, and methodological issues impacting on generalization of research results are also discussed.

Reid, J. B. (1975). The child who steals. In G. R. Patterson, J. B. Reid, R. Jones, & R. E. Conger (Eds.), *A social learning approach to family intervention: Vol. 1. The socially aggressive child* (pp. 135–138). Eugene, OR: Castalia.
In a practical and straightforward way, Reid emphasizes the importance of parent cooperation and consistent labeling and consequation of each event in the treatment of children who steal. In conjunction with a definition of stealing, this article outlines eight points of a very attractive treatment approach.

Renshaw, D. C. (1977). Stealing and school. *Pointer, 21*(3), 9–13.
Renshaw outlines 23 factors related to stealing and discusses their application to schools. She emphasizes the importance of guilt and shame as inhibitors of unacceptable behavior. The importance of strong consequation for initial stealing is stressed.

Weger, R. M. (1985). Stealing. In J. Grimes & A. Thomas (Eds.), *Psychological approaches: Vol. 2. Problems of children and adolescents* (pp. 83–134). Des Moines, IA: Iowa Department of Public Instruction.
This article is an extensive overview of over 100 references regarding the scope, definition, etiology, assessment, and treatment of stealing.

BIBLIOGRAPHY: PARENTS

There is little available that is written *for* parents. Some parents, depending on their sophistication and reading ability, would profit from the following sources.

Ginott, H. G. (1965). *Between parent and child.* New York: MacMillan.

Ginott, H. G. (1969). *Between parent and teenager.* New York: Avon.
Since stealing is often accompanied by other behavioral and/or emotional concerns, these classic and companion child management texts should be helpful. They use a most readable question-and-answer format and, albeit short, have a section specific to stealing.

Reid, J. B. (1975). The child who steals. In G. R. Patterson, J. B. Reid, R. Jones, & R. E. Conger (Eds.), *A social learning approach to family intervention: Vol. 1. The socially aggressive child* (pp. 135–138). Eugene, Oregon: Castalia.
In a practical and straight-forward way, Reid emphasizes the importance of parent cooperation and consistent labeling and consequation of each event in the treatment of children who steal. In conjunction with a definition of stealing, this article outlines eight points of a very attractive treatment approach.

Weger, R. M. (1985). Stealing. In J. Grimes & A. Thomas (Eds.), *Psychological approaches: Vol. 2. Problems of children and adolescents* (pp. 83–134). Des Moines, IA: Iowa Department of Public Instruction.
This article is an extensive overview of over 100 references regarding the scope, definition, etiology, assessment, and treatment of stealing.

Children and Stepfamilies

Susan Kupisch
Austin Peay State University

BACKGROUND

> "We are here to enroll the children in school. I'm Steve Jones; this is my wife Sally Thomas and our kids Jason Marshall, Debbie Thomas, Mark Jones, and Beth Greenlee. Would you like a schedule of our living arrangements?"

One dramatic change in our culture in recent years has been the emergence, as a common pattern, of the family unit experiencing stages of disruption and reorganization. It is estimated that almost half the children under age 18 will spend some time in a single-parent home and that 1 in 5 children will live in a stepfamily. One half million adults become new stepparents each year. Currently the national divorce rate is near 50%; and 80% of divorced adults remarry within 4 years. Estimating that 60% of them have children, single-parent and remarriage families constitute nearly 45% of all families with children (Visher & Visher, 1982a). Considering the elderly population, less than 25% of all homes are composed of the biological unit of mother, father, and their offspring.

The stepfamily represents normal adaptation to a changing society. It is a part of family evolution in the twentieth century. For clarification, a *stepfamily* is defined as a family in which at least one adult has a child prior to the couple union. The children, who predate the current marriage, may live with the couple, visit periodically, or be members jointly of two households. Both adults may have had children prior to the marriage, or just one of them. There are several important differences between the stepfamily and the traditional family, as cited by Visher and Visher (1978): (a) parent-child relationship predates the marriage; (b) one parent lives elsewhere or is deceased; (c) children are often members of two households; (d) most stepfamily members have experienced loss of previous family members; (e) no legal relationship exists between stepparent and child.

Because the "real" family for the U.S. culture is the first-marriage family, societal institutions have not yet adequately accommodated the stepfamily. Some religious groups sanction only the first marriage and most do not fully support alternative choices. Legally, stepparents do not have protected parental rights nor an authorized voice in decision making with the stepchildren. Although they are considered in loco parentis, their assumption of the role is voluntary and can be terminated at will (Hayes & Hayes, 1986). Socially, they have no commonly accepted place in family rituals, school functions, or previously established friendship groups. Rules of etiquette are not formally established. Thus, it has been called a family with no history.

Unresolved loss of original family members is a significant factor in the lives of remarried families (Hayes & Hayes, 1986) and can limit personal and family development. In particular, the pattern of attachments and losses disrupts some children's normal developmental cycle. Critical issues for members of stepfamilies according to Hayes & Hayes (1986), are renewed self-acceptance, mourning, acceptance of new expectancies, and negotiation of new roles and relationships.

DEVELOPMENT

Stepfamily Adjustments

To accommodate these differences, the roles taken by family members, the routines they arrange, and the expectations for one another usually change (Capaldi & McCrae, 1979). Lang (1985) has shown that families that make a success of adjustment to stepfamily life generally do not expect a normal family with Mom, Dad, and the kids gathered happily around the hearth. The boundaries of the home contract and expand as children move in and out to accommodate schedules and household needs. Space is used for multiple purposes — a bedroom for the weekend becomes a den during the weekdays and a playroom for the summer. Roles for adults and children are not as well defined as in the intact family, in which adults are parents and children assume subordinate status. In the stepfamily, children may relate to the same adult in different ways. Mary might be viewed as mother for one child, as a friend by another, and as an enemy by a third.

Stepfamilies also find that the patterns of living are not as simple as previously experienced (Prosen & Farmer, 1982), and that it takes longer than imagined to restabilize — approximately 4 to 5 years. From the beginning, there are members in multiple roles trying to adjust to one another, in contrast to the intact family in which there are two persons, then three in serial progression. Instead of starting a new phase of life, marriage may interrupt an ongoing phase for the adults as well as the children. For example, the remarriage of parents may come when a teenage daughter is struggling with her own sexuality or when a new wife is mothering young children but also having to manage teenagers who are only a few years younger. These complications compound marital problems and strain personal relationships within the family.

Many families feel that "time out" from the usual schedule, vacations, and traditional family gatherings such as Thanksgiving dinner help solidify the family and build feelings of unity. But with children crossing household lines, family traditions are often broken. For the stepfamily, the holiday dinner, the vacation at the beach, and the weekend break easily become issues for interfamily dispute and negotiation. As the stepfamily attempts to build new traditions and rituals to solidify the unit, anxieties arise owing to the destruction of the old ones (Reiss & Huffman, 1981). Movement toward new family identity further signals loss of the old family.

In this time of few public role models, stepfamilies appear to be self-conscious and less spontaneous than the traditional family in making decisions (Berman, 1980). They appear to be cautious and questioning about what is right and wrong with their living routines. Perhaps feeling guilty about past mistakes, such as undergoing divorce or putting children through difficult times, many stepparents perceive their image to be compromised. Many such families attempt to hide their status or pretend that they function as a nuclear family in order not to appear deviant. For example, it is not uncommon for the custodial mother to insist that the children use the stepfather's surname to spare anticipated embarrassment. This tells the children that they have something to hide, a status that is not well accepted.

Remarriage requires that family members blend a host of personal habits, previous disappointments, needs, and expectancies into some kind of organized unit. They may find others in the family unsupportive or even resentful because of religious beliefs, loyalty to the ex-spouse, or a multitude of other personal reasons. For the stepfamily, lifestyles, values, and attitudes must be meshed quickly in order for the new family to become functional and mutually supportive. Blending is complex because of the number of people involved, their various developmental levels, and their extended family histories.

Effects of Remarriage on the Family

Research studies of stepfamily life have produced ambiguous results, although the 1980s appear to be an era of interest in such dynamics. Much of the earlier work focused upon overall adjustment many years after remarriage, with little attention given to the children's ages or to the quality of the adjustment. Remarriages ending in divorce were not included in the samples. Many studies were based upon a small number of families seeking counseling; thus they cannot be considered typical of the stepfamily population.

On the positive side, some researchers have reported that stepchildren experience no higher incidences of juvenile delinquency or mental illness (Bohannan, 1970) and are rated as happy and academically successful as children from intact families (Bohannan & Erickson, 1978). Duberman's 1973 research showed that stepkin rated their relationships with others in the family as positive and satisfying. Lutz (1983) found that the better the stepsibling relationship, the better the family integration. National surveys have found no social or emotional differences between teenagers brought up in stepfather families and those of natural parent homes (Wilson et al., 1975; Santrock et al., 1982).

Other authors have expressed concern about the high divorce rate of remarried couples with children. Langher and Michael (1963) believed that children living in the stepfamily tended to experience more stress than those living in single-parent homes. Touliatos and Lindholm (1980) found that teachers rated children from stepfamilies as having more conduct problems at school than those from intact homes.

Feelings of sadness and anger, owing to the loss of contact with the absent parent, and conflicts about parent loyalty plague many stepchildren (Visher & Visher, 1979). It is not uncommon for a child who had become both friend and confidant to a single parent after divorce to have to abandon the roles when the parent remarries. For many, adjustment to the stepfamily means the readjustment to yet another family structure in a brief period of time. Also,being expected to love a new stepparent can create confusion for a youth whose identity incorporates two biological parents.

Children whose identity remains with the absent parent and who have greater anxiety about abandonment by the guardian parent are prone to emotional difficulties when that parent remarries (Tessman, 1978). It appears that for most children, discipline controversies and feelings of divided loyalties between parents are the most stressful issues of stepfamily living (Lutz, 1983).

Stepmothers in counseling have stated that they feel used and unappreciated by the new children. Feeling that they have little voice in decision-making while forced to discipline behavior, stepmothers have expressed frustration with their ambivalent roles (Nadler, 1976). Boverman and Irish (1962) found the stepparent role more difficult for stepmothers than for stepfathers. For example, Wallerstein and Kelly (1980) found that adolescent girls tended to compete more with stepmothers than boys did with stepfathers. The second-mother role is particularly difficult for stepmothers of adolescent females. Some have expressed that the attributed "wicked stepmother" characteristics tend to be incorporated into their self-concept.

Feelings of being an outsider in the family are expressed by stepfathers in counseling (Stern, 1978). As one who provides financial support, the new adult in the nest sometimes meets with rebuff when his values are shared. Older children and adolescents tend to compare the stepfather with the natural father and are resentful, whereas the stepfather is usually more readily accepted by the 6- to 10-year-old boy (Hetherington et al., 1982). Stepfathers may perceive themselves as cast in the role of scapegoat in the family dynamics. They, too, have not escaped myths associated with their role, although the many stories of the cruel stepfather who abuses the children for his own needs usually appear in adult literature and are not promoted in children's fairy tales, as is the case of the stepmother image.

Case study data reflect that stepparents express conflicts over alimony, child support, visitations, discipline of children, names to be used, nonacceptance of relatives, and sexual tension in the home (Visher & Visher, 1979). Feelings of guilt, resentment, and anger may be more prevalent in the newly established stepfamily than previously assumed (Visher & Visher, 1982b). Owing to the limited tradition, establishing a viable unit may involve more concentrated effort than required in the first-marriage family.

PUTTING THE STEPFAMILY IN PERSPECTIVE

Stepfamily Myths

Although we assume that people learn best by experience, there is little evidence that the experience of a previous marriage better prepares adults to handle remarriage. Coleman and Ganony (1985) believe that many adults hold certain myths about remarriage that set them up for later difficulty.

1. Consider everyone else first: It is frequently believed that keeping others in the family happy will guarantee one's own happiness. In a stepfamily there are many to please and it is not always possible to juggle everyone's needs and wants.

2. Keep disappointments to yourself: Most remarried adults feel that failure in a second marriage would be disastrous. They have an intense fear of failure and rejection because of sensitivity to the previous loss and tend to keep criticisms to themselves.

3. What is mine is mine and what is yours is yours: It is believed that sharing resources in the stepfamily causes many difficulties among the children and ex-spouses. However, maintaining separateness further distances members within the new family unit and maintains old boundaries.

4. Children of divorce are unhappy: Because of the behavioral problems associated with family adjustment periods, some stepparents assume that the children will never be the same again. They stop trying to foster healthy family relationships. However, often only time is required to mediate tension in the first part of the transition period.

5. Love me, love my child: Instant love is not probable in most situations. Respect and willingness to work on relationships is more realistic for the couple with stepchildren.

6. I'll make it all up to you: Parents sometimes want desperately to make up for the pain of divorce, only to be shunned by the kids. Trying to be the perfect new parent doesn't work in solving problems associated with the absent parent and the dissolution of the former family.

Not only do new stepparents and stepchildren but also family, friends, ex-spouses, and clergy buy many of these myths. Friendly but poor advice can run afoul of these and other fallacies.

Stepfamily Tasks for Adjustment

The following tasks appear to be critical in accomplishing a satisfactory level of functioning in the new family unit established by remarriage.

1. Finding realistic, appropriate role models: Roles are ill defined in the new family and this affects both self-concept and self-esteem. Often there are unrealistic expectations as to the appropriate roles for immediate

and extended family members. For example, although adults may choose to replace mates through remarriage, parents are not replaceable. The stepparent does not actually replace the absent parent. Likewise, assuming that the stepparent's role is the same as the parent's role may not be justified. Good stepparenting for the older child is not analogous to good parenting. These new roles must be negotiated within the new family unit and allowed time to develop.

2. Redefining financial and social obligations: Support for children traverses marriage lines, and deciding how to share and budget available resources requires sensitive attention. Dissolution of a marriage does not dissolve the obligation to provide for the welfare of the children, but often allotments are tied to emotional issues. It has been found that resentment over support payments is a major issue for parents and stepparents. Likewise, social networks formed prior to the divorce should not be dissolved immediately. The children need to interact with extended family and family friends. Former friends and relatives continue to be a part of the new family system but may have difficulty with changes in living styles, interactions, and roles. These financial and social pressures have frequently been cited as reasons for divorce of remarried couples with children (Messinger, 1976).

3. Arranging custody and visitation patterns: Conflict between parents may reflect continued struggles of the former marriage. Regular contact with the absent parent is critical, but allowing the child meaningful interaction with both parents requires logistic planning, flexibility, and continued open communication across households. This communication frequently is sacrificed by impulses to gain revenge or hurt the other parent, allowing the child to be caught in the middle of the contest.

4. Establishing consistent leadership and discipline: The responsibility for parenting crosses households and it is difficult to maintain consistent and reasonable discipline patterns. What is handled permissively by one parent or stepparent may be punished by another. With more figures of authority, expectations for behavior become more confused for the child. Conflicts over discipline and child rearing rank first on the list of problems in stepfamily units (Messinger, 1976). It is also an issue at school, where stress reactions are often reflected in behavior problems during times of family disruption.

5. Dispelling myths and tempering idealism: Remarriage does not automatically erase the hurt of divorce or death, and love of stepchildren is not instantaneous. Strong relationships require the resources of time and patience within this blend of families. After a few months many stepparents realize that the superparent image wears thin and that love may develop very slowly or not at all. The lessons of the first marriage are not the lessons of the new family. Members face a reorganization process that takes 4 to 5 years to stabilize.

6. Forming emotional bonds within the new family: More emotional bonds are expected within these multiple homes. The ability to achieve these attachments may require more adaptability than is expected in the intact family. The couple bond is particularly crucial for continuance of the stepfamily, and it is important for the children's sense of security. There is significantly more pressure on this bond than in the first marriage. Given the parent-child bonds that predate the couple relationship, intimacy and time for sharing become difficult tasks.

7. Dealing with sexuality in the home: There are more intrafamily sexual issues in the stepfamily with the loosening of relationship boundaries. Early attachment bonds are limited; thus the older child or adolescent isn't firmly acknowledged as "my child." Also, the new couple demonstrates more sexual behavior in the home, which is observed by the children. A way to gain affection and attention, therefore, may be translated into "act like the adults." Incest between stepfather and stepdaughter is reported to be more prevalent than between biological father and daughter, although data are limited (Meiselman, 1978).

The critical job of the stepfamily is to establish a new pattern of family relationships — one that will allow the children to maintain frequent and positive interaction with the natural parents and relatives while strengthening the foundation of the new family unit. Conflict and mistrust among members appear to diminish their ability to adapt to needed changes, reducing the probability of accomplishing the complex tasks outlined above. Developmentally, the family is at a different level than the first-marriage family, which is organized at a young adult phase in which children are gradually added to the unit at infancy. For the stepfamily, members are of various ages when the unit is formed and the developmental levels may not mesh. For the child, the family reorganization disrupts the normal developmental sequence, and we do not yet understand the long-term psychological impact.

School psychologists can be helpful in detouring families around some common roadblocks and traps that might diminish the likelihood of attaining the goals of family stability and satisfaction. Use of group sessions with adults in transition and with children experiencing family reorganization can be a dynamic vehicle for awareness and positive change. Group sessions can be educational as well as therapeutic, focusing upon common problems inherent in the new family formation.

The following issues are suggested as topics for a series of short sessions with stepparents and/or stepchildren. Each issue can be discussed in terms of the general effects on families with time given for the expression of individual experiences within the group. For some individuals, the issues may become a focus of continued counseling. It is important to understand the unique stressors experienced by these families in order to aid them in problem resolution.

ALTERNATIVE ACTIONS

Preparing for Remarriage

A critical time for counseling and negotiation is prior to the event itself, although few couples with children want to discuss factors that might disrupt the relationship at that time. While working with a family through a divorce or death adjustment, it may be appropriate to suggest future considerations whenever marriage is in the picture. Several early problems in a second marriage relate to unresolved issues in the first-marriage family. Being aware of typical trouble signs helps us recognize the stress when it appears.

1. Grieving and letting go: Closing the chapter and emotionally detaching from the ex-spouse is difficult. Unsuccessful attempts show up in continual arguing and talking negatively about the ex-spouse in front of the children.

2. Courting the family: Marriage is a lifestyle arrangement and in the case of the stepfamily several people are involved. Children need to be realistically included in activities designed to help family members know each other. Without such preparation of children a new marriage is headed for a serious disturbance as the children demonstrate frustration with the unpredictability and lack of control over their lives.

3. Clarifying expectations: What each one expects from the others is critical as a new family blends. Discussing interests, dislikes, and so forth helps each member feel more secure with the dynamics of the new unit.

4. Finding space to live: Each member needs personal space that is respected. The questions of privacy, sharing, and who rules must be negotiated among the parents and siblings from the beginning.

5. Coping with anxieties and uncertainties: Children need to know what is occurring, when, and under what circumstances in order to experience order and predictability. With many changes in family dynamics, it behooves parents to be clear and consistent in communicating what is going on. Anxieties can be lessened by including the children in decision processes.

Guidelines for Stepparents

The following issues address common roadblocks for stepparents that interfere with the child's adjustment to the new family. Parental and stepparental stability greatly enhance a child's overall adjustment and feeling of comfort with family reorganization.

1. Accept being a stepparent: A stepparent cannot replace the biological parent and attempting to do so may create confusion and resentment for the child. The new adult in the family can help clarify an appropriate role by assuming a caring, noncompetitive place in the structure, allowing plenty of personal space. Forced intimacy brings further resentment, as it heightens comparisons with the absent parent.

2. Accept the mate's ex-spouse: Realistically, remarriage is not an experience of starting over. Each mate brings into the marriage a history of intimate relationships that cannot be erased from memory. With children, communication with ex-spouses is required by the necessity of arranging schedules and will continue to be for many years.

3. Allow children time with the absent parent: The child's desire to be with and love the separated parent need not be threatening to the new stepparent. Children usually have emotional bonds with both biological parents and need to feel their love is permanent. Feeling that they must choose between parent and stepparent creates loyalty conflicts that are disastrous for the stepparent. But shared parenting protects the remarriage by decreasing loss experiences and reducing parent competition.

4. Share time with all children: It is tempting for the stepparent who does not have custody of the children from a previous relationship to transfer feelings to the children of a new spouse. Stepchildren may be seen as substitutes when parents are reacting to the loss of offspring. At the other end of the continuum are those who feel that the new children cannot match the natural offspring. In these cases, the children may be ostracized by the stepparent and a relationship not be given the chance to evolve. Being available to all children in the multiple family units and understanding their unique personalities is important for all concerned.

5. Allow relationships to evolve: With extended family involvements prior to remarriage, stepparents need to realize that unlearning as well as relearning is necessary during transition periods. Children may go through a resistance phase before they are receptive to establishing a close relationship. Pushing emotional closeness appears to increase resistance, delaying the desired acceptance.

6. Develop patient discipline: The stepparent is probably more critical of the stepchild's behavior than is the parent in the absence of long-term attachment. Parental protectiveness may increase during the first phase of remarriage as the parent guards against stepparent power. Since children may need time to work through feelings of resentment toward the new intruder, rapport is critical prior to correction of wrongdoing. If a foundation of caring is not established, discipline will be viewed as punitive and unfair.

7. Arrange family meetings: Open communication is needed within the family experiencing new demands and adjustments. The periodic family meetings to hash over feelings and reactions serves as an appropriate vehicle for release of tension and for problem solving. The unit gradually becomes a network of support and comfort, where trust and caring grows.

Guidelines for Stepchildren

Children have the capacity to work on problems associated with their disappointments and frustration. Brief group sessions emphasizing common issues of stepfamily living can offer permission to discuss the events and the feelings associated with them as well as offer help with developing good coping and problem-solving skills. The following points highlight critical stepfamily issues for children.

1. Express feelings and thoughts honestly: Feelings of fear, anger, and sadness are not uncommon during times of family change and uncertainty. Although it may be difficult for children to recognize and acknowledge feelings about family, support people can communicate a willingness to listen and reassure.

2. Ask parents about expectations: Anxieties and frustration can be significantly reduced by preparing for

events. As expectancies change they need to be communicated to children to avoid inappropriate and resistant behavior. Having experienced several significant life changes, children in remarried units may have a special need for structure, reassurance, and anxiety reduction strategies.

3. Realize that marriage and divorce are adult decisions: Many children assume some responsibility for the parents' divorce, feeling that they were not worthy of parental love. Some children, also, feel that they have a choice in a parent's remarriage; thus, they attempt to intervene in the couple's affair. Children may feel that if they cause a stepparent to leave, the absent parent will rejoin the unit. Helping children understand the adult nature of such decisions can diminish inappropriate fantasies.

4. Accepting a stepparent doesn't mean disloyalty to an absent parent: Many children feel they must choose between parent and stepparent. They assume that accepting and liking a stepparent will anger the absent parent and parental love will be taken away. Since the media show families with two parent figures, children may be confused about their feelings for added adults. Love can extend to many adults, since there is not a limited capacity for caring.

5. You can be a member of two households: When parents separate and form two households, it is difficult for some children to understand that they have a a place in each. Their place can be defined emotionally as well as physically by engaging the children in family plans and in protecting physical space. Competition between households and comparison of goods need to be discouraged. Different does not mean worse.

6. Love takes time: Children need to be permitted the time to develop the respect and love for new family members. Given opportunities to spend time together and know one another, they will usually experience flourishing emotional relationships. Frequently, children feel that if attachment is not instant, the stepparent is at fault. With heightened sensitivity, disappointments can negatively color initial impressions. Stepsiblings invading space can become a big issue reflecting resentments. Sharing time and giving the benefit of doubt are necessary factors in the reorganization of family life.

Other issues for children include fears of abandonment, discipline from stepparents, not seeing the absent parent enough, and adjusting to new roles. Coping with the many changes is stressful for most children for at least a year.

Assessment Considerations

For a comprehensive assessment of a child's current level of functioning, background history is essential, and the best method for gathering data is an extensive parent interview. Particularly in the case of children in stepfamily relationships it may be important to know at what developmental periods the family disruptions and reorganizations occurred and the nature and quality of adjustments to the changes. Academically and socially, the children may reflect family life turmoil and stresses through their behavior at school. Sudden changes in concentration, work performance, rate of learning, peer interaction, impulse control, and emotional tone are frequently noted in such children. Experts suggest that change in a given period of time is cumulative and related to physical and emotional stress reactions within the next year. Lags and spurts in learning may be associated with family adjustments as readily as with emotional problems and learning deficits. Self-esteem may alter as the child processes an identity apart from the original family.

The school psychologist must become highly skilled in clinical interviewing in these circumstances. The process of having a parent complete a standard family history form and sending it to the school administrative office rarely is appropriate for understanding stepfamily life and developmental issues. Although knowledge of events is important, assessing the impact of such events is critical. The following areas should be included in the family interview (questioning should proceed from the general to the specific, as exemplified in the revised Vineland Adaptive Behavior Scales format).

1. Family constellation: age when major changes occurred, and sequential view of changes in structure and regroupings.
2. Frequency and amount of significant change in child's life
3. Living, visitation, and custody arrangements
4. Reactions to family disruption and remarriage
5. Typical behavioral reaction to stress
6. Significant emotional attachments
7. Relationship with absent parent and extended family
8. Acceptance of new family members
9. Disciplinary arrangements between and with households
10. Other stressful life events

The Kinetic Family Drawing (Burns, 1982) is a helpful technique for gaining insight into the family dynamics as perceived by the child. The child is asked simply to draw a picture of the family doing something and given a blank sheet of paper. The family as pictorially represented on paper denotes the child's family identity. Who is included and not included, their positions within the unit, activities engaged in, and barriers between them are significant, according to Burns (1982), in interpreting the child's view of family life. The technique is easy to administer, and although not quantitatively scored, it adds qualitatively to overall personality assessment.

For a child experiencing the early phases of stepfamily living, insecurity and sensitivity about self and others abound. Rapport usually is heightened when the child feels accepted by the examiner.

SUMMARY

Stepfamilies need to be understood as to the unique dynamics and conditions of their lives. As with other special target groups,supportive counseling strategies can be used to facilitate awareness and problem solving.

Support groups, educational workshops, and bibliotherapy are but a few methods appropriate for persons experiencing the reorganization of the family unit. As advocates for these families, we can push for recognition of steprelationships and discover ways to appropriately involve them in the mainstream of community and school life.

We can go further with prevention. We can honestly confront our attitudes held about families and the ways we choose to interact with them. Do we help to demythicize the stepfamily? Are we active in suggesting new ways to involve families or do we stick with the "tried and true" Dad's Night?

The point can be made that the stepfamily deserves equal status as a legitimate family form. Currently, this is not the case. The real family for the U.S. culture is considered to be the first-marriage family. What can we do to help? School psychologists are psychoeducational specialists and advocates. Let's hear it for both roles.

REFERENCES

Berman, C., (1980). *Making it as a stepparent.* New York: Doubleday.

Bohannan, P. (1970). *Divorce and after.* New York: Doubleday

Bohannan, P., & Erickson, R. (1978). Stepping in. *Psychology Today, 11,* 53–59.

Bowerman, C. E., & Irish, D. P. (1962). Some relationships of stepchildren to their parents. *Marriage and Family Living, 24,* 113–121.

Burns, C. (1982). Self growth in families. New York: Brunner/Mazel.

Capaldi, F., & McCrae, B. (1979). *Stepfamilies.* New York: New Viewpoints.

Coleman, M., & Ganong, L. (1985). Remarriage myths: Implications for the helping professions. *Journal of Counseling and Development, 64,* 116–120.

Currier, C. (1983). *Learning to step together.* Palo Alto: Stepfamily Association of America.

Duberman, L. (1973). Stepkin relationships. *Journal of Marriage and the Family, 35,* 283–292.

Fisher, B.,& Sprenhle, D. (1978). Therapists' perception of healthy family functioning. *International Journal of Family Counseling, 6,* 9–18.

Gardner, R. (1982). *The boys and girls book about stepfamilies.* New York: Bantam.

Hayes, R., & Hayes, B. (1986). Remarriage families: Counseling parents, stepparents, and their children. *Counseling and Human Development [Special issue], 18*(7), 1–8.

Hetherington, M. E., Cox, M., & Cox, R. (1982). Effects of divorce on parents and children. In M. E. Lamb (Ed.), *Nontraditional families.* Hillsdale, NJ: Erlbaum.

Jones, S. M. (1978). Divorce and remarriage. *Journal of Divorce, 2,* 217–227.

Lang, S. (1985, June). Stepfamilies. *Self.*

Langher, T. S., & Michael, S. T. (1963). *Life stress and mental health.* New York: Free Press.

Lutz, D. (1983). The stepfamily: An adolescent perspective. *Family Relations, 32,* 367–375.

Meiselman, K. (1978). *Incest.* San Francisco: Jossey-Bass.

Messinger, L. (1976). Remarriage between divorced people with children from previous marriages: A proposal for preparation for remarriage. *Journal of Marriage and Family Counseling, 2*(2), 192–200.

Nadler, J. H. (1976). *The psychological stress of the stepmother.* Dissertation; California School of Professional Psychology, Los Angeles.

Prosen, S. S., & Farmer, J. H. (1982). Understanding stepfamilies: Issues and implications for counselors. *Personnel and Guidance Journal, 60,* 393–397.

Ransom, J. W., Schlesinger, S., & Derdyn, A. P. (1979). A stepfamily information. *American Journal of Orthopsychiatry, 49*(1), 36–43.

Reiss, D., & Huffman, H. A. (1981). *The American family: Dying or developing.* New York: Plenum.

Rice, F. P. (1978), *Stepparenting.* New York: Condor.

Roosevelt, R., & Lofas, J. (1976). *Living in step.* New York: McGraw-Hill.

Rosenbaum, J. & Rosenbaum, V. (1977). *Stepparenting.* Corte Madero, CA: Chandler and Sharp.

Santrock, J. W., Worshak, R., Lindbergh, C., & Meadows, L. (1982). Children's and parents' observed social behavior in stepfather families. *Child Development, 53,* 472–480.

Skeen, P., Cove, R., & Robinson, B. (1985). Stepfamilies: A review of the literature with suggestions for practitioners. *Journal of Counseling and Development, 64,* 121–125.

Stern, P. N. (1978). Stepfather families: Integration around child discipline. *Issues in Mental Health Nursing, l*(2), 3.

Tessman, L. (1978). *Children of parting parents.* New York: Jason Aronson.

Touliatos, J., & Lindholm, B. W. (1980). Teacher's perceptions of behavior problems in children from intact, single parent, and stepparent families. *Psychology in the Schools, 17,* 264–69.

Visher, E. B., & Visher, J. S. (1978). Major areas of difficulty for stepparent couples. *International Journal of Family Counseling, 6,* 70–80.

Visher, E. B., & Visher, J. S. (1979). *Stepfamilies: A guide to working with stepparents and stepchildren.* New York: Brunner/Mazel.

Visher, E. B., & Visher, J. S. (1982a). Stepfamilies in the 1980's. In L. Messinger (Ed.) *Therapy with remarriage families.* Rockville, MD: Aspen Systems.

Visher, J. S. & Visher, E. B. (1982b). Stepfamilies and stepparenting. In F. Walsh (Ed.), *Normal family processes.* New York: Guilford.

Wallerstein, J. & Kelly, J. (1980). *Surviving the breakup.* New York: Basic Books.

Wilson, K. L., Zurcher, L. A., McAdams, D. C., Curtis, R. L. (1975). Stepfathers and stepchildren: An exploratory analysis from two national surveys. *Journal of Marriage and the Family, 37,* 526–536.

BIBLIOGRAPHY: PROFESSIONALS

Currier, C. (1982). *Learning to step together.* Baltimore: Stepfamily Association of America.
A leader's manual for educators and metal health practitioners leading courses or workshops for couples or children in stepfamilies. Complete with handout suggestions.

Einstein, E. (1982). *Stepfamilies: Living, loving, and learning.* New York: Macmillan.
This important book presents the developmental passages of the stepfamily through experiences of the author (a stepchild and twice a stepmother), interviews with more than 50 other stepfamilies, and discussions with professionals who work with them. This highly readable book won a national media award from the American Psychological Association.

Ricci, I. (1980). *Mom's house, dad's house: Making shared custody work.* New York: Macmillan.
An excellent book illustrating how parents can make two homes positive and nurturing after divorce, serving the best interests of their children.

Rice, P. (1979). *Stepparenting.* New York: Condor.
The author describes common coping strategies for a stepparent or stepchild. Suggestions for healthy adjustment are provided.

Visher, E., & Visher, J. (1979). *Stepfamilies: Myths and realities.* Secacus, NC: Citadel.
A source book for those working with stepfamilies, as it provides the basic information concerning structure, concerns, problems, and myths.

BIBLIOGRAPHY: STEPPARENTS

Berman, C. (1980). *Making it as a stepparent.* New York: Bantam Books.
This book draws from the real-life experience of stepparents and addresses problems and how to prevent and resolve them. Other areas cover the shock of instant parenthood, money, the shared baby, holidays, dealing with the ex-family, discipline and rules, weekends, visits, disliking your stepchild, sex issues, myths, and Santa Claus parents.

Jensen, L. & Jensen, J. (1981). *Stepping into stepparenting: A practical guide.* Palo Alto, CA: R & E Research Association.
Written for new stepparents, the book highlights common dilemmas and suggestions for preventing more serious problems. It is appropriate for bibliotherapy and group discussions.

Juroe, D. J., & Juroe, B. B. (1983). *Successful stepparenting.* Palo Alto, CA: Stepfamily Association of America.
Two professional counselors offer a resourceful collection of guidelines, based on their personal experiences and training, for the responsibilities and rewards of successful stepparenting. Their informative advice provides valuable insights. It is religion-oriented.

Lewis, H. C. (1980). *All about families the second time around.* Palo Alto, CA: Stepfamily Association of America.
The messages in this illustrated book, although written simply enough for young children, are meant for people of all ages. A gentle, yet direct exploration of feelings, fears, dilemmas, and roles in families of remarriage. Designed to be used by parents and children together as a workbook.

Visher, E., & Visher, J. (1982). *How to win as a stepfamily.* Palo Alto, CA: Stepfamily Association of America.
Highly practical "how-to-succeed" guide for stepfamilies. Drawing on over 40 years of personal and professional experience with stepfamilies, the authors emphasize the personal satisfaction and growth in emotional relationships that can come from stepfamily life.

BIBLIOGRAPHY: CHILDREN

Berman, C. (1982). *What am I doing in a stepfamily?* Palo Alto, CA: Stepfamily Association of America.
With compassion and humor, this illustrated book touches the issues relevant to the young stepchild, including the most important question, Where do I fit in? Its candid look at the sensitive issues involved in the breakup and reorganization of families helps reassure the children about their feelings and thoughts.

Burt, M. S., & Burt, R. (1983). *What's special about our stepfamily?* Palo Alto, CA: Stepfamily Association of America.
This unique book is designed to help young people express their feelings about suddenly becoming a member of a new and different family. A true reader–participation book, it includes fill-in-the-blank questions and space to write down thoughts, with a special "Advice to Parents and Stepparents" section.

Craven, L. (1982). *Stepfamilies: New patterns of harmony.* Palo Alto, CA: Stepfamily Association of America.
A book for teenagers dealing with issues such as loyalty, family role conflicts, and discipline difficulties. Included is a sensitively handled section on sexuality in stepfamilies. Offers practical, down-to-earth advice while exploring the special problems, feelings, and concerns of adolescents growing up in a stepfamily.

Gardner, R. (1982). *The boys and girls book about stepfamilies.* Palo Alto, CA: Stepfamily Association of America.
A warm and honest book that provides reassurance and answers to many of the important questions children ask about stepfamilies. The emphasis throughout is one honesty about feelings and on learning to communicate them in appropriate and constructive ways.

Getzoff, A., & McClenahan, C. (1983). *Stepkids: A survival guide for teenagers in stepfamilies.* Palo Alto, CA: Stepfamily Association of America.
Packed with solid, realistic advice and usually aware of the teenager's point of view, this book will be helpful to even the most well-adjusted stepchildren.

Children and Stress

Ellis P. Copeland
University of Northern Colorado

BACKGROUND

Addressing childhood poverty in the United States, Howe (1986) has demonstrated that our children are losing ground as efforts made to provide them with healthful and rewarding lives are declining just when their need for such efforts are growing. Howe noted that nearly one of every four children under age 6 years is poor, a disportionately large number of these children being black or Latino. U. S. census data indicate that the divorce rate has more than doubled from 1970 to 1981, and more than tripled since 1960. It is now estimated that 40–50% of children born in the 1980s will undergo marital disruption and spend part of their childhood in a single-parent household (Hetherington & Parks, 1986). And, perhaps most distressing, divorce and poverty are only two of the numerous stressors that affect our children and adolescents today.

With both children and adolescents, life stress, defined by self-reported responses to a list of life changes, has been related to the prevalence of medical problems (Greene, Walker, Hickson, & Thompson, 1985), mental and emotional adjustment (Vincent & Rosenstock, 1979), and delinquent behavior (Vaux & Ruggiero, 1983). Such a focus on life changes has come to dominate the research on stress, despite growing evidence that this approach is not as strong a predictor of health and psychological outcomes as previously believed (Tolman & Rose, 1985). However, the life change research has provided an important part of the picture in understanding child and adolescent stress.

Direct Stress and Illness Model

Hans Selye (1956) pioneered most of the early research on the stress response. Selye defined stress as the nonspecific response of the body to any demand made upon it. An external stimulus that evokes a stress response is a stressor. Stimuli might include death of a parent, moving to a new home, or less evident external stressors such as sugar or caffeine intake. Selye noted that individuals may interpret or react to stimuli differently, but his original definition of stress was interpreted in a more normative sense and has guided much of our recent literature. The Schedule of Recent Life Events (Holmes & Rahe, 1967), which established a link between stress and adverse health and remains the most widely used list of stressful life events, was modeled after the ideas presented by Selye (1956).

Cognitive Appraisal of Stressful Events

In an expanded view, Magnusson and Ekehammar (1978) noted that researchers should be examining both *perception* of and *reactions* to stressful situations. A similar view is found in the writings of Richard S. Lazarus in his stress and coping paradigm, circa 1950. Lazarus (1981) viewed stress and coping as a process orientation that involves three separate but partly interdependent levels of analysis: social, psychological, and physiological. Lazarus believes that one must integrate these components in order to determine the degree to which a stressful event causes an individual to experience stress. Lazarus uses the term *cognitive appraisal* to describe how the individual perceives the stressful situation. Appraisals are placed into three categories — harm or loss, threat, or challenge. The term *transaction* indicates the reciprocal nature of human, environment, and person-to-person encounters.

Rutter (1979) supported the Lazarus concepts of cognitive appraisal and transactions when he noted that "the way all of us respond to another person is determined to a considerable extent by what the other person is like" (p. 56). Where teachers are depressed and/or irritable, they do not take it out on all children to the same extent; the target children tend to be the temperamentally difficult ones. Although such a result has not been empirically demonstrated in the classroom, support for the idea can be found in research by Rutter, Quinton, and Yule (1977). They found children with adverse temperamental characteristics to be twice as likely as other children to be the target of parental criticism.

Adaptation Models of Stress and Coping

Langner and Micheal (1963) found that at successively greater levels of stress, lower socioeconomic-status (lower SES) persons have higher risks of impairment than middle or upper SES persons. In other words, even when life stress is held constant, members of disadvantaged groups exhibit more psychological distress or impairment than their advantaged counterparts. This differential response to stress on the part of the disadvantaged has been termed *psychological vulnerability* or *psychological reactivity* (Kessler, 1979). Furthermore, it has been hypothesized that the psychological vulnerability of disadvantaged persons can be explained by the joint occurrence of high levels of life stress and poor access to or lack of psychological or social resources for coping with stress (Kessler and Essex, 1982).

Thus, a comprehensive model of the stress experience of children and adolescents would need to consider perception of and reaction to situational stress, genetic factors and individual skills, cognitive and social factors, self-esteem, and social supports. Furthermore, developmental stress must be taken into consideration, together with the evaluation of coping resources in the individual and the environment. The development and use of such a model would be both descriptive and preventive. Although such a model could be developed by examining all stressors and mediating or buffering variables, two models, which possess the major descriptive and preventive components, are available.

Albee's (1981) model of stress defines prevention as the reduction in the incidence of disorder in accordance with the equation in Figure 1.

FIGURE 1

George Albee's (1981) Model of Prevention

$$\text{Incidence of Emotional Distress} = \frac{\text{Organic Factors and Stress}}{\text{Social Competence and Self-Esteem and Support Groups}}$$

The idea of Albee's model is to reduce items in the numerator such as unnecessary stressors in the school and to strengthen components in the denominator by, for example, increasing a child's ability to develop friendships.

Patterson and McCubbin's (1985) model (Figure 2) is a family stress model designed to address global and situational perceptions, stress and strain (defined as constant demand such as a chronic illness in the family or a handicapped sibling) and resistance capabilities. Proper perception of the stress and use of appropriate resources for coping would lead to positive adjustment.

Conceptual Base and Assumptions

The conceptual base for the present analysis is derived both from a developmental perspective and from the interdisciplinary models of stress and coping. A developmental perspective (to be addressed in the next section) must be maintained at all times because of the differential cognitive and emotional capabilities of children from the preschooler to the late adolescent. The developmental perspective does not specifically address stress, yet it offers a context for understanding stress and coping during these periods.

Before proceeding further, it would appear helpful to summarize some assumptions about stress in children and adolescents based on past research: (a) stress can be beneficial or harmful depending on its context and how it is perceived; (b) the effects of stress vary from person to person and each individual may develop particular symptoms or styles of handling stress; (c)some environments, structures, and so forth are more stressful than others; (d) gender and related constitutional factors play a significant role as to how stress is handled; (e) stress is cumulative and progressive, and improved resources and coping patterns are necessary to reduce adverse effects; and (f) stress appraisal and coping capabilities increase with age and cognitive development.

DEVELOPMENT

Coleman's (1974) focal theory provides an appropriate context for discussing children's and adolescents' reactions to and perceptions of stressful events at different age levels. Studying boys and girls aged 11, 13, 15, and 17, he found attitudes to issues or relationships to be unequal at different stages of the preadolescent-to-adolescent process. Focal theory was proposed because "at different ages particular relationship patterns come into focus, in the sense of being most prominent, but no pattern is specific to one age only" (Coleman, 1978, p. 8). In a similar vein, Eisenberg and Harris (1984) found social competence to be a developmental phenomenon that builds on itself, but that competency at one age may or may not mean competency at another.

Cognition of Stress

Roosman (1986), studying distressing events and coping behaviors of children in the 6- to 11-year range, found that only 38% of her sample understood the meaning of the word *stress* (88% were 9 years old or older). All of the children in her sample understood feeling upset/bad/distressed. When the children reported two distressing experiences, rejection events were the most frequently reported for each age group, with the exception of the 10- to 11-year-olds. In fact, a decreasing linear age trend was noted for the report of rejection. The 10- to 11-year-olds reported rejection, conflict, loss, disobedience, and failure events about equally.

According to Piaget's paradigm (Inhelder & Piaget, 1968), the adolescent years are the time when young people develop the capacity to leave concrete thought and develop the capacity for abstract thinking. Yet, when Miller and Shields (1980) compared the habituation rates of young adults (22–30 years) to those of 13-year-olds, they found that the adolescents required significantly more trials than the adults to habituate to both stressful and neutral stimuli. Copeland and Kelly (1986) found 14-year-olds to perceive significantly less stress than either 15-year-olds or 16-year-olds. So, the question as to how cognitive change, during the adolescent years, amplifies stress or facilitates coping remains unanswered.

Gender and Stress

Family discord and disruption has previously been found to have a more detrimental effect on boys than girls (Rutter, 1970; Wolkind & Rutter, 1973), thus, leading to the conclusion that "it has been well established that males are more vulnerable to physical stresses; and they appear in some respects to be also more susceptible to psychological traumata" (Rutter, 1979, p. 57). Yet with advancing age this gender difference tends to disappear and by late adolescence the stress level for girls accelerates. "The data consistently show preadolescent males to have higher rates of mental illness, while by late adolescence females appear to have as high if not higher rates of mental illness than males" (Gove & Herb, 1975, p. 256).

Lipsitz (1981) believes that early adolescence (11–14 years of age) is a critical time of development when young people seek definition yet often find confusion. Puberty appears to have different meaning for boys and girls. According to Peterson (1981), boys look forward to the immediate life changes while girls are far more ambivalent. Barker and Gump (1964) pointed to

FIGURE 2

J. Patterson and H. McCubbin (1985) Family Stress Model

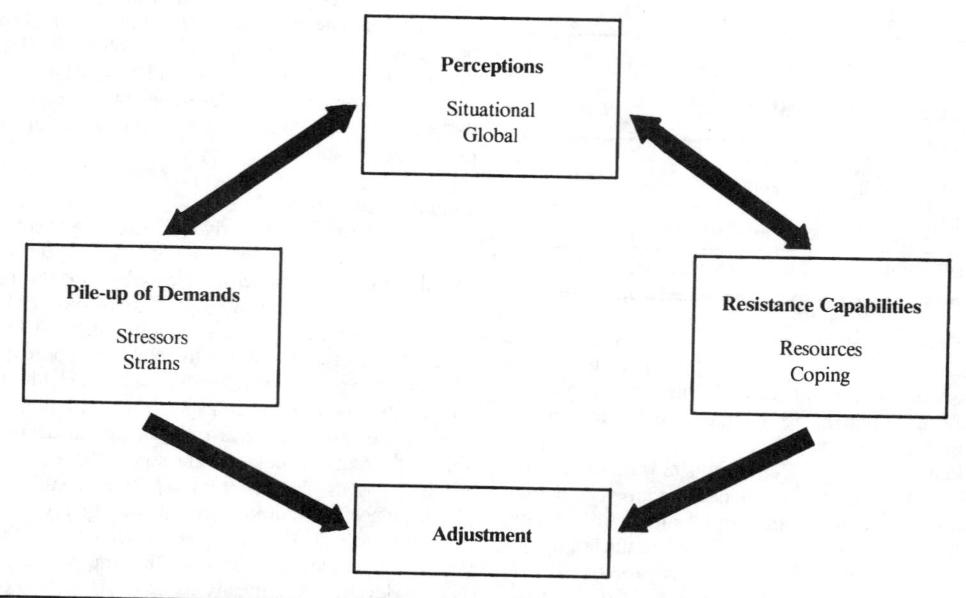

the effects of increased school size as a major change in the experience of adolescence. For the early adolescent, this change in school environment was found to be particularly stressful for females (Simmons, Blyth, Van Cleave, & Bush, 1979). Without intervention, these variables may account for the significantly greater life stress reported by females in high school (Burke & Weir, 1978).

Johnson and McCutcheon (1980) concluded that gender plays an important role in determining the effects of life stress in early adolescence. Furthermore, they pointed to the cumulative effects of stress and locus of control. General maladjustment was associated with an external locus of control; however, this finding was restricted to females. They speculated that "accumulation of negative events may have its greatest impact on the physical health of males and on the psychological adjustment of females" (Johnson & McCutcheon, 1980, p. 120).

Academic Stress and External Conditions

Examining academically related stress among early adolescents and midadolescents in England and the United States, West, Wills, and Sharp (1982) found the extent of stress to be very similar across cultures. The responses of 300 U. S. and 400 English adolescents were factor-analyzed, and four identical factors emerged from the data in both countries: parental stress, peer stress, importance of school, and fear of failure. The amount of variance accounted for by the four factors for the two cultures were very similar, with the exception of peer stress, which was significantly greater in the U. S. sample.

External conditions affect not only individual children but whole school populations. "Schools in communities characterized by a high percentage of single parent families, where frequent television use is more common among students, and where students feel they have less money than they need, are schools that are also relatively unhealthy" (Perry, 1982, p. 76). Perry referred to such a condition as "relative deprivation" (p. 76). So a child in a single-parent family in such a community has not only lost the broader protection of the two-parent family, but has possibly lost aspects of a protective school structure. A child in such a community, experiencing economic deprivation, runs the greatest risk of leaving school early and failing to graduate from high school (McLanahan, 1985); a process that may lead to persistent poverty and increased "psychological vulnerability" or "reactivity," where stressor variables are augmented.

PUTTING CHILDHOOD STRESS IN PERSPECTIVE

Assessment

Unlike adults, and perhaps late adolescents, children and early adolescents are subject to many events over which they have little control. The problem for the psychologist becomes one of not only assessing the impact but properly assessing the stress or stressor. The dominant problem with assessing the effects of adolescent stress is the typical failure of studies to incorporate important features of the stress process into the analysis (e.g., social structure, social resources, and coping). The retrospective correlational designs further preclude the unambiguous determination of cause and effect between life stress and behavioral variables. It is also possible that a third variable may account for the correlation between life change and illness or delinquency variables.

As noted earlier, the study of stress by questionnaire was advanced by Holmes and Rahe (1967), who developed the Schedule of Recent Life Events. Since the Holms and Rahe scale, a number of stress questionnaires for adolescents have been developed and their measures of life changes have significantly correlated with illness and delinquency. To date, these questionnaires either assign weights predetermined by professionals, assign weights established by middle- to upper-middle class group of adolescents, allow an individual to establish his or her own values, or give an equal weight to all events reported. Furthermore, Johnson and McCutcheon (1980) and Swearingen and Cohen (1985) have developed instruments that assess both positive and negative effects of life events. In general, their results show that the positive events fail to buffer the distress.

No questionnaire can be inclusive of all forms of adolescent stress, yet rate of occurrence should be an issue. For example, most adolescents report school problems more often than any other form of psychosocial stress (Andreasen & Wasek, 1980), yet only a few items are focused on school issues on the more popular adolescent stress questionnaires. A 50-item questionnaire by Dobson (1980) is an exception. Dobson's questionnaire is totally devoted to school stressors, but it lacks basic psychometric properties.

By way of summary in respect to self-report adolescent stress questionnaires, it can be said that each method has demonstrated a link between adolescent stress and illness, delinquency, or school problems. Yet the need for theoretical and methodological advancement is evident. To begin, a method limiting responding to only those events occurring in the past year, worded in a negative or distress manner, weighted on the basis of a combination of normative weights and individual values, and dealing with more commonly occurring stress (e.g., examination pressures) would appear to be an improvement. Further, external variables such as social strain, social structure, resources, and available support systems need to be taken into consideration.

Child Stress

Little research has been conducted to examine stress form a child's point of view (Rossman, 1986). Our knowledge, to date, essentially comes from outsider information, either from a parent or third party. Olson (1977) argued persuasively that information from several perspectives, though different, is useful in studying relationships. Hopefully this is the case, as Rossman (1986) found little congruence between parents' reports of stressful events and events their children found stressful. Consistent over the age range of 6–11, "the number of parent–child matches was only slightly above the number expected by chance alone" (p. 14). Similar parent–child discrepancies have been found in studies of adolescents identification of sources of stress; for example, a study involving rape worries and reactions (Mann, 1981) and a second one examining the stressful and nonstressful aspects of living in a stepfamily (Lutz, 1983).

Chandler (1986) questioned the use of children's self-reports and parents' reports and encouraged the use of behavior rating scales. He has developed the Stress Response Scale (SRS) to aid teachers and school psychologists in the assessment of a child's emotional status. In yet another variation, Abidin (1983) developed the Parenting Stress Index (PSI) as a screening and diagnostic technique that measures the magnitude of stress in the parent–child system. Although the scale has been found most useful in the first three years of life, it has been used with children up to 10 years of age.

Hassles and Social Support

A recent controversy highlighted in the *American Psychologist* has centered around the concept of *hassles* as a measure of life stress. Kanner, Coyne, Schaefer, and Lazarus (1981) introduced the Hassles Scale as a measure of stress symptoms and a prediction of pathology. Lazarus and DeLongis (1983) defined hassles as the "irritating, frustrating, distressing demands and troubled relationships that plague us day in and day out" (p. 247). Dohrenwend, Dohrenwend, Dobson, and Shrout (1984) noted that the measurement of hassles "almost guarantees positive correlations between stress and illness outcomes, but contributes little except confusion to our understanding of the role of environmentally induced stress in psychological distress and disorder" (p. 228). The problem of confounded measures was raised and the need to purify the independent variable by making it independent of psychological response was proposed as a solution. Lazarus, DeLongis, Folkman, and Gruen (1985) rebutted by arguing that some confounding is inevitable and that the appraisal process, part of cognitive theory, should not and cannot be removed in the measurement of psychological distress and stress. Dohrenwend and Shrout (1985) rebutted their rebuttal by reviewing alternative social psychological models of the life stress process.

The Lazarus–Dohrenwends debate has been centered around adult variables, yet support for the hassles concept as well as the strain concept (Patterson & McCubbin, 1985) is found in child and adolescent research. Rossman (1986) left children's reports of stressors open-ended and found the incidents that the elementary school age children most often reported were of the daily hassle variety. Eme, Maisiak, and Goodale (1979) studied middle-class adolescents and found their three most worrisome problems were physical appearance, career, and grades. Again, more focus on hassles and strains than specific environmental or life change stressors.

For the lower SES person, "psychological vulnerability" or "psychological reactivity" (Kessler, 1979) can perhaps best be explained by the hassle and strain concepts. "Females, unmarried persons, those with lower education and lower income, and married women all have higher distress scores and significantly less available emotional support" (Thoits, 1984, pp. 401, 403).

Thus, children of relatively disadvantaged, lower-status persons should display more psychological distress, undergo more undesirable experiences, and obtain less social and emotional support. So the hassles and strain variables experienced by such relatively disadvantaged children appear to be more compounding than confounding.

ALTERNATIVE ACTIONS

When children or adolescents find their physical environment unacceptable, distress occurs and they must cope. They may then take either an active or passive role to recreate homeostasis. Mental health professionals have proposed a number of ways to facilitate their adjustment in this process, and their methods generally take either a direct focus (stress management) or indirect focus (support group development).

Direct Methods of Stress Management

McManus (1985) divided signs of stress into body/physiological, behavioral, and emotional/psychological. Techniques for managing stress are placed into body/physiological, cognitive/behavioral, and emotional/psychological categories. His techniques are most accessible to middle and upper SES children. Yet, the present author questions the availability of these resources to the lower SES children. And, to what extent can the "average" child learn to use the techniques and resources and carry out the coping strategies purportedly available?

The most evident behavioral strategies appropriate for facilitating coping with stress appear to be operant conditioning, modeling, and cognitive restructuring. Rossman (1986) noted that younger children might be inclined to use more behavioral strategies inasmuch as their experience and cognitive abilities with problem solving are not as extensive as those of older children. Furthermore, behavioral strategies allow younger children to see direct reward of successful coping with a stressful event. Still, behavioral strategies may be even more successful for the older children because of their decreased egotism that allows them to see the consequences of (successful or unsuccessful coping with) stressful events within their family or peer group.

Dohrenwend and Dohrenwend (1978) saw two conditions that they believed would mediate the impact of unfortunate life events. The first condition was the anticipating of the noxious stimuli. The second condition was the individual's ability to perceive control of the noxious event (an internal locus of control). Thus, it appears behavioral interventions may be necessary to create a more internal process that can buffer the impact of a noxious event.

Lazarus (1966) proposed that stimuli that have been appraised as threatening may subsequently be reappraised as benign. Such a situation may result if the person perceives the stimuli as less threatening or has the ability to cope with the stimuli. Thus, daily stressful situations may bring about the appraisal/reappraisal process. For the 6- to 7-year-olds and 8-to 9-year-olds in the Rossman (1986) study, distraction/avoidance behaviors were the most frequently identified coping strategies for the initial stressful event reported. However, in later reports, all the children in her sample identified several strategies in dealing with distressing events, including approaching the problem in some way either with or without peer or parent help, and avoidance. The reappraisal process of daily stressful events was evident in her study, but greater use of a support network was not. Girls showed a significant decline with age in asking for parental help and both sexes decreased the use of peers in later childhood. Thus, the need to learn cognitive strategies for daily stressful situations is evident. Sanchez-Craig (1984) has demonstrated that preadolescents can be trained to reappraise and develop more adequate behavior for coping.

The result of the stress management intervention is that a child or adolescent becomes more capable of adapting to life change and more capable of making the life transitions with reduced distress. With these goals achieved, increased self-esteem, and social competence should follow.

Indirect Methods of Reducing Distress

Developing a child's social skills and social competence, especially a disadvantaged or handicapped student's, is considered to be an indirect method of reducing stress because the assumption is made that social deficiencies thwart adjustment to stress (Albee, 1981). Although the importance of social skills in children has been repeatedly underscored in the literature (Brockman, 1985), programs for children before 1982 generally yielded discouraging results (Durlak, 1983). Programs by Shure and Spivack (1978) and Stevens and Pihl (1982) were exceptions as they have demonstrated gains in both problem solving and measures of adjustment. The problem, however, may not have been with the programs but with the assessment of the specific skill deficits (Bellack, 1979). Gresham (1985) recently addressed the classification issue in a far more positive manner and offered a number of "effective" social skills training strategies. He presented a structured learning approach to social skills training based upon a directive teaching model as the most efficient and effective strategy.

The family also plays a vital role in problem-solving and in social skills development. Reiss and Oliveri (1980) found that "problem-solving behavior reflects a fundamental conception, by the family, that the social world in which they live is ordered by a coherent set of principles which they can discover and master" (p. 435). Guidabaldi (1986) found children of intact-families to have superior performance on 21 of 27 social competence criteria and 8 of 9 academic competence criteria. Thus, a breakdown in family structure appears to reduce social competence and capacity for problem solving. Kurdek, Blisk, and Siesky (1981) persuasively argued for a strong cognitive component, focused on internal rather than external factors, in services designed to help children accept and understand their parents' divorce. Such an approach would also appear useful to intact families that lack fundamental order.

Schools exercise a powerful formative influence on

children's psychological development (Cowen, 1983) and they can exert an important protective effect (Rutter, 1979). But the questions arise, What makes a good school? and Can/Should schools facilitate normal development of children from deprived and disadvantaged homes? To answer these questions, mental health professionals and/or public school professionals must develop sensitive ways to assess the impact of various dimensions of the school environment. Reynolds, Gutkin, Elliott, and Witt (1984) present a comprehensive discussion of the various methods used to assess the classroom, teacher–pupil interactions, the classroom climate, and the organizational climate. Within an ecological systems approach, the study of the environment (school factors) is as important as the school environment should identify facilitative factors that can be enhanced or expanded and debilitative factors that should be eliminated.

According to Felner, Farber, and Primavera (1983), the presence of high levels of social support not only facilitates successful coping efforts, but it may lead to more adequate and satisfactory levels of social support as a network effect spreads. However, events such as moves and shifts in parents' marital status clearly change a child's social support network. For example, divorce not only stresses a child, but it further increases distressing demands (hassles) and, perhaps most significant, forces the child to reorganize or reconstruct her or his social network and support system. A parent who overprotects or overindulges during this period may further exacerbate the problem. Some children with higher levels of adaptive skills may successfully adjust and reconstruct an appropriate network. However, many others will clearly need secondary intervention so that the "stress buffering" effects of social support can be maintained.

SUMMARY

Stress was originally conceptualized as physiological arousal induced by environmental stimuli. Thus a great deal of research has centered on specific "stressors" and how they relate to health and psychological outcomes. This research has consistently shown low to moderate correlations between life events and maladaptive behavior; even though cognitive skills, coping resources, and social skills were not taken into consideration. At present, life events research for children is examining the separate perspectives of parents, self-reports, and third parties. Hopefully, these surprisingly different perceptions will add to our knowledge of life events. Another development has been to examine not only major life events, but daily hassles. Perhaps it is not only the intensity of stressors but their frequency and duration that have adverse impact.

Rossman (1986) demonstrated that daily hassles were the stressful events that were recalled by children when asked about their experience of distress. In older children and adolescents, the study of daily hassles and strains (e.g., chronically ill parents) needs further study. Present research has shown variables such as examination pressures, peer pressure, appearance, and career choice to be particularly stressful in our culture. Gender differences also need to be further examined from a developmental perspective, as boys seemingly need the greatest attention in the earlier years, girls showing either a delayed reaction or a decreased ability to cope upon reaching adolescence.

Although a number of stress researchers appear to view the environment as static, it is not. Adjustment requires the child/adolescent to make numerous life transitions (Felner et al., 1983). In the case of lower-SES children, such transitions are typically more numerous and they may find that stressful demands increase and intensify. Such a scenario limits these children's ability to recognize stress and create the proper shifts to adapt or cope.

When a specific stress reaction occurs, stress management is a viable option. Yet, upon examination of the cognitive components of stress management, the internal locus of control variable, or the perception that one has control over one's environment, continues to be seen to facilitate adaptation and coping. Coping resources are also very important and they can be enhanced within the family or school environment. Then an additional task is to prevail upon the child to use his or her resources properly.

REFERENCES

Abidin, R. R. (1983). *Parenting stress index-manual.* Charlottesville, VA: Pediatric Psychology Press.

Albee, G. (1981). Politics, power, prevention and social change. In J. Joffee & G. Albee (Eds.), *Prevention through political action and social change* (pp. 5–25). University Press of New England.

Andreasen, N. C., & Wasek, P. (1980). Adjustment disorders in adolescents and adults. *Archives of General Psychiatry, 37,* 1166–1170

Barker, R. G., & Gump, P. V. (1964). *Big school, small school.* Stanford: Stanford University Press.

Bellack, A. S. (1979). Behavioral assessment of social skills. In A. S. Bellack & M. Hersen (Eds.), *Research and practice in social skill training.* New York: Plenum.

Brockman, M. P. (1985). Best practices in assessment of social skills and peer interaction. In A. Thomas and J. Grimes (Eds.), *Best practices in school psychology* (pp. 31–41). Kent, OH: The National Association of School Psychologists.

Burke, R. J., & Weir, T. (1978). Sex differences in adolescent life stress, social support, and well-being. *Journal of Psychology, 98,* 277–288.

Chandler, L. (1986). *Using the stress response scale in psychoeducational assessment.* Paper presented at the annual convention of the National Association of School Psychologists. Hollywood, FL.

Coleman, J. C. (1974). *Relationships in adolescence.* London: Routledge and Kegan Paul.

Coleman, J. C. (1978). Current contradictions in adolescent theory. *Journal of Youth and Adolescence, 7,* 1–11.

Copeland, E. P., & Kelly, M. (1986). *Stress, locus of control and perceived abusive parenting styles as predictors of adolescent delinquency.* Paper presented at the annual conference of the Rocky Mountain Psychological Association, Denver, CO.

Cowen, E. L. (1983). Primary prevention in mental health: Past, present and future. In R. D. Felner, L. A. Jason, J. N. Moritsugu, & S. S. Farber (Eds.), *Preventive psychology; Theory, research and practice* (pp. 11–25). New York: Pergamon.

Dobson, C. B. (1980). Sources of sixth form stress. *Journal of Adolescence, 3,* 65–75.

Dohrenwend, B. P., & Shrout, P. E. (1985). "Hassles" in the conceptualization and measurement of life stress variables. *American Psychologist, 40,* 780–785.

Dohrenwend, B. S., & Dohrenwend, B. P. (1978). Some issues in research on stressful life events. *Journal of Nervous and Mental Disease, 166,* 7–15.

Dohrenwend, B. S., & Dohrenwend, B. P., Dodson, M., & Shrout, P. E. (1984). Symptoms, hassles, social supports, and life events: Problem of confounded measures. *Journal of Abnormal Psychology, 93,* 222–230.

Durlak, J. A. (1983). Social problem-solving as a primary prevention strategy. In R. D. Felner, L. A. Jason, J. N. Moritsugu, & S. S. Farber (Eds.), *Preventive psychology: Theory, research and practice* (pp. 31–48). New York: Pergamon.

Eisenberg, N. & Harris, J. D. (1984). Social competence: A developmental perspective. *School Psychology Review, 13*(3), 267–277.

Eme, R., Maisiak, R., & Goodale, W. (1979). Seriousness of adolescent problems. *Adolescence, 14*(53), 43–99.

Felner, R. D., Farber, S. S., & Primavera, J. (1983). Transitions ipd stressful life events: A model for primary prevention. In R. D. Felner, L. A. Jason, J. N. Moritsugu, & S. S. Farber (Eds.), *Preventive psychology: Theory, research and practice* (pp. 199–215). New York: Pergamon.

Garmezy, N., & Rutter, M. (1983). *Stress, coping and development in children.* New York: McGraw-Hill.

Greene, J. W., Walker, L. S., Hickson, G. & Thompson, J. (1985). Stressful life events and somatic complaints in adolescents. *Pediatrics, 75,* 19–22.

Gove, W. R., & Herb, T. R. (1975). Stress and mental illness among the young: A comparison of the sexes. *Social Forces, 53,* 256–265.

Gresham, F. (1985). Best practices in social skills training. In A. Thomas & J. Grimes (Eds.), *Best practices in school psychology* (pp. 181–192). Kent, OH: The National Association of School Psychologists.

Guidabaldi, J. (1986). *Long-term impact of divorce on children: Report on two- and three-year follow-up samples.* Paper presented at the annual conference of the National Association of School Psychologists, Hollywood, FL.

Hetherington, E. M., & Parke, R. D. (1986). *Child psychology: A contemporary viewpoint* (3rd ed.). New York: McGraw-Hill.

Holmes, T. H., & Rahe, R. H. (1967). The social readjustment rating scale. *Journal of Psychomatic Research, 11,* 213–218.

Howe, H. (1986). The prospect for children in the United States. *Communique, 14*(8), 3.

Inhelder, B., & Piaget, J. (1968). *The growth of logical thinking from childhood to adolescence: An essay on the construction of formal operation structure.* New York: Basic Books.

Johnson, J. H., & McCutcheon, S. (1980). Assessing life stress in older children and adolescents: Preliminary findings with the life events checklist. In I. G. Sarason & C. D. Spielberger (Eds.), *Stress and anxiety* (pp. 111–125). Hemisphere.

Kanner, A. D., Coyne, J. C., Schaefer, C., & Lazarus, R. S. (1981). Comparison of two modes of stress management: Daily hassles and uplifts versus major life events. *Journal of Behavioral Medicine, 4,* 1–39.

Kessler, R. C. (1979). A strategy for studying differential vulnerability to the psychological consequences of stress. *Journal of Health and Social Behavior, 20,* 100–108.

Kessler, R. C., & Essex, M. (1982). Marital status and depression: The importance of coping resources. *Social Forces, 61,* 484–507.

Kurdek, L. A., Blisk, D., & Siesky, A. E. (1981). Correlates of children's long term adjustment to their parents' divorce. *Developmental Psychology, 17*(5), 565–579.

Langner, T. S., & Micheal, S. T. (1963). *Life stress and mental health.* New York: Free Press.

Lazarus, R. S. (1966). *Psychological stress and the coping process.* New York: McGraw-Hill.

Lazarus, R. S. (1981). The stress and coping paradigm. In C. Eisdorder, D. Cohen, A. Kleinman, & P. Maxim (Eds.), *Models for clinical psychopathology* (pp. 177–214). New York: Spectrum.

Lazarus, R. S., & DeLongis, A. (1983). Psychological stress and coping in aging. *American Psychologist, 38,* 245–254.

Lazarus, R. S., DeLongis, A., Folkman, S., & Gruen, R. (1985). Stress and adaptational outcomes: The problem of confounded measures. *American Psychologist, 40,* 770–779.

Lipsitz, J. (1981). *Early adolescence: Social psychological issues.* Paper presented at the annual conference of the Association for Supervision and Curriculum Development, Saint Louis.

Lutz, P. (1983). The stepfamily: An adolescent perspective. *Family Relations, 32,* 367–375.

Magnusson, D., & Ekehammar, B. (1978).Perceptions of and reactions to stressful situations. *Journal of Personality and Social Psychology, 31*(6), 1147–1154.

Mann, E. M. (1981). Self-reported stresses of adolescent rape victims. *Journal of Adolescent Health Care, 2,* 29–33.

McLanahan, S. (1985). Family structure and the reproduction of poverty. *American Journal of Sociology, 90*(4), 873–901.

McManus, J. L. (1985). Understanding and managing stress. In T. N. Fairchild (Ed.), *Crisis intervention strategies for school-based helpers.* Springfield, IL: Thomas.

Miller, E. M., & Shields, S. A. (1980). Skin conductance response as a measure of adolescents' emotional reactivity. *Psychological Reports, 46,* 587–590.

Olson, P. H. (1977).Insiders' and outsiders' views of relationships: Research studies. In G. Levinger & H. L. Raush (Eds.), *Close relationships: Perspectives on the meaning of intimacy.* Amherst: University of Massachusetts Press.

Patterson, J. M., & McCubbin, H. I. (1985). *A family stress model for family medicine research.* Paper presented at the conference on research on the family system in family medicine, San Antonio.

Perry, C. L. (1982). Adolescent health: An educational–ecological perspective. In T. J. Coates, A. C. Petersen, & C. L. Perry (Eds.), *Promoting adolescent health; A dialog on research and practice* (pp. 73–86). New York: Academic.

Peterson, A. C. (1981). Biological development in adolescence. In C. D. Moore (Ed.), *Adolescence and stress* (pp. 34–41). Rockville, MD: National Institute of Mental Health.

Reiss, D., & Oliveri, M. E. (1980). Family paradigm and family coping: A proposal for linking the family's intrinsic adaptive capacities to its responses to stress. *Family Relations, 29,* 431–444.

Reynolds, C. R., Gutkin, T. B., Elliott, S. N., & Witt,J. C. (1984). *School psychology: Essentials of theory and practice.* New York: Wiley.

Rossman, B. B. R. (1986). *Child and parent perceptions of child distressing events and coping behaviors.* Paper presented at the annual conference of the Rocky Mountain Psychological Association, Denver, CO.

Rutter, M. (1970). Sex differences in children's responses to family stress. In E. J. Anthony & C. Koupernick (Eds.), *The child and his family* (pp. 165–196). New York: Wiley.

Rutter, M. (1979). Protective factors in children's responses to stress and disadvantage. In J. E. Rolf (Ed.), *social competence in children* (pp. 49–74). University Press of New England.

Rutter, M., Quinton, D., & Yule, B. (1977). *Family pathology and disorder in children.* London: Wiley.

Sanchez-Craig, B. M. (1976). Cognitive and behavioral coping strategies in the reappraisal of stressful social situations. *Journal of Counseling Psychology, 23*(1), 7–12.

Selye, H. (1956). *The stress of life.* New York: McGraw-Hill.

Shure, M. B., & Spivack, G. (1978). *Problem-solving techniques in childrearing.* San Francisco: Jossey-Bass.

Simmons, R., Blyth, D. A., Van Cleave, E. E., & Bush, D. M. (1979). Entry into early adolescence: The impact of school structure, puberty, and early dating on self-esteem. *American Sociological Review, 44,* 948–967.

Stevens, R., & Pihl, R. O. (1982). The remediation of the student at-risk for failure. *Journal of Clinical Psychology, 38*(2), 298–301.

Swearingen, E. M., and Cohen,L. H. (1985). Life events and Psychological distress: A prospective study of young adolescents. *Developmental Psychology, 21*(6), 1045–1054.

Thoits, P. A. (1984). Explaining distributions of psychological vulnerability: Lack of social support in the face of life stress. *Social Forces, 63*(2), 453–481.

Tolman, R., & Rose, S. D. (1985). Coping with stress: A multimodal approach. *Social Work, 30*(2), 151–158.

Vaux, A., & Ruggiero, M. (1983). Stressful life change and delinquent behavior. *American Journal of Community Psychology, 11*(2), 169–183.

Vincent, K. R., & Rosenstock, H. A. (1979). The relationship between stressful life events and hospitalized adolescent psychiatric patients. *Journal of Clinical Psychiatry, 28,* 262–264.

West, C. K., Wills, C. L. & Sharp, A. (1982). Academic stress among early and mid adolescents in England and in the United States. *Journal of Early Adolescence, 2,* 145–150.

Wolkind, S. N. & Rutter, M. (1973). Children who have been "in care": An epidemiological study. *Journal of Child Psychology and Psychiatry, 14,* 97–105.

BIBLIOGRAPHY: PROFESSIONALS

Chandler, L. A. (1985). *Children under stress: Understanding emotional adjustment reactions* (2nd ed.). Springfield, IL: Thomas.
Written primarily for teachers and counselors in the schools to illuminate the characteristics of, and helping techniques for, dependent, impulsive, passive–aggressive, and repressed responses of children under stress. The implications for assessment and treatment are discussed.

Felner, R. D., Farber, S. S., & Primavera, J. (1983). Transitions and stressful life events: A model for primary prevention. In R. D. Felner, L. A. Jason, J. N. Moritsugu, & S. S. Farber (Eds.),Preventive psychology: Theory, research and practice (pp. 199–215). New York: Pergamon.

Although written from a lifespan perspective, the concept of life transitions has particular relevance to the developmental aspects of stress and coping. Long-term adjustment is discussed as well as coping resources and strategies.

Lazarus, R., & Folkman, S. (1984). *Stress, appraisal, and coping.* New York: Springer.
Perhaps the most extensive coverage of the appraisal reappraisal process in which appraisals are placed in the context of harm or loss, threat, or challenge. The transaction process is discussed as a more realistic method of evaluating the effects of life events on the individual and vice-versa.

McManus, J. L. (1985). Understanding and managing stress. In T. N. Fairchild (Ed.), *Crisis intervention strategies for school-based helpers.* Springfield, IL: Thomas.
McManus presents a model of stress, signs of stress, evaluation of stress, and techniques for managing stress. He uses the body/physiological, cognitive/behavioral, and emotional/psychological concept as his framework.

Pelletier, K. R. (1977). *Mind as healer, mind as slayer.* New York: Delta.
A holistic approach to recognizing and preventing stress disorder. The chapters on the nature of stress are excellent for those who lack background in psychophysiology. Methods of controlling stress are presented.

BIBLIOGRAPHY: PARENTS

Arent, R. P. (1984). *Stress and your child.* Englewood Cliffs, NJ: Prentice-Hall.
Recognizes that children seldom talk to parents about problems with stress and proposes an individual approach to the problem, taking into consideration the parents' needs and the child's. The book covers infancy to adolescence and discusses parenting skills and child management.

Charlesworth, E. A., & Nathan, R. G. (1984). *Stress management: A comprehensive guide to wellness.* New York: Ballantine Books.
A number of self-help books are on the market, yet few are as comprehensive as this one. The book discusses a variety of strategies including relaxation, imagery, and very specific stress management techniques. More for the parent than the child, yet a less distressed parent indirectly helps the child.

Curran, D. (1985). *Stress and the healthy family.* Minneapolis: Winston.
Data having been collected from therapists, counselors, and parents, the most common family stress was found to be problems of money, followed closely by behavior and discipline problems. This is a "how they" book in the sense that the focus is on how healthy families view their stressors and assess their strengths for positive resolution.

Kersey, K. (1985). *Helping your child handle stress.* Washington, DC: Acropolis.
A good advice book that encourages parents to listen and help their children cope with stresses they may be too immature to handle. The book takes the perspective of building coping skills so the child becomes a better manager of his or her life.

Children and Study Skills

Maribeth Gettinger and Susan N. Knopik
University of Wisconsin-Madison

BACKGROUND

Helping students become independent learners is a major objective of education. Teaching students to use appropriate study skills facilitates their becoming independent learners. Educators often assume that students entering middle or high school have acquired basic study skills. However, research has shown that study skills are neither naturally acquired nor specifically taught in school. According to the 1983 report of the National Commission on Excellence in Education entitled "A Nation at Risk" (cited in Davenport, 1984), "in most schools the teaching of study skills is haphazard and unplanned. Instruction in effective study work skills, which are essential if school and independent time is to be used efficiently, should be introduced in the early grades and continued throughout the student's schooling."

Being able to study effectively is crucial to a student's success in school. Large numbers of capable students at all levels experience failure and frustration in school not because they lack ability, but because they lack sufficient study skills. A 1983 College Board report (cited in Davenport, 1984) noted that "when polled about problems they expect during high school, ninth graders anticipate a 'big problem' improving study skills (24%), second only to pressure to get good grades (42%)." In fact, prominent among the explanations given by students themselves for scholastic failure in high school is lack of study skills.

Given the importance of study skills, greater attention should be given to classrooms to help students develop proficiency in their use. There are several compelling pedagogical as well as affective reasons for focusing on study skills. First, study skills are necessary for learning; they are "tools" for solving learning problems that students encounter in school and elsewhere in their lives. If students are to retain what they are taught, they must develop good study skills. Second, effective study skills offer students a means of increasing their sense of personal direction or control. Students who have developed a repertoire of study skills often experience feelings of increased competence and confidence as they learn. They are more likely to approach their schoolwork with a positive and expectant rather than a negative and anxious attitude. There is one additional reason for focusing on study skills. Study skills are often conceptualized as "life skills," applicable to many activities outside of school, such as careers, athletics, and social situations. Thus, for many students, motivation for learning is enhanced when they acquire skills that can be directly and immediately applied to activities besides school-related tasks.

The purpose of this chapter is to provide an overview of study skills for school psychologists. A discussion of what is meant by study skills and what is considered normal development of study skills is presented in the first section. The next section puts the topic of study skills in perspective by describing formal and informal assessment techniques for evaluating study skills and offering a conceptual framework that can be used in developing interventions for teaching or remediating study skills. The following section focuses on alternative actions in specific areas of study skills, examining research findings and successful classroom practices in each area and offering general guidelines for teaching study skills.

DEVELOPMENT

The literature on study skills points to the need for a definition of study skills that encompasses both the mechanical, or skill-based, aspects of study and the self-directional aspects. A skill-based perspective views study skills as learned abilities for acquiring knowledge. They are basic learning tools that, when developed and applied, enable a learner to acquire and retain knowledge effectively and efficiently. A broad definition of study skills views them as processes for learning — competencies associated with acquiring, recording, organizing, synthesizing, remembering, and using information in the classroom. More specifically, they include skills such as listening and reading, notetaking, outlining, managing time, and test taking.

Study skills, whether conceptualized as learning processes or specific skills, can be organized in terms of four general stages of study that are common to all learners. Table 1 delineates these four stages and lists the study skills or behaviors associated with each stage. The first stage of studying — processing information — entails taking in information from books, lectures, or discussions. The second stage entails organizing, synthesizing, and recording material. Stage 3 involves practicing or remembering the organized information. All of the preceding skills culminate in the fourth stage, which is the recall and application of information. Success in performing this step depends on how thoroughly information has been processed, organized, and rehearsed.

A self-direction approach to study skills emphasizes personality characteristics associated with academic performance rather than particular study skills. Specifically, the following emotional or behavioral patterns are associated with effective study: ability to concentrate, positive self-concept, ability to establish and achieve goals, interest in learning, and skill in managing frustration and conflicts. It is upon this dual concept of study skills (skill-based and self-direction) that the following suggestions for evaluation and intervention are based.

PUTTING STUDY SKILLS IN PERSPECTIVE

One of the first steps in gaining a perspective on study skills is to assess students' skills and attitudes related to studying. There are a number of formal instruments specifically designed for this assessment. Table 2 provides a brief description of several of these inventories.

Robyak (1977) has suggested that a distinction should be made between the knowledge of and the use of study skills. For example, responses to the instruments in Table 2 typically indicate how frequently a student uses particular study methods. Thus, scores are interpreted as a measure of how much the student currently uses the study skills. However, knowledge scores can also be obtained by following a procedure similar to one used by Weigel and Weigel (1968) with the Survey of Study Habits and Attitudes (Brown & Holtzman, 1967). Their procedure involves administering the survey under two sets of directions: The first time students complete the survey, they respond to the items according to how frequently they perform the behavior, thus assessing their current use of study skills. The second time they complete the survey, they answer the items as an "ideal" student would. These scores reflect students' knowledge of study skills.

There are many instruments available for evaluating knowledge and/or use of study skills, but aside from general interest inventories and scales such as the Myers-Briggs Type Indicator (Myers-Briggs, 1962), there are few instruments available that measure the self-direction aspects of study. The scope of diagnosis of study skills, however, is not limited to formal tests and should include other forms of assessment, such as observation and student interviews. It is often more efficient to conduct informal assessments, particularly in evaluating students' capacity for self-direction or their classroom application of study techniques.

Students' use of study methods can best be assessed by observing them while they are engaged in studying. Contrived situations on published surveys may not be as effective as observation for assessing actual study behaviors. Robinson (1975) recommends that observations should be made relative to the objectives of a given instructional situation. Students can be observed working independently or in response to specific questions or assignments. Student interviews are also effective assessment tools in that they afford the opportunity to discuss individually with students their particular abilities and attitudes toward study. McCabe (1982), McLoughlin and Lewis (1986), and Robinson (1975) provide examples of questions and interviewing techniques designed to assess study skills. They also provide examples of instruments, such as checklists, time-use charts, study skills questionnaires, and daily journals, that engage students in the active process of assessing their own study skills.

Additional informal methods of assessing study skills include work samples and criterion-referenced measures. For example, questions regarding information located on library card indexes are relevant to assessing

TABLE 1

Stages of Study and Associated Study Skills

Stage 1: Acquiring or processing information	Stage 2: Synthesizing, organizing, information	Stage 3: Rehearsing or remembering information	Stage 4: Recalling or applying information
Listening	Underlining	Reviewing	Taking tests
Reading:	Notetaking	Discussing	Preparing reports
Skimming	Outlining		
Scanning	Listing		
Studying	Questioning		

TABLE 2

Study Skills Inventories

Test name	Publisher	Description
CAI Study Skills	Effective Study Materials P.O. Box 603 San Marcos, TX	Measures knowledge of study behavior and scholastic motivation. Grade 12; 55 minutes.
Cornell Learning and Study Skills Inventory	Psychologists and Educators 211 W. State St. Jacksonville, IL	Measures specific competencies necessary for learning. Grades 7–12; 30–50 minutes.
Effective Study Test	Effective Study Materials P.O. Box 603 San Marcos, TX	Tests knowledge of study practices rather than personal practices. Grades 8–12; 35–45 minutes.
Study Skills Survey	Effective Study Materials P.O. Box 603 San Marcos, TX	Assesses organization, study techniques, and motivation. Grades 9–12; 15–20 minutes.
Study Skills Test	McGraw-Hill 1221 Avenue of the Americas New York, NY	Evaluates study skills, habits, and attitudes. Grades 11–12; 20–25 minutes.
Survey of Study Habits and Attitudes	Psychological Corporation 757 Third Avenue New York, NY	Assesses study habits and attitudes. Grades 7–12; 20–25 minutes.
Test of Library Study Skills	Larlin Corporation P.O. Box 1523 Marietta, GA	Grades 2–5, 4–9, 8–12; 50 minutes
Watson-Glaser Critical Thinking Appraisal	Psychological Corporation 757 Third Avenue New York, NY	Grades 9–12; 50–60 minutes.

students' ability to locate information that may enhance their studying; notetaking abilities can be assessed by playing a recording of a lecture or radio program and having the student take notes; textbook usage skills can be identified by having a student locate various subject areas within a textbook or look up references for further information. Finally, teachers themselves are a good source of information concerning students' study skills. They have had the greatest opportunity to get to know students, to evaluate the motivational and self-directional aspects of study, and to observe study performance in many academic areas and different situations.

In sum, the perspective on study skills presented

here is a comprehensive one that addresses both the knowledge of and the use of study strategies, as well as more global attitudes or learner characteristics related to academic performance. This type of assessment framework will enable school psychologists to develop alternative actions based on students' specific needs. This model stresses that intervention should match the type of study skill deficits as well as particular needs and styles of learners. Aside from a few isolated studies, there is little systematic research specifying the relationship among particular study skills, personality factors, instructional techniques, and increased performance. The following section attempts to delineate what has been documented concerning effective study skills training.

ALTERNATIVE ACTIONS

School psychologists are often called upon to generate interventions to remediate study skill deficits among children and adolescents. Educators and students have traditionally believed that common study techniques, such as underlining, notetaking, or outlining, help students perform better in school. Research, however has failed to document consistent benefits of specific techniques or that one technique is superior to others (Armbruster & Anderson, 1981). An important conclusion emerging from this research is that any study technique is helpful if it enables the student to process information effectively and efficiently. Although there is no simple formula for improving study skills that will apply to all students, educational psychologists have found that the key to effective studying is in building good habits, such as organization and time management, devising a system that works for the individual student, and using it effectively and consistently. The effectiveness of the study techniques described below depends on how much each is used and whether the way each is used matches the demands of the task and the needs of the student. For example, with notetaking, students may merely copy parts of a text and take notes randomly *or* they may use their own words, elaborate on the text, and take notes in an organized fashion. How students take notes and what they do with notetaking affect the results of their study, not the activity of notetaking itself. In other words, students often have to be trained to use a technique effectively and to employ one that best fits the task they are studying.

Many school psychologists and teachers are not familiar with specific study strategies. In spite of research supporting the teachability of study skills, school psychologists may not facilitate the acquisition of effective study skills in classrooms. For example, school psychologists and teachers with whom psychologists often consult may fail to explain and demonstrate how to read an assignment, how to take notes or outline, how to organize and schedule study time, or how to take tests. This underscores the need for educators to acquaint themselves with the broad range of study skills and to initiate a systematic instructional approach that incorporates the development and application of these skills into the curriculum. To address that need, we present below a number of different study methods, a list of appropriate commercial materials, and some general guidelines for study skills instruction.

Study Methods

Several writers suggest that students must master certain skills, such as locating main ideas and supporting details, understanding paragraph structure, synthesizing material, and identifying key words and phrases, before instruction with any particular study method can be successful. In addition to prerequisite skills, consideration should also be given to the method of teaching the study system. Students usually will not learn how to use a study method from didactic instruction alone. Instruction must also include practice exercises with carefully selected materials (at the student's independent reading level, with low vocabulary or conceptual difficulty, and initially in only one content area) that are guided to completion through teacher–student interaction. The key to mastering any of these study methods seems to be direct instruction with numerous opportunities for guided practice that are distributed over an extended period of time.

Several study methods have been designed to help students read and study assigned material. The SQ3R method (Robinson, 1961) is probably the most widely used of all study methods, especially for social studies and science content areas. In fact, it seems to be most effective when taught in the context of specific content. The SQ3R method involves five steps:

1. Survey. Quickly scan the reading assignment (look at headings, visual aids, summaries).
2. Question. Formulate questions by turning headings into who, what, where, how, and why questions.
3. Read. Read to answer the questions generated in the previous step.
4. Recite. Try to answer questions without looking at the book or notes.
5. Review. Immediately review the lesson to organize ideas and enhance retention.

Additional study methods have been developed that are similar to SQ3R in that each provides a systematic approach or structure for studying. Some of these are (a) Bergman's T-SQUARE (1975): Take the textbook, survey, question, underline, answer, review, and expand; (b) Eanet and Manzo's REAP (1976): Read, encode or put into own language, annotate by writing notes, and ponder to process or think about the message; (c) Thomas and Robinson's PQ4R (1977): Preview, question, read, reflect, recite, and review; (d) Pauk's (1963) EVOKER method for use with prose, poetry, and drama: Explore or review the entire selection, note and look up new vocabulary, read orally, determine key ideas, evaluate, and recapitulate; and (e) Edwards's (1973) PANORAMA method, which consists of a preparatory stage (determine purpose, adapt rate to purpose, formulate necessary questions), an intermediate stage (overview, read, annotate), and a concluding stage (memorize, assess.)

Time Management

Effective studying requires efficient time management skills. One of the simplest yet most important study skills is the ability to schedule specific time for studying. A regular plan will help students organize and retain what they are studying. Even students in the elementary grades can be helped by teachers, parents, or school psychologists to plan an overall study time schedule. A time-use chart is an effective tool for helping students become aware of how their time is spent each week and, subsequently, planning study time. A student can build a study plan starting on a monthly level (focusing on exams and long-term assignments), then weekly (listing weekly goals, scheduling project sections to be completed, designating selected weekdays for review and assignment completion), and then daily (identifying an optimal study period for each subject, building breaks into the study school, and setting realistic goals for daily study blocks).

Bandt, Meara, and Schmidt (1974) have offered suggestions for helping students set up a realistic and effective weekly timetable. Using a weekly timetable format, they suggest that students first fill in fixed events like class hours or after-school activities. Second, "life-support" activities (eating, sleeping, and transportation time) that routinely require a standard daily amount of time are added. Third, daily learning or study time is blocked in to facilitate keeping up-to-date on each week's work. As a fourth step, students are encouraged to identify unrestricted free time that they can use to reward themselves for using the scheduled study time effectively. It is important that they resolve to give up this time *only* if they do not achieve their learning goals and to use it *only* for studying if they have to give it up. Fifth, they must check to be sure that there is some time left over to accommodate unexpected time commitments. Once they are satisfied with the schedule, it is recommended that students try it out for a week and, at the end of the week, revise and continue to revise the schedule as necessary.

A weekly timetable enables students to adapt their lifestyles to the demands of school. Once they have scheduled a reasonable block of time for study, then they may prepare a second, more detailed daily schedule to organize study time. To do this, students should make a list of all the things that need to be done each day. The following guidelines may help students convert this list into a plan of action for the day's work: (a) Schedule difficult tasks for times they are typically most alert and set specific time limits for particular projects or assignments; (b) save routine tasks for a time when they are typically most fatigued; (c) divide lengthy assignments into short units (for example, if 20 spelling words have been assigned, break this down into 5 words per day or per study session); (d) spend no more than 15 minutes at a time on memorization (5 minutes for elementary students); (e) schedule study time according to principles of learning (for example, study a subject as soon as possible after class with a brief review just before the next class session; overlearn by frequent short periods of review); (f) vary and intersperse the type of study tasks (reading, writing, memorization); (g) reward or deprive yourself of rewards for using or failing to use time effectively; (h) be flexible enough to leave a project when studying it ineffectively, but compensate with extra time later in the week; and (i) plan periodic study breaks.

Test Taking

Graham and Robinson (1984) offer a comprehensive set of strategies to help students prepare for and take tests. First, students should find out about the test beforehand. Knowing information such as the type of questions the test will ask influences what and how to study. Therefore, answers to the following questions should be sought as soon as possible after a test has been announced: What topics will be included? Which specific notes and readings will be covered? How many and what types of questions, such as multiple choice, true/false, fill-in, or essay, will be asked? How much time will be allowed to complete the test? How much will the test count toward the final grade?

Graham and Robinson recommend several techniques for studying for exams. They suggest that students (a) construct a list of difficult areas and schedule review for them; (b) break material to be reviewed into small sections (each topic on an exam should be studied separately and reviewed at least twice before the test); (c) develop possible exam questions; and (d) outline answers to potential questions. Finally, when taking the exam, students are encouraged to give the test a quick reading before they begin. In addition Graham and Robinson recommend budgeting time, reading and following directions carefully, and varying one's approach to match different kinds of questions. Carman and Adams (1972) have incorporated these and other suggestions for taking tests into a system known as SCORER: schedule time, use clue words for questions, omit difficult questions initially, read questions carefully, estimate answers, and review responses.

Specific Skills

Additional study skills, such as listening, outlining, taking notes, or underlining, can be taught directly as isolated skills or in conjunction with academic content. The specific skills described below may serve either one or both of two functions: an encoding function, in which material that is heard or read is transformed into a personally meaningful form, and an external memory device function for later review, whereby retention of material is greatly enhanced by having the content organized. No attempt is made to review all of the literature related to each skill, however, some key generalizations are drawn from the research and listed as recommendations for school psychologists and teachers.

Listening

1. Establish a purpose for listening. Children may need to be taught how to identify those situations that call for focusing of attention (lectures, explanations), appreciative listening (guest speakers), analytical listening (oral reports), or marginal listening (music, dramatic presentations).

2. Develop with children a personalized checklist that they can consult prior to listening activities. The checklist should include self-oriented questions such as "Am I ready to focus my attention on the speaker?"; "Am I ready now to think about what the speaker is going to say?"; and "Am I going to listen carefully so I can ask questions when the speaker says things I may not understand?".

3. Provide a preview, study guide, or outline to organize students' listening.

4. Intersperse questions during listening activities, such as lectures or demonstrations, to facilitate students' active responding.

5. Encourage students to listen for organizational cues or signal words in lectures, such as "first, second, third," or "to summarize."

Notetaking

1. Notes should be written in students' own words.

2. Students should develop a consistent format, such as an outline format or a columnar format, for notetaking, including consistent abbreviations.

3. Notes should be labeled (topic, date).

4. Students should review notes as soon as possible after class sessions.

5. Notes should be precise and short.

6. Teachers may illustrate an entire lecture or lesson on the board with a model of effective and efficient notes.

Underlining

1. Finish reading before underlining.

2. Restrict the amount of underlining.

3. Augment underlining with marginal comments and coding systems.

4. Use teacher-provided underlining initially to focus attention on underlined material and facilitate review; then encourage student-generated underlining to enhance comprehension and retention.

Outlining

1. Teachers can provide partially completed outlines and instruct students to complete them; this technique can gradually increase in difficulty until the teacher provides only the structural arrangement.

2. Use headings in textbooks to indicate levels of subordination in outlining.

3. Use less complex outlining strategies than hierarchical outlining for younger or disabled learners: (a) pictorial outlining, which requires students to draw symbols or pictures representing material they have read; (b) topic outlining, which requires students to locate and underline the theme sentence in each paragraph or, in order to reduce rote underlining of first sentences, generate one question per paragraph; and (c) critical outlining, in which the teacher poses a specific question before students read a passage and students identify parts of the text that contain information related to that question.

4. Practice in outlining can be structured at first and gradually lead to student independence.

Commercial Materials

Table 3 provides a description of selected commercial materials that school psychologists, teachers, or parents may find helpful in teaching elementary and secondary level students various study skills and strategies.

General Guidelines

Brown, Campione, and Day (1981) have provided some useful guidelines for teaching effective studying. First, the more students know about the study task (for example, memorizing dates for a history test), the more effective their studying will be. Thus, students should be taught how to analyze the study task and how to choose the appropriate study strategy. Second, effective learners use organizational cues in material, such as headings, overviews, and summaries. Therefore, instruction in study skills might teach students about the components of study materials and how to identify and use them while studying. For example, early on children need to learn about the various parts of their textbooks (index, table of contents, glossary, chapter summaries, headings), effective use of which is an important skill that can help students organize information acquired from books. Third, it is helpful for students to know about the role of motivation, ability, and background knowledge in studying and, likewise, how to increase motivation, work with their strengths and weaknesses, and apply their existing knowledge. Fourth, instruction in effective studying may need to emphasize how, why, and when to use study strategies. Instruction should be based on a specific systematic strategy, inform students of the purpose of the strategy, and teach them how to monitor and evaluate their use of the strategy.

Several systematic programs for teaching the development and application of study skills have been described in the literature. Successful programs are characterized by some common elements that collectively represent general guidelines for teaching or remediating study skills. Thus, in addition to incorporating the guidelines provided by Brown et al. (1981), an effective study skills program should address the following:

1. Study skills should be presented as processes for learning. Thus, a part of learning study skills ought to involve learning about how one learns.

2. Learning by doing is the best way to acquire study skills.

3. It is important to remember that a study skill, like any other skill, requires repetition if the student is to gain mastery.

4. Instruction in study skills must involve the student in developing an organized program that is commensurate with his or her skill level and cognitive abilities.

5. A considerable part of study skills instruction ought to take place during class time and should be integrated with the regular curriculum. The most effective way to learn study skills is to learn and use them in a functional setting.

6. There is a place for the use of commercial materials in learning study skills, but overreliance on them can be detrimental.

TABLE 3

Commercial materials for Teaching Study Skills

Material	Publisher	Description
Developing Effective Study Skills	United Learning 6633 W. Howard St. Niles, IL	Includes six filmstrips and workbooks that teach notetaking, writing reports, following directions, and remembering. Grades 4–8.
High School Study Skills	United Learning 6633 W. Howard St. Niles, IL	Multimedia kit including eight units: homework, reading strategies for content areas, notetaking, test taking, and reports.
HM Study Skills Program	NASSP 1904 Association Dr. Reston, VA	Provides 12 activity-oriented units, each of which helps teachers integrate study skills instruction with existing curriculum. Grades 5–10.
Into Studying	Scholastic 904 Sylvan Englewood Cliffs, NJ	Workbook with emphasis on reading and writing skills. Grades 7–9.
Learning How to Learn	Developmental Learning P.O. Box 4000 Allen, TX	Consists of five resource manuals that focus on skills in studying, reading, writing, listening, teaching. Grades 7–12.
Let's Learn to Study	Guidance Associates 1526 Gilpin Wilmington, DE	Two-part filmstrip program designed to introduce students to the benefits of learning and applying study skills. Grades 7–12.
Listening and Notetaking Skills	Educational Activities P.O. Box 392 Freeport, NY	Consists of 10 cassette tapes and activity books that teach students how to prepare for listening, how to grasp main ideas, and how to write summaries/outlines. Grades 7–12.
Primary Thinking Box	Benefic 10300 Roosevelt Westchester, IL	Multimedia kit covers five content areas and emphasizes thinking skills. Activities include filmstrips and cassettes as well as teacher-oriented methods. Grades K–3.
Setting the Pace	Charles Merrill 1300 Alum Creek Dr. Columbus, OH	Consists of 10 cassette tapes and a student workbook that provide exercises to improve reading speed, comprehension, and study skills. Grades 9–12.
Study Skills Series	Media Materials Box 368 Baltimore, MD	Consists of five filmstrips and activity workbooks; following directions, outlining, reading tables, graphs, and taking tests. Grades 4–7.
Test Taking Techniques	Educational Activities P.O. Box 392 Freeport, NY	Consists of four cassette tapes and 10 activity books that teach ways to approach test situations and help establish positive attitudes toward taking tests. Grades 6–12.

7. The teacher must provide time for students to try out new skills and provide feedback about their effectiveness in using a new study skill.

SUMMARY

Because study skills are universal in application, they are as basic to the learning process as other academic skills that children and adolescents are taught in school. School psychologists and teachers have a responsibility to teach study skills, rather than erroneously assume that students already know how to study. Teachers in every classroom can be encouraged to provide opportunities for using study skills and strategies. The principles of effective study can (and should) be built into every lesson. The best materials are those that the student must contend with on a daily basis within a classroom and across the total curriculum. Study skills are important for elementary as well as secondary level students. Therefore, efficient study skills should be developed during the elementary grades and reinforced and applied as students progress through school. Study skills are of sufficient importance for academic achievement and student motivation that they deserve concerted attention from school psychologists. Study skills represent a viable area in which school psychologists can be involved in the instruction of study skills in respect to research and practice, teacher consultation, assessment procedures, curriculum development, and parent training.

What specifically can school psychologists do to help improve students' study skills? With sufficient knowledge in the area of study skills, school psychologists can be involved in a range of activities such as having regular and frequent consultation and communication with teachers and students to relay new study tips and techniques, conducting evaluations of students' study skills on either an individual or classwide basis to help target specific study skills for training, assisting a school district in developing a comprehensive curriculum or program for teaching study skills at all grade levels, and providing in-service training for teachers on how to implement study skills training. School psychologists can assist directly in the training of study skills by helping teachers incorporate the guidelines and techniques discussed in this chapter into the kinds of exercises, assignments, and tests that they already employ.

Not only do teachers need to gain a deeper understanding of the learning process and learn how to teach study skills to their students, but parents also need to understand the concepts and cooperate in assisting their children with study techniques. Furthermore, both teachers and parents need to reinforce the process that students learn in any direct study skills instruction. There are several ways of promoting effective study skills through the cooperation and support of parents, such as making study time a regular part of the day, minimizing common household noises and distractions during study time, providing materials needed for study time, or going over assignments with children. Therefore, school psychologists can also be involved in parent training activities such as holding "study workshops" for parents and students that illustrate the types of assignments that will be made during the school year as well as study methods for accomplishing them.

Clearly, school psychologists have a responsibility to work with schools, parents, and students toward fostering effective study skills. Deficiency in study skills can contribute to academic failure as well as low motivation and inability to benefit from even the most optimal instruction. Therefore, study skills (assessment as well as instruction or remediation) represent a critical area for school psychological services.

REFERENCES

Armbruster, B. B., & Anderson, T. H. (1981). Research synthesis on study skills. *Educational Leadership, 39,* 154–156.

Bandt, P. L., Meara, N. M., & Schmidt, L. D. (1974). *A time to learn: A guide to academic and personal effectiveness.* New York: Holt, Rinehart, & Winston.

Bergman, F. L. (1975). T-SQUARE for studying. *Journal of Reading, 19,* 167–169.

Brown, A. L., Campione, J. C., & Day, J. D. (1981). Learning to learn: On training students to learn from texts. *Educational Researcher, 10,* 14–21.

Brown, W. F., & Holtzman, W. H. (1967). *Survey of study habits and attitudes.* New York: Psychological Corporation.

Carman, R. A., & Adams, W. R. (1972). *Study skills: A student's guide for survival.* New York: Wiley.

Davenport, E. (1984). Study skills: Tools of the trade to make studying easier and more efficient. *Early Years, 15,* 43–44.

Eanet, M. G., & Manzo, A. V. (1976). REAP — A strategy for improving reading/writing skills. *Journal of Reading, 19,* 647–652.

Edwards, P. (1973). PANORAMA: A study technique. *Journal of Reading, 17,* 134–140.

Graham, K. G., & Robinson, H. A. (1984). *Study skills handbook: A guide for all teachers.* Newark, DE: International Reading Association.

McCabe, D. (1982). Developing study skills: The LD high school student. *Academic Therapy, 18,* 197–201.

McLoughlin, J. A., & Lewis, R. B. (1986).Assessing special students. Columbus, OH: Merrill.

Myers-Briggs, I. (1962). *Myers-Briggs Type Indicator.* Princeton, NJ: Educational Testing Service.

Pauk, W. (1963). On scholarship: Advice to high school students. *Reading Teacher, 17,* 73–78.

Robinson, F. P. (1961). *Effective study* (4th ed.). New York: Harper & Row.

Robinson, H. A. (1975). *Teaching reading and study strategies: The content areas.* Boston: Allyn & Bacon.

Robyak, J. E. (1977). A revised study skills model: Do some of them practice what we teach? *Personnel and Guidance Journal, 56,* 171–175.

Thomas, E. L., & Robinson, H. A. (1977). *Improving reading in every class* (2nd ed.). Boston: Allyn & Bacon.

Weigel, R. G., & Weigel, V. M. (1968). The relationship of knowledge and usage of study skills techniques to academic performance. *Journal of Educational Research, 56,* 78–80.

BIBLIOGRAPHY: PROFESSIONALS

Askov, E.N., & Kamm, K. (1982). *Study skills in the content areas.* Boston: Allyn & Bacon.
A text suitable for teachers of academic and nonacademic content areas. Its focus is on skills that should be taught and applied in Grades 3–12. The authors draw heavily on samples from textbooks to demonstrate how to teach study skills as part of content areas.

Bragstad, B. J., & Stumpf, S. M. (1982). *A guidebook for teaching study skills and motivation.* Boston: Allyn & Bacon.
Presents ideas, classroom presentations, activities, and materials appropriate for all school professionals for developing effective study skills. Each chapter is organized to present an introduction to the content and concepts, descriptions of learning experiences, suggestions for evaluating students' mastery of study skills, and an annotated list of references.

Devine, T. G. (1981). *Teaching study skills.* Boston: Allyn & Bacon.
Describes ways teachers can assist students in acquiring study skills. Chapters address content area skills, general thinking, reading, and studying methods, as well as specific skills such as notetaking, outlining, preparing reports, and using library resources. Each chapter concludes with an "idea box" of successful teaching activities.

Graham, K. G., & Robinson, H. A. (1984). *Study skills handbook: A guide for all teachers.* Newark, DE: International Reading Association.
This handbook offers practical suggestions for the development of study strategies. Several features of this book enhance its value for professionals who want to improve their competence in helping students become more effective in studying. The authors describe each strategy in detail and offer suggestions for developing and teaching that strategy.

BIBLIOGRAPHY: PARENTS

Cohn, M. (1979). *Helping your teen-age student: What parents can do to improve reading and study skills.* New York: Dutton.
Written especially for parents of junior and senior high school students, this book offers several good suggestions that parents can implement to foster effective study skills at home. In addition, ideas are provided for motivating teenage students to read and study more.

Duckett, J. C. (1983). *Helping children develop good study habits: A parent's guide.* Washington, DC: National Institute of Education.
A brief, but succinct guide containing suggestions regarding what parents can do and provide to facilitate the improvement of their children's study habits.

Hahn, J. (1985). *Have you done your homework? A parent's guide to helping teenagers succeed in school.* New York: Wiley.
A concise book that tells parents what it takes for students to be successful in school and provides techniques to make maximum achievement possible. The first two chapters discuss establishing a relationship with adolescents and keys to motivation. Subsequent chapters deal with general study strategies.

Whitman, R. (1984). *Home team: Over 60 home learning tips from the American Federation of Teachers.* Washington, DC: American Federation of Teachers.
A three-page publication packed with ways parents can improve their children's learning practices. Also includes suggestions relating to specific subject areas. Available in English or Spanish.

BIBLIOGRAPHY: CHILDREN

Carman, R. A., & Adams, W. R. (1972). *Study skills: A student's guide for survival.* New York: Wiley.
A programmed self-teaching guide aimed at teaching high school students basic academic survival skills, such as reading, writing papers, taking exams, notetaking, etc. The individualized, self-paced nature of this book makes it appropriate for either individual study or a formal study skills course.

Kalina, S. (1975). *How to sharpen your study skills.* New York: Lothrop, Lee & Shepard.
This illustrated book is written for elementary students. The content addresses general study techniques (notetaking, taking tests, homework, etc.) as well as specific content area study strategies (math, science, English, social studies). The writing style and illustrations make this an enjoyable resource for younger students.

Kesselman-Turkel, J., & Peterson, F. (1981). *Study smarts: How to learn more in less time.* Chicago: Contemporary Books.
Includes 31 brief chapters that provide concise and practical suggestions to students concerning a wide range of study skills (taking notes, skimming, remembering, preparing for exams). The style of presentation is very readable, and most students should find the techniques and advice helpful.

Phipps, R. (1983). *The successful student's handbook: A step-by-step guide to study, reading, and thinking skills.* Seattle: University of Washington Press.
This handbook is written for high school students. It is a self-instructional guide for developing basic study skills including notetaking, outlining, writing papers, taking tests. The book concludes with a helpful checklist summarizing effective study skills and behaviors. Exercises and examples are offered throughout the text.

Children and Suicide

William O. Hahn
Behavior Management Consultants, New Kensington, Pennsylvania

BACKGROUND

It is estimated that every 90 minutes, a child or adolescent commits suicide in the United States. Suicide among the young has become the third leading cause of death. Experts disagree whether the adolescent suicide rate is increasing or has plateaued; however, it is known that the rate has more than doubled over the past 20 years (Smith & Crawford, 1986).

Childhood and adolescent suicide is an obvious concern of the school psychologist, an estimated 10% to 25% of any high school population being considered to be at risk sometime during the school year. However, knowing the rate and statistics of suicide is not enough. The school psychologist must have the resources available to respond to a suicidal crisis, to assess suicide potential, and, most important, to be able to establish suicide prevention programs. Suicides among the young are preventable; in fact, programs have been developed that not only prevent adolescent suicides, but also prevent suicide attempts (Joan, 1986).

Contrary to popular belief, the study of youth suicide is not new. Youth suicide was studied in the nineteenth century and found to increase with age, and to be more prevalent in towns than in the countryside (Pfeffer, 1986). During this era, the most notable study of youth suicide occurred in 1910, when the Vienna Psychoanalytic Society met to discuss Dr. Baer's publication, *Suicide in Childhood.* Among those attending this conference were Freud, Adler and Rank. While no conclusions were reached concerning the motives for youth suicide, several relevant causes were presented, including death of a family member, child conflict with family members, suggestions stimulated by the suicide of a significant other, and suicide presented in the media (Oppenheim, 1910). As Berman (1986) has pointed out, the issues and focus of this conference were identical to our recent concerns regarding youth suicide. Most of these studies of the past, including Durkheim's classic *Suicide* (1951), have suggested that childhood suicide occurs only after a child has reached an age of reason, usually during the latency period (ages 5–12). In fact, current national health statistics are not kept on suicide under the age of 10, because according to developmental theory children under 10 do not realize the finality of death. However, more recent studies have established that suicides and attempts occur in children as young as 2½ years (Rosenthal, 1981). Pfeffer (1986) pointed out that while actual suicides are relatively rare in children under the age of 12, suicidal ideation, threats, and attempts are fairly common.

In order to stem this tide of rising youth suicide, researchers have been investigating common risk factors. Cohen-Sandler et al. (1982) have found that suicidal children, as opposed to children diagnosed only as depressed, experienced an increased and significantly greater amount of stress as they became older. Included in these life stressors were such specific chaotic or disruptive family events as addition of a third adult to the family, birth of a sibling, and parents' divorce. These suicidal children were also found to have been first-born, and upon entering school to have experienced a significant number of losses of some type. These losses included the loss of a significant other, the loss of psychological well-being or physical well-being, or the loss of an idealized state or status. These losses often resulted in a decrease of self-esteem and an increase in anger or rage. These children also tended to worry more about the death of family members (Pfeffer et al., 1979). Thus, suicide can be seen as an attempt by a child to alter an intolerable situation, a cry for help, or an attempt to gain love and affection from the parents.

In adolescents (12–18 years), suicidal risk factors are similar to those of children; however, as can be expected with the turmoil of this stage, these factors are more varied and more plentiful. Wieczorek (1984) lists the following as clues to the causes of suicide among adolescents.

1. Loss of a significant other
2. Recent suicide of a peer or family member
3. Legal difficulties caused by delinquent behavior, drugs, or alcohol abuse
4. Unwanted pregnancy
5. Family stress, either psychological or financial
6. Recent and frequent changes in school, home, or work environments.
7. Difficulties in relationships with friends, family, and co-workers
8. Depression and withdrawal
9. Disorientation, disorganization, and isolation (p. 114)

Other authors have offered more exhaustive lists of suicide clues; however, almost all the clues to adolescent suicide presented center around those listed above. Feldman (1984) offers this observation concerning suicidal adolescents:

> Adolescents who are suicidal often come from families in which there was the death of a parent during their childhood. Suicidal adolescents often have a neglectful, a rejecting, or a psychiatrically ill parent, a parent who committed suicide, or parents who are divorced or separated. These adolescents may blame themselves for their parents' unavailability and may harbor feelings that they must be unworthy for their parents not to care. (p. 106)

Pfeffer and associates (1979, 1980, 1984) have demonstrated that there is a reliable association between parents who are suicidal and children who are suicidal. It appears that the children learn that suicidal behavior can be used as a means of diminishing or coping with stress. There have also been studies that investigated the possibility of genetic involvement in the development of suicidal behavior in children. Pfeffer (1986) stated, "There is a strong suggestion, therefore, that genetic factors may be responsible for increasing risk for certain mental disorders and suicidal behavior" (p. 132).

Finally, Pfeffer (1986) highlighted five components, which she feels characterizes the families of suicidal children. These components are "lack of generational boundaries, severely conflicted spouse relationships, parental feelings projected onto the child, a symbiotic parent–child relationship, and an inflexible family system" (p. 153).

Thus far, the background of youth suicide has been explored, along with the characteristics of the children, adolescents, and families who are at risk. The remainder of this chapter will explore youth suicide in respect to the stage of development of the youth at risk, the roles of schools and school psychologists in working with suicidal students and in responding to suicides, and finally, methods that can be used on a broad scale to prevent possible youth suicides.

DEVELOPMENT

Preschool Children (Ages 2–5)

For many years, depression and suicide were thought to be nonexistent in young children. In fact, as previously mentioned, actual suicides among young children is rare; however, that is not true of suicide attempts and ideation. One reason suggested for the lack of actual suicides in the young is the child's inability to utilize lethal methods. Rosenthal (1984) studied preschool children, and found that the usual methods were poisoning, burning, jumping from high places, running into traffic, drowning, and head banging. Usually a child is rescued or prevented from reaching a lethal effect by these means. At times, many of these methods may be considered "accidents," thus masking the child's desperate cry for help.

In studying children and emotional disorders, Toolan (1981) suggested that "children evidence depression, schizophrenia, and other illnesses with different symptomatology at different developmental levels" (p. 312). Toolan feels that young children can be depressed and suicidal, and yet present a different "clinical picture" than a depressed or suicidal adolescent. Rosenthal (1984), in his study of suicidal preschoolers found that over half the children lived in foster homes. Rosenthal also noted that these children had profound feelings of abandonment and despair, yearned to be reunited, and hoped to resolve their painful loss. Paulson and associates (1978) found that suicidal preschoolers tended to feel that their parents didn't care and had perceptions of real or imagined rejection by peers and serious (later) school failures.

Toolan (1975) offered the following as possible dynamics for suicide in childhood: anger towards parents that is internalized in the form of guilt feelings and depression; a manipulation to gain love or to punish others; a sign of distress; a reaction to feelings of inner disintegration; and a desire to join a dead relative.

Pfeffer (1986) indicated that young children at risk will talk about killing themselves, and will make suicidal attempts such as running into traffic, hanging, or ingesting poison. The literature on assessment and recognition of suicidal preschool children is limited; however, the most feasible methods of determining the risk level of these children are exploring with them their feelings (using "sad and happy faces" and "three wishes"), discussing their understanding of death, watching them at play, talking about their dreams or imaginary friends, and gathering a history of life stressors and any previous attempts.

Latency-Age Children (Ages 5–12)

There has been a recent trend within the field of suicidology towards studying the suicidal patterns of older, preadolescent children. Pfeffer and her associates (1980) found that one-third of these latency-age children randomly selected for an outpatient psychiatric evaluation had some type of suicidal activity. Children in this age group that are at risk often have stressful family situations, which include problems with communication and/or a parent with psychopathology. As an example, Pfeffer (1981) stated, "A child may identify with his mother's depression and may feel helplessly unable to escape from this painful affect" (p. 156). Latency-age children will experience and evidence the same symptoms of depression and suicidal ideation as preschool children; however, these symptoms are usually cognitively and developmentally more advanced than those of the preschool child. One area in which suicidal behavior in latency-age children may be most evident is play. Specific themes of play first become visible in preschool children, and are manifested during the latency period. Since suicidal inclination is usually the result of chronic and increasing levels of stress or anxiety, it will be evidenced in a child's play. Play is thought to provide children with the opportunity to cope with anxiety and resolve conflicts. However, in suicidal children, the level of their distress is so intense that the play does not resolve the issues, but allows the children to act out their feelings of self-destruction. Pfeffer (1978) offers an example of a child whose play often included dropping or throwing of dolls or objects from heights. The toys would then be found and "rescued." This child later attempted suicide by jumping from a window. Other types of play offered by Pfeffer as clues to suicidal behavior include repetitive dangerous or reckless behavior, repeated misuse or destruction of toys, and repeated fantasies of being superhuman. Obviously, an important factor in all of these examples is the degree of involvement and the number of occurrences. All children will occasionally imagine being a superhero or will break toys; however, as these themes or activities become more repetitive and involved, the risk of a suicide attempt increases. Pfeffer has offered this additional observation: "It may be that in latency age children, as in adults, the more specific the methods contemplated, the greater the possibility of an actual attempt occurring" (p. 244). She also recommends exploring the presence of suicidal thoughts or actions in the parents.

Other factors evident in this age group of suicidal children include a tendency towards high degrees of isolation, emotional detachment, insensitivity to the affectional needs of others, and rejection by peers. All of these can lead to feelings of hopelessness, and hopelessness has been found to be a key element in adult suicide. In children, these feelings of hopelessness can lead to acting-out behavior, causing more isolation and rejection (French, 1975; Paulson, 1978).

Segal (1975) offered these warning signs that a latency-age child's depression may become suicidal: lack of self-confidence, a low opinion of oneself and one's abilities; loss of competence and feelings of defeat; withdrawing into oneself, (including spending more time alone) and a loss in interest in the future. Other signs include acting out of negative attitudes, hostile behavior and head banging, and finally, changes in eating or sleeping habits.

Adolescence (Ages 12–18)

As a child gets older, the potential for suicide increases. In the adolescent population, suicide is the third leading cause of death. One adolescent dies from suicide every 90 minutes, and one adolescent attempts suicide every minute. Suicide among adolescents has had considerable more research and involvement by the mental health community. As one might expect, many of the symptoms and characteristics of suicidal children are also evident in the suicidal adolescent. Maris (1985) has pointed out that adolescent suicides have intense, repeated depressions and a profound sense of hopelessness, use guns, are socially isolated, and see death as the only true escape from intolerable problems. Tishler and associates (1981) reported: "The decision of the adolescent to attempt suicide appears to be the combination of long standing problems as well as the impact of a recent precipitating event" (p. 91). Their study presented adolescent suicide as a developmental problem resulting from three states: (a) a previous history of problems, (b) an increase of problems associated with adolescence, and (c) an intense period of problems.

Shneidman (1985) has identified four broad areas that can be considered forewarnings of suicide and are applicable to adolescents. These areas are verbal statements, behavioral clues, situational clues, and syndromatic clues. Verbal statements can be very direct, as "I would be better off dead," or more indirect "What's the use?" Behavioral clues include previous attempts, writing a will, and sudden mood changes. Situational clues involve significant losses, major disappointments, or other areas in which failure or rejection is involved. Syndromatic clues refer to the syndrome of developmental stages reported by Tishler.

While these may be repetitious of other indicators offered, it is significant that the American Association of Suicidology (1977) listed these five "danger signs": (a) suicide threat or statement indicating a desire to die, (b) previous attempt, (c) severe depression, (d) marked changes in personality or behavior, and (e) making a will or giving prize possessions away.

While there is no typical adolescent suicide, profiles of those who unsuccessfully attempt suicide indicate that 90% are female and that they are often first-born. This birth order position frequently results in a decrease in parental attention and feelings of rejection. These teens usually have a very close, almost symbiotic, relationship with their mother, whereas, the father is often absent or not actively involved. As a result of this relationship, such a child cannot express anger towards her mother, because of the fragile mother–daughter relationship. Usually there are parental difficulties such as divorce. This often places the child in the role of the mother's ally, rather than being independent. This child often has difficulties asking for help, and being the oldest, she is often required to take care of the siblings. If she has a boyfriend, she will foster a highly dependent relationship, making the boyfriend "everything." This often causes the relationship to dissolve, adding to her feelings of rejection. The suicide attempt may be the result of desperation, rather than manipulation, because the daughter sees no way out (Cantor, 1986).

In contrast, the profile of those who actually commit suicide is somewhat different. These adolescents are usually male, although this probability is changing. He is usually a younger child in the family, who has been left home often by the parents as an infant. He has few friends, tries to please, but feels he gets little recognition. He is a loner, and feels isolated. Sixty-five percent of all teen suicides involve guns; yet studies have shown that if a highly lethal method of suicide to which a suicidal person is predisposed is taken away, he or she will most likely not choose another method. Therefore, it is advisable to eliminate any access a suicidal person has to firearms, and it is quite possible that if firearms are not easily available to teenagers, many will not become suicides (Cantor, 1986).

Three instruments that school psychologists may find useful with adolescents,especially older adolescents, are the Beck Depression Inventory (Beck, 1978a), the Beck Suicide Intent Scale (Beck, 1978c), and the Beck Hopelessness Scale (Beck, 1978b).

It is the responsibility of the school psychologist to utilize the available information and to determine what, if any, intervention needs to be taken on behalf of a potential suicide. If a clinician has established that a suicidal potential exists, the lethality of this potential and the availability of methods must be considered. If a plan for suicide has been revealed, and the child or adolescent is capable of acting on the plan, she or he should be considered to be at risk. If in addition to these factors there have been past attempts, a family background characteristic of suicidal children, and/or behavior changes, the individual must be regarded as highly at risk. Davis (1985) offered this suggestion: "The two primary questions to be answered by the suicide evaluation are (a) In your professional opinion, is the child or adolescent at risk for attempting suicide? and (b) What interventions are necessary given the answer to question 1?" (p. 320). Davis then suggested that hospitalization is necessary for those in imminent danger, the less imminent dangers requiring less restrictive therapeutic involvement. The level of family dynamics and community resources are also important considerations. Hafen and Frandsen (1986) proposed these questions in assessing the level of risk:

1. Do you have a plan for committing suicide?
2. Have you ever tried to commit suicide before?
3. How do you feel about the fact that you failed to complete your suicide before?
4. Has something recently happened that really troubled you?
5. Do you drink or use drugs?
6. Do you often feel hostile?
7. How long have you been thinking about suicide?
8. Do you know anyone who has committed suicide?

(pp. 136–143)

In summary, developing children offer different clues to their level of suicidal potential, the risk of suicide increasing with age. In general, it can be stated that suicidal inclination is a response to long-term stress, poor family dynamics, and the inability to cope. Thus suicide becomes the only apparent alternative. Families that are at risk often have had another suicidal family member, a family crisis, or a symbiotic relationship. The psychologist's response to the suicidal child should be based upon the degree of potential and the lethality of any suicide plan. However, in all cases, some type of response is necessary.

PUTTING CHILD AND ADOLESCENT SUICIDE IN PERSPECTIVE

As the result of suicide or the threat of suicide, other

school personnel will look to the school psychologist for assistance. A review of the research available on suicidal potential suggests a role for projective techniques and other instruments in predicting at-risk behavior. There are also avenues that can be utilized beyond hospitalization, crisis intervention, and outpatient referral. In addition, the school and the psychologist must be ready to assist in the return of a student who has attempted suicide to the mainstream population. Finally, one should be able to adequately deal with the aftermath of a successful suicide, both with students and faculty.

Essentially, in situations in which there is the imminent danger of suicide, hospitalization is the preferred choice. However, if this is not possible,or the danger is less imminent, arrangements should be made so that the suicidal individual is not alone. Follow-up by a mental health professional should be arranged as soon as possible. After the crisis has subsided, it is important for a psychologist or counselor who has intervened to meet with the child or adolescent, just to reaffirm professional concern. If this does not occur, the child may feel that a crisis is necessary to get any attention. Faculty who are involved with the suicidal child should be in-serviced or met with in order to "calm any fears," and to provide support and guidance. While it may not be within the realm of the psychologists' duties to provide ongoing family therapy, it is often helpful to provide some follow-up, to ensure that recommendations are being carried out.

Another avenue of investigation of suicidal potential in children is the use of projective techniques. However, very little actual research has been done in this area. It is obvious that a central emotional theme that would appear to the professional would be extensive feelings of hopelessness (Beck et al., 1985). It is widely accepted that suicidal people display the "Three H's": hopelessness, helplessness, and haplessness (the feeling that everything happens to them). Other themes that may be present are the ideas of being unloved and unwanted. Often there will be little, if any, identification with family members, and possibly an obsession with death. Suicidal children may visualize themselves as dead and their parents overcome with sorrow and grief. Stories or fantasies that have to do with bodily emptiness and loss of some meaningful relationship, has been shown to be an important theme in childhood suicide (Toolan, 1968).

Karon (1981) feels that the Thematic Apperception Test can be very useful in evaluating suicidal potential. He states, "It may even reveal suicidal dangers under circumstances which are now remote, but may not be remote at some future time in the patient's life" (p. 99). Karon proposed that the principles of interpretation are very simple: Suicide is predicted by suicide stories. Vogel (1968) confirmed this view by comparing suicidal and nonsuicidal individuals, finding that suicidal patients did give overt suicidal stories, in which protagonists actually kill themselves.

Often psychologists will utilize projective drawings in working with children. Hammer (1968) presented an example of a suicidal individual "acting out" his intentions in the drawing of a person. Wohl and Kaufmann (1985) presented a drawing of a tree by an 11-year-old, who stated that the tree was about to die; the actual drawing had people hanging from it. Hutt (1969) suggested that on the Bender Gestalt Test suicidal rumination is evidenced by the intrusion of design 6 into design 5.

Richman (1986) utilizes the Machover Figure Drawing Test with suicidal clients and their families. He has found that the presence of slash lines is a major feature evident in the creations of those with self-destruction impulses. He states, "These lines are prominent in the drawings of the majority of the persons I have seen who are suicidal, and in the drawings of at least one of the relatives" (p. 87). He also claims that these slash lines are often presented as articles of clothing, collars, or cuffs.

Pfeffer and associates (1982), in a study of suicidal children, found no correlation between scores on the WISC-R and WRAT and a level of suicidal potential. The mean Full Scale IQ for her study was 99, with a range of IQ scores from 44 to 133.

Among other methods developed to assess suicide potential are interview techniques and self-report scales. However, most of these instruments have not been well validated by research and do not seem popular among professionals. Corder and Haizlip (1983) have developed a checklist for screening suicidal children. This checklist has questions for the parent and for the child. Unfortunately, further studies on this instrument have not been completed.

Pfeffer (1986) has developed the Child Suicide Potential Scale, which can be used for children aged 6–12. The scale consists of nine parts, and elicits information concerning the child's emotions,behaviors, family history, ego functioning, and concepts of death. The nine sections of the scale are the following (p. 198).

1. Spectrum of suicidal behavior
2. Spectrum of assaultive behavior
3. Precipitating events
4. General psychopathology (recent)
5. General psychopathology (past)
6. Family background
7. Concept of death scale
8. Assessment of current ego function
9. Ego defenses

At present, research is still incomplete on these scales; however, they do provide the clinician with a concise, structured method of obtaining information.

In the aftermath of a suicide, "honesty is the best policy." Hewett (1980) provides six guidelines in explaining a suicide to children:

1. Be honest, explain it in simple straight-forward language.

2. Listen carefully. Answer questions as best possible, and listen to what is implied by the questions.

3. Be consistent and repeat whenever necessary, so the children will understand.

4. If told something different from what they saw, they may begin to distrust their own perceptions of reality; or if they realize the falsehood, they may become angry at those who are lying to them.
5. Talk about the deceased. Talking will help the children see that it wasn't their fault.
6. Involve them in what is happening.

Additional suggestions for helping children cope with death can be found in the chapter on reactions to death in this volume.

In schools, there has been considerable debate concerning the appropriate actions to take after a suicide. Brent (1986) argues that little attention should be given to the act openly. He feels that such activities as memorial services, assemblies, and so forth are stimuli for "students at risk" to contemplate the act. He also feels that such activities provide "students at risk" with an avenue to gain more attention and to foster the idea "they'll all miss me when I'm gone." Brent suggests that an alternative to this type of action is to have mental health professionals meet after a suicide with those students considered at risk. One obvious drawback to this type of plan is the assumption that the school personnel will know those "students at risk." It is highly conceivable that some students may become suicidal, but not fit into the profile and not be known. An alternative to this type of plan is to meet with the students in small groups, such as classes. If the assembly approach is used, time should be allowed for those students who wish to meet and discuss their feelings. In utilizing any of these methods, it may also be advisable to provide a "drop-in" counseling service for the students.

ALTERNATIVE ACTIONS

Obviously, the best approach to the prevention of youth suicide is proactive rather than reactive intervention. Preventing youth suicide can begin in the elementary years, with a focus on building self-esteem, helping children understand death, and teaching children to be problem solvers. In the upper elementary and middle schools, the emotional and cognitive levels of the students will allow a more open discussion of suicide and general mental health (Berkovitz, 1985). In the high schools, it is important to offer open and frank discussion of suicide and other topics. It is also important to remember that a suicidal youngster will most often confide in a peer, and that the peers need to know what to do (Ross, 1980). There are many programs available; suggestions include: *Preventing Teenage Suicide: The Living Alternative Handbook* by Polly Joan and *Adolescent Suicide Prevention Program,* developed by the Fairfax County (Virginia) Public School System.

Berkovitz (1985) presented these five elements as necessary to effective suicide prevention programs:

1. General mental health atmosphere of the individual school and district;
2. Optimum psychological services staff;
3. Suicide prevention program;
4. Intervention program;
5. Postvention program (p. 171)

Berkowitz added that without the first two items "it is questionable if the last three elements can be as effective" (p. 171).

In addition to educating the students in suicide prevention, the entire school staff and parents should also be given instruction in prevention (Peck, 1982).

Some school districts have found it beneficial to develop programs based on industries' Employee Assistance Programs. Student Assistance Programs provide walk-in counseling and crisis intervention, with set guidelines for referral and follow-up. The counselors are school personnel who are trained to deal effectively with the wide range of adolescent problems. Related programs include peer counseling, in which concerned adolescents are trained to counsel, or "buddy systems," in which students are teamed with other new students or troubled adolescents. A final crisis intervention technique is to install a school district hotline for after hours. The hotline can be staffed by an answering service with teachers or counselors who rotate being "on call." A system such as this, along with the student assistance program is relatively inexpensive for the district and can be very effective in helping adolescents.

SUMMARY

Youth suicide is possible from preschool to adolescence, the danger increasing with age. Research has been able to establish many factors that contribute to youth suicide and that can aid in identifying those "at risk." The profile or characteristics of those "at risk" have differences depending upon age. These characteristics are all identifiable by appropriately trained staff. Procedures for intervening with a child "at risk" are dependent upon the level of danger and lethality of the situation.

Schools have tended to take a reactive attitude towards suicide, mobilizing only at or after a crisis or a completed suicide. However, some schools have developed more proactive approaches, which include student assistance programs, hotlines, curricula, and extensive in-service instruction. It is obvious that a proactive approach is the best method of suicide prevention.

Cantor (1986) has presented these recommendations for the overall prevention of youth suicide:

1. Education and school mental health programs. She has maintained that these type of programs could effectively reduce suicides by 20%.
2. Limit lethal agents, most notably through gun control. She reported that 65% of all completed youth suicides are by handguns. It is estimated that gun control could reduce suicides by another 20%.
3. Reduce medications by prescription to less lethal doses. This could reduce suicides by another 10%. By enacting these three strategies, youth suicide could be cut in half. The first recommendation requires action at the local level; the latter require action at the national level.

REFERENCES

Ackerly, W. C. (1967). Latency-age children who threaten or attempt to kill themselves. *Journal of the American Academy of Child Psychiatry, 6,* 242–261.

American Association of Suicidology. (1977). *Suicide and how to prevent it.* West Point, PA: Merck, Sharpe, & Dohme.

American Psychological Association. (1984). *Publication Manual of the American Psychological Association* (3rd ed.). Washington, DC: Author.

Baucom, J. Q. (1986). *Fatal choice.* Chicago: Moody.

Beck, A. T. (1978a). *Beck Depression Inventory.* Center for Cognitive Therapy, Room 602, 133 South 36th St., Philadelphia, PA 19104.

Beck, A. T. (1978b). *Beck Hopelessness Scale.* Center for Cognitive Therapy, Room 602, 133 South 36th St., Philadelphia, PA 19104.

Beck, A. T. (1978c). *Suicide Intent Scale.* Center for Cognitive Therapy, Room 602, 133 South 36th St., Philadelphia, PA 19104.

Beck, A. T., Steer, R. A., Kovacs, M., & Garrison, B. (1985). Hopelessness and eventual suicide: A 10-year prospective study of patients hospitalized with suicidal ideation. *American Journal of Psychiatry, 142,* 559–563.

Berent, I. (1981). *The algebra of suicide.* New York: Human Sciences.

Berkovitz, I. H. (1985). The role of schools in child, adolescent, and youth suicide prevention. In M. L. Peck, N. C. Farberow, & R. E. Litman (Eds.), *Youth suicide,* New York: Springer.

Berman, A. L. (1986). A critical look at our adolescence: Notes on turning 18 (and 75). *Suicide and Life-Threatening Behavior, 16,* 1–12.

Brent, D. (1986, May). *Report of study in Allegheny County on adolescent suicide.* Paper presented at Suicide in the Schools, Pittsburgh, PA.

Cantor, P. (1986, May). *Prevention, intervention, and postvention: National trends.* Paper presented at Suicide in the Schools, Pittsburgh, PA.

Cohen-Sandler, R., Berman, A., & King, R. A. (1982). Life stress and symptomatology: Determinants of suicidal behavior in children. *Journal of the American Academy of Child Psychiatry, 21*(2), 178–186.

Corder, B. F., & Haizlip, T. M. (1983). Recognizing suicidal behavior in children. *Resident and Staff Physician, 29,* 18–23.

Crumley, F. E. (1979). Adolescent suicide attempts. *Journal of the American Medical Association, 241,* 2404–2407.

Davis, J. M. (1985). Suicidal crises in schools. *School Psychology Review, 14,* 313–324.

Durkheim, E. (1951). *Suicide.* New York: Macmillan.

Eth, S., Pynoos, R. S., & Carlson, G. A. (1984). An unusual case of self-inflicted death in childhood. *Suicide and Life Threatening Behavior, 14,* 157–165.

Fairfax County Public Schools. (1985). *The adolescent suicide prevention program.* Available from Fairfax County Public Schools, 10210 Layton Hall Drive, Fairfax, VA 22030.

Feldman, R. P. (1984). Some special aspects of suicide in adolescence and youth. In N. Linzen (Ed.), *Suicide: The will to live vs. the will to die* (pp.101–112). New York: Human Sciences.

French, A. P., & Steward, M. J. (1975). Family dynamics, childhood depression, and attempted suicide in a 7-year old boy: A case study. *Suicide, 5,* 29–37.

Gernsbacher, L. M. (1985). *The suicide syndrome: Origins, manifestations, and alleviation of human self-destructiveness.* New York: Human Sciences.

Hafen, B. Q., & Frandsen, K. J. (1986). *Youth suicide: Depression and loneliness.* Provo, UT: Behavioral Health Associates.

Hammer, E. F. (1968). Projective drawings. In A. I. Rabin (Ed.), *Projective techniques in personality assessment.* New York: Springer.

Hammer, E. F. (1971). *The clinical application of projective drawings.* Springfield, IL: Thomas.

Hewett, J. H. (1980). *After suicide.* Philadelphia: Westminster.

Hutt, M. L. (1969). *The Hutt adaptation of the Bender–Gestalt test.* New York: Grune and Stratton.

Joan, P. (1986). *Preventing teenage suicide: The living alternative handbook.* New York: Human Sciences.

Karon, B. P. (1981). The Thematic Apperception Test (TAT). In A. I. Rabin (Ed.), *Assessment with projective techniques: A concise introduction.* New York: Springer.

Mack, J. E., & Hickler, H. (1981). *Vivienne: The life and suicide of an adolescent girl.* Boston: Little, Brown.

Maris, R. (1985). The adolescent suicide problem. *Suicide and Life-Threatening Behavior, 15,* 91-109.

McBrien, R. J. (1983, September). Are you thinking of killing yourself? Controlling students' suicidal thoughts. *School Counselor,* pp. 75–82.

Oppenheim, D. E. (1910). A report on Dr. Baer¢s publication *Suicide in Childhood. Minutes of the Vienna Psychoanalytic Society, 2,* 479–497.

Orbach, I., & Glaubman, H. (1979). The concept of death and suicidal behavior in young children. *Journal of the American Academy of Child Psychiatry, 18,* 668–678.

Orbach, I., Gross, Y., & Glaubman, H. (1981). Some common characteristics of latency-age suicidal children: A tentative model based on case study analysis. *Suicide and Life-Threatening Behavior, 11,* 180–190.

Paulson, M. J., Stone, D., & Sposto, R. A. (1978). Suicide potential and behavior in children ages 4 to 12. *Suicide and Life-Threatening Behavior, 8,* 225–242.

Peck, M. L., Farberow, N. C., & Litman, R. E. (1985). *Youth Suicide.* New York: Springer.

Pfeffer, C. R. (1978). Clinical observations of play of hospitalized suicidal children. *Suicide and Life-Threatening Behavior, 9,* 235–244.

Pfeffer, C. R. (1981). Suicidal behavior of children: A review with implications for research and practice. *American Journal of Psychiatry, 138,* 154–159.

Pfeffer, C. R. (1982). Interventions for suicidal children and their parents. *Suicide and Life-Threatening Behavior, 12,* 240–248.

Pfeffer, C. R. (1986). *The suicidal child.* New York: Guilford.

Pfeffer, C. R., Conte, H. R., Plutchik, R., & Jerrett, I. (1979). Suicidal behavior in latency-aged children: An empirical study. *Journal of the American Academy of Child Psychiatry, 18,* 679–692.

Pfeffer, C. R., Conte, H. R., Plutchik, R., & Jerrett, I. (1980). Suicidal behavior in latency-age children: An empirical study: An outpatient population. *Journal of the American Academy of Child Psychiatry, 19,* 703–710.

Pfeffer, C. R., Solomon, G., Plutchik, R., Mizruchi, M. S., & Weiner, A. (1982). Suicidal behavior in latency-age psychiatric in-patients: A replication and cross-validation. *Journal of the American Academy of Child Psychiatry, 21,* 564–569.

Pfeffer, C. R., Zuckerman, S., Plutchik, R., & Mizruchi, M. S. (1984). Suicidal behavior in normal school children: A comparison with child psychiatric in-patients. *Journal of the American Academy of Child Psychiatry, 23,* 416–423.

Poland, S. (1986). Suicide prevention in the public school: What can the school psychologist do? *Communique, 14,* 8–9.

Richman, J. (1978). Symbiosis, empathy, suicidal behavior, and the family. *Suicide and Life-Threatening Behavior, 8,* 139–149.

Richman, J. (1986). *Family therapy for suicidal people.* New York: Springer.

Rosenthal, P. A., & Rosenthal, S. (1984). Suicidal behavior by preschool children. *American Journal of Psychiatry, 141,* 520–525.

Ross, C. P. (1980). Mobilizing schools for suicide prevention. *Suicide and Life-Threatening Behavior, 10,* 239–244.

Ross, C. P. (1985). Teaching children the facts of life and death: Suicide prevention in the schools. In M. L. Peck,N. C. Farberow, & R. E. Litman, *Youth Suicide.* New York: Springer.

Santostefano, S., Rieder, C., & Berk, S. A. (1984). The structure of fantasized movement in suicidal children and adolescents. *Suicide and Life-Threatening Behavior, 14,* 3–16.

Schneidman, E. (1985). *Definition of suicide.* New York: Wiley.

Segal, J. (1975). Little boy little girl blue. *Family Health, 62,* 36–39.

Shaffer, D. (1986). Developmental factors in child and adolescent suicide. In M. Rutter, C. Rand & P. Read (Eds.), *Depression in young people: Developmental and clinical perspectives.* New York: Guilford.

Smith, K., & Crawford, S. (1986). Suicidal behavior among "normal" high school students. *Social & Life Threatening Behavior, 16,* 313–325.

Tishler, C. L., McKenry, P. C., & Morgan, K. C. (1981). Adolescent suicide attempts: Some significant factors. *Suicide and Life-Threatening Behavior, 11,* 86–92.

Toolan, J. (1968). Suicide and suicide attempts in childhood and adolescence. In M. Resnik (Ed.), *Suicidal behaviors: Diagnostic and management.* Boston: Little, Brown.

Toolan, J. (1975). Suicide in children and adolescents. *American Journal of Psychotherapy, 29,* 339–344.

Toolan, J. (1981). Depression and suicide in children: An overview, *American Journal of Psychotherapy, 35*(3), 311–322.

Vogel, R. B. (1968). A projective study of dynamic factors in attempted suicide (Doctoral dissertation, Michigan State University). *Dissertation Abstracts, 28,* 4303B.

Wenz, F. (1983). *Preventing self-destructive behavior among children and adolescents in the classroom.* Available from Fredrich V. Wenz, 114 Wakerobin Circle, Spartanburg, SC 2930l.

Wenz, F. (1984). *Children and suicide.* Available from Fredrich V. Wenz, 114 Wakerobin Circle, Spartanburg, SC 2930l.

Wieczorek, R. (1984). Adolescent suicide: Prevention and treatment. In N. Linzer (Ed.), *Suicide: The will to live vs. the will to die* (pp. 113–121). New York: Human Services.

Wohl, A., & Kaufman, B. (1985). *Silent screams and hidden cries.* New York: Brunner/Mazel.

BIBLIOGRAPHY: PROFESSIONALS

Fairfax County Public Schools. (1985). *The adolescent suicide prevention program.* Available form Fairfax County Public Schools, 10310 Layton Hall Drive, Fairfax, VA 22030.
Provides a detailed program from rationale, through organization and planning, to evaluation and review.

Joan, p. (1986). *Preventing teenage suicide: The living alternative handbook.* New York: Human Sciences.
Offers a program that has been developed for use with populations of middle school and high school age. The book has specific five-day programs, with "Goals and Means."

Peck, M. L., Farberow, N. C., & Litman, R. E. (1985). *Youth suicide.* New York: Springer.
This editorial work discusses psychodynamic issues, treatment issues, and methods of prevention.

Pfeffer, C. R. (1986). *The suicidal child.* New York: Guilford.
The most up-to-date work on the subject of child suicide; Pfeffer is the leading expert on childhood suicide. The text explores suicidal behavior, analyzes risk factors, and provides methods of assessment and treatment.

Richman, J. (1986). *Family therapy for suicidal people.* New York: Springer.
Reviews the origins of the suicidal crisis and provides methods of assessment and therapeutic interventions. This text is important in recognizing a suicidal youth as a "family problem."

BIBLIOGRAPHY: PARENTS

Baucom, J. Q. (1986). *Fatal choice.* Chicago: Moody.
Provides an excellent, easy-to-read overview of the problem of adolescent suicide, and offers methods that parents can institute to prevent suicide.

Bolton, I. M. (1983). *My son, my son.* Atlanta: Bolton.
This book represents the reactions of a mother (who is a counselor) to her son's suicide. This book provides excellent suggestions for dealing with the aftermath of suicide.

Hewett, J. H. (1980). *After suicide.* Philadelphia: Westminster.
Offers suggestions for both professionals and nonprofessionals in dealing with the aftermath of suicide.

Mack, J. E., & Hickler, H. (1981). *Vivienne: The life and suicide of an adolescent girl.* Boston: Little, Brown.
Discusses the true life story of a girl who commits suicide. the authors are able to bring in examples of Vivienne's diary to show her progression towards suicide. This book would also be appropriate for adolescents.

Children and Teasing

Robert D. Clark
National College of Education

BACKGROUND

> "I don't care what they call me," he said confidently, "So long as they don't call me what they used to call me at school." Ralph was fairly interested. "What was that?" The fat boy glanced over his shoulder, then leaned toward Ralph. He whispered, "They used to call me 'Piggy'." Ralph shrieked with laughter. He jumped up. "Piggy! Piggy!" "Ralph — please!" Piggy clasped his hands in apprehension. "I said I didn't want — " "Piggy! Piggy!" (Golding, 1954, p. 9)

The above excerpt from William Golding's classic novel *Lord of the Flies* serves to illustrate in a succinct and poignant way a number of points about children's teasing. The first is that the exchange between Ralph and Piggy exemplifies a type of teasing, that has as its purpose disparaging or "lording over" another. Second, the passage shows how Piggy, the victim, hands over the information used in the teasing episode by Ralph, the teaser. Third, the information that Piggy provides is an aspect of personal appearance over which he has little, if any, control. Fourth, the teasing occurs in a setting, in context, that could not be provided here, but that must be fully studied in order to understand the nature of the exchange. And, finally, if it is not already clear from Piggy's mournful plea, being the victim of teasing can be a very painful and scarring experience.

Teasing Defined

Keith-Spiegel (1972) commented about the myriad of labels, the imprecision of the terminology, and the lack of operational definitions for humor. Her way of characterizing humor as a "brier patch of terminology" (Keith-Spiegel, 1972, p. 14) might be an understatement when applied to the construct *teasing.* Reviewing the literature creates a challenge for the researcher. There is a considerable variety of synonyms for the term; in fact, the term rarely appears in literature apart from some other term. From a review of literature in sociology, anthropology, psychology, and education there were gleaned 66 terms or synonyms for teasing. These terms are found and grouped in Table 1.

The terms are grouped in Table 1 based on three definitions for teasing found in Webster's dictionary: (a) "to annoy or harass by persistent mocking or poking fun"; (b) "to urge persistently"; (c) "to tantalize or excite sexually in an unfulfilling way" (Guralnik, 1980, p. 1459). The first definition is perhaps the most commonly understood or accepted. Contained in this first grouping in Table 1 are several terms that are more widely used in the literature: disparaging, joking, kidding, and ridiculing. Each of these four terms could be used in place of teasing and would convey perhaps more precisely the semantic meaning of Definition 1. The remaining 42 terms under Definition 1 appeared in the literature reviewed as synonyms for teasing. The extensiveness of the list underscores the difficulty with definition and theory construction in this area. Definitions 2 and 3 (Table 1) are less widely discussed in the literature, but examples and instances of their occurrence among children and adults will be illustrated. There are, therefore, three cases or functional types of teasing that will be discussed in this chapter: *teasing-as-ridicule, teasing-as-encouragement,* and *teasing-as-enticement.*

Teasing-as-Ridicule (T-RID). As noted above, four terms are often used interchangeably in the literature: disparaging, joking, kidding, and ridiculing. The disparaging and ridiculing forms convey nearly the identical meaning — to make fun of, to put down, or to degrade in some way. Joking and kidding, however, convey in general a less harsh meaning. They may be defined as "anything that is done by one or more persons to arouse laughter in others" (Lundberg, 1969, p. 22). The joking and kidding forms of teasing communicate less malice in the exchange than do disparaging/ridiculing forms. The

TABLE 1

Teasing Synonyms Found in Professional Literature

Definition 1: "to mock or annoy"		Definition 2: "urge persistently"	Definition 2: "to tantalize or excite"
Annoying	Kidding	Cajoling	Alluring
Badgering	Laughing at	Coaxing	Arousing
Bantering	Making fun of	Drawing out	Attracting
Belittling	Mocking	Flattering	Baiting
Castigating	Name calling	Goading	Challenging
Chaffing	Parodying	Importuning	Deceiving
Criticizing	Persecuiting	Wheedling	Disappointing
Debasing	Playing with	Urging	Enticing
Degrading	Poking fun at		Exciting
Demeaning	Punning		Humoring
Deprecating	Putting down		Tantalizing
Deriding	Quizzing		Tempting
Disparaging	Razzing		
Dressing down	Ribbing		
Harassing	Ridiculing		
Hazing	Satirizing		
Heckling	Scapegoating		
Humiliating	Shaming		
Insulting	Taunting		
Jesting	Terrorizing		
Jibing	Tormenting		
Joking	Troubling		
Joshing	Victimizing		

distinctions between the synonymous terms for T-RID should not obscure the fact that the goal of the exchange is to provoke laughter in those who witness the interaction and in at least one of the participants. Finally, "the mirth-producing event — namely, disparagement — is thoroughly negative. There is nothing positive about the critical behavioral exchange" (Zillmann, 1983, p. 92). Most of the present discussion will focus on T-RID because of the greater emphasis it commands in the literature and because, to some degree, the other two types of teasing are subsumed under it.

There are few studies in the literature on Western societies that address the prevalence of T-RID apart from other behaviors such as physical aggression or fighting. However, three reports were found that provide information on teasing that was relatively free of conflation with other behaviors. Dallinger and Prince (1984) asked college students of both sexes to report how often they teased people and were teased themselves. They derived five categories of teasing by function, namely teasing for fun or affection, hurting, compliance, jealousy, and revenge. T-RID seems to best fit their second category, hurting. They reported that about 10% of the examples provided by their subjects fell into that category. When they asked how many of the students used teasing to hurt or embarrass, 20% of the sample responded that they had. No information is provided on differential incidence of teasing or victimization by sex of respondent.

Olweus (cited in Collins, 1986), in his research on teasing and bullying in schools, reported that 20% of the school-aged boys were involved. Half (10%) were perpetrators and half (10%) were victims. This study focused primarily on physical aggression, but it reported that behaviors such as T-RID usually preceded physical altercations. A 1984 National Association of Secondary School Principals study (cited in Collins, 1986) reported that 25% of the school-aged population, both male and female, feared being subjected to bullying and related teasing.

Yates (1986) reported that bullying and T-RID represent a serious problem in Japanese schools. Groups of school-aged children were reported to be victimizing and terrorizing other students verbally and physically. These activities are blamed for high rates of school absenteeism and several suicides.

Among primitive, non-Western tribal peoples, T-RID is widespread. Howell (1973), in the only publication devoted exclusively to teasing apart from other aggressive or social relationships, reported extensively on the ritualized, formal, and *expected* T-RID interactions among tribal peoples all over the world. There are strict rules to follow, defined roles to play, and texts that are to be utilized. The T-RID interactions occur between close friends and family members of both sexes, and there is clear understanding of the intent and purposes of the interactions. There are limited examples of these more formal, ritualized behaviors in Western societies, two of which are intersex teasing (Sykes, 1966), which will be addressed below, and "playing the dozens" among blacks (Baugh, 1983).

"Playing the dozens" or "doing the dozens" (Baugh, 1983) has been recognized as a form of ritualized exchange among blacks for some time. In the dozens, "males, and occasionally females, hurl ritual insults at one another, involving their mothers as target of the verbal assault" (Baugh, 1983, p. 26). These exchanges, Baugh reported, are reserved for intimates. These intimates understand the play and can predict the responses of the participants. To play with a nonintimate would be dangerous because there would be no way to predict the other's reaction.

Teasing-as-Encouragement (T-ENC). The second definition for teasing is "to encourage; to urge persistently." This notion underlying this definition is not often associated with that of the first definition of teasing. However, there are instances of its occurrence in the literature. The subjects in a study conducted by Dallinger and Prince (1984) reported that they both experienced and practiced instances of T-ENC, which the authors called "compliance gaining" (p. 4). This study revealed that about 20% of all the episodes of reported teasing were of the T-ENC variety. When the authors in a follow-up study asked another set of subjects what types of teasing behaviors they engaged in, about 25% of the subjects reported they often used this type of T-ENC. However, the subjects further reported that their attempts at gaining compliance met with limited success.

Finally, an instance of the coaxing type of teasing was reported in the autobiography of John D. McKee (1974), a newspaperman who was born with cerebral palsy. He was not expected to live, but he triumphed over his handicaps at the "encouragement" of his parents and family members. He did not take his first step until he was 6 years old. He often fell and only with great effort could rise to his feet. This excerpt illustrates one of those instances of T-ENC. "Why don't you sit on the floor, Jack? Anything that falls up we'll hand down to you" (p. 207). This kind of T-ENC took place in the supportive and nurturing atmosphere of his home. It illustrates not only his determination to succeed but the gentle way teasing was used and how he profited from it. As mentioned earlier, teasing cannot be understood apart from the context in which it occurs.

It is perhaps likely that T-ENC can only be effective when the teasers and the teased are very close and involved in a secure and trusting relationship such as a family. This is the context too for the participants in that special type of ritualized T-RID situation in primitive societies described above. Intimacy and personal knowledge of the participants are keys in this form of teasing.

Teasing-As-Enticing (T-ENT). The definition of this type of teasing is "to tantalize or excite sexually in an unfulfilling way" (Guralnik, 1980, p. 1459). The notion of the sexual tease can be traced to Freudian psychology. Mathis (1970) articulated this position as, "a little bit of the sexual tease is found in the average woman's personality" (p. 21). To him the sexual tease is any woman who by her wiles and physical flirtations attempts to incite physical desire in a man without serious intentions of fulfilling the desire thus aroused. He goes further and offers illustrations from clinical practice of the variety of motives for the sexual teases. In each characterization, a man is the victim of an alluring woman. Others have likewise explicated this position. Shoham, in her provocatively titled book *Sex as bait: EVE, Casanova, and Don Juan* (1983), makes the point of female coquettishness even more strongly than Mathis. This position holds that biologically and genetically the woman's role is to allure the victim, man, by her sexuality. The fulfillment of this union is held off until the very last moment when she is assured her mate will provide for her.

In light of more recent conceptualizations of male/female relationships (e.g., Chafetz, 1984), Goldstein and McGhee's (1972) statement about humor research can be just as serviceably applied here: "Psychoanalytic theory is limited in its capacity to stimulate further advancement along many important dimensions" (p. xix). Thus, it is necessary to turn elsewhere for enlightenment.

Handelman and Kapferer (1972) stated that "joking, or indeed any form of expressive behavior, is not only conditioned by the structure of the social context in which it occurs, but is also mediated and modified by the emergent form of joking activity itself" (p. 484). It is generally accepted that sexual teasing does occur. It is further understood that both sexes participate in this exchange equally. Syke's (1966) observations in a Glasgow printing factory are instructive here. He reported that sexual teasing among the factory workers was stratified along age and sex lines. Overt public displays of petting, kissing, and obscenities were common between younger women and older men. Between young men and young women, conversely, behavior was much more subdued in public. Private behavior was another matter. Young women shunned the older men in private, whereas young men were permitted much more license. The outwardly bawdy teasing, both physical and verbal, rather than inviting intimacy, seemed to inhibit it.

Decades of research with non-Western cultures has demonstrated that sexual teasing occurs for both sexes, serves to minimize hostility, and enables prospective sexual partners to "explore" their sexual relationship without having to enter into a premature, unwise marriage (see Christensen, 1963; Howell, 1973). Thus, T-ENT or sexual teasing, like the other two types, is a form of communication among members of a community. It may serve to reduce tension and to enable prospective partners to learn about each other with minimum risk.

A Theory of Teasing

The theory offered here is intended as a first step in a process of theory development, because teasing is often subsumed under other headings and categories. However, from the above review, some consistencies and patterns can be delineated. Figure 1 shows a conceptualization that places teasing within a theoretical structure.

FIGURE 1

Teasing as an aspect of human communication

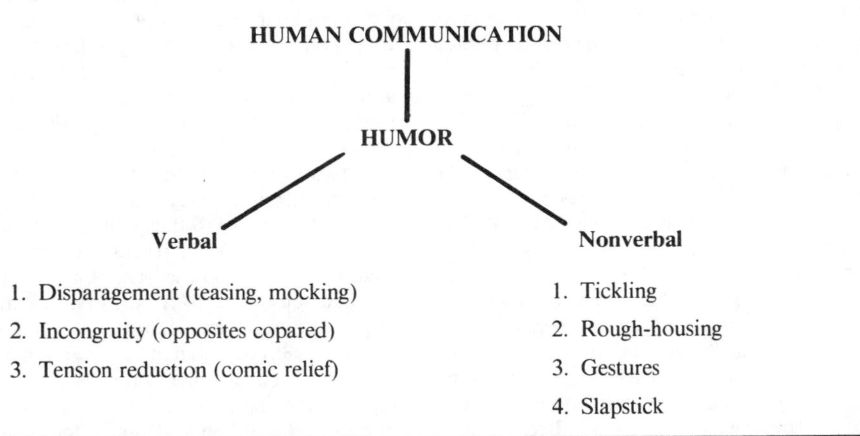

1. Disparagement (teasing, mocking)
2. Incongruity (opposites copared)
3. Tension reduction (comic relief)

1. Tickling
2. Rough-housing
3. Gestures
4. Slapstick

First teasing can be considered an instance of interpersonal expression. Communication can be verbal and nonverbal, but this discussion excludes nonverbal communication. Verbal teasing is related to language development. Because teasing is often associated with laughter, as in the passage from *Lord of the Flies*,it follows that teasing is contained within a theory of humor. Finally, though, the laughter that is concomitant with teasing is not the joyful kind but is often directed *at* someone: witness the expressions "poking fun at" and "laughing at." Thus,teasing is considered an aspect of disparagement humor.

There have been as many as 18 theories of humor proposed (McGhee & Goldstein, 1983). A detailed discussion here is not necessary since that is available elsewhere. However, three theories of humor are relevant: the superiority theory, the incongruity theory, and the tension reduction theory. The superiority theory postulates that laughing at someone establishes and reaffirms the status heirarchy (Chapman, 1983; Gruner, 1978). It is represented as the disparagement theory (Raskin, 1985; Zillmann, 1983) in Figure 1. The incongruity theory posits that humor is a consequence of the discrepancy between two mental representations, one expected and the other unexpected. the resolution of the incongruity (getting the joke) leads to laughter (Suls, 1983). The tension reduction theory or release theory (Raskin, 1985) stems from Freud's writings early in this century. Freud's explanations have since fallen into disfavor (Goldstein & McGhee, 1972), but the theory is now subsumed under an arousal theory that states that anticipation of the joke heightens arousal, which is released with the getting of the joke.

The disparagement theory (Zillman, 1983) is based on the dichotomy of sentiment and is sometimes called the dispositional theory of humor. The dichotomy occurs when both negative and positive elements are present when one witnesses an instance of disparagement. Simply stated, the stronger the animosity felt toward the disparaged person or thing, the greater the enjoyment of the event. The greater the positive feeling toward the disparaged person or thing, the less the enjoyment of it.

DEVELOPMENT

Teasing, Language Development, and Humor

Teasing Innate. Freud (cited in Suls, 1983) believed that the "cathartic" evocative aspect of humor and its expression is innately programmed in the individual. The expression of humor by the individual is disguised by symbolism. The symbols mask the true hostility, or as termed here T-RID, in humor. Freud was the first to point out the sexual and aggressive content in jokes. However, the cathartic function of humor, the release of accumulated hostility, has not been supported by research to date (Suls, 1983). Although Freud's theory has prompted much research, it has not been substantiated.

No other theorists reviewed support a truly innate theory of humor development. Beyond the basic intact, normally functioning individual all other theories support the view that the development of humor and teasing arises out of day-to-day interchange in social contexts. The laugh, the smile, and language expression itself are believed to be innately programmed into the organism, but all other forms of interaction are acquired or learned. It would seem more fruitful (Buckalew & Coffield, 1978; Chapman, 1983; Fine, 1983) to study the development of teasing behavior in social contexts.

Teasing, Language, and Cognitive Development. Language development arises when infants are exposed to and imitate people in their environment. Imitation of sounds and behaviors begins very early in their development. These behaviors are reinforced and they in fact begin to "play" with the sounds of words on their own.

McGhee (1976, 1983) proposed that humor development and cognitive development are parallel stages. The reader is referred to other sources for further details of the theory (McGhee, 1976). What is relevant is that McGhee and others (Brodzinsky, 1975; Brodzinsky, Tew & Palkovitz, 1979; Suls, 1983) have reported substantiation of this stage theory for humor development through the first 7 or 8 years of life. Very little study of humor in adolescents has yet been done.

The major points about the comprehension and appreciation of humor are relevant to the present discussion. Children below the age of 2 years begin to play with words in violating semantic categories by deliberately mislabeling objects (e.g., "box" for "shoe") and gleefully playing with adults in these one- and two-word games. In the next stage they begin to realize that words have reality apart form the objects and begin phonetic game patterns. At this stage, children begin to form incongruity humor, incompatible opposites. The following interchange might occur between parent and child: "Why does Daddy wear a tie?" — "Because it's a custom," to which the child teases, "Is Daddy a custom?" The first forms of humor concern those objects or concepts to which the child is not strongly attached (nontendentious). It is at the next stage, between 3 and 7 years of age, that children develop tendentious humor and true teasing behaviors. This means that children as early as preschool years exhibit "patterns of response of disparagement" (McGhee, 1983, p. 116). By this stage children have developed preferences (dispositions) for objects and persons such that criticism, teasing, and disparagement of these persons and things causes the children discomfort (when the affront is "against" their preferred thing or person) or enjoyment (when the affront "favors" their preferred thing or object).

An example will facilitate the understanding of this point. Billy, Tommy, and Carl are playing. Billy likes Carl but Tommy does not. While playing Carl falls and gets mud on his face, Tommy calls Carl a "mud face" and makes him cry. Billy gets angry and takes his toys and goes home with Carl. McGhee (1983) believes that this outcome could have been predicted on the basis of a knowledge of the preferences (dispositions) of the children in question.

Comprehension and appreciation of humor seem to develop differently and this has implications for teasing behavior (Brodzinsky, 1975; Brodzinsky et al., 1979; McGhee, 1971, 1976). Comprehension of humor is related to levels of cognitive development and problem-solving style. More reflective and cognitively advanced children comprehend humor earlier and better than more impulsive children. Comprehension improves with age, but appreciation of humor does not seem to be related to cognitive ability. In fact, more mirth may be shown by impulsive children (Brodzinsky et al., 1979). This has implications for the ways children respond to humor and disparagement in school. Impulsive and cognitively less adept children may show more response to others' misfortunes. Furthermore, this group may create situations in which others are subject to ridicule so that they can enjoy the results. This would seem to be a fruitful area of research.

Teasing and Families. Children develop the disposition to appreciation and creation of disparaging, T-RID situations by their preschool years. Thus, there are critical periods in respect to teasing well before most children are exposed to a larger peer group. The interactions among family members, therefore, as in most other aspects of children's lives, plays the pivotal role in teasing.

Kessler (1966) speculated that in families "teasing is not an uncommon way of demonstrating affection" (p. 436), but a child has difficulty in sorting out the ridicule from the warmth. What results, she surmised, is that the child is left "hurt, confused, angry, and with little defense except to retort in kind" (p. 437). Apparently, her speculations have received empirical support. Floyd (cited in Collins, 1986) has studied bullies in school who tease, taunt, and bully other vulnerable children. Floyd reported that the "bully at school is usually the victim at home" (p. 8). When a victim is not readily available, these bullies strive to create one. Floyd's explanation for the bully's behavior is that they torment victims who remind them of their own humiliation at home.

Bandura and Walters (1970) studied adolescent aggression in boys and found many of the same characteristics reported by Floyd. They reported that the aggressive boys lack a close, affectional relationship with a parent, particularly a father. The parents of these boys "resorted more freely to such methods as ridicule, physical punishment, and deprivation of privileges" (p. 100). It seems likely, then, that teasing, especially T-RID, is learned largely at home.

There is some evidence to support the notion that girls who are ridiculed in the home are much more likely to become less interested in school work, to become sexually active at an earlier age, and ultimately to become pregnant out of wedlock and to drop out of school (Chilman, 1983; Janus, 1981).

Teasing's Victims. Though this topic has not had much specific research, some characteristics can be drawn from the literature. The opening quote from Golding (1954) illustrates some of the characteristics of victims. They are usually persons who are perceived as the least able to defend themselves and as the least threatening to the bully ("How different", 1971). As Piggy does for Ralph, the victim sometimes provides the information or occasion for T-RID to the bully or teaser. It is as if the victim has hung out a "kick me" sign. Floyd (cited in Collins, 1986) pointed out that bullies are attracted to victims as if in some strange symbiotic, parasitic relationship. The participants are seemingly helpless to extricate themselves from the relationship. This can happen in families (Kessler, 1966) as well as in peer relationship ("Trouble," 1985).

Victims, however, should not be blamed for the pain that is foisted on them by others. As Floyd (cited in Collins, 1986) and Yates (1986) have reported, those in need of a victim will make one if one is not otherwise provided.

Teasing: Sex and Racial Differences. Boys are reported to engage in physical and verbal assaults more frequently than girls in sexually mixed play groups (Barnett & Fiscella, 1985). When interacting in same-sex social groups, boys also exhibit more kidding and teasing (Fine, 1983). Boys also are reported to be adept at T-RID toward girls (Coveney, Jackson, Jeffreys, Kaye, & Mahoney, 1984). Finally, girls are reported to be more vulnerable to such intersex teasing because of their inherently lower status in families and peer groups (Constantine & Martinson, 1981).

Teasing and enjoyment of disparagement humor has been explored in relation to different reference groups (RG) (LaFave, 1972), but most of the work has been conducted with adults. In general, it is necessary to determine an individual's identification with a RG prior to evaluating the appreciation of disparaging humor. Membership in a racial, sexual, or ethnic group does not necessarily mean an individual will be psychologically disposed to that group in reference to evaluation of appreciation of humor directed against that RG. Buckalew and Coffield (1978) found that black males tended to rate racially or sexually demeaning jokes as funnier than male or female whites, or female blacks. Zillman (1983) reported on a study in which black, Mexican-American and white children at three age levels, 3, 5, and 7 years, were asked to rate funniness of degrading accidents for same and different RGs. Only white children (3-year and 5-year age groups) found it funnier to see a child of another, racial or ethnic group degraded than to see a child of their own kind so treated. The difference was even greater for white males than females. Finally, Peterson (1975) reported that among a mixed racial teaching staff, blacks, especially black males, were much more adept at using joking and teasing to explore social boundaries. White males had the most difficulty in these teasing situations.

PUTTING TEASING IN PERSPECTIVE

Teasing has not been researched as a construct separate from humor and physical aggression. As a result the terminology is vague and not adequately operationalized. One of the first needs for the practitioner and the researcher is a consistent, clear definition of teasing that is separate from humor, physical aggression, and other forms of communication. The separation of teasing into different functional categories, namely teasing as ridicule, encouragement, or enticement should promote an appreciation and recognition of teasing as a separate construct.

The development of verbal teasing behavior needs to be better understood. Some tentative conclusions have been reported in the literature: (a) As early as 3 years of age children form dispositions toward people and things; (b) based on these dispositions they are able to appreciate, react to, and practice disparagement or T-RID behavior. However much more needs to be learned about the development of this awareness, its malleability, and the relationship to cognitive and language development.

Data on incidence of teasing show that about 20% of the school-age population has experienced teasing, likely T-RID, at some time. This figure seems exceedingly low, to judge from clinical observations and personal accounts (Milgram & Sciarra, 1974). Dallinger and Prince (1984) found that virtually 100% of their sample of college students reported incidents of teasing. Again, it is likely that teasing, whether T-RID, T-ENC, or T-ENT, has been lumped with some other construct such as physical aggression and the reported data mask the true frequency of the experience.

Some conclusions about teasers and victims of teasing also have been reported: It is likely that those who use T-RID have been victims of T-RID themselves. They pass on hurt they have experienced to others, who then become victims. There is some evidence that there is a cycle of victimization among school-age populations (Floyd, cited in Collins, 1986). More needs to be known about these partners in victimization to better understand and thus intervene to break the cycle.

Race, sex, and ethnicity play a role in teasing behavior. Some tentative observations are offered. A special kind of T-RID, the dozens, is practiced among predominantely young black males (Baugh, 1983). This is a ritualized game among intimates and does not have a known counterpart in the white community. This is a different form of teasing than T-RID. It is likely that there are other racial or ethnic groups who have similar rituals. It would be important for school professionals to know about such practices. Several studies have reported that white males enjoy the disparagement of others much more than the disparagement of their own cohort group. No other group including white females showed this differential reaction. Teased females suffer more than males because of their lower social role (Chafetz, 1984). Research is needed to clarify the role of race, sex, and disparagement appreciation and enactment.

Sexual teasing or T-ENT presents an interesting and distinct phenomenon. It cannot be neatly placed in the context of humor theory, though it clearly is a form of communication. Psychoanalytic theory aside, T-ENT is practiced, sometimes vigorously, by both sexes. Anthropological studies note its prevalence in many societies. The mechanisms that govern its practice, especially in adolescence, need to be studied.

Finally, the roles of context and supportive environment need to be explored. It appears that some victims victimize others through teasing. The role of environment in the promotion and support of all types of teasing is yet another aspect of teasing that begs for further investigation.

ALTERNATIVE ACTIONS

A good problem solver is likely, first, a good problem finder. This means that it is important for school psychologists to learn as much as possible about the variables that pertain to clients and their social settings prior to deciding on any course of action. Therefore, the reader's first action must be to determine what role(s) to play and at what level(s) of intervention. The following are some suggestions in regard to teasing behavior.

Primary Prevention

The goal of primary prevention is to preclude problems from arising. There are several actions that can be taken to prevent the harmful effects of teasing. First, teachers can be informed through routine consultations or more formally through in-service instruction of the present knowledge, sparce as it is, about teasing. For example, children come to schools with well-developed preferences (propositions) about many things including their classmates. Instruments such as sociograms can be used to learn about these preferences so that teachers can head off potential confrontations before they occur. McGhee (1983) believes that through content analyses of sociograms and other preference instruments the incidence of teasing can be predicted and minimized.

Research has shown that boys are more likely to engage in teasing and other forms of aggression than girls. This predisposition is mitigated to some degree by cognitive ability and learning style. Impulsive boys (Brodzinsky, 1975; McGhee, 1983) are likely to tease more and to be involved in more boisterous play and joking. Armed with this knowledge, teachers can arrange groupings and small group activities to separate those who might have difficulty.

Floyd (cited in Collins, 1986) has identified some characteristics of victims of teasing and their abusers. Victims have been found to be shy and withdrawn, physically somewhat smaller, timid, lacking in self-confidence, and likely not to strike back when challenged. Through assertiveness training prior to major incidents, these children can learn how to avoid trouble situations and what to do when presented with one (Hokanson, 1970). Likewise, abusers can be identified for group and individual counseling prior to any major confrontations.

Parenting and appropriate modeling are extremely important for appropriate child development (Bandura & Walters, 1970; Staub, 1975). Education of parents regarding child-rearing practices can serve to encourage parents to develop nurturing, positive, warm, ridicule-free relationships with their children.

Secondary and Tertiary Prevention

The goals of secondary and tertiary prevention are to minimize the impact and duration of occurrences of teasing. The actions and interventions used in primary prevention can be applied, but because children are already involved in undesirable activities, other measures are necessary.

Measures can be undertaken with teachers to insure that they are aware of the prestigious position they hold in their students' lives. If teachers ridicule children, it can have a devastating impact on their sense of selves.

Walters (1970) has pointed out that there can be serious consequences for witnessing students when children who are powerful and are looked up to are not punished for teasing or bullying. The punishment needs to be fair and humane, but it also must be made known to the other children so they will connect it with the offense. If offenders are not punished, weaker children might imitate the model and develop behavior that they would not have under a more disciplined regimen.

SUMMARY

Teasing is recognized as a type of communication between people, but there is little agreement on operational definitions. Ridicule, joking, and kidding are terms that are often used interchangeably with teasing. Three functional definitions for teasing have been presented — teasing as ridicule, as encouragement, and as enticement. Teasing was also discussed in the context of a disparagement theory of humor.

It is likely that everyone suffers teasing at one time or another, (Dallinger & Prince, 1983). However, because teasing is often confounded with aggression or some aspect of humor, its true prevalence is not known.

Special cases of teasing, "playing the dozens" and sexual teasing, seem to be rooted in more ancient, formalized rituals that have had careful study by other disciplines than psychology. The psychological dimensions of teasing especially teasing-as-ridicule have still to be adequately studied. Teasing-as-ridicule is rarely presented as a positive experience, except, perhaps, for the teaser. Even that exception is called into question because teasers are most likely victims themselves. It appears that the cycle of victim prey on victim cannot change without some outside intervention.

The negative impact of teasing on children in particular can be ameliorated through intervention by school psychologists. Appropriate interventions are discussed at the primary, secondary, and tertiary levels.

REFERENCES

Bandura, A., & Walters, R. H. (1970). Adolescent aggression. In E. I. Megargee & J. E. Hokanson (Eds.), *The dynamics of aggression* (pp.89–100). New York: Harper & Row.

Barnett, L. M., & Fiscella, J. (1985). A child by any other name . . . A comparison of the playfulness of gifted and nongifted children. *Gifted Child Quarterly, 29,* 61–66.

Baugh, J. (1983). *Black street speech: Its history, structure, and survival.* Austin, TX: University of Texas Press.

Brodzinsky, D. M. (1975). the role of conceptual tempo and stimulus characteristics in children's humor development. *Developmental Psychology, 11,* 843–850.

Brodzinsky, D. M., Tew, J. D., & Palkovitz, R. (1979). Control of humorous affect in relation to children's conceptual tempo. *Developmental Psychology, 15,* 275–279.

Buckalew, L. W., & Coffield, K. E. (1978). Relationship of reference group to perception of humor. *Perceptual and Motor Skills, 47,* 143–146.

Chafetz, J. D. (1984). *Sex and advantage: A comparative, macro-structural theory of sex stratification.* Towowa, NJ: Rowman & Allanheld.

Chapman, A. J. (1983). Humor and laughter in social interaction and some implications for humor research. In P. E. McGhee & J. H. Goldstein (Eds.), *Handbook of humor research: Vol. 1. Basic issues* (pp.133–157). New York: Springer-Verlag.

Chilman, C. S. (1983). *Adolescent sexuality in a changing American society: Social and psychological perspectives for the human services professions* (2nd ed.). New York: Wiley.

Christensen, J. B. (1963). Utani! Joking, sexual license and social obligation among the Luguru. *American Anthropologist, 63,* 1314–1327.

Collins, G. (1986, June 20). Bullies trying to beat something in their own lives, science finds. *Chicago Tribune,* Section 5, p. 8.

Constantine, L. L., & Martinson, F. M. (Eds.). (1981). *Children and sex! New findings, new perspectives.* Boston: Little, Brown.

Coveny, L., Jackson, M., Jeffreys, S., Kaye, L., & Mahoney, P. (1984). *The sexuality papers: Male sexuality and the social control of women.* London: Hutchinson.

Dallinger, J. M., & Prince, N. (1984). *Teasing: Goals and responses* (Report No. CS 504 788). Paper presented at the meeting of the Speech Communication Association, Chicago. (ERIC Document Reproduction Service No. ED 251 879)

Fine, G. A. (1983). Sociological approaches to the study of humor. In P. E. McGhee & J. H. Goldstein (Eds.), *Handbook of humor research: Vol. l. Basic issues* (pp. 157–186). New York: Springer-Verlag.

Golding, W. (1954). *Lord of the flies.* New York: Capricorn.

Goldstein, J. H., & McGhee, P. E. (Eds.). (1972). *The psychology of humor: Theoretical perspectives and empirical issues.* New York: Academic.

Gruner, C. R. (1978). *Understanding laughter: The workings of wit and humor.* Chicago: Nelson-Hall.

Guralnik, D. B. (Ed.). (1980). *Webster's new world dictionary.* Cleveland, OH: Collins.

Handelman, D., & Krapferer, B. (1972). Forms of joking activity: A comparative approach. *American Anthropologist, 74,* 484–495.

Hokanson, J. E. (1970). Psychophysical evaluation of the catharsis hypothesis. In E. I. Megargee & J. E. Hokanson (Eds.), *The dynamics of aggression.* New York: Harper & Row.

How different is my child? Why do they tease my child? (1971). *The Exceptional Parent, 1*(2), 23–26.

Howell, R. W. (1973). *Teasing relationships.* An Addison-Wesley Module in Anthropology, No. 46, Reading, MA: Addison-Wesley.

Janus, S. (1981). *The death of innocence: How our children are endangered by the new sexual freedom.* New York: Morrow.

Keith-Spiegel, P. (1972). Early conceptions of humor: Varieties and issues. In J. H. Goldstein & P. E. McGhee (Eds.), *The psychology of humor: Theoretical perspectives and empirical issues* (pp. 3–39). New York: Academic.

Kessler, J. W. (1966). *Psychopathology of childhood.* Englewood Cliffs, NJ: Prentice-Hall.

LaFave, L. (1972). Humor judgments as a function of reference groups and identification classes. In J. H. Goldstein & P. E. McGhee (Eds.), *The psychology of humor: Theoretical perspectives and empirical issues* (pp. 195–210). New York: Academic.

Lundberg, C. C. (1969). Person-focused joking! Pattern and function. *Human Organization, 28,* 22–28.

Mathis, J. L. (1970). The sexual tease. *Medical Aspects of Human Sexuality. 4*(12), 21–25.

McGhee, P. E. (1971). Cognitive development and children's comprehension of humor, *Child Development, 42,* 123–138.

McGhee, P. E. (1976). Children's appreciation of humor: A test of the cognitive congruity principle. *Child Development, 47,* 420–426.

McGhee, P. E. (1983). Humor development: Toward a life span approach. In P. E. McGhee & J. H. Goldstein (Eds.), *Handbook of humor research: Vol. 1. Basic issues* (pp. 109–134). New York: Springer-Verlag.

McGhee, P. E., & Goldstein, J. H. (Eds.). (1983). *Handbook of humor research: Vol. 1. Basic issues.* New York: Springer-Verlag.

McKee, J. D. (1974). Selection from "Two legs to stand on." In J. I. Milgram & D. J. Sciarra (Eds.), *Childhood revisited* (pp.198–208). New York: Macmillan.

Milgram, J. I., & Sciarra, D. J. (Eds.). (1974). *Childhood revisited.* New York: Macmillan.

Peterson, J. H., Jr. (1975). Black–white joking relationships among newly-integrated faculty. *Integrated Education, 13,* 33–37.

Raskin, V. (1985, October). Jokes: A linguist explains his new semantic theory of humor. *Psychology Today,* pp. 34–39.

Shoham, S. G. (1983). *Sex as bait: Eve, Casanova, and Don Juan.* St. Lucia, Queensland, Australia: University of Queensland Press.

Staub, E. (1975). To rear a prosocial child: Reasoning, learning by doing, and learning by teaching others. In D. J. DePalma & J. M. Foley (Eds.), *Moral development: Current theory and research* (pp. 113–135). Hillside, NJ: Lawrence Erlbaum.

Suls, J. (1983). Cognitive processes in humor appreciation. In P. E. McGhee & J. H. Goldstein (Eds.), *Handbook of humor research: Vol. 1. Basic issues* (pp. 39–57). New York: Springer-Verlag.

Sykes, A. J. M. (1966). Joking relationships in an industrial setting. *American Anthropologist, 68,* 188–193.

The trouble began as soon as school started: Teasing and the disabled child. (1985). *Exceptional Child. 15,* 36–44.

Walters, R. H. (1970). Implications of laboratory studies of aggression for the control and regulation of violence. In E. I. Megargee & J. E. Hokanson (Eds.), *The dynamics of aggression* (pp. 124–131). New York: Harper & Row.

Yates, R. E. (1985, November 24). Japanese twist bullying into a brutal art. *Chicago Tribune,* Section 5, p.1.

Zillmann, D. (1983). Disparagement humor. In P. E. McGhee & J. H. Goldstein (Eds.), *Handbook of humor research: Vol. 1. Basic issues* (pp. 85–107). New York: Springer-Verlag.

BIBLIOGRAPHY: PROFESSIONALS

Dallinger, J. M., & Prince, N. (1984). *Teasing: Goals and responses* (Report No. CS 504 788). Paper presented at the meeting of the Speech Communication Association, Chicago. (ERIC Document Reproduction Service No. ED 251 879)
One of the few recent studies to focus specifically on teasing separately from humor, aggression, or related subjects. Three different studies were conducted with college-age students focusing on the purposes of teasing and the reaction to it.

Dinkmeyer, D., & Dinkmeyer, D. (1982). *Developing understanding of self and others* (DUSO-2). Circle Pines, MN: American Guidance Service.
A counseling kit of activities and materials developed to help teachers and other professionals help children deal with developmental and other life situations.

Heinz, R. S. (1974). *A biography for young children: Birth through eight years — Affective domain.* (Report No. PS 012 374). Flagstaff, AZ: Northern Arizona University, College of Education. (ERIC Document Reproduction Service No. ED 206 402).
An annotated bibliography of literature for young children with 504 citations. The topics range from anger, loneliness, perseverance to *teasing,* trust, and work values. A good single source of recommended readings for children and parents.

Howell, R. W. (1973). *Teasing relationships.* An Addison-Wesley Module in Anthropology. No. 46. Reading, MA: Addison-Wesley.
A brief monograph that explores the ways in which actually and nominally close relationships are symbolized through teasing. A useful summary of cross-national conceptions and actual instances of teasing relationships. Focuses very little on children's behavior, however.

Zillmann, D. (1983). Disparagement humor. In P. E. McGhee, & J. H. Goldstein (Eds.), *Handbook of humor research: Vol. 1, Basic issues* (pp. 85–107). New York: Spring-Verlag.
Chapter focuses on theoretical development of disparagement humor. Provides an overview of theoretical discussions and explanations of humor which is aimed *at* someone.

BIBLIOGRAPHY: PARENTS AND CHILDREN

Blume, J. (1986). *Letters to Judy: What your kids wish they could tell you.* New York: Putnam's.
For children from primary to high school age. Letters written by readers of Judy Blume books with comments from the author provide a view of children's worlds not often revealed. The letters talk particularly of the pressure and harassment the children suffer.

Blume, J. (1974). *Blubber.* Scarsdale, NY: Bradbury.
For children 12 years old and younger. The story of a young child who is taunted by peers because of overweight. It provides children with a look at prejudice that is all too real.

Miles, M. (1970). *Gertrude's pocket.* New York: Little, Brown.
For children 9 years old and younger. Gertrude is continually teased by Wilson, a classmate and her brother's friend. One day he trips her and she rips her new dress. In an argument she rips his shirt, his only shirt. She feels guilty and reluctantly does something about it.

Turkle, B. (1969). *My friend, Obadish.* New York: Viking.
For children 9 years old and younger. Also available from Viking (1971) in filmstrip and audio cassette.
A story about a young Quaker boy in nineteenth century Nantucket who frees a trapped sea gull that has been following him and causing the other boys to tease him.

Wise, W. (1961). *The cowboy surprise.* New York: Putnam's.
For children in grades 1–3. Two children meet a famous cowboy hero and find to their surprise that he, like them, has to wear glasses.

Children and Television

Theodore A. Ridder
Belding Area Schools, Michigan

BACKGROUND

Children spend as much as 30 hours a week watching television. By the time they graduate from high school they have spent 12,000 hours with the school curriculum and 18,000 hours with the TV curriculum (Moody, 1980). While there are positive aspects to the influence television exerts, the bulk of the literature seems to focus on the negative aspects. It seems reasonable for school psychologists to be most concerned with those aspects as well. Parents, who seem to feel powerless to control access to television (Charren & Sandler, 1984), sometimes point to the educational value of certain programs. Interviews with children, however, suggest that little time is spent watching such programs. They speak mostly about specific characters, specific situation comedies, specific crime dramas, and cartoons (Dorr, 1983). Over half of the nominations for "one favorite show" on a 1978 survey of 4,000 children were accounted for by seven shows: *Charlie's Angels, Happy Days, The Incredible Hulk, Hardy Boys, Baby, I'm Back, Good Times,* and *Three's Company.* While over 99% of the respondents were acquainted with *Charlie's Angels,* only 25% had ever heard of *Nova* (Mielke, Chen, Clarke, & Myerson-Katz, 1978).

Neil Postman, in his book *The Disappearance of Childhood* (1982), argues that childhood, as we know it, is a fairly recent historical development. He links the prolonged special status of children with the advent of printing and the consequent necessity for an extended period of formal education. Television, he points out, has the potential to replace the printed word as the primary medium for communicating cultural knowledge. Such a change could, in his view, herald a return to the medieval concept of children beyond the age of reason as simply adults who are not yet fully grown.

Postman's sobering vision may seem outrageous, but major sociological changes often evolve through introduction of apparently innocuous technology. An accurate prediction of the affects of introducing gun powder into Western culture would probably have been seen as preposterous at the time. Television impacts on the social and emotional development of children (Bandura, 1977). It is altering the nature of the routine demand for attention control in the environment of many children (Anderson & Bryant, 1983). The emphasis television places on the visual or simultaneous could actually be producing fundamental changes in the habitual thinking processes of children (Singer, 1983).

DEVELOPMENT

TV Violence, Aggressive Behavior, and Sterilization

As early as 1963 Albert Bandura demonstrated that the aggressive behavior of children could be affected by allowing them to view other children performing aggressive acts followed by differential consequences. Building on this early research, Bandura derived general principles that explain the development of motivation and new behavior through the modeling process (Bandura, 1977). Consistent with reinforcement theory, the probability of imitation is related to the viewer's perception of the modeled behavior as having produced success or failure. Bandura also introduced the concept of identification as an important predictor of imitation and related it to the observer's impression of the model as being a generally successful or powerful person. It is in this regard that he pointed to the capability of television to program a context that provides models with incredible, even invincible power. Occasionally school psychologists have the opportunity to observe the strength of some children's identification with such superheroes as Rambo or The Incredible Hulk.

A 1982 project funded by the National Institute of Mental Health (NIMH) produced the following conclusion:

> Recent research confirms the earlier findings of a causal relationship between viewing television violence and aggressive behavior . . . The scientific support for the causal relationship derives from the convergence of findings from many studies, the great majority of which demonstrate a positive relationship between television violence and later aggressive behavior. (pp. 89–90)

The 1972 report of the U.S. Surgeon General's Scientific Advisory Committee on Television and Social Behavior, from which Bandura was excluded at the request of the industry, and to which the NIMH study was a follow-up, presented a less decisive conclusion. According to Doerken (1983)

> Interestingly enough, a subsequent . . . hearing on the Report's conclusions revealed that the majority of non-network participants felt the data sufficiently strong to warrant a "causal relationship" between TV aggression and violence in society. It was the network representatives on the Advisory Committee who exerted power over the summary by requesting the "modest" findings. (p. 52)

The Surgeon General's spoken testimony was considerably stronger than the report. He too labeled the relationship causal and drew attention to a phenomenon referred to as sterilization (U.S. Senate, 92nd Congress, 1972). Through this technique those aspects of violent action that elicit negative emotional response are systematically withheld or minimized to render the violence less repulsive. Only weak and impersonal victims are included to prevent strong identification with the victim. Violence is shown primarily between strangers rather than intimates. Camera angles are arranged and techniques such as "cutting away" are employed to insure that the viewer does not have to witness the emotionally unsettling details of the violent act. Sterilization works so subtly that people tend to notice it only by contrast. An example of unsterilized violence occurred in the Washington Redskins versus New York Giants game in 1985 when Joe Theismann's leg was broken.

Sterilization appears to be even more harmful than the presentation of unsterilized violence (Huesmann, 1982). It may enable a process that resembles the systematic desensitization procedure used by behavior therapists to treat phobias (Lazarus, 1971). Just as very gradual introduction of the aversive elements is the key to successful systematic desensitization therapy (Lazarus, 1964), very gradual desterilization could be expected to yield progressive reduction of the emotional discomfort associated with viewing graphic violence. It seems improbable that the movie *A Clockwork Orange,* which recently played on Home Box Office, produced the degree of emotional discomfort in audiences that it produced when originally released in 1972. Another 13 years of gradual desterilization might bring a day when audiences would no longer experience major discomfort viewing an event such as Theismann's injury.

Formal Features, Attention, and School Learning

While *content* refers to the information or message a program provides, the term *formal features* refers to the techniques or methods employed. They include tight framing of faces, rapid scene changes, zooms, pans, fades, background music, animation, special effects, motion sequences, volume fluctuation, nonhuman voices, and numerous other tools of the medium.

There is little question that formal features, especially segment length, can and do function to enhance the attention of children (Anderson & Bryant, 1983; Krull, 1983; Lesser, 1972). The probability of looking away from television during the first two or three seconds after making eye contact is quite high. The probability of looking away after 15 seconds of continuous viewing is much lower and remains stable thereafter. This phenomenon is called *attentional inertia* (Anderson & Lorch, 1983). It appears to sustain cognitive involvement over gaps in comprehension or interruptions in content. The time required to reach maximum attentional inertia is longer for younger children (Krull, 1983). Older children appear to have learned to recognize, and tune out more quickly, the formal elements that signal for them low probability of comprehension or interest. Such formal features include adult voices and framed adult head and shoulder shots that signal news broadcasts, documentaries, and talk shows. Signals of high probability of comprehension are formal features such as nonhuman or children's voices, upbeat background music, and animation (Huston & Wright, 1983). This suggests that TV may be providing children with considerable practice at tuning out teacher surrogates long before entering kindergarten.

Contrary to the implication in journalist Marie Winn's popular book *The Plug-In Drug* (1977), attentional inertia and formal features do not really keep children mesmerized with their eyes glued to the screen. When given the opportunity to play with toys simultaneously, which is the way they "watch" in their homes, most children look away from the TV much of the time (Alwitt, Anderson, Lorch, & Levin, 1980; Anderson & Levin, 1976).

It was demonstrated that the availability of toys, which decreased attention to television, did not necessarily interfere with comprehension (Lorch, Anderson, & Levin, 1979). This finding created a paradox, because it was clear that children could not have responded correctly on the comprehension questions presented unless eye contact had been on the screen at the exact moment when the corresponding bit of information was presented. The dilemma spotlighted the role of auditory cuing, an important mechanism through which the production, rather than the viewer, controls attention. It appears that, while formal *visual* production techniques contribute to the duration of attention once eye contact has been established, re-initiation of eye contact and subsequent comprehensibility is largely accomplished by strategic *auditory* cuing to the critical content or plot elements (Anderson & Lorch, 1983; Bryant, Zillmann, & Brown, 1983). Simply stated, children are routinely warned by enticing auditory stimuli immediately prior to critical plot elements to insure that comprehension is not completely lost. If children develop habitual dependence upon such cuing or highlighting, the implications for success in a traditional classroom are obvious. Not only would important content be missed through failure to sustain constant attention, but eventually, comprehensibility would be completely lost because enhanced vigilance would not be cued at the crucial points in the presentation.

Unfortunately, auditory attention to television content has received little research focus. Friedlander (1975), however, does confirm anecdotal impressions that children appear strikingly insensitive to the meaningfulness of dialogue on television.

Researchers in the area of children's television viewing usually define attention as eye contact or, occasionally, as channel selection. Some cognitive psychologists might consider this method naive. There is basis for believing that the process of attending for purposes of gaining information may be fundamentally different from the process of attending for purposes of being entertained (Eysenck, 1984; Flavell, 1979; Huston & Wright, 1983; Salomon, 1983). If this is true, then the practice of utilizing the formal features of commercial, entertainment programming to educate, as is done by *Sesame Street,* may actually be confusing children regarding which processes to employ when.

Cohen and Salomon (1979) interpreted the finding of their study, that Israeli children learned more from a television program than did a comparable group of U.S. children, as being a function of the greater experience Israeli children have with TV as an educational medium and less as entertainment. It was concluded that the Israeli children attended more constantly and employed memory strategies while doing so. If children typically process television programs with little of what Gavriel Salomon (1983) would call "AIME — the amount of invested mental effort in nonautomatic elaboration of material" (p. 186), they are relying upon already well-mastered, early, cognitive skills and thereby are missing the opportunity to further develop higher-order skills such as inference making. Furthermore, there is some reason to believe that heavy viewers may approach a different medium such as print in the same way (Morgan, 1980; Watkins, Cojuc, Mill, Kwaitek, & Tan, 1981).

Most programming for children is too fast-moving to allow for any reflection or development of long-term associative sequences. In addition, some of the increased hyperactive and aggressive behavior that has been associated with viewing certain high-action programming, such as the *Gong Show,* may simply be a function of heightened arousal produced by the frenetic pace (Dorr, 1982; Rice, Huston, & Wright, 1982; Zillmann, 1982). Foreigners have been noted to describe the pace of novel stimulus presentation, the movement, the intercutting, and the increased volume of U.S. commercial television as almost painful. While *Mister Rogers' Neighborhood* and certain other PBS programs appear to be exceptions, *Sesame Street,* with its very brief segments, rapid pace, and emphasis on rote associative learning, is representative of the standard fare in programming for children (Singer, 1983).

Motivation, Emotional Development, and School Adjustment

Heavy viewers of cartoons were rated by their teachers as low on enthusiasm for schoolwork (Zuckerman, Singer, & Singer, 1980). A persistent link is indicated between aggressive behavior or expressions of anger at school and the viewing of action–adventure programming, news broadcasts, and *Sesame Street* (Singer, 1983). At best, heavy television viewing appears to interfere with positive school adjustment by displacing activities such as reading and homework (Morgan & Gross, 1982).

While the comparison between TV and addictive drugs (Mandler, 1978; Winn, 1977) suggests sensationalism, there is some point to the analogy. Television does share some characteristics with pleasurable drugs. Both constitute alternatives to more demanding activities while providing instant gratification, excitement, and escape. There are indications that television viewing is frequently used as a substitute for active thought. The lively presentation allows little time for reflection and preempts attention from unpleasant private fantasy (Singer, 1983). Perhaps children reveal more than they realize when they answer the question, "What did you do last night?" by saying, "Oh, nothin', I watched television."

The probability that a specific behavior will occur is not only a function of the reinforcement schedule but also of the response effort involved (Mowrer, 1960). Whether a child will shovel the driveway depends not only on the payment but also on the length of the driveway. The response effort involved in watching television is very low, yet the reward is often high (Salomon, 1983). This simple fact provides some insight into how television has changed the contingencies in the natural environment of children. Prior to the advent of television children seeking escape from boredom had fewer alternatives to development of the concentration necessary to follow complex adult speech.

Routinely the reduced reinforcement needed to maintain an established behavior is interpreted as resulting from the conditioned reinforcement value acquired by the stimulus feedback the behavior itself creates (Bijou & Baer, 1966). This occurs, however, only after many repetitions of the behavior. Children often do not develop an instant appreciation for complex undertakings that require concentration and deferral of gratification. If alternatives requiring less effort and yielding equivalent rewards is made available, it seems logical to conclude that the motivation for building appreciation for complex, high-effort activities diminishes. In TV children have a source of excitement that makes no demand for reciprocity and does not withdraw when ignored.

Television also appears to make motivating children more difficult to the extent that it reduces the availability of novel experiences for use as rewards or incentives. The fact that relatively few Americans viewed the second moon landing (Cater & Strickland, 1975) suggests that TV has the power to satiate. More convincing is the casual observation of a child introduced to a novel experience only to react with disinterest and describe a similar but more sensational television experience.

Imagination and Children's Perception of Reality

Even most kindergarten children seem to realize that television is staged. They do not, however, appear to understand industry distinctions such as "only the names have been changed" or "written and produced by"; nor do they appear to understand the relationships between ratings, advertisement, and income (Dorr, 1983, p. 205). While most children around second grade and above categorize news and sports programs as real and identify animation as fantasy, they evaluate the reality of entertainment programming in general on the basis of the specific characters and actions involved (Dorr, 1983). The lack of clear distinction between actors and their characters lingers until much later (Hawkins, 1977). This confusion can even be detected in adults (Dorr, 1983). Anecdotal reports by actors of having been verbally abused by strangers on the street, because of their roles as particular TV villains, are not uncommon.

Young children rely upon the word "possible" to describe their definition of what is real on TV while adolescents more frequently include the necessity that action must be "probable" or coincide with their own personal experience. It is revealing that the actual judgments of the older children about the reality of specific program content do not reflect these more rigid, professed standards (Dorr, 1983).

To the extent that children are able to accept as real on TV events that they have not experienced in their daily lives, it would follow that they form perceptions or expectancies about social realities on the basis of what they view on television (Gerbner & Gross, 1976; Hawkins & Pingree, 1980). The more subtle influences are difficult to research because they are so pervasive. They include "children's expectations about adults' behavior, including the normativeness of crime, family conflict or its absence, appropriateness of various roles and behaviors, and so forth . . . this social content is embedded in sometimes complex plots" (Collins, 1983, p. 137).

TV operates in an accelerated time frame. Crimes are committed, solved, and prosecuted in one half hour with three commercial breaks. Nowhere other than on *Mr. Rogers' Neighborhood* can a child observe someone change shoes from start to finish in real time perspective. If children are learning to expect things to happen at the same rate as they happen on television, it would be reasonable to expect them to become impatient with the pace of the real world.

There is evidence that gross misperception of external reality is learned by children through television viewing (CBS Broadcasting, 1974; Collins, Wellman, Keniston, & Westby, 1978; Faulkner, 1975; Forbes & Lonner, 1980; Gerbner, Gross, Eleey, Jackson-Beeck, Jeffries-Fox, & Signorielli, 1977a, b). Also, children, more often than adults, fill in missed plot elements with stereotypes of common action sequences (Collins, et al., 1978).

While it might be assumed that television would provide a rich source of content and contribute positively to the development of imagination, research suggests the opposite (Singer, 1983). Because of its attractiveness as an alternative to self-awareness and reflective thought, television may actually substitute for self-generated, imaginative activity. Furthermore, imaginative play has been associated with prosocial behavior

(Singer, 1983). Eron (1982) and McIlwraith (1981) have suggested that in middle childhood imagination is differentiated into positive or playful fantasies and those characterized by fearful or negative emotions. Heavy viewers of action–adventure shows are more likely to experience the latter and to see the world as frightening (Gerbner et al., 1977a, 1977b).

PUTTING CHILDREN'S TELEVISION VIEWING IN PERSPECTIVE

School psychologists should be wary when voicing opposition to unlimited access to television. The topic is quite emotionally toned. Anyone who works in the industry or advertises on TV or teaches media techniques or appreciation may be offended by negative comment. Likewise, any comment that suggests support for censorship can bring on vehement rebuttal. Naturally, parents who suffer from guilt over their failure to exert the control they feel they should over their children's viewing could be expected to react emotionally. Denial of the influence that TV appears to have on children may also come from other practitioners and academicians who either interpret the data differently or are simply overwhelmed by the glut of disorganized and nondefinitive information on the subject and the absence of integrating theory. Psychology has for years recognized and allotted major focus to the impact of parents, siblings, peers, and the school system on the development of children. In spite of the fact that the TV spends more time with some developing children, it is unlikely to rate a chapter in developmental psychology texts in the near future. In the absence of general consensus regarding the importance of television's impact on children, practicing psychologists will have to make difficult individual decisions as to whether it warrants their attention.

When attempting to reduce the negative effects of TV on children, it is critical to recognize age differences in determining which discriminations children can be expected to make. Third graders, for example, might be expected to recognize the relationship between violent behavior and its motivation and to discriminate cold-blooded murder from killing in the process of rescuing hostages. Younger children could not necessarily be expected to do so; and third graders might easily miss the connection if the actions and the indications of motivation were separated by a commercial. Sixth graders, on the other hand, could normally be expected to bridge the comprehension difficulty created by the interruption (Collins, 1973; Collins, Berndt, & Hess, 1974).

ALTERNATIVE ACTIONS

Given enhanced awareness, parents and teachers who wish to will often be able to influence children's viewing behavior through their own resources. To aid in developing awareness, psychologists could formulate specific themes that they might introduce periodically in the course of consulting. They could point out, for example, that the rapid pace of most commercial television programs appears to bring children to heightened levels of arousal and aggressiveness, whereas slow-paced shows such as *Mr. Rogers' Neighborhood* appear to have a calming and socializing effect (Singer & Singer, 1976; Stein & Friedrich, 1975; Tower, Singer, Singer, & Biggs, 1979). they can suggest, in some detail, how heavy television viewing by young children may actually be setting them up to fail in school. Such information, at just the right moment, could provide parents and teachers with specific insights into how television viewing influences children. Opportunities may also arise for psychologists to address community or parent groups on this topic, to recommend reading material, and to refer interested parties to political action groups such as Action for Children's Television.

Television viewing habits should probably be considered as part of most comprehensive interventions with children. For example, cartoon viewing might reasonably be expected to have a negative impact on impulsive, hyperactive, aggressive children. Children who have nightmares and phobias should probably not be watching crime dramas. How TV is handled by children who procrastinate or lack motivation can be important. Exploring how television relates to whatever adjustment problems a given child is having can lead to eliminating TV as a contributing factor. Often viewing is used as a reward activity with intervention programs. In some cases this could resemble the treatment of diabetes with M & Ms.

In attempting to help strengthen a family's commitment to reduce television viewing, emphasis could be placed on other family activities that are being displaced. It is possible that some family members may actually feel jealous of the TV. Encouraging them to express those feelings may help to initiate change. Focusing on quality rather than volume of viewing may also be useful. If viewers can be taught to perform concurrent evaluation, much commercial programming may lose appeal (Anderson, 1983).

Case studies investigating how families actually view television suggest that much viewing is incidental to other activities and relates more to the time of day than to the program (Anderson, 1983). Such viewing usually appears to be motivated solely by the absence of other activity. When unplanned viewing is frequent, it may make sense to confront the phenomenon directly.

An actual intervention could begin with the family agreeing, first, to eliminate all unplanned viewing. Spontaneously turning on the TV and spinning the channel selector rather than consulting a guide constitutes a situation in which other possible activities, especially reading, are most probably being replaced. Selection under these circumstances is under maximum influence of attention-grabbing formal features (Bryant et al., 1983). During a second phase of the intervention, all viewing might be assessed a fee. Minimal fees could be assessed where the viewer can cite significant educational or personal growth value to viewing the program. Greater fees might be assessed where only amusement value can be cited and even greater fees for programs involving high levels of violence, action, reality distortion, or antisocial role modeling. Children could consistently be required to restate or explain the message. A child's inability to speak coherently about a program could provide both a reason and an explanation for denying future access.

Parents probably need to be reminded that nongraphic violence is still violence. Researchers usually define violence to include any credible overt expression of physical force to compel action against one's will (Liebert, Neale, & Davidson, 1973).

This sort of approach to intervention would require parents to acquire some critical viewing skills, frequently view programs with children so as to evaluate the form and content, and specifically evaluate, through discussion, at least the immediate impact of programs on children. A list of standard message questions, ethical principles, or value statements could be helpful in this process. It would probably be easier to begin with movies airing on television, because they are longer and the message is often easier to extract. For example the message "the end justifies the means" seems to come through clearly in the James Bond adventures. "Two wrongs *do* make a right" might serve as a subtitle for *Billy Jack*. And "unlimited retaliation" appears to be the *Rambo* principle. "It's only wrong if it can be proven in court," "children are wiser than adults," "work is good," "sharing is fun," and "deferral of gratification requires practice" are other message statements that parents could review in attempting to analyze content.

With assistance many parents will be able to recognize more subtle ways in which television programs may be molding their children's perception of reality. Specific examples, such as the inconsistency between the lifestyle and income of characters on *Miami Vice* or the constantly exhilarating daily lives of the students on *Fame* can help parents to acquire sensitivity to development of subtle, unrealistic expectations by their children. There may be value to drawing attention of parents to certain fairly consistent distortions, such as the tendency to play down the magnitude or irreversibility of negative consequences for any character with whom the viewer identifies.

Anderson (1983) reviews eight TV literacy projects ranging in target population from kindergarten to 12th grade and in intensity from the eight lessons of the American Broadcasting Company (ABC) Project (Singer, Zuckerman, and Singer, 1980) to the 4 years, 40 hours per year of the Idaho Falls ESEA IV-C Project (Idaho Falls School District 91, 1979). While those programs that more obviously spring from an impact mediation philosophy may be more desirable from the point of view of a school psychologist, those that appear to be more academic or truly "literacy-oriented" may be more palatable to school districts. In spite of the apparent value-neutral position of some of these curricula, each includes objectives related to management of viewing time and program selection. Studies have been reasonably successful in demonstrating enhanced knowledge about television resulting from literacy instruction, but have provided no substantial evidence of student change on variables such as program selection, distinguishing fantasy from reality, and volume of viewing (Anderson, 1983).

Identification of alternatives to watching television probably must flow from exploring the situations in which the TV is routinely switched on and should address the question of how to meet the needs that TV is fulfilling. A VCR can make intervention easier to structure by providing greater control over quality and type of programming available to meet the schedule of the family.

SUMMARY

A practicing psychologist probably has to make some judgments that are not necessarily based on overwhelming scientific evidence. In spite of the very guarded Report of the Surgeon General in 1972, the American Medical Association adopted a policy identifying televised violence as an "environmental hazard" threatening the health and welfare of young Americans (Rubinstein, 1983, p. 7). Practitioners should remember that the failure of research to provide definitive evidence for a relationship does not prove that no relationship exists. Proper formulation of the null hypothesis in scientific method should avoid any illusion that negative results prove the absence of a relationship. The earth was round long before science was able to so demonstrate, and repeated failure to do so did not constitute evidence that it was not round. Clean, unambiguous data in the area of television's impact on children is not easy to obtain. A control group without a history of frequent television viewing may simply be impossible to achieve today. Another frustration stems from the fact that the program, not the medium, is usually the critical variable, and the pressure of ratings causes programs to mutate faster than some viruses.

The following judgments are probably defensible, though by no means indisputable: (a) Watching violence on TV can increase the probability of aggressive behavior while decreasing aversion to violence; (b) the rapid pace of most commercial television probably increases the activity level and impulsivity of at least some children; (c) the use of certain formal features and the emphasis of commercial television on entertainment may create a conditioning history that is not conducive to the development of active attention, careful listening skills, or higher cognitive processes; (d) television probably contributes to some perceptions and expectancies about social reality that are both inaccurate and maladaptive; (e) television may satiate children on events and activities that would otherwise function as reinforcers; (f) television provides escape from boredom at little response cost; and (g) viewing displaces some desirable activities such as homework, reading, and imaginative play.

Heavy viewing is inversely related to reading and school achievement (Cal. State Department of Education, 1982). Negative emotional state, aggressive or impulsive behavior, impoverishment of constructive imagination, and school adjustment problems have all been associated with heavy viewing of action–adventure programs (Singer, 1983). Psychologists may actually be able to begin using knowledge of television viewing behavior diagnostically. For example, "preschool children whose play themes reflect specific television references to cartoons, superheroes and action–detective characters are also more likely to be aggressive" (Singer, 1983, p. 282). These children frequently demonstrate maladaptive social behavior and are often rated by teachers as uncooperative, interpersonally unsuccessful, and unhappy. They are less likely to watch *Mr. Rogers' Neighborhood* (Singer & Singer, 1980). Strong identification with television characters has also been associated with aggressive behavior (Eron, 1982). Dorr (1982) suggests that lonely children may watch TV for company, initiating a cyclic pattern wherein the heavy viewing precludes development of appropriate social skills. It certainly appears that much can be learned about the values and reality perceptions of a child by listening to what the child has to say about favorite TV shows, favorite characters, and reasons for viewing.

The influence of commercials, the phenomenon of role stereotyping, and the positive impact of television have not been dealt with in this article owing to space limitations.

REFERENCES

Alwitt, L. F., Anderson, D. R., Lorch, E. P., & Levin, S. R. (1980). Preschool children's visual attention to attributes of television. *Human Communication Research, 7,* 52–67.

Anderson, D. R. (1983). Television literacy and the critical viewer. In J. Bryant & D. Anderson (Eds.), *Children's understanding of television: Research on attention and comprehension* (pp. 297–330). New York: Academic.

Anderson, D. R., & Bryant, J. (1983). Research on children's television viewing: The state of the art. In J. Bryant & D. Anderson (Eds.), *Children's understanding of television: Research on attention and comprehension* (pp. 331–353). New York: Academic.

Anderson, D. R., & Levin, S. R. (1976). Young children's attention to Sesame Street. *Child Development, 47,* 806–811.

Anderson, D. R., & Lorch, E. P. (1983). Looking at television: Action or reaction. In J. Bryant & D. Anderson (Eds.), *Children's understanding of television: Research on attention and comprehension* (pp. 1–33). New York: Academic.

Bandura, A. (1977). *Social learning theory.* Englewood Cliffs, NJ: Prentice-Hall.

Bandura, A., Ross, D., & Ross, S. A. (1963). Vicarious reinforcement and the imitative learning. *Journal of Abnormal & Social Psychology, 67,* 601–607.

Bijou, S. W., & Baer, D. M. (1966). Operant methods in child behavior and development. In W. K. Honig (Ed.), *Operant behavior: Areas of research and application* (pp. 718–789). New York: Meredith.

Bryant, J., Zillmann, D., & Brown, D. (1983). Entertainment features in children's educational television: Effects on attention and information acquisition. In J. Bryant & D. Anderson (Eds.), *Children's understanding of television: Research on attention and comprehension* (pp. 221–240). New York: Academic.

California State Department of Education. (1980). *Student achievement in California schools: 1979–80 annual report.* Sacramento, CA: Author.

Cater, D., & Strickland, S. (1975). *TV violence and the child: The evolution and fate of the surgeon general's report.* New York: Russell Sage Foundation.

Charren, P., & Sandler, M. W. (1983). *Changing channels.* Reading, MA: Addison-Wesley.

Cohen, A. A., & Salomon, G. (1979). Children's literate television viewing: Surprises and possible explanations. *Journal of Communication, 29*(3), 156–163.

Collins, W. A. (1973). The effect of temporal separation between motivation, aggression and consequences: A developmental study. *Developmental Psychology, 8*(2), 215–221.

Collins, W. A. (1983). Interpretation and inference in children's television viewing. In J. Bryant & D. Anderson (Eds.), *Children's understanding of television: Research on attention and comprehension* (pp. 125–150). New York: Academic.

Collins, W. A., Berndt, T. J., & Hess, V. L. (1974). Observational learning of motives and consequences for television aggression: A developmental study. *Child Development, 45,* 799–802.

Collins, W. A., Wellman, H., Keniston, A., & Westby, S. (1978). Age-related aspects of comprehension and inference from a televised dramatic narrative. *Child Development, 49,* 389–399.

Columbia Broadcasting System, Broadcast Group, Office of Social Research, Department of Economics and Research. (1974). *A study of messages received by children who viewed an episode of "Fat Albert and the Cosby Kids."* New York: Author.

Doerken, M. (1983). *Classroom combat: Teaching and television.* Englewood Cliffs, NJ: Educational Technology Publications.

Dorr, A. L. (1982). Television and affective development and functioning. In D. Pearl, L. Bouthilet, & J. Lazar (Eds.), *Television and behavior: Ten years of scientific progress and implications for the eighties* (Vol. 2). (DHHS Publication No. ADM 82-1196, pp. 68–77). Washington, DC: U.S. Government Printing Office.

Dorr, A. (1983). No shortcuts to judging reality. In J. Bryant & D. Anderson (Eds.), *Children's understanding of television: Research on attention and comprehension* (pp. 199–220). New York: Academic.

Eron, L. D. (1982). Parent–child interaction, television violence and aggression of children. *American Psychologist, 37*(2), 197–211.

Eysenck, M. W. (1984). *A handbook of cognitive psychology.* London: Erlbaum.

Faulkner, G. (1975). Media and identity: The Asian adolescent's dilemma. In C. Husbard (Ed.), *White media and black Britain.* London: Arrow.

Flavell, J. H. (1979). Metacognition and cognitive monitoring: A new area of cognitive–developmental inquiry. *American Psychologist, 34,* 906–911.

Forbes, N. E., & Lonner, W. J. (1980, March). *The coming of television to rural Alaska: Attitudes, expectations and effects.* Paper presented at the Television in the Developing World Conference, Winnipeg.

Friedlander, B. Z. (1975). Automated evaluation of selective listening in language-impaired and normal infants and young children. In B. F. Friedlander, G. M. Starrett, & G. E. Kirk (Eds.), *Exceptional infant* (Vol. 3, pp.124–136). New York: Brunner-Mazel.

Gerbner, G., & Gross, L. (1976). Living with television: The violence profile. *Journal of Communication, 26*(2), 173–199.

Gerbner, G., Gross, L., Eleey, M., Jackson-Geeck, M., Jeffries-Fox, S., & Signorielli, N. (1977a). TV violence profile No. 8. *Journal of Communication, 27,* 171–180.

Gerbner, G., Gross, L., Eleey, M., Jackson-Geeck, M., Jeffries-Fox, S., & Signorielli, N. (1977b). *Violence profile No. 8: Trends in network television drama and viewer conceptions of social reality 1967–1976.* Philadelphia: University of Pennsylvania, Annenberg School of Communications.

Hawkins, R. P. (1977). The dimensional structure of children's perceptions of television reality. *Communication Research, 4*(3), 299–320.

Hawkins, R. P., & Pingree, S. (1980). Some processes in the cultivation effect. *Communication Research, 7*(2), 193–226.

Huesmann, L. R. (1982). Television violence and aggressive behavior. In D. Pearl, L. Bouthilet, & J. Lazar (Eds.), *Television and behavior: Ten years of scientific progress and implications for the eighties* (Vol. 2). (DHHS Publication No. ADM 82–1196, pp. 126–137). Washington, DC: U.S. Government Printing Office.

Huston, A. C., & Wright, J. C. (1983). Children's processing of television: The informative functions of formal features. In J. Bryant & D. Anderson (Eds.), *Children's understanding of television: Research on attention and comprehension* (pp. 35–68). New York: Academic.

Idaho Falls School District 91. (1979). *The way we see it handbook.* Idaho Falls: Author.

Krull, R. (1983). Children learning to watch television. In J. Bryant & D. Anderson (Eds.), *Children's understanding of television: Research on attention and comprehension* (pp. 103–123). New York: Academic.

Lazarus, A. (1964). Crucial procedural factors in desensitization therapy. *Behavior Research and Therapy, 2,* 65–70.

Lazarus, A. (1971). *Behavior therapy and beyond.* New York: McGraw-Hill.

Lesser, G. (1972). The experience of Sesame Street. *Harvard Educational Review, 42*(2), 232–272.

Liebert, R. M., Neale, J. M., & Davidson, E. S. (1973). *The early window: Effects of television on children and youth.* New York: Pergamon.

Lorch, E. P., Anderson, D. R., & Levin, S. R. (1979). The relationship of visual attention to children's comprehension of television. *Child Development, 50,* 722–727.

Mandler, J. (1978). *Four arguments for the elimination of television.* New York: Morrow.

McIlwraith, R. D. (1981). *Fantasy life and media use patterns of adults and children.* Unpublished doctoral dissertation, University of Manitoba.

Mielke, K., Chen, M., Clarke, H., & Myerson-Katz, B. (1978). *Survey of television viewing interests among eight-to-twelve-year-olds.* New York: Children's Television Workshop.

Moody, K. (1980). *Growing up on television: The TV effect: A report to parents.* New York: Times Books.

Morgan, M. (1980). Television viewing and reading: Does more equal better? *Journal of Communication, 30,* 159–165.

Morgan, M., & Gross, L. (1982). Television and educational achievement and aspirations. In D. Pearl, L. Bouthilet, & J. Lazar (Eds.), *Television and behavior: Ten years of scientific progress and implications for the eighties* (Vol. 2). (DHHS Publication No. ADM 82-1196, pp. 78–90). Washington, DC: U.S. Government Printing Office.

Mowrer, O. H. (1960). *Learning theory and behavior.* New York: Wiley.

National Institute of Mental Health. (1982). *Television and behavior: Ten years of scientific progress and implications for the eighties* (Vol. 1). (DHHS Publication No. ADM 82-1195). Washington, DC: U.S. Government Printing Office.

Postman, N. (1982). *The disappearance of childhood,* New York: Delacorte.

Rice, M. L., Huston, A. C., & Wright, J. C. (1982). The forms of television: Effects on children's attention, comprehension, and social behavior. In D. Pearl, L. Bouthilet, & J. Lazar (Eds.), *Television and behavior: Ten years of scientific progress and implications for the eighties* (Vol. 2). (DHHS Publication No. ADM 82-1196, pp. 24–39). Washington, DC: U.S. Government Printing Office.

Rubinstein, E. A. (1983). Television violence approaches to prevention and control. In J. Sprafkin, C. Swift, & R. Hess (Eds.), *Rx television: Enhancing the preventive impact of TV* (pp. 1–27). New York: Haworth.

Salomon, G. (1983). Television watching and mental effort: A social psychological view. In J. Bryant & D. Anderson (Eds.), *Children's understanding of television: Research on attention and comprehension* (pp. 181–198). New York: Academic.

Singer, D. G., & Singer, J. L. (1976). Family television viewing habits and the spontaneous play of preschool children. *American Journal of Orthopsychiatry, 46*(3), 496–502.

Singer, D. G., & Singer, J. L. (1980). Television viewing and aggressive behavior in preschool children: A field study. In F. Wright, C. Bahn, & R. W. Rieber (Eds.), *Forensic psychology and psychiatry* (Vols. 347, pp. 289–303). New York: New York Academy of Sciences.

Singer, D. G., Zuckerman, D. M., & Singer, J. L. (1980). Helping elementary school children learn about TV. *Journal of Communication, 30*(3), 84–93.

Singer, J. L., & Singer, D. G. (1983). Implications of childhood television viewing for cognition, imagination, and emotion. In J. Bryant & D. Anderson (Eds.), *Children's understanding of television: Research on attention and comprehension* (pp. 265–291). New York: Academic.

Stein, A. H., & Friedrich, L. K. (1975). The effects of television content on young children. In A. Pick (Ed.), *Minnesota symposium on child psychology* (Vol. 9). Minneapolis: University of Minnesota Press.

Tower, R. B., Singer, D. G., Singer, J. L., & Biggs, A. (1979). Differential effects of television programming on preschoolers' cognition, imagination, and social play. *American Journal of Orthopsychiatry, 49,* 265–281.

United States Senate, 92nd Congress. (1972, 2nd session, Mar. 21, 22, 23, & 24). *Hearings before the Subcommittee on Communications of the Committee on Commerce: Surgeon General's Report by the Scientific Advisory Committee on Television and Social Behavior* (Serial No. 95–52). Washington, DC: U.S. Government Printing Office.

United States Surgeon General's Scientific Advisory Committee on Television and Social Behavior. (1972). *Television and growing up: The impact of televised violence* (PHS Publication No. ADM 72-600612). Washington, DC: U.S. Government Printing Office.

Watkins, B., Cojuc, J. R., Mill, S., Kwaitek, K., & Tan, Z. (1981, July). *Children's use of TV and real life story structure and content as a function of age and prime-time television viewing.* First annual report to the Spencer Foundation. University of Michigan, Children's Media Project.

Winn, M. (1977). *The Plug-In Drug.* New York: Viking.

Zillmann, D. (1982). Cognitive and affective influences: Television viewing and arousal. In D. Pearl, L. Bouthilet, & J. Lazar (Eds.), *Television and behavior: Ten years of scientific progress and implications for the eighties* (Vol. 2). (DHHS Publication No. ADM 82-1196, pp. 53–67). Washington, DC: U.S. Government Printing Office.

Zuckerman, D. M., Singer, D. G., & Singer, J. L. (1980). Television viewing and children's reading and related classroom behavior. *Journal of Communication, 30*(1), 166–174.

BIBLIOGRAPHY: PROFESSIONALS

Bandura, A. (1977). *Social learning theory.* Englewood Cliffs, NJ: Prentice-Hall.
This book provides a detailed and research-based explanation of the modeling process, especially as it applies to television. It provides the professional with clear and concise language for explaining social learning and could probably be read profitably by some parents.

Bryant, J., & Anderson, D. (Eds.). (1983). *Children's understanding of television: Research on attention and comprehension,* New York: Academic.
This volume includes chapters by many of the most prominent authors in the field of children and television. It provides an excellent summary of research, trends, conclusions, and speculation.

National Institute of Mental Health. (1982). *Television and behavior: Ten years of scientific progress and implications for the eighties* (Vols. 1, 2). (DHHS Publication Nos. ADM 82-1195 & ADM 82-1196). Washington, DC: U.S. Government Printing Office.
This publication provides an invaluable summary of the overall findings in Volume 1 and the more detailed technical reviews by various authors in Volume 2.

Ploghoft, M. E., & Anderson, J. A. (1982). *Teaching critical television viewing skills: An integrated approach.* Springfield, IL: Charles C Thomas.
This book resulted from the Idaho Falls project previously cited. It is quite extensive and provides detailed guidance on how to integrate critical viewing skills into the regular curriculum.

Singer, D. G., Singer, J. L., & Zuckerman, D. M. (1981). *Getting the most out of TV.* Santa Monica, CA: Goodyear.
This is a commercial publication of the eight lessons developed and field tested by the authors as part of the ABC project previously cited. The lesson plans are highly detailed, easy to follow, and include classroom materials and permission to reproduce. The target population is grades three through six but adaptation for grades seven and eight would not be difficult.

BIBLIOGRAPHY: PARENTS

DeFranco, E. (1980). *TV on/off: Better family use of television.* Santa Monica, CA: Goodyear.
This is a very practical book written at an easy reading level. It could be of considerable help to a family attempting to reduce or gain better control of viewing within the home.

Kaye, E. (1979). *The ACT guide to children's television: Or how to treat TV with TLC* (rev. ed.). Boston, MA: Beacon.
This work could be helpful to parents who want to learn how to more effectively mediate the impact of television on their children. Action for Children's Television (ACT) is a citizen organization dedicated to improving the quality and reducing the volume of television viewed by children. They disseminate information, lobby, and petition regulatory agencies. The philosophy of the organization is not to impose censorship, but to persuade networks to devote more time to educational and informational programs specifically for children. For information write to: ACT, 46 Austin Street, Newtonville, MA 02160.

Postman, N. (1985). *Amusing ourselves to death.* New York: Viking Penguin.
In this book Postman does not specifically focus on childhood. He explores the manner in which conversion from a print culture to a television culture impacts on the basic nature of social dialogue. He describes a shift from the serious, coherent, and rational to the dangerous, absurd, and nonsensical.

Winn, M. (1977). *The Plug-In Drug.* New York: Viking.
While this book could be described as speculative, perhaps even sensational, it might be useful in heightening parental awareness of some of the possible negative influences television exerts on children.

Children and Temper Tantrums

Theo Lexmond
Barry Intermediate School District, Hastings, Michigan

BACKGROUND

There are few sights as unsettling to parents, few sights that leave parents feeling as helpless and bewildered as that of their typically mild-mannered youngster in the throes of a severe tamper tantrum. While many parents anticipating the onslaught of the "terrible two's" have a notion of what to expect with the onset of tantrum behavior, they are often astonished at the inventiveness demonstrated by their youngsters when tantrums develop.

The wide range of behaviors reported in the literature to have been exhibited by children during temper tantrums can be arranged along a continuum extending from least to most severe. The severity of a given child's tantrum pattern will depend on factors such as the child's temperament and the behaviors the child has been modeled in. Most youngsters who exhibit tantrum behavior will develop a predictable pattern of responses that includes at least some of the behaviors found along the following continuum (by no means all-inclusive) reported to have been exhibited by children during tantrums: verbal behaviors such as pouting, whining, crying, name calling, and screaming; physical outbursts such as throwing ones-self to the floor, destroying one's clothing, and running wildly about; injurious behaviors such as biting, kicking, punching, and scratching; and self-injurious behaviors such as head banging and holding one's breath to the point of fainting (Barrow, 1968; Hawkins, Peterson, Schweid, & Bijou, 1966; Krumboltz & Krumboltz, 1972; Patterson, 1976, chap. 14).

Review of the literature revealed no studies that attempt, either as a primary focus or by-product of their execution, to provide an estimate of the number of youngsters in the general population who exhibit severe tantrum behavior at some point during childhood. One study, conducted to assess the relative efficacy of four behavioral treatment procedures for temper tantrums, however, provided data regarding the frequency and average length of tantrums for 38 children between 2½ and 6 years of age who had been identified as experiencing severe tantrum difficulties (Ames, 1976). Prior to any attempt at intervention, the 38 subjects, divided into four experimental groups, had been exhibiting tantrums at a mean rate of 2 to 3.5 per day. The average length of tantrums across the four experimental groups, prior to intervention, ranged from 2.5 to 8.5 minutes per incident. The specific number of tantrums per day and the length of tantrums for each of the 38 individual subjects participating in the study was not reported.

The occurrence of severe temper tantrums may have a detrimental effect on a child's growth and development in many respects (Barrow, 1968; Murray, 1976; Williams, 1959; Zarske, 1982). Most obviously affected is the parent–child relationship. Tantrum behavior is aversive to everyone involved. As the range of stimuli that set off a child's tantrum pattern grows, parents limit the contact they have with their child in an effort to limit opportunities for tantrums. At times the relationship may become so strained that parents will avoid contact with their child even when the youngster is playing quietly or otherwise behaving appropriately, for fear of introducing the slightest frustration and unwittingly setting off a tantrum. Similarly affected are the tantrum-prone child's interactions with siblings and peers. A child who cannot tolerate frustration makes a very poor playmate. Because children soon learn to avoid a tantrum-prone youngster, desperately needed opportunities to make friendships and to learn tolerance of frustration are lost.

Severe tantrum behavior that grows unchecked in the home may also begin to occur in school, in stores, or in other public places. Tantrums in school result in interrupted learning and gaps in acquisition of basic skills. Tantrums in public places cause embarrassed and frustrated parents to restrict a child's opportunities to go out in public. The net result is fewer chances for experiential learning in the world outside the home.

In any setting, the home, the daycare center, the school, or elsewhere, the amount of tension among all individuals functioning in that environment is exacerbated by the presence of a tantrum-prone youngster. In circumstances in which financial worries, marital discord, or other problems have already infused the atmosphere with tension, the addition of childhood tantrums may strain a social system past the breaking point.

While temper tantrums most typically occur in toddlers and young children, vestiges of tantrum behavior may be retained through adolescence and into adulthood, causing disruption in marital life and the workplace, long after its first occurrence. It is therefore imperative that tantrums be controlled at an early age and that appropriate means of expressing frustration and obtaining goals be acquired.

When approached for help by someone responsible for the care of a tantrum-prone child, a psychological consultant should be prepared to complete the following tasks: (a) explain how temper tantrums develop in children; (b) gather background information necessary for devising an effective intervention plan; (c) propose an appropriate intervention plan and teach caregivers how to implement it; (d) monitor the results of the intervention.

Each of these tasks will be considered in turn. The differences between normal and aberrant temper tantrum development will be explained. An interview guide for collecting necessary background information will be presented. And five intervention strategies — differential reinforcement, time-out, planned ignoring, paradoxical intervention, and chaining and fading — will be discussed.

DEVELOPMENT

Between the ages of 12 months and 4 years children frequently develop temper tantrum behavior in the course of normal growth and maturation. The initial emergence of tantrums is not a signal that a problem exists. To the contrary, the first appearance of tantrum behavior in an infant or toddler is a sign of growth toward greater autonomy and expressive capability. To recognize the difference between tantrum behavior that represents an advance in normal development and that which is an aberration in the growth process, it is necessary to examine carefully the forces that influence the developmental process in young children.

Normal Development

During infancy, children express their needs and wants by crying, smiling, babbling, gurgling, and grabbing at objects that interest them. Locomotion is limited to rolling over and crawling about within a strictly limited area. Soon, however, the restrictions of infancy give way to the emerging freedom of toddlerhood. Most babies begin walking with assistance and forming their first words by about 1 year of age. Within the next 9-12 months the ability to walk unaided and run develop. In addition, vocabulary may reach 20 words or more, accompanied by the ability to produce two and three word phrases. A great expansion in mobility and expressive capacity has occurred in a very short time. It is at this stage in a child's life, when the youngster is bursting with a newfound sense of autonomy and the capacity to explore virtually everything in sight, that verbal rule training by parents begins in earnest. Verbal rule training, the barrage of necessary do's and don'ts that make organized family life possible, is often a bitter pill for toddlers to swallow. Though vocabulary is developing quickly, the ability to use words to express abstractions such as feelings of frustration or anger takes time to learn. Toddlers, faced by a burgeoning list of verbal rules and behavioral consequences, find it natural to revert to crying and screaming as a means for expressing frustration when their capacity to use language is just beginning to grow. An outburst of temper by a frustrated toddler is a healthy sign that verbal rules and limits to autonomy have been encountered and acknowledged. Crying or screaming by an angry toddler communicates frustration in a way that is familiar to the youngster (Barrow, 1968).

Temper tantrum behavior is a normal response to frustration in toddlers who lack the more complete repertoire of avenues for expressing themselves that are accessible to older children. The majority of toddlers who develop temper tantrum behavior learn that tantrums serve only temporarily as a means of expressing frustration with demands and restrictions placed upon them. In the course of normal development, tantrum behavior wanes as the frustration tolerance of tantrum-prone youngsters improves and more efficient ways of expressing frustration, such as putting specific complaints into words, are learned.

Aberrant Development

Temper tantrum behavior becomes an aberration in development when a tantrum-prone youngster learns to use tantrums as something other than a means of expressing frustration. Some children are taught, by the responses to tantrum behavior of significant adults around them, that tantrums can serve a much larger purpose. They learn to use tantrums to accomplish otherwise unobtainable goals, and they learn to use tantrums to gain attention beyond the amount they are used to receiving (Dreikurs & Soltz, 1964; Krumboltz & Krumboltz, 1972; Martin & Iagulli, 1974; Sailor, Guess, Rutherford, & Baer, 1968; Williams, 1959; Zeilberger, Sampen, & Sloane, 1968). When accomplishing goals and gaining attention becomes the object of a child's tantrums, emotional and communicative development becomes arrested as the frequency of tantrum behavior increases and crowds out opportunities to learn new methods for expressing needs and obtaining goals.

The discernment between normal, healthy, expressive tantrum behavior and aberrant, unhealthy, manipulative tantrum behavior is made by assessing the extent to which tantrums have become goal-oriented and are used to control the environment. Tantrum behavior that results, for example, in a child's being given treats that would not otherwise be received, in staying awake past the normal bedtime, in gaining exclusive control over toys that must otherwise be shared, or in accompanying adults on excursions when they would otherwise have had to stay home is goal-oriented behavior that has exceeded the bounds typical of normal growth and development. Problem tantrum behavior is the result of an interplay between children's natural developmental processes occurring and the influence of behavioral reinforcement by caregivers on the way children express frustration. Many toddlers revert, for a time, to crying and screaming to express their frustrations while more efficient, less painful means of expression are being learned. Problems arise when adults attempt to control and placate a tantrum-engulfed child by offering rewards for a return to silence. Soon, however, the tables are turned and the child learns to offer adults the removal of silence in order to control the presentation of desired consequences such as attention, etc.

A child who has learned to manipulate the environment by using tantrums may soon generalize this behavior beyond the home to other settings. When goal-oriented tantrums have generalized and become persistent across environments, only a significant change in the response of caregivers towards the youngster will alter the destructive tantrum process and allow a return to normal emotional and communicative development.

PUTTING TEMPER TANTRUMS IN PERSPECTIVE

The specific circumstances of a severe temper tantrum problem vary widely from one case to another. It is important, therefore, to gather situation-specific information prior to the design of an intervention strategy. Completion of a structured interview with one or more of a referred child's caregivers, and if possible, an observation of the referred child in a setting where tantrums frequently occur, is recommended. In Table 1, a structured interview for use with the caregivers of a tantrum-prone child is provided. It is designed to be copied from this volume and used as a recording tool during interviews.

ALTERNATIVE ACTIONS

After the necessary background information has been obtained, a psychological consultant is faced with the task of developing an intervention strategy that meets the requirements of the presenting situation. In cases in which tantrum behavior is not a long-standing, entrenched pattern and tantrums have not become manipulative or goal-oriented, an explanation of the developmental and behavioral dynamics involved provides an effective intervention approach. Caregivers who possess a clear understanding of the forces involved in instances of tantrum behavior are better equipped to handle their own feelings of confusion and misgiving that often accompany the occasion of tantrums in a youngster. In addition, they are prepared to counter the development of a chronic, manipulative tantrum problem.

In the case of tantrum behavior that is long-standing, entrenched, goal-oriented and manipulative, however, an active intervention plan must be prepared. A successful intervention strategy for dealing with chronic tantrums typically contains both an extinction and a reward component. The extinction component curbs the provision of reinforcement that tantrums are designed to achieve; the reward component reinforces behaviors that are inconsistent with tantrums and fosters alternative ways of expressing frustration, gaining attention, and accomplishing goals. In the following paragraphs two extinction procedures (timeout and planned ignoring), a reward procedure (differential reinforcement), and two strategies that combine features of extinction and reward (chaining/fading and paradoxical intervention) will each be presented in turn. These five procedures are the building blocks used to construct individualized intervention plans for coping with severe temper tantrum problems.

Timeout

In the psychological literature the most frequently cited intervention strategy for dealing with temper tantrum difficulties is timeout. Timeout procedures have been designed for use by caregivers in the home (Hawkins, Peterson, Schweid, & Bijou, 1966; Patterson, 1976, chap. 14; Zeilberger, Sampen, & Sloane, 1968), in school (Carlson, Arnold, Becker, & Madsen, 1968), and in other public settings such as restaurants and stores (Murray, 1976). Thorough preparation for the use of timeout procedures with children requires an examination of the ethical and procedural issues involved in its application. While such a discussion lies beyond the scope of this chapter, review of documents delineating the differences between various types of timeout procedures and the applicability of each procedure to specific situations is encouraged prior to the design of a timeout intervention plan for temper tantrum control (Harris, 1985; Hobbs & Forehand, 1977; McDonough & Forehand, 1973).

Timeout is defined by Hall and Hall (1980c) as "a procedure for decreasing a specific unwanted behavior by removing a person from the opportunity to receive attention and other rewards whenever he or she engages in that specific undesired behavior" (pp. 3–4). Patterson (1976, chap. 14) provides an example of a timeout approach designed for the treatment of temper tantrums that illustrates well the sequence of events typical of this technique:

1. Parents are taught to become aware of behavioral signals that a tantrum may soon begin. In Patterson's example, parents learn that whining by their child after a request has been denied may signal the start of a tantrum.
2. Parents hold a conference with their child to explain the timeout procedure and show the child how it works.
3. Whenever the child's whining begins and a tantrum seems imminent, the child is told to go to timeout and is placed in the bathroom or a similar isolated area for 2 minutes. No one is to interact with the youngster during this timeout period.
4. If the child does not go to the timeout area when told to do so, an extra minute must be spent in timeout after the child has been placed in the designated area.
5. An additional minute is also added to the timeout period if the child is noisy while in timeout.
6. When the timeout session has been completed, the youngster may return to whatever activity he or she was engaged in prior to the tantrum occurrence. The child is not to be lectured and no mention of the tantrum should be made.

In practice, the use of a timeout procedure to the exclusion of other procedures is not encouraged. An extinction technique such as timeout should always be paired with an appropriate reward approach. In Patterson's case example, a gold star chart was used to provide reinforcement each time the youngster complied peacefully with parents' denial of a request.

Many variations of this basic approach to timeout are possible. The variation chosen will depend on the specific demands of the presenting situation, the capabilities of caregivers to carry out a given treatment regimen, and the creativity of the psychological consultant and caregivers involved. As in any behavioral treatment, the principle of consistency must be honored above all others. Once a timeout procedure has been implemented, it must be administered every time the child's tantrum sequence starts. If consistency of application is not monitored and ensured, the effectiveness of intervention will be compromised.

Planned Ignoring

The extinction techniques timeout and planned ignoring are closely related in theory but are procedurally quite different. The purpose of planned ignoring, as with timeout, is to deny the extra attention and achieve-

TABLE 1.

Interview for Caregivers of a Tantrum-Prone Child

A. Child and family characteristics
   1. Name and age of the tantrum-prone child.
   2. Was the achievement of verbal and motor developmental milestones delayed or accelerated?
   3. Is there a history of health problems?
   4. Names and ages of the child's siblings:
   5. Who is the child's primary caregiver?
   6. Who are the child's secondary caregivers? (Persons such as spouse, boyfriend or girlfriend of primary caregiver, older sibling, baby sitter, and grandparent or other relative who accept significant responsibility for care and well-being of the child.)

B. Exclusion of alternative causes for excessive crying and tantrum-like behavior.
   1. Determine if the child is overtired. (An overtired child handles frustration very poorly.)
      a. When does the child wake up each morning?
      b. When is the child's bedtime?
      c. Does the child take naps during the day?
   2. Is the child teething? (The first tooth may appear at about six months of age. Teething may continue through two years of age.)
   3. Does the child show signs of partial or generalized seizure activity?
      (According to informational pamphlets published by the Epilepsy Foundation of America (1981), absent-mindedness, lethargy, irritability, and behaviors such as rapid blinking, chewing, or aimless movements of the head or limbs are just some of the behavioral descriptors that have been associated with seizure activity. Similar behavioral descriptors may be associated with the occurrence of temper tantrums. If seizure activity is suspected, a thorough medical evaluation is warrented.)
   4. Is the child receiving any type of medication that may, as a side effect, exacerbate or cause behavior associated with temper tantrum outbursts?

C. Description of tantrum behavior
   1. What specific behaviors does the child engage in during a temper tantrum? List:
   2. Is the child self-injurious during temper tantrums?
   3. Does the child attempt to injure others or destroy property during tantrums?
   4. How often do tantrums occur?
   5. How long do tantrums last?
   6. How long has the child been exhibiting severe tantrum behaviors?

D. Situational factors associated with tantrum behavior
   1. In what specific settings do tantrums occur? (For example, do tantrums occur in the home, school, church, grocery store, or other public settings? List:
   2. Do tantrums occur more often in some rooms of the home than others? (Are tantrums restricted to the kitchen and bedroom, for example, or do they occur throughout the home?) List:
   3. At what specific times are tantrums most likely to occur? (For example, do tantrums occur consistently at mealtime, bedtime, time for parents to go to work or siblings to leave for school?) List:
   4. Is the occurrence of tantrums widely generalized across caregivers or do they occur only in the company of specific caregivers? List caregivers who have experienced the child's tantrums:
   5. What behaviors signal that a tantrum is coming? (Clues such as abrupt silence, pouting, watery eyes, or loud refusal to comply with a request may be consistent precursors to tantrum outbursts.) List the signal behaviors observed in their order of occurrence:
   6. Describe the typical response of caregivers to the child when a tantrum is occurring. How do caregivers interact with the child during a tantrum? (Note verbal interaction such as threats of punishment, scolding or pleading with the child and physical interaction such as holding, cuddling, or spanking the child.) List caregiver responses:
   7. When a tantrum is completed, is the child punished in any way?
   8. How do the child's brothers and sisters respond during and after a tantrum? List sibling responses:
   9. Have caregivers come to restrict their own and the tantrum-prone child's activities because of the child's tantrum behaviors? (Are caregivers reluctant to take the child grocery shopping, to church, to the park, or on other outings because of concern over tantrum outbursts?)

(Table 1 continued)

10. Does the child, by throwing a tantrum, get to do things he or she would not otherwise be allowed to do? (Have tantrum behaviors become goal-oriented? Does the child use tantrums to manipulate the environment?) List examples of goals the child has obtained by exhibiting tantrum behavior:

E. Tantrum occurrence in school
   1. If tantrums occur in school, how do school personnel such as the child's teacher, principal, and school secretary typically respond to tantrums?
   2. How do the child's classmates respond during and after a tantrum?
   3. Is there an aide available in the school building who could be trained in the use of intervention techniques?

---

ment of goals that maintains tantrum behavior. In a timeout procedure the child is removed from the reinforcing environment when tantrum behavior starts. Removal from the environment requires either a command from the caregiver or physical guidance to the designated timeout area. In either case, some attention is awarded the child as a result of tantrum initiation. In planned ignoring the child is not sent aside. Instead, caregivers divert all their attention from the youngster as soon as tantrum warning behaviors appear. The advantage is that interactions between caregivers and the tantrum-prone child that maintain tantrum behavior are minimized to the greatest extent possible.

Planned ignoring procedures have often been described as an integral part of treatment programs for temper tantrum difficulties (Ames, 1976; Barrow, 1968; Dreikurs & Soltz, 1964; Hall & Hall, 1980; Krumboltz & Krumboltz, 1972; Williams, 1959). The planned ignoring component of a treatment program typically contains the following steps:

1. Caregivers learn to identify warning behaviors that signal a tantrum is coming.
2. Caregivers are taught to withdraw all attention from a tantrum-prone youngster as soon as tantrum warning behavior appears. Withdrawal of attention includes breaking off all eye and voice contact with the child.
3. The youngster is not allowed to accomplish any goal through the use of a tantrum.
4. When the child's tantrum has ceased, caregivers again attend to the child as usual. No scolding for the tantrum nor mention of the tantrum is made. Normal activity is resumed.

Caregivers who find it impossible to remain in the presence of a tantrum-engulfed child may alter the planned ignoring procedure by removing themselves from the scene. If the attention of the caregiver is indeed the key ingredient maintaining tantrum behavior, removal of the caregiver from the scene of the tantrum will have the same effect as ignoring the youngster: the caregiver's attention is denied.

The use of a planned ignoring procedure is recommended for the treatment of children whose tantrum sequence is primarily verbal. Tantrum responses such as whining, crying, and screaming can be effectively treated by planned ignoring. Tantrum behaviors that are physical may also be treated, but they are much more difficult to ignore effectively. Children who become self-injurious during tantrums should not be treated by a planned ignoring approach. Instead, a modified timeout procedure that allows for monitoring and direct intervention during the tantrum sequence should be employed.

Differential Reinforcement

The use of an extinction procedure to reduce tantrum behavior should be paired with a reward procedure to encourage more appropriate means of expressing needs and obtaining goals. Differential reinforcement techniques have been reported by various authors to have been effectively used to encourage the growth of appropriate expressive skills (Ames, 1976; Hall & Hall, 1980b; Hawkins, Peterson, Schweid, & Bijou, 1966; Patterson, 1976, chap. 14; Walle, Hobbs, & Caldwell, 1984; Zeilberger, Sampen, & Sloane, 1968).

The range of differential reinforcement techniques available is extensive. Some examples of commonly used strategies include systematic attention, social reinforcement, behavioral charting, and material reinforcers. The use of systematic attention and social reinforcement techniques as described by Hall and Hall (1980b) and Ames (1976) requires that caregivers be taught to identify and reinforce desirable behaviors such as complying with parental requests, sharing toys with other children, or using words to express frustration. Caregivers must learn to reward the occurrence of these behaviors with positive attention, praise, and positive physical contact. Patterson (1976, chap. 14) advocates the use of a chart to track gradual improvement in a youngster's ability to take no for an answer. Each time a tantrum-prone child minds a caregiver without whining or throwing a tantrum the child is allowed to place a gold star on a chart designed to graphically demonstrate improvements in ability to mind and follow instructions. Points may be accumulated toward the goal of earning some larger reinforcer at a later time.

When tantrums have become an entrenched problem, caregivers may cease to provide attention to the tantrum-prone youngster, even when the child is behaving appropriately, out of fear of upsetting the child and causing a tantrum to erupt. The adage "leave well enough alone" is frequently applied in such cases. Convincing caregivers to behave in a fashion that contradicts this time-honored philosophy may, at times, be a considerable challenge for the psychological consultant. In order for tantrum suppression achieved by the use of extinction procedures to be effective in the long term, however, caregivers must learn to actively encourage the growth of new communication strategies to fill the void left by foregone tantrums which previously had been relied upon for expressing frustration and obtaining goals.

Chaining and Fading Procedure for Bedtime Tantrums

Milan, Mitchell, Berger, and Pierson (1982) developed a procedure for dealing with the problem of children who throw tantrums at bedtime that may be more effective than the planned ignoring strategies commonly used in the past. The approach, chaining and fading of a positive bedtime routine, can be divided into three stages. First, caregivers determine their child's naturally occurring time for falling asleep. The child is dressed for bed at the usual time, but instead of forcing immediate retirement, parents do not put the youngster to bed until he or she has fallen asleep naturally. This stage is carried out for about 1 week or until a consistent time for the child's falling asleep of its own accord emerges. Second, a chain of activities involved in bedtime preparation is devised. The chain might include such activities as using the toilet, taking a bath, putting on pajamas, climbing into bed, reading a bedtime story. Parents are instructed to implement the chain as soon as signs of sleepiness are observed when the child's natural sleep time is reached. The chain is followed in exactly the same order each evening and social praise is provided as each link in the chain is completed (including awakening in the morning). Once the bedtime routine is firmly established, the third stage, gradually fading the start of the bedtime preparation chain backwards until it begins at the target bedtime, is initiated.

The chaining and fading procedure has been found to be highly effective in reducing the occurrence of tantrums. Another benefit of the approach is the extent to which positive social interaction and the opportunity for reinforcement are built into the bedtime preparation chain. In addition to extinguishing tantrum behavior, therefore, this approach provides an appropriate means for a child to attain parental attention.

Paradoxical Intervention

A recent development from the field of family counseling that has been shown in specific cases to be effective in controlling tantrum behavior is paradoxical intervention (Madanes, 1981; Zarske, 1982). The fundamental strategy behind the paradoxical approach, according to Zarske (1982), is that of "prescribing the symptom." He states, "when using the paradoxical directive clients are asked to perform the very behavior which they are seeking to eliminate" (Zarske, 1982, p. 324).

In Zarske's case example, paradoxical intervention was used with a 5-year-old cerebral palsied boy of normal intelligence who was experiencing severe tantrum problems both at home and in school. Monitoring during a 5-day baseline period prior to the onset of treatment revealed that the child exhibited tantrums at an average rate of six per day with a mean duration of 11 minutes 13 seconds per tantrum. The intervention consisted of two stages. In the first stage of treatment, the child's parents and his school aide helped him select a place at home and in school where tantrums could be indulged. Then, at the onset of a tantrum, the child was to go to the designated area and have the tantrum. He was to be accompanied by an adult who was instructed to *encourage* the child to go on with the tantrum. This stage of treatment lasted 2 weeks and resulted in a sharp drop in the daily frequency of tantrums. In the second stage of paradoxical intervention the child was told by his caregivers that he would still be allowed to have tantrums in the designated areas, but he would no longer need to be accompanied by an adult. The youngster was encouraged by his caregivers to have as many tantrums as he pleased, at any time he wished to have them. This second stage of intervention also lasted 2 weeks and resulted in complete extinction of tantrum behavior both at home and in school. Follow-up at 1- and 2-month intervals after conclusion of the treatment revealed a total absence of tantrums.

The basic rationale behind the use of paradoxical intervention is as follows: The change in caregivers' behavior from discouragement to encouragement of temper tantrums causes the tantrums to lose their manipulative power; the child is required, upon making this discovery, to seek alternative means of expressing frustration and obtaining goals.

While results attributed to the use of paradoxical intervention are indeed dramatic, Zarske cautions against practitioner application of the approach without proper background and preparatory experience. Additional reading and instruction in the use of paradoxical techniques is recommended prior to attempts at implementation.

SUMMARY

Among the wide range of emotional, learning, and behavioral problems brought to the attention of psychological consultants working with school-aged children, severe tantrums stand out as one of the most readily observable difficulties of all. As opposed to many problems that consultants face, there is seldom any difficulty in reaching a consensus among parents, school personnel, and the consultant on an operational determination of whether tantrum behavior has become severe, manipulative and entrenched. The fact that tantrums are highly disruptive and readily observable provides, from the consultant's point of view, the following benefits: Caregivers become highly motivated to change their own behavior if the change will have an impact on the child's tantrum activity; the effects of intervention are immediately apparent to all individuals involved; and child management skills found by caregivers to be effective in tantrum treatment can be transferred to use with other youngsters or other problems that arise. For these reasons, intervention in the lives of children experiencing severe tantrum difficulties, if carefully designed and monitored, has a high probability of achieving both short- and long-term success.

Each of the intervention strategies discussed in this chapter has been shown to be effective in tantrum treatment. Even the use of a differential reinforcement strategy without an extinction procedure can be highly effective in reducing tantrum frequency and severity (Ames, 1976). The choice of an appropriate mix of intervention techniques will depend on the specific demands of cases presented.

Often the factor that determines whether a behavioral intervention will succeed or fail is not the design of the intervention but how carefully it is introduced and monitored. Use of the caregiver interview, behavioral observations, and review of available treatment strategies will yield an appropriate intervention design. The success of the design, however, depends on the consultant's patience and skill in modeling treatment strategies for caregivers and providing careful monitoring and feedback.

REFERENCES

Ames, S. M. (1976). Four behavior therapy techniques for treating temper tantrums in young children: A comparative outcome study. *Dissertation Abstracts International, 37,* 5821B. (University Microfilms No. 77-10,742)

Barrow, L. (1968). *Tantrums, jealousy and the fears of children.* Sydney, Australia: A. H. & A. W. Reed.

Carlson, C. S., Arnold, C. R., Becker, W. C., & Madsen, C. H. (1968). The elimination of tantrum behavior of a child in an elementary classroom. *Behavior Research and Therapy, 6,* 117–119.

Dreikurs, R., & Soltz, V. (1964). *Children: The challenge.* New York: Hawthorn.

Epilepsy Foundation of America. (1981a). *How to recognize and classify seizures.* Landover, MD: Author.

Epilepsy Foundation of America. (1981b). *Seizure recognition and observation: A guide for allied health professionals.* Landover, MD: Author.

Hall, R. V., & Hall, M. C. (1980a). *How to use planned ignoring.* Lawrence, KS: H & H Enterprises.

Hall, R. V., & Hall, M. C. (1980b). *How to use systematic attention and approval.* Lawrence, KS: H & H Enterprises.

Hall, R. V., & Hall, M. C. (1980c). *How to use timeout.* Lawrence, KS: H & H Enterprises.

Harris, K. R. (1985). Definitional, parametric, and procedural considerations in timeout interventions and research. *Exceptional Children, 51,* 279–288.

Hawkins, R. P., Peterson, R. F., Schweid, E., & Bijou, S. W. (1966). Behavior therapy in the home: Amelioration of problem parent–child relations with the parent in a therapeutic role. *Journal of Experimental Child Psychology, 4,* 99–107.

Hobbs, S. A., & Forehand, R. (1977). Important parameters in the use of timeout with children: A re-examination. *Journal of Behavior Therapy and Experimental Psychiatry, 8,* 365–370.

Krumboltz, J. D., & Krumboltz, H. B. (1972). *Changing children's behavior.* Englewood Cliffs, NJ: Prentice-Hall.

MacDonough, T. S., & Forehand, R. (1973). Response-contingent timeout: Important parameters in behavior modification with children. *Journal of Behavior Therapy and Experimental Psychiatry, 4,* 231–236.

Madanes, C. (1981). *Strategic family therapy.* San Francisco: Jossey-Bass.

Martin, J. A. & Iagulli, D. M. (1974). Elimination of middle-of-the-night tantrums in a blind, retarded child. *Behavior Therapy, 5,* 420–422.

Milan, M. A., Mitchell, Z. P., Berger, M. I., & Pierson, D. F. (1982). Positive routines: A rapid alternative to extinction for elimination of bedtime tantrum behavior. *Child Behavior Therapy, 3*(1), 13–25.

Murray, M. F. (1976). Modified timeout procedures for controlling tantrum behaviors in public places. *Behavior Therapy, 7,* 412–413.

Patterson, G. R. (1976). *Living with children* (rev. ed., chap. 14). Champaign, IL: Research Press.

Sailor, W., Guess, D., Rutherford, G., & Baer, D. M. (1968). Control of tantrum behavior by operant techniques during experimental verbal training. *Journal of Applied Behavior Analysis, 1,* 237–243.

Walle, D. L., Hobbs, S. A., & Caldwell, H. S. (1984). Sequencing of parent training procedures: Effects on child noncompliance and treatment acceptability. *Behavior Modification, 8*(1), 540–552.

Williams, C. D. (1959). The elimination of tantrum behavior by extinction procedures. *Journal of Abnormal Social Psychology, 59,* 269.

Zarske, J. A. (1982). The treatment of temper tantrums in a cerebral palsied child: A paradoxical intervention. *School Psychology Review, 11*(3), 324–328.

Zeilberger, J., Sampen, S. E., & Sloane, H. N., Jr. (1968). Modification of a child's problem behaviors in the home with a mother as therapist. *Journal of Applied Behavior Analysis, 1,* 47–53.

BIBLIOGRAPHY: PROFESSIONALS

Ames, S. M. (1976). Four behavior therapy techniques for treating temper tantrums in young children: A comparative outcome study. *Dissertation Abstracts International, 37,* 5821B. (University Microfilms No. 77-10, 742)

Four behavior therapy techniques: time out, time out with contingent social isolation, time out with differential reinforcement, and differential reinforcement were used in the treatment of temper tantrums with 38 children (aged 2½ to 6 years). The treatment groups were compared with each other and with a waiting list control group on the basis of various behavioral measures and rating scales. The relative effectiveness and ethical implications of these behavioral treatment approaches are discussed.

Harris, K. R. (1985). Definitional, parametric, and procedural considerations in timeout interventions and research. *Exceptional Children, 51,* 279–288.
The various parameters that must be considered when planning a timeout intervention are discussed. In addition, five general types of timeout are delineated and arranged along a continuum of relative restrictiveness based upon the extent to which the subject is removed from the reinforcing environment.

Milan, M. A., Mitchell, Z. P., Berger, M. I., & Pierson, D. F. (1982). Positive routines: A rapid alternative to extinction for elimination of bedtime tantrum behavior. *Child Behavior Therapy, 3*(1), 13–25.
Three children (ranging in age from 2.1 to 15.5 years) were treated for severely disruptive bedtime temper tantrums by a chaining and fading procedure. The procedure proved effective in seriously reducing tantrum behavior for all three children. Follow-up contacts made at 1 year past treatment termination for two of the children and at 2 years past treatment termination for the third child revealed successful generalization and maintenance of treatment objectives.

Zarske, J. A. (1982). The treatment of temper tantrums in a cerebral palsied child: A paradoxical intervention. *School Psychology Review, 11*(3), 324–328.
A two-stage model of paradoxical intervention was employed to reduce tantrum behavior in a 5-year-old cerebral palsied boy. The results were highly successful. The preparation requirements for implementation of the paradoxical technique and the limitations of the technique are discussed.

BIBLIOGRAPHY: PARENTS

Barrow, L. (1968). *Tantrums, jealousy and the fears of children.* Sydney, Australia: A. H. & A. W. Reed.
This booklet in Barrow's Child Psychology in Outline series provides an excellent brief discussion of temper tantrum development in young children. Case examples are presented that feature parents' descriptions of tantrum problems experienced and dealt with in their own families. Planned ignoring is the primary treatment strategy advocated by Barrow for severe tantrum difficulties.

Dreikurs, R., & Soltz, V. (1964). *Children: The challenge.* New York: Hawthorn.
Dreikurs' and Soltz's book is a readable guide for parents and covers a wide variety of child-rearing issues. Unfortunately, temper tantrum concerns did not receive a separate chapter, but are dealt with in parts of five different chapters scattered throughout the book. Despite this drawback, the authors present a number of vignettes that illustrate well how tantrums can be dealt with successfully by a planned ignoring procedure.

Hall, R. V., & Hall, M. C. (1980). *How to use planned ignoring. How to use systematic attention and approval. How to use time out.* Lawrence, KS: H & H Enterprises.
These three booklets are part of a self-instructional series prepared by Hall and Hall for parents and teachers interested in learning to apply behavioral principles in situations they encounter. The booklets come complete with worksheets, example situations, and clear explanations of the behavioral principles involved in the use of the intervention techniques considered.

Patterson, G. R. (1976). *Living with children* (rev. ed., chap. 14). Champaign, IL: Research Press.
Patterson's brief chapter devoted to temper tantrums reviews behaviors typically produced by tantrum-prone children and describes how to proceed in setting up a simple timeout program for controlling tantrums in the home.

Children and Temperament

Hedy Teglasi
University of Maryland–College Park

BACKGROUND

The study of temperament attempts to delineate the essential foundations of individuality based on built-in tendencies. There is wide consensus that temperament represents the part of personality that appears in the first 2 years of life and continues to influence the course of development over time and that it is largely genetically determined (Buss & Plomin, 1975, 1984; Plomin, 1983). While temperament is the property of the child and resists change, the expression of temperament is modified by interaction with the environment. Furthermore, the functional significance of a temperamental attribute varies with age.

Although the concept is centuries old, the scientific study of temperamental attributes began only recently. Thomas, Chess, and their colleagues (Thomas, Chess, Birch, Herzig, 1963; Thomas, Chess & Birch, 1968) launched a systematic research program that became a very important stimulus to research on temperament and is referred to as the New York Longitudinal Study (NYLS). They sought to identify personality traits inherent in the child that were both related to problems in early childhood and likely to lead to later problems or maladjustment.

Temperament refers to a characteristic style in respect to *how* an individual approaches and responds to people and situations rather than to *what* (content of behavior) that person does, or to *why* that person engages in an activity (motivation, purpose, or goal) or to the person's capacities, abilities, or talents (Thomas & Chess, 1977). However, the concept of style may overlap with content because individuals choose activities that are compatible with their temperament (Buss & Plomin, 1984; Stevenson & Graham, 1982).

The study of temperament is useful in explaining the striking individual differences in the observed behavior of babies and young children that cannot be attributed to socialization (Brazelton, 1973; Buss & Plomin, 1975) and derives its importance from the following findings: (a) certain combinations of temperamental attributes are associated with a substantially increased risk of developing emotional and/or behavioral disorders during childhood (Bates, Maslin, & Frankel, 1985; Thomas & Chess, 1977, 1980; Wolkind & DeSalis, 1982) and into adulthood (Thomas & Chess, 1982), (b) Temperamental attributes are related to interpersonal interactions and adjustment at home (Dunn & Kendrick, 1980; Graham, Rutter, & George, 1973; Hinde, Easton, Mellor, & Tamplin, 1982) and at school (Billman & McDevitt, 1980; Hinde, Stevenson-Hinde, & Tamplin, 1985; Keogh, 1982).

Temperament influences the nature of a child's life experiences in three basic ways: (a) Temperament dictates the *selection* of activities and environments. People select environments that are comfortable and consistent with temperamental characteristics. Differences in emotional reactivity are related to preferences for situations differing in degree of stimulation (Strelau, 1983). Highly reactive individuals will avoid high levels of arousal, stress, or risk. People with a high activity level seek environments that are fast-paced, and sociable people seek out other people (Buss & Plomin, 1984) (b) A child's behavioral characteristics, in part, shape the responses of others (Dunn & Kendrick, 1982; Keogh, 1982). These reactions further amplify the individuality of the child's experiences and provide a basis for further development. (c) The impact of similar environments and life experiences is not the same for children who differ on a variety of temperamental characteristics. There is evidence of "resilience" in some children who thrive despite adverse environmental conditions (Bowlby, 1973).

Although the utility of the temperament concept does not rest on the assumption of a genetic origin of temperament, some researchers have focused on documenting the heritability of dimensions of temperament (Buss & Plomin, 1984). While there appears to be genetic influence in some temperamental traits, differences in behavior emerge as a function of the interaction between the individual and the environment. Inherited traits are not necessarily stable throughout development, because genes that influence temperament in early childhood may not completely overlap with those that affect temperament in later childhood (Buss & Plomin, 1984). The problems involved in assessing the continuity of temperamental attributes have been summarized by Dunn (1980). Whereas temperamental variables at ages 3, 4, and 5 years have generally shown significant associations with the subsequent development of emotional/behavioral disorders, those in the first 2 years of life often have not (Cameron, 1978; Thomas & Chess, 1982).

Children who fall at the extremes of one or more of the temperament dimensions identified in the NYLS are likely to be at odds with parents, teachers, and other children. Eight of these temperamental characteristics as well as their associated interactional difficulties are described below.

Dimensions of Temperament

Quality of Mood. The amount of smiling, pleasant, joyful, and friendly behavior, as contrasted with unpleasant, moody, complaining, fussy, and unfriendly behavior, is defined as quality of mood. Negative mood is *not* related to depression, nor is it pathological, but a manifestation of style.

During the first half-year of life, negative mood is seen as a general tendency to exhibit distress. Subsequently, distress differentiates into fear and anger. Children are typically described as either fearful or angry but not both (Buss & Plomin, 1984).

The negative mood of a baby is likely to cause parents to feel inadequate and describe their baby as "difficult" (Bates, 1980). As they get older, children can display negative mood in two ways: by being worried, serious, timid, anxious, and whining; or by being aggressive, angry, or argumentative. The angry child tends to have frequent temper tantrums and antagonistic interactions. Timid or anxious children tend to remain excessively dependent on caretakers or may be hard to soothe if their distress is intense. Parental tolerance for timidity and fearfulness tends to wane as a child gets older, despite the child's continued susceptibility to negative mood (Stevenson-Hinde & Simpson, 1982).

Threshold of Responsiveness. The intensity of stimulation needed to provoke a response is defined as the threshold of responsiveness. A child with a low threshold is sensitive to sound, lights, temperature, feel of clothes, and physical discomfort, as well as textures and smells of food. An infant with a low threshold may cry in the bath if it is too hot or cold, may refuse new foods, and may even react to changes such as a haircut in a family member.

A preschooler with a low threshold often says, "I don't like it" or "It bothers me." Sensitivity to taste and texture of food may result in rejection of a familiar food when there is a minor substitution in the recipe or if it's not presented on the plate in the customary way. A child's behavior may provoke constant power struggles particularly if the parents view her or him as manipulative or demanding rather than as sensitive.

Intensity of Reaction. Intensity of reaction is the energy level of the response for both positive and negative emotions. A highly intense child expresses protest by screaming with anger, when a less intense child may frown, grumble, or sulk. Similarly, an intense child expresses happiness with exuberance and may roar with laughter, whereas a child with low intensity would smile or grin.

The difficulties associated with intensity depend on

other temperamental attributes. Negative mood expressed intensely (temper tantrums) can be hard to tolerate, whereas exuberance in the expression of positive emotions may be viewed favorably. Intense young children were high on both friendly and hostile interactions with parents (Hinde et al., 1982). Parents of intense children, particularly if the intensity is combined with negative mood, tendency to withdraw, and poor adaptability, can feel overwhelmed, or even afraid of their child's intensity. They may be reluctant to set limits or do things that trigger a tantrum.

Intense reactions may result in a child being viewed as loud, opinionated, or bossy. Emotional reactions may appear out of proportion to the provocation and the intensity can become wearing on others.

Activity Level. A child's activity level is the extent to which he or she is in motion during routine activities such as eating, dressing, playing, or even sleeping. Highly active children may have "run before they walked." Such children are "restless" during quiet activities when not absorbed. A highly active child virtually never sits still and responds at a high frequency, always touching things, talking, etc.

Active children at 42 and 50 months have been found to have more tantrums, make more refusals, and seek attention more than do less active children (Stevenson-Hinde & Simpson, 1982). Active infants are less "cuddly" and sleep less than average as toddlers; they are described as "getting into everything." When older, they have difficulty sitting in their seats at school and may engage in rough play with other children.

A low activity level is generally not regarded as a problem during infancy, but an older child may be viewed as lacking in energy, initiative, and drive.

Distractibility. Distractibility is the degree to which extraneous stimuli interfere with ongoing behavior. A distractible baby stops fussing when given a pacifier, stops crying when picked up. The child's distractibility in early infancy is viewed as "soothability," which is seen as a positive trait. In late childhood, distractibility can show itself by frequent changes of activity during play, topic changes during discussions, or apparent "absent mindedness" when something intrudes into ongoing activity.

A highly distractible child is greatly influenced by the immediacy of the environmental stimulation or even by internal stimulation. Such a child will be "captured" by the strongest stimulus present and has difficulty voluntarily focusing attention. This child can attend for a long time to TV or puzzles because these stimuli may be strong enough to screen out sources of distraction. Lego blocks with notches may rivet attention because, unlike wooden ones, they provide cues (structure) so that each step leads to the next.

As babies and preschoolers, highly distractible children do not seem difficult. However, when they get older, such children have problems at home, school, and in social situations. Parents describe such children as lacking in responsibility, dawdling in the morning, not completing chores on schedule, and not listening. Much to the dismay of parents, these children often do not keep promises because their susceptibility to environmental stimulation may override a previous commitment. Such children may not be able to choose from among a variety of items in a store because they find everything appealing.

In school, they may have difficulty concentrating in a "busy" classroom, can't work "independently," don't "follow directions," and have problems organizing their work or managing their time. They appear to be "unmotivated," but the problem is that they cannot focus their attention when other stimuli impinge. Problems with peer relationships arise owing to their difficulty staying in tune with others. Distractible children may be described as "uncaring," for when caught up in the stimulation of the moment, they may not be aware of others' feelings.

Attention Span/Persistence. Persistence (attention span) is the continuation of activity in the face of obstacles or requests to stop. While persistence is related to distractibility, they are different concepts. A distractible child can be persistent if other stimuli are not strong enough to divert attention from an ongoing activity. A persistent child will insist on continuing an activity despite requests from parents or teachers to stop and will return to the task after an interruption.

Both the high and the low extremes of attention span/persistence can be problematic at different ages. High persistence is related to difficulty changing an activity abruptly; a child may throw a tantrum when asked to come to dinner while absorbed in play or may protest when a teacher requests a change of activity. On the other hand, absorption in games or puzzles and the ability to stay with activities for a long time is viewed as positive. Such children tend to do homework carefully, watch others intently to learn skills, and practice an activity until it is mastered. The stubborn form of persistence (that is, not taking *no* for an answer) involves some aspects of intensity, quality of mood, and low distractibility, in addition to high attention span/persistence (Rowe & Plomin, 1977). Underachievers may be characterized by a combination of low persistence and high distractibility.

Approach or Withdrawal. The approach/withdrawal dimension describes initial response to unfamiliar situations, persons, or tasks. A child may look frightened and hang back in new situations or may hide when unexpected company arrives. A baby may protest when left with strangers either by clinging or throwing a tantrum. Withdrawal responses may also be shown by infants by tuning out their attention or by negative initial reactions to new experiences such as foods or a bath. In older children, withdrawal responses are shown by initial reactions to a new peer group or new academic subjects. Low threshold may increase the likelihood of initial withdrawal from physical stimuli such as noises, new foods, places, and activities.

Parents of a child who avoids new experiences are

faced with decisions about how much to encourage their child to approach unfamiliar situations. Children who are allowed to avoid new situations may not get a chance to learn needed skills and may miss the opportunity to get accustomed to these situations. The cumulative effect of withdrawal can lower confidence, thus increasing future tendencies to withdraw. If the child is gently introduced to new experiences at a tolerable pace (depending on adaptability), the adverse impact of a tendency to avoidance can be minimized. An older child with a moderate tendency to withdraw might be cautious before joining a conversation or game. Depending on the extent of the withdrawal tendency, such caution may be a positive trait, and the opposite extreme of approaching new things with little reflection might be problematic.

Adaptability. Adaptability is the capacity to get used to new or altered situations after the initial reaction. An adaptable child accepts new foods after initial rejection and takes changes of routine in stride. The initial response (approach–avoidance) reflects how the child handles novelty; adaptability reflects adjustment in situations that are routine.

A poorly adaptable child takes a very long time to get used to unfamiliar situations or to changes in routine. Transitions such as entering school may remain difficult for a long time. The poorly adaptable child's trouble with transitions is due to difficulty in getting used to new ideas or situations and not to problems with leaving another activity, as is true for the child with high persistence. Poorly adaptable children remain focused on one idea and cannot change their expectations. They may refuse a present because it is not exactly what was expected. A moderately adaptable child may accept the gift after initial protest.

Temperament Dimension Composites

The issue of how to reduce separate temperamental variables to a smaller number of factors or summary measures is approached differently depending on the goal of the researchers. Those who aim to study the relationship of temperament to personality development rely primarily on factor analysis, letting the factors "speak for themselves," whereas investigators who are more clinically oriented have developed composite measures, such as the "difficult child index" (Hertzig, 1982; Thomas & Chess, 1977), "temperament risk scores" (Cameron, 1978), or "temperamental adversity index" (Rutter, 1978), the components of which are selected on the basis of utility for predicting the development of emotional–behavioral problems. Generally, clusters or patterns of characteristics have proved better predictors than any single attribute. However, for any given individual, the most powerful connection between temperament and adjustment may lie in a single variable. The most widely used cluster of temperamental traits draws on the concept of the "difficult child," which incorporates the child's characteristics that present challenges for parents and other caregivers (see Hubert, Wachs, Peters-Martin, & Gandour, 1982, for a review of how measures of difficultness meet psychometric standards).

The *difficult* child is characterized by high intensity of reactions, withdrawal vis-a-vis new situations and new stimuli, slow adaptation, and negative mood. Roughly 10% of children possess this combination of temperaments. These children exhibit eating and sleeping problems, resist new places or activities, don't get accustomed to changes in routine, and are generally characterized by crying,worrying, or intense anger. A less difficult category of children described as *slow to warm up* is characterized by low activity level, withdrawal orientation, moderately low adaptability, moderately negative mood, and a somewhat lower intensity of reaction than that which characterizes difficult children. About 15% of children fall into this category and appear similar to children who are described as temperamentally "inhibited" (Kagan, Reznick, & Snidman, 1986). Children who are *slow to warm up* take a long time to get involved in new activities and new situations but feel very comfortable in familiar surroundings. They may be better adjusted to school a couple of months into the academic year than in the beginning.

Most of the composite measures of difficulty are broadly similar. *Emotionality* as a general temperamental feature plays a prominent role in every measure of temperament. Buss and Plomin's assessment (1975, 1984) of emotionality incorporates the Thomas and Chess temperamental dimensions of negative mood, low threshold of response, withdrawal orientation, poor adaptability, and high intensity. Rothbart and Derryberry (1981) focused on the central concepts of *reactivity* and *self-regulation,* which have implications for understanding several of the temperamental dimensions proposed by Thomas and Chess. Reactivity is associated with threshold, intensity, soothability (distractibility), and activity. The purpose of self-regulation is the control of stimulation to promote optimal arousal for efficient intellectual and emotional functioning. Approach and withdrawal represent such attempts at self-regulation. Some people withdraw from environments that are overstimulating; other people seek excitement or variation (Fulker, Eysenck, & Zuckerman, 1980). Adaptability is related to self-regulation or modulation of arousal as a way of coping with initial responses. A child who does not calm easily after stimulation may be poorly adaptable. Reactive children who are easily distressed and hard to soothe tend to be characterized as "difficult" (Bates, 1986; Daniels, Plomin & Greenhalgh, 1983).

The temperamental characteristics of high activity level and marked distractibility, while not included in most composite measures, are frequent sources of difficulty for parents, teachers, and children. Extremely active and distractible children may be diagnosed as having an attention deficit disorder. Factor analyses indicate that high activity, marked distractibility, and low attention span/persistence contribute to the temperamental dimension of impulsivity (Lerner et al., 1982; Rowe & Plomin, 1977).

A high activity level increases the problems associated with high distractibility because increased motion without apparent purpose frequently makes a child appear "wild." Such a child responds quickly and when overstimulated may lash out at others. Children who become "caught up in the moment" may cheat at games because of the inability to balance the interpersonal aspect of the situation with the competitive exigencies of the game. Often highly active and distractible children display persistence and refuse to stop an absorbing activity.

Impulsive children have difficulty monitoring their behavior and "forget" important school assignments. Parents may find that their child often seems "revved up" and hard to reach or discipline. They may resort to harsh, punitive measures to "grab" the child's attention. Impulsive children may do better with more structure and reduced stimulation. Although they get wild on the playground or in the classroom, they may do well in a one-to-one or small-group situation. On the positive side, these children display exuberance are are often quick-witted when they are bright. At the extreme end of this spectrum, a child who has trouble paying attention to almost anything, does not follow instructions, and is always interrupting.

Two additional temperamental dimensions that may be composites of those discussed above are helpful in understanding individual differences in children. *Task orientation* appears to be composed of high persistence, low distractibility, and moderate activity (Keogh, 1982). Children with low task orientation may be considered by the teacher to be uninterested, unwilling to learn, and inattentive. *Sociability,* which consists of a tendency to enjoy interaction with other people (Buss & Plomin, 1984), may be related to approach response, positive mood, and adaptability (Keogh, 1982). Because of their orientation toward others, sociable children are likely to develop good social skills and to respond warmly. Such children tend to smile more, be more responsive to others, and share activities more than their less sociable counterparts, thus providing social rewards for others. Person and task orientation are not mutually exclusive; one can be absorbed in tasks of interest, yet be sociable as the occasion demands.

DEVELOPMENT

Development reflects the constantly evolving interactional process between the individual and the environment. The key to the influence of temperament on development is the match or "goodness of fit" between the inborn tendencies of the individual and environmental demands, opportunities, and supports (Thomas & Chess, 1980). When environmental demands are consonant with the predisposition of the child, development proceeds optimally. However, an environment that places demands for adaptation that are beyond the child's capacity undermines development. Continuous friction and antagonism with parents and teachers result in the development of emotional and behavioral problems such as nightmares, school refusals, overreaction to feedback, distrust, and poor self-image (Thomas & Chess, 1977, 1980).

A child with a difficult temperament need not develop emotional–behavioral problems with proper management. For example, Carl (Thomas & Chess, 1986), a "difficult" youngster who exhibited intense negative reactions to anything new, but grew up in a very stable and supportive family, school, and social environment rarely exhibited his negative temperamental attributes past the age of 5 years. Occasionally, a new environmental demand such as piano lessons evoked a typical intense negative response followed by slow adaptation and eventual enjoyment of the new activity. When he went to college and was faced with a host of new situations and demands, his temperamentally difficult traits reappeared in full force. He was constantly irritable, couldn't motivate himself to study, and had a negative attitude about his courses and other students. After discussions with the family and professional consultation, he reduced the demands by limiting extracurricular activities and social contacts. As he gradually adapted, his distress disappeared and he was able to expand his social contacts and extracurricular activities. Transitions will continue to cause temporary problems for Carl, since his negative temperamental traits will probably re-emerge at these times.

Identical patterns of temperamental traits can be acceptable in one setting but not in another. Even after extensive professional guidance, middle-class parents seem unable to accept the individuality of children who are temperamentally distractible and nonpersistent (Thomas et al., 1968). Such parents stubbornly continue to make demands on their children (e.g., to sit still and concentrate for long periods of time) that are at odds with their capacity. Thus, the prevailing values and expectations of one's environment determine the acceptability of various temperamental traits and influence the goodness of fit.

The continuous and sequential interplay among temperaments, abilities, and environment determine the course of development. The nature of the interaction between a person and the environment can be substantially altered as new abilities emerge (e.g., Piaget, 1963) and as new demands to master developmental tasks are imposed (e.g., Erikson, 1963, 1968). A poor fit can be dramatically improved by the appearance of a special talent such as a musical or artistic ability, and a previously good fit can be altered when new age-appropriate environmental demands (e.g., increasing importance of abstract or conceptual thinking) outstrip the child's capacity.

PUTTING CHILDREN AND TEMPERAMENT IN PERSPECTIVE

The evolution of child–environment interaction is affected by many simultaneous influences such as those described below, which determine the course of development jointly with temperament.

1. The level of intelligence and other special abilities contribute to the capacity of the child to meet environmental demands. Children with "difficult" temperaments who have a physical handicap or mild mental retardation have been found to be at an even greater risk

for developing behavioral problems than their nonhandicapped counterparts (Thomas & Chess, 1977).

2. Cognitive style represents an interweaving of affective, temperamental, and motivational components; like temperament, it does not appear to be easily modified by training and operates across a broad range of situations (Messick, 1976). Definitions of cognitive style seem to overlap with aspects of temperament (Kogan, 1971) and a "goodness of fit" approach between cognitive style and environment has been proposed (Witkin, 1973). Nevertheless, research on temperament and cognition (both intelligence and cognitive style) have proceeded independently of each other.

3. The cumulative impact of past interactions with the environment promotes the development of self-concept and self-evaluative standards. These cognitive schemata then act as structures through which subsequent experiences are processed. Cognitions can be short-term notions such as attributions of causes of ongoing events or long-term constructs that put immediate events into perspective by rooting them in the context of goals, aspirations, and philosophical attitudes. A highly emotionally reactive person can moderate the intensity of immediate emotional reactions with the help of appropriate cognitions.

4. Gender may influence children's match with their environment. In the absence of evidence of early-appearing gender differences in emotionality, the difference between boys and girls in older children's rates of expression of anger and fear is assumed to be the result of socialization (Buss & Plomin, 1984). Custom may allow greater expression of different aspects of temperament such as shyness, dependency, activity level, or aggression according to gender (see Stevenson-Hinde & Hinde, 1986).

5. Environmental factors that determine expectations for achievement and standards of behavior influence development. The amount of support for individuality and the freedom of choice available in the environment can influence adjustment. For individuals who select careers, hobbies, and even friends on the basis of compatibility with their temperamental style, the availability of appropriate opportunities enhances the goodness of their fit with the environment. Young children are typically allowed to exercise few choices, but opportunities to select activities and situations increase with age. Other variables that might contribute to the determination of the fit between the individual and the environment are the presence of siblings (with their unique temperaments) and the "match" between the child's and parents' temperaments (e.g., a highly reactive child will do better with a calm parent). Children differ in their vulnerability to the impact of the environment so these variables operate selectively.

ALTERNATIVE ACTIONS

In determining the appropriate intervention to resolve a problem, the first consideration is to ascertain whether the problem is based on a mismatch between environmental demands and temperament, whether it represents an attempt to manipulate, or is a combination of the two. A behavior that is purely an expression of temperament can become manipulative if it is mishandled. For example, a child with negative mood whose parents struggle to make him "happy" could use his "moods" to manipulate parents. The cardinal rule regarding intervention is to support a child with behavior problems due to temperament and to alter contingencies for behaviors that are primarily manipulative. When dealing with a temperamentally difficult child, parents and teachers are more likely to be objective rather than respond with irritation if the following are kept in mind: (a) A child who behaves in a way that upsets parents and teachers does not necessarily *intend* to do this; (b) temperament is a relatively durable trait and generally must be managed rather than changed; (c) misbehavior caused by temperament–environment mismatch should not be punished.

When working with parents and teachers, it is important for the professional to convey an understanding of the emotional impact of the child's behavior. Parents and teachers might also be told that what they are doing might be satisfactory for a child with different temperamental traits. Thus, the *intent* of the teachers' and parents' approach can be separated from its *impact.*

The assessment of temperament relies on concrete descriptive material from a variety of functionally similar life situations (Thomas & Chess, 1977). Global labels such as "difficult" are meaningless unless situations in which a child is difficult are specified. Temperament must be defined in the context within which the behavior occurs; assessment of temperament must be individually tailored to the extent that children differ in their life experiences. As children get older, their lives become more individualized, and the temperamental roots of behavior may be more difficult to assess. Difficulties can arise from one problematic temperamental trait or from the joint impact of several attributes.

Parents and teachers can be helped to identify temperamental characteristics of their charges by the availability of short questionnaire forms that expedite the delineation of temperament (e.g., Bates, Freeland, & Lounsbury, 1979; Carey & McDevitt, 1978; Hegvik, McDevitt, & Carey, 1982; McDevitt & Carey, 1978; Thomas & Chess, 1977). However, a consideration of an individual's life circumstances must also be included. While questionnaires are generally more efficient, better predictions come from well-conducted interview-based assessments.

In the management of a child with difficult temperamental attributes, the goal is not to accept all the youngster's behavior in all situations but to reduce or eliminate the adverse impact of temperament. The aims of intervention strategies are: (a) avoidance of demands or expectations that are substantially dissonant with the child's temperament; (b) enforcing schedules and activities that will minimize the undesirable consequences of the child's temperament.

The ultimate goal of management techniques is for the child to learn self-understanding and ways of coping with temperamental difficulties. There is a progression from a great deal of parental and teacher effort, involvement, guidance, and supervision, which for a "difficult" child is likely to go well beyond what is required for other children, to gradually increasing self-direction on the part of the maturing child.

The following discussion provides specific guidelines for managing children with one or more difficult temperamental characteristics that are consistent with the literature (Thomas & Chess, 1977, 1980; Turecki, 1985) and the author's experience.

Structure. Despite detailed explanations of what is expected, some children cannot manage their own behavior and sustain effort without continued supervision and guidance. One cannot simply tell a distractible child to "clean your room" but may start with a request to "put library books on the bottom shelf." After providing feedback, the next task can be given. Elaborate behavior management programs provide the structure and supervision required in monitoring the behavior.

Teachers may stand physically close to a distractible child when giving instructions and may need to keep gently reminding the child to return to the task.

Not having a predictable routine can make an overactive distractible child even more wild and can increase the adjustment problems of the poorly adaptable child. A fearful child is comforted by an established routine.

Prevention. Understanding the child's temperament and anticipating the situations in which difficulties will arise can help parents and teachers avoid confrontations and minimize dissonance between the child and the environment. Changes in routine for a poorly adaptable child can be planned to allow time for adjustment. Parents and teachers need to anticipate how long a distractible child can stay on task without frustration and provide short breaks.

An active, distractible child may expend so much effort struggling to pay attention in school that parents may wish to ease up on their expectations at home. Parents may decide that maintaining a tidy home with artwork and breakables is not worth the conflict with a very active child. Early intervention may be needed to prevent the escalating sequence that results in the "wild" behavior often seen in active, distractible children. It is necessary to intervene before they are out of control by removing them from the situation, distracting them, or allowing them to "blow off steam."

A sensitive child may benefit from reduced stimulation. A light-sensitive child who wakes at dawn needs blackout shades. A child who is especially sensitive to the taste and texture of foods should be provided with a balanced meal of familiar foods. New foods can be introduced gradually, with familiar alternatives provided as a back-up.

A persistent child who finds it difficult to stop an activity abruptly needs time to disengage. Parents can prevent a tantrum by giving notice a few minutes before switching an activity or by allowing the child to bring the activity to another setting ("let's bring the puzzle or doll along").

Preparation. When parents and teachers cannot modify the environment or their demands to suit a child's needs, they can help prepare the child for upcoming stressful events. Poorly adaptable children and those with a tendency toward initial withdrawal do not like surprises and welcome being able to anticipate changes of routine. Such children benefit from being told of upcoming sequences of events. Parents can explain what will happen on a trip, discuss when company will arrive, or role-play an anticipated visit to the doctor's office.

Teaching Coping Skills and Self-Understanding. When children are old enough, discussions about their sensitivities or about their reactions to change may be helpful. Parents can label their reactions with a nonjudgmental attitude and convey understanding. As children get older, they can label their own reactions and verbalize their needs. A poorly adaptable child can say "I need more time to get used to it." A persistent child who is pulled away from an absorbing activity can learn to express frustration without tantrums.

Children who are taught to recognize that their problems lie in initial reactions may be encouraged to persevere long enough to enjoy activities, once they have ceased to be novel. Nonpersistent children can learn to break up tasks into small components and take breaks during a difficult task. Distractible children can do homework in a quiet place away from interfering stimuli. Children with a high activity level can learn to channel their energies, and those with intense reactions can learn to understand the impact of their intensity on others.

Acceptance. Parents or teachers may feel that unless they attempt to "change" a child's irritating behavior, they are guilty of reinforcing them. However, there is not much one can do to change negative mood quality or high intensity. In fact, it is damaging to require a child to "cheer up," because such admonitions convey that the child's natural mood state is unacceptable. The key lies in the recognition that negative mood quality is not a manifestation of unhappiness but a reflection of temperamental style so that subtle expressions of happy feelings can be appreciated. Similarly, a child's intensity, while jarring at times, must simply be tolerated. Children whose innate tendencies are constantly challenged may not develop the self-esteem necessary to cope with their adverse temperamental characteristics.

Building Relationships. Because parents and teachers are human, there are inevitable frictions and irritations elicited by some temperamental characteristics. Yet criticism and hostility should not be allowed to pervade their relationships with temperamentally difficult children. Parents can capitalize on situations that are pleasant, such as car rides or calm times before going to bed. Enjoyable activities in which a child's temperament is an asset should be planned to help solidify the bond between parents and child. Teachers can be alert for situations that bring out the "best" in a child.

Creative approaches can be used to promote a

warm relationship with children. One parent, who felt she was constantly "badgering" her bright but distractible daughter to get ready on time for school, to do homework, and to practice piano, was wondering about the impact of all this on their relationship. She approached her daughter prior to bedtime as follows: "There's something on my mind and I'd like to talk to you about it by first telling you a story that has something to do with us. A mother keeps yelling at her 7-year-old daughter to do . . . . The mother is wondering if maybe she's expecting too much from her child. Maybe she should put off piano lessons for another year; maybe mother worries too much about the daughter's homework; maybe . . . . What do you think is the right thing to do? The girl replied: "I know what you're talking about. I think the daughter wants her mother to keep reminding her to do her homework and to practice piano. The daughter knows her mother loves her and that sometimes she *has* to yell."

Sometimes it takes a great deal of patience and perseverance to promote a solid relationship with a "difficult" child. However, the impact of inevitable frictions that arise from difficult temperamental qualities can be put into proper perspective in the context of a basically positive relationship.

SUMMARY

Temperament refers to inborn characteristics of an individual that appear early in life, are genetically influenced, and are resistant to modification. The functional significance and the expression of a temperamental quality change with development and with fluctuating environmental circumstances. The "goodness of fit" between the child's temperamental qualities and environmental expectations and opportunities is the cornerstone of development.

REFERENCES

Bates, J. E. (1986). The measurement of temperament. In R. Plomin & J. Dunn (Eds.), *The study of temperament: Changes, continuities and challenges.* Hillsdale, NJ: Erlbaum.

Bates, J. E., Freeland, C. A. B., & Lounsbury, M. L. (1979). Measurement of infant difficultness. *Child Development, 50,* 794–803.

Bates, J. E. (1980). The concept of difficult temperament. *Merrill-Palmer Quarterly, 26,* 299–319.

Bates, J. E., Maslin, C. A., & Frankel, K. A. (1985). Attachment security, mother–child interaction and temperament as predictors of behavior problem ratings at age three years. *Monographs of the Society for Research in Child Development.*

Billman, J., & McDevitt, S. C. (1980). Convergence of parent and observer ratings of temperament with observations of peer interaction at nursery school *Child Development, 51,* 395–400.

Brazelton, T. B. (1973). Neonatal Behavior Assessment Scale. *Little Club Clinics in Developmental Medicine,* No. 50. London: William Heinemann Medical Books: Lippin.

Buss, A. H., & Plomin, R. A. (1975). *A temperamental theory of personality development.* New York: Wiley Interscience.

Buss, A. H., & Plomin, R. A. (1984). *Temperament: Early developing personality traits.* New Jersey: Erlbaum.

Cameron, J. R. (1978). Parental treatment, children's temperament, and the risk of childhood behavior problems. Initial temperament, parental attitudes, and the incidence and form of behavioral problems. *American Journal of Orthopsychiatry, 110,* 651–661.

Carey, W. B., & McDevitt, S. C. (1978). Revision of the infant temperament questionnaire. *Pediatrics, 61,* 735–739.

Daniels, D., Plomin, R., & Greenhalgh, J. (1983). Correlates of difficult temperament in infancy. *Child Development, 55,* 1184–1194.

Dunn, J., & Kendrick, C. (1980). Studying temperament and parent–child interaction: Comparison of interview and direct observation. *Developmental Medical Child Neurology, 22,* 494–496.

Dunn, J., & Kendrick, C. (1982). Temperamental differences, family relationships, and young children's response to change within the family. *Temperamental differences in infants and young children* (Ciba Foundation Symposium, 89). London: Pitman Books.

Erikson, E. H. (1963). *Childhood and society.* New York: Norton.

Erikson, E. H. (1968). *Identity, youth and crisis.* New York: Norton.

Fulker, D. W., Eysenck, H. J., & Zuckerman, M. (1980). A genetic and environmental analysis of sensation seeking. *Journal of Research in Personality, 14,* 261–281.

Graham, P., Rutter, M., & George, S. (1973). Temperamental characteristics as predictors of behavioral disorders in children. *American Journal of Orthopsychiatry, 43,* 328–339.

Hegvik, R. L., McDevitt, S. C., & Carey, W. B. (1982). The middle childhood temperament questionnaire. *Developmental and behavioral Pediatrics, 3,* 197–200.

Hertzig, M. (1982). Temperament and neurological status. In M. Rutter (Ed.), *Behavioral syndromes of brain dysfunction in childhood.* New York: Guilford.

Hinde, R. A., Easton, D. F., Meller, R. E., & Tamplin, A. M. (1982). Temperamental characteristics of 3–4-year-olds and mother–child interaction. In R. Porter & G. M. Collins (Eds.), *Temperamental differences in infants and young children.* London: Pitman.

Hinde, R. A., Stevenson-Hinde, J., & Tamplin, A. (1985). Characteristics of 3–4 year olds assessed at home and interactions in preschool. *Developmental Psychology, 21,* 130–140.

Hubert, N. C., Wachs, T. D., Peters-Martin, P., & Gandour, M. J. (1982). The study of early temperament: Measurement and conceptual issues. *Child Development, 53,* 571–600.

Kagan, J., Reznick, J. S., & Snidman, N. (1986). Temperamental inhibition in early childhood. In R. Plomin & J. Dunn (Eds.), *The study of temperament: Changes, continuities and challenges.* Hillsdale, NJ: Erlbaum.

Keogh, B. K. (1982). Children's temperament and teachers decisions. In R. Porter & G. M. Collins (Eds.), *Temperamental differences in infants and young children.* London: Pitman.

Kogan, N. (1971). Educational implications of cognitive style. In G. S. Lesser (Ed.), *Psychological and educational practice.* Glenview, IL: Scott, Foresman.

Lerner, R. M., Palermo, M., Spiro, A., & Nesselroade, J. R. (1982). Assessing the dimensions of temperamental individuality across the life span: The Dimensions of Temperament Survey (DOTS). *Child Development, 53,* 149–159.

Matheny, A. P. (1980). Bayley's Infant Behavioral Record: Behavioral components and twin analyses. *Child Development, 51,* 1157–1167.

McCall, R. B. (1986). Issues of stability and continuity in temperament research. In R. Plomin & J. Dunn (Eds.), *The study of temperament: Changes, continuities and challenges.* Hillsdale, NJ: Erlbaum.

McDevitt, S. C., & Carey, W. B. (1978). The measurement of temperament in 3 to 7 year old children. *Journal of Child Psychology and Psychiatry, 19,* 245–253.

Messick, S. (1976). Personality consistencies in cognition and creativity. In S. Messick & Associates (Eds.), *Individuality in learning.* San Francisco: Jossey-Bass.

Moss, H. A., & Sussman, E. J. (1980). Longitudinal study of personality development. In O. G. Brim, Jr., & J. Kagan (Eds.), *Constancy and change in human development.* Cambridge: Harvard University Press.

Piaget, J. (1963). *The origins of intelligence in children.* New York: International University Press.

Plomin, R. (1983). Childhood temperament. In B. B. Lahey & A. E. Kazdin (Eds.), *Advances in clinical child psychology, 6,* New York: Plenum.

Pullis, M. E., & Cadwell, J. (1982). The influence of children's temperament characteristics on teacher's decision strategies. *American Educational Research Journal, 19,* 165–181.

Rothbart, M. K., & Derryberry, D. (1981). Development of individual differences in temperament. In M. E. Lamb & A. L. Brown (Eds.), *Advances in developmental psychology (Vol. 1).* Hillsdale, NJ: Erlbaum.

Rowe, D. C., & Plomin, R. (1977). Temperament in early childhood. *Journal of Personality Assessment, 41,* 150–156.

Rutter, M. (1977). Individual differences. In M. Rutter & L. Hersov (Eds.), *Child psychiatry: Modern approaches.* Oxford: Blackwell Scientific.

Stevenson, J., & Graham, P. (1982). Temperament: A consideration of concepts and methods. In R. Porter & G. M. Collins (Eds.), *Temperamental differences in infants and young children.* London: Pitman.

Stevenson-Hinde, J., & Hinde, R. A. (1986). Changes in associations between characteristics and interactions. In R. Plomin & J. Dunn (Eds.), *The study of temperament: Changes, continuities and challenges.* Hillsdale, NJ: Erlbaum.

Strelau, J. (1983). *Temperament-personality-activity.* New York: Academic.

Thomas, A., & Chess, S. (1977). *Temperament and development.* New York: Brunner/Mazel.

Thomas, A., & Chess, S. (1980). *the dynamics of psychological development.* New York: Brunner/Mazel.

Thomas, A., & Chess, S. (1982). Temperament and follow-up to adulthood. In R. Porter & G. M. Collins (Eds.), *Temperamental differences in infants and young children.* London: Pitman.

Thomas, A., & Chess, S. (1986). The New York Longitudinal Study: From infancy to early adult life. In R. Plomin & J. Dunn (Eds.), *The study of temperament: Changes, continuities and challenges.* Hillsdale, NJ: Erlbaum.

Thomas, A., Chess, S., & Birch, H. (1968). *Temperament and behavior disorders in children.* New York: New York University Press.

Thomas, A., Chess, S., Birch, H., Hertzig, M., & Korn, S. (1963). *Behavioral individuality in early childhood.* New York: New York University Press.

Torgensen, A. M., & Kringlen, E. (1978). Genetic aspects of temperamental differences in infants: A study of same-sexed twins. *Journal of the American Academy of Child Psychiatry, 17,* 433–444.

Turecki, S., & Tonner, L. (1985). *The difficult child.* New York: Bantam Books.

Witkin, H. A. (1973). A cognitive style perspective on evaluation and guidance. In *Measurement for self-understanding and personal development.* Princeton: Educational Testing Service.

Wolkind, S. N., & De Salis,W. (1982). Infant temperament, maternal health and child behavioral problems. In R. Porter & G. Collins (Eds.), *Temperamental differences in infants and young children* (Ciba Foundation Symposium, 89). London: Pitman.

BIBLIOGRAPHY: PARENTS

Turecki, S., & Tonner, L. (1985). *The difficult child.* New York: Bantam Books.

Intended primarily for parents of children who are temperamentally difficult to raise, this book helps parents identify and understand the temperamental bases of unconstructive interactions with children. Guidelines for assessment of temperament and management techniques are provided.

Children and Thumbsucking

William R. Jenson, Thomas J. Kehle, and Elaine Clark
University of Utah

BACKGROUND

Thumbsucking is a common problem that affects many children and is disturbing to both parents and teachers. It is difficult to estimate the exact number of children who engage in thumb or finger sucking or to specifically judge the effects of the behavior. However, rough estimates place the number of children given to thumbsucking at approximately 40 million. Thumbsucking is clearly the most frequent habit disorder of childhood (Nunn, 1978).

Thumbsucking has been with us for a long time, and will undoubtedly continue to be a problem for both children and adults. The changing views of this behavior throughout history are of interest. There are frequent examples in both paintings and sculptures of early Renaissance children with a finger or thumb in their mouths. The finger or thumb in the mouth symbolized a feeling of safety and serene tranquillity in children. It was not until the end of the nineteenth century that thumbsucking was viewed as a problematic behavior with serious side effects (as reviewed by Kimball, 1983). From 1914 to 1921, the federal government published a series of "Infant Care" booklets on child care that warned against letting children engage in autoerotic behavior such as thumbsucking and masturbation. The booklet suggested that children's hands be bound in the crib to prevent the damaging behavior. Later, Freudian interpretations of sexuality in children placed an emphasis on the oral phase of psychosexual development and finger sucking. The oral phase of development is assumed to occur around 18–24 months of age. Stimulation of the child's oral erogenous zones by objects such as fingers and thumbs was thought to relieve sexual tension. The response becomes pathological if the child fixates or regresses to the oral state instead of developing normally through the higher psychosexual stages.

Interestingly, at almost the same time that the Freudian argument was being presented, the father of behaviorism, J. B. Watson, when conditioning emotional reactions in the infant "Little Albert," found that thumbsucking appeared to block the effects of noxious stimuli (Watson and Rayner, 1920). Little Albert, then on the verge of tears, would start to suck his thumb and become impervious to the stimuli that produced the conditioned emotional response. Thumbsucking appeared to have a prophylactic effect on conditioned emotional stress for Little Albert.

Contemporary thought concerning thumbsucking is benign in contrast to that of the early part of the nineteenth century. Parents are counseled to be less interfering and more tolerant of a young child's thumbsucking. However, questions still exist for many parents and psychologists about the exact definition of finger sucking, the normality of finger sucking, the possible harmful side effects of this behavior, and, if needed, how the behavior can best be treated. The rest of this chapter will address each of these questions.

Finger and Thumb Sucking Defined

The term *finger sucking* is used interchangeably with the term *thumbsucking* in the research and clinical literature. Clearly, the most common form of finger sucking involves thumbsucking as a subclass. Any finger can be sucked but the common fingers that are sucked include index fingers or more than one finger at a time. However, most of the research and popular literature uses the term thumbsucking to refer to finger sucking in general. In this chapter, when the term thumbsucking is used, it will be used to refer to the general class of all finger sucking.

Most common definitions of thumbsucking allude to the behavior as a daytime habit disorder. Such definitions refer to thumbsucking as any observed instance of children putting any part of their thumb or finger into the mouth or touching their lips (e.g., Lloyd, Kauffman, & Weygant, 1982; Nwachukwu, 1980). However, there are other instances or special cases of thumbsucking that should be considered by school psychologists. First, thumbsucking is termed *primary* when the child has never had a significant amount of time without thumbsucking; it is called *secondary* if the child ceased thumbsucking for a period of time, but recommenced after a stressful event such as an injury, loss of a parent, or a divorce. This regression to thumbsucking is generally a transitory phase, unlike primary thumbsucking. Second, thumbsucking can occur in the daytime or at night. Diurnal and nocturnal thumbsucking can occur in the same child, with the diurnal thumbsucking responding to one type of treatment and the nocturnal thumbsucking requiring a different type of treatment. Third, thumbsucking may be related to other habit disorders such as nail biting. A child may start off sucking a finger or thumb and have the behavior slowly evolve into nail biting (see the chapter, "Nail Biting" in this volume for a more thorough discussion). Fourth, some thumbsucking behaviors are directly related to self-stimulatory types of mouthing or hand-biting behaviors in developmentally disabled children. These self-stimulatory mouthing and biting behaviors can also start as simple thumbsucking and evolve into more serious behaviors.

DEVELOPMENT

The prevalence of thumbsucking varies with the age of the child, and there is disagreement in the research literature with regard to prevalence. Thumbsucking appears to be developmental and decreases in frequency as children get older. One survey of 2,650 infants and children found that approximately half of the group under the age of 16 years had at one time sucked their thumbs (Traisman & Traisman, 1958). Another study (Honzik and McKee, 1962), found that the percentages varied with the age of the child — 42% of 2-year-olds, 46% of 3-year-olds, and 37% of 4-year-olds sucked their thumbs. The percentage drops significantly after age 6 years — approximately 10% of children in the age range of 6–11 years are thumbsuckers (Roberts and Baird, 1971). After age 12, the percentage again drops to less than 2–5%, depending on age (Achenbach & Edelbrock, 1981). Thumbsucking generally appears between the 4th and 10th month of infancy and peaks between the 3rd or 4th year of childhood, although extreme cases have been reported. For example, a letter was sent to Ann Lander's advice column from a 32-year-old housewife who described herself as ashamed and suffering from a thumbsucking problem for years. Ann Landers advised her correspondent that though the problem was not harmful, if she wanted to stop, she should see a behavior therapist and go to work on it (Landers, 1983).

Some researchers have found thumbsucking to be more prevalent among girls. For example, the Achenbach and Edelbrock study (1981) of child behavior problems found slightly more females than males exhibiting the problem before age 12. However, other studies have not found a significant sex difference in the prevalence of thumbsucking (Nunn, 1978).

The Causes of Thumbsucking

A great deal of speculation surrounds the causes of thumbsucking in children. Early Freudian interpretations of thumbsucking as an autoerotic behavior associated with the oral stage of psychosexual development have already been mentioned. Other early interpretations (Levy, 1928) suggested that thumbsucking was caused by interrupting the feeding of a young infant. This interruption could be caused by a spontaneous withdrawal from feeding because of a too rapidly flowing breast or bottle, a forced withdrawal from sucking after too short a feeding time, or a change in feeding schedules. According to Levy, a child that is full after feeding falls asleep in a satisfied condition. However, an infant who is not satisfied after feeding may resort to thumbsucking for satisfaction.

Some speculation also exists that thumbsucking may be a function of how the baby is fed. One study (Davis, Sears, Miller, & Brodbeck, 1948) compared 60 babies fed by using a bottle, cup, or breast and found no significant difference in the oral activities of these three groups. However, babies fed by the breast method did have stronger sucking reflexes than the other two groups.

Gessell and Ilg (1937) have pointed out that thumbsucking may play a role in reducing the irritations that develop during teething behavior in infants. The infant may reduce local irritations by mouthing a fist or a thumb weeks or months before the eruption of teeth. The successive teething episodes appear to make infants put their hands in the mouth far more frequently than at other times. The degree of thumbsucking may markedly decrease or be eliminated between teething episodes in those who later become chronic thumbsuckers.

Behavioral interpretations of the causes of thumbsucking assume that it is a habit disorder that has been conditioned or learned. Little or no emphasis is placed on underlying causes, and a major focus is placed on direct interventions to change thumbsucking. Leading behavioral clinicians (Azrin & Nunn, 1973) assume that "habits begin as normal behaviors induced by physical injury, psychological stress, or imitation, or as normal movements which gradually blend in with daily activities and increase in frequency. When such movements become extremely frequent and/or continue beyond the trauma period, they are classified as a habit" (Nunn, 1978, p. 353).

Possibly one of the most modern demonstrations of thumbsucking behavior was the broadcast on November 9, 1983, on the Public Broadcasting System science program NOVA. This program dramatically showed an in utero infant, several weeks before birth, put its thumb up to its mouth and appear to suck. This demonstration appears to discredit Freudian, behavioral, feeding, and teething explanations of thumbsucking and may demonstrate an early reflexive behavior for sucking in infants. Thumbsucking, like many other complex behaviors, may not have a single cause.

Thumbsucking and Other Problems

Simple thumbsucking has been assumed to be correlated with a number of childhood psychological problems such as anxiety, stress-related problems, and difficulty in psychological adjustment. However, the evidence from psychological research indicates that there is not a significant difference in the incidence of thumbsucking between children referred for psychological problems and children who have never been referred (Achenbach & Edelbrock, 1978). One study found a negative correlation between thumbsucking and behavior problems in preschoolers (Heinstein, 1973). Another study found that children who sucked their thumbs were actually less distractible than children who did not suck their thumbs (Lester, Bierbrauer, & Selfridge, 1976). Overall, thumbsucking appears *not* to be a symptom or manifestation of major behavioral or psychological problems in childhood. However, social censure and embarrassment by peers can result if children continue to suck their thumbs into middle childhood in public places such as classrooms (Lloyd, Kauffman, & Weygant, 1982).

Another concern is that thumbsucking may cause dental problems. Heredity is an important variable in developing sound dental structures and a good bite, and in avoiding malocclusions even if a child thumbsucks. However, the incidence of malocclusion is higher in chronical thumbsuckers (Murray and Anderson, 1969; Traisman and Traisman, 1958). The incidence of dental problems at age 12 is essentially equal in children who never sucked their thumbs and in children who quit the habit before age 6 (Telzrow, 1981). However, among children whose habit of thumbsucking has extended into middle childhood there is a higher probability of developing dental problems (Azrin, Nunn, & Frantz-Renshaw, 1980; Wright, Schaefer, & Solomons, 1971).

Other medical problems that can be associated with thumbsucking include local infections on the thumb or finger due to sores, multiple ulcers on the tongue, and a flattening and wrinkling of the thumb.

The more severe forms of self-stimulatory thumbsucking that occur in developmentally delayed populations can affect a child's social functioning and learning ability. It appears that if an autistic or mentally retarded child vigorously engages in thumbsucking, it precludes attending to other environmental stimuli and interferes with learning. For example, Freeman, Moss, Somerset, and Ritvo (1977) found that reducing severe thumbsucking behavior in a 2-year-old autistic child correspondingly improved his social behavior on the hospital ward. Of particular interest was a dramatic improvement in the child's IQ scores when thumbsucking was reduced.

Some theorists have suggested that other problematic behaviors may occur if thumbsucking is directly reduced through treatment procedures. It is assumed that "symptom substitution" behaviors such as nail biting or enuresis may occur if the underlying problems that cause thumbsucking are not treated. One case study reported a marked increase in enuretic behavior in a 4-year-old female when thumbsucking was directly reduced through behavior modification procedures (Ottenbacher & Ottenbacher, 1981). However, more commonly, just the opposite results have been reported. Some behaviors that are related to thumbsucking may show a positive response generalization effect when thumbsucking behavior is successfully treated. Altman, Grahs, and Friman (1982) reported the dramatic spontaneous reduction of hair pulling in a 3-year-old female when thumbsucking behavior was mildly punished. Problematic symptom substitution is not commonly reported by most researchers as a serious side effect when thumbsucking is directly treated.

PUTTING THUMBSUCKING IN PERSPECTIVE

Most of the information about thumbsucking behavior in children is obtained from reports by parents and teachers in interviews or behavior checklists. When children are interviewed about the behavior some information can be gained by asking them when and in what environments they suck their thumbs. However, it is generally useless to ask why they suck their thumbs, because the answer is generally "I don't know." The most useful data that can be gathered from a parent involve the following interview questions: (a) How old is the child (unless the behavior is severe and damaging, a program should not be started before a child is 4 years old)? (b) How long has thumbsucking been a problem and what is its current frequency? (c) Is its onset correlated with any specific traumatic event such as a divorce or serious illness? (d) Does it interfere with the child's adjustment (i.e., is he or she ridiculed by other children)? (e) What has been tried in the past to stop the sucking? (f) At what times in the day or night does the problem occur? (h) In what environments does the problem occur (i.e., stressful, nocturnal, boring)? (i) Is there any event that immediately precedes thumbsucking (antecedent stimulus analysis)? The times, environments, and antecedent events are of particular importance in the assessment of the condition. The following case exemplifies the importance of environmental antecedents.

Case Study

Jason was a 4-year-old boy who chronically sucked his thumb and the family dentist suggested that it was beginning to cause dental problems. His parents were concerned that the sucking was a way that Jason managed stress and that stopping him might produce a negative psychological reaction. However, when they observed Jason for a week, they found that he most frequently sucked his thumb in front of the television and when he was sleepy. Instead of stressful environments, he appeared to suck in less stimulating or boring circumstances. Of particular interest was the parents' observation that he always picked up his blanket "Silky" and rubbed it between his fingers just before he put his thumb in his mouth. Jason's parents and the psychologist decided that instead of starting a direct intervention for thumbsucking, they would try to contract to see if Jason would give up Silky. The theory was that if they could stop the antecedent blanket-holding behavior, they might be able to reduce or stop the thumbsucking.

At first Jason refused to contract to give up Silky. In fact, his thumbsucking and blanket holding actually increased when the offer was made to trade Silky for a reasonable toy of his choice. However, Jason looked at toy catalogs for approximately 2 weeks and one Saturday announced that he would trade Silky for the Millennium Falcon (a 40-dollar Star Wars toy). The parents agreed, and the exchange was made. Interestingly, Jason never again sucked his thumb. It appears that rubbing Silky had, in fact, been a conditioned stimulus that set the occasion for thumbsucking and by removing the blanket the thumbsucking stopped. In addition, Jason showed no signs of psychological stress or disturbed behavior as a result of giving up Silky or stopping his thumbsucking (Morgan and Jenson, in press).

Other approaches also exist for assessment of thumbsucking. Two interesting approaches include the Behavioral Seal and self-recording.

Behavioral Seal

The Behavioral Seal was developed to assess thumbsucking when it is difficult or impossible to observe the child (Hughes, Hughes, & Dial, 1978, 1979). The seal is essentially a square piece of masking tape with a hole in the middle. Under the masking tape is litmus paper (nitrazine-phenapthazine paper, E. R. Squibb) that shows through the hole. The seal is fixed to the child's thumb (see Figure 1) and the litmus paper lies between the thumbnail and the masking tape. Thumbsucking turns the litmus paper blue through the action of the saliva in the mouth. Other substances turn the litmus paper different colors. For example, water (depending on the pH of a particular city's water) turns it gray, food grease turns it brownish yellow, and urine turns it yellow. Prolonged sucking, such as nocturnal sucking, turns

FIGURE 1

Illustration of the Behavioral Seal placed on the thumb

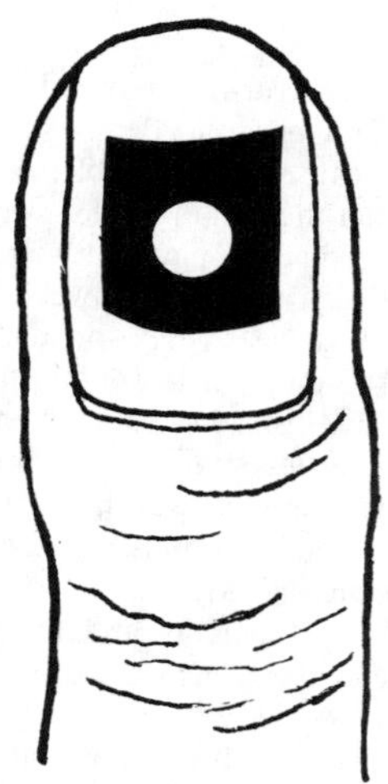

the paper white. The Behavioral Seal has been used successfully in conjunction with other behavior management techniques to successfully reduce thumbsucking (Hughes, Hughes, & Dial, 1979). It allows assessment of thumbsucking without constant monitoring or reliance on a self-report. However, some caution should be shown, since the exact safety of prolonged sucking on litmus paper has not been established for children.

Self-Recording

Having motivated children collect or self-report the frequency of their own thumbsucking behavior is both an assessment and intervention technique. The self-recorded data can be used to determine the frequency of thumbsucking in a number of environments that are difficult to observe. The very act of self-recording (writing down the incident) disrupts the behavioral chain that leads to sucking and consequently can significantly reduce thumbsucking. For example, Cohen, Monty, and Williams (1980) had a 10-year-old thumbsucking female record the frequency of sucking incidents across 5-minute intervals in the evening. The girl wrote each instance of sucking down on a sheet of paper. Thumbsucking dropped from 37% of the time in baseline to 6% in the last self-reporting phase. Agreement between the girl's self-recording and the mother's recording of the behavior was 90%.

Self-recording has been used with a number of problems that include academic off-task, talk-outs, eating problems, and others. The problem with the technique is that the child involved must be motivated to change the behavior or the accuracy of the assessment data may be in doubt. In addition, the changes that result from self-recording are generally temporary and require some types of additional treatment to make them permanent. However, self-recording is an excellent technique to help a child gain initial mastery over a difficult habit such as thumbsucking.

ALTERNATIVE ACTIONS

The treatments and actions that have been used for thumbsucking behavior are diverse in their types and effectiveness. The basic techniques that have scientific validity will be discussed in respect to the settings in which they have been implemented, and to their limitations.

Traditional Verbal Psychotherapy

Buxbaum (1979) has reported a case study of a 6-year-old girl who was treated with psychotherapy for several problems, one of which was thumbsucking. The girl, Joan, masturbated, missed school, had poor sleeping habits and urination problems. The assumed cause was a strong oral fixation and her dislike of her younger brother. Treatment focused on making Joan conscious of her aggressive impulses and letting her express them in actions and words. In addition, her home life was changed to help her deal with her jealousy towards her brother. After therapy started, there was an initial increase in thumbsucking, then it stopped.

However, systematic research studies evaluating the effectiveness of traditional counseling and psychotherapy techniques are rare. Most current studies indicate that these techniques produce little or no benefit in effectively stopping thumbsucking (Foster & Stebbins, 1929; Haryett, Hansen, Davidson, & Sandilands, 1967). In comparison to other researched treatment approaches, counseling and psychotherapy approaches are relatively expensive and generally take a long time, so their use is not recommended.

Hypnosis

The use of hypnosis may be a promising technique for the treatment of thumbsucking. It has been used by Tilton (1980) to treat an 8-year-old boy who exhibited thumbsucking, enuresis, and encopresis problems. Tilton employed a television hypnosis technique in which the child was instructed to imagine a television screen and tune in on his favorite program. This image was then used to introduce the hypnotic suggestion of stopping the problematic behaviors. In this study, the hypnotic procedures did succeed in reducing thumbsucking behaviors.

The research on hypnosis for the treatment is very limited; however, the treatment may be justified because the expense and time commitment may be less than other more traditional procedures. It also appears that children may enjoy hypnosis and the imagery process if it is done properly with a well-trained school psychologist.

Differential Reinforcement of Other Behavior (DRO)

The DRO technique has also been called omission training or reinforcement of zero rates of behavior. Essentially, the DRO technique is a schedule of reinforcement in which the child is reinforced if thumbsucking does not occur for a certain period of time. For example, Lowitz and Suib (1978) used the DRO technique, first in a laboratory setting and then in the home with an 8-year-old girl whose thumbsucking was resulting in dental malocclusions. At the start of laboratory treatment, the DRO schedule of reinforcement gave the girl a penny for each minute that she did not have her thumb in her mouth. Slowly the time for not sucking her thumb was increased both in the laboratory and at home, until her mother made only periodic spot checks. In addition, a star was placed on her chart if the girl had a perfect day or night of no thumbsucking. The star chart reinforcement contingency stipulated that the girl could get her ears pierced after 60 stars had been collected on the chart. The overall percentage of daytime thumbsucking for the girl dropped from 100% of the time to only 1.7%, with a corresponding decrease in nocturnal thumbsucking.

A similar study with DRO was done by Hughes, Hughes, and Dial (1979), who used the Behavioral Seal. In this study, a 4-year-old girl, Hillary, was reinforced with verbal statements and candy if she had not sucked her thumb for a 15-minute interval. The parents observed Hillary or looked at the color of the seal to determine if she had sucked her thumb during the previous 15-minute interval. If sucking had occurred, the seal was simply replaced. If it had not occurred, she was reinforced with a verbal statement and a small piece of hard candy. The Behavioral Seal was also used at night; however, Hillary was not awakened to receive a reinforcer. The data from this study showed that thumbsucking dropped from rates of approximately 10 thumbsucking responses per day to zero rates for both daytime and nocturnal thumbsucking.

In a classroom, DRO procedures were used by a teacher to give social reinforcement for behaviors that were incompatible with thumbsucking (i.e., hands folded on the desk, writing in a notebook) for three 8-year-old girls (Skiba, Pettigrew, & Alden, 1971). The results indicated that for all three girls, thumbsucking was reduced during the contingent social reinforcement procedures. Teachers and parents should be cautious about just ignoring thumbsucking as a way of treating the behavior. Since thumbsucking appears to be intrinsically reinforcing, ignoring it may not work. In fact, there can be actual increases in thumbsucking because a thumbsucking child may be trying to gain an adult's attention (extinction burst) or is simply bored. As in the Skiba et al. study (1971), replacement behaviors that are incompatible with thumbsucking should always be socially reinforced to help avoid these problems.

The major advantage of the DRO technique is that it is a positive approach that does not use punishment. It can also be easily used in both the classroom and the home, with a teacher or parent implementing the program. These authors suggest that after a baseline collection of the frequency of thumbsucking, the DRO technique be used as the first treatment before more costly or aversive techniques are employed.

Response Cost and Time Out Techniques

The response cost procedure is a punishment procedure in which something (e.g., tokens, television, academic materials) is taken away from a child for inappropriate behavior. Time out is also a punishment technique, in which a child is placed in a boring environment (e.g., room corner, chair, or time out room) for inappropriate behavior such as thumbsucking. However, some forms of time out, such as contingent observation, involve the child's observation of his/her materials or toys being taken away for a brief time. This type of time out procedure is very similar to the basic response cost procedure.

Time out from TV viewing was used to reduce thumbsucking in the laboratory in the case of a 5-year-old boy; cartoons were turned off whenever he had his thumb in his mouth (Baer, 1962). In the home, Ross (1975) and Clowes-Hollins and King (1982) used both parents and siblings to assign thumbsucking children 5-minute time outs from television if they were caught sucking. In both studies, thumbsucking was significantly reduced, and in one of the studies (Ross, 1975), the results were generalized to nocturnal thumbsucking with the aid of a bad-tasting substance painted on the thumb. Contingent bedtime story reading has also been successfully used as a response cost technique to reduce bedtime thumbsucking in three girls (aged 3, 6, and 8). With this procedure, the mother would read the story as long as the girls did not suck their thumbs. However, when sucking started the story was interrupted for a brief period of time, which greatly reduced the thumbsucking in the girls.

Response cost has also been successfully used by Lloyd, Kauffman, and Weygant (1982) to reduce thumbsucking in classroom situations. These investigators gave two 7-year-old thumbsuckers, who were in self-contained classes for the learning-disabled, a stack of colored paper (chits) at the beginning of each day. However, each time a child was observed to be thumbsucking a chit was removed from the stack. If the children had enough chits at the end of the day, they could turn them in for a special reinforcing activity that they had previously selected. Large reductions in thumbsucking were obtained for both girls, as well as a generalized decrease in related behaviors (object mouthing and head rubbing).

Response cost and time out are appropriate and effective procedures for thumbsucking. The response cost procedure of Lloyd et al. is particularly easy for teachers to use. However, care must be taken with response cost procedures that a child not lose everything, or go into the "hole," nor be placed in a boring time out environment that may result in an increase in thumbsucking because of a lack of stimulation.

Bad-Tasting and Aversive Substances

Bad-tasting substances (e.g., Don't; Stop-zit; Thum; or a combination of cayenne pepper extract and citric acid) have been painted on thumbs to deter sucking. This technique is only marginally effective (Azrin, Nunn, & Frantz-Renshaw, 1980; Lassen & Fluet, 1978) and is best used in combination with other techniques such as DRO or response cost. Bad-tasting substances also have the negative side effect of getting into a child's eye if they rub them after sucking, while sleeping, or during crying.

Other aversive substances have been used for very severe forms of self-stimulatory or self-injurious thumbsucking. Drabman, Ross, Lynd, and Cordua (1978) held an ice cube to the lips (to a count of three) of a 2-year-old retarded, blind child who chewed or sucked his fingers. Jenson, Rovner, Cameron, and Petersen (1985) used a spray mist of room temperature tapwater to reduce the self-injurious hand mouthing and biting in an autistic girl. However, aversive substances should be employed only in the most severe cases and with full parental consent and by a staff who are well trained.

Response Blocking, or Prevention

This technique is a form of punishment or mild restraint. Response blocking, or prevention, is more effective for nocturnal than for daytime sucking, when more effective techniques can be employed. Lassen and Fluet (1978) used a thin cotton glove to eliminate the nocturnal thumbsucking of a 10-year-old girl. Similarly, Van Houten and Rolider (1984) succeeded in reducing nocturnal thumbsucking in two boys by first using a boxing glove, then fading to absorbent cotton worn on the thumb, then to a fingertip bandage.

More severe forms of response blocking, such as the use of stainless steel spurred bars cemented to the upper mollars (Haryett, Hansen, & Davidson, 1970), or air splints (inflatable plastic finger splints) (Ball, Campbell, & Barkemeyer, 1980), have been used for finger sucking and thumbsucking. However, these are very intrusive methods, with significant negative side effects.

Overcorrection

The use of overcorrection is a behavior-reducing procedure in which a child is required to repeat a behavior many times following an instance of misbehavior. For example, Doke and Epstein (1975) used an oral overcorrection procedure in which a 4-year-old child was required to brush her teeth for 2 minutes, with Listerine mouth wash, for each instance of thumbsucking. The overcorrection technique was effective, particularly when it was coupled with a verbal warning. In addition, there was reduction in thumbsucking of a boy in the same class who merely observed the overcorrection procedures with the other child.

The advantage of overcorrection is that the repeated behavior, such as teeth brushing, is educative. The child learns to brush his or her teeth better. The technique can also be used in both home or school. However, the major disadvantage of this technique is that it requires the supervision of an adult, which can be time-consuming.

Habit Reversal

This technique developed for habit disorders by Azrin and Nunn (1973) is, overall, possibly the most effective technique for reducing thumbsucking (Azrin, Nunn, & Frantz-Renshaw, 1980). Actually the habit reversal is a collection of many separate procedures that is taught in a single treatment session (1–2 hours). The rest of the treatment is then conducted at home. Habit reversal includes (a) an annoyance review (the child lists all the problems created by thumbsucking); (b) heightened awareness training (the child acts out the thumbsucking response, particularly the stimulus antecedents to sucking); (c) competing response reactions training (the child is taught to make a fist in which the fingers grip the thumb; this is done for 1–3 minutes as a corrective measure in instances of thumbsucking or when any antecedent behavior occurs); and (d) social support (parents and concerned persons are encouraged to give the child social reinforcement for not sucking and for making progress with the program.

Habit reversal was compared with use of a bad-tasting substance on the thumb to assess each treatment's effectiveness. The habit reversal reduced thumbsucking 88% the first day of treatment, 95% the second day of treatment, and 89% at 20 months follow-up. The bad-tasting substance reduced thumbsucking by approximately 40% at 20 months follow-up in the control children. The major advantages of habit reversal are its effectiveness and that it can be conducted both at home or school. The major disadvantage is the complexity of the steps.

SUMMARY

Thumbsucking is the most common form of childhood habit disorder, affecting approximately 40 million children in the United States. Thumb and finger sucking appear to be developmental in that children outgrow the problem as they get older. The exact cause of thumbsucking is not known; however, there are probably several separate causes. The negative effects of thumbsucking are generally fairly mild. It is not correlated with other severe forms of psychological or behavioral disorders. The major negative side effects of this behavior include dental malocclusions and ridicule from peers. However, more severe forms of thumbsucking that are self-stimulatory can interfere with social adjustment and learning, particularly in developmentally disabled children.

There have been several researched treatment approaches to thumbsucking behavior in children. Traditional psychotherapy and counseling techniques are not very effective in reducing sucking behavior and are not warranted because of their long treatment times and great expense. Hypnosis is a promising treatment technique, but more research is needed to determine its effectiveness. Differential reinforcement of zero rates of behavior (DRO) is probably the treatment of choice because of its primarily positive approach and demonstrated effectiveness. However, other behavior management techniques such as response cost, time out, response blocking, and overcorrection have been demonstrated to be effective with resistive forms of thumbsucking. Other approaches such as bad-tasting substances are only marginally effective. Possibly, the most effective treatment designed to eliminate or reduce thumbsucking is the habit reversal procedure, which is a collection of several techniques.

REFERENCES

Achenbach, T. M., & Edelbrock, C. S. (1981). Behavioral problems and competencies reported by parents of normal and disturbed children age four through sixteen. *Monograhs of the Society for Research in Child Development, 46,* 1–82.

Altman, K., Grahs, C., & Friman, P. (1982). Treatment of unobserved trichotillomania by attention–reflection and punishment of a covariant. *Journal of Behavior Therapy and Experimental Psychiatry, 13,* 337–340.

Azrin, N. H., & Nunn, R. G. (1973). Habit reversal: A method for eliminating nervous habits and tics. *Behavior Research and Therapy, 11,* 619–628.

Azrin, N. H., Nunn, R. G., & Frantz-Renshaw, S. (1980). Habit reversal treatment of thumbsucking. *Behavioral Research and Therapy, 18,* 395–399.

Baer, D. (1962). Laboratory control of thumbsucking with withdrawal and representation of reinforcement. *Journal of Experimental Analysis of Behavior, 5,* 525–528.

Ball, T. S., Campbell, R., & Barkemeyer, R. (1980). Air splints applied to control self-injurious finger sucking in profoundly retarded individuals. *Journal of Behavior Therapy and Experimental Psychiatry, 11,* 276–271.

Buxbaum, E. (1979). *Troubled children in a troubled world.* New York: International Universities Press.

Clowes-Hollins, V., & King, N. (1982). Parents and siblings as behavior modifiers in the control of a common developmental problem (thumbsucking). *Journal of Clinical and Child Psychology, 11,* 231–233.

Cohen, R., Monty, H., & Williams, D. (1980). Management of thumbsucking using self-recording with parent as observer and experimenter. *Perceptual and Motor Skills, 50,* 136.

Davis, H. V., Sears, R. R., Miller, H. C., & Brodbeck, A. J. (1948). Effects of cup, bottle, and breast feeding on the oral activities of newborn infants. *Pediatrics, 2,* 549–558.

Doke, L. A., & Epstein, L. H. (1975). Oral overcorrection: Side effects and extended applications. *Journal of Experimental Child Psychology, 20,* 496–511.

Drabman, R. S., Ross, J. M., Lynd, R. S., Cordua, G. D. (1978). Retarded children as observers, mediators, and generalization programmers using an icing procedure. *Behavior Modification, 2,* 371–385.

Foster, S., & Stebbins, D. (1929). Problems presented and results of treatment in 150 cases seen at the habit clinic for pre-school children in Boston. *Mental Hygiene, 13,* 529–541.

Freeman, B. J., Moss, D., Somerset, T., & Ritvo, E. (1977). Thumbsucking in an autistic child overcome by overcorrection. *Journal of Behavior Therapy and Experimental Psychiatry, 8,* 211–212.

Gessell, A., & Ilg, F. L. (1937). *Feeding behavior of infants.* Philadelphia: Lippincott.

Haryett, R. D., Hansen, F. C., & Davidson, P. O. (1970). Chronic thumbsucking: A second report on the treatment and its psychological effects. *American Journal of Orthodontics, 57,* 164–178.

Haryett, R. D., Hansen, F. C., Davidson, P. O., & Sandilands, M. L. (1967). Chronic thumbsucking: The psychologic effects and the relative effectiveness of various methods of treatment. *American Journal of Orthodontics, 53,* 569–585.

Heinstein, M. L. (1973). Influence of breast feeding on children's behavior. In A. Davids (Ed.), *Issues in abnormal behavior* (pp. 77–84), Belmont, CA: Wadsworth.

Honzik, M. P., & McKee, J. P. (1962). The sex difference in thumbsucking. *Journal of Pediatrics, 61,* 726–732.

Hughes, H., Hughes, A., & Dial, H. (1978). A behavioral seal: An apparatus alternative to behavioral observation of thumbsucking. *Behavior Research Methods and Instrumentation, 10,* 460–461.

Hughes, H., Hughes, A., & Dial, H. (1979). Home based treatment of thumbsucking: Omission training with edible reinforcers and a Behavioral Seal. *Behavior Modification, 3,* 179–186.

Jenson, W. R., Rovner, L., Cameron, S., & Petersen, B. P. (1985). The use of a spray bottle plus a startle response to reduce chronic self-injury in an autistic girl: A fading technique. *Journal of Behavior Therapy and Experimental Psychiatry, 16,* 77–80.

Kimball, S. (1983). *Everything you always wanted to know, but was afraid to ask about thumbsucking.* Unpublished paper, University of Utah, Department of Educational Psychology, Salt Lake City.

Landers, A. (1983, November 17). For what it's worth. *Salt Lake City Tribune.*

Lassen, M., & Fluet, N. (1978). Elimination of nocturnal thumbsucking by glove wearing. *Journal of Behavior Therapy and Experimental Psychiatry, 9,* 85.

Lester, G., Bierbrauer, B., & Selfridge, B. (1976). Distractibility, intensity of reaction time, and non-nutrituve sucking. *Psychological Reports, 39,* 1212–1214.

Levy, D. (1928). Finger sucking and accessory movements in early infancy. *American Journal of Psychiatry, 84,* 881–918.

Lloyd, J. W., Kauffman, J. M., & Weygant, A. D. (1982). Effects of response cost contingencies on thumbsucking and elated behaviors in the classroom. *Educational Psychology, 2,* 167–173.

Lowitz, G. H., & Suib, M. R. (1978). Generalized control of persistent thumbsucking by differential reinforcement of other behaviors. *Journal of Behavior Therapy and Experimental Psychiatry, 9,* 343–346.

Morgan, D., & Jenson, W. R. (in press). *Teaching behaviorally disordered children: Preferred strategies.* Columbus, OH: Merrill.

Murray, A. B., & Anderson, D. O. (1969). The association of incisor protrusion with digit sucking and allergic nasal itching. *Journal of Allergy, 44,* 239–247.

Nunn, R. G. (1978). Maladaptive habits and tics. *Psychiatric Clinics of North America, 1,* 349–361.

Nwachukwu, F. J. (1980). Control of thumbsucking in the classroom. *Psychological Reports, 47,* 1076–1078.

Ottenbacher, K., & Ottenbacher, M. (1981). Symptom substitution: A case study. *American Journal of Psychoanalysis, 41,* 173–175.

Roberts, J., & Baird, J. T. (1971). *Parent ratings of behavior patterns of children.* DHEW Publication, No. (HSM) 72-1010, Washington, DC: U.S. Government Printing Office.

Ross, J. A. (1975). Parents modify thumbsucking: A case study. *Journal of Behavior Therapy and Experimental Psychiatry, 6,* 248–249.

Skiba, E. A., Pettigrew, L. E., & Alden, S. E. (1971). A behavioral approach to the control of thumbsucking in the classroom. *Journal of Applied Behavior Analysis, 4,* 121–125.

Telzrow, R. W. (1981). Habit patterns. In S. Gabel (Ed.), *Behavioral problems in childhood. A primary care approach* (pp. 309–320). New York: Grune and Stratton.

Tilton, P. (1980). Hypnotic treatment of a child with thumbsucking, enuresis, and encopresis. *American Journal of Clinical Hypnosis, 22,* 238–240.

Traisman, A. S., & Traisman, H. S. (1958). Thumbsucking and finger sucking: A study of 2,650 infants and children. *Journal of Pediatrics, 55,* 566–572.

Van Houten, R., & Rolider, A. (1984). The use of response prevention to eliminate nocturnal thumbsucking. *Journal of Applied Behavior Analysis, 17,* 509–520.

Watson, J. B., & Rayner, R. (1920). Conditioned emotional responses. *Journal of Experimental Psychology, 3,* 1–4.

Wright, L., Schaefer, A. B., & Solomons, G. (1979). *Encyclopedia of Pediatric Psychology,* Baltimore, MD: University Park.

BIBLIOGRAPHY: PROFESSIONALS

Azrin, N. H., Nunn, R. G., & Frantz-Renshaw, S. (1980). Habit reversal treatment of thumbsucking. *Behavior Research and Therapy, 18,* 395–399.
Presents the research on habit reversal as a treatment procedure for thumbsucking. It gives a detailed description of how to implement the procedures for professionals. Habit reversal is probably one of the most successful overall treatments for thumbsucking.

Hughes, H., Hughes, A., & Dial, H. (1979). Home-based treatment of thumbsucking: Omission training with edible reinforcers and a behavioral seal. *Behavior Modification, 3,* 179–186.
A good article for professionals for two reasons. First, the behavioral seal is an excellent assessment procedure for thumbsucking when a child cannot be constantly observed. Second, the intervention used in the study is a non-punishment-based omission training procedure.

Jenson, W. R., Rovner, L., Cameron, S., & Petersen, B. P. (1985). The use of a spray bottle plus a startle response to reduce chronic self-injury in an autistic girl: A fading technique. *Journal of Behavior Therapy and Experimental Psychiatry, 16,* 77–80.
Good for professionals who have an interest in thumbsucking and mouthing as a self-stimulatory behavior in developmentally disabled populations. The paper presents clear approaches for the use of mild punishment procedures and the generalization of these procedures for fingersucking and mouthing.

Lewis, M., Shilton, P., & Fuqua, W. (1981). Parent control of nocturnal thumbsucking. *Journal of Behavior Therapy and Experimental Psychiatry, 12,* 87–90.
Nocturnal thumbsucking can be particularly difficult to control because of the lack of procedures available and the fact that the child is sleeping. This paper outlines the difficulty in using a response blocking procedure for nocturnal thumbsucking. It is a good paper to read before starting such a procedure.

Lloyd, J. W., Kauffman, J. M., & Weygant, A. D. (1982). Effects of response cost contingencies on thumbsucking and elated behaviors in the classroom. *Educational Psychology, 2,* 167–173.
For school psychologists this paper is excellent because it focuses on thumbsucking in the classroom. The paper presents an easy-to-implement response cost procedure. In addition, the need for proper generalization procedures to ensure treatment effectiveness is stressed.

BIBLIOGRAPHY: PARENTS

Azrin, N. H., & Nunn, R. G. (1977). *Habit control: Stuttering, nail biting, and other nervous habits.* New York: Simon & Schuster.
This is a how-to-do-it book geared for parents and professionals. The basic step-by-step procedures outlined in the book are designed for habits in general; however, they can be effectively applied to thumbsucking in children. The therapeutic approach given in the book is a multicomponent, habit reversal approach.

Children and Troubled Families

Janet L. Graden
University of Cincinnati

Sandra L. Christenson
University of Minnesota

BACKGROUND

Children who are members of troubled families are at risk for developing a wide range of behavioral and psychological problems (Rutter, 1985). School psychologists, as they come in contact with children experiencing severe problems in school, are in a position to help these children and their families. Troubled families may experience multiple problems, including chaotic, ineffective family interaction patterns, and psychological problems of one or more members. There is no single national statistic available that indicates the number of children and adolescents living in troubled or dysfunctional families, but the extent of this situation may be revealed by the large number of social service agencies that are designed to provide services for various family problems. Given the established link between home problems and school functioning (Apter, 1982; Hetherington & Martin, 1979), the vastness of the problem and the task of educating children in troubled families is unquestioned.

A Family Systems Perspective

The merits of a system or ecological orientation in working with children (Anderson, 1983; Christenson, Abery, & Weinberg, 1986), particularly with children from troubled families (Apter, 1982) is well documented. According to a family systems perspective, problems are seen as a result of the interaction between a child and critical aspects of his or her surrounding environment, or system. Problems are not viewed as a disease or deficit within the child, but rather as a lack of balance in the system. Systems theorists believe that what are typically described as emotional or behavior disorders of children result from discrepancies between a child's skills and abilities and the expectations or demands of the environment. Thus, children's symptomatic behavior is understood and addressed only within the various environmental contexts in which it occurs. Understanding a child's behavior involves recognizing family, sibling, peer, and school relationships and the linkages between these relationships.

In viewing children's problems from a systems perspective, it is impossible to state whether the "cause" or "problem" is at home or school, because reciprocal influences exist between the two contexts. This concept of complex reciprocal influences, called transaction, is contrasted with simple linear relationships, and is a central concept in a systems perspective. Put simply, every action of a family member is seen as a reaction to some other behavior, and is in turn an action that triggers other behaviors. A child influences, and is also influenced by, the environments in which he or she lives. This principle of a systems perspective can be illustrated by visualizing the interdependency of parts of a mobile, in which even subtle movement in one part has an impact on the entire mobile.

In sum, the systems perspective provides a framework for organizing and understanding children's behavior in its context. It is accepted that there are multiple influences on children's behavior; single causes or simple linear cause–effect relationships for explaining behavior are seen as limited. Because an individual's behavior is a function of environmental influences, systems-oriented school psychologists do not speak of "within individual" problems — for the child, teacher, or parent. Rather, they speak of the child's total system, the relationships *within* a system, such as the child within home or the child within school, and the interrelationships *between* systems. Systems thinkers act as problem solvers by mobilizing significant members of the child's various systems in order to enhance the child's learning, adaptation, and general development.

School Problems Related to Family Functioning

Many school-related problems of children and youth have been clinically and empirically associated with maladaptive family functioning (Rutter, 1985). Among the most salient of children's problems that have been demonstrated to be related to family functioning are conduct problems, aggression, and delinquency (Garbarino, Schellenback, & Sebes, 1986; Patterson & Stouthamer-Zoeber, 1984); eating disorders, such as anorexia, and other psychosomatic disorders (Kog & Vandereycken, 1985; Minuchin, Rosman, & Baker, 1978); drug abuse (Jurich, Polson, Jurich, & Bates, 1985); depression and suicidal gestures (McConville, 1983); school phobia (Lavigne & Burns, 1981); hyperactivity (Barkley, 1981); and child abuse, including sexual abuse (Egeland, Sroufe, & Erickson, 1983; Garbarino et al., 1986). When school psychologists encounter children with any of these problems, a consideration of the relationship of family factors to the referral concern is indicated. However, to say that family factors are *related* to these problems should not be misinterpreted as placing *blame* on families and parents. In a family systems view, blame is seen as a useless construct because several factors are interrelated in contributing to and

---

We gratefully acknowledge the extremely valuable editorial review by Dr. James W. Maddock, Associate Professor, Family Social Science, University of Minnesota.

maintaining problems, including social system factors (stress, support systems), parenting variables, and also children's contribution to their own development (Belsky, 1984). Understanding the relationships among factors serves to guide intervention efforts, not to assign blame.

Children who experience any of the problems noted above or who are labeled emotionally disturbed are likely to be characterized by some of the following clusters of problems described by Apter (1982). These are: *poorly developed impulse control,* including low frustration tolerance, difficulty in delaying gratification, disruptive outbursts, and aggression; *low self-image,* including a view of self as bad or stupid, a negative view of the future, and a lack of success experiences; *poorly developed modulation of emotion,* including difficulty in expressing, understanding, or dealing appropriately with emotions; *relationship problems,* including fear of closeness, avoidance of contact, overdependence or manipulation of others, and poor social skills; *special learning problems,* including specific problems in learning of undetermined origin, and negative academic experiences; and *limited play skills,* including limited repertoire, and difficulty in playing alone or in groups. For children exhibiting these problems and characteristics, it is important to assess the extent to which family variables are involved.

The School's Role and Responsibility

One of the prevalent myths in schools is that students' learning and behavior problems are due, almost exclusively, to either within-student characteristics or home problems. Christenson, Ysseldyke, Wang, and Algozzine (1983) found that 97% of elementary school teachers' attributions for referred students' problems were student or home causes; only 3% were ascribed to teacher or school factors. This reliance on internal or home attributions is very problematic in that these attributions may be seen as allowing educators to abdicate their teaching responsibility, with the source of the problem and responsibility for solutions being seen as out of their control. Another concern is that the use of internal student attributions for children's problems serves to perpetuate the notion of "curing" the student. Apter (1982) contended that "one major implication of an ecological [or systems] orientation is that we must give up our search for a magical answer to the problems presented by troubled children. Instead we must learn to think in terms of troubled systems and increase our understanding of the reciprocal person–environment interaction patterns" (p. 71).

The school's responsibility to children from troubled families is *to teach* — both academic and social skills. Given the strong tendency to use internal or home attributions for students' problems, an attitude change by educators may be needed. School psychologists are in an ideal position to assist educators and parents to solve problems in more creative ways to enhance children's functioning in various contexts. Children's two primary feedback sources are teachers and parents. When there is inconsistency between home and school beliefs, rules, and expectations, an imbalance in a child's total system occurs, resulting in confusion and problems (Apter, 1982). The primary responsibility of school psychologists in working with children from troubled families should be to mobilize resources to assist such children to develop socially competent behavior. In this way, schools can be an important factor in enhancing the development of children, even if they are members of troubled families.

DEVELOPMENT

Functional and Dysfunctional Family Development

In the family therapy literature, there is no single view of "normal" in contrast with "abnormal" family functioning (Walsh, 1982). Families are complex entities in which various behaviors may be functional and various forms may be adaptable. What is "normal" in families may differ as a function of such factors as the family's stage of development (McGoldrick & Carter, 1982), and cultural, ethnic, or socioeconomic factors (Walsh, 1982). What constitutes a "normal family" also may take various forms, such as single-parent families and blended families. Yet many school psychologists may hold their own values regarding what is normal or dysfunctional. School psychologists need to be aware of their possible stereotyping, differing cultural perspectives, and value judgments regarding what constitutes a normal family, and to recognize that a family's view of acceptable functioning may be legitimately different from theirs.

Although there is no single view of a normal functioning family, there are some commonly agreed-upon dimensions and characteristics of effective and healthy family functioning, and likewise, dimensions of dysfunction in families. Characteristics of family functioning that differentiate untroubled/functional from troubled/dysfunctional families are listed in Table 1 and are briefly described here. For a more thorough discussion of variables of family functioning see Goldenberg and Goldenberg (1985) and L'Abate, Ganahl, & Hansen (1986).

Various family researchers have attempted to identify the characteristics of healthy and dysfunctional family functioning (Beavers, 1982; Olson, Sprenkle, & Russell, 1979), with different family theorists focusing on different critical dimensions of the family. The *structure* of the family relationships is one important variable emphasized in most family therapy approaches. Structure refers to how lines of power, communication, and interrelationships are drawn in families. In an adequately functioning family, the parent/marital subsystem is well defined, and the parents work together to make decisions, discipline the children, and carry out family tasks. In troubled families, there often is a problem in the marital relationship, and one child (or more) is viewed as "triangulated" into the marital conflict, thus diverting attention away from the marital conflict and onto the problematic child. The child exhibiting the problem is seen as the scapegoat or "identified patient" for the structural problem in the family system.

TABLE 1

Characteristics of Untroubled and Troubled Families

Untroubled families	Troubled families
Structure	
Clear boundaries between parent and child subsystems	Unclear boundaries between parent and child subsystems (triangulation)
Clear power hierarchy	Unclear power hierarchy
Clear roles	Unclear or rigid roles
Process	
Effective problem solving	Ineffective problem solving
Effective conflict resolution	Ineffective conflict resolution, high level of conflict, escalation of conflict
Responsiveness to change	Too much or too little change (chaotic or rigid)
Communication	
Clear, direct, open	Indirect, confused, inconsistent
Warmth, empathy, closeness, support	Too much or too little closeness (enmeshed or disengaged), hostile, neglectful
Discipline	
Authoritative yet democratic	Too much or too little control (punitive, authoritarian or lax, permissive)
Consistent discipline	Inconsistent discipline

There are several variables to be considered in family *process.* Some basic tenets of family systems theory are that (a) families, like all systems, attempt to maintain a balance of stability and change; and related to this phenomenon, (b) all behavior in the family, even seemingly problematic behavior by children, serves some purpose or function within the family system in maintaining this balance. In other words, a child's problem behavior is seen as functional and as serving a purpose for that family. Also related to family process are problem-solving strategies. Troubled families engage in ineffective problem solving and repeat maladaptive patterns of relating to each other and dealing with problems. In the face of crises, conflicts are escalated and repeated over time, rather than being resolved. A third family process variable is reaction to change. All families are faced with external stress and change and differ in how they respond and cope. Dysfunctional families are characterized by Olson et al. (1979) as either undergoing too much change (chaotic), or too little change (rigid).

Family *communication* patterns are another important aspect of family functioning. In troubled families, members do not communicate openly, honestly, and directly with each other; instead they communicate indirectly, perhaps through their behavior or through another member. Children in troubled families may not feel that their parents understand them, parents may not feel that their children listen to them, and family members in general may not feel supported by the family. Communication patterns are related to the interrelationships and structures of the family. According to Olson's model, troubled families are marked by either too much closeness (enmeshment), or too little closeness, (disengagement). At the extreme of disengagement, families can also be hostile, neglectful, and abusive.

Family *discipline* and *rules* differentiate troubled from untroubled families. All families formulate rules, whether explicit or implicit, consistent or inconsistent. Troubled families are at either extreme of discipline styles, exercising either too much or too little control, or are inconsistent, sometimes being overly punitive and at other times being overly permissive.

These family functioning variables provide a basic framework for assessing family factors related to problems of children and adolescents in school. It also is important to understand how family factors are related to problems experienced by children in schools.

Relationship of Family Functioning and Child Development

Family therapists adhere to the principle that one family member's overt problem cannot be understood separately from the context of the entire family system — that a problem of one member signals a problem in the family system. As stated by Satir (1981, p. 69) "the symptom of any family member at a given time is seen as a comment on a dysfunctional family system." The family factors previously described as characterizing troubled families have been empirically demonstrated to relate to different significant problems of children.

Marital discord is one factor that has been shown consistently to relate to several problems for children and adolescents (Mash, 1984; Porter & O'Leary, 1980; Rutter, 1985). In longitudinal studies, a high level of family discord has been found to be one of the strongest predictors of poor behavioral, psychological, and academic outcomes (Chess & Thomas, 1984; Werner & Smith, 1982). Problems in family structure characterize many troubled families, including those of anorectics, in which there is triangulation and enmeshment (Minuchin et al., 1978). Families of children with conduct disorders, including several behavior problems, aggression, and delinquency, display high levels of conflict, poor discipline, ineffective communication, poor conflict resolution, and low levels of warmth and support (Patterson & Stouthamer-Zoeber, 1984). Children or adolescents at risk for suicide perceive low levels of warmth, caring, or understanding in their homes (McConville, 1983). For many children, school phobia is related to overdependency or enmeshment with one parent, usually the mother (Lavigne & Burns, 1981).

PUTTING CHILDREN AND TROUBLED FAMILIES IN PERSPECTIVE

Assessment of Family Factors

Close contact with and understanding of a child's family system are necessary but neglected components of assessment. For children from troubled families, family assessment is *essential.* Without such assessment, a child's behavior can be misinterpreted, and the resulting misdiagnosis can perpetuate the behavior. In a sense, the child becomes the scapegoat for troubled systems. Family assessment approaches and procedures have been described in detail by Brassard (1986), and some essential features are presented here.

First, school psychologists must decide what family information is needed and how to gather the information. The reason for referral serves as the basis for making these decisions, and the family assessment is tailored to provide data on the referral question. There is some standard information, however, that applies to many referral concerns, is well within school psychologists' expertise to assess, and is necessary when operating from a systems perspective. This information includes *parents' perceptions* of the child's functioning in home, school, and community, and the school's concern for the child; *parents' knowledge* of the child's or adolescent's development, of parenting techniques, and of the school's expectations for the child's behavior and school performance; *parent's expectations* about the child's behavior and school performance and the school's role in teaching the child; *parent's attitude* toward the child, schooling, and the value of education; and *family information* with respect to degree of commitment to work on the referral concern, and information about family members, unusual family stress, communication patterns, degree of support of conflict, type of discipline, family rules, how disagreements are handled, previous family responses to the referral concern, coping strategies of the family, and degree of involvement with the child.

Family interviews, questionnaires, and commercially published self-report scales are available to assist the school psychologist in obtaining these data (see Brassard, 1986). As this family information is gathered, the school psychologist must assess how these factors influence the presenting problem for the child in the school, particularly in relation to the onset and severity of the problem.

School psychologists must maintain a systems perspective as a framework for conducting assessment of family factors. It is not helpful to use family information to shift the focus from the child's problem to the family's problem. Family assessments should be conducted to determine the best intervention strategy for the child, not to assess the functionality of the family. Like all assessment, family assessment should be intervention-oriented.

Guidelines for Working With Children From Troubled Families

Schools, and school psychologists in particular, are concerned about prevention of learning, behavioral, and emotional problems of children and adolescents; in fact, schools have been identified as primary mental health centers (Apter, 1982; Hobbs, 1975). School psychologists are in an ideal position to develop a network of mental health services for students, but in doing so they risk becoming overinvolved and overextended. To guard against this, school psychologists must limit their intervention to providing services that are directed toward ultimately benefiting the child, and set appropriate boundaries for their services.

School psychologists operating from a systems perspective are interested in the various systems in which the child interacts. Consequently, to help the child, they may intervene with persons in the school and/or family system as agents of change. Employing a systems perspective as a framework for providing services to students enables school psychologists to (a) broaden their interaction with the child beyond testing and other artificial contacts; (b) identify targets of intervention within the educational setting and the family environment; (c) reinforce the notion of multiple causality of individual behavior; and (d) increase the probability of accurate problem identification and effective intervention for the child. The school psychologist's goals are to develop interventions that consider the needs of all members of the child's system and to coordinate home and school interventions so that the child responds successfully in specific social contexts (Garbarino, 1982).

The psychologist must be sensitive to boundary issues between home and school (Power & Bartholomew, 1985). School psychologists need to establish rapport in a supportive, nonthreatening way with each system and to serve as a bridge, coordinator, and consultant to the systems involved with the child. However, they must guard against becoming part of a particular alliance or coalition (Guerin & Katz, 1984). Additionally, school psychologists need to know "when to let go," — they can easily become overinvolved with children and their families, and must be aware of which aspects of intervention are in and which are out of their control. School psychologists must remember that families construct their own sense of reality (Reiss, 1981) and that this reality may be in conflict with that of the school. Families can decide *not* to follow through on any recommendations, despite the clarity of presentation, support given, and agreement at a conference.

As a guideline, school psychologists need to focus their primary attention on improving educational opportunities and social relationships for a child in the *school setting.* Their goal is to mobilize all resources so that parents can parent and teachers can teach more effectively. School psychologists need to be cautious about overcompensating for a child's troubled family system. When school professionals unwittingly become entangled or overinvolved in the family system they can actually perpetuate family problems (Coppersmith, 1983; Lynch, 1981). School psychologists must be knowledgeable about how they choose to interact with families and about the impact of their actions on the entire family system.

ALTERNATIVE ACTIONS

Appropriate Actions

Emphasizing the importance of recognizing family factors in a child's problems implies that school psychologists will undertake action to help the child and the family. However, within the context of the school situation, certain kinds of family interventions, such as family therapy, are not appropriate (Anderson, 1983; Fine & Holt, 1983; Petrie & Piersel, 1982). Adopting a family systems orientation is seen as favorable, and various interventions that follow from such a systems view are seen as appropriate and are recommended.

The view adopted in this chapter is that interventions developed by the school psychologist should ultimately be directed toward benefiting the child, although to help the child the school psychologist will intervene with others, such as parents and teachers. This focus of enhancing the child's functioning in the school serves to guide the appropriate actions taken. The major responsibility of the school psychologist is to support the child in the school and enhance his or her competency and skills in that setting. All other activities the school psychologist engages in, such as family interventions, are implemented only to meet this goal.

A consultative service delivery framework is seen as the most appropriate organizing principle for guiding school psychologists' activities with troubled families because it is consistent with their other roles and responsibilities. In consultation (see Gutkin & Curtis, 1982), the child is the client, and the consultant (school psychologist) helps the child through the consultee (teacher and/or parent) by helping *them* in the problem-solving effort to see how they can help the child. Thus, consultation is an indirect service to the child, in that it increases the competence of those who deal directly with the child, as opposed to a direct service, such as child or family counseling. Various appropriate family-oriented interventions for school psychologists, both indirect and direct, are included in Table 2, and aspects of the interventions are discussed below.

Indirect service techniques are recognized as a way to serve more students, prevent more problems, and provide more ecologically sound interventions by altering the environments in which children live. Consultation with teachers and parents should be a primary activity of psychologists in working with children of troubled families. In consultation, school psychologists help the family and/or teacher to systematically go through a process of problem solving, of designing, implementing, and evaluating interventions in the school and/or home. Another appropriate indirect service is parent training or education to enhance parents' skills in the areas of discipline, communication, problem solving, and behavior management (Fleishman, Horne, & Arthur, 1983; Forehand & McMahon, 1981; Kramer, 1985). School psychologists can serve as a resource to their schools in helping others understand the importance of family factors, providing in-service instruction for teachers on family issues, and advocating family-oriented policies and programs at the school and district

TABLE 2

Alternative Actions for Intervening With Children and Troubled Families

Indirect service to child/family	Direct service to child/family
Consultation with parent(s) of child	Individual child counseling
Consultation with teacher(s) of child	Group child counseling
Home–school contracting	Social skills training (child)
Parent education and/or training	Individual family counseling
In-service instruction to teachers	Group family counseling
Advocacy of family issues/ policies	Family-oriented assessment
Program development	
Liaison activities with other agencies	
Referral to outside agency	

level. Finally, an appropriate action for school psychologists working with children from very troubled families is to refer them for outside services, provide supportive services in school, and to serve as a liaison between the school and outside agencies.

Direct services to children often are those for which school psychologists are best trained and see the most consistent with their current activities. Direct services that are appropriate in serving children from troubled families include supportive services to the child designed to facilitate school adjustment and build competence and skills in problem areas. These child-directed services include individual or group counseling, and specific skills training, such as social skills interventions. School-based counseling should be focused on developing competence within the school domain regardless of the difficult family situation. School psychologists in this role can help build a child's competence and increase the likelihood of success, even if the family remains troubled. Research on "invulnerable" children who develop competently, despite being at risk because of several factors including family discord, has shown that having positive social skills and a positive orientation toward the future are important factors that serve to "protect" children against poor outcomes (Garmezy, 1981; Werner & Smith, 1982). By assisting children to develop these positive coping skills, school psychologists may serve a crucial role in preventing more serious problems for students from troubled families.

Depending upon several situational factors, it may be appropriate for school psychologists to provide limited family interventions and/or counseling, but not therapy, to individual family units or groups of families (Anderson, 1983; Golden, 1983). Counseling is differentiated from therapy in that counseling is focused on skill enhancement and problem solving, whereas therapy is focused on intensive restructuring of dysfunctional families. In considering whether direct family intervention by the school psychologist is appropriate, school psychologists need to consider their training, their role description, the severity of the family's problem, and the relationship between the home and school problem(s). The adequacy of the school psychologist's training is a critical factor to consider when providing family intervention. Even if family intervention is indicated, school psychologists ethically cannot provide it unless they have specific training for that activity. Finally, as school psychologists engage in the direct service activity of assessment, they can incorporate a family systems orientation into their assessment (Anderson, 1983; Brassard, 1986).

Referral for Family Therapy

In many instances, it will be apparent to school psychologists from their assessment of family factors that a problem requires interventions that are beyond the scope of what it is appropriate to provide in school. Then, making an *effective* referral is important to increase the likelihood that the family will actually obtain the needed outside service. Several authors (Amatea & Fabrick, 1984; Brassard, 1986; Zins & Hopkins, 1981) have proposed similar guidelines for making an effective referral for outside service. First, it is important to establish a positive relationship with the family so that they will trust the referring professional's judgment and listen to the suggestion to seek therapy. Next, it is critical to know the agencies and/or therapists to whom the family is referred. For example, if the family is being referred for *family* therapy, the therapist should be specifically trained as a family therapist. (A list of practitioners who are certified as family therapists by the American Association for Marriage and Family Therapy can be obtained through the address noted in the annotated bibliography.) The family should be provided basic information about fees, hours, location and other aspects of the agency and services. In making the actual recommendation of therapy to the family, the school psychologist needs to motivate them to follow up on the suggestion and to understand possible benefits and outcomes.

Once the family has started therapy with an outside agency, the school psychologist's role is to serve as a liaison, providing relevant school information if a release of information is obtained, and to monitor school interventions. It is important for the school psychologist to keep family therapy issues separate from school issues and to focus primarily on the child's functioning in school, allowing the family and their therapist to work on family issues.

SUMMARY

In this chapter, adopting a family systems orientation for viewing problems, understanding family functioning and how family factors can affect children's problems, and applying knowledge of family variables toward helping children attain academic and social competence in school have been emphasized as important for school psychologists in helping children and troubled families. School psychologists need to recognize the impact that troubled families can have on children. Yet, this impact cannot be seen as either a cause for students' problems or an excuse not to intervene in their problems. School psychologists should intervene with families to the extent they can within their role. But they must recognize that for most situations with troubled families the most appropriate action is to support the child in school-related concerns, consult with the family and the teacher(s), implement school and home interventions, and when appropriate refer the troubled family for outside therapeutic assistance.

In summary, the following points were emphasized in the chapter:

1. Many commonly occurring and serious problems of children and adolescents are related to difficulties in family functioning. Therefore, it is important to adopt a family systems perspective for understanding children's problems.

2. In a family systems perspective, all family members are seen to influence each other in complex ways. What happens in the family affects the child exhibiting the problem, and the child, in turn, affects others in the family. Also, problems are seen as serving some purpose for the functioning of the family.

3. Although there is no single conception of normal family functioning, troubled families can be distinguished from more adequately functioning families in the areas of family structure and relationships, communication and interaction patterns, problem-solving, rules, and discipline.

4. Research has demonstrated that difficulties in family functioning are related to a variety of serious problems for children and adolescents, such as conduct problems, suicidal gestures, and eating disorders. Consequently, school psychologists need to assess family factors as they relate to the problems of referred students.

5. Appropriate actions depend on the severity of a child's problem, the extent of family involvement, the role boundaries of the school psychologist, and the training of the school psychologist. In general, consultation, child support services, and liaison services are seen as most appropriate for the school psychologist; other options including direct service to the family being appropriate in limited circumstances. Family therapy in the schools is *not* recommended.

REFERENCES

Amatea, E. S., & Fabrick, F. (1984). Moving a family into therapy: Critical referral issues for the school counselor. *School Counselor,* 285–294.

Anderson, C. (1983). An ecological developmental model for a family orientation in school psychology. *Journal of School Psychology, 21,* 179–189.

Apter, S. J. (1982). *Troubled children, troubled systems.* New York: Pergamon.

Barkley, R. A. (1981). Hyperactivity. In E. J. Mash & L. G. Terdal (Eds.), *Behavioral assessment of childhood disorders* (pp. 127–184). New York: Guilford.

Beavers, W. R. (1982). Healthy, midrange, and severely dysfunctional families. In F. Walsh (Ed.), *Normal family process* (pp. 45–66). New York: Guilford.

Belsky, J. (1984). The determinants of parenting: A process model. *Child Development, 55,* 83–96.

Brassard, M. (1986). Family assessment approaches and procedures. In H. M. Knoff (Ed.), *The assessment of child and adolescent personality* (pp. 399–449). New York: Guilford.

Christenson, S., Abery, B., & Weinberg, R.A. (1986). An alternative model for the delivery of psychology in the school community. In S. N. Elliott and J. C. Witt (Eds.), *The delivery of psychological services in the schools: Concepts, processes, and issues.* Hillsdale, NJ: Erlbaum.

Christenson, S., Ysseldyke, J. E., Wang, J. J., & Algozzine, B. (1983). Teachers' attributions for problems that result in referral for psychoeducational evaluation. *Journal of Educational Research, 76,* 174–180.

Coppersmith, E. I. (1983). The family and public service systems: An assessment method. In J. C. Hansen (Ed.), *Diagnosis and assessment in family therapy* (pp. 83–99). Rockville, MD: Aspen.

Egeland, B., Sroufe, L. A., & Erickson, M. (1983). The developmental consequences of different patterns of maltreatment. *Child Abuse and Neglect: The International Journal, 7,* 459–469.

Fine, M. J., & Holt, P. (1983). Intervening with school problems: A family systems perspective. *Psychology in the Schools, 20,* 59–66.

Fleishman, M. J., Horne, A. M., & Arthur, J. L. (1983). *Troubled families: A treatment program.* Champaign, IL: Research Press.

Forehand, R. L., & McMahon, R. J. (1981). *Helping the noncompliant child: A clinician's guide to parent training.* New York: Guilford.

Garbarino, J. (1982). *Children and families in the social environment.* New York: Aldine.

Garbarino, J., Schellenbeck, C. J., Sebes, J., & associates (1986). *Troubled youth, troubled families.* San Francisco: Jossey-Bass.

Garmezy, N. (1981). Children under stress: Perspectives on antecedents and correlates of vulnerability and resistance of psychopathology. In A. I. Rabin, J. Aronoff, A. M. Barclay, & R. A. Zucker (Eds.), *Further explorations in personality* (pp.196–269). New York: Wiley.

Golden, L. (1983). Brief family interventions in a school setting. *Elementary School Guidance and Counseling, 17,* 288-293.

Goldenberg, I., & Goldenberg, H. (1985). *Family therapy: An overview* (2nd ed.). Monterey, CA: Brooks/Cole.

Guerin, P., & Katz, A. (1984). The theory in therapy of families with school related problems: Triangles and hypothesis testing model. In B. F. Okun (Ed.), *Family therapy with school related problems* (pp. 28–45). Rockville, MD: Aspen.

Gutkin, T. B., & Curtis, M. J. (1982). School based consultation: Theory and techniques. In C. R. Reynolds and T. B. Gutkin (Eds.), *Handbook of school psychology* (pp. 796–828). New York: Wiley.

Hetherington, E. M., & Martin, B. (1979). Family interaction. In H. C. Quay and J. S. Werry (Eds.), *Psychopathological disorders of childhood* (2nd ed.) (pp. 247–302). New York: Wiley.

Hobbs, N. (1975). *The futures of children.* San Francisco, CA: Jossey-Bass.

Jurich, A. P., Polson, C. J., Jurich, J. A., & Bates, R. A. (1985). Family factors in the lives of drug users and abusers. *Adolescence, 20,* 143–159.

Kog, E., & Vandereycken, W. (1985). Family characteristics of anorexia nervosa and bulimia: A review of research literature. *Clinical Psychology Review, 5,* 159–180.

Kramer, J. J. (1985). Best practices in parent training. In A. Thomas & J. Grimes (Eds.), *Best practices in school psychology* (pp.263–273). Kent, OH: National Association of School Psychologists.

L'Abate, L., Ganahl, G., & Hansen, J. C. (1986). *Methods of family therapy.* Englewood Cliffs, NJ: Prentice-Hall.

Lavigne, J. V., & Burns, W. J. (1981). *Pediatric psychology: An introduction for pediatricians and psychologists.* New York: Grune & Stratton.

Lynch, C. (1981). On not getting caught up in the family's system. In J. C. Hansen & D. Rosenthal (Eds.), *Strategies and techniques in family therapy* (pp. 259–265). Springfield, IL: Thomas.

Mash, E. J. (1984). Families with problem children. *New Directions for Child Development, 24,* 65–84.

McConville, B. (1983). Depression and suicide in children and adolescents. In P. D. Steinhauer & G. Rae-Grant (Eds.), *Psychological problems of the child in the family* (2nd ed.) (pp. 277–292). New York: Basic Books.

McGoldrick, M., & Carter, E. A. (1982). The family life cycle. In F. Walsh (Ed.), *Normal family process* (pp. 167–195). New York: Guilford.

Minuchin, S., Rosman, B. L., & Baker, L. (1978). *Psychosomatic families: Anorexia nervosa in context.* Cambridge, MA: Harvard University Press.

Olson, D. H., Sprenkle, D. H., & Russell, C. S. (1979). Circumplex model of marital and family systems: I. Cohesion and adaptability dimensions, family types, and clinical adaptations. *Family Process, 18,* 3–28.

Patterson, G. R., & Stouthamer-Zoeber, M. (1984). The correlation of family management practices and delinquency. *Child Development, 55,* 1299–1307.

Petrie, P., & Piersel, W. C. (1982). Family therapy. In C. R. Reynolds & T. B. Gutkin (Eds.), *Handbook of school psychology* (pp. 580–590). New York: Wiley.

Porter, B., & O'Leary, K. D. (1980). Marital discord and childhood behavior problems. *Journal of Abnormal Child Psychology, 8,* 287–295.

Power, T. J., & Bartholomew, K. L. (1985). Getting unstuck in the middle: A case study in family school system consultation. *School Psychology Review, 14,* 222–229.

Reiss, D. (1981). *The family's construction of reality.* Cambridge, MA: Harvard University Press.

Rutter, M. (1985). Family and school influences on behavior development. *Journal of Child Psychology and Psychiatry, 26,* 349–368.

Satir, V. M. (1981). The family as a treatment unit. In J. C. Hansen & D. Rosenthal (Eds.), *Strategies and techniques in family therapy* (pp. 69–73). Springfield, IL: Thomas.

Walsh, F. (1982). Conceptualizations of normal family functioning. In F. Walsh (Ed.), *Normal family process* (pp.3-44). New York: Guilford.

Werner, E. E., & Smith, R. S. (1982). *Vulnerable, but invincible: A longitudinal study of resilient children and youth.* New York: McGraw-Hill.

Zins, J. E., & Hopkins, R. A. (1981). Referral out: Increasing the number of kept appointments. *School Psychology Review, 10,* 107–111.

BIBLIOGRAPHY: PROFESSIONALS

Apter, S. J. (1982). *Troubled children, troubled systems.* New York: Pergamon.
Apter describes several models for serving troubled children in schools. He argues for the adoption of the ecological perspective, which views children's problems as a "failure-to-match" in the interaction between children and the systems (school, family, community) in which they interact. The book is comprehensive, providing information on educational planning (the total school concept), ecological interventions, working with families, mainstreaming, and prevention.

Okun, B. F. (Ed.). (1984). *Family therapy with school related problems.* Rockville, MD: Aspen.
Contains several useful chapters for school psychologists in understanding children's school-related problems from a systems perspective. Critical family systems variable are presented, including reciprocal influences and the concept of the child, parent, and school becoming triangulated in conflict. Particularly recommended are chapters by Okun (an overview), Guerin and Katz (the concept of triangles in relationships), and Horne and Walker (application of a social learning approach to families).

Source of information regarding certified family therapists:

The American Association for Marriage and Family Therapy
1717 K. Street N. W. #407
Washington, D. C. 20006
202/429-1825

BIBLIOGRAPHY: PARENTS AND TEACHERS

Curran, D. (1983). *Traits of a healthy family.* Minneapolis, MN: Winston.
Describes the results of a survey of varied mental health professionals and educators about the traits of a healthy family: The 15 traits of a healthy family are described in a very readable, understandable, and often delightfully humorous way.

Patterson, G. R. (1975). *Families: Applications of social learning to family life.* Champaign, IL: Research Press.
Although an older book, *Families* is a basic, easily understood reference source describing social learning theory from a behavioral perspective. Behavior change, behavior management skills, principles of reinforcement, and dealing with common problems are described. Patterson has continued with extensive research on families of children with behavior problems, and his work remains a useful reference for both practitioners and parents. Accompanying support materials for parent training are available.

Satir, V. (1972). *Peoplemaking.* Palo Alto, CA: Science and Behavior Books.
Considered a classic in the family therapy literature, *Peoplemaking* describes the development and maintenance of healthy relationships for individuals, particularly between parents and children. Roles, communication styles, the development of self-esteem, and interactional patterns for functional and dysfunctional families are presented. The book describes family functioning in an interesting, supportive, and nonthreatening way for parents.

Children and Vision

David Happe and Alan Koenig
Iowa Braille and Sight Saving School

BACKGROUND

Educational professionals are called upon as potential sources of insight and expertise on a wide array of subjects. The topic of vision is among these, and with good reason. Vision's status as a major learning channel alone makes knowledge and appreciation of this sense necessary in considering a child's needs. For the special education professional, vision has added significance; a consideration of visual functioning is required by the rules and regulations of PL 94-142 as a part of a comprehensive evaluation; more and more visually handicapped are being served in regular education settings; improved neonatal care of high-risk infants has the potential for saving the lives of increasing numbers of children with multiple handicaps (including vision);

many children have abnormalities of visual structures or functioning that may not technically constitute visual impairments but do complicate the consideration of educational needs; and the low incidence of actual visual handicaps often means that educators and support staff working with visually handicapped learners have little, if any, prior experience with this population. In order to help meet the needs of children whose vision is in question the school psychologist needs a basic understanding of terms, definitions, and the psychoeducational implications of conditions affecting the eye or nervous system that impair a child's vision.

Definitions

The definitions used to delineate status of visual functioning can be grouped into two major categories; legal and functional. Legal definitions are primarily used in documenting the presence of a visual impairment for tax and social security benefits. A child is said to be legally blind if visual acuity is measured as 20/200 or less in the better eye with the best correction, or if the visual field subtends an angle of 20 degrees or less.

Since legal definitions indicate little about how a child performs visually on a day-to-day basis, functional definitions are used in educational settings to indicate a child's primary mode of learning: tactual or visual. A functionally blind student has no useable vision and employs tactual information as the primary mode of learning. Braille reading is the mode of reading, if applicable. A functionally partially sighted or low-vision student possesses some degree of useable vision and uses vision as the primary learning mode. Print reading from regular print, regular print with magnification, or large print is taught, if appropriate. Some students use a combination of tactual and visual information, although one is generally dominant. Auditory information is also a critical means of learning for visually impaired students, regardless of whether they are primarily tactual or visual learners.

Definitions in this field have caused a great deal of confusion over the years. The definition of visual impairment given in PL 94-142 is purely a functional definition, containing no mention of the level of visual acuity, although some decrease in acuity or field is presumed. School records or medical reports may contain references to either functional or legal definitions without specifying which is being used. In order to consider a child's needs, further supporting information or observation of the child should be obtained in order to prevent misclassification.

In order to prevent confusion in this chapter, the term *visually impaired* will be used in a general sense to describe the total group of children. When it is necessary to differentiate between groups, *blind* will be used to refer to children with no useable vision and *low-vision* will refer to those with some degree of useable vision.

Prevalence of Visual Impairment

It has been estimated that 20% of the general population have some type of visual defect. However, a large majority of these defects are refractive errors, which are correctable with regular prescription lenses (Reynolds & Birch, 1977). Statistics further indicate that 1 in 1,000 children of school age have a visual impairment that interferes with learning to some degree. Barraga (1983) reported that over three-fourths of visually impaired children have some level of useable vision. Abnormalities of the optic nerve are the most common visual problem among children, but other common eye disorders in children, according to these records, include congenital cataracts, albinism, myopia, macular pathologies, glaucoma, retinopathy of prematurity, and corneal pathologies (Faye, Padula, Padula, Gurland, Greenberg, & Hood, 1984).

Identifying Eye Problems in the School

All professionals who have contact with children should be alert to signs of potential eye problems. The National Society for the Prevention of Blindness has identified signs of possible eye trouble in children. These are listed in Table 1. The recognition of any of these signs calls for a referral to the school nurse. The nurse will typically carry out a screening of visual acuity if poor vision is a concern and inspect the eyes. Any significant loss in acuity, apparent dysfunction of the visual system, or infection of the eye or surrounding tissue warrants a referral to an optometrist or ophthamologist.

Role of Vision in Learning

From infancy, visual curiosity about the environment entices the newborn to move, explore, and learn. As remarked by Barraga (1973), "through the visual sense a greater quantity and more refined quality of information is available than can be acquired through any other one sense" (p. 119). Vision provides the learner with details of form, size, color, and spatial relationships of objects, while hearing only provides cues (Lowenfeld, 1973). Also, vision provides the ability to examine objects immediately in their totality, while touch necessitates the examination of bits of an object, which must later be integrated into a whole. Barraga (1973) summarized the importance of the role of vision in learning: "Often called the primary sensory channel or extension of the human being beyond his own body, vision is the mediator for other sensory impressions and acts as a stabilizer between man and the external world" (p. 119).

It has been estimated that 80% of school work requires acuity of near vision (Hanninen, 1979), such as reading and completing math worksheets. Other activities, such as copying information from the chalkboard and catching a ball, require distance acuity. Also, most of the incidental learning of young children occurs through the visual channel (Barraga, 1983). Given the vital role of vision in learning, it is imperative that correctable refractive errors be eliminated as early as possible. Timely screenings throughout the school years and referrals to eye care professionals when necessary will take care of the large majority of refractive errors in school-age children.

For children with low vision, learning is still very possible through the visual channel, although modifica-

TABLE 1

Indicators of Eye Problems

Behavior
- Rubs eyes excessively
- Shuts or covers one eye; tilts head or thrusts head forward
- Difficulty in reading or other close work
- Blinks more than usual or is irritable when doing close work
- Unable to see distant objects clearly
- Squints eyelids together or frowns

Appearance
- Crossed eyes
- Red-rimmed, encrusted, or swollen eyelids
- Inflamed or watery eyes
- Recurring styes

Complaints
- Eyes itch, burn, or feel scratchy
- Cannot see well
- Dizziness, headaches, or nausea following close eye work
- Blurred or double vision

tions in teaching methods may need to be made to promote optimal learning. Central to the education of a low-vision student is the efficient use of remaining vision. When accurate visual interpretations are not possible, it is often necessary to pair visual observations with accompanying sources of tactual and auditory information to develop rich concepts. However, through stimulation and training of remaining vision, the efficiency with which sight can be used in the learning process will increase.

Common Visual Impairments and Their Psychoeducational Implications

A number of factors will impair to some degree a child's visual functioning. Fortunately, corrective lenses are all that is required in most cases. The psychoeducational outcome of actual visual impairments will be related to the degree of vision loss, age at onset of the loss, and other impairments associated with the loss of visual functioning. The individual whose vision loss is total or nearly so will require highly specialized educational services. Early intervention, braille reading instruction, orientation and mobility training, and education in daily living skills may be needed.

Individuals who possess low vision, both those with uncorrectable impairments and those with an uncorrected loss, are worthy of special note for the school psychologist. Children who possess a level of vision that allows them to function at some skills but not others, or under some lighting conditions but not others, present something of an enigma to peers, parents, and teachers. When expected to behave as if sighted, low-vision children will frequently fail to meet the expectations of others. Treated as if blind, they will be held back or made more dependent upon others than is necessary.

The development of a healthy self-concept may suffer immensely as they struggle to appreciate their own skills and limitations in the face of uncertain expectations. Children with low vision may reject the use of low-vision aids such as magnifiers or monoculars because these things mark them as different from their peers. The low-vision child may require supportive counseling and it is imperative that educators, peers, and family members be well educated with respect to the child's vision, including the variability of functioning.

Over 60% of visually handicapped students have additional impairments (Silberman, 1981), which may include congenital anomalies, developmental delays, mental disability, and motor and language impairment. In considering the total needs of such children the impact of these impairments and their interactions with the vision loss will need to be considered. The school psychologist needs a basic understanding of the common causes of impaired visual functioning and their psychoeducational implications. The following discussion provides a brief overview of conditions that interfere with vision; more detailed information can be obtained from Jose (1983).

Refractive Errors. Refractive errors are the most common cause of eye problems and are almost always treatable through the use of corrective lenses. Refractive errors are the result of a failure of the eye to focus light rays properly on the retina. If the focal point falls in front of the retina, the result is myopia (nearsightedness) and the individual can see near objects clearly but not distant objects. If the focal point falls behind the retina (hyperopia, or farsightedness), the individual can see distant objects clearly but not near objects as the result.

In schools undiagnosed refractive errors are a common problem. Vision loss may be so gradual that affected children are unaware of the change and if the condition is myopia, performance on paper-and-pencil tasks may not suffer noticeably. Another problem that sometimes arises, and may involve the school psychologist, is refusal by both intolerant preschoolers and socially sensitive adolescents to wear eyeglasses.

Astigmatism. Astigmatism is caused by imperfect curvature of the cornea or lens of the eye, resulting in images that are focused at several points rather than just one. Vision is distorted or blurred and corrective lenses may be required. Astigmatism may occur along with near- or far-sightedness.

The need for eyeglasses among children with correctable refractive errors or astigmatism cannot be met financially by all parents, and educational professionals should be aware of possible resources. A variety of public assistance programs as well as many local service organizations provide help. Lions Clubs, in particular, target vision problems for their aid programs.

Amblyopia/Strabismus. Amblyopia (lazy eye) refers to a condition in which the visual input from one eye is suppressed and essentially only one eye is being used. This condition may be the result of a significant difference in the acuity of the eyes or, more commonly, the eyes may not be properly aligned. The latter condition is referred to as strabismus. One or both eyes may be turned outward (exotropia) or inward (esotropia). A muscle imbalance or other inability of the eyes to fuse is the cause.

Strabismus and amblyopia are commonly seen in children with congenital disorders such as Down syndrome. These children's vision will depend upon the soundness of the nonsuppressed input. Depending upon the specific cause of amblyopia, treatment may involve corrective lenses, patching the "good" eye to force use of the "weak" eye, or surgery to correct a muscle imbalance. Unfortunately, the course of treatment is not always clear-cut and parents may be advised by different medical professionals that each of the potential treatments is the best choice. School psychologists will not be able to render medical advice but may be able to help parents through the decision-making process.

Retinopathy of Prematurity. Retinopathy of prematurity is the term applied to a retinal condition that has previously been called retrolental fibroplasia (RLF). Premature neonates who are administered high levels of oxygen at birth are sometimes affected. The condition is occasionally seen in full-term infants, but this is exceptional. Retinal development is abnormal, with overvascularization of the retina and development of fibrous tissue in the retina and vitreous.

The effects on a child's vision are highly variable and may range from a moderate degree of myopia to complete retinal detachment. Corneal scarring, nystagmus, strabismus, glaucoma, and cataracts may also be associated with this condition. Premature infants requiring oxygen therapy are at risk of development delay, mental handicap, motor dysfunction, and later learning disorders irrespective of involvement of the visual system.

Retinitis Pigmentosa. Retinitis pigmentosa is a genetic disorder resulting in gradual deterioration of visual functioning owing to the destruction of the receptor cells of the eyes. The rods are typically lost first and night blindness and losses in peripheral vision are early signs of this disorder. As the condition advances, the individual may have difficulty in adapting to changes in lighting conditions and develop very restricted visual fields. Total blindness or stabilized vision with restricted fields may be the result.

Retinitis pigmentosa can be an emotionally devastating condition. The continuous changing of visual functioning, the loss of mobility, and variability of functioning with lighting conditions can be extremely frustrating. Victims must go through a series of adjustments as they see themselves losing the ability to perform tasks and needing to learn new adaptive skills.

Albinism. Albinism is a congenital condition that interferes with the normal production of bodily pigment. Ocular albinism is confined to the eye. The pupil appears pink rather than black because of decreased pigmentation of the retina, and the iris is translucent. The individual's ability to tolerate light may be reduced, and abnormal macular development, decreased acuity, high refractive errors, nystagmus, and photophobia may accompany albinism. The condition is not progressive and visual functioning tends to be stable although refractive errors associated with growth and aging can result in changes in vision.

Children affected by albinism are at risk for the emotional and self-esteem difficulties related to low vision and may also be subject to teasing and social rejection related to their physical appearance.

Cataracts. A cataract is an opacity or clouding of the lens of the eye. In children, cataracts may be congenital or may develop as a result of injury or illness. Congenital cataracts may be associated with nystagmus, strabismus, refractive error, amblyopia, and photophobia, and they frequently occur in association with rubella, Down syndrome, Marfan syndrome, diabetes, or glaucoma.

Glaucoma. Glaucoma is abnormally high pressure in the fluid of the eye, which may cause damage to the optic nerve. In young children the eyeball is somewhat elastic and enlargement of the eye can result. Surgery performed to correct problems of fluid drainage of the eye is a common treatment in infantile glaucoma. In young children this condition may occur with other conditions affecting the eye.

Microphthalmia and Anophthalmia. Microphthalmia is a congenital condition characterized by an abnormally small eyeball. In anophthalmia the eye tissue is absent or present as vestigial tissue only. Microphthalmia is often accompanied by other eye disorders such as cataracts, high myopia, nystagmus, and corneal opacities. The cause of microphthalmia is often prenatal infection, such as rubella or toxoplasmosis. These infectious agents have significant, related risk factors.

Optic Atrophy. Optic atrophy is degeneration of the optic nerve that results in varying degrees of visual loss and associated defects such as impaired color vision, decreased acuity, photophobia, and peripheral field loss. Head trauma, tumors of the eye or brain, and certain central nervous system disorders are the common causes. Psychoeducational implications are related to the visual loss and effects of the neurological trauma.

Cortical Blindness. Cortial blindness is the result of pathology of the visual cortex. The eyes themselves are not affected but the areas of the brain that receive and interpret information from the eyes are damaged or dysfunctional. The pattern of visual loss is dependent upon the degree and complexity of the cortical damage. Again, psychoeducational implications include the impact of the vision loss and effects related to the brain trauma.

Other Visual Conditions. There are several visual conditions that do not necessarily constitute visual impairments or, more accurately, visual handicaps and will most likely not require special programming from a teacher of the visually impaired. The first condition is the loss of vision in one eye. If vision is normal in the other eye, the student would not even fall within the category of legally visually impaired. Functionally, there will be a loss of depth perception, but children in most cases make spontaneous, unconscious adjustments for this loss during the developmental years. In those cases in which such adjustments are not made spontaneously, the student may be best served by an occupational therapist rather than a teacher of the visually impaired. If in doubt, however, a teacher of the visually impaired should be included on the assessment team in order to get appropriate input.

Students with visual perceptual difficulties are occasionally referred for special programming for the visually impaired. However, if visual acuity is normal, programming from other specialists is the appropriate course of action.

There are two aspects related to educationally insignificant refractive errors that should be considered. First, in some cases even with the best correction, students may still have very minor refractive errors in the 20/30 to 20/60 range. If such a level of distance acuity does not interfere in any way with normal daily functioning, no handicap exists, but in some special cases, a student may begin to experience difficulty with near-point work at the 20/60 level. If this occurs, consultation with a low-vision specialist is recommended. Second, minor refractive errors do not automatically necessitate special modifications to a child's program, and in most cases none would be necessary. Again, if any doubt exists, consultation with a teacher of the visually impaired would be appropriate.

A final condition, color blindness, should not be considered a visual impairment if visual acuity is normal. However, a student with color blindness may require some special adaptations in educational programming, especially in the early years when colors play such a vital role in learning. If a child who has normal acuity and adequate cognitive ability is not developing adequate discrimination and identification of colors in preschool or kindergarten, color testing should be initiated. Perhaps the most appropriate first step might be some diagnostic teaching with the primary colors in order to eliminate the possibility of less than adequate teaching methods. Thereafter, formal color tests, such as the Ishihara plates, should be administered. If a child is found to have a color deficiency, teachers and parents should be alerted and appropriate expectations outlined.

Interpreting Eye Reports

When evaluative information regarding a child is being considered, it is rarely the case that a specialist in the field of vision is a participant. A brief overview of the kind of information presented in reports from eye care professionals may make the task of interpretation somewhat less intimidating. While reports may vary in form, most contain information on visual acuities and, if necessary, the prescription for glasses. Others may include the etiology and prognosis and, occasionally, information on the visual fields.

Distance visual acuities are typically presented in fractional units, such as 20/20 or 20/100. Normal visual acuity is 20/20, indicating that this person sees at 20 feet what the normal eye sees at 20 feet. A student with 20/100 vision, on the other hand, sees at 20 feet what the normal eye sees at 100 feet. For students in the general population, reports from an eye care specialist will generally be presented with the number 20 as the numerator. Current practice in low vision, however, uses a numerator of 10, which means that testing occurred at 10 feet rather than 20 feet. Therefore, an eye report on a low-vision student may contain an acuity measure of 10/300, indicating that the student sees at 10 feet what a normal eye would see at 300. If conversion to a "20" measurement will increase interpretability, simply multiply the numerator and denominator by whatever number is necessary to yield 20 in the numerator. In the case of 10/300 we would multiply both by 2, yielding 20/600. For students who have very low vision or are functionally blind, distance acuities may be specified with notations such as HM (hand movements at x inches), LProj (light projection), LP (light perception), and NIL or NLP (no light perception).

Near vision acuities are rarely reported for the typical student. However, near acuities are critical for low-vision students. The commonly accepted practice among low-vision specialists is to specify the size of print in meters or points that can be read by the student *in conjunction with* the distance from the page. For example, a student who reads 1-M print at 10 inches could read common newspaper-size print at a relatively comfortable distance. Figure 1 shows various sizes of print. When examining a low-vision specialist's report of near acuities, it is imperative to have access to such a card in order to make interpretations meaningful. On some occasions, a near acuity may be presented in the fractional form, such as 20/30. This is not the preferred practice in low vision, since it does not specify the distance at which the material was read — when the distance is not given, one must presume a normal working distance of 12–16 inches.

Another common set of numbers in an eye report may look like this: +4.00 1.00 ×1.50 or –.50 2.50 axis .75. These numbers report the student's refractive correction and are necessary for an optician who is fitting a pair of glasses. Perhaps the most important information for the psychologist is the first number. If the sign is positive, the student is farsighted; if negative, the student is nearsighted.

Information on etiologies and prognoses and their related educational implications will require reference to a book on ophthalmology or low vision (e.g., Jose, 1983) or consultation with an educator who specializes in education of the visually impaired. In most cases, the eye care professional who examined the child will provide consultation and interpretation of findings. Consultation with a vision specialist is critical if a low-vision aid has been prescribed to increase visual functioning. A training program will be necessary in order for the aid to be used most efficiently, and educators working with the child will need to understand the appropriate use of the aid.

FIGURE 1

Example of Near Vision Test Card

NEAR VISION TEST CARD

			DISTANCE EQUIVALENT	METRIC PRINT SIZE	
GAME			20/360	6M	
CRANE			20/200	3.5 M	
TOLD	26	(18 Pt)	20/120	2 M	
LEFT	387		20/100	1.6 M	J10
DOT	49	(12 Pt)	20/80	1.4 M	
BAKE	28	(9 Pt)	20/60	1 M	J6
CODE	63		20/50	.8 M	
BOTH	94	(6 Pt)	20/40	.7 M	
NEAR	86	(4 Pt)	20/30	.5 M	J1
PRINT	92		20/20	.35 M	

18 Point Large Type Grades 1 - 3
14 Point Average Book Print Grades 4 - 7
12 Point Magazines, Books Grades 8 - 12
9 Point Magazines, Paper Back Books, Typing
7 Point Newspaper

Near vision should be measured with best distance correction, and with reading add if patient is presbyopic.

In cases of subnormal vision, the distance equivalent is used to calculate the add for reading:

$$\frac{\text{denominator}}{\text{numerator}} = \text{D of add for 1 M print.}$$

LOW VISION LENS SERVICE
New York Association for the Blind
111 East 59th Street, New York, N.Y. 10022 ©1972 LHNV-2
Printed in U.S.A

Note: Copyright 1972 by New York Association for the Blind. Reprinted by permission. Vision Test Card has been reduced. Not intended for actual use.

DEVELOPMENT

Normal development is a highly variable, individualized process. The effects of an intact, properly functioning visual system on this process are immense, yet we are often unable to precisely define or predict the impact of abnormal structure or function of the visual system on the course of a child's development. Research has been concentrated primarily on totally blind samples and, therefore, the impact of less severe forms of visual difficulty have not been as well studied. The low incidence of visual impairment makes the selection of a random sample for study nearly impossible, and much research has utilized subjects from residential schools. The high rate of coincident handicaps makes it difficult to delineate the effects of visual handicaps versus other limitations that an individual may possess. With these limitations to our base of knowledge in mind, some of the major factors relating to development and vision will be discussed.

Cognitive Development

Normal cognitive development is a process that is dependent upon children's genetically determined capabilities, experience in their environment, and the nurturance, guidance, and education provided to them. This is a resilient process, and a slight degree of vision loss will not appreciably affect its course. It is with those children whose sensory experiences are significantly distorted or diminished that cognitive development may follow an apparently abnormal progression. A severe visual impairment diminishes the young child's range and variety of experiences, control of the environment, and ability to move about and explore. It is not possible to adequately experience extremes of size or of dangerous or delicate objects, and color may be lost to experience entirely (Warren, 1984).

These factors build a strong expectation of abnormal cognitive development. However, our ability to convincingly demonstrate developmental lags or persistent cognitive deficits has been severely impaired by inadequate research paradigms and poorly adapted tactual analogs of visually directed tasks (Warren, 1984).

The school psychologist, charged with the assessment of intellectual development, is left in a quandry. The assessment of visually handicapped learners is addressed elsewhere at length (Robinson, 1983; Silberman, 1981; Swallow, 1980), and a cautious, patient, and far-reaching approach is advised.

One element of cognition and mental status deserves further note. The effects of combined visual and mental impairments appear to interact synergistically. A visually impaired child with even a mild mental handicap is often severely impaired in communication, motor, social, and adaptive skills. The argument has been advanced that the blind child does not derive benefit from the organization of the environment which is perceived visually. The blind child must conceptually construct that which is simply made available to the sighted child through vision. The mental construct of something as simple as a checkerboard requires an appreciation of size, number, shape, array, and alternation along an unknowable dimension (color). The sighted child needs none of this to appreciate the playing surface and engage in the game.

Language Development

The study of language development in the visually impaired has again concentrated upon blind subjects. The conventional wisdom held that, despite some differences in early language development, by age 5 or 6 years the language of blind children is essentially indistinguishable from that of sighted children. However, more recent research has pointed out persistent deficiencies in the language of blind children.

The blind child is more likely to parrot the language usage of others, make self-references, misuse pronouns, and change the topic of conversation than sighted children. Detailed observations of language interaction between mothers and children have shown that mothers tend to provide labels for immediate objects and actions to blind children but not the same level of description of the encountered objects and events that is provided to sighted children. As a result, the child is both handicapped in the ability to experience the world and deprived of the information that might serve to compensate for the lack of sensory input, and language development suffers (Warren, 1984).

Development of Functional Low Vision

Development of visual skills in children with low vision has been assumed to proceed in a sequence similar to that of normal vision although more slowly (Barraga, 1983), an assumption that research and practice has largely substantiated. However, Barraga cautions that development of the use of residual low vision may not occur spontaneously as it does in children with unimpaired vision, and a program of visual stimulation will most likely be necessary. Based on a successful series of research studies in the 1960s, Barraga and her colleagues at the University of Texas and the American Printing House for the Blind developed a comprehensive program designed to assess and develop functional low-vision skills (Barraga, 1980). This program was based on the normal sequence of visual development as outlined by Barraga (1983) in Table 2.

In practice, functional low-vision skills should be assessed in low-vision children on a regular basis, and a program of visual stimulation and training developed and implemented. The *Program to Increase Efficiency in Visual Functioning: Diagnostic Assessment Procedure* (Barraga, 1980) is a key resource in this endeavor. An instrument designed to assess lower-level visual skills in multiply handicapped low-vision students is offered by Smith and Cote (1982). Administration of these instruments requires the expertise of an educator trained to work with low-vision students, so consultation will most likely be required during the assessment and training phases.

Social and Emotional Development

While there is no "typical" pattern of social and emotional development among individuals with visual impairments, there are certain broad behavioral tendencies observed within the visually impaired population (Tuttle, 1984). Immaturity, egocentrism, social withdrawal, passivity, and dependence are frequently seen among the visually impaired. In large part, the child's inability to fully benefit from the modeling of prosocial behavior, the limits that the impairment places on participation, and the helpfulness, in excess of actual needs, that is often provided by caregivers account for these tendencies. Certain developmental characteristics of the blind child may also contribute to these tendencies. For example, social smiling appears later in development in blind children and their smiling tends to be less intense and animated than that of sighted children. The long-term impact of this developmental difference is unknown, but it could have an effect on the social interplay of the child with parents, siblings, peers, and others.

Within a school setting it is important for teachers and peers to be well educated to the skills and abilities of the visually impaired child as well as to the child's limitations. When the expectations of these important others match the visually impaired child's skills, the opportunity for maximum social involvement and positive emotional development will be enhanced. Means of involving a visually handicapped child in the fullest possible range of school activities, and methods of adapting activities to the child, should be taught to teachers and peers alike. It is extremely important that this be viewed as an ongoing process, responding to the normal developmental changes in child and school activities.

From the perspective of handicapped children, certain special abilities may be needed. These children must be able to recognize their own need for assistance and be able to request appropriate help. The adolescent who will never be able to drive will need to develop social and communication skills for asking peers for rides or be dependent upon parents and siblings. The child who has independent travel skills in a given environment may still need to learn to accept the assistance of a sighted guide when time is not available for independent travel.

TABLE 2

Sequence of Visual Development

Developmental Age	Visual Responses and Capabilities
0–1 month	Attends to light and possible visual forms; weak ciliary muscles and limited fixation ability, so objects appear out of focus.
1–2 months	Follows moving objects and lights; attends to novelty and complex patterns; stares at faces; begins binocular coordination.
2–3 months	Eyes fixate, converge, and focus; discriminates faces and yellow, orange, and red color waves.
3–4 months	Eye movements smoother and acuity improving; manipulates and looks at objects.
4–5 months	Eyes shift focus from objects to body parts; attempts to reach for and move to objects; visually explores environment; recognizes familiar faces and objects; tracks objects across entire field of vision.
5–6 months	Reaches and grasps objects, indicating eye–hand coordination.
6–7 months	Shifts visual attention from object to object; reaches and rescues dropped objects; fluid eye movements.
7–8 months	Manipulates objects, looking at results; watches movements and scribbles.
9–10 months	Visual acuity good, accommodation smooth; looks for hidden objects even around corners; imitates facial expressions; plays looking games.
11 months to 1½ years	All optical skills refined and acuity good; fits objects together and marks spontaneously.
1½–2 years	Matches objects, points to objects in books; imitates strokes and actions.
2–2½ years	Visually inspects objects in distance; imitates movements of objects; matches colors and like forms; increased visual memory span; orders objects by color; regards and reaches simultaneously.
2½–3 years	Matches geometric forms; draws crude circle; inserts circle, square, and triangle; puts pegs in holes; puts two puzzle pieces together.
3–4 years	Matches identical shaped objects by size; good depth perception; discriminates line length; copies a cross; discriminates most basic forms.
4–5 years	Refined eye–hand coordination; colors, cuts, and pastes; draws square; perceives detail in objects and pictures

Note: From *Visual handicaps and learning, Revised edition* (p. 79) by N. C. Barraga, 1983, Austin, TX: Exceptional Resources. Copyright 1983 by Exceptional Resources. Reprinted by permission.

PUTTING CHILDREN'S VISUAL IMPAIRMENT IN PERSPECTIVE

The educational concerns involving the visually impaired constitute an area of expertise typically not possessed by school psychologists. As a result, the first and often greatest need is for further information. The needed information will vary greatly with the presenting problem, and a consideration of the entire realm of possible concerns is beyond the scope of this chapter. Local educators of the visually handicapped, state departments of education, state schools for the visually impaired, eye care professionals, and colleagues experienced in this field can all be valuable sources of information. Sources listed in this chapter's annotated bibliography provide a starting point for research into vision concerns, including a list of national organizations that provide a variety of information and resource services.

The school psychologist may be involved in the entire gamut of possible actions regarding vision problems from initiating a medical referral to assessment of a child with impaired vision to participating in the special education placement process. Perhaps the question most frequently asked of educational professionals regarding vision is whether a child experiencing academic difficulties can see properly. A referral to the school nurse for screening is usually all that is needed. When further assessment is necessary, familiarity with local medical personnel, particularly an awareness of those who work well with children, can be helpful.

When assessment of a visually impaired child is the immediate task of the school psychologist, it may be necessary to seek out appropriate resources or assistance in designing an appropriate evaluation. When educational placement for a visually impaired child is at issue, knowledge of the child's capacities, visual and otherwise, the services available, and the accommodations that can be made is critical for all participants in the process. It is all too easy, when dealing with low-incidence conditions, to defer to experts in the area. Informed decision making by the diagnostic–educational team requires a full appreciation of the child's condition and psychoeducational needs by all members.

When vision services are provided on an itinerant basis, the teacher of the visually impaired may not have an awareness of the locally available options for assistance, the quality of each option, or an appreciation of those intangible factors that can promote or limit the provision of best services within a given school. School psychologists may be able to provide guidance to the decision-making process through their knowledge of such local school system variables.

The sheer breadth of the topic of vision makes it impossible to address all possible needs for action by the school psychologist. Questions regarding visual functioning do not fall within the school psychologist's normal range of expertise, but school psychologists should have a means of pursuing the knowledge necessary to assist in serving children.

SUMMARY

There are, in education, many areas in which the school psychologist may be solicited for information but not be expected to be expert. In these areas the lack of expertise is understandable and forgivable. Ignorance does not call one's stature into question. Vision is such an area and the school psychologist may function in an admirable, or even exemplary, fashion in day-to-day work with a rudimentary knowledge of the sense of sight. The most common form of visual defect, refractive error, occurs in one in every five children. These are usually treatable with prescription lenses and no special action will be required of the school psychologist. Occasionally, however, there is a need for the many people dealing with a child to have a greater appreciation of this field. In one of every 1,000 children, there exists an educationally significant visual impairment that interferes with the learning process. This chapter has provided a starting point for the school psychologist in need of resources to expand upon knowledge and serve children more effectively.

REFERENCES

Barraga, N. C. (1973). *Utilization of sensory-perceptual abilities.* In B. Lowenfeld (Ed.), *The visually handicapped child in school* (pp. 117–154). New York: John Day.

Barraga, N. C. (1980). *Program to develop efficiency in visual functioning: Diagnostic assessment procedure.* Louisville, KY: American Printing House for the Blind.

Barraga, N. C. (1983). *Visual handicaps and learning.* Austin, TX: Exceptional Resources.

Faye, E. E., Padula, W. V., Padula, J. B., Gurland, J. E., Greenberg, J. L., & Hood, C. M. (1984). The low vision child. In E. E. Faye (Ed.), *Clinical low vision.* Boston: Little, Brown.

Hanninen, K. A. (1979). *Teaching the visually handicapped* (2nd ed.). Detroit: Blindness Publications.

Jose, R. T. (Ed.). (1983). *Understanding low vision.* New York: American Foundation for the Blind.

Lowenfeld, B. (Ed.). (1973). *The visually handicapped child in school.* New York: John Day.

Reynolds, M. C., & Birch, J. W. (1977). *Teaching exceptional children in all America's schools: A first course for teachers and principals.* Reston, VA: Council for Exceptional Children.

Robinson, G. (1985). Best practices in the assessment of visual impairment. In Thomas, A., & Grimes, J. (Eds.), *Best practices in school psychology* (pp. 369–379). Kent, OH: National Association of School Psychologists.

Silberman, R. K. (1981). Assessment and evaluation of visually handicapped students. *Journal of Visual Impairment and Blindness, 75,* 109–114.

Smith, J. A., & Cole, K. S. (1982). *Look at me: A resource manual for the development of residual low vision in multiply handicapped children.* Philadelphia: Pennsylvania College of Optometry Press.

Swallow, R. (1981). Fifty assessment instruments commonly used with blind and partially seeing individuals. *Journal of Visual Impairment and Blindness, 75,* 65–72.

Tuttle, D. W. (1984). *Self-esteem and adjusting with blindness: The process of responding to life's demands.* Springfield, IL: Thomas.

Warren, D. H. (1984). *Blindness and early childhood development* (2nd ed.). New York: American Foundation for the Blind.

BIBLIOGRAPHY: PROFESSIONALS

Bradley-Johnson, S. (1986). *Psychoeducational assessment of visually impaired and blind students.* Austin, TX: Pro-Ed.
This text provides a thorough discussion of the issues and procedures in assessment of visually impaired students. Two observational scales will be useful in naturalistic observation prior to assessment. Of particular interest to the psychologist is an extensive compilation and review of appropriate assessment instruments for use with infants, preschoolers, and school-age children.

Jose, R. (1983). *Understanding low vision.* New York: American Foundation for the Blind.
This volume details the consideration of needs in the assessment, training, and education of low-vision individuals. Of particular interest to the school psychologist is a section on psychosocial aspects of low vision.

Swallow, R. (1981). Fifty assessment instruments commonly used with blind and partially seeing individuals. *Journal of Visual Impairment and Blindness, 75,* 65–72.
This useful article reviews considerations in the assessment of the visually impaired. Fifty assessment instruments used with visually impaired children are described and information regarding appropriate age and grade usage, required testing time, and test source is provided.

Warren, D. H. (1984). *Blindness and early childhood development* (2nd ed.). New York: American Foundation for the Blind.
This is an extremely comprehensive text, covering developmental concerns in the areas of cognition, language, personality, perception, socialization, and motor skills among blind children. Intellectual assessment of blind persons is also discussed.

The following organizations provide information regarding vision and visual impairment:

American Council for the Blind
1211 Connecticut Avenue, NW, Suite 506
Washington, DC 20036-2775
(202) 833-1251

American Foundation for the Blind
15 West 16th Street
New York, NY 10011
(212) 620-2000

American Printing House for the Blind
1839 Frankfort Avenue
Louisville, KY 40206
(502) 895-2405

National Federation of the Blind
1800 Johnson Street
Baltimore, MD 21230
(301) 659-9314

National Association for Parents of the Visually Impaired, Inc. (NAPVI)
P.O. Box 180806
Austin, TX 78718
(512) 459-6651

BIBLIOGRAPHY: PARENTS

Ferrell, K. A. (1984). *Parenting preschoolers: Suggestions for raising young blind and visually impaired children.* New York: American Foundation for the Blind.
This easy-to-read booklet discusses a number of common concerns that parents may have through a question/answer format. Practical advice and suggestions are presented in a casual, nonthreatening manner. Single copies are available free from AFB.

Ferrell, K. A. (1985). *Reach out and teach: Meeting the training needs of parents of visually and multiply handicapped young children.* New York: American Foundation for the Blind.
Presents an excellent training guide for parents of preschool visually impaired children, thoroughly covering the major developmental areas. The accompanying *Reachbook* provides meaningful activities in a workbook format. A series of slide shows (purchased separately) supplements and reinforces the written materials. Parents can work through the series independently or with consultation from a professional.

Jastrzembska, Z. (1985). Resources for parents and professionals working with visually handicapped preschoolers. *Education of the Visually Handicapped, 16,* 115–134.
This journal article presents an annotated bibliography of flyers, booklets, curriculums, and books related to preschool visually impaired children. Each entry is cross-referenced for target audience (parents, teachers) and major focus (blind, low vision, deaf–blind, multihandicapped). The source and cost (if available) for obtaining each publication are provided. Some are free.

Kastein, S., Spaulding, I., & Schaif, B. (1980). *Raising the young blind child: A guide for parents and educators.* New York: Human Services Press.
Discusses major developmental skill areas for blind children in three age groups: birth to 22 months, 23 months to 3 years, and 3 to 5 years. Skill areas include language, motor, social/emotional, sensory, self-help, and school readiness.

Lowenfeld, B. (1971). *Our blind children: Growing and learning with them.* Springfield, IL: Thomas.
This frank, thorough book is written for parents of blind children from birth through adolescence. It offers many practical ideas and suggestions for raising a blind child and contains a section titled "Questions Parents Often Ask." Although it is somewhat old, *Our Blind Children* is still an extremely valuable book for both parents and teachers.

BIBLIOGRAPHY: CHILDREN

American Foundation for the Blind, (1984). *A different way of seeing: An open letter to children about people who are visually handicapped.* New York: Author.
This booklet answers many of the common questions that children have about visual impairment and blindness, including such areas as going to school, writing, eating, and traveling from place to place. It is written in a clear, friendly style, with readability estimated at the upper elementary level. Teachers or parents could read this to younger students to stimulate thought and discussion. Single copies available free from AFB.

National Association for Visually Handicapped. *Monocular Mac* (1977). *Larry* (1978). *Cathy* (1979). *Susan* (1979). New York: Author. (Order from NAVH, 305 East 24th St., New York, NY 10011)
This series of books portrays visually impaired children in realistic situations and discusses common school/home activities and adaptations from their points of view. *Monocular Mac* tells how he uses his new monocular, named "Mac," to see things at a distance. *Larry* is an albino who tells about his special sensitivity to sunlight and how he gets along in the regular classroom, as well as introducing his other friends in a special class for visually impaired children. *Cathy* discusses the cataracts she had at birth and the various adaptations she makes to fit into the regular classroom; later, she befriends another visually impaired child who has just moved to her school. Finally, *Susan,* a child with normal vision, has just moved into the neighborhood and found that her next-door-neighbor is visually impaired; at first she does not want to be friends with Maria because she cannot see well but slowly learns that Maria can do many fun things.

The Media Guild (undated). *My friends call me Tony.* Solana Beach, CA: Author. (Order from the Media Guild, P.O. Box 881, Solana Beach, CA 92075)
Tony is a 10-year-old blind student who narrates a film about a typical day in his life. He talks about things such as going to school, cooking, playing hockey, and camping with the Cub Scouts. This 12-minute film is available on a rental or purchase basis and is accompanied by a short discussion guide.

Children and Working Parents

Beth Deemer
Paulding County Schools, Paulding, Ohio

BACKGROUND

Current statistics indicate that dual-earner families now outnumber "traditional" families, with 52% of U.S. households falling into the dual-earner category. Fewer than 30% of U.S. families represent the employed father–homemaker mother setting, formerly regarded as a typical situation (Nock & Kingston, 1984). Employed parents have specific questions about child development, generally regarding the best time for a mother to start a job or return to work. Children's responsibilities are another developmental issue for these families. The most common concerns facing dual-earner and single-working-parent families seem to be centered around relationships, time, and guilt. Relationships between parent and child, parent and parent, and parent and workplace are sources of conflict. Working parents report that they are concerned about "quality time" with their families. Spouses want an opportunity for time to nurture the marriage, without arguing about division of household labor. Single parents have special problems with the time and energy needed to cultivate new relationships. Finally, time becomes an issue in the workplace when parents neglect work because of family demands. Guilt is closely tied to the time issue. Working parents experience guilt about leaving children in the care of others, guilt about struggling relationships, and guilt about compromises between home and work. Alternatives for problem solving include examining these relationships, managing time in better ways, and tempering guilt with realistic expectations.

DEVELOPMENT

Child Development Considerations for Working Parents

Most working parents with young children are faced at some point with deciding when to put a child or children into child care. For some families, economic or job security concerns force a new mother to return to work within weeks of delivery. These parents may worry that secure attachments are endangered and that the infant will grow to prefer the caregiver to the mother and father. The perspectives on an optimal time for a mother to start a job or return to work are as varied as the psychological theories of child development. A traditional psychoanalytic approach would propose that an infant must be securely attached to its mother in order for the infant to develop the ability to love and trust. The psychoanalytically oriented regard nurturing as a biological and instinctive function; thus, leaving a baby in the care of another may spell doom for the mental health of both mother and child. Child development expert Burton White has clearly stated that from 6 to 7 months to the age of 3 years, a child requires a healthy attachment to one person, and that person should be a parent (White, 1980).

Certain research in the area of attachments has not supported this need for a single attachment. Babies initially exhibit signs of attachment between 6 and 10 months of age. Schaffer and Emerson (1964) found that babies form several attachments at about the same time (9–12 months). In later work, Schaffer (1977) disputes the idea of the need for an exclusive mother–infant bond, proposing that once an infant has developed specific attachments, the infant can then form and maintain several at the same time. Babies with several attachments adjust more quickly when their mothers leave; they are less anxious in the presence of other adults (Rutter, 1982). Finally, studies of daycare babies (Kagan, Kearsley, & Zelazo, 1978) indicate that daycare babies and babies at home with their mothers full time do not differ in their preferences for their mother as a secure attachment. Scarr (1984) has suggested that placing a child in daycare during the first 5 months may be optimal. This is a reassuring perspective for parents who work out of necessity and not choice. Scarr reinforces the concept that babies do not show strong preference for others until about 8–10 months, at which time they can form attachments with several familiar people. By waiting for a year or so to place a child in daycare, a mother may inadvertently cause considerably more temporary distress for the child.

Pediatrician T. Berry Brazelton (1985) identifies critical stages in the development of *mothering,* as opposed to merely examining the development of the child. Attachment is a reciprocal process; while an infant may be establishing "trust," a mother is affirming basic self-trust in her own role as caregiver. The initial stages in a building relationship must occur before a mother is ready to relinquish her baby's care to another. Recognizing that every mother–infant pair will vary somewhat, Dr. Brazelton offers reasonable guidelines for return to work. When there is a choice, mothers should avoid returning to work for 4 months. During the first 4 months, the mother learns a great deal about herself and her baby, laying the foundation for her own parenting competency and sense of attachment. Parents should also avoid placing a baby in childcare at time when stranger anxiety is apparent, usually at 7–8 months of age. The age of 9–10 months, once sitting and crawling are developed, can be regarded as a good time for a change of caregivers; 12–16 months may be a poor time, as separation anxiety is common. Finally, 18 months to 2 years is a favorable time for a mother to return to work; walking has been mastered and negativism is disappearing.

Many working families will not have the luxury of a choice regarding timing and childcare. In spite of the varied opinions of doctors, psychologists, and researchers, there is agreement that all children can thrive with a warm and caring attachment, be it parent or other caregiver.

Developmental Considerations in Responsibilities for Children

Working parents may have concerns about placing too many or too few responsibilities on children. Certainly children vary in rate of development, but there are guidelines to indicate the ages at which children can assume responsibility for aspects of self-care. Generally, 3-year-olds can undress completely, toilet with some assistance, and dress with assistance. They use water faucets independently and wash hands and face without help. In addition, 3-year-olds can put away pajamas and pick up toys, empty wastebaskets, fold small laundry items, and clear dishes from the table, wiping up spills. Gracious acceptance of a less than perfect performance will be required on the part of the parent. A 4-year-old dresses with minimal supervision, other than help with difficult fasteners, cares for toileting needs, and bathes with some assistance (Brigance, 1978). Appropriate duties include picking up clutter, putting dirty clothes in the hamper, and putting clean clothes in drawers. As coordination and attention to task build, children of 5 and 6 can set the table, put away clean dishes, and help with dusting. Feeding and caring for a pet are reasonable duties. A 7-year-old may clean bathroom sinks and tubs, empty garbage, sweep walks, clean the inside of the car, and prepare cereal and sandwiches. Middle elementary school children are capable of all laundry tasks and basic cooking skills. Parents who intend to leave children alone at home should use these responsibility guidelines to determine readiness for some self-care.

The practice of leaving children alone at home before or after school is receiving a great deal of attention. There are an estimated 2 million "latchkey" children between the ages of 7 and 13. The physical and emotional well-being of these children is of great concern and depends heavily on parental guidance and community support. The decision to allow a child to stay alone at home is a serious one. Parents must consider situations likely to affect children: safety risks, increased responsibility, emotions like fear and loneliness, and peer pressure. The child's maturity level, attitude about being independent, sense of responsibility, and level of common sense are factors for parents to assess. Resources such as *Keys for Kids,* by the Cooperative Extension Service of The Ohio State University, are designed for parents who are considering self-care for a child. This type of parent–child workshop format includes tools to help evaluate a child's problem-solving skills and developmental readiness for being alone at home. Parents must gauge each child's level of maturity and ability to cope effectively with self-care.

PUTTING WORKING PARENTS IN PERSPECTIVE

Since 1980, more than half of U.S. families have been dual-earner or single-working parent households. This fact emphasizes that dealing with the problems of working parents is the norm. The situation is neither unique nor poorly understood. Examining the advantages to dual-earner families and the evidence (more appropriately the lack of evidence) regarding detrimental effects to children can help put the decision whether both parents will work in perspective. The most common benefit for families with two working parents is generally economic. Whether the decision is made by choice or necessity, the advantages of additional income are undeniable. Working parents take comfort in their ability to provide for basic needs and enriching experiences. Family stress is reduced when money is less of an issue. More subtle are the advantages of a possibly enhanced involvement of fathers as parents, a sense of self-fulfillment at work for mothers, increased independence on the part of the children, and a decline in sex role stereotyping.

Contemporary families depend on the father to assume a more equitable and significant role in child rearing. Fathers are becoming more involved in physical care of children and in planning other child care. Both parents are regarded as attachment figures who can provide security (Scarr, 1984). Crosby (1982) has demonstrated that mothers who are not working but wish they were are frustrated and depressed. These women reported feelings of entrapment, loneliness, and lack of self-confidence. On the other hand, working mothers who like their jobs are happier than at-home mothers (Hetherington, Cox, & Cox, 1982). In traditional families, mothers who do not work seem to thrive on the dependence of their children. The need to be needed extends into the early adolescent years; as children approach adolescence and seek independence, a mother may feel neglected or unappreciated (Goodman, 1979). Children of working parents have the opportunity to experience broader definitions of sex roles. Hoffman (1983) has reviewed the literature and reported that the daughters of employed mothers are more self-confident and have higher grades than the daughters of mothers who are not employed. (A less positive finding, however, was that sons of employed mothers were inclined to be less self-confident and less academically inclined.) As mothers and fathers are both seen in a variety of roles, children are exposed less to traditional sex roles. Either parent can be responsive, nurturing, understanding, independent, decisive, and aggressive (Ryglewicz & Thaler, 1980).

Much of the research on maternal employment focuses on possible ill effects for children, including deficiencies in infant behavior, school achievement and adjustment, and children's attitudes as well as adolescent delinquency. In 1982, the National Academy of Science published a comprehensive review of the literature regarding working mothers. A basic finding in that report indicates that there are no consistently reported effects of maternal employment on any aspect of child development. Researching this issue is vastly complex because parents work for different reasons in diverse settings with children who are at various stages of development (Kamerman & Hayes, 1982). Heins (1983) cites a lack of evidence to support the notion that a mother in the home guarantees quality motherhood, and notes that there is little proof that maternal employment has deleterious effects. There is another side to the investigation of the role of the working versus the nonworking mother. Time studies comparing nonworking mothers to working mothers, in terms of direct interaction between mothers and children, indicate that mothers at home spend most of their time with household chores and television. Children at home spend about 5% of their waking time in direct interaction with their mothers. Employed mothers spend as much time as mothers at home in reading or playing with children (Ziegler, 1983). Thus, research does not support the notion that outside employment by both parents is a detriment to children, nor are children automatically better off with a full-time mother in the home.

Maintaining perspective is a necessary part of being a working parent. First, it is important to recognize that families with a mother at home full time are not typical; second, for many families, work is not a matter of choice. Next, there is no firm evidence to suggest that the children of working parents suffer as a result of this arrangement. In fact, there may be advantages for children in respect to greater self-confidence and independence, along with a more flexible definition of sex roles.

ALTERNATIVE ACTIONS

The concerns of working parents are diverse and complex. A course of action for a specific problem must first include identification of the relationship involved:- parent and child or children, parent and parent, parent and workplace. Each situation can be analyzed and addressed in terms of time and guilt, with alternative actions designed to approach a reasonable compromise between the ideal and the unbearable.

Relationships

Parents and Children. The ideal relationship between parent and child rests upon their involvement with each other — their interacting in warm, personal, and interested ways (Silberman & Wheelan, 1980). Involvement with a parent is the necessary first step in children's learning to be responsible to themselves and others. By identifying with parents, children learn to make better choices about their own behavior. Furthermore, relationships with caring and involved adults indicate to children that they are worthwhile.

Silberman and Wheelan (1980) described a continuum of emotional involvement in a relationship, with disengagement and overinvolvement at each extreme. Disengagement is a function of emotional distance and avoidance; the message is "Leave me alone" and is sent by limiting communication. A disengaged parent is silent at dinner or in the car, tuning out questions and rarely offering support or encouragement; parent-to-child interaction is reduced to expressions of disapproval. Disengaged parents can be rigid and demanding or weak and permissive, but usually they are disillusioned about family life.

Often the spouse is overinvolved. Overinvolvement is emotional entanglement; the parent uses the child for comfort or security. Often the message is "I live through you" (Silberman and Wheelan, 1980, p. 142). In this situation, the parent may have inadequate relationships with other adults and thus seek a dependent type of friendship with the child. The child's own needs are not separated from the parent's; rescue becomes a common pattern of behavior. Occasionally, overinvolvement may be a response to the guilt felt by a working parent. In an effort to compensate for being less available, a parent may invest heavily in a child's happiness by assuming many of the child's responsibilities or indulging every passing want.

Quality contacts, according to Silberman and Wheelan, are those touching the central region of the continuum between disengagement and overinvolvement. They suggest that parents first identify undeveloped areas of activity between parent and child. Disengaged parents are urged to communicate about themselves by offering information about life experiences, attitudes, or childhood memories. Overinvolved parents need to practice active listening, resisting mind-reading and quick judgments. Parents may be led into thinking that quality time must be spent engaged in some sort of unique and stimulating activity. While it is true that thought and effort go into building these contacts, the setting is largely unimportant. Time in the car or bedtime rituals are regular opportunities for private time. The quality of any relationship is improved by positive expectations. By deliberately and clearly communicating an attitude of approval and satisfaction, parents can foster an atmosphere that promotes compromise and acceptance.

Parent to Parent Relationships. The relationships of working parents are influenced by a number of factors, two critical issues appearing frequently: sharing household responsibilities and finding time for meaningful and involved interaction. Research supports the fact that women who work full time continue to work an additional 35 hours a week doing household chores. Comparatively, men who have preschool children and employed wives spend about 13 hours a week on home work in the home (Cowan, 1983). The type of work men do at home is definitely related to sex role and to the perceived importance of the task (Bird, Bird, & Scruggs, 1984). Approximating the ideal situation requires a compromise in expectations: Adjusted families lower their standards for clean houses and home-cooked meals. Because these are areas associated with women's roles, women feel guiltier than men. Women who can assuage this guilt do it in stages. Initially there exists a belief that one can be and do everything for everyone. Next comes the beginning of self-acceptance and the realization that no one can be everywhere and do everything. Finally, there comes the freedom to choose and prioritize, as women find they do not want to be and do everything (Curran, 1985).

In her survey of 450 men and women, Curran reported that one of the most common causes of family